A-Z MINI LONDON

KT-555-204

Key to Map Pages		Streets, etc.	128-343
Large Scale Map Pages	4-27	Index to Hospitals	344-348
Map Pages	28-125	Index to Stations	349-352
Congestion Charging Zone	126-127	Underground Map	back cover

REFERENCE

Motorway	M1	Church or Chapel	†
A Road	A2	Fire Station	■
B Road	B519	Hospital	Ⓗ
Dual Carriageway		House Numbers A & B Roads only	40 23
One-way Traffic flow on A Roads is indicated by a heavy line on the driver's left. All one-way streets are shown on Large Scale Pages 4-27	→	Information Centre	🄸
		National Grid Reference	539
Junction Names	MARBLE ARCH	Police Station	▲
Pedestrianized Road		Post Office	★
Restricted Access		River Bus Stop	Ⓡ
Railway	Tunnel / Level Crossing	Toilet with facilities for the Disabled	▽ ▽
Stations:		Educational Establishment	◥
National Rail Network	⚉	Hospital or Hospice etc.	◥
Docklands Light Railway	DLR	Industrial Building	◥
Underground Station	●	Leisure & Recreational Facility	◥
Congestion Charging Zone Large Scale Pages only.		Place of Interest	◥
		Public Building	◥
Map Continuation	Large Scale City Centre 84 8	Shopping Centre or Market	◥
Car Park Selected	🅿	Other Selected Building	◥

SCALE

Map Pages 28-125	Map Pages 4-11
1:21477 Approx. 3 inches to 1 mile	1:10560 6 inches to 1 mile
0 ⅛ ¼ Mile	0 1/16 ⅛ Mile
0 100 200 300 Metres	0 100 200 Metres
4.66 cm to 1 km 7.49 cm to 1 mile	9.47 cm to 1km 15.24 cm to 1 mile

Copyright of Geographers' A-Z Map Company Ltd.

Head Office : Fairfield Road, Borough Green, Sevenoaks, Kent TN15 8PP
Tel: 01732 781000 (Enquiries & Trade Sales)   01732 783422 (Retail Sales)

Ordnance Survey® This product includes mapping data licensed from Ordnance Survey ® with the permission of the Controller of Her Majesty's Stationery Office.

© Crown Copyright 2005. All rights reserved. Licence number 100017302

www.a-zmaps.co.uk   Copyright © Geographers' A-Z Map Co. Ltd.   Edition 5 2005

Every possible care has been taken to ensure that, to the best of our knowledge, the information contained in this atlas is accurate at the date of publication. However, we cannot warrant that our work is entirely error free and whilst we would be grateful to learn of any inaccuracies, we do not accept any responsibility for loss or damage resulting from reliance on information contained within this publication.

2 KEY TO MAP PAGES

2 A5

Kingsbury — M1 — A1

HENDON — **HORNSEY**

Golders Green — Highgate

| 28 | 29 | 30 | 31 | 32 | 33 | 34 |

Neasden — Cricklewood

HAMPSTEAD

| 42 | 43 | 44 | 45 | 46 | 47 | 48 |

WILLESDEN — **CAMDEN TOWN** — **ISLIN**

Kensal Green — Kilburn — **MARYLEBONE** — **FINS**

| 56 | 57 | 58 | 59 | 60 | 61 | 62 |

LARGE SC
WEST Holborn
END *SECTI*

ACTON

Shepherd's Bush

| 70 | 71 | 72 | 73 | 74 | 75 | 76 |

PADDINGTON

KENSINGTON — Westminster — **LAM**

CHISWICK — **HAMMERSMITH** — **CHELSEA**

| 84 | 85 | 86 | 87 | 88 | 89 | 90 |

BARNES — **FULHAM** — **BATTERSEA**

PUTNEY — **CLAPHAM** — **BRIX**

| 98 | 99 | 100 | 101 | 102 | 103 | 104 |

WANDSWORTH

Roehampton

Richmond Park — Balham

| 112 | 113 | 114 | 115 | 116 | 117 | 118 |

Tooting

WIMBLEDON — **STREATHAM**

MITCHAM

| SCALE | 0 | 1 | 2 Miles |
| | 0 | 1 | 2 | 3 Kilometres |

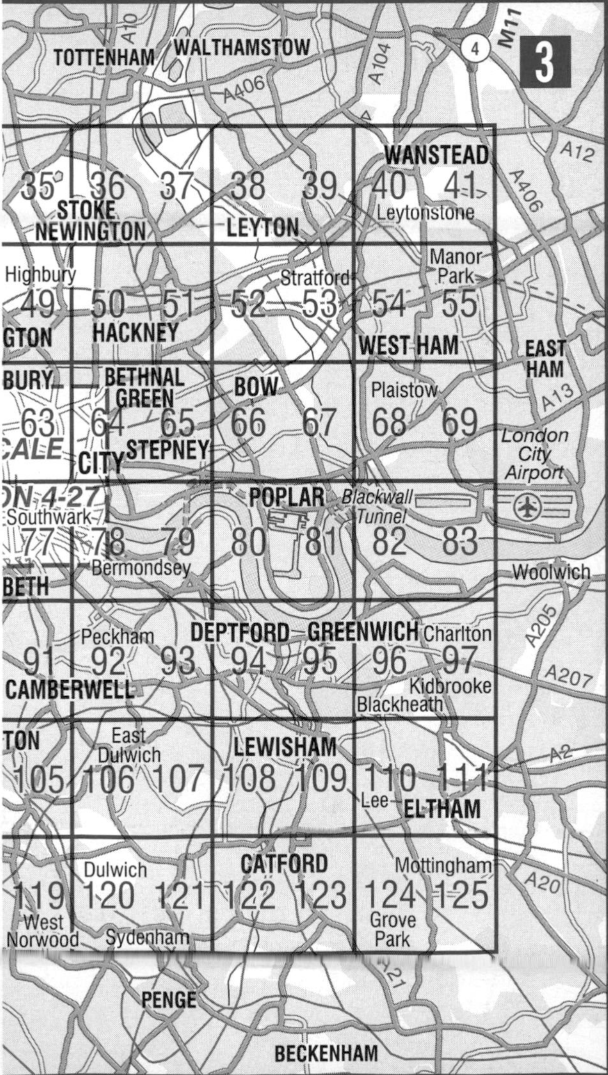

3

TOTTENHAM WALTHAMSTOW

M11

4

A10

A104

A406

A12

A406

35 36 37 38 39 40 41
STOKE
NEWINGTON
LEYTON
WANSTEAD
Leytonstone

Highbury
Stratford
Manor
Park

49 50 51 52 53 54 55
GTON HACKNEY
WEST HAM

EAST
HAM

A13

BURY
BETHNAL
GREEN
BOW
Plaistow

63 64 65 66 67 68 69
CALE
STEPNEY
London
City
Airport

CITY
POPLAR Blackwall
Tunnel

N 4-27
Southwark
77 78 79 80 81 82 83
Bermondsey
Woolwich

BETH

A205

Peckham DEPTFORD GREENWICH Charlton
91 92 93 94 95 96 97
CAMBERWELL
Kidbrooke
Blackheath
A207

TON
East
Dulwich
LEWISHAM
105 106 107 108 109 110 111
Lee ELTHAM

A2

Dulwich CATFORD Mottingham
119 120 121 122 123 124 125
West
Norwood Sydenham
Grove
Park
A20

PENGE

BECKENHAM

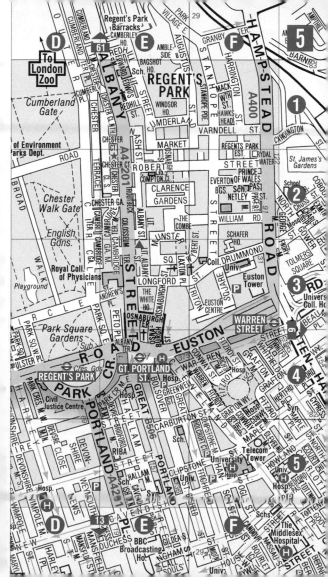

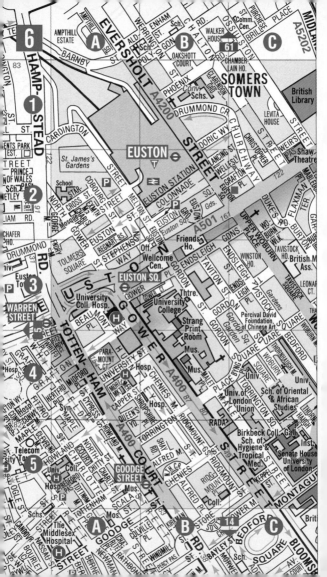

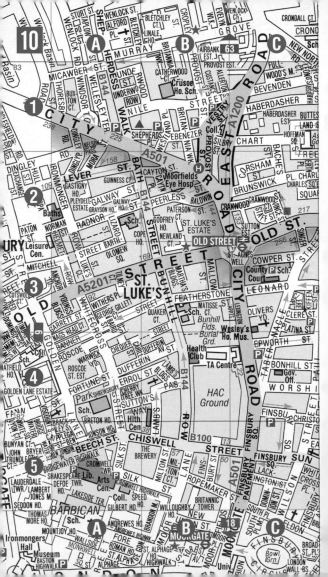

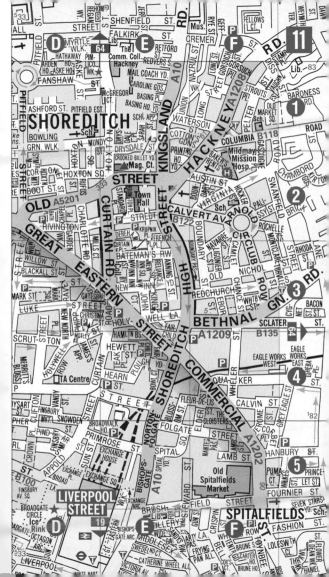

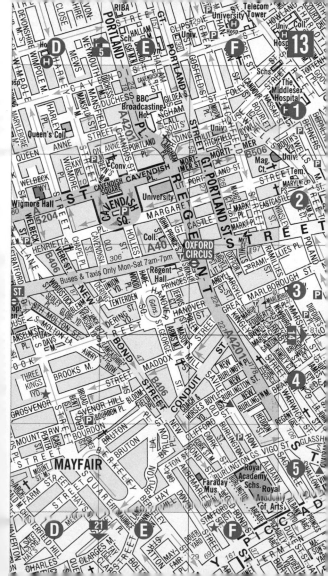

13

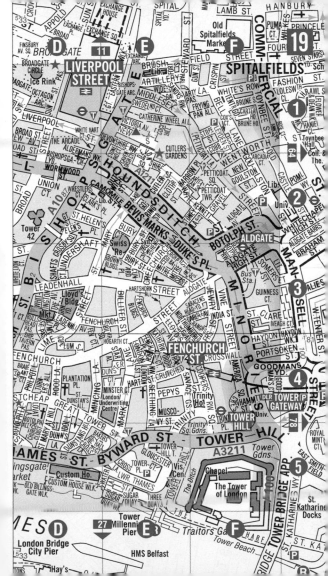

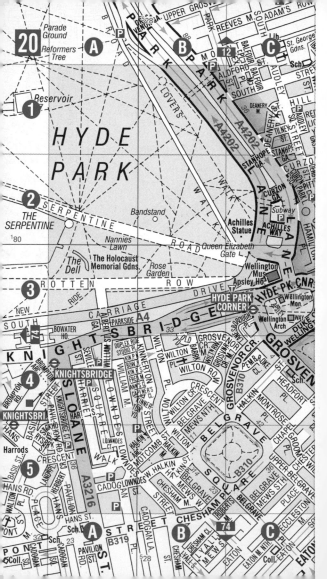

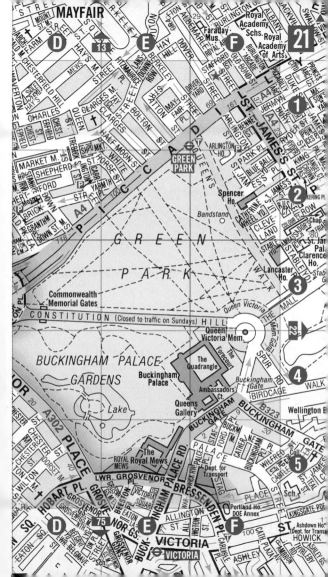

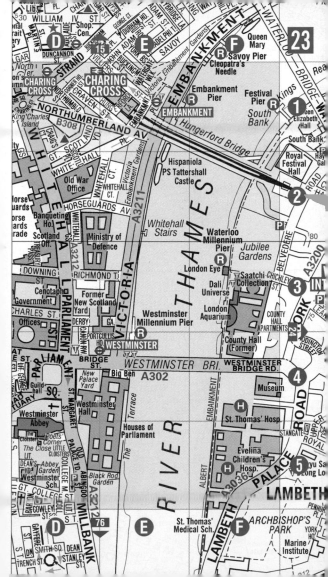

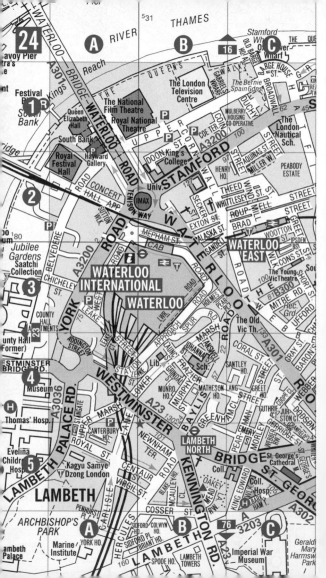

24

RIVER THAMES

Stamford Wharf

OLD BARGE
AGE HOUSE
ST.
THE QUEE
OXO Tower Wharf

Savoy Pier
Savoy
Pier
tra's

531

Kings

WATERLOO BRIDGE

Reach

QUEEN'S WALK

The Bernie Spain Gdns

GABRIEL'S WHARF

16

BROADWALK

KIN REA
STR

1R

Festival Pier

South Bank

The London Television Centre

The National Film Theatre

Queen Elizabeth Hall

Royal National Theatre

UPPER

GROUND

CORNWALL

MULBERRY HOUSING CO-OPERATIVE

A3200 100

DUCHY

62 A 45

The London Nautical Sch.

Royal Festival Hall

South Bank

P

Hayward Gallery

CUT TEN

COIN

St

DOON

King's College

COE TER

STAMFORD

A3200 100

AQUINAS ST.

STREET

PEABODY ESTATE

Univ.

HENRY HO.

97

MILLER W.

STREET

ROAD

CONCERT HALL APP.

TENISON WAY

IMAX

THEED

WHITTLESEY

ST.

WINDMILL ST.

ROUPELL

BRAD

STREET

Jubilee Gardens

Saatchi Collection

180

BELVEDERE

CHICHELEY

A3200

SECKER

EXTON ST.

ALASKA ST.

SANDEL

MEPHAM ST.

CAB

THEED

ST.

MELL

ROAD

WOOTTON

STREET

ST.

IPSDEN

WATERLOO EAST

3

SUTTON WLK

ROAD

i

WATERLOO INTERNATIONAL

WATERLOO

The Young Vic Theatre

100

B300

MITRE RD.

UFFORD

Rec. Grd.

A301

COUNTY HALL ATMENTS

28

LEAKE

STREET

WESTMINSTER

P

ROAD

ROAD

LWR.

SPUR

MARSH

HOLMES

PEAR

GRAY ST.

The Old Vic Th.

CORAL ST.

A301

BARON

4

nty Hall Former)

Museum

ADDINGTON STREET

STATION

LOWER

APPROACH

CAUSE

BRAD

SOHANNA

GORNDAL

FRAZIER

Sch.

MASKELL

SANTLEY HO.

WEBBER

RO.

WESTMINSTER

A23

BRIDGE RD.

MUNRO ST.

MURPHY

MATHESON HO.

LANG

GREET

GUTHRIE

STON

GERRIDGE

ST.

DODSON

WHITG

H

Thomas' Hosp.

BAYLIS

GREENHAMCL

EMERY

MAN

MORLEY

ST.

1300

TOT

PEAR

ST. GEORGE'S

UPPER

MARSH

ST.

CANTERBURY HO.

NEWNHAM TER.

LAMBETH NORTH

Coll

St. George's Cathedral

ROYAL

ST.

Evelina Childr Hosp

5

Kagyu Samye Dzong London

CENTAUR

VIRGIL ST.

BLAKEY HO.

MCAULEY

CL

OAKEY

MEAD

RW.

KING EDWD.

Edward Coll. Hosp.

H

BARK HAM

ST

BRIDGE

A 3203

LAMBETH PALACE RD.

A3036

LAMBETH

PENHURST

CARLISLE

HERCULES RD.

UPPER

KENNINGTON RD.

A23

A302

ARCHBISHOP'S PARK

mbeth Palace

Marine Institute

York Ho.

A

SIDFORD PL.

BRIANT HO.

COLWYN HO.

SIDFORD HO.

B

LAMBETH TOWERS

160

SPODE HO.

COSSER

ST.

76

C

Imperial War Museum

ST. GEORG

KENNINGTON RD.

Geraldi Mary Harmsw Park

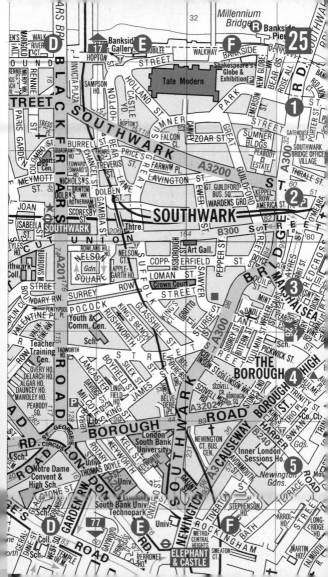

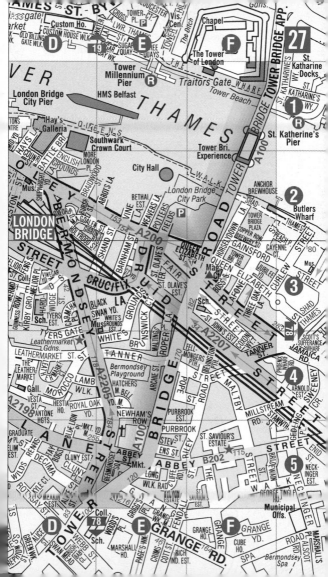

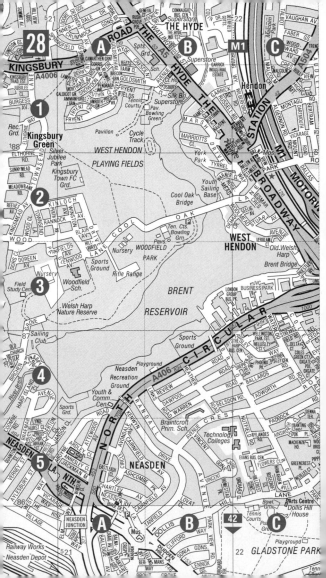

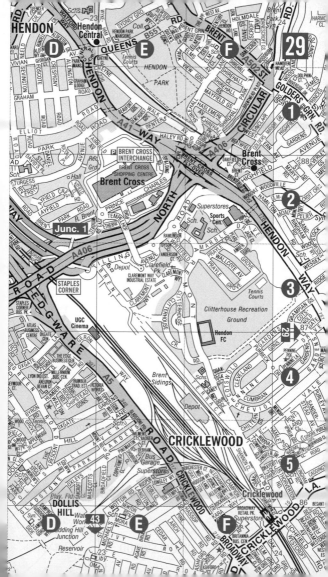

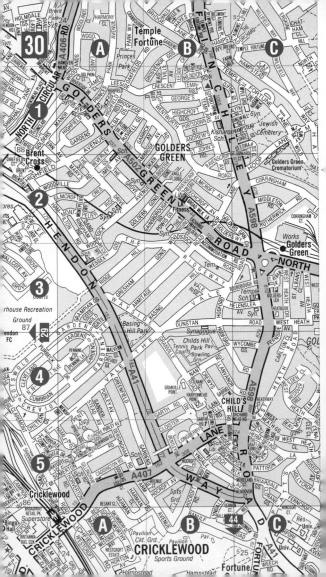

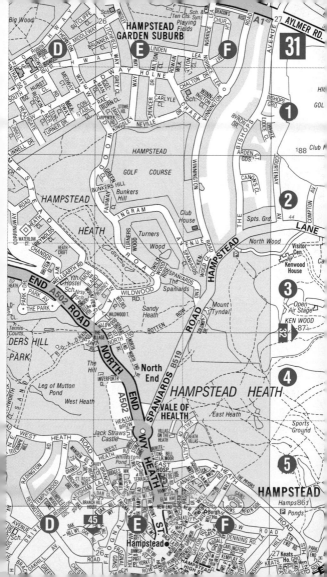

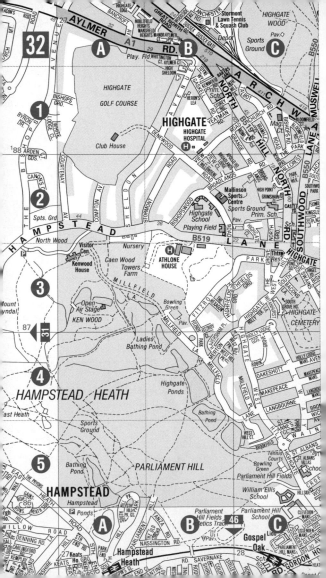

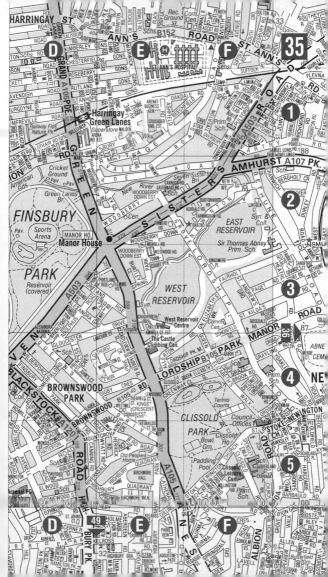

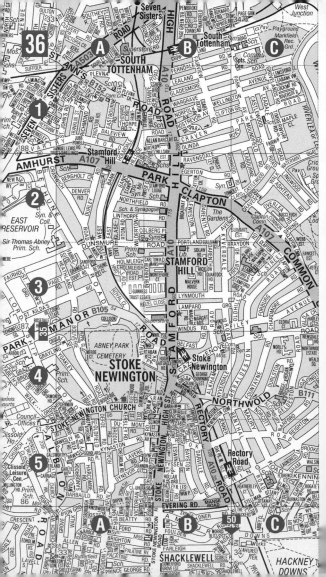

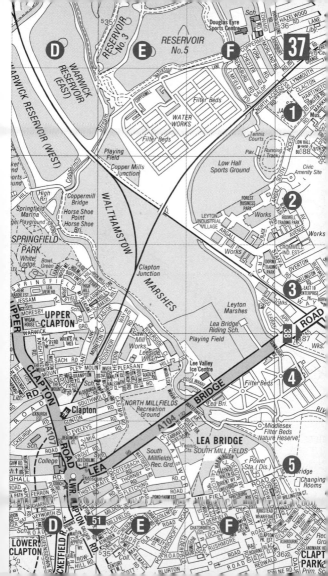

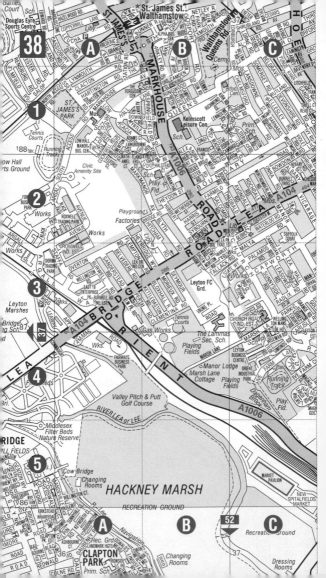

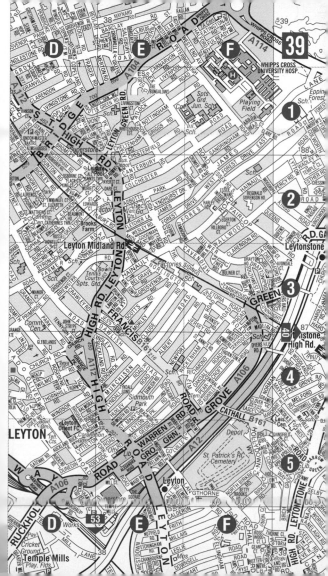

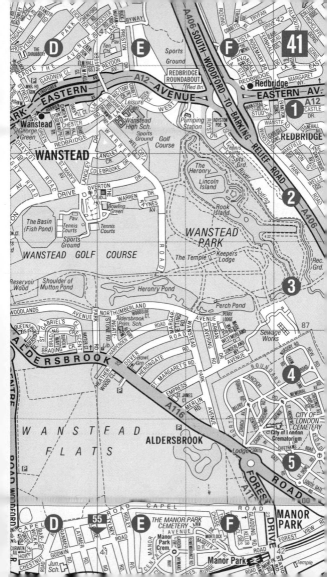

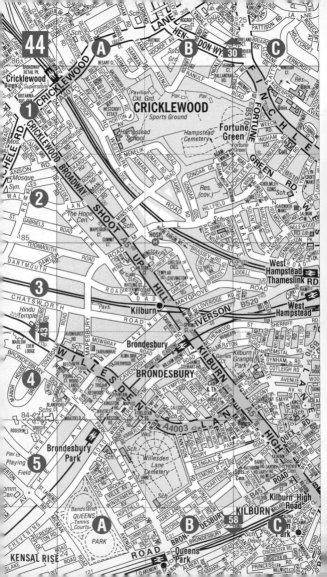

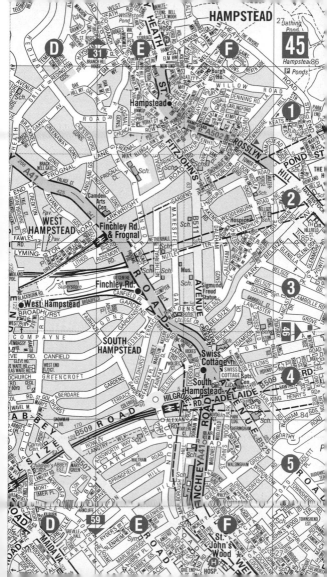

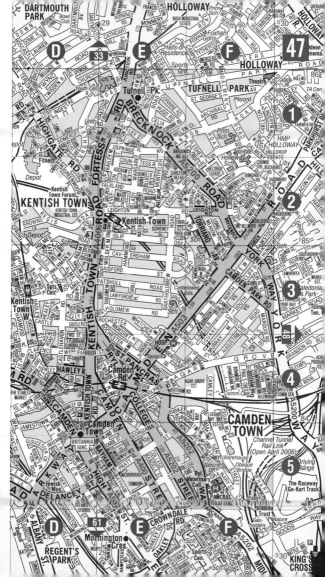

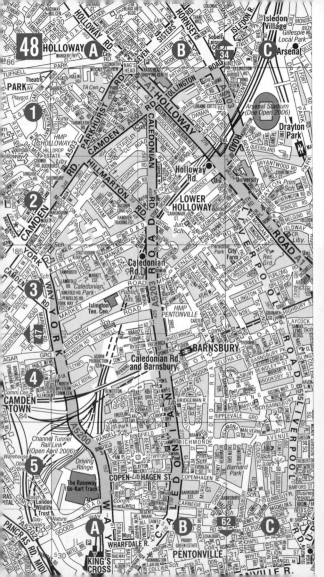

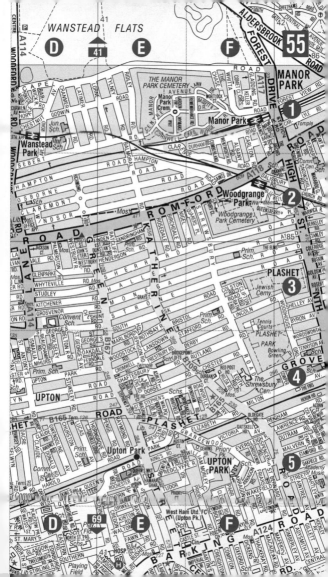

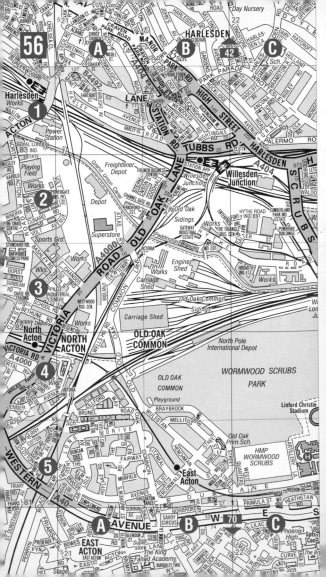

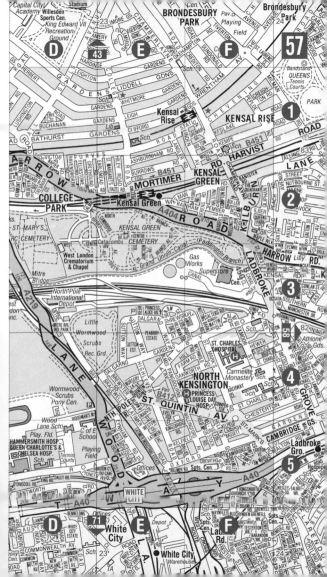

57

Capital City Academy
Willesden Sports Cen.
King Edward VII Recreation Ground
stadium

BRONDESBURY PARK
Pav.
Playing Field
THERTON AV.
Brondesbury Park

D 43 **E** **F**

1
QUEENS PARK
Bandstand
Tennis Courts

LIDDELL GDNS
WHITMORE
LEIGH
CLIFFORD
Sch.
Lib.

Kensal Rise
KENSAL RISE
ROAD
KESLAKE

KEMPE
Sch. B451
HARVIST
ALLING
RD

HARROW
VICTOR
PURVES
FESTWICK
FELIXSTOWE
HILEY
BURROWS
HAZEL
B451
KENSAL GREEN
RD
MORTIMER
COLLEGE PARK
Kensal Green

LANE
STREET
NUTBOURNE ST.
WYNE
HAVOCK

2
HUXLEY
SIXTH
MAPLE
SYCME
KILB
LADBROKE

ST MARY'S RC CEMETERY
North
West London Crematorium & Chapel
Catacombs
KENSAL GREEN CEMETERY
CENTRE
RAINHAM
A404 ROAD
Grand Union Canal (Paddington Branch)
Gas Works
Superstore
CANAL

HARROW RD
Lib.
KENSAL RD

3
CONLAN ST
OCTAVIA
SOUTHERN
ROW
MANCHESTER DR.
WORNINGTON
Sch.

Mitre Bridge
North Pole International Depot
MITRE BRI.
IND.PARK
Little Wormwood Scrubs Rec. Grd.
DALGARNO
SUTTON WAY
PEABODY ESTATE
SUTTON EST.
GARDENS
PRINCESS ALICE HO.
SHREWSBURY
Sch.
HEWER
ST. CHARLES HOSPITAL
Carmelite Monastery
Sch.

4
82 RNING
Sch.
Athlone Gds.
GROVE

A219
LANE
WOOD
Wood Lane Sch.
Play. Fld.
SMITH
POLE
HAMMERSMITH HOSP.
QUEEN CHARLOTTE'S & CHELSEA HOSP.
Tennis Courts
Playing Field
Offices
C of E School
ST. QUINTIN
B412
Pav.
NORTH KENSINGTON
PRINCESS LOUISE DAY HOSP.
EVELYN
KINGSBRIDGE
OXFORD
ST. CHARLES
CHESTERTON
ST. MARK'S
CAMBRIDGE GS.
Ladbroke Gro.
Hospice

5

Wormwood Scrubs Pony Cen.
WOODMAN'S M.
PIONEER
DENTWORTH
WHITE CITY ESTATE
Sch.
Offices
A40 WAY
A40
WHITE City
Spts. Cen.
WALMER RD
CROWTHORW
KINGSWORTH
GOODRICH
WESLEY
TALBOT
GRENFELL
Spts. Cen.
Lath. Rd.

D 71 **E** **F**
White City
COMMONWEALTH AV.
Sch. 23
Depot
White City Warehouse

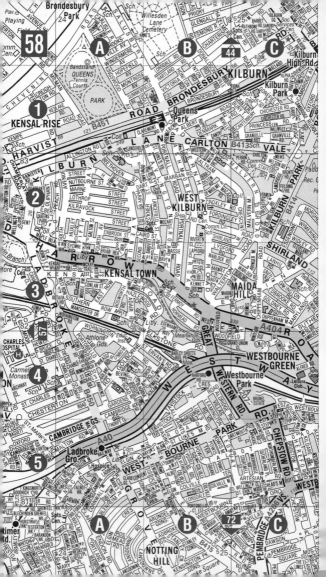

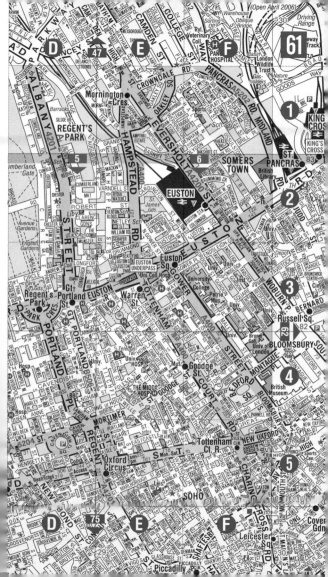

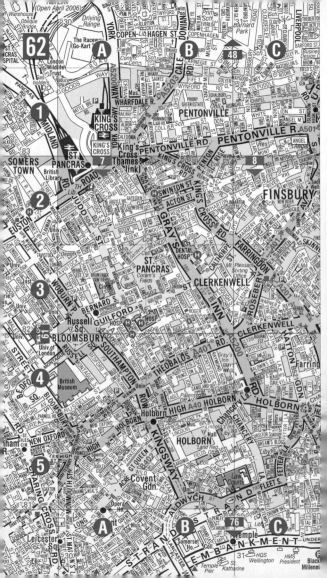

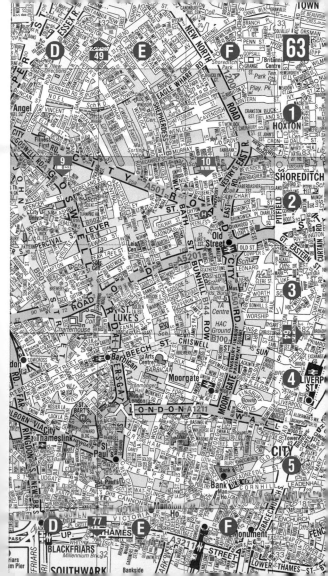

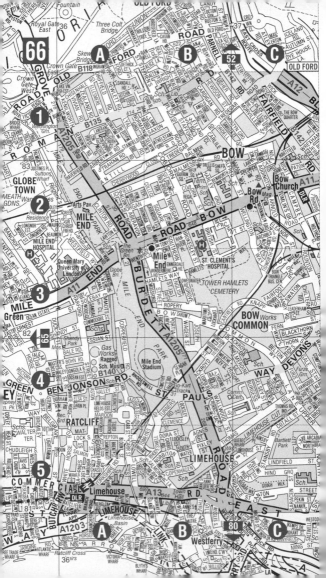

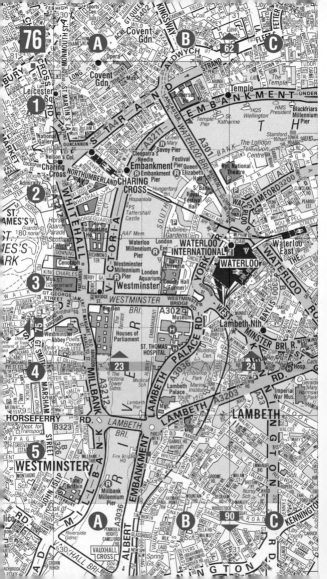

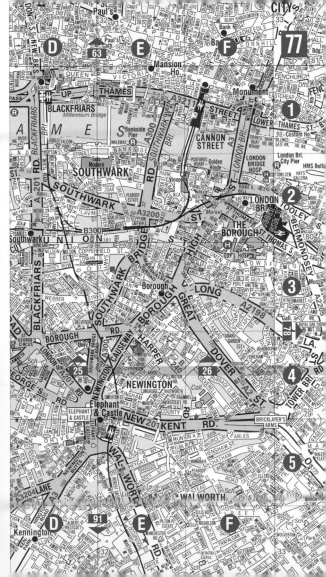

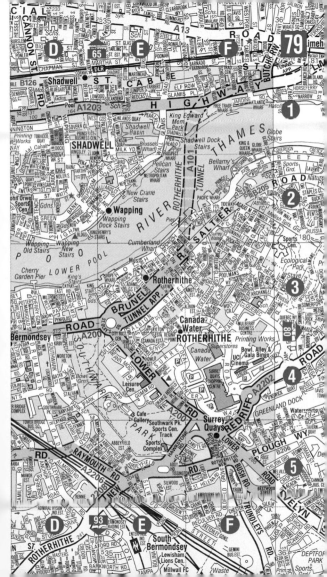

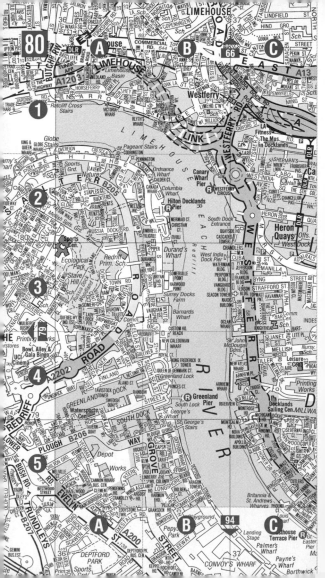

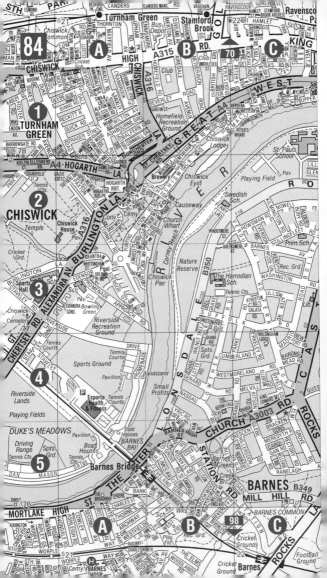

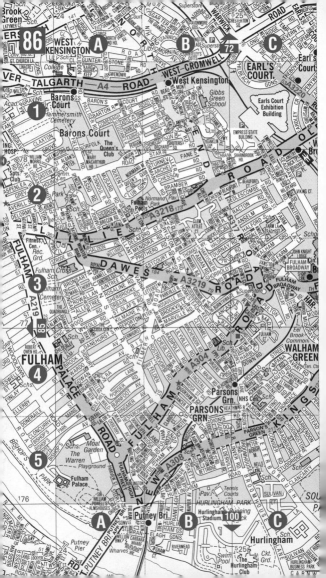

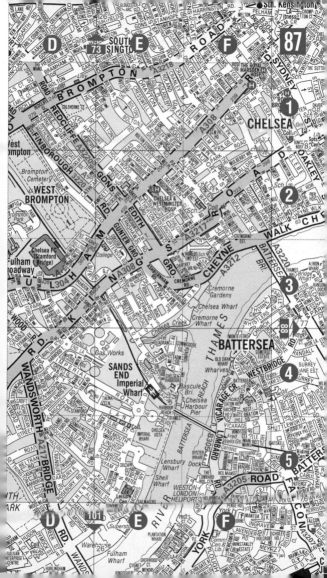

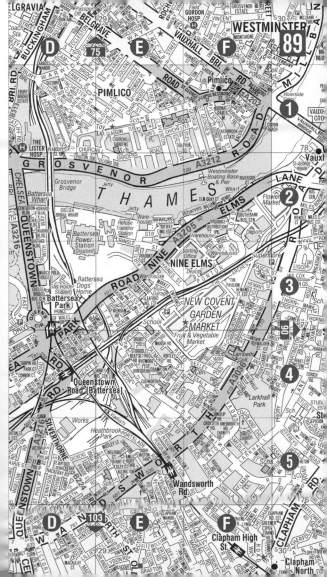

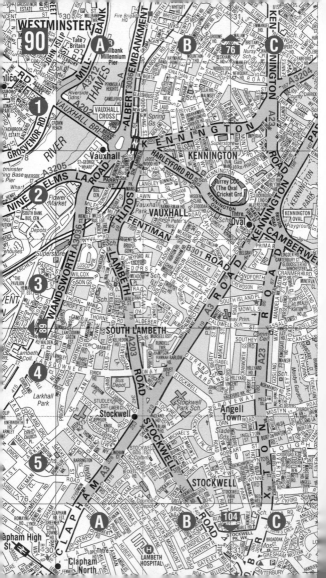

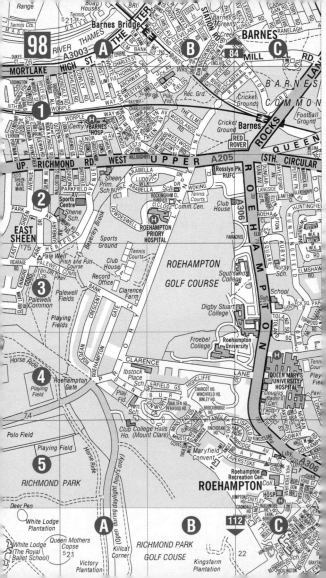

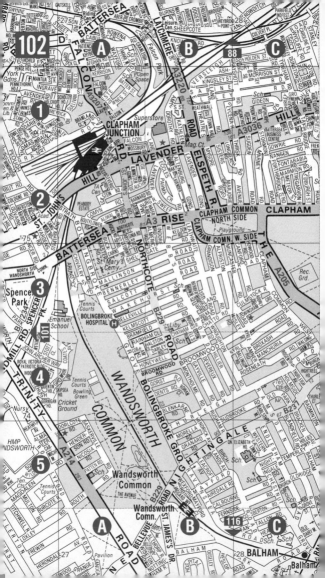

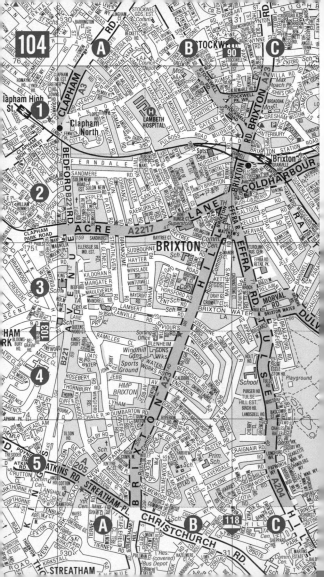

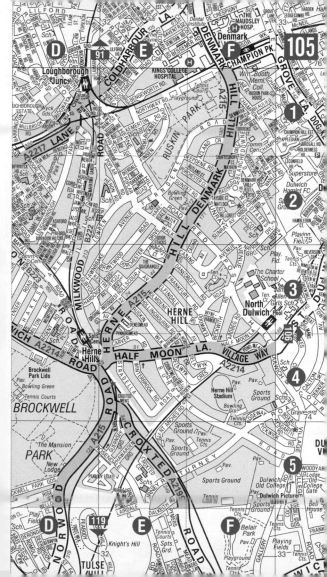

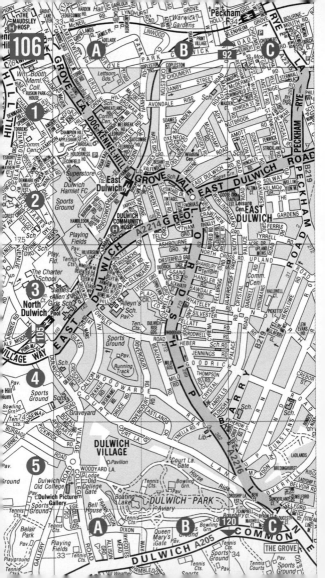

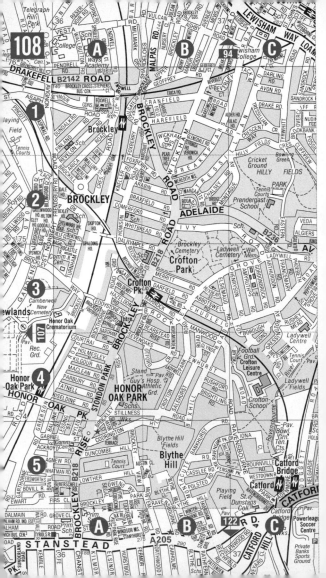

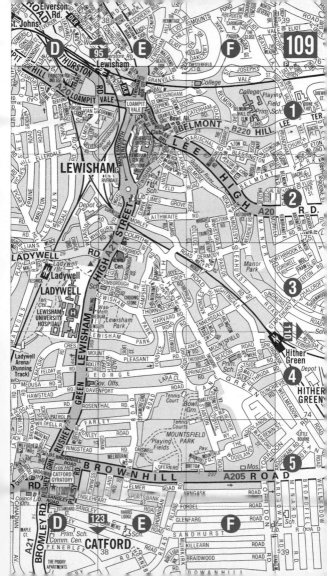

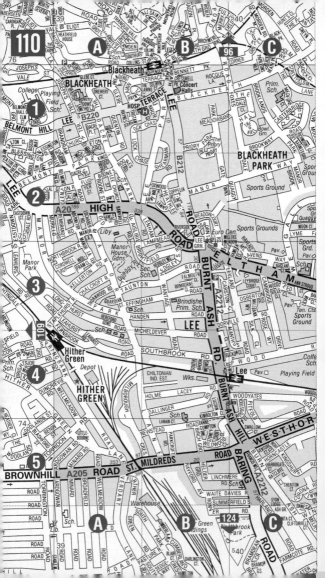

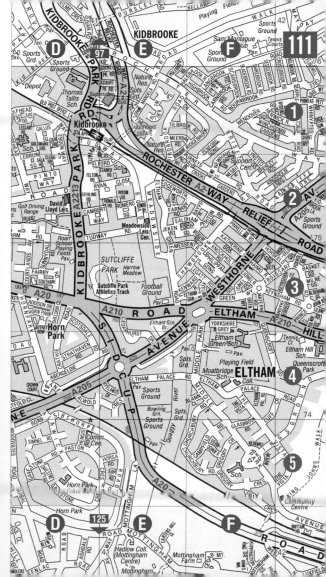

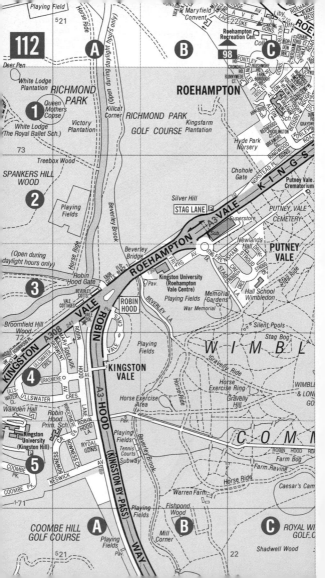

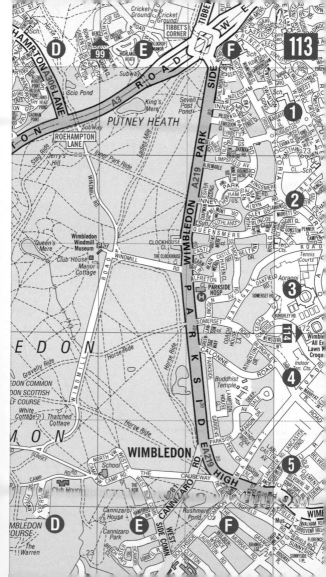

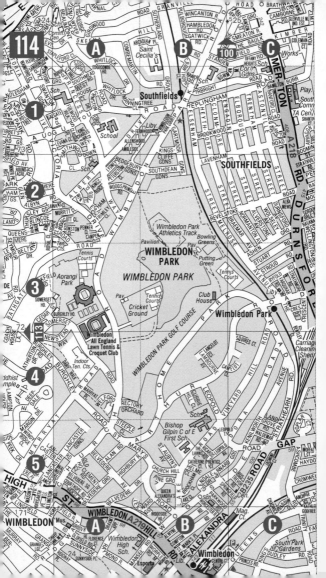

114

Saint Cecilia's

Southfields

100

MERTON

SOUTHFIELDS

DURNSFORD RD.

A218

School

Liby

Wimbledon Park
Athletics Track

Bowling Greens

Putting Green

WIMBLEDON PARK

WIMBLEDON PARK

Pavilion

Tennis Courts

Tennis Courts

Aorangi Park

Club House

Pav.

Cricket Ground

Tennis Courts

Wimbledon Park

Liby

113

Wimbledon
All England
Lawn Tennis &
Croquet Club

WIMBLEDON PARK GOLF COURSE

Carriage Cleaning Shed

Indoor Ten. Cts.

RECTORY ORCHARD

Bishop Gilpin C of E First Sch.

Sch.

GAP

A235 ROAD

Catherine Prentice

Queen Alexandra's Ct.

Bishop Gilpin C of E First Sch.

HIGH

WIMBLEDON

Wimbledon Mus.

WIMBLEDON A219 HILL

Wimbledon
High Sch.

Esporta

A218

ALEXANDRA

Wimbledon

South Park Gardens

Mag. Ct.

A B C

1 2 3 4 5

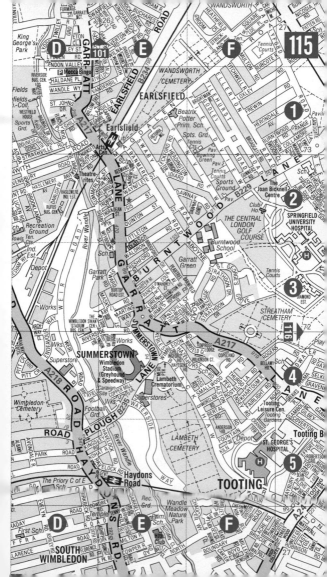

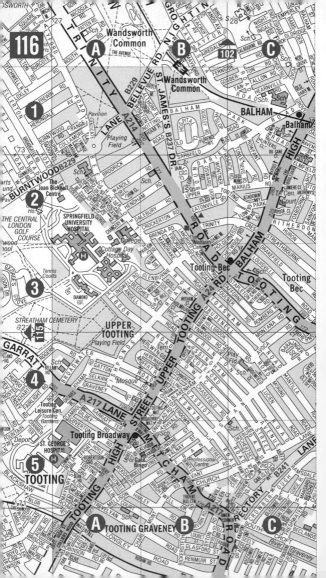

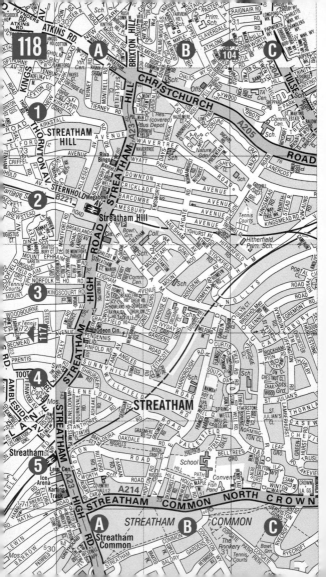

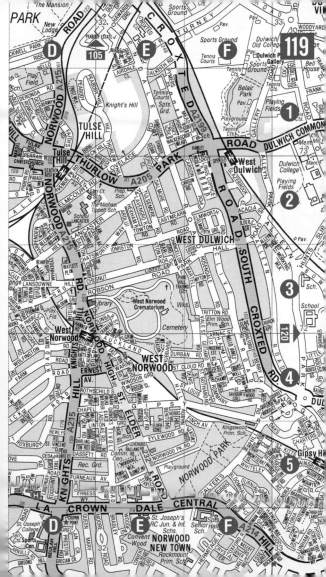

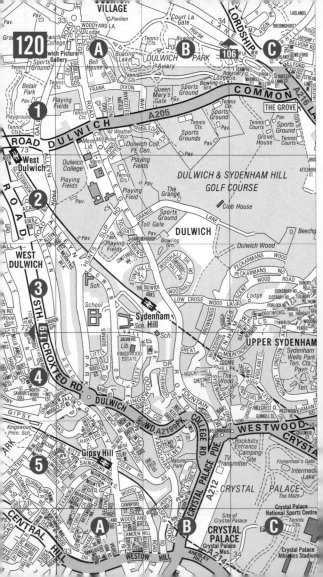

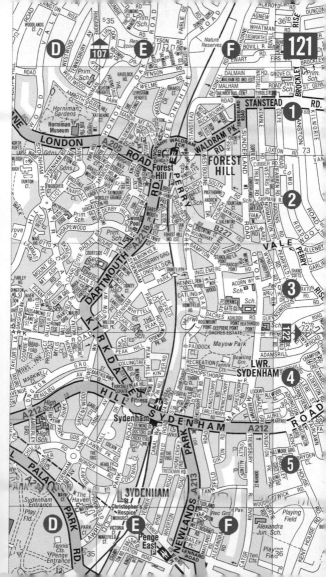

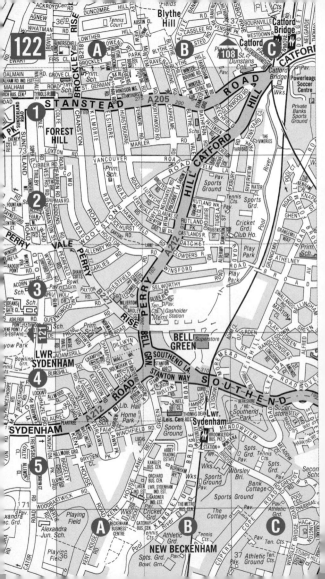

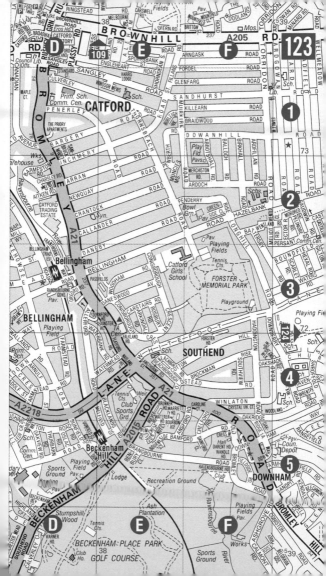

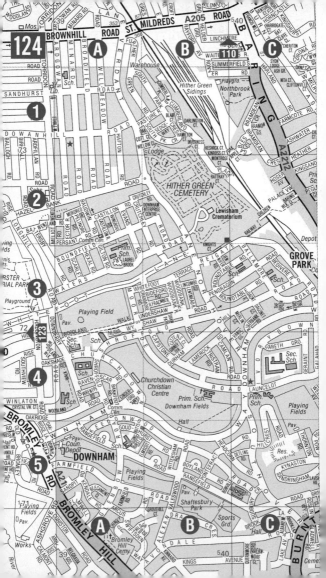

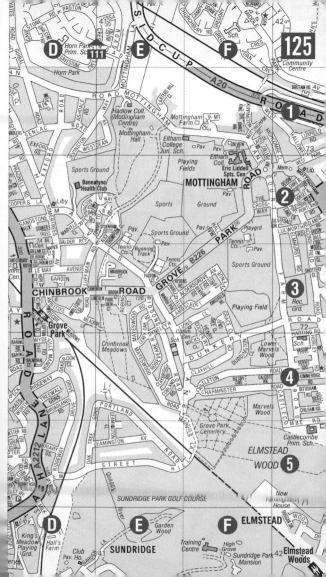

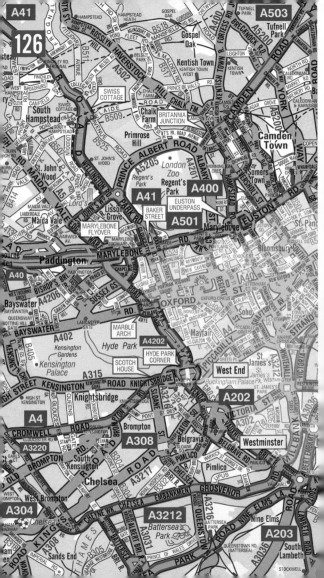

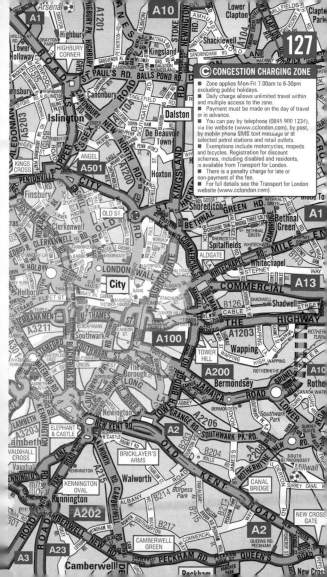

© **CONGESTION CHARGING ZONE**

■ Zone applies Mon-Fri 7.00am to 6-30pm excluding public holidays.
■ Daily charge allows unlimited travel within and multiple access to the zone.
■ Payment must be made on the day of travel or in advance.
■ You can pay by telephone (0845 900 1234), via the website (www.cclondon.com), by post, by mobile phone SMS text message or at selected petrol stations and retail outlets.
■ Exemptions include motorcycles, mopeds and bicycles. Registration for discount schemes, including disabled and residents, is available from Transport for London.
■ There is a penalty charge for late or non-payment of the fee.
■ For full details see the Transport for London website (www.cclondon.com).

INDEX

Including Streets, Places & Areas, Industrial Estates,

Selected Flats & Walkways, Junction Names and

Selected Places of Interest.

HOW TO USE THIS INDEX

1. Each street name is followed by its Postcode District (or, if outside the London Postcodes, by its Locality Abbreviation(s)) and then by its map reference;
e.g. **Abbeville Rd.** SW4 . . . . 4E **103** is in the SW4 Postcode District and is to be found in square 4E on page **103**. The page number is shown in bold type.

2. A strict alphabetical order is followed in which Av., Rd., St., etc. (though abbreviated) are read in full and as part of the street name; e.g. **Abbotsleigh Rd.** appears after **Abbots La.** but before **Abbots Mnr.**

3. Streets and a selection of flats and walkways too small to be shown on the maps, appear in the index with the thoroughfare to which it is connected shown in brackets;
e.g. **Abady Ho.** SW1 . . . . 5F **75** (off Page St.)

4. Addresses that are in more than one part are referred to as not continuous.

5. Places and areas are shown in the index in **BLUE TYPE** and the map reference is to the actual map square in which the town centre or area is located and not to the place name shown on the map; e.g. **ALDERSBROOK** 4D **41**

6. An example of a selected place of interest is **Admiralty Arch** 1C **22** (2F **75**)

7. Junction names are shown in the index in **BOLD TYPE**; e.g. **ANGEL** 1C **62**

8. Map references for entries that appear on large scale pages **4-27** are shown first, with small scale map references shown in brackets; e.g. **Abbey Orchard St.** SW1 . . . . 5B **22** (4F **75**)

GENERAL ABBREVIATIONS

All. : Alley	**Ent.** : Enterprise	**Pal.** : Palace
App. : Approach	**Est.** : Estate	**Pde.** : Parade
Arc. : Arcade	**Fld.** : Field	**Pk.** : Park
Av. : Avenue	**Flds.** : Fields	**Pas.** : Passage
Bk. : Back	**Gdn.** : Garden	**Pav.** : Pavilion
Blvd. : Boulevard	**Gdns.** : Gardens	**Pl.** : Place
Bri. : Bridge	**Gth.** : Garth	**Pct.** : Precinct
B'way. : Broadway	**Ga.** : Gate	**Prom.** : Promenade
Bldg. : Building	**Gt.** : Great	**Quad.** : Quadrant
Bldgs. : Buildings	**Grn.** : Green	**Ri.** : Rise
Bus. : Business	**Gro.** : Grove	**Rd.** : Road
C'way. : Causeway	**Hgts.** : Heights	**Rdbt.** : Roundabout
Cen. : Centre	**Ho.** : House	**Shop.** : Shopping
Chu. : Church	**Ho's.** : Houses	**Sth.** : South
Chyd. : Churchyard	**Ind.** : Industrial	**Sq.** : Square
Circ. : Circle	**Info.** : Information	**Sta.** : Station
Cir. : Circus	**Junc.** : Junction	**St.** : Street
Cl. : Close	**La.** : Lane	**Ter.** : Terrace
Coll. : College	**Lit.** : Little	**Twr.** : Tower
Comn. : Common	**Lwr.** : Lower	**Trad.** : Trading
Cnr. : Corner	**Mnr.** : Manor	**Up.** : Upper
Cott. : Cottage	**Mans.** : Mansions	**Va.** : Vale
Cotts. : Cottages	**Mkt.** : Market	**Vw.** : View
Ct. : Court	**Mdw.** : Meadow	**Vs.** : Villas
Cres. : Crescent	**Mdws.** : Meadows	**Vis.** : Visitors
Cft. : Croft	**M.** : Mews	**Wlk.** : Walk
Dr. : Drive	**Mt.** : Mount	**W.** : West
E. : East	**Mus.** : Museum	**Yd.** : Yard
Emb. : Embankment	**Nth.** : North	

Beck : **Beckenham**
Brom : **Bromley**
Chst : **Chislehurst**

Ilf : **Ilford**
King T : **Kingston Upon Thames**

Wfd G : **Woodford Green**

---

02 Cen. NW3 . . . . 3E **45**
198 Gallery 4D **105**
(off Railton Rd.)

A

Abady Ho. SW1 . . . . 5F **75**
(off Page St.)
Abberley M. SW4 . . . . . 1D **103**
Abbess Cl. SW2 . . . . . 1D **119**
Abbeville M. SW2 . . . . 2F **103**
Abbeville Rd.
SW4 . . . . 4E **103**
Abbey Bus. Cen.
. . . . 4E **89**
Abbey Cl. E5 . . . . 1C **50**
SW8 . . . . 4F **89**
Abbey Ct. NW8 . . . . 1E **59**
(off Abbey Rd.)
SE17 . . . . 1E **91**
(off Macleod St.)
Abbey Dr. SW17 . . . . . 5C **116**
Abbey Est. NW8 . . . . . . 5D **45**
Abbeyfield Est. SE16 . . 5E **79**
Abbeyfield Rd. SE16 . . 5E **79**
(not continuous)
Abbey Gdns. NW8 . . . . . 1A **59**
SE16 . . . . 5C **78**
W6 . . . . 2A **86**
Abbey Ho. E15 . . . . 1A **68**
(off Baker's Row)
NW8 . . . . 2E **59**
(off Garden Rd.)
Abbey La. E15 . . . . 1F **67**
Abbey La. Commercial Est.
E15 . . . . 1A **68**
Abbey Life Ct. E16 . . . . 4D **69**
Abbey Lodge NW8 . . . . 2A **60**
(off Park Rd.)
Abbey M. E17 . . . . 1C **38**
Abbey Orchard St.
SW1 . . . . 5B **22** (4F **75**)
Abbey Orchard St. Est.
SW1 . . . . 5C **22** (4F **75**)
(not continuous)
Abbey Rd. E15 . . . . 1F **67**
NW6 . . . . 4D **45**
NW8 . . . . 5D **45**
Abbey St. E13 . . . . 3C **68**
SE1 . . . . 5E **27** (4B **78**)
Abbey Trad. Est.
SE26 . . . . 5B **122**
Abbot Ct. SW8 . . . . 3A **90**
(off Hartington Rd.)
Abbot Ho. E14 . . . . 1D **81**
(off Cmylin St.)
Abbotsbury Cl. E15 . . . 1E **67**
W14 . . . . 3A **72**
Abbotsbury M. SE15 . . 1E **107**
Abbotsbury Rd. W14 . . 3A **72**

Abbotshade Rd. SE16 . . 2F **79**
Abbotshall Rd. SE6 . . . 1F **123**
Abbot's Ho. W14 . . . . . 4B **72**
(off St Mary Abbots Ter.)
Abbots La.
SE1 . . . . 2E **27** (2A **78**)
Abbotsleigh Rd.
SW16 . . . . 4E **117**
Abbots Mnr. SW1 . . . . . 5D **75**
Abbots Pk. SW2 . . . . . 1C **118**
Abbot's Pl. NW6 . . . . . . 5D **45**
Abbot's Rd. E6 . . . . 5F **55**
Abbots Ter. N8 . . . . 1A **34**
Abbotstone Rd.
SW15 . . . . 1E **99**
Abbot St. E8 . . . . 3B **50**
Abbots Wlk. W8 . . . . . . 4D **73**
Abbotswell Rd. SE4 . . 3B **108**
Abbotswood Rd.
SE22 . . . . 2A **106**
SW16 . . . . 3F **117**
Abbott Rd. E14 . . . . 4E **67**
(not continuous)
Abbotts Cl. N1 . . . . 3E **49**
Abbotts Ho. SW1 . . . . . 1F **89**
(off Aylesford St.)
Abbotts Pk. Rd. E10 . . . 2E **39**
Abbotts Wharf E14 . . . 5C **66**
(off Stainsby Pl.)
Abchurch La.
EC4 . . . . 4C **18** (1F **77**)
(not continuous)
Abchurch Yd.
EC4 . . . . 4B **18** (1F **77**)
Abdale Rd. W12 . . . . . . 2D **71**
Abel Ho. SE11 . . . . 2C **90**
(off Kennington Rd.)
Aberavon Rd. E3 . . . . . 2A **66**
Abercorn Cl. NW8 . . . . . 2E **59**
Abercorn Ho. SE10 . . . . 3D **95**
(off Tarves Way)
Abercorn Mans. NW8 . . 1E **59**
(off Abercorn Pl.)
Abercorn Pl. NW8 . . . . . 2E **59**
Abercorn Way SE1 . . . . 1C **92**
Abercrombie St.
SW11 . . . . 5A **88**
Aberdale Ct. SE16 . . . . 3F **79**
(off Garter Way)
Aberdare Gdns. NW6 . . 4D **45**
Aberdeen Ct. W9 . . . . . 3E **59**
(off Maida Va.)
Aberdeen La. N5 . . . . . . 2E **49**
Aberdeen Mans. WC1 . . 3D **7**
(off Kenton St.)
Aberdeen Pk. N5 . . . . . 2E **49**
Aberdeen Pl. NW8 . . . . 3F **59**
Aberdeen Rd. N5 . . . . . 1E **49**
NW10 . . . . 2B **42**
Aberdeen Sq. E14 . . . . 2B **80**
Aberdeen Ter. SE3 . . . . 5F **95**
Aberdeen Wharf E1 . . . 2D **79**
(off Wapping High St.)
Aberdour St. SE1 . . . . . 5A **78**

Aberfeldy Ho. SE5 . . . . 3D **91**
(not continuous)
Aberfeldy St. E14 . . . . . 4E **67**
(not continuous)
Aberford Gdns. SE18 . . 4F **97**
Abergeldie Rd.
SE12 . . . . 4D **111**
Abernethy Rd. SE13 . . 2A **110**
Abersham Rd. E8 . . . . . 2B **50**
Abingdon W14 . . . . 5B **72**
(off Kensington Village)
Abingdon Cl. NW1 . . . . . 3F **47**
SE1 . . . . 5B **78**
(off Bushwood Dr.)
Abingdon Ct. W8 . . . . . 4C **72**
(off Abingdon Vs.)
Abingdon Gdns. W8 . . . 4C **72**
Abingdon Ho. E2 . . . . . . 3F **11**
(off Boundary St.)
Abingdon Lodge W8 . . . 4C **72**
Abingdon Rd. W8 . . . . . 4C **72**
Abingdon St.
SW1 . . . . 5D **23** (4A **76**)
Abingdon Vs. W8 . . . . . 4C **72**
Abinger Gro. SE8 . . . . . 2B **94**
Abinger Ho. SE1 . . . . . . 4B **26**
(off Gt. Dover St.)
Abinger M. W9 . . . . 3C **58**
Abinger Rd. W4 . . . . . . 4A **70**
Ablett St. SE16 . . . . . . 1E **93**
Abney Gdns. N16 . . . . . 4B **36**
Abney Pk. Ter. N16 . . . . 4B **36**
(off Cazenov Rd.)
Aboyne Rd. NW10 . . . . . 5A **28**
SW17 . . . . 3F **115**
Abyssinia Cl. SW11 . . . 2A **102**
Abyssinia Rd.
SW11 . . . . 2A **102**
Acacia Bus. Cen.
E11 . . . . 5A **40**
Acacia Cl. SE8 . . . . 5A **80**
Acacia Gdns. NW8 . . . . 1F **59**
Acacia Gro. SE21 . . . . 2F **119**
Acacia Pl. NW8 . . . . . . 1F **59**
Acacia Rd. E11 . . . . 4A **40**
E17 . . . . 1A **38**
NW8 . . . . 1F **59**
Academy Apartments
E8 . . . . 2D **51**
(off Dalston La.)
E8 . . . . 2D **51**
(off Institute Pl.)
Academy Bldgs. N1 . . . 1D **11**
(off Fanshaw St.)
Academy Ct. E2 . . . . . . 2E **65**
(off Kirkwall Pl.)
Academy Gdns. W8 . . . 3C **72**
Academy Ho. E3 . . . . . 4D **67**
(off Violet Rd.)
Acanthus Dr. SE1 . . . . 1C **92**
Acanthus Rd. SW11 . . . 1C **102**
Accommodation Rd.
NW11 . . . . 3B **30**

Acfold Rd. 4D **87**
Achilles Cl. SE1 . . . . . . 1C **92**
Achilles Ho. E2 . . . . 1D **65**
(off Old Bethnal Grn. Rd.)
Achilles Rd. NW6 . . . . . . 2C **44**
Achilles Statue
. . . . 2C 20 (2C **74**)
Achilles St. SE14 . . . . . . 3A **94**
Achilles Way
W1 . . . . 2C 20 (2C **74**)
Acklam Rd. W10 . . . . . . 4A **58**
(not continuous)
Ackmar Rd. SW6 . . . . . . 4C **86**
Ackroyd Dr. E3 . . . . . . 4B **66**
Ackroyd Rd. SE23 . . . . . 5F **107**
Acland Cres. SE5 . . . 1F **105**
Acland Ho. SW9 . . . . . . 4B **90**
Acland Rd. NW2 . . . . . . 3D **43**
Acme Ho. E14 . . . . 4E **67**
Acol Cl. NW6 . . . . 4C **44**
Acol Rd. NW6 . . . . 4C **44**
Acorn Ct. E6 . . . . 4F **55**
Acorn Gdns. W3 . . . . . . 4A **56**
Acorn Pde. SE15 . . . . . . 3D **93**
Acorn Production Cen.
N7 . . . . 4A **48**
Acorn Wlk. SE16 . . . . . . 2A **80**
Acorn Way SE23 . . . . . 3F **121**
Acre Dr. SE22 . . . . 2C **106**
Acre Rd. SW19 . . . . . . 5F **115**
Acris St. SW18 . . . . . . 3E **101**
Acton Ho. E8 . . . . 5B **50**
(off Lee St.)
Acton La. NW10 . . . . . . 1A **56**
Acton M. E8 . . . . 5B **50**
Acton Pk. Est. W3 . . . . . 3A **70**
Acton St. WC1 . . . 2F 7 (2B **62**)
Acton Va. Ind. Pk.
W3 . . . . 3B **70**
Acuba Rd. SW18 . . . . . 2D **115**
Ada Ct. N1 . . . . 5E **49**
(off Packington St.)
W9 . . . . 2E **59**
Ada Gdns. E14 . . . . 5F **67**
E15 . . . . 5B **54**
Ada Ho. E2 . . . . 5C **50**
(off Ada Pl.)
Adair Rd. W10 . . . . 3A **58**
Adair Twr. W10 . . . . 3A **58**
(off Appleford Rd.)
Ada Kennedy Ct.
SE10 . . . . 3E **95**
(off Greenwich Sth. St.)
Adam & Eve Ct. W1 . . . . 2A **14**
Adam & Eve M. W8 . . . . 4C **72**
Adam Cl. SE6 . . . . 4B **122**
Adam Ct. SE11 . . . . 5D **77**
(off Opal St.)
SW7 . . . . 5E **73**
(off Gloucester Rd.)
Adams Ct. E17 . . . . 1A **38**
EC2 . . . . 2C 18 (5A **64**)
Adams Gdns. Est.
SE16 . . . . 3E **79**
Adams Ho. E14 . . . . 5F **67**
(off Aberfeldy St.)
Adams M. SW17 . . . . . 2B **116**
Adamson Rd. E16 . . . . . 5C **68**
NW3 . . . . 4F **45**

Adams Pl. E14 . . . . 2D **81**
(off Nth. Colonnade, The)
N7 . . . . 2B **48**
Adamsrill Rd. SE26 . . . . 4F **121**
Adam's Row
W1 . . . . 5C 12 (1C **74**)
Adam St.
WC2 . . . . 5E 15 (1A **76**)
Adam Wlk. SW6 . . . . . . 3E **85**
Ada Pl. E2 . . . . 5C **50**
Adare Wlk. SW16 . . . . . 3B **118**
Ada Rd. SE5 . . . . 3A **92**
Adastral Ho. WC1 . . . . . . 5F 7
(off New North St.)
Ada St. E8 . . . . 5D **51**
Ada Workshops E8 . . . . 5D **51**
Adderley Gro.
SW11 . . . . 3C **102**
Adderley St. E14 . . . . . . 5E **67**
Addey Ho. SE8 . . . . 3B **94**
Addington Ct.
SW14 . . . . 1A **98**
Addington Gro.
SE26 . . . . 4A **122**
Addington Ho. SW9 . . . . 5B **90**
(off Stockwell Rd.)
Addington Rd. E3 . . . . . 2C **66**
E16 . . . . 3A **68**
N4 . . . . 1C **34**
Addington Sq. SE5 . . . . 2F **91**
(not continuous)
Addington St.
SE1 . . . . 4A 24 (3B **76**)
Addis Ho. E1 . . . . 4E **65**
(off Lindley St.)
Addisland Ct. W14 . . . . . 3A **72**
(off Holland Vs. Rd.)
Addison Av. W11 . . . . . . 2A **72**
Addison Bri. Pl. W14 . . . 5B **72**
Addison Cres. W14 . . . . 4A **72**
(not continuous)
Addison Dr. SE12 . . . . . 3D **111**
Addison Gdns. W14 . . . . 4F **71**
Addison Gro. W4 . . . . . . 4A **70**
Addison Ho. NW8 . . . . . 2F **59**
(off Grove End Rd.)
Addison Pk. Mans.
W14 . . . . 4F **71**
(off Richmond Way)
Addison Pl. W11 . . . . . . 2A **72**
Addison Rd. E11 . . . . . . 1C **40**
W14 . . . . 3A **72**
Addle Hill
EC4 . . . . 3E 17 (5D **63**)
Addlestone Ho. W10 . . . . 4E **57**
(off Sutton Way)
Addle St.
EC2 . . . . 2A 18 (5E **63**)
Addy Ho. SE16 . . . . 5E **79**
Adela Ho. W6 . . . . 1E **85**
(off Queen Caroline St.)
Adelaide Av. SE4 . . . . . 2B **108**
Adelaide Cl. SW9 . . . . . 2C **104**
Adelaide Ct. NW8 . . . . . 1E **59**
(off Abbey Rd.)
Adelaide Gro. W12 . . . . 2C **70**
Adelaide Ho. E15 . . . . . 1B **68**
SE5 . . . . 5A **92**
W11 . . . . 5B **58**
(off Portobello Rd.)

Adelaide Rd. E10 . . . . . 5D **39**
NW3 . . . . 4F **45**
SW18 . . . . 3C **100**
Adelaide St.
WC2 . . . . 5D 15 (1A **76**)
Adela St. W10 . . . . 3A **58**
Adelina Gro. E1 . . . . . . 4E **65**
Adelina M. SW12 . . . . . 1F **117**
Adelina Yd. E1 . . . . 4E **65**
(off Adelina Gro.)
Adeline Pl.
WC1 . . . . 1C 14 (4F **61**)
Adelphi Ct. E8 . . . . 4B **50**
(off Celandine Dr.)
SE16 . . . . 3F **79**
(off Garter Way)
W4 . . . . 2A **84**
Adelphi Ter.
WC2 . . . . 5E 15 (1A **76**)
Adelphi Theatre 5E **15**
(off Strand)
Adeney Cl. W6 . . . . 2F **85**
Aden Gro. N16 . . . . 1F **49**
Aden Ho. E1 . . . . 4F **65**
(off Duckett St.)
Adenmore Rd. SE6 . . . . 5C **108**
Aden M. SW12 . . . . 3F **117**
Aden Ter. N16 . . . . 1F **49**
Adeyfield Ho. EC1 . . . . . 2C **10**
(off Cranwood St.)
Adie Rd. W6 . . . . 4E **71**
Adine Rd. E13 . . . . 3D **69**
Adler St. E1 . . . . 5C **64**
Adley St. E5 . . . . 2A **52**
Admiral Ct. SW10 . . . . . 4E **87**
(off Admiral Sq.)
W1 . . . . 1B **12**
(off Blandford St.)
Admiral Ho. SW1 . . . . . . 5E **75**
(off Willow Pl.)
Admiral Hyson Ind. Est.
SE16 . . . . 1D **93**
Admiral M. W10 . . . . . . 3F **57**
Admiral Pl. SE16 . . . . . . 2A **80**
Admirals Ct. SE1 . . . . . . 2F **27**
(off Horselydown La.)
Admiral's Ga. SE10 . . . . 4D **95**
Admiral Sq. SW10 . . . . . 4E **87**
Admiral St. SE8 . . . . . . 5C **94**
Admirals Wlk. NW3 . . . . 5E **31**
Admirals Way E14 . . . . . 3C **80**
Admiralty Arch
. . . . 1C 22 (2F **75**)
Admiralty Cl. SE8 . . . . . 3C **94**
Admiral Wlk. W9 . . . . . . 4C **58**
Adolf St. SE6 . . . . 4D **123**
Adolphus Rd. N4 . . . . . . 4D **35**
Adolphus St. SE8 . . . . . 3B **94**
Adpar St. W2 . . . . 4F **59**
Adrian Av. NW2 . . . . . . 3D **29**
Adrian Boult Ho. E2 . . . . 2D **65**
(off Mansford St.)
Adrian Ho. N1 . . . . 5B **48**
(off Barnsbury Est.)
SW8 . . . . 3A **90**
(off Wyvil Rd.)
Adrian M. SW10 . . . . . . 2D **87**
Adriatic Bldg. E14 . . . . . 1A **80**
(off Horseferry Rd.)
Adriatic Ho. E1 . . . . 3F **65**
(off Ernest St.)

Adron Ho. *SE16* *5E 79*
   (off Millender Wlk.)
Adstock Ho. *N1* *4D 49*
   (off Sutton Est., The)
Advance Rd. *SE27* *4E 119*
Adventurers Ct. *E14* *1F 81*
   (off Newport Av.)
Adys Lawn *NW2* *3D 43*
Ady's Rd. *SE15* *1B 106*
Aegean Apartments
   E16 . . . . *1C 82*
   (off Western Gateway)
Aegon Ho. *E14* *4D 81*
   (off Lanark Sq.)
Affleck St. *N1* . . . . . *1F 7 (1B 62)*
Afghan Rd. *SW11* *5A 88*
Afsil Ho. *EC1* *1C 16*
   (off Viaduct Bldgs.)
Aftab Ter. *E1* *3D 65*
   (off Tent St.)
Agamemnon Rd.
   NW6 . . . . *1B 44*
Agar Gro. *NW1* *4E 47*
Agar Gro. Est. *NW1* *4F 47*
Agar Pl. *NW1* *4E 47*
Agar St.
   WC2 . . . . . *5D 15 (1A 76)*
Agate Cl. *E16* *5F 69*
Agate Rd. *W6* *4E 71*
Agatha Cl. *E1* *2D 79*
Agave Rd. *NW2* *1E 43*
Agdon St. *EC1* . . . *3D 9 (3D 63)*
Agincourt Rd. *NW3* *1B 46*
Agnes Ho. *W11* *1F 71*
   (off St Ann's Rd.)
Agnes Rd. *W3* *2B 70*
Agnes St. *E14* *5B 66*
Agnew Rd. *SE23* *5F 107*
Aigburth Mans. *SW9* *3C 90*
   (off Mowll St.)
Aileen Wlk. *E15* *4B 54*
Ailsa St. *E14* *4E 67*
Ainger M. *NW3* *4B 46*
   (off Ainger Rd., not continuous)
Ainger Rd. *NW3* *4B 46*
Ainsdale *NW1* *1F 5*
   (off Harrington St.)
Ainsdale Dr. *SE1* *1C 92*
Ainsley St. *E2* *2D 65*
Ainslie Wlk. *SW12* *5D 103*
Ainsty Est. *SE16* *3F 79*
Ainsty St. *SE16* *3E 79*
Ainsworth Cl. *NW2* *5C 28*
   SE15 . . . . *5A 92*
Ainsworth Ho. *NW8* *5D 45*
   (off Ainsworth Way)
Ainsworth Rd. *E9* *4E 51*
Ainsworth Way *NW8* *5E 45*
Aintree Av. *E6* *5F 55*
Aintree Est. *SW6* *3A 86*
   (off Aintree St.)
Aintree St. *SW6* *3A 86*
Aird Ho. *SE1* *5F 25*
   (off Rockingham St.)
Airdrie Cl. *N1* *4B 48*
Airedale Av. *W4* *5B 70*
Airedale Av. Sth. *W4* *1B 84*
Airedale Rd. *SW12* *5B 102*
Airlie Gdns. *W8* *2C 72*
Air St. *W1* . . . . *5A 14 (1E 75)*

Aisgill Av. *W14* *1B 86*
   (not continuous)
Aislibie Rd. *SE12* *2A 110*
Aiten Pl. *W6* *5C 70*
Aithan Ho. *E14* *5B 66*
   (off Copenhagen Pl.)
Aitken Cl. *E8* *5C 50*
Aitken Rd. *SE6* *2D 123*
Ajax Ho. *E2* *1D 65*
   (off Old Bethnal Grn. Rd.)
Ajax Rd. *NW6* *1B 44*
Akbar Ho. *E14* *5D 81*
   (off Cahir St.)
Akehurst St. *SW15* *4C 98*
Akenside Rd. *NW3* *2F 45*
Akerman Rd. *SW9* *5D 91*
Akintaro Ho. *SE8* *2B 94*
   (off Alverton St.)
Alamaro Lodge
   SE10 . . . . *4B 82*
Aland Ct. *SE16* *4A 80*
Alan Hocken Way
   E15 . . . . *1A 68*
Alan Preece Ct. *NW6* . . . *4F 43*
Alan Rd. *SW19* *5A 114*
Alanthus Cl. *SE12* *4C 110*
Alaska Bldgs. *SE1* *5A 78*
Alaska St.
   SE1 . . . . *2B 24 (2C 76)*
Alastor Ho. *E14* *4E 81*
   (off Strattondale Ho.)
Albacore Cres.
   SE13 . . . . *4D 109*
Alba Gdns. *NW11* *1A 30*
Alba M. *SW18* *2C 114*
Alban Highwalk *EC2* *2A 18*
   (not continuous)
Albany *W1* . . . . . *5F 13 (1E 75)*
Albany Ct. *E10* *2C 38*
   NW8 . . . . *1F 59*
   (off Abbey Rd.)
   NW10 . . . . *2D 57*
   (off Trenmar Gdns.)
Albany Courtyard
   W1 . . . . *5A 14 (1E 75)*
Albany Mans. *SW11* *3A 88*
Albany M.
   BR1: Brom *5C 124*
   N1 . . . . *4C 48*
   SE5 . . . . *2E 91*
Albany Pl. *N7* *1C 48*
Albany Rd. *E10* *2C 38*
   E12 . . . . *1F 55*
   E17 . . . . *1A 38*
   N4 . . . . *1C 34*
   SE5 . . . . *2E 91*
   SW19 . . . . *5D 115*
Albany St.
   NW1 . . . . *1E 5 (1D 61)*
Albany Ter. *NW1* *4E 5*
Alba Pl. *W11* *5B 58*
Albatross Way *SE16* *3F 79*
Albemarle *SW19* *2F 113*
Albemarle Ho. *SE8* *5B 80*
   (off Foreshore)
   SW9 . . . . *1C 104*
Albemarle St.
   W1 . . . . *5E 13 (1D 75)*
Albemarle Way
   EC1 . . . . *4D 9 (3D 63)*

Alberta Est. *SE17* *1D 91*
   (off Alberta St.)
Alberta Ho. *E14* *2E 81*
   (off Gaselee St.)
Alberta St. *SE17* *1D 91*
Albert Av. *SW8* *3B 90*
Albert Barnes Ho.
   SE1 . . . . *4E 77*
   (off New Kent Rd.)
Albert Bigg Point *E15* . . . *1E 67*
   (off Godfrey St.)
Albert Bri. *SW8* *3A 88*
Albert Bri. Rd. *SW11* *3A 88*
Albert Carr Gdns.
   SW16 . . . . *5A 118*
Albert Cl. *E9* *5D 51*
Albert Cotts. *E1* *4C 64*
   (off Deal St.)
Albert Ct. *E7* *1C 54*
   SW7 . . . . *4F 73*
Albert Ct. Ga. *SW7* *3B 74*
   (off Knightsbridge)
Albert Dr. *SW19* *2A 114*
Albert Emb.
   SE1 . . . . *5F 23 (4B 76)*
   (Lambeth Pal. Rd.)
   SE1 . . . . *1A 90*
   (Vauxhall Bri.)
Albert Gdns. *E1* *5F 65*
Albert Ga.
   SW1 . . . . *3A 20 (3B 74)*
Albert Gray Ho.
   SW10 . . . . *3F 87*
   (off Worlds End Est.)
Albert Hall Mans.
   SW7 . . . . *3F 73*
   (not continuous)
Albert Memorial *3F 73*
Albert M. *E14* *1A 80*
   (off Northey St.)
   N4 . . . . *3B 34*
   SE4 . . . . *2A 108*
   W8 . . . . *4E 73*
Albert Pal. Mans.
   SW11 . . . . *4D 89*
   (off Lurline Gdns.)
Albert Pl. *W8* *4D 73*
Albert Rd. *E10* *4E 39*
   E16 . . . . *2F 83*
   E17 . . . . *1C 38*
   N4 . . . . *3B 34*
   N15 . . . . *1A 36*
   NW6 . . . . *1B 58*
Albert Sq. *E15* *2A 54*
   SW8 . . . . *3B 90*
Albert Starr Ho. *SE8* *5F 79*
   (off Bush Rd.)
Albert St. *NW1* *5D 47*
Albert Studios *SW11* *4B 88*
Albert Ter. *NW1* *5C 46*
   W6 . . . . *1C 84*
   (off Beavor La.)
Albert Ter. M. *NW1* *5C 46*
Albert Westcott Ho.
   SE17 . . . . *1D 91*
   (off Middleton Rd.)
Albery Theatre *4D 15*
   (off St Martin's La.)

Albion Av. SW8 . . . . 5F **89**
Albion Bldgs. *N1* *1A **62***
    (off Albion Yd.)
Albion Cl. W2 . . . . 1A **74**
Albion Ct. *W6* *5D **71***
    (off Albion Pl.)
Albion Dr. E8 . . . . 4B **50**
Albion Est. SE16 . . . . . 3F **79**
Albion Gdns. W6 . . . . . 5D **71**
Albion Ga. *W2* *1A **74***
    (off Albion St., not continuous)
Albion Gro. N16 . . . . . . 1A **50**
Albion Ho. *SE8* *3C **94***
    (off Watsons St.)
Albion M. N1 . . . . 5C **48**
  W2 . . . . 1A **74**
  W6 . . . . 5D **71**
Albion Pde. N16 . . . . . . 1F **49**
Albion Pl.
  EC1 . . . . 5D **9** (4D **63**)
  EC2 . . . . 1C **18** (4F **63**)
  W6 . . . . 5D **71**
Albion Rd. N16 . . . . 1F **49**
Albion Sq. E8 . . . . 4B **50**
    (not continuous)
Albion St. SE16 . . . . . . 3E **79**
  W2 . . . . 5A **60**
Albion Ter. E8 . . . . 4B **50**
Albion Vs. Rd.
  SE26 . . . . 3E **121**
Albion Wlk. *N1* *1A **62***
    (off York Way)
Albion Way
  EC1 . . . . 1F **17** (4E **63**)
  SE13 . . . . 2E **109**
Albion Wharf SW11 . . . 3A **88**
Albion Yd. E1 . . . . 4D **65**
  N1 . . . . 1A **62**
Albon Ho. *SW18* *4D **101***
    (off Neville Gill Cl.)
Albrighton Rd. SE22 . . 1A **106**
Albury Ho. *SE1* *4E **25***
    (off Boyfield St.)
Albury M. E12 . . . . 4E **41**
Albury St. SE8 . . . . 2C **94**
Albyn Rd. SE8 . . . . 4C **94**
Alcester Cres. E5 . . . . . 4D **37**
Alconbury Rd. E5 . . . . . 4C **36**
Aldam Pl. N16 . . . . 4B **36**
Aldbourne Rd. W12 . . . 2B **70**
    (not continuous)
Aldbridge St. SE17 . . . . 1A **92**
Aldburgh M.
  W1 . . . . 2C **12** (5C **60**)
    (not continuous)
Aldbury Ho. *SW3* *5A **74***
    (off Marlborough St.)
Aldebert Ter. SW8 . . . . . 3A **90**
Aldeburgh Cl. E5 . . . . . 4D **37**
Aldeburgh Pl. *SE10* . . . *5C **82***
    (off Aldeburgh St.)
Aldeburgh St. SE10 . . . 1C **96**
Alden Av. E15 . . . . 2B **68**
Aldenham Ho. *NW1* . . . *1A **6***
    (off Aldenham St.)
Aldenham St.
  NW1 . . . . 1A **6** (1E **61**)
Alden Ho. *E8* *5D **51***
    (off Duncan Rd.)
Aldensley Rd. W6 . . . . . 4D **71**

Alderbrook Rd.
  SW12 . . . . 4D **103**
Alderbury Rd. SW13 . . . 2C **84**
Alder Cl. SE15 . . . . 2B **92**
Alder Gro. NW2 . . . . . . 4C **28**
Alder Ho. NW3 . . . . 3B **46**
  SE4 . . . . 1C **108**
  SE15 . . . . *2B **92***
    (off Cator St.)
Alder Lodge SW6 . . . . . 4E **85**
Aldermanbury
  EC2 . . . . . . 2A **18** (5E **63**)
Aldermanbury Sq.
  EC2 . . . . . . 1A **18** (4E **63**)
Aldermans Wlk.
  EC2 . . . . . . 1D **19** (4A **64**)
Aldermoor Rd. SE6 . . . 3B **122**
Alderney Ho. *N1* *3E **49***
    (off Arran Wlk.)
Alderney Rd. E1 . . . . . . 3F **65**
Alderney St. SW1 . . . . . 5D **75**
Alders, The SW16 . . . . 4E **117**
ALDERSBROOK 4D **41**
Aldersbrook Rd. E11 . . 4D **41**
  E12 . . . . 4D **41**
Alders Cl. E11 . . . . 4D **41**
Aldersford Cl. SE4 . . . 3F **107**
Aldersgate St.
  EC1 . . . . 5F **9** (4E **63**)
Aldersgrove Av.
  SE9 . . . . 3F **125**
Aldershot Rd. NW6 . . . . 5B **44**
Alderson St. W10 . . . . . 3A **58**
Alderton Cl. NW10 . . . . 5A **28**
Alderton Cres. NW4 . . . 1D **29**
Alderton Rd. SE24 . . . 1E **105**
Alderton Way NW4 . . . 1D **29**
Alderville Rd. SW6 . . . . 5B **86**
Alderwick Ct. *N7* *3B **48***
    (off Cornelia St.)
Aldford Ho. *W1* *1B **20***
    (off Park St.)
Aldford St.
  W1 . . . . 1C **20** (2C **74**)
ALDGATE 5B **64**
Aldgate *E1* *2F **19***
    (off Whitechapel High St.)
  EC3 . . . . . . 3E **19** (5A **64**)
Aldgate Av.
  E1 . . . . 2F **19** (5B **64**)
Aldgate Barrs E1 . . . . . 2F **19**
Aldgate High St.
  EC3 . . . . . . 3F **19** (5B **64**)
Aldgate Triangle *E1* . . *5C **64***
    (off Coke St.)
Aldham Ho. *SE14* *5B **94***
    (off Malpas Rd.)
Aldine Ct. *W12* *3E **71***
    (off Aldine St.)
Aldine Pl. W12 . . . . 3E **71**
Aldine St. W12 . . . . 3E **71**
Aldington Ct. *E8* *4C **50***
    (off London Flds. W. Side)
Aldington Rd. SE18 . . . 4F **83**
Aldis M. SW17 . . . . 5A **116**
Aldis St. SW17 . . . . 5A **116**
Aldred Rd. NW6 . . . . . . 2C **44**
Aldren Rd. SW17 . . . . . 3E **115**
Aldrich Ter. SW18 . . . . 2E **115**

Aldrick Ho. *N1* *5B **48***
    (off Barnsbury Est.)
Aldridge Rd. Vs.
  W11 . . . . 4B **58**
Aldridge Rd.
  SW16 . . . . 5E **117**
Aldsworth Cl. W9 . . . . . 3D **59**
Aldworth Gro. SE13 . . . 4E **109**
Aldworth Rd. E15 . . . . . 4A **54**
Aldwych WC2 . . . 4F **15** (5B **62**)
Aldwych Ct. *E8* *4B **50***
    (off Middleton Rd.)
Aldwych Theatre 3F **15**
    (off Aldwych)
Aldwyn Ho. *SW8* *3A **90***
    (off Davidson Gdns.)
Alestan Beck Rd. E16 . . 5F **69**
Alexa Ct. W8 . . . . 5C **72**
Alexander Av. NW10 . . . 4D **43**
Alexander Evans M.
  SE23 . . . . 2F **121**
Alexander Fleming Mus.
   . . . . 5F **59**
    (off Praed St.)
Alexander Ho. *E14* . . . *4C **80***
    (off Tiller Rd.)
Alexander M. W2 . . . . . 5D **59**
Alexander Pl. SW7 . . . . 5A **74**
Alexander Rd. N19 . . . . 5A **34**
Alexander Sq. SW3 . . . . 5A **74**
Alexander St. W2 . . . . . 5C **58**
Alexander Studios
  SW11 . . . . *2F **101***
    (off Haydon Way)
Alexandra Av. SW11 . . . 4C **88**
  W4 . . . . 3A **84**
Alexandra Cl. SE8 . . . . 2B **94**
Alexandra Cotts.
  SE14 . . . . 4B **94**
Alexandra Ct. *SW7* . . . *4E **73***
    (off Queen's Ga.)
  W2 . . . . *1D **73***
    (off Moscow Rd.)
  W9 . . . . *3E **59***
    (off Maida Va.)
Alexandra Cres.
  BR1: Brom 5B **124**
Alexandra Dr. SE19 . . . 5A **120**
Alexandra Gdns. W4 . . . 3A **84**
Alexandra Gro. N4 . . . . 3D **35**
Alexandra Ho. *E16* . . . *2D **83***
    (off Wesley Av.)
  W6 . . . . *1E **85***
    (off Queen Caroline St.)
Alexandra Mans.
  SW3 . . . . *2F **87***
    (off King's Rd.)
Alexandra M. SW19 . . . 5B **114**
Alexandra National Ho.
  N4 . . . . 3D **35**
Alexandra Pl. NW8 . . . . 5E **45**
Alexandra Rd. E10 . . . . 5E **39**
  E17 . . . . 1B **38**
  NW8 . . . . 5E **45**
  SE26 . . . . 5F **121**
  SW14 . . . . 1A **98**
  SW19 . . . . 5B **114**
  W4 . . . . 3A **70**
Alexandra St. E16 . . . . . 4C **68**
  SE14 . . . . 3A **94**

Alexandra Ter. E14..... 1D *95*
(off Westferry Rd.)
Alexandra Wlk.
SE19....................5A *120*
Alexandra Yd. E9......5F *51*
Alexis St. SE16......5C *78*
Alfearn Rd. E5......1E *51*
Alford Ct. N1..........1A *10*
(off Shepherdess Wlk.,
not continuous)
Alford Ho. N6......1E *33*
Alford Pl. N1...1A 10 (1E *63*)
Alfreda St. SW11......4D *89*
Alfred Ho. E9..........2A *52*
(off Homerton Rd.)
E12..................4F *55*
(off Tennyson Av.)
Alfred M. W1....5B 6 (4F *61*)
Alfred Nunn Ho.
NW10..................5B *42*
Alfred Pl. WC1...5B 6 (4F *61*)
Alfred Rd. E15........2B *54*
W2....................4C *58*
Alfred St. E3..........2B *66*
Alfreton Cl. SW19.....3F *113*
Alfriston Rd. SW11....3B *102*
Algar Ho. SE1.........4D *25*
Algarve Rd. SW18....1D *115*
Algernon Rd. NW4.....1C *28*
NW6..................5C *44*
SE13.................2D *109*
Algiers Rd. SE13.....2C *108*
Alice Gilliatt Ct. W14...2B *86*
(off Star Rd.)
Alice La. E3..........5B *52*
Alice Owen Technology Cen.
EC1..................1D *9*
(off Goswell Rd.)
Alice Shepherd Ho.
E14....................3E *81*
(off Manchester Rd.)
Alice St. SE1...5D 27 (4A *78*)
(Decima St.)
SE1.........5D 27 (4A *78*)
(Rothsay St.)
Alice Thompson Cl.
SE12..................2E *125*
Alice Walker Cl.
SE24..................2D *105*
Alison Ct. SE1........1C *92*
Aliwal M. SW11.......2A *102*
Aliwal Rd. SW11......2A *102*
Alkerden Rd. W4......1A *84*
Alkham Rd. N16.......4B *36*
Allan Barclay Cl. N15...1B *36*
Allanson Ct. E10......4C *38*
(off Leyton Grange Est.)
Allard Gdns. SW4.....3F *103*
Allardyce St. SW4....2B *104*
Allcott Ho. W12.......5D *57*
(off Du Cane Rd.)
Allcroft Rd. NW5.....2C *46*
Allenby Rd. SE23....3A *122*
Allen Ct. E17.........1C *38*
(off Yunus Khan Cl.)
Allendale Cl. SE5....5F *91*
SE26..................5F *121*
Allen Edwards Dr.
SW8....................4A *90*

Allenford Ho. SW15....4B *98*
(off Tunworth Cres.)
Allen Rd. E3..........1B *66*
N16..................1A *50*
Allensbury Pl. NW1....4F *47*
Allen St. W8..........4C *72*
Allenswood SW19.....1A *114*
Allerford Rd. SE6....3D *123*
Allerton Ho. N1........1B *10*
(off Fairbank Est.)
Allerton Rd. N16......4E *35*
Allerton St.
N1...............1B 10 (2F *63*)
Allerton Wlk. N7.....4B *34*
Allestree Rd. SW6....3A *86*
Alleyn Cres. SE21....2F *119*
Alleyn Ho. SE1.......5C *26*
(off Burbage Cl.)
Alleyn Pk. SE21......2F *119*
Alleyn Rd. SE21......3F *119*
Allfarthing La.
SW18..................4D *101*
Allgood St. E2.......1B *64*
Allhallows La.
EC4............5B 18 (1F *77*)
Allhallows Rd. E6.....4F *69*
Alliance Rd. E13.....5E *69*
Allied Ind. Est. W3....3A *70*
Allied Way W3........3A *70*
Allingham M. N1......1E *63*
(off Allingham St.)
Allingham St. N1......1E *63*
Allington Cl. SW19....5F *113*
Allington Ct. SW1.....5E *21*
(off Allington St.)
SW8..................5E *89*
Allington Rd. NW4....1D *29*
W10..................2A *58*
Allington St.
SW1...........5E 21 (4D *75*)
Allison Cl. SE10......4E *95*
Allison Gro. SE21....1A *120*
Alliston Ho. E2........2B *64*
(off Gibraltar Wlk.)
Allitsen Rd. NW8......1A *60*
(not continuous)
All Nations Ho. E8....4D *51*
(off Martello St.)
Allnutt Way SW4......3F *103*
Alloa Rd. SE8.........1F *93*
Allom Ho. W11........1A *72*
(off Clarendon Rd.)
Allonby Ho. E14......4A *66*
(off Aston St.)
Alloway Rd. E3.......2A *66*
Allport Ho. SE5......1F *105*
(off Denmark Hill)
Allport M. E1.........3E *65*
(off Hayfield Pas.)
All Saints Cl. SW8....4A *90*
All Saints Ct. E1......1E *79*
(off Johnson St.)
SW11..................3D *89*
(off Prince of Wales Dr.)
All Saints Dr. SE3...5A *96*
(not continuous)
All Saints Ho. W11....4B *58*
(off All Saints Rd.)
All Saints Pas.
SW18.................3C *100*

All Saints Rd. W11....4B *58*
All Saints St. N1.....1B *62*
All Saints Twr. E10...2D *39*
Allsop Pl.
NW1..............4A 4 (3B *60*)
All Souls Av. NW10...1D *57*
All Souls' Pl.
W1.............1E 13 (4D *61*)
Allwood Cl. SE26....4F *121*
Alma Birk Ho. NW6....4A *44*
Almack Rd. E5........1E *51*
Alma Gro. SE1........5B *78*
Alma Pl. NW10.......2D *57*
Alma Rd. SW18.......2E *101*
Alma Sq. NW8........1E *69*
Alma St. E15.........3F *53*
NW5..................3D *47*
Alma Ter. E3..........5B *52*
(off Beale Rd.)
SW18..................5F *101*
W8....................4C *72*
Almeida St. N1.......5D *49*
Almeida Theatre......5D *49*
(off Almeida St.)
Almeric Rd. SW11.....2B *102*
Almington St. N4......3B *34*
Almond Cl. SE15......5C *92*
Almond Rd. SE16......5D *79*
Almorah Rd. N1.......4F *49*
Alnwick Rd. E16......5E *69*
SE12.................4D *111*
Alperton St. W10......3B *58*
Alphabet Sq. E3......4C *66*
Alpha Bus. Cen. E17...1R *38*
Alpha Cl. NW1........3A *60*
Alpha Gro. E14.......3C *80*
Alpha Ho. NW6.......1C *58*
NW8..................3A *60*
(off Ashbridge St.)
SW4..................2B *104*
Alpha Pl. NW6........1C *58*
SW3..................2A *88*
Alpha Rd. SE14.......4B *94*
Alpha St. SE15........5C *92*
Alpine Gro. E9........4E *51*
Alpine Rd. E10........4D *39*
SE16.................5E *79*
Alric Av. NW10........4A *42*
Alroy Rd. N4..........2C *34*
Alsace Rd. SE17......1A *92*
Alscot Rd.
SE1..............5F 27 (5B *78*)
(not continuous)
SE1..................4B *78*
Alscot Way SE1.......5B *78*
Alston Rd. SW17......4F *115*
Altenburg Gdns.
SW11.................2B *102*
Althea St. SW6.......5D *87*
Althorpe M. SW11.....4F *87*
Althorp Rd. SW17.....1B *116*
Altima Ct. SE22......2C *106*
Altior Cl. N6..........1E *33*
Alton Rd. SW15.......1C *112*
Alton St. E14.........4D *67*
Aluna Ct. SE15.......1E *107*
Alvanley Gdns. NW6...2D *45*
Alverstone Av.
SW19.................2C *114*

Alverstone Ho. SE11 . . . 2C **90**
Alverstone Rd. NW2 . . . 4E **43**
Alverton St. SE8 . . . . . . 1B **94**
   (not continuous)
Alvey St. SE17 . . . . 1A **92**
Alvington Cres. E8 . . . . 2B **50**
Alwold Cres. SE12 . . . 4D **111**
Alwyne La. N1 . . . . 4D **49**
Alwyne Pl. N1 . . . . 3E **49**
Alwyne Rd. N1 . . . . 4E **49**
  SW19 . . . . 5B **114**
Alwyne Sq. N1 . . . . 3E **49**
Alwyne Vs. N1 . . . . 4D **49**
Alyth Gdns. NW11 . . . 1C **30**
Alzette Ho. E2 . . . . 1F **65**
   (off Mace St.)
Amazon St. E1 . . . . 5C **64**
Ambassadors Ct. E8 . . . 4B **50**
   (off Holly St.)
  SW1 . . . . 2A **22**
Ambassador Sq. E14 . . 5D **81**
Ambassadors Theatre
  . . . . 4C **14**
   (off West St.)
Ambergate St. SE17 . . . 1D **91**
Amber Gro. NW2 . . . . . 3F **29**
Amberley Gro.
  SE26 . . . . 5D **121**
Amberley Rd. E10 . . . . 2C **38**
  W9 . . . . 4C **58**
Amber Wharf E2 . . . . . 5B **50**
   (off Nursery La.)
Amblecote Cl. SE12 . . 3D **125**
Amblecote Mdws.
  SE12 . . . . 3D **125**
Amblecote Rd.
  SE12 . . . . 3D **125**
Ambler Rd. N4 . . . . 5D **35**
Ambleside
  BR1: Brom 5F **123**
  NW1 . . . . 1E **5**
  SW19 . . . . 1A **114**
Ambleside Av.
  SW16 . . . . 4F **117**
Ambleside Cl. E9 . . . . . 2E **51**
  E10 . . . . 2D **39**
Ambleside Gdns.
  SW16 . . . . 5F **117**
Ambleside Point
  SE15 . . . . 3E **93**
   (off Tustin Est.)
Ambleside Rd. NW10 . . 4B **42**
Ambrosden Av.
  SW1 . . . . 5A **22** (4E **75**)
Ambrose Av. NW11 . . . 2A **30**
Ambrose Ho. E14 . . . . . 4C **66**
   (off Selsey St.)
Ambrose M. SW11 . . . . 5B **88**
Ambrose St. SE16 . . . . 5D **79**
Ambrose Wlk. E3 . . . . . 1C **66**
Amelia Ho. W6 . . . . 1E **85**
   (off Queen Caroline St.)
Amelia St. SE17 . . . . . . 1E **91**
Amen Cnr.
  EC4 . . . . 3E **17** (5D **63**)
  SW17 . . . . 5B **116**
Amen Ct.
  EC4 . . . . 3E **17** (5D **63**)
America Sq.
  EC3 . . . . 4F **19** (1B **78**)

America St.
  SE1 . . . . 2F **25** (2E **77**)
Amerland Rd.
  SW18 . . . . 3B **100**
Amersham Gro.
  SE14 . . . . 3B **94**
Amersham Rd. SE14 . . 4B **94**
Amersham Va. SE14 . . 3B **94**
Amery Gdns. NW10 . . 5E **43**
Amery Ho. SE17 . . . . . . 1A **92**
   (off Kinglake St.)
Amesbury Av. SW2 . . 2A **118**
Amesbury Twr. SW8 . . 5E **89**
Ames Cotts. E14 . . . . . . 4A **66**
   (off Maroon St.)
Ames Ho. E2 . . . . 1F **65**
   (off Mace St.)
Amethyst Rd. E15 . . . . 1F **53**
AMF Bowling 1E **109**
Amherst Ho. SE16 . . . . 3F **79**
   (off Wolfe Cres.)
Amhurst Pde. N16 . . . . 2B **36**
   (off Amhurst Pk.)
Amhurst Pk. N16 . . . . . 2F **35**
Amhurst Pas. E8 . . . . . 1C **50**
Amhurst Rd. E8 . . . . . . 2D **51**
  N16 . . . . 1B **50**
Amhurst Ter. E8 . . . . . . 1C **50**
Amias Ho. EC1 . . . . 3F **9**
   (off Central St.)
Amiel St. E1 . . . . 3E **65**
Amies St. SW11 . . . . . . 1B **102**
Amigo Ho. SE1 . . . . 5C **24**
   (off Morley St.)
Amina Way SE16 . . . . . 4C **78**
Amity Rd. E15 . . . . 4B **54**
Ammanford Grn.
  NW9 . . . . 1A **28**
Ammonite Ho. E15 . . . . 4B **54**
Amner Rd. SW11 . . . . . 4C **102**
Amor Rd. W6 . . . . 4E **71**
Amory Ho. N1 . . . . 5B **48**
   (off Barnsbury Est.)
Amott Rd. SE15 . . . . . . 1C **106**
Amoy Pl. E14 . . . . 1C **80**
   (not continuous)
Ampthill Est. NW1 . . . . 1E **61**
Ampthill Sq.
  NW1 . . . . 1A **6** (1E **61**)
Ampton Pl.
  WC1 . . . . 2F **7** (2B **62**)
Ampton St.
  WC1 . . . . 2F **7** (2B **62**)
Amroth Cl. SE23 . . . . . 1D **121**
Amroth Grn. NW9 . . . . 1A **28**
Amstel Ct. SE15 . . . . . . 3B **92**
   (off Garnies Cl.)
Amsterdam Rd. E14 . . 4E **81**
Amundsen Ct. E14 . . . . 1C **94**
   (off Napier Av.)
Amwell Ct. Est. N4 . . . . 4E **35**
Amwell St.
  EC1 . . . . 1B **8** (2C **62**)
Amyruth Rd. SE4 . . . . . 3C **108**
Anatola Rd. N19 . . . . . . 4E **33**
Anchor SW18 . . . . 2D **101**
Anchorage Cl.
  SW19 . . . . 5C **114**
Anchorage Ho. E14 . . . 1F **81**
   (off Clove Cres.)

Anchorage Point E14 . . 3B **80**
   (off Cuba St.)
Anchorage Point Ind. Est.
  SE7 . . . . 4E **83**
Anchor & Hope La.
  SE7 . . . . 4D **83**
Anchor Brewhouse
  SE1 . . . . 2F **27** (2B **78**)
Anchor Ct. SW1 . . . . . . 5F **75**
   (off Vauxhall Bri. Rd.)
Anchor Ho. E16 . . . . . . 4B **68**
   (off Barking Rd.)
  E16 . . . . 5E **69**
   (off Prince Regent La.)
  EC1 . . . . 3F **9**
   (off Old St.)
Anchor M. SW12 . . . . . 4D **103**
Anchor Retail Pk. E1 . . 3E **65**
Anchor Rd. E12 . . . . . . 4F **41**
Anchor St. SE16 . . . . . . 5D **79**
Anchor Ter. E1 . . . . 3E **65**
Anchor Wharf E3 . . . . . 4D **67**
   (off Yeo St.)
Anchor Yd.
  EC1 . . . . 3A **10** (3E **63**)
Ancill Cl. W6 . . . . 2A **86**
Ancona Rd. NW10 . . . . 1C **56**
Andalus Rd. SW9 . . . . 1A **104**
Andaman Ho. E1 . . . . . 4A **66**
   (off Duckett St.)
Anderson Cl. W3 . . . . . 5A **56**
Anderson Ct. NW2 . . . . 3E **29**
Anderson Ho. E14 . . . . 1E **81**
   (off Woolmore St.)
  SW17 . . . . 5F **115**
  W12 . . . . 5D **57**
   (off Du Cane Rd.)
Anderson Rd. E9 . . . . . 3F **51**
Anderson Sq. N1 . . . . . 5D **49**
   (off Gaskin St.)
Anderson St. SW3 . . . . 1B **88**
Anderton Cl. SE5 . . . . . 1F **105**
Andover Av. E16 . . . . . . 5F **69**
Andover Pl. NW6 . . . . . 1D **59**
Andover Rd. N7 . . . . . . 4B **34**
Andoversford Ct.
  SE15 . . . . 2A **92**
   (off Bibury Cl.)
Andre St. E8 . . . . 2C **50**
Andrew Borde St.
  WC2 . . . . 2C **14** (5F **61**)
Andrew Ct. SE23 . . . . . 2F **121**
Andrewes Gdns. E6 . . . 5F **69**
Andrewes Highwalk
  EC2 . . . . 1A **18**
Andrewes Ho. EC2 . . . . 1A **18**
Andrew Pl. SW8 . . . . . . 3F **89**
Andrew Reed Ho.
  SW18 . . . . 5A **100**
   (off Linstead Way)
Andrews Crosse WC2 . . 3B **16**
Andrews Ho. NW3 . . . . 4B **46**
   (off Fellows Rd.)
Andrew's Rd. E8 . . . . . . 5D **51**
Andrew St. E14 . . . . 5E **67**
Andrews Wlk. SE17 . . . 2D **91**
Anerley Hill SE19 . . . . . 5B **120**
Aneurin Bevan Ho.
  NW2 . . . . 4D **29**
Anfield Cl. SW12 . . . . . 5E **103**

ANGEL 1C 62
Angela Davies Ind. Est.
SE24. . . . . 2D 105
Angel All. E1 . . . . 5B 64
(off Whitechapel High St.)
Angel Cen., The N1 . . . . 1C 8
Angel Ct.
EC2. . . . . 2C 18 (5F 63)
SW1 . . . . . . 2A 22 (2E 75)
Angel Ga. EC1 . . . . 1E 9
(not continuous)
Angelina Ho. SE15 . . . . 4C 92
(off Goldsmith Rd.)
Angelis Apartments
N1. . . . . 1E 9
(off Graham St.)
Angell Pk. Gdns.
SW9 . . . . 1C 104
Angell Rd. SW9 . . . . . 1C 104
ANGELL TOWN 4C 90
Angell Town Est.
SW9 . . . . 5C 90
Angel M. E1 . . . . 1D 79
N1. . . . . 1C 62
SW15 . . . . 5C 98
Angel Pas.
EC4 . . . . . 5B 18 (1F 77)
Angel Pl. SE1 . . 3B 26 (3F 77)
Angel Sq. EC1 . . . . . . 1D 63
Angel St. EC1 . . 2F 17 (5E 63)
Angel Wlk. W6 . . . . . . 5E 71
Angel Yd. N6 . . . . 3C 32
Angerstein Bus. Pk.
SE10 . . . . 5C 82
Angerstein La. SE3 . . . 4B 96
Anglebury W2. . . . . . . 5C 58
(off Talbot Rd.)
Angler's La. NW5 . . . . 3D 47
Anglesea Ter. W6 . . . . 4D 71
Anglesey Ho. E14 . . . . 5C 66
(off Lindfield St.)
Angles Rd. SW16 . . . . 4A 118
Anglia Ho. E14 . . . . . . 5A 66
(off Salmon La.)
Anglian Rd. E11 . . . . . 5F 39
Anglo Rd. E3 . . . . 1B 66
Angrave Ct. E8 . . . . . . 5B 50
(off Scriven St.)
Angrave Pas. E8 . . . . . 5B 50
Angus Ho. SW2. . . . . . 5F 103
Angus Rd. E13 . . . . . . 2E 69
Angus St. SE14 . . . . . 3A 94
Anhalt Rd. SW11 . . . . 3A 88
Anley Rd. W14 . . . . . . 3F 71
Annabel Cl. E14 . . . . . 5D 67
Anna Cl. E8 . . . . 5B 50
Annandale Rd. SE10 . . 2B 96
W4 . . . . 1A 84
Anna Neagle Cl. E7 . . 1C 54
Anne Compton M.
SE12 . . . . 5B 110
Anne Goodman Ho.
E1. . . . . 5E 65
(off Jubilee St.)
Annesley Cl. NW10 . . . 5A 28
Annesley Ho. SW9 . . . . 4C 90
Annesley Rd. SE3 . . . . 4D 97
Annesley Wlk. N19 . . . 4E 33
Anne St. E13 . . . . 3C 68

Annette Cres. N1 . . . . 4E 49
Annette Rd. N7 . . . . . . 5B 34
(not continuous)
Annie Besant Cl. E3 . . 5B 52
Anning St.
EC2 . . . . 3E 11 (3A 64)
Annis Rd. E9 . . . . 3A 52
Ann La. SW10 . . . . 2F 87
Ann Moss Way SE16 . . 4E 79
Ann's Cl. SW1 . . . . . . 4A 20
Ann's Pl. E1 . . . . 1F 19
Ann Stroud Ct. SE12 . . 3C 110
Ansar Gdns. E17 . . . . 1B 38
Ansdell Rd. SE15 . . . . 5E 93
Ansdell St. W8 . . . . . . 4D 73
Ansdell Ter. W8 . . . . . 4D 73
Ansell Ho. E1 . . . . 4E 65
(off Mile End Rd.)
Ansell Rd. SW17 . . . . . 3A 116
Anselm Rd. SW6 . . . . . 2C 86
Ansford Rd.
BR1: Brom 5E 123
Ansleigh Pl. W11 . . . . 1F 71
Anson Ho. E1 . . . . 3A 66
(off Shandy St.)
SW1 . . . . 2E 89
(off Churchill Gdns.)
Anson Rd. N7 . . . . 1E 47
NW2 . . . . 1D 43
Anstey Ho. E9 . . . . . . 5E 51
(off Templecombe Rd.)
Anstey Rd. SE15 . . . . 1C 106
Anstice Cl. W4 . . . . . . 3A 84
Antenor Ho. F2 . . . . . 1D 65
(off Old Bethnal Grn. Rd.)
Anthony Cope Ct. N1 . . 1C 10
(off Chart St.)
Anthony Ho. NW8 . . . . 3A 60
(off Ashbridge St.)
Anthony St. E1 . . . . . . 5D 65
Antigua Wlk. SE19 . . . 5F 119
Antilles Bay E14 . . . . 3E 81
Antill Rd. E3 . . . . 2A 66
Antill Ter. E1 . . . . 5F 65
Antoine Hgts. SE1 . . . 4D 27
Anton St. E8 . . . . 2C 50
Antony Ho. SE14. . . . . 3F 93
(off Barlborough St.)
SE16 . . . . 5E 79
(off Raymouth Rd.)
Antrim Gro. NW3 . . . . 3B 46
Antrim Ho. E3. . . . . . 5B 52
(off Birdsfield La.)
Antrim Mans. NW3. . . 3B 46
Antrim Rd. NW3. . . . . 3B 46
Apex Ind. Est. NW10 . . 3B 56
Aphrodite Ct. E14. . . . 5C 80
(off Homer Dr.)
Apollo Bldg. E14 . . . . 5C 80
Apollo Bus. Cen. SE8 . . 1F 93
Apollo Ct. E1 . . . . . . 1C 78
(off Thomas More St.)
SW9 . . . . 4C 90
(off Southey Rd.)
Apollo Ho. E2 . . . . . . 1D 65
(off St Jude's Rd.)
N6 . . . . 2D 32
SW10 . . . . 3F 87
(off Milman's St.)
Apollo Pl. E11 . . . . . . 5A 40
SW10 . . . . 3F 87

Apollo Theatre
Soho 4B 14
(off Shaftesbury Av.)
Victoria 4E 75
(off Wilton Rd.)
Apothecary St.
EC4 . . . . 3D 17 (5D 63)
Appach Rd. SW2 . . . . 3C 104
Apple Blossom Ct.
SW8 . . . . 3F 89
(off Pascal St.)
Appleby Cl. N15 . . . . 1F 35
Appleby Rd. E8 . . . . . 4C 50
E16 . . . . 5B 68
Appleby St. E2 . . . . . 1B 64
Appledore Cl.
SW17 . . . . 2B 116
Appleford Ho. W10 . . . 3A 58
(off Bosworth Rd.)
Appleford Rd. W10 . . . 3A 58
Applegarth Ho. SE1 . . 3E 25
SE15. . . . . 3C 92
(off Bird in Bush Rd.)
Applegarth Rd. W14 . . 4F 71
Applegarth Rd. W14 . . 4F 71
Apple Rd. E11 . . . . . . 5A 40
Appleshaw Ho. SE5 . . 1A 106
Appleton Rd. SE9 . . . . 1F 111
Apple Tree Yd.
SW1 . . . . 1A 22 (2E 75)
Applewood Cl. NW2. . . 5D 29
Applewood Dr. E13 . . . 3D 69
Appold St.
EC2 . . . . 5D 11 (4A 64)
Apprentice Way E5 . . 1D 51
Approach, The NW4 . . 1F 29
W3 . . . . 5A 56
Approach Cl. N16. . . . 1A 50
Approach Rd. E2 . . . . 1E 65
April Ct. E2. . . . . 1C 64
(off Teale St.)
April Glen SE23 . . . . 3F 121
April St. E8. . . . . 1B 50
Apsley Cen., The
NW2 . . . . 4C 28
Apsley House. 3C 20
Apsley Ho. E1. . . . . . 4E 65
(off Stepney Way)
NW8 . . . . 1F 59
(off Finchley St.)
Apsley Way NW2 . . . . 4C 28
W1 . . . . . . 3C 20 (3C 74)
(not continuous)
Aquarius Bus. Pk.
NW2 . . . . 3C 28
(off Priestley Way)
Aquila St. NW8 . . . . . 1F 59
Aquinas St.
SE1 . . . . 2C 24 (2C 76)
Arabella Dr. SW15 . . . 2A 98
Arabian Ho. E1. . . . . . 3A 66
(off Ernest St.)
Arabin Rd. SE4. . . . . 2A 108
Aragon Ho. E16 . . . . 2C 82
(off Capulet M.)
Aragon Twr. SE8. . . . . 5B 80
Aral Ho. E1. . . . . 3F 65
(off Ernest St.)
Arapiles Ho. E14 . . . . 5F 67
(off Blair St.)
Arbery Rd. E3. . . . . . 2A 66

Arbon Ct. *N1* *5E 49*
   (off Linton St.)
Arbor Ct. *N16* *4F 35*
Arboretum St. *E3* *3F 49*
   (off Dove Rd.)
Arborfield Cl. *SW2* . . . 1B 118
Arborfield Ho. *E14* *1C 80*
   (off E. India Dock Rd.)
Arbour Ho. *E1* *5F 65*
   (off Arbour Sq.)
Arbour Sq. *E1* *5F 65*
Arbury Ter. *SE26* 3C 120
Arbuthnot Rd. *SE14* . . . *5F 93*
Arbutus St. *E8* *5B 50*
Arcade, The *EC2* *1D 19*
   N7 . . . . *1A 48*
   (off Macready Pl.)
Arcadia Ct. *E1* *2F 19*
Arcadia St. *E14* *5C 66*
Archangel St. *SE16* . . . *3F 79*
Archbishop's Pl.
   SW2 . . . . *5B 104*
Archdale Ct. *W12* *2D 71*
Archdale Ho. *SE1* *5D 27*
   (off Long La.)
Archdale Rd. *SE22* . . . 3B 106
Archel Rd. *W14* *2B 86*
Archer Ho. *SE14* *4A 94*
   SW11 . . . . *4F 87*
   W11 . . . . *1B 72*
   (off Westbourne Gro.)
Archers Lodge *SE16* *1C 92*
   (off Culloden Cl.)
Archer Sq. *SE14* *2A 94*
Archer St.
   W1 . . . . 4B 14 *(1F 75)*
Archery Cl. *W2* *5A 60*
Archery Steps *W2* *1A 74*
   (off St George's Flds.)
Arches, The *NW1* *4D 47*
   SW8 . . . . *3F 89*
   WC2 . . . . *1E 23*
   (off Villiers St.)
Arches Leisure Cen. 2A 96
Archibald M.
   W1 . . . . 5D 13 *(1C 74)*
Archibald Rd. *N7* *1F 47*
Archibald St. *E3* *2C 66*
Archie St.
   SE1 . . . . 4E 27 *(3A 78)*
Arch St. *SE1* *4E 77*
ARCHWAY *4E 33*
Archway Bus. Cen.
   N19 . . . . *5F 33*
Archway Cl. *N19* *4E 33*
   SW19 . . . . 3D 115
   W10 . . . . *4F 57*
Archway Leisure Cen.
   . . . . *4E 33*
Archway Mall *N19* *4E 33*
Archway M. *SW15* . . . 2A 100
   (off Putney Bri. Rd.)
Archway Rd. *N6* *1C 32*
   N19 . . . . *1C 32*
Archway St. *SW13* *1A 98*
Arcola St. *E8* *2B 50*
Arcola Theatre 1B 50
Arctic St. *NW5* *2D 47*
Arcus Rd.
   BR1: Brom 5A 124

Ardbeg Rd. *SE24* 3F 105
Arden Ct. Gdns. *N2* . . . *1F 31*
Arden Cres. *E14* *5C 80*
Arden Est. *N1* *1A 64*
Arden Ho. *N1* 1D 11
   SE11 . . . . *5B 76*
   (off Black Prince Rd.)
   SW9 . . . . *5A 90*
   (off Grantham Rd.)
Ardent Ho. *E3* *1A 66*
   (off Roman Rd.)
Ardfillan Rd. *SE6* 1F 123
Ardgowan Rd. *SE6* . . . 5A 110
Ardilaun Rd. *N5* 1E 49
Ardleigh Rd. *N1* 3A 50
Ardley Cl. *NW10* 5A 28
   SE6 . . . . 3A 122
Ardlui Rd. *SE27* 2E 119
Ardmere Rd. *SE13* 4F 109
Ardoch Rd. *SE6* 2F 123
Ardshiel Cl. *SW15* 1F 99
Ardwell Rd. *SW2* 2A 118
Ardwick Rd. *NW2* 1C 44
Arena Bus. Cen. *N4* . . . 1E 35
Arena Ind. Est. *N4* 1D 35
Ares Ct. *E14* *5C 80*
   (off Homer Dr.)
Arethusa Ho. *E14* *5C 80*
   (off Cahir St.)
Argall Av. *E10* 2F 37
Argall Way *E10* 3F 37
Argon M. *SW6* 3C 86
Argos Ct. *SW9* *4C 90*
   (off Caldwell St.)
Argos Ho. *E2* *1D 65*
   (off Old Bethnal Grn. Rd.)
Argosy Ho. *SE8* 5A 80
Argyle Ho. *E14* 4E 81
Argyle Pl. *W6* 5D 71
Argyle Rd. *E1* 3F 65
   E15 . . . . 1A 54
   E16 . . . . 5D 69
Argyle Sq.
   WC1 . . . . 1E 7 *(2A 62)*
Argyle St.
   WC1 . . . . 1D 7 *(2A 62)*
Argyle Wlk. *WC1* *2A 62*
Argyle Way *SE16* 1C 92
Argyll Cl. *SW9* 1B 104
Argyll Mans. *SW3* 2F 87
   W14 . . . . *5A 72*
   (off Hammersmith Rd.)
Argyll Rd. *W8* 3C 72
Argyll St. *W1* . . . 3F 13 *(5E 61)*
Arica Ho. *SE16* *4D 79*
   (off Slippers Pl.)
Arica Rd. *SE4* 2A 108
Ariel Ct. *SE11* 5D 77
Ariel Rd. *NW6* 3C 44
Ariel Way *W12* 2E 71
Aristotle Rd. *SW4* . . . 1F 103
Ark, The *W6* *1F 85*
   (off Talgarth Rd.)
Arkindale Rd. *SE6* 3E 123
Arkley Cres. *E17* 1B 38
Arkley Rd. *E17* 1B 38
Arklow Ho. *SE17* 2F 91
Arklow Rd. *SE14* 2A 94
Arklow Rd. Trad. Est.
   SE14 . . . . 2A 94

Arkwright Ho. *SW2* . . . *5A 104*
   (off Streatham Pl.)
Arkwright Rd. *NW3* 2E 45
Arlesey Cl. *SW15* 3A 100
Arlesford Rd. *SW9* . . . 1A 104
Arlingford Rd. *SW2* . . . 3C 104
Arlington Av. *N1* 5E 49
   (not continuous)
Arlington Cl. *SE13* 3F 109
Arlington Ho. *EC1* *1C 8*
   (off Arlington Way)
   SE8 . . . . *2B 94*
   (off Evelyn St.)
   SW1 . . . . 1F 21 *(2E 75)*
   W12 . . . . *2D 71*
   (off Tunis Rd.)
Arlington Lodge
   SW2 . . . . 2B 104
Arlington Pl. *SE10* 3E 95
Arlington Rd. *NW1* 5D 47
Arlington Sq. *N1* 5E 49
Arlington St.
   SW1 . . . . 1F 21 *(2E 75)*
Arlington Way
   EC1 . . . . 1C 8 *(2C 62)*
Armada Ct. *SE8* 2C 94
Armadale Rd. *SW6* 3C 86
Armada St. *SE8* *2C 94*
   (off McMillan St.)
Armagh Rd. *E3* 5B 52
Arminger Rd. *W12* 2D 71
Armitage Rd. *NW11* . . . 3A 30
   SE10 . . . . 1B 96
Armour Cl. *N7* 3B 48
Armoury Rd. *SE8* 5D 95
Armoury Way *SW18* . . . 3C 100
Armsby Ho. *E1* *4E 65*
   (off Stepney Way)
Armstrong Rd. *SW7* . . . 4F 73
   W3 . . . . 2B 70
Arnal Cres. *SW18* 5A 100
Arncliffe *NW6* 1D 59
Arndale Wlk. *SW18* . . . 3D 101
Arne Ho. *SE11* *1B 90*
   (off Worgan St.)
Arne St. *WC2* . . . 3E 15 *(5A 62)*
Arne Wlk. *SE3* 2B 110
Arneway St. *SW1* 4F 75
Arnewood Cl. *SW15* . . . 1C 112
Arngask Rd. *SE6* 5F 109
Arnhem Pl. *E14* 4C 80
Arnhem Way *SE22* 3A 106
Arnhem Wharf *E14* 4B 80
Arnold Cir.
   E2 . . . . 2F 11 *(2B 64)*
Arnold Est.
   SE1 . . . . 4F 27 *(3B 78)*
   (not continuous)
Arnold Ho. *SE3* *3E 97*
   (off Shooters Hill Rd.)
   SE17 . . . . *1D 91*
   (off Doddington Gro.)
Arnold Mans. *W14* . . . 2B 86
   (off Queen's Club Gdns.)
Arnold Rd. *E3* 2C 66
Arnot Ho. *SE5* *3E 91*
   (off Comber Gro.)
Arnott Cl. *W4* 5A 70
Arnould Av. *SE5* 2F 105
Arnside St. *SE17* 2F 91

Arnulf St. SE6. . . . . . . 4D 123
Arnulls Rd. SW16 . . . . . . 5D 119
Arodene Rd. SW2. . . . . . 4B 104
Arragon Rd. E6 . . . . 5F 55
  SW18 . . . . 1C 114
Arran Ct. NW10 . . . . 5A 28
Arran Dr. E12 . . . . 3F 41
Arran Ho. E14. . . . . 2E 81
  (off Raleana Rd.)
Arran Rd. SE6 . . . . 2D 123
Arran Wlk. N1. . . . . 4E 49
Arrol Ho.
  SE1 . . . . 5A 26 (4E 77)
Arrow Ct. SW5 . . . . 5C 72
  (off W. Cromwell Rd.)
Arrowhead Ct. E11 . . . . . 1F 39
Arrow Rd. E3 . . . . 2D 67
Arrows Ho. SE15 . . . . 3E 93
  (off Clifton Way)
Arrowsmith Ho. SE11. . . . 1B 90
  (off Wickham St.)
Arsenal FC 5D 35
Artemis Ct. E14 . . . . 5C 80
  (off Homer Dr.)
Artesian Cl. NW10 . . . . . 4A 42
Artesian Rd. W2. . . . . . . 5C 58
Artesian Wlk. E11 . . . . . . 5A 40
Arthingworth St. E15 . . . . 5A 54
Arthur Ct. SW11 . . . . 4C 88
  W2 . . . . 5D 59
  (off Queensway)
  W10. . . . . 5F 57
  (off Silchester Rd.)
Arthur Deakin Ho. E1 . . . 4C 64
  (off Hunton St.)
Arthurdon Rd. SE4 . . . . 3C 108
Arthur Henderson Ho.
  SW6 . . . . 5B 86
  (off Fulham Rd.)
Arthur Horsley Wlk.
  E7 . . . . 2C 54
  (off Twr. Hamlets Rd.)
Arthur Rd. N7 . . . . 1B 48
  SW19 . . . . 5B 114
Arthur St.
  EC4. . . . . 4C 18 (1F 77)
Artichoke Hill E1 . . . . . . 1D 79
Artichoke M. SE5 . . . . . . 4F 91
  (off Artichoke Pl.)
Artichoke Pl. SE5 . . . . . . 4F 91
Artillery Ho. E15. . . . . . . 3A 54
Artillery La.
  E1. . . . . 1E 19 (4A 64)
  W12 . . . . 5C 56
Artillery Pas. E1 . . . . 1F 19
Artillery Pl.
  SW1 . . . . 5B 22 (4F 75)
Artillery Row
  SW1 . . . . 5B 22 (4E 75)
Artisan Ct. E8 . . . . 3C 50
Artisan M. NW10 . . . . 2F 57
  (off Warfield Rd.)
Artisan Quarter
  NW10 . . . . 2F 57
  (off Wellington Rd.)
Artizan St. E1 . . . . 2F 19
Arts Theatre 4D 15
  (off St Martin's St.)
Arundel Bldgs. SE1 . . . . . 4A 78
  (off Swan Mead)

Arundel Cl. E15 . . . . 1A 54
  SW11 . . . . 3A 102
Arundel Ct. SE16 . . . . 1D 93
  (off Varcoe Rd.)
  SW3 . . . . 1A 88
  (off Jubilee Pl.)
  SW13 . . . . 2D 85
  (off Arundel Ter.)
Arundel Gdns. W11 . . . . . 1B 72
Arundel Gt. Ct.
  WC2. . . . . 4A 16 (1B 76)
Arundel Gro. N16. . . . . . . 2A 50
Arundel Mans. SW6. . . . . 4B 86
  (off Kelvedon Rd.)
Arundel Pl. N1 . . . . 3C 48
Arundel Sq. N7. . . . . 3C 48
Arundel St.
  WC2. . . . . 4A 16 (1B 76)
Arundel Ter. SW13. . . . . . 2D 85
Arvon Rd. N5 . . . . 2C 48
  (not continuous)
Asbridge Ct. W6. . . . . . . 4D 71
  (off Dalling Rd.)
Ascalon Ho. SW8. . . . . . . 3E 89
  (off Thessaly Rd.)
Ascalon St. SW8 . . . . . . 3E 89
Ascham St. NW5 . . . . . . 2E 47
Ascot Ct. NW8 . . . . 2F 59
  (off Grove End Rd.)
Ascot Ho. NW1. . . . . 1E 5
  W9 . . . . 3C 58
  (off Harrow Rd.)
Ascot Lodge NW6 . . . . . . 5D 45
Ascot Rd. N15. . . . . 1F 35
  SW17 . . . . 5C 116
Ashanti M. E8. . . . . 2E 51
Ashbee Ho. E2 . . . . 2E 65
  (off Portman Pl.)
Ashbourne Ct. E5. . . . . . 1A 52
Ashbourne Gro.
  SE22 . . . . 2B 106
  W4 . . . . 1A 84
Ashbridge Rd. E11. . . . . 2A 40
Ashbridge St. NW8 . . . . 3A 60
Ashbrook Rd. N19 . . . . . 3F 33
Ashburn Gdns. SW7. . . . 5E 73
Ashburnham Gro.
  SE10. . . . . 3D 95
Ashburnham Mans.
  SW10 . . . . 3E 87
  (off Ashburnham Rd.)
Ashburnham Pl.
  SE10. . . . . 3D 95
Ashburnham Retreat
  SE10. . . . . 3D 95
Ashburnham Rd.
  NW10 . . . . 2E 57
  SW10 . . . . 3E 87
Ashburnham Twr.
  SW10 . . . . 3F 87
  (off Worlds End Est.)
Ashburton Ent. Cen.
  SW15 . . . . 4E 99
Ashburton Gro. N7 . . . . . 1C 48
Ashburton Rd. W9. . . . . . 3B 58
  (off Fernhead Rd.)
Ashburton Rd. E16. . . . . . 5C 68
Ashburton Ter. E13. . . . . 1C 68
Ashbury Pl. SW19 . . . . . . 5E 115

Ashbury Rd. SW11. . . . . . 1B 102
Ashby Ct. NW8 . . . . 3F 59
  (off Pollitt Dr.)
Ashby Gro. N1 . . . . 4E 49
  (not continuous)
Ashby Ho. N1 . . . . 4E 49
  (off Essex Rd.)
  SW9 . . . . 5D 91
Ashby M. SE4. . . . . 5B 94
  SW2 . . . . 3A 104
  (off Prague Pl.)
Ashby Rd. SE4 . . . . 5B 94
Ashby St. FC1 . . . . 2E 9 (2D 63)
Ashchurch Gro.
  W12 . . . . 4C 70
Ashchurch Pk. Vs.
  W12 . . . . 4C 70
Ashchurch Ter.
  W12 . . . . 4C 70
Ashcombe Pk. NW2 . . . . 5A 28
Ashcombe Rd.
  SW19 . . . . 5C 114
Ashcombe St. SW6 . . . . 5D 87
Ashcroft Ho. SW8 . . . . . . 4E 89
  (off Wadhurst Rd.)
Ashcroft Sq. W6 . . . . 5E 71
Ashdale Ho. N4 . . . . 2F 35
Ashdale Rd. SE12 . . . . . 1D 125
Ashdene SE15 . . . . 3D 93
Ashdon Rd. NW10 . . . . . 5B 42
Ashdown Cres.
  NW5 . . . . 2C 46
Ashdown Ho. SW1 . . . . . 5A 22
Ashdown Wlk. E14. . . . . . 5C 80
  (off Copeland Dr.)
Ashdown Way
  SW17 . . . . 2C 116
Ashenden SE17 . . . . 5E 77
  (off Deacon Way)
Ashenden Rd. E5 . . . . . . 2A 52
Ashen Gro. SW19. . . . . . 3C 114
Ashentree Ct.
  EC4 . . . . 3C 16
Asher Way E1. . . . . 1C 78
Ashfield Ct. SW9 . . . . . . 5A 90
  (off Clapham Rd.)
Ashfield Ho. W14. . . . . . 1B 86
  (off W. Cromwell Rd.)
Ashfield Rd. N4 . . . . 1E 35
  W3 . . . . 2B 70
Ashfield St. E1 . . . . 4D 65
Ashfield Yd. E1. . . . . 4E 65
Ashford Cl. E17 . . . . 1B 38
Ashford Ct. NW2. . . . . . . 1F 43
Ashford Ho. SE8 . . . . . . 2B 94
  SW9 . . . . 2D 105
Ashford Pas. NW2 . . . . . 1F 43
Ashford Rd. NW2 . . . . . . 1F 43
Ashford St.
  N1 . . . . 1D 11 (2A 64)
Ash Gro. E8 . . . . 5D 51
  (not continuous)
  NW2 . . . . 1F 43
  SE12. . . . . 1C 124
Ashgrove Ct. W9 . . . . 4C 58
  (off Elmfield Way)
Ashgrove Ho. SW1 . . . . . 1F 89
  (off Lindsay Sq.)
Ashgrove Rd.
  BR1: Brom 5F 123

Ash Ho. *E14* *3E 81*
   (off E. Ferry Rd.)
SE1 . . . . *5B 78*
   (off Longfield Est.)
W10 . . . . *3A 58*
   (off Heather Wlk.)
Ashington Ho. *E1* *3D 65*
   (off Barnsley St.)
Ashington Rd. SW6 . . . . . 5B 86
Ashlake Rd. SW16 . . . . 4A 118
Ashland Pl.
  W1 . . . . .5B 4 (4C 60)
Ashleigh Commercial Est.
  SE7 . . . . 4E 83
Ashleigh Point SE23 . . . 3F 121
Ashleigh Rd. SW14 . . . . 1A 98
Ashley Ct. *SW1* *4E 75*
   (off Morpeth Ter.)
Ashley Cres. SW11 . . . 1C 102
Ashley Gdns.
  SW1 . . . . 5A 22 (4E 75)
   (not continuous)
Ashley Pl.
  SW1 . . . . 5F 21 (4E 75)
Ashley Rd. E7 . . . . 4E 55
  N19 . . . . .3A 34
  SW19 . . . . .5D 115
Ashlin Rd. E15 . . . . 1F 53
Ashlone Rd. SW15 . . . . . 1E 99
Ashmead Bus. Cen.
  E16 . . . . 3F 67
Ashmead Ho. *E9* *2A 52*
   (off Homerton Rd.)
Ashmead M. SE8 . . . . . . 5C 94
Ashmead Rd. SE8 . . . . . 5C 94
Ashmere Gro. SW2 . . . 2A 104
Ash M. NW5 . . . . 2E 47
Ashmill St. NW1 . . . . 4A 60
Ashmole Pl. SW8 . . . . . . 2B 90
   (not continuous)
Ashmole St. SW8 . . . . . . 2B 90
Ashmore *NW1* *4F 47*
   (off Agar Gro.)
Ashmore Cl. SE15 . . . . . 3B 92
Ashmore Ho. *W14* *4A 72*
   (off Russell Rd.)
Ashmore Rd. W9 . . . . . . 1B 58
Ashmount Est. N19 . . . . 2F 33
Ashmount Rd. N19 . . . . . 2E 33
Ashness Rd. SW11 . . . 3B 102
Ashpark Ho. *E14* *5B 66*
   (off Norbiton Rd.)
Ash Rd. E15 . . . . 2A 54
Ashtead Rd. E5 . . . . 2C 36
Ashton Hgts. SE23 . . . . 1E 121
Ashton Ho. SW9 . . . . . . 3C 90
Ashton Rd. E15 . . . . 2F 53
Ashton St. E14 . . . . 1E 81
Ash Tree Ho. *SE5* *3E 91*
   (off Pitman St.)
Ashurst Gdns. SW2 . . . 1C 118
Ashvale Rd. SW17 . . . . 5B 116
Ashville Rd. E11 . . . . . . 4F 39
Ashwater Rd. SE12 . . . 1C 124
Ashwin St. E8 . . . . 3B 50
Ashworth Cl. SE5 . . . . . . 5F 91
Ashworth Mans. *W9* . . . *2D 59*
   (off Elgin Av.)
Ashworth Rd. W9 . . . . . 2D 59

Aske Ho. N1 . . . . 1D 11
   (not continuous)
Asker Rd. N7 . . . . 1A 48
Aske St. N1 . . . . 1D 11 (2A 64)
Askew Cres. W12 . . . . . . 3B 70
Askew Est. *W12* *2B 70*
   (off Uxbridge Rd.)
Askew Rd. W12 . . . . 3B 70
Askham Ct. W12 . . . . . . 2C 70
Askham Rd. W12 . . . . . . 2C 70
Askill Dr. SW15 . . . . . . 3A 100
Asland Rd. E15 . . . . 5A 54
Aslett St. SW18 . . . . . . 5D 101
Asmara Rd. NW2 . . . . . . 2A 44
Asmuns Hill NW11 . . . . . 1C 30
Asmuns Pl. NW11 . . . . . 1B 30
Asolando Dr.
  SE17 . . . . *5E 77*
Aspect Ct. *E14* *3E 81*
   (off Manchester Rd.)
Aspen Cl. N19 . . . . 4E 33
Aspen Gdns. W6 . . . . . . 1D 85
Aspen Ho. *SE15* *2E 93*
   (off Sharratt St.)
Aspenlea Rd. W6 . . . . . . 2F 85
Aspen Lodge *W8* *4D 73*
   (off Abbots Wlk.)
Aspen Way E14 . . . . 1D 81
Aspern Gro. NW3 . . . . . . 2A 46
Aspinall Rd. SE4 . . . . . . 1F 107
   (not continuous)
Aspinden Rd. SE16 . . . . 5D 79
Aspley Rd. SW18 . . . . . 3D 101
Assam St. *E1* *5C 64*
   (off White Chu. La.)
Assata M. N1 . . . . 3D 49
Assembly Pas. E1 . . . . . 4E 65
Association Gallery, The
  . . . . *3D 11*
   (off Leonard St.)
Astbury Bus. Pk.
  SE15 . . . . 4E 93
Astbury Ho. *SE11* *4C 76*
   (off Lambeth Wlk.)
Astbury Rd. SE15 . . . . . 4E 93
Astell St. SW3 . . . . 1A 88
Aste St. E14 . . . . 3E 81
Astey's Row N1 . . . . 4E 49
Astle St. SW11 . . . . 5C 88
Astley Av. NW2 . . . . 2E 43
Astley Ho. *SE1* *1B 92*
   (off Rowcross St.)
  SW13 . . . . *2D 85*
   (off Wyatt Dr.)
  W2 . . . . *4C 58*
   (off Alfred Rd.)
Aston Ho. SW8 . . . . 4F 89
  W11 . . . . .1B 72
   (off Westbourne Gro.)
Aston St. E14 . . . . 4A 66
Aston Ter. SW12 . . . . . 4D 103
Astonville St. SW18 . . . 1C 114
Astor Ct. *E16* *5E 69*
   (off Ripley Rd.)
  SW6 . . . . *3E 87*
   (off Maynard Cl.)
Astoria, The *1C 24*
   (off Falconberg M.)
Astoria Ct. *E8* *4B 50*
   (off Queensbridge Rd.)

Astoria Mans.
  SW16 . . . . 3A 118
Astoria Wlk. SW9 . . . . . 1C 104
Astra Ho. *SE14* *2B 94*
   (off Arklow Rd.)
Astrop M. W6 . . . . 4E 71
Astrop Ter. W6 . . . . 3E 71
Astwood M. SW7 . . . . . . 5E 73
Atalanta St. SW6 . . . . . . 3F 85
Athelden Rd.
  SW18 . . . . 1D 115
Atheley St. SE6 . . . . 3C 122
Athelstane Gro. E3 . . . . 1B 66
Athelstane M. N4 . . . . . 3C 34
Athelstan Gdns. NW6 . . 4A 44
Athenaeum Ct. N5 . . . . . 1E 49
Athena Pl. *EC4* *2C 16*
   (off St Andrew St.)
Athenia Ho. *E14* *5F 67*
   (off Blair St.)
Athenlay Rd. SE15 . . . . 3F 107
Athens Gdns. *W9* *3C 58*
   (off Harrow Rd.)
Atherden Rd. E5 . . . . . . 1E 51
Atherfold Rd.
  SW9 . . . . 1A 104
Atherstone Ct. *W2* *4D 59*
   (off Delamere Ter.)
Atherstone M. SW7 . . . . 5E 73
Atherton Dr. SW19 . . . . 4F 113
Atherton Leisure Cen.
  . . . . 3B 54
Atherton M. E7 . . . . 3B 54
Atherton Rd. E7 . . . . 3B 54
  SW13 . . . . 3C 84
Atherton St. SW11 . . . . 5A 88
Athlone Cl. E5 . . . . 2D 51
Athlone Ho. *E1* *5E 65*
   (off Sidney St.)
  Athlone Ho. SW2 . . . . 5B 104
Athlone Rd. SW2 . . . . . 5B 104
Athlone St. NW5 . . . . . . 3C 46
Atholl Ho. *W9* *2E 59*
   (off Maida Va.)
Athol Sq. E14 . . . . 5E 67
Atkin Bldg. *WC1* *5A 8*
   (off Raymond Bldgs.)
Atkinson Ct. E10 . . . . . . 2D 39
   (off Kings Cl.)
Atkinson Ho. *E2* *1C 64*
   (off Pritchards Rd.)
  E13 . . . . *3B 68*
   (off Sutton Rd.)
  SE17 . . . . *5F 77*
   (off Catesby St.)
Atkinson Rd. E16 . . . . . 4E 69
Atkins Rd. E10 . . . . 1D 39
  SW12 . . . . 5E 103
Atlanta Ho. *SE16* *4A 80*
   (off Brunswick Quay)
Atlantic Ct. *E14* *1F 81*
   (off Jamestown Way)
Atlantic Ho. *E1* *4A 66*
   (off Harford St.)
  SW9 . . . . 2C 104
Atlantic Wharf E1 . . . . . 1F 79
Atlas Bus. Cen. NW2 . . 3D 29
Atlas Gdns. SE7 . . . . . . 5E 83
Atlas M. E8 . . . . 3B 50
  N7 . . . . 3B 48

Atlas Rd. E13 . . . . 1C 68
  NW10 . . . . 2A 56
Atlas Wharf E9 . . . . 3C 52
Atley Rd. E3 . . . . 5C 52
Atney Rd. SW15 . . . . . 2A 100
Atrium Apartments
  N1 . . . . 5F 49
   (off Felton St.)
Atterbury Rd. N4 . . . . . 1C 34
Atterbury St. SW1 . . . . . 5A 76
Attewood Av. NW10 . . . . 5A 28
Attilburgh Ho. SE1 . . . . . 5F 27
   (off Abbey St.)
Attleborough Ct.
  SE23 . . . . 2C 120
Attneave St.
  WC1 . . . . 2B 8 (2C 62)
Atwater Rd. SW2 . . . . . 1C 118
Atwell Cl. E10 . . . . 1D 39
Atwell Rd. SE15 . . . . . . 5C 92
Atwood Ho. W14 . . . . . . 5B 72
   (off Beckford Cl.)
Atwood Rd. W6 . . . . 5D 71
Aubert Ct. N5 . . . . 1D 49
Aubert Pk. N5 . . . . 1D 49
Aubert Rd. N5 . . . . 1D 49
Aubrey Beardsley Ho.
  SW1 . . . . 5E 75
   (off Vauxhall Bri. Rd.)
Aubrey Mans. NW1 . . . . 4A 60
   (off Lisson St.)
Aubrey Moore Point
  E15 . . . . 1E 67
   (off Abbey La.)
Aubrey Pl. NW8 . . . . 1E 59
Aubrey Rd. N8 . . . . 1A 34
  W8 . . . . 2B 72
Aubrey Wlk. W8 . . . . . . 2B 72
Auburn Cl. SE14 . . . . . . 3A 94
Aubyn Hill SE27 . . . . . 4E 119
Aubyn Sq. SW15 . . . . . . 3C 98
Auckland Hill SE27 . . . 4E 119
Auckland Ho. W12 . . . . . 1D 71
   (off White City Est.)
Auckland Rd. E10 . . . . . 5D 39
  SW11 . . . . 2A 102
Auckland St. SE11 . . . . . 1B 90
Auden Pl. NW1 . . . . 5C 46
   (not continuous)
Audley Cl. SW11 . . . . . 1C 102
Audley Dr. E16 . . . . 2D 83
Audley Rd. NW4 . . . . . . 1C 28
Audley Sq.
  W1 . . . . 1C 20 (2C 74)
Audrey St. E2 . . . . 1C 64
Augurs La. E13 . . . . 2D 69
Augusta St. E14 . . . . . . 5D 67
Augustine Rd. W14 . . . . . 4F 71
Augustus Cl. W12 . . . . . 3D 71
Augustus Ct. SW16 . . . 2F 117
Augustus Ho. NW1 . . . . . 1F 5
   (off Augustus St.)
Augustus Rd. SW19 . . . 1F 113
Augustus St.
  NW1 . . . . 1E 5 (1D 61)
Aulton Pl. SE11 . . . . . . 1C 90
Auriga M. N1 . . . . 2F 49
Auriol Ho. W12 . . . . 2D 71
   (off Ellerslie Rd.)
Auriol Rd. W14 . . . . 5A 72

Aurora Bldg. E14 . . . . . . 2E 81
   (off Blackwall Way)
Aurora Ho. E14 . . . . 5D 67
   (off Kerbey St.)
Austen Ho. NW6 . . . . . . 2C 58
   (off Cambridge Rd.)
Austin Cl. SE23 . . . . . . 5A 108
Austin Ct. E6 . . . . 5E 55
  SE15 . . . . 1C 106
   (off Philip Wlk.)
Austin Friars
  EC2 . . . . 2C 18 (5F 63)
   (not continuous)
Austin Friars Pas.
  EC2 . . . . 2C 18
Austin Friars Sq.
  EC2 . . . . 2C 18
Austin Ho. SE14 . . . . . . 3B 94
   (off Achilles St.)
Austin Rd. SW11 . . . . . . 4C 88
Austin St. E2 . . . 2F 11 (2B 64)
Austin Ter. SE1 . . . . 5C 24
   (off Morley St.)
Australian War Memorial
. . . . 3C 20
   (off Duke of Wellington Pl.)
Australia Rd. W12 . . . . . 1D 71
Austral St. SE11 . . . . . . 5D 77
Autumn Cl.
  SW19 . . . . 5E 115
Autumn St. E3 . . . . 5C 52
Avalon Rd. SW6 . . . . . . 4D 87
Avarn Rd. SW17 . . . . . 5B 116
Avebury Ct. N1 . . . . 5F 49
   (off Imber St.)
Avebury Rd. E11 . . . . . . 3F 39
Avebury St. N1 . . . . 5F 49
Aveline St. SE11 . . . . . . 1C 90
Ave Maria La.
  EC4 . . . . 3E 17 (5D 63)
Avenell Mans.
  N5 . . . . 1D 49
Avenell Rd. N5 . . . . 5D 35
Avenfield Ho. W1 . . . . . . 4A 12
   (off Park La.)
Avening Rd. SW18 . . . . 5C 100
Avening Ter.
  SW18 . . . . 5C 100
Avenons Rd. E13 . . . . . . 3C 68
Avenue, The E11 . . . . . . 1D 41
  NW6 . . . . 5F 43
  SE10 . . . . 3F 95
  SW4 . . . . 3C 102
  SW18 . . . . 5A 102
  W4 . . . . 4A 70
Avenue Cl. NW8 . . . . . . 5A 46
Avenue Ct. NW2 . . . . . . 5B 30
  SW3 . . . . 5B 74
   (off Draycott Av.)
Avenue Gdns. SW14 . . . 1A 98
Avenue Ho. NW8 . . . . . . 1A 60
   (off Allitsen Rd.)
  NW10 . . . . 4F 45
   (off Avenue Rd.)
Avenue Lodge NW8 . . . . 4F 45
   (off Avenue Rd.)
Avenue Mans. NW3 . . . . 2D 45
   (off Finchley Rd.)
Avenue Pk. Rd.
  SE27 . . . . 2D 119

Avenue Rd. E7 . . . . 1D 55
  N6 . . . . 2E 33
  N15 . . . . 1F 35
  NW3 . . . . 4F 45
  NW8 . . . . 4F 45
  NW10 . . . . 1B 56
Averill St. W6 . . . . 2F 85
Avery Farm Row
  SW1 . . . . 5C 74
Avery Row
  W1 . . . . 4D 13 (1D 75)
Aviary Cl. E16 . . . . 4B 68
Avignon Rd. SE4 . . . . . 1F 107
Avington Ct. SE1 . . . . . . 5A 78
   (off Old Kent Rd.)
Avis Sq. E1 . . . . 5F 65
Avoca Rd. SW17 . . . . . 4C 116
Avocet Cl. SE1 . . . . 1C 92
Avon Ct. SW15 . . . . . . 3A 100
  W9 . . . . 4C 58
   (off Elmfield Way)
Avondale Av. NW2 . . . . . 5A 28
Avondale Ct. E11 . . . . . . 3A 40
  E16 . . . . 4A 68
Avondale Cres.
  IG4: Ilf. 1F 41
Avondale Ho. SE1 . . . . . 1C 92
   (off Avondale Sq.)
Avondale Pk. Gdns.
  W11 . . . . 1A 72
Avondale Pk. Rd.
  W11 . . . . 1A 72
Avondale Pavement
  SE1 . . . . 1C 92
Avondale Ri. SE15 . . . . 1B 106
Avondale Rd. E16 . . . . . 4A 68
  E17 . . . . 2C 38
  N15 . . . . 1D 35
  SE9 . . . . 2F 125
  SW14 . . . . 1A 98
  SW19 . . . . 5D 115
Avondale Sq. SE1 . . . . . 1C 92
Avon Ho. W8 . . . . 4C 72
   (off Allen St.)
  W14 . . . . 5B 72
   (off Kensington Village)
Avonhurst Ho. NW2 . . . . 4A 44
Avonley Rd. SE14 . . . . . 3E 93
Avonmore Gdns.
  W14 . . . . 5B 72
Avonmore Pl. W14 . . . . . 5A 72
Avonmore Rd. W14 . . . . 5A 72
Avonmouth St.
  SE1 . . . . 5F 25 (4E 77)
Avon Pl. SE1 . . . 4A 26 (3E 77)
Avon Rd. SE4 . . . . 1C 108
Avro Ho. SW8 . . . . 3D 89
   (off Havelock Ter.)
Axminster Rd. N7 . . . . . 5A 34
Aybrook St.
  W1 . . . . 1B 12 (4C 60)
Aycliffe Rd. W12 . . . . . . 2C 70
Ayerst Ct. E10 . . . . 2E 39
Aylesbury Ho. SE15 . . . . 2C 92
   (off Friary Est.)
Aylesbury Rd. SE17 . . . . 1F 91
Aylesbury St.
  EC1 . . . . 4D 9 (3D 63)
  NW10 . . . . 5A 28

Aylesford Ho. *SE1* *4C 26*
(off Long La.)
Aylesford St. SW1 . . . . . . 1F **89**
Aylesham Cen., The
SE15 . . . . *5E 9*
Aylestone Av. NW6 . . . . . 4F **43**
Aylmer Ct. N2 . . . . 1B **32**
Aylmer Ho. SE10 . . . . 1F **95**
Aylmer Pde. N2 . . . . 1B **32**
Aylmer Rd. E11 . . . . 3B **40**
N2 . . . . 1A **32**
W12 . . . . 3B **70**
Aylton Est. SE16 . . . . 3E **79**
Aylward Rd. SE23 . . . . . 2F **121**
Aylward St. E1 . . . . 5E **65**
(Jamaica St.)
E1 . . . . 5E **65**
(Jubilee St.)
Aylwin Est.
SE1 . . . . 5E **27** (4A **78**)
Aynhoe Mans.
W14 . . . . *5F 71*
(off Aynhoe Rd.)
Aynhoe Rd. W14 . . . . 5F **71**
Ayres Cl. E13 . . . . 2C **68**
Ayres St.
SE1 . . . . 3A **26** (3E **77**)
Ayrsome Ho. N16 . . . . . . 5A **36**
Ayrton Gould Ho. *E2* . . . *2F 65*
(off Roman Rd.)
Ayrton Rd. SW7 . . . . 4F **73**
Aysgarth Rd. SE21 . . . . 5A **106**
Ayshford Ho. *E2* *2D 65*
(off Viaduct St.)
Ayston Ho. *SE16* *5F 79*
(off Plough Way)
Ayton Ho. *SE5* *3F 91*
(off Edmund St.)
Aytoun Pl. SW9 . . . . 5B **90**
Aytoun Rd. SW9 . . . . 5B **90**
Azalea Ho. *SE14* *3B 94*
(off Achilles St.)
Azania M. NW5 . . . . 3D **47**
Azenby Rd.
SE15 . . . . 5B **92**
Azof St. SE10 . . . . 5A **82**
Azov Ho. *E1* *3A 66*
(off Commodore St.)
Azure Ho. *E2* *2C 64*
(off Buckfast St.)

B

Baalbec Rd. N5 . . . . 2D **49**
Babington Ct. WC1 . . . . . 5F **7**
Babington Ho. *SE1* *3A 26*
(off Disney St.)
Babington Rd.
SW16 . . . . 5F **117**
Babmaes St.
SW1 . . . . 5B **14** (1F **75**)
Bacchus Wlk. *N1* *1A 64*
(off Regan Way)
Bache's St.
N1 . . . . 1C **10** (2F **63**)
Back All. EC3 . . . . 3E **19**
Bk. Church La. E1 . . . . . . 5C **64**
Back Hill EC1 . . 4C **8** (3C **62**)
Backhouse Pl. SE17 . . . . 5A **78**

Back La. N8 . . . . 1A **34**
NW3 . . . . 1E **45**
Back Passage *EC1* *5E 9*
(off Long La.)
Bacon Gro. SE1 . . . . 4B **78**
Bacon's College Sports Cen.
. . . . 2A **80**
Bacons La. N6 . . . . 3C **32**
Bacon St.
E1 . . . . 3F **11** (3B **64**)
E2 . . . . 3B **64**
Bacton NW5 . . . . 2C **46**
Bacton St. E2 . . . . 2E **65**
Baddesley Ho. *SE11* . . . *1B 90*
(off Jonathan St.)
Baddow Wlk. *N1* *5E 49*
(off New Nth. Rd.)
Baden Pl.
SE1 . . . . 3B **26** (3F **77**)
Baden Powell Ho.
SW7 . . . . *5E 73*
(off Queen's Ga.)
Badger Ct. NW2 . . . . 5E **29**
Badminton M. E16 . . . . . 2C **82**
Badminton Rd.
SW12 . . . . 4C **102**
Badric Ct. SW11 . . . . . . 5F **87**
Badsworth Rd. SE5 . . . . . 4E **91**
Baffin Way E14 . . . . 2E **81**
Bagley's La. SW6 . . . . . . 4D **87**
Bagnigge Ho. *WC1* *2B 8*
(off Margery St.)
Bagshot Ho. NW1 . . . . . . 1E **5**
Bagshot St. SE17 . . . . . . 1A **92**
Baildon *E2* *1E 65*
(off Cyprus St.)
Baildon St. SE8 . . . . 3B **94**
Bailey Cotts. *E14* *4A 66*
(off Maroon St.)
Bailey Ho. *SW10* *3D 87*
(off Coleridge Gdns.)
Bailey M. SW2 . . . . 3C **104**
Bailey Pl. SE26 . . . . 5F **121**
Bainbridge St.
WC1 . . . . 2C **14** (5F **61**)
Baird Cl. E10 . . . . 3C **38**
Baird Gdns. SE19 . . . . . 4A **120**
Baird Ho. *W12* *1D 71*
(off White City Est.)
Baird St. EC1 . . 3A **10** (3E **63**)
Baizdon Rd. SE3 . . . . . . 5A **96**
Baker Ho. *WC1* *4E 7*
(off Colonnade)
Baker Pas. NW10 . . . . . . 5A **42**
Baker Rd. NW10 . . . . . . 5A **42**
Bakers Av. E17 . . . . 1D **39**
Baker's Fld. N7 . . . . 1A **48**
Bakers Hall Ct.
EC3 . . . . 5D **19**
Bakers Hill E5 . . . . 3E **37**
Baker's La. N6 . . . . 1B **32**
Baker's M.
W1 . . . . 2B **12** (5C **60**)
Bakers Pas. *NW3* *1E 45*
(off Heath St.)
Baker's Rents
E2 . . . . 2F **11** (2B **64**)
Baker's Row E15 . . . . . . 1A **68**
EC1 . . . . 4B **8** (3C **62**)
BAKER STREET 4B **60**

Baker St.
NW1 . . . . 4A **4** (3B **60**)
W1 . . . . 4A **4** (3B **60**)
Baker's Yd. EC1 . . . . 4B **8**
Bakery Cl. SW9 . . . . 3B **90**
Bakery Pl. SW11 . . . . . . 2B **102**
Balaam Leisure Cen.
. . . . 3C **68**
Balaam St. E13 . . . . 3C **68**
Balaclava Rd. SE1 . . . . . 5B **78**
Bala Grn. *NW9* *1A 28*
(off Ruthin Cl.)
Balchen Rd. SE3 . . . . . . 5F **97**
Balchier Rd. SE22 . . . . . 4D **107**
Balcombe Ho. *NW1* *3A 60*
(off Taunton Pl.)
Balcombe St.
NW1 . . . . 5A **4** (3B **60**)
Balcorne St. E9 . . . . 4E **51**
Balder Ri. SE12 . . . . 2D **125**
Balderton Flats *W1* *3C 12*
(off Balderton St.)
Balderton St.
W1 . . . . 3C **12** (5C **60**)
Baldock St. E3 . . . . 1D **67**
Baldrey Ho. *SE10* *1B 96*
(off Blackwall La.)
Baldry Gdns. SW16 . . . . 5B **118**
Baldwin Cres. SE5 . . . . . 4E **91**
Baldwin Ho. SW2 . . . . . 1C **118**
Baldwins Gdns.
EC1 . . . . 5B **8** (4C **62**)
Baldwin St.
EC1 . . . . 2B **10** (2F **63**)
Baldwin Ter. N1 . . . . 1E **63**
Balearic Apartments
E16 . . . . 1C **82**
(off Western Gateway)
Bale Rd. E1 . . . . 4A **66**
Balfern Gro. W4 . . . . 1A **84**
Balfern St. SW11 . . . . . . 5A **88**
Balfe St. N1 . . . . 1A **62**
Balfour Ho. *W10* *4F 57*
(off St Charles Sq.)
Balfour M.
W1 . . . . 1C **20** (2C **74**)
Balfour Pl. SW15 . . . . . . 2D **99**
W1 . . . . 5C **12** (1C **74**)
Balfour Rd. N5 . . . . 1E **49**
Balfour St. SE17 . . . . 5F **77**
Balfron Twr. E14 . . . . 5E **67**
BALHAM 1C **116**
Balham Continental Mkt.
SW12 . . . . *1D 117*
(off Shipka Rd.)
Balham Gro. SW12 . . . . . 5C **102**
Balham High Rd.
SW12 . . . . 3C **116**
SW17 . . . . 3C **116**
Balham Hill SW12 . . . . . 5D **103**
Balham Leisure Cen.
. . . . 2D **117**
Balham New Rd.
SW12 . . . . 5D **103**
Balham Pk. Rd.
SW12 . . . . 1B **116**
Balham Sta. Rd.
SW12 . . . . 1D **117**
Balin Ho. *SE1* *3B 26*
(off Long La.)

Balkan Wlk. E1 . . . . 1D 79
Balladier Wlk. E14 . . . . . 4D 67
Ballamore Rd.
  BR1: Brom 3C 124
Ballance Rd. E9 . . . . 3F 51
Ballantine St. SW18 . . 2E 101
Ballantrae Ho. NW2 . . . 1B 44
Ballard Ho. SE10 . . . . . . 2D 95
  (off Thames St.)
Ballards Rd. NW2 . . . . . 4C 28
Ballast Quay SE10 . . . . 1F 95
Ballater Rd. SW2 . . . . . 2A 104
Ball Ct. EC3 . . . . 3C 18
  (off Cornhill)
Ballina St. SE23 . . . . . . 5F 107
Ballin Ct. E14 . . . . 3E 81
  (off Stewart St.)
Ballingdon Rd.
  SW11 . . . . 4C 102
Balliol Rd. W10 . . . . 5E 57
Balloch Rd. SE6 . . . . . . 1F 123
Ballogie Av. NW10 . . . . 1A 42
Ballow Cl. SE5 . . . . 3A 92
Balls Pond Pl. N1 . . . . . 3F 49
Balls Pond Rd. N1 . . . . 3F 49
Balman Ho. SE16 . . . . . 5F 79
  (off Rotherhithe New Rd.)
Balmer Rd. E3 . . . . 1B 66
Balmes Rd. N1 . . . . 5F 49
Balmoral Apartments
  W2 . . . . 4A 60
  (off Praed St.)
Balmoral Cl. SW15 . . . . 4F 99
Balmoral Ct. SE12 . . . . 4D 125
  SE16 . . . . 2F 79
  (off King & Queen Wharf)
  SE17 . . . . 1F 91
  (off Lytham St.)
  SE27 . . . . 4E 119
Balmoral Gro. N7 . . . . . 3B 48
Balmoral Ho. E14 . . . . . 4D 81
  (off Lanark Sq.)
  E16 . . . . 2D 83
  (off Keats Av.)
  W14 . . . . 5A 72
  (off Windsor Way)
Balmoral M. W12 . . . . . 4B 70
Balmoral Rd. E7 . . . . . . 1E 55
  E10 . . . . 4D 39
  NW2 . . . . 3D 43
Balmore Cl. E14 . . . . . . 5E 67
Balmore St. N19 . . . . . . 4D 33
Balmuir Gdns. SW15 . . 2E 99
Balnacraig Av. NW10 . . 1A 42
Balniel Ga. SW1 . . . . . . 1F 89
Balsam Ho. E14 . . . . . . 1D 81
  (off E. India Dock Rd.)
Baltic Apartments
  E16 . . . . 1C 82
  (off Western Gateway)
Baltic Ct. SE16 . . . . 3F 79
Baltic Ho. SE5 . . . . 5E 91
Baltic Pl. N1 . . . . 5A 50
Baltic St. E.
  EC1 . . . . 4F 9 (3E 63)
Baltic St. W.
  EC1 . . . . 4F 9 (3E 63)
Baltimore Ho. SE11 . . . 5C 76
  (off Hotspur St.)
Balvaird Pl. SW1 . . . . . 1F 89

Balvernie Gro.
  SW18 . . . . 5B 100
Balvernie M. SW18 . . . 5C 100
Bamber Rd. SE15 . . . . . 4B 92
Bamborough Gdns.
  W12 . . . . 3E 71
Bamford Ct. E15 . . . . . . 2D 53
  (off Clays La.)
Bamford Rd.
  BR1: Brom 5E 123
Bampton Rd. SE23 . . . . 3F 121
Banbury Ct. WC2 . . . . . 4D 15
Banbury Ho. E9 . . . . 4F 51
Banbury Rd. E9 . . . . 4F 51
Banbury St. SW11 . . . . 5A 88
Banchory Rd. SE3 . . . . . 3D 97
Bancroft Av. N2 . . . . . . 1A 32
Bancroft Ct. SW8 . . . . . 3A 90
  (off Allen Edwards Dr.)
Bancroft Ho. E1 . . . . . . 3E 65
  (off Cephas St.)
Bancroft Rd. E1 . . . . . . 2E 65
Banfield Rd. SE15 . . . . 1D 107
Bangalore St. SW15 . . . 1E 99
Banim St. W6 . . . . 5D 71
Banister Ho. E9 . . . . 2F 51
  SW8 . . . . 3A 90
  (off Wadhurst Rd.)
  W10 . . . . 2A 58
  (off Bruckner St.)
Banister M. NW6 . . . . . 4D 45
Banister Rd. W10 . . . . . 2F 57
Bank, The N6 . . . . 3D 33
Bank End
  SE1 . . . . 1A 26 (2E 77)
Bankfoot Rd.
  BR1: Brom 4A 124
Bankhurst Rd. SE6 . . . . 5B 108
Bank La. SW15 . . . . 3A 98
Bank of England
  . . . . 3B 18 (5F 63)
Bank of England Mus.
  . . . . 3C 18
Bank of England Offices
  EC4 . . . . 3F 17
Banks Ho. SE1 . . . . 5F 25
  (off Rockingham St.)
Bankside SE1 . . 5F 17 (1E 77)
  (not continuous)
Bankside Art Gallery
  . . . . 5E 17 (1D 77)
Bankside Way SE19 . . . 5A 120
Bank St. E14 . . . . 2D 81
Bankton Rd. SW2 . . . . . 2C 104
Bankwell Rd. SE13 . . . . 2A 110
Bannatyne's Health Club
  Grove Park 2D 125
Bannerman Ho. SW8 . . 2B 90
Banner St.
  EC1 . . . . 4A 10 (3E 63)
Banning St. SE10 . . . . . 1A 96
Bannister Cl. SW2 . . . . 1C 118
Bannister Ho. SE14 . . . 2F 93
  (off John Williams Cl.)
Banqueting House
  . . . . 2D 23 (2A 76)
Banstead St. SE15 . . . . 1E 107
Banting Ho. NW2 . . . . . 5C 28
Bantock Ho. W10 . . . . . 2A 58
  (off Third Av.)

Bantry Ho. E1 . . . . 3F 65
  (off Ernest St.)
Bantry St. SE5 . . . . 3F 91
Banyard Rd. SE16 . . . . . 4D 79
Baptist Gdns.
  NW5 . . . . 3C 46
Barandon Rd. W11 . . . . 1F 71
  (off Grenfell Rd.)
Barandon Wlk. W11 . . . 1F 71
Barbanel Ho. E1 . . . . . . 3E 65
  (off Cephas St.)
Barbara Brosnan Ct.
  NW8 . . . . 1F 59
Barhauld Rd. N16 . . . . . 5A 36
Barber Beaumont Ho.
  E1 . . . . 2F 65
  (off Bancroft Rd.)
Barbers All. E13 . . . . . . 2D 69
Barbers Rd. E15 . . . . . . 1D 67
Barbican Arts Cen.
  . . . . 5A 10 (4E 63)
Barbican Cinema 5A 10
  (in Arts Cen.)
Barbican Theatre 5A 10
  (off Silk St.)
Barbican Trade Cen.
  EC1 . . . . 5A 10
  (off Beech St.)
Barb M. W6 . . . . 4E 71
Barbon All. EC2 . . . . . . 2E 19
  (off Houndsditch)
Barbon Cl.
  WC1 . . . . 5E 7 (4B 62)
Barchard St. SW18 . . . 3D 101
Barchester St. E14 . . . . 4D 67
Barclay Cl. SW6 . . . . . . 3C 86
Barclay Ho. E9 . . . . 4E 51
  (off Well St.)
Barclay Path E17 . . . . . 1E 39
Barclay Rd. E11 . . . . . . 3B 40
  (not continuous)
  E13 . . . . 3E 69
  E17 . . . . 1E 39
  SW6 . . . . 3C 86
Barcombe Av. SW2 . . . 2A 118
Bardell Ho. SE1 . . . . . . 3C 78
  (off Parkers Row)
Bardolph Rd. N7 . . . . . 1A 48
Bard Rd. W10 . . . . 1F 71
Bardsey Pl. E1 . . . . 3E 65
  (off Mile End Rd.)
Bardsey Wlk. N1 . . . . . . 3E 49
  (off Douglas Rd. Nth.)
Bardsley Ho. SE10 . . . . 2E 95
  (off Bardsley La.)
Bardsley La. SE10 . . . . 2E 95
Barents Ho. E1 . . . . 3F 65
  (off White Horse La.)
Barfett St. W10 . . . . 3B 58
Barfield Rd. E11 . . . . . . 3B 40
Barfleur La. SE8 . . . . . . 5B 80
Barford St. N1 . . . . 5C 48
Barforth Rd. SE15 . . . . 1D 107
Barge Ho. St.
  SE1 . . . . 1D 24 (2C 76)
Bargery Rd. SE6 . . . . . . 1D 123
Bargrove Cres. SE6 . . . 2B 122
Barham Ho. SE17 . . . . . 1A 92
  (off Kinglake St.)
Baring Cl. SE12 . . . . . . 2C 124

Baring Ho. *E14* 5C **66**
    (off Canton St.)
Baring Rd. SE12 . . . . 5C **110**
Baring St. N1 . . . . 5F **49**
Barker Dr. NW1 . . . . 4E **47**
Barker M. SW4 . . . . 2D **103**
Barkers Arc. W8 . . . . 3D **73**
Barker St. SW10 . . . . 2E **87**
Barker Wlk. SW16 . . . . . . 3F **117**
Barkham Ter. SE1 . . . . 5C **24**
Barking Rd. E6 . . . . 1E **69**
    E13 . . . . 1E **69**
    E16 . . . . 4B **68**
    (not continuous)
Bark Pl. W2 . . . . 1D **73**
Barkston Gdns. SW5 . . . . 5D **73**
Barkway Ct. *N4* 4E **35**
    (off Queen's Dr.)
Barkwith Ho. *SE14* 2F **93**
    (off Cold Blow La.)
Barkworth Rd. SE16 . . . . 1D **93**
Barlborough St. SE14 . . . . 3F **93**
Barlby Gdns. W10 . . . . 3F **57**
Barlby Rd. W10 . . . . 4F **57**
Barleycorn Way E14 . . . . 1B **80**
Barley Mow Pas. EC1 . . . . 5E **9**
    W4 . . . . 1A **84**
Barley Shotts Bus. Pk.
    W10 . . . . 4B **58**
Barling *NW1* 3D **47**
    (off Castlehaven Rd.)
Barlings Ho. *SE4* 2F **107**
    (off Frendsbury Rd.)
Barlow Dr. SE18 . . . . 4F **97**
Barlow Ho. *N1* 1B **10**
    (off Fairbank Est.)
    SE16 . . . . 5D **79**
    (off Rennie Est.)
    W11 . . . . 1A **72**
    (off Walmer Rd.)
Barlow Pl.
    W1 . . . . 5E **13** (1D **75**)
Barlow Rd. NW6 . . . . 3B **44**
Barlow St. SE17 . . . . 5F **77**
Barmeston Rd. SE6 . . . . 2D **123**
Barmouth Rd. SW18 . . . . 4E **101**
Barnabas Rd. E9 . . . . 2F **51**
Barnaby Ct. *SE16* 3C **78**
    (off Scott Lidgett Cres.)
Barnaby Pl. *SW7* 5F **73**
    (off Old Brompton Rd.)
Barnard Gro. E15 . . . . 4B **54**
Barnard Ho. *E2* 2D **65**
    (off Ellsworth St.)
Barnard Lodge *W9* 4C **58**
    (off Admiral Wlk.)
Barnard M. SW11 . . . . . . 2A **102**
Barnardo Gdns. E1 . . . . . . 1F **79**
Barnardo St. E1 . . . . 5F **65**
Barnard Rd. SW11 . . . . . . 2A **102**
Barnards Ho. *SE16* 3B **80**
    (off Wyatt Cl.)
Barnard's Inn EC1 . . . . . . 1B **16**
Barnbrough *NW1* 5E **47**
    (off Camden St.)
Barnby Sq. E15 . . . . 5A **54**
Barnby St. E15 . . . . 5A **54**
    NW1 . . . . 1A **6** (1B **61**)
Barn Cl. *NW5* 2F **47**
    (off Torriano Av.)

Barn Elms Athletic Track
    . . . . 5D **85**
Barn Elms Pk. SW15 . . . . 1E **99**
BARNES 5B **84**
Barnes Av. SW13 . . . . 3C **84**
Barnes Cl. E12 . . . . 1F **55**
Barnes Ct. E16 . . . . 4E **69**
    N1 . . . . 4C **48**
Barnes High St.
    SW13 . . . . 5B **84**
Barnes Ter. SE8 . . . . 1B **94**
Barnet Gro. E2 . . . . 2C **64**
Barnett St. E1 . . . . 5D **65**
Barney Cl. SE7 . . . . 1E **97**
Barn Fld. NW3 . . . . 2B **46**
Barnfield Cl. N4 . . . . 2A **34**
    SW17 . . . . 3F **115**
Barnfield Pl. E14 . . . . 5C **80**
Barnham St.
    SE1 . . . . 3E **27** (3A **78**)
BARNSBURY 4B **48**
Barnsbury Est. N1 . . . . . . 5B **48**
    (not continuous)
Barnsbury Gro. N7 . . . . . . 4B **48**
Barnsbury Pk. N1 . . . . 4C **48**
Barnsbury Rd. N1 . . . . 1C **62**
Barnsbury Sq. N1 . . . . 4C **48**
Barnsbury St. N1 . . . . 4C **48**
Barnsbury Ter. N1 . . . . 4B **48**
Barnsdale Av. E14 . . . . . . 5D **81**
Barnsdale Rd. W9 . . . . . . 3B **58**
Barnsley St. E1 . . . . 3D **65**
Barnstable La.
    SE13 . . . . 2E **109**
Barnstaple Ho. *SE10* . . . 3D **95**
    (off Devonshire Dr.)
    SE12 . . . . 3B **110**
    (off Taunton Rd.)
Barnston Wlk. *N1* 5E **49**
    (off Popham St.)
Barn St. N16 . . . . 4A **36**
Barnwell Ho. *SE5* 4A **92**
    (off St Giles Rd.)
Barnwell Rd. SW2 . . . . . . 3C **104**
Barnwood Cl. W9 . . . . 3D **59**
Baroness Rd.
    E2 . . . . 1F **11** (2B **64**)
Baronsclere Ct. N6 . . . . . . 2E **33**
BARONS COURT 1A **86**
Baron's Ct. Rd. W14 . . . . 1A **86**
Barons Court Theatre
    . . . . 1A **86**
    (off Comeragh Rd.)
Barons Keep W14 . . . . . . 1A **86**
Baronsmead Rd.
    SW13 . . . . 4C **84**
Baron's Pl.
    SE1 . . . . 4C **24** (3C **76**)
Baron St. N1 . . . . 1C **62**
Baron Wlk. E16 . . . . 4B **68**
Barque M. SE8 . . . . 2C **94**
Barratt Ho. *N1* 4D **49**
    (off Sable St.)
Barratt Ind. Pk. E3 . . . . . . 3E **67**

Barret Ho. NW6 . . . . 5C **44**
    SW9 . . . . 1B **104**
    (off Benedict Rd.)
Barrett Ho. *SE17* 1E **91**
    (off Browning St.)
Barrett's Gro. N16 . . . . . . 2A **50**
Barrett St.
    W1 . . . . 3C **12** (5C **60**)
Barrhill Rd. SW2 . . . . 2A **118**
Barriedale SE14 . . . . 5A **94**
Barrie Est. W2 . . . . 1F **73**
Barrie Ho. *W2* 1E **73**
    (off Lancaster Ga.)
Barrier App. SE7 . . . . 4F **83**
Barrier Point Rd.
    E16 . . . . 2E **83**
Barringer Sq. SW17 . . . . 4C **116**
Barrington Cl. NW5 . . . . . 2C **46**
Barrington Ct. SW4 . . . . . 5A **90**
Barrington Rd. SW9 . . . . 1D **105**
Barrow Ct. *SE6* 1B **124**
    (off Cumberland Pl.)
Barrowgate Rd. W4 . . . . . 1A **84**
Barrow Hill Est. *NW8* . . 1A **60**
    (off Barrow Hill Rd.)
Barrow Hill Rd. NW8 . . . . 1A **60**
Barrow Rd. SW16 . . . . . . 5F **117**
Barry Av. N15 . . . . 1B **36**
Barry Ho. *SE16* 5D **79**
    (off Rennie Est.)
Barry Rd. SE22 . . . . 4C **106**
Barset Rd. SE15 . . . . 1E **107**
    (not continuous)
Barston Rd. SE27 . . . . . . 3E **119**
Barstow Cres. SW2 . . . . 1B **118**
Barter St.
    WC1 . . . . 1E **15** (4A **62**)
Bartholomew Cl.
    EC1 . . . . 1E **17** (4E **63**)
    SW18 . . . . 2E **101**
Bartholomew Ct. *E14* . . 1F **81**
    (off Newport Av.)
    EC1 . . . . 3A **10**
    (off Old St.)
Bartholomew La.
    EC2 . . . . 3C **18** (5F **63**)
Bartholomew Pl. EC1 . . . 1F **17**
Bartholomew Rd.
    NW5 . . . . 3E **47**
Bartholomew Sq. E1 . . . . 3D **65**
    EC1 . . . . 3A **10** (3E **63**)
Bartholomew St. SE1 . . . 4F **77**
Bartholomew Vs.
    NW5 . . . . 3E **47**
Bartle Rd. W11 . . . . 5A **58**
Bartlett Cl. E14 . . . . 5C **66**
Bartlett Ct.
    EC4 . . . . 2C **16** (5C **62**)
Bartletts Pas. *EC4* 2C **16**
    (off Fetter La.)
Barton Cl. E9 . . . . 2E **51**
    SE15 . . . . 1D **107**
Barton Ct. W14 . . . . 1A **86**
    (off Baron's Ct. Rd.)
Barton Ho. *N1* 4D **49**
    (off Sable St.)
    SW6 . . . . 1D **101**
    (off Wandsworth Bri. Rd.)
Barton Rd. W14 . . . . 1A **86**

Barton St.
SW1 . . . . 5D **23** (4A **76**)
Bartonway NW8 . . . . . . *5F 45*
(off Queen's Ter.)
Bartram Rd. SE4 . . . . . 3A **108**
Bartrip St. E9 . . . . 3B **52**
Barville Cl. SE4 . . . . . 2A **108**
Barwell Ho. E2 . . . . *3C 64*
(off Menotti St.)
Barwick Rd. E7 . . . . 1D **55**
Bascombe St. SW2 . . . . 4C **104**
Baseline Bus. Studios
W11 . . . . *1F 71*
(off Barandon Wlk.)
Basevi Way SE8 . . . . . . 2C **94**
Bashley Rd. NW10 . . . . 3A **56**
Basildon Ct. W1 . . . . . . *5C 4*
(off Devonshire Rd.)
Basil Gdns. SE27 . . . . . 5E **119**
Basil Ho. SW8 . . . . *3A 90*
(off Wyvil Rd.)
Basil St.
SW3 . . . . 5A **20** (4B **74**)
Basin App. E14 . . . . . 5A **66**
Basing Ct. SE15 . . . . . 4B **92**
Basingdon Way SE5 . . 2F **105**
Basinghall Av.
EC2 . . . . 2B **18** (5F **63**)
Basinghall St.
EC2 . . . . 2B **18** (5F **63**)
Basing Hill NW11 . . . . 3B **30**
Basing Ho. Yd.
E2 . . . . 1E **11** (2A **64**)
Basing Pl. E2 . . 1E **11** (2A **64**)
Basing St. W11 . . . . . . 5B **58**
Basire St. N1 . . . . 5E **49**
Baskerville Gdns.
NW10 . . . . 1A **42**
Baskerville Rd.
SW18 . . . . 5A **102**
Basket Gdns. SE9 . . . . 3F **111**
Baslow Wlk. E5 . . . . . . 1F **51**
Basnett Rd. SW11 . . . . 1C **102**
Basque Ct. SE16 . . . . . . *3F 79*
(off Garter Way)
Bassano St. SE22 . . . . 3B **106**
Bassein Pk. Rd. W12 . . 3B **70**
Bassett Rd. E7 . . . . . . 1F **55**
W10 . . . . 5F **57**
Bassett St. NW5 . . . . . 3C **46**
Bassingbourn Ho. N1 . . *4C 48*
(off Sutton Est., The)
Bassingham Rd.
SW18 . . . . 5E **101**
Bassishaw Highwalk
EC2 . . . . 1A **18**
Basswood Cl. SE15 . . . 1D **107**
Basterfield Ho. EC1 . . . . *4F 9*
(off Golden La. Est.)
Bastion Highwalk
EC2 . . . . 1F **17**
Bastion Ho. EC2 . . . . . . 1A **18**
(off London Wall)
Bastwick St.
EC1 . . . . 3F **9** (3E **63**)
Basuto Rd. SW6 . . . . . . 4C **86**
Batavia Ho. SE14 . . . . . 3A **94**
(off Batavia Rd.)
Batavia M. SE14 . . . . . . 3A **94**
Batavia Rd. SE14 . . . . . 3A **94**

Batchelor St. N1 . . . . . . 5C **48**
Bateman Ho. SE17 . . . . *2D 91*
(off Otto St.)
Bateman's Bldgs.
W1 . . . . 3B **14**
Bateman's Row
EC2 . . . . 3E **11** (3A **64**)
Bateman St.
W1 . . . . 3B **14** (5F **61**)
Bates Point E13 . . . . . . *5C 54*
(off Pelly Rd.)
Bate St. E14 . . . . 1B **80**
Bath Cl. SE15 . . . . 3D **93**
Bath Ct. EC1 . . . . 4B **8**
SE26 . . . . *3C 120*
(off Droitwich Cl.)
Bathgate Rd. SW19 . . . 3F **113**
Bath Gro. E2 . . . . *1C 64*
(off Horatio St.)
Bath Ho. E2 . . . . *3C 64*
(off Ramsey St.)
SE1 . . . . *5D 26*
(off Bath Ter.)
Bath Pl. EC2 . . 2D **11** (2A **64**)
W6 . . . . 1E **85**
(off Peabody Est.)
Bath Rd. E7 . . . . 3F **55**
W4 . . . . 5A **70**
Baths App. SW6 . . . . . 3B **86**
Bath St.
EC1 . . . . 2A **10** (2E **63**)
Bath Ter. SE1 . . 5F **25** (4E **77**)
Bathurst Gdns.
NW10 . . . . 1D **57**
Bathurst Ho. W12 . . . . *1D 71*
(off White City Est.)
Bathurst M. W2 . . . . . . 5F **59**
Bathurst St. W2 . . . . . . 1F **73**
Batley Pl. N16 . . . . 5B **36**
Batley Rd. N16 . . . . 5B **36**
Batman Cl. W12 . . . . . . 2D **71**
Batoum Gdns. W6 . . . . 4E **71**
Batson Ho. E1 . . . . *5C 64*
(off Fairclough St.)
Batson St. W12 . . . . . . 3C **70**
Battenberg Wlk.
SE19 . . . . 5A **120**
Batten Cotts. E14 . . . . . *4A 66*
(off Maroon St.)
Batten Ho. SW4 . . . . . 3E **103**
W10 . . . . *2A 58*
(off Third Av.)
Batten St. SW11 . . . . . 1A **102**
Battersby Rd. SE6 . . . . 2F **123**
BATTERSEA 4C **88**
Battersea Bri. Rd.
SW11 . . . . 3A **88**
Battersea Bus. Cen.
SW11 . . . . 1C **102**
Battersea Chu. Rd.
SW11 . . . . 4F **87**
Battersea High St.
SW11 . . . . 4F **87**
(not continuous)
Battersea Pk. 3B **88**
Battersea Pk. Children's Zoo
. . . . 3C **88**
Battersea Pk. Equestrian Cen.
. . . . 5A **88**

Battersea Pk. Rd.
SW8 . . . . 5A **88**
SW11 . . . . 5A **88**
Battersea Ri. SW11 . . . 3A **102**
Battersea Sports Cen.
. . . . 1F **101**
Battersea Sq. SW11 . . . 4F **87**
Battishill St. N1 . . . . . . 4D **49**
Battlebridge Ct. N1 . . . . *1A 62*
(off Wharfdale Rd.)
Battle Bri. La.
SE1 . . . . 2D **27** (2A **78**)
Battle Bri. Rd. NW1 . . . 1A **62**
Battle Cl. SW19 . . . . . . 5E **115**
Battledean Rd. N5 . . . . 2D **49**
Battle Ho. SE15 . . . . . . *2C 92*
(off Haymerle Rd.)
Batty St. E1 . . . . 5C **64**
Baudwin Rd. SE6 . . . . 2A **124**
Baulk, The SW18 . . . . . 5C **100**
Bavaria Rd. N19 . . . . . . 4A **34**
(not continuous)
Bavent Rd. SE5 . . . . . . 5E **91**
Bawdale Rd. SE22 . . . . 3B **106**
Bawtree Rd. SE14 . . . . 3A **94**
Baxendale St. E2 . . . . . 2C **64**
Baxter Rd. E16 . . . . 5E **69**
N1 . . . . 3F **49**
Bay Ct. E1 . . . . *3F 65*
(off Frimley Way)
Bayer Ho. EC1 . . . . *4F 9*
(off Golden La. Est.)
Bayes Cl. SE26 . . . . . . 5E **121**
Bayes Ct. NW3 . . . . *4B 46*
(off Primrose Hill Rd.)
Bayfield Ho. SE4 . . . . . *2F 107*
(off Coston Wlk.)
Bayfield Rd. SE9 . . . . . 2F **111**
Bayford M. E8 . . . . *4D 51*
(off Bayford St.)
Bayford Rd. NW10 . . . . 2F **57**
Bayford St. E8 . . . . 4D **51**
Bayford St. Bus. Cen.
E8 . . . . *4D 51*
(off Sidworth St.)
Bayham Pl. NW1 . . . . . 5E **47**
Bayham Rd. W4 . . . . . . 4A **70**
Bayham St. NW1 . . . . . 5E **47**
Bayley St.
WC1 . . . . 1B **14** (4F **61**)
Baylis Rd.
SE1 . . . . 4B **24** (3C **76**)
Baynes M. NW3 . . . . . . 3F **45**
Baynes St. NW1 . . . . . . 4E **47**
Bayonne Rd. W6 . . . . . 2A **86**
Bayston Rd. N16 . . . . . 5B **36**
BAYSWATER 1E **73**
Bayswater Rd. W2 . . . . 1D **73**
Baythorne St. E3 . . . . . 4B **66**
Bayton Ct. E8 . . . . *4C 50*
(off Lansdowne Dr.)
Baytree Cl. SW2 . . . . . 2B **104**
Baytree Rd. SW2 . . . . . 2B **104**
Bazalgette Ho. NW8 . . . *3F 59*
(off Orchardson St.)
Bazeley Ho. SE1 . . . . . *4D 25*
(off Library St.)
Bazely St. E14 . . . . 1E **81**
BBC Broadcasting House
. . . . 1E **13** (4D **61**)

BBC Television Cen. . . . 1E 71
BBC Worldwide 5E 57
 (off Wood La.)
Beacham Cl. SE7 . . . . . 1F 97
Beachborough Rd.
 BR1: Brom 4E 123
Beachcroft Rd. E11 . . . . 5A 40
Beachcroft Way
 N19 . . . . 3F 33
Beach Ho. SW5 . . . . . . 1C 86
 (off Philbeach Gdns.)
Beachy Rd. E3 . . . . 4C 52
Beacon Bingo Hall 1F 43
Beacon Ga. SE14 . . . . . 1F 107
Beacon Hill N7 . . . . 2A 48
Beacon Ho. E14 . . . . . . 1D 95
 (off Burrells Wharf Sq.)
 SE5 . . . . 3A 92
 (off Southampton Way)
Beacon Rd. SE13 . . . . . 4F 109
Beaconsfield Cl.
 SE3 . . . . 2C 96
Beaconsfield Rd.
 E10 . . . . 4E 39
 E16 . . . . 3B 68
 E17 . . . . 1B 38
 NW3 . . . . 3B 42
 SE3 . . . . 3B 96
 SE9 . . . . 2F 125
 SE17 . . . . 1F 91
Beaconsfield Ter. Rd.
 W14 . . . . 4A 72
Beaconsfield Wlk.
 SW6 . . . . 4B 86
Beacontree Rd. E11 . . . 3B 40
Beadman Pl. SE27 . . . . 4D 119
Beadman St. SE27 . . . . 4D 119
Beadnell Rd. SE23 . . . . 1F 121
Beadon Rd. W6 . . . . . . 5E 71
Beak St. W1 . . . . 4A 14 (1E 75)
Beale Pl. E3 . . . . 1B 66
Beale Rd. E3 . . . . 5B 52
Beames Rd. NW10 . . . . 5A 42
Beaminster Ho. SW8 . . 3B 90
 (off Dorset Rd.)
Beamish Ho. SE16 . . . . 5D 79
 (off Rennie Est.)
Beanacre Cl. E9 . . . . . . 3B 52
Bear All.
 EC4 . . . . 2D 17 (5D 63)
Beardell St. SE19 . . . . . 5B 120
Beardsfield E13 . . . . . . 1C 68
Bear Gdns.
 SE1 . . . . 1F 25 (2E 77)
Bear La. SE1 . . . 1E 25 (2D 77)
Bearstead Ri. SE4 . . . . 3B 108
Bear St. WC2 . . . 4C 14 (1F 75)
Beaton Cl. SE15 . . . . . . 4B 92
Beatrice Cl. E13 . . . . . . 3C 68
Beatrice Ho. W6 . . . . . . 1C 85
 (off Queen Caroline St.)
Beatrice Pl. W8 . . . . . . 4D 73
Beatrice Rd. E17 . . . . . . 1C 38
 N4 . . . . 2C 34
 SE1 . . . . 5C 78
Beatrix Ho. SW5 . . . . . 1D 87
 (off Old Brompton Rd.)
Beatson Wlk. SE16 . . . . 2A 80
 (not continuous)
Beattie Ho. SW8 . . . . . 4E 89

Beatty Ho. E14 . . . . . . 3C 80
 (off Admirals Way)
 NW1 . . . . 3F 5
 (off Drummond St.)
 SW1 . . . . 1E 89
 (off Dolphin Sq.)
Beatty Rd. N16 . . . . 1A 50
Beatty St. NW1 . . . . . . 1E 61
Beauchamp Pl. SW3 . . 4A 74
Beauchamp Rd. E7 . . . 4D 55
Beauchamp St.
 EC1 . . . . 1B 16 (4C 62)
Beauchamp Ter.
 SW15 . . . . 1D 99
Beauclerc Rd. W6 . . . . 4D 71
Beauclerk Ho.
 SW16 . . . . 3A 118
Beaufort Cl. SW15 . . . . 5D 99
Beaufort Ct. E14 . . . . . 3C 80
 (off Admirals Way)
 SW6 . . . . 2C 86
Beaufort Gdns. NW4 . . 1E 29
 SW3 . . . . 4A 74
Beaufort Ho. E16 . . . . . 2D 83
 (off Fairfax M.)
 SW1 . . . . 1E 89
 (off Aylesford St.)
Beaufort M. SW6 . . . . . 2B 86
Beaufort St. SW3 . . . . . 2F 87
Beaufort Ter. E14 . . . . . 1E 95
 (off Ferry St.)
Beaufoy Ho. SE27 . . . . 3D 119
 SW8 . . . . 3B 90
 (off Rita Rd.)
Beaufoy Wlk. SE11 . . . . 5B 76
Beaulieu Av. E16 . . . . . 2D 83
 SE26 . . . . 4D 121
Beaulieu Cl. SE5 . . . . . 1F 105
Beaulieu Lodge E14 . . . 4F 81
 (off Schooner Cl.)
Beaumaris Grn. NW9 . . 1A 28
Beaumont W14 . . . . . . 5B 72
 (off Kensington Village)
Beaumont Av. W14 . . . 1B 86
Beaumont Bldgs.
 WC2 . . . . 3E 15
 (off Martlett Ct.)
Beaumont Ct. E1 . . . . . 2A 66
 E5 . . . . 5D 37
 W1 . . . . 5C 4
 (off Beaumont St.)
Beaumont Cres. W14 . . 1B 86
Beaumont Gdns.
 NW3 . . . . 5C 30
Beaumont Gro. E1 . . . . 3F 65
Beaumont Ho. E10 . . . . 2D 39
 E15 . . . . 5B 54
 (off John St.)
Beaumont Lodge E8 . . 3C 50
 (off Greenwood Rd.)
Beaumont M.
 W1 . . . . 5C 4 (4C 60)
Beaumont Pl.
 W1 . . . . 3A 6 (3E 61)
Beaumont Ri. N19 . . . . 3F 33
Beaumont Rd. E10 . . . . 2D 39
 (not continuous)
 E13 . . . . 2D 69
 SW19 . . . . 5A 100

Beaumont Sq. E1 . . . . . 4F 65
Beaumont St.
 W1 . . . . 5C 4 (4C 60)
Beaumont Ter. SE13 . . . 5A 110
 (off Wellmeadow Rd.)
Beaumont Wlk. NW3 . . 4B 46
Beauvale NW1 . . . . 4C 46
 (off Ferdinand St.)
Beauval Rd. SE22 . . . . 4B 106
Beaux Arts Bldg., The
 N7 . . . . 5A 34
Beavor Gro. W6 . . . . . . 1C 84
 (off Beavor La.)
Beavor La. W6 . . . . 1C 84
Beccles St. E14 . . . . . . 5B 66
Bechervaise Ct. E10 . . 3D 39
 (off Leyton Grange Est.)
Bechtel Ho. W6 . . . . . . 5F 71
 (off Hammersmith Rd.)
Beck Cl. SE13 . . . . 4D 95
Beckenham Bus. Cen.
 BR3: Beck 5A 122
Beckenham Hill Est.
 BR3: Beck 5D 123
Beckenham Hill Rd.
 BR3: Beck, Lon 5D 123
 SE6 . . . . 5D 123
Beckers, The N16 . . . . . 1C 50
Becket Ho. E16 . . . . . . 2D 83
 (off Constable Av.)
 SE1 . . . . 4B 26
Becket St.
 SE1 . . . . 5B 26 (4F 77)
Beckett Cl. NW10 . . . . . 3A 42
 SW16 . . . . 2F 117
Beckett Ho. E1 . . . . 4E 65
 (off Jubilee St.)
 SW9 . . . . 5A 90
Beckfoot NW1 . . . . 1A 6
 (off Ampthill Est.)
Beckford Cl. W14 . . . . . 5B 72
Beckford Ho. N16 . . . . . 2A 50
Beckford Pl. SE17 . . . . 1E 91
Beckham Ho. SE11 . . . 5B 76
Becklow Gdns. W12 . . . 3C 70
 (off Becklow Rd.)
Becklow M. W12 . . . . . 3C 70
 (off Becklow Rd.)
Becklow Rd. W12 . . . . . 3B 70
 (not continuous)
Beck Rd. E8 . . . . 5D 51
Beckton Rd. E16 . . . . . 4B 68
Beckway St. SE17 . . . . 5A 78
 (not continuous)
Beckwith Ho. E2 . . . . . 1D 65
 (off Wadeson St.)
Beckwith Rd. SE24 . . . 3F 105
Beclands Rd. SW17 . . . 5C 116
Becmead Av. SW16 . . . 4F 117
Becondale Rd.
 SE19 . . . . 5A 120
Becquerel Ct. SE10 . . . 4B 82
Bective Pl. SW15 . . . . . 2B 100
Bective Rd. E7 . . . . 1C 54
 SW15 . . . . 2B 100
Bedale St.
 SE1 . . . . 2B 26 (2F 77)
Beddalls Farm Ct. E6 . . 4F 69
Bedefield
 WC1 . . . . 2E 7 (2A 62)

Bede Ho. *SE4* 4B 94
(off Clare Rd.)
Bedford Av.
WC1 . . . . 1C 14 (4F 61)
Bedfordbury
WC2 . . . . 4D 15 (1A 76)
Bedford Cl. W4 . . . . 2A 84
Bedford Cnr. W4 . . . . . . 5A 70
(off South Pde.)
Bedford Ct.
WC2 . . . . 5D 15 (1A 76)
(not continuous)
Bedford Ct. Mans.
WC1 . . . . 1C 14
Bedford Gdns. W8 . . . . 2C 72
Bedford Hill SW12 . . 1D 117
SW16 . . . . 1D 117
Bedford Ho. SW4 . . . . 2A 104
(off Solon New Rd. Est.)
Bedford M. SE6 . . . . . 2D 123
BEDFORD PARK 4A 70
Bedford Pk. Cnr. W4 . . 5A 70
Bedford Pk. Mans.
W4 . . . . 5A 70
Bedford Pas. SW6 . . . . 3A 86
(off Dawes Rd.)
W1 . . . . 5A 6 (4E 61)
Bedford Pl.
WC1 . . . . 5D 7 (4A 62)
SW16 . . . . 1D 117
Bedford Rd. N8 . . . . . . 1F 33
SW4 . . . . 2A 104
W4 . . . . 4A 70
Bedford Row
WC1 . . . . 5A 8 (4B 62)
Bedford Sq.
WC1 . . . . 1C 14 (4F 61)
Bedford St.
WC2 . . . . 4D 15 (1A 76)
Bedford Ter. SW2 . . . . 3A 104
Bedford Way
WC1 . . . . 4C 6 (3F 61)
Bedgebury Gdns.
SW19 . . . . 2A 114
Bedgebury Rd. SE9 . . 2F 111
Bedivere Rd.
BR1: Brom 3C 124
Bedlam M. SE11 . . . . . 5C 76
(off Walnut Tree Wlk.)
Bedmond Ho. SW3 . . . 1A 88
(off Ixworth Pl.)
Bedser Cl. SE11 . . . . . . 2B 90
Bedwell Ho. SW9 . . . . . 5C 90
Beeby Rd. E16 . . . . 4D 69
Beech Av. W3 . . . . 2A 70
Beech Cl. SE8 . . . . 2C 94
SW15 . . . . 5C 98
SW19 . . . . 5E 113
Beech Ct. W9 . . . . 4C 58
(off Elmfield Way)
Beech Cres. Ct. N5 . . . 1D 49
Beechcroft Av. NW11 . . 2B 30
Beechcroft Cl.
SW16 . . . . 5B 118
Beechcroft Ct. NW11 . . 2B 30
(off Beechcroft Av.)
Beechcroft Rd.
SW17 . . . . 2A 116
Beechdale Rd. SW2 . . 4B 104
Beechdene SE15 . . . . . 4D 93
(off Carlton Gro.)

Beechen Pl. SE23 . . . . 2F 121
Beeches Rd. SW17 . . . 3A 116
Beechey Ho. E1 . . . . . . 2D 79
(off Watts St.)
Beechfield Rd. N4 . . . . 1E 35
SE6 . . . . 1B 122
Beech Gdns. EC2 . . . . . 5F 9
(off Beech St.)
Beech Ho. SE16 . . . . . . 3E 79
(off Ainsty Est.)
Beechmont Cl.
BR1: Brom 5A 124
Beechmore Rd.
SW11 . . . . 4B 88
Beecholme Est. E5 . . . . 5D 37
Beech St. EC2 . . . 5F 9 (4E 63)
Beech Tree Cl. N1 . . . . 4C 48
Beechwood Cl. SW4 . . . 2A 84
Beechwood Gro. W3 . . 1A 70
Beechwood Ho. E2 . . . . 1C 64
(off Teale St.)
Beechwood Rd. E8 . . . . 3B 50
Beechwoods Ct.
SE19 . . . . 5B 120
Beechworth Cl. NW3 . . 4A 44
Beechworth Cl. NW3 . . 4C 30
Beecroft La. SE4 . . . . . 3A 108
Beecroft M. SE4 . . . . . 3A 108
Beecroft Rd. SE4 . . . . 3A 108
Beehive Cl. E8 . . . . 4B 50
Beehive Pl. SW9 . . . . . 1C 104
Beemans Row
SW18 . . . . 2E 115
Bee Pas. EC3 . . . . 3D 19
(off Lime St.)
Beeston Cl. E8 . . . . 2C 50
Beeston Ho. SE1 . . . . . 5B 26
(off Burbage Cl.)
Beeston Pl.
SW1 . . . . 5E 21 (4D 75)
Beethoven St. W10 . . . 2A 58
Begbie Rd. SE3 . . . . . . 4E 97
Begonia Wlk. W12 . . . . 5B 56
Beira St. SW12 . . . . . . 5D 103
Bekesbourne St. E14 . . 5A 66
Beldanes Lodge
NW10 . . . . 4C 42
Belfast Rd. N16 . . . . . . 4B 36
Belfont Wlk. N7 . . . . . . 1A 48
(not continuous)
Belford Ho. E8 . . . . 5B 50
Belfort Rd. SE15 . . . . . 5E 93
Belfry Cl. SE16 . . . . . . 1D 93
Belfry Rd. E12 . . . . 4F 41
Belgrade Rd. N16 . . . . 1A 50
Belgrave Ct. E2 . . . . . . 1D 65
(off Temple St.)
E13 . . . . 3E 69
E14 . . . . 1B 80
(off Westferry Cir.)
SW8 . . . . 3E 89
(off Ascalon St.)
Belgrave Gdns. NW8 . . 5D 45
Belgrave Hgts. E11 . . . 3C 40
Belgrave Ho. SW9 . . . . 3C 90
Belgrave M. Nth.
SW1 . . . . 4B 20 (3C 74)
Belgrave M. Sth.
SW1 . . . . 5C 20 (4C 74)
Belgrave M. W. SW1 . . 5B 20

Belgrave Pl.
SW1 . . . . 5C 20 (4C 74)
Belgrave Rd. E10 . . . . . 3E 39
E11 . . . . 4C 40
E13 . . . . 3E 69
E17 . . . . 1C 38
SW1 . . . . 5D 75
SW13 . . . . 3B 84
Belgrave Sq.
SW1 . . . . 5B 20 (4C 74)
Belgrave St. E1 . . . . . . 4F 65
Belgrave Yd.
SW1 . . . . 5D 21
BELGRAVIA 4C 74
Belgravia Ct. SW1 . . . . 4D 75
(off Ebury St.)
Belgravia Gdns.
BR1: Brom 5A 124
Belgravia Ho. SW1 . . . 5B 20
(off Halkin Pl.)
SW4 . . . . 4F 103
Belgravia Workshops
N19 . . . . 4A 34
(off Marlborough Rd.)
Belgrove St.
WC1 . . . . 1E 7 (2A 62)
Belham Wlk. SE5 . . . . . 4F 91
Belinda Rd. SW9 . . . . . 1D 105
Belitha Vs. N1 . . . . 4B 48
Bella Best Ho. SW1 . . . 1D 89
(off Westmoreland Ter.)
Bellamy Cl. E14 . . . . . . 3C 80
W14 . . . . 1B 86
Bellamy Ho. SW17 . . . 4F 115
Bellamy's Ct. SE16 . . . 2F 79
(off Abbotshade Rd.)
Bellasis Av. SW2 . . . . 2A 118
Bell Dr. SW18 . . . . 5A 100
Bellefields Rd.
SW9 . . . . 1B 104
Bellenden Rd. SE15 . . 4B 92
Belleville Rd.
SW11 . . . . 3A 102
Bellevue Pde.
SW17 . . . . 1B 116
Bellevue Pl. E1 . . . . . . 3E 65
Bellevue Rd. SW13 . . . 5C 84
SW17 . . . . 1A 116
Bellew St. SW17 . . . . . 3E 115
Bellfield Cl. SE3 . . . . . . 3C 96
Bellflower Cl. E6 . . . . . 4F 69
Bell Gdns. E10 . . . . 3C 38
(off Church Rd.)
Bellgate M. NW5 . . . . . 1D 47
BELL GREEN 4A 122
Bell Grn. SE26 . . . . 4B 122
Bell Grn. La. SE26 . . . 5B 122
Bell Ho. SE10 . . . . 2E 95
(off Haddo St.)
Bellina M. NW5 . . . . . . 1D 47
BELLINGHAM 3C 122
Bellingham Grn.
SE6 . . . . 3C 122
Bellingham Rd.
SE6 . . . . 3D 123
Bellingham Trad. Est.
SE6 . . . . 3D 123
Bell Inn Yd.
EC3 . . . . 3C 18 (5F 63)

Bell La. E1 . . . . . . 1F **19** (4B **64**)
E16 . . . . 2B **82**
Bellmaker Ct. E3 . . . . 4C **66**
Bell Mdw. SE19 . . . . . . 5A **120**
Bell Moor NW3 . . . . *5E **31***
(off E. Heath Rd.)
Bello Cl. SE24 . . . . 5D **105**
Bellot Gdns. SE10 . . . . . 1A **96**
(off Bellot St.)
Bellot St. SE10 . . . . 1A **96**
Bells All. SW6 . . . . 5C **86**
Bellsize Ct. NW3 . . . . . . 2F **45**
Bell St. NW1 . . . . 4A **60**
SE18 . . . . 4F **97**
Belltrees Gro.
SW16 . . . . 5B **118**
Bell Wharf La.
EC4 . . . . . . 5A **18** (1E **77**)
Bellwood Rd. SE15 . . . 2F **107**
Bell Yd. WC2 . . 3B **16** (5C **62**)
Bell Yd. M.
SE1 . . . . . . 4E **27** (3A **78**)
Belmont Cl. SW4 . . . . . 1E **103**
Belmont Ct. N5 . . . . 1E **49**
NW11 . . . . 1B **30**
Belmont Gro. SE13 . . . . 1F **109**
W4 . . . . 5A **70**
Belmont Hall Ct.
SE13 . . . . 1F **109**
Belmont Hill SE13 . . . . 1E **109**
Belmont M. SW19 . . . . . 2F **113**
Belmont Pde. NW11 . . . . 1B **30**
Belmont Pk. SE13 . . . . . 2F **109**
Belmont Pk. Cl.
SE13 . . . . 2A **110**
Belmont Pk. Rd. E10 . . . 1D **39**
Belmont Rd. SW4 . . . . . 1E **103**
Belmont St. NW1 . . . . . . 4C **46**
Belmore Ho. N7 . . . . 2F **47**
Belmore La. N7 . . . . 2F **47**
Belmore St. SW8 . . . . . . 4F **89**
Beloe Cl. SW15 . . . . 2C **98**
Belsham St. E9 . . . . 3E **51**
Belsize Av. NW3 . . . . . . 3F **45**
Belsize Ct. Garages
NW3 . . . . *2F **45***
(off Belsize La.)
Belsize Cres. NW3 . . . . . 2F **45**
Belsize Gro. NW3 . . . . . 3A **46**
Belsize La. NW3 . . . . . . 3F **45**
Belsize M. NW3 . . . . 3F **45**
Belsize Pk. NW3 . . . . . . 3F **45**
Belsize Pk. Gdns.
NW3 . . . . 3F **45**
Belsize Pk. M. NW3 . . . . 3F **45**
Belsize Pl. NW3 . . . . 2F **45**
Belsize Rd. NW6 . . . . . . 5D **45**
Belsize Sq. NW3 . . . . . . 3F **45**
Belsize Ter. NW3 . . . . . . 3F **45**
Beltane Dr. SW19 . . . . . 3F **113**
Belthorn Cres.
SW12 . . . . 5E **103**
Belton Rd. E7 . . . . 4D **55**
E11 . . . . 1A **54**
NW2 . . . . 3C **42**
Belton Way E3 . . . . 4C **66**
Beltran Rd. SW6 . . . . . . 5D **87**
Belvedere, The
SW10 . . . . *4E **87***
(off Chelsea Harbour)

Belvedere Av. SW19 . . . 5A **114**
Belvedere Bldgs.
SE1 . . . . 4E **25** (3D **77**)
Belvedere Ct. N1 . . . . . *5A **50***
(off De Beauvoir Cres.)
NW2 . . . . *3F **43***
(off Willesden La.)
SW15 . . . . 2E **99**
Belvedere Dr.
SW19 . . . . 5A **114**
Belvedere Gro.
SW19 . . . . 5A **114**
Belvedere M. SE3 . . . . . 3D **97**
SE15 . . . . 1E **107**
Belvedere Pl.
SE1 . . . . 4E **25** (3D **77**)
SW2 . . . . 2B **104**
Belvedere Rd. E10 . . . . 3A **38**
SE1 . . . . 3A **24** (2B **76**)
Belvedere Sq.
SW19 . . . . 5A **114**
Belvoir Rd. SE22 . . . . . 5C **106**
Bembridge Ho. NW6 . . . . 4A **44**
Bembridge Ho. *SE8* . . . *5B **80***
(off Longshore)
SW18 . . . . *4D **101***
(off Iron Mill Rd.)
Bemersyde Point *E13* . . 2D **69**
(off Dongola Rd.)
Bemerton Est. N1 . . . . . 4A **48**
Bemerton St. N1 . . . . . . 5B **48**
Bemish Rd. SW15 . . . . . 1F **99**
Benbow Ct. *W6* *4E **71***
(off Benbow Rd.)
Benbow Ho. *SE8* 2C **94**
(off Benbow St.)
Benbow Rd. W6 . . . . 4D **71**
Benbow St. SE8 . . . . . . 2C **94**
Benbury Cl.
BR1: Brom 5E **123**
Bence Ho. *SE8* *4A **80***
(off Rainsborough Av.)
Bendall M. NW1 . . . . . . *4A **60***
(off Bell St.)
Bendemeer Rd.
SW15 . . . . 1F **99**
Benden Ho. *SE13* . . . *3E **109***
(off Monument Gdns.)
Bendish Rd. E6 . . . . 4F **55**
Bendon Valley
SW18 . . . . 5D **101**
Benedict Rd. SW9 . . . . . 1B **104**
Ben Ezra Ct. *SE17* *5E **77***
(off Asolando Dr.)
Benfleet Ct. E8 . . . . 5B **50**
Bengal Ct. *EC3* *3C **18***
(off Birchin La.)
Bengal Ho. E1 . . . . *4F **65***
(off Duckett St.)
Bengeworth Rd.
SE5 . . . . 1E **105**
Benham Cl. SW11 . . . . . 1F **101**
Benham Ho. *SW10* . . . *3D **87***
(off Coleridge Gdns.)
Benham's Pl. NW3 . . . . . 1E **45**
Benhill Rd. SE5 . . . . 3F **91**
Benhurst Ct. SW16 . . . . 5C **118**
Benhurst La. SW16 . . . . 5C **118**
Benin St. SE13 . . . . 5F **109**
Benjamin Cl. E8 . . . . 5C **50**

Benjamin Franklin House
. . . . *1D **23***
(off Craven St.)
Benjamin St.
EC1 . . . . 5D **9** (4D **63**)
Ben Jonson Ct. N1 . . . . 1A **64**
Ben Jonson Ho. EC2 . . . 5A **10**
Ben Jonson Pl. EC2 . . . 5A **10**
Ben Jonson Rd. E1 . . . . 4F **65**
Benledi St. E14 . . . . 5F **67**
Bennelong Cl. W12 . . . . 1D **71**
Bennerley Rd. SW11 . . 3A **102**
Bennet's Hill
EC4 . . . . 4E **17** (1E **77**)
Bennet St.
SW1 . . . . 1F **21** (2E **75**)
Bennett Ct. SE3 . . . . . . 5B **34**
Bennett Gro. SE13 . . . . 4D **95**
Bennett Ho. *SW1* *5F **75***
(off Page St.)
Bennett Pk. SE3 . . . . . . 1B **110**
Bennett Rd. E13 . . . . . . 3E **69**
N16 . . . . 1A **50**
SW9 . . . . 5C **90**
Bennett St. W4 . . . . 2A **84**
Bennett's Yd. SW1 . . . . 4F **75**
Benn St. E9 . . . . 3A **52**
Bensbury Cl. SW15 . . . . 5D **99**
Ben Smith Way SE16 . . . 4C **78**
Benson Av. E6 . . . . 1E **69**
Benson Ho. E2 . . . . *3F **11***
(off Ligonier St.)
SE1 . . . . *2C **24***
(off Hatfields)
Benson Quay E1 . . . . . . 1E **79**
Benson Rd. SE23 . . . . . 1E **121**
Bentfield Gdns. SE9 . . . 3F **125**
Benthal Rd. N16 . . . . . . 4C **36**
Bentham Ct. *N1* *4E **49***
(off Ecclesbourne Rd.)
Bentham Ho. SE1 . . . . . 5B **26**
Bentham Rd. E9 . . . . . . 3F **51**
Bentinck Cl. NW8 . . . . . 1A **60**
Bentinck Ho. *W12* *1D **71***
(off White City Est.)
Bentinck M.
W1 . . . . 2C **12** (5C **60**)
Bentinck St.
W1 . . . . 2C **12** (5C **60**)
Bentley Cl. SW19 . . . . . 3C **114**
Bentley Ct. *SE13* *2E **109***
(off Whitburn Rd.)
Bentley Dr. NW2 . . . . . . 5B **30**
Bentley Ho. *SE5* *4A **92***
(off Peckham Rd.)
Bentley Rd. N1 . . . . 3A **50**
Bentons La. SE27 . . . . . 4E **119**
Benton's Ri. SE27 . . . . . 5F **119**
Bentworth Ct. E2 . . . . . . *3C **64***
(off Granby St.)
Bentworth Rd. W12 . . . . 5D **57**
Benville Ho. *SW8* *3B **90***
(off Oval Pl.)
Benwell Rd. N7 . . . . 1C **48**
Benwick Cl. SE16 . . . . . 5D **79**
Benworth St. E3 . . . . . . 2B **66**
Benyon Ct. *N1* *5A **50***
(off De Beauvoir Est.)
Benyon Ho. *EC1* *1C **8***
(off Myddelton Pas.)

Benyon Rd. N1 . . . . 5F 49
Berberis Ho. E3 . . . . . 4C 66
(off Gale St.)
Berber Pl. E14 . . . . 1C 80
Berber Rd. SW11 . . . 3B 102
Berenger Twr. SW10 . . . 3F 87
(off Worlds End Est.)
Berenger Wlk.
SW10 . . . . 3F 87
(off Worlds End Est.)
Berens Rd. NW10 . . . . 2F 57
Beresford Rd. N5 . . . . . 2F 49
Beresford Ter. N5 . . . . . 2F 49
Rerestede Rd. W6 . . . 1B 84
Bere St. E1 . . . . 1F 79
Bergen Ho. SE5 . . . . . 5E 91
(off Carew St.)
Bergen Sq. SE16 . . . . . 4A 80
Berger Rd. E9 . . . . 3F 51
Berghem M. W14 . . . . 4F 71
Bergholt Cres. N16 . . 2A 36
Bergholt M. NW1 . . . . 4E 47
Berglen Ct. E14 . . . . . . 5A 66
Bering Sq. E14 . . . . . . 1C 94
Bering Wlk. E16 . . . . . 5F 69
Berisford M. SW18 . . 4E 101
Berkeley Ct. NW1 . . . . . 4A 4
NW10 . . . . 1A 42
NW11 . . . . 2B 30
(off Ravenscroft Av.)
Berkeley Gdns. W8 . . 2C 72
Berkeley Ho. SE8 . . . 1B 94
(off Grove St.)
Berkeley M.
W1 . . . . 3A 12 (5B 60)
Berkeley Rd. E12 . . . . 2F 55
N8 . . . . 1F 33
N15 . . . . 1F 35
SW13 . . . . 4C 84
Berkeley Sq.
W1 . . . . 5E 13 (1D 75)
Berkeley St.
W1 . . . . 5E 13 (1D 75)
Berkeley Twr. E14 . . . 2B 80
(off Westferry Cir.)
Berkeley Wlk. N7 . . . . 4B 34
(off Durham Rd.)
Berkley Gro. NW1 . . 4C 46
Berkley Rd. NW1 . . . . 4B 46
Berkshire Ho. SE6 . . 4C 122
Berkshire Rd. E9 . . . . 3B 52
Bermans Way NW10 . . 1A 42
BERMONDSEY 3C 78
Bermondsey Sq.
SE1 . . . . . . 5E 27 (4A 78)
Bermondsey St.
SE1 . . . . 2D 27 (2A 78)
Bermondsey Trad. Est.
SE16 . . . . 1E 93
Bermondsey Wall E.
SE16 . . . . 3C 78
Bermondsey Wall W.
SE16 . . . . 3C 78
Bernard Angell Ho.
SE10 . . . . 2F 95
(off Trafalgar Rd.)
Bernard Ashley Dr.
SE7 . . . . 1D 97
Bernard Cassidy St.
E16 . . . . 4B 68

Bernard Gdns.
SW19 . . . . 5B 114
Bernard Mans. WC1 . . 4D 7
(off Bernard St.)
Bernard Rd. N15 . . . . 1B 36
Bernard Shaw Ct.
NW1 . . . . 4E 47
(off St Pancras Way)
Bernard St.
WC1 . . . . . . 4D 7 (3A 62)
Bernard Sunley Ho.
SW9 . . . . 3C 90
(off Sth. Island Pl.)
Bernays Gro. SW9 . . 2B 104
Berners Ho. N1 . . . . . 1C 62
(off Barnsbury Est.)
Berners M.
W1 . . . . . . 1A 14 (4E 61)
Berners Pl.
W1 . . . . . . 2A 14 (5E 61)
Berners Rd. N1 . . . . . 5D 49
Berners St.
W1 . . . . . . 1A 14 (4E 61)
Berner Ter. E1 . . . . . . 5C 64
Bernhardt Cres. NW8 . . 3A 60
Berridge M. NW6 . . . . 2C 44
Berridge Rd. SE19 . . 5F 119
Berriman Rd. N7 . . . . 5B 34
Berry Cotts. E14 . . . . . 5A 66
(off Maroon St.)
Berryfield Rd. SE17 . . 1D 91
Berry Ho. E1 . . . . 3D 65
(off Headlam St.)
Berry La. SE21 . . . . . 4F 119
Berryman's La.
SE26 . . . . 4F 121
Berry Pl. EC1 . . 2E 9 (2D 63)
Berry St. EC1 . . 3E 9 (3D 63)
Bertal Rd. SW17 . . . . 4F 115
Berthon St. SE8 . . . . . 3C 94
Bertie Rd. NW10 . . . . 3C 42
SE26 . . . . 5F 121
Bertram Rd. NW4 . . . . 1C 28
Bertram St. N19 . . . . . 4D 33
Bertrand Ho. SW16 . . 3A 118
(off Leigham Av.)
Bertrand St. SE13 . . . 1D 109
Berwick Ct. SE1 . . . . . 4A 26
Berwick Ho. E16 . . . . 5D 68
Berwick St.
W1 . . . . . . 2A 14 (5E 61)
Berwyn Rd. SE24 . . . . 1D 119
Beryl Rd. W6 . . . . 1F 85
Besant Ct. NW2 . . . . . 5A 30
Besant Ct. N1 . . . . 2F 49
Besant Ho. NW8 . . . . . 5E 45
(off Boundary Rd.)
Besant Pl. SE22 . . . . 2B 106
Besant Rd. NW2 . . . . . 1A 44
Besant Wlk. N7 . . . . . 4B 34
Besford Ho. E2 . . . . . . 1C 64
(off Pritchard's Rd.)
Besley St. SW16 . . . . 5E 117
Bessborough Gdns.
SW1 . . . . 1F 89
Bessborough Pl.
SW1 . . . . 1F 89
Bessborough Rd.
SW15 . . . . 1C 112

Bessborough St.
SW1 . . . . 1F 89
Bessemer Ct. NW1 . . . 4E 47
(off Rochester Sq.)
Bessemer Pk. Ind. Est.
SE24 . . . . 2D 105
Bessemer Rd. SE5 . . 5E 91
Bessingham Wlk.
SE4 . . . . 2F 107
(off Aldersford Cl.)
Besson St. SE14 . . . . 4E 93
Bessy St. E2 . . . . 2E 65
Bestwood St. SE8 . . . 5F 79
(off Rotherhithe New Rd.)
Beswick M. NW6 . . . . 3D 45
Beta Pl. SW4 . . . . 2B 104
Bethal St. SE1 . . . . . . 2E 27
Bethel Cl. NW4 . . . . . 1F 29
Bethell Av. E16 . . . . . 3B 68
Bethersden Ho. SE17 . . 1A 92
(off Kinglake St.)
Bethlehem Ho. E14 . . 1B 80
(off Limehouse C'way.)
BETHNAL GREEN 2D 65
Bethnal Green Cen. for
Sports & Performing Arts
. . . . 2E 65
Bethnal Green Mus. of
Childhood 2E 65
Bethnal Grn. Rd.
E1 . . . . 3F 11 (3B 64)
E2 . . . . 3F 11 (3B 64)
Bethune Cl. N16 . . . . 3A 36
Bethune Rd. N16 . . . . 2F 35
NW10 . . . . 3A 56
Bethwin Rd. SE5 . . . . 3D 91
Betsham Ho. SE1 . . . . 3B 26
(off Newcomen St.)
Betterton Ho. WC2 . . . 3E 15
(off Betterton St.)
Betterton St.
WC2 . . . . . . 3D 15 (5A 62)
Bettons Pk. E15 . . . . . 5A 54
Bettridge Rd. SW6 . . 5B 86
Betts Ho. E1 . . . . 1D 79
(off Betts St.)
Betts M. E17 . . . . 1B 38
Betts Rd. E16 . . . . 1D 83
Betts St. E1 . . . . 1D 79
Betty Brooks Ho. E11 . . 5F 39
Betty May Gray Ho.
E14 . . . . 5E 81
(off Pier St.)
Beulah Hill SE19 . . . . 5D 119
Beulah Rd. E17 . . . . . 1D 39
Bevan Ho. WC1 . . . . . 5F 7
(off Boswell St.)
Bevan St. N1 . . . . 5E 49
Bev Callender Cl.
SW8 . . . . 1D 103
Bevenden St.
N1 . . . . 1C 10 (2F 63)
Beveridge Rd.
NW10 . . . . 4A 42
Beverley Cl. SW11 . . 2F 101
SW13 . . . . 5C 84
Beverley Cotts.
SW15 . . . . 3A 112
Beverley Ct. SE4 . . . . 1B 108
(not continuous)

Beverley Gdns.
NW11 . . . . 2A **30**
SW13 . . . . 1B **98**
Beverley Ho.
BR1: Brom 5F **123**
(off Brangbourne Rd.)
Beverley La. SW15 . . . . 3B **112**
Beverley Path SW13 . . 5B **84**
Beverley Rd. E6 . . . . . . 2F **69**
SW13 . . . . 1B **98**
W4 . . . . 1B **84**
Beversbrook Rd. N19 . . 5F **33**
Beverstone Rd.
SW2 . . . . 3B **104**
Beverston M. W1 . . . . . 1A **12**
Bevill Allen Cl.
SW17 . . . . 5B **116**
Bevin Cl. SE16 . . . . 2A **80**
Bevin Ct. WC1 . . . 1A **8** (2B **62**)
Bevington Path SE1 . . . 4F **27**
Bevington Rd. W10 . . . 4A **58**
Bevington St. SE16 . . . 3C **78**
Bevin Ho. E2 . . . . 2E **65**
(off Butler St.)
Bevin Sq. SW17 . . . . . 3B **116**
Bevin Way
WC1 . . . . 1B **8** (1C **62**)
Bevis Marks
EC3 . . . . . . 2E **19** (5A **64**)
Bew Ct. SE22 . . . . 5C **106**
Bewdley St. N1 . . . . 4C **48**
Bewick M. SE15 . . . . . . 3D **93**
Bewick St. SW8 . . . . . . 5D **89**
Bewley Ho. E1 . . . . 1D **79**
(off Bewley St.)
Bewley St. E1 . . . . 1E **79**
Bewlys Rd. SE27 . . . . . 5D **119**
Bexhill Rd. SE4 . . . . . . 4B **108**
Bexhill Wlk. E15 . . . . . . 5A **54**
Bexley Ho. SE4 . . . . . . 2A **108**
Bianca Rd. SE15 . . . . . . 2C **92**
Bibury Cl. SE15 . . . . . . 2A **92**
(not continuous)
Bickenhall Mans. W1 . . 5A **4**
(not continuous)
Bickenhall St.
W1 . . . . 5A **4** (4B **60**)
Bickersteth Rd.
SW17 . . . . 5B **116**
Bickerton Rd. N19 . . . . 4E **33**
Bickley Rd. E10 . . . . . . 2D **39**
Bickley St. SW17 . . . . 5A **116**
Bicknell Ho. E1 . . . . 5C **64**
(off Ellen St.)
Bicknell Rd. SE5 . . . . . 1E **105**
Bidborough St.
WC1 . . . . 2D **7** (2A **62**)
Biddenham Ho. SE16 . . 5F **79**
(off Plough Way)
Bidder St. E16 . . . . 3A **68**
(not continuous)
Biddesden Ho. SW3 . . 5B **74**
(off Cadogan St.)
Biddestone Rd. N7 . . . 1B **48**
Biddulph Mans. W9 . . 2D **59**
(off Elgin Av.)
Biddulph Rd. W9 . . . . 2D **59**
Bideford Ho.
BR1: Brom 3B **124**
Bidwell St. SE15 . . . . . 4D **93**

Big Ben 4E **23** (3A **76**)
Biggerstaff Rd. E15 . . . 5E **53**
Biggerstaff St. N4 . . . . 4C **34**
Biggs Row SW15 . . . . . 1F **99**
Big Hill E5 . . . . 3D **37**
Bigland St. E1 . . . . 5D **65**
Bignold Rd. E7 . . . . . . 1C **54**
Bigwood Ct. NW11 . . . 1D **31**
Bigwood Rd.
NW11 . . . . 1F **31**
Bilberry Ho. E3 . . . . 4C **66**
(off Watts Gro.)
Billingford Cl.
SE4 . . . . 2F **107**
Billing Ho. E1 . . . . 5F **65**
(off Bower St.)
Billingley NW1 . . . . 5E **47**
(off Pratt St.)
Billing Pl. SW10 . . . . . . 3D **87**
Billing Rd. SW10 . . . . . 3D **87**
Billingsgate Fish Market
. . . . 2D **81**
Billing St. SW10 . . . . . . 3D **87**
Billington Rd.
SE14 . . . . 3F **93**
Billiter Sq. EC3 . . . . . . 3E **19**
Billiter St.
EC3 . . . . . . 3E **19** (5A **64**)
Billson St. E14 . . . . 5E **81**
Bilsby Gro. SE9 . . . . . 4F **125**
Bilton Towers W1 . . . . 3A **12**
(off Gt. Cumberland Pl.)
Bina Gdns. SW5 . . . . . 5E **73**
Binbrook Ho. W10 . . . . 4E **57**
(off Sutton Way)
Binden Rd. W12 . . . . . 4B **70**
Binfield Ho.
SW4 . . . . 4A **90**
Bingfield St. N1 . . . . . . 5A **48**
(not continuous)
Bingham Ct. N1 . . . . . . 4D **49**
(off Halton Rd.)
Bingham Pl.
W1 . . . . 5B **4** (4C **60**)
Bingham St. N1 . . . . . . 3F **49**
Bingley Rd. E16 . . . . . . 5E **69**
Binley Ho. SW15 . . . . . 4B **98**
Binney St.
W1 . . . . 3C **12** (5C **60**)
Binnie Ct. SE10 . . . . . . 3D **95**
(off Greenwich High Rd.)
Binnie Ho. SE1 . . . . 5F **25**
(off Bath Ter.)
Binns Rd. W4 . . . . 1A **84**
Binns Ter. W4 . . . . 1A **84**
Bircham Path SE4 . . . . 2F **107**
(off Aldersford Cl.)
Birch Cl. E16 . . . . 4A **68**
N19 . . . . 4E **33**
SE15 . . . . 5C **92**
Birchdale Rd. E7 . . . . . 2E **55**
Birchen Cl. NW9 . . . . . 4A **28**
Birchen Gro. NW9 . . . . 4A **28**
Birches, The E12 . . . . . 1F **55**
SE7 . . . . 2D **97**
Birchfield Ho. E14 . . . . 1C **80**
(off Birchfield St.)
Birchfield St. E14 . . . . . 1C **80**
Birch Gro. E11 . . . . 1A **54**
SE12 . . . . 5B **110**

Birch Ho. SE14 . . . . . . 4B **94**
SW2 . . . . 4C **104**
(off Tulse Hill)
W10 . . . . 3A **58**
(off Droop St.)
Birchington Ct. NW6 . . 5D **45**
(off W. End La.)
Birchington Ho. E5 . . . 2D **51**
Birchington Rd. N8 . . . 1F **33**
NW6 . . . . 5C **44**
Birchin La.
EC3 . . . . . . 3C **18** (5F **63**)
Birchlands Av.
SW12 . . . . 5B **102**
Birchmere Lodge
SE16 . . . . 1D **93**
(off Sherwood Gdns.)
Birchmere Row SE3 . . 5B **96**
Birchmore Hall N5 . . . 1E **35**
Birchmore Wlk. N5 . . . 5E **35**
Birch Va. Ct. NW8 . . . . 3F **59**
(off Pollitt Dr.)
Birchwood Dr. NW3 . . 5D **31**
Birchwood Rd.
SW17 . . . . 5D **117**
Birdbrook Ho. N1 . . . . . 4E **49**
(off Popham Rd.)
Birdbrook Rd. SE3 . . . 2E **111**
Birdcage Wlk.
SW1 . . . . . . 4F **21** (3E **75**)
Birdhurst Rd. SW18 . . 3E **101**
Bird in Bush BMX Track
. . . . 3D **93**
(off Bird in Bush Rd.)
Bird in Bush Rd.
SE15 . . . . 3C **92**
Bird-in-Hand Pas.
SE23 . . . . 2E **121**
Bird in Hand Yd.
NW3 . . . . 1E **45**
(off Holly Bush Va.)
NW3 . . . . 1E **45**
(Perrin's Ct.)
Birdlip Cl. SE15 . . . . . . 2A **92**
Birdsall Ho. SE5 . . . . 1A **106**
Birdsfield La. E3 . . . . . 5B **52**
Bird St. W1 . . . 3C **12** (5C **60**)
Birkbeck College 5C **6**
Birkbeck Hill SE21 . . . 1D **119**
Birkbeck M. E8 . . . . . . 2B **50**
Birkbeck Pl. SE21 . . . . 2E **119**
Birkbeck Rd. E8 . . . . . . 2B **50**
SW19 . . . . 5D **115**
Birkbeck St. E2 . . . . . . 2D **65**
Birkdale Cl. SE16 . . . . . 1D **93**
Birkenhead St.
WC1 . . . . 1E **7** (2A **62**)
Birkhall Rd. SE6 . . . . . 1F **123**
Birkwood Cl. SW12 . . 5F **103**
Birley Lodge NW8 . . . . 1F **59**
(off Acacia Rd.)
Birley St. SW11 . . . . . . 5C **88**
Birnam Rd. N4 . . . . 4B **34**
Birrell Ho. SW9 . . . . . . 5B **90**
(off Stockwell Rd.)
Birse Cres. NW10 . . . . 5A **28**
Birstall Rd. N15 . . . . . . 1A **36**
Biscay Ho. E1 . . . . 3F **65**
(off Mile End Rd.)
Biscayne Av. E14 . . . . . 2F **81**

Biscay Rd. W6 . . . . 1F 85
Biscoe Way SE13 . . . . . 1F 109
Biscott Ho. E3 . . . . 3D 67
Bisham Gdns. N6 . . . . . . 3C 32
Bishopsgate Chu. Yd.
EC2 . . . . 4A 64
Bishop King's Rd.
W14 . . . . 5A 72
Bishop's Av. E13. . . . . . . 5D 55
Bishop's Av., The N2 . . . 2F 31
Bishop's Bri. Rd. W2 . . . 5D 59
Bishops Cl. N19 . . . . 5E 33
Bishops Ct. EC4 . . . . 2D 17
W2 . . . . 5D 59
(off Bishop's Bri. Rd.)
WC2 . . . . 2B 16
Bishopsdale Ho.
NW6 . . . . 5C 44
(off Kilburn Va.)
Bishopsgate
EC2 . . . . 3D 19 (5A 64)
Bishopsgate Arc. EC2. . . 1E 19
Bishopsgate Institute &
Libraries 1E 19
(off Bishopsgate)
Bishops Gro. N2 . . . . 1A 32
Bishops Ho. SW8 . . . . . . 3A 90
(off Sth. Lambeth Rd.)
Bishop's Mans. SW6 . . . . 5F 85
(not continuous)
Bishops Mead SE5 . . . . . 3E 91
(off Camberwell Rd.)
Bishop's Pk. Rd.
SW6 . . . . 5F 85
Bishops Rd. N6 . . . . 1C 32
SW6 . . . . 4A 86
SW11 . . . . 3A 88
Bishop's Ter. SE11 . . . . . 5C 76
Bishopsthorpe Rd.
SE26 . . . . 4F 121
Bishop St. N1 . . . . 5E 49
Bishop's Way E2 . . . . 1D 65
Bishops Wood Almshouses
E5 . . . . 1D 51
(off Lwr. Clapton Rd.)
Bishopswood Rd. N6 . . . 2B 32
Bishop Way NW10 . . . . . 4A 42
Bishop Wilfred Wood Cl.
SE15 . . . . 5C 92
Bishop Wilfred Wood Ct.
E13 . . . . 1E 69
(off Pragel St.)
Bissextile Ho. SE13 . . . . 5D 95
Bisson Rd. E15 . . . . 1E 67
Bittern Ct. SE8 . . . . 2C 94
Bittern Ho. SE1 . . . . 4F 25
(off Gt. Suffolk St.)
Bittern St.
SE1 . . . . 4F 25 (3E 77)
Blackall St.
EC2 . . . . 3D 11 (3A 64)
Blackbird Yd. E2 . . . . 2B 64
Black Boy La. N15 . . . . . 1E 35
Blackburne's M.
W1 . . . . 4B 12 (1C 74)
Blackburn Rd. NW6 . . . . 3B 45
Blackett St. SW15 . . . . . 1F 99
Blackford's Path
SW15 . . . . 5C 98

Blackfriars Bri.
SE1 . . . . 5D 17 (1D 77)
Blackfriars Ct. EC4. . . . . 4D 17
Black Friars La.
EC4 . . . . 4D 17 (5D 63)
(not continuous)
Blackfriars Pas.
EC4 . . . . 4D 17 (1D 77)
Blackfriars Rd.
SE1 . . . . 1D 25 (3D 77)
Blackfriars Underpass
EC4 . . . . 4D 17 (1C 76)
BLACKHEATH 5B 96
Blackheath Av. SE10 . . . 3F 95
Blackheath Bus. Est.
SE10 . . . . 5B 96
(off Blackheath Hill)
Blackheath Concert Halls
. . . . 1B 110
Blackheath Gro. SE3 . . . 5B 96
Blackheath Hill SE10 . . . 4E 95
BLACKHEATH PK. 2C 110
Blackheath Pk. SE3 . . . . 1B 110
Blackheath Ri. SE13 . . . . 5E 95
(not continuous)
Blackheath Rd. SE10 . . . 4D 95
BLACKHEATH VALE. 5B 96
Blackheath Va. SE3 . . . . 5A 96
Blackheath Village
SE3 . . . . 5B 96
Black Horse Ct. SE1 . . . . 5C 26
Blackhorse Rd. SE8 . . . . 2A 94
Blacklands Est. SE6 . . . . 4E 123
Blacklands Ter. SW3 . . . 5B 74
Black Lion La. W6 . . . . . 5C 70
Black Lion M. W6 . . . . . . 5C 70
Blackmans Yd. E2 . . . . . 3C 64
(off Grimsby St.)
Blackmore Ho. N1 . . . . . 5B 48
(off Barnsbury Est.)
Black Path E10 . . . . 2A 38
Blackpool Rd. SE15 . . . . 5D 93
Black Prince Rd. SE1 . . . 5B 76
SE11 . . . . 5B 76
Blackshaw Rd.
SW17 . . . . 4E 115
Blacks Rd. W6 . . . . 1E 85
Blackstock M. N4 . . . . . . 4D 35
Blackstock Rd. N4 . . . . . 4D 35
N5 . . . . 4D 35
Blackstone Est. E8 . . . . . 4C 50
Blackstone Rd. NW2 . . . 2E 43
Black Swan Yd.
SE1 . . . . 3E 27 (3A 78)
Blackthorn Ct. E11 . . . . . 1F 53
(off Hall Rd.)
Blackthorne Ct. SE15 . . . 3B 92
(off Cator St.)
Blackthorn St. E3 . . . . . . 3C 66
Blacktree M. SW9 . . . . . 1C 104
BLACKWALL 2E 81
Blackwall La. SE10 . . . . . 1A 96
Blackwall Trad. Est.
E14 . . . . 4E 67
Blackwall Tunnel E14 . . . 2F 81
(not continuous)
Blackwall Tunnel App.
E14 . . . . 5E 67

Blackwall Tunnel
Northern App.
E3 . . . . 1C 66
E14 . . . . 1C 66
Blackwall Tunnel
Southern App.
SE10 . . . . 4A 82
Blackwall Way E14. . . . . 2E 81
Blackwater Cl. E7. . . . . . 1B 54
Blackwater Ho.
NW8 . . . . 4F 59
(off Church St.)
Blackwater St. SE22. . . . 3B 106
Blackwell Cl. E5. . . . . . . 1F 51
Blackwell Ho. SW4 . . . . 4F 103
Blackwood Ho. E1 . . . . . 3D 65
(off Collingwood St.)
Blackwood St. SE17 . . . 1F 91
Blade M. SW15 . . . . 2B 100
Bladen Ho. E1. . . . . 5F 65
(off Dunelm St.)
Blades Ct. SW15 . . . . . . 2B 100
W6 . . . . 1D 85
(off Lower Mall)
Blades Ho. SE11 . . . . . . 2C 90
(off Kennington Oval)
Bladon Ct. SW16 . . . . . . 5A 118
Blagdon Rd. SE13 . . . . . 4D 109
Blagrove Rd. W10 . . . . . 4A 58
Blair Av. NW9 . . . . 2A 28
Blair Cl. N1. . . . . 3E 49
Blair Ct. NW8 . . . . 5F 45
SE6. . . . . 1B 124
Blairderry Rd. SW2 . . . . 2A 118
Blairgowrie Ct. E14 . . . . 5F 67
(off Blair St.)
Blair Ho. SW9 . . . . 5B 90
Blair St. E14. . . . . 5E 67
Blake Ct. NW6 . . . . 2C 58
(off Malvern Rd.)
SE16. . . . . 1D 93
(off Stubbs Dr.)
Blake Gdns. SW6. . . . . . 4D 87
Blake Hall Cres. E11 . . . 3C 40
Blake Hall Rd. E11. . . . . 2C 40
Blake Ho. E14 . . . . 3C 80
(off Admirals Way)
SE1 . . . . 5B 24 (4C 76)
SE8. . . . . 2C 94
(off New King St.)
Blakeley Cotts.
SE10 . . . . 3F 81
Blakemore Rd.
SW16 . . . . 3A 118
Blakeney Cl. E8 . . . . 2C 50
NW1 . . . . 4F 47
Blakenham Rd.
SW17 . . . . 4B 116
Blaker Ct. SE7 . . . . 3E 97
(not continuous)
Blake Rd. E16 . . . . 3B 68
Blaker Rd. E15. . . . . 1E 67
Blakes Cl. W10 . . . . 4E 57
Blake's Rd. SE15 . . . . . . 3A 92
Blanchard Way E8 . . . . . 3C 50
Blanchedowne SE5. . . . . 2F 105
Blanche St. E16 . . . . 3B 68
Blandfield Rd.
SW12 . . . . 5C 102

Blandford Ct. *N1* 4A **50**
  (off St Peter's Way)
NW6 . . . . 4F **43**
Blandford Ho. *SW8* 3B **90**
  (off Richborne Ter.)
Blandford Rd. *W4* 4A **70**
Blandford Sq. *NW1* 3A **60**
Blandford St.
  W1 . . . . 2A **12** (5B **60**)
Bland Ho. *SE11* 1B **90**
  (off Vauxhall St.)
Bland St. *SE9* 2F **111**
Blann Cl. *SE9* 4F **111**
Blantyre St. *SW10* 3F **87**
Blantyre Twr. *SW10* 3F **87**
  (off Blantyre St.)
Blantyre Wlk. *SW10* 3F **87**
  (off Worlds End Est.)
Blashford *NW3* 4B **46**
  (off Adelaide Rd.)
Blashford St. *SE13* 5F **109**
Blasker Wlk. *E14* 1D **95**
Blaxland Ho. *W12* 1D **71**
  (off White City Est.)
Blazer Ct. *NW8* 2F **59**
  (off St John's Wood Rd.)
Blechynden Ho. *W10* . . . 5F **57**
  (off Kingsdown Cl.)
Blechynden St. *W10* 1F **71**
Bledlow Ho. *NW8* 3F **59**
  (off Capland St.)
Bleeding Heart Yd.
  EC1 . . . . 1C **16**
Blegborough Rd.
  SW16 . . . . 5E **117**
Blemundsbury *WC1* 5F **7**
  (off Dombey St.)
Blendon Row *SE17* 5F **77**
  (off Townley St.)
Blendworth Point
  SW15 . . . . 1D **113**
Blenheim Cl. *SE12* 1D **125**
Blenheim Cl. *N19* 4A **34**
  SE16 . . . . 2F **79**
  (off King & Queen Wharf)
Blenheim Cres. *W11* 1A **72**
Blenheim Gdns. *NW2* . . . 3E **43**
  SW2 . . . . 4B **104**
Blenheim Gro. *SE15* . . . 5C **92**
Blenheim Ho. *E16* 2D **83**
  (off Constable Av.)
Blenheim Pas. *NW8* 1E **59**
  (not continuous)
Blenheim Rd. *E6* 2F **69**
  E15 . . . . 1A **54**
  NW8 . . . . 1E **59**
  W4 . . . . 4A **70**
Blenheim St.
  W1 . . . . 3D **13** (5D **61**)
Blenheim Ter. *NW8* 1E **59**
Blenkarne Rd.
  SW11 . . . . 4B **102**
Blessington Cl.
  SE13 . . . . 1F **109**
Blessington Rd.
  SE13 . . . . 1F **109**
Bletchley Ct. *N1* 1B **10**
  (not continuous)
Bletchley St.
  N1 . . . . 1A **10** (1F **63**)

Bletsoe Wlk. *N1* 1E **63**
Blick Ho. *SE16* 4E **79**
  (off Neptune St.)
Blincoe Cl. *SW19* 2F **113**
Bliss Cres. *SE13* 5D **95**
Blissett St. *SE10* 4E **95**
Bliss M. *W10* 2A **58**
Blisworth Ho. *E2* 5C **50**
  (off Whiston Rd.)
Blithfield St. *W8* 4D **73**
Bloemfontein Av.
  W12 . . . . 2D **71**
Bloemfontein Rd.
  W12 . . . . 1D **71**
Bloemfontein Way
  W12 . . . . 2D **71**
Blomfield Ct. *W9* 3E **59**
  (off Maida Va.)
Blomfield Mans.
  W12 . . . . 2E **71**
  (off Stanlake Rd.)
Blomfield Rd. *W9* 4D **59**
Blomfield St.
  EC2 . . . . 1C **18** (4F **63**)
Blomfield Vs. *W2* 4D **59**
Blondel St. *SW11* 5C **88**
Blondin St. *E3* 1C **66**
Bloomburg St. *SW1* 5F **75**
Bloomfield Ct. *N6* 1C **32**
Bloomfield Ho. *E1* 4C **64**
  (off Old Montague St.)
Bloomfield Pl. *W1* 4E **13**
Bloomfield Rd. *N6* 1C **32**
Bloomfield Ter. *SW1* . . . 1C **88**
Bloom Gro. *SE27* 3D **119**
Bloomhall Rd. *SE19* . . . 5F **119**
Bloom Pk. Rd. *SW6* 3B **86**
BLOOMSBURY
  . . . . 5D **7** (4A **62**)
Bloomsbury Ct. *WC1* . . . 1E **15**
Bloomsbury Ho.
  SW4 . . . . 4F **103**
Bloomsbury Pl.
  SW18 . . . . 3E **101**
  WC1 . . . . 5E **7** (4A **62**)
Bloomsbury Sq.
  WC1 . . . . 1E **15** (4A **62**)
Bloomsbury St.
  WC1 . . . . 1C **14** (4F **61**)
Bloomsbury Theatre 3B **6**
Bloomsbury Way
  WC1 . . . . 1D **15** (4A **62**)
Blore Cl. *SW8* 4F **89**
Blore Ct. *W1* 3B **14**
Blore Ho. *SW10* 3D **87**
  (off Coleridge Gdns.)
Blossom St.
  E1 . . . . 4E **11** (3A **64**)
Blount Ho. *E14* 4A **66**
  (off Maroon St.)
Blount St. *E14* 5A **66**
Bloxam Gdns. *SE9* 3F **111**
Bloxhall Rd. *E10* 3B **38**
Blucher Rd. *SE5* 3E **91**
Blue Anchor La.
  SE16 . . . . 5C **78**
Blue Anchor Yd. *E1* 1C **78**
Blue Ball Yd.
  SW1 . . . . 2F **21** (2E **75**)
Bluebell Av. *E12* 2F **55**

Bluebell Cl. *E9* 5E **51**
  SE26 . . . . 4B **120**
Blue Elephant Theatre
  . . . . 3E **91**
  (off Bethwin Rd.)
Bluegate M. *E1* 1D **79**
Blue Lion Pl.
  SE1 . . . . 5D **27** (4A **78**)
Blueprint Apartments
  SW12 . . . . 5D **103**
  (off Balham Gro.)
Blue Water *SW18* 2D **101**
Blundell Cl. *E8* 2C **50**
Blundell St. *N7* 4A **48**
Blurton Rd. *E5* 1E **51**
Blyth Cl. *E14* 5F **81**
Blythe Cl. *SE6* 5B **108**
BLYTHE HILL 5B **108**
Blythe Hill *SE6* 5B **108**
Blythe Hill La. *SE6* 5B **108**
Blythe Hill Pl. *SE23* . . . 5A **108**
Blythe Ho. *SE11* 2C **90**
Blythe M. *W14* 4F **71**
Blythendale Ho. *E2* . . . 1C **64**
  (off Mansford St.)
Blythe Rd. *W14* 4F **71**
  (not continuous)
Blythe St. *E2* 2D **65**
Blythe Va. *SE6* 1B **122**
Blyth Hill Pl. *SE23* . . . 5A **108**
  (off Brockley Pk.)
Blyth Rd. *E17* 2B **38**
Blyth's Wharf *E14* 1A **80**
Blythwood Rd. *N4* 2A **34**
Boades M. *NW3* 1F **45**
Boadicea St. *N1* 5B **48**
Boardman Pl. *E14* 2E **81**
Boarley Ho. *SE17* 5A **78**
  (off Massinger St.)
Boathouse Cen., The
  W10 . . . . 3F **57**
  (off Canal Cl.)
Boathouse Wlk.
  SE15 . . . . 3B **92**
  (not continuous)
Boat Lifter Way *SE16* . . . 5A **80**
Boat Quay *E16* 1E **83**
Bob Anker Cl. *E13* 2C **68**
Bobbin Cl. *SW4* 1E **103**
Bob Marley Way
  SE24 . . . . 2C **104**
Bocking St. *E8* 5D **51**
Boddicott Cl. *SW19* . . . 2A **114**
Boddington Ho. *SE14* . . 4E **93**
  (off Pomeroy St.)
  SW13 . . . . 2D **85**
  (off Wyatt Dr.)
Bodeney Ho. *SE5* 4A **92**
  (off Peckham Rd.)
Boden Ho. *E1* 4C **64**
  (off Woodseer St.)
Bodington Ct. *W12* 3F **71**
Bodley Mnr. Way
  SW2 . . . . 5C **104**
Bodmin St. *SW18* 1C **114**
Bodney Rd. *E8* 2D **51**
Bogart Ct. *E14* 1C **80**
  (off Premiere Pl.)
Bohemia Pl. *E8* 3E **51**
Bohn Rd. *E1* 4A **66**

Boileau Rd. SW13 . . . . . 3C 84
Boisseau Ho. E1 . . . . 4E 65
    (off Stepney Way)
Bolden St. SE8 . . . . 5D 95
Boldero Pl. NW8 . . . . . . 3A 60
    (off Gateforth St.)
Boleyn Ho. E16 . . . . 2C 82
    (off Southey M.)
Boleyn Rd. E6 . . . . 1F 69
  E7 . . . . 4C 54
  N16 . . . . 2A 50
Bolina Rd. SE16 . . . . . . 1E 93
Bolingbroke Gro.
  SW11 . . . . 2A 102
Bolingbroke Rd. W14 . . 4F 71
Bolingbroke Wlk.
  SW11 . . . . 4F 87
Bolney Ga. SW7 . . . . . . 3A 74
Bolney St. SW8 . . . . 3B 90
Bolsover St.
  W1 . . . . 4E 5 (3D 61)
Bolt Ct. EC4 . . . . 3C 16
Bolton Cres. SE5 . . . . . . 3D 91
Bolton Gdns. NW10 . . . 1F 57
  SW5 . . . . 1D 87
Bolton Gdns. M.
  SW10 . . . . 1E 87
Bolton Ho. SE10 . . . . . . 1A 96
    (off Trafalgar Rd.)
Bolton Pl. NW8 . . . . 5D 45
    (off Bolton Rd.)
Bolton Rd. E15 . . . . 3B 54
  NW8 . . . . 5D 45
  NW10 . . . . 5A 42
Boltons, The SW10 . . . . 1E 87
Boltons Ct. SW5 . . . . . . 1D 87
    (off Old Brompton Rd.)
Boltons Pl. SW5 . . . . . . 1E 87
Bolton St.
  W1 . . . . 1E 21 (2D 75)
Bolton Studios SW10 . . 1E 87
    (off Durham Rd.)
Bolton Wlk. N7 . . . . 4B 34
    (off Durham Rd.)
Bombay Ct. SE16 . . . . . . 3E 79
    (off St Marychurch St.)
Bombay St. SE16 . . . . . . 5D 79
Bomore Rd. W11 . . . . . . 1A 72
Bonar Rd. SE15 . . . . 3C 92
Bonchurch Rd. W10 . . . 4A 58
Bond Ct. EC4 . . 4B 18 (1F 77)
Bond Ho. NW6 . . . . 1B 58
    (off Rupert Rd.)
  SE14 . . . . 3A 94
    (off Goodwood Rd.)
Bonding Yd. Wlk.
  SE16 . . . . 4A 80
Bond St. E15 . . . . 2A 54
  W4 . . . . 5A 70
Bondway SW8 . . . . 2A 90
Bonfield Rd. SE13 . . . . . 2E 109
Bonham Rd. SW2 . . . . . 3B 104
Bonheur Rd. W4 . . . . . . 3A 70
Bonhill St.
  EC2 . . . . 4C 10 (3F 63)
Bonita M. SE4 . . . . 1F 107
Bon Marche Ter. M.
  SE27 . . . . 4A 120
    (off Gypsy Rd.)
Bonner Rd. E2 . . . . 1E 65
Bonner St. E2 . . . . 1E 65

Bonneville Gdns.
  SW4 . . . . 4E 103
Bonnington Ho. N1 . . . . 1B 62
Bonnington Sq.
  SW8 . . . . 2B 90
Bonny St. NW1 . . . . 4E 47
Bonsor Ho. SW8 . . . . . . 4E 89
Bonsor St. SE5 . . . . 3A 92
Bonville Rd.
  BR1: Brom 5B 124
Booker Cl. E14 . . . . 4B 66
Boones Rd. SE13 . . . . . . 2A 110
Boone St. SE13 . . . . 2A 110
Boord St. SE10 . . . . 4A 82
Boothby Rd. N19 . . . . . . 4F 33
Booth Cl. E9 . . . . 5D 51
Booth La. EC4 . . . . 4F 17
Booth's Pl.
  W1 . . . . 1A 14 (4E 61)
Boot St. N1 . . 2D 11 (2A 64)
Border Cres. SE26 . . . . . 5D 121
Border Rd. SE26 . . . . . . 5D 121
Bordon Wlk. SW15 . . . . 5C 98
Boreas Wlk. N1 . . . . 1E 9
Boreham Av. E16 . . . . . . 5C 68
Boreham Cl. E11 . . . . . . 3E 39
Boreman Ho. SE10 . . . . 2E 95
    (off Thames St.)
Borland Rd. SE15 . . . . . 2E 107
Borneo St. SW15 . . . . . . 1E 99
BOROUGH, THE
  . . . . 4A 26 (3F 77)
Borough High St.
  SE1 . . . . 4A 26 (3E 77)
Borough Mkt. SE1 . . . . . 2B 26
Borough Rd.
  SE1 . . . . 5E 25 (4D 77)
Borrett Cl. SE17 . . . . 1E 91
Borrodaile Rd.
  SW18 . . . . 4D 101
Borrowdale NW1 . . . . . . 2F 5
    (off Robert St.)
Borthwick M. E15 . . . . . 1A 54
Borthwick Rd. E15 . . . . . 1A 54
  NW9 . . . . 1B 28
Borthwick St. SE8 . . . . . 1C 94
Bosbury Rd. SE6 . . . . . . 3E 123
Boscastle Rd. NW5 . . . . 5D 33
Boscobel Ho. E8 . . . . . . 3D 51
Boscobel Pl. SW1 . . . . . 5C 74
Boscobel St. NW8 . . . . . 3F 59
Boscombe Av. E10 . . . . . 2F 39
Boscombe Cl. E5 . . . . . . 2A 52
Boscombe Rd.
  SW17 . . . . 5C 116
  W12 . . . . 2C 70
Boss Ho. SE1 . . . . 3F 27
    (off Boss St.)
Boss St. SE1 . . 3F 27 (3B 78)
Boston Gdns. W4 . . . . . . 2A 84
Boston Pl. NW1 . . . . 3B 60
Boston Rd. E6 . . . . 2F 69
  E17 . . . . 1C 38
Bosun Cl. E14 . . . . 3C 80
Boswell Ct. W14 . . . . . . 4E 71
    (off Blythe Rd.)
  WC1 . . . . 5E 7 (4A 62)
Boswell Ho. WC1 . . . . . . 5E 7
    (off Boswell St.)

Boswell St.
  WC1 . . . . 5E 7 (4A 62)
Bosworth Ho. W10 . . . . 3A 58
    (off Bosworth Rd.)
Bosworth Rd. W10 . . . . 3A 58
Botha Rd. E13 . . . . 4D 69
Bothwell Cl. E16 . . . . . . 4B 68
Bothwell St. W6 . . . . . . 2F 85
Botolph All. EC3 . . . . . . 4D 19
Botolph La.
  EC3 . . . . 5D 19 (1A 78)
Botts M. W2 . . . . 5C 58
Boughton Ho. SE1 . . . . . 3B 26
    (off Tennis St.)
Boulcott St. E1 . . . . 5F 65
Boulevard, The SW6 . . . 4E 87
  SW17 . . . . 2C 116
  SW18 . . . . 2D 101
Boulogne Ho. SE1 . . . . . 5F 27
    (off Abbey St.)
Boulter Ho. SE14 . . . . . 4E 93
    (off Kender St.)
Boundaries Rd.
  SW12 . . . . 2B 116
Boundary Av. E17 . . . . . 2B 38
Boundary Ho. SE5 . . . . . 3E 91
Boundary La. E13 . . . . . 2F 69
  SE17 . . . . 2E 91
Boundary Pas.
  E1 . . . . 3F 11 (3B 64)
Boundary Rd. E13 . . . . . 1E 69
  E17 . . . . 2B 38
  NW8 . . . . 5D 45
  SW19 . . . . 5F 115
Boundary Row
  SE1 . . . . 3D 25 (3D 77)
Boundary St.
  E2 . . . . 2F 11 (2B 64)
Boundfield Rd. SE6 . . . . 3A 124
Bourbon Ho. SE6 . . . . . . 5E 123
Bourchier St.
  W1 . . . . 4B 14 (1F 75)
    (not continuous)
Bourdon Pl. W1 . . . . 4E 13
Bourdon St.
  W1 . . . . 5D 13 (1D 75)
Bourke Cl. NW10 . . . . . . 3A 42
  SW4 . . . . 4A 104
Bourlet Cl.
  W1 . . . . 1F 13 (4E 61)
Bournbrook Rd. SE3 . . . 1F 111
Bourne Est.
  EC1 . . . . 5B 8 (4C 62)
Bourne M.
  W1 . . . . 3C 12 (5C 60)
Bournemouth Cl.
  SE15 . . . . 5C 92
Bournemouth Rd.
  SE15 . . . . 5C 92
Bourne Pl. W4 . . . . 1A 84
Bourne Rd. E7 . . . . 5B 40
  N8 . . . . 1A 34
Bournes Ho. N15 . . . . . . 1A 36
    (off Chisley Rd.)
Bourneside Gdns.
  SE6 . . . . 5E 123
Bourne St. SW1 . . . . 5C 74
Bourne Ter. W2 . . . . 4D 59
Bournevale Rd.
  SW16 . . . . 4A 118

Bournville Rd. SE6....5C **108**
Bousfield Rd. SE14....5F **93**
Boutflower Rd.
 SW11.............2A **102**
Boutique Hall SE13...2E **109**
Bouverie M. N16.....4A **36**
Bouverie Pl. W2......5F **59**
Bouverie Rd. N16....3A **36**
Bouverie St.
 EC4.........3C **16** (5C **62**)
Boveney Rd. SE23....5F **107**
Bovill Rd. SE23......5F **107**
Bovingdon Cl. N19....4E **33**
Bovingdon Rd. SW6...4D **87**
BOW................2B **66**
Bowater Cl. SW2....4A **104**
Bowater Ho. EC1........*4F 9*
 (off Golden La. Est.)
 SW1.............3A **20**
Bowater Pl. SE3.....3D **97**
Bowater Rd. SE18....4F **83**
Bow Bri. Est. E3.....2D **67**
Bow Brook, The E2....*1F 65*
 (off Mace St.)
Bow Chyd. EC4........3A **18**
BOW COMMON.......4C **66**
Bow Comn. La. E3....3B **66**
Bowden St. SE11.....1C **90**
Bowditch SE8.........5B **80**
 (not continuous)
Bowdon Rd. E17......2C **38**
Bowen Dr. SE21......3A **120**
Bowen St. E14.......5D **67**
Bower Av. SE10......4A **96**
Bowerdean St. SW6...4D **87**
Bower Ho. SE14.......*4F 93*
 (off Besson St.)
Bowerman Av. SE14...2A **94**
Bowerman Ct. N19.....*4F 33*
 (off St John's Way)
Bower St. E1.........5F **65**
Bowes-Lyon Hall E16..*2C 82*
 (off Wesley Av.,
 not continuous)
Bowes Rd. W3.......1A **70**
Bowfell Rd. W6......2E **85**
Bowhill Cl. SW9......3C **90**
Bowie Cl. SW4.......5F **103**
Bow Ind. Pk. E15.....4C **52**
BOW INTERCHANGE...1D **67**
Bowland Rd. SW4....2F **103**
Bowland Yd. SW1.....4A **20**
Bow La. EC4....3A **18** (5E **63**)
Bowl Ct. EC2....4E **11** (3A **64**)
Bowles Rd. SE1......2C **92**
Bowley Cl. SE19.....5B **120**
Bowley Ho. SE16.....4C **78**
Bowley La. SE19.....5B **120**
Bowling Grn. Cl.
 SW15.............5D **99**
Bowling Grn. La.
 EC1.........3C **8** (3C **62**)
Bowling Grn. Pl.
 SE1.........3B **26** (3F **77**)
Bowling Grn. St.
 SE11.............2C **90**
Bowling Grn. Wlk.
 N1.........1D **11** (2A **64**)
Bow Locks E3........3E **67**
Bowman Av. E16......1B **82**

Bowman M. SW18....1B **114**
Bowman's Bldgs.
 NW1.............*4A 60*
 (off Penfold Pl.)
Bowmans Lea SE23...5E **107**
Bowman's M. E1.....1C **78**
 N7..............5A **34**
Bowman's Pl. N7.....*5A 34*
Bowmore Wlk. NW1...4F **47**
Bowness Cl. E8.......*3B 50*
 (off Beechwood Rd.)
Bowness Cres.
 SW15............5A **112**
Bowness Ho. SE15....*3E 93*
 (off Hillbeck Cl.)
Bowness Rd. SE6....5D **109**
Bowood Rd. SW11....3C **102**
Bow Quarter, The E3..1C **66**
Bow Rd. E3..........2B **66**
Bowry Ho. E14.......*4B 66*
 (off Wallwood St.)
Bowspring Point E14..*4C 80*
 (off Westferry Rd.)
Bow St. E15.........2A **54**
 WC2.......3E **15** (5A **62**)
Bow Triangle Bus. Cen.
 E3..............3C **66**
Bowyer Ho. N1........*1A 64*
 (off Mill Row)
Bowyer Pl. SE5......3E **91**
Bowyer St. SE5......3E **91**
Boxall Rd. SE21.....4A **106**
Boxley St. E16......2D **83**
Boxmoor Ho. W11.....*2F 71*
 (off Queensdale Cres.)
Box Tree Ho. SE8....2A **94**
Boxworth Gro. N1....5B **48**
Boyce Ho. SW16......5E **117**
 W10...............*2B 58*
 (off Bruckner St.)
Boyce Way E13......3C **68**
Boydell Ct. NW8.....4F **45**
 (not continuous)
Boyd Rd. SW19......5F **115**
Boyd St. E1.........5C **64**
Boyfield St.
 SE1.........4E **25** (3D **77**)
Boyland Rd.
 BR1: Brom......5B **124**
Boyle St. W1....4F **13** (1E **75**)
Boyne Rd. SE13.....1E **109**
Boyne Ter. M. W11....2B **72**
Boyson Rd. SE17.....2F **91**
 (not continuous)
Boyson Wlk. SE17....2F **91**
Boyton Cl. E1.......3F **65**
Boyton Ho. NW8......*1F 59*
 (off Wellington Rd.)
Brabant Ct. EC3.....4D **19**
Brabazon St. E14....5D **67**
Brabner Ho. E2.......*2C 64*
 (off Wellington Row)
Brabourne Cl. SE19..5A **120**
Brabourn Gro. SE15..5E **93**
Bracer Ho. N1........*1A 64*
 (off Whitmore Est.)
Bracewell Rd. W10...4E **57**
Bracey M. N4........4A **34**
Bracey St. N4.......4A **34**
Bracken Av. SW12...4C **102**

Brackenbury N4......*3C 34*
 (off Osborne Rd.)
Brackenbury Gdns.
 W6..............4D **71**
Brackenbury Rd. W6..4D **71**
Brackenfield Cl. E5...5D **37**
Bracken Gdns.
 SW13............5C **84**
Bracken Ho. E3.......*4C 66*
 (off Devons Rd.)
Brackley Av. SE15...1E **107**
Brackley Ct. NW8.....*3F 59*
 (off Pollitt Dr.)
Brackley Rd. W4....1A **84**
Brackley St.
 EC1.......5A **10** (3E **63**)
Brackley Ter. W4....1A **84**
Bracklyn Ct. N1......1F **63**
 (not continuous)
Bracklyn St. N1......1F **63**
Bracknell Gdns.
 NW3.............1D **45**
Bracknell Ga. NW3...2D **45**
Bracknell Way NW3...1D **45**
Bradbeer Ho. E2......*2E 65*
 (off Cornwall Av.)
Bradbourne St. SW6..5C **86**
Bradbury M. N16......*2A 50*
 (off Bradbury St.)
Bradbury St. N16....2A **50**
Braddyll St. SE10....1A **96**
Bradenham SE17.....*2F 91*
 (off Bradenham Cl.)
Bradenham Cl. SE17..2F **91**
Braden St. W9.......3D **59**
Bradfield Ct. NW1....*4D 47*
 (off Hawley Rd.)
Bradfield Rd. E16....3C **82**
Bradford Cl. SE26....4D **121**
Bradford Ho. W14.....*4F 71*
 (off Spring Va. Ter.)
Bradford Rd. W3....3A **70**
Bradgate Rd. SE6....4D **109**
Brading Cres. E11...4D **41**
Brading Rd. SW2.....5B **104**
Brading Ter. W12....4C **70**
Bradiston Rd. W9....2B **58**
Bradley Cl. N7......3A **48**
Bradley Ho. SE16.....*5E 79*
 (off Raymouth Rd.)
Bradley M. SW17....1B **116**
Bradley Rd. SE19....5E **119**
Bradley's Cl. N1......1C **62**
Bradmead SW8......3D **89**
Bradmore Pk. Rd.
 W6..............5D **71**
Bradshaw Cl. SW19...5C **114**
Bradshaw Cotts. E14..*5A 66*
 (off Repton St.)
Bradstock Ho. E9.....4F **51**
Bradstock Rd. E9....3F **51**
Brad St. SE1....2C **24** (2C **76**)
Bradwell Ho. NW6....*5D 45*
 (off Mortimer Cres.)
Brady Ho. SW8.......*4E 89*
 (off Corunna Rd.)
Brady St. E1........3D **65**
Braemar SW15.......*4F 99*
Braemar Av. NW10...5A **28**
 SW19............2C **114**

Braemar Cl. *SE16* 1D **93**
  (off Masters Dr.)
Braemar Ct. SE6. . . . . . .1B **124**
Braemar Ho. *W9*. 2E **59**
  (off Maida Va.)
Braemar Rd. E13 . . . . . . .3B **68**
Braeside
  BR3: Beck. 5C **122**
Braes St. N1. . . . . .4D **49**
Braganza St. SE17 . . . . . .1D **91**
Braham Ho. SE11. . . . . . .1B **90**
Braham Mus. *3B 78*
  (off Maguire St.)
Braham St. E1. . .3F **19** (5B **64**)
Braid Av. W3. . . . . .5A **56**
Braid Ho. *SE10*. *4E 95*
  (off Blackheath Hill)
Braidwood Pas. *EC1*. . . .*5F 9*
  (off Aldersgate St.)
Braidwood Rd. SE6. . . .1F **123**
Braidwood St.
  SE1 . . . . . . .2D **27** (2A **78**)
Brailsford Rd. SW2 . . . .3C **104**
Braintree Ho. *E1*. *3E 65*
  (off Malcolm Rd.)
Braintree St. E2 . . . . .2E **65**
Braithwaite Ho. *EC1*. . . .*3B 10*
  (off Bunhill Row)
Braithwaite Twr. *W2*. . . .*4F 59*
  (off Hall Pl.)
Bramah Grn. SW9 . . . . . .4C **90**
Bramah Tea & Coffee Mus.
  . . . . .3F **27** (2E **77**)
Bramalea Cl. N6. . . . . . . .1C **32**
Bramall Cl. E15. . . . . .2B **54**
Bramall Ct. *N7*. *2B 48*
  (off George's Rd.)
Bramber WC1. . . . . .2D **7**
Bramber Rd. W14 . . . . . . .2B **85**
Bramble Gdns. W12. . . . .1B **70**
Bramble Ho. *E3* *4C 66*
  (off Devons Rd.)
Brambles, The
  SW19. . . . .*5B 114*
  (off Woodside)
Brambling Ct. *SE8* *2B 94*
  (off Abinger Gro.)
Bramcote Gro. SE16. . . .1E **93**
Bramcote Rd. SW15 . . . .2D **99**
Bramdean Cres.
  SE12. . . . . .1C **124**
Bramdean Gdns.
  SE12. . . . . .1C **124**
Bramerton NW6 . . . .*4F 43*
  (off Willesden La.)
Bramerton St. SW3 . . . . .2A **88**
Bramfield Ct. *N4*. *4E 35*
  (off Queens Dr.)
Bramfield Rd.
  SW11. . . . . .4A **102**
Bramford Rd. SW18. . . .2E **101**
Bramham Gdns.
  SW5 . . . . .1D **87**
Bramhope La. SE7. . . . . .2D **97**
Bramlands Cl.
  SW11. . . . . .1A **102**
Bramley Cres. SW8 . . . . .3F **90**
Bramley Ho. SW15. . . . . .*4B 98*
  (off Tunworth Cres.)
  W10. . . . . .5F **57**

Bramley Rd. W10. . . . . . .5F **57**
  (not continuous)
Brampton *WC1*. *1F 15*
  (off Red Lion Sq.)
Brampton Cl. E5. . . . . . . .4D **37**
Brampton Gdns. N15 . . . .1E **35**
Brampton Rd. E6 . . . . . . .2F **69**
  N15. . . . . .1E **35**
Bramshaw Rd. E9. . . . . . .3F **51**
Bramshill Gdns.
  NW5. . . . . .5D **33**
Bramshill Rd. NW10 . . . .1B **56**
Bramshot Av. SE7 . . . . . .2C **96**
Bramshurst *NW8* *5D 45*
  (off Abbey Rd.)
Bramston Rd. NW10 . . . .1C **56**
  SW17 . . . . .3E **115**
Bramwell Ho.
  SE1 . . . . . . .5A **26** (4E **77**)
  SW1 . . . . .1D **89**
  (off Churchill Gdns.)
Bramwell M. N1. . . . . .5B **48**
Brancaster Ho. *E1* *2F 65*
  (off Moody St.)
Brancaster Rd.
  SW16 . . . . .3A **118**
Branch Hill NW3. . . . . . . .5E **31**
Branch Hill Ho. NW3. . . . .5D **31**
Branch Pl. N1. . . . . .5F **49**
Branch Rd. E14 . . . . .1A **80**
Branch St. SE15. . . . . . . .3A **92**
Brand Cl. N4 . . . . .3D **35**
Brandlehow Rd.
  SW15. . . . . .2B **100**
Brandon Est. SE17. . . . . .2D **91**
Brandon Ho.
  BR3: Beck. *5D 123*
  (off Beckenham Hill Rd.)
Brandon Mans. *W14* . . .2A **86**
  (off Queen's Club Gdns.)
Brandon M. EC2 . . . . .1B **18**
Brandon Rd. N7 . . . . .4A **48**
Brandon St. SE17. . . . . . .5E **77**
  (not continuous)
Brandram M. *SE13*. *2A 110*
  (off Brandram Rd.)
Brandram Rd. SE13 . . . .1A **110**
Brandreth Rd.
  SW17 . . . . .2D **117**
Brand St. SE10. . . . . .3E **95**
Brangbourne Rd.
  BR1: Brom. 5E **123**
Brangton Rd. SE11 . . . . .1B **90**
Brangwyn Ct. *W14*. *4A 72*
  (off Blythe Rd.)
Branksea St. SW6 . . . . . .3A **86**
Branksome Ho. *SW8* . . .*3B 90*
  (off Meadow Rd.)
Branksome Rd.
  SW2 . . . . .3A **104**
Branscombe *NW1*. *5E 47*
  (off Plender St.)
Branscombe St.
  SE13. . . . . .1D **109**
Bransdale Cl. NW6 . . . . . .5C **44**
Brantwood Ho. *SE5* *3E 91*
  (off Wyndam Est.)
Brantwood Rd.
  SE24 . . . . .3E **105**
Brasenose Dr. SW13 . . .2E **85**

Brassett Point *E15*. *5A 54*
  (off Abbey Rd.)
Brassey Ho. *E14*. *5D 81*
  (off Cahir St.)
Brassey Rd. NW6. . . . . . .3B **44**
Brassey Sq. SW11 . . . . .1C **102**
Brassie Av. W3. . . . . .5A **56**
Brass Talley All.
  SE16. . . . . .3F **79**
Brasted Cl. SE26 . . . . . .4E **121**
Brathay *NW1* *1A 6*
  (off Ampthill Est.)
Brathway Rd. SW18. . . .5C **100**
Bratley St. E1 . . . . .3C **64**
Bravington Pl. W9 . . . . . .3B **58**
Bravington Rd. W9. . . . . .1B **58**
Bravingtons Wlk. *N1* . . .*1E 7*
  (off York Way)
Brawne Ho. *SE17*. *2D 91*
  (off Brandon St.)
Braxfield Rd. SE4. . . . . .2A **108**
Braxted Pk. SW16 . . . . .5B **118**
Bray NW3 . . . . .4A **46**
Brayards Rd. SE15. . . . . .5D **93**
Brayards Rd. Est.
  SE15 . . . .*5E 93*
  (off Brayards Rd.)
Braybrook St. W12. . . . . .4B **56**
Brayburne Av.
  SW4 . . . . .5E **89**
Bray Cl. SW16 . . . . .3A **118**
Bray Cres. SE16 . . . . .3F **79**
Braydon Rd. N16 . . . . . . .3C **36**
Bray Dr. E16. . . . . .1B **82**
Brayfield Ter. N1 . . . . .4C **48**
Brayford Sq. E1 . . . . .5E **65**
Bray Pas. E16. . . . . .1C **82**
Bray Pl. SW3 . . . . .5B **74**
Bread St.
  EC4 . . . . .3A **18** (5E **63**)
  (not continuous)
Breakspears M. SE4 . . . .5B **94**
Breakspears Rd.
  SE4 . . . . .2B **108**
Breamore Cl. SW15. . . .1C **112**
Breamore Ho. *SE15*. . . .*3C 92*
  (off Friary Est.)
Bream's Bldgs.
  EC4 . . . . .2B **16** (5C **62**)
Bream St. E3 . . . . .4C **52**
Breasley Cl. SW15. . . . . .2D **99**
Brechin Pl. SW7. . . . . . . .5E **73**
Brecknock Rd. N7 . . . . . .2F **47**
  N19. . . . . .1E **47**
Brecknock Rd. Est.
  N19. . . . . .1E **47**
Brecon Grn. NW9 . . . . . .1A **28**
Brecon Ho. *W2*. *5E 59*
  (off Hallfield Est.)
Brecon M. NW5 . . . . .2F **47**
Brecon Rd. W6. . . . . .2A **86**
Bredel Ho. *E14*. *4C 66*
  (off St Paul's Way)
Bredgar SE13 . . . . .3D **109**
Bredgar Rd. N19 . . . .*1E 46*
Bredinghurst Cl. SE20. . .5E **121**
Bredinghurst SE22 . . . . .5C **106**
Bredin Ho. SW10. . . . . . .3D **87**
  (off Coleridge Gdns.)
Breer St. SW6 . . . . .1D **101**

Breezers Ct. E1. . . . . 1C 78
     (off Highway, The)
Breezer's Hill E1. . . . . 1C 78
Bremner Rd. SW7 . . . . . . 4E 73
Brenchley Gdns.
  SE23. . . . . 4E 107
Brenda Rd. SW17. . . . . . 2B 116
Brendon Av. NW10. . . . . . 1A 42
Brendon St. W1 . . . . 5A 60
Brenley Gdns. SE9 . . . . . . 2F 111
Brenley Ho. SE1. . . . . 3B 26
     (off Tennis St.)
Brennand Ct. N19. . . . . . . 5E 33
Brent Ct. NW11. . . . . 2F 29
BRENT CROSS 2F 29
Brent Cross Fly-Over
  NW2. . . . . 2F 29
  NW4. . . . . 2F 29
Brent Cross Gdns.
  NW4. . . . . 1F 29
BRENT CROSS INTERCHANGE
  . . . . 1E 29
Brent Cross Shop. Cen.
  NW4. . . . . 2E 29
Brentfield Gdns.
  NW2. . . . . 2E 29
Brentfield Ho. NW10. . . . . 4A 42
Brentfield Rd. NW10. . . . . 4A 42
Brent Grn. NW4. . . . . 1E 29
Brent Ho. E9. . . . . 3E 51
     (off Frampton Pk. Rd.)
Brenthouse Rd. E9. . . . . . 4E 51
Brenthurst Rd. NW10. . . . . 3B 42
Brentmead Pl. NW11. . . . . 1F 29
Brent New Ent. Cen.
  NW10. . . . . 3B 42
Brenton St. E14 . . . . 5A 66
Brent Pk. Rd. NW4. . . . . . 2D 29
  NW9 . . . . 2D 29
     (not continuous)
Brent Rd. E16. . . . . 5C 68
Brent St. NW4. . . . . 1F 29
Brent Ter. NW2. . . . . 3E 29
     (not continuous)
Brent Trad. Cen.
  NW10. . . . . 2A 42
Brent Vw. Rd. NW9 . . . . . 1C 28
Brentwood Ho. SE18. . . . . 3F 97
     (off Portway Gdns.)
Brentwood Lodge
  NW4 . . . . 1F 29
     (off Holmdale Gdns.)
Bressenden Pl.
  SW1. . . . . 5E 21 (4D 75)
Breton Highwalk EC1 . . . 5A 10
     (off Golden La.)
Breton Ho. EC2. . . . . 5A 10
  SE1. . . . . 5F 27
     (off Abbey St.)
Brett Cl. N16. . . . . 4A 36
Brettell St. SE17. . . . . 1F 91
Brett Ho. Cl. SW15. . . . . . 5F 99
Brettinghurst SE1. . . . . . . 1C 92
     (off Avondale Sq.)
Brett Pas. E8. . . . . 2D 51
Brett Rd. E8 . . . . 2D 51
Brewer's Grn. SW1. . . . . . 5B 22
Brewer's Hall Gdn.
  EC2. . . . . 1A 18
     (off London Wall)

Brewer St.
  W1. . . . . 4A 14 (1E 75)
Brewery, The
  EC2. . . . . 5B 10 (4E 63)
Brewery Ind. Est., The
  N1. . . . . 1A 10
     (off Wenlock Rd.)
Brewery Rd. N7 . . . . 4A 48
Brewery Sq.
  EC1 . . . . 3D 9 (3D 63)
  SE1 . . . . 2F 27
Brewhouse La. E1 . . . . . . 2D 79
  SW15. . . . . 1A 100
Brewhouse Wlk.
  SE16. . . . . 2A 80
Brewhouse Yd.
  EC1. . . . . 3D 9 (3D 63)
Brewster Gdns. W10 . . . . 4E 57
Brewster Ho. E14. . . . . . . 1B 80
     (off Three Colt St.)
  SE1. . . . . 5B 78
     (off Dunton Rd.)
Brewster Rd. E10. . . . . . . 3D 39
Briant Ho. SE1 . . . . 5B 24
Briant St. SE14. . . . . 4F 93
Briar Ct. SW15. . . . . 2D 99
Briardale Gdns.
  NW3 . . . . 5C 30
Briar Rd. NW2 . . . . 1E 43
Briar Wlk. SW15. . . . . 2D 99
  W10 . . . . 3A 58
Briarwood Rd. SW4 . . . . . 3F 103
Briary Cl. NW3. . . . . 4A 46
Briary Ct. E16. . . . . 5B 68
Briary Gdns.
  BR1: Brom 5D 125
Brickbarn Cl. SW10 . . . . . 3E 87
     (off King's Barn)
Brick Ct. EC4. . . 3B 16 (5C 62)
Brickfield Rd.
  SW19. . . . . 4D 115
Brick La. E1 . . . . 4B 64
  E2. . . . . 2F 11 (2B 64)
Brick Lane Music Hall
  . . . . 2F 83
BRICKLAYER'S ARMS
  . . . . 5F 77
Bricklayers Arms Bus. Cen.
  SE1. . . . . 5A 78
Brick St. W1 . . . 2D 21 (2D 75)
Brickwood Cl. SE26 . . . . 3D 121
Brideale Cl. SE15. . . . . . . 2B 92
Bride La. EC4. . . 3D 17 (5D 63)
Bridel M. N1 . . . . 5D 49
     (off Colebrook Row)
Brides Pl. N1. . . . . 4A 50
     (off De Beauvoir Rd.)
Bride St. N7 . . . . 3B 48
Bridewain St.
  SE1. . . . . 5F 27 (4B 78)
     (not continuous)
Bridewell Pl. E1 . . . . 2D 79
  EC4. . . . . 3D 17 (5D 63)
Bridford M.
  W1. . . . . 5E 5 (4D 61)
Bridge, The SW8 . . . . 3D 89
     (off Queenstown Rd.)
Bridge App. NW1. . . . . . . 4C 46
Bridge Av. W6 . . . . 5E 71

Bridge Av. Mans. W6. . . . 1E 85
     (off Bridge Av.)
Bridge Cl. W10. . . . . 5F 57
Bridge Ct. E10 . . . . 3B 38
  E14. . . . . 1F 81
     (off Newport Av.)
Bridgefoot SE1. . . . . 1A 90
Bridge Gdns. N16. . . . . . . 1F 49
Bridge Ho. E9. . . . . 3F 51
     (off Shepherds La.)
  NW3 . . . . 4C 46
     (off Adelaide Rd.)
  NW10 . . . . 1F 57
     (off Chamberlayne Rd.)
  SE4. . . . . 2B 108
  SW1. . . . . 1D 89
     (off Ebury Bri.)
  W2. . . . . 4F 59
     (off Nth. Wharf Rd.)
Bridgehouse Ct. SE1 . . . . 4D 25
     (off Blackfriars Rd.)
Bridge Ho. Quay E14 . . . . 2E 81
Bridgeland Rd. E16. . . . . . 1C 82
Bridge La. NW11. . . . . 1B 30
  SW11. . . . . 4A 88
Bridge Leisure Cen., The
  . . . . 4B 122
Bridgeman Ho. E9 . . . . . . 4E 51
     (off Frampton Pk. Rd.)
Bridgeman Rd. N1. . . . . . 4B 48
Bridgeman St. NW8. . . . . 1A 60
Bridge Mdws. SE14 . . . . . 2F 93
Bridgend Rd. SW18. . . . . 2E 101
Bridgen Ho. E1. . . . . 5D 65
     (off Nelson St.)
Bridgepark SW18. . . . . . 3C 100
Bridge Pl. SW1 . . . . 5D 75
Bridgepoint Lofts E7. . . . . 4E 55
Bridgeport Pl. E1. . . . . . . 2C 78
Bridge Rd. E15. . . . . 4F 53
  E17. . . . . 2B 38
  NW10 . . . . 3A 42
Bridges Ct. SW11. . . . . . . 1F 101
     (not continuous)
Bridges Ho. SE5. . . . . 3F 91
     (off Elmington Est.)
Bridgeside Ho. N1. . . . . . . 1E 63
     (off Wharf Rd.)
Bridges Pl. SW6. . . . . 4B 86
Bridge St.
  SW1. . . . . 4D 23 (3A 76)
Bridge Ter. E15. . . . . 4F 53
Bridgetown Cl.
  SE19. . . . . 5A 120
Bridge Vw. W6 . . . . 1E 85
Bridgewalk Hgts. SE1 . . . 3C 26
     (off Weston St.)
Bridgewater Highwalk
  EC2. . . . . 5F 9
Bridgewater Rd. E15. . . . . 5E 53
Bridgewater Sq.
  EC2. . . . . 5F 9 (4E 63)
Bridgewater St.
  EC2. . . . . 5F 9 (4E 63)
Bridge Way NW11 . . . . . . 1B 30
Bridgeway St. NW1 . . . . . 1E 61
Bridge Wharf E2 . . . . 1F 65
Bridge Yd.
  SE1. . . . . 1C 26 (2F 77)
Bridgford St. SW18 . . . . . 3E 115

Bridgnorth Ho. *SE15* . . . 2C **92**
(off Friary Est.)
Bridgwater Ho. *W2*. 5E **59**
(off Hallfield Est.)
Bridle La.
W1. . . . . 4A **14** (1E **75**)
Bridport *SE17* 1F **91**
(off Date St.)
Bridport Ho. *N1*. 5F **49**
(off Bridport Pl.)
Bridport Pl. N1 . . . . 5F **49**
(not continuous)
Bridstow Pl. W2. . . . . . 5C **58**
Brief St. SE5. . . . . 4D **91**
Brierfield *NW1* 5E **47**
(off Arlington Rd.)
Brierley Rd. E11. . . . . . . 1F **53**
SW12 . . . . 2E **117**
Brierly Gdns. E2. . . . . . . 1E **65**
Brigade St. *SE3* 5B **96**
(off Tranquil Va.)
Briggeford Cl. E5 . . . . . 4C **36**
Briggs Ho. *E2* 1F **11**
(off Chambord St.)
Brightfield Rd.
SE12. . . . . 3A **110**
Brightling Rd. SE4. . . . . 4B **108**
Brightlingsea Pl. E14. . . 1B **80**
Brightman Rd.
SW18 . . . . 1F **115**
Brighton Av. E17. . . . . . . 1B **38**
Brighton Bldgs. *SE1* . . . 5D **27**
(off Tower Bri. Rd.)
Brighton Gro. SE14 . . . . 4A **94**
Brighton Rd. N16. . . . . . 1A **50**
Brighton Ter. SW9 . . . . . 2B **104**
Brightside Rd. SE13. . . 4F **109**
Bright St. E14. . . . . 5D **67**
Brightwell Cres.
SW17. . . . . 5B **116**
Brig M. SE8 . . . . 2C **94**
Brigstock Ho. SE5. . . . . 5E **91**
Brill Pl. NW1 . . . . 1C **6** (1F **61**)
Brimsdown Ho. E3 . . . . . 3D **67**
Brimstone Ho. *E15*. . . . 4A **54**
(off Victoria St.)
Brindley Ho. *W2*. 4C **58**
(off Alfred Rd.)
Brindley St. SE14. . . . . . 4B **94**
Brindley Way
BR1: Brom 5C **124**
Brinklow Ho. *W2*. 4D **59**
(off Torquay St.)
Brinkworth Way E9. . . . . 3B **52**
Brinsley Ho. *E1*. 5E **65**
(off Tarling St.)
Brinsley St. E1 . . . . 5D **65**
Brinton Wlk. SE1. . . . . . 2D **25**
Brion Pl. E14 . . . . 4E **67**
Brisbane Ho. *W12*. 1D **71**
(off White City Est.)
Brisbane Rd. E10. . . . . . 4D **39**
Brisbane Road Stadium
. . . . 5D **39**
Brisbane St. SE5. . . . . . 3F **91**
Briscoe Cl. E11. . . . . . . 4B **40**
Briscoe Rd. SW19 . . . . 5F **115**
Briset Rd. SE9 . . . . 1F **111**
Briset St. EC1. . . 5D **9** (4D **63**)
Briset Way N7. . . . . 4B **34**

Bristol Gdns. SW15 . . . . 5E **99**
W9. . . . . 3D **59**
Bristol Ho. *SE11*. 4C **76**
(off Lambeth Wlk.)
Bristol M. W9. . . . . 3D **59**
Bristol Rd. E7. . . . . 3E **55**
Bristowe Cl. SW2. . . . . 4C **104**
Bristow Rd. SE19. . . . . 5A **120**
Britain & London Vis. Cen.
. . . . 1B **22**
(off Regent St.)
Britain at War Experience
. . . . 2D **27**
Britannia Bri. *E14* 5B **66**
(off Commercial Rd.)
Britannia Bus. Cen.
NW2. . . . . 1F **43**
Britannia Cl. SW4. . . . . 2F **103**
Britannia Ga. E16. . . . . 2C **82**
BRITANNIA JUNC. 5D **47**
Britannia Leisure Cen.
. . . . 5F **49**
Britannia Rd. E14. . . . . 5C **80**
SW6. . . . . 3D **87**
(not continuous)
Britannia Row N1. . . . . . 5D **49**
Britannia St.
WC1. . . . . 1F **7** (2B **62**)
Britannia Wlk.
N1 . . . . 1B **10** (1F **63**)
(Murray Gro.)
N1 . . . . 1B **10** (2F **63**)
(Nile St.)
Britannia Way *SW6*. . . . 3D **87**
(off Britannia Rd.)
Britannic Highwalk
EC2. . . . . 1B **18**
(off Moor La.)
Britannic Twr. EC2. . . . . 5B **10**
British Cartoon Cen., The
. . . . 4E **7**
(off Bernard St.)
British Genius Site 3C **88**
British Gro. W4 . . . . 1B **84**
British Gro. Pas. W4 . . . 1B **84**
British Gro. Sth. W4 . . . 1B **84**
(off British Gro. Pas.)
British Library
. . . . 1C **6** (2F **61**)
British Mus. . . 1D **15** (4A **62**)
British St. E3 . . . . 2B **66**
British Telecom Cen.
EC1. . . . . 2F **17**
British Wharf Ind. Est.
SE14. . . . . 1F **93**
Britley Ho. *E14*. 5B **66**
(off Copenhagen Pl.)
Brittain Ho. SE9 . . . . . 1F **125**
Brittany Point SE11. . . . 5C **76**
Britten Cl. NW11. . . . . . 3D **31**
Britten Ct. E15. . . . . 1F **67**
Britten St. SW3 . . . . 1A **88**
Britten Cl. SE6. . . . . . . 5F **109**
Britton St.
EC1. . . . . 4D **9** (3D **63**)
BRIXTON 2D **104**
Brixton Academy 1C **104**
(off Stockwell Rd.)
Brixton Hill SW2 . . . . . 5A **104**

Brixton Hill Ct. SW2. . . . 3B **104**
Brixton Hill Pl. SW2. . . . 5A **104**
Brixton Oval SW2. . . . . 2C **104**
Brixton Recreation Cen.
. . . . 1C **104**
(off Brixton Sta. Rd.)
Brixton Rd. SE11. . . . . . 2C **90**
SW9 . . . . 2C **104**
Brixton Sta. Rd.
SW9 . . . . 1C **104**
Brixton Water La.
SW2. . . . . 3B **104**
Broadbent Cl. N6. . . . . . 3D **33**
Broadbent St.
W1. . . . . 4D **13** (1D **75**)
Broadbridge Cl. SE3 . . . 3C **96**
Broad Comn. Est.
N16. . . . . 3C **36**
(off Osbaldeston Rd.)
Broad Ct.
WC2. . . . . 3E **15** (5A **62**)
Broadfield NW6 . . . . . . 3D **45**
Broadfield Cl. NW2 . . . . 5E **29**
Broadfield La. NW1 . . . . 4A **48**
Broadfield Rd. SE6 . . . 5A **110**
Broadfields Way
NW10 . . . . 2B **42**
Broadford Ho. *E1*. 3A **66**
(off Commodore St.)
Broadgate EC2. . . . . . . 1D **19**
Broadgate Circ.
EC2 . . . . 1D **19** (4A **64**)
Broadgate Ice Rink. . . . 1D **19**
Broadgate Rd. E16. . . . 5F **69**
Broadgates Ct. *SE11* . . 1C **90**
(off Cleaver St.)
Broadgates Rd.
SW18 . . . . 1F **115**
Broadhinton Rd.
SW4 . . . . 1D **103**
Broadhurst Cl. NW6 . . . 3E **45**
Broadhurst Gdns.
NW6 . . . . 3D **45**
Broadlands Av.
SW16 . . . . 2A **118**
Broadlands Cl. N6. . . . . 2C **32**
SW16 . . . . 2A **118**
Broadlands Lodge
N6. . . . . 2B **32**
Broadlands Rd.
BR1: Brom 4D **125**
N6. . . . . 2B **32**
Broad La.
EC2 . . . . 5D **11** (4A **64**)
N8. . . . . 1B **34**
Bradley St. NW8. . . . . . 4F **59**
Broadley Ter. NW1. . . . . 3A **60**
Broadmayne *SE17* 1F **91**
(off Portland St.)
Broadmead SE6 . . . . . 3C **122**
W14 . . . . 5A **72**
Broadoak Ct. SW9 . . . . 1C **104**
Broadoak Ho. *NW6* . . . 5D **45**
(off Mortimer Cres.)
Broad Sanctuary
SW1 . . . . 4C **22** (3F **75**)
Broadstone Ho. *SW8* . . 3B **90**
(off Dorset Rd.)
Broadstone Pl.
W1. . . . . 1B **12** (4C **60**)

Broad St. Av.
EC2 . . . . 1D **19** (4A **64**)
Broad St. Pl. EC2 . . . . . . 1C **18**
Broad Wlk.
NW1 . . . . 1C **4** (5C **46**)
SE3 . . . . 5E **97**
W1 . . . . 5A **12** (1B **74**)
Broad Wlk., The W8 . . 2D **73**
Broadwalk Ct. W8 . . . . 2C **72**
Broadwalk Ho.
EC2 . . . . 5D **11** (3A **64**)
SW7 . . . . 3E **73**
(off Hyde Pk. Ga.)
Broad Wlk. La.
NW11 . . . . 2B **30**
Broadwall
SE1 . . . . 1C **24** (3E **77**)
Broadwater Rd.
SW17 . . . . 4A **116**
Broadway E13 . . . . 1D **69**
E15 . . . . 4F **53**
SW1 . . . . 4B **22** (4F **75**)
Broadway, The N8 . . 1A **34**
NW9 . . . . 1B **28**
SW13 . . . . 1B **84**
Broadway Arc. W6 . . . . 5E **71**
(off Hammersmith B'way.)
Broadway Cen., The
W6 . . . . 5E **71**
Broadway Chambers
W6 . . . . 5E **71**
(off Hammersmith B'way.)
Broadway Ho.
BR1: Brom 5F **123**
(off Bromley Rd.)
E8 . . . . 5D **51**
(off Ada St.)
Broadway Mkt. E8 . . 5D **51**
SW17 . . . . 4B **116**
Broadway Mkt. M.
E8 . . . . 5C **50**
Broadway M. E5 . . . . . 2B **36**
Broadway Pde. N8 . . 1A **34**
Broadway Retail Pk.
NW2 . . . . 1F **43**
Broadway Shop. Mall
SW1 . . . . 5B **22** (4F **75**)
Broadway Squash &
Fitness Cen. 5F **71**
(off Chalk Hill Rd.)
Broadway Theatre, The
Catford 5D **109**
Broadwick St.
W1 . . . . 4A **14** (1E **75**)
Broadwood Ter. W8 . . 5B **72**
Broad Yd. EC1 . . 4D **9** (3D **63**)
Brocas Cl. NW3 . . . . . . 4A **46**
Brockbridge Ho.
SW15 . . . . 4B **98**
Brocket Ho. SW8 . . . . . 5F **89**
Brockham Cl. SW19 . . 5B **114**
Brockham Dr. SW2 . . . 5B **104**
Brockham Ho. NW1 . . . . 5E **47**
(off Bayham St.)
SW2 . . . . 5B **104**
(off Brockham Dr.)
Brockham St.
SE1 . . . . 5A **26** (4E **77**)
Brockill Cres. SE4 . . . 2A **108**

Brocklebank Ind. Est.
SE7 . . . . 5C **82**
Brocklebank Rd. SE7 . . 5D **83**
SW18 . . . . 5E **101**
Brocklehurst St.
SE14 . . . . 3F **93**
BROCKLEY 2F **107**
Brockley Cross SE4 . . 1A **108**
Brockley Cross Bus. Cen.
SE4 . . . . 1A **108**
Brockley Footpath
SE4 . . . . 3A **108**
(not continuous)
SE15 . . . . 2E **107**
Brockley Gdns. SE4 . . 5B **94**
Brockley Gro. SE4 . . . 3B **108**
Brockley Hall Rd.
SE4 . . . . 3A **108**
Brockley Jack Theatre
. . . . 3A **108**
Brockley M. SE4 . . . . . 3A **108**
Brockley Pk. SE23 . . . 5A **108**
Brockley Ri. SE23 . . . 1A **122**
Brockley Rd. SE4 . . . . 1B **108**
Brockley Vw. SE23 . . . 5A **108**
Brockley Way SE4 . . . . 3F **107**
Brockman Ri.
BR1: Brom 4F **123**
Brockmer Ho. E1 . . . . . 1D **79**
(off Crowder St.)
Brock Pl. E3 . . . . 3D **67**
Brock Rd. E13 . . . . 4D **69**
Brock St. SE15 . . . . . . 1E **107**
Brockway Cl. E11 . . . . . 4A **40**
Brockweir E2 . . . . 1E **65**
(off Cyprus St.)
Brockwell Ho. SE11 . . . 2B **90**
(off Vauxhall St.)
Brockwell Pk. 4D **105**
Brockwell Pk. Gdns.
SE24 . . . . 5C **104**
Brockwell Pk. Lido . . 4D **105**
Brockwell Pk. Row
SW2 . . . . 5C **104**
Brodia Rd. N16 . . . . . . 5A **36**
Brodie Ho. SE1 . . . . . . 1B **92**
(off Cooper's Rd.)
Brodie Rd. SW17 . . . . 2A **116**
Broken Wharf
EC4 . . . . 4F **17** (1E **77**)
Brokesley St. E3 . . . . . 2B **66**
Broke Wlk. E8 . . . . 5B **50**
Bromar Rd. SE5 . . . . . 1A **106**
Bromell's Rd. SW4 . . . 2E **103**
Bromfelde Rd. SW4 . . . 1F **103**
Bromfelde Wlk. SW4 . . 5F **89**
Bromfield St. N1 . . . . . 5C **48**
Bromhead Rd. E1 . . . . . 5E **65**
(off Jubilee St.)
Bromhead St. E1 . . . . . 5E **65**
Bromleigh Ct. SE23 . . 2C **120**
Bromleigh Ho. SE1 . . . . 5F **27**
(off Abbey St.)
BROMLEY 2D **67**
Bromley Hall Rd.
E14 . . . . 4E **67**
Bromley High St. E3 . . 2D **67**

Bromley Hill
BR1: Brom 5A **124**
Bromley Pl.
W1 . . . . 5F **5** (4E **61**)
Bromley Rd.
BR1: Brom 1D **123**
E10 . . . . 1D **39**
SE6 . . . . 1D **123**
Bromley St. E1 . . . . 4F **65**
BROMPTON 4A **74**
Brompton Arc. SW3 . . 4A **20**
Brompton Cotts.
SW10 . . . . 2E **87**
(off Hollywood Rd.)
Brompton Oratory . . . 4A **74**
Brompton Pk. Cres.
SW6 . . . . 2D **87**
Brompton Pl. SW3 . . . 4A **74**
Brompton Rd.
SW1 . . . . 4A **20** (5A **74**)
SW3 . . . . 4A **20** (5A **74**)
Brompton Sq. SW3 . . . 4A **74**
Bromwich Av. N6 . . . . . 4C **32**
Bromyard Av. W3 . . . . . 1A **70**
Bromyard Ho. SE15 . . . 3D **93**
(off Commercial Way)
Bromyard Leisure Cen.
. . . . 2A **70**
Bron Ct. NW6 . . . . 5C **44**
BRONDESBURY 4B **44**
Brondesbury Ct. NW2 . 3F **43**
Brondesbury M. NW6 . 4C **44**
BRONDESBURY PARK
. . . . 5A **44**
Brondesbury Pk.
NW2 . . . . 3D **43**
NW6 . . . . 4E **43**
Brondesbury Rd.
NW6 . . . . 1B **58**
Brondesbury Vs.
NW6 . . . . 1B **58**
Bronsart Rd. SW6 . . . . 3A **86**
Bronte Cl. E7 . . . . 1C **54**
Bronte Ct. W14 . . . . 4F **71**
(off Girdler's Rd.)
Bronte Ho. N16 . . . . . . 2A **50**
NW6 . . . . 2C **58**
SW4 . . . . 5E **103**
Bronti Cl. SE17 . . . . . . 1E **91**
Bronwen Ct. NW8 . . . . . 2F **59**
(off Grove End Rd.)
Bronze St. SE8 . . . . 3C **94**
Brookbank Rd.
SE13 . . . . 1C **108**
Brook Cl. SW17 . . . . . 2C **116**
Brook Ct. E11 . . . . 5A **40**
E15 . . . . 2D **53**
(off Clays La.)
SE12 . . . . 3E **125**
Brookdale Rd. SE6 . . . 5D **109**
(not continuous)
Brook Dr. SE11 . . . . . . 4C **76**
Brooke Ho. SE14 . . . . . 4A **94**
Brookehowse Rd.
SE6 . . . . 2C **122**
Brooke Rd. E5 . . . . 5A **36**
N16 . . . . 5B **36**
Brooke's Ct.
EC1 . . . . 5B **8** (4C **62**)
Brooke's Mkt. EC1 . . . . 5C **8**

Brooke St.
EC1 . . . . . . 1B **16** (4C **62**)
Brookfield N6 . . . . 5C **32**
Brookfield Pk. NW5 . . 5D **33**
Brookfield Rd. E9 . . . . 3A **52**
W4 . . . . 3A **70**
Brook Gdns. SW13 . . 1B **98**
Brook Ga.
W1 . . . . . . .5A **12** (1B **74**)
BROOK GREEN 5F **71**
Brook Grn. W6 . . . . . . 4F **71**
Brook Grn. Flats
W14 . . . . 4F **71**
(off Dunsany Rd.)
Brook Ho. W6 . . . . 5F **71**
(off Shepherd's Bush Rd.)
Brook Ho's. NW1 . . . . . 1E **61**
(off Cranleigh St.)
Brooking Rd. E7 . . . . . 2C **54**
Brooklands Av.
SW19 . . . . 2D **115**
Brooklands Ct. NW6 . . 4B **44**
Brooklands Pk. SE3 . . 1C **110**
Brooklands Pas. SW8 . . 4F **89**
Brook La.
BR1: Brom 5C **124**
SE3 . . . . 5D **97**
Brook Lodge NW11 . . . 1F **29**
(off Nth. Circular Rd.)
Brookmarsh Ind. Est.
SE10 . . . . 3D **95**
Brook M. WC2 . . . . . . 3C **14**
Brook M. Nth. W2 . . . . 1E **73**
Brookmill Rd. SE8 . . . . 4C **94**
Brook Rd. NW2 . . . . . . 4B **28**
Brooksbank St. E9 . . . 3E **51**
Brooksby M. N1 . . . . . 4C **48**
Brooksby St. N1 . . . . . 4C **48**
Brooksby's Wlk. E9 . . . 2F **51**
Brooks Ct. SW8 . . . . . 3E **89**
Brooks Farm 2D **39**
Brookside Rd. N19 . . . 4E **33**
NW11 . . . . 1A **30**
Brooks Lodge N1 . . . . . 1A **64**
(off Hoxton St.)
Brooks M.
W1 . . . . . . .4D **13** (1D **75**)
Brook Sq. SE18 . . . . . . 4F **97**
Brooks Rd. E13 . . . . . . 5C **54**
Brook St. W1 . . 4D **13** (1D **75**)
W2 . . . . 1F **73**
Brooksville Av. NW6 . . 5A **44**
Brookview Rd.
SW16 . . . . 5E **117**
Brookville Rd. SW6 . . . 3B **86**
Brookway SE3 . . . . . . 1C **110**
Brookwood Av. SW13 . . 5B **84**
Brookwood Ho. SE1 . . . 4E **25**
(off Webber St.)
Brookwood Rd.
SW18 . . . . 1B **114**
Broome Way SE5 . . . . 3F **91**
Broomfield E17 . . . . . . 2B **38**
NW1 . . . . 4C **46**
(off Ferdinand St.)
Broomfield Ct. SE16 . . . 4C **78**
(off Ben Smith Way)
Broomfield Ho. SE17 . . 5A **78**
(off Massinger St.)
Broomfield St. E14 . . . 4C **66**

Broomgrove Rd.
SW9 . . . . 5B **90**
Broomhill Rd.
SW18 . . . . 3C **100**
Broomhouse La.
SW6 . . . . 5C **86**
(not continuous)
Broomhouse Rd.
SW6 . . . . 5C **86**
Broomsleigh Bus. Pk.
SE26 . . . . 5B **122**
Broomsleigh St.
NW6 . . . . 2B **44**
Broomwood Rd.
SW11 . . . . 4D **102**
Broseley Gro. SE26 . . 5A **122**
Brougham Rd. E8 . . . . 5C **50**
Brougham St. SW11 . . 5B **88**
Brough Cl. SW8 . . . . . 3A **90**
Broughton Dr. SW9 . . 2C **104**
Broughton Gdns. N6 . . 1E **33**
Broughton Rd. SW6 . . 5D **87**
Broughton St. SW8 . . . 5D **89**
Broughton St. Ind. Est.
SW11 . . . . 5C **88**
Browne Ho. SE8 . . . . . 3C **94**
(off Deptford Chu. St.)
Brownfield Area E14 . . 5D **67**
Brownfield St. E14 . . . 5D **67**
Browning Cl. W9 . . . . . 3E **59**
Browning Ho.
N16 . . . . 1A **50**
(off Shakspeare Wlk.)
SE14 . . . . 2F **93**
(off Loring Rd.)
W12 . . . . 5E **57**
(off Wood La.)
Browning M.
W1 . . . . . . .1C **12** (4D **61**)
Browning Rd. E11 . . . 2B **40**
Browning St. SE17 . . . 1E **91**
Brownlow Ho. SE16 . . 3C **78**
(off George Row)
Brownlow M.
WC1 . . . . . . .4A **8** (3B **62**)
Brownlow Rd. E7 . . . . 1C **54**
E8 . . . . 5B **50**
NW10 . . . . 4A **42**
Brownlow St.
WC1 . . . . . . 1A **16** (4B **62**)
Browns Arc. W1 . . . . . 5A **14**
(off Regent St.)
Brown's Bldgs.
EC3 . . . . . . 3E **19** (5A **64**)
Browns La. NW5 . . . . 2D **47**
Brown St. W1 . . . . . . 5B **60**
BROWNSWOOD PARK
. . . . 4D **35**
Brownswood Rd. N4 . . 5D **35**
Broxash Rd. SW11 . . . 4C **102**
Broxbourne Rd. E7 . . . 5C **40**
Broxholme Ho. SW6 . . 4D **87**
(off Harwood Rd.)
Broxholm Rd. SE27 . . 3C **118**
Broxted Rd. SE6 . . . . 2B **122**
Broxwood Way NW8 . . 5A **46**
Bruce Cl. W10 . . . . . . 4F **57**

Bruce Hall M.
SW17 . . . . 4C **116**
Bruce Ho. W10 . . . . . . 4F **57**
Bruce Rd. E3 . . . . 2D **67**
NW10 . . . . 4A **42**
Bruckner St. W10 . . . . 2A **58**
Brudenell Rd.
SW17 . . . . 3B **116**
Bruford Ct. SE8 . . . . . 2C **94**
Bruges Pl. NW1 . . . . . 4E **47**
(off Randolph St.)
Brune Ho. E1 . . . . 1F **19**
Brunei Gallery
. . . . 5C **6** (4F **61**)
. . . . 3E **79**
Brunel Engine House Mus.
. . . . 3E **79**
Brunel Est. W2 . . . . . . 4C **58**
Brunel Ho. E14 . . . . . . 1D **95**
(off Ship Yd.)
Brunel Rd. E17 . . . . . . 1A **38**
SE16 . . . . 3F **79**
W3 . . . . 4A **56**
Brunel St. E16 . . . . . . 5B **68**
Brune St. E1 . . 1F **19** (4B **64**)
Brunlees Ho. SE1 . . . . 5F **25**
(off Bath Ter.)
Brunner Cl. NW11 . . . . 1D **31**
Brunner Ho. SE6 . . . . 4E **123**
Brunner Rd. E17 . . . . . 1A **38**
Brunswick Cen.
WC1 . . . . 3D **7** (3A **62**)
Brunswick Cl. Est.
EC1 . . . . 2D **9** (2D **63**)
Brunswick Ct. EC1 . . . . 2D **9**
(off Tompion St.)
SE1 . . . . 4E **27** (3A **78**)
SW1 . . . . 5F **75**
(off Regency St.)
Brunswick Gdns.
W8 . . . . 2C **72**
Brunswick Ho. E2 . . . . 1B **64**
(off Thurtle Rd.)
SE16 . . . . 4A **80**
(off Brunswick Quay)
Brunswick Mans. WC1 . . 3E **7**
(off Handel St.)
Brunswick M. SW16 . . 5F **117**
W1 . . . . 2A **12** (5B **60**)
Brunswick Pk. SE5 . . . 4A **92**
Brunswick Pl.
N1 . . . . 2C **10** (2F **63**)
NW1 . . . . 4C **4** (3C **60**)
(not continuous)
Brunswick Quay SE16 . . 4F **79**
Brunswick Rd. E10 . . . 3E **39**
E14 . . . . 5E **67**
Brunswick Sq.
WC1 . . . . 3E **7** (3A **62**)
Brunswick Vs. SE5 . . . 4A **92**
Brunton Pl. E14 . . . . . 5A **66**
Brushfield St.
E1 . . . . 5E **11** (4A **64**)
Brushwood Cl. E14 . . . 4D **67**
Brussels Rd. SW11 . . . 2F **101**
Bruton La.
W1 . . . . 5E **13** (1D **75**)
Bruton Pl.
W1 . . . . 5E **13** (1D **75**)
Bruton St.
W1 . . . . 5E **13** (1D **75**)

Brutus Ct. *SE11* 5D *77*
(off Kennington La.)
Bryan Av. NW10. . . . . . . .4D *43*
Bryan Ho. NW10 . . . . . . .4D *43*
SE16. . . . . .3B *80*
Bryan Rd. SE16 . . . . .3B *80*
Bryan's All. SW6 . . . . . . .5D *87*
Bryanston Ct. W1 . . . . . .2A *12*
(not continuous)
Bryanstone Rd. N8 . . . . .1F *33*
Bryanston Mans.
W1 . . . . .5A *4*
(off York St.)
Bryanston M. E.
W1 . . . . .1A *12* (4B *60*)
Bryanston M. W.
W1 . . . . .2A *12* (4B *60*)
Bryanston Pl. W1 . . . . . .4B *60*
Bryanston Sq.
W1 . . . . .2A *12* (5B *60*)
Bryanston St.
W1 . . . . .3A *12* (5B *60*)
Bryant Ct. *E2* 1B *64*
(off Whiston Rd.,
not continuous)
Bryant St. E15. . . . . .4F *53*
Bryantwood Rd. N7 . . . . .2C *48*
Bryce Ho. *SE14*. 2F *93*
(off John Williams Cl.)
Brydale Ho. *SE16* 5F *79*
(off Rotherhithe New Rd.)
Bryden Cl. SE26 . . . . . . .5A *122*
Brydges Pl.
WC2 . . . . . . .5D *15* (1A *76*)
Brydges Rd. E15 . . . . . . .2F *53*
Brydon Wlk. N1 . . . . .5A *48*
Bryer Ct. EC2 . . . . .5F *9*
Bryett Rd. N7 . . . . .5A *34*
Bryher Ct. *SE11* 1C *90*
(off Sancroft St.)
Brymay Cl. E3. . . . . .1C *66*
Brynmaer Rd.
SW11 . . . . .4B *88*
Bryony Rd. W12. . . . . . . .1C *70*
Buccleugh Ho. E5. . . . . . .2C *36*
Buchanan Ct. SE16. . . . . .5F *79*
(off Worgan St.)
Buchanan Gdns.
NW10. . . . . .1D *57*
Buchan Rd. SE15 . . . . . .1E *107*
Bucharest Rd.
SW18 . . . . .5E *101*
Buckden Cl. SE12. . . . . . .4C *110*
Buckfast St. E2. . . . . .2C *64*
Buck Hill Wlk. W2. . . . . . .1F *73*
Buckhold Rd. SW18 . . . . .4C *100*
Buckhurst Ho. N7. . . . . . .2F *47*
Buckhurst St. E1. . . . . . . .3D *65*
Buckingham Arc.
WC2 . . . . .5E *15*
Buckingham Chambers
SW1 . . . . .5E *75*
(off Greencoat Pl.)
Buckingham Ga.
SW1 . . . . . . .5F *21* (4E *75*)
Buckingham La.
SE23 . . . . .5A *108*
Buckingham Mans.
NW6 . . . . .2D *45*
(off W. End La.)

Buckingham M. N1 . . . . .3A *50*
NW10. . . . . .1B *56*
SW1 . . . . .5F *21*
Buckingham Palace
. . . . .4E *21* (3D *75*)
Buckingham Pal. Rd.
SW1 . . . . . . .5E *21* (5D *75*)
Buckingham Pl.
SW1 . . . . . . .5F *21* (4E *75*)
Buckingham Rd. E10. . . . .5D *39*
E11 . . . . .1E *41*
E15 . . . . .2B *54*
N1 . . . . .3A *50*
NW10. . . . . .1B *56*
Buckingham St.
WC2 . . . . . . .1E *23* (1A *76*)
Buckland Ct. *N1*. 1A *64*
(off St John's Est.)
Buckland Cres. NW3 . . . .4F *45*
Buckland Rd. E10. . . . . . .4E *39*
Buckland St. N1 . . . . .1F *63*
Bucklebury *NW1* 3F *5*
(off Stanhope St.)
Bucklers All. SW6 . . . . . .2B *86*
(not continuous)
Bucklersbury
EC4 . . . . .3B *18* (5F *63*)
Bucklersbury Pas.
EC4 . . . . .5F *63*
Buckle St. E1. . . . . .5B *64*
Buckley Cl. SE23 . . . . . . .5D *107*
Buckley Ct. NW6. . . . . . . .4B *44*
Buckley Rd. NW6 . . . . . . .4B *44*
Buckmaster Cl.
SW9 . . . . .1C *104*
(off Stockwell Pk. Rd.)
Buckmaster Ho. N7 . . . . .1B *48*
Buckmaster Rd.
SW11 . . . . .2A *102*
Bucknall St.
WC2 . . . . . . .2C *14* (5A *62*)
Bucknell Cl. SW2. . . . . . .2B *104*
Buckner Rd. SW2 . . . . . . .2B *104*
Bucknill Ho. *SW1*. 1D *89*
(off Ebury Bri. Rd.)
Buckridge Ho. EC1. . . . . . .5B *8*
(off Portpool La.)
Buckstone Cl. SE23 . . . . .4E *107*
Buck St. NW1. . . . . .4D *47*
Buckters Rents SE16 . . . .2A *80*
Buckthorne Rd. SE4. . . . .3A *108*
Bude Cl. E17 . . . . .1B *38*
Budge Row
EC4. . . . . .4B *18* (1F *77*)
Budge's Wlk. *W2*. 2E *73*
(off Broad Wlk., The)
Budleigh Ho. SE15. . . . . .3C *92*
(off Bird in Bush Rd.)
Buer Rd. SW6 . . . . .5A *86*
Bugsby's Way SE7 . . . . . .5B *82*
SE10. . . . . .5B *82*
Bulbarrow *NW8* 5D *45*
(off Abbey Rd.)
Bulinga St. SW1. . . . . . . .5A *76*
(off John Islip St.)
Bullace Row SE5 . . . . . . .5F *91*
Bullard's Pl. E2. . . . . .2F *65*
Bulleid Way SW1. . . . . . .5D *75*
Bullen Ho. E1. . . . . .3D *65*
(off Collingwood St.)

Bullen St. SW11. . . . . . . .5A *88*
Buller Cl. SE15. . . . . .3C *92*
Buller Rd. NW10 . . . . . . .2F *57*
Bullingham Mans.
W8. . . . . .3C *72*
(off Pitt St.)
Bull Inn Ct. WC2. . . . . . . .5E *15*
Bullivant St. E14 . . . . . . .1E *81*
Bull Rd. E15. . . . . .1B *68*
Bulls Gdns. SW3 . . . . . . .5A *74*
(not continuous)
Bulls Head Pas. EC3 . . . .3D *19*
Bull Wharf La.
EC4 . . . . .4A *18* (1E *77*)
Bull Wharf Wlk. *EC4* 5A *18*
(off Bull Wharf La.)
Bull Yd. SE15. . . . . .4C *92*
Bulmer M. W11 . . . . .1C *72*
Bulmer Pl. W11 . . . . .2C *72*
Bulow Est. SW6. . . . . . . .4D *87*
(off Pearscroft Rd.)
Bulstrode Pl.
W1. . . . . .1C *12* (4C *60*)
Bulstrode St.
W1. . . . . .2C *12* (5C *60*)
Bulwer Ct. E11. . . . . .3F *39*
Bulwer Ct. Rd. E11. . . . . .3F *39*
Bulwer Rd. E11. . . . . .2F *39*
Bulwer St. W12 . . . . .2E *71*
Bunbury Ho. SE15 . . . . . .3C *92*
(off Fenham Rd.)
Bungalows, The E10 . . . . .1E *39*
Bunhill Row
EC1. . . . . .3B *10* (3F *63*)
Bunhouse Pl. SW1. . . . . . .1C *88*
Bunkers Hill NW11. . . . . .2E *31*
Bunning Way N7 . . . . . . .4A *48*
Bunsen Ho. *E3* 1A *66*
(off Grove Rd.)
Bunsen St. E3. . . . . .1A *66*
Bunyan Ct. EC2. . . . . .5F *9*
Buonaparte M. SW1 . . . . .1F *89*
Burbage Cl.
SE1. . . . . .5B *26* (4F *77*)
Burbage Ho. N1 . . . . .5F *49*
(off Poole St.)
SE14 . . . . .2F *93*
(off Samuel Cl.)
Burbage Rd. SE21 . . . . . .4E *105*
SE24 . . . . .4E *105*
Burcham St. E14 . . . . . . .5D *67*
Burchell Ho. *SE11* 1B *90*
(off Jonathan St.)
Burchell Rd. E10 . . . . . . .3D *39*
SE15. . . . . .4D *93*
Burcote Rd. SW18 . . . . . .5F *101*
Burden Ho. SW8 . . . . . . .3A *90*
(off Thorncroft St.)
Burden Way E11 . . . . . . .4D *41*
Burder Cl. N1 . . . . .3A *50*
Burder Rd. N1 . . . . .3A *50*
Burdett M. NW3 . . . . . . .3F *45*
W2. . . . . .5D *59*
Burdett Rd. E3 . . . . .3A *66*
E14. . . . . .3A *66*
Burfield Cl. SW17. . . . . . .4F *115*
Burford Rd. E6 . . . . .2F *69*
E15 . . . . .5F *53*
SE6. . . . . .2B *122*
Burford Wlk. SW6 . . . . . .3E *87*

Burge Rd. E7 . . . . 1F 55
Burges Gro. SW13 . . . . 3D 85
Burgess Av. NW9 . . . . . 1A 28
Burgess Bus. Pk. SE5 . . 3F 91
Burgess Hill NW2 . . . . . 1C 44
Burgess Pk. Kart Track
. . . . 2F 91
Burgess Rd. E15 . . . . . 1A 54
Burgess St. E14 . . . . . . 4C 66
Burge St.
   SE1 . . . . 5C 26 (4F 77)
Burgh House 1F 45
Burghill Rd. SE26 . . . . 4A 122
Burghley Hall Cl.
   SW19 . . . . 1A 114
Burghley Ho. SW19 . . . 3A 114
Burghley Rd. E11 . . . . . 3A 40
   NW5 . . . . 1D 47
   SW19 . . . . 4F 113
Burghley Twr. W3 . . . . . 1B 70
Burgh St. N1 . . . . 1D 63
Burgon St.
   EC4 . . . . 3E 17 (5D 63)
Burgos Gro. SE10 . . . . . 4D 95
Burgoyne Rd. N4 . . . . . 1D 35
   SW9 . . . . 1B 104
Burke Cl. SW15 . . . . . . 2A 98
Burke Lodge E13 . . . . . 2D 69
Burke St. E16 . . . . 4B 68
   (not continuous)
Burland Rd. SW11 . . . . 3B 102
Burleigh Ho. SW3 . . . . . 2F 87
   (off Beaufort St.)
   W10 . . . . 4A 58
   (off St Charles Sq.)
Burleigh Pl. SW15 . . . . . 3F 99
Burleigh St.
   WC2 . . . . 4F 15 (1B 76)
Burleigh Wlk. SE6 . . . . 1E 123
Burley Ho. E1 . . . . 5F 65
   (off Chudleigh St.)
Burley Rd. E16 . . . . 5E 69
Burlington Arc.
   W1 . . . . 5F 13 (1E 75)
Burlington Cl. W9 . . . . . 3C 58
Burlington Gdns.
   SW6 . . . . 5A 86
   W1 . . . . 5F 13 (1E 75)
Burlington La. W4 . . . . . 3A 84
Burlington M. SW15 . . . 3B 100
Burlington Pl. SW6 . . . . 5A 86
Burlington Rd. SW6 . . . . 5A 86
Burma M. N16 . . . . 1F 49
Burma Rd. N16 . . . . 1F 49
Burmarsh NW5 . . . . 3C 46
Burma Ter. SE19 . . . . . 5A 120
Burmester Rd.
   SW17 . . . . 3E 115
Burnaby St. SW10 . . . . . 3E 87
Burnand Ho. W14 . . . . . 4F 71
   (off Redan St.)
Burnard Pl. N7 . . . . 2B 48
Burnaston Ho. E5 . . . . . 5C 36
Burnbury Rd. SW12 . . . 1E 117
Burne Jones Ho.
   W14 . . . . 5A 72
Burnell Wlk. SE1 . . . . . 1B 92
   (off Abingdon Cl.)
Burness Cl. N7 . . . . 3B 48
Burne St. NW1 . . . . 4A 60

Burnett Cl. E9 . . . . 2E 51
Burnett Ho. SE13 . . . . . 5E 95
   (off Lewisham Hill)
Burney St. SE10 . . . . . . 3E 95
Burnfoot Av. SW6 . . . . . 4A 86
Burnham NW3 . . . . 4A 46
Burnham Cl. SE1 . . . . . . 5B 78
Burnham Ct. W2 . . . . . . 1D 73
   (off Moscow Rd.)
Burnham Est. E2 . . . . . . 2E 65
   (off Burnham St.)
Burnham St. E2 . . . . 2E 65
Burnham Way SE26 . . . 5B 122
Burnhill Cl. SE15 . . . . . 3D 93
Burnley Rd. NW10 . . . . . 2B 42
   SW9 . . . . 5B 90
Burnsall St. SW3 . . . . . . 1A 88
Burns Cl. SW19 . . . . . . 5F 115
Burns Ho. E2 . . . . 2E 65
   (off Cornwall Av.)
   SE17 . . . . 1D 91
   (off Doddington Gro.)
Burnside Cl. SE16 . . . . . 2F 79
Burns Rd. NW10 . . . . . . 5B 42
   SW11 . . . . 5B 88
Burnt Ash Hgts.
   BR1: Brom 5D 125
Burnt Ash Hill SE12 . . . 4B 110
   (not continuous)
Burnt Ash La.
   BR1: Brom 5C 124
Burnt Ash Rd. SE12 . . . 3B 110
Burnthwaite Rd. SW6 . . 3B 86
Burntwood Cl.
   SW18 . . . . 1A 116
Burntwood Grange Rd.
   SW18 . . . . 1F 115
Burntwood La.
   SW17 . . . . 3E 115
Burntwood Vw.
   SE19 . . . . 5B 120
Buross St. E1 . . . . 5D 65
Burrage Ct. SE16 . . . . . 5F 79
   (off Worgan St.)
Burrard Ho. E2 . . . . 1E 65
   (off Bishop's Way)
Burrard Rd. E16 . . . . . . 5D 69
   NW6 . . . . 2C 44
Burr Cl. E1 . . . . 2C 78
Burrell St.
   SE1 . . . . 1D 25 (2D 77)
Burrells Wharf Sq.
   E14 . . . . 1D 95
Burrell Towers E10 . . . . 2C 38
Burrhill Ct. SE16 . . . . . . 4F 79
   (off Worgan St.)
Burroughs Cotts. E14 . . 4A 66
   (off Halley St.)
Burrow Ho. SW9 . . . . . . 5C 90
   (off Stockwell Pk. Rd.)
Burrow Rd. SE22 . . . . . 2A 106
Burrows M.
   SE1 . . . . 3D 25 (3D 77)
Burrows Rd. NW10 . . . . 2F 57
Burrow Wlk. SE21 . . . . 5E 105
Burr Rd. SW18 . . . . . . 1C 114
Bursar St. SE1
   . . . . 2D 27 (2A 78)
Burslem St. E1 . . . . 5C 64
Burstock Rd. SW15 . . . 2A 100

Burston Rd. SW15 . . . . 3F 99
Burtley Cl. N4 . . . . 3E 35
Burton Bank N1 . . . . 4F 49
   (off Yeate St.)
Burton Ct. SW3 . . . . 1B 88
   (off Franklin's Row,
      not continuous)
Burton Gro. SE17 . . . . . 1F 91
Burton Ho. SE16 . . . . . . 3D 79
   (off Cherry Gdn. St.)
Burton La. SW9 . . . . 5C 90
   (not continuous)
Burton Pl.
   WC1 . . . . 2C 6 (2F 61)
Burton Rd. NW6 . . . . . . 4B 44
   SW9 . . . . 5D 91
   (Akerman Rd.)
   SW9 . . . . 5C 90
   (Evesham Wlk.)
Burton St.
   WC1 . . . . 2C 6 (2F 61)
Burtonwood Ho. N4 . . . . 2F 35
Burtop Rd. Est.
   SW17 . . . . 3E 115
Burt Rd. E16 . . . . 2E 83
Burtt Ho. N1 . . . . 1D 11
   (off Aske St.)
Burwash Ho. SE1 . . . . . 4C 26
   (off Kipling Est.)
Burwell Cl. E1 . . . . 5D 65
Burwell Rd. E10 . . . . . . 3A 38
Burwell Rd. Ind. Est.
   E10 . . . . 3A 38
Burwell Wlk. E3 . . . . . . 3C 66
Burwood Ho. SW9 . . . . 2D 105
Burwood Pl. W2 . . . . . . 5A 60
Bury Cl. SE16 . . . . 2F 79
Bury Ct. EC3 . . . 2E 19 (5A 64)
Bury Pl.
   WC1 . . . . 1D 15 (4A 62)
Bury St. EC3 . . . 3E 19 (5A 64)
   SW1 . . . . 1A 22 (2E 75)
Bury Wlk. SW3 . . . . 5A 74
Busbridge Ho. E14 . . . . 4C 66
   (off Brabazon St.)
Busby Ho. SW16 . . . . . 4E 117
Busby M. NW5 . . . . 3F 47
Busby Pl. NW5 . . . . 3F 47
Bushbaby Cl.
   SE1 . . . . 5D 27 (4A 78)
Bushberry Rd. E9 . . . . . 3A 52
Bush Cotts. SW18 . . . . 3C 100
Bush Ct. W12 . . . . 3F 71
Bushell Cl. SW2 . . . . . 2B 118
Bushell St. E1 . . . . 2C 78
Bushey Down SW12 . . . 2D 117
Bushey Hill Rd. SE5 . . . 4A 92
Bushey Rd. E13 . . . . . . 1E 69
   N15 . . . . 1A 36
Bush Ind. Est. N19 . . . . 5E 33
Bush La. EC4 . . . 4B 18 (1F 77)
Bushnell Rd. SW17 . . . 2D 117
Bush Rd. E8 . . . . 5D 51
   E11 . . . . 2B 40
   SE8 . . . . 5F 79
   (off Rotherhithe New Rd.)
Bush Theatre 3E 71
Bushwood E11 . . . . 3B 40

Bushwood Dr.—Caleb St.

Bushwood Dr. SE1 . . . . 5B **78**
Business Design Cen.
. . . . 5C **48**
(off Upper St.)
Butcher Row E1 . . . . . . 1F **79**
E14 . . . . 1F **79**
Butchers Rd. E16 . . . . . 5C **68**
Bute Gdns. W6 . . . . 5F **71**
Bute St. SW7 . . . . 5F **73**
Bute Wlk. N1 . . . . 3F **49**
Butfield Ho. E9 . . . . 3E **51**
(off Stevens Av.)
Butler Ho. E2 . . . . 2E **65**
(off Bacton St.)
E14 . . . . 5B **66**
(off Burdett St.)
SW9 . . . . 4D **91**
(off Lothian Rd.)
Butler Pl.
SW1 . . . . 5B **22** (4F **75**)
Butler Rd. NW10 . . . . . 4B **42**
Butlers & Colonial Wharf
SE1 . . . . 3F **27**
(off Shad Thames)
Butler St. E2 . . . . 2E **65**
Butlers Wharf SE1 . . . . 3F **27**
(off Gainsford St.)
Butley Ct. E3 . . . . 1A **66**
(off Ford St.)
Butterfield Cl. SE16 . . . 3D **79**
Butterfields E1 . . . . 1E **39**
Butterfly Wlk. SE5 . . . . 4F **91**
(off Denmark Hill)
Buttermere NW1 . . . . . 1E **5**
(off Augustus St.)
Buttermere Cl. E15 . . . . 1F **53**
SE1 . . . . 5B **78**
Buttermere Ct. NW8 . . 5F **45**
(off Boundary Rd.)
Buttermere Dr.
SW15 . . . . 3A **100**
Buttermere Wlk. E8 . . . 3B **50**
Butterwick W6 . . . . 5F **71**
Butterworth Ter.
SE17 . . . . 1E **91**
(off Sutherland Wlk.)
Buttesland St.
N1 . . . . 1C **10** (2F **63**)
Butts Rd.
BR1: Brom 5A **124**
Buxhall Cres. E9 . . . . . 3B **52**
Buxted Rd. E8 . . . . 4B **50**
SE22 . . . . 2A **106**
Buxton Ct. E11 . . . . 2B **40**
N1 . . . . 1A **10**
Buxton M. SW4 . . . . . . 5F **89**
Buxton Rd. E6 . . . . 2F **69**
E15 . . . . 2A **54**
N19 . . . . 3F **33**
NW2 . . . . 3D **43**
SW14 . . . . 1A **98**
Buxton St. E1 . . . . 3B **64**
Byam St. SW6 . . . . 5E **87**
Byards Ct. SE16 . . . . . . 5F **79**
(off Worgan St.)
Bye, The W3 . . . . 5A **56**
Byelands Cl. SE16 . . . . 2F **79**
Byfeld Gdns. SW13 . . . 4C **84**
Byfield Cl. SE16 . . . . . . 3B **80**
Byford Cl. E15 . . . . 4A **54**

Bygrove St. E14 . . . . . . 5D **67**
(not continuous)
Byne Rd. SE26 . . . . 5E **121**
Byng Pl.
WC1 . . . . 4C **6** (3F **61**)
Byng Rd. E14 . . . . 3C **80**
Byrne Rd. SW12 . . . . . 1D **117**
Byron Av. E12 . . . . 3F **55**
Byron Cl. E8 . . . . 5C **50**
SE26 . . . . 4A **122**
SW16 . . . . 5A **118**
Byron Ct. NW6 . . . . 4E **45**
(off Fairfax Rd.)
SE22 . . . . 1C **120**
W9 . . . . 3C **58**
(off Lanhill Rd.)
WC1 . . . . 3F **7**
(off Mecklenburgh Sq.)
Byron Dr. N2 . . . . 1F **31**
Byron M. NW3 . . . . 1A **46**
W9 . . . . 3C **58**
Byron Rd. E10 . . . . 3D **39**
NW2 . . . . 4D **29**
Byron St. E14 . . . . 5E **67**
Bythorn St. SW9 . . . . . 1B **104**
Byton Rd. SW17 . . . . . 5B **116**
Byward St.
EC3 . . . . 5E **19** (1A **78**)
Bywater Ho. SE18 . . . . 4F **83**
Bywater Pl. SE16 . . . . . 2A **80**
Bywater St. SW3 . . . . . 1B **88**
Byway E11 . . . . 1E **41**
Bywell Pl. W1 . . . . 1F **13**
Byworth Wlk. N19 . . . . 3A **34**

C

Cabbell St. NW1 . . . . . 4A **60**
Cable Ho. WC1 . . . . 1B **8**
(off Gt. Percy St.)
Cable Pl. SE10 . . . . 4E **95**
Cable St. E1 . . . . 1C **78**
Cable Trade Pk. SE7 . . 5E **83**
Cabot Ct. SE16 . . . . . . 5F **79**
(off Worgan St.)
Cabot Sq. E14 . . . . 2C **80**
Cabot Way E6 . . . . 5F **55**
Cabul Rd. SW11 . . . . . . 5A **88**
Caci Ho. W14 . . . . 5B **72**
(off Kensington Village)
Cactus Cl. SE15 . . . . . . 5A **92**
Cactus Wlk. W12 . . . . . 5B **56**
Cadbury Way SE16 . . . 4B **78**
Caddington Rd. NW2 . . 5A **30**
Cadell Cl. E2 . . . . 1B **64**
Cade Rd. SE10 . . . . 4F **95**
Cader Rd. SW18 . . . . . . 4E **101**
Cadet Dr. SE1 . . . . 5B **78**
Cadet Pl. SE10 . . . . 1A **96**
Cadiz St. SE17 . . . . 1E **91**
Cadley Ter. SE23 . . . . . 2E **121**
Cadman Cl. SW9 . . . . . 3D **91**
Cadmore Ho. N1 . . . . . . 4D **49**
(off Sutton Est., The)
Cadmus Cl. SW4 . . . . . 1F **103**
Cadmus Ct. SW9 . . . . . 4C **90**
(off Southey Rd.)
Cadnam Lodge E14 . . . 4E **81**
(off Schooner Cl.)

Cadnam Point
SW15 . . . . 1D **113**
Cadogan Cl. E9 . . . . . . 4B **52**
Cadogan Ct. SW3 . . . . 5B **74**
(off Draycott Av.)
Cadogan Gdns. SW3 . . 5B **74**
Cadogan Ga. SW3 . . . . 5B **74**
Cadogan Ho. SW3 . . . . 2F **87**
(off Beaufort St.)
Cadogan La.
SW1 . . . . 5B **20** (4C **74**)
Cadogan Mans. SW3 . . 5B **74**
(off Cadogan Gdns.)
Cadogan Pl.
SW1 . . . . 5A **20** (4B **74**)
Cadogan Sq.
SW1 . . . . 5A **20** (4B **74**)
Cadogan Ter. E9 . . . . . 3B **52**
Cadoxton Av. N15 . . . . 1B **36**
Caedmon Rd. N7 . . . . . 1B **48**
Caernarvon Ho. E16 . . 2D **83**
(off Audley Dr.)
W2 . . . . 5E **59**
(off Hallfield Est.)
Caesar Ct. E2 . . . . 1F **65**
(off Palmer's Rd.)
Cafe Gallery 4E **79**
Cahill St.
EC1 . . . . 4A **10** (3E **63**)
Cahir St. E14 . . . . 5D **81**
Caird St. W10 . . . . 2A **58**
Cairncross M. N8 . . . . . 1A **34**
(off Felix Av.)
Cairnfield Av. NW2 . . . 5A **28**
Cairns Rd. SW11 . . . . . 3A **102**
Caister Ho. N7 . . . . 3B **48**
Caister Ho. E15 . . . . . . 5B **54**
(off Caistor Pk. Rd.)
Caistor M. SW12 . . . . . 5D **103**
Caistor Pk. Rd. E15 . . . 5B **54**
Caistor Rd. SW12 . . . . 5D **103**
Caithness Ho. N1 . . . . . 5B **48**
(off Twyford St.)
Caithness Rd. W14 . . . 4F **71**
Calabria Rd. N5 . . . . . . 3D **49**
Calais Ga. SE5 . . . . 4D **91**
Calais St. SE5 . . . . 4D **91**
Calbourne Rd.
SW12 . . . . 5B **102**
Calcott Ct. W14 . . . . . . 4A **72**
(off Blythe Rd.)
Calcott Wlk. SE9 . . . . . 4F **125**
Calcraft Ho. E2 . . . . . . 1E **65**
(off Bonner Rd.)
Caldecot Rd. SE5 . . . . 5E **91**
Caldecott Way E5 . . . . 5F **37**
Calder Ct. SE16 . . . . . . 2B **80**
Calderon Ho. NW8 . . . 1A **60**
(off Townshend Est.)
Calderon Pl. W10 . . . . 4E **57**
Calderon Rd. E11 . . . . . 1E **53**
Caldervale Rd. SW4 . . 3F **103**
Caldew St. SE5 . . . . . . 3F **91**
Caldicot Grn. NW9 . . . 1A **28**
Caldwell Ho. SW13 . . . 3E **85**
(off Trinity Chu. Rd.)
Caldwell St. SW9 . . . . . 3B **90**
Caldy Wlk. N1 . . . . 4E **49**
Caleb St. SE1 . . . 3F **25** (3E **77**)

160 Mini London

Caledonia Ho. *E14* *5A 66*
(off Salmon La.)
Caledonian Rd.
N1 . . . . .1E **7** (1A **62**)
N7 . . . . .1B **48**
Caledonian Sq.
NW1 . . . . .3F **47**
Caledonia Wharf
E14 . . . . .5F **81**
Caledonia St.
N1 . . . . .1E **7** (1A **62**)
Cale St. SW3 . . . . .1A **88**
Caletock Way SE10 . .1B **96**
Calgarth *NW1* *1A* **6**
(off Ampthill Est.)
Calgary Ct. *SE16* *3E* **79**
(off Canada Est.)
Caliban Twr. *N1* *1A 64*
(off Arden Est.)
Calico Ho. *EC4* *3A 18*
(off Well Ct.)
Calico Row SW11 . . . . .1E **101**
Callaby Ter. N1 . . . . . .3F **49**
Callaghan Cl. SE13 . .2A **110**
Callahan Cotts. *E1* *4E 65*
(off Lindley St.)
Callander Rd. SE6 . . .2D **123**
Callcott Ct. NW6 . . . . .4B **44**
Callcott Rd. NW6 . . . . .4B **44**
Callcott St. W8 . . . . . . .2C **72**
Callendar Rd. SW7 . . .4F **73**
Callingham Cl. E14 . . .4B **66**
Callis Rd. E17 . . . . .1B **38**
Callow St. SW3 . . . . . .2F **87**
Cally Swimming Pool
. . . . .5B **48**
Calmington Rd. SE5 . .2A **92**
Calmont Rd.
BR1: Brom 5F **123**
Calonne Rd. SW19 . . .4F **113**
Calshot Ho. *N1* *1B 62*
(off Calshot St.)
Calshot St. N1 . . .1F **7** (1B **62**)
Calstock *NW1* *5E 47*
(off Royal College St.)
Calstock Ho. *SE11* *1C 90*
(off Kennings Way)
Calthorpe St.
WC1 . . . . .3A **8** (3B **62**)
Calton Rd. SE21 . . . . .4A **106**
Calverley Cl.
BR3: Beck. 5D **123**
Calverley Gro. N19. . . . .3F **33**
Calvert Av.
E2. . . . . .2E **11** (2A **64**)
Calvert Ho. *W12* *1D 71*
(off White City Est.)
Calverton *SE5* *2A 92*
(off Albany Rd.)
Calvert Rd. SE10 . . . .1B **96**
Calvert's Bldgs.
SE1 . . . . . . .2B **26** (2F **77**)
Calvert St. NW1 . . . . . .5C **46**
Calvin St. E1 . . .4F **11** (3B **64**)
Calydon Rd. SE7 . . . .1D **97**
Calypso Cres. SE15 . . . . .3B **92**
Calypso Way SE16 . . . . .4B **80**
Camarthen Grn. NW9 . .1A **28**
Cambalt Rd. SW15 . . . . .3F **99**

Cambay Ho. *E1* *3A 66*
(off Harford St.)
Camber Ho. SE15. . . . .2E **93**
Camberley Ho. NW1 . . .1E **5**
Cambert Way SE3 . . .2D **111**
CAMBERWELL 4F **91**
Camberwell Chu. St.
SE5 . . . . .4F **91**
Camberwell Glebe
SE5 . . . . .4A **92**
CAMBERWELL GREEN
. . . . .4F **91**
Camberwell Grn.
SE5 . . . . .4F **91**
Camberwell Gro. SE5. . .4F **91**
Camberwell Leisure Cen.
. . . . .4F **91**
Camberwell New Rd.
SE5 . . . . .2C **90**
Camberwell Pl. SE5. . . .4E **91**
Camberwell Rd. SE5 . . .2E **91**
Camberwell Sta. Rd.
SE5 . . . . .4E **91**
Camberwell Trad. Est.
SE5 . . . . .4D **91**
Camborne Rd.
SW18 . . . . .5C **100**
Cambourne M. W11 . . .5A **58**
Cambray Rd. SW12 . . .1E **117**
Cambria Ho. *E14* *5D 66*
(off Salmon La.)
SE26 . . . .*4C 120*
(off High Level Dr.)
Cambrian Cl. SE27 . . .3D **119**
Cambrian Grn. *NW9* . . .*1A 28*
(off Snowden Dr.)
Cambrian Rd. E10 . . . .2C **38**
Cambria Rd. SE5 . . . . .1E **105**
Cambria St. SW6 . . . . .3D **87**
Cambridge Arc. *E9* *4E 51*
(off Elsdale St.)
Cambridge Av. NW6. . .1C **58**
NW10 . . . . .2E **57**
Cambridge Cir.
WC2 . . . . . . .3C **14** (5F **61**)
Cambridge Cl. E17. . . . .1B **38**
Cambridge Ct. *E2*. *1D 65*
(off Cambridge Heath Rd.)
N16. . . . .*2A 36*
(off Amhurst Pk.)
NW6 . . . . .1C **58**
W2 . . . .*4A 60*
(off Edgware Rd.)
W6 . . . .*5E 71*
(off Shepherd's Bush Rd.)
Cambridge Cres. E2. . . .1D **65**
Cambridge Dr. SE12 . . .3C **110**
Cambridge Gdns.
NW6 . . . . .1C **58**
W10. . . . . .5F **57**
Cambridge Ga.
NW1 . . . . .3D **5** (3D **61**)
Cambridge Ga. M.
NW1 . . . . .3E **5** (3D **61**)
Cambridge Gro. W6. . . .5D **71**
Cambridge Heath Rd.
E1. . . . . .4D **65**
Cambridge Ho. *W6* *5D 71*
(off Cambridge Gro.)
Cambridge Pk. E11 . . .2C **40**

Cambridge Pk. Rd.
E11. . . . . .2C **40**
(off Lonsdale Rd.)
Cambridge Pl. W8. . . . .3D **73**
Cambridge Rd. E11 . . .1B **40**
NW6 . . . . .1C **58**
(not continuous)
SW11 . . . . .4B **88**
SW13 . . . . .5B **84**
Cambridge Sq. W2. . . . .5A **60**
Cambridge St. SW1. . . .5D **75**
Cambridge Ter.
NW1 . . . . .2D **5** (2D **61**)
Cambridge Ter. M.
NW1 . . . . .2E **5** (2D **61**)
Cambridge Theatre. . . .*3D 15*
(off Earlham St.)
Cambus Rd. E16 . . . . .4C **68**
Cam Ct. SE15 . . . . .2B **92**
Camden Arts Cen. 2D **45**
Camden Ct. *NW1* *4E 47*
(off Rousden St.)
Camden Gdns.
NW1 . . . . .4D **47**
Camden High St.
NW1 . . . . .4D **47**
Camden Hill Rd.
SE19 . . . . .5A **120**
Camden Ho. SE8 . . . . .1B **94**
Camdenhurst St. E14. . .5A **66**
Camden La. N7. . . . . . .2F **47**
Camden Lock Market
. . . .*4D 47*
(off Camden Lock Pl.)
Camden Lock Pl.
NW1 . . . . .4D **47**
Camden Market *5D 47*
(off Dewsbury Ter.)
Camden M. NW1 . . . . . .4E **47**
Camden Pk. Rd.
NW1 . . . . .3F **47**
Camden Pas. N1 . . . . . .5D **49**
(not continuous)
Camden Peoples Theatre
. . . .*3F 5*
(off Hampstead Rd.)
Camden Rd. E11 . . . . . .1D **41**
E17. . . . . .1B **38**
N7. . . . . .1A **48**
NW1 . . . . .4E **47**
Camden Row SE3. . . . .5A **96**
Camden Sq. NW1 . . . . .4F **47**
(not continuous)
SE15 . . . . .4B **92**
Camden St. NW1 . . . . .4E **47**
Camden Studios
NW1 . . . .*5E 47*
(off Camden St.)
Camden Ter. NW1. . . . .3F **47**
CAMDEN TOWN 5D **47**
Camden Wlk. N1 . . . . . .5D **49**
(not continuous)
Cameford Ct. SW2 . . . .5A **104**
Camelford *NW1* *5E 47*
(off Royal College St.)
Camelford Ct. *W11* *5A 58*
Camelford Ho. SE1 . . . .1A **90**
Camelford Wlk. W11 . . .5A **58**
Camellia Ho. *SE8*. *3B 94*
(off Idonia St.)

Camellia St. SW8......3A **90**
(not continuous)
Camelot Cl. SW19......4B **114**
Camel Rd. E16......2F **83**
Camera Pl. SW10......2F **87**
Cameret Ct. W11......3F **71**
(off Holland Rd.)
Cameron Ho. NW8......1A **60**
(off St John's Wood Ter.)
SE5......3E **91**
Cameron Pl. E1......5D **65**
SW16......2C **118**
Cameron Rd. SE6......2B **122**
Cameron Ter. SE12......3D **125**
Camerton Cl. E8......3B **50**
Camilla Rd. SE16......5D **79**
Camlan Rd.
BR1: Brom......4B **124**
Camlet St.
E2......3F **11** (3B **64**)
Camley St. NW1......4F **47**
Camomile St.
EC3......2E **19** (5A **64**)
Campana Rd. SW6......4C **86**
Campania Bldg. E1......1F **79**
(off Jardine Rd.)
Campbell Bldg. SE1......1F **79**
Campbell Cl. SW16......4F **117**
Campbell Ct. SE21......1C **120**
SW7......4E **73**
(off Gloucester Rd.)
Campbell Gordon Way
NW2......1D **43**
Campbell Ho. SW1......1E **89**
(off Churchill Gdns.)
W12......1D **71**
(off White City Est.)
Campbell Rd. E3......2C **66**
E15......1B **54**
Campbell Wlk. N1......5A **48**
(off Outram Pl.)
Campdale Rd. N7......5F **33**
Campden Gro. W8......3C **72**
Campden Hill W8......3C **72**
Campden Hill Ct. W8......3C **72**
Campden Hill Gdns.
W8......2C **72**
Campden Hill Ga.
W8......3C **72**
Campden Hill Mans.
W8......2C **72**
(off Edge St.)
Campden Hill Pl.
W11......2B **72**
Campden Hill Rd.
W8......2C **72**
Campden Hill Sq.
W8......2B **72**
Campden Ho. NW6......4F **45**
(off Harben Rd.)
W8......2C **72**
(off Sheffield Ter.)
Campden Ho. Cl. W8......3C **72**
Campden Ho's. W8......2C **72**
Campden Ho. Ter.
W8......2C **72**
(off Kensington Ch. St.)
Campden St. W8......2C **72**
Campen Cl. SW19......2A **114**
Camperdown St. E1......5B **64**

Campfield Rd. SE9......5F **111**
Campion Rd. SW15......2E **99**
Campion Ter. NW2......5F **29**
Camplin St. SE14......3F **93**
Camp Rd. SW19......5D **113**
(not continuous)
Campshill Pl. SE13......3E **109**
Campshill Rd.
SE13......3E **109**
Camp Vw. SW19......5D **113**
Campus Rd. E17......1B **38**
Cam Rd. E15......5F **53**
Canada Est. SE16......4E **79**
Canada Gdns. SE13......3E **109**
Canada Ho. SE16......4A **80**
(off Brunswick Quay)
Canada Memorial......3F **21**
(off Green Pk.)
Canada Pl. E14......2D **81**
(off Up. Bank St.)
Canada Sq. E14......2D **81**
Canada St. SE16......3F **79**
Canada Way W12......1D **71**
Canada Wharf SE16......2B **80**
Canadian Av. SE6......1D **123**
Canal App. SE8......1A **94**
Canal Blvd. NW1......3F **47**
CANAL BRIDGE......2C **92**
Canal Bldg. N1......1E **63**
(off Shepherdess Wlk.)
Canal Cl. E1......3A **66**
W10......3F **57**
Canal Gro. SE15......2D **93**
Canal Mkt. NW1......4D **47**
(off Castlehaven Rd.)
Canal Path E2......5B **50**
Canalside Activity Cen.
......3F **57**
Canal St. SE5......2F **91**
Canal Wlk. N1......5F **49**
SE26......5E **121**
Canal Way N1......1D **57**
Canberra Rd. SE7......2E **97**
Cancell Rd. SW9......4C **90**
Candahar Rd. SW11......5A **88**
Candida Ct. NW1......4D **47**
Candid Ho. NW10......2D **57**
(off Trenmar Gdns.)
Candle Gro. SE15......1D **107**
Candlelight Ct. E15......3B **54**
(off Romford Rd.)
Candler St. N15......1F **35**
Candover St.
W1......1F **13** (4E **61**)
Candy St. E3......5B **52**
Caney M. NW2......4F **29**
Canfield Gdns. NW6......4D **45**
Canfield Ho. N15......1A **36**
(off Albert Rd.)
Canfield Pl. NW6......3E **45**
Canford Rd. SW11......3C **102**
Canham Rd. W3......3A **70**
CANN HALL......1A **54**
Cann Hall Rd. E11......1A **54**
Cann Ho. W14......4A **72**
(off Russell Rd.)
Canning Cross SE5......5A **92**
Canning Ho. W12......1D **71**
(off Australia Rd.)

Canning Pas. W8......4E **73**
(not continuous)
Canning Pl. W8......4E **73**
Canning Pl. M. W8......4E **73**
(off Canning Pl.)
Canning Rd. E15......1A **68**
N5......5D **35**
CANNING TOWN......5B **68**
CANNING TOWN......5A **68**
Cannizaro Rd.
SW19......5E **113**
Cannock Ho. N4......2E **35**
Cannon Ct. EC1......3E **9**
(off Brewhouse Yd.)
Cannon Dr. E14......1C **80**
Cannon Hill NW6......2C **44**
Cannon Ho. SE11......5B **76**
(off Beaufoy Wlk.)
Cannon La. NW3......5F **31**
Cannon Pl. NW3......5F **31**
Cannons Health Club
Cannon St......5B **18**
Fulham......4F **85**
Willesden Green......4E **43**
Cannon St.
EC4......3F **17** (5E **63**)
Cannon St. Rd. E1......5D **65**
Cannon Wharf Bus. Cen.
SE8......5A **80**
Cannon Workshops
E14......1C **80**
(off Cannon Dr.)
Canon All. EC4......3F **17**
Canon Beck Rd.
SE16......3E **79**
Canonbie Rd. SE23......5E **107**
CANONBURY......3E **49**
Canonbury Bus. Cen.
N1......5E **49**
Canonbury Ct. N1......4D **49**
(off Hawes St.)
Canonbury Cres. N1......4E **49**
Canonbury Gro. N1......4E **49**
Canonbury Hgts. N1......3F **49**
(off Dove Rd.)
Canonbury La. N1......4D **49**
Canonbury Pk. Nth.
N1......3E **49**
Canonbury Pk. Sth.
N1......3E **49**
Canonbury Pl. N1......3D **49**
Canonbury Rd. N1......3D **49**
Canonbury Sq. N1......4D **49**
Canonbury St. N1......4E **49**
Canonbury Vs. N1......4D **49**
Canon Row
SW1......4D **23** (3A **76**)
(not continuous)
Canon's Cl. N2......2F **31**
Canons Ct. E15......1A **54**
Canon St. N1......5E **49**
Canrobert St. E2......1D **65**
Cantelowes Rd. NW1......3F **47**
Canterbury Av.
IG1: Ilf......2F **41**
Canterbury Cl. SE5......5E **91**
(off Lilford Rd.)

Canterbury Ct. *NW6* 1C **58**
   (off Canterbury Rd.)
SE12 . . . . 3D **125**
SW9 . . . . 3C **90**
Canterbury Cres.
SW9 . . . . 1C **104**
Canterbury Gro.
SE27 . . . . 4C **118**
Canterbury Ho.
SE1 . . . . 5A **24** (4B **76**)
SE15 . . . . 2E **93**
Canterbury Ind. Pk.
SE1 . . . . 2E **93**
Canterbury Pl. SE17 . . 1D **91**
Canterbury Rd. E10 . . . 2E **39**
NW6 . . . . 1B **58**
   (not continuous)
Canterbury Ter. *NW6* . . 1C **58**
Cantium Retail Pk.
SE1 . . . . 2C **92**
Canton St. E14 . . . . . . 5C **66**
Cantrell Rd. E3 . . . . . . 3B **66**
Canute Gdns. SE16 . . . 5F **79**
Canvey St.
SE1 . . . . 1F **25** (2E **77**)
Cape Henry Cl. *E14* . . . 1F **81**
   (off Jamestown Way)
Cape Ho. *E8* 3B **50**
   (off Dalston La.)
Capel Ct. *EC2* 3C **18**
   (off Bartholomew La.)
Capel Ho. *E9* 4E **51**
   (off Loddiges Rd.)
Capel Rd. E7 . . . . 1D **55**
E12 . . . . 1D **55**
Capener's Cl. SW1 . . . . 4A **20**
Capern Rd. SW18 . . . . 1E **115**
Cape Yd. E1 . . . . 1C **78**
Capital E. Apartments
E16 . . . . 1C **82**
   (off Western Gateway)
Capital Wharf E1 . . . . . 2C **78**
Capland Ho. *NW8* 3F **59**
   (off Capland St.)
Capland St. NW8 . . . . . 3F **59**
Caple Ho. *SW10* 3E **87**
   (off King's Rd.)
Caple Rd. NW10 . . . . . 1B **56**
Capper St.
WC1 . . . . 4A **6** (3E **61**)
Capstan Ct. *E1* 1E **79**
   (off Wapping Wall)
Capstan Ho. *E14* 1F **81**
   (off Clove Cres.)
E14 . . . . 5E **81**
   (off Stebondale St.)
Capstan Rd. SE8 . . . . . 5B **80**
Capstan Sq. E14 . . . . . 3E **81**
Capstan Way SE16 . . . 2A **80**
Capstone Rd.
BR1: Brom 4B **124**
Capulet M. E16 . . . . . . 2C **82**
Capworth St. E10 . . . . . 3C **38**
Caradoc Cl. W2 . . . . . . 5C **58**
Caradoc St. SE10 . . . . 1A **96**
Caradon Cl. E11 . . . . . 3A **40**
Caranday Vs. *W11* 2F **71**
   (off Norland Rd.)
Caravel St. E14 . . . . . . 4C **80**
Caravel M. SE8 . . . . . . 2C **94**
Caraway Cl. E13 . . . . . . 4D **69**

Caraway Hgts. *E14* 1E **81**
   (off Poplar High St.)
Carbis Rd. E14 . . . . . . 5B **66**
Carbrooke Ho. *E9* 5E **51**
   (off Templecombe Rd.)
Carburton St.
W1 . . . . 5E **5** (4D **61**)
Cardale St. E14 . . . . . . 3E **81**
Carden Rd. SE15 . . . . . 1D **107**
Cardiff Ho. *SE15* 2C **92**
   (off Friary Est.)
Cardigan Pl. SE3 . . . . . 5F **95**
Cardigan Rd. E3 . . . . . 1B **66**
SW13 . . . . 5C **84**
Cardigan St. SE11 . . . . 1C **90**
Cardigan Wlk. *N1* 4E **49**
   (off Ashby Gro.)
Cardinal Bourne St.
SE1 . . . . 5C **26** (4F **77**)
Cardinal Cap All.
SE1 . . . . 2E **77**
Cardinal Ct. *E1* 1C **78**
   (off Thomas More St.)
Cardinal Hinsley Cl.
NW10 . . . . 1C **56**
Cardinal Pl. SW15 . . . . 2F **99**
Cardinals Way N19 . . . 3F **33**
Cardine M. SE15 . . . . . 3D **93**
Cardington St.
NW1 . . . . 1A **6** (2E **61**)
Cardozo Rd. N7 . . . . . . 2A **48**
Cardross Ho. *W6* 4D **71**
   (off Cardross St.)
Cardross St. W6 . . . . . 4D **71**
Cardwell Rd. N7 . . . . . . 1A **48**
Career Ct. *SE16* 3F **79**
   (off Christopher Cl.)
Carew Cl. N7 . . . . 4B **34**
Carew Ct. *SE14* 2F **93**
   (off Samuel Cl.)
Carew St. SE5 . . . . 5E **91**
Carey Ct. SE5 . . . . 3E **91**
Carey Gdns. SW8 . . . . 4E **89**
Carey La.
EC2 . . . . 2F **17** (5E **63**)
Carey Mans. *SW1* 5F **75**
   (off Rutherford St.)
Carey Pl. SW1 . . . . 5F **75**
Carey St.
WC2 . . . . 3A **16** (5B **62**)
Carfax Pl. SW4 . . . . . . 2F **103**
Carfree Cl. N1 . . . . 4C **48**
Cargill Rd. SW18 . . . . . 1D **115**
Carholme Rd. SE23 . . . 1B **122**
Carinthia Ct. *SE16* 5A **80**
   (off Plough Way)
Carisbrooke Gdns.
SE15 . . . . 3B **92**
Carker's La. NW5 . . . . . 2D **47**
Carleton Gdns. N19 . . . 2E **47**
Carleton Rd. N7 . . . . . . 2F **47**
Carleton Vs. NW5 . . . . 2E **47**
Carlile Cl. E3 . . . . 1B **66**
Carlingford Rd. NW3 . . 1F **45**
Carlisle Av.
EC3 . . . . 3F **19** (5B **64**)
M0 . . . . 5A **55**
Carlisle Gdns. IG1: Ilf. . . 1F **41**
Carlisle La.
SE1 . . . . 5A **24** (4B **76**)

Carlisle Mans. *SW1* 5E **75**
   (off Carlisle Pl.)
Carlisle Pl.
SW1 . . . . 5F **21** (4E **75**)
Carlisle Rd. E10 . . . . . . 3C **38**
N4 . . . . 2C **34**
NW6 . . . . 5A **44**
Carlisle St.
W1 . . . . 3B **14** (5F **61**)
Carlisle Wlk. E8 . . . . . . 3B **50**
Carlisle Way SW17 . . . 5C **116**
Carlos Pl.
W1 . . . . 5C **12** (1C **74**)
Carlow St. NW1 . . . . . . 1E **61**
Carlson Ct. SW15 . . . . 2D **100**
Carlton Cl. NW3 . . . . . . 4C **30**
Carlton Ct. SW9 . . . . . . 4D **91**
W9 . . . . 1D **59**
   (off Maida Va.)
Carlton Dr. SW15 . . . . . 3F **99**
Carlton Gdns.
SW1 . . . . 2B **22** (2F **75**)
Carlton Gro. SE15 . . . . 4D **93**
Carlton Hill NW8 . . . . . 1D **59**
Carlton Ho. *NW6* 1C **58**
   (off Canterbury Ter.,
   not continuous)
SE16 . . . . 3F **79**
   (off Wolfe Cres.)
Carlton Ho. Ter.
SW1 . . . . 2B **22** (2F **75**)
Carlton Lodge *N4* 2C **34**
   (off Carlton Rd.)
Carlton Mans. N16 . . . . 3B **36**
   NW6 . . . . 4C **44**
   (off W. End La.)
W9 . . . . 2D **59**
Carlton M. *NW6* 2C **44**
   (off West Cotts.)
NW6 . . . . 2C **58**
   (West Kilburn)
Carlton Rd. E11 . . . . . . 3B **40**
E12 . . . . 1F **55**
N4 . . . . 2C **34**
Carlton Sq. E1 . . . . 3F **65**
   (not continuous)
Carlton St.
SW1 . . . . 5B **14** (1F **75**)
Carlton Ter. SE26 . . . . . 3E **121**
Carlton Ter. St. E7 . . . . 4E **55**
Carlton Twr. Pl. SW1 . . 4B **74**
Carlton Va. NW6 . . . . . 1B **58**
Carlton Vs. SW15 . . . . 3A **100**
Carlwell St. SW17 . . . . 5A **116**
Carlyle Cl. N2 . . . . 1E **31**
NW10 . . . . 5A **42**
Carlyle Ct. *SW6* 4D **87**
   (off Imperial Rd.)
   SW10 . . . . 4E **87**
   (off Chelsea Harbour Dr.)
Carlyle Ho. N16 . . . . . . 5A **36**
SE5 . . . . 3E **91**
SW3 . . . . 2F **87**
Carlyle M. E1 . . . . 3F **65**
Carlyle Pl. SW15 . . . . . 2F **99**
Carlyle Rd. E12 . . . . . . 1F **55**
Carlyle's House 2A **88**
   (off Cheyne Row)
Carlyle Sq. SW3 . . . . . 1F **87**
Carmalt Gdns. SW15 . . 2E **99**
Carmarthen Pl.
SE1 . . . . 3D **27** (3A **78**)

Carmel Ct. *W8* *3D 73*
(off Holland St.)
Carmelite St.
EC4 . . . . 4C 16 (1C 76)
Carmel Lodge *SW6* . . . *2C 86*
(off Lillie Rd.)
Carmen St. E14 . . . . . . 5D 67
Carmichael Cl.
SW11 . . . . 1F 101
Carmichael Cl.
SW13 . . . . 5B 84
(off Grove Rd.)
Carmichael Ho. *E14* . . . 1E 81
(off Poplar High St.)
Carmichael M.
SW18 . . . . 5F 101
Carminia Rd. SW17 . . . 2D 117
Carnaby St.
W1 . . . . 3F 13 (5E 61)
Carnac St. SE27 . . . . . 4F 119
Carnarvon Rd. E10 . . . . 1E 39
E15 . . . . 3B 54
Carnbrook Rd. SE3 . . . . 1F 111
Carnegie Ho. SW19 . . . 3F 113
Carnegie Pl. SW19 . . . . 3F 113
Carnie Lodge SW17 . . . 3D 117
Carnival Ho. *SE1* *3F 27*
(off Gainsford St.)
Carnoustie Dr. *N1* 4B 48
(not continuous)
Carnwath Rd. SW6 . . . . 1C 100
Carolina Cl. E15 . . . . . . 2A 54
Caroline Cl. SW16 . . . . . 3B 118
W2 . . . . *1D 73*
(off Bayswater Rd.)
Caroline Cl. SE6 . . . . . 4F 123
Caroline Gdns.
E2 . . . . . . 1E 11 (2A 64)
SE15 . . . . 3D 93
Caroline Ho. *W6* *1E 85*
(off Queen Caroline St.)
Caroline Pl. SW11 . . . . . 5C 88
W2 . . . . 1D 73
Caroline Pl. M. W2 . . . . 1D 73
Caroline St. E1 . . . . . . 5F 65
Caroline Ter. SW1 . . . . 5C 74
Caroline Wlk. *W6* *2A 86*
(off Lillie Rd.)
Carol St. NW1 . . . . . . 5E 47
Caronia St. *SE16* *5A 80*
(off Plough Way)
Carpenter Ho. *E14* . . . 4C 66
(off Burgess St.)
NW11 . . . . 1E 31
Carpenters Bus. Pk.
E15 . . . . 4D 53
Carpenters Ct. *NW1* . . *5E 47*
(off Pratt St.)
Carpenters M. N7 . . . . 2A 48
Carpenters Pl. SW4 . . . 2F 103
Carpenter's Rd. E15 . . 3C 52
Carpenter St.
W1 . . . . . . 5D 13 (1D 75)
Carradale Ho. *E14* . . . *5E 67*
(off St Leonard's Rd.)
Carrara Cl. SE24 . . . . . 2C 104
SW9 . . . . 2D 105
Carrara M. E8 . . . . . . 3C 50
Carrara Wharf SW6 . . . 1A 100
Carriage Dr. E. SW11 . . 3C 88

Carriage Dr. Nth.
SW11 . . . . 2C 88
(Carriage Dr. E.)
SW11 . . . . 3B 88
(Parade, The)
Carriage Dr. Sth.
SW11 . . . . 4B 88
(not continuous)
Carriage Dr. W.
SW11 . . . . 3B 88
Carriage Pl. N16 . . . . . 5F 35
SW16 . . . . 5E 117
Carrick Ho. *N7* 3B 48
(off Caledonian Rd.)
SE11 . . . . 1C 90
Carrick M. SE8 . . . . . . 2C 94
Carrington Ct.
SW11 . . . . 2A 102
(off Barnard Rd.)
Carrington Gdns. E7 . . 1C 54
Carrington Ho. *W1* . . . 2D 21
(off Carrington St.)
Carrington St.
W1 . . . . . . 2D 21 (2D 75)
Carrol Cl. NW5 . . . . . . 1D 47
Carroll Cl. E15 . . . . . . 2B 54
Carroll Ho. *W2* *1F 73*
(off Craven Ter.)
Carronade Ct. *N7* . . . 2B 48
Carron Cl. E14 . . . . . . 5D 67
Carroun Rd. SW8 . . . . 3B 90
Carr St. E14 . . . . 4A 66
Carslake Rd.
SW15 . . . . 4E 99
Carson Rd. E16 . . . . . 3C 68
SE21 . . . . 2F 119
Carstairs Rd. SE6 . . . . 3E 123
Carston Cl. SE12 . . . . 3B 110
Carswell Rd. SE6 . . . . 5E 109
Carter Ct. EC4 . . . . . . 3D 17
Carteret Ho. *W12* 1D 71
(off White City Est.)
Carteret St.
SW1 . . . . . . 4B 22 (3F 75)
Carteret Way SE8 . . . . 5A 80
Carter Ho. E1 . . . . . . 1F 19
EC4 . . . . . . 3E 17 (5D 63)
Carter La.
EC4 . . . . . . 3E 17 (5D 63)
Carter Pl. SE17 . . . . . 1E 91
Carter Rd. E13 . . . . . 5D 55
SW19 . . . . 5F 115
Carters Cl. *NW5* *2F 47*
(off Torriano Av.)
Carters Hill Cl. SE9 . . . 1E 125
Carters La. SE23 . . . . 2A 122
Carter St. SE17 . . . . . 2E 91
Carter's Yd. SW18 . . . 3C 100
Carthew Rd. W6 . . . . . 4D 71
Carthew Vs. W6 . . . . . 4D 71
Carthusian St.
EC1 . . . . . . 5F 9 (4E 63)
Cartier Circ. E14 . . . . 2D 81
Carting La.
WC2 . . . . . 5E 15 (1A 76)
Cartmel *NW1* 1F 5
(off Hampstead Rd.)
Carton Ho. *SE16* 4C 78
(off Marine St.)
W11 . . . . 1F 71
(off St Ann's Rd.)

Cartwright Gdns.
WC1 . . . . . . 2D 7 (2A 62)
Cartwright Ho. *SE1* . . . 4E 77
(off County St.)
Cartwright St. E1 . . . . 1B 78
Cartwright Way
SW13 . . . . 3D 85
Carvel Ho. *E14* 1E 95
(off Manchester Rd.)
Carver Rd. SE24 . . . . 4E 105
Cary Rd. E11 . . . . . . 1A 54
Carysfort Rd. N16 . . . . 5F 35
Casby Ho. *SE16* 4C 78
(off Marine St.)
Cascades Twr. E14 . . . 2B 80
Casella Rd. SE14 . . . . 3F 93
Casewick Rd. SE27 . . . 5C 118
Casey Cl. NW8 . . . . . 2A 60
Casimir Rd. E5 . . . . . 4E 37
Casino Av. SE24 . . . . 3E 105
Caspian Ho. *E1* 4F 65
(off Shandy St.)
Caspian St. SE5 . . . . 3F 91
Caspian Wlk. E16 . . . . 5F 69
Casselden Ho. NW10 . . 4A 42
Cassell Ho. *SW9* 5A 90
(off Stockwell Gdns. Est.)
Cassidy Rd. SW6 . . . . 3C 86
(not continuous)
Cassiobury Rd. E17 . . . 1A 38
Cassland Rd. E9 . . . . 4F 51
Casslee Rd. SE6 . . . . 5B 108
Casson Ho. *E1* 4C 64
(off Spelman St.)
Castalia Sq. E14 . . . . 3E 81
Castellain Mans. *W9* . . 3D 59
(off Castellain Rd.,
not continuous)
Castellain Rd. W9 . . . . 3D 59
Castellane Cl. SE8 . . . 3C 94
Castello Av. SW15 . . . 3E 99
CASTELNAU 2D 85
Castelnau SW13 . . . . 4C 84
Castelnau Gdns.
SW13 . . . . 2D 85
Castelnau Mans.
SW13 . . . . 2D 85
(off Castelnau, not continuous)
Castelnau Row
SW13 . . . . 2D 85
Casterbridge *NW6* . . . 5D 45
(off Abbey Rd.)
W11 . . . . 5B 58
(off Dartmouth Cl.)
Casterbridge Rd.
SE3 . . . . 1C 110
Casterton St. E8 . . . . 3D 51
Castillon Rd. SE6 . . . . 2A 124
Castlands Rd. SE6 . . . 2B 122
Castleacre *W2* 5A 60
(off Hyde Pk. Cres.)
Castle Baynard St.
EC4 . . . . . . 4E 17 (1D 77)
Castlebrook Cl. SE11 . . 5D 77
Castle Climbing Cen., The
. . . . 4E 35
Castle Cl. E9 . . . . . . 2A 52
SW19 . . . . 3F 113
Castlecombe Dr.
SW19 . . . . 5F 99

Castlecombe Rd.
SE9 . . . . 4F 125
Castle Ct. EC3 . . . . . . 3C 18
(off Birchin La.)
SE26 . . . . 4A 122
Castle Dr. IG4: IIf 1F 41
Castleford Ct. NW8 . . . 3F 59
(off Henderson Dr.)
Castlehaven Rd.
NW1 . . . . 4D 47
Castle Ho. SE1 . . . . . . 5E 77
(off Walworth Rd.)
SW8 . . . . 3A 90
(off Sth. Lambeth Rd.)
Castle Ind. Est. SE17 . . 5E 77
Castle La.
SW1 . . . . 5A 22 (4E 75)
Castlemaine SW11 . . . 5B 88
Castlemain St. E1 . . . . 4D 65
Castle Mead SE5 . . . . 3E 91
Castle M. NW1 . . . . . . 3D 47
SW17 . . . . 4A 116
Castle Pl. NW1 . . . . . . 3D 47
W4 . . . . 5A 70
Castle Point E13 . . . . . 1E 69
(off Boundary Rd.)
Castlereagh St. W1 . . . 5B 60
Castle Rd. NW1 . . . . . 3D 47
Castle St. E6 . . . . 1E 69
Castleton Ho. E14 . . . . 5E 81
(off Pier St.)
Castleton Rd. SE9 . . . . 4F 125
Castletown Rd. W14 . . 1A 86
Castleview Cl. N4 . . . . 4E 35
Castle Way SW19 . . . . 3F 113
Castle Wharf E14 . . . . 1A 82
(off Orchard Pl.)
Castlewood Rd. N15 . . 1C 36
N16 . . . . 1C 36
Castle Yd. N6 . . . . 2C 32
SE1 . . . . . . 1E 25 (2D 77)
Castor La. E14 . . . . . . 1D 81
Caterham Rd. SE13 . . . 1F 109
Catesby Ho. E9 . . . . . . 4E 51
(off Frampton Pk. Rd.)
Catesby St. SE17 . . . . 5F 77
CATFORD 5D 109
Catford Art Gallery . . . 5D 109
Catford B'way.
SE6 . . . . 5D 109
CATFORD GYRATORY
. . . . 5D 109
Catford Hill SE6 . . . . . 1B 122
Catford Island SE6 . . . 5D 109
Catford M. SE6 . . . . . . 5D 109
Catford Rd. SE6 . . . . . 5C 108
Catford Trad. Est.
SE6 . . . . 2D 123
Cathall Leisure Cen. . . . 4A 40
Cathall Rd. E11 . . . . . . 4F 39
Cathay Ho. SE16 . . . . . 3D 79
Cathay St. SE16 . . . . . 3D 79
Cathcart Hill N19 . . . . . 5E 33
Cathcart Rd. SW10 . . . 2D 87
Cathcart St. NW5 . . . . 3D 47
Cathedral Lodge EC1 . . 5F 9
(off Aldersgate St.)
Cathedral Mans.
SW1 . . . . 5E 75
(off Vauxhall Bri. Rd.)

Cathedral Piazza
SW1 . . . . 5F 21 (4E 75)
Cathedral St.
SE1 . . . . 1B 26 (2F 77)
Catherall Rd. N5 . . . . . 5E 35
Catherine Ct.
SW19 . . . . 5B 114
Catherine Griffiths Ct.
EC1 . . . . 3C 8
(off Northampton Rd.)
Catherine Gro. SE10 . . 4A 95
Catherine Ho. N1 . . . . . 5A 50
(off Whitmore Est.)
Catherine Pl.
SW1 . . . . 5F 21 (4E 75)
Catherine St.
WC2 . . . . 4F 15 (1B 76)
Catherine Wheel All.
E1 . . . . 1E 19 (4A 64)
(not continuous)
Catherine Wheel Rd.
TW8 . . . . 2F 21
Catherine Wheel Yd.
SW1 . . . . 2F 21
Catherwood Ct.
N1 . . . . 1B 10
(off Murray Gro.,
not continuous)
Cathles Rd. SW12 . . . 4D 103
Cathnor Rd. W12 . . . . 3D 71
Catling Cl. SE23 . . . . . 3E 121
Cato St. SE16 . . . . 1C 92
Cato Rd. SW4 . . . . 1F 103
Cator Rd. SE26 . . . . . . 5F 121
Cator St. SE15 . . . . . . 3B 92
(E. Surrey Gro.)
SE15 . . . . 2B 92
(Ebley Cl.)
Cato St. W1 . . . . 4A 60
Catton St.
WC1 . . . . 1F 15 (4B 62)
Caudwell Ter.
SW18 . . . . 4F 101
Caughley Ho. SE11 . . . 4C 76
(off Lambeth Wlk.)
Caulfield Rd.
SE15 . . . . 5D 93
Causeway, The
SW18 . . . . 3D 101
(not continuous)
SW19 . . . . 5E 113
Causton Cotts. E14 . . . 5A 66
Causton Ho. SE5 . . . . . 2E 91
Causton Rd. N6 . . . . . . 2D 33
Causton St. SW1 . . . . . 5F 75
Cautley Av. SW4 . . . . . 3E 103
Cavalry Gdns.
SW15 . . . . 3B 100
Cavan Ho. E3 . . . . 6B 52
Cavaye Pl. SW10 . . . . . 1E 87
Cavell Ho. N1 . . . . 5A 50
(off Colville Est.)
Cavell St. E1 . . . . 4D 65
Cavendish Av. NW8 . . . 1F 59
Cavendish Cl. NW6 . . . 3B 44
NW8 . . . . 2F 59
Cavendish Ct. EC3 . . . 2E 19
(off Bromley Rd.)
Cavendish Dr. E11 . . . . 3F 39
Cavendish Gdns.
SW4 . . . . 4E 103

Cavendish Ho.
NW8 . . . . 1F 59
(off Wellington Rd.)
Cavendish Mans. EC1 . . 4B 8
(off Rosebery Av.)
NW6 . . . . 2C 44
Cavendish M. Nth.
W1 . . . . 5E 5 (4D 61)
Cavendish M. Sth.
W1 . . . . 1E 13 (4D 61)
Cavendish Pde.
SW4 . . . . 4D 103
(off Clapham Comn. Sth. Side)
Cavendish Pl. SW4 . . . 3F 103
W1 . . . . 2E 13 (5D 61)
Cavendish Rd. N4 . . . . 1D 35
NW6 . . . . 4A 44
SW12 . . . . 4D 103
Cavendish Sq.
W1 . . . . 2E 13 (5D 61)
Cavendish St. N1 . . . . . 1F 63
Cavendish Ter. E3 . . . . 2B 66
Cave Rd. E13 . . . . 2D 69
Caversham Ho.
SE15 . . . . 2C 92
(off Haymerle Rd.)
Caversham Rd. NW5 . . 3E 47
Caversham St.
SW3 . . . . 2B 88
Caverswall St. W12 . . . 5E 57
Cavour Ho. SE17 . . . . . 1D 91
(off Alberta Est.)
Cawnpore St. SE19 . . . 5A 120
Caxton Cl. SW11 . . . . . 5A 88
Caxton Gro. E3 . . . . . . 2C 66
Caxton Rd. SW19 . . . . 5E 115
W12 . . . . 3F 71
Caxton St.
SW1 . . . . 5B 22 (4E 75)
Caxton St. Nth. E16 . . . 5B 68
Caxton Wlk.
WC2 . . . . 3C 14 (5F 61)
Cayenne Ct.
SE1 . . . . 3F 27 (3B 78)
Cayton Pl. EC1 . . . . . . 2B 10
Cayton St.
EC1 . . . . 2B 10 (2F 63)
Cazenove Rd. N16 . . . . 4B 36
Cearns Ho. E6 . . . . 5F 55
Cecil Ct. NW6 . . . . 4D 45
SW10 . . . . 2E 87
(off Fawcett St.)
WC2 . . . . . 5D 15 (1A 76)
Cecile Pk. N8 . . . . 1A 34
Cecilia Rd. E8 . . . . 2B 50
Cecil Rhodes Ho.
NW1 . . . . 1F 61
(off Goldington St.)
Cecil Rd. E11 . . . . 5B 40
E13 . . . . 5C 54
NW10 . . . . 5A 42
Cecil Sharp House 5C 46
Cedar Cl. E3 . . . . 5B 52
SE21 . . . . 1E 119
Cedar Ct. N1 . . . . 4E 49
SE1 . . . . 4D 27
(off Royal Oak Yd.)
SE7 . . . . 2E 97
SW19 . . . . 3F 113
Cedar Hgts. NW2 . . . . . 3B 44

Cedar Ho. *E14* *3E 81*
   (off Manchester Rd.)
SE14 . . . . *4F 93*
SE16 . . . . *3F 79*
   (off Woodland Cres.)
W8 . . . . *4D 73*
   (off Marloes Rd.)
Cedarhurst Dr. SE9 . . . *3E 111*
Cedar Mt. SE9 . . . . . . *1F 125*
Cedarne Rd. SW6 . . . . . *3D 87*
Cedar Pl. SE7 . . . . *1E 97*
Cedar Rd. NW2 . . . . . . *1E 43*
Cedars, The E15 . . . . . . *4B 54*
Cedars Av. E17 . . . . . . *1C 38*
Cedars Cl. SE13 . . . . . *1F 109*
Cedars M. SW4 . . . . . . *2D 103*
   (not continuous)
Cedars Rd. E15 . . . . . . *3A 54*
SW4 . . . . *1D 103*
SW13 . . . . *5C 84*
Cedar Tree Gro.
  SE27 . . . . *5D 119*
Cedar Way NW1 . . . . . . *4F 47*
Cedar Way Ind. Est.
  NW1 . . . . *4F 47*
Cedra Ct. N16 . . . . *3C 36*
Celandine Cl. E14 . . . . . *4C 66*
Celandine Dr. E8 . . . . . . *4B 50*
Celandine Way E15 . . . . *2A 68*
Celbridge M. W2 . . . . . . *4D 59*
Celestial Gdns.
  SE13 . . . . *2F 109*
Celia Ho. *N1* *1A 64*
   (off Arden Est.)
Celia Rd. N19 . . . . *1E 47*
Celtic St. E14 . . . . *4D 67*
Cemetery La. SE7 . . . . . *2F 97*
Cemetery Rd. E7 . . . . . . *2B 54*
Cenacle Cl. NW3 . . . . . . *5C 30*
Cenotaph . . . . . *3D 23 (3A 76)*
Centaur St.
  SE1 . . . . *5A 24 (4B 76)*
Central Av. E11 . . . . *4F 39*
E12 . . . . *5F 41*
SW11 . . . . *3B 88*
Central Bus. Cen.
  NW10 . . . . *2A 42*
Central Church Sports Club
  . . . . *2F 121*
Central Cir. NW4 . . . . . . *1D 29*
Central Hill SE19 . . . . . *5E 119*
Central Ho. E15 . . . . *1D 67*
Central Mall *SW18.* . . *4D 101*
   (off South Mall)
Central Mans. *NW4* . . . *1D 29*
   (off Watford Way)
Central Markets (Smithfield)
  . . . . *1D 17*
Central Pk. Rd. E6 . . . . . *1F 69*
Central St Martins College of
  Art & Design *1F 15*
Central Sq. NW11 . . . . . *1D 31*
Central St.
  EC1 . . . . *1F 9 (2E 63)*
Central Wharf *E14* *5C 66*
   (off Thomas Rd.)
Centre Av. NW10 . . . . . . *2E 57*
W3 . . . . *2A 70*
Centre Ct. Shop. Cen.
  SW19 . . . . *5B 114*

Centre Dr. E7 . . . . *1E 55*
Cen. for the Magic Arts, The
  . . . . *3A 6*
   (off Stephenson Way)
Centre Hgts. NW3 . . . . . *4F 45*
   (off Finchley Rd.)
Centrepoint WC2 . . . . . . *2C 14*
Centre Point SE1 . . . . . *1C 92*
Centre Point Ho.
  WC2 . . . . *2C 14*
   (off St Giles High St.)
Centre Rd. E7 . . . . *4C 40*
E11 . . . . *4C 40*
Centre St. E2 . . . . *1D 65*
Centric Cl. NW1 . . . . . . *5C 46*
Centurion Bldg.
  SW8 . . . . *2D 89*
Centurion Cl. N7 . . . . . . *4B 48*
Centurion La. E3 . . . . . . *5B 52*
Century Cl. NW4 . . . . . . *1F 29*
Century Ho. SW15 . . . . . *2F 99*
Century M. E5. . . . . *1E 51*
Century Yd. SE23 . . . . . *2E 121*
Cephas Av. E1 . . . . *3E 65*
Cephas Ho. *E1* *3E 65*
   (off Doveton St.)
Cephas St. E1. . . . . *3E 65*
Cerise Rd. SE15 . . . . . . *4C 92*
Cerney M. W2. . . . . *1F 73*
Cervantes Ct. W2. . . . . . *5D 59*
Cester St. E2 . . . . *5C 50*
Ceylon Rd. W14 . . . . . . *4F 71*
Chabot Dr. SE15 . . . . . *1D 107*
Chadacre Ct. E15 . . . . . *5C 54*
   (off Vicars Cl.)
Chadacre Ho. SW9 . . . *2D 105*
   (off Loughborough Pk.)
Chadbourn St. E14 . . . . *4D 67*
Chadd Grn. E13 . . . . . . *5C 54*
   (not continuous)
Chadston Ho. *N1* *4D 49*
   (off Halton Rd.)
Chadswell WC1 . . . . *2E 7*
   (off Cromer St.)
Chadwell St.
  EC1 . . . . *1C 8 (2C 62)*
Chadwick Av. SW19 . . . *5C 114*
Chadwick Pl. SW15 . . . . *5B 98*
Chadwick Rd. E11 . . . . . *1A 40*
NW10 . . . . *5B 42*
SE15 . . . . *5B 92*
Chadwick St.
  SW1 . . . . . *5B 22 (4F 75)*
Chadwin Rd. E13 . . . . . . *4D 69*
Chadworth Ho. *EC1* *2F 9*
   (off Lever St.)
N4 . . . . *3E 35*
Chagford St.
  NW1 . . . . . . *4A 4 (3B 60)*
Chailey St. E5. . . . . *5E 37*
Chalbury Wlk. N1 . . . . . . *1B 62*
Chalcot Cres. NW1 . . . . *5B 46*
Chalcot Gdns. NW3 . . . . *3B 46*
Chalcot M. SW16 . . . . . *3A 118*
Chalcot Rd. NW1 . . . . . . *4C 46*
Chalcot Sq. NW1 . . . . . . *4C 46*
   (not continuous)
Chalcroft Rd. SE13 . . . . *3A 110*
Chaldon Rd. SW6 . . . . . *3A 86*
Chale Rd. SW2 . . . . . . *4A 104*

Chalfont Ct. NW1 . . . . . . *4A 4*
   (off Baker St.)
Chalfont Ho. SE16 . . . . . *4D 79*
   (off Keetons Rd.)
Chalford NW3 . . . . *3E 45*
   (off Finchley Rd.)
Chalford Rd. SE21 . . . . *4F 119*
CHALK FARM *4C 46*
Chalk Farm Rd. NW1 . . . *4C 46*
Chalk Hill Rd. W6 . . . . . . *5F 71*
Chalk Rd. E13 . . . . *4D 69*
Chalkwell Ho. *E1* *5F 65*
   (off Pitsea St.)
Challenge Cl.
  NW10 . . . . *5A 42*
Challenger Ho. E14 . . . . *1A 80*
   (off Victory Pl.)
Challice Way SW2 . . . . . *1B 118*
Challoner Cres. W14 . . . *1B 86*
Challoner St. W14 . . . . . *1B 86*
Chalmers Wlk. SE17 . . . . *2D 91*
   (off Hillingdon St.)
Chalsey Rd. SE4 . . . . . . *2B 108*
Chalton Dr. N2 . . . . *1F 31*
Chalton Ho. NW1 . . . . . . *1B 6*
   (off Chalton St.)
Chalton St.
  NW1 . . . . . . *1B 6 (1E 61)*
   (not continuous)
Chamberlain Cotts.
  SE5 . . . . *4F 91*
Chamberlain Ho. *E1*. . . . *1E 79*
   (off Cable St.)
NW1 . . . . *1C 6*
SE1 . . . . *4B 24*
   (off Westminster Bri. Rd.)
Chamberlain St.
  NW1 . . . . *4B 46*
Chamberlayne Mans.
  NW10 . . . . *2F 57*
   (off Chamberlayne Rd.)
Chamberlayne Rd.
  NW10 . . . . *5E 43*
Chamberlens Garages
  W6 . . . . *5D 71*
   (off Dalling Rd.)
Chambers, The
  . . . . *4E 87*
   (off Chelsea Harbour Dr.)
Chambers La. NW10 . . . . *4D 43*
Chambers Rd. N7 . . . . . . *1A 48*
Chambers St. SE16 . . . . *3C 78*
Chamber St. E1 . . . . *1B 78*
Chambers Wharf
  SE16 . . . . *3C 78*
Chambon Pl. W6 . . . . . . *5C 70*
Chambord St.
  E2. . . . . *2F 11 (2B 64)*
Chamomile Ct. E17 . . . . *1C 38*
   (off Yunus Khan Cl.)
Champion Cres.
  SE26 . . . . *4A 122*
Champion Gro. SE5 . . . . *1F 105*
Champion Hill SE5 . . . . *1F 105*
Champion Hill Est.
  SE5 . . . . *1A 106*
Champion Hill Stadium
  . . . . *2A 106*
Champion Pk. SE5 . . . . . *5F 91*
Champion Rd. SE26 . . . *4A 122*

Champlain Ho. W12.... 1D 71
(off White City Est.)
Champness Cl.
SE27 .... 4F 119
Chancel Ind. Est.
NW10 .... 2B 42
Chancellor Gro.
SE21 .... 2E 119
Chancellor Ho. E1 ..... 2D 79
(off Green Bank)
Chancellor Pas. E14.... 2C 80
Chancellors Ct. WC1 ... 5F 7
Chancellor's Rd. W6 ... 1E 85
Chancellor's St. W6 ... 1E 85
Chancellors Wharf
W6 .... 1E 85
Chancel St.
SE1 .... 2D 25 (2D 77)
Chancery Bldgs. E1 .... 1D 79
(off Lowood St.)
Chancery La.
WC2............ 1A 16 (5C 62)
Chancery M. SW17 .... 2A 116
Chance St.
E1 .... 3F 11 (3B 64)
E2 .... 3F 11 (3B 64)
Chandler Av. E16 ..... 4C 68
Chandler Ho. NW6.... 5B 44
(off Willesden La.)
WC1 .... 4E 7
(off Colonnade)
Chandlers Ct. SE12 ... 1D 125
Chandlers M. E14..... 3C 80
Chandler St. E1 ...... 2D 79
Chandlers Way
SW2 .... 5C 104
Chandler Way SE15 ... 3A 92
(Innis St.)
SE15 .... 2A 92
(St George's Way)
Chandlery, The SE1 ... 5C 24
(off Gerridge St.)
Chandlery Ho. E1..... 5C 64
(off Bk. Church La.)
Chandos Pl.
WC2.......... 5D 15 (1A 76)
Chandos Rd. E15 ..... 2F 53
NW2 .... 2E 43
NW10 .... 3A 56
Chandos St.
W1............ 1E 13 (4D 65)
Chandos Way NW11... 3D 31
Change All.
EC3............ 3C 18 (5F 63)
Channel Ga. Rd.
NW10 .... 2A 56
Channel Ho. E14 ..... 4A 66
(off Aston St.)
Channel Islands Est.
N1 .... 3E 49
(off Guernsey Rd.)
Channelsea Path E15 .. 5F 53
Channelsea Rd. E15... 5F 53
Chantrey Rd. SW9 .... 1B 104
Chantry Cl. W9....... 3C 58
Chantry Cres. NW10 .. 3B 42
Chantry Sq. W8 ...... 4D 73
Chantry St. N1....... 5D 49
Chant Sq. E15........ 4F 53
Chant St. E15........ 4F 53

Chapel Av. E12 .... 5F 41
Chapel Cl. NW10 ..... 2B 42
Chapel Ct.
SE1........... 3B 26 (3F 77)
Chapel Ho. St. E14 ... 1D 95
Chapelier Ho.
SW18 .... 2C 100
Chapel Mkt. N1 ...... 1C 62
Chapel of St John the
Evangelist......... 5F 19
(in Tower of London)
Chapel of St Peter & St Paul
.... 2F 95
(in Old Royal Naval College)
Chapel Path E11 ..... 1D 41
(off Woodbine Pl.)
Chapel Pl.
EC2......... 2D 11 (2A 64)
N1................. 1C 62
W1........... 3D 13 (5D 61)
Chapel Rd. SE27 ..... 4D 119
Chapel Side W2....... 1D 73
Chapel St. NW1 ...... 4A 60
SW1.......... 5C 20 (4C 74)
Chapel Way N7 ...... 5B 34
Chapel Yd. SW18..... 3D 101
(off Wandsworth High St.)
Chaplin Cl.
SE1........... 3C 24 (3C 76)
Chaplin Rd. E15...... 1B 68
NW2 .... 3C 42
Chapman Ho. E1 ..... 5D 65
(off Bigland St.)
Chapman Pl. N4...... 4D 35
Chapman Rd. E9 ..... 3B 52
Chapmans Pk. Ind. Est.
NW10 .... 3B 42
Chapman Sq.
SW19 .... 2F 113
Chapman St. E1...... 1D 79
Chapone Pl.
W1........... 3B 14 (5F 61)
Chapter Chambers
SW1 .... 5F 75
(off Chapter St.)
Chapter House
.... 3F 17 (5D 63)
Chapter Rd. NW2..... 2C 42
SE17............... 1D 91
Chapter St. SW1...... 5F 75
Charcot Ho. SW15 .... 4B 98
Charcroft Ct. W14..... 3F 71
(off Minford Gdns.)
Chardin Ho. SW9..... 4C 90
(off Gosling Way)
Chardin Rd. W4...... 5A 70
Chardmore Rd. N16... 3C 36
Charecroft Way W12 .. 3F 71
W14.............. 3F 71
Charfield Ct. W9 ..... 3D 59
(off Shirland Rd.)
Charford Rd. E16..... 4C 68
Chargeable La. E13.... 3B 68
Chargeable St. E16.... 3B 68
Chargrove Cl. SE16 ... 3F 79
Charing Cross SW1 ... 1D 22
Charing Cross Rd.
WC2............ 2C 14 (5F 61)
Charing Cross Sports Club
.... 2F 85

Charing Cross Underground
Shop. Cen. WC2 .... 5D 15
Charing Ho. SE1...... 3C 24
(off Windmill Wlk.)
Chariot Cl. E3....... 5C 52
Charlbert Ct. NW8 .... 1A 60
(off Charlbert St.)
Charlbert St. NW8 .... 1A 60
Charlecote Gro.
SE26 .... 3D 121
Charles II Pl. SW3..... 1B 88
Charles II St.
SW1............ 1B 22 (2F 75)
Charles Auffray Ho.
E1 .... 4E 65
(off Smithy St.)
Charles Barry Cl.
SW4 .... 1E 103
Charles Coveney Rd.
SE15 .... 4B 92
Charles Darwin Ho.
E2 .... 2D 65
(off Canrobert St.)
Charles Dickens Ho.
E2 .... 2C 64
(off Mansford St.)
Charlesfield SE9...... 3E 125
Charles Flemwell M.
E16 .... 2C 82
Charles Gardner Ct.
N1................. 1C 10
(off Haberdasher Est.)
Charles Haller St.
SW2 .... 5C 104
Charles Harrod Ct.
SW13 .... 2E 85
(off Somerville Av.)
Charles Ho. W14..... 5B 72
(off Kensington High St.)
Charles La. NW8 ..... 1A 60
Charles MacKenzie Ho.
SE16............... 5C 78
(off Linsey St.)
Charles Pl.
NW1.......... 2A 6 (2E 61)
Charles Rd. E7....... 4E 55
Charles Rowan Ho.
WC1............... 2B 8
(off Margery St.)
Charles Simmons Ho.
WC1............... 2B 8
(off Margery St.)
Charles Sq.
N1 .... 2C 10 (2F 63)
Charles Sq. Est. N1 ... 2C 10
Charles St. E16...... 2E 83
SW13 .... 5A 84
W1.......... 1D 21 (2D 75)
Charleston St. SE17... 5E 77
Charles Townsend Ho.
EC1............... 3D 9
(off Skinner St.)
Charles Uton Ct. E8 .. 1C 50
Charles Whincup Rd.
E16............... 2D 83
Charlesworth Ho.
E14 .... 5B 66
(off Dod St.)
Charlesworth Pl.
SW13 .... 1A 98

Charleville Cir.
SE26 . . . . 5C 120
Charleville Mans.
W14 . . . . 1A 86
(off Charleville Rd.)
Charleville Rd. W14. . . 1A 86
Charlie Chaplin Wlk.
SE1 . . . . 2A 24
(off Waterloo Rd.)
Charlmont Rd.
SW17 . . . . 5A 116
Charlotte Ct. N8 . . . . . 1F 33
SE1 . . . . 5A 78
(off Old Kent Rd.)
W6 . . . . 5C 70
(off Invermead Cl.)
Charlotte Despard Av.
SW11 . . . . 4C 88
Charlotte Ho. E16. . . . . 2D 83
(off Fairfax M.)
W6 . . . . 1E 85
(off Queen Caroline St.)
Charlotte M.
W1 . . . . 5A 6 (4E 61)
W10 . . . . 5F 57
W14 . . . . 5A 72
Charlotte Pl. SW1. . . . 5E 75
W1 . . . . 1A 14 (4E 61)
Charlotte Rd.
EC2 . . . . . . 2D 11 (2A 64)
SW13 . . . . 4B 84
Charlotte Row SW4 . . 1E 103
Charlotte St.
W1 . . . . 5A 6 (4E 61)
Charlotte Ter. N1 . . . . 5B 48
Charlow Cl. SW6 . . . . . 5E 87
CHARLTON 3F 97
Charlton Athletic FC . . 1E 97
Charlton Chu. La.
SE7 . . . . 1E 97
Charlton Ct. E2 . . . . . 5B 50
Charlton Dene SE7 . . . 3E 97
Charlton Ga. Bus. Pk.
SE7 . . . . 5E 83
Charlton House. 2F 97
Charlton King's Rd.
NW5 . . . . 2F 47
Charlton La. SE7. . . . . 5F 83
Charlton Lido 3F 97
Charlton Pk. La. SE7 . . 3F 97
Charlton Pk. Rd. SE7 . . 2F 97
Charlton Pl. N1. . . . . . 1D 63
Charlton Rd. NW10 . . . 5A 42
SE3 . . . . 3C 96
SE7 . . . . 3C 96
Charlton Way SE3. . . . 4A 96
Charlwood Ho's. SW1 . . 5F 75
(off Vauxhall Bri. Rd.)
Charlwood Ho's. WC1 . . 2E 7
(off Midhope St.)
Charlwood Pl. SW1 . . . 5E 75
Charlwood Rd. SW15 . . 2F 99
Charlwood St. SW1 . . . 1E 88
(not continuous)
Charlwood Ter. SW15 . . 2F 99
Charmans Ho. SW8 . . . 3A 90
(off Wandsworth Rd.)
Charminster Rd.
SE9 . . . . 4F 125
Charmouth Ho. SW8 . . 3B 90

Charnock Ho. W12. . . . 1D 71
(off White City Est.)
Charnock Rd. E5 . . . . . 5D 37
Charnwood Gdns.
E14 . . . . 5C 80
Charnwood St. E5 . . . . 4D 37
Charrington St. NW1 . . 1F 61
Charsley Rd. SE6. . . . 2D 123
Charter Ct. N4 . . . . . . 3C 34
Charterhouse 4E 9
(off Charterhouse M.)
Charter Ho. WC2 . . . . . 3E 15
(off Crown Ct.)
Charterhouse Bldgs.
EC1 . . . . 4E 9 (3E 63)
Charterhouse M.
EC1 . . . . 5E 9 (4D 63)
Charterhouse Rd. E8 . . 1C 50
Charterhouse Sq.
EC1 . . . . 5E 9 (4D 63)
Charterhouse St.
EC1 . . . . 1C 16 (4C 62)
Charteris Rd. N4 . . . . . 3C 34
NW6 . . . . 5B 44
Charters Cl. SE19. . . . 5A 120
Chartes Ho. SE1 . . . . . 5E 27
(off Stevens St.)
Chartfield Av. SW15 . . 3D 99
Chartfield Sq. SW15 . . 3F 99
Chartham Ct. SW9 . . . 1C 104
(off Canterbury Cres.)
Chartham Gro.
SE27 . . . . 3D 119
Chartham Ho. SE1 . . . . 5C 26
(off Weston St.)
Chart Ho. E14 . . . . 1D 95
(off Burrells Wharf Sq.)
Chartley Av. NW2 . . . . 5A 28
Chartridge SE17 . . . . . 2F 91
(off Westmoreland Rd.)
Chart St. N1. . . 1C 10 (2F 63)
Charwood SE16 . . . . . 4C 118
Chase, The E16 . . . . . 1F 55
SW4 . . . . 1D 103
Chase Cen., The
NW10 . . . . 2A 56
Chasefield Rd.
SW17 . . . . 4B 116
Chaseley St. E14 . . . . 5A 66
Chasemore Ho. SW6 . . 3A 86
(off Williams Cl.)
Chase Rd. NW10 . . . . 3A 56
Chase Rd. Trad. Est.
NW10 . . . . 3A 56
Chaston Pl. NW5 . . . . 2C 46
(off Grafton Ter.)
Chater Ho. E2 . . . . 2F 65
(off Roman Rd.)
Chateris Community
Sports Cen. 5C 44
Chatfield Rd. SW11 . . 1E 101
Chatham Cl. NW11 . . . 1C 30
Chatham Pl. E9 . . . . . 3E 51
Chatham Rd. SW11 . . . 4B 102
Chatham St. SE17 . . . . 5F 77
Chats Palace Arts Cen.
. . . . 2F 51
Chatsworth Av.
BR1: Brom 4D 125
Chatsworth Ct. W8 . . . 5C 72
(off Pembroke Rd.)

Chatsworth Est. E5 . . . 1F 51
Chatsworth Ho. E16 . . . 2D 83
(off Wesley Av.)
Chatsworth Lodge
W4 . . . . 1A 84
(off Bourne Pl.)
Chatsworth Pl. NW2 . . 3E 43
Chatsworth Rd. E5 . . . 5E 37
E15 . . . . 2B 54
NW2 . . . . 3E 43
(not continuous)
Chatsworth Way
SE27 . . . . 3D 119
Chatterton M. N4 . . . . 5D 35
(off Chatterton Rd.)
Chatterton Rd. N4 . . . 5D 35
Chatto Rd. SW11 . . . . 3B 102
Chaucer Ct. N16. . . . . 1A 50
Chaucer Dr. SE1. . . . . 5B 78
Chaucer Ho. SW1 . . . . 1E 89
(off Churchill Gdns.)
Chaucer Mans. W14 . . 2A 86
(off Queen's Club Gdns.)
Chaucer Rd. E7 . . . . . 3C 54
E11 . . . . 1C 40
SE24 . . . . 3C 104
Chaucer Theatre. 2F 5
(off Braham St.)
Chaucer Way SW19 . . 5F 115
Chaulden Ho. EC1 . . . . 2C 10
(off Cranwood St.)
Chauntler Cl. E16. . . . 5D 69
Cheadle Ct. NW8 . . . . 3F 59
(off Henderson Dr.)
Cheadle Ho. E14 . . . . . 5B 66
(off Copenhagen Pl.)
Cheam St. SE15 . . . . 1E 107
Cheapside
EC2 . . . . . . 3A 18 (5E 63)
Chearsley SE17 . . . . . 5E 77
(off Deacon Way)
Cheddington Ho. E2 . . 5C 50
(off Whiston Rd.)
Chedworth Cl. E16 . . . 5B 68
Cheesemans Ter.
W14 . . . . 1B 86
(not continuous)
Cheetham Rd. E12 . . . 5F 41
Chelford Rd.
BR1: Brom 5F 123
Chelmer Rd. E9 . . . . . 2F 51
Chelmsford Cl. W6 . . . 2F 85
Chelmsford Ho. N7 . . . 1B 48
(off Holloway Rd.)
Chelmsford Rd. E11 . . 3F 39
E17 . . . . 1C 38
Chelmsford Sq.
NW10 . . . . 5E 43
CHELSEA 1A 88
Chelsea Bri. SW1 . . . . 2D 89
Chelsea Bri. Bus. Cen.
SW8 . . . . 3D 89
Chelsea Bri. Rd.
SW1 . . . . 1C 88
Chelsea Bri. Wharf
SW8 . . . . 2D 89
Chelsea Cinema 1A 88
Chelsea Cloisters
SW3 . . . . 5A 74
Chelsea Cl. NW10 . . . 5A 42

Chelsea College of
    Art & Design 1A 88
Chelsea Cres. NW2 . . 3B 44
Chelsea Emb. SW3 . . 2A 88
SW10 . . . . 4E 87
Chelsea Farm Ho. Studios
    SW10 . . . . 2F 87
    (off Moravian Pl.)
Chelsea FC 3D 87
Chelsea Gdns. SW1 . . 1C 88
Chelsea Ga. SW1 . . . . 1C 88
    (off Ebury Bri. Rd.)
Chelsea Harbour
    SW10 . . . . 4E 87
Chelsea Harbour Design Cen.
    SW10 . . . . 4E 87
    (off Chelsea Harbour Dr.)
Chelsea Harbour Dr.
    SW10 . . . . 4E 87
Chelsea Lodge SW3 . . 2B 88
    (off Tite St.)
Chelsea Mnr. Ct.
    SW3 . . . . 2A 88
Chelsea Mnr. Gdns.
    SW3 . . . . 1A 88
Chelsea Mnr. St.
    SW3 . . . . 1A 88
Chelsea Pk. Gdns.
    SW3 . . . . 2F 87
Chelsea Physic Garden
    . . . . 2B 88
Chelsea Reach Twr.
    SW10 . . . . 3F 87
    (off Worlds End Est.)
Chelsea Sports Cen. . 1A 88
Chelsea Sq. SW3 . . . . 1F 87
Chelsea Studios
    SW6 . . . . 3D 87
    (off Fulham Rd.)
Chelsea Towers SW3 . . 2A 88
    (off Chelsea Mnr. Gdns.)
Chelsea Village SW6 . . 3D 87
    (off Fulham Rd.)
Chelsea Vista SW6 . . . 5E 87
Chelsea Wharf SW10 . . 3F 87
    (off Lots Rd.)
Chelsfield Gdns.
    SE26 . . . . 3E 121
Chelsfield Ho. SE17 . . 5A 78
    (off Massinger St.)
Chelsham Rd. SW4 . . 1F 103
Cheltenham Gdns. E6 . . 1F 69
Cheltenham Rd. E10 . . 1E 39
    SE15 . . . . 2E 107
Cheltenham Ter.
    SW3 . . . . 1B 88
Chelverton Rd. SW15 . . 2F 99
Chelwood Ho. W2 . . . . 5F 59
    (off Gloucester Sq.)
Chelwood Wlk. SE4 . . 2A 108
Chenappa Cl. E13 . . . . 2C 68
Cheney Ct. SE23 . . . . 1F 121
Cheneys Rd. E11 . . . . 5A 40
Chenies, The NW1 . . . . 1F 61
    (off Pancras Rd.)
Chenies Ho. W4 . . . . . 2B 84
    (off Corney Reach Way)
Chenies M.
    WC1 . . . . 4B 6 (3F 61)
Chenies Pl. NW1 . . . . 1F 61

Chenies St.
    WC1 . . . . 5B 6 (4F 61)
Cheniston Gdns. W8 . . 4D 72
Chepstow Cl. SW15 . . 3A 100
Chepstow Cnr. W2 . . . 5C 58
    (off Chepstow Pl.)
Chepstow Ct. W11 . . . 1C 72
    (off Chepstow Vs.)
Chepstow Cres. W11 . . 1C 72
Chepstow Pl. W2 . . . . 5C 58
Chepstow Rd. W2 . . . . 5C 58
Chepstow Vs. W11 . . . 1B 72
Chequers Ct. EC1 . . . . 4A 10
    (off Chequer St.)
Chequers Ho. NW8 . . . 3A 60
    (off Jerome Cres.)
Chequer St.
    EC1 . . . . 4A 10 (3E 63)
    (not continuous)
Cherbury Ct. N1 . . . . . 1F 63
    (off St John's Est.)
Cherbury St. N1 . . . . . 1F 63
Cheriton Cl. SE12 . . . . 5C 110
Cheriton Sq. SW17 . . 2C 116
Cherry Cl. SW2 . . . . . 5C 104
Cherry Ct. W3 . . . . . . 2A 70
Cherry Gdn. Ho.
    SE16 . . . . 3D 79
    (off Cherry Gdn. St.)
Cherry Gdn. St. SE16 . . 3D 79
Cherry Laurel Wlk.
    SW2 . . . . 4B 104
Cherry Orchard SE7 . . 2E 97
Cherry Tree Cl. E9 . . . 5E 51
Cherry Tree Ct. NW1 . . 4E 47
    (off Camden St.)
    SE7 . . . . 2E 97
Cherry Tree Dr.
    SW16 . . . . 3A 118
Cherry Tree Rd. E15 . . 5A 54
Cherry Tree Ter. SE1 . . 4E 27
    (off Whites Grounds)
Cherry Tree Wlk.
    EC1 . . . . 4A 10 (3E 63)
Cherrywood Cl. E3 . . . 2A 66
Cherrywood Dr.
    SW15 . . . . 3F 99
Chertsey Rd. E11 . . . . 4F 39
Chertsey St. SW17 . . 5C 116
Cherwell Ho. NW8 . . . . 3F 59
    (off Church St. Est.)
Cheryls Cl. SW6 . . . . . 4D 87
Cheseman St. SE26 . . 3D 121
Chesham Cl. SW1 . . . . 5B 20
Chesham Flats W11 . . . 4C 12
    (off Brown Hart Gdns.)
Chesham M. SW1 . . . . 5B 20
Chesham Pl.
    SW1 . . . . 5B 20 (4C 74)
    (not continuous)
Chesham Rd. SW19 . . 5F 115
Chesham St.
    SW1 . . . . 5B 20 (4C 74)
Cheshire Cl. SE4 . . . . 5B 94
Cheshire Ct. EC4 . . . . 3C 16
    (off Fleet St.)
Cheshire St. E2 . . . . . 3B 64
Chesholm Rd. N16 . . . 5A 36
Cheshunt Ho. NW6 . . . 5D 45
    (off Mortimer Cres.)

Cheshunt Rd. E7 . . . . 3D 55
Chesil Ct. E2 . . . . 1E 65
    SW3 . . . . 2A 88
Chesilton Rd. SW6 . . . 4B 86
Chesley Gdns. E6 . . . . 1F 69
Chesney Ct. W9 . . . . . 3C 58
    (off Shirland Rd.)
Chesney Ho. SE13 . . . 2F 109
    (off Mercator Rd.)
Chesney St. SW11 . . . 4C 88
Chessington Ho.
    SW8 . . . . 5F 89
Chessington Mans.
    E10 . . . . 2C 38
    E11 . . . . 2A 40
Chesson Rd. W14 . . . . 2B 86
Chester Cl.
    SW1 . . . . 4D 21 (3D 75)
    SW13 . . . . 1D 99
Chester Cl. Nth.
    NW1 . . . . 1E 5 (2D 61)
Chester Cl. Sth.
    NW1 . . . . 2E 5 (2D 61)
Chester Cotts. SW1 . . 5C 74
    (off Bourne St.)
Chester Ct.
    NW1 . . . . 1E 5 (2D 61)
    SE5 . . . . 3F 91
    (off Lomond Gro.)
    SE8 . . . . 1F 93
Chester Cres. E8 . . . . 2B 50
Chesterfield Cl.
    SE13 . . . . 5F 95
Chesterfield Gdns.
    N4 . . . . 1D 35
    SE10 . . . . 4F 95
    W1 . . . . 1D 21 (2D 75)
Chesterfield Gro.
    SE22 . . . . 3B 106
Chesterfield Hill
    W1 . . . . 1D 21 (2D 75)
Chesterfield Ho. W1 . . 1C 20
    (off Chesterfield Gdns.)
Chesterfield M. N4 . . . 1D 35
Chesterfield Rd. E10 . . 1E 39
Chesterfield St.
    W1 . . . . 1D 21 (2D 75)
Chesterfield Wlk.
    SE10 . . . . 4F 95
Chesterfield Way
    SE15 . . . . 3E 93
Chesterford Gdns.
    NW3 . . . . 1D 45
Chesterford Ho. SE18 . . 4F 97
    (off Tellson Av.)
Chester Ga.
    NW1 . . . . 2D 5 (2D 61)
Chester Ho.
    SE8 . . . . 2B 94
    SW1 . . . . 5D 75
    (off Eccleston Pl.)
    SW9 . . . . 3C 90
    (off Brixton Rd.)
Chesterman Ct.
    W4 . . . . 3A 84
    (off Corney Reach Way)
Chester M.
    SW1 . . . . 5D 21 (4D 75)
Chester Pl.
    NW1 . . . . 1D 5 (2D 61)

Chester Rd. E7 . . . . 4F 55	Cheylesmore Ho.	Chillington Dr.
E11 . . . . 1D 41	SW1 . . . . 1D 89	SW11 . . . . 2F 101
E16 . . . . 3A 68	(off Ebury Bri. Rd.)	Chillingworth Rd. N7 . . 2C 48
E17 . . . . 1F 37	Cheyne Cl. NW4 . . . . . . 1E 29	Chiltern Ct. NW1 . . . . . . 4A 4
N19 . . . . 4D 33	Cheyne Ct. SW3 . . . . . . 2B 88	(off Baker St.)
NW1 . . . . . . 2C 4 (2C 60)	Cheyne Gdns.	SE14 . . . . 3E 93
SW19 . . . . 5E 113	SW3 . . . . 2A 88	(off Avonley Rd.)
Chester Row SW1 . . . . 5C 74	Cheyne M. SW3 . . . . . . 2A 88	Chiltern Gdns.
Chester Sq. SW1 . . . . 5C 74	Cheyne Pl. SW3 . . . . . . 2B 88	NW2 . . . . 5F 29
Chester Sq. M.	Cheyne Row SW3 . . . . . 2A 88	Chiltern Rd. E3 . . . . . . 3C 66
SW1 . . . . 5D 21	Cheyne Wlk. NW4 . . . . . 1E 29	Chiltern St.
Chester St. E2 . . . . . . 3C 64	SW3 . . . . 2A 88	W1 . . . . 5B 4 (4C 60)
SW1 . . . . . . 5C 20 (4C 74)	(not continuous)	Chilthorne Cl. SE6 . . . . 5B 108
Chester Ter.	SW10 . . . . 3F 87	Chilton Gro. SE8 . . . . . . 5F 79
NW1 . . . . 1D 5 (2D 61)	Chichele Rd. NW2 . . . . 2F 43	Chiltonian Ind. Est.
(not continuous)	Chicheley St.	SE12 . . . . 4B 110
Chesterton Cl.	SE1 . . . . 3A 24 (3B 76)	Chilton St. E2 . . . . 3B 64
SW18 . . . . 3C 100	Chichester Cl. SE3 . . . . 3E 97	Chilver St. SE10 . . . . . . 1B 96
Chesterton Rd. E13 . . . 2C 68	Chichester Ct. NW1 . . . . 4E 47	Chilworth M. W2 . . . . . . 5F 59
W10 . . . . 4F 57	(off Royal Coll. St.)	Chilworth M. W2 . . . . . . 5F 59
Chesterton Sq. W8 . . . 5C 72	Chichester Ho. NW6 . . . 1C 58	Chilworth St. W2 . . . . . . 5E 59
Chesterton Ter. E13 . . . 2C 68	SW9 . . . . 3C 90	Chimney Ct. E1 . . . . . . 2D 79
Chester Way SE11 . . . . 5C 76	(off Brixton Rd.)	(off Brewhouse La.)
Chestnut All. SW6 . . . . 2B 86	Chichester M. SE27 . . . 4C 118	China Ct. E1 . . . . 2D 79
Chestnut Av. E7 . . . . . . 1D 55	Chichester Rents	(off Asher Way)
E12 . . . . 4F 41	WC2 . . . . 2B 16	China Hall M. SE16 . . . . 4E 79
Chestnut Cl. N16 . . . . . 4F 35	Chichester Rd. E11 . . . . 5A 40	China M. SW2 . . . . . . 5B 104
SE6 . . . . 5E 123	NW6 . . . . 1C 58	China Walk SE11 . . . . . 5B 76
SE14 . . . . 4B 94	W2 . . . . 4D 59	China Wharf SE1 . . . . . 3C 78
SW16 . . . . 4C 118	Chichester St. SW1 . . . . 1E 89	Chinbrook Cres.
Chestnut Ct. SW6 . . . . . 2B 86	Chichester Way E14 . . . . 5F 81	SE12 . . . . 3D 125
W8 . . . . 4D 73	Chicksand Ho. E1 . . . . . 4C 64	Chinbrook Rd. SE12 . . 3D 125
(off Abbots Wlk.)	(off Chicksand St.)	Ching Ct. WC2 . . . . 3D 15
Chestnut Dr. E11 . . . . . 1C 40	Chicksand St. E1 . . . . . . 4B 64	(off Monmouth St.)
Chestnut Gro.	(not continuous)	Chingley Cl.
SW12 . . . . 5C 102	Chiddingstone SE13 . . . 3E 109	BR1: Brom 5A 124
Chestnut Ho. W4 . . . . . . 5A 70	Chiddingstone St.	Chinnock's Wharf
(off Orchard, The)	SW6 . . . . 5C 86	E14 . . . . 1A 80
Chestnut Pl. SE26 . . . . 4B 120	Chigwell Hill E1 . . . . 1D 79	(off Narrow St.)
Chestnut Rd. SE27 . . . 3D 119	Chilcombe Ho. SW15 . . . 5C 98	Chipka St. E14 . . . . 3E 81
Chestnuts, The N5 . . . . 1E 49	(off Fontley Way)	(not continuous)
(off Highbury Grange)	Chilcot Cl. E14 . . . . 5D 67	Chipley St. SE14 . . . . . . 2A 94
Chettle Cl. SE1 . . . . . . 5B 26	Childebert Rd.	Chippendale Ho.
Chettle Ct. N8 . . . . 1C 34	SW17 . . . . 2D 117	SW1 . . . . 1D 89
Chetwode Ho. NW8 . . . . 3A 60	Childeric Rd. SE14 . . . . 3A 94	(off Churchill Gdns.)
(off Grendon St.)	Childerley St. SW6 . . . . . 4A 86	Chippendale St. E5 . . . . 5F 37
Chetwode Rd.	Childers St. SE8 . . . . . . 2A 94	Chippenham Gdns.
SW17 . . . . 3B 116	Child La. SE10 . . . . 4B 82	NW6 . . . . 2C 58
Chetwood Wlk. E6 . . . . 4F 69	(off School Bank Rd.)	Chippenham M. W9 . . . . 3C 58
(off Greenwich Cres.)	Children's Discovery Cen.	Chippenham Rd. W9 . . . 3C 58
Chetwynd Rd. NW5 . . . 1D 47	. . . . 4F 53	Chipperfield Ho.
Cheval Pl. SW7 . . . . . . 4A 74	CHILD'S HILL 5C 30	SW3 . . . . 1A 88
Cheval St. E14 . . . . . . 4C 80	Childs Hill Wlk. NW2 . . . 5B 30	(off Ixworth Pl.)
Chevening Rd. NW6 . . . 1F 57	(off Cricklewood La.)	Chipstead Gdns.
SE10 . . . . 1B 96	Child's M. SW5 . . . . 5C 72	NW2 . . . . 4D 29
Cheverell Ho. E2 . . . . . 1C 64	(off Child's Pl.)	Chipstead St. SW6 . . . . 4C 86
(off Pritchard's Rd.)	Child's Pl. SW5 . . . . 5C 72	Chip St. SW4 . . . . 1F 103
Cheverton Rd. N19 . . . . 3F 33	Child's St. SW5 . . . . 5C 72	Chisenhale Rd. E3 . . . . 1A 66
Chevet St. E9 . . . . 2A 52	Child's Wlk. SW5 . . . . . . 5C 72	Chisholm Ct. W6 . . . . . . 1C 84
Chevington NW2 . . . . . 3B 44	(off Child's St.)	Chisledon Wlk. E9 . . . . . 3B 52
Cheviot Ct. SE14 . . . . . 2E 93	Chilham Ho.	(off Osborne Rd.)
(off Avonley Rd.)	SE1 . . . . 5C 26 (4F 77)	Chisley Rd. N15 . . . . . . 1A 36
Cheviot Gdns.	SE15 . . . . 2E 93	Chiswell Sq. SE3 . . . . . 5D 97
NW2 . . . . 4F 29	Chilham Rd. SE9 . . . . . 4F 125	Chiswell St.
SE27 . . . . 4D 119	Chilianwallan Memorial	EC1 . . . . 5B 10 (4E 63)
Cheviot Ga. NW2 . . . . . 4A 30	. . . . 2C 88	SE5 . . . . 3F 91
Cheviot Ho. E1 . . . . 5D 65	Chillerton Rd.	(off Edmund St.)
(off Commercial Rd.)	SW17 . . . . 5C 116	CHISWICK 1A 84
Cheviot Rd. SE27 . . . . 5C 118	Chillingford Ho.	Chiswick Comn. Rd.
Chevron Cl. E16 . . . . . . 5C 68	SW17 . . . . 4E 115	W4 . . . . 5A 70

Chiswick Community
   Sports Hall. 3A 84
Chiswick High Rd.
   W4. . . . . 1A 84
Chiswick House 2A 84
Chiswick La. W4 . . . . 1A 84
Chiswick La. Sth.
   W4. . . . . 2B 84
Chiswick Mall W4 . . . 2B 84
   W6. . . . . 2B 84
Chiswick Sq. W4 . . . . 2A 84
Chiswick Wharf W4 . . 2B 84
Chitty St. W1. . . . 5A 6 (4E 61)
Chivalry Rd.
   SW11. . . . . 3A 102
Chobham Gdns.
   SW19. . . . . 2F 113
Chobham Rd. E15. . . . 2F 53
Chocolate Studios
   N1. . . . . 1B 10
     (off Shepherdess Pl.)
Cholmeley Cres. N6. . . 2D 33
Cholmeley Lodge N6 . . 3D 33
Cholmeley Pk. N6 . . . . 3D 33
Cholmley Gdns. NW6. . 2C 44
Cholmondeley Av.
   NW10. . . . . 1C 56
Choppin's Ct. E1 . . . . . 2D 79
Chopwell Cl. E15 . . . . . 4F 53
Choumert Gro. SE15 . . 5C 92
Choumert M. SE15. . . . 5C 92
Choumert Rd. SE15 . . 1B 106
Choumert Sq. SE15 . . . 5C 92
Chow Sq. E8. . . . . 2B 50
Chrisp Ho. SE10 . . . . . 2A 96
     (off Maze Hill)
Chrisp St. E14 . . . . 4D 67
     (not continuous)
Christchurch Av.
   NW6 . . . . 5F 43
Christ Chu. Ct.
   NW10 . . . . 5A 42
Christchurch Ct. EC4 . . 2E 17
     (off Warwick La.)
Christchurch Hill
   NW3 . . . . 5F 31
Christchurch Ho.
   SW2 . . . . 1B 118
     (off Christchurch Rd.)
Christchurch Pas.
   NW3 . . . . 5E 31
Christchurch Pl. SW8 . . 5F 89
Christchurch Rd. N8. . . 1A 34
   SW2 . . . . 1B 118
Christchurch Sq. E9 . . . 5E 51
Christchurch St. SW3 . . 2B 88
Christchurch Ter.
   SW3 . . . . 2B 88
     (off Christchurch St.)
Christchurch Way
   SE10. . . . . 1A 96
Christian Ct. SE16 . . . . 2B 80
Christian Pl. E1 . . . . . . 5C 64
     (off Burslem St.)
Christian St. E1 . . . . . . 5C 64
Christie Ct. N19 . . . . . . 4A 34
Christie Ho. SE10 . . . . . 1B 96
     (off Blackwall La.)
Christie Rd. E9 . . . . . . 3A 52
Christina Sq. N4. . . . . . 3D 35

Christina St.
   EC2. . . . . . . 3D 11 (3A 64)
Christopher Cl. SE16 . . 3F 79
Christopher Pl.
   NW1. . . . . . . 1C 6 (2F 61)
Christophers M. W11. . . 2A 72
Christopher St.
   EC2. . . . . . . 4C 10 (3F 63)
Chryssell Rd. SW9. . . . 3C 90
Chubworthy St. SE14 . . 2A 94
Chudleigh Rd. NW6. . . 4F 43
   SE4. . . . . 3B 108
Chudleigh St. E1. . . . . . 5F 65
Chulsa Rd. SE26 . . . . . 5D 121
Chumleigh Gdns.
   SE5. . . . . 2A 92
     (off Chumleigh St.)
Chumleigh St. SE5. . . . 2A 92
Church App. SE21. . . . . 3F 119
Church Av. E12 . . . . . . 5F 41
   NW1. . . . . 3D 47
Churchbury Rd. SE9. . . 5F 111
Church Cloisters EC3. . . 5D 19
Church Cl. W8. . . . . 3D 73
     (off Rotherhithe St.)
Church Cres. E9 . . . . . . 4F 51
Churchcroft Cl.
   SW12. . . . . 5C 102
Churchdown
   BR1: Brom. 4A 124
CHURCH END. 3A 42
Church Entry EC4. . . . . 3E 17
Churchfield Mans.
   SW6. . . . . 5B 86
     (off New Kings Rd.)
Churchfields SE10 . . . . 2E 95
Church Gth. N19. . . . . . 4F 33
     (off St John's Gro.)
Church Ga. SW6. . . . . . 1A 100
Church Grn. SW9. . . . . 4C 90
Church Gro. SE13 . . . . 3D 109
Church Hill SW19. . . . . 5B 114
Church Ho. EC1. . . . . . . 3E 9
     (off Compton St.)
   SW1. . . . . 5C 22
     (off Gt. Smith St.)
Churchill Ct. N4. . . . . . 2C 34
Churchill Gdns. SW1 . . 1E 89
Churchill Gdns. Rd.
   SW1. . . . . 1D 89
Churchill Mus.
   (Cabinet War Rooms)
   . . . . 3C 22 (3F 75)
Churchill Pl. E14 . . . . . 2D 81
Churchill Rd. E16. . . . . 5F 69
   NW2. . . . . 3D 43
   NW5. . . . . 1D 47
Churchill Wlk. E9 . . . . . 2E 51
Church La. E11. . . . . . . 3A 40
   SW17. . . . . 5B 116
Churchley Rd.
   SE26. . . . . 4D 121
Church Mead SE5. . . . . 3E 91
     (off Camberwell Rd.)
Churchmead Rd.
   NW10. . . . . 3C 42
Church Mt. N2. . . . . 1F 31
Church Pas. EC2. . . . . . 2A 18
     (off Guildhall Yd.)

Church Path E11. . . . . . 1C 40
   N5. . . . . 2D 49
   NW10. . . . . 4A 42
   SW14. . . . . 1A 98
     (not continuous)
Church Pl.
   SW1. . . . . . . 5A 14 (1E 75)
Church Ri. SE23. . . . . . 2F 121
Church Rd. E10 . . . . . . 3C 38
   E12. . . . . 2F 55
   N1. . . . . 3E 49
   N6. . . . . 1C 32
   NW10. . . . . 4A 42
   SW13. . . . . 5B 84
   SW19. . . . . 5A 114
Church Rd. Almshouses
   E10. . . . . 4D 39
     (off Church Rd.)
Church Rd. Ind. Est.
   E10. . . . . 3C 38
Church Row NW3. . . . . 1E 45
   SW6 . . . . 3D 87
     (off Park Rd.)
Church St. E15. . . . . . . 5A 54
   NW8 . . . . 4F 59
   W2. . . . . 4F 59
   W4 . . . . 2B 84
Church St. Est. NW8. . . 3F 59
Church St. Nth. E15. . . . 5A 54
Church St. Pas. E15. . . . 5A 54
     (off Church St.)
Church Ter. SE13 . . . . . 1A 110
Church Va. SE23. . . . . . 2F 121
Church Wlk. N6 . . . . . . 5C 32
   N16. . . . . 5F 35
     (not continuous)
   NW2 . . . . 5B 30
   SW13 . . . . 4C 84
   SW15 . . . . 3D 99
Churchward Ho. W14. . 1B 86
     (off Ivatt Pl.)
Churchway
   NW1. . . . . . . 1C 6 (2F 61)
Churchwell Path E9 . . . 2E 51
Churchyard Pas. SE5 . . 5F 91
Churchyard Row
   SE11. . . . . 5D 77
Church Yd. Wlk. W2. . . 4F 59
     (off St Mary's Sq.)
Churnfield N4. . . . . 4C 34
Churston Av. E13 . . . . . 5D 55
Churston Cl. SW2. . . . . 1C 118
Churton Pl. SW1 . . . . . 5E 75
Churton St. SW1 . . . . . 5E 75
Chusan Pl. E14. . . . . . . 5B 66
Chute Ho. SW9. . . . . . . 5C 90
     (off Stockwell Pk. Rd.)
Cibber Rd. SE23 . . . . . 2F 121
Cicada Rd. SW18. . . . . 4E 101
Cicely Ho. NW8. . . . . . . 1F 59
     (off Cochrane St.)
Cicely Rd. SE15 . . . . . . 4C 92
Cinderella Path
   NW11. . . . . 3D 31
Cinderford Way
   BR1: Brom. 4A 124
Cine Lumiere 5F 73
     (off Queensberry Pl.)

Cineworld Cinema
. . . . 3D 101
Cinnabar Wharf Central
E1 . . . . 2C 78
(off Wapping High St.)
Cinnabar Wharf E.
E1 . . . . 2C 78
(off Wapping High St.)
Cinnabar Wharf W.
E1 . . . . 2C 78
(off Wapping High St.)
Cinnamon Cl. SE15 . . . . 3B 92
Cinnamon Row
SW11 . . . . 1E 101
Cinnamon St. E1 . . . . . . 2D 79
Cinnamon Wharf *SE1* . . . 3B 78
(off Shad Thames)
Circa Apartments
NW1 . . . . 4C 46
Circle, The NW2 . . . . . . 5A 28
SE1 . . . . 3F 27
(off Queen Elizabeth St.)
Circus Lodge NW8 . . . . 2F 59
(off Circus Rd.)
Circus M. *W1* 4B 60
(off Enford St.)
Circus Pl.
EC2. . . . . 1C 18 (4F 63)
Circus Rd. NW8 . . . . . . 2F 59
Circus St. SE10 . . . . . . 3E 95
Cirencester St. W2. . . . . 4D 59
Cissbury Ho. SE26 . . . 3C 120
Cissbury Rd. N15 . . . . . 1F 35
Citadel Pl. SE11. . . . . . 1B 90
Citizen Ho. N7 . . . . 1C 48
Citizen Rd. N7 . . . . 1C 48
Citrus Ho. *SE8* 1B 94
(off Alverton St.)
City Bus. Cen. SE16. . . . 4E 79
City Central Est. *EC1* . . . 2F 9
(off Seward St.)
City Cross Bus. Cen.
SE10 . . . . 5A 82
City Gdn. Row
N1 . . . . 1E 9 (1D 63)
City Harbour *E14* 4D 81
(off Selsdon Way)
City Hgts. *SE1*. 2E 27
(off Weavers La.)
CITY OF LONDON
. . . . 3B 18 (5F 63)
City of London Almshouses
SW9 . . . . 2B 104
City of London Crematorium
E12 . . . . 5F 41
City of London Point
N7 . . . . 3F 47
(off York Way)
City of Westminster College
. . . . 4B 14 (1E 75)
City Pav. *EC1* 5D 9
(off Britton St.)
City Rd. EC1 . . . 1D 9 (1D 63)
City Twr. *EC2* 1B 18
(off Basinghall St.)
City University
. . . . 2D 9 (2D 63)
City University Saddlers
Sports Cen.
. . . . 3E 9 (3D 63)

Cityview SE7. . . . . 2E 97
City Vw. Ct. SE22. . . . . 5C 106
City Wlk. Apartments
EC1 . . . . 2F 9
(off Seward St.)
Clabon M. SW1 . . . . . . 4B 74
Clack St. SE16 . . . . 3E 79
Clacton Rd. E6 . . . . 2F 69
E17 . . . . 1A 38
Claire Ct. NW2 . . . . 3A 44
Claire Pl. E14. . . . . 4C 80
Clairview Rd.
SW16 . . . . 5D 117
Clairville Point
SE23 . . . . 3F 121
(off Dacres Rd.)
Clancarty Rd. SW6. . . . . 5C 86
Clandeboye Ho. *E15* . . . 5B 54
(off John St.)
Clandon Ho. *SE1* 4E 25
(off Webber St.)
Clandon St. SE8. . . . . . 5C 94
Clanricarde Gdns.
W2 . . . . 1C 72
CLAPHAM 2E 103
CLAPHAM COMMON
. . . . 2F 103
Clapham Comn. Nth. Side
SW4 . . . . 2B 102
Clapham Comn. Sth. Side
SW4 . . . . 4D 103
Clapham Comn. W. Side
SW4 . . . . 2B 102
(not continuous)
Clapham Cres. SW4. . . 2F 103
Clapham High St.
SW4 . . . . 2F 103
CLAPHAM JUNCTION
. . . . 1A 102
Clapham Junc. App.
SW11 . . . . 1A 102
Clapham Leisure Cen.
. . . . 1F 103
Clapham Mnr. Ct.
SW4 . . . . 1E 103
Clapham Mnr. St.
SW4 . . . . 1E 103
CLAPHAM PARK 5F 103
Clapham Pk. Est.
SW4 . . . . 4F 103
Clapham Pk. Rd.
SW4 . . . . 2E 103
Clapham Pk. Ter.
SW2 . . . . 3A 104
(off Kings Av.)
Clapham Picturehouse
. . . . 2E 103
Clapham Rd. SW9 . . . . 1A 104
Clapham Rd. Est.
SW4 . . . . 1A 104
Clapton Comn. E5 . . . . 2B 36
(not continuous)
CLAPTON PARK 1F 51
Clapton Pk. Est. E5. . . . 1F 51
Clapton Pas. E5 . . . . . . 2E 51
Clapton Sq. E5 . . . . 2E 51
Clapton St. N16. . . . . . 3C 36
Clapton Way E5 . . . . . . 1C 50
Clara Grant Ho. *E14*. . . 4C 80
(off Mellish St.)

Clara Nehab Ho.
NW11. . . . . 1B 30
(off Leeside Cres.)
Clare Ct. WC1. . . . . 2E 7
(off Judd St.)
Claredale Ho. *E2* 1D 65
(off Claredale St.)
Claredale St. E2. . . . . . 1C 64
Clare Gdns. E7. . . . . . . 1C 54
W11 . . . . 5A 58
Clare La. N1 . . . . 4E 49
Clare Lawn Av.
SW14 . . . . 3A 98
Clare Mkt.
WC2. . . . . . . 3A 16 (5B 62)
Clare M. SW6 . . . . 3D 87
Claremont Cl.
N1 . . . . 1C 8 (1C 62)
SW2 . . . . 1A 118
Claremont Gro.
W4 . . . . 3A 84
Claremont Rd. E7 . . . . 2D 55
E11 . . . . 5F 39
N6 . . . . 2E 33
NW2 . . . . 2F 29
W9 . . . . 1A 58
Claremont Sq.
N1 . . . . 1B 8 (1C 62)
Claremont St. SE10 . . . 2D 95
Claremont Vs. *SE5*. . . . 3F 91
(off Southampton Way)
Claremont Way NW2 . . . 3E 29
(not continuous)
Claremont Way Ind. Est.
NW2 . . . . 3E 29
Clarence Av. SW4. . . . . 5F 103
Clarence Ct. *W6*. 5D 71
(off Cambridge Gro.)
Clarence Cres. SW4. . . 4F 103
Clarence Gdns.
NW1. . . . . 2E 5 (2D 61)
Clarence Ga. Gdns.
NW1 . . . . 4A 4
(off Glentworth St.)
Clarence House 3A 22
Clarence La. SW15 . . . . 4A 98
Clarence M. E5 . . . . . . 2D 51
SE16. . . . . 2F 79
SW12 . . . . 5D 103
Clarence Pl. E5 . . . . . . 2D 51
Clarence Rd. E5. . . . . . 1D 51
E12 . . . . 1E 55
E16 . . . . 3A 68
NW6 . . . . 4B 44
SE8. . . . . 2D 95
SE9 . . . . 2F 125
SW19 . . . . 5D 115
Clarence Ter.
NW1. . . . . 3A 4 (3B 60)
Clarence Wlk. SW4 . . . 5A 90
Clarence Way NW1 . . . 4D 47
Clarendon Cl. E9 . . . . . 4E 51
W2 . . . . 1A 74
Clarendon Ct. NW2 . . . 4E 43
Clarendon Cross
W11 . . . . 1A 72
Clarendon Dr. SW15 . . . 2E 99
Clarendon Flats *W1*. . . 3C 12
(off Balderton St.)
Clarendon Gdns. W9 . . . 3E 59

Clarendon Gro.
  NW1 . . . . 1B **6** (2F **61**)
Clarendon Ho. NW1 . . . . 1A **6**
  (off Werrington St.)
Clarendon M. W2 . . . . . . 1A **74**
Clarendon Pl. W2 . . . . . . 1A **74**
Clarendon Ri. SE13 . . . . 2E **109**
Clarendon Rd. E11 . . . . . 3F **39**
  E17 . . . . 1D **39**
  W11 . . . . 1A **72**
Clarendon St. SW1 . . . . . 1D **89**
Clarendon Ter. W9 . . . . . 3E **59**
Clarendon Wlk. W11 . . 5A **58**
Clarens St. SE6 . . . . . . 2B **122**
Clare Pl. SW15 . . . . 5B **98**
Clare Point NW2 . . . . . . 3F **29**
  (off Whitefield Av.)
Clare Rd. E11 . . . . 1F **39**
  NW10 . . . . 4C **42**
  SE14 . . . . 4B **94**
Clare St. E2 . . . . 1D **65**
Clareville Gro. SW7 . . 5E **73**
Clareville Gro. M.
  SW7 . . . . 5E **73**
Clareville St. SW7 . . . . 5E **73**
Clarewood Ct. W1 . . . . 4B **60**
  (off Seymour Pl.)
Clarewood Wlk.
  SW9 . . . . 2C **104**
Clarges M.
  W1 . . . . . . 1D **21** (2D **75**)
Clarges St.
  W1 . . . . . . 1E **21** (2D **75**)
Claribel Rd. SW9 . . . . . 5D **91**
Claridge Ct. SW6 . . . . . 5B **86**
Clarion Ho. E3 . . . . 1A **66**
  (off Roman Rd.)
SW1 . . . . 1E **89**
  (off Moreton Pl.)
W1 . . . . 3B **14**
  (off St Anne's Ct.)
Clarissa Ho. E14 . . . . 5D **67**
  (off Cordelia St.)
Clarissa St. E8 . . . . . . 5B **50**
Clarke Path N16 . . . . . 3C **36**
Clarke's M.
  W1 . . . . 5C **4** (4C **60**)
Clark Ho. SW10 . . . . . . 3E **87**
  (off Coleridge Gdns.)
Clarkson Rd. E16 . . . . 5B **68**
Clarkson Row NW1 . . . 1E **61**
  (off Mornington Ter.)
Clarkson St. E2 . . . . . 2D **65**
Clark's Pl.
  EC2 . . . . 2D **19** (5A **64**)
Clark St. E1 . . . . 4D **65**
Classic Mans. E9 . . . . 4D **51**
  (off Wells St.)
Claude Rd. E10 . . . . . . 4E **39**
  E13 . . . . 5D **55**
  SE15 . . . . 5D **93**
Claude St. E14 . . . . . . 5C **80**
Claudia Jones Way
  SW2 . . . . 4A **104**
Claudia Pl. SW19 . . . 1A **114**
Claughton Rd. E13 . . . 1E **69**
Clavell St. SE10 . . . . . 2E **95**
Claverdale Rd.
  SW2 . . . . 5B **104**
Clavering Av. SW13 . . 2D **85**

Clavering Ho. SE13 . . 2F **109**
  (off Blessington Rd.)
Clavering Rd. E12 . . . 3F **41**
Claverton St. SW1 . . . 1E **89**
Clave St. E1 . . . . 2E **79**
Claxton Gro. W6 . . . . . 1F **85**
Claxton Path SE4 . . . 2F **107**
  (off Coston Wlk.)
Claybank Gro.
  SE13 . . . . 1D **109**
Claybridge Rd.
  SE12 . . . . 4E **125**
Claybrook Rd. W6 . . . . 2F **85**
Claydon SE17 . . . . 5E **77**
  (off Deacon Way)
Clayhill Cres. SE9 . . . 4F **125**
Claylands Pl. SW8 . . . 3C **90**
Claylands Rd. SW8 . . . 2B **90**
Claypole Ct. E17 . . . . . 1C **38**
  (off Yunus Khan Cl.)
Claypole Rd. E15 . . . . 1E **67**
Clays La. E15 . . . . 2D **53**
Clays La. Cl. E15 . . . . . 2D **53**
Clay St. W1 . . . . 1A **12** (4B **60**)
Clayton Cres. N1 . . . . . 5A **48**
Clayton Dr. SE8 . . . . . 1A **94**
Clayton Ho. E9 . . . . . . 4E **51**
  (off Frampton Pk. Rd.)
SW13 . . . . 3E **85**
  (off Trinity Chu. Rd.)
Clayton M. SE10 . . . . . 4F **95**
Clayton Rd. SE15 . . . . 4C **92**
Clayton St. SE11 . . . . . 2C **90**
Clearbrook Way E1 . . . 5E **65**
Clearwater Ter. W11 . . 3A **72**
  (off Lorne Gdns.)
Clearwell Dr. W9 . . . . . 3D **59**
Cleaver Ho. NW3 . . . . . 4B **46**
  (off Adelaide Rd.)
Cleaver Sq. SE11 . . . . . 1C **90**
Cleaver St. SE11 . . . . . 1C **90**
Cleeve Hill SE23 . . . . 1D **121**
Cleeve Way SW15 . . . . 5B **98**
Cleeve Workshops E2 . 2E **11**
  (off Boundary Rd.)
Clegg Ho. SE3 . . . . . . 2D **111**
SE16 . . . . 4E **79**
  (off Moodkee St.)
Clegg St. E1 . . . . 2D **79**
  E13 . . . . 1C **68**
Cleland Ho. E2 . . . . . . 1E **65**
  (off Sewardstone Rd.)
Clematis St. W12 . . . . . 1C **70**
Clem Attlee Ct. SW6 . . 2B **86**
Clem Attlee Pde.
  SW6 . . . . 2B **86**
  (off Nth. End Rd.)
Clemence St. E14 . . . . 4B **66**
Clement Av. SW4 . . . . 2F **103**
Clement Cl. NW6 . . . . . 4E **43**
Clement Ho. SE8 . . . . . 5A **80**
W10 . . . . 4E **57**
  (off Dalgarno Gdns.)
Clementina Rd. E10 . . 3B **38**
Clement Rd. SW19 . . . 5A **114**
Clement's Av. E16 . . . . 1C **82**
Clement's Inn
  WC2 . . . . . 3A **16** (5B **62**)
Clement's Inn Pas.
  WC2 . . . . 3A **16**

Clements La.
  EC4 . . . . 4C **18** (1F **77**)
Clement's Rd. SE16 . . 4C **78**
Clemson Ho. E8 . . . . . 5B **50**
Clennam St.
  SE1 . . . . . . 3A **26** (3E **77**)
Clenston M.
  W1 . . . . . . 2A **12** (5B **60**)
Cleopatra's Needle
  . . . . 5F **15** (2A **76**)
Clephane Rd. N1 . . . . . 3E **49**
Clephane Rd. Nth.
  N1 . . . . 3E **49**
Clephane Rd. Sth.
  N1 . . . . 3F **49**
Clere Pl. EC2 . . 3C **10** (3F **63**)
Clere St. EC2 . . 3C **10** (3F **63**)
CLERKENWELL
  . . . . 3B **8** (3C **62**)
Clerkenwell Cl.
  EC1 . . . . 3C **8** (3C **62**)
  (not continuous)
Clerkenwell Grn.
  EC1 . . . . 4C **8** (3C **62**)
Clerkenwell Rd.
  EC1 . . . . 4B **8** (3C **62**)
Clermont Rd. E9 . . . . . 5E **51**
Clevedon Cl. N16 . . . . 5B **36**
Clevedon Mans.
  NW5 . . . . 1C **46**
Clevedon Pas. N16 . . . 4B **36**
Cleve Ho. NW6 . . . . . . 4D **45**
Cleveland Av. W4 . . . . 5B **70**
Cleveland Gdns. N4 . . 1E **35**
  NW2 . . . . 4F **29**
  SW13 . . . . 5B **84**
  W2 . . . . 5E **59**
Cleveland Gro. E1 . . . . 3E **65**
Cleveland Mans.
  SW9 . . . . 3C **90**
  (off Mowll St.)
  W9 . . . . 3C **58**
Cleveland M.
  W1 . . . . 5F **5** (4E **61**)
Cleveland Pl.
  SW1 . . . . . 1A **22** (2E **75**)
Cleveland Rd. N1 . . . . 4F **49**
  SW13 . . . . 5B **84**
Cleveland Row
  SW1 . . . . . 2F **21** (2E **75**)
Cleveland Sq. W2 . . . . 5E **59**
Cleveland St.
  W1 . . . . 4E **5** (3D **61**)
Cleveland Ter. W2 . . . . 5E **59**
Cleveland Way E1 . . . . 3E **65**
Cleveley Cl. SE7 . . . . . 5F **83**
Cleveleys Rd. E5 . . . . 5D **37**
Cleverly Est.
  W12 . . . . 2C **70**
Cleve Rd. NW6 . . . . . . 4D **45**
Cleves Ho. E16 . . . . . . 2C **82**
  (off Southey M.)
Clewer Ct. E10 . . . . . . 3C **38**
  (off Leyton Grange Est.)
Cley Ho. SE4 . . . . 2F **107**
Clichy Est. E1 . . . . 4E **65**
Clichy Ho. E1 . . . . 4E **65**
  (off Stepney Way)
Clifden Rd. E5 . . . . . . 2E **51**

Cliffe Ho. *SE10*. 1B **96**
  (off Blackwall La.)
Clifford Ct. *W2*. 4D **59**
  (off Westbourne Pk. Vs.)
Clifford Dr. SW9. . . . . . 2D **105**
Clifford Gdns. NW10. . . 1E **57**
Clifford Haigh Ho.
  SW6. . . . . 3F **85**
Clifford Ho.
  BR3: Beck. 5D **123**
  (off Calverley Cl.)
  W14. . . . . 5B **72**
  (off Edith Vs.)
Clifford Rd. E16. . . . . . . 3B **68**
  N1. . . . . 5A **50**
Clifford's Inn Pas.
  EC4. . . . . . . 3B **16** (5C **62**)
Clifford St.
  W1. . . . . 5F **13** (1E **75**)
Clifford Way NW10. . . . 1B **42**
Cliffsend Ho. SW9. . . . . 4C **90**
  (off Cowley Rd.)
Cliff Ter. SE8. . . . . 5C **94**
Cliffview Rd. SE13. . . . . 1C **108**
Cliff Vs. NW1. . . . . 3F **47**
Cliff Wlk. E16. . . . . 4B **68**
Clifton Av. W12. . . . . 2B **70**
Clifton Ct. N4. . . . . 4C **34**
  NW8. . . . . 3F **59**
  (off Maida Va.)
  SE15. . . . . 3D **93**
Clifton Cres. SE15. . . . . 3D **93**
Clifton Est. SE15. . . . . . 4D **93**
Clifton Gdns. N15. . . . . 1B **36**
  NW11. . . . . 1B **30**
  W4. . . . . 5A **70**
  (not continuous)
  W9. . . . . 3E **59**
Clifton Ga. SW10. . . . . . 2E **87**
Clifton Gro. E8. . . . . 3C **50**
Clifton Hill NW6. . . . . . . 1D **59**
  NW8. . . . . 1D **59**
Clifton Ho. E2. . . . . 3F **11**
  (off Club Row)
  E11. . . . . 4A **40**
Clifton Pl. SE16. . . . . . . 3F **79**
  W2. . . . . 5F **59**
Clifton Ri. SE14. . . . . . . 3A **94**
  (not continuous)
Clifton Rd. E7. . . . . 3F **55**
  E16. . . . . 4A **68**
  N8. . . . . 1F **33**
  NW10. . . . . 1C **56**
  SW19. . . . . 5F **113**
  W9. . . . . 3E **59**
Clifton St.
  EC2. . . . . . . 4D **11** (3A **64**)
Clifton Ter. N4. . . . . 4C **34**
Clifton Vs. W9. . . . . 4E **59**
Cliftonville Ct. SE12. . . 1C **124**
Clifton Wlk. W6. . . . . 5D **71**
  (off King St.)
Clifton Way SE15. . . . . . 3D **93**
Climsland Ho.
  SE1. . . . . . . 1C **24** (2C **76**)
Clinch Ct. E16. . . . . 4C **68**
  (off Plymouth Rd.)
Clinger Ct. N1. . . . . 5A **50**
  (off Hobbs Pl. Est.)

Clink Exhibition, The
  . . . . 1B **26**
Clink St. SE1. . . 1B **26** (2F **77**)
Clink Wharf
  SE1. . . . . 1B **26**
  (off Clink St.)
Clinton Rd. E3. . . . . 2A **66**
  E7. . . . . 1C **54**
Clipper Cl. SE16. . . . . . 3F **79**
Clipper Ho. E14. . . . . . . 1E **95**
  (off Manchester Rd.)
Clipper Way SE13. . . . . 2E **109**
Clipstone M.
  W1. . . . . 5F **5** (4E **61**)
Clipstone St.
  W1. . . . . 5E **5** (4D **61**)
Clissold Ct. N4. . . . . 4E **35**
Clissold Cres. N16. . . . . 5F **35**
Clissold Leisure Cen.
  . . . . 5F **35**
Clissold Rd. N16. . . . . . 5F **35**
Clitheroe Rd. SW9. . . . . 5A **90**
Clitterhouse Cres.
  NW2. . . . . 3E **29**
Clitterhouse Rd.
  NW2. . . . . 3E **29**
Clive Ct. W9. . . . . 3E **59**
Cliveden Ho. E16. . . . . . 2C **82**
  (off Fitzwilliam M.)
Cliveden Pl. SW1. . . . . . 5C **74**
Clive Ho. SE10. . . . . 2E **95**
  (off Haddo St.)
Clive Lloyd Ho. N15. . . . 1E **35**
  (off Woodlands Pk. Rd.)
Clive Lodge NW4. . . . . . 1F **29**
Clive Pas. SE21. . . . . . . 3F **119**
Clive Rd. SE21. . . . . 3F **119**
  SW19. . . . . 5A **116**
Cloak La.
  EC4. . . . . . . 4A **18** (1E **77**)
Clochar Ct. NW10. . . . . 5B **42**
Clock Ho. E3. . . . . 2E **67**
Clockhouse, The
  SW19. . . . . 3E **113**
Clockhouse Cl.
  SW19. . . . . 2E **113**
Clock Ho. Pde. E11. . . . 1D **41**
Clockhouse Pl.
  SW15. . . . . 4A **100**
Clock Mus., The. 2A **18**
Clock Pl. SE1. . . . . 5D **77**
  (off Newington Butts)
Clock Twr. M. N1. . . . . . 5E **49**
Clock Twr. Pl. N7. . . . . . 3A **48**
Cloister Rd. NW2. . . . . . 5B **30**
Cloisters, The. 5D **23**
Cloisters, The E1. . . . . . 4F **11**
  SW9. . . . . 4C **90**
Cloisters Bus. Cen.
  SW8. . . . . 3D **89**
  (off Battersea Pk. Rd.)
Clonbrock Rd. N16. . . . 1A **50**
Cloncurry St. SW6. . . . . 5F **85**
Clonmel Rd. SW6. . . . . 3B **86**
Clonmore St. SW18. . . . 1B **114**
Clorane Gdns. NW3. . . . 5C **30**
Close, The SE3. . . . . 5F **95**
Cloth Ct. EC1. . . . . 1E **17**
Cloth Fair
  EC1. . . . . . . 1E **17** (4D **63**)

Clothier St.
  E1. . . . . 2E **19** (5A **64**)
Cloth St. EC1. . . . . 5F **9** (4E **63**)
Cloudesdale Rd.
  SW17. . . . . 2D **117**
Cloudesley Pl. N1. . . . . 5C **48**
Cloudesley Rd. N1. . . . . 5C **48**
  (not continuous)
Cloudesley Sq. N1. . . . . 5C **48**
Cloudesley St. N1. . . . . 5C **48**
Clova Rd. E7. . . . . 3B **54**
Clove Cres. E14. . . . . . . 1E **81**
Clove Hitch Quay
  SW11. . . . . 1E **101**
Clovelly Ct. NW2. . . . . . 2E **43**
Clovelly Ho. W2. . . . . . . 5E **59**
  (off Hallfield Est.)
Clovelly Way E1. . . . . . . 5E **65**
Clover Cl. E11. . . . . 4F **39**
Clover M. SW3. . . . . 2B **88**
Clove St. E13. . . . . 3C **68**
Clowders Rd. SE6. . . . . 3B **122**
Cloysters Grn. E1. . . . . 2C **78**
Club Row E1. . . 3F **11** (3B **64**)
  E2. . . . . 3F **11** (3B **64**)
Clunbury St. N1. . . . . . . 1F **63**
Cluny Est.
  SE1. . . . . . . 5D **27** (4A **78**)
Cluny M. SW5. . . . . 5C **72**
Cluny Pl.
  SE1. . . . . . . 5D **27** (4A **78**)
Cluse Ct. N1. . . . . 1E **63**
  (off St Peters St.,
  not continuous)
Clutton St. E14. . . . . 4D **67**
Clyde Ct. NW1. . . . . 1F **61**
  (off Hampden Cl.)
Clyde Flats SW6. . . . . . . 3B **86**
  (off Rhylston Rd.)
Clyde Pl. E10. . . . . 2D **39**
Clydesdale Ho. W11. . . 5B **58**
  (off Clydesdale Rd.)
Clydesdale Rd. W11. . . 5B **58**
Clyde St. SE8. . . . . 2B **94**
Clyde Ter. SE23. . . . . . . 2E **121**
Clyde Va. SE23. . . . . . . 2E **121**
Clyde Wharf E16. . . . . . 2C **82**
Clynes Ho. E2. . . . . 2F **65**
  (off Knottisford St.)
Clyston St. SW8. . . . . . . 5E **89**
Coach & Horses Yd.
  W1. . . . . 4E **13** (1E **75**)
Coach Ho. La. N5. . . . . . 1D **49**
  SW19. . . . . 4F **113**
Coach Ho. M. SE23. . . . 4F **107**
Coach Ho. Yd. NW3. . . . 1E **45**
  (off Heath St.)
  SW18. . . . . 2D **101**
Coachmaker M.
  SW4. . . . . 1A **104**
  (off Fenwick Pl.)
Coach Yd. M. N19. . . . . 3A **34**
Coaldale Wlk. SE21. . . . 5E **105**
Coalecroft Rd. SW15. . . 2E **99**
Coalport Ho. SE11. . . . . 5C **76**
  (off Walnut Tree Wlk.)
Coates Av. SW18. . . . . . 4A **102**
Coate St. E2. . . . . 1C **64**
Cobalt Sq. SW8. . . . . . . 2B **90**
  (off Sth. Lambeth Rd.)

Cobbetts Av. IG4: Ilf . . . 1F 41
Cobbett St. SW8 . . . . 3B 90
Cobble La. N1 . . . . 4D 49
Cobble M. N5 . . . . 5E 35
Cobbold Ct. SW1 . . . . 5F 75
(off Elverton St.)
Cobbold Ind. Est.
NW10 . . . . .3B 42
Cobbold M. W12 . . . . 3B 70
Cobbold Rd. E11 . . . . 5B 40
NW10 . . . . .3B 42
W12 . . . . 3A 70
Cobb's Ct. EC4 . . . . 3E 17
Cobb's Hall W6. . . . . 2F 85
(off Fulham Pal. Rd.)
Cobbsthorpe Vs.
SE26 . . . . 4F 121
Cobb St. E1 . . . 1F 19 (4B 64)
Cobden Ho. E2 . . . . 2C 64
(off Nelson Gdns.)
NW1 . . . . 1E 61
(off Arlington Rd.)
Cobden M. SE26 . . . . 5D 121
Cobden Rd. E11 . . . . 5A 40
Cobham Cl. SW11 . . . . 4A 102
Cobham M. NW1 . . . . . . 4F 47
Cobland Rd.
SE12 . . . . 4E 125
Coborn Rd. E3 . . . . 1B 66
Coborn St. E3 . . . . 2B 66
Cobourg Rd. SE5 . . . . . . 2B 92
Cobourg St.
NW1 . . . . 2A 6 (2E 61)
Coburg Cl. SW1 . . . . 5E 75
Coburg Cres. SW2 . . . . . 1B 118
Coburg Dwellings E1 . . 1E 65
(off Hardinge St.)
Cochrane Cl. NW8 . . . . . 1F 59
(off Cochrane St.)
Cochrane Ct. E10 . . . . . . 3C 38
(off Leyton Grange Est.)
Cochrane Ho. E14 . . . . . . 3C 80
(off Admirals Way)
Cochrane M. NW8 . . . . . . 1F 59
Cochrane St. NW8 . . . . . . 1F 59
Cochrane Theatre 1E 13
(off Southampton Row)
Cockburn Ho. SW1 . . . . . 1F 89
(off Aylesford St.)
Cockerell Rd. E17 . . . . . . 2A 38
Cock Hill E1 . . . . 1E 19 (4A 64)
Cock La.
EC1 . . . . 1D 17 (4D 63)
Cockpit Steps SW1 . . . . 4B 22
Cockpit Theatre 3A 60
(off Gateforth St.)
Cockpit Yd.
WC1 . . . . 5A 8 (4B 62)
Cockspur Ct.
SW1 . . . . 1C 22 (2F 75)
Cockspur St.
SW1 . . . . 1C 22 (2F 75)
Coda Cen., The SW6 . . . 3A 86
Code St. E1 . . . . 3B 64
Codicote Ho. SE8 . . . . . . 5F 79
(off Chilton Gro.)
Codicote Ter. N4 . . . . 4E 35
Codling Cl. E1 . . . . 2C 78
Codrington Ct. E1 . . . . . . 3D 65
SE16 . . . . 1A 80

Codrington Hill
SE23 . . . . 5A 108
Codrington M. W11 . . . . . 5A 58
Cody Rd. E16 . . . . 3F 67
Coffey St. SE8 . . . . 3C 94
Coin St. SE1 . . . 1B 24 (2C 76)
(not continuous)
Coity Rd. NW5 . . . . 3C 46
Cokers La. SE21 . . . . 1F 119
Coke St. E1 . . . . 5C 64
Colas M. NW6 . . . . 5C 44
Colbeck M. SW7 . . . . 5D 73
Colberg Pl. N16 . . . . 2B 36
Colborne Ho. E14 . . . . . . 1C 80
(off E. India Dock Rd.)
Colby M. SE19 . . . . 5A 120
Colby Rd. SE19 . . . . 5A 120
Colchester Rd. E10 . . . . . 2E 39
E17 . . . . 1C 38
Colchester St. E1 . . . . . . 5B 64
Coldbath Sq.
EC1 . . . . 3B 8 (3C 62)
Coldbath St. SE13 . . . . . 4D 95
Cold Blow La. SE14 . . . . . 3F 93
(not continuous)
Coldharbour E14 . . . . 3E 81
Coldharbour La.
SE5 . . . . 1E 105
SW9 . . . . 2C 104
Coldharbour Pl. SE5 . . . . 5E 91
Coldstream Gdns.
SW18 . . . . 4B 100
Colebeck M. N1 . . . . 3D 49
Colebert Av. E1 . . . . 3E 65
Colebert Ho. E1 . . . . 3E 65
(off Colebert Av.)
Colebrook Cl. SW15 . . . . 5F 99
Colebrook Ct. SW3 . . . . . 5A 74
(off Makins St.)
Colebrooke Dr. E11 . . . . . 2E 41
Colebrooke Pl. N1 . . . . . . 5D 49
Colebrooke Row N1 . . . . . 1D 63
Colebrooke Ho. E14 . . . . . 5D 67
(off Ellesmere St.)
Coleby Path SE5 . . . . 3F 91
Colechurch Ho. SE1 . . . . 1C 92
(off Avondale Sq.)
Coleford Rd. SW18 . . . . . 3E 101
Colegrave Rd. E15 . . . . . 2F 53
Colegrove Rd. SE15 . . . . 2B 92
Coleherne Ct. SW5 . . . . . 1D 87
Coleherne Mans.
SW5 . . . . 1D 87
(off Old Brompton Rd.)
Coleherne M. SW10 . . . . 1D 87
Coleherne Rd. SW10 . . . . 1D 87
Colehill Gdns. SW6 . . . . . 5A 86
Colehill La. SW6 . . . . 4A 86
Cole Ho. SE1 . . . . 4C 24
(off Baylis Rd.)
Coleman Ct. SW18 . . . . . 5C 100
Coleman Flds. N1 . . . . . . 5E 49
Coleman Mans. N8 . . . . . 2A 34
Coleman Rd. SE5 . . . . . . 3A 92
Coleman St.
EC2 . . . . 2B 18 (5F 63)
Coleman St. Bldgs.
EC2 . . . . 2B 18
Colenso Rd. E5 . . . . 1E 51
Coleraine Rd. SE3 . . . . . 2B 96

Coleridge Av. E12 . . . . . . 3F 55
Coleridge Cl. SW8 . . . . . 5D 89
Coleridge Ct. W14 . . . . . 4F 71
(off Blythe Rd.)
Coleridge Gdns. NW6 . . . 4E 45
SW10 . . . . 3D 87
Coleridge Ho. SE17 . . . . 1E 91
(off Browning St.)
SW1 . . . . 1E 89
(off Churchill Gdns.)
Coleridge La. N8 . . . . 1A 34
Coleridge Rd. N4 . . . . . . 4C 34
N8 . . . . 1F 33
Coleridge Sq. SW10 . . . . 3E 87
(off Coleridge Gdns.)
Coles Grn. Ct. NW2 . . . . . 4C 28
Coles Grn. Rd. NW2 . . . . 3C 28
Coleshill Flats SW1 . . . . 5C 74
(off Pimlico Rd.)
Colestown St. SW11 . . . . 5A 88
Cole St. SE1 . . . 4A 26 (3E 77)
Colet Ct. W6 . . . . 5F 71
(off Hammersmith Rd.)
Colet Flats E1 . . . . 5A 66
(off Troon St.)
Colet Gdns. W14 . . . . . . 5F 71
Colet Ho. SE17 . . . . 1D 91
(off Doddington Gro.)
Colette Ct. SE16 . . . . . . 3F 79
(off Eleanor Cl.)
Coley St. WC1 . . . 4A 8 (3B 62)
Colfe & Hatcliffe Glebe
SE13 . . . . 3D 109
(off Lewisham High St.)
Colfe Rd. SE23 . . . . 1A 122
Colin Dr. NW9 . . . . 1B 28
Colinette Rd. SW15 . . . . 2E 99
Colin Rd. NW10 . . . . 3C 42
Colin Winter Ho. E1 . . . . 3E 65
(off Nicholas Rd.)
Coliseum Theatre 5D 15
(off St Martin's La.)
Coliston Pas. SW18 . . . . 5C 100
Coliston Rd. SW18 . . . . . 5C 100
Collamore Av. SW18 . . . . 1A 116
Collard Pl. NW1 . . . . 4D 47
Collards Almshouses
E17 . . . . 1E 39
(off Maynard Rd.)
College App. SE10 . . . . . 2E 95
College Cl. E9 . . . . 2E 51
College Ct. NW3 . . . . 3F 45
(off College Cres.)
SW3 . . . . 1B 88
(off West Rd.)
W6 . . . . 1E 85
(off Queen Caroline St.)
College Cres. NW3 . . . . . 3E 45
College Cross N1 . . . . . . 4C 48
College E. E1 . . . . 4B 64
College Gdns. IG4: Ilf . . . 1F 41
SE21 . . . . 1A 120
SW17 . . . . 2A 116
(not continuous)
College Gro. NW1 . . . . . . 5E 47
College Hill
EC4 . . . . 4A 18 (1E 77)
College La. NW5 . . . . 1D 47
College Mans. NW6 . . . . 5A 44
(off Winchester Av.)

College M. *N1* 4C **48**
  (off College Cross,
  not continuous)
  SW1 . . . . 5D **23**
  SW18 . . . . 3D **101**
College of Arms 4F **17**
College Pde. *NW6* . . . 5A **44**
COLLEGE PARK 2D **57**
College Pk. Cl.
  SE13 . . . . 2F **109**
College Pl. *NW1* 5E **47**
  SW10 . . . . 3E **87**
College Point *E15* . . . 3B **54**
College Rd. *E17* 1E **39**
  NW10 . . . . 1E **57**
  SE19 . . . . 5A **106**
  SE21 . . . . 5A **106**
College Row *E9* 2F **51**
College St.
  EC4 . . . . 4A **18** (1E **77**)
College Ter. *E3* 2B **66**
College Vw. *SE9* . . . 1F **125**
College Yd. *NW5* . . . 1D **47**
Collent St. *E9* 3E **51**
Collerston Ho. *SE10* . . 1B **96**
  (off Armitage Rd.)
Colless Rd. *N15* 1B **36**
Collett Rd. *SE16* 4C **78**
Collier St. *N1* 1B **62**
Collingbourne Rd.
  W12 . . . . 2D **71**
Collingham Gdns.
  SW5 . . . . 5D **73**
Collingham Pl. *SW5* . . 5D **73**
Collingham Rd. *SW5* . 5D **73**
Collington St. *SE10* . . 1F **95**
Collingtree Rd.
  SE26 . . . . 4E **121**
Collingwood Ho. *E1* . . 3D **65**
  (off Darling Row)
  SE16 . . . . 3D **79**
  (off Cherry Gdn. St.)
  SW1 . . . . 1F **89**
  (off Dolphin Sq.)
  W1 . . . . 5F **5**
  (off Clipstone St.)
Collingwood Rd. *E17* . 1C **38**
Collingwood St. *E1* . . 3D **65**
Collins St. *E8* 3C **50**
Collins Ho. *E14* 1E **81**
  (off Newby Pl.)
  E15 . . . . 5B **54**
  (off John St.)
  SE10 . . . . 1B **96**
  (off Armitage Rd.)
Collinson Ct. *SE1* . . . 4F **25**
  (off Gt. Suffolk St.)
Collinson Ho. *SE15* . . 3C **92**
  (off Peckham Pk. Rd.)
Collinson St.
  SE1 . . . . 4F **25** (3E **77**)
Collinson Wlk.
  SE1 . . . . 4F **25** (3E **77**)
Collins Rd. *N5* 1E **49**
Collins Sq. *SE3* 5B **96**
Collins St. *SE3* 5A **96**
  (not continuous)
Collin's Yd. *N1* 5D **49**
Collison Pl. *N16* 3A **36**
Coll's Rd. *SE15* 4E **93**

Collyer Pl. *SE15* 4C **92**
Colman Rd. *E16* 4E **69**
Colmans Wharf *E14* . . 4D **67**
  (off Morris Rd.)
Colmar Cl. *E1* 3F **65**
Colmore M. *SE15* . . . 4D **93**
Colnbrook St.
  SE1 . . . . 5D **25** (4D **77**)
Colne Rd. *E5* 1A **52**
Colne St. *E13* 2C **68**
Cologne Rd. *SW11* . . 2F **101**
Colombo St.
  SE1 . . . . 2D **25** (2D **77**)
Colombo Street Sports Cen. &
  Community Cen.
  . . . . 2D **25**
  (off Colombo St.)
Colomb St. *SE10* . . . 1A **96**
Colonial Ct. *N7* 5B **34**
Colonnade
  WC1 . . . . 4E **7** (3A **62**)
Colonnade, The *SE8* . . 5B **80**
Colonnades, The *W2* . 5D **59**
Colonnades Wlk. *SW1* . 5D **75**
Colosseum Ter. *NW1* . 2E **5**
Colour Ct. *SW1* 2A **22**
Colson Way *SW16* . . 4E **117**
Colstead Ho. *E1* 5D **65**
  (off Watney Mkt.)
Colston Rd. *E7* 3F **55**
Colthurst Cres. *N4* . . 4D **35**
Coltman Ho. *E14* 5A **66**
  (off Maroon St.)
  SE10 . . . . 2E **95**
  (off Welland St.)
Columbas Dr. *NW3* . . 3F **31**
Columbia Point *SE16* . 4E **79**
  (off Surrey Quays Rd.)
Columbia Rd.
  E2 . . . . 1F **11** (2B **64**)
  E13 . . . . 3B **68**
Columbia Road Flower Market
  . . . . 1F **11**
  (off Columbia Rd.)
Columbine Av. *E6* . . . 4F **69**
Columbine Way *SE13* . 5E **95**
Columbus Ct. *SE16* . . 2E **79**
  (off Rotherhithe St.)
Columbus Ct. Yd.
  E14 . . . . 2C **80**
Colva Wlk. *N19* 4D **33**
Colverson Ho. *E1* . . . 4E **65**
  (off Lindley St.)
Colvestone Cres. *E8* . 2B **50**
Colview Ct. *SE9* 1F **125**
Colville Est. *N1* 5A **50**
Colville Ho. *E2* 1E **65**
  (off Waterloo Gdns.)
Colville Ho's. *W11* . . . 5B **58**
Colville M. *W11* 5B **58**
Colville Pl.
  W1 . . . . 1A **14** (4E **61**)
Colville Rd. *E11* 5E **39**
Colville Sq. *W11* 5B **58**
Colville Ter. *W11* 5B **58**

Colvin Cl. *SE26* 5E **121**
Colvin Rd. *E6* 4F **55**
Colwell Rd. *SE22* . . . 3B **106**
Colwick Cl. *N6* 2F **33**
Colwith Rd. *W6* 2E **85**
Colworth Gro.
  SE17 . . . . 5E **77**
Colworth Rd. *E11* . . . 1A **40**
Colwyn Cl. *SW16* . . . 5E **117**
Colwyn Grn. *NW9* . . . 1A **28**
  (off Snowdon Dr.)
Colwyn Ho.
  SE1 . . . . 5B **24** (4C **76**)
Colwyn Rd. *NW2* . . . 5D **29**
Colyer Cl. *N1* 1B **62**
Colyton La. *SW16* . . . 5C **118**
Colyton Rd. *SE22* . . . 3D **107**
Combe, The
  NW1 . . . . 2E **5** (2D **61**)
Combe Av. *SE3* 3B **96**
Combedale Rd. *SE10* . 1C **96**
Combemartin Rd.
  SW18 . . . . 5A **100**
Combe M. *SE3* 3B **96**
Comber Cl. *NW2* . . . 5D **29**
Comber Gro. *SE5* . . . 3E **91**
Comber Ho. *SE5* 3E **91**
Combermere Rd.
  SW9 . . . . 1B **104**
Comberton Rd. *E5* . . 4D **37**
Comedy Store 5B **14**
  (off Oxendon St.)
Comedy Theatre 5B **14**
  (off Panton St.)
Comeragh M. *W14* . . 1A **86**
Comeragh Rd. *W14* . . 1A **86**
Comerell Pl. *SE10* . . 1B **96**
Comerford Rd. *SE4* . . 2A **108**
Comet Cl. *E12* 1F **55**
Comet Pl. *SE8* 3C **94**
  (not continuous)
Comet St. *SE8* 3C **94**
Comfort St. *SE15* . . . 2A **92**
Commercial Dock Path
  SE16 . . . . 4B **80**
  (off Gulliver St.)
Commercial Rd. *E1* . . 5C **64**
  E14 . . . . 5A **66**
Commercial St.
  E1 . . . . 4F **11** (3B **64**)
Commercial Way
  SE15 . . . . 3B **92**
Commerell St. *SE10* . . 1A **96**
Commodity Quay *E1* . . 1B **78**
Commodore St. *SE8* . . 4C **94**
  (off Albyn Rd.)
Commodore Ho. *E14* . . 1E **81**
  (off Poplar High St.)
  SW18 . . . . 1E **101**
Commodore Sq.
  SW10 . . . . 4E **87**
Commodore St. *E1* . . 3A **66**
Common, The *E15* . . . 3A **54**
Commondale *SW15* . . 1E **99**
Commonfield La.
  SW17 . . . . 5A **116**
Common Mile Cl.
  SW4 . . . . 3F **103**
Common Rd. *SW13* . . 1D **99**
  W4 . . . . 5A **70**

Commonwealth Av.
W12 . . . . 1D 71
(not continuous)
Commonwealth Conference Cen.
. . . . 2A 22 (2E 75)
Commonwealth Institute
. . . . 4B 72
Community La. N7 . . . . . 2F 47
Community Rd. E15 . . . 2F 53
Como Rd. SE23 . . . . . 2A 122
Compass Ct. SE1 . . . . 2F 27
(off Shad Thames.)
Compass Hu. SW18 . . . 2D 101
Compass Point E14 . . . 1B 80
(off Grenade St.)
Compayne Gdns.
NW6 . . . . 4D 45
Compton Av. E6 . . . . . . 1F 69
N1 . . . . 3D 49
N6 . . . . 2A 32
Compton Cl. E3 . . . . . 4C 66
NW1 . . . . 2E 5
NW11 . . . . 5F 29
SE15 . . . . 3C 92
Compton Ct. SE19 . . . 5A 120
Compton Pas.
EC1 . . . . 3E 9 (3D 63)
Compton Pl.
WC1 . . . . 3D 7 (3A 62)
Compton Rd. N1 . . . . . 3D 49
NW10 . . . . 2F 57
SW19 . . . . 5B 114
Compton St.
EC1 . . . . 3E 9 (3D 63)
Compton Ter. N1 . . . . . 3D 49
Comus Ho. SE17 . . . . . 5A 78
(off Comus Pl.)
Comus Pl. SE17 . . . . . 5A 78
Comyn Rd. SW11 . . . . 2A 102
Comyns Cl. E16 . . . . . 4B 68
Conant Ho. SE11 . . . . . 2D 91
(off St Agnes Pl.)
Conant M. E1 . . . . . . 1C 78
Concanon Rd. SW2 . . 2B 104
Concert Hall App.
SE1 . . . . . . 2A 24 (2B 76)
Concordia Wharf E14 . . 2E 81
(off Coldharbour)
Condell Rd. SW8 . . . . 4E 89
Conder St. E14 . . . . . 5A 66
Condray Pl. SW11 . . . . 3A 88
Conduit Av. SE10 . . . . 4F 95
Conduit Ct. WC2 . . . . . 4D 15
Conduit M. W2 . . . . . . 5F 59
Conduit Pas. W2 . . . . . 5F 59
(off Conduit St.)
Conduit Pl. W2 . . . . . . 5F 59
Conduit St.
W1 . . . . 4E 13 (1D 75)
Conewood St. N5 . . . . 5D 35
Coney Acre SE21 . . . . 1E 119
Coney Way SW8 . . . . . 2B 90
Congers Ho. SE8 . . . . 3C 94
Congreve Ho. N16 . . . 2A 50
Congreve St. SE17 . . . 5A 78
Congreve Wlk. E16 . . . 4F 69
(off Fulmer Rd.)
Conifer Gdns.
SW16 . . . . 3A 118

Conifer Ho. SE4 . . . . . 2B 108
(off Brockley Rd.)
Coniger Rd. SW6 . . . . 5C 86
Coningham Ct. SW10 . . 3E 87
(off King's. Rd.)
Coningham M. W12 . . . 2C 70
Coningham Rd.
W12 . . . . 3D 71
Coningsby Ho. N4 . . . . 2D 35
Conington Rd. SE13 . . 5D 95
Conisborough Cres.
SE6 . . . . 3E 123
Conisbrough NW1 . . . . 5E 47
(off Bayham St.)
Coniston NW1 . . . . . . 1F 5
(off Harrington St.)
Coniston Cl. SW13 . . . 3B 84
Coniston Ct. SE16 . . . . 3F 79
(off Eleanor Cl.)
W2 . . . . 5A 60
(off Kendal St.)
Conistone Way N7 . . . 4A 48
Coniston Gdns. NW9 . . 1A 28
Coniston Ho. E3 . . . . . 3B 66
(off Southern Gro.)
SE5 . . . . 3E 91
(off Wyndham St.)
Coniston Rd.
BR1: Brom 5A 124
Coniston Wlk. E9 . . . . 2E 51
Conlan St. W10 . . . . . 3A 58
Conley Rd. NW10 . . . . 3A 42
Conley St. SE10 . . . . . 1A 96
Connaught Bri. E16 . . . 2F 83
Connaught Bus. Cen.
NW9 . . . . 1B 28
Connaught Cl. E10 . . . . 4F 37
W2 . . . . 5A 60
(off Connaught St.)
Connaught Ho.
NW10 . . . . 2D 57
(off Trenmar Gdns.)
W1 . . . . 5D 13
(off Davies St.)
Connaught Lodge N4 . . 2C 34
(off Connaught Rd.)
Connaught M. NW3 . . . 1A 46
SE11 . . . . 5C 76
(off Walcot Sq.)
SW6 . . . . 4A 86
Connaught Pl. W2 . . . . 1B 74
Connaught Rd. E11 . . . 3F 39
E16 . . . . 2F 83
E17 . . . . 1C 38
N4 . . . . 2C 34
NW10 . . . . 5A 42
Connaught Rdbt.
E16 . . . . 1F 83
(off Victoria Dock Rd.)
Connaught Sq. W2 . . . 5B 60
Connaught St. W2 . . . . 5A 60
Connell Ct. SE14 . . . . 2F 93
(off Myers La.)
Connor Cl. E11 . . . . . . 2A 40
Connor Ct. SW11 . . . . 4D 89
Conrad Ho. E14 . . . . . 1A 80
(off Victory Pl.)
E16 . . . . 2D 83
(off Wesley Av.)

Conrad Ho. N16 . . . . . 2A 50
(off Matthias Rd.)
SW8 . . . . 3A 90
(off Wyvil Rd.)
Consort Ho. E14 . . . . . 1D 95
(off St Davids Sq.)
W2 . . . . 1D 73
(off Queensway)
Consort Lodge NW8 . . 5B 46
(off Prince Albert Rd.)
Consort Rd. SE15 . . . . 4D 93
Cons St. SE1 . . . 3C 24 (3C 76)
Constable Av. E16 . . . . 2D 83
Constable Cl. NW11 . . . 1D 31
Constable Ct. SE16 . . . 1D 93
(off Stubbs Dr.)
Constable Ho. NW3 . . . 4B 46
SE21 . . . . 3A 120
Constance Allen Ho.
W10 . . . . 5F 57
(off Bridge Cl.)
Constance St. E16 . . . . 2F 83
Constant Ho. E14 . . . . 1D 81
(off Harrow La.)
Constantine Ct. E1 . . . 5C 64
(off Fairclough St.)
Constantine Rd.
NW3 . . . . 1A 46
Constitution Hill
SW1 . . . . 3D 21 (3D 75)
Content St. SE17 . . . . 5F 77
Convent Gdns. W11 . . . 5A 58
Conway Gro. W3 . . . . . 4A 56
Conway Ho. E14 . . . . . 5C 80
(off Cahir St.)
Conway M. W1 . . . . . . 4F 5
Conway Rd. NW2 . . . . 4E 29
Conway St.
W1 . . . . 4F 5 (3E 61)
(not continuous)
Conybeare NW3 . . . . . 4A 46
Conyer's Rd. SW16 . . . 5F 117
Conyer St. E3 . . . . . . 1A 66
Cook Ct. SE16 . . . . . . 2E 79
(off Rotherhithe St.)
Cookes Cl. E11 . . . . . . 4B 40
Cookham Cres. SE16 . . 3F 79
Cookham Ho. E2 . . . . . 3F 11
(off Montclare St.)
Cook's Rd. E15 . . . . . 1D 67
SE17 . . . . 2D 91
Coolfin Rd. E16 . . . . . 5C 68
Coolhurst Rd. N8 . . . . 1F 33
Cool Oak La. NW9 . . . 2A 28
Coomassie Rd. W9 . . . 3B 58
Coombe Ho. N7 . . . . . 2F 47
Coombe Lodge SE7 . . . 2E 97
Coombe Pk.
KT2: King T. 5A 112
Coomber Ho. SW6 . . . 1D 101
(off Wandsworth Bri. Rd.)
Coombe Rd. NW10 . . . 5A 28
SE26 . . . . 4D 121
W4 . . . . 1A 84
Coombs St.
N1 . . . . 1E 9 (1D 63)
Coomer M. SW6 . . . . . 2B 86
Coomer Pl. SW6 . . . . . 2B 86
Coomer Rd. SW6 . . . . . 2B 86

Cooper Cl.
SE1 . . . . 4C 24 (3C 76)
Cooper Ct. E15 . . . . . . 2D 53
Cooper Ho. NW8 . . . . . . 3F 59
(off Lyons Cl.)
Cooper Rd. NW4 . . . . . . 1F 29
NW10 . . . . 2B 42
Coopersale Rd. E9 . . . . . 2F 51
Coopers Cl. E1 . . . . 3E 65
Coopers Ct. E3 . . . . 3B 66
(off Eric St.)
Coopers La. E10 . . . . . . 3D 39
NW1 . . . . 1F 61
(not continuous)
SE12 . . . . 2D 125
Coopers Lodge SE1 . . . . 3F 27
(off Tooley St.)
Cooper's Rd. SE1 . . . . . . 1B 92
Coopers Row
EC3 . . . . 4F 19 (1B 78)
Coopers Wlk. E15 . . . . . 2A 54
Cooper's Yd. SE19 . . . . . 5A 120
Cope Ho. EC1 . . . . 2A 10
Copeland Ho. SE11 . . . . 4C 76
(off Lambeth Wlk.)
SW17 . . . . 4F 115
Copeland Rd. E17 . . . . . 1D 39
SE15 . . . . 5C 92
Copeman Cl. SE26 . . . . . 5E 121
Copenhagen Ho. N1 . . . 5B 48
(off Barnsbury Est.)
Copenhagen Pl. E14 . . . 5B 66
(not continuous)
Copenhagen St. N1 . . . . 5A 48
Cope Pl. W8 . . . . 4C 72
Cope St. SE16 . . . . 5F 79
Copford Wlk. N1 . . . . . . 5E 49
(off Popham St.)
Copgate Path SW16 . . . . 5B 118
Copleston M. SE15 . . . . 5B 92
Copleston Pas. SE5 . . . . 5B 92
Copleston Rd. SE15 . . . . 1B 106
Copley Cl. SE17 . . . . 2E 91
Copley Pk. SW16 . . . . . . 5B 118
Copley St. E1 . . . . 4F 65
Coppelia Rd. SE3 . . . . . . 2B 110
Copperas St. SE8 . . . . . . 2D 95
Copperbeech Cl.
NW3 . . . . 2F 45
Copperfield Ho. SE1 . . . . 3C 78
(off Wolseley St.)
W1 . . . . 5C 4
(off Marylebone High St.)
W11 . . . . 2F 71
(off St Ann's Rd.)
Copperfield Rd. E3 . . . . . 3A 66
Copperfield St.
SE1 . . . . 3E 25 (3D 77)
Coppermead Cl.
NW2 . . . . 5E 29
Copper Mill La.
SW17 . . . . 4E 115
Coppermill La. E17 . . . . . 1E 37
(not continuous)
Copper Row SE1 . . . . . . 1A 62
Copperworks, The
N1 . . . . 1A 62
(off Railway St.)

Coppice Dr. SW15 . . . . . 4D 99
Coppock Cl. SW11 . . . . . 5A 88
Copse Cl. SE7 . . . . 2D 97
Coptain Ho. SW18 . . . . . 2C 100
Copthall Av.
EC2 . . . . 2C 18 (5F 63)
(not continuous)
Copthall Bldgs. EC2 . . . . 2C 18
Copthall Cl.
EC2 . . . . 2B 18 (5F 63)
Copthorne Av.
SW12 . . . . 5F 103
Coptic St.
WC1 . . . . 1D 15 (4A 62)
Coral Apartments
E16 . . . . 1C 82
(off Western Gateway)
Coral Ho. E1 . . . . 3A 66
(off Harford St.)
Coral Row SW11 . . . . . . 1E 101
Coral St. SE1 . . . 4C 24 (3C 76)
Coram Ho. W4 . . . . 1A 84
(off Wood St.)
WC1 . . . . 3D 7
Coram St.
WC1 . . . . 4D 7 (3A 62)
Corbden Cl. SE15 . . . . . 4B 92
Corbet Ct.
EC3 . . . . 3C 18 (5F 63)
Corbet Ho. N1 . . . . 1C 62
(off Barnsbury Est.)
Corbet Pl. E1 . . 5F 11 (4B 64)
Corbett Ct. SE26 . . . . . . 4B 122
Corbett Ho. SW10 . . . . . 2E 87
(off Cathcart Rd.)
Corbett Rd. E11 . . . . 1E 41
Corbetts La. SE16 . . . . . 5E 79
(not continuous)
Corbetts Pas. SE16 . . . . 5E 79
(off Corbetts La.)
Corbetts Wharf SE16 . . . 3D 79
(off Bermondsey Wall E.)
Corbicum E11 . . . . 2A 40
Corbidge Ct. SE8 . . . . . . 2D 95
(off Glaisher St.)
Corbiere Ho. N1 . . . . 5F 49
(off De Beauvoir Est.)
Corbridge Cres. E2 . . . . 1D 65
Corbyn St. N4 . . . . 3A 34
Corby Way E3 . . . . 3C 66
Cordelia Cl. SE24 . . . . . 2D 105
Cordelia Ho. N1 . . . . 1A 64
(off Arden Est.)
Cordelia St. E14 . . . . 5D 67
Cording St. E14 . . . . 4D 67
Cordwainers Ct. E9 . . . . 4E 51
(off St Thomas's Sq.)
Cordwainers Wlk.
E13 . . . . 1C 68
Cord Way E14 . . . . 4C 80
Cordwell Rd. SE13 . . . . . 3A 110
Corelli Ct. SW5 . . . . 5C 72
(off W. Cromwell Rd.)
Corelli Rd. SE3 . . . . 5F 97
Corfe Ho. SW8 . . . . 3B 90
(off Dorset Rd.)
Corfield St. E2 . . . . 2D 65
Coriander Av. E14 . . . . . 5F 67
Corinne Rd. N19 . . . . . . 1E 47
Corker Wlk. N7 . . . . 4B 34

Cork Sq. E1 . . . . 2D 79
Cork St. W1 . . . 5F 13 (1E 75)
Cork St. M. W1 . . . . 5F 13
Cork Tree Ho. SE27 . . . . 5D 119
(off Lakeview Rd.)
Corlett St. NW1 . . . . 4A 60
Cormont Rd. SE5 . . . . . . 4D 91
Cormorant Ct. SE8 . . . . . 2B 94
(off Pilot Cl.)
Cormorant Lodge E1 . . . 2C 78
(off Thomas More St.)
Cormorant Rd. E7 . . . . . 2B 54
Cornbury Ho. SE8 . . . . . 2B 94
(off Evelyn St.)
Cornelia St. N7 . . . . 3B 48
Cornell Bldg. E1 . . . . 5C 64
(off Coke St.)
Corner Fielde SW2 . . . . . 1B 118
Corner Grn. SE3 . . . . 5C 96
Corner Ho. St. WC2 . . . . 1D 23
Corney Reach Way
W4 . . . . 3A 84
Corney Rd. W4 . . . . 2A 84
Cornflower Ter.
SE22 . . . . 4D 107
Cornford Gro.
SW12 . . . . 2D 117
Cornhill EC3 . . 3C 18 (5F 63)
Cornick Ho. SE16 . . . . . . 4D 79
(off Slippers Pl.)
Cornish Ho. SE17 . . . . . 2D 91
(off Brandon Est.)
Cornmill La. SE13 . . . . . 1E 109
Cornmow Dr. NW10 . . . . 2B 42
Cornthwaite Rd. E5 . . . . 5E 37
Cornwall Av. E2 . . . . 2E 65
Cornwall Cres. W11 . . . . 5A 58
Cornwall Gdns.
NW10 . . . . 3D 43
SW7 . . . . 4D 73
Cornwall Gdns. Wlk.
SW7 . . . . 4D 73
Cornwall Gro. W4 . . . . . . 1A 84
Cornwallis Ct. SW8 . . . . 4A 90
(off Lansdowne Grn.)
Cornwallis Ho. SE16 . . . 3D 79
(off Cherry Gdn. St.)
W12 . . . . 1D 71
(off India Way)
Cornwallis Rd. N19 . . . . 4A 34
Cornwallis Sq. N19 . . . . 4A 34
Cornwall Mans.
SW10 . . . . 3E 87
(off Cremorne Rd.)
W14 . . . . 4F 71
(off Blythe Rd.)
Cornwall M. Sth.
SW7 . . . . 4E 73
Cornwall M. W. SW7 . . . 4D 73
Cornwall Rd. N4 . . . . 2C 34
N15 . . . . 1F 35
SE1 . . . . 1B 24 (2C 76)
Cornwall Sq. SE11 . . . . . 1D 91
(off Seaton Cl.)
Cornwall St. E1 . . . . 1D 79
Cornwall Ter.
NW1 . . . . 4A 4 (3B 60)
Cornwall Ter. M. NW1 . . 4A 4
Corn Way E11 . . . . 5F 39
Cornwell Cres. E7 . . . . . 1E 55

Cornwood Dr. E1. . . . . . . 5E 65
Corona Bldg. E14. . . . . . 2E 81
(off Blackwall Way)
Corona Rd. SE12 . . . . . . 5C 110
Coronation Av.
  N16. . . . . 1B 50
Coronation Ct. E15. . . . . 3B 54
  W10 . . . . 4E 57
(off Brewster Gdns.)
Coronation Rd. E13 . . . . . 2E 69
Coroners Ct. NW1. . . . . . 5F 47
(off Camley St.)
Coronet Cinema 2C 72
(off Notting Hill Ga.)
Coronet St.
  N1 . . . . 2D 11 (2A 64)
Corporation Row
  EC1 . . . . 3C 8 (3C 62)
Corporation St. E15 . . . . 1A 68
  N7 . . . . 2A 48
Corrance Rd. SW2 . . . . 2A 104
Corringham Ct.
  NW11 . . . . 2C 30
Corringham Ho. E1. . . . . 5F 65
(off Pitsea St.)
Corringham Rd.
  NW11 . . . . 2C 30
Corringway NW11 . . . . . 2D 31
Corris Grn. NW9 . . . . . . 1A 28
Corry Dr. SW9 . . . . 2D 105
Corry Ho. E14. . . . . 1D 81
(off Wade's Pl.)
Corsehill St. SW16 . . . . 5E 117
Corsham St.
  N1 . . . . 2C 10 (2F 63)
Corsica St. N5 . . . . 3D 49
Corsley Way E9 . . . . . . 3B 52
(off Osborne Rd.)
Cortayne Rd. SW6 . . . . . 5B 86
Cortis Rd. SW15 . . . . . . 4D 99
Cortis Ter. SW15 . . . . . . 4D 99
Corunna Rd. SW8. . . . . . 4E 89
Corunna Ter. SW8. . . . . . 4E 89
Corvette Sq. SE10. . . . . . 2F 95
Coryton Path W9 . . . . . . 3B 58
(off Ashmore Rd.)
Cosbycote Av. SE24 . . . 3E 105
Cosgrove Ho. E2. . . . . . 5C 50
(off Whiston St.)
Cosmo Pl.
  WC1 . . . . 5E 7 (4A 62)
Cosmur Cl. W12. . . . . . . 4B 70
Cossall Wlk. SE15 . . . . 5D 93
Cossar M. SW2 . . . . . . 3C 104
Cosser St.
  SE1 . . . . 5B 24 (4C 76)
Costa St. SE15 . . . . 5C 92
Coston Wlk. SE4 . . . . . 2F 107
Cosway Mans. NW1 . . . . 4A 60
(off Shroton St.)
Cosway St. NW1. . . . . . . 4A 60
Cotall St. E14. . . . . 4C 66
Coteford St. SW17 . . . . 4B 116
Cotesbach Rd. E5. . . . . . 5E 37
Cotes Ho. NW8. . . . . . . 3A 60
(off Broadley St.)
Cotham St. SE17 . . . . . . 5F 77
Cotherstone Rd.
  SW2 . . . . 1B 118
Cotleigh Rd. NW6 . . . . . 4C 44

Cotman Cl. NW11. . . . . . 1E 31
  SW15 . . . . 4F 99
Cotman Ho. NW8 . . . . . . 1A 60
(off Townshend Est.)
Cotswold Ct. EC1 . . . . . . 3F 9
Cotswold Gdns. E6 . . . . . 2F 69
  NW2 . . . . 4F 29
Cotswold Ga. NW2 . . . . . 3A 30
Cotswold M. SW11 . . . . . 4F 87
Cotswold St. SE27 . . . . 4D 119
Cottage Cl. E1 . . . . 3E 65
(off Hayfield Pas.)
Cottage Grn. SE5 . . . . . . 3F 91
Cottage Gro. SW9 . . . . . 1A 104
Cottage Pl. SW3. . . . . . . 4A 74
Cottage Rd. N7. . . . . 2B 48
Cottage St. E14 . . . . 1D 81
Cottage Wlk. N16. . . . . . 5B 36
Cottesbrook St. SE14. . . 3A 94
Cottesloe Ho. NW8 . . . . 3A 60
(off Jerome Cres.)
Cottesloe M. SE1. . . . . . 5C 24
(off Emery St.)
Cottesloe Theatre 1B 24
(in Royal National Theatre)
Cottesmore Ct. W8 . . . . 4D 73
(off Stanford Rd.)
Cottesmore Gdns.
  W8 . . . . 4D 73
Cottingham Rd. SW8 . . . 3B 90
Cottington St. SE11 . . . . 1C 90
Cottle Way SE16 . . . . . . 3D 79
(off Paradise St.)
Cotton Av. W3 . . . . 5A 56
Cotton Cl. E11 . . . . 4A 40
Cotton Hill
  BR1: Brom 4E 123
Cotton Ho. SW2 . . . . . . 5A 104
Cotton Row SW11 . . . . . 1E 101
Cottons Cen.
  SE1 . . . . 1D 27 (2A 78)
Cotton's Gdns.
  E2. . . . . 1E 11 (2A 64)
Cottons La.
  SE1. . . . . 1C 26 (2F 77)
Cotton St. E14. . . . . 1E 81
Cottrell Ct. SE10. . . . . . 5B 82
Cottrill Gdns. E8 . . . . . . 3D 51
Coulgate St. SE4 . . . . . 1A 108
Coulson St. SW3 . . . . . . 1B 88
Coulter Rd. W6 . . . . 4D 71
Councillor St. SE5 . . . . . 3E 91
Counter Ct. SE1 . . . . . . 2B 26
(off Borough High St.)
Counter St.
  SE1 . . . . 2D 27 (2A 78)
Countess Rd. NW5 . . . . . 2E 47
County Gro. SE5 . . . . . . 4E 91
County Hall Apartments
  SE1 . . . . 3F 23
County Hall (Former)
  . . . . 3F 23 (3B 76)
County St. SE1 . . . . 4F 77
Courland Gro. SW8 . . . . 4F 89
Courland St. SW8. . . . . . 4F 89
Courtauld Ho. E2. . . . . . 5C 50
(off Goldsmith's Row)
Courtauld Institute Galleries
  . . . . 4F 15
Courtauld Rd. N19 . . . . . 3A 34

Court Cl. NW8. . . . . 4F 45
(off Boydell Ct.,
not continuous)
Courtenay Av. N6 . . . . . . 2A 32
Courtenay M. E17 . . . . . 1A 38
Courtenay Pl. E17 . . . . . 1A 38
Courtenay Rd. E11. . . . . 5B 40
Courtenay Sq. SE11. . . . 1C 90
Courtenay St. SE11 . . . . 1C 90
Court Farm Rd. SE9 . . . 2F 125
Courtfield Gdns.
  SW5 . . . . 5D 73
Courtfield Ho. EC1 . . . . . 5B 8
(off Baldwins Gdns.)
Courtfield M. SW5 . . . . . 5E 73
Courtfield Rd. SW7 . . . . 5E 73
Court Gdns. N7. . . . . 3C 48
(not continuous)
Courthill Rd. SE13 . . . . 2E 109
Courthope Ho. SE16. . . . 4E 79
(off Lower Rd.)
  SW8 . . . . 3A 90
(off Hartington Rd.)
Courthope Rd. NW3. . . . 1B 46
  SW19 . . . . 5A 114
Courtland Rd. E6 . . . . . . 5F 55
Courtlands Av.
  SE12 . . . . 3D 111
Court La. SE21 . . . . 4A 106
Court La. Gdns.
  SE21 . . . . 5A 106
Courtleigh NW11 . . . . . . 1B 30
Courtmead Cl. SE24. . . . 4E 105
Courtnell St. W2 . . . . . . 5C 58
Courtney Ct. N7. . . . . . . 2C 48
Courtney Ho. W14 . . . . . 4A 72
(off Russell Rd.)
Courtney Rd. N7. . . . . . . 2C 48
Courtrai Rd. SE23 . . . . . 4A 108
Court Royal SW15 . . . . 3A 100
Courtside N8. . . . . 1F 33
  SE26 . . . . 3D 121
Court St. E1. . . . . 4D 65
Courtville Ho. W10 . . . . 2A 58
(off Third Av.)
Courtyard, The E3 . . . . . 1C 66
  EC3. . . . . 3C 18
(in Royal Exchange)
  N1. . . . . 4B 48
  NW1 . . . . 4C 46
Courtyard Theatre, The
  King's Cross 1A 62
(off York Way)
Cousin La.
  EC4. . . . . 5B 18 (1F 77)
Couthurst Rd. SE3 . . . . . 2D 97
Coutt's Cres. NW5 . . . . . 5C 32
Couzens Ho. E3 . . . . . . 4B 66
(off Weatherley Cl.)
Covell Ct. SE8 . . . . 3C 94
COVENT GARDEN
  . . . . 4E 15 (1A 76)
Covent Garden
  . . . . 4E 15 (1A 76)
Covent Gdn.
  WC2. . . . . 4F 15 (1A 76)
Coventry Cl. NW6. . . . . . 1C 58
Coventry Cross E3 . . . . . 3E 67
Coventry Hall SW16. . . . 5A 118
Coventry Rd. E1. . . . . . . 3D 65

Coventry St.
W1 . . . . 5B **14** (1F **75**)
Coverdale Rd. NW2 . . . 4F **43**
W12 . . . . 3D **71**
Coverley Cl. E1 . . . . 4C **64**
Coverley Point SE11 . . . *5B 76*
(off Tyers St.)
Coverton Rd. SW17 . . 5A **116**
Covington Way
SW16 . . . . 5B **118**
(not continuous)
Cowcross St.
EC1 . . . . 5D **9** (4D **63**)
Cowdenbeath Path
N1 . . . . 5B **48**
Cowden St. SE6 . . . . . 4C **122**
Cowdrey Rd. SW19 . . 5D **115**
Cowick Rd. SW17 . . 4B **116**
Cowley La. E11 . . . . . . 5A **40**
Cowley Rd. E11 . . . . . . 1D **41**
SW9 . . . . 4C **90**
(not continuous)
SW14 . . . . 1A **98**
W3 . . . . 2B **70**
Cowley St.
SW1 . . . . 5D **23** (4A **76**)
Cowling Cl. W11 . . . . . . 2A **72**
Cowper Av. E6 . . . . 4F **55**
Cowper Ho. SE17 . . . . . *1E 91*
(off Browning St.)
SW1 . . . . *1F 89*
(off Aylesford St.)
Cowper Rd. N16 . . . . . . 2A **50**
SW19 . . . . 5E **115**
Cowper's Ct. EC3 . . . . *3C 18*
(off Birchin La.)
Cowper St.
EC2 . . . . 3C **10** (3F **63**)
Cowper Ter. W10 . . . . . 4A **57**
Cowthorpe Rd. SW8 . . 4F **89**
Cox Ho. W6 . . . . 2A **86**
(off Field Rd.)
Coxmount Rd. SE7 . . . . 1F **97**
Cox's Ct. E1 . . . . 1F **19**
Coxson Way
SE1 . . . . 4F **27** (3B **78**)
Cox's Wlk. SE21 . . . . 1C **120**
Crabtree Cl. E2 . . . . . . 1B **64**
Crabtree Ct. E15 . . . . . 2D **53**
Crabtree La. SW6 . . . . 3E **85**
(not continuous)
Crabtree Wlk. SE15 . . *4B 92*
(off Peckham Rd.)
Crace St. NW1 . . 1B **6** (2F **61**)
Craddock St. NW5 . . . . 3C **46**
Crafts Council & Gallery
. . . . 1C **62**
Cragie Ho. SE1 . . . . . . *5B 78*
(off Balaclava Rd.)
Craigerne Rd. SE3 . . . . 3D **97**
Craignair Rd. SW2 . . . 5C **104**
Craig's Ct.
SW1 . . . . 1D **23** (2A **76**)
Craik Ct. NW6 . . . . *1B 58*
(off Carlton Va.)
Crail Row SE17 . . . . . . 5F **77**
Cramer St.
W1 . . . . 1C **12** (4C **60**)
Crammond Cl. W6 . . . . 2A **86**
Crampton Ho. SW8 . . . 4E **89**

Crampton Rd. SE20 . . 5E **121**
Crampton St. SE17 . . . 5E **77**
Cranberry La. E16 . . . . 3A **68**
Cranbourn All.
WC2 . . . . *4C 14*
(off Cranbourn St.)
Cranbourne Gdns.
NW11 . . . . 1A **30**
Cranbourne Pas.
SE16 . . . . 3D **79**
Cranbourne Rd. E12 . . 2F **55**
E15 . . . . 1E **53**
Cranbourn Ho. SE16 . . *3D 79*
(off Marigold St.)
Cranbourn St.
WC2 . . . . 4C **14** (1F **75**)
Cranbrook NW1 . . . . . . *5E 47*
(off Camden St.)
Cranbrook Est. E2 . . . . 1F **65**
Cranbrook Rd. SE8 . . . 4C **94**
W4 . . . . 1A **84**
Cranbrook St. E2 . . . . . 1F **65**
Crandley Ct. SE8 . . . . . 5A **80**
Crane Ct. EC4 . . . . 5C **62**
Crane Gro. N7 . . . . 3C **48**
Crane Ho. E3 . . . . *1A 66*
(off Roman Rd.)
SE15 . . . . 4B **92**
Crane Mead SE16 . . . . 5F **79**
(not continuous)
Crane St. SE10 . . . . . . 1F **95**
SE15 . . . . 4B **92**
Cranfield Ct. SE27 . . 3E **119**
Cranfield Cl. W1 . . . . . 4A **60**
(off Homer St.)
Cranfield Ho. WC1 . . . . 5D **7**
Cranfield Rd. SE4 . . . 1B **108**
Cranfield Row SE1 . . . 5C **24**
Cranford Cotts. E1 . . . . *1F 79*
(off Cranford St.)
Cranford St. E1 . . . . . . 1F **79**
Cranford Way N8 . . . . . 1B **34**
Cranhurst Rd. NW2 . . . 2E **43**
Cranleigh Ho's. NW1 . . *1E 61*
(off Cranleigh St.)
Cranleigh M. SW11 . . . 5A **88**
Cranleigh St. NW1 . . . 1E **61**
CRANLEY GARDENS . . 1D **33**
Cranley Gdns. SW7 . . . 1E **87**
Cranley M. SW7 . . . . . 1E **87**
Cranley Pl. SW7 . . . . . 5F **73**
Cranley Rd. E13 . . . . . 4D **69**
Cranmer Ct. SW3 . . . . 5A **74**
SW4 . . . . 1F **103**
Cranmere Ct. SE5 . . . . 4E **91**
Cranmer Ho. SW9 . . . . *3C 90*
(off Brixton Rd.)
Cranmer Rd. E7 . . . . . 1D **55**
SW9 . . . . 3C **90**
Cranmer Ter. SW17 . . 5F **115**
Cranmore Rd.
BR1: Brom 3B **124**
Cranston Est. N1 . . . . . 1F **63**
Cranston Rd. SE23 . . . 1A **122**
Cranswick Rd. SE16 . . 1D **93**
Crantock Rd. SE6 . . . . 2D **123**
Cranwell Cl. E3 . . . . . . 3D **67**
Cranwich Rd. N16 . . . . 2F **35**
Cranwood Ct. EC1 . . . . 2C **10**

Cranwood St.
EC1 . . . . 2C **10** (2F **63**)
Cranworth Gdns.
SW9 . . . . 4C **90**
Craster Rd. SW2 . . . . 5B **104**
Crathie Rd. SE12 . . . . 4D **111**
Craven Cl. N16 . . . . . . 2C **36**
Craven Cottage 4F **85**
Craven Ct. NW10 . . . . 5A **42**
Craven Gdns.
SW19 . . . . 5C **114**
Craven Hill W2 . . . . . . 1E **73**
Craven Hill Gdns. W2 . . 1E **73**
(not continuous)
Craven Hill M. W2 . . . . 1E **73**
Craven Lodge W2 . . . . *1E 73*
(off Craven Hill)
Craven M. SW11 . . . . 1C **102**
Craven Pk. NW10 . . . . 5A **42**
Craven Pk. M. NW10 . . 4A **42**
Craven Pk. Rd. N15 . . 1B **36**
NW10 . . . . 5A **42**
Craven Pas. WC2 . . . . *1D 23*
(off Craven St.)
Craven Rd. NW10 . . . . 5A **42**
W2 . . . . 1E **73**
Craven St.
WC2 . . . . 1D **23** (2A **76**)
Craven Ter. W2 . . . . . . 1E **73**
Craven Wlk. N16 . . . . . 2C **36**
Crawford Bldgs. W1 . . . *4A 60*
(off Homer St.)
Crawford Est. SE5 . . . . 5E **91**
Crawford Mans. W1 . . . *4A 60*
(off Crawford St.)
Crawford M.
W1 . . . . 1A **12** (4B **60**)
Crawford Pas.
EC1 . . . . 4C **8** (3C **62**)
Crawford Pl. W1 . . . . . 5A **60**
Crawford Point E16 . . . *5B 68*
(off Wouldham Rd.)
Crawford Rd. SE5 . . . . 4E **91**
Crawford St.
W1 . . . . 1A **12** (4A **60**)
Crawley Rd. E10 . . . . . 3D **39**
Crawshay Ct. SW9 . . . 4C **90**
Crawthew Gro.
SE22 . . . . 2B **106**
Crayford Cl. E6 . . . . . . 5F **69**
Crayford Ho. SE1 . . . . *4C 26*
(off Long La.)
Crayford Rd. N7 . . . . . 1F **47**
Crayle Ho. EC1 . . . . . . *3E 9*
(off Malta St.)
Crealock St. SW18 . . . 4D **101**
Creasy Est. SE1 . . . . . 4A **78**
Crebor St. SE22 . . . . . 4C **106**
Credenhill Ho. SE15 . . 3D **93**
Credenhill St.
SW16 . . . . 5E **117**
Crediton Hill NW6 . . . . 2D **45**
Crediton Rd. E16 . . . . 5C **68**
NW10 . . . . 5F **43**
Credon Rd. E13 . . . . . 1E **69**
SE16 . . . . 1D **93**
Creechurch La.
EC3 . . . . 3E **19** (5A **64**)
(not continuous)
Creechurch Pl. EC3 . . . 3E **19**

Creed Ct. E1 . . . . 2A 66
EC4 . . . . 3E 17
Creed La.
EC4 . . . . 3E 17 (5D 63)
Creek Ho. W14 . . . . . . 4A 72
(off Russell Rd.)
Creek Rd. SE8 . . . . 2C 94
SE10 . . . . 2C 94
Creekside SE8 . . . . 3D 95
Creeland Gro. SE6 . . . . 1B 122
Crefeld Cl. W6 . . . . 2A 86
Creighton Av. E6 . . . . . . 1F 69
Creighton Cl. W12 . . . . . 1C 70
Creighton Rd. NW6 . . . . 1F 57
Cremer Bus. Cen.
E2 . . . . 1F 11
(off Cremer St.)
Cremer Ho. SE8 . . . . . . 3C 94
(off Deptford Chu. St.)
Cremer St.
E2 . . . . 1F 11 (1B 64)
Cremorne Est. SW10 . . . 2F 87
Cremorne Rd. SW10 . . . . 3E 87
Creon Ct. SW9 . . . . 3C 90
(off Caldwell St.)
Crescent EC3 . . 4F 19 (1B 78)
Crescent, The E17 . . . . . 1A 38
NW2 . . . . 5D 29
SW13 . . . . 5B 84
SW19 . . . . 3C 114
W3 . . . . 5A 56
Crescent Arc. SE10 . . . . 2E 95
(off Creek Rd.)
Crescent Ct. SW4 . . . . . 3F 103
(off Park Hill)
Crescent Ct. Bus. Cen.
E16 . . . . 3F 67
Crescent Gdns.
SW19 . . . . 3C 114
Crescent Gro. SW4 . . . . 2E 103
Crescent Ho. EC1 . . . . . 4F 9
(off Golden La. Est.)
SE13 . . . . 5D 95
Crescent La. SW4 . . . . . 2E 103
Crescent Pl. SW3 . . . . . 5A 74
Crescent Rd. E6 . . . . . . 5E 55
E10 . . . . 4D 39
E13 . . . . 5C 54
N8 . . . . 1F 33
Crescent Row
EC1 . . . . 4F 9 (3E 63)
Crescent Stables
SW15 . . . . 3A 100
Crescent St. N1 . . . . . . 4B 48
Crescent Way SE4 . . . . . 1C 108
Crescent Wharf E16 . . . . 3D 83
Crescent Wood Rd.
SE26 . . . . 3C 120
Cresford Rd. SW6 . . . . . 4C 87
Crespigny Rd. NW4 . . . . 1D 29
Cressal Ho. E14 . . . . . . 4C 80
(off Tiller Rd.)
Cresset Rd. E9 . . . . 3E 51
Cresset St. SW4 . . . . . . 1F 103
Cressfield Cl. NW5 . . . . 2C 46
Cressida Rd. N19 . . . . . 3E 33
Cressingham Rd.
SE13 . . . . 1E 109
Cressington Cl. N16 . . . . 2A 50
Cress M. BR1: Brom . . . 5F 123

Cresswell Gdns. SW5 . . . 1E 87
Cresswell Pk. SE3 . . . . . 1B 110
Cresswell Pl. SW10 . . . . 1E 87
Cressy Ct. E1 . . . . 4E 65
W6 . . . . 4D 71
Cressy Ho's. E1 . . . . . . 4E 65
(off Hannibal Rd.)
Cressy Pl. E1 . . . . 4E 65
Cressy Rd. NW3 . . . . . . 2B 46
Cresta Ho. NW3 . . . . . . 4F 45
(off Finchley Rd.)
Crestfield St.
WC1 . . . . 1E 7 (2A 62)
Crest Rd. NW2 . . . . 4B 28
Crestway SW15 . . . . . . 4C 98
Creswick Wlk. E3 . . . . . 2C 66
Crewe Pl. NW10 . . . . . . 2B 56
Crewkerne Ct. SW11 . . . 4F 87
(off Bolingbroke Wlk.)
Crews St. E14 . . . . 5C 80
Crewys Rd. NW2 . . . . . . 4B 30
SE15 . . . . 5D 93
Crichton St. SW8 . . . . . 5E 89
Cricketers Ct. SE11 . . . . 5D 77
(off Kennington La.)
Cricketers M. SW18 . . . . 3D 101
Cricketers Wlk.
SE26 . . . . 5E 121
Cricketfield Rd. E5 . . . . 1D 51
Cricket La.
BR3: Beck 5A 122
Cricklade Av. SW2 . . . . 2A 118
CRICKLEWOOD 2F 43
Cricklewood B'way.
NW2 . . . . 5E 29
Cricklewood La. NW2 . . . 1F 43
Cridland St. E15 . . . . . . 5B 54
Crieff Rd. SW18 . . . . . . 4E 101
Criffel Av. SW2 . . . . . . 2F 117
Crimscott St.
SE1 . . . . 5E 27 (4A 78)
Crimsworth Rd. SW8 . . . 4F 89
Crinan St. N1 . . . . 1A 62
Cringle St. SW8 . . . . . . 3E 89
Cripplegate St.
EC2 . . . . 5A 10 (4E 63)
Crispe Ho. N1 . . . . 5B 48
(off Barnsbury Est.)
Crispian Cl. NW10 . . . . 1A 42
Crispin St. E1 . . 1F 19 (4B 64)
Crisp Rd. W6 . . . . 1E 85
Cristowe Rd. SW6 . . . . . 5B 86
Criterion Ct. E8 . . . . . . 4B 50
(off Middleton Rd.)
Criterion M. N19 . . . . . . 4F 33
Criterion Theatre 5B 14
(off Piccadilly)
Crockerton Rd.
SW17 . . . . 2B 116
Croft, The NW10 . . . . . 1B 56
Croft Ct. SE13 . . . . 4E 109
Croftdown Rd. NW5 . . . . 5C 32
Crofters Ct. SE8 . . . . . . 5A 80
(off Croft St.)
Crofters Way NW1 . . . . . 5F 47
Croft Ho. W10 . . . . 2A 58
(off Third Av.)
Croftongate Way
SE4 . . . . 3A 108

Crofton Leisure Cen.
. . . . 4C 108
CROFTON PARK 3B 108
Crofton Pk. Rd. SE4 . . . 4B 108
Crofton Rd. E13 . . . . . . 3D 69
SE5 . . . . 4A 92
Crofton Ter. E5 . . . . 2A 52
Crofts Ho. E2 . . . . 1C 64
(off Teale St.)
Crofts St. E1 . . . . 1C 78
Croft St. SE8 . . . . 5A 80
Croftway NW3 . . . . 1C 44
Crogsland Rd. NW1 . . . . 4C 46
Cromartie Rd. N19 . . . . 2F 33
Cromarty Ct. SW2 . . . . . 3B 104
Cromarty Ho. E1 . . . . . . 4A 66
(off Ben Jonson Rd.)
Crombie M. SW11 . . . . . 5A 88
Crome Rd. NW10 . . . . . 3A 42
Cromer Rd. E10 . . . . . . 2F 39
SW17 . . . . 5C 116
Cromer St.
WC1 . . . . 2D 7 (2A 62)
Cromer Ter. E8 . . . . 2C 50
Cromer Vs. Rd.
SW18 . . . . 4B 100
Cromford Path E5 . . . . . 1F 51
Cromford Rd. SW18 . . . 3C 100
Crompton Ct. SW3 . . . . 5A 74
Crompton Ho. SE1 . . . . . 4E 77
(off County St.)
W2 . . . . 3F 59
(off Hall Pl.)
Crompton St. W2 . . . . . . 3F 59
Cromwell Av. N6 . . . . . . 3D 33
W6 . . . . 1D 85
Cromwell Cl. E1 . . . . . . 2C 78
Cromwell Cres. SW5 . . . 5C 72
Cromwell Gdns. SW7 . . . 4F 73
Cromwell Gro. W6 . . . . . 4E 71
Cromwell Highwalk
EC2 . . . . 5A 10
Cromwell Ind. Est.
E10 . . . . 3A 38
Cromwell Lodge E1 . . . . 3E 65
(off Cleveland Gro.)
Cromwell M. SW7 . . . . . 5F 73
Cromwell Pl. EC2 . . . . . 5A 10
(off Beech St.)
N6 . . . . 3D 33
SW7 . . . . 5F 73
Cromwell Rd. E7 . . . . . . 4E 55
E17 . . . . 1E 39
SW5 . . . . 5C 72
SW7 . . . . 5C 72
SW9 . . . . 4D 91
SW19 . . . . 5C 114
Cromwell Twr. EC2 . . . . 5A 10
Crondace Rd. SW6 . . . . 4C 86
Crondall Ct. N1 . . . . . . 1C 10
Crondall Ho. SW15 . . . . 5C 98
Crondall St.
N1 . . . . 1C 10 (1F 63)
Crone Ct. NW6 . . . . 1B 58
(off Denmark Rd.)
Cronin St. SE15 . . . . . . 3B 91
Crooked Billet Yd.
E2 . . . . 2E 11 (2A 64)
Crooke Rd. SE8 . . . . . . 1A 94
Crookham Rd. SW6 . . . . 4B 86

Croombs Rd.—Culford Rd.

Croombs Rd. E16 . . . . . 4E 69
Croom's Hill SE10 . . . . . 3E 95
Croom's Hill Gro.
  SE10 . . . . 3E 95
Cropley Ct. N1 . . . . . . 1F 63
  (off Cropley St.,
  not continuous)
Cropley St.
  N1 . . . . 1B 10 (1F 63)
Cropthorne Ct. W9 . . . . 2E 59
Crosby Ct.
  SE1 . . . . 3B 26 (3F 77)
Crosby Ho. E7 . . . . 3C 54
  E14 . . . . 4E 81
    (off Manchester Rd.)
Crosby Rd. E7 . . . . 3C 54
Crosby Row
  SE1 . . . . 4B 26 (3F 77)
Crosby Sq.
  EC3 . . . . 3D 19 (5A 64)
Crosby Wlk. E8 . . . . . . 3B 50
  SW2 . . . . 5C 104
Crosby Way SW2 . . . . . 5C 104
Crosier Cl. SE3 . . . . . . 4F 97
Crosland Pl.
  SW11 . . . . 1C 102
Cross Av. SE10 . . . . . . 2F 95
Crossbrook Rd. SE3 . . . 5F 97
Cross Cl. SE15 . . . . . . 5D 93
Crossfield Ho. W11 . . . . 1A 72
    (off Mary Pl.)
Crossfield Rd. NW3 . . . 3F 45
Crossfield St. SE8 . . . . 3C 94
    (not continuous)
Crossford St. SW9 . . . . 5B 90
Cross Keys Cl.
  W1 . . . . 1C 12 (4C 60)
Cross Keys Sq. EC1 . . . 1F 17
    (off Little Britain)
Crossleigh Ct. SE14 . . . 3B 94
    (off New Cross Rd.)
Crosslet St. SE17 . . . . . 5F 77
Crosslet Va. SE10 . . . . 4D 95
Crossley St. N7 . . . . . . 3E 48
Crossmount Ho. SE5 . . . 3E 91
    (off Bowyer St.)
Cross Rd. SE5 . . . . 5A 92
Cross St. N1 . . . . 5D 49
  SE5 . . . . 1F 105
  SW13 . . . . 5A 84
Crossthwaite Av.
  SE5 . . . . 2F 105
Crosswall
  EC3 . . . . 4F 19 (1B 78)
Crossway N16 . . . . 2A 50
Crossway, The SE9 . . . . 2F 125
Crossway Ct. SE4 . . . . . 5A 94
Crossways Ter. E5 . . . . 1E 51
Croston St. E8 . . . . 5C 50
CROUCH END 2F 33
Crouch End Hill N8 . . . . 2F 33
Crouch Hall Ct. N19 . . . 3A 34
Crouch Hall Rd. N8 . . . 1F 33
Crouch Hill N4 . . . . 1A 34
  N8 . . . . 1A 34
Crouch Hill Recreation Cen.
  . . . . 2A 34

Crouchman's Cl.
  SE26 . . . . 3B 120
Crowborough Rd.
  SW17 . . . . 5C 116
Crowder St. E1 . . . . . . 1D 79
Crowfield Ho. N5 . . . . . 1E 49
Crowfoot Cl. E9 . . . . . . 2B 52
Crowhurst Cl. SW9 . . . . 5C 90
Crowhurst Ho.
  SW9 . . . . 5B 90
    (off Aytoun Rd.)
Crowland Ho. NW8 . . . . 5E 45
    (off Springfield Rd.)
Crowland Rd. N15 . . . . 1B 36
Crowland Ter. N1 . . . . . 4F 49
Crowline Wlk. N1 . . . . . 3E 49
Crowmarsh Gdns.
  SE23 . . . . 5E 107
Crown Cl. E3 . . . . 5C 52
  NW6 . . . . 3D 45
Crown Cl. Bus. Cen.
  E3 . . . . 5C 52
    (off Crown Cl.)
Crown Ct. EC2 . . . . 3A 18
  SE12 . . . . 4D 111
  WC2 . . . . 3E 15 (5A 62)
Crown Dale SE19 . . . . . 5D 119
Crowndale Ct. NW1 . . . . 1F 61
    (off Crowndale Rd.)
Crowndale Rd. NW1 . . . 1E 61
Crownfield Rd. E15 . . . . 1F 53
Crown Hill Rd. NW10 . . 5B 42
Crown La. NW16 . . . . . 5C 118
Crown La. Gdns.
  SW16 . . . . 5C 118
Crown Lodge SW3 . . . . 5A 74
    (off Elystan St.)
Crown M. E1 . . . . 4F 65
    (off White Horse La.)
  E13 . . . . 5E 55
  W6 . . . . 5C 70
Crown Office Row
  EC4 . . . . 4B 16 (1C 76)
Crown Pas.
  SW1 . . . . 2A 22 (2E 75)
Crown Pl.
  EC2 . . . . 5D 11 (4A 64)
    (not continuous)
  NW5 . . . . 3D 47
  SE16 . . . . 1D 93
Crown Point SE19 . . . . 5D 119
Crown Reach SW1 . . . . 1F 89
Crownstone Ct.
  SW2 . . . . 3C 104
Crownstone Rd.
  SW2 . . . . 3C 104
Crown St. SE5 . . . . 3E 91
Crown Wharf E14 . . . . . 2E 81
    (off Coldharbour)
  SE8 . . . . 1B 94
    (off Grove St.)
Crows Rd. E15 . . . . 2F 67
Crowther Cl. SW6 . . . . . 2B 86
    (off Bucklers All.)
Crowthorne Cl.
  SW18 . . . . 5B 100
Crowthorne Rd. W10 . . 5F 57
Croxley Rd. W9 . . . . . . 2B 58
Croxted Cl. SE21 . . . . . 5E 105
Croxted M. SE24 . . . . . 4E 105

Croxted Rd. SE21 . . . . 5E 105
  SE24 . . . . 5E 105
Croxteth Ho. SW8 . . . . 5F 89
Croydon Ho. SE1 . . . . . 3C 24
    (off Wootton St.)
Croydon Rd. E13 . . . . . 3B 68
Crozier Ho. SE3 . . . . . . 1D 111
  SW8 . . . . 3B 90
    (off Wilkinson St.)
Crozier Ter. E9 . . . . . . 2F 51
Crucifix La.
  SE1 . . . . 3E 27 (3A 78)
Cruden Ho. SE17 . . . . . 2D 91
    (off Brandon Est.)
Cruden St. N1 . . . . 5D 49
Cruikshank Ho. NW8 . . 1A 60
    (off Townshend Rd.)
Cruikshank Rd. E15 . . . 1A 54
Cruikshank St.
  WC1 . . . . 1B 8 (2C 62)
Crummock Gdns.
  NW9 . . . . 1A 28
Crusader Ind. Est. N4 . . 1E 35
Crusoe M. N16 . . . . . . 4F 35
Crutched Friars
  EC3 . . . . 4E 19 (1A 78)
Crutchley Rd. SE6 . . . . 2A 124
CRYSTAL PALACE 5B 120
Crystal Palace Athletics
  Stadium 5C 120
Crystal Palace Mus.
  . . . . 5B 120
Crystal Palace National
  Sports Cen. 5C 120
Crystal Palace Pde.
  SE19 . . . . 5B 120
Crystal Pal. Pk. Rd.
  SE26 . . . . 5C 120
Crystal Pal. Rd.
  SE22 . . . . 4B 106
Crystal Ter. SE19 . . . . . 5F 119
Crystal Vw. Ct.
  BR1: Brom 4F 123
Crystal Wharf N1 . . . . . 1D 63
Cuba St. E14 . . . . 3C 80
Cube Ho.
  SE16 . . . . 5F 27 (4B 78)
Cubitt Ho. SW4 . . . . . . 4E 103
Cubitt Steps E14 . . . . . 2C 80
Cubitt St.
  WC1 . . . . 2A 8 (2B 62)
Cubitt's Yd. WC2 . . . . . 4E 15
Cubitt Ter. SW4 . . . . . . 1E 103
CUBITT TOWN 5E 81
Cuddington SE17 . . . . . 5E 77
    (off Deacon Way)
Cudham St. SE6 . . . . . . 5E 109
Cudworth Ho. SW8 . . . . 4E 89
Cudworth St. E1 . . . . . 3D 65
Cuff Cres. SE9 . . . . 4F 111
Cuffley Ho. W10 . . . . . . 4E 57
    (off Sutton Way)
Cuff Point E2 . . . . 1F 11
    (off Columbia Rd.)
Culford Gdns. SW3 . . . 5B 74
Culford Gro. N1 . . . . . . 3A 50
Culford Mans. SW3 . . . 5B 74
    (off Culford Gdns.)
Culford M. N1 . . . . 3A 50
Culford Rd. N1 . . . . . . 4A 50

Culham Ho. *E2* 2F **11**
  (off Palissy St.)
Culling Rd. SE16 . . . . . . 4E **79**
Cullingworth Rd.
  NW10 . . . . 2C **42**
Culloden Cl. SE16 . . . 1C **92**
Cullum St.
  EC3 . . . . 4D **19** (1A **78**)
Cullum Welch Ct.
  N1 . . . . 1C **10**
  (off Haberdasher St.)
Cullum Welch Ho. *EC1* . . . 4F **9**
  (off Goswell Rd.)
Culmore Rd. SE15 . . . 3D **93**
Culmstock Rd.
  SW11 . . . . 3C **102**
Culpeper Ho. E14 . . . . 5A **66**
Culpepper Ct. SE11 . . 5C **76**
  (off Kennington Rd.)
Culross Bldgs. NW1 . . 1A **62**
  (off Battle Bri. Rd.)
Culross Ho. W10 . . . . . . 5F **57**
  (off Bridge Cl.)
Culross St.
  W1 . . . . 5B **12** (1C **74**)
Culverden Rd.
  SW12 . . . . 2E **117**
Culverhouse St. 1F **15**
  (off Red Lion Sq.)
Culverhouse Gdns.
  SW16 . . . . 3B **118**
Culverley Rd. SE6 . . . 1D **123**
Culvert Pl. SW11 . . . . 5C **88**
Culvert Rd. N15 . . . . . 1A **36**
  SW11 . . . . 5B **88**
Culworth Ho. *NW8* . . . 1A **60**
  (off Allitsen Rd.)
Culworth St. NW8 . . . . 1A **60**
Culzean Cl. SE27 . . . . 3D **119**
Cumberland Cl. E8 . . . 3B **50**
Cumberland Ct. SW1 . . 1D **89**
  (off Cumberland St.)
Cumberland Cres.
  W14 . . . . 5A **72**
  (not continuous)
Cumberland Gdns.
  WC1 . . . . 1B **8** (2C **62**)
Cumberland Ga.
  W1 . . . . 4A **12** (1B **74**)
Cumberland Ho.
  E16 . . . . 2C **82**
  (off Wesley Av.)
Cumberland Mans.
  W1 . . . . 5B **60**
  (off George St.)
Cumberland Mkt.
  NW1 . . . . 1E **5** (2D **61**)
Cumberland Mills Sq.
  E14 . . . . 1F **95**
Cumberland Pk. Ind. Est.
  NW10 . . . . 2C **56**
Cumberland Pl.
  NW1 . . . . 1D **5** (2D **61**)
  SE6 . . . . 1B **124**
Cumberland Rd. E12 . . 1F **55**
  E13 . . . . 4D **69**
  SW13 . . . . 4B **84**
Cumberland St. SW1 . . 1D **89**
Cumberland Ter.
  NW1 . . . . 1D **5** (1D **61**)

Cumberland Ter. M.
  NW1 . . . . 1D **5**
  (not continuous)
Cumbrian Gdns. NW2 . . 4F **29**
Cuming Mus. 5E **77**
  (off Walworth Rd.)
Cumming St.
  N1 . . . . 1A **8** (1B **62**)
  (off Robsart St.)
Cumnor Cl. SW9 . . . . . . 5B **90**

Cunard Pl.
  EC3 . . . . 3E **19** (5A **64**)
Cunard Rd. NW10 . . . . 2A **56**
Cunard Wlk. SE16 . . . . 5F **79**
Cundy Rd. E16 . . . . 5F **69**
Cundy St. SW1 . . . . . . 5C **74**
Cunliffe St. SW16 . . . . 5E **117**
Cunningham Ho.
  SE5 . . . . 3F **91**
  (off Elmington Est.)
Cunningham Pl.
  NW8 . . . . 3F **59**
Cupar Rd. SW11 . . . . . . 4C **88**
Cupola Cl.
  BR1: Brom 5D **125**
Cureton St. SW1 . . . . . . 5F **75**
Curlew Ho. *SE4* 2A **108**
  (off St Norbert Rd.)
  SE15 . . . . 4B **92**
Curlew St.
  SE1 . . . . 3F **27** (3B **78**)
Curness St. SE13 . . . . . 2E **109**
Curnick's La. SE27 . . . 4E **119**
Curran Ho. *SW3* 5A **74**
  (off Lucan Pl.)
Curricle St. W3 . . . . . . 2A **70**
Currie Hill Cl.
  SW19 . . . . 4B **114**
Currie Ho. *E14* 5F **67**
  (off Abbott Rd.)
Cursitor St.
  EC4 . . . . 2B **16** (5C **62**)
Curtain Pl.
  EC2 . . . . 3E **11** (2A **64**)
Curtain Rd.
  EC2 . . . . 2E **11** (3A **64**)
Curtis Dr. W3 . . . . 5A **56**
Curtis Fld. Rd.
  SW16 . . . . 4B **118**
Curtis Ho. *SE17* 1F **91**
  (off Morecambe St.)
Curtis St. SE1 . . . . 5B **78**
Curtis Way SE1 . . . . . . 5B **78**
Curve, The W12 . . . . . . 1C **70**
Curwen Av. E7 . . . . 1D **55**
Curwen Rd. W12 . . . . . 3C **70**
Curzon Cinema
  Mayfair 2D **21**
  (off Curzon St.)
  Soho 4C **14**
  (off Shaftesbury Av.)
Curzon Ct. SW6 . . . . . . 4E **87**
  (off Imperial Rd.)
Curzon Cres. NW10 . . . 4A **42**
Curzon Ga.
  W1 . . . . 2C **20** (2C **74**)
Curzon Sq.
  W1 . . . . 2C **20** (2C **74**)
Curzon St.
  W1 . . . . 2C **20** (2C **74**)

Custance Ho. *N1* 1B **10**
  (off Fairbank Est.)
Custance St.
  N1 . . . . 1B **10** (2F **63**)
CUSTOM HOUSE 5E **69**
Custom House
  . . . . 5D **19** (1A **78**)
Custom Ho. Reach
  SE16 . . . . 3B **80**
Custom Ho. Wlk.
  EC3 . . . . 5D **19** (1A **78**)
Cut, The SE1 . . 3C **24** (3C **76**)
Cutbush Ho. N7 . . . . . . 2F **47**
Cutcombe Rd. SE5 . . . . 5E **91**
Cuthbert Harrowing Ho.
  EC1 . . . . 4F **9**
  (off Golden La. Est.)
Cuthbert Ho. *W2* 4F **59**
  (off Hall Pl.)
Cuthbert St. W2 . . . . . . 4F **59**
Cuthill Wlk. SE5 . . . . . . 4F **91**
Cutlers Gdns. EC2 . . . . 1E **19**
Cutlers Sq. E14 . . . . . . 5C **80**
Cutler St. E1 . . 2E **19** (5A **64**)
Cutty Sark 2E **95**
Cutty Sark Gdns.
  SE10 . . . . 2E **95**
  (off King William Wlk.)
Cyclops M. E14 . . . . . . 5C **80**
Cygnet Cl. NW10 . . . . . 2A **42**
Cygnet Ho. SW18 . . . . 1E **101**
Cygnet Ho. Nth. *E14* . . 5D **67**
  (off Chrisp St.)
Cygnet Ho. Sth. *E14* . . 5D **67**
  (off Chrisp St.)
Cygnet St. E1 . . 3F **11** (3B **64**)
Cygnus Bus. Cen.
  NW10 . . . . 2B **42**
Cynthia St. N1 . . 1A **8** (1B **62**)
Cyntra Pl. E8 . . . . 4D **51**
Cypress Gdns. SE4 . . . 3A **108**
Cypress Ho. SE14 . . . . 4F **93**
  SE16 . . . . 3F **79**
  (off Woodland Cres.)
Cypress Pl.
  W1 . . . . 4A **6** (3E **61**)
Cyprus Cl. N4 . . . . 1D **35**
Cyprus Pl. E2 . . . . 1E **65**
Cyprus St. E2 . . . . 1E **65**
  (not continuous)
Cyrena Rd. SE22 . . . . . 4B **106**
Cyril Mans.
  SW11 . . . . 4B **88**
Cyrus Ho. EC1 . . . . 3E **9**
Cyrus St. EC1 . . . . 3E **9**
Czar St. SE8 . . . . 2C **94**

D

Dabbs La. *EC1* 4C **8**
  (off Farringdon Rd.)
Dabin Cres. SE10 . . . . 4E **95**
Dacca St. SE8 . . . . 2B **94**
Dace Rd. E3 . . . . 5C **52**
Dacre Ho. *SW3* 2F **87**
  (off Beaufort St.)
Dacre Pk. SE13 . . . . . . 1A **110**
Dacre Pl. SE13 . . . . . . 1A **110**

Dacre Rd. E11 . . . . 3B 40
  E13 . . . . 5D 55
Dacres Est. SE23 . . . . . 3F 121
Dacres Ho. SW4 . . . . . . 1D 103
Dacres Rd. SE23 . . . . . 2F 121
Dacre St.
  SW1 . . . . 5B 22 (4F 75)
Daffodil St. W12 . . . . 1B 70
Dafforne Rd. SW17 . . . . . 3C 116
Da Gama Pl. E14 . . . . 1C 94
Dagenham Rd. E10 . . . . . 3B 38
Dagmar Ct. E14 . . . . 4E 61
Dagmar Gdns. NW10 . . . 1F 57
Dagmar Pas. N1 . . . . 5D 49
            (off Cross St.)
Dagmar Rd. N4 . . . . 2C 34
  SE5 . . . . 4A 92
Dagmar Ter. N1 . . . . 5D 49
Dagnall St. SW11 . . . . . . 5B 88
Dagnan Rd. SW12 . . . . . 5D 103
Dagobert Ho. E1 . . . . 4E 65
         (off Smithy St.)
Dagonet Gdns.
  BR1: Brom 3C 124
Dagonet Rd.
  BR1: Brom 3C 124
Dahomey Rd. SW16 . . . . 5E 117
Dain Ct. W8 . . . . 5C 72
       (off Lexham Gdns.)
Dainford Cl.
  BR1: Brom 5F 123
Daintry Way E9 . . . . 3B 52
Dairy Cl. NW10 . . . . 5C 42
Dairyman Cl. NW2 . . . . . 5F 29
Dairy M. SW9 . . . . 1A 104
Dairy Wlk. SW19 . . . . . . 4A 114
Daisy Dobbins Wlk.
  N19 . . . . 2A 34
     (off Jessie Blythe La.)
Daisy La. SW6 . . . . 1C 100
Daisy Rd. E16 . . . . 3A 68
Dakin Pl. E1 . . . . 4A 66
Dakota Gdns. E6 . . . . . . 3F 69
Dalberg Rd. SW2 . . . . . 2C 104
      (not continuous)
Dalby Rd. SW18 . . . . . . 2E 101
Dalby St. NW5 . . . . 3D 47
Dalebury Rd. SW17 . . . . 2B 116
Dale Cl. SE3 . . . . 1C 110
Daleham Gdns. NW3 . . . 2F 45
Daleham M. NW3 . . . . . 3F 45
Dalehead NW1 . . . . 1F 5
    (off Hampstead Rd.)
Dale Ho. NW8 . . . . 5E 45
      (off Boundary Rd.)
  SE4 . . . . 2A 108
Dale Lodge N6 . . . . 1E 33
Dalemain M. E16 . . . . . . 2C 82
Dale Rd. NW5 . . . . 2C 46
  SE17 . . . . 2D 91
Dale Row W11 . . . . 5A 58
Daleside Rd. SW16 . . . . 5D 117
Dale St. W4 . . . . 1A 84
Daleview Rd. N15 . . . . . 1A 36
Daley Ho. W12 . . . . 5D 57
Daley St. E9 . . . . 3F 51
Daley Thompson Way
  SW8 . . . . 5D 89
Dalgarno Gdns. W10 . . . 4E 57
Dalgarno Way W10 . . . . 3E 57

Dalgleish St. E14 . . . . . . 5A 66
Daling Way E3 . . . . 5A 52
Dali Universe
         . . . 3F 23 (3B 76)
Dalkeith Ct. SW1 . . . . . . 5F 75
       (off Vincent St.)
Dalkeith Ho. SW9 . . . . . 4D 91
       (off Lothian Rd.)
Dalkeith Rd. SE21 . . . . . 1E 119
Dallas Rd. NW4 . . . . 2C 28
  SE26 . . . . 3D 121
Dallinger Rd. SE12 . . . . 4B 110
Dalling Rd. W6 . . . . 5D 71
Dallington Sq. EC1 . . . . . 3E 9
        (off Berry St.)
Dallington St.
  EC1 . . . . 3E 9 (3D 63)
Dalmain Rd. SE23 . . . . . 1F 121
Dalmeny Av. N7 . . . . 1F 47
Dalmeny Rd. N7 . . . . 5F 33
      (not continuous)
Dalmeyer Rd. NW10 . . . 3B 42
Dalmore Rd. SE21 . . . . . 2E 119
Dalo Lodge E3 . . . . 4C 66
        (off Gale St.)
Dalrymple Rd. SE4 . . . . 2A 108
DALSTON 3B 50
Dalston La. E8 . . . . 3B 50
Dalton Ho. SE14 . . . . . . 2F 93
    (off John Williams Cl.)
  SW1 . . . . 1D 89
      (off Ebury Bri. Rd.)
Dalton St. SE27 . . . . 2D 119
Dalwood St. SE5 . . . . . . 4A 92
Daly Ct. E15 . . . . 2D 53
Dalyell Rd. SW9 . . . . . . 1B 104
Damascene Wlk.
  SE21 . . . . 1E 119
Damask Cres. E16 . . . . . 3A 68
Damer Ter. SW10 . . . . . . 3E 87
Dames Rd. E7 . . . . 5C 40
Dame St. N1 . . . . 1E 63
Damien Ct. E1 . . . . 5D 65
      (off Damien St.)
Damien St. E1 . . . . 5D 65
Damory Ho. SE16 . . . . . 5D 79
     (off Abbeyfield St.)
Danbury St. N1 . . . . 1D 63
Danby Ho. E9 . . . . 4E 51
     (off Frampton Pk. Rd.)
Danby St. SE15 . . . . 1B 106
Dando Cres. SE3 . . . . . . 1D 111
Dandridge Cl. SE10 . . . . 1B 96
Dandridge Ho. E1 . . . . . 5F 11
       (off Lamb St.)
Danebury Av. SW15 . . . . 4A 98
      (not continuous)
Daneby Rd. SE6 . . . . 3D 123
Danehurst St. SW6 . . . . 4A 86
Danemere St. SW15 . . . . 1E 99
Dane Pl. E3 . . . . 1A 66
Danes Ct. NW8 . . . . 5B 46
    (off St Edmund's Ter.)
Danescroft NW4 . . . . 1F 29
Danescroft Av. NW4 . . . . 1F 29
Danescroft Gdns.
  NW4 . . . . 1F 29

Danesdale Rd. E9 . . . . . 3A 52
Danesfield SE5 . . . . 2A 92
      (off Albany Rd.)
Danes Ho. W10 . . . . 4E 57
      (off Sutton Way)
Dane St.
  WC1 . . . . 1F 15 (4B 62)
Daneswood Av. SE6 . . . . 3E 123
Daneville Rd. SE5 . . . . . 4F 91
Dangan Rd. E11 . . . . 1C 40
Daniel Bolt Cl. E14 . . . . 4D 67
Daniel Cl. SW17 . . . . . . 5A 116
Daniel Gdns. SE15 . . . . 3B 92
Daniell Ho. N1 . . . . 1F 63
     (off Cranston Est.)
Daniel Pl. NW4 . . . . 2D 29
Daniels Rd. SE15 . . . . . 1E 107
Dan Leno Wlk. SW6 . . . . 3D 87
Dan Mason Dr. W4 . . . . . 5A 84
Dansey Pl. W1 . . . . 4B 14
Danson Rd. SE17 . . . . . 1D 91
Dante Pl. SE11 . . . . 5D 77
Dante Rd. SE11 . . . . 5D 77
Danube Ct. SE15 . . . . . . 3B 92
     (off Daniel Gdns.)
Danube St. SW3 . . . . 1A 88
Danvers Ho. E1 . . . . 5C 64
     (off Christian St.)
Danvers St. SW3 . . . . . . 2F 87
Da Palma Ct. SW6 . . . . . 2C 86
      (off Anselm Rd.)
Daphne St. SW18 . . . . . 4E 101
Daplyn St. E1 . . . . 4C 64
D'Arblay St.
  W1 . . . . 3A 14 (5E 61)
Darcy Ho. E8 . . . . 5D 51
   (off London Flds. E. Side)
Dare Ct. E10 . . . . 2E 39
Darent Ho.
  BR1: Brom 5F 123
  NW8 . . . . 4F 59
     (off Church St. Est.)
Darenth Rd. N16 . . . . . . 2B 36
Darfield NW1 . . . . 5E 47
      (off Bayham St.)
Darfield Rd. SE4 . . . . . . 3B 108
Darfield Way W10 . . . . . 5F 57
Darfur St. SW15 . . . . . . 1F 99
Darien Ho. E1 . . . . 4F 65
      (off Shandy St.)
Darien Rd. SW11 . . . . . 1F 101
Daring Ho. E3 . . . . 1A 66
      (off Roman Rd.)
Dark Ho. Wlk.
  EC3 . . . . 5D 19 (1F 77)
Darlan Rd. SW6 . . . . 3B 86
Darley Ho. SE11 . . . . . . 1B 90
       (off Laud St.)
Darley Rd. SW11 . . . . . 4B 102
Darling Rd. SE4 . . . . . . 1C 108
Darling Row E1 . . . . 3D 65
Darlington Ct. SE6 . . . . . 1B 124
Darlington Ho. SW8 . . . . 3F 89
     (off Hemans St.)
Darlington Rd.
  SE27 . . . . 5D 119
Darnall Ho. SE10 . . . . . 4E 95
      (off Royal Hill)
Darnaway Pl. E14 . . . . . 4E 67
     (off Aberfeldy St.)

Darnay Ho. SE16 . . . . . . 4C 78
Darnley Ho. *E14* *5A 66*
   (off Camdenhurst St.)
Darnley Rd. E9 . . . . 3E 51
Darnley Ter. W11 . . . . 2F 71
Darrell Rd. SE22 . . . . . . 3C 106
Darren Cl. N14 . . . . 2B 34
Darren Ct. N7 . . . . 1A 48
Darsley Dr. SW8 . . . . 4F 89
Dartford Ho. *SE1* *5B 78*
   (off Longfield Est.)
Dartford St. SE17 . . . . . . 2E 91
Dartington NW1 . . . . 5E 47
   (off Plender St.)
Dartington Ho. *SW8* *5F 89*
   (off Union Gro.)
 W2 . . . . *4D 59*
   (off Senior St.)
Dartle Ct. *SE16* *3C 78*
   (off Scott Lidgett Cres.)
Dartmoor Wlk. *E14* *5C 80*
   (off Charnwood Gdns.)
Dartmouth Cl. W11 . . . . . 5B 58
Dartmouth Ct. SE10 . . . . 4E 95
Dartmouth Gro. SE10 . . . 4E 95
Dartmouth Hill SE10 . . . 4E 95
DARTMOUTH PARK 5D 33
Dartmouth Pk. Av.
 NW5 . . . . 5D 33
Dartmouth Pk. Hill
 N19 . . . . 3D 33
 NW5 . . . . 3D 33
Dartmouth Pk. Rd.
 NW5 . . . . 1D 47
Dartmouth Pl. SE23 . . . . 2E 121
 W4 . . . . 2A 84
Dartmouth Rd. NW2 . . . . . 3F 43
 NW4 . . . . 1C 28
 SE23 . . . . 3D 121
 SE26 . . . . 3D 121
Dartmouth Row SE10 . . . 5E 95
Dartmouth St.
 SW1 . . . . 4C 22 (3F 75)
Dartmouth Ter. SE10 . . . . 4F 95
Dartrey Twr. *SW10* *3E 87*
   (off Worlds End Est.)
Dartrey Wlk. SW10 . . . . . 3E 87
Dart St. W10 . . . . 2A 58
Darville Rd. N16 . . . . 5B 36
Darwen Pl. E2 . . . . 1D 65
Darwin Ct. NW1 . . . . 5D 47
 SE17 . . . . *5F 77*
   (off Barlow St.)
Darwin Ho. *SW1* *2E 89*
   (off Grosvenor Rd.)
Darwin St. SE17 . . . . 5F 77
   (not continuous)
Daryngton Ho. *SW8* *3A 90*
   (off Hartington Rd.)
Dashwood Ho. N8 . . . . . . 1B 34
Dassett Rd. SE27 . . . . . 5D 119
Data Point Bus. Cen.
 E16 . . . . 3F 67
Datchelor Pl. SE5 . . . . . . 4F 91
Datchet Ho. *NW1* *1E 5*
   (off Augustus St.)
Datchet Rd. SE6 . . . . . . 2B 122
Datchworth Ho. *N1* *4D 49*
   (off Sutton Est., The)
Date St. SE17 . . . . 1F 91

Daubeney Rd. E5 . . . . 1A 52
Daubeney Twr. *SE8* *1B 94*
   (off Bowditch)
Dault Rd. SW18 . . . . 4E 101
Dauncey Ho. SE1 . . . . . . 4D 25
Davenant Rd. N19 . . . . . . 4F 33
Davenant St. E1 . . . . 4C 64
Davenport Ho. *SE11* *5C 76*
   (off Walnut Tree Wlk.)
Davenport Rd. SE6 . . . . . 4D 109
Daventry Av. E17 . . . . 1C 38
Daventry St. NW1 . . . . . . 4A 60
Daver Ct. SW3 . . . . 1A 88
Davern Cl. SE10 . . . . 5B 82
Davey Cl. N7 . . . . 3B 48
Davey Rd. E9 . . . . 4E 52
Davey's Ct. WC2 . . . . 4D 15
Davey St. SE15 . . . . 2B 92
Davidge Ho. *SE1* *4C 24*
   (off Coral St.)
Davidge St.
 SE1 . . . . 4D 25 (3D 77)
David Ho. *SW8* *3A 90*
   (off Wyvil Rd.)
David Lee Point E15 . . . . 5A 54
   (off Leather Gdns.)
David Lloyd Leisure
 Kidbrooke 2D 111
 South Kensington . . . 5D 73
   (in Point West)
David M. W1 . . . . . 5A 4 (4B 60)
Davidson Gdns. SW8 . . . 3A 90
Davidson Terraces
 E7 . . . . *2D 55*
   (off Claremont Rd.,
   not continuous)
David's Rd. SE23 . . . . . . 1E 121
David St. E15 . . . . 3F 53
Davies La. E11 . . . . 4A 40
Davies M.
 W1 . . . . 4D 13 (1D 75)
Davies St.
 W1 . . . . 3D 13 (5D 61)
Da Vinci Ct. *SE16* *1D 93*
   (off Rossetti Rd.)
Davis Ho. *W12* *1D 71*
   (off White City Cl.)
Davis Rd. W3 . . . . 2B 70
Davis St. E13 . . . . 1D 69
Davisville Rd. W12 . . . . . 3C 70
Dawes Ho. *SE17* *5F 77*
   (off Orb St.)
Dawes Rd. SW6 . . . . 3A 86
Dawes St. SE17 . . . . 1F 91
Dawlish Av. SW18 . . . . . 2D 115
Dawlish Rd. E10 . . . . 3E 39
 NW2 . . . . 3F 43
Dawnay Gdns.
 SW18 . . . . 2E 115
Dawnay Rd. SW18 . . . . . 2E 115
Dawn Cres. E15 . . . . 5F 53
Dawpool Rd. NW2 . . . . . 4B 28
Dawson Ho. *E2* *2E 65*
   (off Sceptre Rd.)
Dawson Pl. W2 . . . . 1C 72
Dawson Rd. NW2 . . . . 2F 43
Dawson St.
 E2 . . . . 1F 11 (1B 64)
Day Ho. SE5 . . . . 3E 91
   (off Bethwin Rd.)

Daylesford Av. SW15 . . . 2C 98
Daysbrook Rd. SW2 . . . 1B 118
Dayton Gro. SE15 . . . . . 4E 93
Deacon Ho. *SE11* *5B 76*
   (off Black Prince Rd.)
Deacon M. N1 . . . . 4F 49
Deacon Rd. NW2 . . . . 2C 42
Deacon's Ri. N2 . . . . 1F 31
Deacons Ter. *N1* *3E 49*
   (off Harecourt Rd.)
Deacon Way SE17 . . . . . 5E 77
Deal Ho. *SE15* *2F 93*
   (off Lovelinch La.)
Deal Porters Wlk.
 SE16 . . . . 3F 79
Deal Porters Way
 SE16 . . . . 4E 79
Deal St. E1 . . . . 4C 64
Dealtry Rd. SW15 . . . . . . 2E 99
Dean Bradley St. SW1 . . 4A 76
Dean Cl. E9 . . . . 2E 51
 SE16 . . . . 2F 79
Dean Ct. *SW8* *3A 90*
   (off Thorncroft St.)
Deancross St. E1 . . . . . . 5E 65
Deanery M. W1 . . . . 1C 20
Deanery Rd. E15 . . . . . . 3A 54
Deanery St.
 W1 . . . . 1C 20 (2C 74)
Dean Farrar St.
 SW1 . . . . 5C 22 (4F 75)
Dean Ho. *E1* *5E 65*
   (off Tarling St.)
 SE14 . . . . *3A 94*
   (off New Cross Rd.)
Dean Rd. NW2 . . . . 3E 43
Dean Ryle St. SW1 . . . . . 5A 76
Dean's Bldgs. SE17 . . . . 5F 77
Dean's Ct.
 EC4 . . . . 3E 17 (5D 63)
Deans Ga. Cl. SE23 . . . 3F 121
Deanshanger Ho.
 SE8 . . . . *5F 79*
   (off Chilton Gro.)
Dean's M.
 W1 . . . . 2E 13 (5D 61)
Dean Stanley St.
 SW1 . . . . 5D 23 (4A 76)
Deanston Wharf E16 . . . 3D 83
Dean St. E7 . . . . 2C 54
 W1 . . . . 2B 14 (5F 61)
Dean's Yd. SW1 . . . . 5C 22
Dean Trench St.
 SW1 . . . . 5D 23 (4A 76)
Deason St. E15 . . . . 5E 53
Deauville Ct. *SE16* *3F 79*
   (off Eleanor Cl.)
 SW4 . . . . 4E 103
Debdale Ho. *E2* *5C 50*
   (off Whiston Rd.)
De Beauvoir Ct. *N1* *4F 49*
   (off Northchurch Rd.)
De Beauvoir Cres.
 N1 . . . . 5A 50

De Beauvoir Est. N1 . . . . . 5A 50
De Beauvoir Pl. N1 . . . . . . 3A 50
De Beauvoir Rd. N1 . . . . . . 5A 50
De Beauvoir Sq. N1 . . . . . . 4A 50
DE BEAUVOIR TOWN
. . . . 5A 50
Debenham Ct. E8 . . . . . . 5C 50
(off Pownall Rd.)
Debham Ct. NW2 . . . . 5E 29
Debnams Rd. SE16 . . . . . 5E 79
De Bruin Ct. E14 . . . . 1E 95
(off Ferry St.)
Decima St.
SE1 . . . . 5D 27 (4A 78)
Deck Cl. SE16 . . . . 2F 79
De Crespigny Pk.
SE5 . . . . 5F 91
Deeley Rd. SW8 . . . . 4F 89
Deepdale SW19 . . . . 4F 113
Deepdene Gdns.
SW2 . . . . 5B 104
Deepdene Point
SE23 . . . . 3F 121
Deepdene Rd. SE5 . . . . . 2F 105
Deerbrook Rd.
SE24 . . . . 1D 119
Deerdale Rd. SE24 . . . . . 2E 105
Deerfield Cotts. NW9 . . 1B 28
Deerhurst Ho. SE15 . . . . 2C 92
(off Haymerle Rd.)
Deerhurst Rd. NW2 . . . . 3F 43
SW16 . . . . 5B 118
Deeside Rd. SW17 . . . . . 3F 115
Dee St. E14 . . . . 5E 67
Defoe Cl. SE16 . . . . 3B 80
SW17 . . . . 5A 116
Defoe Ho. EC2 . . . . 5A 10
(off Beech St.)
Defoe Pl. EC2 . . . . 5F 9
(off Beech St.)
SW17 . . . . 4B 116
Defoe Rd. N16 . . . . 5A 36
De Frene Rd. SE26 . . . . . 4F 121
Dehar Cres. NW9 . . . . . . 2B 28
Dekker Rd. SE5 . . . . 3F 91
(off Elmington Est.)
Dekker M. SE21 . . . . 4A 106
Delacourt Rd. SE3 . . . . . 3D 97
Delafield Ho. E1 . . . . 5C 64
(off Christian St.)
Delafield Rd. SE7 . . . . . . 1D 97
Delaford Rd. SE16 . . . . . 1D 93
Delaford St. SW6 . . . . . . 3A 86
Delamere St. W2 . . . . . . 4D 59
Delamere Ter. W2 . . . . . . 4D 59
Delancey Pas. NW1 . . . . 5D 47
(off Delancey St.)
Delancey St. NW1 . . . . . 5D 47
Delancey Studios
NW1 . . . . 5D 47
Delany Ho. SE10 . . . . 2E 95
(off Thames St.)
Delarch Ho. SE1 . . . . 4D 25
De Laune St. SE17 . . . . . 1D 91
Delaware Mans. W9 . . . . 3D 59
(off Delaware Rd.)
Delaware Rd. W9 . . . . 3D 59
Delawyk Cres. SE24 . . . . 4E 105
Delfina Studio Trust
SE1 . . . . 3D 27
(off Bermondsey St.)
Delft Way SE22 . . . . 3A 106

Delhi St. N1 . . . . 5A 48
(not continuous)
Delia St. SW18 . . . . 5D 101
Delius Gro. E15 . . . . 1F 67
Della Path E5 . . . . 5C 36
Dell Cl. E15 . . . . 5F 53
Dellow Ho. E1 . . . . 1D 79
(off Dellow St.)
Dellow St. E1 . . . . 1D 79
Dell's M. SW1 . . . . 5E 75
(off Churton Pl.)
Delmaine Ho. E14 . . . . . . 5A 66
(off Maroon St.)
Delmare Cl. SW9 . . . . . . 2B 104
Delme Cres. SE3 . . . . 5D 97
Delmerend Ho. SW3 . . . 1A 88
(off Ixworth Pl.)
Deloraine Ho. SE8 . . . . . . 4C 94
Delorme St. W6 . . . . 2F 85
Delta Bldg. E14 . . . . 5E 67
(off Ashton St.)
Delta Ct. NW2 . . . . 4C 28
Delta Pk. SW18 . . . . 2D 101
Delta Point E2 . . . . 2C 64
Delta St. E2 . . . . 2C 64
Delverton Ho. SE17 . . . . 1D 91
(off Delverton Rd.)
Delverton Rd. SE17 . . . . 1D 91
Delvino Rd. SW6 . . . . 4C 86
De Montfort Pde.
SW16 . . . . 3A 118
De Montfort Rd.
SW16 . . . . 3A 118
De Morgan Rd.
SW6 . . . . 1D 101
Dempster Rd. SW18 . . . 3E 101
Den, The 1E 93
Denbigh Cl. NW10 . . . . . 4A 42
W11 . . . . 1B 72
Denbigh Ct. E6 . . . . 2F 69
Denbigh Ho. SW1 . . . . . . 5A 20
(off Hans Pl.)
W11 . . . . 1B 72
(off Westbourne Gro.)
Denbigh M. SW1 . . . . 5E 75
(off Denbigh St.)
Denbigh Pl. SW1 . . . . . . 1E 89
Denbigh Rd. E6 . . . . 2F 69
W11 . . . . 1B 72
Denbigh St. SW1 . . . . . . 5E 75
(not continuous)
Denbigh Ter. W11 . . . . . . 1B 72
Denby Ct. SE11 . . . . 5B 76
(off Lambeth Wlk.)
Dence Ho. E2 . . . . 2C 64
(off Turin St.)
Denchworth Ho. SW9 . . 5C 90
Dene Cl. SE4 . . . . 1A 108
Denehurst Gdns.
NW4 . . . . 1E 29
Denesmead SE24 . . . . . . 3E 105
Denewood Rd. N6 . . . . . . 1B 32
Denford St. SE10 . . . . 1B 96
(off Glenforth St.)
Dengie Wlk. N1 . . . . 5E 49
(off Basire St.)
Denham Ct. SE26 . . . . . . 3D 121
(off Kirkdale)
Denham Ho. W12 . . . . . . 1D 71
(off White City Est.)

Denham St. SE10 . . . . . . 1C 96
Denholme Rd. W9 . . . . . . 2B 58
Denison Ho. E14 . . . . 5C 66
(off Farrance St.)
Denison Rd. SW19 . . . . . 5F 115
Denland Ho. SW8 . . . . . . 3B 90
(off Dorset Rd.)
Denman Ho. N16 . . . . 4A 36
Denman Pl. W1 . . . . 4B 14
Denman St. SE15 . . . . . . 4B 92
Denman St.
W1 . . . . 5B 14 (1F 75)
Denmark Gro. N1 . . . . . . 1C 62
Denmark Hill SE5 . . . . . . 4F 91
Denmark Hill Est.
SE5 . . . . 2F 105
Denmark Mans. SE5 . . . 5E 91
(off Coldharbour La.)
Denmark Pl. E3 . . . . 2C 66
WC2 . . . . 2C 14 (5F 61)
Denmark Rd. NW6 . . . . . 1B 58
(not continuous)
SE5 . . . . 4E 91
E13 . . . . 4D 69
WC2 . . . . 2C 14 (5F 61)
Denmark Wlk. SE27 . . . . 4E 119
Denmead Ho. SW15 . . . . 4B 98
(off Highcliffe Dr.)
Denne Ter. E8 . . . . 5B 50
Dennett's Rd. SE14 . . . . 4E 93
Denning Cl. NW8 . . . . . . 2E 59
Denning Point E1 . . . . . . 2F 19
(off Commercial St.)
Denning Rd. NW3 . . . . . . 1F 45
Dennington Cl. E5 . . . . . . 4E 37
Dennington Pk. Rd.
NW6 . . . . 3C 44
Dennison Point E15 . . . . 4E 53
Denny Cl. E6 . . . . 4F 69
Denny Cres. SE11 . . . . . . 1C 90
Denny St. SE11 . . . . 1C 90
Densham Ho. NW8 . . . . . 1F 59
(off Cochrane St.)
Densham Rd. E15 . . . . . . 5A 54
Denstone Ho. SE15 . . . . 2C 92
(off Haymerle Rd.)
Dent Ho. SE17 . . . . 5A 78
(off Tatum St.)
Denton NW1 . . . . 3C 46
Denton Ho. N1 . . . . 4D 49
(off Halton Rd.)
Denton Rd. N8 . . . . 1B 34
Denton St. SW18 . . . . . . 4D 101
Denton Way E5 . . . . 5F 37
Dents Rd. SW11 . . . . 4B 102
Denver Rd. N16 . . . . 2A 36
Denwood SE23 . . . . 3F 121
Denyer St. SW3 . . . . 5A 74
Denys Ho. EC1 . . . . 5B 8
(off Bourne Est.)
Denzil Rd. NW10 . . . . . . 2B 42
Deodar Rd. SW15 . . . . . . 2A 100
Depot App. NW2 . . . . . . 1F 43
Depot Rd. W12 . . . . 1E 71
Depot St. SE5 . . . . 2F 91
DEPTFORD 3C 94
Deptford Bri. SE8 . . . . . . 4C 94
Deptford B'way. SE8 . . . 4C 94

Deptford Bus. Pk.
SE15 . . . . 2E 93
Deptford Chu. St.
SE8 . . . . 2C 94
Deptford Creek Bri.
SE8 . . . . 2D 95
(off Creek Rd.)
Deptford Ferry Rd.
E14 . . . . 5C 80
Deptford Grn. SE8 . . . . 2C 94
Deptford High St.
SE8 . . . . 2C 94
Deptford Pk. Bus. Cen.
SE8 . . . . 1A 94
Deptford Strand SE8 . . 5B 80
Deptford Trad. Est.
SE8 . . . . 1A 94
Deptford Wharf SE8 . . 5B 80
De Quincey Ho. SW1 . . 1E 89
(off Lupus St.)
De Quincey M. E16 . . . 2C 82
Derby Ga.
SW1 . . . . 3D 23 (3A 76)
(not continuous)
Derby Hill SE23 . . . . . 2E 121
Derby Hill Cres.
SE23 . . . . 2E 121
Derby Ho. SE11 . . . . . . 5C 76
(off Walnut Tree Wlk.)
Derby Lodge WC1 . . . . . 1F 7
(off Britannia St.)
Derby Rd. E7 . . . . 4F 55
E9 . . . . 5F 51
Derbyshire St. E2 . . . . 2C 64
(not continuous)
Derby St. W1 . . 2C 20 (2C 74)
Dereham Ho. SE4 . . . . 2F 107
(off Frendsbury Rd.)
Dereham Pl.
EC2 . . . . 2E 11 (2A 64)
Derek Walcott Cl.
SE24 . . . . 3D 105
Dericote St. E8 . . . . . . 5D 51
Dering St.
W1 . . . . 3D 13 (5D 61)
Dering Yd.
W1 . . . . 3D 13 (5D 61)
Derinton Rd. SW17 . . . 4B 116
Dermody Gdns.
SE13 . . . . 3F 109
Dermody Rd. SE13 . . . 3F 109
Deronda Est. SW2 . . . 1D 119
Deronda Rd. SE24 . . . 1D 119
Derrick Gdns. SE7 . . . 4E 83
Derry St. W8 . . . . 3D 73
Dersingham Rd. NW2 . . 5A 30
Derwent NW1 . . . . 2F 5
(off Robert St.)
Derwent Av. NW9 . . . . 1A 28
SW15 . . . . 4A 112
Derwent Ct. SE16 . . . . 3F 79
(off Eleanor Cl.)
Derwent Gro. SE22 . . 2B 106
Derwent Ho. E3 . . . . . . 3B 66
(off Southern Gro.)
SW7 . . . . 5F 73
(off Cromwell Rd.)
Derwent Ri. NW9 . . . . . 1A 28
Derwent St. SE10 . . . . 1A 96
Desborough Cl. W2 . . . 4D 59

Desborough Ho.
W14 . . . . 2B 86
(off Nth. End Rd.)
Desborough St. W2 . . . 4D 59
(off Cirencester St.)
Desenfans Rd.
SE21 . . . . 4A 106
Desford Rd. E16 . . . . . 3A 68
Design Mus. 3B 78
Desmond St. SE14 . . . 2A 94
Desmond Tutu Dr.
SE23 . . . . 1B 122
Despard Rd. N19 . . . . . 3E 33
Dethick Ct. E3 . . . . 5A 52
Detling Ho. SE17 . . . . . 5A 78
(off Congreve St.)
Detling Rd.
BR1: Brom 5C 124
Detmold Rd. E5 . . . . . . 4E 37
Devas St. E3 . . . . 3D 67
Devenay Rd. E15 . . . . . 4B 54
Deventer Cres.
SE22 . . . . 3A 106
De Vere Gdns. W8 . . . 3E 73
Deverell St.
SE1 . . . . 5B 26 (4F 77)
De Vere M. W8 . . . . . . 4E 73
(off De Vere Gdns.)
Devereux Ct. WC2 . . . . 3B 16
Devereux La. SW13 . . . 3D 85
Devereux Rd. SW11 . . 4B 102
Devitt Ho. E14 . . . . 1D 81
(off Wade's Pl.)
Devizes St. N1 . . . . 5F 49
Devon Gdns. N4 . . . . . 1D 35
Devonia Rd. N1 . . . . . . 1D 63
Devon Mans. SE1 . . . . 3F 27
(off Tooley St.)
Devonport W2 . . . . 5A 60
Devonport Ho. W12 . . . 3D 71
Devonport Rd. W12 . . . 2D 71
(not continuous)
Devonport St. E1 . . . . . 5F 65
Devonshire Cl. E15 . . . 1A 54
W1 . . . . 5D 5 (4D 61)
Devonshire Ct. E1 . . . . 2E 65
(off Bancroft Rd.)
WC1 . . . . 5E 7
(off Boswell St.)
Devonshire Dr. SE10 . . 3D 95
Devonshire Gro.
SE15 . . . . 2D 93
Devonshire Hall E9 . . . 3E 51
(off Frampton Pk. Rd.)
Devonshire Ho. E14 . . 5C 80
(off Westferry Rd.)
NW6 . . . . 3B 44
(off Kilburn High Rd.)
SE1 . . . . 5F 25
(off Bath Ter.)
SW1 . . . . 1F 89
(off Lindsay Sq.)
Devonshire M. SW10 . . 2F 87
(off Park Wlk.)
W4 . . . . 1A 84
Devonshire M. Nth.
W1 . . . . 5D 5 (4D 61)
Devonshire M. Sth.
W1 . . . . 5D 5 (4D 61)

Devonshire M. W.
W1 . . . . 4C 4 (3C 60)
Devonshire Pas. W4 . . 1A 84
Devonshire Pl. NW2 . . 5C 30
W1 . . . . 4C 4 (3C 60)
W8 . . . . 4D 73
Devonshire Pl. M.
W1 . . . . 4C 4 (4C 60)
Devonshire Rd. E16 . . 5D 69
E17 . . . . 1C 38
SE9 . . . . 2F 125
SE23 . . . . 1E 121
W4 . . . . 1A 84
**Devonshire Road
Nature Reserve** 5F 107
Devonshire Row
EC2 . . . . 1E 19 (4A 64)
Devonshire Row M.
W1 . . . . 4E 5
Devonshire Sq.
EC2 . . . . 1E 19 (5A 64)
Devonshire St.
W1 . . . . 5C 4 (4C 60)
W4 . . . . 1A 84
Devonshire Ter. W2 . . 5E 59
Devons Rd. E3 . . . . . . 2D 67
Devon St. SE15 . . . . . . 2D 93
Devon Wharf E14 . . . . 4E 67
De Walden Ho. NW8 . . 1A 60
(off Allitsen Rd.)
De Walden St.
W1 . . . . 1C 12 (4C 60)
Dewar St. SE15 . . . . . 1C 106
Dewberry Gdns. E6 . . . 4F 69
Dewberry St. E14 . . . . 4E 67
Dewey Rd. N1 . . . . 1C 62
Dewey St. SW17 . . . . . 5B 116
Dewhurst Rd. W14 . . . 4F 71
Dewsbury Rd. NW10 . . 2C 42
Dewsbury Ter. NW1 . . . 5D 47
D'Eynsford Rd. SE5 . . 4F 91
Dhonau Ho. SE1 . . . . . 5B 78
(off Longfield Est.)
Diadem Ct. W1 . . . . . . 2B 14
Dial Wlk., The W8 . . . . 3D 73
(off Broad Wlk., The)
Diamond Est. SW17 . . 3A 116
Diamond Ho. E3 . . . . . . 1A 66
(off Roman Rd.)
Diamond St. SE15 . . . . 3A 92
Diamond Ter. SE10 . . . 4E 95
Diamond Way SE8 . . . 2C 94
Diana Cl. SE8 . . . . 2B 94
Diana Ho. SW13 . . . . . 4B 84
**Diana, Princess of Wales
Memorial Fountain** . . 3F 73
**Diana, Princess of Wales
Memorial Walk** 2D 73
(in Kensington Gardens)
Dibden Ho. SE5 . . . . . 3A 92
Dibden St. N1 . . . . 5E 49
Dibdin Ho. W9 . . . . 1D 59
Dicey Av. NW2 . . . . . . 1E 43
Dickens Est. SE1 . . . . . 3C 78
SE16 . . . . 4C 78
Dickens Ho. 4A 8
Dickens Ho. NW6 . . . . 2C 58
(off Malvern Rd.)
NW8 . . . . 3F 59
(off Fisherton St.)

Dickens Ho. SE17 . . . . . . 1D **91**
(off Doddington Gro.)
WC1 . . . . 3D **7**
Dickens M. EC1 . . . . 5D **9**
(off Turnmill St.)
Dickenson Ho. N8 . . . . . . 1B **34**
Dickenson Rd. N8 . . . . . . 2A **34**
Dickens Rd. E6 . . . . 1F **69**
Dickens Sq.
SE1 . . . . 5A **26** (4E **77**)
Dickens St. SW8 . . . . . . 5D **89**
Dickinson Ct. EC1 . . . . 3E **9**
(off Brewhouse Yd.)
Dicksee Ho. NW8 . . . . . . 3F **59**
(off Lyons Pl.)
Dickson Ho. E1 . . . . 5D **65**
(off Philpot St.)
Dieppe Cl. W14 . . . . 1B **86**
Digby Bus. Cen. E9 . . . . . 3F **51**
(off Digby Rd.)
Digby Cres. N4 . . . . 4E **35**
Digby Mans. W6 . . . . 1D **85**
(off Hammersmith Bri. Rd.)
Digby Rd. E9 . . . . 3F **51**
Digby St. E2 . . . . 2E **65**
Diggon St. E1 . . . . 4F **65**
Dighton Ct. SE5 . . . . 2E **91**
Dighton Rd. SW18 . . . . . 3E **101**
Dignum St. N1 . . . . 1C **62**
Digswell Rd. N7 . . . . 3C **48**
Dilhorne Cl. SE12 . . . . . 3D **125**
Dilke St. SW3 . . . . 2B **88**
Dillwyn Cl. SE26 . . . . . . 4A **122**
Dilston Gro. SE16 . . . . . . 5E **79**
Dilton Gdns. SW15 . . . . . 1C **112**
Dimes Pl. W6 . . . . 5D **71**
Dimond Cl. E7 . . . . 1C **54**
Dimsdale Wlk. E13 . . . . . . 1C **68**
Dimson Cres. E3 . . . . 2C **66**
Dingle Gdns. E14 . . . . . . 1C **80**
Dingley La. SW16 . . . . . . 2F **117**
Dingley Pl.
EC1 . . . . 1A **10** (2E **63**)
Dingley Rd.
EC1 . . . . 2F **9** (2E **63**)
Dingwall Gdns.
NW11 . . . . 1C **30**
Dingwall Rd. SW18 . . . . . 5E **101**
Dinmont Est. E2 . . . . 1C **64**
Dinmont Ho. E2 . . . . 1C **64**
(off Pritchard's Rd.)
Dinmont St. E2 . . . . 1D **65**
Dinmore Ho. E9 . . . . 5E **51**
(off Templecombe Rd.)
Dinnington Ho. E1 . . . . . . 3D **65**
(off Coventry Rd.)
Dinsdale Rd. SE3 . . . . . . 2B **96**
Dinsmore Rd. SW12 . . . 5D **103**
Dinton Ho. NW8 . . . . 3A **60**
(off Lilestone St.)
Dinton Rd. SW19 . . . . . . 5F **115**
Diprose Lodge
SW17 . . . . 4F **115**
Dirleton Rd. E15 . . . . 5B **54**
Disbrowe Rd.
W6 . . . . 2A **86**
Discovery Bus. Pk.
SE16 . . . . 4C **78**
(off St James's Rd.)

Discovery Ho. E14 . . . . . . 1E **81**
(off Newby Pl.)
Discovery Wlk. E1 . . . . . . 2D **79**
Disney Pl.
SE1 . . . . 3A **26** (3E **77**)
Disney St.
SE1 . . . . 3A **26** (3E **77**)
Disraeli Gdns.
SW15 . . . . 2B **100**
Disraeli Rd. E7 . . . . 3C **54**
SW15 . . . . 2A **100**
Diss St. E2 . . . . . 1F **11** (2B **64**)
Distaff La.
EC4 . . . . 4F **17** (1E **77**)
Distillery La. W6 . . . . 1E **85**
Distillery Rd. W6 . . . . 1E **85**
Distin St. SE11 . . . . 5C **76**
Ditch All. SE13 . . . . 4D **95**
Ditchburn St. E14 . . . . . . 1E **81**
Dittisham Rd. SE9 . . . . . 4F **125**
Divisional Rd. E12 . . . . . . 4F **41**
Divis Way SW15 . . . . 4D **99**
(off Dover Pk. Dr.)
Dixon Clark Ct. N1 . . . . . 3D **49**
Dixon Ho. W10 . . . . 5F **57**
(off Darfield Way)
Dixon Rd. SE14 . . . . 4A **94**
Dixon's All. SE16 . . . . . . 3D **79**
Dobree Av. NW10 . . . . . . 4D **43**
Dobson Cl. NW6 . . . . 4F **45**
Dobson Ho. SE5 . . . . 3F **91**
(off Edmund St.)
SE14 . . . . 2F **93**
(off John Williams Cl.)
Doby Ct. EC4 . . . . 4A **18**
Dock Cotts. E1 . . . . 1E **79**
(off Highway, The)
Dockers Tanner Rd.
E14 . . . . 4C **80**
Dockhead SE1 . . . . 3B **78**
Dockhead Wharf SE1 . . . . 4F **27**
(off Shad Thames)
Dock Hill Av. SE16 . . . . . 2F **79**
Docklands Sailing Cen.
. . . . 4C **80**
Dockley Rd. SE16 . . . . . . 4C **78**
Dockley Rd. Ind. Est.
SE16 . . . . 4C **78**
(off Dockley Rd.)
Dock Offices SE16 . . . . . . 4E **79**
(off Surrey Quays Rd.)
Dock Rd. E16 . . . . 1B **82**
Dockside Rd. E16 . . . . . . 1F **83**
Dock St. E1 . . . . 1C **78**
Doctor Johnson Av.
SW17 . . . . 3D **117**
Doctors Cl. SE26 . . . . . . 5E **121**
Docwra's Bldgs. N1 . . . . . 3A **50**
Dodbrooke Rd.
SE27 . . . . 3C **118**
Dodd Ho. SE16 . . . . 5D **79**
(off Rennie Est.)
Doddington Gro.
SE17 . . . . 2D **91**
Doddington Pl. SE17 . . . . 2D **91**
Dodson St.
SE1 . . . . 4C **24** (3C **76**)
Dod St. E14 . . . . 5B **66**
Dog & Duck Yd. WC1 . . . . 5F **7**
Doggett Rd. SE6 . . . . . . 5C **108**

Dog Kennel Hill
SE22 . . . . 1A **106**
Dog Kennel Hill Est.
SE22 . . . . 1A **106**
(off Albrighton Rd.)
Dog La. NW10 . . . . 1A **42**
Doherty Rd. E13 . . . . 3C **68**
Dolben Ct. SE8 . . . . 5B **80**
Dolben St.
SE1 . . . . 2D **25** (2D **77**)
(not continuous)
Dolby Rd. SW6 . . . . 5B **86**
Dolland Ho. SE11 . . . . . . 1B **90**
(off Newburn St.)
Dolland St. SE11 . . . . . . 1B **90**
Dollar Bay Ct. E14 . . . . . 3E **81**
(off Lawn Ho. Cl.)
DOLLIS HILL 4D **29**
Dollis Hill Av. NW2 . . . . . 5D **29**
Dollis Hill La. NW2 . . . . . 1B **42**
Dolman Rd. W4 . . . . 5A **70**
Dolman St. SW4 . . . . 2B **104**
Dolphin Cl. SE16 . . . . . . 3F **79**
Dolphin Ct. NW11 . . . . . . 1A **30**
SE8 . . . . 2B **94**
(off Wotton Rd.)
Dolphin Ho. SW18 . . . . . 2D **101**
Dolphin La. E14 . . . . 1D **81**
Dolphin Sq. SW1 . . . . . . 1E **89**
W4 . . . . 3A **84**
Dolphin Twr. SE8 . . . . . . 2B **94**
(off Abinger Gro.)
Dombey Ho. SE1 . . . . 3C **78**
(off Wolseley St.)
W11 . . . . 2F **71**
(off St Ann's Rd.)
Dombey St.
WC1 . . . . 5F **7** (4B **62**)
(not continuous)
Domecq Ho. EC1 . . . . 3E **9**
(off Dallington St.)
Dome Hill Pk. SE26 . . . . 4B **120**
Domelton Ho.
SW18 . . . . 4D **101**
(off Iron Mill Rd.)
Domett Cl. SE5 . . . . 2F **105**
Domfe Pl. E5 . . . . 1E **51**
Domingo St.
EC1 . . . . 3F **9** (3E **63**)
Dominica Cl. E13 . . . . . . 1F **69**
Dominion Ct. E8 . . . . 4B **50**
(off Middleton Rd.)
Dominion Ho. E14 . . . . . 1D **95**
(off St Davids Sq.)
Dominion St.
EC2 . . . . 5C **10** (4F **63**)
Dominion Theatre 2C **14**
(off Tottenham Ct. Rd.)
Donald Hunter Ho.
E7 . . . . 2D **55**
(off Woodgrange Rd.)
Donald Rd. E13 . . . . 5D **55**
Donaldson Rd. NW6 . . . . 5B **44**
Donato Dr. SE15 . . . . . . 2A **92**
Doncaster Gdns. N4 . . . . 1E **35**
Donegal Ho. E1 . . . . 3D **65**
(off Cambridge Heath Rd.)
Donegal St. N1 . . . . 1B **62**
Doneraile Ho. SW1 . . . . . 1D **89**
(off Ebury Bri. Rd.)

Doneraile St. SW6 . . . . . . 5F **85**
Dongola Rd. E1 . . . . 4A **66**
   E13 . . . . 2D **69**
Dongola Rd. W. E13 . . . . . . 2D **69**
Donkey All. SE22 . . . . . 5C **106**
Donkin Ho. *SE16* *5D 79*
Donmar Warehouse Theatre
   . . . . *3D 15*
   (off Earlham St.)
Donnatt's Rd. SE14 . . . . . 4B **94**
Donne Ct. SE24 . . . . 4E **105**
Donne Ho. *E14* *5C 66*
   (off Dod St.)
   SE14 . . . . *2F 93*
   (off Samuel Cl.)
Donnelly Ct. *SW6* *3A 86*
   (off Dawes St.)
Donne Pl. SW3 . . . . 5A **74**
Donnington Ct. *NW1* . . . *4D 47*
   (off Castlehaven Rd.)
   NW10 . . . . 4D **43**
Donnington Mans.
   NW10 . . . . *5E 43*
   (off Donnington Rd.)
Donnington Rd.
   NW10 . . . . 4D **43**
Donoghue Cotts. *E14* . . . *4A 66*
   (off Galsworthy Av.)
Donovan Ct. *SW10* *1F 87*
   (off Drayton Gdns.)
Donovan Ho. *E1* *1E 79*
   (off Cable St.)
Don Phelan Cl. SE5 . . . . . 4F **91**
Doon St. SE1 . . 2B **24** (2C **76**)
Dora Ho. *E14* *5B 66*
   (off Rhodeswell Rd.)
   W11 . . . . *1F 71*
   (off St Ann's Rd.)
Dorando Cl. W12 . . . . . . 1D **71**
Doran Mnr. *N2* *1B 32*
   (off Gt. North Rd.)
Doran Wlk. E15 . . . . 4E **53**
Dora Rd. SW19 . . . . . . 5C **114**
Dora St. E14 . . . . 5B **66**
Dora Way SW9 . . . . 5C **90**
Dorchester Ct. *N1* *4D 50*
   (off Englefield Rd.)
   NW2 . . . . 5F **29**
   SE24 . . . . 3E **105**
Dorchester Dr. SE24 . . 3E **105**
Dorchester Gro. W4 . . . . 1A **84**
Dorchester Ter. *NW2* . . . *5F 29*
   (off Needham Ter.)
Dordrecht Rd. W3 . . . . . . 2A **70**
Doreen Av. NW9 . . . . 3A **28**
Doreen Capstan Ho.
   E11 . . . . *5A 40*
   (off Apollo Pl.)
Doria Rd. SW6 . . . . 5B **86**
Doric Ho. *E2* *1F 65*
   (off Mace St.)
Doric Way
   NW1 . . . . 1B **6** (2F **61**)
Doris Emmerton Ct.
   SW11 . . . . 2E **101**
Doris Rd. E7 . . . . 4C **54**
Dorking Cl. SE8 . . . . 2B **94**
Dorking Ho.
   SE1 . . . . 5C **26** (4F **77**)

Dorlcote Rd. SW18 . . . . 5A **102**
Dorman Way NW8 . . . . . . 5F **45**
Dorma Trad. Pk.
   E10 . . . . 3F **37**
Dormay St. SW18 . . . . . 3D **101**
Dormer Cl. E15 . . . . 3B **54**
Dormstone Ho. *SE17* . . . *5A 78*
   (off Beckway St.)
Dornberg Cl. SE3 . . . . . . 3C **96**
Dornberg Rd. SE3 . . . . . 3D **97**
Dorncliffe Rd. SW6 . . . . . 5A **86**
Dorney NW3 . . . . 4A **46**
Dornfell St. NW6 . . . . 2B **44**
Dornton Rd. SW12 . . . . 2D **117**
Dorothy Rd. SW11 . . . . . 1B **102**
Dorrell Pl. SW9 . . . . 1C **104**
Dorrien Wlk. SW16 . . . . . 2F **117**
Dorrington St.
   EC1 . . . . 5B **8** (4C **62**)
Dorrit Ho. *W11* *2F 71*
   (off St Ann's Rd.)
Dorrit St.
   SE1 . . . . 3A **26** (3E **77**)
Dorryn Ct. SE26 . . . . 5F **121**
Dors Cl. NW9 . . . . 3A **28**
Dorset Bldgs.
   EC4 . . . . 3D **17** (5D **63**)
Dorset Cl.
   NW1 . . . . 5A **4** (4B **60**)
Dorset Ct. *N1* *4A 50*
   (off Hertford Rd.)
Dorset Ho. *NW1* *5A 4*
   (off Gloucester Pl.)
Dorset M.
   SW1 . . . . 5D **21** (4D **75**)
Dorset Pl. E15 . . . . 3F **53**
Dorset Ri.
   EC4 . . . . 3D **17** (5D **63**)
Dorset Rd. E7 . . . . 4E **55**
   SE9 . . . . 2F **125**
   SW8 . . . . 3A **90**
Dorset Sq.
   NW1 . . . . 4A **4** (3B **60**)
Dorset St.
   W1 . . . . 1A **12** (4B **60**)
Dorton Cl. SE15 . . . . 3A **92**
Dorville Cres. W6 . . . . . . 4D **71**
Dorville Rd. SE12 . . . . . 3B **110**
Doughty Ct. *E1* *2D 79*
   (off Prusom St.)
Doughty Ho. *SW10* *2E 87*
   (off Netherton Gro.)
Doughty M.
   WC1 . . . . 4F **7** (3B **62**)
Doughty St.
   WC1 . . . . 3F **7** (3B **62**)
Douglas Cl. *NW6* *4C 44*
   (off Quex Rd.)
Douglas Est. *N1* *3E 49*
   (off Oransay Rd.)
Douglas Eyre Sports Cen.
   . . . . 1F **37**
Douglas Johnstone Ho.
   SW6 . . . . *2B 86*
   (off Clem Attlee Ct.)
Douglas M. NW2 . . . . 5A **30**
Douglas Path *E14* *1E 95*
   (off Manchester Rd.)
Douglas Pl. *SW1* *5F 75*
   (off Douglas St.)

Douglas Rd. E16 . . . . 4C **69**
   N1 . . . . 4E **49**
   NW6 . . . . 5B **44**
Douglas Rd. Nth. N1 . . . . 3E **49**
Douglas Rd. Sth. N1 . . . . 3E **49**
Douglas St. SW1 . . . . . . 5F **75**
Douglas Waite Ho.
   NW6 . . . . 4C **44**
Douglas Way SE8 . . . . . . 3C **94**
   (Octavius St.)
   SE8 . . . . 3B **94**
   (Stanley St.)
Doulton Ho. *SE11* *4B 76*
   (off Lambeth Wlk.)
Doulton M. NW6 . . . . 3D **45**
Dounesforth Gdns.
   SW18 . . . . 1D **115**
Douro Pl. W8 . . . . 4D **73**
Douro St. E3 . . . . 1C **66**
Douthwaite Sq. E1 . . . . . 2C **78**
Dove App. E6 . . . . 4F **69**
Dove Commercial Cen.
   NW5 . . . . 2E **47**
Dovecote Gdns.
   SW14 . . . . 1A **98**
Dove Ct. EC2 . . . . 3B **18**
Dovedale Bus. Est.
   SE15 . . . . *5C 92*
   (off Blenheim Gro.)
Dovedale Rd. SE22 . . . 3D **107**
Dovehouse St. SW3 . . . . 1F **87**
Dove M. SW5 . . . . 5E **73**
Dove Rd. N1 . . . . 3E **49**
Dove Row E2 . . . . 5C **50**
Dover Pk. Dr. SW15 . . . . 4D **99**
Dover Patrol SE3 . . . . . . 5D **97**
Dover Rd. E12 . . . . 4E **41**
   SE19 . . . . 5F **119**
Dover St. W1 . . . 5E **13** (1D **75**)
Dover Yd. W1 . . . . 1F **21**
Doves Yd. N1 . . . . 5C **48**
Dovet Ct. SW9 . . . . 4B **90**
Doveton Ho. *E1* *3E 65*
   (off Doveton St.)
Doveton St. E1 . . . . 3E **65**
Dove Wlk. SW1 . . . . 1C **88**
Dovey Lodge *N1* *4C 48*
   (off Bewdley St.)
Dowanhill Rd. SE6 . . . . 1F **123**
Dowdeswell Cl.
   SW15 . . . . 2A **98**
Dowding Ho. *N6* *2C 32*
   (off Hillcrest)
Dowdney Cl. NW5 . . . . . . 2E **47**
Dowe Ho. SE3 . . . . 1A **110**
Dowes Ho. SW16 . . . . . 3A **118**
Dowgate Hill
   EC4 . . . . 1D **19** (1F **77**)
Dowland St. W10 . . . . . . 2A **58**
Dowlas St. SE5 . . . . 3A **92**
Dowler Ho. *E1* *5C 64*
   (off Burslem St.)

Downbury M.
SW18 . . . . 3C **100**
Dowderry Rd.
BR1: Brom 3F **123**
Dowend Ct. SE15 . . . . . 2A **92**
(off Longhope Cl.)
Downer's Cott.
SW4 . . . . 2E **103**
Downey Ho. E1 . . . . 3F **65**
(off Globe Rd.)
Downfield Cl. W9 . . . . . . 3D **59**
DOWNHAM 5F **123**
Downham Ct. N1 . . . . . . 4F **49**
(off Downham Rd.)
Downham Ent. Cen.
SE6 . . . . 2B **124**
Downham La.
BR1: Brom 5F **123**
Downham Rd. N1 . . . . . . 4F **49**
Downham Way
BR1: Brom 5F **123**
Downing St.
SW1 . . . . 3D **23** (3A **76**)
Downland Ct. E11 . . . . . 4A **40**
Down Pl. W6 . . . . 5D **71**
Downs Ct. Pde. E8 . . . . . 2D **51**
(off Amhurst Rd.)
Downsell Rd. E15 . . . . . 1E **53**
Downshire Hill NW3 . . . 1F **45**
Downside Cres. NW3 . . . 2A **46**
Downs La. E5 . . . . 1D **51**
Downs Pk. Rd. E5 . . . . . 2B **50**
E8 . . . . 2B **50**
Downs Rd. E5 . . . . 1C **50**
Down St. W1 . . 2D **21** (2D **75**)
Down St. M.
W1 . . . . 2D **21** (2D **75**)
Downton Av. SW2 . . . . . 2A **118**
Downtown Rd. SE16 . . . 3A **80**
Dowrey St. N1 . . . . 5C **48**
Dowson Cl. SE5 . . . . . . 2F **105**
Dowson Ho. E1 . . . . 5F **65**
(off Bower St.)
Doyce St.
SE1 . . . . 3F **25** (3E **77**)
Doyle Gdns. NW10 . . . . 5C **42**
Doyle Ho. SW13 . . . . . . 3E **85**
(off Trinity Chu. Rd.)
D'Oyley St. SW1 . . . . . . 5C **74**
Doynton St. N19 . . . . . . 4D **33**
Draco Ga. SW15 . . . . . . 1E **99**
Draco St. SE17 . . . . 2E **91**
Dragonfly Cl. E13 . . . . . 2D **69**
Dragon Rd. SE15 . . . . . . 2A **92**
Dragon Yd.
WC1 . . . . 2E **15** (5A **62**)
Dragoon Rd.
SE8 . . . . 1B **94**
Drake Cl. SE16 . . . . 3F **79**
Drake Ct. SE1 . . . . 4A **26**
(off Swan St.)
W12 . . . . 3E **71**
(off Scott's Rd.)
Drakefell Rd. SE4 . . . . . 1A **108**
SE14 . . . . 5F **93**
Drakefield Rd.
SW17 . . . . 3C **116**
Drake Hall E16 . . . . 2D **83**
(off Wesley Av.)

Drake Ho. E1 . . . . 4E **65**
(off Stepney Way)
E14 . . . . 1A **80**
(off Victory Pl.)
SW1 . . . . 2F **89**
(off Dolphin Sq.)
Drakeland Ho. W9 . . . . . 3B **58**
(off Fernhead Rd.)
Drakeley Ct. N5 . . . . . . 1D **49**
Drake Rd. SE4 . . . . 1C **108**
Drakes Ct. SE23 . . . . . . 1E **121**
Drakes Courtyard
NW6 . . . . 4B **44**
Drake St.
WC1 . . . . . . 1F **15** (4B **62**)
Draper Ho. SE1 . . . . 5D **77**
(off Elephant & Castle)
Draper Pl. N1 . . . . 5D **49**
(off Dagmar Ter.)
Drapers Gdns.
EC2 . . . . 2C **18** (5F **63**)
Drapers Rd. E15 . . . . . . 1F **53**
Drappers Way SE16 . . . . 5C **78**
Drawdock Rd. SE10 . . . . 3F **81**
Draxmont SW19 . . . . . . 5A **114**
Draycot Rd. E11 . . . . . . 1D **41**
Draycott Av. SW3 . . . . . 5A **74**
Draycott Cl. NW2 . . . . . 5F **29**
SE5 . . . . 3F **91**
(not continuous)
Draycott M. SW6 . . . . . . 5B **86**
(off Laurel Bank Gdns.)
Draycott Pl. SW3 . . . . . 5B **74**
Draycott Ter. SW3 . . . . . 5B **74**
Drayford Cl. W9 . . . . . . 3B **58**
Dray Gdns. SW2 . . . . . . 3B **104**
Draymans M. SE15 . . . . 5B **92**
Drayson M. W8 . . . . 3C **72**
Drayton Gdns. SW10 . . . 1E **87**
Drayton Ho. E11 . . . . . . 3F **39**
SE5 . . . . 3F **91**
(off Elmington Rd.)
Drayton Pk. N5 . . . . 1C **48**
Drayton Pk. M. N5 . . . . . 2C **48**
Drayton Rd. E11 . . . . . . 3F **39**
NW10 . . . . 5B **42**
Dreadnought St.
SE10 . . . . 4A **82**
Dreadnought Wharf
SE10 . . . . 2D **95**
(off Thames St.)
Dresden Cl. NW6 . . . . . 3D **45**
Dresden Ho. SE11 . . . . . 5B **76**
(off Lambeth Wlk.)
Dresden Rd. N19 . . . . . . 3E **33**
Dressington Av.
SE4 . . . . 4C **108**
Drewery Ct. SE3 . . . . . . 1A **110**
Drewett Ho. E1 . . . . 5C **64**
(off Christian St.)
Drew Ho. SW16 . . . . . . 3A **118**
Drew Rd. E16 . . . . 2F **83**
(not continuous)
Drewstead Rd.
SW16 . . . . 2F **117**
Driffield Rd. E3 . . . . 1A **66**
Drill Hall Arts Cen. 5B **6**
(off Chenies St.)
Drinkwater Ho. SE5 . . . . 3F **91**
(off Picton St.)

Drive, The N7 . . . . 3B **48**
(not continuous)
NW10 . . . . 5B **42**
NW11 . . . . 2A **30**
SW6 . . . . 5A **86**
Drive Mans. SW6 . . . . . 5A **86**
(off Fulham Rd.)
Driveway, The E17 . . . . . 1D **39**
(off Hoe St.)
Dr Johnson's House . . . 3C **16**
(off Pemberton Row)
Droitwich Cl. SE26 . . . . 3C **120**
Dromore Rd.
SW15 . . . . 4A **100**
Dron Ho. E1 . . . . 4E **65**
(off Adelina Gro.)
Droop St. W10 . . . . 2F **57**
Drovers Pl. SE15 . . . . . . 3E **93**
Druce Rd. SE21 . . . . . . 4A **106**
Druid St. SE1 . . 3E **27** (3A **78**)
Drummond Cres.
NW1 . . . . 1B **6** (2F **61**)
Drummond Ga. SW1 . . . 1F **89**
Drummond Ho. E2 . . . . . 1C **64**
(off Goldsmiths Row)
Drummond Rd. E11 . . . . 1E **41**
SE16 . . . . 4D **79**
Drummond St.
NW1 . . . . 3F **5** (3E **61**)
Drum St. E1 . . . . 5B **64**
Drury Ho. SW8 . . . . 4E **89**
Drury La.
WC2 . . . . 2E **15** (5A **62**)
Drury Lane Theatre 3F **15**
(off Catherine St.)
Drury Way NW10 . . . . . 2A **42**
Dryad St. SW15 . . . . . . 1F **99**
Dryburgh Ho. SW1 . . . . 1D **89**
(off Abbots Mnr.)
Dryburgh Rd. SW15 . . . 1D **99**
Dryden Ct. SE11 . . . . . . 5D **77**
Dryden Mans. W14 . . . . 2A **86**
(off Queen's Club Gdns.)
Dryden Rd. SW19 . . . . . 5E **115**
Dryden St.
WC2 . . . . 3E **15** (5A **62**)
Dryfield Wlk. SE8 . . . . . 2C **94**
Drylands Rd. N8 . . . . . . 1A **34**
Drysdale Dwellings
E8 . . . . 2B **50**
(off Dunn St.)
Drysdale Ho. N1 . . . . . . 1E **11**
(off Drysdale St.)
Drysdale Pl.
N1 . . . . 1E **11** (2A **64**)
Drysdale St.
N1 . . . . 1E **11** (2A **64**)
Dublin Av. E8 . . . . 5C **50**
Ducal St. E2 . . . . 2B **64**
Du Cane Cl. W12 . . . . . 5E **57**
Du Cane Ct. SW17 . . . . 1C **116**
Du Cane Rd. W12 . . . . . 5B **56**
Ducavel Ho. SW2 . . . . . 1B **118**
Duchess M.
W1 . . . . 1E **13** (4D **61**)
Duchess of Bedford Ho.
W8 . . . . 3C **72**
(off Duchess of Bedford's Wlk.)
Duchess of Bedford's Wlk.
W8 . . . . 3C **72**

Duchess St.
W1 . . . . 1E **13** (4D **61**)
Duchess Theatre 4F **15**
(off Catherine St.)
Duchy St.
SE1 . . . . 1C **24** (2C **76**)
(not continuous)
Ducie St. SW4 . . . . . . 2B **104**
Duckett M. N4 . . . . . . 1D **35**
Duckett Rd. N4 . . . . . . 1C **34**
Duckett St. E1 . . . . 3F **65**
Duck La. W1 . . . . 3B **14**
Du Cros Rd. W3 . . . . . . 2A **70**
DUDDEN HILL 2D **43**
Dudden Hill La.
NW10 . . . . 1B **42**
Dudden Hill Pde.
NW10 . . . . 1B **42**
Duddington Cl.
SE9 . . . . 4F **125**
Dudley Ct. W1 . . . . . . 5B **60**
(off Up. Berkeley St.)
WC2 . . . . 2D **15** (5A **62**)
Dudley Ho. W2 . . . . . . 4F **59**
(off Nth. Wharf Rd.)
Dudley M. SW2 . . . . . 4C **104**
Dudley Rd. NW6 . . . . . 1A **58**
SW19 . . . . 5C **114**
Dudley St. W2 . . . . . . 4F **59**
Dudlington Rd. E5 . . . . 4E **37**
Dudmaston M.
SW3 . . . . 1F **87**
(off Fulham Rd.)
Dudrich M. SE22 . . . . 3B **106**
Duffell Ho. SE11 . . . . . 1B **90**
(off Loughborough St.)
Dufferin Av. EC1 . . . . . 4B **10**
Dufferin Ct. EC1 . . . . . 4B **10**
(off Dufferin St.)
Dufferin St.
EC1 . . . . . . 4A **10** (3E **63**)
Duff St. E14 . . . . 5D **67**
Dufour's Pl.
W1 . . . . 3A **14** (5E **61**)
Dugard Way SE11 . . . 5D **77**
Duggan Dr.
BR7: Chst 5F **125**
Duke Humphrey Rd.
SE3 . . . . 4A **96**
Duke of Wellington Pl.
SW1 . . . . . . 3C **20** (3D **74**)
Duke of York Column
(Memorial) 2C **22**
Duke of York Sq.
SW3 . . . . 5B **74**
Duke of York's Theatre
. . . . 5D **15**
(off St Martin's La.)
Duke of York St.
SW1 . . . . . . 1A **22** (2E **75**)
Duke Rd. W4 . . . . 1A **84**
Duke's Av. W4 . . . . . . 1A **84**
Dukes Ct. SE13 . . . . . 5E **95**
SW14 . . . . 5A **84**
Duke's Head Yd. N6 . . 3D **33**
Duke Shore Wharf
E14 . . . . 1B **80**
Duke's Ho. SW1 . . . . . 5F **75**
(off Vincent St.)
Dukes La. W8 . . . . . . 3D **73**

Duke's La. Chambers
W8 . . . . 3D **73**
(off Dukes La.)
Duke's La. Mans.
W8 . . . . 3D **73**
(off Dukes La.)
Duke's M. W1 . . . . . . 2C **12**
Duke's Pl.
EC3 . . . . . . 3E **19** (5A **64**)
Dukes Point N6 . . . . . 3D **33**
(off Dukes Head Yd.)
Duke's Rd.
WC1 . . . . . . 2C **6** (2F **61**)
Dukesthorpe Rd.
SE26 . . . . 4F **121**
Duke St.
SW1 . . . . . . 1A **22** (2E **75**)
W1 . . . . 2C **12** (5C **60**)
Duke St. Hill
SE1 . . . . 1C **26** (2F **77**)
Duke St. Mans. W1 . . . 3C **12**
(off Duke St.)
Duke's Yd.
W1 . . . . 4C **12** (1C **74**)
Dulas St. N4 . . . . 3B **34**
Dulford St. W11 . . . . . 1A **72**
Dulka Rd. SW11 . . . . 3B **102**
Dulverton NW1 . . . . . . 5E **47**
(off Royal College St.)
Dulverton Mans.
WC1 . . . . 4A **8**
DULWICH 2A **120**
Dulwich Bus. Cen.
SE23 . . . . 1F **121**
Dulwich Comn.
SE21 . . . . 1A **120**
SE22 . . . . 1A **120**
Dulwich Hamlet FC . . 2A **106**
Dulwich Lawn Cl.
SE22 . . . . 3B **106**
Dulwich Leisure Cen.
. . . . 2C **106**
Dulwich Oaks, The
SE21 . . . . 3B **120**
Dulwich Picture Gallery
. . . . 5F **105**
Dulwich Ri. Gdns.
SE22 . . . . 3B **106**
Dulwich Rd. SE24 . . . 3C **104**
Dulwich Upper Wood
Nature Pk. 5B **120**
DULWICH VILLAGE . . 5A **106**
Dulwich Village
SE21 . . . . 4F **105**
Dulwich Wood Av.
SE19 . . . . 4A **120**
Dulwich Wood Pk.
SE19 . . . . 4A **120**
Dumain Ct. SE11 . . . . . 5D **77**
(off Opal St.)
Dumbarton Ct. SW2 . . 4A **104**
Dumbarton Rd.
SW2 . . . . 4A **104**
Dumont Rd. N16 . . . . . 5A **36**
Dumpton Pl. NW1 . . . . 4C **46**
Dunbar Rd. E7 . . . . . . 3C **54**
Dunbar St. SE27 . . . . 3E **119**
Dunbar Wharf E14 . . . . 1B **80**
(off Narrow St.)
Dunboyne Rd. NW3 . . 2B **46**

Dunbridge Ho. SW15 . . 4B **98**
(off Highcliffe Dr.)
Dunbridge St. E2 . . . . 3C **64**
Duncan Gro. W3 . . . . . 5A **56**
Duncan Ho. NW3 . . . . 4B **46**
(off Fellows Rd.)
SW1 . . . . 1E **89**
(off Dolphin Sq.)
Duncannon Ho. SW1 . . 1F **89**
(off Lindsay Sq.)
Duncannon St.
WC2 . . . . . . 5D **15** (1A **76**)
Duncan Rd. E8 . . . . . . 5D **51**
Duncan St. N1 . . . . . . 1D **63**
Duncan Ter. N1 . . . . . 1D **63**
(not continuous)
Dunch St. E1 . . . . 5D **65**
Duncombe Hill
SE23 . . . . 5A **108**
Duncombe Rd. N19 . . . 3F **33**
Duncrievie Rd.
SE13 . . . . 4F **109**
Dundalk Ho. E1 . . . . . 5E **65**
(off Clark St.)
Dundalk Rd. SE4 . . . . 1A **108**
Dundas Ho. E2 . . . . . . 1E **65**
(off Bishop's Way)
Dundas Rd. SE15 . . . . 5E **93**
Dundee Ct. E1 . . . . . . 2D **79**
(off Wapping High St.)
Dundee Ho. W9 . . . . . 2E **59**
(off Maida Va.)
Dundee Rd. E13 . . . . . 1D **69**
Dundee St. E1 . . . . . . 2D **79**
Dundee Wharf E14 . . . 1B **80**
Dundonald Ho. E14 . . . 3D **81**
(off Admirals Way)
Dundonald Rd. NW10 . . 5F **43**
Dundry Ho. SE26 . . . . 3C **120**
Dunedin Rd. E10 . . . . . 5D **39**
Dunelm Gro. SE27 . . . 3E **119**
Dunelm St. E1 . . . . . . 5F **65**
Dunfield Gdns. SE6 . . . 5D **123**
Dunfield Rd. SE6 . . . . 5D **123**
(not continuous)
Dunford Rd. N7 . . . . . 1B **48**
Dungarvan Av. SW15 . . 2C **98**
Dunhill Point SW15 . . 1C **112**
Dunkeld Ho. E14 . . . . . 5F **67**
(off Abbott Rd.)
Dunkery Rd. SE9 . . . . 4F **125**
Dunkirk St. SE27 . . . . 4E **119**
Dunlace Rd. E5 . . . . . . 1E **51**
Dunlin Ho. SE16 . . . . . 5F **79**
(off Tawny Way)
Dunloe Ct. E2 . . . . 1B **64**
Dunloe St. E2 . . . . 1B **64**
Dunlop Pl. SE16 . . . . . 4D **78**
Dunmore Point E2 . . . . 2F **11**
(off Gascoigne Pl.)
Dunmore Rd. NW6 . . . 5A **44**
Dunmow Ho. SE11 . . . . 1B **90**
(off Newburn St.)
Dunmow Rd. E15 . . . . 1F **53**
Dunmow Wlk. N1 . . . . 5E **49**
(off Popham St.)
Dunmore Gro. E17 . . . 5A **80**
(not continuous)
Dunnico Ho. SE17 . . . . 1A **92**
(off East St.)

Dunn's Pas. WC1 . . . . . . 2E 15
Dunn St. E8 . . . . 2B 50
Dunollie Pl. NW5 . . . . . 2E 47
Dunollie Rd. NW5 . . . . . 2E 47
Dunoon Gdns. SE23 . . 5F 107
Dunoon Ho. N1 . . . . 5B 48
  (off Bemerton Est.)
Dunoon Rd. SE23 . . . . . 5E 107
Dunraven Rd. W12 . . . . 2C 70
Dunraven St.
  W1 . . . . 4A 12 (1B 74)
Dunsany Rd. W14 . . . . . 4F 71
Dunsford Way
  SW15 . . . . 4D 99
Dunsmure Rd. N16 . . . . 3A 36
Dunstable M.
  W1 . . . . 5C 4 (4C 60)
Dunstan Ho's. E1 . . . . . 4E 65
  (off Stepney Grn.)
Dunstan Rd. NW11 . . . . 3B 30
Dunstan's Gro.
  SE22 . . . . 4D 107
Dunstan's Rd. SE22 . . . 5C 106
Dunster Ct.
  EC3 . . . . 4E 19 (1A 78)
Dunster Gdns. NW6 . . . 4B 44
Dunster Ho. SE6 . . . . . 3E 123
Dunsterville Way
  SE1 . . . . 4C 26 (3F 77)
Dunston Rd. E8 . . . . . . 5B 50
  SW11 . . . . 5C 88
Dunston St. E8 . . . . . . 5A 50
Dunton Ct. SE23 . . . . . 2D 121
Dunton Rd. E10 . . . . . . 2D 39
  SE1 . . . . 1B 92
Duntshill Rd. SW18 . . . 1D 115
Dunworth M. W11 . . . . . 5B 58
Duplex Ride
  SW1 . . . . 4A 20 (3B 74)
Dupree Rd. SE7 . . . . . . 1D 97
Durand Gdns. SW9 . . . . 4B 90
Durands Wlk. SE16 . . . . 3B 80
Durant St. E2 . . . . 1C 64
Durban Ho. W12 . . . . . . 1D 71
  (off White City Est.)
Durban Rd. E15 . . . . . . 2A 68
  SE27 . . . . 4E 119
Durdans Ho. NW1 . . . . . 4D 47
  (off Farrier St.)
Durell Ho. SE16 . . . . . . 3F 79
  (off Wolfe Cres.)
Durford Cres. SW15 . . 1D 113
Durham Ct. NW6 . . . . . 1C 58
  (off Kilburn Pk. Rd.,
  not continuous)
Durham Hill
  BR1: Brom 4B 124
Durham Ho. St. WC2 . . 5E 15
Durham Pl. SW3 . . . . . 1B 88
Durham Rd. E12 . . . . . 1F 55
  E16 . . . . 3A 68
  N7 . . . . 4B 34
Durham Row E1 . . . . . 4F 65
Durham St. SE11 . . . . . 1B 90
Durham Ter. W2 . . . . . 5D 59
Durham Yd. E2 . . . . . . 2D 65
Durley Rd. N16 . . . . . . 2A 36
Durlston Rd. E5 . . . . . . 4C 36
Durnford Ho. SE6 . . . . 3E 123

Durnford St. N15 . . . . . 1A 36
  SE10 . . . . 2E 95
Durning Rd. SE19 . . . . 5F 119
Dunsford Av. SW19 . . . 2C 114
Durnsford Rd.
  SW19 . . . . 2C 114
Durrell Rd. SW6 . . . . . 4B 86
Durrels Ho. W14 . . . . . 5B 72
  (off Warwick Gdns.)
Durrington Rd. E5 . . . . 1A 52
Durrington Twr.
  SW8 . . . . 5E 89
Durrisdeer Ho. NW2 . . 1B 44
  (off Lyndale)
Dursley Cl. SE3 . . . . . . 5E 97
Dursley Gdns. SE3 . . . 4F 97
Dursley Rd. SE3 . . . . . 5E 97
Durward St. E1 . . . . . . 4D 65
Durweston M. W1 . . . . 5A 4
Durweston St.
  W1 . . . . 1A 12 (4B 60)
Dutch Yd. SW18 . . . . . 3C 100
Dutton St. SE10 . . . . . 4E 95
Dye Ho. La. E3 . . . . . . 5C 52
Dyer's Bldgs.
  EC1 . . . . 1B 16 (4C 62)
Dyers Hall Rd. E11 . . . 3A 40
Dyers Hall Rd. E11 . . . 4F 39
Dyers La. SW15 . . . . . 2D 99
Dylan Rd. SE24 . . . . . . 2D 105
Dylways SE5 . . . . 2F 105
Dymes Path SW19 . . . 2F 113
Dymock St. SW6 . . . . . 1D 101
Dyneley Rd. SE12 . . . . 3E 125
Dyne Rd. NW6 . . . . . . 4A 44
Dynevor Rd. N16 . . . . . 5A 36
Dynham Rd. NW6 . . . . 4C 44
Dyott St.
  WC1 . . . . 2C 14 (5F 61)
Dysart St.
  EC2 . . . . 4D 11 (3F 63)
Dyson Ct. NW2 . . . . . . 3E 29
Dyson Ho. SE10 . . . . . 1B 96
  (off Blackwall La.)
Dyson Rd. E11 . . . . . . 1A 40
  E15 . . . . 3B 54

E

Eade Rd. N4 . . . . 2E 35
Eagle Cl. SE16 . . . . . . 1E 93
Eagle Ct.
  EC1 . . . . 5D 9 (4D 63)
Eagle Hill SE19 . . . . . 5F 119
Eagle Ho. E1 . . . . 3D 65
  (off Headlam St.)
  N1 . . . . 1F 63
  (off Eagle Wharf Rd.)
Eagle Lodge NW11 . . . 2B 30
Eagle M. N1 . . . . 3A 50
Eagle Pl. SW1 . . . . . . 5A 14
  SW7 . . . . 1E 87
Eagle St.
  WC1 . . . . 1F 15 (4B 62)
Eagle Wharf Ct. SE1 . . 2F 27
  (off Lafone St.)
Eagle Wharf E. E14 . . . 1A 80
  (off Narrow St.)
Eagle Wharf Rd. N1 . . . 1E 63

Eagle Wharf W. E14 . . . 1A 80
  (off Narrow St.)
Eagle Works E. E1 . . . 4F 11
Eagle Works W.
  E1 . . . . 4F 11 (3B 64)
Ealdham Sq. SE9 . . . . 2E 111
Eamont Ct. NW8 . . . . . 1A 60
  (off Eamont St.)
Eamont St. NW8 . . . . . 1A 60
Eardley Cres. SW5 . . . 1C 86
Eardley Rd. SW16 . . . . 5E 117
Earldom Rd. SW15 . . . 2E 99
Earlham St. E11 . . . . . 2B 40
Earlham Gro. E7 . . . . . 2B 54
Earlham St.
  WC2 . . . . 3C 14 (5A 62)
Earl Ho. NW1 . . . . 3A 60
  (off Lisson Gro.)
Earlom Ho. WC1 . . . . . 2B 8
  (off Margery St.)
EARL'S COURT 1C 86
Earls Court
  Exhibition Building
  . . . . 1C 86
Earl's Ct. Gdns. SW5 . . 5D 73
Earls Ct. Rd. SW5 . . . . 4C 72
  W8 . . . . 4C 72
Earl's Ct. Sq. SW5 . . . 1D 87
Earlsferry Way N1 . . . . 4A 48
  (not continuous)
EARLSFIELD 1E 115
Earlsfield Rd. SW18 . . 1E 115
Earlsmead Rd. NW10 . . 2E 57
Earls Ter. W8 . . . . 4B 72
Earlsthorpe M.
  SW12 . . . . 4C 102
Earlsthorpe Rd.
  SE26 . . . . 4F 121
Earlstoke St.
  EC1 . . . . 1D 9 (2D 63)
Earlston Gro. E9 . . . . . 5D 51
Earl St. EC2 . . . . . 5D 11 (4F 63)
  (not continuous)
Earls Wlk. W8 . . . . 4C 72
Earlswood Cl. SE10 . . . 2A 96
Earlswood St. SE10 . . . 1A 96
Early M. NW1 . . . . 5D 47
Earnshaw St.
  WC2 . . . . 2C 14 (5F 61)
Earsby St. W14 . . . . . . 5A 72
  (not continuous)
Eashing Point
  SW15 . . . . 1D 113
  (off Wanborough Dr.)
Easleys M.
  W1 . . . . 2C 12 (5C 60)
East 10 Ent. Pk. E10 . . 3A 38
EAST ACTON 1B 70
E. Acton Arc. W3 . . . . 5A 56
E. Acton Ct. W3 . . . . . 1A 70
E. Acton La. W3 . . . . . 2A 70
E. Arbour St. E1 . . . . . 5F 65
East Bank N16 . . . . . . 2A 36
East Block SE1 . . . . . . 3A 24
  (off York Rd.)
Eastbourne M. W2 . . . 5E 59
Eastbourne Rd. E15 . . 5A 54
  N15 . . . . 1A 36
  SW17 . . . . 5C 116
Eastbourne Ter. W2 . . . 5E 59

Eastbrook Rd. SE3 . . . . . . 4D 97
Eastbury Gro. W4 . . . . 1A 84
Eastbury Ter. E1 . . . . 3F 65
Eastcastle St.
  W1 . . . . 2F 13 (5E 61)
Eastcheap
  EC3 . . . . 4D 19 (1A 78)
E. Churchfield Rd.
  W3 . . . . 2A 70
Eastcombe Av. SE7 . . . . 2D 97
Eastcote St. SW9 . . . . . . 5B 90
E. Cross Cen. E15 . . . . . 3C 52
E. Cross Route E3 . . . . . 4B 52
  E9 . . . . 2B 52
    (Homerton)
  E9 . . . . 4B 52
    (Old Ford)
  E15 . . . . 2B 52
Eastdown Ct. SE13 . . . . 2F 109
Eastdown Ho. E8 . . . . . . 1C 50
Eastdown Pk. SE13 . . . . 2F 109
EAST DULWICH 2B 106
E. Dulwich Gro.
  SE22 . . . . 3A 106
E. Dulwich Rd.
  SE22 . . . . 2B 106
    (not continuous)
Eastern Av. E11 . . . . 1D 41
  IG4: Ilf. 1F 41
Eastern Gateway E16 . . 1E 83
Eastern Quay Apartments
  E16 . . . . 2D 83
    (off Portsmouth M.)
Eastern Rd. E13 . . . . 1D 69
  E17 . . . . 1E 39
  SE4 . . . . 2C 108
E. Ferry Rd. E14 . . . . . . 5D 81
Eastfields Av. SW18 . . . 2C 100
Eastfield St. E14 . . . . . . 4A 66
East Gdns. SW17 . . . . . 5A 116
EAST HAM 2F 69
E. Ham Ind. Est. E6 . . . 3F 69
E. Harding St.
  EC4 . . . . 2C 16 (5C 62)
E. Heath Rd. NW3 . . . . . 5E 31
East Hill SW18 . . . . 3D 101
E. India Bldgs. E14 . . . 1C 80
E. India Ct. SE16 . . . . . 3E 79
    (off St Marychurch St.)
E. India Dock Ho.
  E14 . . . . 5E 67
E. India Dock Rd.
  E14 . . . . 5C 66
Eastlake Ho. NW8 . . . . . 3F 59
    (off Frampton St.)
Eastlake Rd. SE5 . . . . . . 5E 91
Eastlands Cres.
  SE21 . . . . 4B 106
East La. SE16 . . . . 3C 78
    (Chambers St.)
  SE16 . . . . 3C 78
    (Scott Lidgett Cres.)
Eastlea M. E16 . . . . 3A 68
Eastleigh Cl. NW2 . . . . . 5A 28
Eastleigh Wlk. SW15 . . 5C 98
East Lodge E16 . . . . . . 2C 82
    (off Wesley Av.)
E. London Crematorium
  E13 . . . . 2B 68

Eastman Ho. SW4 . . . . . 4E 103
Eastman Rd. W3 . . . . . . 3A 70
East Mascalls SE7 . . . . . 2E 97
Eastmearn Rd.
  SE21 . . . . 2E 119
Eastmoor Pl. SE7 . . . . . . 4F 83
Eastmoor St. SE7 . . . . . . 4F 83
East Mt. St. E1 . . . . 4D 65
    (not continuous)
Eastney St. SE10 . . . . . . 1F 95
Easton St.
  WC1 . . . . 3B 8 (3C 62)
East Parkside
  SE10 . . . . 3A 82
East Pas. EC1 . . . . 5F 9
East Pl. SE27 . . . . 4E 119
East Point SE1 . . . . 1C 92
E. Poultry Av.
  EC1 . . . . 1D 17 (4D 63)
East Rd. E15 . . . . 5A 54
  N1 . . . . 2B 10 (2F 63)
  SW3 . . . . 1C 88
East Row E11 . . . . 1C 40
  W10 . . . . 3A 58
Eastry Ho. SW8 . . . . . . 3A 90
    (off Hartington Rd.)
E. Sheen Av. SW14 . . . . 2A 98
EAST SHEEN 2A 98
East Smithfield
  E1 . . . . 5F 19 (1B 78)
East St. SE17 . . . . 1E 91
E. Surrey Gro. SE15 . . . 3B 92
E. Tenter St. E1 . . . . 5B 64
East Va. W3 . . . . 2B 70
Eastville Av. NW11 . . . . 1B 30
Eastwell Ho. SE1 . . . . . . 5C 26
Eastwood Cl. N7 . . . . . . 2C 48
Eatington Rd. E10 . . . . . 1F 39
Eaton Cl. SW1 . . . . 5C 74
Eaton Dr. SW9 . . . . 2D 105
Eaton Ga. SW1 . . . . 5C 74
Eaton Ho. E14 . . . . 1B 80
    (off Westferry Cir.)
Eaton La.
  SW1 . . . . 5E 21 (4D 75)
Eaton Mans. SW1 . . . . . 5C 74
    (off Bourne St.)
Eaton M. Nth.
  SW1 . . . . 5C 20 (5C 74)
Eaton M. Sth. SW1 . . . . 5C 74
Eaton M. W. SW1 . . . . . 5C 74
Eaton Pl.
  SW1 . . . . 5C 20 (5C 74)
Eaton Row SW1 . . . . . . 4D 75
Eaton Sq.
  SW1 . . . . 5C 20 (5C 74)
Eaton Ter. E3 . . . . 2A 66
  SW1 . . . . 5C 74
Eaton Ter. M. SW1 . . . . 5C 74
    (off Eaton Ter.)
Eatonville Rd.
  SW17 . . . . 2B 116
Eatonville Vs.
  SW17 . . . . 2B 116
Ebbisham Dr. SW8 . . . . 2B 90
Ebbsfleet Rd. NW2 . . . . 2A 44
Ebdon Way SE3 . . . . . . 1D 111
Ebenezer Ho. SE11 . . . . 5D 77

Ebenezer Mussel Ho.
  E2 . . . . 1E 65
    (off Patriot Sq.)
Ebenezer St.
  N1 . . . . 1B 10 (2F 63)
Ebley Cl. SE15 . . . . 2B 92
Ebner St. SW18 . . . . . . 3D 101
Ebony Ho. E2 . . . . 2C 64
    (off Buckfast St.)
Ebor Cotts. SW15 . . . . . 3A 112
Ebor St. E1. . . 3F 11 (3B 64)
Ebsworth St.
  SE23 . . . . 5F 107
Eburne Rd. N7 . . . . 5A 34
Ebury Bri. SW1 . . . . 1D 89
Ebury Bri. Est. SW1 . . . 1D 89
Ebury Bri. Rd. SW1 . . . 1C 88
Ebury M. SE27 . . . . 3D 119
  SW1 . . . . 5D 75
Ebury M. E. SW1 . . . . . 4D 75
Ebury Sq. SW1 . . . . 5C 74
Ebury St. SW1 . . . . 5C 74
Ecclesbourne Rd. N1 . . 4E 49
Eccles Rd. SW11 . . . . . 2B 102
Eccleston Bri. SW1 . . . 5D 75
Eccleston Ho.
  SW2 . . . . 4C 104
Eccleston M.
  SW1 . . . . 5C 20 (4C 74)
Eccleston Pl. SW1 . . . . 5D 75
Eccleston Sq. SW1 . . . . 5D 75
Eccleston Sq. M.
  SW1 . . . . 5D 75
Eccleston St. SW1 . . . . 4D 75
Eckford St. N1 . . . . 1C 62
Eckington Ho. N15 . . . . 1F 35
    (off Fladbury Rd.)
Eckstein Rd. SW11 . . . . 2A 102
Eclipse Rd. E13 . . . . . . 4D 69
Ecology Cen. and
  Arts Pavilion 2A 66
Ector Rd. SE6 . . . . 2A 124
Edans Ct. W12 . . . . 3B 70
Edbrooke Rd. W9 . . . . . 3C 58
Eddisbury Ho. SE26 . . . 3C 120
Eddiscombe Rd.
  SW6 . . . . 5B 86
Eddystone Rd. SE4 . . . . 3A 108
Eddystone Twr. SE8 . . . 1A 94
Edenbridge Cl. SE16 . . 1D 93
    (off Masters Dr.)
Edenbridge Rd. E9 . . . . 4F 51
Eden Cl. NW3 . . . . 4C 30
  W8 . . . . 4C 72
Edencourt Rd.
  SW16 . . . . 5D 117
Eden Gro. E17 . . . . 1D 39
  N7 . . . . 2B 48
Edenham Way W10 . . . 3B 58
Eden Ho. NW8 . . . . 3A 60
    (off Church St.)
Edenhurst Av. SW6 . . . 1B 100
Eden Lodge NW6 . . . . . 4F 43
Eden M. SW17 . . . . 3E 115
Eden Rd. E17 . . . . 1D 39
  SE27 . . . . 4D 119
Edensor Gdns. W4 . . . . 3A 84
Edensor Rd. W4 . . . . . . 3A 84
Edenvale St. SW6 . . . . . 5E 87
Eden Way E3 . . . . 5B 52

Edgar Ho. *E9* 2A **52**
   (off Homerton Rd.)
E11 . . . . 2C **40**
SW8 . . . . 3A **90**
   (off Wyvil Rd.)
Edgar Kail Way
SE22 . . . . 2A **106**
Edgarley Ter. SW6 . . . . 4A **86**
Edgar Rd. E3 . . . . 2D **67**
Edgcott Ho. *W10* 4E **57**
   (off Sutton Way)
Edge Bus. Cen., The
NW2 . . . . 4D **29**
Edgecombe Ho. SE5. . . 5A **92**
SW19 . . . . 1A **114**
Edgecot Gro. N15. . . . . . 1A **36**
Edgehill Ho. SW9. . . . . 5D **91**
Edgeley La. SW4 . . . . . 1F **103**
Edgeley Rd. SW4 . . . . 1F **103**
Edgel St. SW18 . . . . . . 2D **101**
Edge St. W8 . . . . 2C **72**
Edgeworth Ho. *NW8* 5E **45**
   (off Boundary Rd.)
Edgeworth Rd. SE9. . . 2E **111**
Edgson Ho. *SW1* 1D **89**
   (off Ebury Bri. Rd.)
Edgware Rd. NW2 . . . . 3D **29**
W2 . . . . 3A **12** (3F **59**)
Edinburgh Cl. E2. . . . . . 1E **65**
Edinburgh Ct. *SE16*. . . . 2F **79**
   (off Rotherhithe St.)
Edinburgh Ga. SW1 . . . 3B **74**
Edinburgh Ho. *W9* 2D **59**
   (off Maida Va.)
Edinburgh Rd. E13. . . . 1D **69**
E17 . . . . 1C **38**
   (not continuous)
Edington NW5. . . . . 3C **46**
Edison Bldg. E14 . . . . . 3C **80**
Edison Ct. SE10 . . . . . . 4B **82**
Edison Rd. N8. . . . . . . 1F **33**
Edis St. NW1. . . . . 5C **46**
Edith Brinson Ho.
E14 . . . . 5F **67**
   (off Oban St.)
Edith Cavell Cl. N19. . . 2A **34**
Edith Gro. SW10. . . . . . 2E **87**
Edith Ho. *W6* 1E **85**
   (off Queen Caroline St.)
Edithna St. SW9. . . . . 1A **104**
Edith Neville Cotts.
NW1 . . . . *1B 6*
   (off Drummond Cres.)
Edith Ramsay Ho. *E1*. . 4A **66**
   (off Duckett St.)
Edith Rd. E6 . . . . 4F **55**
E15 . . . . 2F **53**
SW19 . . . . 5D **115**
W14 . . . . 5A **72**
Edith Row SW6 . . . . . . 4D **87**
Edith St. E2. . . . . 1C **64**
Edith Summerskill Ho.
SW6 . . . . *3B 86*
   (off Clem Attlee Est.)
Edith Ter. SW10 . . . . . . 3E **87**
Edith Vs. W14. . . . . . . 5B **72**
Edith Yd. SW10 . . . . . . 3E **87**
Edmeston Cl. E9. . . . . . 3A **52**
Edmond Cl. SE14 . . . . 4E **93**

Edmonton Ct. *SE16*. . . . 4E **79**
   (off Canada Est.)
Edmund Halley Way
SE10. . . . . 3A **82**
Edmund Ho. SE17 . . . . 2D **91**
Edmundsbury Ct. Est.
SW9 . . . . 2B **104**
Edmund St. SE5 . . . . . 3F **91**
Ednam Ho. *SE15* 2C **92**
   (off Haymerle Rd.)
Edna St. SW11. . . . . . . 4A **88**
Edred Ho. *E9* 1A **52**
   (off Lindisfarne Way)
Edrich Ho. SW4 . . . . . . 4A **90**
Edric Ho. *SW1* 5F **75**
   (off Page St.)
Edric Rd. SE14. . . . . . . 3F **93**
Edward VII Mans.
NW10 . . . . 2F **57**
   (off Chamberlayne Rd.)
Edward Bond Ho. *WC1*. . . 2E **7**
   (off Cromer St.)
Edward Cl. NW2 . . . . . . 1F **43**
Edward Ct. E16. . . . . . . 4C **68**
Edward Dodd Ct. *N1*. . . 1C **10**
   (off Haberdasher St.)
Edward Edward's Ho.
SE1 . . . . 2D **25**
Edwardes Pl. W8 . . . . . 4B **72**
Edwardes Sq. W8. . . . . 4B **72**
Edward Ho. SE11 . . . . . 1B **90**
   (off Newburn St.)
Edward Mann Cl. *E1*. . . 5F **65**
   (off Caroline St.)
Edward M.
NW1 . . . . 1E **5** (2D **61**)
Edward Pl. SE8 . . . . . . 2B **94**
Edward Rd. E17 . . . . . . 1F **37**
Edward Robinson Ho.
SE14 . . . . 3F **93**
   (off Reaston St.)
Edward's Cotts. N1 . . . 3D **49**
Edward's La. N16. . . . . 4A **36**
Edwards M. N1. . . . . . . 4C **48**
W1. . . . . 3B **12** (5C **60**)
Edward Sq. N1. . . . . . . 5B **48**
SE16. . . . . 2A **80**
Edward St. E16. . . . . . . 3C **68**
   (not continuous)
SE8 . . . . 2B **94**
SE14 . . . . 3A **94**
Edward Temme Av.
E15 . . . . 4B **54**
Edward Tyler Rd.
SE12 . . . . 2E **125**
Edwina Gdns.
IG4: Ilf 1F **41**
Edwin Ho. SE15. . . . . . 3C **92**
Edwin's Head Ho. 1A **52**
Edwin St. E1. . . . . 3E **65**
E16. . . . . 4C **68**
Edwyn Ho. *SW18*. 4D **101**
   (off Neville Gill Cl.)
Effie Pl. SW6 . . . . 3C **86**
Effie Rd. SW6. . . . . 3C **86**
Effingham Rd. SE12. . . 3A **110**
Effort St. SW17 . . . . . 5A **116**
Effra Ct. *SW2* *3B 104*
   (off Brixton Hill)
Effra Pde. SW2. . . . . . 3C **104**

Effra Rd. SW2 . . . . . . 2C **104**
SW19 . . . . 5D **115**
Effra Rd. Retail Pk.
SW2 . . . . 3C **104**
Egbert St. NW1 . . . . . . 5C **46**
Egbury Ho. *SW15*. 4B **98**
   (off Tangley Gro.)
Egeremont Rd. SE13. . 5D **95**
Egerton Ct. E11. . . . . . 2F **39**
Egerton Cres. SW3. . . . 5A **74**
Egerton Dr. SE10 . . . . 4D **95**
Egerton Gdns. NW10 . . 5E **43**
SW3 . . . . 5A **74**
Egerton Gdns. M.
SW3 . . . . 4A **74**
Egerton Pl. SW3. . . . . . 4A **74**
Egerton Rd. N16. . . . . . 2B **36**
Egerton Ter. SW3 . . . . 4A **74**
Egham Cl. SW19 . . . . . 2A **114**
Egham Rd. E13 . . . . . . 4D **69**
Eglantine Rd. SW18. . . 3E **101**
Eglington Ct. SE17 . . . 2E **91**
Egliston M. SW15 . . . . 1E **99**
Egliston Rd. SW15. . . . 1E **99**
Eglon M. NW1 . . . . 4B **46**
Egmont St. SE14. . . . . 3F **93**
Egremont Ho. *SE13* . . . 5D **95**
   (off Russett Way)
Egremont Rd. SE27 . . . 3C **118**
Egret Ho. SE16 . . . . . . 5F **79**
   (off Tawny Way)
Eider Cl. E7 . . . . 2B **54**
Eider Ct. *SE8* *2B 94*
   (off Pilot Cl.)
Eisenhower Dr. E6 . . . . 4F **69**
Elaine Gro. NW5 . . . . . 2C **46**
Elam Cl. SE5 . . . . 5D **91**
Elam St. SE5 . . . . 5D **91**
Elan Ct. E1 . . . . 4D **65**
Eland Ho. *SW1* 5F **21**
   (off Bressenden Pl.)
Eland Rd. SW11. . . . . . 1B **102**
Elba Pl. SE17 . . . . 5E **77**
Elbe St. SW6 . . . . 5E **87**
Elborough St. SW18. . . 1C **114**
Elbourne Ct. *SE16*. 4F **79**
   (off Worgan St.)
Elbourn Ho. *SW3*. 1A **88**
   (off Cale St.)
Elbury Dr. E16 . . . . 5C **68**
Elcho St. SW11 . . . . . . 3A **88**
Elcot Av. SE15 . . . . 3D **93**
Elder Av. N8 . . . . 1A **34**
Elderberry Gro.
SE27 . . . . 4E **119**
Elderfield Ho. E14 . . . . 1C **80**
Elderfield Pl. SW17. . . 4D **117**
Elderfield Rd. E5 . . . . . 1F **51**
Elderflower Way E15 . . 4A **54**
Elder Gdns. SE27 . . . . 5E **119**
Elder Rd. SE27. . . . . . . 4E **119**
Elder St. E1 . . . . . 5F **11** (3B **64**)
   (not continuous)
Elderton Rd. SE26 . . . 4A **122**
Elder Wlk. *N1*. *5D 49*
   (off Popham St.)
Elderwood Pl. SE27 . . . 5E **119**
Eldon Ho. NW6 . . . . . . 5C **44**
Eldon Gro. NW3 . . . . . 2F **45**
Eldon Rd. W8. . . . . 4D **73**

Eldon St. EC2... 1C 18 (4F 63)
Eldridge Ct. SE16...... 4C 78
Eleanor Cl. SE16...... 3F 79
Eleanor Gro. SW13.... 1A 98
Eleanor Ho. W6...... 1E 85
   (off Queen Caroline St.)
Eleanor Rathbone Ho.
  N6...... 2F 33
   (off Avenue Rd.)
Eleanor Rd. E8...... 3D 51
  E15...... 3B 54
Eleanor St. E3...... 2C 66
Electra Bus. Pk. E16... 4F 67
Electric Av. SW9.... 2C 104
Electric La. SW9.... 2C 104
   (not continuous)
Elektron Ho. E14...... 1F 81
ELEPHANT & CASTLE
                4D 77
Elephant & Castle
  SE1...... 5D 77
Elephant & Castle Superbowl
               5E 77
   (off Walworth Rd.)
Elephant La. SE16.... 3E 79
Elephant Rd. SE17.... 5E 77
Elfindale Rd. SE24.... 3E 105
Elford Cl. SE3...... 2D 111
Elford M. SW4...... 3E 103
Elfort Rd. N5...... 1C 48
Elfrida Cres. SE6.... 4C 122
Elf Row E1...... 1E 79
Elgar Av. NW10...... 3A 42
   (not continuous)
Elgar Cl. E13...... 1E 69
  SE8...... 3C 94
Elgar Ct. W14...... 4A 72
   (off Blythe Rd.)
Elgar Ho. NW6...... 4E 45
   (off Fairfax Rd.)
  SW1...... 1D 89
   (off Churchill Gdns.)
Elgar St. SE16...... 4A 80
Elgin Av. W9...... 3B 58
  W12...... 4D 71
Elgin Cl. W12...... 3D 71
Elgin Ct. W9...... 3D 59
Elgin Cres. W11...... 1A 72
Elgin Est. W9...... 3C 58
   (off Elgin Av.)
Elgin Ho. E14...... 5D 67
   (off Ricardo St.)
Elgin Mans. W9...... 2D 59
Elgin M. W11...... 5A 58
Elgin M. Nth. W9...... 2D 59
Elgin M. Sth. W9...... 2D 59
Elgood Cl. W11...... 1A 72
Elgood Ho. NW8...... 1F 59
   (off Wellington Rd.)
Elham Ho. E5...... 2D 51
Elia M. N1...... 1D 9 (1D 63)
Elias Pl. SW8...... 2C 90
Elia St. N1...... 1E 9 (1D 63)
Elim Est.
  SE1...... 5D 27 (4A 78)
Elim St. SE1...... 5C 26 (4F 77)
   (not continuous)
Elim Way E13...... 2B 68
Eliot Bank SE23...... 2D 121
Eliot Cotts. SE3...... 5A 96

Eliot Ct. SW18...... 4D 101
Eliot Gdns. SW15.... 2C 98
Eliot Hill SE13...... 5E 95
Eliot M. NW8...... 1E 59
Eliot Pk. SE13...... 5E 95
Eliot Pl. SE3...... 5A 96
Eliot Va. SE3...... 5F 95
Elizabeth Av. N1...... 5E 49
Elizabeth Barnes Ct.
  SW6...... 5D 87
   (off Marinefield Rd.)
Elizabeth Bri. SW1.... 5D 75
Elizabeth Cl. E14.... 5D 67
  W9...... 3F 59
Elizabeth Ct. SW1.... 5C 22
  SW10...... 2F 87
   (off Milman's St.)
Elizabeth Fry M. E8.. 4D 51
Elizabeth Gdns. W3.. 2B 70
Elizabeth Ho. SE11... 5C 76
   (off Reedworth St.)
  W6...... 1E 85
   (off Queen Caroline St.)
Elizabeth Ind. Est.
  SE14...... 2F 93
Elizabeth M. NW3.... 3A 46
Elizabeth Newcomen Ho.
  SE1...... 3B 26
   (off Newcomen St.)
Elizabeth Rd. E6.... 5F 55
  N15...... 1A 36
Elizabeth Sq. SE16... 1A 80
   (off Sovereign Cres.)
Elizabeth St. SW1.... 5C 74
Elkington Point SE11.. 5C 76
   (off Lollard St.)
Elkington Rd. E13.... 3D 69
Elkstone Rd. W10.... 4B 58
Ellaline Rd. W6...... 2F 85
Ella M. NW3...... 1B 46
Elland Ho. E14...... 5B 66
   (off Copenhagen Pl.)
Elland Rd. SE15...... 2E 107
Ella Rd. N8...... 2A 34
Ellenborough Ho.
  W12...... 1D 71
   (off White City Est.)
Ellenborough Pl.
  SW15...... 2C 98
Ellen St. E1...... 5C 64
Ellen Terry Ct. NW1.. 4D 47
   (off Farrier St.)
Ellen Wilkinson Ho.
  E2...... 2F 65
   (off Usk St.)
  SW6...... 2B 86
   (off Clem Attlee Ct.)
Ellerby St. SW6...... 4F 85
Ellerdale Cl. NW3.... 1E 45
Ellerdale Rd. NW3.... 2E 45
Ellerdale St. SE13.... 2D 109
Ellerslie Gdns. NW10. 5C 42
Ellerslie Rd. W12.... 2D 71
Ellerslie Sq. Ind. Est.
  SW2...... 3A 104
Ellerton Rd. SW13... 4C 84
  SW18...... 1F 115
Ellery Ho. SE17...... 5F 77
Ellery St. SE15...... 5D 93
Ellesmere Cl. E11.... 1B 40

Ellesmere Ct. W4.... 1A 84
Ellesmere Rd. E3.... 1A 66
  NW10...... 2C 42
Ellesmere St. E14.... 5D 67
Ellingfort Rd. E8.... 4D 51
Ellingham Rd. E15... 1F 53
  W12...... 3C 70
Ellington Ho.
  SE1...... 5A 26 (4E 77)
Ellington St. N7...... 3C 48
Elliot Cl. E15...... 4A 54
Elliot Ho. W1...... 4A 60
   (off Cato St.)
Elliot Rd. NW4...... 1D 29
Elliott Rd. SW9...... 4D 91
  W4...... 5A 70
Elliott's Pl. N1...... 5D 49
Elliott Sq. NW3...... 4A 46
Elliotts Row SE11... 5D 77
Ellis Cl. NW10...... 3D 43
Ellisfield Dr. SW15... 5C 98
Ellis Franklin Ct.
  NW8...... 1E 59
   (off Abbey Rd.)
Ellis Ho. SE17...... 1F 91
   (off Brandon St.)
Ellison Ho. SE13.... 5D 95
   (off Lewisham Rd.)
Ellison Rd. SW13.... 5B 84
Ellis St. SW1...... 5C 74
Ellora Rd. SW16..... 5F 117
Ellsworth St. E2.... 2D 65
Ellwood Ct. W9...... 3D 59
   (off Clearwell Dr.)
Elm Bank Gdns.
  SW13...... 5A 84
Elmbourne Rd.
  SW17...... 3D 117
Elmbridge Wlk. E8... 4C 50
Elm Cl. E11...... 1D 41
  N19...... 4E 33
  NW4...... 1F 29
Elm Ct. EC4...... 3B 16
  SE13...... 1F 109
  W9...... 4C 58
   (off Admiral Wlk.)
Elmcourt Rd. SE27... 2D 119
Elmcroft N6...... 2E 33
Elmcroft Av. NW11... 2B 30
Elmcroft Cres. NW11. 2A 30
Elmcroft St. E5...... 1E 51
Elmer Ho. NW1...... 4A 60
   (off Penfold St.)
Elmer Rd. SE6...... 5E 109
Elmfield Av. N8...... 1A 34
Elmfield Rd. E17.... 1F 37
  SW17...... 2C 116
Elmfield Way W9..... 4C 58
Elm Friars Wlk.
  NW1...... 4F 47
Elm Grn. W3...... 5A 56
Elmgreen Cl. E15.... 5A 54
Elm Gro. N8...... 1A 34
  NW2...... 1F 43
  SE15...... 5B 92
Elm Gro. Rd. SW13... 4C 84
Elm Hall Gdns. E11... 1D 41
   (not continuous)

Elm Ho. *E14* *3E 81*
   (off E. Ferry Rd.)
  W10 . . . . *3A 58*
   (off Briar Wlk.)
Elmhurst Mans.
  SW4 . . . . 1F 103
Elmhurst Rd. E7 . . . . 4D 55
  SE9 . . . . 2F 125
Elmhurst St. SW4 . . . . . . 1F 103
Elmington Est. SE5 . . . . . 3F 91
Elmington Rd. SE5 . . . . . . 3F 91
Elmira St. SE13 . . . . 1D 109
Elm La. SE6 . . . . 2B 122
Elm Lodge SW6 . . . . 4E 85
Elmore Ho. SW9 . . . . 5D 91
Elmore Rd. E11 . . . . 5E 39
Elmore St. N1 . . . . 4E 49
Elm Pk. SW2 . . . . 4B 104
Elm Pk. Av. N15 . . . . 1B 36
Elm Pk. Chambers
  SW10 . . . . 1F 87
   (off Fulham Rd.)
Elm Pk. Gdns. SW10 . . . . . 1F 29
  SW10 . . . . 1F 87
Elm Pk. Ho. SW10 . . . . . . 1F 87
Elm Pk. La. SW3 . . . . 1F 87
Elm Pk. Mans. SW10 . . . . 2E 87
   (off Park Wlk.)
Elm Pk. Rd. E10 . . . . 3A 38
  SW3 . . . . 2F 87
Elm Pl. SW7 . . . . 1F 87
Elm Quay Ct. SW8 . . . . . . 2F 89
Elm Rd. E7 . . . . 3B 54
  E11 . . . . 4F 39
  E17 . . . . 1E 39
Elm Row NW3 . . . . 5E 31
Elms, The E12 . . . . 3F 55
  SW13 . . . . 1B 98
Elms Av. NW4 . . . . 1F 29
Elmscott Rd.
  BR1: Brom 5A 124
Elms Cres. SW4 . . . . 4E 103
Elmshaw Rd. SW15 . . . . . 3C 98
Elmslie Point E3 . . . . 4B 66
   (off Leopold St.)
Elms M. W2 . . . . 1F 73
Elms Rd. SW4 . . . . 3E 103
ELMSTEAD 5F 125
Elmstone Rd. SW6 . . . . . . 4C 86
Elm St. WC1 . . . . . 4A 8 (3B 62)
Elm Ter. NW2 . . . . 5C 30
  NW3 . . . . 1A 46
Elmton Ct. NW8 . . . . 3F 59
   (off Cunningham Pl.)
Elmton Way E5 . . . . 5C 36
Elm Tree Cl. NW8 . . . . 2F 59
Elm Tree Ct. NW8 . . . . 2F 59
   (off Elm Tree Rd.)
  SE7 . . . . 2E 97
Elm Tree Rd. NW8 . . . . . . 2F 59
Elm Wlk. NW3 . . . . 4C 30
Elm Way NW10 . . . . 1A 42
Elmwood Ct. E10 . . . . 3C 38
   (off Goldsmith Rd.)
  SW11 . . . . 4D 89
Elmwood Ho. NW10 . . . . 1D 57
   (off All Souls Av.)
Elmwood Rd. SE24 . . . . 3F 105
Elmworth Gro. SE21 . . . . 2F 119
Elnathan M. W9 . . . . 3D 59

Elphinstone Ct.
  SW16 . . . . 5A 118
Elphinstone St. N5 . . . . . . 1D 49
Elrington Rd. E8 . . . . 3C 50
Elsa Cotts. E14 . . . . 4A 66
   (off Hatley St.)
Elsa St. E1 . . . . 4A 66
Elsdale St. E9 . . . . 3E 51
Elsden M. E2 . . . . 1E 65
Elsenham St. SW18 . . . . 1B 114
Elsham Rd. E11 . . . . 5A 40
  W14 . . . . 3A 72
Elsham Ter. W14 . . . . 4A 72
   (off Elsham Rd.)
Elsie La. Ct. W2 . . . . 4C 58
   (off Westbourne Pk. Vs.)
Elsiemaud Rd. SE4 . . . . . 3B 108
Elsie Rd. SE22 . . . . 2B 106
Elsinore Gdns. NW2 . . . . . 5A 30
Elsinore Ho. N1 . . . . 5C 48
   (off Denmark Gro.)
  SE5 . . . . 5E 91
   (off Denmark Rd.)
  W6 . . . . 1F 85
   (off Fulham Pal. Rd.)
Elsinore Rd. SE23 . . . . . 1A 122
Elsley Rd. SW11 . . . . 1B 102
Elspeth Rd. SW11 . . . . . . 2B 102
Elstead Ho. SW2 . . . . 5B 104
   (off Redlands Way)
Elsted St. SE17 . . . . 5F 77
Elstow Grange NW6 . . . . . 4F 43
Elswick Rd. SE13 . . . . 5D 95
Elswick St. SW6 . . . . 5E 87
Elsworthy Ri. NW3 . . . . . . 4A 46
Elsworthy Rd. NW3 . . . . . 5A 46
Elsworthy Ter. NW3 . . . . . 4A 46
Elsynge Rd. SW18 . . . . . 3F 101
ELTHAM 5F 111
Eltham Grn. SE9 . . . . 3F 111
Eltham Grn. Rd.
  SE9 . . . . 2E 111
Eltham Hill SE9 . . . . 3F 111
Eltham Pal. Rd.
  SE9 . . . . 4E 111
Eltham Rd. SE9 . . . . 3B 110
  SE12 . . . . 3B 110
Elthiron Rd. SW6 . . . . 4C 86
Elthorne Rd. N19 . . . . 4F 33
  NW9 . . . . 2A 28
Elthorne Way NW9 . . . . . . 1A 28
Elthruda Rd. SE13 . . . . . 4F 109
Elton Ho. E3 . . . . 5B 52
   (off Candy St.)
Elton Pl. N16 . . . . 2A 50
Eltringham St.
  SW18 . . . . 2E 101
Elvaston M. SW7 . . . . 4E 73
Elvaston Pl. SW7 . . . . 4E 73
Elveden Rd. SE24 . . . . . . 3D 105
Elver Gdns. E2 . . . . 2C 64
Elverson Rd. SE8 . . . . 5D 95
Elverton St. SW1 . . . . 5F 75
Elvino Rd. SE26 . . . . 5A 122
Elvis Rd. NW2 . . . . 3E 43
Elwin St. E2 . . . . 2C 64
Elwood St. N5 . . . . 5D 35
Elworth Ho. SW8 . . . . 3B 90
   (off Oval Pl.)
Elwyn Gdns. SE12 . . . . . . 5C 110

Ely Cotts. SW8 . . . . 3B 90
Ely Ct. EC1 . . . . 1C 16
  NW6 . . . . 1C 58
   (off Chichester Rd.)
Ely Ho. SE15 . . . . 3C 92
   (off Friary Est.)
Elyne Rd. N4 . . . . 1C 34
Ely Pl. EC1 . . . . . . 1C 16 (4C 62)
Ely Rd. E10 . . . . 1E 39
Elysium Pl. SW6 . . . . 5B 86
   (off Elysium St.)
Elysium St. SW6 . . . . 5B 86
Elystan Pl. SW3 . . . . 1A 88
Elystan St. SW3 . . . . 5A 74
Elystan Wlk. N1 . . . . 5C 48
Embankment SW15 . . . . . 5F 85
   (not continuous)
Embankment Gdns.
  SW3 . . . . 2B 88
Embankment Pl.
  WC2 . . . . 1E 23 (2A 76)
Embassy Ct. NW8 . . . . . . 1F 59
   (off Wellington Rd.)
Embassy Ho. NW6 . . . . . . 4D 45
Embassy Theatre 4F 45
   (off College Cres.)
Emba St. SE16 . . . . 3C 78
Emberton SE5 . . . . 2A 92
   (off Albany Rd.)
Emberton Ct. EC1 . . . . 2D 9
   (off Tompion St.)
Embleton Rd. SE13 . . . . 2D 109
Emden St. SW6 . . . . 4D 87
Emerald Cl. E16 . . . . 5F 69
Emerald Rd. NW10 . . . . . 5A 42
   (not continuous)
Emerald St.
  WC1 . . . . 5F 7 (4B 62)
Emerson Ho.
  SE1 . . . . 1F 25 (2E 77)
Emery Hill St. SW1 . . . . . 4E 75
Emery St.
  SE1 . . . . 5C 24 (4C 76)
Emery Theatre 5D 67
   (off Annabel Cl.)
Emily Pl. N7 . . . . 1C 48
Emily St. E16 . . . . 5B 68
   (off Jude St.)
Emlyn Gdns. W12 . . . . 3A 70
Emlyn Rd. W12 . . . . 3A 70
Emmanuel Cl. E10 . . . . . . 2D 39
Emmanuel Ho. SE11 . . . . 5C 76
Emmanuel Rd.
  SW12 . . . . 1E 117
Emma Rd. E13 . . . . 1B 68
Emma St. E2 . . . . 1D 65
Emminster NW6 . . . . 5D 45
   (off Abbey Rd.)
Emmott Cl. E1 . . . . 3A 66
  NW11 . . . . 1E 31
Emperor's Ga. SW7 . . . . . 4E 73
Empingham Ho. SE8 . . . . 5F 79
   (off Chilton Ho.)
Empire Cinema 4C 14
   (off Leicester Sq.)
Empire Sq. N7 . . . . 5A 34
Empire Wharf E3 . . . . 5A 52
   (off Old Ford Rd.)
Empire Wharf Rd.
  E14 . . . . 5F 81

Empress App. SW6 . . . . . 1C 86
Empress Av. E12. . . . . 4E 41
Empress M. SE5 . . . . 5E 91
Empress Pl. SW6 . . . . 1C 86
Empress State Bldg.
  SW6 . . . . 1C 86
Empress St. SE17 . . . . 2E 91
Empson St. E3 . . . . 3D 67
Emsworth Ct.
  SW16 . . . . 3A 118
Emsworth St. SW2 . . . . . . 2B 118
Emu Rd. SW8 . . . . 5D 89
Enbrook St. W10 . . . . 2A 58
Enclave, The SW13 . . . . . . 5B 84
Endeavour Way
  SW19 . . . . 4D 115
Endell St.
  WC2 . . . . 2D 15 (5A 62)
Enderby St. SE10 . . . . 1F 95
Endlesham Rd.
  SW12 . . . . 5C 102
Endsleigh Gdns.
  WC1 . . . . 3B 6 (3F 61)
Endsleigh Pl.
  WC1 . . . . 3C 6 (3F 61)
Endsleigh St.
  WC1 . . . . 3C 6 (3F 61)
Endwell Rd. SE4 . . . . 5A 94
Endymion Rd. N4 . . . . 2C 34
  SW2 . . . . 4B 104
Energen Cl. NW10 . . . . 3A 42
Energize Fitness Club
  . . . . 1A 86
  (in Hammersmith &
   West London College)
Enfield Cloisters N1 . . . . 1D 11
  (off Fanshaw St.)
Enfield Ho. SW9 . . . . 5A 90
  (off Stockwell Rd.)
Enfield Rd. N1 . . . . 4A 50
Enford St. W1 . . . . 4B 60
Engadine St. SW18 . . . . . 1B 114
Engate St. SE13 . . . . 2E 109
Engine Ct. SW1 . . . . 2A 22
  (off Ambassador's Ct.)
England's La. NW3 . . . . . . 3B 46
Englefield NW1 . . . . 2F 5
  (off Clarence Gdns.)
Englefield Rd. N1 . . . . 4F 49
Engleheart Rd. SE6 . . . . . 5D 109
Englewood Rd.
  SW12 . . . . 4D 103
English Grounds
  SE1 . . . . 2D 27 (2A 78)
English St. E3 . . . . 3B 66
Enid St. SE16 . . . . 5F 27 (4B 78)
Enmore Gdns. SW14 . . . . . 3A 98
Enmore Rd. SW15 . . . . 2E 99
Ennerdale NW1 . . . . 1F 5
  (off Varndell St.)
Ennerdale Ct. E11 . . . . 2C 40
  (off Cambridge Rd.)
Ennerdale Dr. NW9 . . . . . . 1A 28
Ennerdale Ho. E3 . . . . 3B 66
Ennerdale Rd. SE13 . . . . 3F 109
Ennis Ho. E14 . . . . 5D 67
  (off Vesey Path)
Ennismore Av. W4 . . . . 5B 70
Ennismore Gdns.
  SW7 . . . . 3A 74

Ennismore Gdns. M.
  SW7 . . . . 4A 74
Ennismore M. SW7 . . . . . . 4A 74
Ennismore St. SW7 . . . . . . 4A 74
Ennis Rd. N4 . . . . 3C 34
Ensbury Ho. SW8 . . . . 3B 90
  (off Carroun Rd.)
Ensign Ho. E14 . . . . 3C 80
  (off Admirals Way)
Ensign Ind. Cen. E1 . . . . . 1C 78
  (off Ensign St.)
Ensign St. E1 . . . . 1C 78
Ensor M. SW7 . . . . 1F 87
Enterprise Bus. Pk.
  E14 . . . . 3D 81
Enterprise Cen., The
  BR3: Beck. 5A 122
  (off Cricket La.)
Enterprise Ho. E9 . . . . 4E 51
  (off Tudor Gro.)
  E14 . . . . 1D 95
  (off St Davids Sq.)
Enterprise Ind. Est.
  SE16 . . . . 1E 93
Enterprise Row N15 . . . . . 1B 36
Enterprise Way
  NW10 . . . . 2B 56
  SW18 . . . . 2C 100
Enterprize Way SE8 . . . . . 5B 80
Epcot M. NW10 . . . . 2F 57
Epirus M. SW6 . . . . 3C 86
Epirus Rd. SW6 . . . . 3B 86
Epping Cl. E14 . . . . 5C 80
Epping Pl. N1 . . . . 3C 48
Epple Rd. SW6 . . . . 4B 86
Epsom Rd. E10 . . . . 1E 39
Epworth St.
  EC2 . . . . 4C 10 (3F 63)
Equity Sq. E2 . . . . 2B 64
  (off Shacklewell St.)
Erasmus St. SW1 . . . . 5F 75
Erconwald St. W12 . . . . . . 5B 56
Eresby Ho. SW7 . . . . 3A 74
  (off Rutland Ga.)
Eresby Pl. NW6 . . . . 4C 44
Erica Ho. SE4 . . . . 1B 108
Erica St. W12 . . . . 1C 70
Eric Cl. E7 . . . . 1C 54
Ericcson Cl. SW18 . . . . . . 3C 100
Eric Fletcher Ct. N1 . . . . . 4E 49
  (off Essex Rd.)
Eric Liddell Sports Cen.
  . . . . 1C 124
Eric Rd. E7 . . . . 1C 54
  NW10 . . . . 3B 42
Eric Shipman Ter. E13 . . . 3C 68
  (off Balaam St.)
Ericson Ho. SE13 . . . . 2F 109
  (off Blessington Rd.)
Eric St. E3 . . . . 3B 66
  (not continuous)
Eric Wilkins Ho. SE1 . . . . 1C 92
  (off Old Kent Rd.)
Eridge Rd. W4 . . . . 4A 70
Erlanger Rd. SE14 . . . . . . 4F 93
Erlich Cotts. E1 . . . . 4E 65
  (off Sidney St.)
Ermine Rd. N15 . . . . 1B 36
  SE13 . . . . 2D 109
Ernest Av. SE27 . . . . 4D 119

Ernest Harriss Ho.
  W9 . . . . 3C 58
  (off Elgin Av.)
Ernest St. E1 . . . . 3F 65
Ernshaw Pl. SW15 . . . . . . 3A 100
Eros 5B 14 (1F 75)
Eros Ho. Shops
  SE6 . . . . 5D 109
  (off Brownhill Rd.)
Erpingham Rd. SW15. . . . 1E 99
Errington Rd. W9 . . . . 3B 58
Errol St. EC1 . . . . 4A 10 (3E 63)
Erskine Hill NW11 . . . . 1C 30
Erskine Ho. SW1 . . . . 1E 89
  (off Churchill Gdns.)
Erskine M. NW3 . . . . 4B 46
  (off Erskine Rd.)
Erskine Rd. NW3 . . . . 4B 46
Esam Way SW16 . . . . 5C 118
Escott Gdns. SE9 . . . . 4F 125
Esher Gdns. SW19 . . . . . . 2F 113
Eskdale NW1 . . . . 1F 5
  (off Stanhope St.)
Esk Rd. E13 . . . . 3D 68
Esmar Cres. NW9 . . . . 2C 28
Esmeralda Rd. SE1 . . . . . . 5C 78
Esmond Ct. W8 . . . . 4D 73
  (off Thackeray St.)
Esmond Gdns. W4 . . . . . . 5A 70
Esmond Rd. NW6 . . . . 5B 44
  W4 . . . . 5A 70
Esmond St. SW15 . . . . . . 2A 100
Esparto St. SW18 . . . . . . 5D 101
Esporta Health & Fitness
  Finchley Rd. 3E 45
  (in O2 Centre)
  Grove Park 4A 84
  Islington 5D 49
  Wandsworth 2D 101
  Wimbledon 5B 114
Esprit Ct. E1 . . . . 1F 19
  (off Brune St.)
Essendine Rd. W9 . . . . 2C 58
Essex Ct. EC4 . . . . 3B 16
  SW13 . . . . 5B 84
Essex Gdns. N4 . . . . 1D 35
Essex Gro. SE19 . . . . 5F 119
Essex Ho. E14 . . . . 5D 67
  (off Girauld St.)
Essex Mans. E11 . . . . 2F 39
Essex Pk. M. W3 . . . . 2A 70
Essex Rd. E10 . . . . 1E 39
  E17 . . . . 1A 38
  N1 . . . . 5D 49
  NW10 . . . . 4A 42
Essex Rd. Sth. E11 . . . . . . 2F 39
Essex St. E7 . . . . 2C 54
  WC2 . . . . 3B 16 (5C 62)
Essex Vs. W8 . . . . 3C 72
Essex Wharf E5 . . . . 4F 37
Essian St. E1 . . . . 4A 66
Estate Way E10 . . . . 3B 38
Estcourt Rd. SW6 . . . . 3B 86
Estella Ho. W11 . . . . 1F 71
  (off St Ann's Rd.)
Estelle Rd. NW3 . . . . 1B 46
Esterbrooke St. SW1 . . . . 5F 75
Este Rd. SW11 . . . . 1A 102
Esther Rd. E11 . . . . 2A 40
Estoria Cl. SW2 . . . . 5C 104

Estorick Collection of Modern
Italian Art 3D 49
Estreham Rd. SW16 . . . . 5F 117
Eswyn Rd. SW17 . . . . 4B 116
Etal Ho. N1 . . . . 4D 49
(off Sutton Est., The)
Etcetera Theatre 4D 47
(off Camden High St.)
Etchingham Rd. E15 . . . . 1E 53
Eternit Wlk. SW6 . . . . 4E 85
Ethelbert St. SW12 . . . . 1D 117
Ethelburga St. SW11 . . . . 4A 88
Ethelburga St.
SW11 . . . . 4A 88
(off Maskelyne Cl.)
Ethelden Rd. W12 . . . . 2D 71
Ethel Rd. E16 . . . . 5D 69
Ethel St. SE17 . . . . 5E 77
Etheridge Rd. NW4 . . . . 2E 29
Etherow St. SE22 . . . . 5C 106
Etherstone Grn.
SW16 . . . . 4C 118
Etherstone Rd.
SW16 . . . . 4C 118
Ethnard Rd. SE15 . . . . 2D 93
Etloe Ho. E10 . . . . 3C 38
Etloe Rd. E10 . . . . 4C 38
Eton Av. NW3 . . . . 4F 45
Eton Cl. SW18 . . . . . . 5D 101
Eton Coll. Rd. NW3 . . . . 3B 46
Eton Ct. NW3 . . . . 4F 45
Eton Garages NW3 . . . . 3A 46
Eton Gro. SE13 . . . . . . 1A 110
Eton Hall NW3 . . . . . . 3B 46
Eton Ho. N5 . . . . 1D 49
(off Leigh Rd.)
Eton Mnr. Ct. E10 . . . . 4C 38
(off Leyton Grange Est.)
Eton Pl. NW3 . . . . 4C 46
Eton Ri. NW3 . . . . 3B 46
Eton Rd. NW3 . . . . 4B 46
Eton Vs. NW3 . . . . 3B 46
Etta St. SE8 . . . . 2A 94
Ettrick St. E14 . . . . 5E 67
(not continuous)
Eugene Cotter Ho.
SE17 . . . . 5F 77
(off Tatum St.)
Eugenia Rd. SE16 . . . . 5E 79
Euro Cl. NW10 . . . . 3C 42
Eurolink Bus. Cen.
SW2 . . . . 3C 104
Europa Pl. EC1 . . 2F 9 (2E 63)
Eustace Bldg. SW8 . . . . 2D 89
Eustace Ho. SE11 . . . . 5B 76
(off Old Paradise St.)
Eustace Rd. E6 . . . . . . 2F 69
SW6 . . . . 3C 86
Euston Cen.
NW1 . . . . 3F 5 (3E 61)
(not continuous)
Euston Gro. NW1 . . . . . 2B 6
(off Euston Sq.)
Euston Rd.
NW1 . . . . 4F 5 (3D 61)
(not continuous)
Euston Sq. NW1 . . . . . 2F 61
Euston Sta. Colonnade
NW1 . . . . 2B 6 (2F 61)

Euston St.
NW1 . . . . 2A 6 (2E 61)
Euston Twr.
NW1 . . . . 3F 5 (3E 61)
Evandale Rd. SW9 . . . . 5C 90
Evangelist Ho. EC4 . . . . 3D 17
(off Black Friars La.)
Evangelist Rd.
NW5 . . . . 1D 47
Evans Bus. Cen.
NW2 . . . . 5C 28
Evans Cl. E8 . . . . 3B 50
Evans Ho. SW8 . . . . . . 3F 89
(off Wandsworth Rd.)
W12 . . . . 1D 71
(off White City Est.)
Evans Rd. SE6 . . . . . . 2A 124
Evanston Gdns.
IG4: Ilf 1F 41
Evelina Mans. SE5 . . . . 3F 91
Evelina Rd. SE15 . . . . 1E 107
Evelyn Ct. E8 . . . . 1C 50
N1 . . . . 1B 10
(off Evelyn Wlk.,
not continuous)
Evelyn Denington Ct.
N1 . . . . 4D 49
(off Sutton Est., The)
Evelyn Fox Ct. W10 . . . . 4E 57
Evelyn Gdns. SW7 . . . . 1E 87
Evelyn Ho. SE14 . . . . 4A 94
(off Loring Rd.)
W12 . . . . 3B 70
(off Cobbold Rd.)
Evelyn Lowe Est.
SE16 . . . . 4C 78
Evelyn Mans. SW1 . . . . 5F 21
(off Carlisle Pl.)
W14 . . . . 2A 86
(off Queen's Club Gdns.)
Evelyn Rd. E16 . . . . . . 2C 82
SW19 . . . . 5D 115
Evelyn St. SE8 . . . . . . 5A 80
Evelyn Wlk.
N1 . . . . 1B 10 (1F 63)
Evelyn Yd.
W1 . . . . 2B 14 (5F 61)
Evenwood Cl. SW15 . . . 3A 100
Everard Ho. E1 . . . . . . 5C 64
(off Boyd St.)
Everatt Cl. SW18 . . . . . 4B 100
Everdon Rd. SW13 . . . . 2C 84
Everest Pl. E14 . . . . . . 4E 67
Everett Ho. SE17 . . . . . 1F 91
(off East St.)
Evergreen Sq. E8 . . . . 4B 50
Everilda St. N1 . . . . . . 5B 48
Evering Rd. E5 . . . . . . 5B 36
N16 . . . . 5B 36
Everington St. W6 . . . . 2F 85
(not continuous)
Everitt Rd. NW10 . . . . 2A 56
Everleigh St. N4 . . . . . 3B 34
Eve Rd. E11 . . . . 1A 54
E15 . . . . 1A 68
Eversholt St.
NW1 . . . . 1A 6 (1E 61)
Evershot Rd. N4 . . . . . 3B 34
Eversleigh Rd. E6 . . . . 5F 55
SW11 . . . . 1B 102

Eversley Ho. E2 . . . . . . 2C 64
(off Gossett St.)
Eversley Pk. SW19 . . . 5D 113
Eversley Rd. SE7 . . . . 2D 97
Everthorpe Rd.
SE15 . . . . 1B 106
Everton Bldgs.
NW1 . . . . 2F 5 (2E 61)
Evesham Ho. E2 . . . . . 1E 65
(off Old Ford Rd.)
NW8 . . . . 5E 45
(off Abbey Rd.)
Evesham Rd. E15 . . . . 4B 54
Evesham St. W11 . . . . 1F 71
Evesham Wlk. SE5 . . . . 5F 91
SW9 . . . . 5C 90
Evesham Way
SW11 . . . . 1C 102
Ewald Rd. SW6 . . . . . 5B 86
Ewart Pl. E3 . . . . 1B 66
Ewart Rd. SE23 . . . . . 5F 107
Ewe Cl. N7 . . . . 3A 48
Ewelme Rd. SE23 . . . . 1E 121
Ewen Cres. SW2 . . . . 5C 104
Ewen Henderson Ct.
SE14 . . . . 3A 94
(off Goodwood Rd.)
Ewen Ho. N1 . . . . 5B 48
(off Barnsbury Est.)
Ewer St. SE1 . . 2F 25 (2E 77)
Ewhurst Cl. E1 . . . . . . 4E 65
Ewhurst Rd. SE4 . . . . 4B 108
Exbury Ho. E9 . . . . . . 4E 51
SW1 . . . . 1F 89
(off Rampayne St.)
Exbury Rd. SE6 . . . . . 2C 122
ExCeL 1D 83
Excel Ct. WC2 . . . . . . 5C 14
Excel Marina E16 . . . . . 1C 82
Excelsior Gdns. SE13 . . 5E 95
Excelsior Ind. Est.
SE15 . . . . 2E 93
Excel Waterfront E16 . . 1D 83
Exchange Arc.
EC2 . . . . 5E 11 (4A 64)
Exchange Bldg. E1 . . . . 4F 11
(off Commercial St.)
Exchange Ct.
WC2 . . . . 5E 15 (1A 76)
Exchange Ho. EC2 . . . . 5E 11
SW1 . . . . 5F 75
(off Vauxhall Bri. Rd.)
Exchange Mans.
NW11 . . . . 2B 30
Exchange Pl.
EC2 . . . . 5D 11 (4A 64)
Exchange Sq.
EC2 . . . . 5D 11 (4A 64)
Exchange St.
EC1 . . . . 2F 9 (2E 63)
Exeter Ct. NW6 . . . . . . 1C 58
(off Cambridge Rd.)
Exeter Ho. SE15 . . . . . 2C 92
(off Friary Est.)
SW15 . . . . 4E 99
W2 . . . . 5E 59
(off Hallfield Est.)
Exeter Mans. NW2 . . . . 3A 44
Exeter M. NW6 . . . . . . 3D 45
SW6 . . . . 3C 86

Exeter Rd. E16 . . . . 4C 68
E17 . . . . 1C 38
NW2 . . . . 2A 44
Exeter St.
WC2 . . . . 4E 15 (1A 76)
Exeter Way SE14 . . . . . 3B 94
Exford Gdns. SE12 . . . . 1D 125
Exford Rd. SE12 . . . . 2D 125
Exhibition Cl. W12 . . . . 1E 71
Exhibition Rd.
SW7 . . . . 3F 73
Exmoor Ho. E3 . . . . . . 1A 66
(off Gernon Rd.)
Exmoor M. W10 . . . . . 3F 57
Exmouth Ho. E14 . . . . . 5D 81
(off Cahir St.)
EC1 . . . . 3B 8
(off Pine St.)
Exmouth Mkt.
EC1 . . . . 3B 8 (3C 62)
Exmouth M.
NW1 . . . . 2A 6 (2E 61)
Exmouth Pl. E8 . . . . . . 4D 51
Exmouth Rd. E17 . . . . . 1B 38
Exmouth St. E1 . . . . . . 5E 65
Exning Rd. E16 . . . . . . 3B 68
Exonbury NW8 . . . . . . 5D 45
(off Abbey Rd.)
Exon St. SE17 . . . . 1A 92
Export Ho. SE1 . . . . . . 4E 27
(off Tower Bri. Rd.)
Express Newspapers
SE1 . . . . 1D 25
(off Blackfriars Rd.)
Exton St.
SE1 . . . . . . 2B 24 (2C 76)
Eyhurst Cl. NW2 . . . . . 4C 28
Eylewood Rd. SE27 . . . . 5E 119
Eynella Rd. SE12 . . . . 5B 106
Eynham Rd. W12 . . . . . 5E 57
Eynsford Ho. SE1 . . . . . 4B 26
(off Crosby Row)
SE15 . . . . 2E 93
SE17 . . . . 5A 78
(off Beckway St.)
Eyot Gdns. W6 . . . . . . 1B 84
Eyot Grn. W4 . . . . 1B 84
Eyre Cl. NW8 . . . . 1F 59
Eyre St. Hill
EC1 . . . . 4B 8 (3C 62)
Eythorne Rd. SW9 . . . . 4C 90
Ezra St. E2 . . . . 2B 64

Fairburn Ho. W14 . . . . . 1B 86
(off Ivatt Pl.)
Fairby Ho. SE1 . . . . . . 5B 78
(off Longfield Est.)
Fairby Rd. SE12 . . . . . 3D 111
Faircharm Trad. Est.
SE8 . . . . 3D 95
Fairchild Cl. SW11 . . . . 5F 87
Fairchild Ho. E9 . . . . . 4E 51
(off Frampton Pk. Rd.)
N1 . . . . 1D 11
(off Fanshaw St.)
Fairchild Pl. EC2 . . . . . 4E 11
Fairchild St.
EC2 . . . . 3E 11 (3A 64)
Fairclough St. E1 . . . . . 5C 64
Fairdale Gdns.
SW15 . . . . 2D 99
Fairfax Gdns. SE3 . . . . 4E 97
Fairfax Mans. NW3 . . . . 3E 45
(off Finchley Rd.)
Fairfax M. E16 . . . . . . 2D 83
SW15 . . . . 2E 99
Fairfax Pl. NW6 . . . . . . 4A 45
W14 . . . . 4A 72
Fairfax Rd. NW6 . . . . . 4E 45
W4 . . . . 4A 70
Fairfield E1 . . . . 4E 65
(off Redman's Rd.)
NW1 . . . . 5E 47
(off Arlington Rd.)
Fairfield Av. NW4 . . . . . 1D 29
Fairfield Ct. NW10 . . . . 5C 42
Fairfield Dr. SW18 . . . . 3D 101
Fairfield Gdns. N8 . . . . 1A 34
Fairfield Gro. SE7 . . . . 2F 97
Fairfield Rd. E3 . . . . . . 1C 66
N8 . . . . 1A 34
Fairfield St. SW18 . . . . 3D 101
Fairfoot Rd. E3 . . . . . . 3C 66
Fairford SE6 . . . . 1C 122
Fairford Ho. SE11 . . . . 5C 76
Fairhazel Gdns. NW6 . . 3D 45
Fairhazel Mans.
NW6 . . . . 4E 45
(off Fairhazel Gdns.)
Fairholme Rd. W14 . . . . 1A 86
Fairholt Cl. N16 . . . . . . 3A 36
Fairholt Rd. N16 . . . . . 3F 35
Fairholt St. SW7 . . . . . 4A 74
Fairland Rd. E15 . . . . . 3B 54
Fairlawn SE7 . . . . 3E 97
Fairlawn Cl. SE7 . . . . . 3E 97
(not continuous)
Fairlawn Mans. SE14 . . 4F 93
Fairlawn Pk. SE26 . . . . 5A 122
Fairlie Gdns. SE23 . . . . 5E 107
Fairlight Av. NW10 . . . . 1A 56
(not continuous)
Fairlight Ct. NW10 . . . . 1A 56
Fairlight Rd. SW17 . . . . 4F 115
Fairlop Ct. E11 . . . . . . 3F 39
Fairlop Rd. E11 . . . . . . 2F 39
Fairmead Gdns.
IG4: Ilf 1F 41
Fairmead Ho. E9 . . . . . 1A 52
Fairmead Rd. N19 . . . . 5F 33
Fairmile Av. SW16 . . . . 5F 117
Fairmont Av. E14 . . . . . 2F 81
Fairmount Rd. SW2 . . . 4B 104

Fairstead Wlk. N1 . . . . 5E 49
(off Popham St.)
Fair St. SE1 . . . . . 3E 27 (3A 78)
Fairthorn Rd. SE7 . . . . 1C 96
Fairview Cl. SE26 . . . . 5A 122
Fairview Ho. SW2 . . . . 5B 104
Fairview Pl. SW2 . . . . . 5B 104
Fairview Rd. N15 . . . . . 1B 36
Fairway, The W3 . . . . . 5A 56
Fairwall Ho. SE5 . . . . . 4A 92
Fairway Cl. NW11 . . . . 2E 31
Fairway Ct. SE16 . . . . . 3F 79
(off Christopher Cl.)
Fairways Bus. Pk.
E10 . . . . 4A 38
Fairweather Rd.
N16 . . . . 1C 36
Fairwyn Rd. SE26 . . . . 4A 122
Fakruddin St. E1 . . . . . 3C 64
Falcon WC1 . . . . 5E 7
(off Old Gloucester St.)
Falconberg Ct.
W1 . . . . 2C 14 (5F 61)
Falconberg M.
W1 . . . . 2C 14 (5F 61)
Falcon Cl.
SE1 . . . . 1E 25 (2D 77)
Falcon Ct.
EC4 . . . . 3C 16 (5C 62)
N1 . . . . 1E 9
(off City Gdn. Row)
Falconer Wlk. N7 . . . . . 4B 34
Falconet Ct. E1 . . . . . . 2D 79
(off Wapping High St.)
Falcon Gro. SW11 . . . . 1A 102
Falcon Highwalk EC2 . . 1F 17
Falcon Ho. E14 . . . . . . 1D 95
(off St Davids Sq.)
Falcon La. SW11 . . . . . 1A 102
Falcon Lodge W9 . . . . 4C 58
(off Admiral Wlk.)
Falcon Pk. Ind. Est.
NW10 . . . . 1A 42
Falcon Point
SE1 . . . . 5E 17 (1D 77)
Falcon Rd. SW11 . . . . 5A 88
Falcon St. E13 . . . . . . 3B 68
Falcon Ter. SW11 . . . . 1A 102
Falcon Way E14 . . . . . 5D 81
Falconwood Ct. SE3 . . . 5B 96
(off Montpelier Row)
Falkirk Ct. SE16 . . . . . 2F 79
(off Rotherhithe St.)
Falkirk Ho. W9 . . . . . . 1D 59
(off Maida Va.)
Falkirk St.
N1 . . . . 1E 11 (1A 64)
Falkland Ho. SE6 . . . . . 4E 123
W8 . . . . 4D 73
W14 . . . . 1B 86
(off Edith Vs.)
Falkland Pl. NW5 . . . . . 2E 47
Falkland Rd. NW5 . . . . 2E 47
Fallodon Ho. W11 . . . . 4B 58
(off Tavistock Cres.)
Fallow Ct. SE16 . . . . . . 1C 92
(off Argyle Way)
Fallsbrook Rd.
SW16 . . . . 5E 117
Falmouth Cl. SE12 . . . . 3B 110

F

F1 City Go-Kart Circuit
. . . . 2E 83
(off Connaught Bri.)
Faber Gdns. NW4 . . . . . 1C 28
Fabian Rd. SW6 . . . . . . 3B 86
Facade, The SE23 . . . . 2E 121
Factory Rd. E16 . . . . . . 2F 83
Fairacres SW15 . . . . . . 2B 98
Fairbairn Grn.
SW9 . . . . 4D 91
Fairbank Est.
N1 . . . . 1B 10 (1F 63)
Fairbridge Rd. N19 . . . . 4F 33
Fairburn Ct. SW15 . . . . 3A 100

Falmouth Gdns.
  IG4: Ilf 1F **41**
Falmouth Ho. *SE11* 1C **90**
  (off Seaton Cl.)
  W2 . . . . 1A **74**
  (off Clarendon Pl.)
Falmouth Rd.
  SE1 . . . . 5A **26** (4E **77**)
Falmouth St. E15 . . . . 2F **53**
Falmouth Way E17 . . . . . 1B **38**
Falstaff Ct. *SE11* 5D **77**
  (off Opal St.)
Falstaff Ho. *N1* 1D **11**
  (off Crondall St.)
Fambridge Cl. SE26 . . . . 4B **122**
Fane Ho. E2 . . . . 5E **51**
Fane St. W14 . . . . 2B **86**
Fan Mus., The 3E **95**
Fann St. EC1 . . . . . . 4F **9** (3E **63**)
  EC2 . . . . 4F **9** (3E **63**)
  (not continuous)
Fanshaw St.
  N1 . . . . 1D **11** (2A **64**)
Fanthorpe St. SW15 . . . . 1E **99**
Faraday Cl. N7 . . . . 3B **48**
Faraday Ho. E14 . . . . 1B **80**
  (off Brightlingsea Pl.)
  SE1 . . . . 4A **26**
  (off Cole St.)
Faraday Lodge SE10 . . . . 4B **82**
Faraday Mans. *W14* 2A **86**
  (off Queen's Club Gdns.)
Faraday Mus.
  . . . . 5F **13** (1E **75**)
Faraday Rd. E15 . . . . 3B **54**
  SW19 . . . . 5C **114**
  W10 . . . . 4A **58**
Faraday Way SE18 . . . . . 4F **83**
Fareham St.
  W1 . . . . 2B **14** (5F **61**)
Faringford Rd. E15 . . . . . 4A **54**
Fariweather Ho. N7 . . . . . 1A **48**
Farjeon Ho. *NW6* 4F **45**
  (off Hilgrove Rd.)
Farjeon Rd. SE3 . . . . 4F **97**
Farleigh Pl. N16 . . . . 1B **50**
Farleigh Rd. N16 . . . . 1B **50**
Farley Ct. *NW1* 4B **4**
  (off Allsop Pl.)
Farley Ho. SE26 . . . . 3D **121**
Farley Rd. SE6 . . . . 5D **109**
Farlington Pl. SW15 . . . . 5D **99**
Farlow Rd. SW15 . . . . . . 1F **99**
Farlton Rd. SW18 . . . . . . 1D **115**
Farm Av. NW2 . . . . 5A **30**
  SW16 . . . . 4A **118**
Farm Cl. SW6 . . . . 3C **86**
Farmcote Rd. SE12 . . . . . 1C **124**
Farmdale Rd. SE10 . . . . . 1C **96**
Farmer Rd. E10 . . . . 3D **39**
Farmer's Rd. SE5 . . . . 3D **91**
Farmer St. W8 . . . . 2C **72**
Farmfield Rd.
  BR1: Brom 5A **124**
Farmilo Rd. E17 . . . . 2B **38**
Farm La. SW6 . . . . 2C **86**
  (not continuous)
Farm La. Trad. Est.
  SW6 . . . . 2C **86**
Farmleigh Ho. SW9 . . . . 3D **105**

Farm Pl. W8 . . . . 2C **72**
Farm Rd. E12 . . . . 4F **41**
  NW10 . . . . 5A **42**
Farmstead Rd. SE6 . . . . 4D **123**
Farm St. W1 . . . . . 5D **13** (1D **75**)
Farm Wlk. NW11 . . . . . . 1B **30**
Farnaby Ho. *W10* 2B **58**
  (off Bruckner St.)
Farnaby Rd. SE9 . . . . 2E **111**
Farnan Rd. SW16 . . . . . 5A **118**
Farnborough Ho.
  SW15 . . . . 1C **112**
Farncombe St. SE16 . . . . 3C **78**
Farndale Ct. SE18 . . . . . . 3F **97**
Farndale Ho. *NW6* 5D **45**
  (off Kilburn Va.)
Farnell M. SW5 . . . . 1D **87**
Farnham Ho. *NW1* 3A **60**
  (off Harewood Av.)
Farnham Pl.
  SE1 . . . . 2E **25** (2D **77**)
Farnham Royal SE11 . . . 1B **90**
Farningham Ho. N4 . . . . . 2F **35**
Farnley Ho. SW8 . . . . 5F **89**
Farnsworth Ct. *SE10* . . . 4B **82**
  (off Greenroof Way)
Farnworth Ho. *E14* 5F **81**
  (off Manchester Rd.)
Faroe Rd. W14 . . . . 4F **71**
Farquhar Rd. SE19 . . . . . 5B **120**
  SW19 . . . . 3C **114**
Farrance St. E14 . . . . 5C **66**
Farrell Ho. *E1* 5E **65**
  (off Ronald St.)
Farrell Ho. SE23 . . . . . . 2A **122**
Farrer Ho. SE8 . . . . 3C **94**
Farriers Ho. *EC1* 4A **10**
  (off Errol St.)
Farriers M. SE15 . . . . . . 1E **107**
Farrier St. NW1 . . . . 4D **47**
Farrier Wlk. SW10 . . . . . 2E **87**
Farringdon La.
  EC1 . . . . 4C **8** (3C **62**)
Farringdon Rd.
  EC1 . . . . 3B **8** (3C **62**)
  EC4 . . . . 1D **17** (4D **63**)
Farrins Rents SE16 . . . . 2A **80**
Farrow La. SE14 . . . . 3E **93**
Farrow Pl. SE16 . . . . 4A **80**
Farthingale Wlk. E15 . . . 4F **53**
Farthing All. SE1 . . . . 3C **78**
Farthing Flds. E1 . . . . 2D **79**
Fashion & Textile Mus.
  . . . . 3E **27**
Fashion St.
  E1 . . . . 1F **19** (4B **64**)
Fassett Rd. E8 . . . . 3C **50**
Fassett Sq. E8 . . . . 3C **50**
Faulkners All.
  EC1 . . . . 5D **9** (4D **63**)
Faulkner St. SE14 . . . . . . 4E **93**
Faunce Ho. *SE17* 2D **91**
  (off Doddington Gro.)
Faunce St. SE17 . . . . 1D **91**
Favart Rd. SW6 . . . . 4C **86**
Faversham Ho. *NW1* . . . 5E **47**
  (off Bayham Pl.)
  SE17 . . . . 1A **92**
  (off Kinglake St.)

Faversham Rd. SE6 . . . . 5B **108**
Fawcett Cl. SW11 . . . . . . 5F **87**
  SW16 . . . . 5C **118**
Fawcett Est. E5 . . . . 3C **36**
Fawcett Rd. NW10 . . . . . 4B **42**
Fawcett St. SW10 . . . . . . 2E **87**
Fawe Pk. M. SW15 . . . . 2B **100**
Fawe Pk. Rd. SW15 . . . . 2B **100**
Fawe St. E14 . . . . 4D **67**
Fawkham Ho. *SE1* 5B **78**
  (off Longfield Est.)
Fawley Ct. *SE1* 5F **81**
  (off Millennium Dr.)
Fawley Rd. NW6 . . . . 2D **45**
Fawnbrake Av. SE24 . . . 3D **105**
Fawn Rd. E13 . . . . 1E **69**
Fawood Av. NW10 . . . . . 4A **42**
Faygate Rd. SW2 . . . . . . 2B **118**
Fayland Av. SW16 . . . . . 5E **117**
Fazeley Ct. *W9* 4C **58**
  (off Elmfield Way)
Fearnley Ho. SE5 . . . . 5A **92**
Fearon St. SE10 . . . . 1C **96**
Feathers Pl. SE10 . . . . . . 2F **95**
Featherstone Av.
  SE23 . . . . 2D **121**
Featherstone St.
  EC1 . . . . 3B **10** (3F **63**)
Featley Rd. SW9 . . . . . . 1D **105**
Felbridge Cl. SW16 . . . . 4C **118**
Felbridge Ho. SE22 . . . . 1A **106**
Felday Rd. SE13 . . . . 4D **109**
Felden St. SW6 . . . . 4B **86**
Feldman Cl. N16 . . . . 3C **36**
Felgate M. W6 . . . . 5D **71**
Felix Av. N8 . . . . 1A **34**
Felixstowe Rd.
  NW10 . . . . 2D **57**
Felix St. E2 . . . . 1D **65**
Fellbrigg Rd. SE22 . . . . . 3B **106**
Fellbrigg St. E1 . . . . 3D **65**
Fellmongers Path
  SE1 . . . . 4F **27**
Fellows Ct.
  E2 . . . . 1F **11** (1B **64**)
  (not continuous)
Fellows Ho. NW3 . . . . . . 4F **45**
Felltram M. *SE7* 1C **96**
  (off Felltram Way)
Felltram Way SE7 . . . . . . 1C **96**
Felmersham Cl.
  SW4 . . . . 2A **104**
Felsberg Rd. SW2 . . . . . 4A **104**
Felsham M. *SW15* 1F **99**
  (off Felsham Rd.)
Felsham Rd. SW15 . . . . . 1E **99**
Felstead Gdns. E14 . . . . 1E **95**
Felstead Rd. E9 . . . . 3B **52**
  E11 . . . . 2C **40**
Felstead St. E9 . . . . 3B **52**
Felstead Wharf E14 . . . . 1E **95**
Felsted Rd. E16 . . . . 5F **69**
Felton Ho. *N1* 5F **49**
  (off Branch Pl.)
  SE3 . . . . 2D **111**
Felton St. N1 . . . . 5F **49**
Fenchurch Av.
  EC3 . . . . 3D **19** (5A **64**)
Fenchurch Bldgs.
  EC3 . . . . 3E **19** (5A **64**)

Fenchurch Pl.
EC3 . . . . 4E 19 (5A 64)
Fenchurch St.
EC3 . . . . 4D 19 (1A 78)
Fen Ct. EC3 . . . . 4D 19 (5A 64)
Fendall St.
SE1 . . . . 5E 27 (4A 78)
. . . . (not continuous)
Fendt Cl. E16 . . . . 5B 68
Fenelon Pl. W14 . . . . 5B 72
Fenham Rd. SE15 . . . . . . 3C 92
Fen La. SW13 . . . . 4D 85
Fennel Cl. E16 . . . . 3A 68
Fennor Cl. SE16 . . . . 5D 79
. . . . (off Watts St.)
Fenner Ho. E1 . . . . 2D 79
. . . . (off Watts St.)
Fenner Sq. SW11 . . . . . . 1F 101
Fenning St.
SE1 . . . . 3D 27 (3A 78)
Fenn St. E9 . . . . 2F 51
Fenstanton N4 . . . . 3B 34
. . . . (off Marquis Rd.)
Fen St. E16 . . . . 1B 82
Fentiman Rd. SW8 . . . . . . 2A 90
Fenton Cl. E8 . . . . 3B 50
SW9 . . . . 5B 90
Fenton House 1E 45
. . . . (off Windmill Hill)
Fenton Ho. SE14 . . . . 3A 94
Fentons Av. E13 . . . . 2D 69
Fenton St. E1 . . . . 5D 65
Fenwick Gro. SE15 . . . . . 1C 106
Fenwick Pl. SW9 . . . . . . 1A 104
Fenwick St. SE15 . . . . . . 1C 106
Ferdinand Ho. NW1 . . . . . 4C 46
. . . . (off Ferdinand Pl.)
Ferdinand Pl. NW1 . . . . . . 4C 46
Ferdinand St. NW1 . . . . . . 4C 46
Ferguson Cen., The
E17 . . . . 1A 38
Ferguson Cl. E14 . . . . 5C 80
Ferguson Dr. W3 . . . . 5A 56
Ferguson Ho. SE10 . . . . . . 4E 95
Fergus Rd. N5 . . . . 2D 49
Fermain Ct. E. N1 . . . . . . 5A 50
. . . . (off De Beauvoir Est.)
Fermain Ct. Nth. N1 . . . . . 5A 50
. . . . (off De Beauvoir Est.)
Fermain Ct. W. N1 . . . . . . 5A 50
. . . . (off De Beauvoir Est.)
Ferme Pk. Rd. N8 . . . . . . 1A 34
Fermor Rd. SE23 . . . . . . 1A 122
Fermoy Rd. W9 . . . . 3B 58
Fernbank M. SW12 . . . . . 4E 103
Fernbrook Cres.
SE13 . . . . 4A 110
. . . . (off Leahurst Rd.)
Fernbrook Rd. SE13 . . . . 3A 110
Ferncliff Rd. E8 . . . . 2C 50
Fern Cl. N1 . . . . 1A 64
Fern Ct. SE14 . . . . 5F 93
Ferncroft Av. NW3 . . . . . . 5C 30
Ferndale Community
Sports Cen. 1B 104
Ferndale Rd. E7 . . . . 4D 55
E11 . . . . 4A 40
N15 . . . . 1B 36
SW4 . . . . 2A 104
SW9 . . . . 2A 104
Ferndene Rd. SE24 . . . . . 2E 105

Ferndown Lodge E14 . . . 4E 81
. . . . (off Manchester Rd.)
Ferndown Rd. SE9 . . . . . 5F 111
Fernhall Dr. IG4: Ilf. 1F 41
Fernhead Rd. W9 . . . . . . 1B 58
Fernholme Rd.
SE15 . . . . 3F 107
Fernhurst Rd. SW6 . . . . . 4A 86
Fernlea Rd. SW12 . . . . . 1D 117
Fernsbury St.
WC1 . . . . 2B 8 (2C 62)
Fernshaw Cl. SW10 . . . . . 2E 87
Fernshaw Rd. SW10 . . . . . 2E 87
Fernside NW11 . . . . 4C 30
Fernside Rd. SW12 . . . . . 1D 116
Ferns Rd. E15 . . . . 3B 54
Fern St. E3 . . . . 3C 66
Fernthorpe Rd.
SW16 . . . . 5E 117
Ferntower Rd. N5 . . . . 2E 49
Fern Wlk. SE16 . . . . 1C 92
Fernwood SW19 . . . . . . 1B 114
Fernwood Av. SW16 . . . . 4F 117
Ferranti Cl. SE18 . . . . . . 4F 83
Ferrers Rd. SW16 . . . . . 5F 117
Ferrey M. SW9 . . . . 5C 90
Ferriby Cl. N1 . . . . 4C 48
Ferrier Ind. Est.
SW18 . . . . 2D 101
. . . . (off Ferrier St.)
Ferrier Point E16 . . . . . . 4C 68
. . . . (off Forty Acre La.)
Ferrier St. SW18 . . . . . . 2D 101
Ferrings SE21 . . . . 3A 120
Ferris Rd. SE22 . . . . 2C 106
Ferron Rd. E5. . . . . 5D 37
Ferrybridge Ho.
SE11 . . . . 4C 76
. . . . (off Lambeth Wlk.)
Ferry Ho. E5. . . . . 3D 37
. . . . (off Harrington Rd.)
Ferry La. SW13 . . . . 2B 84
Ferry Rd. SW13 . . . . 3C 84
Ferry St. E14 . . . . 1E 95
Festing Rd. SW15 . . . . . . 1F 99
Festival Ct. E8 . . . . 4B 50
. . . . (off Holly St.)
Festoon Way E16 . . . . . . 1F 83
Fetter La.
EC4 . . . . 3C 16 (5C 62)
. . . . (not continuous)
Fettes Ho. NW8 . . . . 1F 59
. . . . (off Wellington Rd.)
Ffinch St. SE8 . . . . 3C 94
Field Cl. NW2 . . . . 4C 28
Field Ct. SW19 . . . . 3C 114
WC1 . . . . 1A 16 (4B 62)
Fieldgate Mans. E1 . . . . 4C 64
. . . . (off Fieldgate St.,
. . . . not continuous)
Fieldgate St. E1 . . . . 4C 64
Field Ho. NW6 . . . . 2F 57
. . . . (off Harvist Rd.)
Fieldhouse Rd.
SW12 . . . . 1E 117
Fielding Ho. NW6 . . . . . . 2D 08
W4 . . . . 2A 84
. . . . (off Devonshire St.)
Fielding M. SW13 . . . . . . 2D 85
. . . . (off Jenner Pl.)

Fielding Rd. W4 . . . . 4A 70
W14 . . . . 4F 71
Fieldings, The SE14 . . . . 1E 121
Fielding St. SE17 . . . . . . 2E 91
Field Point E7 . . . . 1C 54
Field Rd. E7 . . . . 1B 54
W6 . . . . 1A 86
Fields Est. E8 . . . . 4C 50
Fieldside Rd.
BR1: Brom 5F 123
Field St. WC1 . . . 1F 7 (2B 62)
Fieldsway Ho. N5 . . . . . . 2C 48
Fieldview SW18 . . . . 1F 115
Fieldway Cres. N5 . . . . . . 2C 48
Fife Rd. E16 . . . . 4C 68
Fife Ter. N1 . . . . 1B 62
Fifield Path SE23 . . . . . . 3F 121
Fifth Av. W10 . . . . 2A 58
Fig Tree Cl. NW10 . . . . . . 5A 42
Figure Ct. SW3. . . . . 1B 88
. . . . (off West Rd.)
Filey Av. N16 . . . . 3C 36
Filigree Cl. SE16 . . . . . . 2B 80
Fillebrook Rd. E11 . . . . . 3F 39
Filmer Chambers
SW6 . . . . 4A 86
. . . . (off Filmer Rd.)
Filmer Rd. SW6 . . . . 4A 86
Filton Ct. SE14 . . . . 3E 93
. . . . (off Farrow La.)
Finborough Ho.
SW10 . . . . 2E 87
. . . . (off Finborough Rd.)
Finborough Rd.
SW10 . . . . 1D 87
Finborough Theatre, The
. . . . 2D 87
. . . . (off Finborough Rd.)
Finch Av. SE27 . . . . 4F 119
Finchdean Ho. SW15 . . . 5B 98
Finch Ho. SE8 . . . . 3D 95
. . . . (off Bronze St.)
Finch La.
EC3 . . . . 3C 18 (5F 63)
Finchley Pl. NW8 . . . . . . 1F 59
Finchley Rd. NW2 . . . . . 1B 30
NW3 . . . . 1C 44
NW8 . . . . 5F 45
NW11 . . . . 1B 30
Finch Lodge W9 . . . . 4C 58
. . . . (off Admiral Wlk.)
Finch M. SE15 . . . . 4B 92
Finch's Ct. E14 . . . . 1D 81
Finden Rd. E7 . . . . 2E 55
Findhorn St. E14 . . . . . . 5E 67
Findon Cl. SW18 . . . . . . 4C 100
Findon Rd. W12 . . . . 3C 70
Fingal St. SE10 . . . . 1B 96
Fingest Ho. NW8 . . . . . . 3A 60
. . . . (off Lilestone St.)
Finland Rd. SE4 . . . . 1A 108
Finland St. SE16 . . . . . . 4A 80
Finlay St. SW6 . . . . 4F 85
Finmere Ho. N4 . . . . 2E 35
Finnemore Ho. N1 . . . . . 5E 49
. . . . (off Britannia Row)
Finn Ho. N1 . . . . 1C 10
. . . . (off Bevenden St.)
Finnis St. E2 . . . . 2D 65
FINSBURY 3F 9 (2C 62)

Finsbury Av.
  EC2. . . . . 1C **18** (4F **63**)
            (not continuous)
Finsbury Av. Sq. EC2. . . 5D **11**
Finsbury Cir.
  EC2. . . . . 1C **18** (4F **63**)
Finsbury Est.
  EC1 . . . . 2C **8** (2C **62**)
Finsbury Leisure Cen.
  . . . . 3F **9** (2E **63**)
Finsbury Mkt.
  EC2 . . . . 4D **11** (3A **64**)
            (Clifton St.)
  EC2 . . . . 5D **11** (4A **64**)
            (Pindar St.)
Finsen Rd. SE5. . . . . . . 2E **105**
Finstock Rd. W10. . . . . . 5F **57**
Finwhale Ho. E14. . . . . . 4D **81**
            (off Glengall Gro.)
Fiona Ct. NW6 . . . . 1C **58**
Firbank Cl. E16. . . . . . . 4F **69**
Firbank Rd. SE15. . . . . . 5D **93**
Fircroft Rd. SW17 . . . . 2B **116**
Firecrest Dr. NW3 . . . . . 5D **31**
Firefly Gdns. E6 . . . . . . 3F **69**
Fir Gro. Rd. SW9. . . . . . 5C **90**
Firhill Rd. SE6 . . . . . . 4C **122**
Fir Ho. W10 . . . . 3A **58**
            (off Droop St.)
Firle Ho. W10 . . . . 4E **57**
            (off Sutton Way)
Firs, The E6 . . . . 4F **55**
  SE26. . . . . 5D **121**
            (Border Rd.)
  SE26. . . . . 5E **121**
            (Waverley Ct.)
Firsby Rd. N16. . . . . 3C **36**
Firs Cl. SE23 . . . . 5A **108**
First Av. E13. . . . . 2C **68**
  SW14 . . . . 1A **98**
  W3 . . . . 2B **70**
  W10. . . . . 3B **58**
First St. SW3 . . . . 5A **74**
Firth Gdns. SW6. . . . . . . 4A **86**
Firth Ho. E2 . . . . 2C **64**
            (off Barnet Gro.)
Firtree Cl. SW16. . . . . . 5E **117**
Fir Trees Cl. SE14. . . . . . 3E **93**
            (off Avonley Rd.)
Fir Trees Cl. SE16 . . . . . 2A **80**
Fisher Athletic FC 2F **79**
Fisher Ho. E1 . . . . 1E **79**
            (off Cable St.)
  N1. . . . . 5C **48**
            (off Barnsbury Est.)
Fishermans Dr. SE16 . . . . 3F **79**
Fisherman's Pl. W4 . . . . . 2B **84**
Fisherman's Wlk.
  E14. . . . . 2C **80**
Fisher's Cl. SW16. . . . . . 3F **117**

Fishers Ct. SE14. . . . . . . 4F **93**
Fisher's La. W4 . . . . 5A **70**
Fisher St. E16 . . . . 4C **68**
  WC1 . . . . 1F **15** (4B **62**)
Fisherton St. NW8 . . . . . 3F **59**
Fishmongers Hall Wharf
  EC4. . . . . 5B **18**
Fishponds Rd.
  SW17 . . . . 4A **116**
Fish St. Hill
  EC3. . . . . 5C **18** (1F **77**)
Fish Wharf
  EC3. . . . . 5C **18** (1F **77**)
Fisons Rd. E16. . . . . 2C **82**
Fitness First Health Club
  Islington 1D **9** (1D **63**)
  Lewisham 1E **109**
  Tooting Bec 3C **116**
            (off Balham High Rd.)
Fitrooms 2B **86**
Fitzalan St. SE11 . . . . . . 5C **76**
Fitzgeorge Av. W14 . . . . . 5A **72**
Fitzgerald Av. SW14 . . . . 1A **98**
Fitzgerald Ct. E10 . . . . . 3D **39**
            (off Leyton Grange Est.)
Fitzgerald Ho. E14. . . . . . 5D **67**
            (off E. India Dock Rd.)
  SW9. . . . . 5C **90**
  SW14 . . . . 1A **98**
Fitzgerald Rd. E11 . . . . . 1C **40**
  SW14 . . . . 1A **98**
Fitzhardinge Ho. W1 . . . . 2B **12**
            (off Portman Sq.)
Fitzhardinge St.
  W1. . . . . 2B **12** (5C **60**)
Fitzhugh Gro. SW18. . . . 4F **101**
Fitzjames Av. W14. . . . . . 5A **72**
Fitzjohn's Av. NW3. . . . . 1E **45**
Fitzmaurice Ho.
  SE16. . . . . 5D **79**
            (off Rennie Est.)
Fitzmaurice Pl.
  W1. . . . . 1E **21** (2D **75**)
Fitzneal St. W12. . . . . . . 5B **56**
FITZROVIA. 5E **5**
Fitzroy Cl. N6. . . . . 3B **32**
Fitzroy Ct. N6 . . . . 3B **32**
  W1 . . . . 4A **6**
Fitzroy Ho. E14. . . . . 4B **66**
            (off Wallwood St.)
  SE1 . . . . 1B **92**
            (off Coopers La.)
Fitzroy M. W1. . . . . 4F **5**
Fitzroy Pk. N6. . . . . 3B **32**
Fitzroy Rd. NW1 . . . . 5C **46**
Fitzroy Sq. W1 . . . 4F **5** (3E **61**)
Fitzroy St. W1 . . . 4F **5** (3E **61**)
            (not continuous)
Fitzroy Yd. NW1. . . . . . . 5C **46**
Fitzsimmons Ct.
  NW10 . . . . 5A **42**
Fitzwarren Gdns. N19 . . . 3E **33**
Fitzwilliam Hgts.
  SE23 . . . . 2E **121**
Fitzwilliam M. E16. . . . . . 2C **82**
Fitzwilliam Rd.
  SW4 . . . . 1E **103**
Five Bell All. E14. . . . . . . 5B **66**
            (off Three Colt St.)
Fives Ct. SE11. . . . . 4D **77**
Fiveways Rd. SW9. . . . . . 5C **90**

Flack Ct. E10 . . . . 2D **39**
Fladbury Rd. N15. . . . . . 1F **35**
Fladgate Rd. E11. . . . . . 1A **40**
Flamborough Ho.
  SE15 . . . . 4C **92**
            (off Clayton Rd.)
Flamborough St.
  E14. . . . . 5A **66**
Flamborough Wlk.
  E14. . . . . 5A **66**
            (off Flamborough St.)
Flamingo Ct. SE8. . . . . . 3C **94**
            (off Hamilton St.)
Flamstead Ho. SW3. . . . . 1A **88**
            (off Cale St.)
Flamsteed Rd. SE7. . . . . 1F **97**
Flanchford Rd. W12. . . . . 4B **70**
Flanders Ct. E17 . . . . . . 2A **38**
Flanders Mans. W4 . . . . . 5B **70**
Flanders Rd. W4 . . . . . . 5A **70**
Flanders Way E9 . . . . . . 3F **51**
            (not continuous)
Flank St. E1 . . . . 1C **78**
Flansham Ho. E14. . . . . . 5B **66**
            (off Clemence St.)
Flask Wlk. NW3 . . . . 1E **45**
Flatford Ho. SE6. . . . . . 4E **123**
Flatiron Yd. SE1. . . . . . . 2A **26**
            (off Union St.)
Flavell M. SE10 . . . . 1A **96**
Flaxman Ct. W1. . . . . . . 3B **14**
  WC1 . . . . 2C **6**
            (off Flaxman Ter.)
Flaxman Ho. W4 . . . . . . 1A **84**
            (off Devonshire St.)
Flaxman Leisure Cen.
  . . . . 5E **91**
Flaxman Rd. SE5. . . . . . 1D **105**
Flaxman Ter.
  WC1 . . . . 2C **6** (2F **61**)
Flecker Ho. SE5 . . . . 3F **91**
            (off Lomond Gro.)
Fleece Wlk. N7. . . . . 3A **48**
Fleetbank Ho. EC4 . . . . . 3C **16**
            (off Salisbury Sq.)
Fleet Bldg. EC4 . . . . 2D **17**
Fleetfield WC1 . . . . 1E **7**
            (off Birkenhead St.)
Fleet Ho. E14. . . . . 1A **80**
            (off Victory Pl.)
Fleet Pl. EC4. . . . 2D **17** (5D **63**)
            (not continuous)
Fleet Rd. NW3 . . . . 2A **46**
Fleet Sq. WC1 . . . 2A **8** (2B **62**)
Fleet St. EC4. . . . 3B **16** (5C **62**)
Fleet St. Hill E1 . . . . 3C **64**
Fleetway WC1 . . . . 1E **7**
            (off Birkenhead St.)
Fleetwood Cl. E16. . . . . . 4F **69**
Fleetwood Rd. NW10. . . . 2C **42**
Fleetwood St. N16. . . . . . 4A **36**
Fleming Cl. W9 . . . . 3C **58**
Fleming Ct. W2 . . . . 4F **59**
            (off St Mary's Sq.)
Fleming Ho. N4 . . . . 3E **35**
  SE16. . . . . 3C **78**
            (off George Row)
Fleming Lodge W9. . . . . . 4C **58**
            (off Admiral Wlk.)
Fleming Rd. SE17 . . . . . . 2D **91**

Flemming Cl. SW10 . . . . 2E **87**
  (off Park Wlk.)
Flempton Rd. E10 . . . . . 3A **38**
Fletcher Bldgs. WC2 . . . . 3E **15**
  (off Martlett Ct.)
Fletcher Ho. SE15 . . . . . 3E **93**
  (off Clifton Way)
Fletcher La. E10 . . . . . . 2E **39**
Fletcher Path SE8 . . . . . 3C **94**
Fletcher St. E1 . . . . 1C **78**
Fletching Rd. E5 . . . . . . 5E **37**
  SE7 . . . . 2E **97**
Fleur-de-Lis St.
  E1 . . . . 4E **11** (3B **64**)
Fleur Gates SW19 . . . . . 5F **99**
Flimwell Cl.
  BR1: Brom 5A **124**
Flinders Ho. E1 . . . . . . 2D **79**
  (off Green Bank)
Flint Cl. E15 . . . . 4B **54**
Flintmill Cres. SE3 . . . . 5F **97**
  (not continuous)
Flinton St. SE17 . . . . . . 1A **92**
Flint St. SE17 . . . . 5F **77**
Flitcroft St.
  WC2 . . . . 3C **14** (5F **61**)
Flitton Ho. N1 . . . . 4D **49**
  (off Sutton Est., The)
Flock Mill Pl. SW18 . . 1D **115**
Flockton St. SE16 . . . . . 3C **78**
Flodden Rd. SE5 . . . . . . 4E **91**
Flood St. SW3 . . . . 1A **88**
Flood Wlk. SW3 . . . . . . 2A **88**
Flora Cl. E14 . . . . 5D **67**
Flora Gdns. W6 . . . . . . 5D **71**
  (off Albion Gdns.)
Floral Pl. N1 . . . . 2F **49**
Floral St.
  WC2 . . . . 4D **15** (1A **76**)
Florence Cantwell Wlk.
  N19 . . . . 2A **34**
  (off Jessie Blythe La.)
Florence Ct. E5 . . . . . . 5C **36**
  N1 . . . . 4D **49**
  (off Florence St.)
  SW19 . . . . 5A **114**
  W9 . . . . 2E **59**
  (off Maida Va.)
Florence Ho. SE16 . . . . 1D **93**
  (off Rotherhithe New Rd.)
  W11 . . . . 1F **71**
  (off St Ann's Rd.)
Florence Mans. NW4 . . 1D **29**
  (off Vivian Av.)
Florence Nightingale Mus.
  . . . . 4F **23** (3B **76**)
Florence Rd. E6 . . . . . . 5E **55**
  E13 . . . . 1C **68**
  N4 . . . . 2B **34**
  (not continuous)
  SE14 . . . . 4B **94**
  SW19 . . . . 5D **115**
Florence St. E16 . . . . . . 3B **68**
  N1 . . . . 4D **49**
Florence Ter. SE14 . . . . 4B **94**
  SW15 . . . . 3A **112**
Florence Way
  SW12 . . . . 1B **116**
Flores Ho. E1 . . . . 4F **65**
  (off Shandy St.)

Florey Lodge W9 . . . . . 4C **58**
  (off Admiral Wlk.)
Florfield Pas. E8 . . . . . . 3D **51**
  (off Florfield Rd.)
Florfield Rd. E8 . . . . . . 3D **51**
Florian SE5 . . . . 4A **92**
Florian Rd. SW15 . . . . . 2A **100**
Florida St. E2 . . . . 2C **64**
Florin Ct. SE1 . . . . 4F **27**
  (off Tanner St.)
Floris Pl. SW4 . . . . 1E **103**
Florys Ct. SW19 . . . . . . 1A **114**
Floss St. SW15 . . . . . . 5E **85**
Flower & Dean Wlk.
  E1 . . . . 1F **19** (4B **64**)
Flower M. NW11 . . . . . . 1A **30**
Flowerpot Cl. N15 . . . . . 1B **36**
Flowers Cl. NW2 . . . . . . 5C **28**
Flowersmead SW17 . . . . 2C **116**
Flowers M. N19 . . . . . . 4E **33**
Flower Wlk., The
  SW7 . . . . 3E **73**
Floyd Rd. SE7 . . . . 1E **97**
Fludyer St. SE13 . . . . . . 2A **110**
Flynn Ct. E14 . . . . 1C **80**
  (off Garford St.)
Foley Ho. E1 . . . . 5E **65**
  (off Tarling St.)
Foley St. W1 . . . . . 1F **13** (4E **61**)
Folgate St.
  E1 . . . . 5E **11** (4A **64**)
  (not continuous)
Foliot Ho. N1 . . . . 1B **62**
  (off Priory Grn. Est.)
Foliot St. W3 . . . . 5A **56**
Follett Ho. SW10 . . . . . 3F **87**
  (off Worlds End Est.)
Follett St. E14 . . . . 5E **67**
Follingham Ct. N1 . . . . . 1E **11**
  (off Drysdale Pl.)
Folly M. W11 . . . . 5B **58**
Folly Wall E14 . . . . 3E **81**
Fonda Ct. E14 . . . . 1C **80**
  (off Premiere Pl.)
Fontarabia Rd.
  SW11 . . . . 2C **102**
Fontenelle Gdns.
  SE5 . . . . 4A **92**
Fontenoy Ho. SE11 . . . . 5D **77**
  (off Kennington La.)
Fontenoy Rd. SW12 . . . 2D **117**
Fonthill M. N4 . . . . 4B **34**
Fonthill Rd. N4 . . . . 3B **34**
Fontley Way SW15 . . . . 5C **98**
Footpath, The SW15 . . . 4C **98**
Forber Ho. E2 . . . . 2F **65**
  (off Cornwall Av.)
Forbes Cl. NW2 . . . . . . 5C **28**
Forbes St. E1 . . . . 5C **64**
Forburg Rd. N16 . . . . . . 3C **36**
Ford Cl. E3 . . . . 1A **66**
Fordel Rd. SE6 . . . . 1E **123**
Fordham St. E1 . . . . . . 5C **64**
Fordingley Rd. W9 . . . . . 2B **58**
Fordington Ho.
  SE26 . . . . 3C **120**
Fordmill Rd. SE6 . . . . . 2C **122**
Ford Rd. E3 . . . . 1B **66**
Fords Pk. Rd. E16 . . . . . 4C **68**
Ford Sq. E1 . . . . 4D **65**

Ford St. E3 . . . . 5A **52**
  E16 . . . . 5B **68**
Fordwych Rd. NW2 . . . . 1A **44**
Fordyce Rd. SE13 . . . . . 4E **109**
Foreign St. SE5 . . . . . . 5D **91**
Foreland Ho. W11 . . . . . 1A **72**
  (off Walmer Rd.)
Foreshore SE8 . . . . 5B **80**
Forest Bus. Pk. E10 . . . . 2F **37**
Forest Cl. E11 . . . . 1C **40**
  SE23 . . . . 2D **121**
Forest Cft. SE23 . . . . . . 2D **121**
Forest Dr. E12 . . . . 5F **41**
Forest Dr. E. E11 . . . . . 2F **39**
Forest Dr. W. E11 . . . . . 2E **39**
Forester Ho. E14 . . . . . . 1A **80**
  (off Victory Pl.)
Forester Rd. SE15 . . . . . 1D **107**
FOREST GATE 2C **54**
Forest Ga. Retreat
  E7 . . . . 2C **54**
  (off Odessa Rd.)
Forest Glade E11 . . . . . 1A **40**
Forest Gro. E8 . . . . 3B **50**
FOREST HILL 2E **121**
Forest Hill Bus. Cen.
  SE23 . . . . 2E **121**
  (off Clyde Va.)
Forest Hill Ind. Est.
  SE23 . . . . 2E **121**
Forest Hill Pool 2E **121**
Forest Hill Rd.
  SE22 . . . . 3D **107**
Forestholme Cl.
  SE23 . . . . 2E **121**
Forest La. E7 . . . . 2A **54**
  E15 . . . . 2A **54**
Forest Lodge SE23 . . . . 3E **121**
  (off Dartmouth Rd.)
Forest Point E7 . . . . . . 2D **55**
  (off Windsor Rd.)
Fore St. EC2 . . . . . 1A **18** (4E **63**)
  EC2 . . . . 1B **18** (4F **63**)
Forest Rd. E7 . . . . 1C **54**
  E8 . . . . 3B **50**
  E11 . . . . 2F **39**
Forest Side E7 . . . . 1D **55**
Forest Vw. E11 . . . . 2B **40**
Forest Vw. Av. E10 . . . . 1F **39**
Forest Vw. Rd. E12 . . . . 1F **55**
Forest Way N19 . . . . . . 4E **33**
Forfar Rd. SW11 . . . . . . 4C **88**
Forge Pl. NW1 . . . . 3C **46**
Forges Rd. E12 . . . . . . 4F **41**
Forman Pl. N16 . . . . . . 1B **50**
Formby Ct. N7 . . . . 2C **48**
  (off Morgan Rd.)
Formosa Ho. E1 . . . . . . 3A **66**
  (off Ernest St.)
Formosa St. W9 . . . . . . 3D **59**
Formunt Cl. E16 . . . . . . 4B **68**
Forres Gdns. NW11 . . . . 1C **30**
Forrester Path
  SE26 . . . . 4E **121**
Forset St. W1 . . . . 5A **60**
Forster Ho.
  BR1: Brom 4F **123**

Forster Rd. E17 . . . . 1A 38
  SW2 . . . . 5A 104
Forston St. N1 . . . . 1E 63
Forsyth Gdns. SE17 . . . 2D 91
Forsyth Ho. E9 . . . . 4E 51
  (off Frampton Pk. Rd.)
  SW1 . . . . 1E 89
  (off Tachbrook St.)
Fortescue Av. E8 . . . . . . 4D 51
Fortess Gro. NW5 . . . . . 2E 47
Fortess Rd. NW5 . . . . . . 2D 47
Fortess Wlk. NW5 . . . . . 2D 47
Fortess Yd. NW5 . . . . . . 1D 47
Forthbridge Rd.
  SW11 . . . . 2C 102
Fortis Cl. E16 . . . . 5E 69
Fortnam Rd. N19 . . . . . . 4F 33
Fort Rd. SE1 . . . . 5B 78
Fortrose Cl. E14 . . . . . . 5F 67
Fortrose Gdns. SW2 . . 1A 118
Fort St. E1 . . . 1E 19 (4A 64)
  E16 . . . . 2D 83
Fortuna Cl. N7 . . . . 3B 48
Fortune Ct. E8 . . . . 4B 50
  (off Queensbridge Rd.)
Fortunegate Rd.
  NW10 . . . . 5A 42
FORTUNE GREEN 1C 44
Fortune Grn. Rd.
  NW6 . . . . 1C 44
Fortune Ho. EC1 . . . . . . 4A 10
  (off Fortune St.)
  SE11 . . . . 5C 76
  (off Marylee Way)
Fortune St.
  EC1 . . . . 4A 10 (3E 63)
Fortune Theatre 3E 15
  (off Russell St.)
Fortune Way NW10 . . . 2C 56
Forty Acre La. E16 . . . . 4C 68
Forum Magnum Sq.
  SE1 . . . . 3A 24
  (off York Rd.)
Forward Bus. Cen., The
  E16 . . . . 3F 67
Fosbrooke Ho. SW8 . . 3A 90
  (off Davidson Gdns.)
Fosbury M. W2 . . . . 1D 73
Foscote Ct. W9 . . . . 3C 58
  (off Foscote M.)
Foscote M. W9 . . . . 3C 58
Foscote Rd. NW4 . . . . . 1D 29
Foskett Rd. SW6 . . . . . 5B 86
Fossdene Rd. SE7 . . . . 1D 97
Fossil Rd. SE13 . . . . . 1C 108
Foss Rd. SW17 . . . . . . 4F 115
Foster Ct. E16 . . . . 1B 82
  (off Tarling Rd.)
  NW1 . . . . 4E 47
  (off Royal College St.)
Foster Ho. SE14 . . . . . . 4B 94
Foster La.
  EC2 . . . . 2F 17 (5E 63)
Foster Rd. E13 . . . . 3C 68
  W3 . . . . 1A 70
  W4 . . . . 1A 84
Foster's Way SW18 . . . 1D 115
Fothergill Cl. E13 . . . . . 1C 68
Foubert's Pl.
  W1 . . . . 3F 13 (5E 61)

Foulden Rd. N16 . . . . . . 1B 50
Foulden Ter. N16 . . . . . . 1B 50
Foulis Ter. SW7 . . . . 1F 87
Foulser Rd. SW17 . . . . 3B 116
Founders Ct. EC2 . . . . . 2B 18
Founders Ho. SW1 . . . . 1F 89
  (off Aylesford St.)
Foundling Ct. WC1 . . . . 3D 7
  (off Brunswick Cen.)
Foundling Mus., The
  . . . . 3E 7 (3A 62)
Foundry Cl. SE16 . . . . . 2A 80
Foundry Ho. E14 . . . . . . 4D 67
  (off Morris Rd.)
Foundry M. NW1 . . . . . . 3A 6
Foundry Pl. E1 . . . . 4E 65
  (off Redman's Rd.)
  SW18 . . . . 5D 101
Fountain Cl.
  EC4 . . . . . . 4B 16 (1C 76)
  SE23 . . . . 2F 121
  SW1 . . . . 5D 75
  (off Buckingham Pal. Rd.)
Fountain Dr. SE19 . . . . 4B 120
Fountain Grn. Sq.
  SE16 . . . . 3C 78
Fountain Ho. NW6 . . . . 4A 44
  W1 . . . . 1B 20
  (off Park St.)
Fountain M. N5 . . . . 1E 49
  (off Highbury Grange)
  NW3 . . . . 3B 46
Fountain Pl. SW9 . . . . . 4C 90
Fountain Rd. SW17 . . . 5F 115
Fountain Sq. SW1 . . . . . 5D 75
Fountayne Rd. N16 . . . . 4C 36
Fount St. SW8 . . . . 3F 89
Fournier St.
  E1 . . . . 5F 11 (4B 64)
Fourscore Mans. E8 . . 4C 50
  (off Shrubland Rd.)
Four Seasons Cl. E3 . . 1C 66
Fourth Av. W10 . . . . 3A 58
Fovant Ct. SW8 . . . . 5E 89
Fowey Cl. E1 . . . . 2D 79
Fowey Ho. SE11 . . . . . . 1C 90
  (off Kennings Way)
Fowler Cl. SW11 . . . . . . 1F 101
Fowler Ho. N15 . . . . 1F 35
  (off South Gro.)
Fowler Rd. E7 . . . . 1C 54
  N1 . . . . 5D 49
Fowlers M. N19 . . . . 4E 33
Fownes St. SW11 . . . . . 1A 102
Fox & Knot St. EC1 . . . 5E 9
Foxberry Rd. SE4 . . . . . 1A 108
Foxborough Gdns.
  SE4 . . . . 3C 108
Foxbourne Rd.
  SW17 . . . . 2C 116
Fox Cl. E1 . . . . 3E 65
  E16 . . . . 4C 68
Foxcombe Cl. E6 . . . . . 1F 69
Foxcombe Rd.
  SW15 . . . . 1C 112
Foxcote SE5 . . . . 1A 92
Foxcroft WC1 . . . . 1A 8
  (off Penton Ri.)
Foxes Dale SE3 . . . . . . 1C 110

Foxfield NW1 . . . . 5D 47
  (off Arlington Rd.)
Foxglove St. W12 . . . . . 1B 70
Foxham Rd. N19 . . . . . . 5F 33
Foxhole Rd. SE9 . . . . . . 3F 111
Foxley Cl. E8 . . . . 2C 50
Foxley Rd. SW9 . . . . . . 3C 90
Foxley Sq. SW9 . . . . . . 4D 91
Foxmore St. SW11 . . . . 4B 88
Fox Rd. E16 . . . . 4B 68
Foxwell M. SE4 . . . . 1A 108
Foxwell St. SE4 . . . . 1A 108
Foxwood Rd. SE3 . . . . . 2B 110
Foyle Rd. SE3 . . . . 2B 96
Framfield Rd. N5 . . . . . . 2D 49
Framlingham Cl.
  E5 . . . . 4E 37
Frampton NW1 . . . . 4F 47
  (off Wrotham Rd.)
Frampton Ho. NW8 . . . 3F 59
  (off Frampton St.)
Frampton Pk. Est. E9 . . 4E 51
Frampton Pk. Rd. E9 . . 3E 51
Frampton St. NW8 . . . . 3F 59
Francemary Rd.
  SE4 . . . . 3C 108
Frances Ct. E17 . . . . . . 1C 38
Franche Ct. Rd.
  SW17 . . . . 3E 115
Francis Barber Cl.
  SW16 . . . . 5B 118
Franciscan Rd.
  SW17 . . . . 5B 116
Francis Chichester Way
  SW11 . . . . 4C 88
Francis Cl. E14 . . . . 5F 81
Francis Ct. EC1 . . . . 5D 9
  SE14 . . . . 2F 93
  (off Myers La.)
Francis Ho. E17 . . . . . . 1B 38
  N1 . . . . 5A 50
  (off Colville Est.)
  SW10 . . . . 3D 87
  (off Coleridge Gdns.)
Francis M. SE12 . . . . . . 5C 110
Francis Rd. E10 . . . . . . 3E 39
Francis St. E15 . . . . 2A 54
  SW1 . . . . 5A 22 (5E 75)
Francis Ter. N19 . . . . . . 5E 33
Francis Wlk. N1 . . . . 5B 48
Franconia Rd. SW4 . . . 3F 103
Frank Beswick Ho.
  SW6 . . . . 2B 86
  (off Clem Attlee Ct.)
Frank Burton Cl. SE7 . . 1D 97
Frank Dixon Cl.
  SE21 . . . . 5A 106
Frank Dixon Way
  SE21 . . . . 1A 120
Frankfurt Rd. SE24 . . . . 3E 105
Frankham Ho. SE8 . . . . 3C 94
  (off Frankham St.)
Frankham St. SE8 . . . . 3C 94
Frank Ho. SW8 . . . . 3A 90
  (off Wyvil Rd.)
Frankland Cl. SE16 . . . . 4D 79
Frankland Rd. SW7 . . . 4F 73
Franklin Bldg. E14 . . . . 3C 80
Franklin Cl. SE13 . . . . . 4D 95
  SE27 . . . . 3D 119

Franklin Ho. *E1* 2D **79**	Fremont St. E9. . . . . 5D **51**
(off Watts St.)	(not continuous)
Franklin Pl. SE13. . . . . . . 4D **95**	French Ordinary Ct.
Franklin Sq. W14. . . . . . . 1B **86**	EC3. . . . . 4E **19**
Franklin's Row SW3. . . . 1B **88**	French Pl. E1. . . 2E **11** (2A **64**)
Franklin St. E3. . . . . 2D **67**	Frendsbury Rd. SE4. . . 2A **108**
N15. . . . . 1A **36**	Frensham Dr. SW15. . . 3B **112**
Franklyn Rd. NW10 . . . 3B **42**	(not continuous)
Frank Soskice Ho.	Frensham St. SE15. . . . . 2C **92**
SW6 . . . . 2B **86**	Frere St. SW11 . . . . 5A **88**
(off Clem Attlee Ct.)	Freshfield Av. E8 . . . . . . 4B **50**
Frank St. E13 . . . . 3C **68**	Freshfield Cl. SE13 . . . 2F **109**
Frank Whymark Ho.	Freshford St. SW18 . . . 3E **115**
SE16. . . . . 3E **79**	Freshwater Cl.
(off Hupack St.)	SW17 . . . . 5C **116**
Fransfield Gro.	Freshwater Ct. *W1*. . . . 4A **60**
SE26. . . . . 3D **121**	(off Crawford St.)
Frans Hals Ct. E14 . . . . . 4F **81**	Freshwater Rd.
Franthorne Way	SW17 . . . . 5C **116**
SE6. . . . . 2D **123**	Freston Rd. W10 . . . . . . 1F **71**
Fraser Cl. E6. . . . . 5F **69**	W11. . . . . 1F **71**
Fraser Ct. *E14*. 1E **95**	Freswick Ho. *SE8* 5F **79**
(off Ferry St.)	(off Chilton Gro.)
Fraser Rd. E17. . . . . 1D **39**	Freud Mus., The. 3E **45**
Fraser St. W4. . . . . 1A **84**	Frewell Ho. *EC1* 5B **8**
Frazier St.	(off Bourne Est.)
SE1 . . . . 4B **24** (3C **76**)	Frewin Rd. SW18. . . . . 1F **115**
Frean St. SE16. . . . . 4C **78**	Friar M. SE27. . . . . . . 3D **119**
Frearson Ho. *WC1* 1A **8**	Friars Av. SW15. . . . . . 3B **112**
(off Penton Ri.)	Friars Cl. SE1 . . . . 2E **25**
Freda Corbet Cl.	Friars Gdns. W3. . . . . . . 5A **56**
SE15 . . . . 3C **92**	Friars Mead E14. . . . . . . 4E **81**
Frederica St. N7. . . . . . . 4B **48**	Friars Pl. La. W3 . . . . . 1A **70**
Frederick Charrington Ho.	Friars Rd. E6 . . . . 5F **55**
E1 . . . . 3E **65**	Friar St. EC4 . . 3E **17** (5D **63**)
(off Wickford St.)	Friars Way W3 . . . . 5A **56**
Frederick Cl. W2 . . . . . . 1B **74**	Friary Cl. SW1 . . . . 2A **22**
Frederick Cl. *SW3* 5B **74**	Friary Est. SE15. . . . . . . 2C **92**
(off Duke of York Sq.)	(not continuous)
Frederick Cres.	Friary Rd. SE15 . . . . 3C **92**
SW9 . . . . 3D **91**	W3 . . . . 5A **56**
Frederick Rd. SE17 . . . . 2D **91**	Friday St.
Frederick's Pl.	EC4. . . . . . . 4F **17** (1E **77**)
EC2. . . . . 3B **18** (5F **63**)	Frideswide Pl. NW5. . . . 2E **47**
Frederick Sq. SE16 . . . . 1A **80**	Frieghtliners City Farm
(off Sovereign Cres.)	. . . . 3C **48**
Frederick's Row	Friendly Pl. SE13. . . . . . 4D **95**
EC1. . . . . 1D **9** (2D **63**)	Friendly Pl. SE8. . . . . . . 5C **94**
Frederick St.	Friendly St. M. SE8 . . . . 5C **94**
WC1. . . . . 2F **7** (2B **62**)	Friendship Ho. *SE1* 4E **25**
Frederick Ter. E8 . . . . . . 4B **50**	(off Belvedere Pl.)
Frederic M. SW1 . . . . . . 4A **20**	Friendship Way E15. . . . 5E **53**
Frederic St. E17. . . . . . . 1A **38**	Friends House. 2B **6**
Fred Styles Ho. SE7. . . . 2E **97**	Friend St.
Fred White Wlk. N7 . . . . 3A **48**	EC1. . . . . 1D **9** (2D **63**)
Freedom St. SW11. . . . . 5B **88**	Friern Rd. SE22. . . . . . 5C **106**
Freegrove Rd. N7. . . . . . 2A **48**	Frigate Ho. *E14* 5E **81**
(not continuous)	(off Stebondale St.)
Freeling Ho. *NW8* 5F **45**	Frigate M. SE8 . . . . 2C **94**
(off Dorman Way)	Frimley Cl. SW19. . . . . 2A **114**
Freeling St. N1. . . . . 4B **48**	Frimley St. *E1* 3F **65**
(Carnoustie Dr.)	(off Frimley Way)
N1. . . . . 4A **48**	Frimley Way E1 . . . . 3F **65**
(Pembroke St.)	Frinstead Ho. *W10* 1F **71**
Freemantle St. SE17 . . . 1A **92**	(off Freston Rd.)
Freemasons Rd. E16. . . . 4D **69**	Frinton Rd. E6 . . . . 2F **69**
Free Trade Wharf E1. . . . 1F **79**	N15. . . . . 1A **36**
Freke Rd. SW11. . . . . . 1C **102**	Friston St. SW6. . . . . . . 5D **87**
Fremantle Ho. *E1*. 3D **65**	Frith Rd. NW8. . . . . 3F **59**
(off Somerford St.)	(off Frampton St.)
Frith Rd. E11. . . . . 1E **53**
Frith St. W1. . . . . 3B **14** (5F **61**)
Frithville Ct. *W12*. 2E **71**
(off Frithville Gdns.)
Frithville Gdns.
W12 . . . . 2E **71**
Frobisher Ct. *SE10*. 2F **95**
(off Old Woolwich Rd.)
SE23. . . . . 2D **121**
W12 . . . . 3E **71**
(off Lime Gro.)
Frobisher Cres. EC2. . . . 5A **10**
(off Beech St.)
Frobisher Gdns. E10 . . . 2D **39**
Frobisher Ho. *E1*. 2D **79**
(off Watts St.)
SW1 . . . . 2F **89**
(off Dolphin Sq.)
Frobisher Pas. E14 . . . . 2C **80**
Frobisher Pl. Pioneer Cen.
SE15. . . . . 4E **93**
Frobisher Rd. SE10. . . . 2A **96**
Frogley Rd. SE22. . . . . 2B **106**
Frogmore SW18. . . . . . 3C **100**
Frogmore Ind. Est.
N5. . . . . 2E **49**
Frognal NW3. . . . . 1E **45**
Frognal Cl. NW3. . . . . . . 2E **45**
Frognal Ct. NW3. . . . . . . 3E **45**
Frognal Gdns. NW3 . . . 1E **45**
Frognal La. NW3 . . . . . . 2D **45**
Frognal Pde. NW3 . . . . . 3E **45**
Frognal Ri. NW3 . . . . . . 5E **31**
Frognal Way NW3 . . . . . 1E **45**
Froissart Rd. SE9. . . . . 3F **111**
Frome Ho. SE15. . . . . . 2D **107**
Frome St. N1 . . . . 1E **63**
Frontenac NW10 . . . . . . 4D **43**
Frostic Wlk. E1. . . . . 4C **64**
Froude St. SW8 . . . . 5D **89**
Fruiterers Pas. *EC4* 5A **18**
(off Queen St. Pl.)
Fryday Gro. M.
SW12 . . . . 5E **103**
(off Weir Rd.)
Fryent Cres. NW9. . . . . . 1A **28**
Fryent Flds. NW9. . . . . . 1A **28**
Fryent Gro. NW9 . . . . . . 1A **28**
Fry Ho. E6. . . . . 4E **55**
Frying Pan All. E1 . . . . . 1F **19**
Fry Rd. E6. . . . . 4F **55**
NW10 . . . . 5B **42**
Fulbeck Ho. *N7* 3B **48**
(off Sutterton St.)
Fulbeck Rd. N19. . . . . . . 1E **47**
Fulbourne St. E1. . . . . . . 4D **65**
Fulbrook M. N19 . . . . . . 1E **47**
Fulcher Ho. *N1*. 5A **50**
(off Colville St.)
SE8. . . . . 1B **94**
Fulford St. SE16. . . . . . . 3D **79**
FULHAM 5A **86**
FULHAM BROADWAY
. . . . 3C **86**
Fulham B'way. SW6. . . . 3C **86**
Fulham B'way. Shop. Cen.
SW6 . . . . 3C **86**
(off Fulham B'way.)
Fulham Pal. Rd. SW6. . . 4C **86**
Fulham FC. SW6. . . . . . 4F **85**

Fulham High St.
SW6 . . . . 5A **86**
Fulham Palace 5A **86**
Fulham Pal. Rd.
SW6 . . . . 1E **85**
W6 . . . . 1E **85**
Fulham Pk. Gdns.
SW6 . . . . 5B **86**
Fulham Pk. Rd. SW6 . 5B **86**
Fulham Pools 2A **86**
Fulham Rd. SW3 . . . . 3D **87**
SW6 . . . . 5A **86**
SW10 . . . . 3D **87**
(not continuous)
Fuller Cl. *E2* *3C **64***
(off Cheshire St.)
Fuller's Griffin Brewery &
Vis. Cen. 2B **84**
Fullerton Rd. SW18 . . 3D **101**
Fullwood's M.
N1 . . . . 1C **10** *(2F 63)*
Fulmar Rd. *SE16* *5F 79*
(off Tawny Way)
Fulmead St. SW6 . . . . 4D **87**
Fulmer Ho. *NW8* *3A 60*
(off Mallory St.)
Fulmer Rd. E16 . . . . . 4F **69**
Fulneck *E1* *4E 65*
(off Mile End Rd.)
Fulready Rd. E10 . . . . 1F **39**
Fulthorp Rd. SE3 . . . . 5B **96**
Fulton M. *W2* *1E 73*
Fulwood Pl.
WC1 . . . . . . 1A **16** *(4B 62)*
Fulwood Wlk.
SW19 . . . . 1A **114**
Funland *5B 14*
(in Trocadero Cen)
Furber St. *W6* 4D **71**
Furley Ho. *SE15* *3C 92*
(off Peckham Pk. Rd.)
Furley Rd. SE15 . . . . . 3C **92**
Furlong Rd. N7 . . . . . 3C **48**
Furmage St. SW18 . . . 5D **101**
Furneaux Av. SE27 . . . 5D **119**
Furness Ho. *SW1* *1D 89*
(off Abbots Mnr.)
Furness Rd. NW10 . . . 1C **56**
SW6 . . . . 5D **87**
Furnival Mans. *W1* . . . *1F 13*
(off Wells St.)
Furnival St.
EC4 . . . . 2B **16** *(5C 62)*
Furrow La. E9 . . . . . . 2E **51**
Fursecroft *W1* *5B 60*
(off George St.)
Further Grn. Rd.
SE6 . . . . 5A **110**
FURZEDOWN 5D **117**
Furzedown Dr.
SW17 . . . . 5D **117**
Furzedown Rd.
SW17 . . . . 5D **117**
Furzefield Rd. SE3 . . . 2D **97**
Furze St. E3 . . . . 4C **66**
Fusion Health & Leisure Cen.
. . . . 5D **77**
Fye Foot La. *EC4* *4F 17*
*(off Queen Victoria St.,
not continuous)*

Fyfield *N4* *4C 34*
(off Six Acres Est.)
Fyfield Ct. E7 . . . . . . 3C **54**
Fyfield Rd. SW9 . . . . 1C **104**
Fynes St. SW1 . . . . . 5F **75**

G

Gable Ct. SE26 . . . . . 4D **121**
Gables Cl. SE5 . . . . . 4A **92**
SE12 . . . . 1C **124**
Gabriel Ho. SE11 . . . . 5B **76**
Gabrielle Ct.
NW3 . . . . 3F **45**
Gabriel M. NW2 . . . . 4B **30**
Gabriel St. SE23 . . . . 5F **107**
Gabriels Wharf
SE1 . . . . . 1B **24** *(2C 76)*
Gad Cl. E13 . . . . 2D **69**
Gaddesden Ho. *EC1* . . . *2C 10*
(off Cranwood St.)
Gadebridge Ho. *SW3* . . *1A 88*
(off Cale St.)
Gadsbury Cl. NW9 . . . 1B **28**
Gadsden Ho. *W10* *3A 58*
(off Hazlewood Cres.)
Gadwall Cl. E16 . . . . . 5D **69**
Gage Brown Ho. *W10* . *5F 57*
(off Bridge Cl.)
Gage Rd. E16 . . . . . . 4A **68**
Gage St. WC1 . . . . . 5E **7** *(4A 62)*
Gainford Ho. *E2* *2D 65*
(off Ellsworth St.)
Gainford St. N1 . . . . . 5C **48**
Gainsborough Ct.
SE16 . . . . *1D 93*
(off Stubbs Dr.)
SE21 . . . . 2A **120**
W12 . . . . 3E **71**
Gainsborough Gdns.
NW3 . . . . 5F **31**
NW11 . . . . 2B **30**
Gainsborough Ho.
E14 . . . . *1A 80*
(off Victory Pl.)
SW1 . . . . *5F 75*
(off Erasmus St.)
Gainsborough Mans.
W14 . . . . *2A 86*
(off Queen's Club Gdns.)
Gainsborough Rd.
E11 . . . . 2A **40**
E15 . . . . 2A **68**
W4 . . . . 5B **70**
Gainsborough St. E9 . . 3B **52**
Gainsborough Studios E.
N1 . . . . *5F 49*
(off Poole St.)
Gainsborough Studios Nth.
N1 . . . . *5F 49*
(off Poole St.)
Gainsborough Studios Sth.
N1 . . . . *5F 49*
(off Poole St.)
Gainsborough Studios W.
N1 . . . . *5F 49*
(off Poole St.)

Gainsfield Ct. E11 . . . 5A **40**
Gainsford St.
SE1 . . . . 3F **27** *(3B 78)*
Gairloch Ho. *NW1* *4F 47*
(off Stratford Vs.)
Gairloch Rd. SE5 . . . . 5A **92**
Gaisford St. NW5 . . . . 3E **47**
Gaitskell Ct. SW11 . . . 5A **88**
Gaitskell Ho. E6 . . . . . 5F **55**
SE17 . . . . *2A 92*
(off Villa St.)
Gala Bingo
Camberwell 3E **91**
Stratford 5F **53**
Surrey Quays 4F **79**
Galahad Rd.
BR1: Brom 4C **124**
Galata Rd. SW13 . . . . 3C **84**
Galatea Sq. SE15 . . . . 1D **107**
Galaxy Bldg. *E14* *5C 80*
(off Crews St.)
Galaxy Ho. *EC2* *3C 10*
(off Leonard St.)
Galbraith St. E14 . . . . 4E **81**
Galena Arches *W6* *5D 71*
(off Galena Rd.)
Galena Ho. *W6* *5D 71*
(off Galena Rd.)
Galena Rd. W6 . . . . . 5D **71**
Galen Pl.
WC1 . . . . . . 1E **15** *(4A 62)*
Galesbury Rd.
SW18 . . . . 4E **101**
Gales Gdns. E2 . . . . . 2D **65**
Gale St. E3 . . . . 4C **66**
Galgate Cl. SW19 . . . . 1F **113**
Galleon Cl. SE16 . . . . 3F **79**
Galleon Ho. *E14* *5E 81*
(off Glengarnock Av.)
Gallery Ct. *SE1* *4B 26*
(off Pilgrimage St.)
SW10 . . . . *2E 87*
(off Gunter Gro.)
Gallery Rd. SE21 . . . . 1F **119**
Galleywall Rd. SE16 . . 5D **79**
Galleywall Rd. Trad. Est.
SE16 . . . . *5D 79*
(off Galleywall Rd.)
Galleywood Ho. *W10* . . *4E 57*
(off Sutton Way)
Gallia Rd. N5 . . . . . . 2D **49**
Gallions Ct. SE7 . . . . . 5D **83**
Galliver Pl. E5 . . . . . . 1D **51**
Gallon Cl. SE7 . . . . . . 5E **83**
Galloway Rd. W12 . . . 2C **70**
Gallus Sq. SE3 . . . . . 1D **111**
Galsworthy Av. E14 . . . 4A **66**
Galsworthy Cl. NW2 . . 1A **44**
Galsworthy Cres. SE3 . 4E **97**
Galsworthy Ho. *W11* . . *5A 58*
(off Elgin Cres.)
Galsworthy Rd. NW2 . . 1A **44**
Galsworthy Ter. N16 . . 5A **36**
Galton St. W10 . . . . . 2A **58**
Galveston Ho. *E1* *3A 66*
(off Harford St.)
Galveston Rd.
SW15 . . . . 3B **100**
Galway Cl. *SE16* *1D 93*
(off Masters Dr.)

Galway Ho. *E1* 4F **65**
  (off White Horse La.)
EC1 . . . . 2A **10**
Galway St.
  EC1 . . . . 2A **10** (2E **63**)
Gambetta St. SW8 . . . 5D **89**
Gambia St.
  SE1 . . . . . . 2E **25** (2D **77**)
Gambier Ho. *EC1* 2A **10**
  (off Mora St.)
Gambole Rd. SW17 . . . 4A **116**
Gamlen Rd. SW15 . . . . 2F **99**
Gamuel Cl. E17 . . . . . . 1C **38**
Gandhi Cl. E17 . . . . . . 1C **38**
Gandolfi St. SE15 . . . . 2A **92**
Ganton St.
  W1 . . . . 4F **13** (1E **75**)
Gap Rd. SW19 . . . . . . 5C **114**
Garbett Ho. *SE17* 2D **91**
  (off Doddington Gro.)
Garbutt Pl.
  W1 . . . . 5C **4** (4C **60**)
Garden Cl. SE12 . . . . . 3D **125**
SW15 . . . . 5E **99**
Garden Ct. EC4 . . . . . . 4B **16**
Garden Ho., The *W6* . . . 2F **85**
  (off Bothwell St.)
Garden La.
  BR1: Brom 5D **125**
SW2 . . . . 1B **118**
Garden M. W2 . . . . 1C **72**
Garden Pl. E8 . . . . 5B **50**
Garden Wlk. NW8 . . . . . 2E **59**
Garden Row
  SE1 . . . . . . 5D **25** (4D **77**)
Garden Royal SW15 . . . 4F **99**
Gardens, The SE22 . . . 2C **106**
Garden St. E1 . . . . 4F **65**
Garden Ter. SW1 . . . . . 1F **89**
SW7 . . . . 5F **73**
  (off Trevor Pl.)
Garden Vw. E7 . . . . . . 1E **55**
Garden Wlk.
  EC2 . . . . . . 2D **11** (2A **64**)
Gardiner Av. NW2 . . . . . 2E **43**
Gardner Cl. E11 . . . . . . 1D **41**
Gardner Ct. *EC1* 3D **9**
  (off Brewery Sq.)
N5 . . . . 1E **49**
Gardner Ind. Est.
  SE26 . . . . 5B **122**
Gardner Rd. E13 . . . . . 3D **69**
Gardners La.
  EC4 . . . . . . 4F **17** (1E **77**)
Gardnor Rd. NW3 . . . . . 1F **45**
Gard St. EC1 . . . 1E **9** (2D **63**)
Gareth Ct. SW16 . . . . . 3F **117**
Gareth Gro.
  BR1: Brom 4C **124**
Garfield Ct. *NW6* 4A **44**
  (off Willesden La.)
Garfield M. SW11 . . . . 1C **102**
Garfield Rd. E13 . . . . . 3B **68**
SW11 . . . . 1C **102**
SW19 . . . . 5E **115**
Garford St. E14 . . . . . . 1C **80**
Gergerny St. NW10 . . . 1D **57**
  (off Elgar Av.)
Garland Ct. *E14* 1C **80**
  (off Premiere Pl.)

Garlick Hill
  EC4 . . . . . . 4A **18** (1E **77**)
Garlies Rd. SE23 . . . . 3A **122**
Garlinge Rd. NW2 . . . . 3B **44**
Garnault M. EC1 . . . . . . 2C **8**
Garnault Pl.
  EC1 . . . . 2C **8** (2C **62**)
Garner St. E2 . . . . 1C **64**
Garnet Ho. *E1* 2E **79**
  (off Garnet St.)
Garnet Rd. NW10 . . . . . 3A **42**
Garnet St. E1 . . . . 1E **79**
Garnett Rd. NW3 . . . . . 2B **46**
Garnham St. N16 . . . . . 4B **36**
Garnham St. N16 . . . . . 4B **36**
Garnies Cl. SE15 . . . . . 3B **92**
Garrad's Rd. SW16 . . . 3F **117**
Garrard Wlk. NW10 . . . 3A **42**
Garratt Cl. SW18 . . . . 5D **101**
Garratt La. SW17 . . . . 3E **115**
SW18 . . . . 4D **101**
Garratt Ter. SW17 . . . . 4A **116**
Garraway Ct. *SW13* . . . 3E **85**
  (off Wyatt Dr.)
Garrett Cl. W3 . . . . 4A **56**
Garrett Ho. *SE1* 3D **25**
  (off Burrows M.)
W12 . . . . 5D **57**
  (off Du Cane Rd.)
Garrett St.
  EC1 . . . . . . 3A **10** (3E **63**)
Garrick Av. NW11 . . . . 1A **30**
Garrick Cl. SW18 . . . . 2E **101**
Garrick Ct. E8 . . . . 4B **50**
  (off Jacaranda Gro.)
Garrick Ho. W1 . . . . . . 2D **21**
W4 . . . . 2A **84**
Garrick Ind. Est.
  NW9 . . . . 1B **28**
Garrick Rd. NW9 . . . . . 1B **28**
Garrick St.
  WC2 . . . . . . 4D **15** (1A **76**)
Garrick Theatre 5D **15**
  (off Charing Cross Rd.)
Garrick Yd. WC2 . . . . . 4D **15**
Garsdale Ter. *W14* . . . 1B **86**
  (off Aisgill Av.)
Garsington M. SE4 . . . 1B **108**
Garson Ho. *W2* 1F **73**
  (off Gloucester Ter.)
Garston Ho. *N1* 4D **49**
  (off Sutton Est., The)
Garter Way SE16 . . . . . 3F **79**
Garth Ho. NW2 . . . . . . 4B **30**
Garthorne Rd. SE23 . . . 5F **107**
Garthorne Road
  Nature Reserve . . . 5F **107**
Garth Rd. NW2 . . . . . . 4B **30**
Gartmoor Gdns.
  SW19 . . . . 1B **114**
Garton Pl. SW18 . . . . . 4E **101**
Gartons Way SW11 . . . 1E **101**
Garvary Rd. E16 . . . . . 5D **69**
Garway Rd. W2 . . . . . . 5D **59**
Gascoigne Pl.
  E2 . . . . 1F **11** (2B **64**)
  (not continuous)
Gascony Av. NW6 . . . . 4C **44**
Gascoyne Ho. E9 . . . . 4A **52**
Gascoyne Rd. E9 . . . . . 4F **51**

Gaselee St. E14 . . . . . . 2E **81**
  (off Baffin Way)
Gaskarth Rd. SW12 . . . 4D **103**
Gaskell Rd. N6 . . . . 1B **32**
Gaskell St. SW4 . . . . . 5A **90**
Gaskin St. N1 . . . . 5D **49**
Gaspar Cl. *SW5* 5D **73**
  (off Courtfield Gdns.)
Gaspar M. SW5 . . . . . . 5D **73**
Gassiot Rd. SW17 . . . . 4B **116**
Gasson Ho. *SE14* 2F **93**
  (off John Williams Cl.)
Gastein Rd. W6 . . . . . . 2F **85**
Gastigny Ho. EC1 . . . . . 2A **10**
Gataker Ho. *SE16* 4D **79**
  (off Slippers Pl.)
Gataker St. SE16 . . . . . 4D **79**
Gatcombe Ho. SE22 . . 1A **106**
Gatcombe Ho. E16 . . . . 2C **82**
N19 . . . . 5F **33**
Gate Cinema 2C **72**
  (off Notting Hill Ga.)
Gateforth St. NW8 . . . . 3A **60**
Gate Hill Ct. *W11* 2B **72**
  (off Ladbroke Ter.)
Gatehouse Sq. SE1 . . . 1A **26**
Gatehouse Theatre 3C **32**
Gateley Ho. *SE4* 2F **107**
  (off Coston Wlk.)
Gateley Rd. SW9 . . . . . 1B **104**
Gate Lodge W9 . . . . . . 4C **58**
  (off Admiral Wlk.)
Gate M. *SW7* 3A **74**
  (off Rutland Ga.)
Gatesborough St.
  EC2 . . . . . . 3D **11** (3A **64**)
Gates Ct. SE17 . . . . . . 1E **91**
Gatesden WC1 . . 2F **7** (2A **62**)
Gateside Rd.
  SW17 . . . . 3B **116**
Gate St. WC2 . . 2F **15** (5B **62**)
Gate Theatre, The 2C **72**
  (off Pembridge Rd.)
Gateway SE17 . . . . . . 2E **91**
Gateway Arc. *N1* 1D **63**
  (off Upper St.)
Gateway Bus. Cen.
  BR3: Beck 5A **122**
Gateway Ind. Est.
  NW10 . . . . 2B **56**
Gateway M. E8 . . . . . . 2B **50**
Gateway Rd. E10 . . . . . 5D **39**
Gateways, The *SW3* . . . 5A **74**
  (off Sprimont Pl.)
Gathorne St. E2 . . . . . . 1F **65**
Gatliff Cl. *SW1* 1D **89**
  (off Ebury Bri. Rd.)
Gatliff Rd. SW1 . . . . . . 1D **89**
  (not continuous)
Gatonby St. SE15 . . . . 4B **92**
Gattis Wharf *N1* 1A **62**
  (off New Wharf Rd.)
Gatton Rd. SW17 . . . . 4A **116**
Gatwick Ho. *E14* 5B **66**
  (off Clemence St.)
Gatwick Rd. SW18 . . . 5B **100**
Gauden Cl. SW4 . . . . . 1F **103**
Gauden Rd. SW4 . . . . . 5F **89**
Gaugin Ct. *SE16* 1D **93**
  (off Stubbs Dr.)

Gaumont Ter. *W12* 3E **71**
(off Lime Gro.)
Gaunt St.
SE1 . . . . 5F **25** (4E **77**)
Gautrey Rd. SE15 . . . . . 5E **93**
Gavel St. SE17 . . . . 5F **77**
Gaverick M. E14 . . . . . . 5C **80**
Gavestone Cres.
SE12 . . . . 5D **111**
Gavestone Rd.
SE12 . . . . 5D **111**
Gaviller Pl. E5 . . . . 1D **51**
Gawber St. E2 . . . . 2E **65**
Gawsworth Cl. E15 . . . 2B **54**
Gaydon Ho. *W2* 4D **59**
(off Bourne Ter.)
Gayfere St.
SW1 . . . . 5D **23** (4A **76**)
Gayford Rd. W12 . . . . . . 3B **70**
Gay Ho. N16 . . . . 2A **50**
Gayhurst *SE17* 2F **91**
(off Hopwood Rd.)
Gayhurst Ho. *NW8* 3A **60**
(off Mallory St.)
Gayhurst Rd. E8 . . . . . . 4C **50**
Gaymead *NW8* 5D **45**
(off Abbey Rd.)
Gaynesford Rd.
SE23 . . . . 2F **121**
Gay Rd. E15 . . . . 1F **67**
Gaysley Ho. *SE11* 5C **76**
(off Hotspur St.)
Gay St. SW15 . . . . 1F **99**
Gayton Cres. NW3 . . . . . 1F **45**
Gayton Rd. NW3 . . . . . . 1F **45**
Gayville Rd. SW11 . . . 4B **102**
Gaywood Cl. SW2 . . . . 1B **118**
Gaywood St.
SE1 . . . . 5E **25** (4D **77**)
Gaza St. SE17 . . . . 1D **91**
Gaze Ho. *E14* 5F **67**
(off Blair St.)
Gean Ct. E11 . . . . 1F **53**
Gearing Cl. SW17 . . . . 4C **116**
Geary Rd. NW10 . . . . . . 2C **42**
Geary St. N7 . . . . 2B **48**
Gedling Pl.
SE1 . . . . 5F **27** (4B **78**)
Geere Rd. E15 . . . . 5B **54**
Gees Ct. W1 . . . 3C **12** (5C **60**)
Gee St. EC1 . . . 3F **9** (3E **63**)
Geffrye Ct. N1 . . . . 1A **64**
Geffrye Est. N1 . . . . . . 1A **64**
Geffrye Mus. 1F **11**
Geffrye St.
E2 . . . . 1F **11** (1B **64**)
Geldart Rd. SE15 . . . . . 3D **93**
Geldeston Rd. E5 . . . . . 4C **36**
Gellatly Rd. SE14 . . . . . 5E **93**
Gemini Bus. Cen.
E16 . . . . 3F **67**
Gemini Bus. Est.
SE14 . . . . 1F **93**
Gemini Ct. *E1* 1C **78**
(off Vaughan Way)
General Wolfe Rd.
SE10 . . . . 4F **95**
Geneva Ct. NW9 . . . . . 1A **28**
Geneva Dr. SW9 . . . . . 2C **104**

Genoa Av. SW15 . . . . . 3E **99**
Genoa Ho. *E1* 3F **65**
(off Ernest St.)
Gentry Gdns. E13 . . . . . 3C **68**
Geoffrey Cl. SE5 . . . . . 5E **91**
Geoffrey Ct. SE4 . . . . . 5B **94**
Geoffrey Gdns.
E6 . . . . 1F **69**
Geoffrey Ho. *SE1* 5C **26**
(off Pardoner St.)
Geoffrey Jones Ct.
NW10 . . . . 5C **42**
Geoffrey Rd. SE4 . . . . 1B **108**
George Beard Rd.
SE8 . . . . 5B **80**
George Belt Ho. *E2* 2F **65**
(off Smart St.)
George St. WC2 . . . . . . 5E **15**
George Downing Est.
N16 . . . . 4B **36**
George Eliot Ho.
SW1 . . . . 5E **75**
(off Vauxhall Bri. Rd.)
George Elliston Ho.
SE1 . . . . 1C **92**
(off Old Kent Rd.)
George Eyre Ho.
NW8 . . . . 1F **59**
(off Cochrane St.)
George Gillett Ct.
EC1 . . . . 3A **10**
George Inn Yd.
SE1 . . . . . . 2B **26** (2F **77**)
George La. SE13 . . . . . 4D **109**
George Lansbury Ho.
NW10 . . . . 4A **42**
George Lindgren Ho.
SW6 . . . . 3B **86**
(off Clem Attlee Ct.)
George Loveless Ho.
E2 . . . . 1F **11**
(off Diss St.)
George Lowe Ct. *W2* . . . 4D **59**
(off Bourne Ter.)
George Mathers Rd.
SE11 . . . . 5D **77**
George M. NW1 . . . . . . 2A **6**
George Peabody Ct.
NW1 . . . . 4A **60**
(off Burne St.)
George Potter Ho.
SW11 . . . . 5F **87**
(off George Potter Way)
George Potter Way
SW11 . . . . 5F **87**
George Row SE16 . . . . . 3C **78**
George's Rd. N7 . . . . . . 2B **48**
George's Sq. SW6 . . . . 2B **86**
(off Nth. End Rd.)
George St. E16 . . . . 5B **68**
(not continuous)
W1 . . . . 2A **12** (5B **60**)
George Tingle Ho.
SE1 . . . . 5F **27**
Georgetown Cl.
SE19 . . . . 5A **120**
Georgette Pl. SE10 . . . . 3E **95**
George Walter Ct.
SE16 . . . . 5E **79**
(off Millender Wlk.)

George Wyver Cl.
SW19 . . . . 5A **100**
George Yd.
EC3 . . . . 3C **18** (5F **63**)
W1 . . . . 4C **12** (1C **74**)
Georgiana St. NW1 . . . . 5E **47**
Georgian Ct. E9 . . . . . . 5E **51**
NW4 . . . . 1D **29**
SW16 . . . . 4A **118**
Georgian Ho. *E16* 4C **82**
(off Capulet M.)
Georgina Gdns. E2 . . . . 2B **64**
Geraint Rd.
BR1: Brom 4C **124**
Geraldine Rd.
SW18 . . . . 3E **101**
Geraldine St.
SE11 . . . . . . 5D **25** (4D **77**)
Gerald M. *SW1* 5C **74**
(off Gerald Rd.)
Gerald Rd. E16 . . . . 3B **68**
SW1 . . . . 5C **74**
Gerard Rd. SW13 . . . . . 4B **84**
Gerards Cl. SE16 . . . . . 1E **93**
Germander Way E15 . . . 2A **68**
Germington Ho. SW18 . . 4F **101**
Gernon Rd. E3 . . . . 1A **66**
Geron Way NW2 . . . . . . 4D **29**
Gerrard Ho. *SE14* 3E **93**
(off Briant St.)
Gerrard Pl.
W1 . . . . 4C **14** (1F **75**)
Gerrard Rd. N1 . . . . 1D **63**
Gerrard St.
W1 . . . . 4C **14** (1F **75**)
Gerridge Ct. *SE1* 5C **24**
(off Gerridge St.)
Gerridge St.
SE1 . . . . 5C **24** (4C **76**)
Gerry Raffles Sq. E15 . . 4F **53**
Gertrude St. SW10 . . . . 2E **87**
Gervase St. SE15 . . . . . 3D **93**
Ghent St. SE6 . . . . 2C **122**
Ghent Way E8 . . . . 3B **50**
Giant Arches Rd.
SE24 . . . . 5E **105**
Gibbings Ho. *SE1* 4E **25**
(off King James St.)
Gibbins Rd. E15 . . . . . . 4E **53**
Gibbon Ho. *NW8* 3F **59**
(off Fisherton St.)
Gibbon Rd. SE15 . . . . . 5E **93**
W3 . . . . 1A **70**
Gibbon's Rents SE1 . . . . 2D **27**
Gibbons Rd. NW10 . . . . 3A **42**
Gibbon Wlk. SW15 . . . . 2C **98**
Gibbs Av. SE19 . . . . . . 5F **119**
Gibbs Cl. SE19 . . . . . . 5F **119**
Gibbs Grn. W14 . . . . . 1B **86**
(not continuous)
Gibbs Grn. Cl. W14 . . . 1B **86**
Gibbs Sq. SE19 . . . . . . 5F **119**
Gibney Ter.
BR1: Brom 4B **124**
Gibraltar Wlk. *E2* 2B **64**
(off Padbury Ct.)
Gibson Cl. E1 . . . . 3E **65**
Gibson Gdns. N16 . . . . . 4B **36**
Gibson Rd. SE11 . . . . . . 5B **76**
Gibsons Hill SW16 . . . . 5D **119**

Gibson Sq. N1 . . . . 5C 48
Gibson St. SE10 . . . . 1A 96
Gideon Rd. SW11 . . . . . 1C 102
Gielgud Theatre 4B 14
(off Shaftesbury Av.)
Giesbach Rd. N19 . . . . . . 4F 33
Giffen Sq. Mkt. SE8 . . . . 3C 94
(off Giffen St.)
Giffin St. SE8 . . . . 3C 94
Gifford Ho. SE10 . . . . . . 1F 95
(off Eastney St.)
SW1 . . . . 1E 89
(off Churchill Gdns.)
Gifford St. N1 . . . . 4A 48
Gift La. E15 . . . . 5A 54
Gilbert Bri. EC2 . . . . 5A 10
(off Gilbert Ho.)
Gilbert Collection 4A 16
(off Lancaster Pl.)
Gilbert Ho. E2 . . . . 2F 65
(off Usk St.)
EC2 . . . . 5A 10
SE8 . . . . 2C 94
SW1 . . . . 1D 89
(off Churchill Gdns.)
SW8 . . . . 3A 90
(off Wyvil Rd.)
SW13 . . . . 3D 85
(off Trinity Chu. Rd.)
Gilbert Pl.
WC1 . . . . 1D 15 (4A 62)
Gilbert Rd. SE11 . . . . . . 5C 76
Gilbert Scott SW18 . . . 4A 100
Gilbert Sheldon Ho.
W2 . . . . 4F 59
(off Edgware Rd.)
Gilbertson Ho. E14 . . . . 4C 80
(off Mellish St.)
Gilbey Rd. SW17 . . . . . 4A 116
Gilby Ho. E9 . . . . 3F 51
Gilda Cres. N16 . . . . 3C 36
Gildea St.
W1 . . . . 1E 13 (4D 61)
Gilden Cres. NW5 . . . . . 2C 46
Giles Coppice SE19 . . . 4B 120
Giles High St.
WC2 . . . . 2C 14 (5F 61)
Giles Ho. SE16 . . . . 4C 78
(off Old Jamaica Rd.)
Gilesmead SE5 . . . . 4F 91
Gilkes Cres. SE21 . . . . 4A 106
Gilkes Pl. SE21 . . . . . . 4A 106
Gillam Ho. SE16 . . . . . . 5E 79
(off Silwood St.)
Gillan Ct. SE12 . . . . 3D 125
Gill Av. E16 . . . . 5C 68
Gillender St. E3 . . . . 3E 67
E14 . . . . 3E 67
Gillespie Rd. N5 . . . . 5C 34
Gillett Av. E6 . . . . 1F 69
Gillett Pl. N16 . . . . 2A 50
Gillett St. N16 . . . . 2A 50
Gillfoot NW1 . . . . 1F 5
(off Hampstead Rd.)
Gillian St. SE13 . . . . . . 3D 109
Gillies St. NW5 . . . . 2C 46
Gilling Ct. NW3 . . . . 3A 46

Gillingham M. SW1 . . . . . 5E 75
Gillingham Rd. NW2 . . . . 5A 30
Gillingham Row
SW1 . . . . 5E 75
Gillingham St. SW1 . . . . 5E 75
Gillison Wlk. SE16 . . . . . 4D 79
Gilman Dr. E15 . . . . 5B 54
Gilman Ho. E2 . . . . 1C 64
(off Pritchard's Rd.)
Gill St. E14 . . . . 5B 66
Gilmore Rd. SE13 . . . . . 2F 109
Gilpin Av. SW14 . . . . . . 2A 98
Gilpin Cl. W2 . . . . 4E 59
(off Porteus Rd.)
Gilpin Rd. E5 . . . . 1A 52
Gilray Ho. W2 . . . . 1F 73
(off Gloucester Ter.)
Gilstead Rd. SW6 . . . . . 5D 87
Gilston Rd. SW10 . . . . . 1E 87
Gilton Rd. SE6 . . . . 3A 124
Giltspur St.
EC1 . . . . 2E 17 (5D 63)
Ginsburg Yd. NW3 . . . . . 1E 45
Gipsy Hill SE19 . . . . 4A 120
Gipsy La. SW15 . . . . 1D 99
Gipsy Moth IV 2E 95
Gipsy Rd. SE27 . . . . 4E 119
Gipsy Rd. Gdns.
SE27 . . . . 4E 119
Giraldo Cl. E14 . . . . 4F 69
Giraud St. E14 . . . . 5D 67
Girdler's Rd. W14 . . . . . . 5F 71
Girdlestone Wlk. N19 . . . 4E 33
Girdwood Rd.
SW18 . . . . 5A 100
Girling Ho. N1 . . . . 5A 50
(off Colville Est.)
Gironde Rd. SW6 . . . . . . 3B 86
Girton Rd. SE26 . . . . . . 5F 121
Girton Vs. W10 . . . . 5F 57
Gisburn Ho. SE15 . . . . . 2C 92
(off Friary Est.)
Gissing Wlk. N1 . . . . 4C 48
Gittens Cl.
BR1: Brom 4B 124
Given Wilson Wlk.
E13 . . . . 1B 68
Gladding Rd. E12 . . . . . . 1F 55
Glade, The SE7 . . . . 3E 97
Gladesmore Community
School & Sports Cen.
. . . . 1C 36
Gladesmore Rd. N15 . . . 1B 36
Gladiator St. SE23 . . . . 5A 108
Glading Ter. N16 . . . . . . 5B 36
Gladsmuir Rd. N19 . . . . . 3E 33
Gladstone Ct. SW1 . . . . . 5F 75
(off Regency St.)
Gladstone Ct. Bus. Cen.
SW8 . . . . 4D 89
(off Pagden St.)
Gladstone Ho. E14 . . . . . 5C 66
(off E. India Dock Rd.)
Gladstone M. NW6 . . . . . 4B 44
Gladstone Pde. NW2 . . . 4E 29
NW2 . . . . 5D 29
Gladstone Pl. E3 . . . . . . 1B 66
Gladstone St.
SE1 . . . . 5D 25 (4D 77)

Gladstone Ter. SE27 . . . 5E 119
(off Bentons La.)
SW8 . . . . 4D 89
Gladwell Rd.
BR1: Brom 5C 124
N8 . . . . 1B 34
Gladwin Ho. NW1 . . . . . . 1A 6
(off Werrington St.)
Gladwyn Rd. SW15 . . . . 1F 99
Gladys Dimson Ho.
E7 . . . . 2B 54
Gladys Rd. NW6 . . . . . . 4C 44
Glaisher St. SE8 . . . . . . 2C 94
Glamis Pl. E1 . . . . 1E 79
Glamis Rd. E1 . . . . 1E 79
Glanville Rd. SW2 . . . . 3A 104
Glasbrook Rd. SE9 . . . . 5F 111
Glaserton Rd. N16 . . . . . 2A 36
Glasford St.
SW17 . . . . 5B 116
Glasgow Ho. W9 . . . . . . 1D 59
(off Maida Va.)
Glasgow Rd. E13 . . . . . . 1D 69
Glasgow Ter. SW1 . . . . . 1E 89
Glasier Ct. E15 . . . . 4A 54
Glass Art Gallery, The
. . . . 3A 78
Glasshill St.
SE1 . . . . 3E 25 (3D 77)
Glass Ho. SE1 . . . . 4D 27
(off Royal Oak Yd.)
Glasshouse Flds. E1 . . . 1F 79
Glasshouse St.
W1 . . . . 5A 14 (1E 75)
Glasshouse Wlk.
SE11 . . . . 1A 90
Glasshouse Yd.
EC1 . . . . 4F 9 (3E 63)
Glasslyn Rd. N8 . . . . 1F 33
Glass St. E2 . . . . 3D 65
Glassworks Studios
E2 . . . . 1E 11
(off Basing Pl.)
Glastonbury Ct. SE14 . . . 3E 93
(off Farrow La.)
Glastonbury Ho.
SE12 . . . . 3B 110
(off Wantage Rd.)
SW1 . . . . 1D 89
(off Abbots Mnr.)
Glastonbury Pl. E1 . . . . . 5E 65
Glastonbury St. NW6 . . . 2B 44
Glaucus St. E3 . . . . 4D 67
Glazbury Rd. W14 . . . . . 5A 72
Glazebrook Cl. SE21 . . . 2F 119
Glebe, The SE3 . . . . 1A 110
SW16 . . . . 4F 117
Glebe Cl. W4 . . . . 1A 84
Glebe Cl. SE3 . . . . 1A 110
(off Glebe, The)
Glebe Ho. SE16 . . . . 4D 79
(off Slippers Pl.)
Glebe Hyrst SE19 . . . . . 4A 120
Glebelands E10 . . . . 4D 39
Glebelands Cl. SE5 . . . . 1A 106
Glebe Rd. E8 . . . . 4B 50
NW10 . . . . 3C 42
SW13 . . . . 5C 84
Glebe St. W4 . . . . 1A 84

Glebe Ter. E3 . . . . 2D 67
W4 . . . . 1A 84
Gledhow Gdns. SW5 . . . . 5E 73
Gledstanes Rd. W14 . . . 1A 86
Glegg Pl. SW15 . . . . . . 2F 99
Glenaffric Av. E14. . . . . 5E 81
Glen Albyn Rd.
SW19 . . . . 2F 113
Glenallan Ho. W14. . . . . 5B 72
(off Nth. End Cres.)
Glenalvon Way SE18 . . . 5F 83
Glenarm Rd. E5 . . . . . . 1E 51
Glenavon Rd. E15 . . . . . 4A 54
Glenbow Rd.
BR1: Brom 5A 124
Glenbrook Rd. NW6. . . . . 2C 44
Glenburnie Rd.
SW17 . . . . 3B 116
Glencairne Cl. E16 . . . . . 4F 69
Glencoe Mans. SW9 . . . . 3C 90
(off Mowll St.)
Glendale Dr. SW19. . . 5B 114
Glendall St. SW9 . . . . . 2B 104
Glendarvon St. SW15. . . 1F 99
Glendower Gdns.
SW14 . . . . 1A 98
Glendower Pl. SW7 . . . . 5F 73
Glendower Rd.
SW14 . . . . 1A 98
Glendown Ho. E8 . . . . . 2C 50
Glendun Ct. W3 . . . . . . 1A 70
Glendun Rd. W3 . . . . . . 1A 70
Gleneagle M. SW16 . . . . 5F 117
Gleneagle Rd.
SW16 . . . . 5F 117
Gleneagles Cl. SE16 . . . 1D 93
Glendon M. SW16. . . . 4A 118
Glendon Rd.
SW16 . . . . 4A 118
Glenelg Rd. SW2 . . . . . 3A 104
Glenfarg Rd. SE6 . . . . . 1E 123
Glenfield Rd. SW12 . . . 1E 117
Glenfinlas Way SE5 . . . 3D 91
Glenforth St. SE10 . . . . 1B 96
Glengall Gro. E14 . . . . . 4D 81
Glengall Pas. NW6 . . . . . 5C 44
(off Priory Pk. Rd.,
not continuous)
Glengall Rd. NW6 . . . . . 5B 44
SE15 . . . . 1B 92
Glengall Ter. SE15 . . . . . 1B 92
Glengarnock Av. E14 . . . 5E 81
Glengarry Rd. SE22 . . . 3A 106
Glenhurst Av. NW5 . . . . 1C 46
Glenilla Rd. NW3 . . . . . 3A 46
Glenister Rd. SE10 . . . . 1B 96
Glenkerry Ho. E14 . . . . 5E 67
(off Burcham St.)
Glenloch Rd. NW3 . . . . 3A 46
Glenluce Rd. SE3 . . . . . 2C 96
Glen M. E17 . . . . 1B 38
Glenmore Rd. NW3 . . . . 3A 46
Glennie Cl. SE22 . . . . . 1C 120
Glennie Ho. SE10 . . . . . 4E 95
(off Blackheath Hill)
Glennie Rd. SE27 . . . . . 3C 118
Glenparke Rd. E7 . . . . . 3D 55
(not continuous)
Glenridding NW1 . . . . . . 1A 6
(off Ampthill Est.)

Glen Rd. E13 . . . . 3E 69
E17 . . . . 1B 38
Glenrosa St. SW6 . . . . . 5E 87
Glenroy St. W12 . . . . . . 5E 57
Glensdale Rd. SE4 . . . . 1B 108
Glenshaw Mans.
SW9 . . . . 3C 90
(off Brixton Rd.)
Glentanner Way
SW17 . . . . 3F 115
Glen Ter. E14 . . . . 3E 81
(off Manchester Rd.)
Glentham Gdns.
SW13 . . . . 2D 85
Glentham Rd. SW13 . . . 2C 84
Glenthorne M. W6 . . . . 5D 71
Glenthorne Rd. W6 . . . . 5D 71
Glenthorpe Av.
SW15 . . . . 2C 98
Glenton Rd. SE13. . . . . 2A 110
Glentworth St.
NW1 . . . . 4A 4 (3B 60)
Glenville Gro. SE8 . . . . 3B 94
Glenville M. SW18 . . . 5D 101
Glenville M. Ind. Est.
SW18 . . . . 5C 100
Glenwood Av. NW9 . . . . 3A 28
Glenwood Rd. N15. . . . . 1D 35
SE6 . . . . 1B 122
Glenworth Av. E14 . . . . 5F 81
Gliddon Dr. E5 . . . . . . 1C 50
Gliddon Rd. W14 . . . . . 5A 72
Global App. E3 . . . . . . 1D 67
Globe, The
SE1 . . . . 4B 26 (3E 77)
Globe Pond Rd.
SE16 . . . . 2A 80
Globe Rd. E1 . . . . 2E 65
E2 . . . . 2E 65
(not continuous)
E15 . . . . 2B 54
Globe Rope Wlk.
E14 . . . . 5D 81
(off E. Ferry Rd.)
Globe St.
SE1 . . . . 5B 26 (4F 77)
Globe Ter. E2 . . . . 2E 65
GLOBE TOWN 2F 65
Globe Town Mkt. E2 . . . 2F 65
Globe Wharf SE16 . . . . 1F 79
Globe Yd. W1 . . . . 3D 13
Gloucester Arc. SW7 . . . 5E 73
Gloucester Av. NW1 . . . 4C 46
Gloucester Cir. SE10 . . . 3E 95
Gloucester Cl. NW10 . . . 4A 42
Gloucester Ct.
EC3 . . . . 5E 19 (1A 78)
NW11 . . . . 2B 30
(off Golders Grn. Rd.)
SE22 . . . . 1C 120
Gloucester Cres.
NW1 . . . . 5D 47
Gloucester Dr. N4 . . . . 4D 35
Gloucester Gdns.
NW11 . . . . 2B 30
W2 . . . . 5E 59
Gloucester Ga. NW1 . . . 1D 61
(not continuous)
Gloucester Ga. M.
NW1 . . . . 1D 61

Gloucester Ho. E16 . . . . 2C 82
(off Gatcombe Rd.)
NW6 . . . . 1C 58
(off Cambridge Rd.)
SW9 . . . . 3C 90
Gloucester M. E10 . . . . 2C 38
W2 . . . . 5E 59
Gloucester M. W. W2. . . 5E 59
Gloucester Pl.
NW1 . . . . 4A 4 (3B 60)
W1 . . . . 5A 4 (3B 60)
Gloucester Pl. M.
W1 . . . . 1A 12 (4B 60)
Gloucester Rd. E10 . . . 2C 38
E11 . . . . 1D 41
SW7 . . . . 4E 73
Gloucester Sq. E2 . . . . 5C 50
W2. . . . . 5F 59
Gloucester St. SW1 . . . 1E 89
Gloucester Ter. W2 . . . 5D 59
Gloucester Wlk. W8. . . . 3C 72
Gloucester Way
EC1 . . . . 2C 8 (2C 62)
Glover Ho. NW6 . . . . . . 4E 45
(off Harben Rd.)
SE15. . . . . 2D 107
Glycena Rd. SW11. . . 1B 102
Glyn Ct. SW16 . . . . . . 3C 118
Glynde M. SW3 . . . . . . 4A 74
(off Walton St.)
Glynde Reach WC1 . . . 2E 7
Glynde St. SE4. . . . . . 4B 108
Glynfield Rd. NW10 . . . 4A 42
Glyn Rd. E5. . . . . 5F 37
Glyn St. SE11. . . . . . . 1B 90
Glynwood Ct. SE23. . . 2E 121
Goater's All. SW6 . . . . 3B 86
(off Dawes Rd.)
Godalming Rd. E14 . . . 4D 67
Godbold Rd. E15 . . . . 3A 68
Goddard Pl. N19. . . . . 5E 33
Godfree Ct. SE1 . . . . . 3B 26
(off Long La.)
Godfrey Ho. EC1. . . . . 2B 10
Godfrey St. E15 . . . . . 1E 67
SW3 . . . . 1A 88
Goding St. SE11. . . . . 1A 90
Godley Cl. SE14 . . . . . 4E 93
Godley Rd. SW18. . . . 1F 115
Godliman St.
EC4 . . . . 3E 17 (5D 63)
Godman Rd. SE15 . . . 5D 93
Godolphin Ho. NW3 . . . 4A 46
(off Fellows Rd.)
Godolphin Pl. W3. . . . . 1A 70
Godolphin Rd. W12 . . . 2D 71
(not continuous)
Godson St. N1 . . . . . . 1E 63
Godstone Ho. SE1 . . . . 5C 26
(off Pardoner St.)
Godwin Cl. N1. . . . . . . 1E 63
Godwin Ct. NW1 . . . . . 1E 61
(off Chalton St.)
Godwin Ho. NW6 . . . . . 1D 59
(off Tollgate Gdns.,
not continuous)
Godwin Rd. E7. . . . . . 1D 55
Goffers Rd. SE3 . . . . . 4A 96
Golborne Gdns. W10 . . 3A 58
Golborne Ho. W10 . . . . 3A 58
(off Adair Rd.)

Golborne M. W10......4A **58**
Golborne Rd. W10......4A **58**
Goldcrest Cl. E16......4F **69**
Golden Cross M.
W11..............*5B 58*
(off Portobello Rd.)
Golden Hind M.
Golden Hind Pl. *SE8*...*5B 80*
(off Grove St.)
Golden La.
EC1............3F **9** (3E **63**)
Golden La. Est.
EC1............4F **9** (3E **63**)
Golden Lane Leisure Cen.
................*4F 9*
(off Golden La. Est.)
Golden Plover Cl.
E16............5C **68**
Golden Sq.
W1........4A **14** (1E **75**)
Golden Yd. NW3.....1E **45**
(off Holly Mt.)
Golders Ct. NW11.....2B **30**
Golders Gdns. NW11...2A **30**
GOLDERS GREEN....1A **30**
Golders Grn. Crematorium
NW11..........2C **30**
Golders Grn. Cres.
NW11..........2B **30**
Golders Grn. Rd.
NW11..........1A **30**
Golderslea NW11.....3C **30**
Golders Mnr. Dr.
NW11..........1F **29**
Golders Pk. Cl.
NW11..........3C **30**
Golders Way NW11...2B **30**
Goldhawk Ind. Est.
W6............4D **71**
Goldhawk M. W12....3D **71**
Goldhawk Rd. W6....5B **70**
W12..........5B **70**
Goldhurst Ter. NW6...4D **45**
Goldie Ho. N19......2F **33**
Golding St. E1......5C **64**
Golding Ter. E1......5C **64**
SW11..........5C **88**
Goldington Bldgs.
NW1..............*5F 47*
(off Royal College St.)
Goldington Cres.
NW1..........1F **61**
Goldington St. NW1...1F **61**
Goldman Cl. E2......3C **64**
Goldmark Ho. SE3....1D **111**
Goldney Rd. W9.....3C **58**
Goldsboro' Rd. SW8...4F **89**
Goldsborough Ho.
E14..............*1D 95*
(off St Davids Sq.)
Goldsmith Av. E12....3F **55**
NW9..........1A **28**
Goldsmith Cl. *WC2*...*2E 15*
(off Stukeley St.)
Goldsmith Rd. E10....3C **38**
SE15............1C 93
Goldsmith's Bldgs.
W3............2A **70**
Goldsmiths Cl. W3....2A **70**
Goldsmiths College ...4A **94**

Goldsmith's Pl. NW6...5D **45**
(off Springfield La.)
Goldsmith's Row E2...1C **64**
Goldsmith's Sq. E2...1C **64**
Goldsmith St.
EC2........2A **18** (5E **63**)
Goldsworthy Gdns.
SE16............1E **93**
Goldthorpe NW1.....5E **47**
(off Camden St.)
Goldwell Ho. SE22...1A **106**
Goldwin Cl. SE14....4E **93**
Goldwing Cl. E16....5C **68**
Gollogly Ter. SE1....1E **97**
Gomm Rd. SE16.....4E **79**
Gondar Gdns. NW6...2B **44**
Gonson St. SE8.....2D **95**
Gonston Cl. SW19....2A **114**
Gonville St. SW6....1A **100**
Gooch Ho. E5......5D **37**
EC1............*5B 8*
(off Portpool La.)
Goodall Ho. SE4.....2F **107**
Goodall Rd. E11.....5E **39**
Goodfaith Ho. *E14*...*1D 81*
(off Simpson's Rd.)
Goodge Pl.
W1........1A **14** (4E **61**)
Goodge St.
W1........1A **14** (4E **61**)
Goodhall St. NW10...2B **56**
(not continuous)
Goodhart Pl. E14....1A **80**
Goodhope Ho. *E14*...*1D 81*
(off Poplar High St.)
Goodinge Cl. N7......3A **48**
Gooding Ho. SE7....1E **97**
Goodman Cres.
SW2..........2A **118**
Goodman Rd. E10....2E **39**
Goodman's Ct. E1....4F **19**
Goodman's Stile E1...5C **64**
Goodmans Yd.
E1............4F **19** (1B **78**)
Goodrich Ct. W10....5F **57**
Goodrich Ho. *E2*....*1E 65*
(off Sewardstone Rd.)
Goodrich Rd. SE22...4B **106**
Goodson Rd. NW10...4A **42**
Goodson St. N1......1C **62**
Goodspeed Ho. *E14*...*1D 81*
(off Simpson's Rd.)
Goods Way NW1.....1A **62**
Goodway Gdns. E14...5F **67**
Goodwill Ho. *E14*...*1D 81*
(off Simpson's Rd.)
Goodwin Cl. SE16....4B **78**
Goodwin Rd. W12....3C **70**
Goodwins Ct.
WC2..........4D **15** (1A **76**)
Goodwin St. N4......4C **34**
Goodwood Cl. *W1*....*5E 5*
(off Devonshire St.)
Goodwood Ho. SE14...4A **94**
(off Goodwood St.)
Goodyear Pl. SE5....2E **91**
Goodyer Ho. *SW1*....*1F 89*
(off Tachbrook St.)
Goodyers Gdns. NW4..1F **29**

Goose Grn. Trad. Est.
SE22............2B **106**
Gophir La.
EC4........4B **18** (1F **77**)
Gopsall St. N1......5F **49**
Gordon Av. SW14....2A **98**
Gordonbrook Rd.
SE4............3C **108**
Gordon Cl. E17......1C **38**
N19............3E **33**
Gordon Ct. W12.....5E **57**
Gordondale Rd.
SW19..........2C **114**
Gordon Gro. SE5....5D **91**
Gordon Ho. E1......1E **79**
(off Glamis Rd.)
SE10............3D **95**
(off Tarves Way)
SW1............4E **75**
(off Greencoat Pl.)
Gordon Ho. Rd. NW5..1C **46**
Gordon Mans. *W14*...*4F 71*
(off Addison Gdns.)
WC1............*4B 6*
(off Torrington Pl.)
Gordon Pl. W8......3C **72**
Gordon Rd. E11.....1C **40**
E15............1E **53**
SE15............5D **93**
Gordon Sq.
WC1..........3B **6** (3F **61**)
Gordon St. E13......2C **68**
WC1..........3B **6** (3F **61**)
Gorefield Ho. NW6....1C **58**
(off Gorefield Pl.)
Gorefield Pl. NW6....1C **58**
Gore Rd. E9........5E **51**
Gore St. SW7......4E **73**
Gorham Ho. *SE16*...*3F 79*
(off Wolfe Cres.)
Gorham Pl. W11.....1A **72**
Goring St. EC3......2E **19**
Gorleston St. W14...5A **72**
(not continuous)
Gorse Cl. E16......5C **68**
Gorsefield Ho. *E14*...*1C 80*
(off E. India Dock Rd.)
Gorse Ri. SW17.....5C **116**
Gorst Rd. NW10....3A **56**
SW11..........4B **102**
Gorsuch Pl.
E2............1F **11** (2B **64**)
Gorsuch St.
E2............1F **11** (1B **64**)
Gosberton Rd.
SW12..........1B **116**
Gosfield St.
W1............1F **13** (4E **61**)
Goslett Yd.
WC2..........3C **14** (5F **61**)
Gosling Ho. *E1*....*1E 79*
(off Sutton St.)
Gosling Way SW9....4C **90**
GOSPEL OAK.......1C **46**
Gosport Rd. E17.....1B **38**
Gosset St. E2......2B 64
Gosterwood St. SE8...2A **94**
Goswell Pl. EC1.....2E **9**
Goswell Rd.
EC1............1D **9** (1D **63**)

Gothic Ct. *SE5* 3E **91**
(off Wyndham Rd.)
Gottfried M. NW5 . . . . . . 1E **47**
Goudhurst Rd.
BR1: Brom 5A **124**
Gough Ho. *N1* 5D **49**
(off Windsor St.)
Gough Rd. E15 . . . . 1B **54**
Gough Sq.
EC4 . . . . 2C **16** (5C **62**)
Gough St.
WC1 . . . . 3A **8** (3B **62**)
Gough Wlk. E14 . . . . 5C **66**
Goulden Ho. SW11 . . . . . 5A **88**
Goulden Ho. App.
SW11 . . . . 5A **88**
Gouldman Ho. *E1* 3E **65**
(off Wyllen Cl.)
Gould Ter. E8 . . . . 2D **51**
Goulston St.
E1 . . . . 2F **19** (5B **64**)
Goulton Rd. E5 . . . . 1D **51**
Gourley Pl. N15 . . . . 1A **36**
Gourley St. N15 . . . . 1A **36**
Govan St. E2 . . . . 5C **50**
Gover Ct. SW4 . . . . 5A **90**
Govier Cl. E15 . . . . 4A **54**
Gowan Av. SW6 . . . . 4A **86**
Gowan Ho. *E2* 2F **11**
(off Chambord St.)
Gowan Rd. NW10 . . . . . . 3D **43**
Gower Cl. SW4 . . . . 4E **103**
Gower Ct.
WC1 . . . . 3B **6** (3F **61**)
Gower Ho. *SE17* 1E **91**
(off Morecambe St.)
Gower M.
WC1 . . . . 1C **14** (4F **61**)
Gower M. Mans. *WC1* . . . 5C **6**
(off Gower M.)
Gower Pl.
WC1 . . . . 3A **6** (3F **61**)
Gower Rd. E7 . . . . 3C **54**
Gower St.
WC1 . . . . 3A **6** (3F **61**)
Gower's Wlk. E1 . . . . 5C **64**
Gowlett Rd. SE15 . . . . . 1C **106**
Gowrie Rd. SW11 . . . . . 1C **102**
Gracechurch St.
EC3 . . . . 4C **18** (1F **77**)
Grace Cl. SE9 . . . . 3F **125**
Gracedale Rd.
SW16 . . . . 5D **117**
Gracefield Gdns.
SW16 . . . . 3A **118**
Gracehill *E1* 4E **65**
(off Hannibal Rd.)
Grace Ho. *SE11* 2B **90**
(off Vauxhall St.)
Grace Jones Cl. E8 . . . . 3C **50**
Grace Path SE26 . . . . . 4E **121**
Grace Pl. E3 . . . . 2D **67**
Graces All. E1 . . . . 1C **78**
Graces M. NW8 . . . . 1E **59**
SE5 . . . . 5F **91**
Grace's Rd. SE5 . . . . 5A **92**
Grace St. E3 . . . . 2D **67**
Gradient, The SE26 . . . 4C **120**
Graduate Pl. SE1 . . . . . . 5D **27**
Grafton Cres. NW1 . . . . . 3D **47**

Grafton Gdns. N4 . . . . . . 1E **35**
Grafton Ho. SE8 . . . . 1B **94**
Grafton M. W1 . . . 4F **5** (3E **61**)
Grafton Pl.
NW1 . . . . 2C **6** (2F **61**)
Grafton Rd. NW5 . . . . . . 2C **46**
Grafton Sq. SW4 . . . . . . 1E **103**
Grafton St.
W1 . . . . 5E **13** (1D **75**)
Grafton Ter. NW5 . . . . . . 2B **46**
Grafton Way
W1 . . . . 4F **5** (3E **61**)
WC1 . . . . 4A **6** (3E **61**)
Grafton Yd. NW5 . . . . . . 3D **47**
Graham Ct. *SE14* 2F **93**
(off Myers La.)
Graham Lodge
NW4 . . . . 1D **29**
Graham Rd. SE8 . . . . 3C **50**
E13 . . . . 3D **68**
NW4 . . . . 1D **29**
Graham St.
N1 . . . . 1F **9** (1D **63**)
Graham Ter. SW1 . . . . . . 5C **74**
Grainger Ct. SE5 . . . . . . 3E **91**
Grampian Gdns.
NW2 . . . . 3A **30**
Grampians, The *W6* 3F **71**
(off Shepherd's Bush Rd.)
Gramsci Way SE6 . . . . . 3D **123**
Granada St. SW17 . . . . . 5B **116**
Granard Av. SW15 . . . . . 3D **99**
Granard Ho. E9 . . . . 3F **51**
Granard Rd. SW12 . . . . 5B **102**
Granary Rd. E1 . . . . 3D **65**
Granary Sq. N1 . . . . 3C **48**
Granary St. NW1 . . . . . . 5F **47**
Granby Pl. *SE1* 4B **24**
(off Station App. Rd.)
Granby St. E2 . . . . 3C **64**
(not continuous)
Granby Ter.
NW1 . . . . 1F **5** (1E **61**)
Grand Av.
EC1 . . . . 5E **9** (4D **63**)
(not continuous)
Grand Central Hgts.
EC1 . . . . 1F **9**
(off Central St.)
Grandfield Ct. W4 . . . . . 2A **84**
Grandison Rd.
SW11 . . . . 3B **102**
Grand Junc. Wharf
N1 . . . . 1E **63**
Grand Pde. N4 . . . . 1D **35**
Grand Pde. M.
SW15 . . . . 3A **100**
Grand Union *W2* 4F **59**
(off Harbet Rd.)
Grand Union Cen.
W10 . . . . 3F **57**
(off West Row)
Grand Union Cl. W9 . . . . 4B **58**
Grand Union Cres.
E8 . . . . 5C **50**
Grand Union Wlk.
NW1 . . . . 4D **47**
(off Kentish Town Rd.)

Grand Vitesse Ind. Cen.
SE1 . . . . 2E **25**
(off Dolben St.)
Grand Wlk. E1 . . . . 3A **66**
Granfield St. SW11 . . . . . 4F **87**
Grange, The *E17* 1A **38**
(off Grange Rd.)
SE1 . . . . 5F **27** (4B **78**)
SW19 . . . . 5F **113**
W14 . . . . 5B **72**
Grange Ct. *NW10* 5A **28**
(off Neasden La.)
WC2 . . . . 3A **16** (5B **62**)
Grangecourt Rd. N16 . . . 3A **36**
Grangefield *NW1* 4F **47**
(off Marquis Rd.)
Grange Gdns. NW3 . . . . . 5D **31**
Grange Gro. N1 . . . . 3E **49**
Grange Ho. NW10 . . . . . 4D **43**
SE1 . . . . 5F **27** (4B **78**)
Grange La. SE21 . . . . . . 2B **120**
Grange Lodge
SW19 . . . . 5F **113**
Grangemill Rd. SE6 . . . . 3C **122**
Grangemill Way
SE6 . . . . 2C **122**
Grange Mus. of
Community History . . 1A **42**
Grange Pk. Rd. E10 . . . . 3D **39**
Grange Pl. NW6 . . . . 4C **44**
Grange Rd. E10 . . . . 3C **38**
E13 . . . . 2B **68**
E17 . . . . 1A **38**
(not continuous)
N6 . . . . 1C **32**
NW10 . . . . 3D **43**
SE1 . . . . 5E **27** (4A **78**)
SW13 . . . . 4C **84**
Grange St. N1 . . . . 5F **49**
Grange Wlk.
SE1 . . . . 5E **27** (4B **78**)
Grange Wlk. M. SE1 . . . 5E **27**
Grange Way NW6 . . . . . 4C **44**
Grangewood St. E6 . . . . 5F **55**
Grange Yd.
SE1 . . . . 5F **27** (4B **78**)
Granite Apartments
E15 . . . . 3F **53**
Granleigh Rd. E11 . . . . . 4A **40**
Gransden Av. E8 . . . . . . 4D **51**
Gransden Ho. SE8 . . . . . 1B **94**
Gransden Rd. W12 . . . . . 3B **70**
Grantbridge St. N1 . . . . . 1D **63**
Grantham Ct. *SE16* 3F **79**
(off Eleanor Cl.)
Grantham Ho. *SE15* 2C **92**
(off Friary Est.)
Grantham Pl.
W1 . . . . 2D **21** (2D **75**)
Grantham Rd. SW9 . . . . 5A **90**
W4 . . . . 3A **84**
Grantley Ho. *SE14* 2F **93**
(off Myers La.)
Grantley St. E1 . . . . 2F **65**
Grant Mus. of Zoology &
Comparative Anatomy
. . . . 4B **6**
Grant Rd. SW11 . . . . . . 2F **101**
Grants Quay Wharf
EC3 . . . . 5C **18** (1F **77**)

Grant St. E13 . . . . 2C 68
N1 . . . . 1C 62
Grant Ter. N16 . . . . 2C 36
(off Castlewood Rd.)
Grantully Rd. W9 . . . . . . 2D 59
Granville Arc. SW9 . . . 2C 104
Granville Ct. N1 . . . . . . 5A 50
N4 . . . . 1B 34
SE14 . . . . 3A 94
(off Nynehead St.)
Granville Gro. SE13 . . . 1E 109
Granville Ho. E14 . . . . . 5C 66
(off E. India Dock Rd.)
Granville Mans. W12 . . 3E 71
(off Shepherd's Bush Grn.)
Granville Pk. SE13 . . . 1E 109
Granville Pl. SW6 . . . . . 3D 87
W1 . . . . 3B 12 (5C 60)
Granville Point NW2 . . . 4B 30
Granville Rd. E17 . . . . . 1D 39
N4 . . . . 1B 34
NW2 . . . . 4B 30
NW6 . . . . 1C 58
(not continuous)
SW18 . . . . 5B 100
Granville Sq. SE15 . . . . 3A 92
WC1 . . . . . . 2A 8 (2B 62)
Granville St.
WC1 . . . . . . 2A 8 (2B 62)
Grape St.
WC2 . . . . 2D 15 (5A 62)
Graphite Sq. SE11 . . . . 1B 90
Grasmere NW1 . . . . 2E 5
(off Osnaburgh St.)
Grasmere Av. SW15 . . 4A 112
Grasmere Ct. SE26 . . . 5C 120
SW13 . . . . 2C 84
(off Verdun Rd.)
Grasmere Point SE15 . . 3E 93
(off Old Kent Rd.)
Grasmere Rd. E13 . . . . 1C 68
SW16 . . . . 5B 118
Grassmount SE23 . . . . 2D 121
Gratton Dr. W14 . . . . . 4A 72
Gratton Ter. NW2 . . . . . 5F 29
Gravel La. E1 . . 2F 19 (5B 64)
Gravely Ho. SE8 . . . . . . 5A 80
(off Chilton Gro.)
Gravenel Gdns.
SW17 . . . . 5A 116
(off Nutwell St.)
Graveney Rd. SW17 . . 4A 116
Gravesend Rd. W12 . . . 1C 70
Gray Ho. SE17 . . . . 1E 91
(off King & Queen St.)
Grayling Cl. E16 . . . . . . 3A 68
Grayling Rd. N16 . . . . . 4F 35
Grayling Sq. E2 . . . . . . 2C 64
(off Nelson Gdns.)
Grayshott Rd. SW11 . . . 5C 88
Gray's Inn 5A 8 (4B 62)
Gray's Inn Bldgs. EC1 . . 4B 8
(off Rosebery Av.)
Gray's Inn Pl.
WC1 . . . . . . 1A 16 (4D 62)
Gray's Inn Rd.
WC1 . . . . 1E 7 (2A 62)
Gray's Inn Sq.
WC1 . . . . . . 5B 8 (4B 62)
Grayson Ho. EC1 . . . . . 2A 10

Grays Ter. E7 . . . . 3E 55
Gray St. SE1 . . . 4C 24 (3C 76)
Grayswood Point
SW15 . . . . 1C 112
Gray's Yd. W1 . . . . 3C 12
Grazebrook Rd. N16 . . . 4F 35
Grazeley Ct. SE19 . . . . 5A 120
Gt. Acre Ct. SW4 . . . . . 2F 103
Gt. Arthur Ho. EC1 . . . . . 4F 9
(off Golden La. Est.)
Gt. Bell All.
EC2 . . . . 2B 18 (5F 63)
Great Brownings
SF21 . . . . 4B 120
Gt. Castle St.
W1 . . . . 2E 13 (5D 61)
Gt. Central St. NW1 . . . 4B 60
Gt. Central Way
NW10 . . . . 1A 42
Gt. Chapel St.
W1 . . . . 2B 14 (5F 61)
Gt. Chart St. SW11 . . . . 2F 101
Gt. Chertsey Rd. W4 . . . 4A 84
Gt. Church La. W6 . . . . 5F 71
Gt. College St.
SW1 . . . . 5D 23 (4A 76)
Great Cft. WC1 . . . . 2E 7
(off Cromer St.)
Gt. Cross Av. SE10 . . . 3F 95
(not continuous)
Gt. Cumberland M.
W1 . . . . 3A 12 (5B 60)
Gt. Cumberland Pl.
W1 . . . . 2A 12 (5B 60)
Gt. Dover St.
SE1 . . . . 4A 26 (3E 77)
Gt. Eastern Ent. Cen.
E14 . . . . 3D 81
Gt. Eastern Rd. E15 . . . 4F 53
Gt. Eastern St.
EC2 . . . . 2D 11 (2A 64)
Gt. Eastern Wlk. EC2 . . 1E 19
Gt. Eastern Wharf
SW11 . . . . 3A 88
Greatfield Cl. N19 . . . . . 1E 47
SE4 . . . . 2C 108
Gt. George St.
SW1 . . . . 4C 22 (3F 75)
Gt. Guildford Bus. Sq.
SE1 . . . . 2F 25 (2E 77)
Gt. Guildford St.
SE1 . . . . 1F 25 (2E 77)
Great Hall 1B 88
Greatham Wlk.
SW15 . . . . 1C 112
Gt. James St.
WC1 . . . . 5F 7 (4B 62)
Gt. Marlborough St.
W1 . . . . 3F 13 (5E 61)
Gt. Maze Pond
SE1 . . . . 2C 26 (2F 77)
(not continuous)
Gt. Newport St.
WC2 . . . . 4D 15 (1A 76)
Gt. New St.
EC4 . . . . 2C 16 (5C 62)
Greatorex Ho. E1 . . . . . 4C 64
(off Spelman St.)
Greatorex St. E1 . . . . . . 4C 64

Gt. Ormond St.
WC1 . . . . 5E 7 (4A 62)
Gt. Percy St.
WC1 . . . . 1A 8 (2B 62)
Gt. Peter St.
SW1 . . . . 5B 22 (4F 75)
Gt. Portland St.
W1 . . . . 4E 5 (3D 61)
Gt. Pulteney St.
W1 . . . . 4A 14 (1E 75)
Gt. Queen St.
WC2 . . . . 3E 15 (5A 62)
Gt. Russell St.
WC1 . . . . 2C 14 (5F 61)
Gt. St Helen's
EC3 . . . . 2D 19 (5A 64)
Gt. St Thomas Apostle
EC4 . . . . 4A 18 (1E 77)
Gt. Scotland Yd.
SW1 . . . . 2D 23 (2A 76)
Gt. Smith St.
SW1 . . . . 5C 22 (4F 75)
Great Spilmans
SE22 . . . . 3A 106
Gt. Suffolk St.
SE1 . . . . 2E 25 (2D 77)
Gt. Sutton St.
EC1 . . . . 4E 9 (3D 63)
Gt. Swan All.
EC2 . . . . 2B 18 (5F 63)
(not continuous)
Gt. Titchfield St.
W1 . . . . 4E 5 (3D 61)
Gt. Tower St.
EC3 . . . . 4D 19 (1A 78)
Gt. Trinity La.
EC4 . . . . 4A 18 (1E 77)
Great Turnstile
WC1 . . . . 1A 16 (4B 62)
Gt. Western Rd. W9 . . . 4B 58
W11 . . . . 4B 58
Gt. West Rd. W4 . . . . . 1B 84
W6 . . . . 1B 84
Gt. Winchester St.
EC2 . . . . 2C 18 (5F 63)
Gt. Windmill St.
W1 . . . . 4B 14 (1F 75)
Great Yd. SE1 . . . . 3E 27
Greaves Cotts. E14 . . . 4A 66
Greaves Pl. SW17 . . . 4A 116
Greaves Twr. SW10 . . . 3E 87
(off Worlds End Est.)
Grebe Cl. E7 . . . . 2B 54
Grebe Ct. E14 . . . . 3E 81
(off River Barge Cl.)
SE8 . . . . 2B 94
(off Dorking Cl.)
Grecian Cres. SE19 . . 5D 119
Greek St. W1 . . . 3C 14 (5F 61)
Greek St. W1 . . . 3C 14 (5F 61)
Green, The
BR1: Brom 3C 124
(not continuous)
E11 . . . . 1D 41
E15 . . . . 3A 54
SW19 . . . . 5F 113
W3 . . . . 5A 56
Greenacre Sq. SE16 . . 3F 79
Grn. Arbour Ct. EC1 . . 2D 17
(off Old Bailey)

Greenaway Gdns.
NW3 . . . . 1D 45
Greenaway Ho. NW8 . . . . 5E 45
(off Boundary Rd.)
WC1 . . . . 2B 8
(off Fernsbury St.)
Green Bank E1 . . . . 2D 79
Greenbay Rd. SE7 . . . . . 3F 97
Greenberry St. NW8 . . . 1A 60
Green Cl. NW11 . . . . 2E 31
Greencoat Mans.
SW1 . . . . 4E 75
(off Greencoat Row)
Greencoat Pl.
SW1 . . . . 5A 22 (5E 75)
Greencoat Row SW1 . . . 4E 75
Greencourt Ho. E1 . . . . . 3F 65
(off Mile End Rd.)
Greencrest Pl. NW2 . . . . 5C 28
Greencroft Cl. E6 . . . . . . 4F 69
Greencroft Gdns.
NW6 . . . . 4D 45
Green Dale SE5 . . . . 2F 105
Grn. Dale Cl. SE22 . . . . . 3A 106
Grn. Dragon Ct. SE1 . . . 1B 26
Grn. Dragon Yd. E1 . . . . 4C 64
Greene Ct. SE14 . . . . 2F 93
(off Samuel Cl.)
Greene Ho. SE1 . . . . 5B 26
(off Burbage Cl.)
Greenend Rd. W4 . . . . . . 3A 70
Greener Ho. SW4 . . . . . . 1F 103
Greenfell Mans. SE8 . . . 2D 95
Greenfield Gdns.
NW2 . . . . 4A 30
Greenfield Ho.
SW19 . . . . 1F 113
Greenfield Rd. E1 . . . . . . 4C 64
N15 . . . . 1A 36
Greengate Lodge
E13 . . . . 1D 69
(off Hollybush St.)
Greengate St. E13 . . . . . 1D 69
Greenham Cl.
SE1 . . . . 4B 24 (3C 76)
Greenham Ho. E9 . . . . . . 5E 51
(off Templecombe Rd.)
E2 . . . . 3D 65
(off Three Colts La.)
Greenhill NW3 . . . . 1F 45
Greenhill Gro. E12 . . . . . 1F 55
Greenhill Pk. NW10 . . . . 5A 42
Greenhill Rd. NW10 . . . . 5A 42
Greenhill's Rents
EC1 . . . . 5D 9 (4D 63)
Greenhills Ter. N1 . . . . . 3F 49
Grn. Hundred Rd.
SE15 . . . . 2C 92
Greenhurst Rd.
SE27 . . . . 5C 118
Greenland Ho. E1 . . . . . . 3A 66
(off Ernest St.)
Greenland M. SE8 . . . . . 1F 93
Greenland Pl. NW1 . . . . 5D 47
Greenland Quay
SE16 . . . . 5F 79
Greenland St. NW1 . . . . 5D 47

Green La. NW4 . . . . 1F 29
Green Lanes N4 . . . . 3E 35
N16 . . . . 1D 35
Greenleaf Cl. SW2 . . . . . 5C 104
Greenleaf Rd. E6 . . . . . . 5E 55
GREEN MAN RDBT. 2B 40
Greenman St. N1 . . . . . . 4E 49
Greenoak Way
SW19 . . . . 4F 113
Green Pk. 3E 21 (3D 75)
Green Point E15 . . . . 3A 54
Greenroof Way
SE10 . . . . 4B 82
(off School Bank Rd.)
Greenscape SE10 . . . . . 4B 82
(not continuous)
Green's Ct. W1 . . . . 4B 14
W11 . . . . 2B 72
(off Lansdowne M.)
Greenshields Ind. Est.
E16 . . . . 3C 82
Greenside Cl. SE6 . . . . . 2F 123
Greenside Rd. W12 . . . . 4C 70
Greenstead Gdns.
SW15 . . . . 3D 99
Greenstone M. E11 . . . . 1C 40
Green St. E7 . . . . 3D 55
E13 . . . . 3D 55
W1 . . . . 4B 12 (1C 74)
Greenstreet Hill
SE14 . . . . 5F 93
Green Ter.
EC1 . . . . 2C 8 (2C 62)
Greenview Cl. W3 . . . . . 2A 70
Green Wlk.
SE1 . . . . 5D 27 (4A 78)
Green Way SE9 . . . . 3F 111
Greenway Cl. N4 . . . . . . 4E 35
Greenwell St.
W1 . . . . 4E 5 (3D 61)
GREENWICH 3E 95
Greenwich Bus. Pk.
SE10 . . . . 3D 95
Greenwich Chu. St.
SE10 . . . . 2E 95
Greenwich Cinema 3E 95
Greenwich Commercial Cen.
SE10 . . . . 3D 95
Greenwich Ct. E1 . . . . . . 5D 65
(off Cavell St.)
Greenwich Cres. E6 . . . . 4F 69
Greenwich Gateway Vis. Cen.
. . . . 2E 95
Greenwich High Rd.
SE10 . . . . 4D 95
Greenwich Ind. Est.
SE7 . . . . 5D 83
Greenwich Mkt. SE10 . . 2E 95
GREENWICH MILLENNIUM
VILLAGE 4B 82
Greenwich Pk. 3F 95
Greenwich Pk. St.
SE10 . . . . 2F 95
Greenwich Quay SE8 . . 2D 95
Greenwich Shop. Pk.
SE7 . . . . 5D 83
Greenwich Sth. St.
SE10 . . . . 4D 95
Greenwich Theatre 3E 95

Greenwich Vw. Pl.
E14 . . . . 4D 81
Greenwich Yacht Club
. . . . 4C 82
Greenwood Ho. SE4 . . . 2F 107
Greenwood Pl. NW5 . . . 2D 47
Greenwood Rd. E8 . . . . . 3C 50
E13 . . . . 1B 68
Greenwood Ter.
NW10 . . . . 5A 42
Green Yd.
WC1 . . . . 3A 8 (3B 62)
Green Yd., The EC3 . . . . 3D 19
Greet Ho. SE1 . . . . 4C 24
Greet St. SE1 . . 2C 24 (2C 76)
Greg Cl. E10 . . . . 1E 39
Gregor M. SE3 . . . . 3C 96
Gregory Cres. SE9 . . . . . 5F 111
Gregory Pl. W8 . . . . 3D 73
Greig Ter. SE17 . . . . 2D 91
Grenada Ho. E14 . . . . . . 1B 80
(off Limehouse C'way.)
Grenada Rd. SE7 . . . . . . 3E 97
Grenade St. E14 . . . . 1B 80
Grenard Cl. SE15 . . . . . . 3C 92
Grendon Ho. E9 . . . . 4E 51
(off Shore Pl.)
N1 . . . . 1B 62
(off Calshot St.)
Grendon St. NW8 . . . . . 3A 60
Grenfell Ho. SE5 . . . . . . 3E 91
Grenfell Rd. W11 . . . . . . 1F 71
Grenfell Twr. W11 . . . . . 1F 71
Grenfell Wlk. W11 . . . . . 1F 71
Grenier Apartments
SE15 . . . . 3D 93
Grenville Ho. E3 . . . . 1A 66
(off Arbery Rd.)
SE8 . . . . 2C 94
(off New King St.)
SW1 . . . . 2F 89
(off Dolphin Sq.)
Grenville M. N19 . . . . . . 3A 34
SW7 . . . . 5E 73
Grenville Pl. SW7 . . . . . 4E 73
Grenville St. N19 . . . . . . 3A 34
Grenville St.
WC1 . . . . 4E 7 (3A 62)
Gresham Gdns.
NW11 . . . . 3A 30
Gresham Lodge E17 . . . 1D 39
Gresham Pl. N19 . . . . . . 4F 33
Gresham Rd. E16 . . . . . . 5D 69
NW10 . . . . 2A 42
SW9 . . . . 1C 104
Gresham St.
EC2 . . . . 2F 17 (5E 63)
Gresham Way
SW19 . . . . 3D 115
Gresley Cl. E17 . . . . 1A 38
Gresley Rd. N19 . . . . 3E 33
Gressenhall Rd.
SW18 . . . . 4B 100
Gresse St.
W1 . . . . 1B 14 (5F 61)
Greswell St. SW6 . . . . . 4F 85
Gretton Ho. E2 . . . . 2E 65
(off Globe Rd.)
Greville Ct. E5 . . . . 1D 51
(off Napoleon Rd.)

Greville Hall NW6 . . . . . 1D **59**	Grindley Ho. E3 . . . . . . 4B **66**	Grosvenor Way E5 . . . . . 4E **37**
Greville Lodge E13 . . . . 5D **55**	(off Leopold St.)	Grosvenor Wharf Rd.
Greville M. NW6 . . . . . . 5D **45**	Grinling Pl. SE8 . . . . . . 2C **94**	E14 . . . . 5F **81**
(off Greville Rd.)	Grinstead Rd. SE8 . . . . 1A **94**	Grotes Bldgs. SE3 . . . . 5A **96**
Greville Pl. NW6 . . . . . . 1D **59**	Grisedale NW1 . . . . 1F **5**	Grote's Pl. SE3 . . . . . . 5A **96**
Greville Rd. NW6 . . . . . 1D **59**	(off Cumberland Mkt.)	Groton Rd. SW18 . . . . 2D **115**
Greville St.	Grittleton Rd. W9 . . . . . 3C **58**	Grotto Ct.
EC1 . . . . . . 1B **16** (4C **62**)	Grizedale Ter. SE23 . . . 2D **121**	SE1 . . . . 3E **25** (3D **77**)
(not continuous)	Grocer's Hall Ct.	Grotto Pas.
Grey Cl. NW11 . . . . 1E **31**	EC2 . . . . . . 3B **18** (5F **63**)	W1 . . . . 5C **4** (4C **60**)
Greycoat Gdns. SW1 . . . 4F **75**	Grocer's Hall Gdns.	GROVE, THE 1C **120**
(off Greycoat St.)	EC2 . . . . 3B **18**	Grove, The E15 . . . . . . 3A **54**
Greycoat Pl.	Groombridge Rd. E9 . . . 4F **51**	N4 . . . . 2D **34**
SW1 . . . . . . 5B **22** (4F **75**)	Groom Cres. SW18 . . . . 5F **101**	N6 . . . . 3C **32**
Greycoat St. SW1 . . . . . 4F **75**	Groome Ho. SE11 . . . . . 5B **76**	N8 . . . . 1F **33**
Greycot Rd.	Groomfield Cl.	NW11 . . . . 2A **30**
BR3: Beck. 5C **122**	SW17 . . . . 4C **116**	Grove Cl. SE23 . . . . . . 1A **122**
Grey Eagle St.	Groom Pl.	Grove Cotts. SW3 . . . . . 2A **88**
E1 . . . . 4F **11** (3B **64**)	SW1 . . . . . . 5C **20** (4C **74**)	(off Chelsea Mnr. St.)
Greyfriars SE26 . . . . . . 3C **120**	Grosse Way SW15 . . . . 4D **99**	W4 . . . . 2A **84**
(off Wells Pk. Rd.)	Grosvenor Av. N5 . . . . . 2E **49**	Grove Ct. NW8 . . . . 2F **59**
Greyfriars Pas.	SW14 . . . . 1A **98**	(off Grove End Rd.)
EC1 . . . . . . 2E **17** (5D **63**)	Grosvenor Cotts.	SW10 . . . . 1E **87**
Greyhound Ct.	SW1 . . . . 5C **74**	(off Drayton Gdns.)
WC2 . . . . . . 4A **16** (1B **76**)	Grosvenor Ct. E10 . . . . 3D **39**	Grove Cres. Rd. E15 . . . 3F **53**
Greyhound La.	NW6 . . . . 5F **43**	Grovedale Rd. N19 . . . . 4F **33**
SW16 . . . . 5A **118**	SE5 . . . . 4E **65**	Grove Dwellings E1 . . . 4E **65**
Greyhound Mans.	Grosvenor Ct. Mans.	Grove End NW5 . . . . . . 1D **47**
W6 . . . . 2A **86**	W2 . . . . 5B **60**	Grove End Gdns.
(off Greyhound Rd.)	(off Edgware Rd.)	NW8 . . . . 1F **59**
Greyhound Rd.	Grosvenor Cres.	Grove End Ho. NW8 . . . 2F **59**
NW10 . . . . 2D **57**	SW1 . . . . . . 4C **20** (3C **74**)	(off Grove End Rd.)
W6 . . . . 2F **85**	Grosvenor Cres. M.	Grove End Rd. NW8 . . . 1F **59**
W14 . . . . 2F **85**	SW1 . . . . . . 4B **20** (3C **74**)	Grove Gdns. NW8 . . . . 2A **60**
Grey Ho. W12 . . . . 1D **71**	Grosvenor Est. SW1 . . . 5F **75**	Grove Grn. Rd. E11 . . . 5E **39**
(off White City Est.)	Grosvenor Gdns. E6 . . . 2F **69**	Grove Hall Ct. NW8 . . . 2E **59**
Greyladies Gdns.	NW2 . . . . 2E **43**	Grovehill Ct.
SE10 . . . . 5E **95**	NW11 . . . . 1B **30**	BR1: Brom. 5B **124**
Greystead Rd. SE23 . . . 5E **107**	SW1 . . . . . . 5D **21** (4D **75**)	Grove Hill Rd. SE5 . . . . 1A **106**
Greystoke Ho. SE15 . . . 2C **92**	SW14 . . . . 1A **98**	Grove Ho. SW3 . . . . . . 2A **88**
(off Peckham Pk. Rd.)	Grosvenor Gdns. M. E.	(off Chelsea Mnr. St.)
Greystoke Pl.	SW1 . . . . 5E **21**	Groveland Ct. EC4 . . . . 3A **18**
EC4 . . . . . . 2B **16** (5C **62**)	Grosvenor Gdns. M. Nth.	Grovelands Cl. SE5 . . . 5A **92**
Greystone Path E11 . . . 2B **40**	SW1 . . . . 5D **21**	Grovelands Rd. N15 . . . 1C **36**
(off Mornington Rd.)	Grosvenor Gdns. M. Sth.	Grove La. SE5 . . . . 4F **91**
Greyswood St.	SW1 . . . . 5E **21**	Grove La. Ter. SE5 . . . . 5F **91**
SW16 . . . . 5D **117**	Grosvenor Ga.	Grove Mans. W6 . . . . . 3E **71**
Grey Turner Ho. W12 . . 5C **56**	W1 . . . . 5B **12** (1C **74**)	(off Hammersmith Gro.)
Grierson Ho. SW16 . . . 4E **117**	Grosvenor Hill	Grove M. W6 . . . . 3E **71**
Grierson Rd. SE23 . . . . 5E **107**	SW19 . . . . 5A **114**	GROVE PARK 3D **125**
Griffin Cl. NW10 . . . . . . 2D **43**	W1 . . . . 4D **13** (1D **75**)	Grove Pk. E11 . . . . 1D **41**
Griffin Ct. W4 . . . . 1B **84**	Grosvenor Hill Ct.	SE5 . . . . 5A **92**
Griffin Ho. E14 . . . . 5D **67**	W1 . . . . 4D **13**	Grove Pk. Rd. SE9 . . . . 3E **125**
(off Ricardo St.)	(off Bourdon St.)	Grove Pas. E2 . . . . 1D **65**
W6 . . . . 5F **71**	Grosvenor Pk. SE5 . . . . 3E **91**	Grove Pl. NW3 . . . . 5F **31**
(off Hammersmith Rd.)	Grosvenor Pk. Rd.	SW12 . . . . 5D **103**
Grigg's Pl. SE1 . . . . 5E **27**	E17 . . . . 1C **38**	Grover Ct. SE13 . . . . . . 5D **95**
Griggs Rd. E10 . . . . 1E **39**	Grosvenor Pl.	Grover Ho. SE11 . . . . . . 1B **90**
Grimaldi Ho. N1 . . . . . . 1B **62**	SW1 . . . . . . 4C **20** (3C **74**)	Grove Rd. E3 . . . . 5F **51**
(off Calshot St.)	Grosvenor Ri. E. E17 . . . 1D **39**	E11 . . . . 2B **40**
Grimsby St. E2 . . . . 3B **64**	Grosvenor Rd. E6 . . . . . 5F **55**	E17 . . . . 1D **39**
Grimsel Path SE5 . . . . . 3D **91**	E7 . . . . 3D **55**	N15 . . . . 1A **36**
Grimshaw Cl. N6 . . . . . 2C **32**	E10 . . . . 3E **39**	NW2 . . . . 3E **43**
Grimston Rd. SW6 . . . . 5B **86**	E11 . . . . 1D **41**	SW13 . . . . 5B **84**
Grimthorpe Ho. EC1 . . . 3D **9**	SW1 . . . . 2D **89**	Grove St. SE8 . . . . 5B **80**
Grimwade Cl. SE15 . . . 1E **107**	Grosvenor Sq.	Grove Ter. NW5 . . . . . . 5D **33**
Grindall Ho. E1 . . . . 3D **65**	W1 . . . . 4C **12** (1C **74**)	Grove Ter. M. NW5 . . . . 5D **33**
(off Darling Row)	Grosvenor St.	Grove Va. SE22 . . . . . . 2B **106**
Grindal St.	W1 . . . . 4D **13** (1D **75**)	Grove Vs. E14 . . . . 1D **81**
SE1 . . . . . . 4B **24** (3C **76**)	Grosvenor Ter. SE5 . . . . 3E **91**	Groveway SW9 . . . . . . 4B **90**

Grummant Rd. SE15 . . . 4B 92
Grundy St. E14 . . . . 5D 67
Guardian Ct. SE12 . . . 3A 110
Guards Memorial
. . . . 2C 22 (2F 75)
Guards' Mus.
. . . . 4A 22 (3E 75)
Gubyon Av. SE24 . . . . 3D 105
Guerin Sq. E3 . . . . 2B 66
Guernsey Gro. SE24 . . 5E 105
Guernsey Ho. N1 . . . . . . 3E 49
(off Douglas Rd. Nth.)
Guernsey Rd. E11 . . . . . 3F 39
N1 . . . . 3E 49
Guibal Rd. SE12 . . . . . 5D 111
Guildford Ct. SW8 . . . . 3A 90
(off Guildford Rd.)
Guildford Gro. SE10 . . . 4D 95
Guildford Rd. SW8 . . . . 4A 90
Guildhall
City 2A 18 (5E 63)
Westminster 3A 76
Guildhall Art Gallery
. . . . 2B 18 (5F 63)
Guildhall Bldgs. EC2 . . 2B 18
. . . . (5F 63)
Guildhall Library
. . . . 2A 18 (5E 63)
Guildhall Offices
EC2 . . . . 2A 18 (5E 63)
Guildhall Yd.
EC2 . . . . 2A 18 (5E 63)
Guildhouse St. SW1 . . . 5E 75
Guild Rd. SE7 . . . . 2F 97
Guilford Pl.
WC1 . . . . 4F 7 (3B 62)
Guilford St.
WC1 . . . . 4D 7 (3A 62)
Guillemot Ct. SE8 . . . . . 2B 94
(off Alexandra Cl.)
Guilsborough Cl.
NW10 . . . . 4A 42
Guinea Ct. E1 . . . . 1C 78
(off Royal Mint St.)
Guinness Cl. E9 . . . . . . 4A 52
Guinness Ct. E1 . . . . . . 3F 19
EC1 . . . . 2A 10
NW8 . . . . 5A 46
SE1 . . . . 3D 27
SW3 . . . . 5B 74
Guinness Sq. SE1 . . . . . 5A 78
Guinness Trust SW3 . . 5B 74
Guinness Trust Bldgs.
SE11 . . . . 1D 91
W6 . . . . 1F 85
(off Fulham Pal. Rd.)
Guinness Trust Est.
E15 . . . . 5B 54
(off John St.)
N16 . . . . 3A 36
Guion Rd. SW6 . . . . 5B 86
Gulland Wlk. N1 . . . . . . 3E 49
(off Church Rd.)
Gulliver's Ho. EC1 . . . . . 4F 9
Gulliver St. SE16 . . . . . . 4A 80
Gulston Wlk. SW3 . . . . . 5B 74
(off Blackland Ter.)
Gun Ho. E1 . . . . 2D 79
(off Wapping High St.)
Gunmaker's La. E3 . . . . 5A 52
E9 . . . . 5A 52

Gunnell Cl. SE26 . . . . . 4C 120
Gunners Rd. SW18 . . . . 2F 115
Gunpowder Sq. EC4 . . . 2C 16
(off Gough Sq.,
not continuous)
Gunstor Rd. N16 . . . . . 1A 50
Gun St. E1 . . . . . 1F 19 (4B 64)
Gunter Gro. SW10 . . . . . 2E 87
Gunterstone Rd.
W14 . . . . 5A 72
Gunthorpe St. E1 . . . . . 4B 64
Gunton Rd. E5 . . . . 5D 37
Gunwhale Cl. SE16 . . . . 2F 79
Gun Wharf E1 . . . . 2E 79
(off Wapping High St.)
Gun Wharf Bus. Cen.
. . . . 5A 52
(off Old Ford Rd.)
Gurdon Ho. E14 . . . . . . 5C 66
(off Dod St.)
Gurdon Rd. SE7 . . . . . . 1C 96
Gurney Cl. E15 . . . . 2A 54
Gurney Ho. E2 . . . . 1C 64
(off Goldsmiths Row)
Gurney Rd. E15 . . . . 2A 54
SW6 . . . . 1E 101
Guthrie Ct. SE1 . . . . 4C 24
Guthrie St. SW3 . . . . . . 1F 87
Gutter La.
EC2 . . . . 2F 17 (5E 63)
Guy Barnett Gro.
SE3 . . . . 1C 110
Guyscliff Rd. SE13 . . . . 3E 109
Guy St. SE1 . . . . . 3C 26 (3F 77)
Gwalior Rd. SW15 . . . . . 2F 99
Gwendolen Av. SW15 . . 3A 100
Gwendolen Cl. SW15 . . . 3F 99
Gwendoline Av. E13 . . . 5D 55
Gwendwr Rd. W14 . . . . . 1A 86
Gwent Ct. SE16 . . . . 2F 79
(off Rotherhithe St.)
Gwilym Maries Ho.
E2 . . . . 2D 65
(off Blythe St.)
Gwyn Cl. SW6 . . . . 3E 87
Gwynne Cl. W4 . . . . 2B 84
Gwynne Ho. E1 . . . . 4D 65
(off Turner St.)
WC1 . . . . 2B 8
(off Lloyd Baker St.)
Gwynne Pl.
WC1 . . . . 2A 8 (2B 62)
Gwynne Rd. SW11 . . . . . 5F 87
Gylcote Cl. SE5 . . . . . . 2F 105

H

Haarlem Rd. W14 . . . . . . 4F 71
Haberdasher Est.
N1 . . . . 1C 10 (2F 63)
Haberdasher Pl.
N1 . . . . 1C 10 (2F 63)
Haberdashers Ct.
SE14 . . . . 1F 107
Haberdasher St.
N1 . . . . 1C 10 (2F 63)
Habington Ho. SE5 . . . . 3F 91
(off Notley St.)
Habitat Cl. SE15 . . . . . . 5D 93

Habitat Sq. SE10 . . . . . . 4B 82
(off Teal St.)
Hackford Rd. SW9 . . . . . 4B 90
Hackford Wlk. SW9 . . . . 4B 90
Hackington Cres.
BR3: Beck 5C 122
HACKNEY 3D 51
Hackney City Farm 1C 64
Hackney Empire Theatre
. . . . 3D 51
Hackney Gro. E8 . . . . . . 3D 51
Hackney Rd.
E2 . . . . 2F 11 (2B 64)
HACKNEY WICK 3B 52
HACKNEY WICK 3A 52
Haddington Ct. SE10 . . . 3D 95
(off Tarves Way)
Haddington Rd.
BR1: Brom 3F 123
Haddo Ho. SE10 . . . . . . 2D 95
(off Haddo St.)
Haddon Ct. W3 . . . . 1B 70
Haddonfield SE8 . . . . . . 5F 79
Haddon Hall St. SE1 . . . 4F 77
(off Rephidim St.)
Haddo St. SE10 . . . . 2D 95
Haden Ct. N4 . . . . 4C 34
Hadfield Ho. E1 . . . . 5C 64
(off Ellen St.)
Hadleigh Cl. E1 . . . . 3E 65
Hadleigh Ho. E1 . . . . . . 3E 65
(off Hadleigh Cl.)
Hadleigh St. E2 . . . . 2E 65
Hadley Ct. N16 . . . . 3C 36
Hadley Gdns. W4 . . . . . 1A 84
Hadley St. NW1 . . . . 3D 47
(not continuous)
Hadlow Ho. SE17 . . . . . 1A 92
(off Kinglake St.)
Hadrian Est. E2 . . . . 1C 64
Hadrian St. SE10 . . . . . . 1A 96
Hadstock Ho. NW1 . . . . . 1C 6
(off Ossulston St.)
Hadyn Pk. Ct. W12 . . . . . 3C 70
(off Curwen Rd.)
Hadyn Pk. Rd. W12 . . . . 3C 70
Hafer Rd. SW11 . . . . . . 2B 102
Hafton Rd. SE6 . . . . 1A 124
HAGGERSTON 4B 50
Haggerston Rd. E8 . . . . . 4B 50
Hague St. E2 . . . . 2C 64
Haig Ho. E2 . . . . 1C 64
(off Shipton St.)
Haig Rd. E. E13 . . . . 2E 69
Haig Rd. W. E13 . . . . 2E 69
Hailes Cl. SW19 . . . . . . 5E 115
Hailsham Av. SW2 . . . . 2B 118
Haimo Rd. SE9 . . . . 3F 111
Hainault Rd. E11 . . . . . . 3E 39
Haines St. SW8 . . . . 3E 89
Hainford Cl. SE4 . . . . . . 2F 107
Hainthorpe Rd.
SE27 . . . . 3D 119
Hainton Cl. E1 . . . . 5D 65
Halberd M. E5 . . . . 4D 37
Halcomb St. N1 . . . . 5A 50
Halcrow St. E1 . . . . 4D 65
Halcyon Wharf E1 . . . . . 2C 78
(off Hermitage Wall)
Haldane Pl. SW18 . . . . . 1D 115

Haldane Rd. E6. . . . . 2F 69
  SW6 . . . . 3B 86
Haldon Rd. SW18. . . . . 4B 100
Hale Ho. SW1 . . . . 1F 89
  (off Lindsay Sq.)
Hale Path SE27 . . . . . 4D 119
Hale Rd. E6. . . . . 3F 69
Hales Prior N1 . . . . 1F 7
  (off Calshot St.)
Hales St. SE8 . . . . 3C 94
Hale St. E14. . . . . 1D 81
Halesworth Cl. E5. . . . . . 4E 37
Halesworth Rd.
  SE13 . . . . 1D 109
Haley Rd. NW4. . . . . 1E 29
Half Moon Cl. EC1 . . . . . 1F 17
Half Moon Cres. N1 . . . 1B 62
  (not continuous)
Half Moon La. SE24 . . . 4E 105
Half Moon Pas.
  E1. . . . . 3F 19 (5B 64)
  (not continuous)
Half Moon St.
  W1. . . . . 1E 21 (2D 75)
Halford Rd. E10 . . . . 1F 39
  SW6 . . . . 2C 86
Haliday Ho. N1 . . . . 3F 49
  (off Mildmay St.)
Haliday Wlk. N1 . . . . 3F 49
Halidon Cl. E9 . . . . 2E 51
Halifax St. SE26 . . . . . 3D 121
Haliwell Ho. NW6 . . . . . 5D 45
  (off Mortimer Cres.)
Halkett Ho. E2 . . . . 5E 51
  (off Waterloo Gdns.)
Halkin Arc.
  SW1 . . . . 5A 20 (4B 74)
Halkin M.
  SW1 . . . . 5B 20 (4C 74)
Halkin Pl.
  SW1 . . . . 5B 20 (4C 74)
Halkin St.
  SW1 . . . . 4C 20 (3C 74)
Hall, The SE3 . . . . 1C 110
Hallam Ct. W1 . . . . 5E 5
  (off Hallam St.)
Hallam Ho. SW1 . . . . 1E 89
  (off Churchill Gdns.)
Hallam M. W1. . . . . 5E 5 (4D 61)
Hallam Rd. SW13 . . . . . 1D 99
Hallam St.
  W1. . . . . 4E 5 (3D 61)
Hallane Ho. SE27 . . . . . 5E 119
Hall Dr. SE26 . . . . 5E 121
Halley Gdns. SE13 . . . . 2F 109
Halley Ho. E2 . . . . 1C 64
  (off Pritchards Rd.)
  SE10 . . . . 1B 96
  (off Armitage Rd.)
Halley Rd. E7 . . . . 3E 55
  E12 . . . . 3E 55
Halley St. E14 . . . . 4A 66
Hallfield Est. W2 . . . . . . 5E 59
  (not continuous)
Hall Ga. NW8 . . . . 2F 59
Halliford St. N1 . . . . 4E 49
Hallings Wharf Studios
  E15 . . . . 5F 53
Halliwell Ct. SE22 . . . . 3C 106
Halliwell Rd. SW2 . . . . 4B 104

Hall Oak Wlk. NW6 . . . . 3B 44
Hall Pl. W2. . . . . 3F 59
  (not continuous)
Hall Rd. E15. . . . . 1F 53
  NW8 . . . . 2E 59
Hall St. EC1. . . . . 1E 9 (2D 63)
Hallsville Rd. E16 . . . . . 5B 68
Hallswelle Rd.
  NW11 . . . . 1B 30
Hall Twr. W2. . . . . 4F 59
  (off Hall Pl.)
Hall Vw. SE9. . . . . 2F 125
Halpin Pl. SE17 . . . . 5F 77
Halsbrook Rd. SE3 . . . 1E 111
Halsbury Ho. N7. . . . . . . 1B 48
  (off Biddestone Rd.)
Halsbury Rd. W12. . . . . 2D 71
Halsey M. SW3 . . . . 5B 74
Halsey St. SW3 . . . . 5B 74
Halsmere Rd. SE5 . . . . 4D 91
Halstead Ct. E17 . . . . . 2B 38
  N1. . . . . 1C 10
  (off Fairbank Est.)
Halstead Rd. E11. . . . . . 1C 40
Halston Cl. SW11. . . . . 4B 102
Halstow Rd. NW10. . . . . 2F 57
  SE10. . . . . 1C 96
Halton Cross St. N1. . . . 5D 49
Halton Mans. N1 . . . . . 4D 49
Halton Pl. N1 . . . . 5E 49
Halton Rd. N1 . . . . 4D 49
Halyard Ho. E14. . . . . . . 4E 81
Hamara Ghar E13. . . . . 1E 55
Hamball Rd. SW4 . . . . 3E 103
Hambledon SE17 . . . . . 2F 91
  (off Villa St.)
Hambledon Ct.
  SE22 . . . . 2A 106
Hambledon Pl.
  SE21 . . . . 1A 120
Hambledon Rd.
  SW18 . . . . 5B 100
Hamble St. SW6 . . . . . 1D 101
Hambley Ho. SE16. . . . . 5D 79
  (off Camilla Rd.)
Hambridge Way
  SW2 . . . . 5C 104
Hambro Rd. SW16 . . . . 5F 117
Hamfrith Rd. E15 . . . . . 3B 54
Hamilton Bldgs. EC2 . . . 4E 11
Hamilton Cl. NW8 . . . . . 2F 59
  SE16. . . . . 3A 80
Hamilton Ct. SE6 . . . . . 1B 124
  SW15 . . . . 1A 100
  W9 . . . . 2E 59
  (off Maida Va.)
Hamilton Gdns. NW8 . . 2E 59
Hamilton Ho. E14 . . . . . 1D 95
  (off St Davids Sq.)
  E14. . . . . 1B 80
  (off Victory Pl.)
  NW8 . . . . 2F 59
  (off Hall Rd.)
  W4 . . . . 2A 84
Hamilton La. N5 . . . . 1D 49
Hamilton Lodge E1 . . . . 3E 65
  (off Cleveland Gro.)
Hamilton M. SW18 . . . . 1C 114
  W1. . . . . 3D 21 (3D 75)
Hamilton Pk. N5 . . . . . . 1D 49

Hamilton Pk. W. N5. . . . 1D 49
Hamilton Pl. N19 . . . . . . 5F 33
  W1. . . . . 2C 20 (2C 74)
Hamilton Rd. E15. . . . . . 2A 68
  NW10 . . . . 2C 42
  NW11 . . . . 2F 29
  SE27 . . . . 4F 119
  W4 . . . . 3F 71
Hamilton Rd. Ind. Est.
  SE27 . . . . 4F 119
  (off Hamilton Rd.)
Hamilton Sq.
  SE1. . . . . 3C 26 (3F 77)
Hamilton St. SE8 . . . . . 2C 94
Hamilton Ter. NW8 . . . . 1D 59
Hamlea Cl. SE12 . . . . . 3C 110
Hamlet, The SE5 . . . . . . 1F 105
Hamlet Cl. SE13. . . . . . 2A 110
Hamlet Ct. SE11 . . . . . . 1D 91
  (off Opal St.)
  W6 . . . . 5C 70
Hamlet Gdns. W6 . . . . . 5C 70
Hamlet Ind. Est. E9 . . . . 4C 52
Hamlet M. SE21 . . . . . 1F 119
Hamlet Sq. NW2 . . . . . 5A 30
Hamlets Way E3. . . . . . 3B 66
Hamlet Way
  SE1. . . . . 3C 26 (3F 77)
Hammelton Grn.
  SW9 . . . . 4D 91
Hammerfield Ho.
  SW3 . . . . 1A 88
  (off Cale St.)
Hammersley Ho.
  SE14 . . . . 3E 93
  (off Pomeroy St.)
HAMMERSMITH 5E 71
Hammersmith Bri.
  W6 . . . . 1D 85
Hammersmith Bri. Rd.
  W6 . . . . 1E 85
HAMMERSMITH BROADWAY
  . . . . 5E 71
Hammersmith B'way.
  W6 . . . . 5E 71
HAMMERSMITH FLYOVER
  . . . . 1E 85
Hammersmith Flyover
  W6 . . . . 1E 85
Hammersmith Gro.
  W6 . . . . 3E 71
Hammersmith Ind. Est.
  W6 . . . . 2E 85
Hammersmith Rd.
  W6. . . . . 5F 71
  W14. . . . . 5F 71
Hammersmith Ter.
  W6 . . . . 1C 84
Hammett St.
  EC3. . . . . 4F 19 (1B 78)
Hammond Ct. E10 . . . . . 4D 39
  (off Crescent Rd.)
Hammond Ho. E14. . . . . 4C 80
  (off Tiller Rd.)
  SE14 . . . . 3E 93
  (off Lubbock St.)
Hammond Lodge W9 . . 4C 58
  (off Admiral Wlk.)
Hammond St. NW5 . . . . 3E 47
Hamond Sq. N1 . . . . . . 1A 64

Ham Pk. Rd. E7 . . . . 4B 54
E15 . . . . 4B 54
Hampden Cl. NW1 . . . . . 1F 61
Hampden Gurney St.
W1 . . . . 3A **12** (5B **60**)
Hampden Ho. NW9 . . . . . 5C 90
Hampden Rd. N19 . . . . . 4F 33
Hampshire Hog La.
W6 . . . . 1D 85
Hampshire St. NW5 . . . . 3F 47
Hampson Way SW8 . . . . 4B 90
HAMPSTEAD 1F 45
Hampstead Gdns.
NW11 . . . . 1C 30
HAMPSTEAD GARDEN
SUBURB 1E 31
Hampstead Grn.
NW3 . . . . 2A 46
Hampstead Gro.
NW3 . . . . 5E 31
Hampstead Heath 4F 31
Hampstead Heath Info. Cen.
. . . . 1C 46
Hampstead High St.
NW3 . . . . 1F 45
Hampstead Hill Gdns.
NW3 . . . . 1F 45
Hampstead La. N6 . . . . . 3F 31
NW3 . . . . 3F 31
Hampstead Mus. *1F 45*
(in Burgh House)
Hampstead Rd.
NW1 . . . . 1F **5** (1E **61**)
Hampstead Sq. NW3 . . . 5E 31
Hampstead Theatre 4F 45
Hampstead Wlk. E3 . . . . 5B 52
Hampstead Way
NW11 . . . . 1B 30
Hampstead W. NW6 . . . . 3C 44
Hampton Cl. NW6 . . . . . 2C 58
Hampton Ct. N1 . . . . . . 3D 49
SE16 . . . . 1F 79
(off King & Queen Wharf)
Hampton Rd. E7 . . . . . . 2D 55
E11 . . . . 3F 39
Hampton St. SE17 . . . . . 5D 77
Ham Yd. W1 . . . . . 4B **14** (1F **75**)
Hanameel St. E16 . . . . . 2C 82
Hana M. E5 . . . . 1D 51
Hanbury Dr. E11 . . . . . . 2B 40
Hanbury Ho. E1 . . . . . . 4C **64**
(off Hanbury St.)
SW8 . . . . 3A **90**
(off Regent's Bri. Gdns.)
Hanbury M. N1 . . . . 5E 49
Hanbury St.
E1 . . . . 5F **11** (4B **64**)
Hancock Nunn Ho.
NW3 . . . . 3B **46**
(off Fellows Rd.)
Hancock Rd. E3 . . . . . . 2E 67
Handa Wlk. N1 . . . . 3F 49
Hand Ct.
WC1 . . . . 1A **16** (4B **62**)
Handel House Mus. *4D 13*
(off Brook St.)
Handel Mans. SW13 . . . . 3E 85
WC1 . . . . 5E **7**
(off Handel St.)
Handel Pl. NW10 . . . . . . 3A 42

Handels Bus. Cen.
SW8 . . . . 2A 90
Handel St.
WC1 . . . . 3D **7** (3A **62**)
Handen Rd. SE12 . . . . . 3A 110
Handforth Rd. SW9 . . . . 3C 90
Handley Gro. NW2 . . . . . 5F 29
Handley Rd. E9 . . . . 4E 51
Hands Wlk. E16 . . . . . . 5C 68
Hanford Cl. SW18 . . . . . 1C 114
Hanford Row SW19 . . . . 5E 113
Hanging Sword All.
EC4 . . . . 3C 16
Hankey Pl.
SE1 . . . . 4C **26** (3F **77**)
Hanley Gdns. N4 . . . . . . 3B 34
Hanley Rd. N4 . . . . 3A 34
Hanmer Wlk. N7 . . . . . . 4B 34
Hannah Barlow Ho.
SW8 . . . . 4B 90
Hannah Mary Way
SE1 . . . . 5C 78
Hannay La. N8 . . . . 2F 33
Hannay Wlk. SW16 . . . . 2F 117
Hannell Rd. SW6 . . . . . 3A 86
Hannen Rd. SE27 . . . . . 3D 119
Hannibal Rd. E1 . . . . . . 4E 65
Hannington Rd.
SW4 . . . . 1D 103
Hanover Av. E16 . . . . . . 2C 82
Hanover Ct. SW15 . . . . . 2B 98
W12 . . . . 2C 70
(off Uxbridge Rd.)
Hanover Flats W1 . . . . . 4C **12**
(off Binney St., not continuous)
Hanover Gdns. SE11 . . . 2C 90
Hanover Ga. NW1 . . . . . 2A 60
Hanover Ga. Mans.
NW1 . . . . 3A **60**
(off Park Rd.)
Hanover Ho. E14 . . . . . . 2B **80**
(off Westferry Cir.)
NW8 . . . . 1A **60**
(off St John's Wood High St.)
SW9 . . . . 1C 104
Hanover Mans.
SW2 . . . . 3C **104**
(off Barnwell Rd.)
Hanover Mead NW11 . . . 1A 30
Hanover Pk. SE15 . . . . . 4C 92
Hanover Pl. E3 . . . . 2B 66
WC2 . . . . 3E **15** (5A **62**)
Hanover Sq.
W1 . . . . 3E **13** (5D **61**)
Hanover Steps W2 . . . . . 5A **60**
(off St George's Flds.)
Hanover St.
W1 . . . . 3E **13** (5D **61**)
Hanover Ter. NW1 . . . . . 2A 60
Hanover Ter. M.
NW1 . . . . 2A 60
Hanover Trad. Est.
N7 . . . . 2A 48
Hanover Yd. N1 . . . . . . 1E **63**
(off Noel Rd.)
Hansard M. W14 . . . . . . 3F 71
Hanscomb M. SW4 . . . . 2E 103
Hans Cres.
SW1 . . . . 5A **20** (4B **74**)

Hansler Rd. SE22 . . . . . 3B 106
Hanson Cl. SW12 . . . . . 5D 103
Hanson Ct. E17 . . . . . . 1D 39
Hanson St. W1 . . 5F **5** (4E **61**)
Hans Pl.
SW1 . . . . 5A **20** (4B **74**)
Hans Rd.
SW3 . . . . 5A **20** (4B **74**)
Hans St.
SW1 . . . . 5A **20** (4B **74**)
Hanway Pl.
W1 . . . . 2B **14** (5F **61**)
Hanway St.
W1 . . . . 2B **14** (5F **61**)
Hanworth Ho. SE5 . . . . . 3D **91**
(off Camberwell New Rd., not continuous)
Harad's Pl. E1 . . . . 1C 78
Harben Pde. NW3 . . . . . 4E **45**
(off Finchley Rd.)
Harben Rd. NW6 . . . . . . 4E 45
Harberson Rd. E15 . . . . 5B 54
SW12 . . . . 1D 117
Harberton Rd. N19 . . . . 3E 33
Harbet Rd. W2 . . . . 4F 59
Harbinger Rd. E14 . . . . . 5D 81
Harbledown Ho. SE1 . . . 4B **26**
(off Manciple St.)
Harbledown Rd. SW6 . . . 4C 86
Harbord Cl. SE5 . . . . . . 5F 91
Harbord Ho. SE16 . . . . . 5F **79**
(off Cope St.)
Harbord St. SW6 . . . . . 4F 85
Harborough Rd.
SW16 . . . . 4B 118
Harbour Av. SW10 . . . . . 4E 87
Harbour Club
Leisure Cen.,The . . 5E 87
Harbour Exchange Sq.
E14 . . . . 3D 81
Harbour Quay E14 . . . . . 2E 81
Harbour Reach SW6 . . . . 4E 87
Harbour Rd. SE5 . . . . . . 1E 105
Harbour Yd. SW10 . . . . . 4E 87
Harbridge Av. SW15 . . . . 5B 98
Harbut Rd. SW11 . . . . . 2F 101
(not continuous)
Harcombe Rd. N16 . . . . 5A 36
Harcourt Bldgs. EC4 . . . 4B 16
Harcourt Rd. E15 . . . . . 1B 68
SE4 . . . . 1B 108
Harcourt St. W1 . . . . . . 4A 60
Harcourt Ter. SW10 . . . . 1D 87
Hardcastle Ho. SE14 . . . 4A **94**
(off Loring Rd.)
Hardel Ri. SW2 . . . . . . 1D 119
Hardel Wlk. SW2 . . . . . 5C 104
Harden Ct. SE7 . . . . . . 5F 83
Harden Ho. SE5 . . . . . . 5A 92
Harden's Manorway
SE7 . . . . 4F 83
(not continuous)
Harders Rd. SE15 . . . . . 5D 93
Hardess St. SE24 . . . . . 1E 105
Harding Cl. SE17 . . . . . 2E 91
Hardinge La. E1 . . . . . . 5E 65
(not continuous)
Hardinge Rd. NW10 . . . . 5D 43
Hardinge St. E1 . . . . . . 1E 79
(not continuous)

Harding Ho. *SW13* 2D **85**
  (off Wyatt Dr.)
Hardington *NW1* 4C **46**
  (off Belmont St.)
Hardman Rd. SE7 . . . . . 1D **97**
Hardwicke M. WC1 . . . . . 2A **8**
Hardwick Ho. *NW8* 3A **60**
  (off Lilestone St.)
Hardwick St.
  EC1 . . . . 2C **8** (2C **62**)
Hardwicks Way
  SW18 . . . . 3C **100**
Hardwidge St.
  SE1 . . . . . . 3D **27** (3A **78**)
Hardy Av. E16 . . . . 2C **82**
Hardy Cl. SE16 . . . . 3F **79**
Hardy Cotts. SE10 . . . . . . 2F **95**
Hardy Ho. SW4 . . . . 5E **103**
Hardy Rd. SE3 . . . . 3B **96**
Hare & Billet Rd.
  SE3 . . . . 4F **95**
Hare Ct. EC4 . . . 3B **16** (5C **62**)
Harecourt Rd. N1 . . . . 3E **49**
Haredale Rd. SE24 . . . . . 2E **105**
Haredon Cl. SE23 . . . . . 5F **107**
Harefield M. SE4 . . . . . . 1B **108**
Harefield Rd. SE4 . . . . . 1B **108**
Hare Marsh E2 . . . . 3C **64**
Hare Pl. *EC4* 3C **16**
  (off Pleydell St.)
Hare Row E2 . . . . 1D **65**
Hare Wlk. N1 . . . . 1A **64**
  (not continuous)
Harewood Av. NW1 . . . . . 3A **60**
Harewood Pl.
  W1 . . . . 3E **13** (5D **61**)
Harewood Row NW1 . . . . 4A **60**
Harfield Gdns. SE5 . . . . 1A **106**
Harfleur Ct. *SE11* 5D **77**
  (off Opal St.)
Harford Ho. *SE5* 2E **91**
  (off Bethwin Rd.)
  W11 . . . . 4B **58**
Harford M. N19 . . . . 5F **33**
Harford St. E1 . . . . 3A **66**
Hargood Rd. SE3 . . . . . . 4E **97**
Hargrave Mans. N19 . . . . 4F **33**
Hargrave Pk. N19 . . . . . . 4E **33**
Hargrave Pl. NW5 . . . . . . 2F **47**
Hargrave Rd. N19 . . . . . . 4E **33**
Hargraves Ho. *W12* 1D **71**
  (off White City Est.)
Hargwyne St. SW9 . . . . . 1B **104**
Haringey Pk. N8 . . . . 1A **34**
Harkness Ho. *E1* 5C **64**
  (off Christian St.)
Harland Rd. SE12 . . . . . 1C **124**
Harlequin Ct. *E1* 1C **78**
  (off Thomas More St.)
  NW10 . . . . 3A **42**
  (off Mitchellbrook Way)
Harlescott Rd. SE15 . . . 2F **107**
HARLESDEN 1B **56**
Harlesden Gdns.
  NW10 . . . . 5B **42**
Harlesden La. NW10 . . . . 5C **42**
Harlesden Plaza
  NW10 . . . . 1B **56**
Harlesden Rd. NW10 . . . . 5C **42**
Harleston Cl. E5 . . . . 4E **37**

Harley Ct. E11 . . . . 2C **40**
Harleyford Ct. *SE11* 2B **90**
  (off Harleyford Rd.)
Harleyford Rd.
  SE11 . . . . 2B **90**
Harleyford St. SE11 . . . . 2C **90**
Harley Gdns. SW10 . . . . 1E **87**
Harley Gro. E3 . . . . 2B **66**
Harley Ho. E11 . . . . 2F **39**
  NW1 . . . . 4C **4**
Harley Pl.
  W1 . . . . 1D **13** (4D **61**)
Harley Rd. NW3 . . . . 4F **45**
  NW10 . . . . 1A **56**
Harley St. W1 . . . 4D **5** (3D **61**)
Harley Vs. NW10 . . . . . . 1A **56**
Harling Ct. SW11 . . . . . . 5B **88**
Harlinger St. SE18 . . . . . 4F **83**
Harlowe Cl. E8 . . . . 5C **50**
Harlowe Ho. *E8* 5B **50**
  (off Clarissa St.)
Harlynwood *SE5* 3E **91**
  (off Wyndham Rd.)
Harman Cl. NW2 . . . . . . 5A **30**
  SE1 . . . . 1C **92**
Harman Dr. NW2 . . . . . . 5A **30**
Harmon Ho. SE8 . . . . . . 5B **80**
Harmont Ho. *W1* 1D **13**
  (off Harley St.)
Harmony Cl. NW11 . . . . . 1A **30**
Harmood Gro. NW1 . . . . 4D **47**
Harmood Ho. *NW1* 4D **47**
  (off Harmood St.)
Harmood Pl. NW1 . . . . . 4D **47**
Harmood St. NW1 . . . . . 3D **47**
Harmsworth M. SE11 . . . 4D **77**
Harmsworth St.
  SE17 . . . . 1D **91**
Harold Ct. *SE16* 3F **79**
  (off Christopher Cl.)
Harold Est. SE1 . . . . 4A **78**
Harold Gibbons Ct.
  SE7 . . . . 2E **97**
Harold Ho. *E2* 1F **65**
  (off Mace St.)
Harold Laski Ho. *EC1* . . 2E **9**
  (off Percival St.)
Harold Maddison Ho.
  SE17 . . . . 1D **91**
  (off Penton Pl.)
Harold Pl. SE11 . . . . 1C **90**
Harold Rd. E11 . . . . 3A **40**
  E13 . . . . 5D **55**
  NW10 . . . . 2B **56**
Haroldstone Rd. E17 . . . 1F **37**
Harold Wilson Ho.
  SW6 . . . . 2B **86**
  (off Clem Attlee Ct.)
Harp All.
  EC4 . . . . . . 2D **17** (5D **63**)
Harp Bus. Cen. *NW2* . . . 3C **28**
  (off Apsley Way)
Harp Bus. Cen., The
  NW2 . . . . 4C **28**
Harpenden Rd. E12 . . . . 4E **41**
  SE27 . . . . 3D **119**
Harpenmead Point
  NW2 . . . . 4B **30**
Harper Ho. SW9 . . . . . . 1D **105**
Harper M. SW17 . . . . . . 3E **115**

Harper Rd.
  SE1 . . . . 5A **26** (4E **77**)
Harp Island Cl.
  NW10 . . . . 4A **28**
Harp La. EC3 . . . 5D **19** (1A **78**)
Harpley Sq. E1 . . . . 3E **65**
Harpsden St. SW11 . . . . 4C **88**
Harpur M.
  WC1 . . . . 5F **7** (4B **62**)
Harpur St.
  WC1 . . . . 5F **7** (4B **62**)
Harraden Rd. SE3 . . . . . 4E **97**
Harrier Av. E11 . . . . 1D **41**
Harriet Cl. E8 . . . . 5C **50**
Harriet Ho. *SW6* 3D **87**
  (off Wandon Rd.)
Harriet St.
  SW1 . . . . 4A **20** (3B **74**)
Harriet Tubman Cl.
  SW2 . . . . 5B **104**
Harriet Wlk.
  SW1 . . . . 4A **20** (3B **74**)
HARRINGAY 1D **35**
Harrington Ct. W10 . . . . 2B **58**
Harrington Gdns.
  SW7 . . . . 5D **73**
Harrington Hill E5 . . . . . 3D **37**
Harrington Ho. *NW1* . . . 1F **5**
  (off Harrington St.)
Harrington Rd. E11 . . . . . 3A **40**
  SW7 . . . . 5F **73**
Harrington Sq.
  NW1 . . . . 1E **61**
Harrington St.
  NW1 . . . . 1F **5** (1E **61**)
  (not continuous)
Harrington Way SE18 . . . 4F **83**
Harriott Cl. SE10 . . . . . . 5B **82**
Harriott Ho. *E1* 4E **65**
  (off Jamaica St.)
Harris Bldgs. *E1* 5C **64**
  (off Burslem St.)
Harris Ho. *SW9* 1C **104**
  (off St James's Cres.)
Harris Lodge SE6 . . . . . 1E **123**
Harrison Ho. *SE17* 1F **91**
  (off Brandon St.)
Harrisons Ct. *SE14* 2F **93**
  (off Myers La.)
Harrison St.
  WC1 . . . . 2E **7** (2A **62**)
Harris St. E17 . . . . 2B **38**
  SE5 . . . . 3F **91**
Harrods 5A **20** (4B **74**)
Harrogate Ct. SE12 . . . . 5C **110**
  SE26 . . . . 3D **120**
  (off Droitwich Cl.)
Harrold Ho. *NW3* 4F **45**
Harroway Rd. SW11 . . . . 5F **87**
Harrowby St. W1 . . . . . . 5A **60**
Harrow Club Sports Cen.
  . . . . 1F **71**
Harrowgate Ho. E9 . . . . . 3F **51**
Harrowgate Rd. E9 . . . . . 3A **52**
Harrow Grn. E11 . . . . . . 5A **40**
Harrow La. *E14* 1B **81**
Harrow Lodge *NW8* 3F **59**
  (off Northwick Ter.)
Harrow Pl.
  E1 . . . . 2E **19** (5A **64**)

Harrow Rd. E6 . . . . 5F **55**
E11 . . . . 5A **40**
NW10 . . . . 2D **57**
W2 . . . . 4A **58**
(not continuous)
W9 . . . . 3A **58**
W10 . . . . 3A **58**
Harrow Rd. Bri. W2 . . . 4E **59**
(off Daventry St.)
Harrow St. NW1 . . . . . . 4A **60**
Harry Hinkins Ho.
SE17 . . . . 1E **91**
(off Bronti Cl.)
Harry Lambourn Ho.
SE15 . . . . 3D **93**
(off Gervase St.)
Hartfield Ter. E3 . . . . . . 1C **66**
Hartham Cl. N7 . . . . . . 2A **48**
Hartham Rd. N7 . . . . . . 2A **48**
Harting Rd. SE9 . . . . 3F **125**
Hartington Ct. SW8 . . . . 4A **90**
Hartington Ho.
SW1 . . . . 1F **89**
(off Drummond Ga.)
Hartington Rd. E16 . . . 5D **69**
E17 . . . . 1A **38**
SW8 . . . . 4A **90**
Hartismere Rd. SW6 . . 3B **86**
Hartlake Rd. E9 . . . . . . 3F **51**
Hartland NW1 . . . . 5E **47**
(off Royal College St.)
Hartland Rd. E15 . . . . . 4B **54**
NW1 . . . . 4D **47**
NW6 . . . . 1B **58**
Hartley Av. E6 . . . . 5F **55**
Hartley Ho. SE1 . . . . . . 5B **78**
(off Longfield Est.)
Hartley Rd. E11 . . . . . . 3B **40**
Hartley St. E2 . . . . 2E **65**
(not continuous)
Hartmann Rd. E16 . . . . 2F **83**
(not continuous)
Hartnoll St. N7 . . . . . . 2B **48**
Harton St. SE8 . . . . . . 4C **94**
Hartop Point SW6 . . . . 3A **86**
(off Pellant Rd.)
Hartshorn All. EC3 . . . . 3E **19**
Hart's La. SE14 . . . . . . 4A **94**
Hart St. EC3 . . . 4E **19** (1A **78**)
Hartswood Gdns.
W12 . . . . 3D **71**
Hartswood Rd. W12 . . . 3B **70**
Hartsworth Cl. E13 . . . 1B **68**
Hartwell Ho. SE7 . . . . . 1D **97**
(off Troughton Rd.)
Hartwell St. E8 . . . . . . 3B **50**
Harvard Ct. NW6 . . . . . 2D **45**
Harvard Ho. SE17 . . . . 2D **91**
(off Doddington Gro.)
Harvard Rd. SE13 . . . . 3E **109**
SE7 . . . . 1E **97**
Harvey Gdns. E11 . . . . 3B **40**
SE7 . . . . 1E **97**
Harvey Ho. E1 . . . . 3D **65**
(off Brady St.)
N1 . . . . 5F **49**
(off Colville Est.)
SW1 . . . . 1F **89**
(off Aylesford St.)
Harvey Lodge W9 . . . . 4C **58**
(off Admiral Wlk.)

Harvey Point E16 . . . . . 4C **68**
(off Fife Rd.)
Harvey Rd. E11 . . . . . . 3A **40**
SE5 . . . . 4F **91**
(not continuous)
Harvey's Bldgs.
WC2 . . . . . . 5E **15** (1A **76**)
Harvey St. N1 . . . . 5F **49**
Harvington Wlk. E8 . . . . 4C **50**
Harvist Est. N7 . . . . . . 1C **48**
Harvist Rd. NW6 . . . . . 1F **57**
Harwood Ct. N1 . . . . . . 5F **49**
(off Colville Est.)
SW15 . . . . 2E **99**
Harwood M. SW6 . . . . . 3C **86**
Harwood Point SE16 . . 3B **80**
Harwood Rd. SW6 . . . . 3C **86**
Harwood Ter. SW6 . . . . 4D **87**
Haseley End SE23 . . . 5E **107**
Haselrigge Rd. SW4 . . 2F **103**
Haseltine Rd. SE26 . . . 4B **122**
Hasker St. SW3 . . . . . . 5A **74**
Haslam Cl. N1 . . . . 4C **48**
Haslam St. SE15 . . . . . 3B **92**
Haslemere Av. NW4 . . . 1F **29**
SW18 . . . . 2D **115**
Haslemere Ind. Est.
SW18 . . . . 2D **115**
Haslemere Rd. N8 . . . . 2F **33**
Haslers Wharf E3 . . . . 5A **52**
(off Old Ford Rd.)
Hassard St. E2 . . . . . . 1B **64**
Hassendean Rd. SE3 . . 2D **97**
Hassett Rd. E9 . . . . . . 3F **51**
Hassocks Cl. SE26 . . . 3D **121**
Hassop Rd. NW2 . . . . . 1F **43**
Hassop Wlk. SE9 . . . . 4F **125**
Hasted Rd. SE7 . . . . . . 1F **97**
Hastings Cl. SE15 . . . . 3C **92**
Hastings Ho. W12 . . . . 1D **71**
(off White City Est.)
WC1 . . . . 2D **7**
(off Hastings St.)
Hastings St.
WC1 . . . . . . 2D **7** (2A **62**)
Hat & Mitre Ct. EC1 . . . 4E **9**
Hatcham M. Bus. Cen.
SE14 . . . . 4F **93**
(off Hatcham Pk. Rd.)
Hatcham Pk. M.
SE14 . . . . 4F **93**
Hatcham Pk. Rd.
SE14 . . . . 4F **93**
Hatcham Rd. SE15 . . . 2E **93**
Hatchard Rd. N19 . . . . 4F **33**
Hatchers M. SE1 . . . . . 4E **27**
Hatchfield Ho. N15 . . . 1A **36**
(off Albert Rd.)
Hatcliffe Almshouses
SE10 . . . . 1A **96**
(off Tuskar St.)
Hatcliffe Cl. SE3 . . . . 1B **110**
Hatcliffe St. SE10 . . . . 1B **96**
Hatfield Cl. SE14 . . . . . 3F **93**
Hatfield Ct. SE3 . . . . . . 3C **96**
Hatfield Ho. EC1 . . . . . 4F **9**
Hatfield Rd. E15 . . . . . 2A **54**
W4 . . . . 3A **70**
Hatfields
SE1 . . . . 1C **24** (2C **76**)

Hathaway Ho.
N1 . . . . 1D **11** (1A **64**)
Hatherley Ct. W2 . . . . . 5D **59**
(off Hatherley Gro.)
Hatherley Gdns. E6 . . . 2F **69**
N8 . . . . 1A **34**
Hatherley Gro. W2 . . . . 5D **59**
Hatherley St. SW1 . . . . 5E **75**
Hathersage Ct. N1 . . . . 2F **49**
Hathorne Cl. SE15 . . . . 5D **93**
Hathway St. SE15 . . . . 5F **93**
Hathway Ter. SE14 . . . . 5F **93**
(off Hathway St.)
Hatley Rd. N4 . . . . 4B **34**
Hatteraick St. SE16 . . . 3E **79**
Hatton Gdn.
EC1 . . . . 5C **8** (4C **62**)
Hatton Pl. EC1 . . 5C **8** (4C **62**)
Hatton Row NW8 . . . . . 3F **59**
(off Hatton St.)
Hatton St. NW8 . . . . . . 3F **59**
Hatton Wall
EC1 . . . . 5C **8** (4C **62**)
Haunch of Venison Yd.
W1 . . . . 3D **13** (5D **61**)
Hauteville Ct. Gdns.
W6 . . . . 4B **70**
(off South Side)
Havana Rd. SW19 . . . . 2C **114**
Havannah St. E14 . . . . 3C **80**
Havelock Cl. W12 . . . . 1D **71**
Havelock Ho. SE23 . . . 1E **121**
Havelock Rd.
SW19 . . . . 5E **115**
Havelock St. N1 . . . . . . 5A **48**
Havelock Ter. SW8 . . . 4D **89**
Havelock Ter. Arches
SW8 . . . . 4D **89**
(off Havelock Ter.)
Havelock Wlk. SE23 . . 1E **121**
Haven Cl. SW19 . . . . . 3F **113**
Haven M. E3 . . . . 4B **66**
N1 . . . . 4C **48**
Havenpool NW8 . . . . . . 5D **45**
(off Abbey Rd.)
Haven St. NW1 . . . . . . 4D **47**
Haverfield Rd. E3 . . . . 2A **66**
Haverhill Rd. SW12 . . 1E **117**
Havering NW1 . . . . 4D **47**
(off Castlehaven Rd.)
Havering St. E1 . . . . . . 5F **65**
Haversham Pl. N6 . . . . 4B **32**
Haverstock Hill NW3 . . 2A **46**
Haverstock Pl. N1 . . . . 1E **9**
(off Haverstock St.)
Haverstock Rd. NW5 . . 2C **46**
Haverstock St.
N1 . . . . 1E **9** (1D **63**)
Havil St. SE5 . . . . 3A **92**
Havisham Ho. SE16 . . . 3C **78**
Hawarden Gro.
SE24 . . . . 5E **105**
Hawarden Hill NW2 . . . 5C **28**
Hawbridge Rd. E11 . . . 3F **39**
Hawes St. N1 . . . . 4D **49**
Hawgood St. E3 . . . . . 4C **66**
Hawke Ho. E1 . . . . 3F **65**
(off Ernest St.)
Hawke Pl. SE16 . . . . . . 3F **79**
Hawke Rd. SE19 . . . . . 5F **119**

Hawkesbury Rd.
SW15 . . . . 3D 99
Hawkesfield Rd.
SE23 . . . . 2A 122
Hawke Twr. SE14 . . . . . . 2A 94
Hawkins Ho. SE8 . . . . . . 2C 94
(off New King St.)
SW1 . . . . 2E 89
(off Dolphin Sq.)
Hawkins Rd. NW10 . . . . 4A 42
Hawkins Way SE6. . . . . . 5C 122
Hawkley Gdns.
SE27 . . . . 2D 119
Hawkshaw Cl. SW2 . . . . 5A 104
Hawkshead NW1 . . . . 1F 5
Hawkshead Rd.
NW10 . . . . 4B 42
W4 . . . . 3A 70
Hawkslade Rd.
SE15 . . . . 3F 107
Hawksley Rd. N16 . . . . . 5A 36
Hawks M. SE10 . . . . 3E 95
Hawksmoor Cl. E6 . . . . . 5F 69
Hawksmoor Ho. E14 . . . 4A 66
(off Aston St.)
Hawksmoor M. E1 . . . . . 1D 79
Hawksmoor Pl. E2 . . . . . 3C 64
(off Cheshire St.)
Hawkstone Rd. SE16 . . . 5E 79
Hawkwell Wlk. N1 . . . . . . 5E 49
(off Maldon Cl.)
Hawkwood Mt. E5 . . . . . 3D 37
Hawley Cres. NW1 . . . . . 4D 47
Hawley M. NW1 . . . . 4D 47
Hawley Rd. NW1 . . . . . . 4D 47
(not continuous)
Hawley St. NW1 . . . . 4D 47
Hawstead Rd. SE6 . . . . . 4D 109
Hawthorn Av. E3 . . . . . . 5B 52
Hawthorn Cres.
SW17 . . . . 5C 116
Hawthorne Cl. N1 . . . . . . 3A 50
Hawthorne Ho. SW1 . . . . 1E 89
(off Churchill Gdns.)
Hawthorn Rd. NW10 . . . . 4C 42
Hawthorn Ter. N19 . . . . . 3F 33
(off Calverley Gro.)
Hawthorn Wlk. W10 . . . . 3A 58
Hawtrey Rd. NW3 . . . . . . 4A 46
Hay Cl. E15 . . . . 4A 54
Haycroft Gdns.
NW10 . . . . 5C 42
Haycroft Rd. SW2 . . . . . 3A 104
Hay Currie St. E14 . . . . . 5D 67
Hayday Rd. E16 . . . . 4C 68
(not continuous)
Hayden's Pl. W11 . . . . . . 5B 58
Haydon Pk. Rd.
SW19 . . . . 5C 114
Haydons Rd. SW19 . . . . 5D 115
Haydon St.
EC3 . . . . 4F 19 (1B 78)
Haydon Wlk.
E1 . . . . 3F 19 (5B 64)
Haydon Way SW11 . . . . . 2F 101
Hayes Ct. SE5 . . . . 3E 91
(off Camberwell New Rd.)
SW2 . . . . 1A 118
Hayes Cres. NW11 . . . . . 1B 30

Haysens Ho.
SW17 . . . . 4E 115
Hayes Gro. SE22 . . . . . . 1B 106
Hayes Pl. NW1 . . . . 3A 60
Hayfield Pas. E1 . . . . 3E 65
Hayfield Yd. E1 . . . . 3E 65
Hay Hill W1 . . . . . 5E 13 (1D 75)
Hayles Bldgs. SE11 . . . . 5D 77
(off Elliotts Row)
Hayles St. SE11 . . . . 5D 77
Hayling Cl. N16 . . . . 2A 50
Haymans Point SE11 . . . 5B 76
Hayman St. N1 . . . . 4D 49
Haymarket
SW1 . . . . 5B 14 (1F 75)
Haymarket Arc. SW1 . . . 5B 14
Haymarket Ct. E8 . . . . . . 4B 50
(off Jacaranda Gro.)
Haymarket Theatre Royal
. . . . 5C 14
(off Haymarket)
Haymerle Ho. SE15 . . . . 2C 92
(off Haymerle Rd.)
Haymerle Rd. SE15 . . . . 2C 92
Hayne Ho. W11 . . . . 2A 72
(off Penzance Pl.)
Haynes Cl. SE3 . . . . 1A 110
Hayne St. EC1 . . . 5E 9 (4D 63)
Hay's Galleria
SE1 . . . . 1D 27 (2A 78)
Hays La.
SE1 . . . . 1D 27 (2A 78)
Hay's M. W1 . . . . 1D 21 (2D 75)
Hay St. E2 . . . . 5C 50
Hayter Ct. E11 . . . . 4D 41
Hayter Rd. SW2 . . . . 3A 104
Hayton Cl. E8 . . . . 3B 50
Hayward Cl. SW4 . . . . . . 5A 90
(off Clapham Rd.)
Hayward Gallery 2A 24
Hayward Gdns.
SW15 . . . . 4E 99
Hayward's Pl.
EC1 . . . . 3D 9 (3D 63)
Haywards Yd. SE4 . . . . . 3B 108
(off Lindal Rd.)
Hazelbank Rd. SE6 . . . . 2F 123
Hazelbourne Rd.
SW12 . . . . 4D 103
Hazel Cl. N19 . . . . 4E 33
Hazeldean Rd. NW10 . . . 4A 42
Hazeldon Rd. SE4 . . . . . 3A 108
Hazel Gro. SE26 . . . . . . 4F 121
Hazelhurst Ct. SE6 . . . . 5E 123
(off Beckenham Hill Rd.)
Hazelhurst Rd.
SW17 . . . . 4E 115
Hazellville Rd. N19 . . . . . 2F 33
Hazelmere Ct. SW2 . . . . 1B 118
Hazelmere Rd. NW6 . . . . 5B 44
Hazel Rd. E15 . . . . 2A 54
NW10 . . . . 2D 57
(not continuous)
Hazel Way SE1 . . . . 5B 78
Hazelwood Ho. SE8 . . . . 5A 80
Hazelwood Rd. E17 . . . . 1A 38
Hazlebury Rd. SW6 . . . . 5D 87
Hazlewell Rd. SW15 . . . . 3E 99

Hazlewood Cl. E5 . . . . . . 5A 38
Hazlewood Cres.
W10 . . . . 3A 58
Hazlewood Twr. W10 . . . 3A 58
(off Golborne Gdns.)
Hazlitt M. W14 . . . . 4A 72
Hazlitt Rd. W14 . . . . 4A 72
Headbourne Ho.
SE1 . . . . 5C 26 (4F 77)
Headcorn Rd.
BR1: Brom 5B 124
Headfort Pl.
SW1 . . . . 4C 20 (3C 74)
Headington Rd.
SW18 . . . . 2E 115
Headlam Rd. SW4 . . . . . 4F 103
(not continuous)
Headlam St. E1 . . . . 3D 65
Headley Ct. SE26 . . . . . . 5E 121
Head's M. W11 . . . . 5C 58
Head St. E1 . . . . 5F 65
(not continuous)
Heald St. SE14 . . . . 4C 94
Healey Ho. SW9 . . . . 3C 90
Healey St. NW1 . . . . 3D 47
Hearn's Bldgs. SE17 . . . . 5F 77
Hearnshaw Ho. E14 . . . . 4A 66
(off Halley St.)
Hearnshaw St. E14 . . . . 5A 66
Hearn St.
EC2 . . . . 4E 11 (3A 64)
Hearnville Rd.
SW12 . . . . 1C 116
Heath Brow NW3 . . . . . . 5E 31
Heath Cl. NW11 . . . . 2D 31
Heathcock Ct. WC2 . . . . 5E 15
(off Exchange Ct.)
Heathcote St.
WC1 . . . . 3F 7 (3B 62)
Heath Cft. NW11 . . . . . . 3D 31
Heath Dr. NW3 . . . . 1D 45
Heathedge SE26 . . . . . . 2D 121
Heather Cl. N7 . . . . 5B 34
SE13 . . . . 5F 109
SW8 . . . . 1D 103
Heather Gdns. NW11 . . . 1A 30
Heather Ho. E14 . . . . . . 5E 67
(off Dee St.)
Heatherley Ct. E5 . . . . . . 5C 36
Heather Rd. NW2 . . . . . . 4B 28
SE12 . . . . 2C 124
Heather Wlk. W10 . . . . . 3A 58
Heatherwood Cl. E12 . . . 4E 41
Heathfield Av. SW18 . . . . 5F 101
Heathfield Cl. E16 . . . . . 4F 69
Heathfield Gdns.
NW11 . . . . 1F 29
SE3 . . . . 5A 96
(off Baizdon Rd.)
SW18 . . . . 4F 101
Heathfield Ho. SE3 . . . . 5A 96
Heathfield Pk. NW2 . . . . 3E 43
Heathfield Rd.
SW18 . . . . 4E 101
Heathfield Sq.
SW18 . . . . 5F 101
Heathfield St. W11 . . . . . 1A 72
(off Portland Rd.)
Heathgate NW11 . . . . . . 1D 31
Heathgate Pl. NW3 . . . . 2B 46

Heath Hurst Rd. NW3.....1A 46
Heathland Rd. N16.....3A 36
Heath La. SE3.....5F 95
(not continuous)
Heathlee Rd. SE3.....2B 110
Heathmans Rd. SW6.....4B 86
Heath Mead SW19.....3F 113
Heathpool Ct. E1.....3D 65
Heath Ri. SW15.....4F 99
Heath Rd. SW8.....5D 89
Heath Royal SW15.....4F 99
Heath Side NW3.....1F 45
Heathside NW11.....3C 30
SE13.....5E 95
Heathstan Rd. W12.....5C 56
Heath St. NW3.....5E 31
Heathview NW5.....1C 46
Heathview Gdns.
SW15.....5E 99
Heath Vs. NW3.....5F 31
Heathville Rd. N19.....2A 34
Heathwall St. SW11.....1B 102
Heathway SE3.....3C 96
Heathway Ct. NW3.....4C 30
Heathwood Gdns.
SE7.....5F 83
Heathwood Point
SE23.....3F 121
Heaton Rd. SE15.....5D 93
Heaven Tree Cl. N1.....3E 49
Heaver Rd. SW11.....1F 101
Hebden Ct. E2.....5B 50
Hebdon Rd. SW17.....3A 116
Heber Mans. W14.....2A 86
(off Queen's Club Gdns.)
Heber Rd. NW2.....2F 43
SE22.....4B 106
Hebron Rd. W6.....4E 71
Heckfield Pl. SW6.....3C 86
Heckford St. E14.....5D 67
(off Grundy St.)
Heckford St. E1.....1F 79
(off Caldwell St.)
Hector Ct. SW9.....3C 90
(off Caldwell St.)
Hector Ho. E2.....1D 65
(off Old Bethnal Grn. Rd.)
Heddington Gro. N7....2B 48
Heddon St.
W1.....4F 13 (1E 75)
(not continuous)
Hedgegate Ct. W11.....5B 58
(off Powis Ter.)
Hedgers Gro. E9.....3A 52
Hedger St. SE11.....5D 77
Hedge Wlk. SE6.....5D 123
Hedgley St. SE12.....3B 110
Hedgley St. SE12.....3B 110
Hedingham Cl. N1.....4E 49
Hedley Ho. E14.....4E 81
(off Stewart St.)
Hedley Row N5.....2F 49
Hedsor Ho. E2.....3F 11
(off Ligonier St.)
Hega Ho. E14.....4E 67
(off Ullin St.)
Heidegger Cres.
SW13.....3D 85
Heigham Rd. E6.....4F 55
Heights, The SE7.....1E 97
Heiron St. SE17.....2D 91

Helby Rd. SW4.....4F 103
Heldar Ct.
SE1.....4C 26 (3F 77)
Helder Gro. SE12.....5B 110
Helena Pl. E9.....5D 51
Helena Rd. E13.....1B 68
E17.....1C 38
NW10.....2D 43
Helena Sq. E1.....1A 80
(off Sovereign Cres.)
Helen Gladstone Ho.
SE1.....3D 25
(off Surrey Row)
Helen Ho. E2.....1D 65
(off Old Bethnal Grn. Rd.)
Helen Mackay Ho.
E14.....5F 67
(off Blair St.)
Helen Peele Cotts.
SE16.....4E 79
(off Lower Rd.)
Helenslea Av. NW11.....3C 30
Helen's Pl. E2.....2E 65
Helen Taylor Ho.
SE16.....4C 78
(off Evelyn Lowe Est.)
Heliport Ind. Est.
SW11.....5F 87
Helix Gdns. SW2.....4B 104
Helix Rd. SW2.....4B 104
Hellings St. E1.....2C 78
Helme Cl. SW19.....5B 114
Helmet Row
EC1.....2A 10 (3E 63)
Helmsdale Ho. NW6.....1D 59
(off Carlton Va.)
Helmsley Pl. E8.....4D 51
Helmsley St. E8.....4D 51
Helperby Rd. NW10.....4A 42
Helsby Ct. NW8.....3F 59
(off Pollitt Dr.)
Helsinki Sq. SE16.....4A 80
Helston NW1.....5E 47
(off Camden St.)
Helston Ct. N15.....1A 36
(off Culvert Rd.)
Helston Ho. SE11.....1C 90
(off Kennings Way)
Helvetia St. SE6.....2B 122
Hemans St. SW8.....3F 89
Hemans St. Est.
SW8.....3F 89
Hemberton Rd.
SW9.....1A 104
Hemingford Rd. N1.....5B 48
Hemingway Cl.
NW5.....1C 46
Hemlington Ho. E14.....4A 66
(off Aston St.)
Hemlock Rd. W12.....1B 70
(not continuous)
Hemming St. E1.....3C 64
Hemp Wlk. SE17.....5F 77
Hemstal Rd. NW6.....4C 44
Hemsworth Ct. N1.....1A 64
Hemsworth St. N1.....1A 64
Hemus Pl. SW3.....1A 88
Hen & Chicken Cts.
EC4.....3B 16
(off Fleet St.)

Hen & Chickens Theatre
.....3D 49
(off St Paul's Rd.)
Henchman St. W12.....5B 56
Henderson Ct. NW3.....2F 45
(off Fitzjohn's Av.)
SE14.....2F 93
(off Myers La.)
Henderson Dr. NW8.....3F 59
Henderson Rd. E7.....3E 55
SW18.....5A 102
Hendham Rd.
SW17.....2A 116
HENDON.....1D 29
Hendon FC.....3F 29
Hendon Ho. NW4.....1F 29
Hendon Pk. Mans.
NW4.....1E 29
Hendon Pk. Row
NW11.....1B 30
Hendon Way NW2.....2F 29
NW4.....1D 29
Hendon Youth Sports Cen.
.....2F 29
Hendre Rd. SE1.....5A 78
Hendrick Av.
SW12.....5B 102
Heneage La.
EC3.....3E 19 (5A 64)
Heneage Pl.
EC3.....3E 19 (5A 64)
Heneage St. E1.....4B 64
Henfield Cl. N19.....3E 33
Hengist Rd. SE12.....5D 111
Hengrave Rd. SE23.....4E 107
Henley Cl. SE16.....3E 79
(off St Marychurch St.)
Henley Ct. NW2.....3F 43
Henley Dr. SE1.....5B 78
Henley Ho. E2.....2F 11
(off Swanfield St.)
Henley Prior N1.....1F 7
(off Affleck St.)
Henley Rd. NW10.....5E 43
Henley St. SW11.....5C 88
Hennel Cl. SE23.....3E 121
Henniker Gdns. E6.....2F 69
Henniker M. SW3.....2F 87
Henniker Point E15.....2A 54
(off Leytonstone Rd.)
Henniker Rd. E15.....2F 53
Henning St. SW11.....4A 88
Henrietta Cl. SE8.....2C 94
Henrietta Ho. N15.....1A 36
(off St Ann's Rd.)
W6.....1E 85
(off Queen Caroline St.)
Henrietta M.
WC1.....3E 7 (3A 62)
Henrietta Pl.
W1.....3D 13 (5D 61)
Henrietta St. E15.....2E 53
WC2.....4E 15 (1A 76)
Henriques St. E1.....5C 64
Henry Cooper Way
SE9.....3F 125
Henry Dickens Ct.
W11.....1F 71
Henry Doulton Dr.
SW17.....4C 116

Henry Ho.
SE1 . . . . 2B **24** (2C **76**)
SW8 . . . . 3A **90**
(off Wyvil Rd.)
Henry Jackson Rd.
SW15 . . . . 1F **99**
Henry Purcell Ho.
E16 . . . . 2D **83**
(off Evelyn Rd.)
Henry Rd. N4 . . . . 3E **35**
Henryson Rd. SE4 . . . . 3C **108**
Henry Tate M.
SW16 . . . . 5C **118**
Henry Wise Ho. SW1 . . . 5F **75**
(off Vauxhall Bri. Rd.)
Hensford Gdns.
SE26 . . . . 4D **121**
Henshall St. N1 . . . . 3F **49**
Henshaw St. SE17 . . . . . 5F **77**
Henslowe Rd. SE22 . . . 3C **106**
Henslow Ho. SE15 . . . . . 3C **92**
(off Peckham Pk. Rd.)
Henson Av. NW2 . . . . . . 2E **43**
Henstridge Pl. NW8 . . . . 5A **46**
Henty Cl. SW11 . . . . 3A **88**
Henty Wlk. SW15 . . . . . 3D **99**
Henwick Rd. SE9 . . . . . 1F **111**
Hepburn M. SW11 . . . . 3B **102**
Hepplestone Cl.
SW15 . . . . 4D **99**
Hepscott Rd. E9 . . . . . . 3C **52**
Hepworth Ct. N1. . . . . . . 5D **49**
(off Gaskin St.)
NW3 . . . . 2A **46**
Hera Ct. E14. . . . . 5C **80**
(off Homer Dr.)
Herald's Pl. SE11. . . . . . 5D **77**
(off Gilbert Rd.)
Herald St. E2 . . . . 3D **65**
Herbal Hill
EC1 . . . . . . 4C **8** (3C **62**)
Herbal Hill Gdns. EC1 . . 4C **8**
(off Herbal Hill)
Herbal Pl. EC1 . . . . 4C **8**
Herbert Cres.
SW1. . . . . . . 5A **20** (4B **74**)
Herbert Gdns. NW10 . . . 1D **57**
Herbert Ho. E1 . . . . 2F **19**
(off Old Castle St.)
Herbert M. SW2 . . . . . . 4C **104**
Herbert Morrison Ho.
SW6 . . . . 2B **86**
(off Clem Attlee Ct.)
Herbert Rd. E12 . . . . 1F **55**
E17 . . . . 2B **38**
NW9 . . . . 1C **28**
Herbert St. E13. . . . . . . 1C **68**
NW5 . . . . 3C **46**
Herbrand Est.
WC1. . . . . 3D **7** (3A **62**)
Herbrand St.
WC1. . . . . 3D **7** (3A **62**)
Hercules Pl. SE14 . . . . . 2A **94**
Hercules Pl. N7 . . . . 5A **34**
(not continuous)
Hercules Rd.
SE1 . . . . 5A **24** (3A **76**)
Hercules St. N7 . . . . 5A **34**
Hercules Wharf E14. . . . 1A **82**
(off Orchard Pl.)

Hercules Yd. N7. . . . . . . 5A **34**
Hereford Bldgs.
SW3 . . . . 2F **87**
(off Old Chu. St.)
Hereford Gdns.
SE13 . . . . 3A **110**
Hereford Ho. NW6 . . . . . 1C **58**
(off Carlton Va.)
SW3 . . . . 4A **74**
(off Ovington Gdns.)
SW10 . . . . 3D **87**
(off Fulham Rd.)
Hereford M. W2 . . . . 5C **58**
Hereford Pl. SE14 . . . . . 3B **94**
Hereford Retreat
SE15 . . . . 3C **92**
Hereford Rd. E11. . . . . . 1D **41**
W2 . . . . 5C **58**
Hereford Sq. SW7 . . . . . 5E **73**
Hereford St. E2 . . . . 3C **64**
Hereward Rd.
SW17 . . . . 4B **116**
Heritage Cl. SW9 . . . . . 1D **105**
Heritage Ct. SE8. . . . . . . 1F **93**
(off Trundley's Rd.)
Heritage Pl. SW18 . . . . 1E **115**
Herlwyn Gdns.
SW17 . . . . 4B **116**
Her Majesty's Theatre
. . . . 1B **22**
(off Haymarket)
Hermes Cl. W9. . . . . 3C **58**
Hermes St. SW2 . . . . . . 4B **104**
SW9 . . . . 4C **90**
(off Southey Rd.)
Hermes St.
N1 . . . . 1B **8** (1C **62**)
Herm Ho. N1 . . . . 3E **49**
Hermiston Av. N8. . . . . . 1A **34**
Hermitage, The
SE13 . . . . 5E **95**
SE23 . . . . 1E **121**
SW13 . . . . 4B **84**
Hermitage Ct. E1 . . . . . . 2C **78**
(off Knighten St.)
NW2 . . . . 5C **30**
Hermitage Gdns.
NW2 . . . . 5C **30**
Hermitage La. NW2. . . . . 5C **30**
Hermitage Rd. N4 . . . . . 2D **35**
SE19 . . . . 5F **119**
Hermitage Rooms 4A **16**
(off Embankment)
Hermitage Row E8 . . . . . 2C **50**
Hermitage St. W2. . . . . . 4F **59**
Hermitage Vs. SW6. . . . . 2C **86**
(off Lillie Rd.)
Hermitage Wall E1. . . . . 2C **78**
Hermitage Waterside
E1 . . . . 2C **78**
(off Thomas More St.)
Hermit Pl. NW6 . . . . 5D **45**
Hermit Rd. E16 . . . . 4B **68**
Hermit St.
EC1 . . . . 1D **9** (2D **63**)
Hermon Hill E11 . . . . 1C **40**
Hermon Rd. NW10 . . . . . 2A **42**
HERNE HILL. 3E **105**
Herne Hill SE24 . . . . . . 4E **105**

Herne Hill
SE24 . . . . 4D **105**
(off Railton Rd.)
Herne Hill Rd. SE24 . . . 1E **105**
Herne Hill Stadium . . . 4F **105**
Herne Pl. SE24 . . . . 3D **105**
Heron Cl. NW10 . . . . . . 3A **42**
Heron Ct. E14. . . . . 4E **81**
(off New Union Cl.)
Herondale Av.
SW18 . . . . 1F **115**
Heron Dr. N4 . . . . 4E **35**
Herongate Rd. E12. . . . . 4E **41**
Heron Ho. E6 . . . . 4F **55**
NW8 . . . . 1A **60**
(off Newcourt St.)
SW11 . . . . 3A **88**
(off Searles Cl.)
Heron Ind. Est. E15 . . . . 1D **67**
Heron Pl. SE16. . . . . 2A **80**
W1. . . . . 2C **12**
(off Thayer St.)
Heron Quay E14 . . . . . . 2C **80**
Heron Rd. SE24 . . . . . . 2E **105**
Herons, The E11 . . . . . . 1B **40**
Heron's Lea N6 . . . . 1B **32**
Herrick Ho. N16. . . . . . . 1F **49**
(off Howard Rd.)
SE5 . . . . 3F **91**
(off Elmington Est.)
Herrick Rd. N5. . . . . 5E **35**
Herrick St. SW1 . . . . 5F **75**
Herries St. W10 . . . . 1A **58**
Herringham Rd. SE7 . . . 4E **83**
Hersant Cl. NW10 . . . . . 5C **42**
Herschell M. SE5 . . . . . 1E **105**
Herschell Rd. SE23 . . . 5A **108**
Hersham Cl. SW15 . . . . 5C **98**
Hertford Av. SW14 . . . . 3A **98**
Hertford Pl.
W1. . . . . 4A **6** (3E **61**)
Hertford Rd. N1 . . . . . . 5A **50**
(not continuous)
Hertford St.
W1. . . . . 2D **21** (2D **75**)
Hertslet Rd. N7 . . . . 5B **34**
Hertsmere Ho. E14 . . . . 1C **80**
(off Hertsmere Rd.)
Hertsmere Rd. E14 . . . . 2C **80**
Hervey Rd. SE3 . . . . 4D **97**
Hesewall Cl. SW4 . . . . . 5E **89**
Hesketh Pl. W11 . . . . . . 1A **72**
Hesketh Rd. E7 . . . . 5C **40**
Heslop Rd. SW12. . . . . . 1B **116**
Hesper M. SW5 . . . . 5D **73**
Hesperus Cl. E14. . . . . . 5D **81**
Hesperus Cres. E14. . . . 5D **81**
Hessel St. E1. . . . . 5D **65**
Hestercombe Av.
SW6 . . . . 5A **86**
Hester Rd. SW11 . . . . . . 3A **88**
Hestia Ho. SE1. . . . . 4D **27**
Heston Ho. SE8 . . . . 4C **94**
Heston St. SE14. . . . . . . 4C **94**
Hetherington Rd.
SW4 . . . . 2A **104**
Hethpool Ho. W2 . . . . . . 3F **59**
(off Hall Pl.)
Hetley Rd. W12 . . . . 2D **71**
Hevelius Cl. SE10 . . . . . 1B **96**

Hever Ho. *SE15* 2F **93**
(off Lovelinch Cl.)
Heversham Ho. SE15 . . . . 2E **93**
Hewer St. W10 . . . . 4F **57**
Hewett St.
EC2 . . . . 4E **11** (3A **64**)
Hewison St. E3 . . . . 1B **66**
Hewitt Rd. N8 . . . . 1C **34**
Hewlett Ho. *SW8* 3D **89**
(off Havelock Ter.)
Hewlett Rd. E3 . . . . 1A **66**
Hexagon, The N6 . . . . . . 3B **32**
Hexal Rd. SE6 . . . . 3A **124**
Hexham Rd. SE27 . . . . . 2E **119**
Heybridge *NW1* 3D **47**
(off Lewis St.)
Heybridge Av.
SW16 . . . . 5B **118**
Heybridge Way E10 . . . . 2A **38**
Heydon Ho. *SE14* 4E **93**
(off Kender St.)
Heyford Av. SW8 . . . . . . 3A **90**
Heyford Ter. SW8 . . . . . . 3A **90**
Heygate St. SE17 . . . . . . 5E **77**
Heylyn Sq. E3 . . . . 2B **66**
Heysham La. NW3 . . . . . 5D **31**
Heysham Rd. N15 . . . . . . 1F **35**
Heythorp St. SW18 . . . . 1B **114**
Heywood Ho. *SE14* 2F **93**
(off Myers La.)
Heyworth Rd. E5 . . . . . . 1D **51**
E15 . . . . 2B **54**
Hibbert Ho. *E14* 4C **80**
(off Tiller Rd.)
Hibbert Rd. E17 . . . . 2B **38**
Hibbert St. SW11 . . . . . 1F **101**
Hichisson Rd. SE15 . . . . 3E **107**
Hickes Ho. NW6 . . . . . . 4F **45**
Hickin Cl. SE7 . . . . 5F **83**
Hickin St. E14 . . . . 4E **81**
Hickleton *NW1* 5E **47**
(off Camden St.)
Hickling Ho. *SE16* 4D **79**
(off Slippers Pl.)
Hickman Cl. E16 . . . . . . 4F **69**
Hickmore Wlk. SW4 . . . . 1F **103**
Hicks Cl. SW11 . . . . . . 1A **102**
Hicks St. SE8 . . . . 1A **94**
Hide Pl. SW1 . . . . 5F **75**
Hider Ct. SE3 . . . . 3E **97**
Hides St. N7 . . . . 3B **48**
Hide Twr. *SW1* 5F **75**
(off Regency St.)
Higgins Ho. *N1* 5A **50**
(off Colville St.)
Higginson Ho. *NW3* 4B **46**
(off Fellows Rd.)
Higgs Ind. Est.
SE24 . . . . 1D **105**
Highbank Way N8 . . . . . 1C **34**
High Bri. SE10 . . . . 1F **95**
Highbridge Ct. *SE14* . . . 3E **93**
(off Farrow La.)
High Bri. Wharf *SE10* . . 1F **95**
(off High Bri.)
Highbrook Rd. SE3 . . . . 1F **111**
HIGHBURY 1D **49**
HIGHBURY CORNER . . . 3D **49**
Highbury Cres. N5 . . . . . 2D **49**
Highbury Est. N5 . . . . . . 2E **49**

Highbury Grange N5 . . . . 1E **49**
Highbury Gro. N5 . . . . . . 2D **49**
Highbury Gro. Ct. N5 . . . 3E **49**
Highbury Hill N5 . . . . . . 5C **34**
Highbury New Pk. N5 . . . 2E **49**
Highbury Pk. N5 . . . . 5D **35**
Highbury Pk. M. N5 . . . . 1E **49**
Highbury Pl. N5 . . . . 3D **49**
Highbury Pool 3D **49**
Highbury Quad. N5 . . . . . 5E **35**
Highbury Rd. SW19 . . . . 5A **114**
Highbury Stadium 5D **35**
Highbury Sta. Rd. N1 . . . 3C **48**
Highbury Ter. N5 . . . . . . 2D **49**
Highbury Ter. M. N5 . . . . 2D **49**
Highclere St. SE26 . . . . 4A **122**
Highcliffe Dr. SW15 . . . . 4B **98**
(not continuous)
Highcliffe Gdns.
IG4: Ilf 1F **41**
Highcombe SE7 . . . . . . 2D **97**
Highcombe Cl. SE9 . . . . 1F **125**
Highcroft Est. N19 . . . . . 2A **34**
Highcroft Gdns.
NW11 . . . . 1B **30**
Highcroft Rd. N19 . . . . . 2A **34**
Highcross Way
SW15 . . . . 1C **112**
Highdown Rd. SW15 . . . 4D **99**
Highfield Av. NW11 . . . . 1F **29**
Highfield Cl. SE13 . . . . . 4F **109**
Highfield Ct. NW11 . . . . 1A **30**
Highfield Gdns.
NW11 . . . . 1A **30**
Highfield Rd. NW11 . . . . 1A **30**
Highfields Gro. N6 . . . . . 3B **32**
HIGHGATE 2C **32**
Highgate Av. N6 . . . . . . 2D **33**
Highgate Cemetery
N6 . . . . 3C **32**
Highgate Cl. N6 . . . . . . 2C **32**
Highgate Edge N2 . . . . . 1A **32**
Highgate Hgts. N6 . . . . . 1E **33**
Highgate High St. N6 . . . 3C **32**
Highgate Hill N6 . . . . . . 3D **33**
N19 . . . . 3D **33**
Highgate Ho. SE26 . . . . 3C **120**
Highgate NW5 . . . . 5C **32**
Highgate Spinney N8 . . . 1F **33**
Highgate Wlk. SE23 . . . . 2E **121**
Highgate W. Hill N6 . . . . 3C **32**
Highgate Wood School
Sports Cen. 1E **33**
High Hill Est. E5 . . . . . . 3D **37**
High Hill Ferry E5 . . . . . 3D **37**
High Holborn
WC1 . . . . 2D **15** (5A **62**)
Highland Cft.
BR3: Beck. 5D **123**
Highland Rd. SE19 . . . . 5A **120**
Highlands Cl. N4 . . . . . . 2A **34**
Highlands Heath
SW15 . . . . 5E **99**
Highland Ter. *SE13* . . . 1D **109**
(off Algernon Rd.)
High Level Dr. SE26 . . . 4C **120**
Highlever Rd. W10 . . . . 4E **57**
High Meads Rd. E16 . . . 5F **69**
Highmore Rd. SE3 . . . . . 3A **96**
High Mt. NW4 . . . . 1C **28**

High Pde., The
SW16 . . . . 3A **118**
High Point N6 . . . . 2C **32**
High Rd. N15 . . . . 1B **36**
NW10 . . . . 3A **42**
High Rd. Leystone
E11 . . . . 5A **40**
High Rd. Leyton E10 . . . 1D **39**
E15 . . . . 1E **53**
High Rd. Leytonstone
E15 . . . . 1A **54**
High Sheldon N6 . . . . . . 1B **32**
Highshore Rd. SE15 . . . . 5B **92**
(not continuous)
Highstone Av. E11 . . . . . 1C **40**
Highstone Ct. *E11* 1C **40**
(off New Wanstead)
Highstone Mans.
NW1 . . . . 4E **47**
(off Camden Rd.)
High St. E11 . . . . 1C **40**
E13 . . . . 1C **68**
E15 . . . . 1E **67**
SW19 . . . . 5F **113**
High St. Colliers Wood
SW19 . . . . 5A **116**
High St. Harlesden
NW10 . . . . 1B **56**
High St. M. SW19 . . . . . 5A **114**
High St. Nth. E12 . . . . . 2F **55**
High Timber St.
EC4 . . . . 4F **17** (1E **77**)
High Trees SW2 . . . . . . 1C **118**
Hightrees Ho.
SW12 . . . . 4C **102**
Highview N6 . . . . 1E **33**
Highway, The E1 . . . . . . 1C **78**
Highway Bus. Pk., The
E1 . . . . 1F **79**
(off Heckford St.)
Highway Trad. Cen., The
E1 . . . . 1F **79**
(off Heckford St.)
Highwood Rd. N19 . . . . . 5A **34**
Highworth St. *NW1* 4A **60**
(off Daventry St.)
Hi-Gloss Cen. SE8 . . . . 1A **94**
Hilary Cl. SW6 . . . . 3D **87**
Hilary Rd. W12 . . . . 5B **56**
(not continuous)
Hilborough Ct. E8 . . . . . 4B **50**
Hilda Rd. E6 . . . . 4F **55**
E16 . . . . 3A **68**
(not continuous)
Hilda Ter. SW9 . . . . 5C **90**
Hildenborough Gdns.
BR1: Brom 5A **124**
Hildreth St. SW12 . . . . . 1D **117**
Hildreth St. M.
SW12 . . . . 1D **117**
Hildyard Rd. SW6 . . . . . 2C **86**
Hiley Rd. NW10 . . . . . . 2E **57**
Hilgrove Rd. NW6 . . . . . 4E **45**
Hiliary Ct. *W12* 3E **71**
(off Titmuss St.)
Hillbeck Cl. SE15 . . . . . 3E **93**
Hillbeck Ho. *SE15* 2E **93**
(off Hillbeck Cl.)
Hillboro Ct. E11 . . . . 2F **39**
Hillbrook Rd. SW17 . . . . 3B **116**

Hillbury Rd. SW17 . . . . . 3D **117**
Hill Cl. NW2 . . . . 5D **29**
   NW11 . . . . 1C **30**
Hillcourt Est. N16 . . . . . . 3F **35**
Hillcourt Rd. SE22 . . . . . 4D **107**
Hillcrest N6 . . . . 2C **32**
   SE24 . . . . 2F **105**
Hillcrest Cl. SE26 . . . . . . 4C **120**
Hill Crest Gdns. NW2 . . . 5C **28**
Hillcrest Rd.
   BR1: Brom 5C **124**
Hilldrop Cres. N7 . . . . . . 2F **47**
Hilldrop Est. N7 . . . . 2F **47**
   (not continuous)
Hilldrop La. N7 . . . . 2F **47**
Hilldrop Rd.
   BR1: Brom 5D **125**
   N7 . . . . 2F **47**
Hillersden Ho. SW1 . . . . . 1D **89**
   (off Ebury Bri. Rd.)
Hillersdon Av. SW13 . . . . 5C **84**
Hillery Cl. SE17 . . . . 5F **77**
Hill Farm Rd. W10 . . . . . 4E **57**
Hillfield Cl. NW3 . . . . 2A **46**
Hillfield Ho. N5 . . . . 2E **49**
Hillfield Rd. NW6 . . . . . . 2B **44**
Hillgate Pl. SW12 . . . . . . 5D **103**
   W8 . . . . 2C **72**
Hillgate St. W8 . . . . 2C **72**
Hillgate Wlk. N6 . . . . 1E **33**
Hill Ho. E5 . . . . 3D **37**
   (off Harrington Hill)
Hill Ho. Rd. SW16 . . . . . 5B **118**
Hilliard Ho. E1 . . . . 2D **79**
   (off Prusom St.)
Hilliards Ct. E1 . . . . 2E **79**
Hillier Ho. NW1 . . . . 4F **47**
   (off Camden Sq.)
Hillier Rd. SW11 . . . . . . 4B **102**
Hillingdon St. SE17 . . . . 2D **91**
Hillman Dr. W10 . . . . 3E **57**
Hillman St. E8 . . . . 3D **51**
Hillmarton Rd. N7 . . . . . . 2A **48**
Hillmead Dr. SW9 . . . . . 2D **105**
Hillmore Ct. SE13 . . . . . . 1F **109**
   (off Belmont Hill)
Hillmore Gro. SE26 . . . . 5A **122**
Hill Path SW16 . . . . 5B **118**
Hill Ri. SE23 . . . . 1D **121**
Hillrise Mans. N19 . . . . . 2A **34**
   (off Warltersville Rd.)
Hillrise Rd. N19 . . . . 2A **34**
Hill Rd. NW8 . . . . 2E **59**
Hillsboro' Rd. SE22 . . . . 3A **106**
Hillsborough Ct.
   NW6 . . . . 5D **45**
   (off Mortimer Cres.)
Hillside N8 . . . . 1F **33**
   NW5 . . . . 5C **32**
   NW10 . . . . 5A **42**
   SE10 . . . . 3F **95**
   (off Crooms Hill)
Hillside Cl. NW8 . . . . 1D **59**
Hillside Est. N15 . . . . 1B **36**
   (not continuous)
   SW2 . . . . 2C **118**
Hillside Pas. SW16 . . . . 2B **118**
Hillside Rd. N15 . . . . 2A **36**
   SW2 . . . . 2B **118**
Hillsleigh Rd. W8 . . . . . . 2B **72**

Hills Pl. W1 . . . . . . 3F **13** (5E **61**)
Hillstowe St. E5 . . . . 5E **37**
Hill St. W1 . . . . . 1C **20** (2C **74**)
Hilltop Ct. NW8 . . . . 4E **45**
   (off Alexandra Rd.)
Hilltop Ho. N6 . . . . 2F **33**
Hilltop Rd. NW6 . . . . 4C **44**
Hill Vw. Gdns.
   NW9 . . . . 1A **28**
Hillway N6 . . . . 4C **32**
   NW9 . . . . 3A **28**
Hill-Wood Ho. NW1 . . . . . 1A **6**
   (off Polygon Rd.)
Hillworth Rd. SW2 . . . . . 5C **104**
Hillyard St. SW9 . . . . . . 4C **90**
Hillyard St. SW9 . . . . . . 4C **90**
Hillyfield Cl. E9 . . . . 2A **52**
Hilly Flds. Cres.
   SE4 . . . . 1C **108**
   SE13 . . . . 1C **108**
Hilsea Point SW15 . . . . . 1D **113**
Hilsea St. E5 . . . . 1E **51**
Hilton Ho. SE4 . . . . 2F **107**
Hilton's Wharf SE10 . . . . 2D **95**
   (off Norman Rd.)
Hilversum Cres.
   SE22 . . . . 3A **106**
Himley Rd. SW17 . . . . . 5A **116**
Hinchinbrook Ho.
   NW6 . . . . 5D **45**
   (off Mortimer Cres.)
Hinckley Rd. SE15 . . . . . 2C **106**
Hind Ct. EC4 . . . . 3C **16** (5C **62**)
Hinde M. W1 . . . . 2C **12**
   (off Hinde St.)
Hinde M. W1 . . . . 2C **12**
Hinde St. W1 . . . . 2C **12** (5C **60**)
Hind Gro. E14 . . . . 5C **66**
Hindhead Cl. N16 . . . . . 3A **36**
Hindhead Point
   SW15 . . . . 1D **113**
Hind Ho. N7 . . . . 1C **48**
   SE14 . . . . 2F **93**
   (off Myers La.)
Hindlip Ho. SW8 . . . . . . 4F **89**
Hindmans Rd. SE22 . . . . 3C **106**
Hindmarsh Cl. E1 . . . . . 1C **78**
Hindon Ct. SW1 . . . . 5E **75**
   (off Guildhouse St.)
Hindrey Rd. E5 . . . . 2D **51**
Hindsley's Pl. SE23 . . . . 2E **121**
Hinstock NW6 . . . . 5D **45**
   (off Belsize Rd.)
Hinton Ct. E10 . . . . 4D **39**
   (off Leyton Grange Est.)
Hinton Rd. SE24 . . . . . . 1D **105**
Hippodrome M. W11 . . . 1A **72**
Hippodrome Pl. W11 . . . 1A **72**
Hiroshima Prom.
   SE7 . . . . 4E **83**
Hitcham Rd. E17 . . . . . . 2B **38**
Hitchin Sq. E3 . . . . 1A **66**
Hithe Gro. SE16 . . . . . . 4E **79**
Hither Farm Rd.
   SE3 . . . . 1E **111**
Hitherfield Rd.
   SW16 . . . . 2B **118**
HITHER GREEN 4A **110**
Hither Grn. La.
   SE13 . . . . 3E **109**

Hitherwood Dr.
   SE19 . . . . 4B **120**
HMP Brixton SW2 . . . . . 4A **104**
HMP Pentonville N7 . . . 3B **48**
HMP Wormwood Scrubs
   W12 . . . . 5C **56**
HMS Belfast . . . 1D **27** (2A **78**)
Hoadly Rd. SW16 . . . . . 3F **117**
Hobart Pl.
   SW1 . . . . . 5D **21** (4D **75**)
Hobbes Wlk. SW15 . . . . 3D **99**
Hobbs Ct. SE1 . . . . 3B **78**
   (off Mill St.)
Hobbs Pl. N1 . . . . 5A **50**
Hobbs Pl. Est. N1 . . . . . 1A **64**
   (off Hobbs Pl.)
Hobbs Rd. SE27 . . . . . . 4E **119**
Hobday St. E14 . . . . 5D **67**
Hobson's Pl. E1 . . . . 4C **64**
Hobury St. SW10 . . . . . 2E **87**
Hocker St. E2 . . 2F **11** (2B **64**)
Hockett Cl. SE8 . . . . 5A **80**
Hockley Av. E6 . . . . 1F **69**
Hockliffe Ho. W10 . . . . . 4E **57**
   (off Sutton Way)
Hockney Ct. SE16 . . . . . 1D **93**
   (off Rossetti Rd.)
Hocroft Av. NW2 . . . . . . 5B **30**
Hocroft Ct. NW2 . . . . . . 5B **30**
Hocroft Rd. NW2 . . . . . . 5B **30**
Hocroft Wlk. NW2 . . . . . 5B **30**
Hodes Row NW3 . . . . . . 1C **46**
Hodford Rd. NW11 . . . . 3B **30**
Hodister Cl. SE5 . . . . . . 3E **91**
Hodnet Gro. SE16 . . . . . 5F **79**
Hoe St. E17 . . . . 1C **38**
Hoever Ho. SE6 . . . . 4E **123**
Hoffman Sq. N1 . . . . 1C **10**
Hofland Rd. W14 . . . . . . 4A **72**
Hogan M. W2 . . . . 4E **59**
Hogan Way E5 . . . . 4C **36**
Hogarth Bus. Pk. W4 . . . 2A **84**
Hogarth Cl. E16 . . . . 4F **69**
Hogarth Ct. E1 . . . . 5C **64**
   (off Batty St.)
   EC3 . . . . 4E **19** (5A **64**)
   NW1 . . . . 4E **47**
   (off St Pancras Way)
   SE19 . . . . 4B **120**
Hogarth Ho. SW1 . . . . . 5F **75**
   (off Erasmus St.)
Hogarth Ind. Est.
   NW10 . . . . 3C **56**
Hogarth La. W4 . . . . 2A **84**
Hogarth Pl. SW5 . . . . . . 5D **73**
   (off Hogarth Rd.)
Hogarth Rd. SW5 . . . . . 5D **73**
Hogarth Rdbt. 2A **84**
Hogarth's House 2A **84**
   (off Hogarth La.)
Hogarth Ter. W4 . . . . . . 2A **84**
Hogshead Pas. E1 . . . . . 1D **79**
   (off Reunion Row)
Holbeach M. SW12 . . . . 1D **117**
Holbeach Rd. SE6 . . . . . 5C **108**
Holbeck Row SE15 . . . . 3C **92**
Holbein Ho. SW1 . . . . . . 1C **88**
   (off Holbein M.)
Holbein M. SW1 . . . . . . 1C **88**
Holbein Pl. SW1 . . . . . . 5C **74**

Holberton Gdns.
NW10 . . . . 2D 57
HOLBORN 1F 15 (4C 62)
Holborn EC1 . . 1B 16 (4C 62)
Holborn Cir.
EC1 . . . . 1C 16 (4C 62)
Holborn Pl. WC1 . . . . . 1F 15
Holborn Rd. E13 . . . . . 3D 69
Holborn Viaduct
EC1 . . . . 1C 16 (4C 62)
Holbrook Cl. N19 . . . . . 3D 33
Holbrooke Ct. N7 . . . . . 5A 34
Holburne Rd. E15 . . . . . 1B 68
Holburne Cl. SE3 . . . . . 4E 97
Holburne Gdns. SE3 . . . 4F 97
Holburne Rd. SE3 . . . . . 4F 97
Holcombe Ho.
SW9 . . . . 1A 104
(off Landor Rd.)
Holcombe Pl. SE4 . . . 1A 108
(off St Asaph Rd.)
Holcombe St. W6 . . . . . 5D 71
Holcroft Ct. W1 . . . . . . 5F 5
Holcroft Rd. SW11 . . . 1F 101
Holcroft Rd. E9 . . . . . . 4E 51
Holdenby Rd. SE4 . . . . 3A 108
Holden Ho. N1 . . . . 5E 49
(off Prebend St.)
SE8 . . . . 3C 94
Holden St. SW11 . . . . . 5C 88
Holdernesse Rd.
SW17 . . . . 3B 116
Holderness Ho. SE5 . . 1A 106
Holderness Way
SE27 . . . . 5D 119
Holford Ho. SE16 . . . . . 5D 79
(off Camilla Rd.)
Holford M. WC1 . . . . . . 1B 8
Holford Pl.
WC1 . . . . 1A 8 (2B 62)
Holford Rd. NW3 . . . . . 5E 31
Holford St.
WC1 . . . . 1B 8 (2B 62)
Holford Yd. WC1 . . . . . . 1B 8
(off Cruikshank St.)
Holgate Av. SW11 . . . . 1F 101
Holgate St. SE7 . . . . . . 4F 83
Holland Dr. SE23 . . . . . 3A 122
Holland Gdns. W14 . . . . 4A 72
Holland Gro. SW9 . . . . . 3C 90
Holland Ho. NW10 . . . . . 1D 57
(off Holland Rd.)
HOLLAND PARK 2B 72
Holland Pk. 3B 72
HOLLAND PARK 3F 71
Holland Pk. W11 . . . . . . 2A 72
Holland Pk. Av. W11 . . . 3A 72
Holland Pk. Gdns.
W14 . . . . 3A 72
Holland Pk. M. W11 . . . 2A 72
Holland Pk. Rd. W14 . . . 4B 72
Holland Pk. Ter. W11 . . . 2A 72
(off Portland Rd.)
Holland Pk. Theatre
(Open Air) 3B 72
(in Holland Pk.)
Holland Pas. N1 . . . . . . 5D 49
(off Basire St.)
Holland Pl. W8 . . . . 3D 73
(off Kensington Chu. St.)

Holland Pl. Chambers
W8 . . . . 3D 73
(off Holland Pl.)
Holland Ri. Ho. SW9 . . . 3B 90
(off Clapham Rd.)
Holland Rd. E15 . . . . . . 2A 68
NW10 . . . . 5C 42
W14 . . . . 3F 71
Holland St.
SE1 . . . . . . 1E 25 (2D 77)
W8 . . . . 3C 72
Holland Vs. Rd.
W14 . . . . 3A 72
Holland Wlk. N19 . . . . . 3F 33
W8 . . . . 2B 72
Hollar Rd. N16 . . . . 5B 36
Hollen St.
W1 . . . . . . 2B 14 (5F 61)
Holles Ho. SW9 . . . . . . 5C 90
Holles St.
W1 . . . . . . 2E 13 (5D 61)
Holley Rd. W3 . . . . 3A 70
Holliday Sq. SW11 . . . 1F 101
(off Fowler Cl.)
Hollies, The E11 . . . . . . 1C 40
(off New Wanstead)
Hollies Way SW12 . . . 5C 102
Hollingbourne Rd.
SE24 . . . . 3E 105
Hollins Ho. N7 . . . . 1A 48
Hollisfield WC1 . . . . 2E 7
(off Cromer St.)
HOLLOWAY 5A 34
Holloway Ho. NW2 . . . . 5E 29
(off Stoll Cl.)
Holloway Rd. E11 . . . . . 5F 39
N7 . . . . 1B 48
N19 . . . . 4F 33
Hollyberry La. NW3 . . . . 1E 45
Hollybush Cl. E11 . . . . . 1C 40
Hollybush Gdns. E2 . . . 2D 65
Hollybush Hill E11 . . . . . 1B 40
NW3 . . . . 1E 45
Hollybush Ho. E2 . . . . . 2D 65
Hollybush Pl. E2 . . . . . . 2D 65
Hollybush Steps
NW3 . . . . 1E 45
(off Holly Mt.)
Hollybush St. E13 . . . . . 2D 69
Holly Bush Va. NW3 . . . 1E 45
Hollybush Wlk.
SW9 . . . . 2D 105
Holly Cl. NW10 . . . . 4A 42
Hollycroft Av. NW3 . . . . 5C 30
Hollydale Rd. SE15 . . . . 4E 93
Holly Dene SE15 . . . . . 4D 93
Hollydown Way E11 . . . 5F 39
Holly Gro. SE15 . . . . . . 5B 92
Holly Hedge Ter.
SE13 . . . . 3F 109
Holly Hill NW3 . . . . 1E 45
Holly Ho. W10 . . . . 3A 58
(off Hawthorn Wlk.)
Holly Lodge Gdns.
N6 . . . . 4C 32
Holly Lodge Mans.
N6 . . . . 4C 32
Holly M. SW10 . . . . 1E 87
Holly Mt. NW3 . . . . 1E 45
Hollymount Cl. SE10 . . . 4E 95

Holly Pk. N4 . . . . 2A 34
(not continuous)
Holly Pk. Est. N4 . . . . . 2B 34
Holly Pl. NW3 . . . . 1E 45
(off Holly Berry La.)
Holly Rd. E11 . . . . 2B 40
W4 . . . . 5A 70
Holly St. E8 . . . . 4B 50
Holly Ter. N6 . . . . 3C 32
Holly Tree Cl. SW19 . . . 1F 113
Holly Tree Ho. SE4 . . . 1B 108
(off Brockley Rd.)
Holly Vw. Cl. NW4 . . . . 1C 28
Holly Village N6 . . . . . . 4D 33
Holly Vs. W6 . . . . 4D 71
(off Wellesley Av.)
Holly Wlk. NW3 . . . . . . 1E 45
Hollywood Bowl
Surrey Quays 4F 79
Hollywood M. SW10 . . . 2E 87
Hollywood Rd. SW10 . . 2E 87
Holman Ho. E2 . . . . 2F 65
(off Roman Rd.)
Holman Hunt Ho. W6 . . 1A 86
(off Field Rd.)
Holman Rd. SW11 . . . . 5F 87
Holmbrook NW1 . . . . . . 1E 61
(off Eversholt St.)
Holmbury Ct. SW17 . . . 3B 116
Holmbury Ho. SE24 . . . 3D 105
Holmbury Vw. E5 . . . . . 3D 37
Holmbush Rd.
SW15 . . . . 4A 100
Holmcote Gdns. N5 . . . 2E 49
Holm Ct. SE12 . . . . . . 3D 125
Holmdale Gdns. NW4 . . 1F 29
Holmdale Rd. NW6 . . . . 2C 44
Holmdale Ter. N15 . . . . 2A 36
Holmdene Av. SE24 . . . 3E 105
Holmead Rd. SW6 . . . . 3D 87
Holme Lacey Rd.
SE12 . . . . 4B 110
Holmesdale Ho.
NW6 . . . . 5C 44
(off Kilburn Va.)
Holmesdale Rd. N6 . . . 2D 33
Holmesley Rd.
SE23 . . . . 4A 108
Holmes Pl. SW10 . . . . . 2E 87
Holmes Place Health Club
Barbican 5F 9
(off Aldersgate St.)
Hammersmith 5F 71
(off Hammersmith Rd.)
Merton 5E 115
St Luke's 4B 10
Holmes Rd. NW5 . . . . . 2D 47
Holmes Ter. SE1 . . . . . 3B 24
Holmewood Gdns.
SW2 . . . . 5B 104
Holmewood Rd.
SW2 . . . . 5A 104
Holmfield Ct. NW3 . . . . 2A 46
Holmleigh Rd. N16 . . . . 3A 36
Holmleigh Rd. Est.
N16 . . . . 3A 36
Holmoak Cl. SW15 . . . . 4B 100
Holm Oak M. SW4 . . . . 3A 104
Holmsdale Ho. E14 . . . 1D 81
(off Poplar High St.)

Holmshaw Cl. SE26 . . . 4A **122**
Holmside Rd.
SW12 . . . . 4C **102**
Holmsley Ho. SW15 . . . 5B **98**
    (off Tangley Gro.)
Holm Wlk. SE3 . . . . . . 5C **96**
Holmwood Vs. SE7 . . . 1C **96**
Holne Chase N2 . . . . . 1E **31**
Holness Rd. E15 . . . . . 3B **54**
Holocaust Memorial Garden
. . . . 3A **20**
Holroyd Rd. SW15 . . . . 2E **99**
Holst Ct. SE1 . . . . 5B **24**
    (off Westminster Bri. Rd.)
Holst Mans. SW13 . . . . 2F **85**
Holsworthy Sq. WC1 . . . 4A **8**
Holt Ct. E15 . . . . 2E **53**
Holt Ho. SW2 . . . . 4C **104**
Holton St. E1. . . . . 3F **65**
Holwood Pl. SW4 . . . . 2F **103**
Holybourne Av.
SW15 . . . . 5C **98**
Holyhead Cl. E3 . . . . . 2C **66**
Holyoake Ct. SE16 . . . . 3B **80**
Holyoak Rd. SE11 . . . . 5D **77**
Holyport Rd. SW6 . . . . 3F **85**
Holyrood M. E16 . . . . . 2C **82**
    (off Badminton M.)
Holyrood St.
SE1 . . . . 2D **27** (2A **78**)
Holywell Cen. 3D **11**
    (off Phipp St.)
Holywell Cl. SE3 . . . . 2C **96**
SE16. . . . . 1D **93**
Holywell La.
EC2 . . . . 3E **11** (3A **64**)
Holywell Row
EC2 . . . . . . 4D **11** (3A **64**)
Homecroft Rd. SE26. . . 5E **121**
Homefield Rd. SE23. . . 3F **121**
Homefield Rd.
SW19 . . . . 5F **113**
W4 . . . . 1B **84**
Homefield St.
N1 . . . . 1D **11** (1A **64**)
Homeleigh Ct.
SW16 . . . . 3A **118**
Homeleigh Rd.
SE15 . . . . 3F **107**
Home Pk. Rd.
SW19 . . . . 4B **114**
Homer Dr. E14 . . . . . . 5C **80**
Home Rd. SW11. . . . . . 5A **88**
Homer Rd. E9. . . . . 3A **52**
Homer Row W1 . . . . . . 4A **60**
Homer St. W1 . . . . 4A **60**
HOMERTON 2F **51**
Homerton Gro. E9 . . . . 2F **51**
Homerton High St.
E9 . . . . 2F **51**
Homerton Rd. E9 . . . . . 2A **52**
Homerton Row E9 . . . . 2E **51**
Homerton Ter. E9 . . . . . 3E **51**
    (not continuous)
Homesdale Rd. E11 . . . 1C **40**
Homestall Rd. SE22 . . . 3E **107**
Homestead Pk. NW2 . . . 5B **28**
Homestead Rd. SW6 . . 3B **86**
Homewoods SW12. . . . 5E **103**
Homildon Ho. SE26 . . . 3C **120**

Honduras St.
EC1. . . . . 3F **9** (3E **63**)
Honeybourne Rd.
NW6 . . . . 2D **45**
Honeybrook Rd.
SW12 . . . . 5E **103**
Honey La. EC2 . . . . . . 3A **18**
Honeyman Cl. NW6 . . . 4F **43**
Honeywell Rd.
SW11 . . . . 4B **102**
Honeywood Rd.
NW10 . . . . 1B **56**
Honiton Gdns. SE15 . . . 5E **93**
    (off Gibbon Rd.)
Honiton Rd. NW6. . . . . 1B **58**
Honley Rd. SE6 . . . . . 5D **109**
HONOR OAK 4E **107**
Honor Oak Crematorium
SE23 . . . . 3F **107**
HONOR OAK PARK . . . 5A **108**
Honor Oak Pk. SE23. . . 4E **107**
Honor Oak Ri. SE23 . . . 4E **107**
Honor Oak Rd.
SE23 . . . . 1E **121**
Hood Ct. EC4 . . . . 3C **16**
Hood Ho. SE5 . . . . 3F **91**
    (off Elmington Est.)
SW1 . . . . 1F **89**
    (off Dolphin Sq.)
Hooke Ho. E3. . . . . 1A **66**
    (off Gernon Rd.)
Hookham Ct. SW8 . . . . 4F **89**
Hooks Cl. SE15 . . . . . 4D **93**
Hooper Rd. E16 . . . . . 5C **68**
Hooper's Ct. SW3. . . . . 3B **74**
Hooper Sq. E1 . . . . 5C **64**
    (off Hooper St.)
Hooper St. E1. . . . . 5C **64**
Hoop La. NW11 . . . . . . 2B **30**
    (not continuous)
Hope Cl. N1 . . . . 3E **49**
SE12. . . . . 3D **125**
Hope Ct. NW10 . . . . . . 2F **57**
    (off Chamberlayne Rd.)
Hopedale Rd. SE7 . . . . 2D **97**
Hopefield Av. NW6 . . . 1A **58**
Hope St. SW11 . . . . . . 1F **101**
Hopetown St. E1 . . . . . 4B **64**
Hopewell St. SE5 . . . . . 3F **91**
Hopewell Yd. SE5 . . . . 3F **91**
    (off Hopewell St.)
Hope Wharf SE16. . . . . 3E **79**
Hop Gdns.
WC2. . . . . . . 5D **15** (1A **76**)
Hopgood St. W12 . . . . 2E **71**
Hopkins Ho. E14 . . . . . 5C **66**
    (off Canton St.)
Hopkins M. E15 . . . . . 5B **54**
Hopkinsons Pl. NW1 . . . 5C **46**
Hopkins St.
W1 . . . . 3A **14** (5E **61**)
Hopping La. N1 . . . . . . 3D **49**
Hop St. SE10 . . . . 5B **82**
    (off School Bank Rd.)
Hopton Rd. SW16 . . . . 5A **118**
Hopton's Gdns. SE1 . . . 1E **25**
Hopton St.
SE1 . . . . 5D **17** (1D **77**)
Hopwood Cl. SW17 . . . 3E **115**
Hopwood Rd. SE17. . . . 2F **91**

Hopwood Wlk. E8. . . . . 4C **50**
Horace Rd. E7 . . . . . . 1D **55**
Horatio Ct. SE16 . . . . . 2E **79**
    (off Rotherhithe St.)
Horatio Ho. E2 . . . . . . 1B **64**
    (off Horatio St.)
W6. . . . . 1F **85**
    (off Fulham Pal. Rd.)
Horatio Pl. E14. . . . . . . 2E **81**
    (off Preston's Rd.)
Horatio St. E2. . . . . . . 1B **64**
Horbury Cres. W11 . . . . 1C **72**
Horbury M. W11. . . . . . 1B **72**
Horder Rd. SW6 . . . . . 4A **86**
Hordle Prom. E.
SE15 . . . . 3B **92**
Hordle Prom. Sth.
SE15 . . . . 3B **92**
    (off Quarley Way)
Horizon Bldg. E14 . . . . 1C **80**
    (off Hertsmere Rd.)
Horizon Way SE7 . . . . 5D **83**
Horle Wlk. SE5 . . . . . . 5D **91**
Horley Rd. SE9 . . . . . 4F **125**
Hormead Rd. W9 . . . . . 3B **58**
Hornbeam Cl. SE11 . . . 5C **76**
Hornbeam Sq. E3. . . . . 5B **52**
Hornblower Cl. SE16 . . . 4A **80**
Hornby Cl. NW3 . . . . . 4F **45**
Hornby Ho. SE11 . . . . . 2C **90**
    (off Clayton St.)
Horncastle Cl. SE12. . . 5C **110**
Horncastle Rd.
SE12. . . . . 5C **110**
Horndean Cl. SW15 . . . 1C **112**
Horner Ho. N1 . . . . 5A **50**
    (off Whitmore Est.)
Horne Way SW15 . . . . 5E **85**
Hornfair Rd. SE7 . . . . . 2E **97**
Horniman Dr. SE23 . . . 1D **121**
Horniman Mus. 1D **121**
Horn La. SE10 . . . . . . 1C **96**
    (not continuous)
Horn Link Way SE10 . . . 5C **82**
HORN PARK. 3D **111**
Horn Pk. Cl. SE12 . . . . 3D **111**
Hornpark La. SE12. . . 3D **111**
Hornsey Club, The 1F **33**
Hornsey La. N6 . . . . . . 3D **33**
Hornsey La. Est. N19 . . . 2F **33**
Hornsey La. Gdns.
N6. . . . . 2E **33**
Hornsey Ri. N19 . . . . . 2F **33**
Hornsey Ri. Gdns.
N19 . . . . 2F **33**
Hornsey Rd. N7 . . . . . . 3A **34**
N19 . . . . 3A **34**
Hornsey St. N7. . . . . . . 2B **48**
HORNSEY VALE 1B **34**
Hornshay St. SE15 . . . . 2E **93**
Hornton Ct. W8 . . . . . . 3C **72**
    (off Kensington High St.)
Hornton Pl. W8 . . . . . . 3D **73**
Hornton St. W8 . . . . . . 3C **72**
Horsa Rd. SE12 . . . . . 5E **111**
Horse & Dolphin Yd.
W1 . . . . 4C **14**
Horseferry Pl. SE10 . . . 2E **95**
Horseferry Rd. E14 . . . 1A **80**
SW1 . . . . 4F **75**

Horseferry Rd. Est.
  SW1 . . . . 5B 22
Horseguards Av.
  SW1 . . . . 2D 23 (2A 76)
Horse Guards Parade
  . . . . 2D 23 (2A 76)
Horse Guards Rd.
  SW1 . . . . . . 2C 22 (2F 75)
Horsell Rd. N5 . . . . . . 2C 48
  (not continuous)
Horselydown La.
  SE1 . . . . 3F 27 (3B 78)
Horselydown Mans.
  SE1 . . . . 3F 27
  (off Lafone St.)
Horsemongers M.
  SE1 . . . . 4A 26
Horse Ride
  SW1 . . . . 2B 22 (2E 75)
Horseshoe Cl. E14 . . . . . 1E 95
  NW2 . . . . 4D 29
Horseshoe Ct. EC1 . . . . . 3E 9
  (off Brewhouse Yd.)
Horseshoe Wharf
  SE1 . . . . 1B 26
  (off Clink St.)
Horse Yd. N1 . . . . 5D 49
  (off Essex Rd.)
Horsfeld Gdns.
  SE9 . . . . 3F 111
Horsfeld Rd. SE9 . . . . . 3F 111
Horsfield Ho. N1 . . . . . . 4E 49
  (off Northampton St.)
Horsford Rd. SW2 . . . . . 3B 104
Horsley St. SE17 . . . . . . 2F 91
Horsman Ho. SE5 . . . . . 2E 91
  (off Bethwin Rd.)
Horsman St. SE5 . . . . . 2E 91
Horsmonden Rd.
  SE4 . . . . 3B 108
Hortensia Ho. SW10 . . . . 3E 87
  (off Gunter Gro.)
Hortensia Rd. SW10 . . . . 3E 87
Horton Av. NW2 . . . . . . 1A 44
Horton Ho. SE15 . . . . . . 2E 93
  SW8 . . . . 3B 90
  W6 . . . . 1A 86
  (off Field Rd.)
Horton Rd. E8 . . . . 3D 51
Horton St. SE13 . . . . . . 1D 109
Horwood Ho. E2 . . . . . . 2D 65
  (off Pott St.)
  NW8 . . . . 3A 60
  (off Paveley St.)
Hosack Rd. SW17 . . . . . 2C 116
Hoser Av. SE12 . . . . . . 2C 124
Hosier La.
  EC1 . . . . 1D 17 (4D 63)
Hoskins Cl. E16 . . . . 5E 69
Hoskins St. SE10 . . . . . . 1F 95
Hospital Rd. E9 . . . . 2F 51
Hospital Way SE13 . . . . . 4F 109
Hotham Rd. SW15 . . . . . 1E 99
Hotham St. E15 . . . . 5A 54
Hothfield Pl. SE16 . . . . . 4E 79
Hotspur St. SE11 . . . . . . 5C 76
Houghton Cl. E8 . . . . . . 3B 50
Houghton St.
  WC2 . . . . 3A 16 (5B 62)
  (not continuous)

Houndsditch
  EC3 . . . . 2E 19 (5A 64)
Houseman Way SE5 . . . . 3F 91
Houses of Parliament
  . . . . 5E 23 (4A 76)
Houston Rd. SE23 . . . . . 2A 122
Hove Av. E17 . . . . 1B 38
Hoveden Rd. NW2 . . . . . 2A 44
Hove St. SE15 . . . . 3E 93
  (off Culmore Rd.)
Howard Bldg. SW8 . . . . . 2D 89
Howard Cl. NW2 . . . . . . 1A 44
Howard Ho. E16 . . . . . . 2D 83
  (off Wesley Av.)
  SE8 . . . . 2B 94
  (off Evelyn St.)
  SW1 . . . . 1E 89
  (off Dolphin Sq.)
  SW9 . . . . 1D 105
  (off Barrington Rd.)
  W1 . . . . 4E 5
  (off Cleveland St.)
Howard M. N5 . . . . 1D 49
Howard Rd. E11 . . . . 5A 40
  N15 . . . . 1A 36
  N16 . . . . 1F 49
  NW2 . . . . 1F 43
Howard's La. SW15 . . . . 2D 99
Howards Rd. E13 . . . . . . 2C 68
Howarth Ct. E15 . . . . . . 2E 53
  (off Clays La.)
Howbury Rd. SE15 . . . . . 1E 107
Howden St. SE15 . . . . . . 1C 106
Howell Ct. E10 . . . . 2D 39
Howell Wlk. SE1 . . . . . . 5D 77
Howick Pl.
  SW1 . . . . 5A 22 (4E 75)
Howie St. SW11 . . . . 3A 88
Howitt Cl. N16 . . . . 1A 50
  NW3 . . . . 3A 46
Howitt Rd. NW3 . . . . 3A 46
Howland Est. SE16 . . . . . 4E 79
Howland Ho. SW16 . . . . . 3A 118
Howland M. E.
  W1 . . . . 5A 6 (4E 61)
Howland St.
  W1 . . . . 5F 5 (4E 61)
Howland Way SE16 . . . . 3A 80
Howlett's Rd. SE24 . . . . . 4E 105
Howley Pl. W2 . . . . 4E 59
Howsman Rd. SW13 . . . . 2C 84
Howson Rd. SE4 . . . . . . 2A 108
How's St. E2 . . . . 1B 64
HOXTON 1A 64
Hoxton Hall Theatre 1A 64
  (off Hoxton Rd.)
Hoxton Mkt. N1 . . . . 2D 11
Hoxton Sq.
  N1 . . . . 2D 11 (2A 64)
Hoxton St.
  N1 . . . . 2E 11 (5A 50)
Hoylake Rd. W3 . . . . 5A 56
Hoyland Cl. SE15 . . . . . . 3D 93
Hoyle Rd. SW17 . . . . . . 5A 116
Hoy St. E16 . . . . 5B 68
HQS Wellington 5B 16
Hubbard Rd. SE27 . . . . . 4E 119
Hubbard St. E15 . . . . . . 5A 54
Huberd Ho. SE1 . . . . . . 5C 26
  (off Manciple St.)

Hubert Gro. SW9 . . . . . . 1A 104
Hubert Ho. NW8 . . . . . . 3A 60
  (off Ashbridge St.)
Hubert Rd. E6 . . . . 2F 69
Hucknall Ct. NW8 . . . . . . 3F 59
  (off Cunningham Pl.)
Huddart St. E3 . . . . 4B 66
  (Ackroyd Dr.)
  E3 . . . . 4B 66
  (Weatherley Cl.)
Huddleston Cl. E2 . . . . . 1E 65
Huddlestone Rd. E7 . . . . 1B 54
  NW2 . . . . 3D 43
Huddleston Rd. N7 . . . . . 5E 33
Hudson Cl. W12 . . . . 1D 71
Hudson Ct. E14 . . . . 1C 94
  (off Maritime Quay)
Hudson's Pl. SW1 . . . . . . 5D 75
Huggin Ct. EC4 . . . . 4A 18
Huggin Hill
  EC4 . . . . 4A 18 (1E 77)
Huggins Pl. SW2 . . . . . . 1B 118
Hughan Rd. E15 . . . . 2F 53
Hugh Astor Ct. SE1 . . . . 5E 25
  (off Keyworth St.)
Hugh Cubitt Ho. N1 . . . . 1B 62
  (off Collier St.)
Hugh Dalton Av. SW6 . . . 2B 86
Hughenden Ho. NW8 . . . . 3A 60
  (off Jerome Cres.)
Hughenden Ter. E15 . . . . 1E 53
Hughes Ct. N7 . . . . 2F 47
Hughes Ho. E2 . . . . 2E 65
  (off Sceptre Ho.)
  SE8 . . . . 2C 94
  (off Benbow St.)
  SE17 . . . . 5D 77
  (off Peacock St.)
Hughes Mans. E1 . . . . . . 3C 64
Hughes M. SW11 . . . . . . 3B 102
Hughes Ter. E16 . . . . . . 4B 68
  (off Clarkson Rd.)
  SW9 . . . . 1D 105
  (off Styles Gdns.)
Hugh Gaitskell Cl.
  SW6 . . . . 2B 86
Hugh Gaitskell Ho.
  N16 . . . . 4B 36
Hugh M. SW1 . . . . 5D 75
Hugh Platt Ho. E2 . . . . . 1D 65
  (off Patriot Sq.)
Hugh St. SW1 . . . . 5D 75
Hugon Rd. SW6 . . . . 1D 101
Hugo Rd. N19 . . . . 1E 47
Huguenot Pl. E1 . . . . 4B 64
  SW18 . . . . 3E 101
Huguenot Sq. SE15 . . . . 1D 107
Hullbridge M. N1 . . . . . . 5F 49
Hull Cl. SE16 . . . . 3F 79
Hull St. EC1 . . . . . . 2F 9 (2E 63)
Hulme Pl.
  SE1 . . . . 4A 26 (3E 77)
Humber Dr. W10 . . . . . . 3F 57
Humber Rd. NW2 . . . . . . 4D 29
  SE3 . . . . 2B 96
Humberstone Rd.
  E13 . . . . 2E 69
Humberton Cl. E9 . . . . . . 2A 52
Humber Trad. Est.
  NW2 . . . . 4D 29

Humbolt Rd. W6 . . . . 2A **86**
Hume Ct. N1 . . . . 4D **49**
   (off Hawes St.)
Hume Ho. W11 . . . . 2F **71**
   (off Queensdale Cres.)
Hume Ter. E16 . . . . 4D **69**
Humphrey St. SE1 . . . . . . 1B **92**
Hungerford Ho. SW1 . . . 2E **89**
   (off Churchill Gdns.)
Hungerford La. WC2 . . . 1E **23**
   (not continuous)
Hungerford Rd. N7 . . . . . 3F **47**
Hungerford St. E1 . . . . . . 5D **65**
Hunsdon Rd. SE14 . . . . . . 3F **93**
Hunslett St. E2 . . . . 2E **65**
Hunstanton Ho. NW1 . . . 4A **60**
   (off Cosway St.)
Hunt Cl. W11 . . . . 2F **71**
   (off Cambridge Gdns.)
Hunter Cl.
  SE1 . . . . 5C **26** (4F **77**)
  SW12 . . . . 1C **116**
Hunter Ho. SE1 . . . . 4E **25**
   (off Lancaster St.)
  SW5 . . . . 1C **86**
   (off Old Brompton Rd.)
  SW8 . . . . 3F **89**
   (off Fount St.)
  WC1 . . . . 3E **7**
   (off Hunter St.)
Hunterian Mus., The . . 2A **16**
   (off Portugal St.)
Hunter Lodge W9 . . . . . . 4C **58**
   (off Admiral Wlk.)
Hunters Cl. SW12 . . . . . 1C **116**
Hunters Mdw. SE19 . . . 4A **120**
Hunter St.
  WC1 . . . . 3E **7** (3A **62**)
Hunter Wlk. E13 . . . . 1C **68**
Huntingdon St. E16 . . . . 5B **68**
  N1 . . . . 4B **48**
Huntingfield Rd.
  SW15 . . . . 2C **98**
Huntley St.
  WC1 . . . . 4A **6** (3E **61**)
Hunton St. E1 . . . . 4C **64**
Hunt's Cl. SE3 . . . . 5C **96**
Hunt's Ct.
  WC2 . . . . 5C **14** (1F **75**)
Hunts La. E15 . . . . 1E **67**
Huntsman St. SE17 . . . . . 5A **78**
Huntspill St. SW17 . . . . . 3E **115**
Hunts Slip Rd.
  SE21 . . . . 3A **120**
Huntsworth M.
  NW1 . . . . 3A **4** (3B **60**)
Hurdwick Pl. NW1 . . . . . 1E **61**
   (off Hampstead Rd.)
Hurleston Ho. SE8 . . . . . . 1B **94**
Hurley Cres. SE16 . . . . . . 3F **79**
Hurley Ho. SE11 . . . . 5D **77**
HURLINGHAM 1D **101**
Hurlingham Bus. Pk.
  SW6 . . . . 1C **100**
Hurlingham Club, The
  . . . . 1C **100**
Hurlingham Ct.
  SW6 . . . . 1B **100**
Hurlingham Gdns.
  SW6 . . . . 1B **100**
Hurlingham Retail Pk.
  SW6 . . . . 1D **101**

Hurlingham Rd.
  SW6 . . . . 5B **86**
Hurlingham Sq.
  SW6 . . . . 1C **100**
Hurlingham Stadium
  . . . . 1B **100**
Hurlock St. N5 . . . . 5D **35**
Huron Rd. SW17 . . . . . . 2C **116**
Huron University 4F **73**
Hurren Cl. SE3 . . . . 1A **110**
Hurry Cl. E15 . . . . 4A **54**
Hurst Av. N6 . . . . 1E **33**
Hurstbourne Ho.
  SW15 . . . . 4B **98**
   (off Tangley Gro.)
Hurstbourne Rd.
  SE23 . . . . 1A **122**
Hurst Cl. NW11 . . . . 1D **31**
Hurst Ct. E6 . . . . 4F **69**
   (off Tollgate Rd.)
Hurstdene Gdns. N15 . . 2A **36**
Hurst Ho. WC1 . . . . 1A **8**
   (off Penton Ri.)
Hurst St. SE24 . . . . 4D **105**
Hurstway Rd. W11 . . . . . 1F **71**
Hurstway Wlk. W11 . . . . 1F **71**
Husborne Ho. SE8 . . . . . 5A **80**
   (off Chilton Gro.)
Huson Cl. NW3 . . . . 4A **46**
Hutchings St. E14 . . . . . . 3C **80**
Hutchings Wharf E14 . . 3C **80**
   (off Hutchings St.)
Hutchins Cl. E15 . . . . 4E **53**
Hutchinson Ho. NW3 . . . 4B **46**
  SE14 . . . . 3E **93**
Hutton Ct. N4 . . . . 3B **34**
   (off Victoria Rd.)
Hutton St.
  EC4 . . . . 4C **16** (5D **63**)
Huxbear St. SE4 . . . . 3B **108**
Huxley Ho. NW8 . . . . 3F **59**
   (off Fisherton St.)
Huxley Rd. E10 . . . . 4E **39**
Huxley St. W10 . . . . 2A **58**
Hyacinth Rd. SW15 . . . 1C **112**
Hyde, The NW9 . . . . 1B **28**
   (not continuous)
Hyde Cl. E13 . . . . 1C **68**
Hyde Cres. NW9 . . . . 1A **28**
Hyde Est. Rd. NW9 . . . . . 1B **28**
Hyde Farm M.
  SW12 . . . . 1F **117**
Hyde Ind. Est., The
  NW9 . . . . 1B **28**
Hyde La. SW11 . . . . 4A **88**
HYDE PARK CORNER
  . . . . 3D **75**
Hyde Pk. Cnr.
  W1 . . . . 3C **20** (3C **74**)
Hyde Pk. Cres. W2 . . . . . 5A **60**
Hyde Pk. Gdns. W2 . . . . 1F **73**
Hyde Pk. Gdns. M.
  W2 . . . . 1F **73**
   (not continuous)
Hyde Pk. Ga. SW7 . . . . . 3E **73**
   (not continuous)
Hyde Pk. Ga. M.
  SW7 . . . . 3E **73**

Hyde Pk. Mans. NW1 . . 4A **60**
   (off Cabbell St.,
   not continuous)
Hyde Pk. Pl. W2 . . . . 1A **74**
Hyde Pk. Sq. W2 . . . . . . 5A **60**
Hyde Pk. Sq. M. W2 . . . 5A **60**
   (off Southwick Pl.)
Hyde Pk. St. W2 . . . . 5A **60**
Hyde Pk. Towers W2 . . 1E **73**
Hyderabad Way E15 . . . 4A **54**
Hyde St. SE8 . . . . 2C **94**
Hyde's Pl. N1 . . . . 4D **49**
Hyde St. SE8 . . . . 2C **94**
Hydethorpe Rd.
  SW12 . . . . 1F **117**
Hyde Va. SE10 . . . . 3E **95**
Hydra Bldg., The
  EC1 . . . . 2C **8**
Hyndewood SE23 . . . . . 3F **121**
Hyndman St. SE15 . . . . . 2D **93**
Hyperion Ho. E3 . . . . 1A **66**
   (off Arbery Rd.)
  SW2 . . . . 4B **104**
Hyson Rd. SE16 . . . . 1D **93**
Hythe Ho. SE16 . . . . 3E **79**
   (off Swan Rd.)
  W6 . . . . 5E **71**
   (off Shepherd's Bush Rd.)
Hythe Rd. NW10 . . . . 2B **56**
Hythe Rd. Ind. Est.
  NW10 . . . . 2C **56**

I

Ian Bowater Ct. N1 . . . . . 1C **10**
   (off East Rd.)
Ian Ct. SE23 . . . . 2E **121**
Ibberton Ho. SW8 . . . . . 3B **90**
   (off Meadow Rd.)
  W14 . . . . 4A **72**
   (off Russell Rd.)
Ibbotson Av. E16 . . . . . . 5B **68**
Ibbott St. E1 . . . . 3E **65**
Iberia Ho. N19 . . . . 2F **33**
Ibex Ho. E15 . . . . 2A **54**
   (off Forest La.)
Ibis Ct. SE8 . . . . 2B **94**
   (off Edward Pl.)
Ibsley Gdns. SW15 . . . 1C **112**
ICA Cinema 2C **22**
   (off Mall, The)
ICA Theatre 2C **22**
   (off Mall, The)
Iceland Rd. E3 . . . . 5C **52**
Ice Wharf Marina N1 . . 1A **62**
   (off New Wharf Rd.)
Ickburgh Est. E5 . . . . 4D **37**
Ickburgh Rd. E5 . . . . 5D **37**
Icknield Ho. SW3 . . . . . . 1A **88**
   (off Cale St.)
Icon Apartments SE1 . . 5D **27**
   (off Cluny Pl.)
Ida St. E14 . . . . 5E **67**
   (not continuous)
Idlecombe Rd.
  SW17 . . . . 5C **116**
Idmiston Rd. E15 . . . . . . 1B **54**
  SE27 . . . . 3E **119**
Idol La. EC3 . . . 5D **19** (1A **78**)

Idonia St. SE8 . . . . 3C **94**
Iffley Rd. W6 . . . . 4D **71**
Ifield Rd. SW10 . . . . 2D **87**
Ifor Evans Pl. E1 . . . . . . 3F **65**
Ightham Ho. SE17 . . . . . 5A **78**
(off Beckway St.)
Ilbert St. W10 . . . . 2F **57**
Ilchester Gdns. W2 . . . 1D **73**
Ilchester Pl. W14 . . . . . 4B **72**
Ildersly Gro. SE21 . . . . 2F **119**
Ilderton Rd. SE16 . . . . . 1E **93**
Ilderton Wharf SE15 . . . 2E **93**
(off Rollins St.)
Ilex Rd. NW10 . . . . 3B **42**
Ilex Way SW16 . . . . . . 5C **118**
Ilford Ho. N1 . . . . 3F **49**
(off Dove Rd.)
Ilfracombe Flats SE1 . . 3A **26**
(off Marshalsea Rd.)
Ilfracombe Rd.
BR1: Brom 3B **124**
Iliffe St. SE17 . . . . 1D **91**
Iliffe Yd. SE17 . . . . 1D **91**
(off Crampton St.)
Ilkeston Ct. E5 . . . . 1F **51**
(off Overbury St.)
Ilkley Rd. E16 . . . . 4E **69**
Ilminster Gdns.
SW11 . . . . 2A **102**
Ilsley Ct. SW8 . . . . 5E **89**
Imani Mans. SW11 . . . . 5F **87**
IMAX Cinema
. . . . 2B **24** (2C **76**)
Imber St. N1 . . . . 5F **49**
Imperial Av. N16 . . . . . . 1A **50**
Imperial College of Science,
Technology & Medicine
Imperial Coll. Rd. . . . 4F **73**
Wilson House 5A **60**
(off Star La.)
Imperial Coll. Rd.
SW7 . . . . 4F **73**
Imperial Ct. N6 . . . . 1E **33**
NW8 . . . . 1A **60**
(off Prince Albert Rd.)
SE11 . . . . 1C **90**
Imperial Ho. E3 . . . . . . 2A **66**
(off Grove Rd.)
E14 . . . . 1B **80**
(off Victory Pl.)
Imperial M. E6 . . . . 1F **69**
Imperial Pde. EC4 . . . . 3D **17**
(off New Bri. St.)
Imperial Rd. SW6 . . . . . 4D **87**
Imperial Sq. SW6 . . . . . 4D **87**
Imperial War Mus.
. . . . 5C **24** (4C **76**)
Imperial Wharf SW6 . . . 5E **87**
Imre Cl. W12 . . . . 2D **71**
Inchmery Rd. SE6 . . . . 2D **123**
Independent Pl. E8 . . . . 2B **50**
Independents Rd.
SE3 . . . . 1B **110**
Inderwick Rd. N8 . . . . . 1B **34**
Indescon Ct. E14 . . . . . 3C **80**
India Pl. WC2 . . . . 4F **15**
India St. EC3 . . . 3F **19** (5B **64**)
India Way W12 . . . . 1D **71**
Indigo M. E14 . . . . 1E **81**
N16 . . . . 5F **35**

Indus Rd. SE7 . . . . 3E **97**
Infirmary Ct. SW3 . . . . 2B **88**
(off West Rd.)
Ingal Rd. E13 . . . . 3C **68**
Ingate Pl. SW8 . . . . 4D **89**
E12 . . . . 3E **41**
Ingelow Ho. W8 . . . . . . 3D **73**
(off Holland St.)
Ingelow Rd. SW8 . . . . . 5D **89**
Ingersoll Rd. W12 . . . . . 2D **71**
Ingestre Pl.
W1 . . . . 3A **14** (5E **61**)
Ingestre Rd. E7 . . . . . . 1C **54**
NW5 . . . . 1D **47**
Ingham Rd. NW6 . . . . . 1C **44**
Inglebert St.
EC1 . . . . 1B **8** (2C **62**)
Ingleborough St.
SW9 . . . . 5C **90**
Ingleby Rd. N7 . . . . 5A **34**
Inglefield Sq. E1 . . . . . 2D **79**
(off Prusom St.)
Inglemere Rd. SE23 . . 3F **121**
Inglesham Wlk. E9 . . . . 3B **52**
Ingleside Gro. SE3 . . . 2B **96**
Inglethorpe St. SW6 . . 4F **85**
Ingleton St. SW9 . . . . . 5C **90**
Inglewood Cl. E14 . . . . 5C **80**
Inglewood Rd. NW6 . . . 2C **44**
Inglis St. SE5 . . . . 4D **91**
Ingoldisthorpe Gro.
SE15 . . . . 2B **92**
Ingram Av. NW11 . . . . . 2E **31**
Ingram Cl. SE11 . . . . . 5B **76**
Ingram Ho. E3 . . . . 5A **52**
Ingrave St. SW11 . . . . . 1F **101**
Ingrebourne Ho.
BR1: Brom 5F **123**
(off Brangbourne Rd.)
NW8 . . . . 4F **59**
(off Broadley St.)
Ingress St. W4 . . . . 1A **84**
Inigo Jones Rd. SE7 . . 3F **97**
Inigo Pl. WC2 . . . . 4D **15**
Inkerman Rd. NW5 . . . . 3D **47**
Inkerman Ter. W8 . . . . 4C **72**
(off Allen St.)
Inman Rd. NW10 . . . . . 5A **42**
SW18 . . . . 5E **101**
Inner Circ.
NW1 . . . . 2B **4** (2C **60**)
Inner Pk. Rd. SW19 . . 1F **113**
Inner Temple 4C **16**
Inner Temple Hall 3B **16**
Inner Temple La.
EC4 . . . . 3B **16** (5C **62**)
Innes Gdns. SW15 . . . 4D **99**
Innis Ho. SE17 . . . . 1A **92**
(off East St.)
Inniskilling Rd. E13 . . . 1E **69**
Innis St. SE15 . . . . 3A **92**
Inn of Court &
City Yeomanry Mus.
. . . . 1A **16**
(off Chancery La.)
Innovation Cen., The
E14 . . . . 3E **81**
(off Marsh Wall)
Inskip Cl. E10 . . . . 4D **39**

Institute of Archaeology
. . . . 3B **6**
(off Gordon Sq.)
Institute of Classical Studies
. . . . 3B **6**
(off Gordon Sq.)
Institute of Contemporary Arts
. . . . 2C **22**
Institute Pl. E8 . . . . 2D **51**
Integer Gdns. E11 . . . . 2F **39**
International Bus. Pk.
E15 . . . . 5F **53**
International Ho. E1 . . . 5F **19**
(off St Katharine's Way)
Inver Cl. E5 . . . . 4E **37**
Inver Ct. W2 . . . . 5D **59**
W6 . . . . 4C **70**
Inverforth Cl. NW3 . . . . 4E **31**
Invergarry Ho. NW6 . . . 1D **59**
(off Carlton Va.)
Inverine Rd. SE7 . . . . . 1D **97**
Invermead Cl. W6 . . . . 4C **70**
Inverness Ct. SE6 . . . . 1B **124**
Inverness Gdns. W8 . . 2D **73**
Inverness M. W2 . . . . . 1D **73**
Inverness Pl. W2 . . . . . 1D **73**
Inverness St. NW1 . . . . 5D **47**
Inverness Ter. W2 . . . . 5D **59**
Inverton Rd. SE15 . . . . 2F **107**
Invicta Plaza
SE1 . . . . 1D **25** (2D **77**)
Invicta Rd. SE3 . . . . . . 3C **96**
Invicta Sq. E3 . . . . 4C **66**
Inville Rd. SE17 . . . . . . 1F **91**
Inville Wlk. SE17 . . . . . 1F **91**
Inwen Ct. SE8 . . . . 1A **94**
Inwood Cl. NW1 . . . . . . 4E **47**
(off Rochester Sq.)
Inworth St. SW11 . . . . . 5A **88**
Inworth Wlk. N1 . . . . . . 5E **49**
(off Popham St.)
Iona Cl. SE6 . . . . 5C **108**
Ion Ct. E2 . . . . 1C **64**
Ionian Bldg. E14 . . . . . 1A **80**
Ionian Ho. E1 . . . . 3F **65**
(off Duckett St.)
Ion Sq. E2 . . . . 1C **64**
Ipsden Bldgs. SE1 . . . . 2C **24**
Ipswich Ho. SE4 . . . . . 3F **107**
Ireland Yd. EC4 . . . . . . 3E **17**
(off St Andrew's Hill)
Irene Rd. SW6 . . . . 4C **86**
Ireton St. E3 . . . . 3C **66**
Iris Ct. SE14 . . . . 4E **93**
(off Briant St.)
Iron Bri. Cl. NW10 . . . . . 2A **42**
Iron Bri. Ho. NW1 . . . . 4B **46**
Iron Mill Pl. SW18 . . . . 4D **101**
Iron Mill Rd. SW18 . . . 4D **101**
Ironmonger La.
EC2 . . . . 3A **18** (5E **63**)
Ironmonger Pas. EC1 . . 2A **10**
(off Ironmonger Row)
Ironmonger Row
EC1 . . . . 2A **10** (2E **63**)
Ironmonger Row Baths
. . . . 2A **10**
(off Ironmonger Row)
Ironmongers Pl. E14 . . 5C **80**
Ironside Cl. SE16 . . . . . 3F **79**

Ironside Ho. E9 . . . . 1A 52
Irvine Ho. N7 . . . . 3B 48
  (off Caledonian Rd.)
Irving Gro. SW9 . . . . 5B 90
Irving Ho. SE17 . . . . 1D 91
  (off Doddington Gro.)
Irving Mans. W14. . . . . . . 2A 86
  (off Queen's Club Gdns.)
Irving M. N1 . . . . 3E 49
Irving Rd. W14 . . . . 4F 71
Irving St.
  WC2 . . . . 5C 14 (1F 75)
Irving Way NW9 . . . . 1C 28
Irwell Est. SE16 . . . . 4E 79
Irwin Gdns. NW10 . . . . . . 5D 43
Isaac Way SE1 . . . . 3A 26
  (off Lant St.)
Isabella Ho. SE11 . . . . . . 1D 91
  (off Othello Cl.)
  W6 . . . . 1E 85
  (off Queen Caroline St.)
Isabella Rd. E9 . . . . 2E 51
Isabella St.
  SE1 . . . . 2D 25 (2D 77)
Isabel St. SW9 . . . . 4B 90
Isambard M. E14 . . . . 4E 81
Isambard Pl. SE16 . . . . . . 2E 79
Isel Way SE22 . . . . 3A 106
Isis Cl. SW15 . . . . 2E 99
Isis Ho. NW8 . . . . 3F 59
  (off Church St. Est.)
Isis St. SW18 . . . . 2E 115
Island Row E14 . . . . 5B 66
Islay Wlk. N1 . . . . 3E 49
  (off Douglas Rd. Sth.)
Isleden Ho. N1 . . . . 5E 49
  (off Prebend St.)
Isledon Rd. N7 . . . . 5C 34
ISLEDON VILLAGE . . 5C 34
Isley Ct. SW8 . . . . 5E 89
ISLINGTON 4D 49
Islington Grn. N1 . . . . 5D 49
Islington High St.
  N1 . . . . 1C 62
  (not continuous)
Islington Mus. 4D 49
Islington Pk. M. N1 . . . . . 4D 49
Islington Pk. St. N1 . . . . 4C 48
Islington Tennis Cen.
  . . . . 3A 48
Islip St. NW5 . . . . 2E 47
Ismailia Rd. E7 . . . . 4D 55
Isom Cl. E13 . . . . 2D 69
Ivanhoe Ho. E3 . . . . 1A 66
  (off Grove Rd.)
Ivanhoe Rd. SE5 . . . . . . 1B 106
Ivatt Pl. W14 . . . . 1B 86
Iveagh Cl. E9 . . . . 5F 51
Iveagh Ct. E1 . . . . 3F 19
Iveagh Ho. SW9 . . . . 5D 91
  SW10 . . . . 3E 87
  (off King's Rd.)
Ive Farm Cl. E10 . . . . . . 4C 38
Ive Farm La. E10 . . . . . . 4C 38
Iveley Rd. SW4 . . . . 5E 89
Iverna Ct. W8 . . . . 4C 72
Iverna Gdns. W8 . . . . 4C 72
Iverson Rd. NW6 . . . . 3B 44
Ives Rd. E16 . . . . 4A 68
Ives St. SW3 . . . . 5A 74

Ivestor Ter. SE23 . . . . . 5E 107
Ivimey St. E2 . . . . 2C 64
Ivinghoe Ho. N7 . . . . 2F 47
Ivor Ct. N8 . . . . 1A 34
  NW1 . . . . 3B 60
  (off Gloucester Pl.)
Ivories, The N1 . . . . 4E 49
  (off Northampton St.)
Ivor Pl. NW1 . . . . . 4A 4 (3B 60)
Ivor St. NW1 . . . . 4E 47
Ivorydown
  BR1: Brom 4C 124
Ivory Ho. E1 . . . . 2B 78
Ivory Sq. SW11 . . . . 1E 101
Ivybridge Ct. NW1 . . . . . 4D 47
  (off Lewis St.)
Ivybridge La.
  WC2 . . . . 5E 15 (1A 76)
Ivychurch La. SE17 . . . . . 1B 92
Ivy Cotts. E14 . . . . 1E 81
Ivy Ct. SE16 . . . . 1C 92
  (off Argyle Way)
Ivydale Rd. SE15 . . . . . 1F 107
Ivyday Gro. SW16 . . . . . 3B 118
Ivy Gdns. N8 . . . . 1A 34
Ivymount Rd.
  SE27 . . . . 3C 118
Ivy Rd. E16 . . . . 5C 68
  E17 . . . . 1C 38
  NW2 . . . . 1E 43
  SE4 . . . . 2B 108
  SW17 . . . . 5A 116
Ivy St. N1 . . . . 1A 64
Ixworth Pl. SW3 . . . . 1A 88

J

Jacana Ct. E1 . . . . 1B 78
  (off Star Pl.)
Jacaranda Gro. E8 . . . . . 4B 50
Jack Clow Rd. E15 . . . . . 1A 68
Jack Dash Ho. E14 . . . . . 3E 81
  (off Lawn Ho. Cl.)
Jack Dash Way E6 . . . . . 3F 69
Jackman Ho. E1 . . . . 2D 79
  (off Watts St.)
Jackman M. NW10 . . . . . 5A 28
Jackman St. E8 . . . . 5D 51
Jackson Cl. E9 . . . . 4E 51
Jackson Ct. E7 . . . . 3D 55
Jackson Rd. N7 . . . . 1B 48
Jacksons La. N6 . . . . 2C 32
Jacksons Lane Theatre
  . . . . 1D 33
  (off Jacksons La.)
Jacks Pl. E1 . . . . 5F 11
  (off Corbet Pl.)
Jack Walker Ct. N5 . . . . 1D 49
Jacobin Lodge N7 . . . . . 2A 48
Jacobs Ho. E13 . . . . 2E 69
  (off New City Rd.)
Jacob St. SE1 . . . . 3C 78
Jacob's Well M.
  W1 . . . . 1C 12 (4C 60)
  (off Sutton Way)
Jacotts Ho. W10 . . . . 3E 57
  (off Grange Rd.)
Jacqueline Creft Ter.
  N6 . . . . 1C 32
  (off Grange Rd.)

Jade Cl. E16 . . . . 5F 69
  NW2 . . . . 2F 29
Jade Ter. NW6 . . . . 4E 45
Jaffray Pl. SE27 . . . . . . 4D 119
Jaggard Way SW12 . . . . 5B 102
Jagger Ho. SW11 . . . . . . 4B 88
  (off Rosenau Rd.)
Jago Wlk. SE5 . . . . 3F 91
Jamaica Rd.
  SE1 . . . . 4F 27 (3B 78)
  SE16 . . . . 3B 78
Jamaica St. E1 . . . . 5E 65
James Allens School
  Swimming Pool . . . 3A 106
James Anderson Ct.
  E2 . . . . 1A 64
  (off Kingsland Rd.)
James Av. NW2 . . . . 2E 43
James Boswell Cl.
  SW16 . . . . 4B 118
James Brine Ho.
  E2 . . . . 1F 11
  (off Ravenscroft St.)
James Campbell Ho.
  E2 . . . . 1E 65
  (off Old Ford Rd.)
James Cl. E13 . . . . 1C 68
  NW11 . . . . 1A 30
James Collins Cl.
  W9 . . . . 3B 58
James Ct. N1 . . . . 5E 49
  (off Raynor Pl.)
James Docherty Ho.
  E2 . . . . 1D 65
  (off Patriot Sq.)
James Hammett Ho.
  E2 . . . . 1F 11
  (off Ravenscroft St.)
James Ho. E1 . . . . 3A 66
  (off Solebay St.)
  SE16 . . . . 3F 79
  (off Wolfe Cres.)
James Joyce Wlk.
  SE24 . . . . 2D 105
James La. E10 . . . . 2E 39
  E11 . . . . 2F 39
James Lind Ho. SE8 . . . . 5B 80
  (off Grove St.)
James Middleton Ho.
  E2 . . . . 2D 65
  (off Middleton St.)
Jameson Ct. E2 . . . . 1E 65
  (off Russia La.)
Jameson Ho. SE11 . . . . . 1B 90
  (off Glasshouse Wlk.)
Jameson Lodge N6 . . . . 1E 33
Jameson St. W8 . . . . 2C 72
James Stewart Ho.
  NW6 . . . . 4B 44
James St.
  W1 . . . . 3C 12 (5C 60)
  WC2 . . . . 3E 15 (1A 76)
James Stroud Ho.
  SE17 . . . . 1E 91
  (off Bronti Cl.)
Jamon Ter. SW14 . . . . . 1A 98
  (off Church Path)
Jamestown Rd. NW1 . . . . 5D 47
Jamestown Way E14 . . . 1F 81
Jamuna Cl. E14 . . . . 4A 66

Jane Austen Hall E16. . . 2D **83**
(off Wesley Av.)
Jane Austen Ho.
SW1 . . . . 1E **89**
(off Churchill Gdns.)
Jane St. E1. . . . . 5D **65**
Janet Adegoke Leisure Cen.
. . . . 1C **70**
Janet St. E14 . . . . 4C **80**
Janeway Pl. SE16 . . . . 3D **79**
Janeway St. SE16 . . . . 3C **78**
Jansen Wlk. SW11 . . 1F **101**
NW10 . . . . 5A **28**
Janson Cl. E15 . . . . . . 2A **54**
NW10 . . . . 5A **28**
Janson Rd. E15 . . . . . . 2A **54**
Japan Cres. N4 . . . . . . 3B **34**
Jardine Rd. E1 . . . . . . 1F **79**
Jarman Ho. E1 . . . . . . 4E **65**
(off Jubilee St.)
SE16 . . . . 5F **79**
(off Hawkstone Rd.)
Jarrett Cl. SW2 . . . . 1D **119**
Jarrow Rd. SE16. . . . . 5E **79**
Jarrow Way E9 . . . . . . 1B **52**
Jarvis Rd. SE22 . . . . 2A **106**
Jasmin Cl. SE12. . . . 4B **110**
Jasmine Ct. SW19 . . . 5C **114**
Jasmin Lodge SE16 . . 1D **93**
(off Sherwood Gdns.)
Jason Ct. SW9 . . . . . . 4C **90**
(off Southey Rd.)
W1 . . . . 2C **12**
Jasper Pas. SE19 . . . 5B **120**
Jasper Rd. E16 . . . . . . 5F **69**
SE19 . . . . 5B **120**
Jasper Wlk. N1 . . . . . . 1B **10**
Java Wharf SE1 . . . . . 3B **78**
(off Shad Thames)
Jay M. SW7 . . . . 3E **73**
Jean Darling Ho.
SW10 . . . . 2F **87**
(off Milman's St.)
Jean Ho. SW17 . . . . . 5A **116**
Jean Pardies Ho. E1. . 4E **65**
(off Jubilee St.)
Jebb Av. SW2 . . . . . . 4A **104**
(not continuous)
Jebb St. E3 . . . . 1C **66**
Jedburgh Rd. E13 . . . 2E **69**
Jedburgh St. SW11 . . 2C **102**
Jeddo M. W12 . . . . 3B **70**
Jeddo Rd. W12 . . . . . . 3B **70**
Jefferson Bldg. E14 . . 3C **80**
Jeffrey Row SE12. . . . 3D **111**
Jeffrey's Pl. NW1 . . . . 4E **47**
Jeffreys Rd. SW4 . . . . 5A **90**
Jeffrey's St. NW1 . . . . 4E **47**
Jeffreys Walk SW4 . . . 5A **90**
Jeger Av. E2 . . . . 5B **50**
Jeken Rd. SE9 . . . . . . 2E **111**
Jelf Rd. SW2 . . . . 3C **104**
Jellicoe Ho. E2. . . . . . . 1C **64**
(off Ropley St.)
NW1 . . . . 3D **61**
Jellicoe Rd. E13 . . . . . 3C **68**
(off Myers La.)
Jemotts Ct. SE14 . . . . . 2F **93**
(off Myers La.)
Jenkinson Ho. E2 . . . . 2F **65**
(off Usk St.)
Jenkins Rd. E13 . . . . . 3D **69**

Jenner Av. W3 . . . . 4A **56**
Jenner Ho. SE3 . . . . . . 2A **96**
(off Restell Cl.)
WC1 . . . . 3E **7**
(off Hunter St.)
Jenner Pl. SW13 . . . . . 2D **85**
Jenner Rd. N16 . . . . . 5B **36**
Jennifer Ho.
SE11 . . . . 5C **76**
(off Reedworth St.)
Jennifer Rd.
BR1: Brom 3B **124**
Jenningsbury Ho.
SW3 . . . . 1A **88**
(off Cale St.)
Jennings Ho. SE10 . . . 1F **95**
(off Old Woolwich Rd.)
Jennings Rd. SE22. . . 4B **106**
Jenny Hammond Cl.
E11 . . . . 5B **40**
Jephson Ct. SW4 . . . . 5A **90**
Jephson Ho. SE17 . . . . 2D **91**
(off Doddington Gro.)
Jephson Rd. E7 . . . . . 4E **55**
Jephson St. SE5 . . . . . 4F **91**
Jephtha Rd.
SW18 . . . . 4C **100**
Jepson Ho. SW6 . . . . . 4D **87**
(off Pearscroft Rd.)
Jerdan Pl. SW6 . . . . . 3C **86**
Jeremiah St. E14 . . . . 5D **67**
Jeremy Bentham Ho.
E2 . . . . 2C **64**
(off Mansford St.)
Jermyn St.
SW1 . . . . . . 1F **21** (2E **75**)
Jermyn Street Theatre
. . . . 5B **14**
(off Jermyn St.)
Jerningham Ct. SE14 . . 4A **94**
Jerningham Rd.
SE14 . . . . 5A **94**
Jerome Cres. NW8. . . . 3A **60**
Jerome Ho. NW1 . . . . . 4A **60**
(off Lisson Gro.)
SW7 . . . . 5F **73**
(off Glendower Pl.)
Jerome St.
E1. . . . . 5F **11** (3B **64**)
Jerrard St. SE13 . . . . 1D **109**
Jerrold St.
N1 . . . . 1E **11** (1A **64**)
Jersey Ho. N1. . . . . . . 3E **49**
Jersey Rd. E11 . . . . . . 3F **39**
E16 . . . . 5E **69**
N1 . . . . 3E **49**
Jersey St. E2 . . . . 2D **65**
Jerusalem Pas.
EC1 . . . . 4D **9** (3D **63**)
Jervis Bay Ho.
E14 . . . . 5F **67**
(off Blair St.)
Jervis Ct. SE10. . . . . . . 4E **95**
(off Blissett St.)
W1 . . . . 3E **13**
Jerviston Gdns.
SW16 . . . . 5C **118**
Jerwood Space Art Gallery
. . . . 3F **25**
Jessam Av. E5 . . . . . . 3D **37**

Jessel Ho. SW1 . . . . . . 5F **75**
(off Page St.)
WC1 . . . . 2D **7**
(off Judd St.)
Jessel Mans. W14 . . . . 2A **86**
(off Queen's Club Gdns.)
Jesse Rd. E10 . . . . 3E **39**
Jessica Rd. SW18 . . . 4E **101**
Jessie Blythe La.
N19 . . . . 2A **34**
Jessie Duffett Ho.
SE5 . . . . 3E **91**
(off Pitman St.)
Jessie Wood Ct.
SW9 . . . . 3C **90**
(off Caldwell St.)
Jesson Ho. SE17 . . . . . 5F **77**
(off Orb St.)
Jessop Ct. N1. . . . . . . 1D **63**
Jessop Rd. SE24 . . . . 2D **105**
Jessop Sq. E14 . . . . . . 2C **80**
(off Heron Quay)
Jevington Way
SE12. . . . . 1D **125**
Jewel House E1 . . . . . . 5F **19**
(in Tower of London)
Jewel Tower 5D **23**
(off College M.)
Jewish Mus.
Camden Town 5D **47**
Jewry St.
EC3. . . . . 3F **19** (5B **64**)
Jew's Row SW18 . . . . 2D **101**
Jews' Wlk. SE26 . . . . 4D **121**
Jeymer Av. NW2 . . . . . 2D **43**
Jeypore Pas. SW18 . . 4E **101**
Jeypore Rd. SW18. . . 5E **101**
Jim Griffiths Ho.
SW6 . . . . 2B **86**
(off Clem Attlee Ct.)
Joan Bicknell Cen., The
. . . . 2F **115**
Joan Cres. SE9 . . . . . . 5F **111**
Joanna Ho. W6. . . . . . . 1E **85**
(off Queen Caroline St.)
Joan St. SE1. . . 2D **25** (2D **77**)
Jocelin Ho. N1 . . . . . . 5B **48**
(off Barnsbury Est.)
Jocelyn St. SE15 . . . . 4C **92**
Jockey's Flds.
WC1. . . . . 5A **8** (4B **62**)
Jodane St. SE8. . . . . . 5B **80**
Jodrell Rd. E3 . . . . . . 5B **52**
Joe Hunte Ct. SE27 . . 5D **119**
Johanna St.
SE1 . . . . 4B **24** (3C **76**)
John Adam St.
WC2. . . . . 5E **15** (1A **76**)
John Aird Ct. W2 . . . . . 4E **59**
(off Howley Pl., not continuous)
John Archer Way
SW18 . . . . 4F **101**
John Ashby Cl. SW2 . . 4A **104**
John Baird Ct. SE26. . . 4E **121**
John Barker Rd. NW6 . . 4A **44**
John Barnes Wlk.
E15 . . . . 3B **54**
John Betts' Ho. W12 . . 4B **70**
John Brent Ho. SE8 . . . 5F **79**
(off Bush Rd.)

John Buck Ho.
NW10 . . . . 5B *42*
John Campbell Rd.
N16 . . . . 2A *50*
John Carpenter St.
EC4 . . . . . . 4D *17* (1D *77*)
John Cartwright Ho.
E2 . . . . 2D *65*
(off Old Bethnal Grn. Rd.)
John Drinkwater Cl.
E11 . . . . 2B *40*
John Fearon Wlk.
W10 . . . . 2A *58*
(off Dart St.)
John Felton Rd.
SE16 . . . . 3C *78*
John Fielden Ho. *E2* . . 2D *65*
(off Canrobert St.)
John Fisher St. E1 . . . . 1C *78*
John Harrison Way
SE10 . . . . 4B *82*
John Horner M. N1 . . . . 1E *63*
John Islip St. SW1 . . . . 5F *75*
John Kennedy Ct. *N1* . . 3F *49*
(off Newington Grn. Rd.)
John Kennedy Ho.
SE16 . . . . 5F *79*
(off Rotherhithe Old Rd.)
John Knight Lodge
SW6 . . . . 3C *86*
John McDonald Ho.
E14 . . . . 4E *81*
(off Glengall Gro.)
John McKenna Wlk.
SE16 . . . . 4C *78*
John Masefield Ho.
N15 . . . . 1F *35*
(off Fladbury Rd.)
John Maurice Cl.
SE17 . . . . 5F *77*
John Orwell Sports Cen.
. . . . 2D *79*
John Parker Sq.
SW11 . . . . 1F *101*
John Parry Ct. *N1* 1A *64*
(off Hare Wlk.)
John Penn Ho. SE14 . . 3B *94*
(off Amersham Va.)
John Penn St. SE13 . . 4D *95*
John Prince's St.
W1 . . . . 2E *13* (5D *61*)
John Pritchard Ho.
E1 . . . . 3C *64*
(off Buxton St.)
John Ratcliffe Ho.
NW6 . . . . 2C *58*
(off Chippenham Gdns.)
John Rennie Wlk. E1 . . 1D *79*
John Roll Way SE16 . . 4C *78*
John Ruskin St.
SE5 . . . . 3D *91*
John Scurr Ho. E14 . . 5A *66*
(off Ratcliffe La.)
John Silkin La. SE8 . . 1F *93*
John's M.
W1 . . . . 1A *9* (2D *60*)
John Smith Av.
SW6 . . . . 3B *86*
John Smith M. E14 . . . 1F *81*
Johnson Cl. E8 . . . . . . 5C *50*

Johnson Ho. *E2* 2C *64*
(off Roberta St.)
NW1 . . . . 1E *61*
(off Cranleigh St.)
NW3 . . . . 4B *46*
(off Adelaide Rd.)
SW1 . . . . 5C *74*
(off Cundy St.)
SW8 . . . . 3F *89*
(off Wandsworth Rd.)
Johnson Lodge W9 . . 4C *58*
(off Admiral Wlk.)
Johnson Mans. W14 . . 2A *86*
(off Queen's Club Gdns.)
Johnson's Ct. EC4 . . . . 5C *62*
Johnson's Pl. SW1 . . . . 1E *89*
Johnson St. E1 . . . . . . 1E *79*
John Spencer Sq. N1 . . 3D *49*
John's Pl. E1 . . . . 5D *65*
Johnston Cl. SW9 . . . . 4B *90*
Johnstone Ho. SE13 . . 1F *109*
(off Belmont Hill)
Johnston Ter. NW2 . . . . 5F *29*
John Strachey Ho.
SW6 . . . . 2B *86*
(off Clem Attlee Ct.)
John St. E15 . . . . 5B *54*
WC1 . . . . 4A *8* (3B *62*)
John Strype St. E10 . . 3D *39*
John Trundle Ct. EC2 . . 5F *9*
John Trundle Highwalk
EC2 . . . . 5F *9*
(off Beech St.)
John Tucker Ho. E14 . . 4C *80*
(off Mellish St.)
John Wesley Highwalk
EC2 . . . . 1F *17*
(off Barbican)
John Wheatley Ho.
SW6 . . . . 2B *86*
(off Clem Attlee Ct.)
John Williams Cl.
SE14 . . . . 2F *93*
John Woolley Cl.
SE13 . . . . 2A *110*
Joiners Arms Yd.
SE5 . . . . 4F *91*
Joiners Pl. N5 . . . . 1F *49*
Joiner St.
SE1 . . . . 2C *26* (2F *77*)
Joiners Yd. *N1* 1E *7*
(off Caledonia St.)
Jonathan St. SE11 . . . . 1B *90*
Jones Ho. E14 . . . . . . 5F *67*
(off Blair St.)
Jones M. SW15 . . . . . . 2A *100*
Jones Rd. E13 . . . . . . 3D *69*
Jones St.
W1 . . . . 5D *13* (1D *75*)
Jonson Ho. *SE1* 5C *26*
(off Burbage Cl.)
Jordan Ct. SW15 . . . . 2F *99*
Jordan Ho. *N1* 5F *49*
(off Colville St.)
SE4 . . . . 2F *107*
(off St Norbert Rd.)
Jordans Ho. NW8 . . . . 3F *59*
(off Capland St.)
Joscoyne Ho. E1 . . . . . 5D *65*
(off Philpot St.)

Joseph Conrad Ho.
SW1 . . . . 5E *75*
(off Tachbrook St.)
Joseph Ct. N16 . . . . . . 1A *36*
(off Amhurst Pk.)
Joseph Hardcastle Cl.
SE14 . . . . 3F *93*
Josephine Av. SW2 . . 3B *104*
Joseph Irwin Ho. E14 . . 1B *80*
(off Gill St.)
Joseph Lister Ct. E7 . . 4C *54*
Joseph Powell Cl.
SW12 . . . . 4E *103*
Joseph Priestley Ho.
E2 . . . . 2D *65*
(off Canrobert St.)
Joseph Ray Rd. E11 . . 4A *40*
Joseph St. E3 . . . . 3B *66*
Joseph Trotter Cl. EC1 . . 2C *8*
Joshua St. E14 . . . . . . 5E *67*
Joslings Cl. W12 . . . . . 1C *70*
Josseline Ct. E3 . . . . . 1A *66*
(off Ford St.)
Joubert St. SW11 . . . . 5B *88*
Jowett St. SE15 . . . . . 3B *92*
Jowitt Ho. *E2* 2F *65*
(off Morpeth St.)
Joyce Page Cl. SE7 . . . 2F *97*
Joyce Wlk. SW2 . . . . . 4C *104*
Jubilee, The SE10 . . . . 3D *95*
Jubilee Bldgs. NW8 . . 5F *45*
Jubilee Cl. NW9 . . . . . . 1A *28*
Jubilee Cres. E14 . . . . 4E *81*
Jubilee Hall Sports Cen.
. . . . 4E *15*
(off Tavistock St.)
Jubilee Ho. SE11 . . . . 5C *76*
(off Reedworth St.)
WC1 . . . . 3F *7*
Jubilee Mans. *E1* 5E *65*
(off Jubilee St.)
Jubilee Mkt. WC2 . . . . 4E *15*
Jubilee Pl. SW3 . . . . . . 1A *88*
Jubilee Pl. Shop. Mall
E14 . . . . 2D *81*
(off Bank St.)
Jubilee Sports Cen. & Baths
. . . . 2B *58*
Jubilee St. E1 . . . . 5E *65*
Jubilee Walkway
SE1 . . . . 5E *17* (1D *77*)
Jubilee Yd. SE1 . . . . . . 3F *27*
Judd St. WC1 . . . 2D *7* (2A *62*)
Jude St. E16 . . . . 5B *68*
Judges Wlk. NW3 . . . . 5E *31*
Juer Ho. *SW11* 3A *88*
(off Juer St.)
Juer St. SW11 . . . . 3A *88*
Julia Ct. E17 . . . . 1D *39*
Julia Garfield M. E16 . . 2D *83*
(not continuous)
Julian Ho. SE21 . . . . . 4A *120*
Julian Pl. E14 . . . . 1D *95*
Julian Tayler Path
SE23 . . . . 2D *121*
Julia St. NW5 . . . . 1C *46*
Juliet Ho. *N1* 1A *64*
(off Arden Est.)
Juliette Rd. E13 . . . . . . 1C *68*

Julius Nyerere Cl.
  N1 . . . . .5B **48**
    (off Copenhagen St.)
  SW11 . . . . .1A **102**
Junction App. SE13 . . 1E **109**
Junction Av. NW10 . . . 3E **57**
Junction M. W2 . . . . . . 5A **60**
Junction Pl. W2 . . . . . . 5F **59**
    (off Praed St.)
Junction Rd. E13 . . . . 1D **69**
  N19 . . . . .1E **47**
Juniper Ct. W8 . . . . . . 4D **73**
    (off St Mary's Pl.)
Juniper Cres. NW1 . . . 4C **46**
Juniper Ho. SE14 . . . . 3E **93**
  W10 . . . . .3A **58**
    (off Fourth Av.)
Juniper St. E1 . . . . 1E **79**
Juno Ct. SW9 . . . . 3C **90**
    (off Caldwell St.)
Juno Way SE14 . . . . . 2F **93**
Juno Way Ind. Est.
  SE14 . . . . .2F **93**
Jupiter Ct. SW9 . . . . . 3C **90**
    (off Caldwell St.)
Jupiter Ho. E14 . . . . . 1D **95**
    (off St Davids Sq.)
Jupiter Way N7 . . . . . . 3B **48**
Jupp Rd. E15 . . . . 4F **53**
Jupp Rd. W. E15 . . . . . 5F **53**
Jura Ho. SE16 . . . . . . 5F **79**
    (off Plough Way)
Jurston Ct. SE1 . . . . . . 4C **24**
Justice Wlk. SW3 . . . . 2A **88**
Justines Pl. E2 . . . . . . 2F **65**
Jutland Cl. N19 . . . . . . 3A **34**
Jutland Ho. SE5 . . . . . 5E **91**
Jutland Rd. E13 . . . . . 3C **68**
  SE6 . . . . .5E **109**
Juxon Ho. EC4 . . . . . . 3E **17**
    (off St Paul's Chyd.)
Juxon St. SE11 . . . . . . 5B **76**
JVC Bus. Pk. NW2 . . . 3C **28**

K

Kambala Rd. SW11 . . 1F **101**
Kangley Bri. Rd.
  SE26 . . . . .5B **122**
Kangley Bus. Cen.
  SE26 . . . . .5B **122**
Karanjia St. NW2 . . . . 3E **43**
Kara Way NW2 . . . . . . 1F **43**
Karen Ter. E11 . . . . . . 4B **40**
Kashmir Rd. SE7 . . . . 3F **97**
Kassala Rd. SW11 . . . 4B **88**
Katherine Cl. SE16 . . . 2F **79**
Katherine Ct. SE23 . . 1D **121**
Katherine Gdns.
  SE9 . . . . .2F **111**
Katherine Rd. E6 . . . . 2E **55**
  E7 . . . . .2E **55**
Katherine Sq. W11 . . . 2A **72**
Kathleen Godfree Ct.
  SW19 . . . . .5C **114**
Kathleen Rd. SW11 . . 1B **102**
Kay Rd. SW9 . . . . 5A **90**
Kay St. E2 . . . . 1C **64**
  E15 . . . . 4F **53**

Kean Ho. SE17 . . . . . . 2D **91**
Kean St.
  WC2 . . . . 3F **15** (5B **62**)
Keats Av. E16 . . . . 2D **83**
Keats Cl. E11 . . . . 1D **41**
  NW3 . . . . .1A **46**
  SE1 . . . . .5B **78**
  SW19 . . . . .5F **115**
Keats Est. N16 . . . . . . 4B **36**
    (off Kyverdale St.)
Keats Gro. NW3 . . . . . 1A **46**
Keats House 1A **46**
Keats Ho. E2 . . . . 2E **65**
    (off Roman Rd.)
  SE5 . . . . .3E **91**
    (off Elmington Est.)
  SW1 . . . . .2E **89**
    (off Churchill Gdns.)
Keats Pl. EC2 . . . . 1B **18**
    (off Moorfields)
Kebbell Ter. E7 . . . . . . 2D **55**
    (off Claremont Rd.)
Keble Pl. SW13 . . . . . 2D **85**
Keble St. SW17 . . . . . 4E **115**
Kedge Ho. E14 . . . . . . 4C **80**
    (off Tiller Rd.)
Kedleston Wlk. E2 . . . 2D **65**
Keedonwood Rd.
  BR1: Brom 5A **124**
Keel Cl. SE16 . . . . 2F **79**
Keel Ct. E14 . . . . 1F **81**
    (off Newport Av.)
Keeley St.
  WC2 . . . . 3F **15** (5B **62**)
Keeling Ho. E2 . . . . . . 1D **65**
    (off Claredale St.)
Keeling Rd. SE9 . . . . . 3F **111**
Keens Cl. SW16 . . . . . 5F **117**
Keen's Yd. N1 . . . . 3D **49**
Keep, The SE3 . . . . . . 5C **96**
Keepier Wharf E14 . . . 1F **79**
    (off Narrow St.)
Keeton's Rd. SE16 . . . 4D **79**
    (not continuous)
Keevil Dr. SW19 . . . . . 5F **99**
Keighley Cl. N7 . . . . . . 2A **48**
Keildon Rd. SW11 . . . 2B **102**
Keir, The SW19 . . . . . 5E **113**
Keir Hardie Ct.
  NW10 . . . . .4B **42**
Keir Hardie Est. E5 . . 3D **37**
Keir Hardie Ho. N19 . . 2F **33**
  W6 . . . . .2E **85**
    (off Fulham Pal. Rd.)
Keith Connor Cl.
  SW8 . . . . .1D **103**
Keith Gro. W12 . . . . . . 3C **70**
Keith Ho. NW6 . . . . . . 1D **59**
    (off Carlton Va.)
Kelbrook Rd. SE3 . . . . 5F **97**
Kelby Ho. N7 . . . . 3B **48**
    (off Sutterton St.)
Kelceda Cl. NW2 . . . . 4C **28**
Kelfield Ct. W10 . . . . . 5F **57**
Kelfield Gdns. W10 . . . 5E **57**
Kelfield M. W10 . . . . . 5F **57**
Kelland Rd. E13 . . . . . 3C **68**
Kellaway Rd. SE3 . . . . 5F **97**
Keller Cres. E12 . . . . . 1F **55**
Kellerton Rd. SE13 . . . 3A **110**

Kellet Ho's. WC1 . . . . . 2E **7**
    (off Tankerton St.)
Kellett Ho. N1 . . . . 5A **50**
    (off Colville St.)
Kellett Rd. SW2 . . . . . 2C **104**
Kellino St. SW17 . . . . 4B **116**
Kellow Ho. SE1 . . . . . . 3B **26**
    (off Tennis St.)
Kell St. SE1 . . . . . . 5E **25** (4D **77**)
Kelly Av. SE15 . . . . . . 3B **92**
Kelly Cl. NW10 . . . . . . 5A **28**
Kelly Ct. E14 . . . . 1C **80**
    (off Garford St.)
Kelly M. W9 . . . . 3B **58**
Kelly St. NW1 . . . . 3D **47**
Kelman Cl. SW4 . . . . . 5F **89**
Kelmore Gro. SE22 . . 2C **106**
Kelmscott Gdns.
  W12 . . . . .4C **70**
Kelmscott Leisure Cen.
  . . . . .1B **38**
Kelmscott Rd.
  SW11 . . . . .3A **102**
Kelross Pas. N5 . . . . . 1E **49**
Kelross Rd. N5 . . . . . . 1E **49**
Kelsall Cl. SE3 . . . . . . 5D **97**
Kelsey St. E2 . . . . 3C **64**
Kelson Ho. E14 . . . . . . 4E **81**
Kelso Pl. W8 . . . . 4D **73**
Kelvedon Ho. SW8 . . . 4A **90**
Kelvedon Rd. SW6 . . . 3B **86**
Kelvin Ct. W11 . . . . . . 1C **72**
Kelvin Gro. SE26 . . . . 3D **121**
Kelvington Rd.
  SE15 . . . . .3F **107**
Kelvin Rd. N5 . . . . 1E **49**
Kember St. N1 . . . . 4B **48**
Kemble Ho. SW9 . . . . 1D **105**
    (off Barrington Rd.)
Kemble Rd. SE23 . . . . 1F **121**
Kemble St.
  WC2 . . . . 3F **15** (5B **62**)
Kemerton Rd. SE5 . . . 1E **105**
Kemeys St. E9 . . . . . . 2A **52**
Kemp Ct. SW8 . . . . . . 3A **90**
    (off Hartington Rd.)
Kempe Ho. SE1 . . . . . . 4F **77**
    (off Burge St.)
Kempe Rd. NW6 . . . . . 1F **57**
Kemp Ho. E2 . . . . 1F **65**
    (off Sewardstone Rd.)
  W1 . . . . .4B **14**
    (off Berwick St.)
Kempis Way SE22 . . . 3A **106**
Kemplay Rd. NW3 . . . 1F **45**
Kemps Ct. W1 . . . . 3B **14**
    (off Hopkins St.)
Kemps Dr. E14 . . . . . . 1C **80**
Kempsford Gdns.
  SW5 . . . . .1C **86**
Kempsford Rd. SE11 . . 5C **76**
    (not continuous)
Kemps Gdns. SE13 . . 3E **109**
Kempson Rd. SW6 . . . 4C **86**
Kempthorne Rd. SE8 . 5B **80**
Kempton Ct. E1 . . . . . . 4D **65**
Kemsing Ho. SE1 . . . . 4C **26**
    (off Long La.)
Kemsing Rd. SE10 . . . 1C **96**
Kemsley SE13 . . . . . . 3D **109**

Kenbrook Ho. W14 . . . . . 4B **72**
Kenbury Gdns. SE5. . . . . 5E **91**
Kenbury Mans. *SE5* *5E 91*
  (off Kenbury St.)
Kenbury St. SE5 . . . . 5E **91**
Kenchester Cl. SW8 . . . . 3A **90**
Kendal *NW1* *1E 5*
  (off Augustus St.)
Kendal Cl. SW9 . . . . 3D **91**
Kendale Rd.
  BR1: Brom 5A **124**
Kendal Ho. E9 . . . . 5E **51**
  N1 . . . . *1B 62*
  (off Priory Grn. Est.)
Kendall Pl.
  W1 . . . . 1B **12** (4C **60**)
Kendal Pl. SW15 . . . . 3B **100**
Kendal Rd. NW10 . . . . . 1C **42**
Kendal Steps *W2* *5A 60*
  (off St George's Flds.)
Kendal St. W2 . . . . 5A **60**
Kender Est. *SE14* *4E 93*
  (off Queen's Rd.)
Kender St. SE14 . . . . 3E **93**
Kendoa Rd. SW4 . . . . . . 2F **103**
Kendon Cl. E11 . . . . 1D **41**
Kendrick Ct. *SE15* *4D 93*
  (off Woods Rd.)
Kendrick M. SW7 . . . . . . 5F **73**
Kendrick Pl. SW7 . . . . . . 5F **73**
Kenilford Rd. SW12 . . . 5D **103**
Kenilworth Av.
  SW19 . . . . 5C **114**
Kenilworth Rd. E3 . . . . . 1A **66**
  NW6 . . . . 5B **44**
Kenley Wlk. W11 . . . . . . 1A **72**
Kenlor Rd. SW17 . . . . . . 5F **115**
Kenmont Gdns.
  NW10 . . . . 2D **57**
Kenmure Rd. E8 . . . . 2D **51**
Kenmure Yd. E8 . . . . 2D **51**
Kennacraig Cl. E16 . . . . 2C **82**
Kennard Ho. SW11 . . . . . 5C **88**
Kennard Rd. E15 . . . . . . 4F **53**
Kennard St. SW11 . . . . . 4C **88**
Kennedy Cl. E13 . . . . . . 1C **68**
Kennedy Cox Ho.
  E16 . . . . 4B **68**
  (off Burke St.)
Kennedy Ho. *SE11* *1B 90*
  (off Vauxhall Wlk.)
Kennedy Wlk. *SE17* . . . *5F 77*
  (off Elsted St.)
Kennet Cl. SW11 . . . . . . 2F **101**
Kennet Ct. *W9* *4C 58*
  (off Elmfield Way)
Kenneth Campbell Ho.
  NW8 . . . . *3F 59*
  (off Orchardson St.)
Kenneth Ct. SE11 . . . . . 5C **76**
Kenneth Cres. NW2 . . . . 2D **43**
Kennet Ho. *NW8* *3F 59*
  (off Church St. Est.)
Kenneth Younger Ho.
  SW6 . . . . *2B 86*
  (off Clem Attlee Ct.)
Kennet Rd. W9 . . . . 3B **58**
Kennet St. E1 . . . . 2C **78**
Kennett Wharf La.
  EC4 . . . . 4A **18**

Kenninghall Rd. E5 . . . . 5C **36**
Kenning Ho. *N1* *5A 50*
  (off Colville Est.)
Kenning St. SE16 . . . . . . 3E **79**
Kennings Way
  SE11 . . . . 1C **90**
KENNINGTON 2C **90**
Kennington Grn.
  SE11 . . . . 1C **90**
Kennington Gro.
  SE11 . . . . 2B **90**
Kennington La. SE11 . . . 1B **90**
KENNINGTON OVAL . . . 2C **90**
Kennington Oval
  SE11 . . . . 2B **90**
Kennington Pal. Ct.
  SE11 . . . . *1C 90*
  (off Sancroft St.)
Kennington Pk. Gdns.
  SE11 . . . . 2D **91**
Kennington Pk. Ho.
  SE11 . . . . *1C 90*
  (off Kennington Pk. Pl.)
Kennington Pk. Pl.
  SE11 . . . . 2C **90**
Kennington Pk. Rd.
  SE11 . . . . 2C **90**
Kennington Rd.
  SE1 . . . . 5B **24** (4C **76**)
  SE11 . . . . 5B **24** (4C **76**)
Kennistoun Ho.
  NW5 . . . . 2E **47**
Kennolees *SE21* *2F 119*
  (off Croxted Rd.)
Kennyland Ct. *NW4* . . . *1D 29*
  (off Hendon Way)
Kenrick Pl.
  W1 . . . . 1B **12** (4C **60**)
KENSAL GREEN 2E **57**
Kensal Ho. *W10* *3F 57*
  (off Ladbroke Gro.)
KENSAL RISE 1F **57**
Kensal Rd. W10 . . . . 3A **58**
KENSAL TOWN 3A **58**
Kensal Wharf W10 . . . . . 3F **57**
KENSINGTON 3D **73**
Kensington Arc. *W8*. . . *3D 73*
  (off Kensington High St.)
Kensington Cen.
  W14 . . . . 5A **72**
  (not continuous)
Kensington Chu. Ct.
  W8 . . . . 3D **73**
Kensington Chu. St.
  W8 . . . . 2C **72**
Kensington Chu. Wlk.
  W8 . . . . 3D **73**
  (not continuous)
Kensington Ct. *SE16*. . . *2F 79*
  (off King & Queen Wharf)
  W8 . . . . 3D **73**
Kensington Ct. Gdns.
  W8 . . . . *4D 73*
  (off Kensington Ct. Pl.)
Kensington Ct. M.
  W8 . . . . *4D 73*
  (off Kensington Ct. Pl.)
Kensington Ct. Pl.
  W8 . . . . 4D **73**
Kensington Gardens . . . 2E **73**

Kensington Gdns. Sq.
  W2 . . . . 5D **59**
  (not continuous)
Kensington Ga. W8 . . . . 4E **73**
Kensington Gore
  SW7 . . . . 3E **73**
Kensington Hall Gdns.
  W14 . . . . 1B **86**
Kensington Hgts. W8. . . 2C **72**
Kensington High St.
  W8 . . . . 4B **72**
  W14 . . . . 4B **72**
Kensington Ho. W14 . . . 3F **71**
Kensington Mall W8 . . . 2C **72**
Kensington Mans.
  SW5 . . . . *1C 86*
  (off Trebovir Rd.,
  not continuous)
Kensington Palace 3D **73**
Kensington Pal. Gdns.
  W8 . . . . 2D **73**
Kensington Pk. Gdns.
  W11 . . . . 1B **72**
Kensington Pk. M.
  W11 . . . . 5B **58**
Kensington Pk. Rd.
  W11 . . . . 5B **58**
Kensington Pl. W8 . . . . . 2C **72**
Kensington Rd. SW7 . . . 3D **73**
  W8 . . . . 3D **73**
Kensington Sports Cen.
  . . . . 1A **72**
Kensington Sq. W8 . . . . 4D **73**
Kensington Village
  W14 . . . . 5B **72**
Kensington W. W14 . . . . 5A **72**
Kensworth Ho. *EC1* . . . *2C 10*
  (off Cranwood St.)
Kent Ct. E2 . . . . 1B **64**
Kent Ho. SE1 . . . . 1B **92**
  SW1 . . . . *1F 89*
  (off Aylesford St.)
  W4 . . . . *1A 84*
  (off Devonshire St.)
Kent Ho. La.
  BR3: Beck. 5A **122**
Kent Ho. Rd. SE26 . . . . 5A **122**
Kentish Bldgs.
  SE1. . . . . 2B **26** (3F **77**)
KENTISH TOWN 2D **47**
Kentish Town Forum . . . 2D **47**
Kentish Town Ind. Est.
  NW5 . . . . 2D **47**
Kentish Town Rd.
  NW1 . . . . 4D **47**
  NW5 . . . . 4D **47**
Kentish Town Sports Cen.
  . . . . 3D **47**
Kentmere Ho. SE15 . . . . 2E **93**
Kenton Ct. *SE26* *4A 122*
  (off Adamsrill Rd.)
  W14 . . . . 4B **72**
Kenton Ho. *E1* *3E 65*
  (off Mantus Cl.)
Kenton Rd. E9. . . . . 3F **51**
Kenton St.
  WC1. . . . . 3D **7** (3A **62**)
Kent Pk. Ind. Est.
  SE15 . . . . 2D **93**
Kent Pas. NW1. . . . . 3B **60**

Kent St. E2 . . . . 1B 64
E13 . . . . 2E 69
Kent Ter. NW1 . . . . 2A 60
Kent Wlk. SW9 . . . . . . 2D 105
Kentwell Cl. SE4 . . . . 2A 108
Kent Wharf SE8 . . . . . . 3D 95
(off Creekside)
Kentwode Grn. SW13 . . 3C 84
Kenward Rd. SE9 . . . . 3E 111
Kenward Way SW11 . . . 5C 88
Kenway Rd. SW5 . . . . . 5D 73
Ken Wilson Ho. E2 . . . . 1C 64
(off Pritchards Rd.)
Kenwood Cl. NW3 . . . . . 3F 31
Kenwood House 3A 32
Kenwood Ho. SW9 . . . . 2D 105
Kenwood Rd. N6 . . . . . 1B 32
Kenworthy Rd. E9 . . . . 2A 52
Kenwrick Ho. N1 . . . . . 5B 48
(off Barnsbury Est.)
Kenwyn Dr. NW2 . . . . . 4A 28
Kenwyn Rd. SW4 . . . . 2F 103
Kenya Rd. E17 . . . . 3F 97
Kenyon Mans. W14 . . . . 2A 86
(off Queen's Club Gdns.)
Kenyon St. SW6 . . . . . 4F 85
Keogh Rd. E15 . . . . 3A 54
Kepler Ho. SE10 . . . . . . 1B 96
(off Armitage Rd.)
Kepler Rd. SW4 . . . . . 2A 104
Keppel Ho. SE8 . . . . . . 1B 94
Keppel Row
SE1 . . . . 2F 25 (2E 77)
Keppel St.
WC1 . . . . 5C 6 (4F 61)
Kerbela St. E2 . . . . 3C 64
Kerbey St. E14 . . . . . . 5D 67
Kerfield Cres. SE5 . . . . 4F 91
Kerfield Pl. SE5 . . . . . . 4F 91
Kerridge Ct. N1 . . . . . . 3A 50
(off Balls Pond Rd.)
Kerrington Ct. W12 . . . 3E 71
(off Uxbridge Rd.)
Kerrison Rd. E15 . . . . . 5F 53
SW11 . . . . 1A 102
Kerry N7 . . . . 3A 48
Kerry Cl. E16 . . . . 5D 69
Kerry Ho. E1 . . . . 5E 65
(off Sidney St.)
Kerry Path SE14 . . . . . 2B 94
Kerry Rd. SE14 . . . . . . 2B 94
Kersey Gdns. SE9 . . . . 4F 125
Kersfield Ho. SW15 . . . 4F 99
Kersfield Rd. SW15 . . . 4F 99
Kershaw Cl. SW18 . . . . 4F 101
Kersley M. SW11 . . . . . 4B 88
Kersley Rd. N16 . . . . . . 4A 36
Kersley St. SW11 . . . . . 5B 88
Kerswell Cl. N15 . . . . . 1A 36
Kerwick Cl. N7 . . . . 4A 48
Keslake Mans. NW10 . . 1F 57
(off Station Rd.)
Keslake Rd. NW6 . . . . . 1F 57
Keston Ho. SE17 . . . . . 1A 92
(off Kinglake St.)
Keston Rd. SE15 . . . . . 1C 106
Kestrel Av. E6 . . . . 4F 69
SE24 . . . . 3D 105
Kestrel Cl. NW10 . . . . . 2A 42

Kestrel Ho. EC1 . . . . . . 1F 9
(off Pickard St.)
Kestrel Pl. SE14 . . . . . . 2A 94
Keswick Av. SW15 . . . 5A 112
Keswick Ct. SE6 . . . . . 1B 124
SE13 . . . . 3D 109
Keswick Ho. SE5 . . . . . 5E 91
Keswick Rd. SW15 . . . 3A 100
Kett Gdns. SW2 . . . . . 3B 104
Kettlebaston Rd. E10 . . 3B 38
Kettleby Ho. SW9 . . . . 1D 105
(off Barrington Rd.)
Ketton Ho. W10 . . . . . . 3E 57
(off Sutton Way)
Kevan Ho. SE5 . . . . 3E 91
Keybridge Ho. SW8 . . . 2A 90
(off Miles St.)
Key Cl. E1 . . . . 3E 65
Keyes Ho. SW1 . . . . . . 1F 89
(off Dolphin Sq.)
Keyes Rd. NW2 . . . . . . 2F 43
Key Ho. SE11 . . . . 2C 90
Keymer Rd. SW2 . . . . 2B 118
Keynsham Gdns.
SE9 . . . . 3F 111
Keynsham Rd. SE9 . . . 3F 111
Keyse Rd. SE1 . . . . 4B 78
Keystone Cres.
N1 . . . . 1E 7 (1A 62)
Keyworth Cl. E5 . . . . . 1A 52
Keyworth Pl. SE1 . . . . . 5E 25
Keyworth St.
SE1 . . . . 5E 25 (4D 77)
Kezia St. SE8 . . . . 1A 94
Khama Rd. SW17 . . . . 4A 116
Khartoum Rd. E13 . . . . 2D 69
SW17 . . . . 4F 115
Khyber Rd. SW11 . . . . 5A 88
Kibworth St. SW8 . . . . . 3B 90
KIDBROOKE 5D 97
Kidbrooke Est. SE3 . . . 1E 111
Kidbrooke Gdns. SE3 . . 5C 96
Kidbrooke Green
Nature Reserve 1E 111
Kidbrooke Gro. SE3 . . . 4C 96
Kidbrooke La. SE9 . . . 2F 111
Kidbrooke Pk. Cl.
SE3 . . . . 4D 97
Kidbrooke Pk. Rd.
SE3 . . . . 4D 97
Kidbrooke Way SE3 . . . 5D 97
Kidderpore Av. NW3 . . . 1C 44
Kidderpore Gdns.
NW3 . . . . 1C 44
Kierbeck Bus. Complex
E16 . . . . 3D 83
Kiffen St.
EC2 . . . . 3C 10 (3F 63)
Kilbrennan Ho. E14 . . . 5E 67
(off Findhorn St.)
KILBURN 1B 58
Kilburn Bri. NW6 . . . . . 5C 44
Kilburn Ga. NW6 . . . . . 1D 59
Kilburn High Rd.
NW6 . . . . 4B 44
Kilburn Ho. NW6 . . . . . 1B 58
(off Malvern Pl.)
Kilburn La. W10 . . . . . . 2F 57
Kilburn Pk. Rd. NW6 . . 2C 58
Kilburn Pl. NW6 . . . . . . 5C 44

Kilburn Priory NW6 . . . 5D 45
Kilburn Sq. NW6 . . . . . 5C 44
Kilburn Va. NW6 . . . . . 5D 45
Kilburn Va. Est. NW6 . . 5D 45
(off Kilburn Va.)
Kilby Ct. SE10 . . . . 4B 82
(off School Bank Rd.)
Kildare Gdns. W2 . . . . . 5C 58
Kildare Rd. E16 . . . . . . 4C 68
Kildare Ter. W2 . . . . . . 5C 58
Kildare Wlk. E14 . . . . . 5C 66
Kildoran Rd. SW2 . . . . 3A 104
Kilgour Rd. SE23 . . . . 4A 108
Kilkie St. SW6 . . . . 5E 87
Killarney Rd.
SW18 . . . . 4E 101
Killearn Rd. SE6 . . . . . 1F 123
Killick St. N1 . . . 1F 7 (1B 62)
Killieser Av. SW2 . . . . 2A 118
Killip Cl. E16 . . . . 5B 68
Killoran Ho. E14 . . . . . . 4E 81
(off Galbraith St.)
Killowen Rd. E9 . . . . . . 3F 51
Killyon Rd. SW8 . . . . . . 5E 89
Killyon Ter. SW8 . . . . . 5E 89
Kilmaine Rd. SW6 . . . . 3A 86
Kilmarsh Rd. W6 . . . . . 5E 71
Kilmington Rd.
SW13 . . . . 2C 84
Kilmore Ho. E14 . . . . . . 5D 67
(off Vesey Path)
Kilmorie Rd. SE23 . . . 1A 122
Kilmuir Ho. SW1 . . . . . 5C 74
(off Bury St.)
Kiln Ct. E14 . . . . 1B 80
(off Newell St.)
Kilner Ho. E16 . . . . 4D 69
(off Freemasons Rd.)
SE11 . . . . 2C 90
(off Clayton St.)
Kilner St. E14 . . . . 4C 66
Kiln M. SW17 . . . . 5F 115
Kiln Pl. NW5 . . . . 2C 46
Kilravock St. W10 . . . . 2A 58
Kimbell Gdns. SW6 . . . 4A 86
Kimbell Pl. SE3 . . . . . . 2E 111
Kimberley Av. E6 . . . . . 1F 69
SE15 . . . . 5D 93
Kimberley Gdns. N4 . . . 1D 35
Kimberley Ho. E14 . . . . 4E 81
(off Galbraith St.)
Kimberley Rd. E11 . . . . 4F 39
E16 . . . . 3B 68
NW6 . . . . 5A 44
SW9 . . . . 5A 90
Kimber Rd. SW18 . . . . 5C 100
Kimble Ho. NW8 . . . . . 3A 60
(off Lilestone St.)
Kimble Rd. SW19 . . . . 5F 115
Kimbolton Cl. SE12 . . . 4B 110
Kimbolton Ct. SW3 . . . 5A 74
(off Fulham Rd.)
Kimbolton Row SW3 . . 5A 74
(off Fulham Rd.)
Kimmeridge Rd.
SE9 . . . . 4F 125
Kimpton Ho. SW15 . . . 5C 98
Kimpton Rd. SE5 . . . . . 4F 91
Kinburn St. SE16 . . . . . 3F 79
Kincaid Rd. SE15 . . . . . 3D 93

Kincardine Gdns. *W9* . . . *3C 58*
(off Harrow Rd.)
Kinder Ho. *N1* *1F 63*
(off Cranston Est.)
Kindersley Ho. *E1* *5C 64*
(off Pinchin St.)
Kinder St. *E1* *5D 65*
Kinefold Ho. *N7* *3A 48*
Kinfauns Rd. *SW2* *2C 118*
King Alfred Av. *SE6* . . *4C 122*
(not continuous)
King & Queen St.
SE17 . . . . *1E 91*
King & Queen Wharf
SE16 . . . . *1F 79*
King Arthur Cl.
SE15 . . . . *3E 93*
King Charles I Island
WC2 . . . . *1D 23*
King Charles Ct.
SE17 . . . . *2D 91*
(off Royal Rd.)
King Charles Ho.
SW6 . . . . *3D 87*
(off Wandon Rd.)
King Charles's Ct.
SE10 . . . . *2C 95*
(off Park Row)
King Charles St.
SW1 . . . . *3C 22 (3F 75)*
King Charles Ter. *E1* . . *1D 79*
(off Sovereign Cl.)
King Charles Wlk.
SW19 . . . . *1A 114*
King Ct. *E10* *2D 39*
King David La. *E1* *1E 79*
Kingdon Ho. *E14* *4E 81*
(off Galbraith St.)
Kingdon Rd. *NW6* *3C 44*
King Edward III M.
SE16 . . . . *3D 79*
King Edward Bldg.
EC1 . . . . *5D 63*
King Edward Mans.
E8 . . . . *5D 51*
(off Mare St.)
King Edward M.
SW13 . . . . *4C 84*
King Edward Rd. *E10* . . *3E 39*
King Edwards Mans.
SW6 . . . . *3C 86*
(off Fulham Rd.)
King Edward's Rd.
E9 . . . . *5D 51*
King Edward St.
EC1 . . . . *2F 17 (5F 63)*
King Edward Wlk.
SE1 . . . . *5C 24 (4C 76)*
Kingfield St. *E14* *5E 81*
Kingfisher Av. *E11* *1D 41*
Kingfisher Ct. *E14* *3E 81*
(off River Barge Cl.)
SE1 . . . . *4A 26*
(off Swan St.)
SW19 . . . . *2F 113*
Kingfisher Ho.
SW18 . . . . *1E 101*
Kingfisher M. *SE13* . . *2C 108*
Kingfisher Sq. *SE8* *2B 94*
(off Clyde St.)

Kingfisher Way
NW10 . . . . *3A 42*
King Frederick IX Twr.
SE16 . . . . *4B 80*
King George IV Ct.
SE17 . . . . *1F 91*
(off Dawes St.)
King George VI Memorial
. . . . *2B 22 (2F 75)*
King George Av. *E16* . . *5E 69*
King George St.
SE10 . . . . *3E 95*
Kingham Cl. *SW18* . . . *5E 101*
W11 . . . . *3A 72*
King Henry's Reach
W6 . . . . *2E 85*
King Henry's Rd.
NW3 . . . . *4A 46*
King Henry's Stairs
E1 . . . . *2D 79*
King Henry M. *N16* . . . *2A 50*
King Henry's Wlk. *N1* . . *3A 50*
King Henry Ter. *E1* . . . *1D 79*
(off Sovereign Cl.)
Kinghorn St.
EC1 . . . . *1F 17 (4E 63)*
King Ho. *W12* *5D 57*
King James Ct. *SE1* . . . *4E 25*
King James St.
SE1 . . . . *4E 25 (3D 77)*
King John Ct.
EC2 . . . . *3E 11 (3A 64)*
King John St. *E1* *4F 65*
King John's Wlk.
SE9 . . . . *5F 111*
(not continuous)
Kinglake Est. *SE17* *1A 92*
Kinglake St. *SE17* *1A 92*
(not continuous)
Kinglet Cl. *E7* *3C 54*
Kingly Ct. *W1* *4A 14*
Kingly St. *W1* . . *3F 13 (5E 61)*
Kingsand Rd. *SE12* . . *2C 124*
Kings Arms Ct. *E1* *4C 64*
Kings Arms Yd.
EC2 . . . . *2B 18 (5F 63)*
Kings Av.
BR1: Brom *5B 124*
SW4 . . . . *1F 117*
SW12 . . . . *1F 117*
King's Bench St.
SE1 . . . . *3E 25 (3D 77)*
King's Bench Wlk.
EC4 . . . . *3C 16 (5C 62)*
Kingsbridge Ct. *E14* . . . *4C 80*
(off Dockers Tanner Rd.)
NW1 . . . . *4D 47*
(off Castlehaven Rd.)
Kingsbridge Rd. *W10* . . *5E 57*
KINGSBURY GREEN . . *1A 28*
Kingsbury Rd. *N1* *3A 50*
NW9 . . . . *1A 28*
Kingsbury Ter. *N1* *3A 50*
Kingsbury Trad. Est.
NW9 . . . . *1A 28*
Kingsclere Cl.
SW15 . . . . *5C 98*
Kingscliffe Gdns.
SW19 . . . . *1B 114*
Kings Cl. *E10* *2D 39*

Kings Coll. Ct. *NW3* . . . *4A 46*
Kings College London
Dental Institute *5F 91*
Hampstead Campus
. . . . *1C 44*
Strand Campus
. . . . *4A 16 (1B 76)*
Waterloo Campus . . . *2B 24*
King's Coll. Rd.
NW3 . . . . *4A 46*
King's College School of
Medicine & Dentistry
. . . . *5E 91*
Kingscote St.
EC4 . . . . *4D 17 (1D 77)*
Kings Ct. *E13* *5D 55*
N7 . . . . *4B 48*
(off Caledonian Rd.)
NW8 . . . . *5B 46*
(off Prince Albert Rd.)
SE1 . . . . *3E 25 (3D 77)*
W6 . . . . *5C 70*
Kings Ct. Nth. *SW3* . . . *1A 88*
Kingscourt Rd.
SW16 . . . . *3F 117*
Kings Ct. Sth. *SW3* . . . *1A 88*
(off Chelsea Mnr. Gdns.)
King's Cres. *N4* *5E 35*
Kings Cres. Est. *N4* . . . *4E 35*
Kingscroft *SW4* *4A 104*
Kingscroft Rd. *NW2* . . . *3B 44*
KING'S CROSS *1A 62*
King's Cross Bri. *N1* *1E 7*
King's Cross Rd.
WC1 . . . . *1F 7 (2B 62)*
Kingsdale Gdns. *W11* . . *2F 71*
Kingsdown Av. *W3* *1A 70*
Kingsdown Cl. *SE16* . . . *1D 93*
(off Masters Dr.)
W10 . . . . *5F 57*
Kingsdown Ho. *E8* *2C 50*
Kingsdown Rd. *E11* *5A 40*
N19 . . . . *4A 34*
Kingsfield Ho. *SE9* . . . *3F 125*
Kingsford St. *NW5* *2B 46*
Kings Gdns. *NW6* *4C 44*
Kings Gth. M. *SE23* . . . *2E 121*
Kingsgate Est. *N1* *3A 50*
Kingsgate Ho. *SW9* . . . *4C 90*
Kingsgate Mans.
WC1 . . . . *1F 15*
(off Red Lion Sq.)
Kingsgate Pde. *SW1* . . *5A 22*
Kingsgate Pl. *NW6* *4C 44*
Kingsgate Rd. *NW6* . . . *4C 44*
Kingsground *SE9* *5F 111*
King's Gro. *SE15* *3D 93*
(not continuous)
Kings Hall Leisure Cen.
. . . . *2E 51*
Kingshall M. *SE13* . . . *1E 109*
Kings Hall Rd.
BR3: Beck. *5A 122*
Kings Head Pas.
SW4 . . . . *2F 103*
(off Clapham Pk. Rd.)
Kings Head Theatre . . . *5D 49*
(off Upper St.)
King's Head Yd.
SE1 . . . . *2B 26 (2F 77)*

Kingshill SE17 . . . . 5E 77
   (off Brandon St.)
Kingshold Rd. E9 . . . . 4E 51
Kingsholm Gdns.
  SE9 . . . . 2F 111
Kings Ho. SE1 . . . . 3A 90
   (off Sth. Lambeth Rd.)
Kingshurst Rd.
  SE12 . . . . 5C 110
Kings Keep SW15 . . . . 3F 99
KINGSLAND 3A 50
Kingsland NW8 . . . . 5A 46
Kingsland Grn. E8 . . . . 3A 50
Kingsland High St.
  E8 . . . . 3B 50
Kingsland Pas. E8 . . . . 3A 50
Kingsland Rd.
  E2 . . . . 2E 11 (2A 64)
  E8 . . . . 2A 64
  E13 . . . . 2E 69
Kingsland Shop. Cen.
  E8 . . . . 3B 50
Kingslawn Cl. SW15 . . . . . 3D 99
Kingsley Ct. NW2 . . . . 3D 43
Kingsley Flats SE1 . . . . . . 5A 78
   (off Old Kent Rd.)
Kingsley Ho. SW3 . . . . 2F 87
   (off Beaufort St.)
Kingsley Mans. W14 . . . . . 2A 86
   (off Greyhound Rd.)
Kingsley M. E1 . . . . 1D 79
  W8 . . . . 4D 73
Kingsley Pl. N6 . . . . 2C 32
Kingsley Rd. E7 . . . . 4C 54
  NW6 . . . . 5B 44
  SW19 . . . . 5D 115
Kingsley St. SW11 . . . . . . 1B 102
Kingsley Way N2 . . . . 1E 31
Kings Mall W6 . . . . 5E 71
Kingsmead Av. NW9 . . . . . 2A 28
Kingsmead Ct. N6 . . . . 2F 33
Kingsmead Ho. E9 . . . . . . 1A 52
Kingsmead Rd.
  SW2 . . . . 2C 118
King's Mead Way
  E9 . . . . 1A 52
Kingsmere Cl.
  SW15 . . . . 1F 99
Kingsmere Pl. N16 . . . . . . 3F 35
Kingsmere Rd.
  SW19 . . . . 2F 113
King's M. SW4 . . . . 3A 104
  WC1 . . . . 4A 8 (3B 62)
Kingsmill NW8 . . . . 1F 59
   (off Kingsmill Ter.)
Kingsmill Ho. SW3 . . . . . . 1A 88
   (off Cale St.)
Kingsmill Ter. NW8 . . . . . . 1F 59
Kingsnorth Ho. W10 . . . . . 5F 57
Kings Pde. NW10 . . . . 5E 43
  W12 . . . . 4C 70
Kings Pas. E11 . . . . 2A 40
King's Pl.
  SE1 . . . . 4F 25 (3E 77)
King Sq. EC1 . . . . 2F 9 (2E 63)
King's Quay SW10 . . . . . . 4E 87
   (off Chelsea Harbour Dr.)
Kings Reach Twr.
  SE1 . . . . 1C 24
Kingsridge SW19 . . . . 2A 114

Kings Rd. E6 . . . . 5E 55
  E11 . . . . 2A 40
  NW10 . . . . 4D 43
  SW6 . . . . 3D 87
  SW10 . . . . 3D 87
  SW14 . . . . 1A 98
  SW19 . . . . 5C 114
King's Scholars' Pas.
  SW1 . . . . 4E 75
   (off Carlisle Pl.)
King Stairs Cl. SE16 . . . . . 3D 79
King's Ter. NW1 . . . . 5E 47
Kingsthorpe Rd.
  SE26 . . . . 4F 121
Kingston By-Pass
  SW15 . . . . 5A 112
  SW20 . . . . 5A 112
Kingston Ho. NW6 . . . . . . 4A 44
Kingston Ho. E. SW7 . . . . . 3A 74
   (off Prince's Ga.)
Kingston Ho. Nth.
  SW7 . . . . 3A 74
   (off Prince's Ga.)
Kingston Ho. Sth.
  SW7 . . . . 3A 74
   (off Ennismore Gdns.)
Kingston Rd. SW15 . . . . . . 2C 112
  SW19 . . . . 2C 112
Kingston Sq. SE19 . . . . . . 5F 119
Kingston University
  Kingston Hill 5A 112
  Roehampton Vale Cen.
  . . . . 3B 112
KINGSTON VALE 4A 112
Kingston Va. SW15 . . . . . . 4A 112
Kingstown St. NW1 . . . . . . 5C 46
   (not continuous)
King St. E13 . . . . 3C 68
  EC2 . . . . 3A 18 (5E 63)
  SW1 . . . . 2A 22 (2E 75)
  W6 . . . . 5C 70
  WC2 . . . . 4D 15 (1A 76)
King St. Cloisters
  W6 . . . . 5D 71
   (off Clifton Wlk.)
Kings Wlk. Shop. Cen.
  SW3 . . . . 1B 88
Kingswater Pl. SW11 . . . . . 3A 88
Kingsway
  WC2 . . . . 2F 15 (5B 62)
Kingsway Mans. WC1 . . . . 5F 7
   (off Red Lion Sq.)
Kingsway Pde. N16 . . . . . . 5F 35
   (off Albion Rd.)
Kingsway Pl. EC1 . . . . 3C 8
   (off Sans Wlk.)
Kingswear Rd. NW5 . . . . . 5D 33
Kings Wharf E8 . . . . 5A 50
   (off Kingsland Rd.)
Kingswood E2 . . . . 1E 65
   (off Cyprus St.)
Kingswood Av. NW6 . . . . . 5A 44
Kingswood Cl. SW8 . . . . . . 3A 90
Kingswood Ct. NW6 . . . . . 4C 44
   (off W. End La.)
Kingswood Dr.
  SE19 . . . . 4A 120
Kingswood Est.
  SE21 . . . . 4A 120
Kingswood Pl. SE13 . . . . . 2A 110

Kingswood Rd.
  E11 . . . . 2A 40
  SW2 . . . . 4A 104
Kings Yd. E15 . . . . 3C 52
  SW15 . . . . 1E 99
   (off Lwr. Richmond Rd.)
Kingthorpe Ter.
  NW10 . . . . 3A 42
Kington Ho. NW6 . . . . 5D 45
   (off Mortimer Cres.)
Kingward Ho. E1 . . . . 4C 64
   (off Hanbury St.)
Kingweston Cl.
  NW2 . . . . 5A 30
King William La.
  SE10 . . . . 1A 96
King William's Ct.
  SE10 . . . . 2F 95
   (off Park Row)
King William St.
  EC4 . . . . 3C 18 (5F 63)
King William Wlk.
  SE10 . . . . 2E 95
   (not continuous)
Kingwood Rd. SW6 . . . . . . 4A 86
Kinloch Dr. NW9 . . . . 2A 28
Kinloch St. N7 . . . . 5B 34
Kinnaird Av.
  BR1: Brom 5B 124
Kinnear Rd. W12 . . . . 3B 70
Kinnerton Pl. Nth.
  SW1 . . . . 4A 20
Kinnerton Pl. Sth.
  SW1 . . . . 4A 20
Kinnerton St.
  SW1 . . . . 4B 20 (3C 74)
Kinnerton Yd. SW1 . . . . . . 4B 20
Kinnoul Rd. W6 . . . . 2A 86
Kinross Ct. SE6 . . . . 1B 124
Kinsale Rd. SE15 . . . . 1C 106
Kinsella Gdns.
  SW19 . . . . 5D 113
Kinsham Ho. E2 . . . . 3C 64
   (off Ramsey St.)
Kintore Way SE1 . . . . 5B 78
Kintyre Ct. SW2 . . . . 5A 104
Kintyre Ho. E14 . . . . 2E 81
   (off Coldharbour)
Kinveachy Gdns.
  SE7 . . . . 1F 97
Kinver Rd. SE26 . . . . 4E 121
Kipling Dr. SW19 . . . . 5F 115
Kipling Est.
  SE1 . . . . 4C 26 (3F 77)
Kipling Ho. E16 . . . . 2D 83
   (off Southampton M.)
  SE5 . . . . 3F 91
   (off Elmington St.)
Kipling St.
  SE1 . . . . 4C 26 (3F 77)
Kippington Dr. SE9 . . . . . . 1F 125
Kirby Est. SE16 . . . . 4D 79
Kirby Gro.
  SE1 . . . . 3D 27 (3A 78)
Kirby St. EC1 . . . . . 5C 8 (4C 62)
Kirkdale SE26 . . . . 2D 121
Kirkdale Cnr. SE26 . . . . . . 4E 121
Kirkdale Rd. E11 . . . . 3A 40
Kirkeby Ho. EC1 . . . . 5B 8
   (off Leather La.)

Kirkland Ho. *E14* *1D* **95**
  (off St Davids Sq.)
  E14. . . . . *1D* **95**
  (off Westferry Rd.)
Kirkland Ter.
  BR3: Beck. *5C* **122**
Kirkland Wlk. *E8* *3B* **50**
Kirkman Pl. *W1* *1B* **14**
Kirkmichael Rd. *E14* . . *5E* **67**
Kirk Rd. *E17* *1B* **38**
Kirkside Rd. *SE3* *2C* **96**
Kirkstall Gdns.
  SW2 . . . . *1A* **118**
Kirkstall Rd. *SW2* . . . *1F* **117**
Kirkstead Ct. *E5* *1F* **51**
Kirkstone *NW1* *1F* **5**
  (off Harrington St.)
Kirk St. *WC1* *4F* **7**
Kirkwall Pl. *E2* *2E* **65**
Kirkwood Pl. *NW1* *4C* **46**
Kirkwood Rd. *SE15* . . . *5D* **93**
Kirtley Ho. *SW8* *4E* **89**
Kirtley Rd. *SE26* *4A* **122**
Kirtling St. *SW8* *3E* **89**
Kirton Cl. *W4* *5A* **70**
Kirton Gdns.
  E2. . . . . *2F* **11** (2B **64**)
Kirton Lodge *SW18* . . *4D* **101**
Kirton Rd. *E13* *1E* **69**
Kirwyn Way *SE5*. *3D* **91**
Kitcat Ter. *E3* *2C* **66**
Kitchener Rd. *E7* *3D* **55**
Kite Pl. *E2* *2C* **64**
  (off Lampern Sq.)
Kite Yd. *SW11* *4B* **88**
  (off Cambridge Rd.)
Kitson Rd. *SE5* *3F* **91**
  SW13. . . . . *4C* **84**
Kittiwake Ct. *SE1* *4A* **26**
  (off Swan St.)
  SE8. . . . . *2B* **94**
  (off Abinger Gro.)
Kitto Rd. *SE14* *5F* **93**
Kiver Rd. *N19* *4F* **33**
Klea Av. *SW4* *4E* **103**
Klein's Wharf *E14*. . . . *4C* **80**
  (off Westferry Rd.)
Knapdale Cl. *SE23* . . . *2D* **121**
Knapmill Rd. *SE6* *2C* **122**
Knapmill Way *SE6*. . . *2D* **123**
Knapp Cl. *NW10*. *3A* **42**
Knapp Rd. *E3*. *3C* **66**
Knapton M. *SW17* . . . *5C* **116**
Knaresborough Dr.
  SW18. . . . . *1D* **115**
Knaresborough Pl.
  SW5 . . . . *5D* **73**
Knatchbull Rd.
  NW10 . . . . *5A* **42**
  SE5. . . . . *5D* **91**
Knebworth Ho. *SW8* . . *5F* **89**
Knebworth Rd. *N16* . . *1A* **50**
Kneller Rd. *SE4* *2A* **108**
Knighten St. *E1* *2D* **79**
Knighthead Point
  E14 . . . . *3C* **80**
Knight Ho. *SE17*. *5A* **78**
  (off Tatum St.)
Knightland Rd. *E5* . . . *4D* **37**
Knightleas Ct. *NW2* . . . *3E* **43**

Knightleys Ct. *E10*. . . . *3A* **38**
  (off Wellington Rd.)
Knighton Pk. Rd.
  SE26 . . . . *5F* **121**
Knighton Rd. *E7*. *5C* **40**
Knightrider Ct.
  EC4. . . . . *4E* **17**
Knightrider St.
  EC4. . . . . . . *4E* **17** (5D **63**)
Knights Arc. *SW1* *4A* **20**
KNIGHTSBRIDGE *3A* **74**
Knightsbridge
  SW1 . . . . *4A* **20** (3B **74**)
  SW7 . . . . *3B* **74**
Knightsbridge Ct.
  SW1 . . . . *4A* **20**
Knightsbridge Grn.
  SW1 . . . . *3B* **74**
  (not continuous)
Knights Cl. *E9*. *2E* **51**
Knights Ct.
  BR1: Brom *3B* **124**
Knights Hill *SE27* . . . *5D* **119**
Knight's Hill Sq.
  SE27 . . . . *4D* **119**
Knights Ho. *SW8* *3A* **90**
  (off Sth. Lambeth Rd.)
Knight's Rd. *E16* *3C* **82**
Knight's Wlk. *SE11* . . . *5D* **77**
  (not continuous)
Knightswood Ct. *N6* . . . *2F* **33**
Knivet Rd. *SW6* *2C* **86**
Knobs Hill Rd. *E15* . . . *5D* **53**
Knockholt Rd. *SE9* . . . *3F* **111**
Knoll Ho. *NW8* *1E* **59**
  (off Carlton Hill)
Knoll Rd. *SW18* *3E* **101**
Knollys Cl. *SW16* . . . *3C* **118**
Knolly's Ho. *WC1*. *3D* **7**
  (off Tavistock Pl.)
Knollys Rd. *SW16* . . . *3B* **118**
Knottisford St. *E2*. . . . *2E* **65**
Knotts Grn. M. *E10* . . . *1D* **39**
Knotts Grn. Rd. *E10*. . *1D* **39**
Knowlden Ho. *E1* *1E* **79**
  (off Cable St.)
Knowle Cl. *SW9* *1C* **104**
Knowles Hill Cres.
  SE13 . . . . *3A* **110**
Knowles Ho. *SW18* . . *4D* **101**
  (off Neville Gill Cl.)
Knowles Wlk. *SW4* . . . *1E* **103**
Knowlton Ho. *SW9*. . . *4C* **90**
  (off Cowley Rd.)
Knowsley Rd. *SW11* . . *5B* **88**
Knox Ct. *SW4* *5A* **90**
Knox Rd. *E7* *3B* **54**
Knox St. *NW1* . . . *5A* **4** (4B **60**)
Knoyle St. *SE14* *2A* **94**
Kohat Rd. *SW19* *5D* **115**
Kossuth St. *SE10* *1A* **96**
Kotree Way *SE1* *5C* **78**
Kramer M. *SW5* *1C* **86**
Kreedman Wlk. *E8* . . . *2C* **50**
Krupnik Pl. *EC2* *2E* **11**
Kubrick Bus. Est. *E7* . . *1D* **55**
  (off Station App.)
Kuhn Way *E7* *2C* **54**
Kylemore Cl. *E6* *1F* **69**
Kylemore Rd. *NW6* . . . *4C* **44**

Kylestrome Ho. *SW1* . . *5C* **74**
  (off Cundy St.)
Kynance M. *SW7* *4D* **73**
Kynance Pl. *SW7* *4E* **73**
Kynaston Av. *N16*. *5B* **36**
Kynaston Rd.
  BR1: Brom *5C* **124**
  N16. . . . . *5A* **36**
Kyrle Rd. *SW11* *4C* **102**
Kyverdale Rd. *N16*. . . . *2B* **36**

L

Laburnum Cl. *SE15* . . . *3C* **93**
Laburnum Ct. *E2* *5B* **50**
  SE16. . . . . *3E* **79**
  (off Albion St.)
Laburnum St. *E2* *5B* **50**
La Caye Apartments
  E14. . . . . *5F* **81**
  (off Glenaffric Av.)
Lacewing Cl. *E13*. *2C* **68**
Lacine Ct. *SE16* *3F* **79**
  (off Christopher Cl.)
Lackington St.
  EC2. . . . . *5C* **10** (4F **63**)
Lackland Ho. *SE1*. *1B* **92**
  (off Rowcross St.)
Lacland Ho. *SW10*. . . . *3F* **87**
  (off Worlds End Est.)
Lacon Ho. *WC1*. *5F* **7**
  (off Theobalds Rd.)
Lacon Rd. *SE22* *2C* **106**
Lacy Rd. *SW15*. *2F* **99**
  (not continuous)
Ladas Rd. *SE27* *4E* **119**
Ladbroke Cres. *W11* . . *5A* **58**
Ladbroke Gdns. *W11* . . *1B* **72**
Ladbroke Gro. *W10* . . . *3F* **57**
Ladbroke Gro. Ho.
  W11 . . . . *1B* **72**
  (off Ladbroke Gro.)
Ladbroke M. *W11* *2A* **72**
Ladbroke Rd. *W11*. . . . *2B* **72**
Ladbroke Sq. *W11*. . . . *1B* **72**
Ladbroke Ter. *W11*. . . . *1B* **72**
Ladbroke Wlk. *W11* . . . *2B* **72**
Ladlands *SE22* *5C* **106**
Ladycroft Rd.
  SE13 . . . . *1D* **109**
Lady Dock Path
  SE16 . . . . *3A* **80**
Ladyfern Ho. *E3*. *4C* **66**
  (off Gail St.)
Lady Margaret Rd.
  N19. . . . . *2E* **47**
  NW5 . . . . *2E* **47**
Lady Micos Almshouses
  E1 . . . . *5E* **65**
  (off Aylward St.)
Ladyship Ter. *SE22* . . *5C* **106**
Ladysmith Av. *E6* *1F* **69**
Ladysmith Rd. *E16*. . . . *2B* **68**
Lady Somerset Rd.
  NW5 . . . . *1D* **47**
LADYWELL *3D* **109**
Ladywell Arena *4D* **109**
Ladywell Cl. *SE4* *3C* **108**
Ladywell Hgts. *SE4* . . *4B* **108**

Ladywell Leisure Cen.
. . . . 3E 109
Ladywell Rd. SE13. . . 3C 108
Ladywell St. E15 . . . . . 5B 54
LA Fitness
 Aldgate 4F 19
  (off Portsoken St.)
 Bayswater 1D 73
  (off Queen's M.)
 Bloomsbury 5F 7
  (off Conduit St.)
 Covent Garden 4F 15
 Golders Green 2B 30
 Gospel Oak 1D 47
 Leadenhall 3E 19
  (off Billiter St.)
 Marylebone
 . . . . 5A 4 (4B 60)
 Piccadilly 5B 14
  (off Regent St.)
 St Pauls. 1F 17
  (off King Edward St.)
 South Kensington . . 5A 74
 Sydenham 4E 121
 Victoria 5F 21
  (off Bressenden Pl.)
 West India Quay . . . 1C 80
Lafone St.
 SE1. . . . . . 3F 27 (3B 78)
Lagado M. SE16 . . . . 2F 79
Laing Ho. SE5. . . . . . . 3E 91
Lainson St. SW18 . . 5C 100
Lairdale Cl. SE21 . . . 1E 119
Laird Ho. SE5. . . . . . . 3E 91
  (off Redcar St.)
Lairs Cl. N7 . . . . 2A 48
Laitwood Rd. SW12 . . 1D 117
Lakanal SE5 . . . . 4A 92
  (off Dalwood St.)
Lake Av. BR1: Brom . 5C 124
Lake Cl. SW19 . . . . . 5B 114
Lake Ho. SE1 . . . . 4F 25
  (off Southwark Bri. Rd.)
Lake Ho. Rd. E11 . . . . 5C 40
Laker Cl. SW4 . . . . . . 4A 90
Laker Ind. Est.
 BR3. . . . . 5A 122
  (off Kent Ho. La.)
Lake Rd. SW19 . . . . . 5B 114
Laker Pl. SW15 . . . . . 4A 100
Lakeside Ct. N4 . . . . . 4E 35
Lakeside Rd. W14 . . . 4F 71
Lakeside Ter. EC2. . . . 5A 10
Lake Vw. Cl. SW1. . . . 5E 21
  (off Bressenden Pl.)
Lake Vw. Est. E3 . . . . 1A 66
Lakeview Rd. SE27 . . 5C 118
Lakis Cl. NW3. . . . . . . 1E 45
Laleham Ho. E2 . . . . . 3F 11
  (off Camlet St.)
Laleham Rd. SE6 . . . 5E 109
Lalor St. SW6. . . . . . . 5A 86
Lambard Ho. SE10 . . . 3E 95
  (off Langdale Rd.)
Lamb Ct. E14 . . . . 1A 80
  (off Narrow St.)
Lamberhurst Ho.
 SE15 . . . . 2E 93
Lamberhurst Rd.
 SE27 . . . . 4C 118

Lambert Jones M. EC2. . . 5F 9
Lambert Rd. E16 . . . . . 5D 69
 SW2 . . . . 3A 104
Lambert St. N1. . . . . . . 4C 48
LAMBETH . . . 5F 23 (4B 76)
Lambeth Bri. SE1. . . . 5A 76
Lambeth Crematorium
 SW17 . . . . 4E 115
Lambeth High St.
 SE1 . . . . 5B 76
Lambeth Hill
 EC4. . . . . . . 4F 17 (1E 77)
Lambeth Palace
 . . . . 5F 23 (4B 76)
Lambeth Pal. Rd.
 SE1. . . . . . . 5F 23 (4B 76)
Lambeth Rd.
 SE1 . . . . . . 5B 24 (5B 76)
Lambeth Towers
 SE11 . . . . 5B 24
Lambeth Wlk. SE11 . . 5B 76
  (not continuous)
Lambfold Ho. N7 . . . . 3A 48
Lamb Ho. SE5 . . . . 3E 91
  (off Elmington Est.)
 SE10 . . . . 2E 95
  (off Haddo St.)
Lamb La. E8. . . . . 4D 51
Lamble St. NW5. . . . . . 2C 46
Lambolle Pl. NW3 . . . 3A 46
Lambolle Rd. NW3 . . . 3A 46
Lambourn Cl. NW5. . . 1E 47
Lambourne Av.
 SW19 . . . . 4B 114
Lambourne Gro.
 SE16 . . . . 1F 93
Lambourne Ho. NW8 . . 4F 59
  (off Broadley St.)
 SE16 . . . . 5F 79
Lambourne Pl. SE3 . . 4D 97
Lambourne Rd. E11 . . 2E 39
Lambourn Rd. SW4 . . 1D 103
Lambrook Ho. SE15 . . 4C 92
Lambrook Ter. SW6 . . 4A 86
Lamb's Bldgs.
 EC1. . . . . 4B 10 (3F 63)
Lamb's Conduit Pas.
 WC1 . . . . 5F 7 (4B 62)
Lamb's Conduit St.
 WC1 . . . . 4F 7 (3B 62)
  (not continuous)
Lambscroft Av. SE9 . . 3E 125
Lambs Health & Fitness
 . . . . 4B 10
Lamb's M. N1 . . . . 5D 49
Lamb's Pas.
 EC1. . . . . 5B 10 (3F 63)
Lamb St. E1. . . . . 5F 11 (4B 64)
Lamb Wlk.
 SE1 . . . . 4D 27 (3A 78)
LAMDA Theatre 5C 72
  (off Logan Pl.)
Lamerock Rd.
 BR1: Brom 5A 124
Lamerton St. SE8. . . . 2C 94
Lamington St. W6 . . . . 5D 71

Lamlash St. SE11 . . . . 5D 77
Lamley Ho. SE10. . . . . 3D 95
  (off Ashburnham Pl.)
Lammas Grn. SE26 . . 3D 121
Lammas Rd. E9 . . . . . 4F 51
 E10 . . . . 4A 38
Lammermoor Rd.
 SW12 . . . . 5D 103
Lamont Rd. SW10 . . . 2F 87
Lamont Rd. Pas.
 SW10 . . . . 2F 87
  (off Lamont Rd.)
Lampard Gro. N16. . . 3B 36
Lampern Sq. E2. . . . . 2C 64
Lampeter Cl. NW9 . . . 1A 28
Lampeter Sq. W6. . . . 2A 86
Lamplighter Cl. E1. . . 3E 65
Lampmead Rd.
 SE12. . . . . 3B 110
Lamp Office Ct.
 WC1 . . . . 4F 7
Lamps Ct. SE5 . . . . . . 3E 91
  (off Thompson's Av.)
Lampton Ho. Cl.
 SW19 . . . . 4F 113
Lanain Ct. SE12 . . . . 5B 110
Lanark Ho. SE1 . . . . . 1C 92
  (off Old Kent Rd.)
Lanark Mans. W9. . . . . 3E 59
  (off Lanark Rd.)
 W12 . . . . 3E 71
  (off Pennard Rd.)
Lanark M. W9. . . . . . . 2E 59
Lanark Pl. W9. . . . . . . 3E 59
Lanark Rd. W9 . . . . . . 1D 59
Lanark Sq. E14 . . . . . 4D 81
Lanbury Rd. SE15 . . . 2F 107
Lancashire Ct. W1. . . 4E 13
Lancaster Av. SE27 . . 2D 119
 SW19 . . . . 5F 113
Lancaster Cl. N1 . . . . 4A 50
 W2 . . . . 1D 73
  (off St Petersburgh Pl.)
Lancaster Ct. SE27 . . 2D 119
 SW6 . . . . 3B 86
 W2 . . . . 1E 73
  (off Lancaster Ga.)
Lancaster Dr. E14. . . . 2E 81
 NW3 . . . . 3A 46
Lancaster Gdns.
 SW19 . . . . 5A 114
Lancaster Ga. W2 . . . 1E 73
Lancaster Gro. NW3. . 3F 45
Lancaster Hall E16. . . 2C 82
  (off Wesley Av,
       not continuous)
Lancaster House 3A 22
Lancaster Lodge
 W11 . . . . 5A 58
  (off Lancaster Rd.)
Lancaster M. SW18. . . 3D 101
 W2 . . . . 1E 73
Lancaster Pl. SW19 . . 5F 113
 WC2. . . . . . . 4F 15 (1B 76)
Lancaster Rd. E7 . . . . 4C 54
 E11 . . . . 4A 40
 N4 . . . . 2B 34
 NW10 . . . . 2C 42
 SW19 . . . . 5F 113
 W11 . . . . 5A 58

Lancaster Stables
NW3 . . . . 3A **46**
Lancaster Ho.
SE1 . . . . 4D **25** (3D **77**)
Lancaster Ter. W2. . . . . . 1F **73**
Lancaster Wlk. W2. . . . . 2E **73**
Lancefield Ct. W10 . . . . 1A **58**
Lancefield Ho.
SE15 . . . . 2D **107**
Lancefield St. W10 . . . . 2B **58**
Lancell St. N16 . . . . 4B **36**
Lancelot Pl. SW7 . . . . . . 3B **74**
Lancer Sq. W8 . . . . 3D **73**
Lancey Cl. SE7 . . . . 5F **83**
Lanchester Ct. W2 . . . . . **5B 60**
(off Seymour St.)
Lanchester Rd. N6 . . . . . 1B **32**
Lancing St.
NW1. . . . . 2B **6** (2F **61**)
Lancresse Ct. N1 . . . . . . **5A 50**
(off De Beauvoir Est.)
Landale Ho. SE16 . . . . . **4E 79**
(off Lower Rd.)
Landcroft Rd. SE22 . . . 3B **106**
Landells Rd. SE22 . . . . 4B **106**
Landford Rd. SW15 . . . . 1E **99**
Landgrove Rd.
SW19 . . . . 5C **114**
Landin Ho. E14 . . . . **5C 66**
(off Thomas Rd.)
Landleys Fld. NW5 . . . . . **2F 47**
(off Long Mdw.)
Landmann Ho. SE16 . . . **5D 79**
(off Rennie Est.)
Landmann Way SE14 . . 1F **93**
Landmark Hgts. E5. . . . . 1A **52**
Landmark Ho. W6 . . . . . **1E 85**
(off Hammersmith Bri. Rd.)
Landon Pl.
SW1. . . . . 5A **20** (4B **74**)
Landon's Cl. E14 . . . . . . 2E **81**
Landon Wlk. E14 . . . . . . 1D **81**
Landor Ho. SE5 . . . . 3F **91**
(off Elmington Est.)
Landor Rd. SW9 . . . . . . 1A **104**
Landor Theatre 1A **104**
Landor Wlk. W12 . . . . . 3C **70**
Landrake NW1 . . . . **5E 47**
(off Plender St.)
Landridge Rd. SW6 . . . . 5B **86**
Landrock Rd. N8 . . . . . . 1A **34**
Landseer Ho. NW8 . . . . . **3F 59**
(off Frampton St.)
SW1 . . . . **5F 75**
(off Herrick St.)
SW11 . . . . 4C **88**
Landseer Rd. N19 . . . . . 5A **34**
(not continuous)
Landulph Ho. SE11 . . . . **1C 90**
(off Kennings Way)
Landward Ct. W1 . . . . . . **5A 60**
(off Harrowby St.)
Lane, The NW8 . . . . 1E **59**
SE3. . . . . 1C **110**
Lane Cl. NW2 . . . . 5D **29**
Lane End SW16 . . . . 1F **90**
Lanercost Cl. SW2 . . . . 2C **118**
Lanercost Rd. SW2 . . . . 2C **118**
Lanesborough Ct. N1 . . . 1D **11**
(off Fanshaw St.)

Lanesborough Pl.
SW1 . . . . 3C **20**
Laneway SW15 . . . . 3D **99**
Laney Ho. EC1 . . . . **5B 8**
(off Leather La.)
Lanfranc Rd. E3 . . . . 1A **66**
Lanfrey Pl. W14 . . . . 1B **86**
Langbourne Av. N6 . . . . 4C **32**
Langbourne Ct. E17 . . . 1A **38**
Langbourne Mans.
N6 . . . . 4C **32**
Langbourne Pl. E14 . . . 1D **95**
Langbrook Rd. SE3 . . . . 1F **111**
Langdale NW1 . . . . **1F 5**
(off Stanhope St.)
Langdale Cl. SE17 . . . . . 2E **91**
Langdale Ho. SW1 . . . . . **1E 89**
(off Churchill Gdns.)
Langdale Rd. SE10 . . . . 3E **95**
Langdale St. E1 . . . . 5D **65**
Langdon Ct. EC1 . . . . . . **1E 9**
(off City Rd.)
NW10 . . . . 5A **42**
Langdon Ho. E14 . . . . . . 5F **67**
Langdon Pk. Rd. N6 . . . 2E **33**
Langdon Way SE1 . . . . . 5C **78**
Langford Cl. E8 . . . . 2C **50**
NW8 . . . . 1E **59**
Langford Ct. NW8 . . . . . 1E **59**
(off Abbey Rd.)
Langford Grn. SE5 . . . 1A **106**
Langford Ho. SE8 . . . . . 2C **94**
Langford Pl. NW8 . . . . . 1E **59**
Langford Rd. SW6 . . . . . 5D **87**
Langham Mans. SW5 . . . **1D 87**
(off Earl's Ct. Sq.)
Langham Pl.
W1 . . . . 1E **13** (4D **61**)
W4 . . . . 2A **84**
Langham St.
W1 . . . . 1E **13** (4D **61**)
Langholm Cl. SW12 . . . 5F **103**
Langhorne Ct. NW8 . . . . **4F 45**
(off Dorman Way)
Lang Ho. SW8 . . . . 3A **90**
(off Hartington Rd.)
Langland Gdns. NW3. . . 2D **45**
Langland Ho. SE5 . . . . . **3F 91**
(off Edmund St.)
Langler Rd. NW10 . . . . . 1E **57**
Langley Ct.
WC2 . . . . 4D **15** (1A **76**)
Langley Cres. E11 . . . . . 2E **41**
Langley Dr. E11 . . . . 2D **41**
Langley Ho. W2 . . . . **4C 58**
(off Alfred Rd.)
Langley La. SW8 . . . . . . 2B **90**
Langley Mans. SW8. . . . 2B **90**
(off Langley La.)
Langley St.
WC2 . . . . 3D **15** (5A **62**)
Langmead St. SE27 . . . 4D **119**
Langmore Ho. E1 . . . . . . **5C 64**
(off Stutfield St.)
Langport Ho. SW9 . . . . . 5D **91**
Langridge Rd. SW17 . . . **1F 99**
Langroyd Rd. SW17 . . . . 2B **116**
Langside Av. SW15 . . . . 2C **98**
Langston Hughes Cl.
SE24 . . . . 2D **105**
Lang St. E1 . . . . 3E **65**

Langthorn Ct.
EC2 . . . . 2B **18** (5F **63**)
Langthorne Ct.
BR1: Brom 4E **123**
Langthorne Rd. E11 . . . . 5E **39**
Langthorne St. SW6 . . . 3F **85**
Langton Cl.
WC1 . . . . 3A **8** (3B **62**)
Langton Ho. SE11 . . . . . **5B 76**
(off Lambeth Wlk.)
Langton Pl. SW18 . . . . . 1C **114**
Langton Ri. SE23 . . . . . 5D **107**
Langton Rd. NW2 . . . . . 5F **29**
SW9 . . . . 3D **91**
Langton St. SW10 . . . . . 2E **87**
Langton Way SE3 . . . . . 4B **96**
Langtry Pl. SW6 . . . . 2C **86**
Langtry Rd. NW8 . . . . . . 5D **45**
Langtry Wlk. NW8 . . . . . 5D **45**
Lanhill Rd. W9 . . . . 3C **58**
Lanier Rd. SE13 . . . . . . 4F **109**
Lannoy Point SW6 . . . . . **3A 86**
(off Pellant Rd.)
Lanrick Ho. E14 . . . . **5F 67**
(off Lanrick Rd.)
Lanrick Rd. E14 . . . . 5F **67**
Lansbury Est. E14 . . . . . 5D **67**
Lansbury Gdns. E14 . . . 5F **67**
Lanscombe Wlk.
SW8 . . . . 4A **90**
Lansdell Ho. SW2 . . . . . **4C 104**
(off Tulse Hill)
Lansdowne Cl. SW11 . . . 1A **72**
(off Lansdowne Ri.)
Lansdowne Cres.
W11 . . . . 1A **72**
Lansdowne Dr. E8 . . . . . 3C **50**
Lansdowne Gdns.
SW8 . . . . 4A **90**
Lansdowne Grn. Est.
SW8 . . . . 4A **90**
Lansdowne Gro.
NW10 . . . . 1A **42**
Lansdowne Hill
SE27 . . . . 3D **119**
Lansdowne La. SE7 . . . . 2F **97**
Lansdowne M. SE7 . . . . 1F **97**
W11 . . . . 2B **72**
Lansdowne Pl.
SE1 . . . . 5C **26** (4F **77**)
Lansdowne Ri. W11 . . . 1A **72**
Lansdowne Rd. E11 . . . . 4B **40**
E17 . . . . 1C **38**
W11 . . . . 1A **72**
Lansdowne Row
W1 . . . . 1E **21** (2D **75**)
Lansdowne Ter.
WC1 . . . . 4E **7** (3A **62**)
Lansdowne Wlk.
W11 . . . . 2B **72**
Lansdowne Way SW8. . . 4F **89**
Lansdowne Wood Cl.
SE27 . . . . 3D **119**
Lansdowne Workshops
SE7 . . . . 1E **97**
Lansdown Rd. E15 . . . . . **5B 54**
Lantern Cl. SW15 . . . . . 2C **98**
Lanterns Ct. E14 . . . . . . 4C **80**
Lant Ho. SE1 . . . . **4F 25**
(off Toulmin St.)

Lant St. SE1 . . . . . 3F **25** (3E **77**)
Lanvanor Rd.
  SE15 . . . . 5E **93**
Lanyard Ho. SE8 . . . . . 5B **80**
Lapford Cl. W9 . . . . . . 3B **58**
Lapse Wood Wlk.
  SE23 . . . . 1D **121**
Lapwing Ct. SE1 . . . . . 4A **26**
  (off Swan St.)
Lapwing Twr. SE8 . . . . 2B **94**
  (off Taylor Cl.)
Lapworth Ct. W2 . . . . . 4D **59**
  (off Delamere Ter.)
Lara Cl. SE13 . . . . 4E **109**
Larch Av. W3 . . . . 2A **70**
Larch Cl. E13 . . . . 3D **69**
  N19 . . . . 4E **33**
  SE8 . . . . 2B **94**
  SW12 . . . . 2D **117**
Larch Ct. SE1 . . . . 4D **27**
  (off Royal Oak Yd.)
  W9 . . . . 4C **58**
  (off Admiral Wlk.)
Larch Ho. SE16 . . . . . . 3E **79**
  (off Ainsty Est.)
  W10 . . . . 3A **58**
  (off Rowan Wlk.)
Larch Rd. E10 . . . . 4C **38**
  NW2 . . . . 1E **43**
Larcom St. SE17 . . . . . 5E **77**
Larden Rd. W3 . . . . . . 2A **70**
Larissa St. SE17 . . . . . 1F **91**
Larkbere Rd. SE26 . . . 4A **122**
Larkhall La. SW4 . . . . 5F **89**
Larkhall Ri. SW4 . . . . . 1E **103**
  (not continuous)
Lark Row E2 . . . . 5E **51**
Larkspur Cl. E6 . . . . . . 4F **69**
Larnach Rd. W6 . . . . . 2F **85**
Larpent Av. SW15 . . . . 3E **99**
Lascelles Cl. E11 . . . . . 4F **39**
Lascelles Ho. NW1 . . . 3A **60**
  (off Harewood Av.)
Lasell St. SE10 . . . . . . 1F **95**
Lasseter Pl. SE3 . . . . . 2A **96**
Latchmere Leisure Cen.
  . . . . 5B **88**
Latchmere Pas.
  SW11 . . . . 5A **88**
Latchmere Rd. SW11 . . 5B **88**
Latchmere St. SW11 . . 5B **88**
Latham Ct. SW5 . . . . . 5C **72**
  (off W. Cromwell Rd.)
Latham Ho. E1 . . . . . . 5F **65**
  (off Chudleigh St.)
Latimer Ho. E9 . . . . . . 3F **51**
  W11 . . . . 1B **72**
  (off Kensington Pk. Rd.)
Latimer Ind. Est.
  W10 . . . . 5E **57**
Latimer Pl. W10 . . . . . 5E **57**
Latimer Rd. E7 . . . . . . 1D **55**
  N15 . . . . 1A **36**
  W10 . . . . 4E **57**
  (not continuous)
Latona Ct. SW9 . . . . . . 3C **90**
  (off Caldwell St.)
Latona Rd. SE15 . . . . . 2C **92**
Lattimer Pl. W4 . . . . . . 3A **84**
Latymer Ct. W6 . . . . . . 5F **71**

Latymer Upper School
  Sports Cen. 1C **84**
Lauderdale House 3D **33**
Lauderdale Ho. SW9 . . 4C **90**
  (off Gosling Way)
Lauderdale Mans.
  W9 . . . . 2D **59**
  (off Lauderdale Rd.,
  not continuous)
Lauderdale Pde. W9 . . 3D **59**
Lauderdale Pl. EC2 . . . 5F **9**
  (off Beech St.)
Lauderdale Rd. W9 . . . 2D **59**
Lauderdale Twr.
  EC2 . . . . 5F **9**
Laud St. SE11 . . . . 1B **90**
Launcelot Rd.
  BR1: Brom 4C **124**
Launcelot St.
  SE1 . . . . . . 4B **24** (3C **76**)
Launceston Pl. W8 . . . 4E **73**
Launch St. E14 . . . . . . 4E **81**
Laundress La. N16 . . . 5C **36**
Laundry La. N1 . . . . . . 5E **49**
Laundry M. SE23 . . . . 5A **108**
Laundry Rd. W6 . . . . . 2A **86**
Laura Pl. E5 . . . . 1E **51**
Laura Ter. N4 . . . . 4D **35**
Laurel Bank Gdns.
  SW6 . . . . 5B **86**
Laurelbrook SE6 . . . . 3A **124**
Laurel Cl. N19 . . . . 4E **33**
  SW17 . . . . 5A **116**
Laurel Gro. SE26 . . . . 4F **121**
Laurel Ho. SE8 . . . . . . 2B **94**
Laurel Rd. SW13 . . . . . 5C **84**
Laurels, The NW10 . . . 5D **43**
Laurel St. E8 . . . . 3B **50**
Laurence Ct. E10 . . . . 2D **39**
Laurence M. W12 . . . . 3C **70**
Laurence Pountney Hill
  EC4 . . . . . . 4B **18** (1F **77**)
Laurence Pountney La.
  EC4 . . . . . . 4B **18** (1F **77**)
Laurie Gro. SE14 . . . . 4A **94**
Laurie Ho. SE1 . . . . . . 5E **25**
  (off St George's Rd.)
Laurier Rd. NW5 . . . . . 5D **33**
Lauriston Ho. E9 . . . . . 4E **51**
  (off Lauriston Rd.)
Lauriston Rd. E9 . . . . . 4E **51**
  SW19 . . . . 5F **113**
Lausanne Rd. SE15 . . 4E **93**
Lavell St. N16 . . . . 1F **49**
Lavender Cl. SW3 . . . . 2F **87**
Lavender Gdns.
  SW11 . . . . 2B **102**
Lavender Gro. E8 . . . . 4C **50**
Lavender Hill SW11 . . 2A **102**
Lavender Ho. SE16 . . . 2F **79**
  (off Rotherhithe St.)
Lavender Pond Nature Pk.
  . . . . 2A **80**
Lavender Rd. SE16 . . . 2A **80**
  SW11 . . . . 1F **101**
Lavender Sq. E11 . . . . 5F **39**
Lavender St. E15 . . . . 3A **54**
Lavender Sweep
  SW11 . . . . 2B **102**
Lavender Ter. SW11 . . 1A **102**

Lavender Wlk.
  SW11 . . . . 2B **102**
Lavendon Ho. NW8 . . . 3A **60**
  (off Paveley St.)
Lavengro Rd. SE27 . . . 2E **119**
Lavenham Rd.
  SW18 . . . . 2B **114**
Lavers Rd. N16 . . . . . . 5A **36**
Laverstoke Gdns.
  SW15 . . . . 5B **98**
Laverton M. SW5 . . . . 5D **73**
Laverton Pl. SW5 . . . . 5D **73**
Lavina Gro. N1 . . . . . . 1B **62**
Lavington Cl. E9 . . . . . 3B **52**
Lavington St.
  SE1 . . . . 2E **25** (2D **77**)
Lavisham Ho.
  BR1: Brom 5C **124**
Lawford Rd. N1 . . . . . . 4A **50**
  NW5 . . . . 3E **47**
Lawless Ho. E14 . . . . . 1E **81**
  (off Bazely St.)
Lawless St. E14 . . . . . 1D **81**
Lawley St. E5 . . . . 1E **51**
Lawn Dr. E7 . . . . 1F **55**
Lawn Ho. Cl. E14 . . . . 3E **81**
Lawn La. SW8 . . . . . . 2A **90**
Lawn Rd. NW3 . . . . . . 2B **46**
Lawns, The SE3 . . . . . 1B **110**
  SW19 . . . . 5B **114**
Lawnside SE3 . . . . . . 3B **110**
Lawn Ter. SE3 . . . . . . 1A **110**
Lawrence Av.
  NW10 . . . . 5A **42**
  N16 . . . . 5B **36**
Lawrence Bldgs.
  N16 . . . . 5B **36**
Lawrence Cl. E3 . . . . . 2C **66**
  W12 . . . . 1D **71**
Lawrence Ct. N16 . . . . 5B **36**
  (off Smalley Rd. Est.)
Lawrence Ho. SW1 . . . 5F **75**
  (off Cureton St.)
Lawrence La.
  EC2 . . . . 2A **18** (5E **63**)
Lawrence Pl. N1 . . . . . 5A **48**
  (off Brydon Wlk.)
Lawrence Rd. E6 . . . . . 5F **55**
  E13 . . . . 5D **55**
  SW3 . . . . 2A **88**
Lawrence Trad. Est.
  SE10 . . . . 5A **82**
Lawrie Pk. Av.
  SE26 . . . . 5D **121**
Lawrie Pk. Cres.
  SE26 . . . . 5D **121**
Lawrie Pk. Gdns.
  SE26 . . . . 4D **121**
Lawrie Pk. Rd.
  SE26 . . . . 5D **121**
Lawson Cl. E16 . . . . . . 4E **69**
  SW19 . . . . 3F **113**
Lawson Ct. N4 . . . . . . 3B **34**
  (off Lorne Rd.)
Lawson Ho. W12 . . . . . 1D **71**
  (off White City Est.)
Law St. SE1 . . . 5C **26** (4F **77**)
Lawton Rd. E3 . . . . . . 2A **66**
  (not continuous)
  E10 . . . . 3E **39**

Laxfield Ct. E8 . . . . 5C 50
   (off Pownall Rd.)
Laxford Ho. SW1 . . . . . . 5C 74
   (off Cundy St.)
Laxley Cl. SE5 . . . . 3D 91
Laxton Pl.
  NW1 . . . . 3E 5 (3D 61)
Layard Rd. SE16 . . . . . . 5D 79
Layard Sq. SE16 . . . . . . 5D 79
Laybourne Ho. E14 . . . . 3C 80
   (off Admirals Way)
Laycock St. N1 . . . . 3C 48
Layfield Cl. NW4 . . . . . . 2D 29
Layfield Cres. NW4 . . . . 2D 29
Layfield Ho. SE10 . . . . . 1C 96
   (off Kemsing Rd.)
Layfield Rd. NW4 . . . . . . 2D 29
Laystall Ct. WC1 . . . . 4B 8
   (off Mount Pleasant)
Laystall St.
  EC1 . . . . 4B 8 (3F 62)
Layton's Bldgs.
  SE1 . . . . 3B 26 (3F 77)
Layzell Wlk. SE9 . . . . . . 1F 125
Lazar Wlk. N7 . . . . 4B 34
Lazenby Ct. WC2 . . . . . . 4D 15
Leabank Sq. E9 . . . . 3C 52
Leabank Vw. N15 . . . . . . 1C 36
Lea Bon Ct. E15 . . . . . . 5B 54
   (off Plaistow Gro.)
Leabourne Rd. N16 . . . . 2C 36
LEA BRIDGE 5F 37
Lea Bri. Ind. Cen.
  E10 . . . . 3A 38
Lea Bri. Rd. E5 . . . . 5E 37
  E10 . . . . 5E 37
Lea Ct. E13 . . . . 2C 68
Leacroft Av. SW12 . . . . 5B 102
Leadale Rd. N15 . . . . . . 1C 36
  N16 . . . . 1C 36
Leadenhall Mkt.
  EC3 . . . . 3D 19 (5A 64)
Leadenhall Pl.
  EC3 . . . . 3D 19 (5A 64)
Leadenhall St.
  EC3 . . . . 3D 19 (5A 64)
Leadenham Ct. E3 . . . . . 3C 66
Leaf Gro. SE27 . . . . 5C 118
Leafy Oak Rd. SE12 . . . . 4E 125
Leagrave St. E5 . . . . 5E 37
Lea Hall Gdns. E10 . . . . 3C 38
Lea Hall Rd. E10 . . . . . . 3C 38
Lea Ho. NW8 . . . . 3A 60
   (off Salisbury St.)
Leahurst Rd. SE13 . . . . . 3F 109
   (not continuous)
LEA INTERCHANGE 2C 52
Leake Ct.
  SE1 . . . . 4A 24 (3B 76)
Leake St.
  SE1 . . . . 3A 24 (3B 76)
   (not continuous)
Lealand Rd. N15 . . . . . . 1B 36
Leamington Av.
  BR1: Brom 5E 125
  E17 . . . . 1C 38
Leamington Cl.
  BR1: Brom 4E 125
Leamington Rd. Vs.
  W11 . . . . 4B 58

Leamore St. W6 . . . . 5E 71
LEAMOUTH 1A 82
Leamouth Rd. E6 . . . . . . 4F 69
  E14 . . . . 5F 67
Leander Ct. SE8 . . . . 4C 94
Leander Rd. SW2 . . . . . 4B 104
Lea Pk. Trad. Est.
  E10 . . . . 2B 38
Leary Ho. SE11 . . . . 1B 90
Leaside Rd. E5 . . . . 3E 37
Leasowes Rd. E10 . . . . . 3C 38
Lea Sq. E3 . . . . 5B 52
Leatherdale St. E1 . . . . . 3E 65
   (Harpley Sq.)
  E1 . . . . 2F 65
   (Portelet Rd.)
Leather Gdns. E15 . . . . . 5A 54
Leatherhead Cl.
  N16 . . . . 3B 36
Leather La.
  EC1 . . . . 5B 8 (4C 62)
   (not continuous)
Leathermarket, The
  SE1 . . . . 4D 27
Leathermarket Ct.
  SE1 . . . . 4D 27 (3A 78)
Leathermarket St.
  SE1 . . . . 4D 27 (3A 78)
Leather St. E1 . . . . 1F 79
Leathwaite Rd.
  SW11 . . . . 2B 102
Leathwell Rd. SE8 . . . . . 5D 95
Lea Vw. Ho. E5 . . . . 3D 37
Leaway E10 . . . . 3F 37
Lebanon Gdns.
  SW18 . . . . 4C 100
Lebanon Rd. SW18 . . . . 3C 100
Lebrun Sq. SE3 . . . . . . 2D 111
Lebus Ho. NW8 . . . . 1A 60
   (off Cochrane St.)
Lechmere Rd. NW2 . . . . 3D 43
Leckford Rd. SW18 . . . . 2E 115
Leckhampton Pl.
  SW2 . . . . 5C 104
Lecky St. SW7 . . . . 1F 87
Leclair Ho. SE3 . . . . . . 1D 111
Leconfield Av. SW13 . . . 1B 98
Leconfield Ho. SE5 . . . . 2A 106
Leconfield Rd. N5 . . . . . 1F 49
Le Cordon Bleu London
  Culinary Arts Institute
  . . . . 1C 12
   (off Marylebone La.)
Leda Ct. SW9 . . . . 3C 90
   (off Caldwell St.)
Ledam Ho. EC1 . . . . 5B 8
   (off Bourne Est.)
Ledbury Ho. SE22 . . . . . 1A 106
  W11 . . . . 5B 58
   (off Colville Rd.)
Ledbury M. Nth.
  W11 . . . . 1C 72
Ledbury M. W. W11 . . . . 1C 72
Ledbury Rd. W11 . . . . . . 5B 58
Ledbury St. SE15 . . . . . . 3C 92
LEE 4E 110
Lee Bri. SE13 . . . . 1E 109
Lee Chu. St. SE13 . . . . . 2A 110
Lee Conservancy Rd.
  E9 . . . . 2B 52

Lee Ct. SE13 . . . . 2F 109
   (off Lee High Rd.)
Leefern Rd. W12 . . . . . . 3C 70
Leegate SE12 . . . . 3B 110
LEE GREEN 3B 110
Lee High Rd. SE12 . . . . 1E 109
  SE13 . . . . 1E 109
Lee Ho. EC2 . . . . 1A 18
   (off Monkwell Sq.)
Leeke St. WC1 . . 1F 7 (2B 62)
Leeland Way NW10 . . . . 1B 42
Lee Pk. SE3 . . . . 2B 110
Leerdam Dr. E14 . . . . . . 4E 81
Lee Rd. SE3 . . . . 1B 110
Lees Ct. W1 . . . . 4B 12
   (off Lees Pl.)
Leeside Ct. SE16 . . . . . . 2F 79
   (off Rotherhithe St.)
Leeside Cres. NW11 . . . 1A 30
Leeson Rd. SE24 . . . . . . 2C 104
Lees Pl. W1 . . . . 4B 12 (1C 74)
Lee St. E8 . . . . 5B 50
Lee Ter. SE3 . . . . 1A 110
  SE13 . . . . 1A 110
Lee Valley Cycle Circuit
  . . . . 2D 53
Lee Valley Ice Cen. 4F 37
Lee Valley Sports Cen.
  . . . . 1D 53
Leeward Ct. E1 . . . . 1C 78
Leeward Gdns.
  SW19 . . . . 5A 114
Leeway SE8 . . . . 1B 94
Leewood Cl. SE12 . . . . . 4B 110
Lefevre Wlk. E3 . . . . 1C 66
Leff Ho. NW6 . . . . 5A 44
Lefroy Ho. SE1 . . . . 4F 25
   (off Southwark Bri. Rd.)
Lefroy Rd. W12 . . . . 3B 70
Legard Rd. N5 . . . . 5D 35
Legatt Rd. SE9 . . . . 3F 111
Leggatt Rd. E15 . . . . 1E 67
Legge St. SE13 . . . . 3E 109
Leghorn Rd. NW10 . . . . 1B 56
Legion Cl. N1 . . . . 4C 48
Legion Ter. E3 . . . . 5B 52
Leicester Ct. W9 . . . . . . 4C 58
   (off Elmfield Way)
  WC2 . . . . 4C 14
Leicester Ho. SW9 . . . . 1D 105
   (off Loughborough Rd.)
Leicester Pl.
  WC2 . . . . 4C 14 (1F 75)
Leicester Rd. E11 . . . . . 1D 41
  NW10 . . . . 4A 42
Leicester Sq.
  WC2 . . . . 5C 14 (1F 75)
Leicester St.
  WC2 . . . . 4C 14 (1F 75)
Leigham Av. SW16 . . . . 3A 118
Leigham Cl. SW16 . . . . . 3B 118
Leigham Ct. Rd.
  SW16 . . . . 2A 118
Leigham Hall Pde.
  SW16 . . . . 3A 118
   (off Streatham High Rd.)
Leigham Va. SW2 . . . . . 3B 118
  SW16 . . . . 3B 118
Leigh Gdns. NW10 . . . . 1E 57

Leigh Orchard Cl.
  SW16 . . . . 3B 118
Leigh Pl. EC1 . . . 5B 8 (4C 62)
Leigh Rd. E10 . . . . 2E 39
  N5 . . . . 1D 49
Leigh St. WC1 . . 2D 7 (2A 62)
Leighton Cres. NW5 . . . . 2E 47
Leighton Gdns.
  NW10 . . . . 1D 57
Leighton Gro. NW5 . . . . 2E 47
Leighton Ho. SW1 . . . . . 5F 75
  (off Herrick St.)
Leighton House Art Gallery &
  Mus. 4B 72
Leighton Mans. W14 . . . 2A 86
  (off Greyhound Rd.)
Leighton Pl. NW5 . . . . . 2E 47
Leighton Rd. NW5 . . . . . 2E 47
Leila Parnell Pl. SE7 . . . 2E 97
Leinster Gdns. W2 . . . . . 5E 59
Leinster M. W2 . . . . 1E 73
Leinster Pl. W2 . . . . 5E 59
Leinster Sq. W2 . . . . 5C 58
  (not continuous)
Leinster Ter. W2 . . . . . . 1E 73
Leithcote Gdns.
  SW16 . . . . 4B 118
Leithcote Path
  SW16 . . . . 3B 118
Leith Mans. W9 . . . . 2D 59
  (off Grantully Rd.)
Leith Yd. NW6 . . . . 5C 44
  (off Quex Rd.)
Lelitia Cl. E8 . . . . 5C 50
Leman Pas. E1 . . . . 5C 64
  (off Leman St.)
Leman St. E1 . . . . 5B 64
Le May Av. SE12 . . . . . . 3D 125
Lemmon Rd. SE10 . . . . . 2A 96
Lemna Rd. E11 . . . . 2B 40
Le Moal Ho. E1 . . . . 4E 65
  (off Stepney Way)
Lemsford Cl. N15 . . . . . . 1C 36
Lemsford Ct. N4 . . . . 4E 35
Lemuel St. SW18 . . . . . . 4E 101
Lena Gdns. W6 . . . . 4E 71
Lenanton Steps E14 . . . . 3C 80
  (off Manilla St.)
Lendal Ter. SW4 . . . . . . 1F 103
Len Freeman Pl.
  SW6 . . . . 2B 86
Lenham Ho. SE1 . . . . 4C 26
  (off Long La.)
Lenham Rd. SE12 . . . . . . 2B 110
Lennard Rd. SE20 . . . . . 5F 121
Lennon Rd. NW2 . . . . . . 2E 43
Lennox Gdns. NW10 . . . . 1B 42
  SW1 . . . . 4B 74
Lennox Gdns. M.
  SW1 . . . . 4B 74
Lennox Lewis Cen.
  E5 . . . . 4E 37
  (off Theydon Rd.)
Lennox Rd. E17 . . . . 1B 38
  N4 . . . . 4B 34
Lens Rd. E7 . . . . 4E 55
Lenthall Ho. SW1 . . . . . . 1E 89
  (off Churchill Gdns.)
enthall Rd. E8 . . . . 4C 50
enthorp Rd. SE10 . . . . . 5B 82

Lentmead Rd.
  BR1: Brom 3B 124
Len Williams Ct.
  NW6 . . . . 1C 58
Leof Cres. SE6 . . . . 5D 123
Leonard Ct.
  WC1 . . . . 3C 6 (3F 61)
Leonard Pl. N16 . . . . 1A 50
Leonard Rd. E7 . . . . 1C 54
Leonard St.
  EC2 . . . . 3C 10 (3F 63)
Leonora Ho. W9 . . . . 3E 59
  (off Lanark Rd.)
Leontine Cl. SE15 . . . . . 3C 92
Leopards Ct. EC1 . . . . . . 5B 8
Leopold Av. SW19 . . . . . 5B 114
Leopold Bldgs. E2 . . . . . 1F 11
  (off Columbia Rd.)
Leopold M. E9 . . . . 5E 51
Leopold Rd. E17 . . . . 1C 38
  NW10 . . . . 4A 42
  SW19 . . . . 4B 114
Leopold St. E3 . . . . 4B 66
Leopold Ter. SW19 . . . . 5B 114
Leo St. SE15 . . . . 3D 93
Leo Yd. EC1 . . . . 4E 9
Leppoc Rd. SW4 . . . . . . 3F 103
Leroy St. SE1 . . . . 5A 78
Lerry Cl. W14 . . . . 2B 86
Lescombe Cl. SE23 . . . . 3A 122
Lescombe Rd. SE23 . . . . 3A 122
Leslie Prince Ct. SE5 . . . 3F 91
Leslie Rd. E11 . . . . 1E 53
  E16 . . . . 5D 69
Lessar Av. SW4 . . . . 4E 103
Lessingham Av.
  SW17 . . . . 4B 116
Lessing St. SE23 . . . . . . 5A 108
Lester Av. E15 . . . . 3A 68
Leswin Pl. N16 . . . . 5B 36
Leswin Rd. N16 . . . . 5B 36
Letchford Gdns.
  NW10 . . . . 2C 56
Letchford M. NW10 . . . . 2C 56
Letchmore Ho. W10 . . . . 3E 57
  (off Sutton Way)
Letchworth St.
  SW17 . . . . 4B 116
Lethbridge Cl. SE13 . . . . 4E 95
Letterstone Rd. SW6 . . . 3B 86
Lettice St. SW6 . . . . 4B 86
Lettsom St. SE5 . . . . 5A 92
Lettsom Wlk. E13 . . . . . 1C 68
Leucha Rd. E17 . . . . 1A 38
Levana Cl. SW19 . . . . . . 1A 114
Levant Ho. E1 . . . . 3F 65
  (off Ernest St.)
Levehurst Ho. SE27 . . . . 5E 119
Levendale Rd.
  SE23 . . . . 2A 122
Levenhurst Way SW4 . . 5A 90
Leven Rd. E14 . . . . 4E 67
Leverett St. SW3 . . . . . . 5A 74
Leverington Pl.
  N1 . . . . 2C 10 (2F 63)
Leverson St. SW16 . . . . 5E 117
Leverstock Ho. SW3 . . . 1A 88
  (off Cale St.)
Lever St. EC1 . . 2E 9 (2D 63)

Leverton Pl. NW5 . . . . . 2E 47
Leverton St. NW5 . . . . . 2E 47
Levison Way N19 . . . . . . 3F 33
Levita Ho. NW1 . . . . 1C 6
  (not continuous)
Lewesdon Cl. SW19 . . . 1F 113
Lewes Ho. SE1 . . . . 3E 27
  (off Druid St.)
  SE15 . . . . 2C 92
  (off Friary Est.)
Leweston Pl. N16 . . . . . . 2B 36
Lew Evans Ho.
  SE22 . . . . 3C 106
Lewey Ho. E3 . . . . 3B 66
  (off Joseph St.)
Lewin Rd. SW14 . . . . . . 1A 98
  SW16 . . . . 5F 117
Lewis Cl. SE16 . . . . 1D 93
  (off Stubbs Dr.)
Lewis Gro. SE13 . . . . . . 2E 109
LEWISHAM 1E 109
Lewisham Bus. Cen.
  SE14 . . . . 2F 93
Lewisham Cen.
  SE13 . . . . 2E 109
Lewisham Crematorium
  SE6 . . . . 2B 124
Lewisham Hgts.
  SE23 . . . . 1E 121
Lewisham High St.
  SE13 . . . . 4D 109
Lewisham Hill SE13 . . . . 5E 95
Lewisham Lions Cen. . . 1E 93
Lewisham Model Mkt.
  SE13 . . . . 2E 109
  (off Lewisham High St.)
Lewisham Pk. SE13 . . . . 3E 109
Lewisham Rd. SE13 . . . . 4D 95
Lewisham St.
  SW1 . . . . 4C 22 (3F 75)
Lewisham Way SE4 . . . . 4B 94
  SE14 . . . . 4B 94
Lewis Ho. E14 . . . . 2E 81
  (off Coldharbour)
Lewis Pl. E8 . . . . 2C 50
Lewis Silkin Ho.
  SE15 . . . . 2E 93
  (off Lovelinch Cl.)
Lewis St. NW1 . . . . 3D 47
  (not continuous)
Lexham Gdns. W8 . . . . . 5C 72
Lexham Gdns. M.
  W8 . . . . 4D 73
Lexham M. W8 . . . . 5C 72
Lexham Wlk. W8 . . . . . . 4D 73
Lexington Apartments
  EC1 . . . . 3C 10 (3F 63)
Lexington St.
  W1 . . . . 4A 14 (1E 75)
Lexton Gdns. SW12 . . . 1F 117
Leybourne Ho. E14 . . . . 5B 66
  (off Dod St.)
  SE15 . . . . 2E 93
Leybourne Rd. E11 . . . . 3B 40
  NW1 . . . . 4D 47
Leyburne Rd. NW1 . . . . 4D 47
Leybridge Ct. SE12 . . . . 3C 110
Leyden Mans. N19 . . . . 2A 34
Leyden St.
  E1 . . . . 1F 19 (4B 64)

Leydon Cl. SE16 . . . . 2F 79
Leyes Rd. E16 . . . . 1F 83
Leyland Ho. E14 . . . . 1D 81
   (off Hale St.)
Leyland Rd. SE12 . . . . 3C 110
Leylands SW18 . . . . 4B 100
Leylang Rd. SE14 . . . . 3F 93
Leys Ct. SW9 . . . . 5C 90
Leysdown Ho. SE17 . . . . . 1A 92
   (off Madron St.)
Leysfield Rd. W12 . . . . . . 4C 70
Leyspring Rd. E11 . . . . . . 3B 40
LEYTON 4E 39
Leyton Bus. Cen. E10 . . . 4C 38
Leyton Ct. SE23 . . . . 1E 121
Leyton Grange Est.
E10 . . . . 3C 38
Leyton Grn. Rd. E10 . . . . 1E 39
Leyton Grn. Twr. E10 . . . 1E 39
   (off Leyton Grn. Rd.)
Leyton Grn. Towers
F10 . . . . 1E 39
   (off Leyton Grn. Rd.)
Leyton Ind. Village
E10 . . . . 2F 37
Leyton Leisure Lagoon
. . . . 2D 39
Leyton Orient FC 5D 39
Leyton Pk. Rd. E10 . . . . . 5E 39
Leyton Rd. E15 . . . . 2E 53
LEYTONSTONE 5A 40
Leytonstone Ho. E11 . . . . 2B 40
   (off Hanbury Dr.)
Leytonstone Rd. E15 . . . . 2A 54
Leyton Way E11 . . . . 2A 40
Leywick St. E15 . . . . 1A 68
Liardet St. SE14 . . . . 2A 94
Liberia Rd. N5 . . . . 3D 49
Liberty Ho. E1 . . . . 1C 78
   (off Ensign St.)
Liberty M. SW12 . . . . 4D 103
Liberty St. SW9 . . . . 4B 90
Libra Rd. E3 . . . . 5B 52
E13 . . . . 1C 68
Library Mans. W12 . . . . . . 3E 71
   (off Pennard Rd.)
Library Pde. NW10 . . . . . . 5A 42
   (off Craven Pk. Rd.)
Library Pl. E1 . . . . 1D 79
Library St.
SE1 . . . . 5D 25 (3D 77)
Lichfield Rd. E3 . . . . 2A 66
E6 . . . . 2F 69
NW2 . . . . 1A 44
Lickey Ho. W14 . . . . 2B 86
   (off Nth. End Rd.)
Lidcote Gdns. SW9 . . . . . 5B 90
Liddell Gdns. NW10 . . . . . 1E 57
Liddell Rd. NW6 . . . . 3C 44
Liddington Rd. E15 . . . . . . 5B 54
Liddon Rd. E13 . . . . 2D 69
Liden Cl. E17 . . . . 2B 38
Lidfield Rd. N16 . . . . 1F 49
Lidgate Rd. SE15 . . . . 3B 92
Lidiard Rd. SW18 . . . . 2F 115
Lidlington Pl. NW1 . . . . . . 1E 61
Lidyard Rd. N19 . . . . 3E 33
Liffords Pl. SW13 . . . . 5B 84
Lifford St. SW15 . . . . 2F 99
Lighter Cl. SE16 . . . . 5A 80

Lighterman Ho. E14 . . . . . 1E 81
Lighterman M. E1 . . . . 5F 65
Lightermans Rd. E14 . . . . 3C 80
Lightermans Wlk.
SW18 . . . . 2C 100
Light Horse Ct. SW3 . . . . 1C 88
   (off Royal Hospital Rd.)
Ligonier St.
E2 . . . . 3F 11 (3B 64)
Lilac Ct. E13 . . . . 5E 55
Lilac Ho. SE4 . . . . 1C 108
Lilac Pl. SE11 . . . . 5B 76
Lilac St. W12 . . . . 1C 70
Lilburne Rd. SE9 . . . . 3F 111
Lilestone Ho. NW8 . . . . . . 3F 59
   (off Frampton St.)
Lilestone St. NW8 . . . . . . 3A 60
Lilford Ho. SE5 . . . . 5E 91
Lilford Rd. SE5 . . . . 5D 91
Lilian Barker Cl.
SE12 . . . . 3C 110
Lilian Cl. N16 . . . . 5A 36
Lilley Cl. E1 . . . . 2C 78
Lillian Rd. SW13 . . . . 2C 84
Lillie Mans. SW6 . . . . 2A 86
   (off Lillie Rd.)
Lillie Rd. SW6 . . . . 2A 86
Lillie Road Fitness Cen.
. . . . 3F 85
Lillieshall Rd. SW4 . . . . . 1D 103
Lillie Yd. SW6 . . . . 2C 86
Lillingston Ho. N7 . . . . . . 1C 48
Lillington Gdns. Est.
SW1 . . . . 5E 75
   (off Vauxhall Bri. Rd.)
Lilliput Ct. SE12 . . . . 3D 111
Lily Cl. W14 . . . . 5F 71
   (not continuous)
Lily Nichols Ho. E16 . . . . 2F 83
   (off Connaught Rd.)
Lily Pl. EC1 . . . . 5C 8 (4C 62)
Lily Rd. E17 . . . . 1C 38
Lilyville Rd. SW6 . . . . 4B 86
Limborough Ho. E14 . . . . 4C 66
   (off Thomas Rd.)
Limburg Rd. SW11 . . . . . 2A 102
Limeburner La.
EC4 . . . . 3D 17 (5D 63)
Lime Cl. E1 . . . . 2C 78
Lime Ct. E11 . . . . 4A 40
   (off Trinity Cl.)
E17 . . . . 1E 39
Lime Gro. W12 . . . . 3E 71
Limeharbour E14 . . . . 4D 81
LIMEHOUSE 5B 66
Limehouse C'way.
E14 . . . . 1B 80
Limehouse Ct. E14 . . . . . 5C 66
Limehouse Cut E14 . . . . . 4D 67
   (off Morris Rd.)
Limehouse Flds. Est.
E14 . . . . 4A 66
Limehouse Link E14 . . . . 5A 66
Lime Kiln Dr. SE7 . . . . . . 2D 97
Limerick Cl. SW12 . . . . . 5E 103
Limerston St. SW10 . . . . . 2E 87
Limes, The SW18 . . . . . . 4C 100
W2 . . . . 1C 72
Limes Av. NW11 . . . . 2A 30
SW13 . . . . 5B 84

Limes Ct. NW6 . . . . 4A 44
   (off Brondesbury Pk.)
Limes Fld. Rd.
SW14 . . . . 1A 98
Limesford Rd. SE15 . . . . . 2F 107
Limes Gdns. SW18 . . . . . 4C 100
Limes Gro. SE13 . . . . 2E 109
Limes St. EC3 . . 4D 19 (1A 78)
Lime St. Pas.
EC3 . . . . 3D 19 (5A 64)
Limes Wlk. SE15 . . . . 2E 107
Lime Tree Ct. E3 . . . . 4C 66
Limetree Ter. SE6 . . . . . . 1B 122
Limetree Wlk.
SW17 . . . . 5C 116
Lime Wlk. E15 . . . . 5A 54
Limpsfield Av.
SW19 . . . . 2F 113
Linacre Cl. SE15 . . . . 1D 107
Linacre Ct. W6 . . . . 1F 85
Linacre Rd. NW2 . . . . 3D 43
Linale Ho. N1 . . . . 1B 10
Linberry Wlk. SE8 . . . . . . 5B 80
Linchmere Rd.
SE12 . . . . 5B 110
Lincoln Av. SW19 . . . . . . 3F 113
Lincoln Cl. N16 . . . . 2F 35
SE12 . . . . 3E 125
Lincoln Ho. SE5 . . . . 3C 90
NW3 . . . . 3B 74
Lincoln M. NW6 . . . . 5B 44
SE21 . . . . 2F 119
Lincoln Rd. E7 . . . . 3F 55
E13 . . . . 3D 69
Lincolns Inn Flds.
WC2 . . . . 2F 15 (5B 62)
Lincoln's Inn Hall
. . . . 2A 16 (5B 62)
Lincoln St. E11 . . . . 4A 40
SW3 . . . . 5B 74
Lincombe Rd.
BR1: Brom 3B 124
Lindal Rd. SE4 . . . . 3B 108
Linden Av. NW10 . . . . 1F 57
Linden Ct. W12 . . . . 2E 71
Linden Gdns. W2 . . . . 1C 72
W4 . . . . 1A 84
Linden Gro. SE15 . . . . . . 1D 107
Linden Ho. SE8 . . . . 2B 94
   (off Abinger Gro.)
Linden Lea N2 . . . . 1E 31
Linden Mans. N6 . . . . 3D 33
   (off Hornsey La.)
Linden M. N1 . . . . 2F 49
W2 . . . . 1C 72
Linden Wlk. N19 . . . . 4E 33
Lindfield Gdns. NW3 . . . . 2D 45
Lindfield St. E14 . . . . 5C 66
Lindisfarne Way E9 . . . . . 1A 52
Lindley Est. SE15 . . . . . . 3C 92
Lindley Ho. E1 . . . . 4E 65
   (off Lindley St.)
SE15 . . . . 3C 92
   (off Peckham Pk. Rd.)
Lindley Rd. E10 . . . . 4E 39
Lindley St. E1 . . . . 4E 65
Lindop Ho. E1 . . . . 3A 66
   (off Mile End Rd.)
Lindore Rd. SW11 . . . . . . 2B 102

Lindo St. SE15 . . . . 5E 93
Lindrop St. SW6 . . . . . . 5E 87
Lindsay Sq. SW1 . . . . . . 1F 89
Lindsell St. SE10 . . . . . . 4E 95
Lindsey M. N1 . . . . 4E 49
Lindsey St.
    EC1 . . . . 5E 9 (4D 63)
Lind St. SE8 . . . . 5C 94
Lindway SE27 . . . . 5D 119
Linfield WC1 . . . . 2F 7
        (off Sidmouth St.)
Linford Christie Stadium
    . . . . 4C 56
Linford St. SW8 . . . . . . 4E 89
Lingard Ho. E14 . . . . . . 4E 81
        (off Marshfield St.)
Lingards Rd. SE13 . . . . 2E 109
Lingfield Ho. SE1 . . . . . 4E 25
Lingfield Rd.
    SW19 . . . . 5F 113
Lingham Ct. SW9 . . . . . . 5A 90
Lingham St. SW9 . . . . . . 5A 90
Ling Rd. E16 . . . . 4C 68
Lings Coppice SE21 . . . 2F 119
Lingwell Rd. SW17 . . . . 3A 116
Lingwood Rd. E5 . . . . . 2C 36
Linhope St. NW1 . . . . . . 3B 60
Link, The NW2 . . . . 3C 28
Linkenholt Mans. W6 . . . 5B 70
        (off Stamford Brook Av.)
Link Ho. E3 . . . . 1D 67
    W10 . . . . 5F 57
        (off Kingsdown Cl.)
Link Rd. E1 . . . . 1C 78
    E12 . . . . 4F 41
Links Rd. NW2 . . . . 4B 28
Link St. E9 . . . . 3E 51
Linksview N2 . . . . 1B 32
        (off Gt. North Rd.)
Links Yd. E1 . . . . 4B 64
        (off Spelman St.)
Linkway N4 . . . . 2E 35
Linkwood Wlk. NW1 . . . . 4F 47
Linley Sambourne House
    . . . . 4C 72
        (off Stafford Ter.)
Linnell Cl. NW11 . . . . . . 1D 31
Linnell Dr. NW11 . . . . . . 1D 31
Linnell Ho. E1 . . . . 5F 11
        (off Folgate St.)
Linnell Rd. SE5 . . . . 5A 92
Linnet M. SW12 . . . . . . 5C 102
Linom Rd. SW4 . . . . 2A 104
Linscott Rd. E5 . . . . 1E 51
Linsey Ct. E10 . . . . 3C 38
        (off Grange Rd.)
Linsey St. SE16 . . . . 5C 78
        (not continuous)
Linslade Ho. E2 . . . . . . 5C 50
    NW8 . . . . 3A 60
        (off Paveley St.)
Linstead Hall SW7 . . . . . 4F 73
        (off Princes Gdns.)
Linstead St. NW6 . . . . . . 4C 44
Linstead Way SW18 . . . . 5A 100
Lintaine Cl. W6 . . . . 2A 86
Linthorpe Rd. N16 . . . . . 2A 36
Linton Cl. SE7 . . . . 1E 97
Linton Gdns. E6 . . . . 5F 69
Linton Gro. SE27 . . . . . 5D 119

Linton Ho. E3 . . . . 4C 66
        (off St Paul's Way)
Linton St. N1 . . . . 5E 49
        (not continuous)
Linver Rd. SW6 . . . . 5C 86
Linwood Cl. SE5 . . . . 5B 92
Lion Cl. SE4 . . . . 4C 108
Lion Ct. E1 . . . . 1F 79
        (off Highway, The)
    N1 . . . . 5B 48
        (off Copenhagen St.)
    SE1 . . . . 2D 27
        (off Magdalen St.)
Lionel Gdns. SE9 . . . . . 3F 111
Lionel Mans. W14 . . . . . 4F 71
        (off Haarlem Rd.)
Lionel M. W10 . . . . 4A 58
Lionel Rd. SE9 . . . . . . 3F 111
Lion Gate M.
    SW18 . . . . 5C 100
Lion Mills E2 . . . . 1C 64
Lions Cl. SE9 . . . . 3F 125
Lion Yd. SW4 . . . . 2F 103
Liphook Cres. SE23 . . . 5E 107
Lipton Rd. E1 . . . . 5F 65
Lisburne Rd. NW3 . . . . . 1B 46
Lisford St. SE15 . . . . . . 4B 92
Lisgar Ter. W14 . . . . . . 5B 72
Liskeard Gdns. SE3 . . . . 4C 96
Liskeard Ho. SE11 . . . . . 1C 90
        (off Kennings Way)
Lisle Cl. SW17 . . . . 4D 117
Lisle Ct. NW2 . . . . 5A 30
Lisle St.
    WC2 . . . . 4C 14 (1F 75)
Lismore SW19 . . . . 5B 114
        (off Woodside)
Lismore Cir. NW5 . . . . . . 2C 46
Lismore Ho. SE15 . . . . . 1D 107
Lismore Wlk. N1 . . . . 3E 49
        (off Clephane Rd. Nth.)
Lissenden Gdns.
    NW5 . . . . 1C 46
        (not continuous)
Lissenden Mans.
    NW5 . . . . 1C 46
Lisson Grn. Est.
    NW8 . . . . 3A 60
        (off Tresham Cres.)
LISSON GROVE 4A 60
Lisson Gro. NW1 . . . . . . 3F 59
    NW8 . . . . 3F 59
Lisson Ho. NW1 . . . . . . 4A 60
        (off Lisson St.)
Lisson St. NW1 . . . . 4A 60
Lister Cl. W3 . . . . 4A 56
Listergate Ct. SW15 . . . . 2E 99
Lister Ho. E1 . . . . 4C 64
    SE3 . . . . 2A 96
        (off Restell Cl.)
Lister Lodge W9 . . . . . . 4C 58
        (off Admiral Wlk.)
Lister Rd. E11 . . . . 3A 40
Liston Rd. SW4 . . . . 1E 103
Listowel Cl. SW9 . . . . . . 3C 90
Listria Pk. N16 . . . . 4A 36
Litcham Ho. E1 . . . . 2F 65
        (off Longnor Rd.)
Litchfield Av. E15 . . . . . . 3A 54
Litchfield Ct. E17 . . . . . . 1C 38

Litchfield Gdns.
    NW10 . . . . 3C 42
Litchfield St.
    WC2 . . . . 4C 14 (1F 75)
Litchfield Way NW11 . . . . 1E 31
Lithos Rd. NW3 . . . . 3D 45
Lit. Albany St.
    NW1 . . . . 2E 5 (2D 61)
        (Albany St.)
    NW1 . . . . 3E 5
        (Longford St.)
Little Angel Theatre 5D 49
        (off Cross St.)
Lit. Argyll St.
    W1 . . . . 3F 13 (5E 61)
Lit. Boltons, The
    SW5 . . . . 1D 87
    SW10 . . . . 1D 87
Little Bornes SE21 . . . . 4A 120
Littlebourne SE13 . . . . 5A 110
Little Britain
    EC1 . . . . 1E 17 (4D 63)
Little Brownings
    SE23 . . . . 2D 121
Littlebury Rd.
    SW4 . . . . 1F 103
Lit. Chester St.
    SW1 . . . . 5D 21 (4D 75)
Little Cloisters
    SW1 . . . . 5D 23 (4A 76)
Lit. College La. EC4 . . . . 4B 18
        (off College St.)
Lit. College St.
    SW1 . . . . 5D 23 (4A 76)
Littlecombe SE7 . . . . . . 2D 97
Littlecombe Cl.
    SW15 . . . . 4F 99
Littlecote Cl. SW19 . . . . 5A 100
Lit. Dean's Yd. SW1 . . . . 5D 23
Little Dimocks
    SW12 . . . . 2D 117
Lit. Dorrit Ct.
    SE1 . . . . 3A 26 (3E 77)
Lit. Edward St.
    NW1 . . . . 1E 5 (2D 61)
Lit. Essex St. WC2 . . . . 4B 16
Littlefield Cl. N19 . . . . . . 1E 47
Lit. George St.
    SW1 . . . . 4D 23 (3A 76)
Little Grn. St. NW5 . . . . . 1D 47
Little Heath SE7 . . . . . . 2F 97
Little Holt E11 . . . . 1C 40
Lit. London Ct. SE1 . . . . 3B 78
        (off Wolseley St.)
Lit. Marlborough St.
    W1 . . . . 3F 13
Lit. Newport St.
    WC2 . . . . 4C 14 (1F 75)
Lit. New St.
    EC4 . . . . 2C 16 (5C 62)
Lit. Portland St.
    W1 . . . . 2E 13 (5E 61)
Lit. Russell St.
    WC1 . . . . 1D 15 (4A 62)
Lit. St James's St.
    SW1 . . . . 2F 21 (2E 75)
Little Sanctuary
    SW1 . . . . 4C 22 (3F 75)
Lit. Smith St.
    SW1 . . . . 5C 22 (4F 75)

Lit. Somerset St.
E1 . . . . 3F **19** (5B **64**)
Lit. Titchfield St.
W1 . . . . 1F **13** (4E **61**)
Littleton Ho. SW1 . . . . 1E **89**
(off Lupus St.)
Littleton St. SW18 . . . . . 2E **115**
Lit. Trinity La.
EC4 . . . . 4A **18** (1E **77**)
Little Turnstile
WC1 . . . . 1F **15** (4B **62**)
Littlewood St13 . . . . . . 4E **109**
Livermere Ct. E8 . . . . 5R **50**
(off Queensbridge Rd.)
Livermere Rd. E8 . . . . 5B **50**
Liverpool Gro. SE17 . . . . . 1E **91**
Liverpool Rd. E10 . . . . 1E **39**
E16 . . . . 4A **68**
N1 . . . . 4C **48**
N7 . . . . 2C **48**
Liverpool St.
EC2 . . . . 1D **19** (4A **64**)
Livesey Mus. for Children
. . . . 2D **93**
Livesey Pl. SE15 . . . . 2C **92**
Livingstone Ct. E10 . . . . . 1E **39**
Livingstone Ho. SE5 . . . . . 3E **91**
(off Wyndham Rd.)
Livingstone Lodge
W9 . . . . 4C **58**
(off Admiral Wlk.)
Livingstone Mans.
W14 . . . . 2A **86**
(off Queen's Club Gdns.)
Livingstone Pl. E14 . . . . . . 1E **95**
Livingstone Rd. E15 . . . . . 5E **53**
E17 . . . . 1D **39**
SW11 . . . . 1F **101**
LivingWell Health Club
. . . . 1D **59**
(within Regents Plaza)
Livonia St.
W1 . . . . 3A **14** (5E **61**)
Lizard St.
EC1 . . . . 2A **10** (2E **63**)
Lizban St. SE3 . . . . 3D **97**
Llandovery Ho. E14 . . . . . 3E **81**
(off Chipka St.)
Llanelly Rd. NW2 . . . . . . 4B **30**
Llanvanor Rd. NW2 . . . . . 4B **30**
Llewellyn St. SE16 . . . . . 3C **78**
Lloyd Baker St.
WC1 . . . . 2A **8** (2B **62**)
(not continuous)
Lloyd's Av.
EC3 . . . . 3E **19** (5A **64**)
Lloyds' Building
. . . . 3D **19** (5A **64**)
Lloyd's Pl. SE3 . . . . 5A **96**
Lloyd Sq.
WC1 . . . . 1B **8** (2C **62**)
Lloyd's Row
EC1 . . . . 2B **8** (2C **62**)
Lloyd St. WC1 . . . 1B **8** (2C **62**)
Lloyds Wharf SE1 . . . . . . 3E **78**
(off Mill St.)
Lloyd Vs. SE4 . . . . 5C **94**
Loampit Hill SE13 . . . . . . 5C **94**
LOAMPIT VALE 1E **109**
Loampit Va. SE13 . . . . 1D **109**

Loanda Cl. E8 . . . . 5B **50**
Loats Rd. SW2 . . . . 4A **104**
Lobelia Cl. E6 . . . . 4F **69**
Locarno Ct. SW16 . . . . . 5E **117**
Lochaber Rd. SE13 . . . . 2A **110**
Lochaline St. W6 . . . . . . 2E **85**
Lochinvar St.
SW12 . . . . 5D **103**
Lochmore Ho. SW1 . . . . . 5C **74**
(off Cundy St.)
Lochnagar St. E14 . . . . . . 4E **67**
Lockbridge Ct. W9 . . . . . . 4C **58**
(off Woodfield Rd.)
Lock Chase SE3 . . . . . . 1A **110**
Locke Ho. SW8 . . . . 4E **89**
(off Wadhurst Rd.)
Lockesfield Pl. E14 . . . . . 1D **95**
Lockgate Cl. E9 . . . . 2B **52**
Lockhart Cl. N7 . . . . 3B **48**
Lockhart Ho. SE10 . . . . . 3D **95**
(off Tarves Way)
Lockhart St. E3 . . . . 3B **66**
Lockington Rd. SW8 . . . . 4D **89**
Lock Keepers Quay
SE16 . . . . 4F **79**
(off Brunswick Quay)
Lockmead Rd. N15 . . . . . 1C **36**
SE13 . . . . 1E **109**
Lock M. NW5 . . . . 3F **47**
(off Northpoint Sq.)
Locksfields SE17 . . . . . . 5F **77**
(off Catesby St.)
Lockside E14 . . . . 1A **80**
(off Narrow St.)
Locksley Est. E14 . . . . . . 5B **66**
Locksley St. E14 . . . . 4B **66**
Lock Vw. Ct. E14 . . . . 1A **80**
(off Narrow St.)
Lockwood Cl. SE26 . . . . 4F **121**
Lockwood Ho. SE11 . . . . 2C **90**
Lockwood Sq. SE16 . . . . 4D **79**
Lockyer Est. SE1 . . . . . . 4C **26**
(not continuous)
Lockyer Ho. SE10 . . . . . . 1B **96**
(off Armitage Rd.)
SW8 . . . . 3F **89**
(off Wandsworth Rd.)
SW15 . . . . 1F **99**
Lockyer St.
SE1 . . . . 4C **26** (3F **77**)
Locton Grn. E3 . . . . 5B **52**
Loddiges Ho. E9 . . . . 4E **51**
Loddiges Rd. E9 . . . . 4E **51**
Loder St. SE15 . . . . 3E **93**
Lodge Av. SW14 . . . . 1A **98**
Lodge Rd. NW8 . . . . 2F **59**
Lodore Gdns. NW9 . . . . . 1A **28**
Lodore St. E14 . . . . 5E **67**
Loftie St. SE16 . . . . 3C **78**
Lofting Rd. N1 . . . . 4B **48**
Loftus Road 2D **71**
Loftus Rd. W12 . . . . 2D **71**
Loftus Vs. W12 . . . . 2D **71**
(off Loftus Rd.)
Logan M. W8 . . . . 5C **72**
Logan Pl. W8 . . . . 5C **72**
Loggetts SE21 . . . . 2A **120**
Lohmann Ho. SE11 . . . . . 2C **90**
(off Kennington Oval)

Lolesworth Cl.
E1 . . . . 1F **19** (4B **64**)
Lollard St. SE11 . . . . 5B **76**
(not continuous)
Loman St.
SE1 . . . . 3E **25** (3D **77**)
(off Richmond St.)
Lomas Dr. E8 . . . . 4B **50**
(off Richmond St.)
Lomas St. E1 . . . . 4C **64**
Lombard Bus. Cen., The
SW11 . . . . 5F **87**
Lombard Ct.
EC3 . . . . 4C **18** (1F **77**)
Lombard La.
EC4 . . . . 3C **16** (5C **62**)
Lombard Rd. SW11 . . . . . 5F **87**
Lombard St.
EC3 . . . . 3C **18** (5F **63**)
Lombard Trad. Est.
SE7 . . . . 5D **83**
Lombard Wall SE7 . . . . . 4D **83**
(not continuous)
Lombardy Pl. W2 . . . . . . 1D **73**
Lomond Gro. SE5 . . . . . . 3F **91**
Lomond Ho. SE5 . . . . . . 3F **91**
Loncroft Rd. SE5 . . . . . . 2A **92**
Londesborough Rd.
N16 . . . . 1A **50**
Londinium Twr. E1 . . . . . . 4F **19**
(off W. Tenter St.)
London Academy of Music &
Dramatic Art 5C **72**
(off Cromwell Rd.)
London Apollo 1E **85**
London Aquarium
. . . . 3F **23** (3B **76**)
London Bri.
EC4 . . . . 5C **18** (2F **77**)
London Bri. St.
SE1 . . . . 1C **26** (2F **77**)
London Bri. Wlk.
SE1 . . . . 1C **26**
(off Duke St. Hill)
London Business School
. . . . 3A **4** (3B **60**)
London Canal Mus. 1A **62**
LONDON CITY AIRPORT
. . . . 1F **83**
London City College
. . . . 2B **24** (2C **76**)
(in Schiller University)
London Coliseum 5D **15**
(off St Martin's La.)
London College of
Fashion, The
Hackney 4E **51**
(off Mare St.)
St Luke's 4F **9** (3E **63**)
London Dungeon 2C **26**
London Eye 3F **23** (3B **76**)
London Flds. E. Side
E8 . . . . 4D **51**
London Flds. W. Side
E8 . . . . 4C **50**
London Fruit Exchange
E1 . . . . 1F **19**
(off Brushfield St.)
London Group Bus. Pk.
NW2 . . . . 3B **28**

London Guildhall University
  Coke St. 5C 64
London Ho. NW8 . . . . . . 1A 60
  (off Avenue Rd.)
  WC1 . . . . 3F 7 (3B 62)
London La. E8 . . . . . . 4D 51
London Master Bakers
  Almshouses E10 . . . . 1D 39
London Metropolitan
  University
  Benwell Rd. 2C 48
  City of London 3F 19
  (off Jewry St.)
  Hornsey St. 2B 48
  Manningtree St.
  . . . . 2F 19 (5C 64)
London M. W2 . . . . 5F 59
London Palladium 3F 13
  (off Argyll St.)
London Planetarium
  . . . . 4B 4 (3C 60)
London Regatta Cen. . . 1F 83
London Rd. E13 . . . . . . 1C 68
  SE1 . . . . 5D 25 (4D 77)
  SE23 . . . . 1D 121
London School of Economics
  & Politics, The
  . . . . . . 3A 16 (5B 62)
London South Bank University
  . . . . . . 5E 25 (4D 77)
London South Bank University
  Sports Cen. 4D 77
  (off Borough Rd.)
London Stock Exchange
  . . . . 2E 17
  (off Paternoster Sq.)
London St.
  EC3 . . . . 4E 19 (1A 78)
  W2 . . . . 5F 59
London Symphony Orchestra
  . . . . 3A 10
  (off St Lukes Cl.)
London Telecom Tower, The
  . . . . 5F 5 (4E 61)
London Television Cen., The
  . . . . . . 1B 24 (2C 76)
London Ter. E2 . . . . . . 1C 64
London Towers Basketball
  Crystal Palace National
  Sports Cen. 5C 120
London Transport Mus.
  . . . . . . 4E 15 (1A 76)
London Wall
  EC2 . . . . . . 1A 18 (4E 63)
London Wall Bldgs.
  EC2 . . . . 1C 18
London Wetland Cen.
  . . . . 4D 85
London Wharf E2 . . . . . 5D 51
  (off Wharf Pl.)
London Wildlife Trust
  . . . . 5F 47
London Wildlife Trust Cen.
  for Wildlife Gardening
  . . . . 1B 106
London Zoo 1C 60
Long Acre
  WC2 . . . . . . 4D 15 (1A 76)
Longbeach Rd.
  SW11 . . . . 1B 102

Longberrys NW2 . . . . . 5B 30
Longbridge Way
  SE13 . . . . 3E 109
Longdown Rd. SE6 . . . 4C 122
Long Dr. W3 . . . . 5A 56
Longfellow Rd. E17 . . . 1B 38
Longfellow Way SE1 . . 5B 78
Longfield Cres.
  SE26 . . . . 3E 121
Longfield Est. SE1 . . . . 5B 78
Longfield SW18 . . . . . 5C 100
Longford Ct. E5 . . . . . . 1F 51
  (off Pedro St.)
Longford St.
  NW1 . . . . 3E 5 (3D 61)
Longford Wlk. SW2 . . . 5C 104
Longhedge Ho.
  SE26 . . . . 4C 120
  (off High Level Dr.)
Longhedge St. SW11 . . 5C 88
Longhill Rd. SE6 . . . . . 2F 123
Longhope Cl. SE15 . . . . 2A 92
Longhurst Rd. SE13 . . 3F 109
Longland Ct. SE1 . . . . . 1C 92
Longlands Ct. W11 . . . 1B 72
  (off Westbourne Gro.)
Long La. EC1 . . 1E 17 (4D 63)
  SE1 . . . . 4B 26 (3F 77)
Longleat Ho. SW1 . . . . 1F 89
  (off Rampayne St.)
Longleigh Ho. SE5 . . . . 4A 92
  (off Peckham Rd.)
Long Lents Ho.
  NW10 . . . . 5A 42
  (off Fitzsimmons Ct.)
Longley Ct. SW8 . . . . . 4A 90
Longley Rd. SW17 . . . 5A 116
Longley St. SE1 . . . . . . 5C 78
Longley Way NW2 . . . . 5E 29
Longman Ho. E2 . . . . . 1F 65
  (off Mace St.)
  E8 . . . . 5B 50
  (off Haggerston Rd.)
Long Mark Rd. E16 . . . 4F 69
Longmead Ho.
  SE27 . . . . 5E 119
Long Mdw. NW5 . . . . . 2F 47
Longmead Rd.
  SW17 . . . . 5B 116
Longmoore St. SW1 . . 5E 75
Longmoor Point
  SW15 . . . . 1D 113
  (off Norley Vale)
Longmore Gdns. SW1
  . . . . 5E 75
  (off Vauxhall Bri. Rd.)
Longnor Est. E1 . . . . . 2F 65
Longnor Rd. E1 . . . . . . 2F 65
Long Pond Rd. SE3 . . . 4A 96
Longridge Ho.
  SE1 . . . . 5A 26 (4E 77)
Longridge Rd. SW5 . . . 5C 72
Long Rd. SW4 . . . . . . 2D 103
Long's Ct. WC2 . . . . . . 5C 14
Longshore SE8 . . . . . . 5B 80

Longshott Ct. SW5 . . . 5C 72
  (off W. Cromwell Rd.)
Longstaff Cres.
  SW18 . . . . 4C 100
Longstaff Rd. SW18 . . 4C 100
Longstone Av. NW10 . . 4B 42
Longstone Ct. SE1 . . . . 4B 26
  (off Gt. Dover St.)
Longstone Rd.
  SW17 . . . . 5D 117
Long St. E2 . . . 1F 11 (2B 64)
Longthorpe Ct. W6 . . . 5C 70
  (off Invermead Cl.)
Longton Av. SE26 . . . . 4C 120
Longton Gro. SE26 . . . 4D 121
Longville Rd. SE11 . . . 5D 77
Long Wlk. SE1 . . . . 5E 27
  SW13 . . . . 5A 84
Long Wall E15 . . . . 2F 67
Longwood Dr. SW15 . . 4C 98
Long Yd. WC1 . . 4F 7 (3B 62)
Lonsdale Av. E6 . . . . . 2F 69
Lonsdale Cl. E6 . . . . . . 3F 69
  SE9 . . . . 3F 125
Lonsdale Ho. W11 . . . . 5B 58
  (off Lonsdale Rd.)
Lonsdale M. W11 . . . . . 5B 58
  (off Lonsdale Rd.)
Lonsdale Pl. N1 . . . . . . 4C 48
Lonsdale Rd. E11 . . . . 1B 40
  NW6 . . . . 5B 44
  SW13 . . . . 4B 84
  W4 . . . . 5B 70
  W11 . . . . 5B 58
Lonsdale Sq. N1 . . . . . 4C 48
Lonsdale Yd. W11 . . . . 1C 72
Lopez Ho. SW9 . . . . . 1A 104
Loraine Cotts. N7 . . . . 1B 48
Loraine Rd. N7 . . . . . . 1B 48
Lord Amory Way E14 . . 3E 81
Lordell Pl. SW19 . . . . . 5E 113
Lorden Wlk. E2 . . . . . . 2C 64
Lord Hills Bri. W2 . . . . 4D 59
Lord Hills Rd. W2 . . . . 4D 59
Lord Holland La.
  SW9 . . . . 5C 90
Lord Napier Pl. W6 . . . 1C 84
Lord North St.
  SW1 . . . . 5D 23 (4A 76)
Lord Roberts M. SW6 . . 3D 87
Lords Cl. SE21 . . . . . . 2E 119
Lord's Cricket Ground
  Marylebone & Middlesex
  County Cricket Clubs
  . . . . 2F 59
Lordship Gro. N16 . . . . 4F 35
Lordship La. SE22 . . . 2B 106
Lordship La. Est.
  SE21 . . . . 5C 106
Lordship Pk. N16 . . . . 4E 35
Lordship Pk. M. N16 . . 4E 35
Lordship Pl. SW3 . . . . 2A 88
Lordship Rd. N16 . . . . 3F 35
Lordship Ter. N16 . . . . 4F 35
Lords Vw. NW8 . . . . . . 2F 59
Loreburn Ho. N7 . . . . . 1B 48
Lorenzo St.
  WC1 . . . . 1F 7 (2B 62)
Loring Rd. SE14 . . . . . 4A 94
Loris Rd. W6 . . . . 4E 71

Lorn Ct. SW9 . . . . 5C 90
Lorne Cl. NW8 . . . . 2A 60
Lorne Gdns. W11 . . . . . . 3F 71
Lorne Ho. E1 . . . . 4A 66
(off Ben Jonson Rd.)
Lorne Rd. E7 . . . . 1D 55
E17 . . . . 1C 38
N4 . . . . 3B 34
Lorn Rd. SW9 . . . . 5B 90
Lorraine Ct. NW1 . . . . . . 4D 47
Lorrimore Rd. SE17 . . . . 2D 91
Lorrimore Sq. SE17 . . . . 2D 91
Lorton Ho. NW6 . . . . 5C 44
(off Kilburn Va.)
Lothair Rd. Nth. N4 . . . . 1D 35
Lothair Rd. Sth. N4 . . . . 2C 34
Lothbury
EC2 . . . . 2B 18 (5F 63)
Lothian Rd. SW9 . . . . . . 4D 91
Lothrop St. W10 . . . . . . 2A 58
Lots Rd. SW10 . . . . 3E 87
Lotus Cl. SE21 . . . . 3F 119
Loubet St. SW17 . . . . . . 5B 116
Loudoun Rd. NW8 . . . . . 5E 45
Loughborough Est.
SW9 . . . . 1D 105
Loughborough Pk.
SW9 . . . . 2D 105
Loughborough Rd.
SW9 . . . . 5C 90
Loughborough St.
SE11 . . . . 1B 90
Lough Rd. N7 . . . . 2B 48
Louisa Cl. E9 . . . . 5F 51
Louisa Gdns. E1 . . . . . . 3F 65
Louisa St. E1 . . . . 3F 65
Louise Aumonier Wlk.
N19 . . . . 2A 34
(off Jessie Blythe La.)
Louise Bennett Cl.
SE24 . . . . 2D 105
Louise De Marillac Ho.
E1 . . . . 4E 65
(off Smithy St.)
Louise White Ho.
N19 . . . . 1F 33
Louisville Rd.
SW17 . . . . 3C 116
Louvaine Rd. SW11 . . . . 2F 101
Lovat Cl. NW2 . . . . 5B 28
Lovat La.
EC3 . . . . 4D 19 (1A 78)
(not continuous)
Lovatt Ct. SW12 . . . . . . 1D 117
Lovegrove St. SE1 . . . . . 1C 92
Lovegrove Wlk. E14 . . . . 2E 81
Lovelace Ho. E8 . . . . . . 5B 50
(off Haggerston Rd.)
Lovelace Rd. SE21 . . . . 2E 119
Love La. EC2 . . 2A 18 (5E 63)
Lovelinch Cl. SE15 . . . . 2E 93
Lovell Ho. E8 . . . . 5C 50
(off Shrubland Rd.)
Lovell Pl. SE16 . . . . 4A 80
Loveridge M. NW6 . . . . . 3B 44
Loveridge Rd. NW6 . . . . 3B 44
Lovers Wlk. SE10 . . . . . 2F 95
W1 . . . . 1B 20 (2C 74)
Love Wlk. SE5 . . . . 5F 91

Low Cross Wood La.
SE21 . . . . 3B 120
Lowden Rd. SE24 . . . . . 2D 105
Lowder Ho. E1 . . . . 2D 79
(off Wapping La.)
Lowe Av. E16 . . . . 4C 68
Lowell Ho. SE5 . . . . 3E 91
(off Wyndham Est.)
Lowell St. E14 . . . . 5A 66
Lwr. Addison Gdns.
W14 . . . . 3A 72
Lwr. Belgrave St.
SW1 . . . . 5D 21 (4D 75)
LOWER CLAPTON 5D 37
Lwr. Clapton Rd. E5. . . . 5D 37
Lwr. Clarendon Wlk.
W11 . . . . 5A 58
(off Clarendon Rd.)
Lwr. Common Sth.
SW15 . . . . 1F 99
Lwr. Grosvenor Pl.
SW1 . . . . 5E 21 (4D 75)
LOWER HOLLOWAY . . . 2B 48
Lwr. James St.
W1 . . . . 4A 14 (1E 75)
Lwr. John St.
W1 . . . . 4A 14 (1E 75)
Lwr. Lea Crossing
E14 . . . . 1A 82
E16 . . . . 1A 82
Lower Mall W6 . . . . 1D 85
Lower Marsh
SE1 . . . . 4B 24 (3C 76)
Lwr. Merton Ri. NW3 . . 4A 46
Lwr. Richmond Rd.
SW15 . . . . 1D 99
Lower Rd.
SE1 . . . . 3B 24 (3C 76)
SE8 . . . . 5F 79
SE16 . . . . 3E 79
(not continuous)
Lwr. Robert St. WC2 . . . 5E 15
(in Robert St.)
Lwr. Sloane St. SW1 . . . 5C 74
LOWER SYDENHAM
. . . . 4F 121
Lwr. Sydenham Ind. Est.
SE26 . . . . 5B 122
Lower Ter. NW3 . . . . . . 5E 31
SE27 . . . . 5D 119
(off Woodcote Pl.)
Lwr. Thames St.
EC3 . . . . 5C 18
Lowerwood Ct. W11 . . . 5A 58
(off Westbourne Pk. Rd.)
Lowestoft Cl. E5 . . . . . . 4E 37
(off Mundford Rd.)
Loweswater Ho. E3 . . . . 3B 66
Lowfield Rd. NW6 . . . . . 4C 44
Low Hall La. E17 . . . . . . 1A 38
Low Hall Mnr. Bus. Cen.
E17 . . . . 1A 38
Lowman Rd. N7 . . . . . . 1B 48
Lowndes Cl. SW1 . . . . . 4C 74
Lowndes Ct.
SW1 . . . . 3A 20 (1D 74)
W1 . . . . 3F 13
Lowndes Pl. SW1 . . . . . 4C 74
Lowndes Sq.
SW1 . . . . 4A 20 (3B 74)

Lowndes St.
SW1 . . . . 5A 20 (4C 74)
Lowood Ho. E1 . . . . 1E 79
(off Bewley St.)
Lowood St. E1 . . . . 1D 79
Lowry Ct. SE16 . . . . 1D 93
(off Stubbs Dr.)
Lowther Gdns. SW7 . . . 3F 73
Lowther Hill SE23 . . . . . 5A 108
Lowther Ho. E8 . . . . 5B 50
(off Clarissa St.)
SW1 . . . . 1E 89
(off Churchill Gdns.)
Lowther Rd. N7 . . . . 2C 48
SW13 . . . . 4D 84
Lowth Rd. SE5 . . . . 4F 91
Loxford Av. E6 . . . . 1F 69
Loxham St.
WC1 . . . . 2E 7 (2A 62)
Loxley Cl. SE26 . . . . 5F 121
Loxley Rd. SW18 . . . . . . 1F 115
Loxton Rd. SE23 . . . . . . 1F 121
Lubbock Ho. E14 . . . . . . 1D 81
(off Poplar High St.)
Lubbock St. SE14 . . . . . 3E 93
Lucan Ho. N1 . . . . 5F 49
(off Colville Est.)
Lucan Pl. SW3 . . . . 5A 74
Lucas Av. E13 . . . . 5D 55
Lucas Cl. NW10 . . . . . . 4C 42
Lucas Ct. SE26 . . . . 5A 122
SW11 . . . . 4C 88
Lucas Ho. SW10 . . . . . . 3D 87
(off Coleridge Gdns.)
Lucas Sq. NW11 . . . . . . 1C 30
Lucas St. SE8 . . . . 4C 94
Lucerne M. W8 . . . . 2C 72
Lucerne Rd. N5 . . . . 1D 49
Lucey Rd. SE16 . . . . . . 4C 78
Lucey Way SE16 . . . . . . 4C 78
Lucien Rd. SW17 . . . . . 4C 116
SW19 . . . . 2D 115
Lucorn Cl. SE12 . . . . . . 4B 110
Lucy Brown Ho. SE1 . . . 2A 26
Ludgate B'way.
EC4 . . . . 3D 17 (5D 63)
Ludgate Cir.
EC4 . . . . 3D 17 (5D 63)
Ludgate Hill
EC4 . . . . 3D 17 (5D 63)
Ludgate Sq.
EC4 . . . . 3E 17 (5D 63)
Ludham NW5 . . . . 2B 46
Ludlow St.
EC1 . . . . 3F 9 (3E 63)
Ludovick Wlk. SW15 . . . 2A 98
Ludwick M. SE14 . . . . . 3A 94
Luffman Rd. SE12 . . . . . 3D 125
Lugard Ho. W12 . . . . . . 2D 71
Lugard Rd. SE15 . . . . . . 5D 93
Luke Ho. E1 . . . . 5D 65
(off Tillman St.)
Luke St. EC2 . . 3D 11 (3A 64)
Lukin St. E1 . . . . 5E 65
Lullingstone Ho.
SE15 . . . . 2E 93
(off Lovelinch Cl.)
Lullingstone La.
SE13 . . . . 4F 109
Lulot Gdns. N19 . . . . . . 4D 33

Lulworth NW1 . . . . . . 4F **47**
  (off Wrotham Rd.)
SE17 . . . . 1F **91**
  (off Portland St.)
Lulworth Ct. N1 . . . . . 4A **50**
  (off St Peter's Way)
Lulworth Ho. SE9 . . . . 3B **90**
Lulworth Rd. SE9 . . . . 2F **125**
SE15 . . . . 5D **93**
Lumiere Bldg., The
  E7 . . . . 2F **55**
  (off Romford Rd.)
Lumiere Ct. SW17 . . . . 2C **116**
Lumina Bldgs. E14 . . . 2E **81**
  (off Prestons Rd.)
Lumley Bldgs.
  WC2 . . . . 5E **15** (1A **76**)
Lumley Flats SW1 . . . . 1C **88**
  (off Holbein Pl.)
Lumley St.
  W1 . . . . 3C **12** (5C **60**)
Lumsdon NW8 . . . . . . 5D **45**
  (off Abbey Rd.)
Lund Point E15 . . . . . . 5E **53**
Lundy Wlk. N1 . . . . . . 3E **49**
Lunham Rd. SE19 . . . . 5A **120**
Luntley Pl. E1 . . . . 4C **64**
  (off Chicksand St.)
Lupin Cl. SW2 . . . . . . 2D **119**
Lupino Ct. SE11 . . . . . 5B **76**
Lupin Point SE1 . . . . . 3B **78**
  (off Abbey St.)
Lupton Cl. SE12 . . . . . 3D **125**
Lupton St. NW5 . . . . . 1E **47**
  (not continuous)
Lupus St. SW1 . . . . . . 1D **89**
Luralda Wharf E14 . . . 1F **95**
Lurgan Av. W6 . . . . . . 2F **85**
Lurline Gdns. SW11 . . 4C **88**
Luscombe Way SW8 . . 3A **90**
Lushington Rd.
  NW10 . . . . 1D **57**
SE6 . . . . 4D **123**
Lushington Ter. E8 . . . 2C **50**
Luther King Cl. E17 . . 1B **38**
Luton Ho. E13 . . . . 3C **68**
  (off Luton Rd.)
Luton Pl. SE10 . . . . . . 3E **95**
Luton Rd. E13 . . . . 3C **68**
Luton St. NW8 . . . . . . 3F **59**
Lutton Ter. NW3 . . . . . 1E **45**
  (off Lakis Cl.)
Luttrell Av. SW15 . . . . 3D **99**
Lutwyche Rd. SE6 . . . 2B **122**
Lutyens Ho. SW1 . . . . 1E **89**
  (off Churchill Gdns.)
Luxborough Ho. W1 . . 5B **4**
  (off Luxborough St.)
Luxborough St.
  W1 . . . . 5B **4** (4C **60**)
Luxborough Twr. W1 . . 5B **4**
Lux Cinema 2D **11**
  (off Hoxton Sq.)
Luxembourg M. E15 . . 2A **54**
Luxemburg Gdns. W6 . . 5F **71**
Luxfield Rd. SE9 . . . . . 1F **125**
Luxford St. SE16 . . . . . 5F **79**
Luxmore St. SE4 . . . . . 4B **94**
Luxor St. SE5 . . . . 1E **105**
Lyall Av. SE21 . . . . . . 4A **120**

Lyall M.
  SW1 . . . . 5B **20** (4C **74**)
Lyall M. W. SW1 . . . . . 4C **74**
Lyall St.
  SW1 . . . . 5B **20** (4C **74**)
Lyal Rd. E3 . . . . 1A **66**
Lycett Pl. W12 . . . . . . 3C **70**
Lyceum Theatre 4F **15**
Lydden Gro. SW18 . . . 5D **101**
Lydden Rd. SW18 . . . . 5D **101**
Lyden Ho. E1 . . . . 2F **65**
  (off Westfield Way)
Lydford NW1 . . . . 5E **47**
  (off Royal College St.)
Lydford Cl. N16 . . . . . 2A **50**
  (off Pellerin Rd.)
Lydford Rd. N15 . . . . . 1F **35**
NW2 . . . . 3E **43**
W9 . . . . 3B **58**
Lydhurst Av. SW2 . . . . 2B **118**
Lydney Cl. SW19 . . . . 2A **114**
Lydon Rd. SW4 . . . . . 1E **103**
Lyford Rd. SW18 . . . . 5F **101**
Lygon Ho. E2 . . . . 2B **64**
  (off Gosset St.)
SW6 . . . . 4A **86**
  (off Fulham Pal. Rd.)
Lygon Pl.
  SW1 . . . . 5D **21** (4D **75**)
Lyham Cl. SW2 . . . . . 4A **104**
Lyham Rd. SW2 . . . . . 3A **104**
Lyly Ho. SE1 . . . . 5C **26**
  (off Burbage Cl.)
Lyme Farm Rd.
  SE12 . . . . 2C **110**
Lyme Gro. E9 . . . . 4E **51**
Lyme Gro. Ho. E9 . . . . 4E **51**
  (off Lyme Gro.)
Lymer Av. SE19 . . . . . 5B **120**
Lyme St. NW1 . . . . . . 4E **47**
Lyme Ter. NW1 . . . . . . 4E **47**
Lyminge Gdns.
  SW18 . . . . 1A **116**
Lymington Lodge E14 . . 4F **81**
  (off Schooner Cl.)
Lymington Rd. NW6 . . 3D **45**
Lympstone Gdns.
  SE15 . . . . 3C **92**
Lynbrook Gro. SE15 . . 3A **92**
Lynch Cl. SE3 . . . . 5B **96**
Lynch Wlk. SE8 . . . . . 2B **94**
  (off Prince St.)
Lyncott Cres. SW4 . . . 2D **103**
Lyncourt SE3 . . . . 5F **95**
Lyncroft Gdns. NW6 . . 2C **44**
Lyncroft Mans. NW6 . . 2C **44**
Lyndale NW2 . . . . 1B **44**
Lyndale Av. NW2 . . . . 5B **30**
Lyndale Cl. SE3 . . . . . 2B **96**
Lynde Ho. SW4 . . . . . 1F **103**
Lyndhurst Cl. NW10 . . 5A **28**
Lyndhurst Cl. NW8 . . . 5F **45**
  (off Finchley Rd.)
Lyndhurst Dr. E10 . . . . 2E **39**
Lyndhurst Gdns. NW3 . . 2F **45**
Lyndhurst Gro. SE15 . . 5A **92**
Lyndhurst Lodge E14 . . 5F **81**
  (off Millennium Dr.)
Lyndhurst Rd. NW3 . . 2F **45**
Lyndhurst Sq. SE15 . . 4B **92**

Lyndhurst Ter. NW3 . . 2F **45**
Lyndhurst Way SE15 . . 4B **92**
Lyndon Yd. SW17 . . . 4E **115**
Lyneham Wlk. E5 . . . . 2A **52**
Lynette Av. SW4 . . . . . 4D **103**
Lyn M. E3 . . . . 2B **66**
N16 . . . . 1A **50**
Lynmouth Rd. E17 . . . 1A **38**
N16 . . . . 3B **36**
Lynne Cl. SE23 . . . . . . 5B **108**
Lynn Ho. SE15 . . . . . . 2D **93**
  (off Friary Est.)
Lynn M. E11 . . . . 4A **40**
Lynn Rd. E11 . . . . 4A **40**
SW12 . . . . 5D **103**
Lynsted Gdns. SE9 . . . 1F **111**
Lynton Cl. NW10 . . . . 2A **42**
Lynton Est. SE1 . . . . . 5C **78**
Lynton Ho. W2 . . . . . . 5E **59**
  (off Hallfield Est.)
Lynton Mans. SE1 . . . 5B **24**
  (off Kennington Rd.)
Lynton Rd. N8 . . . . . . 1F **33**
  (not continuous)
NW6 . . . . 1B **58**
SE1 . . . . 5B **78**
Lynwood Rd. SW17 . . 3B **116**
Lynx Way E16 . . . . 1F **83**
Lyon Ho. NW8 . . . . . . 3A **60**
  (off Broadley St.)
Lyon Ind. Est.
  NW2 . . . . 4D **29**
Lyons Pl. NW8 . . . . . . 3F **59**
Lyon St. N1 . . . . 4B **48**
Lyons Wlk. W14 . . . . . 5A **72**
Lyric Ct. E8 . . . . 4B **50**
  (off Holly St.)
Lyric M. SE26 . . . . 4E **121**
Lyric Rd. SW13 . . . . . 4B **84**
Lyric Theatre
  Hammersmith 5E **71**
  Westminster 4B **14**
  (off Shaftesbury Av.)
Lysander Gro. N19 . . . 3F **33**
Lysander Ho. E2 . . . . . 1D **65**
  (off Temple St.)
Lysander M. N19 . . . . 3E **33**
Lysia Ct. SW6 . . . . 3F **85**
  (off Lysia St.)
Lysias Rd. SW12 . . . . 4D **103**
Lysia St. SW6 . . . . 3F **85**
Lysons Wlk. SW15 . . . 2C **98**
Lytcott Gro. SE22 . . . . 3A **106**
Lytham St. SE17 . . . . . 1F **91**
Lyttelton Cl. NW3 . . . . 4A **46**
Lyttelton Ho. E9 . . . . . 4E **51**
  (off Well St.)
Lyttelton Rd. E10 . . . . 5D **39**
Lyttelton Theatre 1B **24**
  (in Royal National Theatre)
Lytton Cl. N2 . . . . 1F **31**
Lytton Gro. SW15 . . . 3F **99**
Lytton Rd. E11 . . . . . . 2A **40**
Lyveden Rd. SE3 . . . . 3D **97**

M

Mabledon Ct. WC1 . . . 2C **6**
  (off Mabledon Pl.)

Mabledon Pl.
WC1 . . . . 2C 6 (2F 61)
Mablethorpe Rd.
SW6 . . . . 3A 86
Mabley St. E9 . . . . 2A 52
Macarthur Cl. SE1 . . . . . 3C 54
Macarthur Ter. SE7 . . . . 2F 97
Macartney Ho. SE10 . . . 3F 95
(off Chesterfield Wlk.)
SW9 . . . . 4C 90
(off Gosling Way)
Macaulay Ct. SW4 . . . 1D 103
Macaulay Rd. E6 . . . . . . 1F 69
SW4 . . . . 1D 103
Macaulay Sq. SW4 . . . 2D 103
McAuley Cl. SE1 . . . . . . 5B 24
Macauley M. SE13 . . . . . 4E 95
Macbeth Ho. N1 . . . . . . 1A 64
Macbeth St. W6 . . . . . . 1D 85
McCall Cl. SW4 . . . . . . 5A 90
McCall Cres. SE7 . . . . . 1F 97
McCall Ho. N7 . . . . 1A 48
MCC Cricket Mus. and Tours
. . . . 2F 59
Macclesfield Ho. EC1 . . . 2F 9
(off Central St.)
Macclesfield Rd.
EC1 . . . . 1F 9 (2E 63)
Macclesfield St.
W1 . . . . 4C 14 (1F 75)
McCoid Way
SE1 . . . . 4F 25 (3E 77)
McCrone M. NW3 . . . . . . 3F 45
McCullum Rd. E3 . . . . . . 5B 52
McDermott Cl.
SW11 . . . . 1A 102
McDermott Rd.
SE15 . . . . 1C 106
Macdonald Rd. E7 . . . . 1C 54
N19 . . . . 4E 33
McDowall Cl. E16 . . . . . . 4B 68
McDowall Rd. SE5 . . . . . 4E 91
Macduff Rd. SW11 . . . . . 4C 88
Mace Cl. E1 . . . . 2D 79
Mace St. E2 . . . . 1F 65
McEwen Way E15 . . . . . . 5F 53
Macey St. SE10 . . . . . . 2E 95
(off Thames St.)
Macfarlane Rd. W12 . . . 2E 71
Macfarren Pl.
NW1 . . . . 4C 4 (3C 60)
(off Hunton St.)
McGlashon Ho. E1 . . . 3C 64
(off Hunton St.)
McGrath Rd. E15 . . . . . . 2B 54
McGregor Cl. N1 . . . . . . 1E 11
Macgregor Rd. E16 . . . . 4E 69
McGregor Rd. W11 . . . . 5B 58
Machell Rd. SE15 . . . . . 1E 107
McIndoe St. N1 . . . . . . 5F 49
(off Sherborne St.)
Macintosh Ho. W1 . . . . 5C 4
(off Beaumont St.)
McIntosh Ho. SE16 . . . 5E 79
(off Millender Wlk.)
Mackay Ho. W12 . . . 1D 71
(off White City Est.)
Mackay Rd. SW4 . . . 1D 103
McKay Trad. Est.
W10 . . . . 3A 58
Mackennal St. NW8 . . . 1A 60

Mackenzie Cl. W12 . . . 1D 71
Mackenzie Ho. NW2 . . . 5C 28
Mackenzie Rd. N7 . . . 3B 48
Mackenzie Wlk. E14 . . . 2C 80
McKerrell Rd. SE15 . . . 4C 92
Mackeson Rd. NW3 . . . 1B 46
Mackie Rd. SW2 . . . . . 5C 104
Mackintosh La. E9 . . . . 2F 51
Macklin St.
WC2 . . . . 2E 15 (5A 62)
Mackonochie Ho. EC1 . . 5B 8
(off Baldwins Gdns.)
Mackrow Wlk. E14 . . . . . 1E 81
Mack's Rd. SE16 . . . . . 5C 78
Mackworth Ho. NW1 . . . 1F 5
(off Augustus St.)
Mackworth St.
NW1 . . . . 1F 5 (2E 61)
McLaren House SE1 . . . 4D 25
(off St Georges Cir.)
Maclaren M. SW15 . . . . 2E 99
Maclean Rd. SE23 . . . . 4A 108
McLeod Ct. SE22 . . . . 1C 120
McLeod's M. SW7 . . . . 5D 73
Macleod St. SE17 . . . . 1E 91
Maclise Ho. SW1 . . . . . 5A 76
(off Marsham St.)
Maclise Rd. W14 . . . . . 4A 72
McMillan Ho. SE4 . . . 1A 108
(off Arica Rd.)
SE14 . . . . 4A 94
McMillan St. SE8 . . . . . 2C 94
Macmillan Way
SW17 . . . . 4D 117
Macnamara Ho.
SW10 . . . . 3F 87
(off Worlds End Est.)
McNeil Rd. SE5 . . . . . . 5A 92
Maconochies Rd.
E14 . . . . 1D 95
Macquarie Way E14 . . . 5D 81
Macready Ho. W1 . . . 4A 60
(off Crawford St.)
Macready Pl. N7 . . . . . 1A 48
(not continuous)
Macroom Rd. W9 . . . . . 2B 58
Mac's Pl. EC4 . . . . 2B 16
Madame Tussaud's
. . . . 4B 4 (3C 60)
Maddams St. E3 . . . . . 3D 67
Maddocks Ho. E1 . . . 1D 79
(off Cornwall St.)
Maddox St.
W1 . . . . 4E 13 (1D 75)
Madeira Rd. E11 . . . . . 3F 39
SW16 . . . . 5A 118
Madinah Rd. E8 . . . . . . 3C 50
Madison, The SE1 . . . 3B 80
(off Long La.)
Madison Ho. E14 . . . 1B 80
(off Victory Pl.)
Madras Pl. N7 . . . . 3C 48
Madrid St. SW13 . . . . . 4C 84
Madrigal La. SE5 . . . . . 3D 91
Madron St. SE17 . . . 1A 92
Mafeking Av. E6 . . . . . 1F 69
Mafeking Rd. E16 . . . . 3B 68
Magazine Ga. W2 . . . . 2A 74
Magdala Av. N19 . . . . 4E 33

Magdalene Cl. SE15 . . 5D 93
Magdalen Ho. E16 . . . 2D 83
(off Keats Av.)
Magdalen Pas. E1 . . . 1B 78
Magdalen Rd.
SW18 . . . . 1E 115
Magdalen St.
SE1 . . . . 2D 27 (2A 78)
Magee St. SE11 . . . . . 2C 90
Magellan Ct. NW10 . . 4A 42
(off Brentfield Rd.)
Magellan Ho. E1 . . . . 3F 65
(off Ernest St.)
Magellan Pl. E14 . . . . 5C 80
Magnin Cl. E8 . . . . . . 5C 50
Magnolia Cl. E10 . . . . 4C 38
Magnolia Gdns. E10 . . 4C 38
Magnolia Ho. SE8 . . . 2B 94
(off Evelyn St.)
Magnolia Lodge W8 . . 4D 73
(off St Mary's Ga.)
Magnolia Pl. SW4 . . . 3A 104
Magpie All.
EC4 . . . . 3C 16 (5C 62)
Magpie Cl. E7 . . . . . . 2B 54
Magpie Pl. SE14 . . . . 2A 94
Magri Wlk. E1 . . . . . . 4E 65
Maguire St. SE1 . . . . . 3B 78
Mahatma Gandhi Ind. Est.
SE24 . . . . 2D 105
Mahogany Cl. SE16 . . 2A 80
Maida Av. W2 . . . . . . 4E 59
MAIDA HILL 3B 58
MAIDA VALE 2D 59
Maida Va. W9 . . . . . . 1D 59
Maiden La. NW1 . . . . 4F 47
SE1 . . . . 2A 26 (2E 77)
WC2 . . . . 5E 15 (1A 76)
Maiden Pl. NW5 . . . . 5E 33
Maiden Rd. E15 . . . . 4A 54
Maidenstone Hill
SE10 . . . . 4E 95
Maidstone Bldgs. M.
SE1 . . . . 2A 26 (2E 77)
Maidstone Ho. E14 . . 5D 67
(off Carmen St.)
Mail Coach Yd. E2 . . 1E 11
Mais Ho. SE26 . . . . . 2D 121
Maismore St. SE15 . . 2C 92
Maitland Cl. SE10 . . . 3D 95
Maitland Ct. W2 . . . . 1F 73
(off Lancaster Ter.)
Maitland Ho. E2 . . . . 1E 65
(off Waterloo Gdns.)
SW1 . . . . 2E 89
(off Churchill Gdns.)
Maitland Pk. Est.
NW3 . . . . 3B 46
Maitland Pk. Rd.
NW3 . . . . 3B 46
Maitland Pk. Vs.
NW3 . . . . 3B 46
Maitland Pl. E5 . . . . . 1D 51
Maitland Rd. E15 . . . . 3B 54
SE26 . . . . 5F 121
Maize Row E14 . . . . . 1B 80
Major Cl. SW9 . . . . . 1D 105
Major Rd. E15 . . . . . 2F 53
SE16 . . . . 4C 78
Makepeace Av. N6 . . . 4C 32

Makepeace Mans.	**Malmesbury Ter.**	**Mandarin Ct.** NW10 . . . . . 3A **42**
N6 . . . . 4C **32**	E16 . . . . 4B **68**	(off Mitchellbrook Way)
Makins St. SW3 . . . . . . 5A **74**	**Malmsey Ho.** SE11 . . . . 1B **90**	SE8 . . . . 2B **94**
Malabar Ct. W12 . . . . . 1D **71**	**Malmsmead Ho.** E9 . . . . 2B **52**	**Mandarin St.** E14 . . . . . 1C **80**
(off India Way)	(off King's Mead Way)	**Mandela Cl.** W12 . . . . . 1D **71**
Malabar St. E14 . . . . . . 3C **80**	**Malpas Rd.** E8 . . . . 2D **51**	**Mandela Ho.** E2 . . . . . . 2F **11**
Malam Cl. E11 . . . . 5C **76**	SE4 . . . . 5B **94**	(off Virginia Rd.)
Malam Gdns. E14 . . . . . 1D **81**	**Malta Rd.** E10 . . . . 3C **38**	SE5 . . . . 5D **91**
Malbrook Rd. SW15 . . . 2D **99**	**Malta St.** EC1 . . . . 3D **9** (3D **63**)	**Mandela Rd.** E16 . . . . . 5C **68**
Malcolm Ct. E7 . . . . . . 3B **54**	**Maltby St.**	**Mandela St.** NW1 . . . . . 5E **47**
NW4 . . . . 1C **28**	. . . . 4F **27** (3B **78**)	SW9 . . . . 3C **90**
Malcolm Cres. NW4 . . . 1C **28**	**Malthouse Dr.** W4 . . . . 2B **84**	(not continuous)
Malcolm Ho. N1 . . . . . . 1A **64**	**Malthouse Pas.**	**Mandela Way** SE1 . . . . 5A **78**
(off Arden Est.)	SW13 . . . . 5B **84**	**Mandel Ho.** SW18 . . . . 2C **100**
Malcolm Pl. E2 . . . . . . 3E **65**	(off Maltings Cl.)	**Mandeville Cl.** SE3 . . . . 3B **96**
Malcolm Rd. E1 . . . . . . 3E **65**	**Malting Ho.** E14 . . . . . . 1B **80**	**Mandeville Ho.** SE1 . . . 1B **92**
Malcolm Sargent Ho.	(off Oak La.)	(off Rolls Rd.)
E16 . . . . 2D **83**	**Maltings Cl.** SW13 . . . . 5B **84**	SW4 . . . . 3E **103**
(off Evelyn Rd.)	**Maltings Lodge** W4 . . . . 2A **84**	**Mandeville M.** SW4 . . . 2F **103**
Malcolmson Ho. SW1 . . 1F **89**	(off Corney Reach Way)	**Mandeville Pl.**
(off Aylesford St.)	**Maltings Pl.** SE1 . . . . . . 4E **27**	W1 . . . . 2C **12** (5C **60**)
Malden Ct. N4 . . . . 1E **35**	SW6 . . . . 4D **87**	**Mandrake Cl.** SE5 . . . . 5A **38**
Malden Cres. NW1 . . . . 3C **46**	**Malton M.** W10 . . . . . . 5A **58**	**Mandrake Rd.**
Malden Pl. NW5 . . . . . . 2C **46**	**Malton Rd.** W10 . . . . . . 5A **58**	SW17 . . . . 3B **116**
Malden Rd. NW5 . . . . . . 2B **46**	**Maltravers St.**	**Mandrake Way** E15 . . . . 4A **54**
Maldon Cl. E15 . . . . 2A **54**	WC2 . . . . 4A **16** (1B **76**)	**Mandrell Rd.** SW2 . . . . 3A **104**
N1 . . . . 5E **49**	**Malt St.** SE1 . . . . 2C **92**	**Manette St.**
SE5 . . . . 1A **106**	**Malva Cl.** SW18 . . . . . . 3D **101**	W1 . . . . 3C **14** (5F **61**)
Malet Pl. WC1 . . . . 4B **6** (3F **61**)	**Malvern Cl.** W10 . . . . . . 4B **58**	**Manfred Rd.**
Malet St. WC1 . . . . 4B **6** (3F **61**)	**Malvern Ct.** SW7 . . . . . . 5F **73**	SW15 . . . . 3B **100**
Maley Av. SE27 . . . . . . 2D **119**	(off Onslow Sq.)	**Manger Rd.** N7 . . . . . . 3A **48**
Malfort Rd. SE5 . . . . . . 1A **106**	W12 . . . . 3C **70**	**Manilla St.** E14 . . . . . . 3C **80**
Malham Rd. SE23 . . . . . 1F **121**	(off Hadyn Pk. Rd.)	**Manitoba Ct.** SE16 . . . . . 3E **79**
Malham Rd. Ind. Est.	**Malvern Gdns.** NW2 . . . 4A **30**	(off Canada Est.)
SE23 . . . . 1F **121**	**Malvern Ho.** N16 . . . . . 3B **36**	**Manley Ct.** N16 . . . . . . 5B **36**
Malibu Ct. SE26 . . . . . 3D **121**	**Malvern M.** NW6 . . . . . . 2C **58**	**Manley Ho.** SE11 . . . . . 5C **76**
Mall, The E15 . . . . 4F **53**	**Malvern Pl.** NW6 . . . . . . 2B **58**	**Manley St.** NW1 . . . . . . 5C **46**
SW1 . . . . 2C **22** (3E **75**)	**Malvern Rd.** E6 . . . . 5F **55**	**Manneby Prior** N1 . . . . . 1A **8**
Mallams M. SW9 . . . . . 1D **105**	E8 . . . . 4C **50**	(off Cumming St.)
Mallard Cl. E9 . . . . 3B **52**	E11 . . . . 4A **40**	**Manningford Cl.**
NW6 . . . . 1C **58**	NW6 . . . . 1B **58**	EC1 . . . . 1D **9** (2D **63**)
Mallard Ho. NW8 . . . . . 1A **60**	(not continuous)	**Manningtree Cl.**
(off Barrow Hill Est.)	**Malvern Ter.** N1 . . . . . . 5C **48**	SW19 . . . . 1A **114**
Mallards E11 . . . . 2C **40**	**Malwood Rd.** SW12 . . . 4D **103**	**Manningtree St.** E1 . . . . 5C **64**
(off Blake Hall Rd.)	**Malyons Rd.** SE13 . . . . 4D **109**	**Manny Shinwell Ho.**
Mall Chambers W8 . . . . 2C **72**	**Malyons Ter.** SE13 . . . . 3D **109**	SW6 . . . . 2B **86**
(off Kensington Mall)	**Managers St.** E14 . . . . . 2E **81**	(off Clem Attlee Ct.)
Mallet Rd. SE13 . . . . . . 4F **109**	**Manaton Cl.** SE15 . . . . 1D **107**	**Manor, The** SE23 . . . . . 5E **107**
Mall Galleries 1C **22**	**Manbey Gro.** E15 . . . . . 3A **54**	**Manor Av.** E7 . . . . 1E **55**
Mall Gallery WC2 . . . . . 3D **15**	**Manbey Pk. Rd.** E15 . . . 3A **54**	SE4 . . . . 5B **94**
(in Thomas Neals Shop. Mall)	**Manbey Rd.** E15 . . . . . . 3A **54**	**Manor Brook** SE3 . . . . 2C **110**
Malling SE13 . . . . 3D **109**	**Manbey St.** E15 . . . . . . 3A **54**	**Manor Ct.** E10 . . . . 3D **39**
Mallinson Rd.	**Manbre Rd.** W6 . . . . 2E **85**	N2 . . . . 1B **32**
SW11 . . . . 3A **102**	**Manchester Ct.** E16 . . . . 5D **69**	SW2 . . . . 3B **104**
Mallinson Sports Cen.	(off Garvary Rd.)	SW6 . . . . 4D **87**
. . . . 2B **32**	**Manchester Dr.** W10 . . . 3A **58**	SW16 . . . . 3A **118**
Mallon Gdns. E1 . . . . . . 2F **19**	**Manchester Gro.** E14 . . . 1E **95**	**Manor Est.** SE16 . . . . . 5D **79**
(off Commercial St.)	**Manchester Ho.** SE17 . . . 1E **91**	**Manorfield Cl.** N19 . . . . . 1E **47**
Mallord St. SW3 . . . . . . 2F **87**	**Manchester M.** W1 . . . . 1B **12**	(off Fulbrook M.)
Mallory Cl. SE4 . . . . . . 2A **108**	**Manchester Rd.** E14 . . . 1E **95**	**Manor Flds.** SW15 . . . . 4F **99**
Mallory St. NW8 . . . . . . 3A **60**	N15 . . . . 1F **35**	**Manor Gdns.** N7 . . . . . . 5A **34**
Mallow St.	**Manchester Sq.**	SW4 . . . . 5E **89**
EC1 . . . . 3B **10** (3D **63**)	W1 . . . . 2B **12** (5C **60**)	(off Larkhall Ri.)
Mall Rd. W6 . . . . 1D **85**	**Manchester St.**	W4 . . . . 1A **84**
Mall Vs. W6 . . . . 1D **85**	W1 . . . . 1B **12** (4C **60**)	**Manor Gro.** SE15 . . . . . 2E **93**
(off Mall Rd.)	**Manchester St.** 2F **35**	**Manorhall Gdns.** E10 . . . 3C **38**
Malmesbury E2 . . . . . . 1E **65**	**Manchuria Rd.**	**MANOR HOUSE** 2F **35**
(off Cyprus St.)	SW11 . . . . 4C **102**	**MANOR HOUSE** 2E **35**
Malmesbury Rd. E3 . . . 2B **66**	**Manciple St.**	**Manor Ho.** NW1 . . . . . . 4A **60**
E16 . . . . 4A **68**	SE1 . . . . 4B **26** (3F **77**)	(off Marylebone Rd.)

Manor Ho. Ct. W9 . . . . 3E 59
  (off Warrington Gdns.)
Manor Ho. Dr. NW6 . . . . 4F 43
Manor Ho. Gdn.
  E11 . . . . 1D 41
Manor La. SE12 . . . . 3A 110
SE13 . . . . 3A 110
Manor La. Ter.
  SE13 . . . . 2A 110
Manor M. NW6 . . . . . . 1C 58
  (off Cambridge Av.)
SE4 . . . . 5D 94
Manor Mt. SE23 . . . . . 1F 121
Manor Pde. N16 . . . . . 4B 36
NW10 . . . . 1B 56
  (off High St. Harlesden)
MANOR PARK 1F 55
Manor Pk. SE13 . . . . 2F 109
Manor Pk. Crematorium
  E7 . . . . 1E 55
Manor Pk. Pde.
  SE13 . . . . 2F 109
  (off Lee High Rd.)
Manor Pk. Rd. E12 . . . . 1F 55
  (not continuous)
NW10 . . . . 5B 42
Manor Pl. SE17 . . . . . 1D 91
Manor Rd. E10 . . . . . . 2C 38
E15 . . . . 1A 68
E16 . . . . 1A 68
N16 . . . . 4F 35
Manor Way SE3 . . . . 2B 110
Manorway SE7 . . . . . . 5F 83
Manresa Rd. SW3 . . . 1A 88
Mansard Beeches
  SW17 . . . . 5C 116
Mansell St.
  E1 . . . . 3F 19 (5B 64)
Mansel Rd. SW19 . . . 5A 114
Manse Rd. N16 . . . . . . 5B 36
Mansfield Ct. E2 . . . . . 5B 50
  (off Whiston Rd.)
Mansfield Hgts. N2 . . . 1A 32
Mansfield M.
  W1 . . . . . . 1D 13 (4D 61)
Mansfield Pl. NW3 . . . 1E 45
Mansfield Rd. E11 . . . . 1D 41
NW3 . . . . 2B 46
Mansfield St.
  W1 . . . . . . 1D 13 (4D 61)
Mansford St. E2 . . . . . 1C 64
Mansion Cl. SW9 . . . . 4C 90
  (not continuous)
Mansion Cottage
  Vis. Info. Cen. 3A 32
Mansion Gdns. NW3 . . 5D 31
Mansion House
  . . . . 3B 18 (5F 63)
Mansion Ho. Pl.
  EC4. . . . . . . 3B 18 (5F 63)
Mansion Ho. St. EC4 . . 3B 18
Mansions, The SW5 . . 1D 87
Manson M. SW7 . . . . . 5F 73
Manson Pl. SW7 . . . . . 5F 73
Manston NW1 . . . . 4E 47
  (off Agar Gro.)
Manstone Rd. NW2 . . . 2A 44
Manston Ho. W14 . . . . 4A 72
  (off Russell Rd.)
Mantilla Rd. SW17 . . . 4C 116

Mantle Ct. SW18 . . . . 4D 101
  (off Mapleton Rd.)
Mantle Rd. SE4 . . . . . 1A 108
Mantle Way E15 . . . . . 4A 54
Mantua St. SW11 . . . . 1F 101
Mantus Cl. E1 . . . . 3E 65
Mantus Rd. E1 . . . . . . 3E 65
Manville Gdns.
  SW17 . . . . 3D 117
Manville Rd. SW17 . . . 2C 116
Manwood Rd. SE4 . . . 3B 108
Manygates SW12 . . . . 2D 117
Mapesbury Ct. NW2 . . ?A 44
Mapesbury M. NW4 . . . 1C 28
Mapesbury Rd. NW2 . . 4A 44
Mapeshill Pl. NW2 . . . 3E 43
Mapes Ho. NW6 . . . . . 4A 44
Mape St. E2 . . . . 3D 65
  (not continuous)
Maple Av. W3 . . . . 2A 70
Maple Cl. N16 . . . . 1C 36
SW4 . . . . 4F 103
Maple Ct. SE6 . . . . . . 1D 123
Maplecroft Cl. E6 . . . . 5F 69
Mapledene Est. E8 . . . 4C 50
Mapledene Rd. E8 . . . 4B 50
Maple Ho. SE8 . . . . . . 3B 94
  (off Idonia St.)
Maple Leaf Sq. SE16 . . 3F 79
Maple Lodge W8 . . . . 4D 73
  (off Abbots Wlk.)
Maple M. NW6 . . . . . . 1D 59
SW16 . . . . 5B 118
Maple Pl. W1 . . . 5A 6 (3E 61)
Maple Rd. E11 . . . . . . 1A 40
Maples Pl. E1 . . . . 4D 65
Maplestead Rd.
  SW2 . . . . 5B 104
Maple Wik. W10 . . . . . . 5B 104
Maple Wik. W1 . . . 5F 5 (4E 61)
Mapleton Cres.
  SW18 . . . . 4D 101
Mapleton Rd. SW18. . . 4C 100
  (not continuous)
Maple Tree M. SE3. . . 4F 97
Maple Wlk. W10 . . . . . 2F 57
Maplin Rd. E16 . . . . . . 5C 68
Maplin St. E3 . . . . 2B 66
Mapperley Cl. E11 . . . 1B 40
Marabou Cl. E12 . . . . . 2F 55
Marathon Ho. NW1 . . . 5A 4
  (off Marylebone Rd.)
Marban Rd. W9 . . . . . 2B 58
Marble Arch 4A 12
MARBLE ARCH 1B 74
Marble Arch
  W1 . . . . . . 4A 12 (1B 74)
Marble Arch Apartments
  W1 . . . . 5B 60
  (off Harrowby St.)
Marble Dr. NW2 . . . . . 3F 29
Marble Ho. W9 . . . . . . 3B 58
Marble Quay E1 . . . . . 2C 78
Marbles Ho. SE5 . . . . 2E 91
  (off Grosvenor Ter.)
Marcella Rd. SW9 . . . 5C 90
Marchant Cl. SE1 . . . . 1B 92
Marchant Rd. E11 . . . . 4F 39
Marchant St. SE14 . . . 2A 94
Marchbank Rd. W14 . . 2B 86

March Ct. SW15 . . . . . 2D 99
Marchmont St.
  WC1 . . . . 3D 7 (3A 62)
Marchwood Cl. SE5 . . 3A 92
Marcia Rd. SE1 . . . . . 5A 78
Marcilly Rd. SW18 . . . 3F 101
Marcon Ct. E8 . . . . . . 2D 51
  (off Amhurst Rd.)
Marconi Rd. E10 . . . . . 3C 38
Marconi Pl. E8 . . . . . . 3D 51
Marco Polo Ho.
  SW8 . . . . 3D 89
Marco Rd. W6 . . . . . . 4E 71
Marcus Ct. E15 . . . . . 5A 54
Marcus Garvey M.
  SE22 . . . . 4D 107
Marcus Garvey Way
  SE24 . . . . 2C 104
Marcus St. E15 . . . . . 5B 54
SW18 . . . . 4D 101
Marcus Ter. SW18 . . . 4D 101
Marden Ho. E8 . . . . . . 2D 51
Marden Sq. SE16 . . . . 4D 79
Mardyke Ho. SE17 . . . 5F 77
  (off Mason St.)
Maresfield Gdns.
  NW3 . . . . 2E 45
Mare St. E2 . . . . 1D 65
E8 . . . . 2D 51
Margaret Bldgs. N16 . . 3B 36
Margaret Ct. W1 . . . . . 2F 13
Margaret Herbison Ho.
  SW6 . . . . 2B 86
  (off Clem Attlee Ct.)
Margaret Ho. W6 . . . . 1E 85
  (off Queen Caroline St.)
Margaret Ingram Cl.
  SW6 . . . . 2B 86
Margaret Rd. N16 . . . . 3B 36
Margaret St.
  W1 . . . . . . 2E 13 (5D 61)
Margaretta Ter. SW3 . . 2A 88
Margaretting Rd. E12. . 3E 41
Margaret Way IG4: Ilf . . 1F 41
Margaret White Ho.
  NW1 . . . . 1C 6
  (off Chalton St.)
Margate Rd. SW2 . . . 3A 104
Margery Fry Ct. N7 . . . 5A 34
Margery Pk. Rd. E7 . . . 3C 54
Margery St.
  WC1 . . . . . . 2B 8 (2C 62)
Margery Ter. E7 . . . . . 3C 54
  (off Margery Pk. Rd.)
Margin Dr. SW19 . . . . 5F 113
Margravine Gdns. W6 . . 1F 85
Margravine Rd. W6 . . . 1F 85
Marham Gdns.
  SW18 . . . . 1A 116
Maria Cl. SE1 . . . . 5D 79
Marian Ct. E9 . . . . 2E 51
Marian Pl. E2 . . . . 1D 65
Marian St. E2 . . . . 1D 65
Marian Way NW10 . . . 4B 42
Maria Ter. E1 . . . . 4F 65
Maribor SE10 . . . . 3E 95
  (off Burney St.)
Marie Curie SE5 . . . . . 4A 92
Marie Lloyd Gdns.
  N19 . . . . 2A 34

Marie Lloyd Ho. *N1* *1B 10*
    (off Murray Gro.)
Marie Lloyd Wlk. E8 . . . . *3B 50*
Marigold All. SE1 . . . . . . *5D 17*
Marigold St. SE16 . . . . . *3D 79*
Marinefield Rd. SW6 . . . *5D 87*
Marinel Ho. SE5 . . . . . . *3E 91*
Mariners M. E14 . . . . . . *5F 81*
Marine St. SE16 . . . . . . *4C 78*
Marine Twr. SE8 . . . . . . *2B 94*
    (off Abinger Gro.)
Marischal Rd. SE13 . . *1F 109*
Maritime Ind. Est.
  SE7 . . . . *5D 83*
Maritime Quay E14 . . . *1C 94*
Maritime St. E3 . . . . . . *3B 66*
Marius Mans.
  SW17 . . . . *2C 116*
Marius Rd. SW17 . . . . *2C 116*
Marjorie Gro. SW11 . . *2B 102*
Marjorie M. E1 . . . . *5F 65*
Market Ct. W1 . . . . *2F 13*
Market Entrance SW8 . . *3E 89*
Market Est. N7 . . . . *3A 48*
Market La. W12 . . . . . . *3E 71*
Market M.
  W1 . . . . *2D 21 (2D 75)*
Market Pde. E10 . . . . . . *1E 39*
    (off High Rd.)
  N16 . . . . *3C 36*
    (off Oldhill St.)
Market Pav. E10 . . . . . . *5C 38*
Market Pl. SE16 . . . . . . *5C 78*
    (not continuous)
  W1 . . . . . . *2F 13 (5E 61)*
Market Rd. N7 . . . . *3A 48*
Market Row SW9 . . . . . *2C 104*
Market Sq. E14 . . . . *5D 67*
Market Way E14 . . . . . . *5D 67*
Market Yd. M.
  SE1 . . . . . . *5D 27 (3A 78)*
Markham Pl. SW3 . . . . . *1B 88*
Markham Sq. SW3 . . . . *1B 88*
Markham St. SW3 . . . . . *1A 88*
Mark Ho. E2 . . . . *1F 65*
    (off Sewardstone Rd.)
Markhouse Av. E17 . . . . *1A 38*
Markhouse Pas. E17 . . . *1B 38*
    (off Markhouse Rd.)
Markhouse Rd. E17 . . . . *1B 38*
Markland Ho. W10 . . . . . *1F 71*
    (off Darfield Way)
Mark La. EC3 . . *4E 19 (1A 78)*
Markmanor Av. E17 . . . . *2A 38*
Mark Sq.
  EC2 . . . . . . *3D 11 (3A 64)*
Markstone Ho. SE1 . . . *4D 25*
    (off Lancaster St.)
Mark St. E15 . . . . *4A 54*
  EC2 . . . . . . *3D 11 (3A 64)*
Mark Wade Cl. E12 . . . . *3F 41*
Markwell Cl. SE26 . . . . *4D 121*
Markyate Ho. W10 . . . . . *3E 57*
    (off Sutton Way)
Marlborough SW19 . . . *1F 113*
    (off Inner Pk. Rd.)
Marlborough Av. E8 . . . . *5C 50*
    (not continuous)
Marlborough Cl.
  SE17 . . . . *5E 77*

Marlborough Ct. W1 . . . *4F 13*
  W8 . . . . *5C 72*
    (off Pembroke Rd.)
Marlborough Cres.
  W4 . . . . *4A 70*
Marlborough Flats
  SW3 . . . . *5A 74*
    (off Walton St.)
Marlborough Gro.
  SE1 . . . . *1C 92*
Marlborough Hill
  NW8 . . . . *1E 59*
Marlborough House
  . . . . *2A 22 (2E 75)*
Marlborough Ho. E16 . . *2C 82*
    (off Hardy Av.)
  NW1 . . . . *3E 5*
    (off Osnaburgh St.)
Marlborough La. SE7 . . *2E 97*
Marlborough Mans.
  NW6 . . . . *2D 45*
    (off Canon Hill)
Marlborough Pl.
  NW8 . . . . *1E 59*
Marlborough Rd.
  E7 . . . . *4E 55*
  E15 . . . . *1A 54*
  N19 . . . . *4F 33*
    (not continuous)
  SW1 . . . . . . *2A 22 (2E 75)*
Marlborough St.
  SW3 . . . . *5A 74*
Marlborough Yd. N19 . . *4F 33*
Marlbury NW8 . . . . *5D 45*
    (off Abbey Rd.)
Marler Rd. SE23 . . . . . *1A 122*
Marley Ho. W11 . . . . . . *1F 71*
    (off St Ann's Rd.)
Marley Wlk. NW2 . . . . . *2E 43*
Marloes Rd. W8 . . . . . . *4D 73*
Marlow Ct. NW6 . . . . . . *4F 43*
Marlowe Bus. Cen.
  SE14 . . . . *3A 94*
    (off Batavia Rd.)
Marlowe Ct. SW3 . . . . . *5A 74*
    (off Petyward)
Marlowe Ho. SE8 . . . . . *1B 94*
    (off Bowditch)
Marlowe Path SE8 . . . . *2C 94*
Marlowes, The NW8 . . . *5F 45*
Marlow Ho. E2 . . . . *2F 11*
    (off Calvert Av.)
  SE1 . . . . *5F 27*
    (off Maltby St.)
  W2 . . . . *5D 59*
    (off Hallfield Est.)
Marlow Way SE16 . . . . *3F 79*
Marlow Workshops
  E2 . . . . *2F 11*
    (off Virginia Rd.)
Marl Rd. SW18 . . . . . . *2E 101*
Marlton St. SE10 . . . . . *1B 96*
Marmara Apartments
  E16 . . . . *1C 82*
    (off Western Gateway)
Marmion M. SW11 . . . *1C 102*
Marmion Rd. SW11 . . . *2C 102*
Marmont Rd. SE15 . . . . *4C 92*

Marmora Ho. E1 . . . . . . *4A 66*
    (off Ben Jonson Rd.)
Marmora Rd. SE22 . . . *4E 107*
Marne St. W10 . . . . *2A 58*
Marney Rd. SW11 . . . . *2C 102*
Marnfield Cres.
  SW2 . . . . *1C 118*
Marnham Av. NW2 . . . . *1A 44*
Marnock Ho. SE17 . . . . *1F 91*
    (off Brandon St.)
Marnock Rd. SE4 . . . . *3B 108*
Maroon Ho. E14 . . . . . . *4A 66*
Maroon St. E14 . . . . . . *4A 66*
Maroons Way
  SE6 . . . . *5C 122*
Marquess Rd. N1 . . . . . *3F 49*
Marquess Rd. Nth.
  N1 . . . . *3F 49*
Marquess Rd. Sth.
  N1 . . . . *3E 49*
Marquis Ct. N4 . . . . *3B 34*
    (off Marquis Rd.)
Marquis Rd. N4 . . . . *3B 34*
  NW1 . . . . *3F 47*
Marrick Cl. SW15 . . . . . *2C 98*
Marrick Ho. NW6 . . . . . *5D 45*
    (off Mortimer Cres.)
Marriett Ho. SE6 . . . . . *4E 123*
Marriott Rd. E15 . . . . . . *5A 54*
  N4 . . . . *3B 34*
Marriotts Cl. NW9 . . . . . *1B 28*
Marryat Ho. SW1 . . . . . *1E 89*
    (off Churchill Gdns.)
Marryat Pl. SW19 . . . . *4A 114*
Marryat Rd. SW19 . . . *5F 113*
Marryat Sq. SW6 . . . . . *4A 86*
Marsala Rd. SE13 . . . . *2D 109*
Marsden Rd. SE15 . . . *1B 106*
Marsden St. NW5 . . . . . *3C 46*
    (not continuous)
Marshall Cl. SW18 . . . *4E 101*
Marshall Ho. N1 . . . . . . *1F 63*
    (off Cranston Est.)
  NW6 . . . . *1B 58*
    (off Albert Rd.)
  SE1 . . . . *5E 27*
  SE17 . . . . *1F 91*
    (off East St.)
Marshall Rd. E10 . . . . . *5D 39*
Marshall's Pl.
  SE16 . . . . . . *5F 27 (4B 78)*
Marshall St.
  W1 . . . . *3A 14 (5E 61)*
Marshall Street Leisure Cen.
  . . . . *5E 61*
Marshalsea Rd.
  SE1 . . . . . . *3A 26 (3E 77)*
Marsham Ct. SW1 . . . . *5F 75*
Marsham St.
  SW1 . . . . . . *5C 22 (4F 75)*
Marshbrook Cl. SE3 . . *1F 111*
Marsh Cen., The E1 . . . *2F 19*
    (off Whitechapel High St.)
Marsh Ct. E8 . . . . *3C 50*
Marsh Dr. NW9 . . . . *1B 28*
Marshfield St. E14 . . . . *4E 81*
Marsh Ga. Bus. Cen.
  E15 . . . . *5E 53*
Marshgate Cen., The
  E15 . . . . *5D 53*

Marshgate La. E15 . . . . . 4D 53
(not continuous)
Marshgate Sidings
(Bow Depot)
E15 . . . . 5D 53
Marshgate Trad. Est.
E15 . . . . 4D 53
Marsh Hill E9 . . . . 2A 52
Marsh Ho. SW1 . . . . 1F 89
(off Aylesford St.)
SW8 . . . . 4E 89
Marsh La. E10 . . . . 4B 38
Marsh St. E14 . . . . 5D 81
Marsh Wall E14 . . . . 2C 80
Marshwood Ho. NW6 . . 5C 44
(off Kilburn Va.)
Marsland Cl. SE17 . . . . . 1D 91
Marsom Ho. N1 . . . . 1B 10
(off Fairbank Est.)
Marston Cl. NW6 . . . . . . 4E 45
Marston Ho. SW9 . . . . . . 5C 90
Marsworth Ho. E2 . . . . . 2C 50
(off Whiston Rd.)
Martaban Ho. N16 . . . . . 4B 36
Martara M. SE17 . . . . . . 1E 91
Martello St. E8 . . . . 4D 51
Martello Ter. E8 . . . . . . 4D 51
Martell Rd. SE21 . . . . . 3F 119
Martel Pl. E8 . . . . 3B 50
Martha Ct. E2 . . . . 1D 65
Martha Rd. E15 . . . . 3A 54
Martha's Bldgs.
EC1 . . . . 3B 10 (3F 63)
Martha St. E1 . . . . 5E 65
Martin Ct. E14 . . . . 3E 81
(off River Barge Cl.)
Martindale Av. E16 . . . . 1C 82
Martindale Ho. E14 . . . . 1D 81
(off Poplar High St.)
Martindale Rd.
SW12 . . . . 5D 103
Martineau Est. E1 . . . . . 1E 79
Martineau Ho. SW1 . . . . 1E 89
(off Churchill Gdns.)
Martineau M. N5 . . . . . . 1D 49
Martineau Rd. N5 . . . . . 1D 49
Martin Ho.
SE1 . . . . 5A 26 (4E 77)
SW8 . . . . 3A 90
(off Wyvil Rd.)
Martin La.
EC4 . . . . 4C 18 (1F 77)
(not continuous)
Martlett Ct.
WC2 . . . . 3E 15 (5A 62)
Marton Cl. SE6 . . . . . . 3C 122
Marton Rd. N16 . . . . . . 4A 36
Martys Yd. NW3 . . . . . . 1F 45
Marvell Ho. SE5 . . . . . . 3F 91
(off Camberwell Rd.)
Marvels Cl. SE12 . . . . . 2D 125
Marvels La. SE12 . . . . . 2D 125
(not continuous)
Marville Rd. SW6 . . . . . 3B 86
Marvin St. E8 . . . . 3D 51
Mary Adelaide Cl.
SW15 . . . . 4A 112
Mary Ann Gdns. SE8 . . . 2C 94
Mary Datchelor Cl.
SE5 . . . . 4F 91

Mary Flux Ct. SW5 . . . . . 1D 87
(off Bramham Gdns.)
Mary Grn. NW8 . . . . 5D 45
Mary Holben Ho.
SW16 . . . . 5E 117
Mary Ho. W6 . . . . 1E 85
(off Queen Caroline St.)
Mary Jones Ho. E14 . . . . 1C 80
(off Garford St.)
Maryland Ind. Est.
E15 . . . . 2A 54
(off Maryland Rd.)
Maryland Pk. E15 . . . . . 2A 54
(not continuous)
Maryland Point E15 . . . . 3A 54
(off Grove, The)
Maryland Rd. E15 . . . . . 2A 54
Maryland Sq. E15 . . . . . 2A 54
Marylands Rd. W9 . . . . . 3C 58
Maryland St. E15 . . . . . 2F 53
Maryland Wlk. N1 . . . . . 5E 49
(off Popham St.)
Mary Lawrenson Pl.
SE3 . . . . 3C 96
MARYLEBONE
. . . . 5C 4 (4C 60)
Marylebone Cricket Club
Lord's Cricket Ground
. . . . 2F 59
MARYLEBONE FLYOVER
. . . . 4F 59
Marylebone Fly-Over
W2 . . . . 4F 59
Marylebone High St.
W1 . . . . 5C 4 (4C 60)
Marylebone La.
W1 . . . . 1C 12 (4C 60)
Marylebone M.
W1 . . . . 1D 13 (4D 61)
Marylebone Pas.
W1 . . . . 2A 14 (5E 61)
Marylebone Rd.
NW1 . . . . 5A 4 (4A 60)
Marylebone St.
W1 . . . . 1C 12 (4C 60)
Marylee Way SE11 . . . . 5B 76
Mary MacArthur Ho.
E2 . . . . 2F 65
(off Warley St.)
W6 . . . . 2A 86
Maryon M. NW3 . . . . . . 1A 46
Maryon Rd. SE7 . . . . . . 5F 83
SE18 . . . . 5F 83
Mary Pl. W11 . . . . 1A 72
Mary Seacole Cl. E8 . . . 5B 50
Mary Smith Ct. SW5 . . . 5C 72
(off Trebovir Rd.)
Marysmith Ho. SW1 . . . . 1F 89
(off Cureton St.)
Mary St. E16 . . . . 4B 68
N1 . . . . 5E 49
Mary Ter. NW1 . . . . 5D 47
Mary Wharrie Ho.
NW3 . . . . 4B 46
(off Fellows Rd.)
Masbro' Rd. W14 . . . . . 4E 71
Mascalls Ct. SE7 . . . . . 2E 97
Mascalls Rd. SE7 . . . . . 2E 97
Mascotte Rd. SW15 . . . 2F 99
Mascotts Cl. NW2 . . . . . 5D 29

Masefield Ho. NW6 . . . . 2C 58
(off Stafford Rd.)
Mashie Rd. W3 . . . . 5A 56
Maskall Cl. SW2 . . . . . 1C 118
Maskell Rd. SW17 . . . . 3E 115
Maskelyne Cl. SW11 . . . 4A 88
Mason Cl. E16 . . . . 1C 82
SE16 . . . . 1C 92
Mason Ho. E9 . . . . 4E 51
(off Frampton Pk. Rd.)
Mason's Arms M.
W1 . . . . 3E 13 (5D 61)
Mason's Av.
EC2 . . . . 2B 18 (5E 63)
Masons Pl.
EC1 . . . . 1E 9 (2E 63)
Mason St. SE17 . . . . . . 5F 77
Masons Yd.
EC1 . . . . 1E 9 (2D 63)
SW1 . . . . 1A 22 (2E 75)
SW19 . . . . 5F 113
Massey Ct. E6 . . . . 5E 55
(off Florence Rd.)
Massie Rd. E8 . . . . 3C 50
Massingberd Way
SW17 . . . . 4D 117
Massinger St. SE17 . . . . 5A 78
Massingham St. E1 . . . . 3F 65
Mast Ct. SE16 . . . . 5A 80
(off Boat Lifter Way)
Master Gunners Pl.
SE18 . . . . 3F 97
Masterman Ho. SE5 . . . . 3F 91
(off Elmington Est.)
Masterman Rd. E6 . . . . 2F 69
Masters Cl. SW16 . . . . 5E 117
Masters Dr. SE16 . . . . . 1D 93
Masters Lodge E1 . . . . . 5E 65
(off Johnson St.)
Masters St. E1 . . . . 4F 65
Mast Ho. Ter. E14 . . . . . 5C 80
(not continuous)
Mastmaker Ct. E14 . . . . 3C 80
Mastmaker Rd. E14 . . . . 3C 80
Matcham Rd. E11 . . . . . 5A 40
Matham Gro. SE22 . . . . 2B 106
Matheson Lang Ho.
SE1 . . . . 4B 24
Matheson Rd. W14 . . . . 5B 72
Mathews Pk. Av. E15 . . . 3B 54
Mathews Yd.
WC2 . . . . 3D 15 (5A 62)
Mathieson Ct. SE1 . . . . 4E 25
(off King James St.)
Mathison Ho. SW10 . . . 3E 87
(off Coleridge Gdns.)
Matilda Ho. E1 . . . . 2C 78
(off St Katherine's Way)
Matilda St. N1 . . . . 5B 48
Matisse Ct.
EC1 . . . . 3B 10 (3F 63)
Matlock Cl. SE24 . . . . . 2E 105
Matlock Ct. SE5 . . . . . . 2F 105
Matlock Pl. E10 . . . . . . 1E 39
Matlock St. E14 . . . . . . 5A 66
Maton Ho. SW6 . . . . . . 3B 86
(off Estcourt Rd.)
Matrimony Pl. SW4 . . . . 5F 89
Matson Ho. SE16 . . . . . 4D 79
Matthew Cl. W10 . . . . . 3F 57

Matthew Parker St.
SW1 . . . . . . 4C 22 (3F 75)
Matthews Ho. E14 . . . . . 4C 66
(off Burgess St.)
Matthews St. SW11 . . . . 5B 88
Matthias Rd. N16 . . . . . 2A 50
Mattison Rd. N4 . . . . . . 1C 34
Maude Ho. E2. . . . . 1C 64
(off Ropley St.)
Maude Rd. SE5 . . . . 4A 92
Maud Gdns. E13 . . . . . . 5B 54
Maudlins Grn. E1 . . . . . 2C 78
Maud Rd. E10 . . . . 5E 39
E13 . . . . 1B 68
Maud St. E16 . . . . 4B 68
Maud Wilkes Cl.
NW5 . . . . 2E 47
Mauleverer Rd.
SW2 . . . . 3A 104
Maundeby Wlk.
NW10 . . . . 3A 42
Maunsel St. SW1 . . . . . . 5F 75
Maurer Ct. SE10 . . . . . . 4B 82
Mauretania Bldg. E1. . . 1F 79
(off Jardine Rd.)
Maurice Bishop Ter.
N6 . . . . 1C 32
(off View Rd.)
Maurice Ct. E1 . . . . 2F 65
Maurice Drummond Ho.
SE10 . . . . 4D 95
(off Catherine Gro.)
Maurice St. W12 . . . . . . 5D 57
Mauritius Rd. SE10 . . . . 5A 82
Maury Rd. N16 . . . . 4C 36
Maverton Rd. E3 . . . . . . 5C 52
Mavis Wlk. E6. . . . . 4F 69
(off Greenwich Cres.)
Mavor Ho. N1 . . . . 5B 48
(off Barnsbury Est.)
Mawbey Ho. SE1 . . . . . 1B 92
Mawbey Pl. SE1 . . . . . . 1B 92
Mawbey Rd. SE1 . . . . . 1B 92
Mawbey St. SW8 . . . . . 3A 90
Mawdley Ho. SE1 . . . . . 4D 25
Mawson Ct. N1 . . . . 5F 49
(off Gopsall St.)
Mawson Ho. EC1 . . . . . . 5B 8
(off Baldwins Gdns.)
Mawson La. W4 . . . . . . 2B 84
Maxden Ct. SE15 . . . . . 1B 106
Maxilla Wlk. W10 . . . . . . 5F 57
Maxted Rd. SE15 . . . . . 1B 106
Maxwell Ct. SE22 . . . . . 1C 120
SW4 . . . . 3F 103
Maxwell Rd. SW6 . . . . . 3D 87
Maya Cl. SE15 . . . . 5D 93
Mayall Rd. SE24 . . . . . 3D 105
Maybourne Cl.
SE26 . . . . 5D 121
Maybury Ct. W1 . . . . . . 1C 12
(off Marylebone St.)
Maybury Gdns.
NW10 . . . . 3D 43
Maybury M. N6 . . . . 2E 33
Maybury Rd. E13 . . . . . 3E 69
Maybury St. SW17 . . . . 5A 116
Mayday Gdns. SE3 . . . . 5F 97
Maydew Ho. SE16 . . . . . 5E 79
(off Abbeyfield Est.)

Maydwell Ho. E14 . . . . . 4C 66
(off Thomas Rd.)
Mayerne Rd. SE9 . . . . . 3F 111
Mayeswood Rd.
SE12 . . . . 4E 125
MAYFAIR 5D 13 (1D 75)
Mayfair Ho. Regents Pk. Rd.)
Mayfair M. NW1 . . . . . . 4B 46
(off Regents Pk. Rd.)
Mayfair Pl.
W1 . . . . 1E 21 (2D 75)
Mayfield Av. W4. . . . . . . 5A 70
Mayfield Cl. E8 . . . . 3B 50
SW4 . . . . 3F 103
Mayfield Gdns.
NW4 . . . . 1F 29
Mayfield Ho. E2. . . . . . . 1D 65
(off Cambridge Heath Rd.)
Mayfield Mans.
SW15 . . . . 3B 100
Mayfield Rd. E8 . . . . . . 4B 50
E13 . . . . 3B 68
N8 . . . . 1B 34
W12 . . . . 3A 70
Mayfield Rd. Flats
N8 . . . . 1B 34
Mayflower Cl. SE16 . . . . 5F 79
Mayflower Rd. SW9 . . . 1A 104
Mayflower St. SE16 . . . . 3E 79
Mayford NW1 . . . . 1E 61
(not continuous)
Mayford Cl. SW12 . . . . 5B 102
Mayford Rd. SW12 . . . . 5B 102
Maygood St. N1 . . . . . . 1C 62
Maygrove Rd. NW6 . . . . 3B 44
Mayhew Ct. SE5 . . . . . 2F 105
Mayhill Rd. SE7 . . . . . . 2D 97
Maylands Ho. SW3 . . . . 5A 74
(off Elystan St.)
Maynard Cl. SW6 . . . . . 3D 87
Maynard Rd. E17 . . . . . 1E 39
Maynards Quay E1 . . . . 1E 79
Mayne Ct. SE26 . . . . . . 5D 121
Mayo Ho. E1 . . . . 4E 65
(off Lindley St.)
Mayola Rd. E5 . . . . 1E 51
Mayo Rd. NW10 . . . . . . 3A 42
Mayow Rd. SE23 . . . . . 3F 121
SE26 . . . . 4F 121
May Rd. E13 . . . . 1C 68
May's Bldgs. M.
SE10 . . . . 3E 95
Mays Ct. SE10 . . . . 3F 95
WC2 . . . . . . 5D 15 (1A 76)
Maysoule Rd. SW11 . . 2F 101
Mayston M. SE10 . . . . . 1C 96
(off Ormiston Rd.)
May St. W14 . . . . 1B 86
Mayton St. N7 . . . . 5B 34
May Tree Ho. SE4 . . . . . 1B 108
(off Wickham Rd.)
Maytree Wlk. SW2 . . . 2C 118
Mayville Est. N16 . . . . . 2A 50
Mayville Rd. E11 . . . . . 4A 40
May Wlk. E13 . . . . 1D 69
Mayward Ho. SE5 . . . . . 4A 92
(off Peckham Rd.)
May Wynne Ho. E16 . . . 1D 83
(off Murray Sq.)
Maze Hill SE3 . . . . 3B 96
SE10 . . . . 2A 96

Maze Hill Lodge
SE10 . . . . 2F 95
(off Park Vista)
Mazenod Av. NW6 . . . . 4C 44
Meadbank Studios
SW11 . . . . 3A 88
(off Parkgate Rd.)
Mead Cl. NW1 . . . . 3C 46
Meadcroft Rd. SE11 . . . 2D 91
(not continuous)
Meader Ct. SE14 . . . . . 3F 93
Mead Ho. W11 . . . . 2B 72
(off Ladbroke Rd.)
Meadow Bank SE3 . . . 1B 110
Meadowbank NW3 . . . . 4B 46
Meadowbank Cl.
SW6 . . . . 3E 85
Meadowbank Rd.
NW9 . . . . 2A 28
Meadow Cl. SE6. . . . . . 5C 122
Meadow Cl. N1 . . . . . . 1A 64
Meadowcourt Rd.
SE3 . . . . 2B 110
Meadow La. SE12 . . . . 3D 125
Meadow M. SW8 . . . . . 2B 90
Meadow Pl. SW8 . . . . . 3A 90
SW4 . . . . 3A 84
Meadow Rd. SW8 . . . . . 3B 90
Meadow Row SE1 . . . . . 4E 77
Meadows Cl. E10 . . . . . 4C 38
Meadowside SE9 . . . . . 2E 111
Meadowside Leisure Cen.
. . . . 2E 111
Meadowsweet Cl.
E16 . . . . 4F 69
Meadowview Rd.
SE6 . . . . 5B 122
Mead Path SW17 . . . . . 4E 115
Mead Pl. E9 . . . . 3E 51
Mead Row
SE1 . . . . . . 5B 24 (4C 76)
Meads Ct. E15 . . . . 3B 54
Meadway NW11 . . . . . . 1C 30
Meadway, The SE3. . . . 5F 95
Meadway Cl. NW11 . . . 1D 31
Meadway Ga. NW11 . . . 1C 30
Meakin Est.
SE1 . . . . . . 5D 27 (4A 78)
Meanley Rd. E12 . . . . . 1F 55
Meard St.
W1 . . . . 3B 14 (5F 61)
(not continuous)
Meath Ho. SE24. . . . . . 4D 105
(off Dulwich Rd.)
Meath Rd. E15 . . . . 1B 68
Meath St. SW11 . . . . . . 4D 89
Mecca Bingo
Camden. 5D 47
(off Arlington Rd.)
Earlsfield 1D 115
Fulham Broadway. . . 3C 86
(off Vanston Pl.)
Haggerston 1B 64
(off Hackney Rd.)
Islington 4E 49
Kilburn 5C 44
Mecklenburgh Pl.
WC1 . . . . 3F 7 (3B 62)
Mecklenburgh Sq.
WC1 . . . . 3F 7 (3B 62)

Mecklenburgh St.
  WC1 . . . . 3F 7 (3B **62**)
Medburn St. NW1 . . . . . . .1F **61**
Medebourne Cl.
  SE3 . . . . .1C **110**
Mede Ho.
  BR1: Brom 5D **125**
    (off Pike Cl.)
Medfield St. SW15 . . . . .5C **98**
Medhurst Cl. E3 . . . . . . .1A **66**
    (not continuous)
Medlan Rd. E5 . . . . .2E **51**
Medina Gro. N7 . . . . . . .5C **34**
Medina Rd. N7 . . . . .5C **34**
Medland Ho. E14 . . . . . .1A **80**
Medlar St. SE5 . . . . .4E **91**
Medley Rd. NW6 . . . . . . .3C **44**
Medora Rd. SW2 . . . . . .5B **104**
Medusa Rd. SE6 . . . . . .4D **109**
Medway Bldgs. E3 . . . . .1A **66**
    (off Medway Rd.)
Medway Ct. NW11 . . . . . .1D **31**
  WC1 . . . . .2D **7**
    (off Judd St.)
Medway Ho. NW8 . . . . . .3A **60**
    (off Penfold St.)
  SE1 . . . . .4C **26**
    (off Hankey Pl.)
Medway M. E3 . . . . .1A **66**
Medway Rd. E3 . . . . .1A **66**
Medway St. SW1 . . . . . . .4F **75**
Medwin St. SW4 . . . . . .2B **104**
Meerbrook Rd. SE3 . . . .1F **111**
Meeson Rd. E15 . . . . . . .4B **54**
Meeson St. E5 . . . . .1A **52**
Meeson's Wharf E15 . . . .1E **67**
Meeting Fld. Path E9 . . . .3E **51**
Meeting Ho. All. E1 . . . . .2D **79**
Meeting Ho. La.
  SE15 . . . . .4D **93**
Megabowl 2A **118**
Mehetabel Rd. E9 . . . . . .2E **51**
Melba Way SE13 . . . . . .4D **95**
Melbourne Ct. W9 . . . . . .3E **59**
    (off Randolph Av.)
Melbourne Gro.
  SE22 . . . . .2A **106**
Melbourne Ho. W8 . . . . .2C **72**
    (off Kensington Pl.)
Melbourne Mans.
  W14 . . . . .2A **86**
    (off Musard Rd.)
Melbourne M. SE6 . . . .5E **109**
  SW9 . . . . .4C **90**
Melbourne Pl.
  WC2 . . . . .3A **16** (5B **62**)
Melbourne Rd. E10 . . . .2D **39**
Melbourne Sq. SW9 . . . .4C **90**
Melbourne Ter. SW6 . . . .3D **87**
    (off Moore Pk. Rd.)
Melbray M. SW6 . . . . . . .5B **86**
Melbreak Ho. SE22 . . . .1A **106**
Melbury Cl. W8 . . . . .4B **72**
Melbury Dr. SE5 . . . . . . .3A **92**
Melbury Ho. SW8 . . . . . .3B **90**
    (off Richborne Ter.)
Melbury Rd. W14 . . . . . .4B **72**
Melbury Ter. NW1 . . . . . .3A **60**
Melchester W11 . . . . . . .5B **58**
    (off Ledbury Rd.)

Melchester Ho. N19 . . . .5F **33**
    (off Wedmore St.)
Melcombe Ct. NW1 . . . . .5A **4**
    (off Melcombe Pl.)
Melcombe Ho. SW8 . . . .3B **90**
    (off Dorset Rd.)
Melcombe Pl. NW1 . . . .4B **60**
Melcombe Regis Ct.
  W1 . . . . .1C **12**
    (off Weymouth St.)
Melcombe St.
  NW1 . . . . .4A **4** (3B **60**)
Meldon Cl. SW6 . . . . . . .4D **87**
Melfield Gdns. SE6 . . . .4E **123**
Melford Cl. SE1 . . . . . . .5E **27**
    (off Fendall St.)
  SE22 . . . . .1C **120**
    (not continuous)
Melford Pas. SE22 . . . .5C **106**
Melford Rd. E11 . . . . . . .4A **40**
  SE22 . . . . .5C **106**
Melgund Rd. N5 . . . . . . .2C **48**
Melina Ct. SW15 . . . . . .1C **98**
Melina Pl. NW8 . . . . . . .2F **59**
Melina Rd. W12 . . . . . . .3D **71**
Melior Cl. N6 . . . . .1E **33**
Melior Pl.
  SE1 . . . . .3D **27** (3A **78**)
Melior St.
  SE1 . . . . .3D **27** (3A **78**)
Meliot Rd. SE6 . . . . . . .2F **123**
Mellish Flats E10 . . . . . .2C **38**
Mellish Ho. E1 . . . . .5D **65**
    (off Varden St.)
Mellish Ind. Est.
  SE18 . . . . .4F **83**
Mellish St. E14 . . . . .4C **80**
Mellison Rd. SW17 . . . .5A **116**
Mellitus St. W12 . . . . . . .4B **56**
Mell St. SE10 . . . . .1A **96**
Melody La. N5 . . . . .2E **49**
Melody Rd. SW18 . . . . .3E **101**
Melon Pl. W8 . . . . .3C **72**
Melon Rd. E11 . . . . .5A **40**
  SE15 . . . . .4C **92**
Melrose Av. NW2 . . . . . .2D **43**
  SW19 . . . . .2B **114**
Melrose Cl. SE12 . . . . . .1C **124**
Melrose Gdns. W6 . . . . .4E **71**
Melrose Ho. E14 . . . . . . .4D **81**
    (off Lanark Sq.)
  NW6 . . . . .2C **58**
    (off Carlton Va.)
Melrose Rd. SW13 . . . . .5B **84**
  SW18 . . . . .4B **100**
Melrose Ter. W6 . . . . . . .4E **71**
Melthorpe Gdns. SE3 . . .4F **97**
Melton Ct. SW7 . . . . . . .5F **73**
    (not continuous)
Melton St.
  NW1 . . . . .2A **6** (2E **61**)
Melville Ct. SE8 . . . . . . .5A **80**
  W12 . . . . .4D **71**
    (off Goldhawk Rd.)
Melville Ho. SE10 . . . . . .4E **95**
Melville Pl. N1 . . . . .4E **49**
Melville Rd. SW13 . . . . .4C **84**
Melwood Ho. E1 . . . . . . .5D **65**
    (off Watney Mkt.)
Melyn Cl. N7 . . . . .1E **47**

Memel Ct. EC1 . . . . .4F **9**
Memel St. EC1 . . .4F **9** (3E **63**)
Memorial Av. E12 . . . . . .4F **41**
  E15 . . . . .2A **68**
Mendham Ho. SE1 . . . . .5D **27**
    (off Cluny Pl.)
Mendip Cl. SE26 . . . . . .4E **121**
Mendip Ct. SE14 . . . . . .2E **93**
    (off Avonley Rd.)
  SW11 . . . . .1E **101**
Mendip Dr. NW2 . . . . . .4A **30**
Mendip Ho's. E2 . . . . . . .2E **65**
    (off Welwyn St.)
Mendip Rd. SW11 . . . . .1E **101**
Mendora Rd. SW6 . . . . .3A **86**
Menelik Rd. NW2 . . . . . .1A **44**
Menotti St. E2 . . . . .3C **64**
Menteath Ho. E14 . . . . . .5C **66**
    (off Dod St.)
Mentmore Ter. E8 . . . . . .4D **51**
Mepham St.
  SE1 . . . . .2B **24** (2C **76**)
Merbury Cl. SE13 . . . . . .3E **109**
Mercator Pl. E14 . . . . . . .1C **94**
Mercator Rd. SE13 . . . .2F **109**
Mercer Ho. SW1 . . . . . . .1D **89**
    (off Ebury Bri. Rd.)
Merceron Ho's. E2 . . . . .2E **65**
    (off Globe Rd.)
Merceron St. E1 . . . . . . .3D **65**
Mercers Cl. SE10 . . . . . .5B **82**
Mercer's Cotts. E1 . . . . .5A **66**
    (off White Horse Rd.)
Mercers M. N19 . . . . . . .5F **33**
Mercers Pl. W6 . . . . .5F **71**
Mercers Rd. N19 . . . . . .5F **33**
    (not continuous)
Mercer St.
  WC2 . . . . .3D **15** (5A **62**)
Merchant Ct. E1 . . . . . . .2E **79**
    (off Wapping Wall)
Merchants Ho. SE10 . . .1F **95**
    (off Collington St.)
Merchants Row SE10 . . .1F **95**
    (off Hoskins St.)
Merchant St. E3 . . . . . . .2B **66**
Merchiston Rd. SE6 . . . .2F **123**
Mercia Gro. SE13 . . . . .2E **109**
Mercia Ho. SE5 . . . . . . .5E **91**
    (off Denmark Rd.)
Mercier Rd. SW15 . . . . .3A **100**
Mercury Ct. E14 . . . . . . .5C **80**
    (off Homer Dr.)
Mercury Way SE14 . . . . .2F **93**
Mere Cl. SW15 . . . . .5F **99**
Meredith Av. NW2 . . . . . .2E **43**
Meredith Ho. N16 . . . . . .2A **50**
Meredith M. SE4 . . . . . .2B **108**
Meredith St. E13 . . . . . . .2C **68**
  EC1 . . . . .2D **9** (2D **63**)
Meredyth Rd. SW13 . . . .5C **84**
Meretone Cl. SE4 . . . . . .2A **108**
Mereton Mans. SE8 . . . .4C **94**
    (off Brookmill Rd.)
Mereworth Ho. SE15 . . . .2E **93**
Merganser Ct. SE8 . . . . .2B **94**
    (off Edward St.)
Meriden Ct. SW3 . . . . . .1A **88**
    (off Chelsea Mnr. St.)

Meridian Ga. E14 . . . . . . 3D 81
Meridian Ho. SE10 . . . . . 5A 82
(off Azof St.)
SE10 . . . . 3E 95
(off Royal Hill)
Meridian Pl. E14 . . . . . . 3D 81
Meridian Point SE8 . . . . 2D 95
Meridian Rd. SE7 . . . . . . 3F 97
Meridian Sq. E15 . . . . . . 4F 53
Meridian Trad. Est.
SE7 . . . . 5D 83
Merifield Rd. SE9 . . . . . 2E 111
Merivale Rd. SW15 . . . . 2A 100
Merlin Gdns.
BR1: Brom 3C 124
Merlin Ho. SW18 . . . . . 2E 101
Merlin Rd. E12 . . . . 4F 41
Merlins Ct. WC1 . . . . 2B 8
(off Margery St.)
Merlin St.
WC1 . . . . 2B 8 (2C 62)
Mermaid Ct. E8 . . . . 4B 50
(off Celandine Dr.)
SE1 . . . . 3B 26 (3F 77)
SE16 . . . . 3C 80
Mermaid Ho. E14 . . . . . . 1E 81
(off Bazely St.)
Mermaid Twr. SE8 . . . . . 2B 94
(off Abinger Gro.)
Meroe Ct. N16 . . . . 4A 36
Merredene St. SW2 . . . . 4B 104
Merriam Av. E9 . . . . 3B 52
Merrick Sq.
SE1 . . . . 5B 26 (4F 77)
Merriman Rd. SE3 . . . . . 4E 97
Merrington Rd. SW6 . . . . 2C 86
Merritt Rd. SE4 . . . . . . 3B 108
Merritt's Bldgs. EC2 . . . . 4D 11
Merrivale NW1 . . . . 5E 47
(off Camden St.)
Merrow St. SE17 . . . . . . 1F 91
Merrow Wlk. SE17 . . . . . 1F 91
Merryfield SE3 . . . . 5B 96
Merryfield Ho. SE9 . . . . 3E 125
(off Grove Pk. Rd.)
Merryfields Way
SE6 . . . . 5D 109
Merryweather Ct.
N19 . . . . 5E 33
Merthyr Ter. SW13 . . . . . 2D 85
Merton Av. W4 . . . . 5B 70
Merton La. N6 . . . . 4B 32
Merton Ri. NW3 . . . . 4A 46
Merton Rd. E17 . . . . 1E 39
SW18 . . . . 4C 100
(off Seymour Pl.)
Merttins Rd. SE4 . . . . . . 3F 107
SE15 . . . . 3F 107
Meru Cl. NW5 . . . . 1C 46
Mervan Rd. SW2 . . . . . . 2C 104
Messent Rd. SE9 . . . . . . 3E 111
Messina Av. NW6 . . . . . . 4C 44
Messiter Ho. N1 . . . . 5B 48
(off Barnsbury Est.)
Meteor St. SW11 . . . . . . 2C 102
Methley St. SE11 . . . . . . 1C 90
Methwold Rd. W10 . . . . . 4F 57
Metro Bus. Cen., The
SE26 . . . . 5B 122

Metro Central Hgts.
SE1 . . . . 5F 25
Metropolis SE11 . . . . . . 4D 77
(off Oswin St.)
Metropolitan Bus. Cen.
N1 . . . . 4A 50
(off Enfield Rd.)
Metropolitan Cl. E14 . . . . 4C 66
Metropolitan Sta. Bldgs.
W6 . . . . 5E 71
(off Beadon Rd.)
Metropolitan Wharf
E1 . . . . 2E 79
Mews, The IG4: Ilf 1F 41
N1 . . . . 5E 49
SE22 . . . . 3C 106
Mews St. E1 . . . . 2C 78
Mexfield Rd. SW15 . . . . 3B 100
Mexborough NW1 . . . . . . 5E 47
Meymott St.
SE1 . . . . 2D 25 (2D 77)
Meynell Cres. E9 . . . . . . 4F 51
Meynell Gdns. E9 . . . . . . 4F 51
Meynell Rd. E9 . . . . 4F 51
Meyrick Ho. E14 . . . . . . 4C 66
(off Burgess St.)
Meyrick Rd. NW10 . . . . . 3C 42
SW11 . . . . 1F 101
Miah Ter. E1 . . . . 2C 78
Miall Wlk. SE26 . . . . . . 4A 122
Micawber Ct. N1 . . . . . . 1A 10
(off Windsor Ter.)
Micawber Ho. SE16 . . . . 3C 78
(off Llewellyn St.)
Micawber St.
N1 . . . . 1A 10 (2E 63)
Michael Cliffe Ho.
EC1 . . . . 2D 9
Michael Faraday Ho.
SE17 . . . . 1A 92
(off Beaconsfield Rd.)
Michael Manley Ind. Est.
SW8 . . . . 5E 89
(off Clyston St.)
Michael Rd. E11 . . . . . . 3B 40
SW6 . . . . 4D 87
Michaels Cl. SE13 . . . . . 2A 110
Michael Sobell Leisure Cen.
. . . . 5B 34
Michael Stewart Ho.
SW6 . . . . 2B 86
(off Clem Attlee Ct.)
Michelangelo Ct.
SE16 . . . . 1D 93
(off Stubbs Dr.)
Micheldever Rd.
SE12 . . . . 4A 110
Michelle Ct. W3 . . . . . . 1A 70
Michelson Ho. SE11 . . . . 5B 76
(off Black Prince Rd.)
Michigan Ho. E14 . . . . . 4C 80
Mickledore NW1 . . . . . . 1A 6
(off Ampthill Est.)
Micklethwaite Rd.
SW6 . . . . 2C 86
Middle Dartrey Wlk.
SW10 . . . . 3E 87
(off Dartrey Wlk.)
Middlefield NW8 . . . . . . 5F 45
Middle La. N8 . . . . 1A 34

Middle La. M. N8 . . . . . . 1A 34
Middle Pk. Av. SE9 . . . . . 4F 111
Middle Rd. E13 . . . . 1C 68
Middle Row W10 . . . . . . 3A 58
Middlesex County Cricket Club
Lord's Cricket Ground
. . . . 2F 59
Middlesex Ct. W4 . . . . . . 5B 70
Middlesex Filter Beds
Nature Reserve. 5F 37
Middlesex Pas. EC1 . . . . 1E 17
Middlesex Pl. E9 . . . . . . 3E 51
(off Elsdale St.)
Middlesex St.
. . . . 1E 19 (4A 64)
Middlesex University
Archway Campus, The
. . . . 3E 33
Middlesex Wharf E5 . . . . 4E 37
Middle St. EC1 . . . . 5F 9 (4E 63)
Middle Temple 4B 16
Middle Temple Hall 4B 16
(off Middle Temple La.)
Middle Temple La.
EC4 . . . . 3B 16 (5C 62)
Middleton Dr. SE16 . . . . 3F 79
Middleton Gro. N7 . . . . . 2A 48
Middleton Ho. E8 . . . . . . 4C 50
SE1 . . . . 5B 26
(off Burbage St.)
SW1 . . . . 5F 75
(off Causton St.)
Middleton M. N7 . . . . . . 2A 48
Middleton Pl. W1 . . . . . . 1F 13
Middleton Rd. E8 . . . . . . 4B 50
NW11 . . . . 2C 30
Middleton St. E2 . . . . . . 2D 65
Middleton Way
SE13 . . . . 2F 109
Middleway NW11 . . . . . . 1D 31
Middle Yd.
SE1 . . . . 1D 27 (2A 78)
Midford Pl.
W1 . . . . 4A 6 (3E 61)
Midhope Ho. WC1 . . . . . 2E 7
(off Midhope St.)
Midhope St.
WC1 . . . . 2E 7 (2A 62)
Midhurst SE26 . . . . 5E 121
Midhurst Ho. E14 . . . . . . 5B 66
(off Salmon La.)
Midhurst Way E5 . . . . . . 1C 50
Midland Pde. NW6 . . . . . 3D 45
Midland Pl. E14 . . . . 1E 95
Midland Rd. E10 . . . . . . 2E 39
NW1 . . . . 1C 6 (1F 61)
Midland Ter. NW2 . . . . . 5F 29
NW10 . . . . 3A 56
Midmoor Rd. SW12 . . . . 1E 117
Midship Cl. SE16 . . . . . . 2F 79
Midship Point E14 . . . . . 3C 80
(off Quarterdeck, The)
Midstrath Rd. NW10 . . . . 1A 42
Midway Ho. EC1 . . . . . . 1D 9
Midwood Cl. NW2 . . . . . 5D 29
Mighell Av. IG4: Ilf 1F 41
Milborne Gro. SW10 . . . . 1E 87
Milborne St. E9 . . . . 3E 51
Milborough Cres.
SE12 . . . . 4A 110

Milcote St.
SE1 . . . . . . 4D **25** (3D **77**)
Mildenhall Rd. E5 . . . . . 1E **51**
Mildmay Av. N1 . . . . 3F **49**
Mildmay Gro. Nth.
N1 . . . . 2F **49**
Mildmay Gro. Sth.
N1 . . . . 2F **49**
Mildmay Pk. N1 . . . . 2F **49**
Mildmay Pl. N16 . . . . . . 2A **50**
Mildmay Rd. N1 . . . . 2F **49**
Mildmay St. N1 . . . . 3F **49**
MILE END 3B **66**
Mile End Pk. 3A **66**
Mile End Pl. E1 . . . . 3F **65**
Mile End Rd. E1 . . . . . . 4E **65**
E3 . . . . 4E **65**
Mile End Stadium 4A **66**
Miles Bldgs. NW1 . . . . . 4A **60**
(off Penfold Pl.)
Miles Ct. E1 . . . . 5D **65**
(off Tillman St.)
Miles Ho. SE10 . . . . 1A **96**
(off Tuskar St.)
Miles Pl. NW1 . . . . 4F **59**
(off Broadley St.)
Miles St. SW8 . . . . 2A **90**
(not continuous)
Miles St. Bus. Est.
SW8 . . . . 2A **90**
(off Miles St.)
Milfoil St. W12 . . . . 1C **70**
Milford La.
WC2 . . . . 4A **16** (1C **76**)
Milford M. SW16 . . . . . . 3B **118**
Milford Towers SE6 . . . 5D **109**
Milk St. BR1: Brom . . . 5D **125**
EC2 . . . . 3A **18** (5E **63**)
Milkwell Yd. SE5 . . . . . . 4E **91**
Milkwood Rd. SE24 . . . 3D **105**
Milk Yd. E1 . . . . 1E **79**
Millais Ho. SW1 . . . . . . 5A **76**
(off Marsham St.)
Millais Rd. E11 . . . . 1E **53**
Millard Cl. N16 . . . . 2A **50**
Millard Ho. SE8 . . . . 1B **94**
(off Leeway)
Millbank
SW1 . . . . 5D **23** (4A **76**)
Millbank Ct. SW1 . . . . . 5A **76**
(off John Islip St.)
Millbank Twr. SW1 . . . . 5A **76**
Millbank Way SE12 . . . 3C **110**
Millbrook Ho. SE15 . . . . 2C **92**
(off Peckham Pk. Rd.)
Millbrook Pas. SW9 . . . 1D **105**
Millbrook Pl. NW1 . . . . 1E **61**
(off Hampstead Rd.)
Millbrook Rd. SW9 . . . 1D **105**
Mill Ct. E10 . . . . 5E **39**
Millcroft Ho. SE6 . . . . . 4E **123**
(off Melfield Gdns.)
Millender Wlk. SE16 . . . 5E **79**
(off New Rotherhithe Rd.)
Millennium Bridge
. . . . 5E **17** (1D **77**)
Millennium Bus. Cen.
NW2 . . . . 4D **29**
Millennium Cl. E16 . . . . 5D **69**
Millennium Dome 2A **82**

Millennium Dr. E14 . . . . . 5F **81**
Millennium Pl. E2 . . . . . 1D **65**
Millennium Sq.
SE1 . . . . 3F **27** (3B **78**)
Millennium Way
SE10 . . . . 3A **82**
Miller Cl.
BR1: Brom 5D **125**
Miller Rd. SW19 . . . . . . 5F **115**
Miller's Av. E8 . . . . 2B **50**
Millers Mdw. Cl.
SE3 . . . . 2B **110**
Miller's Ter. E8 . . . . 2B **50**
Miller St. NW1 . . . . 1E **61**
(not continuous)
Millers Way W6 . . . . 3E **71**
Millers Wharf Ho. E1 . . . 2C **78**
(off St Katherine's Way)
Miller Wlk.
SE1 . . . . 2C **24** (2C **76**)
Millfield N4 . . . . 4C **34**
Millfield La. N6 . . . . 3A **32**
(not continuous)
Millfield Pl. N6 . . . . 4C **32**
Mill Gdns. SE26 . . . . . . 3C **121**
Millgrove St. SW11 . . . . 4C **88**
Millharbour E14 . . . . . . 3D **81**
Mill Hill SW13 . . . . 5C **84**
Mill Hill Rd. SW13 . . . . 5C **84**
Millhouse Pl. SE27 . . . . 4D **119**
Millicent Rd. E10 . . . . . 3B **38**
Milligan St. E14 . . . . 1B **80**
Milliners Ho. SW18 . . . . 2C **100**
Millington Ho. N16 . . . . 5F **35**
Mill La. NW6 . . . . 2B **44**
Millman M.
WC1 . . . . 4F **7** (3B **62**)
Millman Pl. WC1 . . . . 4A **8**
(off Millman St.)
Millman St.
WC1 . . . . 4F **7** (3B **62**)
Millmark Gro. SE14 . . . . 5A **94**
MILL MEADS 1F **67**
Mill Pl. E14 . . . . 5A **66**
Mill Pond Cl. SW8 . . . . . 3F **89**
Millpond Est. SE16 . . . . 3D **79**
Mill Rd. E16 . . . . 2D **83**
Mill Row N1 . . . . 5A **50**
Mills Ct. EC2 . . . . 3D **11**
(off Curtain Rd.)
Mills Gro. E14 . . . . 5E **67**
Millshot Cl. SW6 . . . . . . 4E **85**
Mills Ho. SW8 . . . . 4E **89**
(off Thessaly Rd.)
Millstream Ho. SE16 . . . 3D **79**
(off Jamaica Rd.)
Millstream Rd.
SE1 . . . . 4F **27** (3B **78**)
Mill St. SE1 . . . . 3B **78**
W1 . . . . 4F **13** (1D **75**)
MILLWALL 5D **81**
Millwall Dock Rd.
E14 . . . . 4C **80**
Millwall FC 1E **93**
Millwood St. W10 . . . . . . 4A **58**
Mill Yd. E1 . . . . 1C **78**
Milman Rd. NW6 . . . . . . 1F **57**
Milman's St. SW10 . . . . . 2F **87**
Milne Gdns. SE9 . . . . . . 3F **111**

Milner Ct. SE15 . . . . 3B **92**
(off Colegrove Rd.)
Milner Pl. N1 . . . . 5C **48**
Milner Rd. E15 . . . . 2A **68**
Milner Sq. N1 . . . . 4D **49**
Milner St. SW3 . . . . 5B **74**
Milo Gdns. SE22 . . . . . 4B **106**
Milo Rd. SE22 . . . . 4B **106**
Milrood Ho. E1 . . . . 4F **65**
(off Stepney Grn.)
Milroy Wlk.
SE1 . . . . 1D **25** (2D **77**)
Milson Rd. W14 . . . . 4F **71**
Milstead Ho. E5 . . . . . . 2D **51**
Milton Av. E6 . . . . 4F **55**
N6 . . . . 2E **33**
Milton Cl. N2 . . . . 1E **31**
SE1 . . . . 5B **78**
Milton Ct.
EC2 . . . . 5B **10** (4F **63**)
SE14 . . . . 2B **94**
(not continuous)
SW18 . . . . 3C **100**
Milton Ct. Rd. SE14 . . . . 2A **94**
Milton Ct. Wlk. EC2 . . . . 5B **10**
(off Silk St.)
Milton Gdn. Est.
N16 . . . . 1F **49**
Milton Gro. N16 . . . . 1F **49**
Milton Ho. E2 . . . . 2E **65**
(off Roman Rd.)
SE5 . . . . 3F **91**
(off Elmington Est.)
Milton Mans. W14 . . . . . 2A **86**
(off Queen's Club Gdns.)
Milton Pk. N6 . . . . 2E **33**
Milton Pl. N7 . . . . 2C **48**
(off Eastwood Cl.)
Milton Rd. N6 . . . . 2E **33**
NW9 . . . . 2C **28**
SE24 . . . . 3D **105**
SW19 . . . . 5E **115**
Milton St.
EC2 . . . . 5B **10** (4F **63**)
Milverton Ho. SE23 . . . 3A **122**
Milverton Rd. NW6 . . . . 4E **43**
Milverton St. SE11 . . . . 1C **90**
Milward St. E1 . . . . 4D **65**
Mimosa Lodge
NW10 . . . . 2B **42**
Mimosa St. SW6 . . . . . . 4B **86**
Minard Rd. SE6 . . . . 5A **110**
Mina Rd. SE17 . . . . 1A **92**
Minchin Ho. E14 . . . . . . 5C **66**
(off Dod St.)
Mincing La.
EC3 . . . . 4D **19** (1A **78**)
Minehead Rd.
SW16 . . . . 5B **118**
Minera M. SW1 . . . . 5C **74**
Minerva Cl. SW9 . . . . . . 3C **90**
(not continuous)
Minerva Rd. NW10 . . . . 2A **56**
Minerva St. E2 . . . . 1D **65**
Minerva Wlk.
EC1 . . . . 2E **17** (5D **63**)
Minet Av. NW10 . . . . . . 1A **56**
Minet Gdns. NW10 . . . . 1A **56**
Minet Rd. SW9 . . . . 5D **91**
Minford Gdns. W14 . . . . 3F **71**

Minford Ho. *W14* *3F 71*
  (off Minford Gdns.)
Mingard Wlk. N7 . . . . . . 4B 34
Ming St. E14. . . . . 1C 80
Miniver Pl. EC4 . . . . 4A 18
Minnow St. SE17 . . . . . . 5A 78
Minnow Wlk. SE17 . . . . . 5A 78
Minories EC3 . . 3F 19 (5B 64)
Minshill St. SW8 . . . . 4F 89
Minson Rd. E9 . . . . 5F 51
Minstead Gdns.
  SW15 . . . . 5B 98
Minster Ct. EC3 . . . . 4E 19
Minster Pavement
  EC3 . . . . 4E 19
  (off Mincing La.)
Minster Rd. NW2 . . . . . . 2A 44
Mint Bus. Pk. E16 . . . . . . 4D 69
Mintern St. N1 . . . . 1F 63
Minton Ho. SE11 . . . . . 5C 76
  (off Walnut Tree Wlk.)
Minton M. NW6 . . . . 3D 45
Mint St. SE1. . . . 3F 25 (3E 77)
Mirabel Rd. SW6 . . . . . . 3B 86
Miranda Cl. E1 . . . . 4E 65
Miranda Rd. N19 . . . . . . 3E 33
Mirfield St. SE7 . . . . 5F 83
Mirror Path SE9 . . . . . . 3E 125
Missenden SE17 . . . . . . 1F 91
  (off Roland Way)
Missenden Ho. NW8 . . . 3A 60
  (off Jerome Cres.)
Mission, The E14 . . . . . . 5B 66
  (off Commercial Rd.)
Mission Pl. SE15 . . . . . . 4C 92
Mistral SE5. . . . . 4A 92
Mitali Pas. E1. . . . . 5C 64
  (not continuous)
Mitcham Ho. SE5 . . . . . . 4E 91
Mitcham La. SW16. . . . . 5E 117
Mitcham Rd. SW17 . . . . 5B 116
Mitchellbrook Way
  NW10 . . . . 3A 42
Mitchell Ho. W12. . . . . . 1D 71
  (off White City Est.)
Mitchell's Pl. SE21. . . . . 4A 106
  (off Aysgarth Rd.)
Mitchell St.
  EC1. . . . . 3F 9 (3E 63)
  (not continuous)
Mitchell Wlk. E6. . . . . . . 4F 69
  (off Neats Ct. Rd.)
Mitchison Rd. N1 . . . . . . 3F 49
Mitford Rd. N19 . . . . 4A 34
Mitre, The E14 . . . . 1B 80
Mitre Bri. Ind. Pk.
  NW10 . . . . 3D 57
Mitre Ct. EC2 . . . . 2A 18
Mitre Rd. E15 . . . . 1A 68
  SE1 . . . . 3C 24 (3C 76)
Mitre Sq.
  EC3 . . . . 3E 19 (5A 64)
Mitre St. EC3 . . 3E 19 (5A 64)
Mitre Way NW10 . . . . . . 3D 57
  W10. . . . . 3D 57
Mitre Yd. SW3 . . . . 5A 74
Moat Dr. E13. . . . . 1E 69
Moatfield NW6 . . . . 4A 44
Moatlands Ho. WC1. . . . . 2E 7
  (off Cromer St.)

Moat Pl. SW9. . . . . 1B 104
Moberley Rd. SW4 . . . . . 5F 103
Mobil Ct. WC2 . . . . 3A 16
  (off Clement's Inn)
Mocatta Ho. E1 . . . . 3D 65
  (off Brady St.)
Modbury Gdns. NW5 . . . 3C 46
Modder Pl. SW15 . . . . . . 2F 99
Model Bldgs. WC1. . . . . . 2A 8
Model Farm Cl. SE9. . . . 3F 125
Modern Ct. EC4 . . . . 2D 17
Modling Ho. E2. . . . . 1F 65
  (off Mace St.)
Moelwyn N7 . . . . 2F 47
Moffat Ct. SW19. . . . . . . 5C 114
Moffat Ho. SE5. . . . . 3E 91
Moffat Rd. SW17 . . . . . . 4B 116
Mohawk Ho. E3 . . . . 1A 66
  (off Gernon Rd.)
Mohmmad Khan Rd.
  E11 . . . . 3B 40
Moland Mead SE16 . . . . 1F 93
  (off Crane Mead)
Molasses Ho. SW11. . . 1E 101
  (off Clove Hitch Quay)
Molasses Row
  SW11 . . . . 1E 101
Molesford Rd. SW6 . . . . 4C 86
Molesworth Ho.
  SE17. . . . . 2D 91
  (off Brandon Est.)
Molesworth St.
  SE13 . . . . 2E 109
Mollis Ho. E3 . . . . 4C 66
  (off Gale St.)
Molly Huggins Cl.
  SW12 . . . . 5E 103
Molton Ho. N1 . . . . 5B 48
  (off Barnsbury Est.)
Molyneux Dr. SW17 . . . . 4D 117
Molyneux St. W1 . . . . . . 4A 60
Monarch Dr. E16 . . . . . . 4F 69
  SW16 . . . . 5C 118
Mona Rd. SE15 . . . . 5E 93
Mona St. E16 . . . . 4B 68
Moncks Row SW18 . . . . 4B 100
Monck St.
  SW1 . . . . 5C 22 (4F 75)
Monclar Rd. SE5 . . . . . . 2F 105
Moncorvo Cl. SW7 . . . . . 3A 74
Moncrieff Cl. E6 . . . . 5F 69
Moncrieff Pl. SE15. . . . . 5C 92
Moncrieff St. SE15. . . . . 5C 92
Monega Rd. E7. . . . . 3E 55
  E12 . . . . 3E 55
Monet Ct. SE16 . . . . 1D 93
  (off Stubbs Dr.)
Moneyer Ho. N1. . . . . . . 1B 10
  (off Fairbank Est.)
Mongers Almshouses
  E9 . . . . 4F 51
  (off Church Cres.)
Monica Shaw Ct.
  NW1 . . . . 1F 61
  (off Purchese St.,
  not continuous)
Monier Rd. E3 . . . . 4C 52
Monk Ct. W12 . . . . 2C 70
Monk Dr. E16 . . . . 1C 82

Monk Pas. E16. . . . . 1C 82
  (off Monk Dr.)
Monkton Ho. E5. . . . . . . 2D 51
  SE16 . . . . 3F 79
  (off Wolfe Cres.)
Monkton St. SE11 . . . . . 5C 76
Monkwell Sq.
  EC2 . . . . 1A 18 (4E 63)
Monmouth Pl. W2 . . . . . 5D 59
  (off Monmouth Rd.)
Monmouth Rd. W2. . . . . 5C 58
Monmouth St.
  WC2. . . . . 3D 15 (5A 62)
Monnery Rd. N19 . . . . . . 5E 33
Monnow Rd. SE1 . . . . . . 1C 92
Monro Way E5 . . . . 1C 50
Monsell Ct. N4 . . . . 5D 35
Monsell Rd. N4 . . . . 5C 34
Monson Rd. NW10. . . . . 1C 56
  SE14 . . . . 3F 93
Montacute Rd.
  SE6 . . . . 5B 108
Montague Av. SE4 . . . . . 2B 108
Montague Cl.
  SE1. . . . . 1B 26 (2F 77)
Montague Ho. E16. . . . . 2D 83
  (off Wesley Av.)
Montague Pl.
  WC1 . . . . 5C 6 (4F 61)
Montague Rd. E8. . . . . . 2C 50
  E11 . . . . 4B 40
  N8. . . . . 1B 34
Montague Sq. SE15 . . . . 3E 93
Montague St.
  EC1. . . . . 1F 17 (4E 63)
  WC1. . . . . 5D 7 (4A 62)
Montagu Mans.
  W1 . . . . 5A 4 (4B 60)
Montagu M. Nth.
  W1. . . . . 1A 12 (4B 60)
Montagu M. Sth.
  W1. . . . . 2A 12 (5B 60)
Montagu M. W.
  W1 . . . . 2A 12 (5B 60)
Montagu Pl.
  W1. . . . . 1A 12 (4B 60)
Montagu Rd. NW4 . . . . . 1C 28
Montagu Row
  W1. . . . . 1A 12 (4B 60)
Montagu Sq.
  W1. . . . . 1A 12 (4B 60)
Montagu St.
  W1. . . . . 2A 12 (5B 60)
Montaigne Cl. SW1 . . . . 5F 75
Montana Gdns.
  SE26 . . . . 5B 122
Montana Rd. SW17 . . . . 3C 116
Montcalm Ho. E14 . . . . . 5B 80
Montcalm Rd. SE7 . . . . . 3F 97
Montclare St.
  E2. . . . . 2F 11 (3B 64)
Monteagle Ct. N1. . . . . . 1A 64
Monteagle Way E5. . . . . 5C 36
  SE15 . . . . 1D 107
Montefiore St. N16 . . . . . 3B 36
Montefiore St. SW8. . . . . 5D 89
Montego Cl. SE24 . . . . . 2C 104
Montem Rd. SE23 . . . . . 5B 108
Montem St. N4. . . . . 3B 34
Montenotte Rd. N8. . . . . 1E 33

Montesquieu Ter.
E16 . . . . 5B **68**
(off Clarkson Rd.)
Montevetro SW11 . . . . 4F **87**
Montford Pl. SE11 . . . . 1C **90**
Montfort Ho. E2 . . . . . . 2E **65**
(off Victoria Pk. Sq.)
E14 . . . . 4E **81**
(off Galbraith St.)
Montfort Pl. SW19 . . 1F **113**
Montgomery Lodge
E1 . . . . 3E **65**
(off Cleveland Gro.)
Montgomery St.
E14 . . . . 2D **81**
Montholme Rd.
SW11 . . . . 4B **102**
Monthope Rd. E1 . . . . 4C **64**
Montolieu Gdns.
SW15 . . . . 3D **99**
Montpelier Gdns. F6. . 2F **69**
Montpelier Gro. NW5 . . 2E **47**
Montpelier M. SW7 . . 4A **74**
Montpelier Pl. E1 . . . . 5E **65**
SW7 . . . . 4A **74**
Montpelier Ri. NW11 . . 2A **30**
Montpelier Rd.
SE15 . . . . 4D **93**
Montpelier Row
SE3 . . . . 5B **96**
Montpelier Sq. SW7 . . 3A **74**
Montpelier St. SW7 . . 4A **74**
Montpelier Ter.
SW7 . . . . 3A **74**
Montpelier Va. SE3 . . 5B **96**
Montpelier Wlk.
SW7 . . . . 4A **74**
Montpelier Way
NW11 . . . . 2A **30**
Montreal Pl.
WC2 . . . . 4F **15** (1B **76**)
Montrell Rd. SW2 . . . 1A **118**
Montrose Av. NW6 . . 1A **58**
Montrose Ct. SE6 . . . 2B **124**
SW7 . . . . 3F **73**
Montrose Ho. E14 . . . 4C **80**
Montrose Pl.
SW1 . . . . 4C **20** (3C **74**)
Montrose Way SE23 . 1F **121**
Montserrat Cl. SE19 . 5F **119**
Montserrat Rd.
SW15 . . . . 2A **100**
Monument, The 4C **18**
(off Monument St.)
Monument Gdns.
SE13 . . . . 3E **109**
Monument St.
EC3 . . . . 4C **18** (1F **77**)
Monza St. E1 . . . . 1E **79**
Moodkee St. SE16 . . . 4E **79**
Moody Rd. SE15 . . . . 4B **92**
Moody St. E1 . . . . 2F **65**
Moon Ct. SE12 . . . . . 2C **110**
Moon St. N1 . . . . 5D **49**
Moorcroft Rd.
SW16 . . . . 3A **118**
Moore Ct. N1 . . . . 5D **49**
(off Gaskin St.)
Moorehead Way
SE3 . . . . 1C **110**

Moore Ho. E1 . . . . 1E **79**
(off Cable St.)
E2 . . . . 2E **65**
(off Roman Rd.)
SE10 . . . . 1B **96**
(off Armitage St.)
Moore Pk. Ct. SW6 . . 3D **87**
(off Fulham Rd.)
Moore Pk. Rd.
SW6 . . . . 3C **86**
Moore St. SE19 . . . . . 5E **119**
Moore St. SW3 . . . . . 5B **74**
Moore Wlk. C7 . . . . . 1C **54**
Moorey Cl. F15 . . . . . 5B **54**
Moorfields
EC2 . . . . 1B **18** (4F **63**)
Moorfields Highwalk
EC2 . . . . 1B **18**
(off Moorfields,
not continuous)
Moorgate
EC2 . . . . 2B **18** (5F **63**)
Moorgate Pl. EC2 . . . . 2B **18**
Moorgreen Ho. EC1 . . 1D **9**
Moorhouse Rd. W2 . . 5C **58**
Moorings, The E16 . . 4E **69**
(off Prince Regent La.)
Moorland Rd. SW9 . . 2D **105**
Moor La. EC2 . . 1B **18** (4F **63**)
(not continuous)
Moor Pl. EC2 . . 1B **18** (4F **63**)
Moorside Rd.
BR1: Brom 3A **124**
Moor St. W1 . . 3C **14** (5F **61**)
Moran Ho. E1 . . . . 2D **79**
(off Wapping La.)
Morant St. E14 . . . . . 1C **80**
Mora Rd. NW2 . . . . . . 1E **43**
Mora St. EC1 . . 2A **10** (2E **63**)
Morat St. SW9 . . . . . . 4B **90**
Moravian Cl. SW10 . . 2F **87**
Moravian Pl. SW10 . . 2F **87**
Moravian St. E2 . . . . . 1E **65**
Moray Ho. E1 . . . . 3A **66**
(off Harford St.)
Moray M. N7 . . . . 4B **34**
Moray Rd. N4 . . . . 4B **34**
Mordaunt Ho. NW10 . 5A **42**
Mordaunt Rd. NW10 . 5A **42**
Mordaunt St. SW9 . . 1B **104**
Morden Hill SE13 . . . 5E **95**
(not continuous)
Morden La. SE13 . . . . 4E **95**
Morden Rd. SE3 . . . . . 5C **96**
Morden Rd. M. SE3 . . 5C **96**
Morden St. SE13 . . . . 4D **95**
Morden Wharf SE10 . . 4A **82**
(off Morden Wharf Rd.)
Morden Wharf Rd.
SE10 . . . . 4A **82**
Mordern Ho. NW1 . . . 3A **60**
(off Harewood Av.)
Mordred Rd. SE6 . . . 2A **124**
Morecambe Cl. E1 . . . 4F **65**
Morecambe St. SE17 . 5E **77**
More Cl. E16 . . . . 5D **68**
W14 . . . . 5A **72**
Moreland Cotts. E3 . . 1C **66**
(off Fairfield Rd.)
Moreland Ct. NW2 . . . 5C **30**

Moreland St.
EC1 . . . . 1E **9** (2D **63**)
Morella Rd. SW12 . . . 5B **102**
More London Pl.
SE1 . . . . 2D **27** (2A **78**)
Moremead Rd. SE6 . . 4B **122**
Morena St. SE6 . . . . . 5D **109**
Moresby Rd. E5 . . . . . 3D **37**
Moresby Wlk. SW8 . . 5E **89**
More's Gdn. SW3 . . . . 2F **87**
(off Cheyne Wlk.)
Moreton Cl. E5 . . . . . . 4D **37**
N15 . . . . 1F **35**
SW1 . . . . 1E **89**
(off Moreton Ter.)
Moreton Ho. SE16 . . . 4D **79**
Moreton Pl. SW1 . . . . 1E **89**
Moreton Rd. N15 . . . . 1F **35**
Moreton St. SW1 . . . . 1E **89**
Moreton Ter. SW1 . . . 1E **89**
Moreton Ter. M. Nth.
SW1 . . . . 1E **89**
Moreton Ter. M. Sth.
SW1 . . . . 1E **89**
Morgan Ho. SW1 . . . . 5E **75**
(off Vauxhall Bri. Rd.)
SW8 . . . . 4E **89**
(off Wadhurst Rd.)
Morgan Mans. N7 . . . . 2C **48**
(off Morgan Rd.)
Morgan Rd. N7 . . . . . . 2C **48**
W10 . . . . 4B **58**
Morgan St. E3 . . . . . . 2A **66**
E16 . . . . 4B **68**
Moriatry Cl. N7 . . . . . 1A **48**
Morie St. SW18 . . . . . 3D **101**
Morieux Rd. E10 . . . . . 3B **38**
Moring Rd. SW17 . . . 4C **116**
Morkyns Wlk. SE21 . . 3A **120**
Morland Cl. NW11 . . . 3D **31**
Morland Ct. W12 . . . . 3D **71**
(off Coningham Rd.)
Morland Est. E8 . . . . . 4C **50**
Morland Gdns.
NW10 . . . . 4A **42**
Morland Ho. NW1 . . . . 1A **6**
(off Werrington St.)
NW6 . . . . 5C **44**
SW1 . . . . 5A **76**
(off Marsham St.)
W11 . . . . 5A **58**
(off Lancaster Rd.)
Morland M. N1 . . . . . . 4C **48**
Morland Rd. E17 . . . . 1F **37**
Morley Ho. N16 . . . . . . 4C **36**
Morley Rd. E10 . . . . . . 3E **39**
E15 . . . . 1B **68**
SE13 . . . . 2E **109**
Morley St.
SE1 . . . . 5C **24** (4C **76**)
Morna Rd. SE5 . . . . . . 5E **91**
Morning La. E9 . . . . . . 3E **51**
Mornington Av.
W14 . . . . 5B **72**
Mornington Cl. NW1 . 1E **61**
(off Mornington Cres.)
Mornington Cres.
NW1 . . . . 1E **61**
Mornington Gro. E3 . . 2C **66**
Mornington M. SE5 . . 4E **91**

Mornington Pl. NW1.... 1E 61
  SE8 .... 3B 94
  (off Mornington Rd.)
Mornington Rd.
  E11 .... 2B 40
  (not continuous)
  SE8 .... 3B 94
Mornington Sports &
  Leisure Cen. 5D 47
  (off Stanmore Pl.)
Mornington St. NW1... 1D 61
Mornington Ter.
  NW1 .... 5D 47
Morocco St.
  SE1 .... 4D 27 (3A 78)
Morocco Wharf *E1* 2D 79
  (off Wapping High St.)
Morpeth Gro. E9 ...... 5F 51
Morpeth Mans. *SW1* . 5E 75
  (off Morpeth St.)
Morpeth Rd. E9....... 5F 51
Morpeth St. E2 .... 2E 65
Morpeth Ter. SW1..... 4E 75
Morrel Ct. *E2* 1C 64
  (off Goldsmiths Row)
Morris Blitz Ct. N16 ... 1B 50
Morris Gdns. SW18 .... 5C 100
Morris Ho. *E2* 2E 65
  (off Roman Rd.)
  NW8 .... 3A 60
  (off Salisbury St.)
Morrish Rd. SW2 ..... 5A 104
Morrison Bldgs. Nth.
  E1 .... 5C 64
  (off Commercial Rd.)
Morrison Ho. *SW2* 1C 118
  (off High Trees)
Morrison Rd. SW9 .... 5C 90
Morrison St. SW11 .... 1C 102
Morris Pl. N4 .... 4C 34
Morris Rd. E14 .... 4D 67
  E15 .... 1A 54
Morriss Ho. *SE16* 3D 79
  (off Cherry Gdn. St.)
Morris St. E1 .... 5D 65
Morse Cl. E13 .... 2C 68
Morshead Mans. *W9* . 2C 58
  (off Morshead Rd.)
Morshead Rd. W9 .... 2C 58
Mortain Ho. *SE16* 5D 79
  (off Roseberry St.)
Morten Cl. SW4 ...... 4F 103
Mortham St. E15 ..... 5A 54
Mortimer Cl. NW2 .... 4B 30
  SW16 .... 2F 117
Mortimer Ct. *NW8* 1E 59
  (off Abbey Rd.)
Mortimer Cres. NW6 .. 5D 45
Mortimer Est. *NW6* ... 5D 45
  (off Mortimer Pl.)
Mortimer Ho. W11 .... 2F 71
  W14 .... 5A 72
  (off Nth. End Rd.)
Mortimer Mkt.
  WC1 .... 4A 6 (3E 61)
Mortimer Pl. NW6 .... 5D 45
Mortimer Rd. N1 ..... 4A 50
  (not continuous)
  NW10 .... 2E 57
Mortimer Sq. W11 .... 1F 71

Mortimer St.
  W1 .... 2E 13 (5E 61)
Mortimer Ter. NW5 .... 1D 47
Mortlake High St.
  SW14 .... 1A 98
Mortlake Rd. E16 ..... 5D 69
Mortlock Cl. SE15 .... 4D 93
Mortlock Ct. E7 ...... 1F 55
Morton M. SW5 ...... 5D 73
Morton Pl. SE1 .... 4C 76
Morton Rd. E15 ...... 4B 54
  N1 .... 4E 49
Morval Rd. SW2 ...... 3C 104
Morven Rd. SW17 .... 3B 116
Morville Ho. *SW18*... 4F 101
  (off Fitzhugh Gro.)
Morville St. E3 .... 1C 66
Morwell St.
  WC1 .... 1B 14 (4F 61)
Moscow Pl. W2 ...... 1D 73
Moscow Rd. W2....... 1C 72
Mosedale *NW1* 2E 5
  (off Cumberland Mkt.)
Moseley Row SE10 ... 5B 82
  (off School Bank Rd.)
Mosque Ter. *E1* 4C 64
  (off Fieldgate St.)
Mosque Twr. *E1* 4C 64
  (off Fieldgate St.)
  E3 .... 1A 66
  (off Ford St.)
Mossbury Rd.
  SW11 .... 1A 102
Moss Cl. E1 .... 4C 64
Mossford St. E3 ...... 3B 66
Mossington Gdns.
  SE16 .... 5E 79
Mossop St. SW3 ..... 5A 74
Mostyn Gdns. NW10.. 2F 57
Mostyn Gro. E3 ...... 1C 66
Mostyn Rd. SW9 ..... 4C 90
Motcomb St.
  SW1 .... 5B 20 (4C 74)
Mothers Sq. *E5* 1D 51
  (off Hana M.)
Motley Av. EC2 .... 4D 11
Motley St. SW8 ...... 5E 89
MOTTINGHAM 2F 125
Mottingham Gdns.
  SE9 .... 1F 125
Mottingham La.
  SE9 .... 1E 125
  SE12 .... 1E 125
Mottingham Rd.
  SE9 .... 2F 125
Moules Ct. SE5....... 3E 91
Moulins Rd. E9....... 4E 51
Moulsford Ho. N7 .... 2F 47
Moundfield Rd. N16... 1C 36
Mounsey Ho. *W10* ... 2A 58
  (off Third Av.)
Mount, The E5 .... 4D 37
  (Alcester Cres.)
  E5 .... 4D 37
  (Muston Rd.)
  NW3 .... 5E 31
Mountacre Cl. SE26.. 4B 120
Mt. Adon Pk. SE22.... 5C 106
Mountague Pl. E14.... 1E 81
Mountain Ho. SE11 ... 5B 76

Mt. Angelus Rd.
  SW15 .... 5B 98
Mt. Ash Rd. SE26 .... 3D 121
Mountbatten Cl.
  SE19 .... 5A 120
Mountbatten Ct.
  SE16 .... 2E 79
  (off Rotherhithe St.)
Mountbatten Ho. *N6*.. 2C 32
  (off Hillcrest)
Mountbatten M.
  SW18 .... 5E 101
Mt. Carmel Chambers
  W8 .... 3C 72
  (off Dukes La.)
Mount Ct. SW15...... 1A 100
Mountearl Gdns.
  SW16 .... 3B 118
Mt. Ephraim La.
  SW16 .... 3F 117
Mt. Ephraim Rd.
  SW16 .... 3F 117
Mountfield Cl. SE6.... 5F 109
Mountfield Ter.
  SE13 .... 5F 109
Mountford Rd. E8..... 2C 50
Mountfort Cres. N1 ... 4C 48
Mountfort Ter. N1..... 4C 48
Mount Gdns. SE26.... 3D 121
Mountgrove Rd. N5 ... 5D 35
Mountjoy Cl. EC2..... 1A 18
  (off Thomas More Highwalk)
Mountjoy Ho. EC2..... 1F 17
Mount Lodge N6....... 1E 33
Mount Mills
  EC1 .... 2E 9 (2D 63)
Mt. Nod Rd. SW16.... 3B 118
Mount Pleasant
  SE27 .... 4E 119
  WC1 .... 4B 8 (3C 62)
Mt. Pleasant Cres.
  N4 .... 3B 34
Mt. Pleasant Hill E5 ... 4D 37
Mt. Pleasant La. E5... 3D 37
Mt. Pleasant Rd.
  NW10 .... 4E 43
  SE13 .... 4D 109
Mt. Pleasant Vs. N4... 2B 34
Mount Rd. NW2 ...... 5D 29
  NW4 .... 1C 28
  SW19 .... 2C 114
Mount Row
  W1 .... 5D 13 (1D 75)
Mountsfield Ct.
  SE13 .... 4F 109
Mounts Pond Rd.
  SE3 .... 5F 95
  (not continuous)
Mount Sq., The NW3 .. 5E 31
Mount St.
  W1 .... 5B 12 (1C 74)
Mount St. M.
  W1 .... 5D 13 (1D 75)
Mount Ter. E1........ 4D 65
Mount Vernon NW3 ... 1E 45
Mountview Cl. NW11... 3D 31
Mount Vw. Rd. N4 .... 2A 34
Mount Vs. SE27...... 3D 119
Mowatt Cl. N19....... 3F 33
Mowbray Rd. NW6.... 4A 44

Mowlem St. E2. . . . . . . 1D 65
Mowll St. SW9 . . . . 3C 90
Moxon Cl. E13 . . . . 1B 68
Moxon St.
W1 . . . . 1B 12 (4C 60)
Moye Cl. E2 . . . . 1C 64
Moyers Rd. E10 . . . . . . 2E 39
Moylan Rd. W6 . . . . . . 2A 86
Moyle Ho. SW1 . . . . . . 1E 89
(off Churchill Gdns.)
Moyne Ho. SW9 . . . . . . 3D 105
Moyser Rd. SW16 . . . . 5D 117
Mozart St. W10 . . . . . . 2B 58
Mozart Ter. SW1. . . . . . 5C 74
Mudlarks Blvd. SE10 . . 4B 82
Mudlarks Way SE10 . . . 4B 82
(not continuous)
Muir Dr. SW18 . . . . 4A 102
Muirfield W3 . . . . 5A 56
Muirfield Cl. SE16 . . . . 1D 93
Muirfield Cres. E14 . . . 4D 81
Muirkirk Rd. SE6 . . . . . 1E 123
Muir Rd. E5 . . . . 1C 50
Mulberry Bus. Cen.
SE16 . . . . 3F 79
Mulberry Cl. NW3 . . . . 1F 45
SE7 . . . . 2F 97
SE22 . . . . 3C 106
SW3 . . . . 2F 87
SW16 . . . . 4E 117
Mulberry Ct. E11. . . . . . 1F 53
(off Langthorne Rd.)
EC1 . . . . 2E 9
(off Tompion St.)
Mulberry Ho. E2 . . . . . . 2E 65
(off Victoria Pk. Sq.)
SE8 . . . . 2B 94
Mulberry Housing Co-operative
SE1 . . . . 1C 24
Mulberry M. SE14 . . . . 4B 94
Mulberry Pl. E14 . . . . . 1E 81
(off Clove Cres.)
SE9 . . . . 2F 111
W6 . . . . 1C 84
Mulberry Rd. E8 . . . . . 4B 50
Mulberry St. E1 . . . . . . 5C 64
Mulberry Wlk. SW3 . . . 2F 87
Mulgrave Rd. NW10. . . 1B 42
SW6 . . . . 2B 86
Mulkern Rd. N19 . . . . . 3F 33
(not continuous)
Mullen Twr. WC1 . . . . . 4B 8
(off Mount Pleasant)
Muller Rd. SW4 . . . . . . 4F 103
Mullet Gdns. E2 . . . . . . 2C 64
Mulletsfield WC1 . . . . . 2E 7
(off Cromer St.)
Mull Wlk. N1 . . . . 3E 49
(off Clephane Rd.)
Mulready Ho. SW1 . . . . 5A 76
(off Marsham St.)
Mulready St. NW8 . . . . 3A 60
Multi Way W3 . . . . 3A 70
Multon Ho. E5 . . . . 4E 51
Multon Rd. SW18 . . . . . 5F 101
Mulvaney Way
SE1 . . . . 4C 26 (3F 77)
(not continuous)
Mumford Ct.
EC2 . . . . 2A 18 (5E 63)

Mumford Rd. SE24 . . . 3D 105
Muncaster Rd.
SW11 . . . . 3B 102
Muncies M. SE6 . . . . . 2E 123
Mundania Ct. SE22 . . . 4D 107
Mundania Rd. SE22 . . . 4D 107
Munday Ho. SE1 . . . . . 5B 26
(off Deverell St.)
Munday Rd. E16 . . . . . . 1C 82
Munden St. W14 . . . . . 5A 72
Mundford Rd. E5 . . . . . 4E 37
Mund St. W14 . . . . 1B 86
Mundy Ho. W10 . . . . . . 2A 58
(off Dart St.)
Mundy St.
N1 . . . . 1D 11 (2A 64)
Munnings Ho. E16 . . . . 2D 83
(off Portsmouth M.)
Munro Ho.
SE1 . . . . 4B 24 (3C 76)
Munro M. W10 . . . . 4A 58
(not continuous)
Munro Ter. SW10 . . . . . 3F 87
Munster Cl. SW6 . . . . . 5B 86
Munster M. SW6 . . . . . 3A 86
Munster Rd. SW6 . . . . . 3A 86
Munster Sq.
NW1 . . . . 2E 5 (2D 61)
Munton Rd. SE17 . . . . . 5E 77
Murchison Rd. E10 . . . . 4E 39
Murdoch Ho. SE16 . . . . 4F 79
(off Moodkee St.)
Murdock Cl. E16. . . . . . 5B 68
Murdock St. SE15 . . . . 2D 93
Murfett Cl. SW19 . . . . . 2A 114
Muriel Ct. E10 . . . . 2D 39
Muriel St. N1 . . . . 1B 62
(not continuous)
Murillo Rd. SE13 . . . . . 2F 109
Murphy Ho. SE1 . . . . . . 5D 25
(off Borough Rd.)
Murphy St.
SE1 . . . . 4B 24 (3C 76)
Murray Gro.
N1 . . . . 1A 10 (1E 63)
Murray M. NW1 . . . . . . 4F 47
Murray Rd. SW19 . . . . 5F 113
Murray Sq. E16 . . . . . . 5D 68
Murray St. NW1 . . . . . . 4F 47
Murray Ter. NW3 . . . . . 1E 45
Mursell Est. SW8 . . . . . 4B 90
Musard Rd. W6 . . . . . . 2A 86
W14 . . . . 2A 86
Musbury St. E1. . . . . . . 5E 65
Muscal W6 . . . . 2A 86
(off Field Rd.)
Muscatel Pl. SE5 . . . . . 4A 92
Muschamp Rd.
SE15 . . . . 1B 106
Muscovy St.
EC3 . . . . 4E 19 (1A 78)
Museum Chambers
WC1 . . . . 1D 15
(off Bury Pl.)
Mus. in Docklands, The
. . . . 1C 80
Museum La. SW7. . . . . 4F 73
Mus. of Classical Archaeology
. . . . 3B 6
(off Gower Pl.)

Mus. of Garden History
. . . . 4B 76
Mus. of London
. . . . 1F 17 (4E 63)
Mus. of the Order of
St John, The 4D 9
(off St John's La.)
Museum Pas. E2 . . . . . 2E 65
Museum St.
WC1 . . . . . . 1D 15 (4A 62)
Musgrave Ct. SW11. . . 4A 88
Musgrave Cres.
SW6 . . . . 3C 86
Musgrove Rd. SE14 . . . 4F 93
Musjid Rd. SW11 . . . . . 5F 87
Muston Rd. E5 . . . . 4D 37
Mustow Pl. SW6 . . . . . 5B 86
Muswell Hill Rd. N6 . . . 1C 32
N10. . . . . 1D 33
Mutrix Rd. NW6 . . . . . . 5C 44
Mutton Pl. NW1 . . . . . . 3C 46
Myatt Rd. SW9. . . . . . . 4D 91
Myatts Flds. Sth.
SW9 . . . . 5C 90
(off St Lawrence Way)
Mycenae Rd. SE3. . . . . 3C 96
Myddelton Pas.
EC1 . . . . 1C 8 (2C 62)
Myddelton Sq.
EC1 . . . . 1C 8 (2C 62)
Myddelton St.
EC1 . . . . 2C 8 (2C 62)
Myddleton Av. N4. . . . . 4E 35
Myddleton Ho. N1. . . . . 1B 8
Myers La. SE14 . . . . . . 2F 93
Mylis Cl. SE26 . . . . 4D 121
Mylius Cl. SE14 . . . . . . 3E 93
Mylne Cl. W6 . . . . 1C 84
Mylne St. EC1 . . . . 1B 8 (2C 62)
Myrdle Ct. E1 . . . . 5C 64
(off Myrdle St.)
Myrdle St. E1 . . . . 4C 64
Myron Pl. SE13 . . . . . . 1E 109
Myrtleberry Cl. E8 . . . . 3B 50
(off Beechwood Rd.)
Myrtle Rd. E17. . . . . . . 1A 38
Myrtle Wlk.
N1 . . . . 1D 11 (1A 64)
Mysore Rd. SW11 . . . . 1B 102
Myton Rd. SE21 . . . . . . 3F 119
Mytton Ho. SW8. . . . . . 3B 90
(off St Stephens Ter.)

N

N1 Shop. Cen. N1 . . . . 1C 62
N16 Fitness Cen. 1F 49
Nadine St. SE7 . . . . 1E 97
Nagasaki Wlk. SE7 . . . 4D 83
NAG'S HEAD 5A 34
Nags Head Ct. EC1 . . . 4A 10
Nags Head Shop. Cen.
N7 . . . . 1B 48
Nainby Ho. SE11 . . . . . 5C 76
(off Hotspur St.)
Nairne Gro. SE24 . . . . 3F 105
Nairn St. E14 . . . . 4E 67
Naish Ct. N1 . . . . 5A 48
(not continuous)

Naldera Gdns. SE3 . . . . 2C **96**
Namba Roy Cl.
SW16 . . . . 4B **118**
Nankin St. E14 . . . . 5C **66**
Nansen Rd.
SW11 . . . . 1C **102**
Nantes Cl. SW18 . . . . 2E **101**
Nantes Pas.
E1 . . . . 5F **11** (4B **64**)
Nant Ct. NW2 . . . . 4B **30**
Nant St. E2 . . . . 2D **65**
Naoroji St.
WC1 . . . . 2B **8** (2C **62**)
Napier Av. E14 . . . . 1C **94**
SW6 . . . . 1B **100**
Napier Cl. SE8 . . . . 3B **94**
W14 . . . . 4A **72**
Napier Ct. N1 . . . . 1F **63**
(off Cropley St.)
SE12 . . . . 3D **125**
SW6 . . . . 1B **100**
(off Ranelagh Gdns.)
Napier Gro. N1 . . . . 1E **63**
Napier Pl. W14 . . . . 4B **72**
Napier Rd. E11 . . . . 1A **54**
E15 . . . . 1A **68**
(not continuous)
NW10 . . . . 2D **57**
W14 . . . . 4B **72**
Napier St. SE8 . . . . 3B **94**
(off Napier Cl.)
Napier Ter. N1 . . . . 4D **49**
Napoleon Rd. E5 . . . . . 5D **37**
Narbonne Av. SW4 . . . 3E **103**
Narborough St. SW6 . . 5D **87**
Narcissus Rd. NW6 . . . 2C **44**
Narford Rd. E5 . . . . 5C **36**
Narrow St. E14 . . . . 1A **80**
Narvic Ho. SE5 . . . . 5E **91**
Narwhal Inuit Art Gallery
. . . . 5A **70**
Nascot St. W12 . . . . 5E **57**
Naseby Cl. NW6 . . . . . . 4E **45**
Naseby Rd. SE19 . . . . 5F **119**
Nash Ct. E14 . . . . 2D **81**
(off Nash Pl.)
Nashe Ho. SE1 . . . . 5B **26**
(off Burbage Cl.)
Nash Ho. SW1 . . . . 1D **89**
(off Lupus St.)
Nash Pl. E14 . . . . 2D **81**
Nash Rd. SE4 . . . . 2A **108**
Nash St. NW1 . . . 1E **5** (2D **61**)
Nasmyth St. W6 . . . . . . 4D **71**
Nassau Rd. SW13 . . . . 4B **84**
Nassau St.
W1 . . . . 1F **13** (4E **61**)
Nassington Rd. NW3 . . 1B **46**
Natal Rd. SW16 . . . . . 5F **117**
Nathan Ho. SE11 . . . . . 5C **76**
(off Reedworth St.)
Nathaniel Cl.
E1 . . . . 1F **19** (4B **64**)
Nathaniel Ct. E17 . . . . . 2A **38**
National Army Mus. . . 2B **88**
National Film Theatre, The
. . . . 1A **24**
National Gallery
. . . . 5C **14** (1F **75**)

National Gallery
(Sainsbury Wing) . . . 5C **14**
(in National Gallery)
National Maritime Mus.
. . . . 2F **95**
National Portrait Gallery
. . . . 5C **14**
National Ter. SE16 . . . . 3D **79**
(off Bermondsey Wall E.)
Natural History Mus. . . 4F **73**
Nautilus Bldg., The
EC1 . . . . 1C **8**
(off Myddelton Pas.)
Naval Ho. E14 . . . . 1F **81**
(off Quixley St.)
Naval Row E14 . . . . 1E **81**
Navarino Gro. E8 . . . . . 3C **50**
Navarino Mans.
E8 . . . . 3C **50**
Navarino Rd. E8 . . . . . . 3C **50**
Navarre St.
E2 . . . . 3F **11** (3B **64**)
Navenby Wlk. E3 . . . . . 3C **66**
Navy St. SW4 . . . . 1F **103**
Naxos Bldg. E14 . . . . . 3B **80**
Nayim Pl. E8 . . . . 2D **51**
Nayland Ho. SE6 . . . . 4E **123**
Naylor Ho. W10 . . . . . . 2A **58**
(off Dart St.)
Naylor Rd. SE15 . . . . . 3D **93**
Nazareth Gdns. SE15 . . 5D **93**
Nazrul St. E2 . . 1F **11** (2B **64**)
Neagle Ho. NW2 . . . . . 5E **29**
(off Stoll Cl.)
Nealden St. SW9 . . . . 1B **104**
Neal St.
WC2 . . . . 3D **15** (5A **62**)
Neal's Yd.
WC2 . . . . 3D **15** (5A **62**)
NEASDEN 5A **28**
Neasden Cl. NW10 . . . . 2A **42**
NEASDEN JUNC. 1A **42**
Neasden La. NW10 . . . . 5A **28**
(not continuous)
NW10 . . . . 5A **28**
Neasden La. Nth.
NW10 . . . . 5A **28**
Neate St. SE5 . . . . 2A **92**
(not continuous)
Neathouse Pl. SW1 . . . 5E **75**
Neatscourt Rd. E6 . . . . 4F **69**
Nebraska St.
SE1 . . . . 4B **26** (3F **77**)
Neckinger
SE16 . . . . 5F **27** (4B **78**)
Neckinger Est.
SE16 . . . . 5F **27** (4B **78**)
Neckinger St. SE1 . . . . 3C **78**
Nectarine Way SE13 . . 5D **95**
Needham Ho. SE11 . . . 1C **90**
(off Marylee Way)
Needham Rd. W11 . . . . 5C **58**
Needham Ter. NW2 . . . 5F **29**
Needleman St. SE16 . . 3F **79**
Needwood Ho. N4 . . . . 3E **35**
Neeld Cres. NW4 . . . . . 1D **29**
Neil Wates Cres.
SW2 . . . . 1C **118**
Nelgarde Rd. SE6 . . . . 5C **108**
Nella Rd. W6 . . . . 2F **85**
Nelldale Rd. SE16 . . . . 5E **79**

Nello James Gdns.
SE27 . . . . 4F **119**
Nelson Cl. NW6 . . . . . . 2C **58**
Nelson Ct.
SE1 . . . . 3E **25** (3D **77**)
SE16 . . . . 2E **79**
(off Brunel Rd.)
Nelson Gdns. E2 . . . . . 2C **64**
Nelson Ho. SW1 . . . . . 2E **89**
(off Dolphin Sq.)
Nelson Mandela Rd.
SE3 . . . . 1E **111**
Nelson Pas.
EC1 . . . . 1A **10** (2E **63**)
Nelson Pl.
N1 . . . . 1E **9** (1D **63**)
Nelson Rd. N8 . . . . 1B **34**
SE10 . . . . 2E **95**
Nelson's Column
. . . . 1D **23** (2A **76**)
Nelson Sq.
SE1 . . . . 3D **25** (3D **77**)
Nelson's Row SW4 . . . 2F **103**
Nelson St. E1 . . . . 5D **65**
E16 . . . . 1B **82**
(not continuous)
Nelsons Yd. NW1 . . . . . 1E **61**
(off Mornington Cres.)
Nelson Ter.
N1 . . . . 1E **9** (1D **63**)
Nelson Wlk. SE16 . . . . 2A **80**
Nepaul Rd. SW11 . . . . . 5A **88**
Nepean St. SW15 . . . . 4C **98**
Neptune Ct. E14 . . . . . 5C **80**
(off Homer Dr.)
Neptune Ho. SE16 . . . . 4E **79**
(off Moodkee St.)
Neptune St. SE16 . . . . 4E **79**
Nesbit Rd. SE9 . . . . . . 2F **111**
Nesbitt Cl. SE3 . . . . . . 1A **110**
Nesham St. E1 . . . . 1C **78**
Ness St. SE16 . . . . 4C **78**
Nestor Ho. E2 . . . . 1D **65**
(off Old Bethnal Grn. Rd.)
Netheravon Rd. W4 . . . 5B **70**
Netheravon Rd. Sth.
W4 . . . . 1B **84**
Netherby Rd. SE23 . . . 5E **107**
Netherfield Rd.
SW17 . . . . 3C **116**
Netherford Rd. SW4 . . 5E **89**
Netherhall Gdns.
NW3 . . . . 3E **45**
Netherhall Way NW3 . . 2E **45**
Netherleigh Cl. N6 . . . 3D **33**
Netherton Gro. SW10 . . 2E **87**
Netherton Rd. N15 . . . . 1F **35**
Netherwood Pl. W14 . . 4F **71**
(off Netherwood Rd.)
Netherwood Rd. W14 . . 4F **71**
Netherwood St. NW6 . . 4B **44**
Netley SE5 . . . . 4A **92**
(off Redbridge Gdns.)
Netley Rd. E17 . . . . 1B **38**
Netley St. NW1 . . 2F **5** (2E **61**)
Nettlecombe NW1 . . . . 4F **47**
(off Agar Gro.)
Nettleden Ho. SW3 . . . 5A **74**
(off Marlborough St.)
Nettlefold Pl. SE27 . . . 3D **119**

Nettleton Ct. *EC2* 1F *17*
(off London Wall)
Nettleton Rd. SE14. . . . . . 4F *93*
Neuchatel Rd. SE6 . . . . 2B *122*
Nevada St. SE10. . . . . . . 2E *95*
Nevern Pl. SW5 . . . . 5C *72*
Nevern Rd. SW5. . . . . . . 5C *72*
Nevern Sq. SW5. . . . . . . 5C *72*
Nevil Ho. *SW9* 5D *91*
(off Loughborough Est.)
Nevill Ct. EC4 . . . . 2C *16*
Neville Cl. E11 . . . . 5B *40*
NW1 . . . . 1F *61*
NW6 . . . . 1B *58*
SE15 . . . . 4C *92*
Neville Ct. *NW8* 1F *59*
(off Abbey Rd.)
Neville Dr. N2. . . . . 1E *31*
Neville Gill Cl.
SW18 . . . . 4C *100*
Neville Rd. E7 . . . . 4C *54*
NW6 . . . . 1B *58*
Nevilles Ct. NW2 . . . . . . 5C *28*
Neville St. SW7 . . . . 1F *87*
Neville Ter. SW7 . . . . 1F *87*
Nevill Rd. N16 . . . . 1A *50*
Nevinson Cl.
SW18 . . . . 4F *101*
Nevis Rd. SW17 . . . . . 2C *116*
Nevitt Ho. *N1* 1F *63*
(off Cranston Est.)
Newall Ho. *SE1* 5A *26*
(off Bath Ter.)
Newarke Ho. SW9 . . . . . . 5D *91*
Newark St. E1 . . . . 4D *65*
(not continuous)
New Atlas Wharf *E14* . . . 4C *80*
(off Arnhem Pl.)
New Baltic Wharf
SE8 . . . . 1A *94*
(off Evelyn St.)
New Barn St. E13 . . . . . . 3C *68*
NEW BECKENHAM . . . 5B *122*
New Bentham Ct. *N1* . . . 4E *49*
(off Ecclesbourne Rd.)
Newbery Ho. *N1* 4E *49*
(off Northampton St.)
Newbold Cotts. E1 . . . . . 5E *65*
Newbolt Ho. *SE17* 1F *91*
(off Brandon St.)
New Bond St.
W1. . . . . 3D *13* (5D *61*)
Newbridge Point
SE23 . . . . 3F *121*
(off Windrush La.)
New Bri. St.
EC4 . . . . 3D *17* (5D *63*)
New Broad St.
EC2 . . . . 1D *19* (4A *64*)
Newburgh St.
W1. . . . . 3A *14* (5E *61*)
New Burlington M.
W1 . . . . 4F *13* (1E *75*)
New Burlington Pl.
W1 . . . . 4F *13* (1E *75*)
New Burlington St.
W1 . . . . 4F *13* (1E *75*)
Newburn Ho. *SE11* 1B *90*
(off Newburn St.)
Newburn St. SE11 . . . . . 1B *90*

Newbury Ho. SW9 . . . . . . 5D *91*
W2 . . . . 5D *59*
(off Hallfield Est.)
Newbury M. NW5 . . . . . . 3C *46*
Newbury St.
EC1 . . . . 1F *17* (4E *63*)
New Bus. Cen., The
NW10 . . . . 2B *56*
New Butt La. SE8 . . . . . . 3C *94*
New Butt La. Nth.
SE8 . . . . 3C *94*
(off Hales St.)
Newby *NW1* 2F *5*
(off Robert St.)
Newby Ho. *E14* 1E *81*
(off Newby Pl.)
Newby Pl. E14 . . . . 1E *81*
Newby St. SW8 . . . . . . 1D *103*
New Caledonian Mkt.
SE1 . . . . 5E *27*
New Caledonian Wharf
SE16 . . . . 4B *80*
Newcastle Cl.
EC4 . . . . 2D *17* (5D *63*)
Newcastle Ct. *EC4* 4A *18*
(off College Hill)
Newcastle Ho. *W1* 5B *4*
(off Luxborough St.)
Newcastle Pl. W2 . . . . . . 4F *59*
Newcastle Row
EC1 . . . . 4C *8* (3C *62*)
New Cavendish St.
W1. . . . . 1C *12* (4C *60*)
New Change
EC4 . . . . 3F *17* (5E *63*)
New Charles St.
EC1 . . . . 1E *9* (2D *63*)
NEW CHARLTON 5E *83*
New Chiswick Pool . . . 3A *84*
New Church Rd.
SE5 . . . . 3E *91*
(not continuous)
New City Rd. E13. . . . . . . 2E *69*
New College Ct.
NW3 . . . . 3E *45*
(off Finchley Rd.)
New College M. N1 . . . . 4C *48*
New College Pde.
NW3 . . . . 3F *45*
(off Finchley Rd.)
Newcombe Gdns.
SW16 . . . . 4A *118*
Newcombe St. W8 . . . . . 2C *72*
Newcomen Rd. E11 . . . . 5B *40*
SW11 . . . . 1F *101*
Newcomen St.
SE1 . . . . 3B *26* (3F *77*)
New Compton St.
WC2 . . . . 3C *14* (5F *61*)
New Concordia Wharf
SE1 . . . . 3C *78*
New Ct. EC4 . . . . 4B *16*
Newcourt Ho. *E2* 2D *65*
(off Pott St.)
Newcourt St. NW8 . . . . . 1A *60*
New Covent Garden Market
. . . . 3F *89*
New Coventry St.
W1 . . . . 5C *14* (1F *75*)
New Crane Pl. E1 . . . . . . 2E *79*

New Crane Wharf *E1* . . . 2E *79*
(off New Crane Pl.)
New Cres. Yd. NW10 . . . 1B *56*
NEW CROSS 3B *94*
NEW CROSS GATE . . . 4F *93*
NEW CROSS GATE . . . 4F *93*
New Cross Rd. SE15 . . 3E *93*
Newdigate Ho. *E14* 5B *66*
(off Norbiton Rd.)
Newell St. E14 . . . . 5B *66*
New End NW3 . . . . 1E *45*
New End Sq. NW3 . . . . . 1F *45*
New End Theatre 5E *31*
Newent Cl. SE15 . . . . . . 3A *92*
New Era Est. *N1* 5A *50*
(off Phillipp St.)
New Fetter La.
EC4 . . . . 2C *16* (5C *62*)
Newfield Ri. NW2 . . . . . . 5C *28*
Newgate St.
EC1 . . . . 2E *17* (5D *63*)
New Globe Wlk.
SE1 . . . . 1F *25* (2E *77*)
New Goulston St.
E1. . . . . 2F *19* (5B *64*)
New Grn. Pl. SE19 . . . . 5A *120*
Newham College of
Further Education
Stratford Campus . . . 4A *54*
Newham Leisure Cen.
. . . . 4E *69*
Newham's Row
SE1 . . . . 4E *27* (4A *78*)
Newham Way E6 . . . . . . 4B *68*
E16 . . . . 4B *68*
Newhaven Gdns.
SE9 . . . . 2F *111*
Newhaven La. E16. . . . . 3B *68*
Newick Rd. E5 . . . . 1D *51*
NEWINGTON 4E *77*
Newington Barrow Way
N7 . . . . 5B *34*
Newington Butts
SE1 . . . . 5D *77*
SE11 . . . . 5D *77*
Newington C'way.
SE1 . . . . 5E *25* (4D *77*)
Newington Ct. Bus. Cen.
SE1 . . . . 5F *25*
Newington Grn. N1. . . . . 2F *49*
N16 . . . . 2F *49*
Newington Grn. Mans.
N16 . . . . 2F *49*
Newington Grn. Rd.
N1 . . . . 3F *49*
Newington Ind. Est.
SE17 . . . . 5E *77*
New Inn B'way.
EC2 . . . . 3E *11* (3A *64*)
New Inn Pas. WC2 . . . . 3A *16*
New Inn Sq. EC2 . . . . . 3E *11*
New Inn St.
EC2 . . . . 3E *11* (3A *64*)
New Inn Yd.
EC2 . . . . 3E *11* (3A *64*)
New Jubilee Wharf
E1 . . . . 2E *79*
(off Wapping Wall)
New Kent Rd. SE1 . . . . . 4E *77*

New Kings Rd. SW6 . . . . . 5B **86**
New King St. SE8 . . . . 2C **94**
Newland Ct. EC1 . . . . 2B **10**
Newland Ho. SE14 . . . . . . *2F 93*
   (off John Williams Cl.)
NEWLANDS 3F **107**
Newlands NW1 . . . . *1F 5*
   (off Harrington St.)
Newlands Pk. SE26 . . . . . 5E **121**
Newlands Quay E1 . . . . . 1E **79**
New London St. EC3 . . . . 4E **19**
New London Theatre . . . *2E 15*
   (off Drury La.)
New Lydenburg
  Commercial Est.
  SE7 . . . . 4E **83**
New Lydenburg St.
  SE7 . . . . 4E **83**
Newlyn NW1 . . . . *5E 47*
   (off Plender St.)
Newman Pas.
  W1 . . . . 1A **14** (4E **61**)
Newman Rd. E13 . . . . . . 2D **69**
Newman's Ct. EC3 . . . . . 3C **18**
Newman's Row
  WC2 . . . . 1A **16** (4B **62**)
Newman St.
  W1 . . . . 1A **14** (4E **61**)
Newman Yd.
  W1 . . . . 2B **14** (5E **61**)
Newmarket Grn.
  SE9 . . . . 5F **111**
Newmill Ho. E3 . . . . 3E **67**
New Mount St. E15 . . . . . 4F **53**
Newnes Path SW15 . . . . 2D **99**
Newnham Ter.
  SE1 . . . . 5B **24** (4C **76**)
New Nth. Pl.
  EC2 . . . . 3D **11** (3A **64**)
New Nth. Rd.
  N1 . . . . 1C **10** (4E **49**)
New Nth. St.
  WC1 . . . . 5F **7** (4B **62**)
Newnton Cl. N4 . . . . 2F **35**
   (not continuous)
New Orleans Wlk.
  N19 . . . . 2F **33**
New Oxford St.
  WC1 . . . . 2C **14** (5F **61**)
New Pk. Pde. SW2 . . . . . *5A 104*
   (off New Pk. Rd.)
New Pk. Rd. SW2 . . . . . 1F **117**
New Pl. Sq. SE16 . . . . . . 4D **79**
New Plaistow Rd.
  E15 . . . . 5A **54**
Newport Av. E13 . . . . . . 3D **69**
  E14 . . . . 1F **81**
Newport Ct.
  WC2 . . . . 4C **14** (1F **75**)
Newport Ho. E3 . . . . *2A 66*
   (off Strahan Rd.)
Newport Pl.
  WC2 . . . . 4C **14** (1F **75**)
Newport Rd. E10 . . . . . . 4E **39**
  SW13 . . . . 4C **84**
Newport St. SE11 . . . . . . 5B **76**
New Priory Ct. NW6 . . . . *4C 44*
   (off Mazenod Av.)
New Providence Wharf
  E14 . . . . 2F **81**

Newquay Ho. SE11 . . . . . 1C **90**
Newquay Rd.
  SE6 . . . . 2D **123**
New Quebec St.
  W1 . . . . 3A **12** (5B **60**)
New Ride
  SW7 . . . . 3A **20** (3A **74**)
New River Ct. N5 . . . . . . 1E **49**
New River Head
  EC1 . . . . 1C **8** (2C **62**)
New River Wlk.
  N1 . . . . 3E **49**
New River Way N4 . . . . . 2F **35**
New Rd. E1 . . . . 4D **65**
  E12 . . . . 4F **41**
  N8 . . . . 1A **34**
New Rochford St.
  NW5 . . . . 2B **46**
New Row
  WC2 . . . . 4D **15** (1A **76**)
New Spitalfields Mkt.
  E10 . . . . 5D **39**
New Spring Gdns. Wlk.
  SE11 . . . . 1A **90**
New Sq.
  WC2 . . . . 2B **16** (5C **62**)
New Sq. Pas. WC2 . . . . . 2B **16**
Newstead Rd. SE12 . . . . 5B **110**
Newstead Way
  SW19 . . . . 4F **113**
New St. EC2 . . . 1E **19** (4A **64**)
New St. Hill
  BR1: Brom 5D **125**
New St. Sq.
  EC4 . . . . 2C **16** (5C **62**)
Newton Cl. E17 . . . . 1A **38**
Newton Gro. W4 . . . . . . 5A **70**
Newton Ho. E1 . . . . *1D 79*
   (off Cornwall St.)
  NW8 . . . . *5D 45*
   (off Abbey Rd.)
Newton Mans. W14 . . . . . *2A 86*
   (off Queen's Club Gdns.)
Newton Pl. E14 . . . . 5C **80**
Newton Point E16 . . . . . . *5B 68*
   (off Clarkson Rd.)
Newton Rd. E15 . . . . 2F **53**
  NW2 . . . . 1E **43**
  W2 . . . . 5D **59**
Newton St.
  WC2 . . . . 2E **15** (5A **62**)
Newton's Yd. SW18 . . . . 3C **100**
New Twr. Bldgs. E1 . . . . 2D **79**
Newtown St. SW11 . . . . . 4D **89**
New Turnstile WC1 . . . . . 1F **15**
New Union Cl. E14 . . . . . 4E **81**
New Union St.
  EC2 . . . . 1B **18** (4F **63**)
New Wanstead E11 . . . . . 1B **40**
New Wharf Rd. N1 . . . . . 1A **62**
New Zealand Way
  W12 . . . . 1D **71**
Next Generation Carlton Club
  . . . . 4C **58**
Nexus Ct. E11 . . . . 3A **40**
Niagra Cl. N1 . . . . 1E **63**
Niagra Ct. SE16 . . . . *4E 79*
   (off Canada Est.)
Nicholas Ct. W4 . . . . *2A 84*
   (off Corney Reach Way)

Nicholas La.
  EC4 . . . . 4C **18** (1F **77**)
   (not continuous)
Nicholas M. W4 . . . . 2A **84**
Nicholas Pas. EC4 . . . . . 3C **18**
Nicholas Rd. E1 . . . . 3E **65**
Nicholas Stacey Ho.
  SE7 . . . . *1D 97*
   (off Frank Burton Cl.)
Nicholay Rd. N19 . . . . . . 3F **33**
   (not continuous)
Nicholl Ho. N4 . . . . 3E **35**
Nichollsfield Wlk. N7 . . . 2B **48**
Nicholls Point E15 . . . . . *5C 54*
   (off Park Gro.)
Nicholl St. E2 . . . . 5C **50**
Nichols Cl. N4 . . . . *3C 34*
   (off Osborne Rd.)
Nichols Ct. E2 . . . . 1B **64**
Nicholson Ho. SE17 . . . . 1F **91**
Nicholson St.
  SE1 . . . . 2D **25** (2D **77**)
Nickleby Ho. SE16 . . . . . *3C 78*
   (off Parkers Row)
Nickols Wlk. SW18 . . . . 2D **101**
Nicolas Ct. E13 . . . . 2D **69**
Nicoll Ct. NW10 . . . . 5A **42**
Nicoll Pl. NW4 . . . . 1D **29**
Nicoll Rd. NW10 . . . . . . 5A **42**
Nicosia Rd. SW18 . . . . . 5A **102**
Niederwald Rd.
  SE26 . . . . 4A **122**
Nigel Ho. EC1 . . . . *5B 8*
   (off Portpool La.)
Nigel Playfair Av.
  W6 . . . . 5D **71**
Nigel Rd. E7 . . . . 2E **55**
  SE15 . . . . 1C **106**
Nigeria Rd. SE7 . . . . 3E **97**
Nightingale Ct. E14 . . . . . *3E 81*
   (off Ovex Cl.)
  N4 . . . . *4B 34*
   (off Tollington Rd.)
  SW6 . . . . *4D 87*
   (off Maltings Pl.)
Nightingale Gro.
  SE13 . . . . 3F **109**
Nightingale Ho. E1 . . . . . *2C 78*
   (off Thomas More St.)
  E2 . . . . *5A 50*
   (off Kingsland Rd.)
  W12 . . . . *5E 57*
   (off Du Cane Rd.)
Nightingale La.
  SW12 . . . . 5B **102**
Nightingale Lodge
  W9 . . . . *4C 58*
   (off Admiral Wlk.)
Nightingale M. E3 . . . . . 1F **65**
  E11 . . . . 1C **40**
  SE11 . . . . 5D **77**
Nightingale Pl.
  SW10 . . . . 2E **87**
   (not continuous)
Nightingale Rd. E5 . . . . . 5D **37**
  NW10 . . . . 1B **56**
Nightingale Sq.
  SW12 . . . . 5C **102**
Nightingale Wlk.
  SW4 . . . . 4D **103**

Nile Cl. N16 . . . . 5B 36
Nile Rd. E13 . . . . 1E 69
Nile St. N1 . . . . 1A 10 (2E 63)
Nile Ter. SE15 . . . . 1B 92
Nimegen Way SE22 . . . 3A 106
Nimrod Ho. E16 . . . . 4D 69
    (off Vanguard Cl.)
Nimrod Pas. N1 . . . . 3A 50
Nimrod Rd. SW16 . . . . . 5D 117
Nina Mackay Cl. E15 . . . 5A 54
NINE ELMS 3E 89
Nine Elms La. SW8 . . . . 3E 89
Nipponzan Myohoji Peace
    Pagoda 2B 88
Nirvana Apartments
    N1 . . . . 5D 49
    (off Islington Grn.)
Nisbet Ho. E9 . . . . 2F 51
Nita Ct. SE12 . . . . 1C 124
Niton St. SW6 . . . . 3F 85
Nobel Ho. SE5 . . . . 5E 91
Noble Ct. E1 . . . . 1D 79
Noblefield Hgts. N2 . . . 1A 32
Noble M. N16 . . . . 5F 35
    (off Albion Rd.)
Noble St. EC2 . . 2F 17 (5E 63)
Noel Coward Ho.
    SW1 . . . . 5E 75
    (off Vauxhall Bri. Rd.)
Noel Ho. NW6 . . . . 4F 45
    (off Harben Rd.)
Noel Rd. E6 . . . . 3F 69
    N1 . . . . 1D 63
Noel St. W1 . . . . 3A 14 (5E 61)
Noel Ter. SE23 . . . . 2E 121
Nolan Way E5 . . . . 1C 50
Norbiton Rd. E14 . . . . . . 5B 66
Norbroke St. W12 . . . . . . 1B 70
Norburn St. W10 . . . . . . 4A 58
Norcombe Ho. N19 . . . . . 5F 33
    (off Wedmore St.)
Norcott Rd. N16 . . . . 4C 36
Norcroft Gdns. SE22 . . . 5C 106
Norden Ho. E2 . . . . 2D 65
    (off Pott St.)
Norfolk Av. N15 . . . . 1B 36
Norfolk Cres. W2 . . . . . . 5A 60
Norfolk Ho. SE3 . . . . . . 2A 96
    (off Restell Cl.)
    SE8 . . . . 4C 94
    SW1 . . . . 5F 75
    (off Page St.)
Norfolk Ho. Rd.
    SW16 . . . . 3F 117
Norfolk Mans. SW11 . . . 4B 88
    (off Prince of Wales Dr.)
Norfolk M. W10 . . . . 4A 58
    (off Blagrove Rd.)
Norfolk Pl. W2 . . . . 5F 59
    (not continuous)
Norfolk Rd. NW8 . . . . . . 5F 45
    NW10 . . . . 4A 42
Norfolk Row SE1 . . . . . . 5B 76
    (not continuous)
Norfolk Sq. W2 . . . . 5F 59
Norfolk Sq. M. W2 . . . . . 5F 59
    (off London St.)
Norfolk St. E7 . . . . 2C 54
Norfolk Ter. W6 . . . . 1A 86
Norgrove St. SW12 . . . . 5C 102

Norland Ho. W11 . . . . . . 2F 71
    (off Queensdale Cres.)
Norland Pl. W11 . . . . . . 2A 72
Norland Rd. W11 . . . . . . 2F 71
Norland Sq. W11 . . . . . . 2A 72
Norland Sq. Mans.
    W11 . . . . 2A 72
    (off Norland Sq.)
Norley Va. SW15 . . . . . 1C 112
Norlington Rd. E10 . . . . 3E 39
    E11 . . . . 3E 39
Normanby Cl. SW15 . . . 3B 100
Normanby Rd.
    NW10 . . . . 1B 42
Norman Ct. N4 . . . . 2C 34
    NW10 . . . . 4C 42
Normand Gdns. W14 . . . 2A 86
    (off Greyhound Rd.)
Normand M. W14 . . . . . . 2A 86
Normand Rd. W14 . . . . . 2B 86
Normandy Cl. SE26 . . . 3A 122
Normandy Ho. E14 . . . . . 3E 81
    (off Plevna St.)
Normandy Rd. SW9 . . . . 4C 90
Normandy Ter. E16 . . . . 5D 69
Norman Gro. E3 . . . . . . 1A 66
Norman Ho. SW8 . . . . . . 3A 90
    (off Wyvil Rd.)
Normanhurst Rd.
    SW2 . . . . 2B 118
Norman Rd. E11 . . . . . . 4F 39
    SE10 . . . . 3D 95
Norman St.
    EC1 . . . . 2A 10 (2E 63)
Normanton Av.
    SW19 . . . . 2C 114
Normanton St. SE23 . . . 2F 121
Normington Cl.
    SW16 . . . . 5C 118
Norrice Lea N2 . . . . 1F 31
Norris Ho. E9 . . . . 5E 51
    (off Handley Rd.)
    N1 . . . . 5A 50
    (off Colville Est.)
    SE8 . . . . 1B 94
    (off Grove St.)
Norris St.
    SW1 . . . . 5B 14 (1F 75)
Norroy Rd. SW15 . . . . . 2F 99
Norstead Pl. SW15 . . . 2C 112
Nth. Access Rd. E17 . . . 1F 37
NORTH ACTON 4A 56
Nth. Acton Rd. NW10 . . 1A 56
Northampton Gro. N1 . . 2F 49
Northampton Pk. N1 . . . 3E 49
Northampton Rd.
    EC1 . . . . 3C 8 (3C 62)
Northampton Row EC1 . . 3C 8
Northampton Sq.
    EC1 . . . . 2D 9 (2D 63)
Northampton St. N1 . . . 4E 49
Nth. Audley St.
    W1 . . . . 3B 12 (5C 60)
North Av. NW10 . . . . . . 2E 57
Nth. Bank NW8 . . . . 2A 60
NORTH BECKTON 4F 69
Nth. Birkbeck Rd.
    E11 . . . . 5F 39
North Block SE1 . . . . . . 3A 24
    (off York Rd.)

Nth. Boundary Rd.
    E12 . . . . 5F 41
Northbourne Rd.
    SW4 . . . . 3F 103
Nth. Branch Av.
    NW10 . . . . 2E 57
Northbrook Rd.
    SE13 . . . . 3A 110
Northburgh St.
    EC1 . . . . 4E 9 (3D 63)
Nth. Carriage Dr. W2 . . 1A 74
    (off Bayswater Rd.)
Northchurch SE17 . . . . . 1F 91
    (not continuous)
Northchurch Rd. N1 . . . 4F 49
    (not continuous)
Northchurch Ter. N1 . . . 4A 50
Nth. Circular Rd.
    NW2 . . . . 5A 28
    NW4 . . . . 2E 29
    NW10 . . . . 2A 42
    NW11 . . . . 1F 29
Nth. Colonnade, The
    E14 . . . . 2C 80
Northcote M. SW11 . . . 2A 102
Northcote Rd. NW10 . . . 4A 42
    SW11 . . . . 3A 102
North Ct. SE24 . . . . 1D 105
    SW1 . . . . 5D 23
    (off Gt. Peter St.)
    W1 . . . . 5A 6 (4E 61)
North Cres. E16 . . . . . . 3F 67
    WC1 . . . . 5B 6 (4F 61)
Northcroft Ct. W12 . . . . 3C 70
North Crofts SE23 . . . 1D 121
Nth. Cross Rd.
    SE22 . . . . 3B 106
Northdene Gdns. N15 . . 1B 36
Northdown St.
    N1 . . . . 1F 7 (1A 62)
North Dr. SW16 . . . . . . 4E 117
NORTH END 4E 31
Nth End NW3 . . . . 4E 31
Nth. End Av. NW3 . . . . . 4E 31
    (not continuous)
Nth. End Cres. W14 . . . 5B 72
Nth. End Ho. W14 . . . . 5A 72
Nth. End Pde. W14 . . . . 5A 72
    (off Nth. End Rd.)
Nth. End Rd. NW11 . . . 3C 30
    W14 . . . . 5A 72
Nth. End Way NW3 . . . . 4E 31
Northern Hgts. N8 . . . . . 2F 33
    (off Crescent Rd.)
Northern Rd. E13 . . . . . 1D 69
Northesk Ho. E1 . . . . . . 3D 65
    (off Tent St.)
Nth. Eyot Gdns. W6 . . . 1B 84
Northey St. E14 . . . . . . 1A 80
Northfield Ho. SE15 . . . 2C 92
Northfield Rd. N16 . . . . 2A 36
Northfields SW18 . . . . 2C 100
Northfields Prospect Bus. Cen.
    SW18 . . . . 2C 100
Northfleet Ho. SE1 . . . . 3B 26
    (off Tennis St.)
Nth. Flock St. SE16 . . . 3C 78
Nth. Flower Wlk. W2 . . 1E 73
    (off Lancaster Wlk.)
North Gdn. E14 . . . . . . 2B 80

North Ga. NW8 . . . . . . 1A 60
  (off Prince Albert Rd.)
Northgate Dr. NW9 . . . . 1A 28
Northgate Ho. E14 . . . . 1C 80
  (off E. India Dock Rd.)
Nth. Gower St.
  NW1 . . . . 2A 6 (2E 61)
North Gro. N6 . . . . 2C 32
N15 . . . . 1F 35
North Hill N6 . . . . 1B 32
Nth. Hill Av. N6 . . . . . . 1C 32
North Ho. SE8 . . . . 1B 94
Northiam WC1 . . . . 2E 7
  (off Cromer St.)
Northiam St. E9 . . . . . . 5D 51
Northington St.
  WC1 . . . . 4A 8 (3B 62)
NORTH KENSINGTON
  . . . . 4F 57
Northlands St. SE5 . . . . 5E 91
Northleach Ct. SE15 . . . 2A 92
  (off Birdlip Cl.)
North Lodge E16 . . . . . 2D 83
  (off Wesley Av.)
North Mall SW18 . . . . 3D 101
  (off Buckhold Rd.)
North M. WC1 . . 4A 8 (3B 62)
Northolme Rd. N5 . . . . . 1E 49
Northover
  BR1: Brom 3B 124
North Pas. SW18 . . . . 3C 100
Northpoint Sq. NW1 . . . 3F 47
Nth. Pole Rd. W10 . . . . 4E 57
Northport St. N1 . . . . . . 5F 49
North Ride W2 . . . . 1A 74
North Ri. W2 . . . . 5A 60
North Rd. N6 . . . . 2C 32
N7 . . . . 3A 48
SW19 . . . . 5E 115
North Row
  W1 . . . . 4A 12 (1B 74)
Nth. Row Bldgs. W1 . . 4B 12
  (off North Row)
North Several SE3 . . . . 5F 95
Nth. Side Wandsworth Comn.
  SW18 . . . . 3F 101
North Sq. NW11 . . . . . . 1C 30
Northstead Rd.
  SW2 . . . . 2C 118
North St. E13 . . . . 1D 69
SW4 . . . . 1E 103
North St. Pas. E13 . . . . 1D 69
Nth. Tenter St. E1 . . . . 5B 64
North Ter. SW3 . . . . . . 4A 74
Northumberland All.
  EC3 . . . . . 3E 19 (5A 64)
  (not continuous)
Northumberland Av.
  E12 . . . . 3E 41
  WC2 . . . . . . 1D 23 (2A 76)
Northumberland Ho.
  SW1 . . . . 1D 23
  (off Northumberland Av.)
Northumberland Pl.
  W2 . . . . 5C 58
Northumberland Rd.
  E17 . . . . 2C 38
Northumberland St.
  WC2 . . . . . . 1D 23 (2A 76)

Northumbria St. E14 . . . 5C 66
Nth. Verbena Gdns.
  W6 . . . . 1C 84
North Vw. SW19 . . . . . 5E 113
Northview N7 . . . . 5A 34
Northview Cres.
  NW10 . . . . 1B 42
North Vs. NW1 . . . . 3F 47
North Wlk. W8 . . . . 1D 73
  (off Bayswater Rd.)
Northway NW11 . . . . . . 1D 31
Northway Rd. SE5 . . . . 1E 105
Northways Pde. NW3 . . 4F 45
  (off College Cres.,
  not continuous)
Nth. Western Commercial
  Cen. NW1 . . . . 4A 48
Northwest Pl. N1 . . . . . 1C 62
North Wharf E14 . . . . . 2E 81
  (off Coldharbour)
Nth. Wharf Rd. W2 . . . . 5A 60
Northwick Cl. NW8 . . . . 3F 59
Northwick Ho. NW8 . . . 3E 59
  (off St John's Wood Rd.)
Northwick Ter. NW8 . . . 3F 59
Northwold Rd. E5 . . . . . 4B 36
N16 . . . . 4B 36
Northwood Est. E5 . . . . 4C 36
Northwood Hall N6 . . . . 2E 33
Northwood Ho.
  SE27 . . . . 4F 119
Northwood Rd. N6 . . . . 2D 33
SE23 . . . . 1B 122
Northwood Way
  SE19 . . . . 5F 119
Nth. Woolwich Rd.
  E16 . . . . 2B 82
Nth. Worple Way
  SW14 . . . . 1A 98
Norton Folgate
  E1 . . . . 5E 11 (4A 64)
Norton Folgate Ho.
  E1 . . . . 5F 11
  (off Puma Ct.)
Norton Ho. E1 . . . . 5D 65
  (off Bigland St.)
E2 . . . . 1F 65
  (off Mace St.)
SW1 . . . . 4F 75
  (off Arneway St.)
SW9 . . . . 5B 90
  (off Aytoun Rd.)
Norton Rd. E10 . . . . . . 3B 38
Norway Ga. SE16 . . . . . 4A 80
Norway Pl. E14 . . . . . . 5B 66
Norway St. SE10 . . . . . 2D 95
Norway Wharf E14 . . . . 5B 66
  (off Norway Pl.)
Norwich Ho. E14 . . . . . 5D 67
  (off Cordelia St.)
Norwich Rd. E7 . . . . . . 2C 54
Norwich St.
  EC4 . . . . . . 2B 16 (5C 62)
Norwood Cl. NW2 . . . . 5A 30
Norwood High St.
  SE27 . . . . 3D 119
Norwood Ho. E14 . . . . . 1D 81
  (off Poplar High St.)
NORWOOD NEW TOWN
  . . . . 5E 119

Norwood Pk. Rd.
  SE27 . . . . 5E 119
Norwood Rd. SE24 . . . 1D 119
SE27 . . . . 2D 119
Notley St. SE5 . . . . 3F 91
Notting Barn Rd.
  W10 . . . . 3F 57
Nottingdale Sq. W11 . . 2A 72
Nottingham Av. E16 . . . 4E 69
Nottingham Ct.
  WC2 . . . . . . 3D 15 (5A 62)
Nottingham Ho.
  WC2 . . . . 3D 15
  (off Shorts Gdns.)
Nottingham Pl.
  W1 . . . . 4B 4 (4C 60)
Nottingham Rd. E10 . . . 1E 39
SW17 . . . . 1B 116
Nottingham St.
  W1 . . . . 5B 4 (4C 60)
Nottingham Ter. NW1 . . 4B 4
NOTTING HILL 1B 72
Notting Hill Ga. W11 . . 2C 72
Nottingwood Ho.
  W11 . . . . 1A 72
  (off Clarendon Rd.)
Nova Bldg. E14 . . . . . . 5C 80
Nova Ct. E. E14 . . . . . . 2E 81
  (off Yabsley St.)
Nova Ct. W. E14 . . . . . 2E 81
  (off Yabsley St.)
Novello St. SW6 . . . . . 4C 86
Novel Sq. SE10 . . . . . . 4B 82
  (off School Bank Rd.)
Nowell Rd. SW13 . . . . . 2C 84
Noyna Rd. SW17 . . . . . 3B 116
Nubia Way
  BR1: Brom 3A 124
Nuding Cl. SE13 . . . . . 1C 108
Nuffield Lodge N6 . . . . 1E 33
  W9 . . . . 4C 58
  (off Admiral Wlk.)
Nugent Rd. N19 . . . . . . 3A 34
Nugent Ter. NW8 . . . . . 1E 59
Nun Ct. EC2 . . . . 2B 18
NUNHEAD 1D 107
Nunhead Cres.
  SE15 . . . . 1D 107
Nunhead Est. SE15 . . . 2D 107
Nunhead Grn. SE15 . . . 1D 107
Nunhead Gro. SE15 . . . 1D 107
Nunhead La. SE15 . . . . 1D 107
Nunhead Pas. SE15 . . . 1C 106
Nursery Cl. SE4 . . . . . . 5B 94
SW15 . . . . 2F 99
Nursery La. E2 . . . . 5B 50
E7 . . . . 3C 54
W10 . . . . 4E 57
Nursery Rd. E9 . . . . . . 3E 51
E12 . . . . 4F 41
SW9 . . . . 2B 104
Nutbourne St. W10 . . . 2A 58
Nutbrook St. SE15 . . . . 1C 106
Nutcroft Rd. SE15 . . . . 3D 93
Nutfield Rd. E15 . . . . . 1E 53
NW2 . . . . 5C 28
SE22 . . . . 2B 106
Nutford Pl. W1 . . . . . . 5B 60
Nuthurst Av. SW2 . . . . 2B 118
Nutley Ter. NW3 . . . . . 3E 45

Nutmeg Cl. E16 . . . . . . 3A 68
Nutmeg La. E14 . . . . . 5F 67
Nuttall St. N1 . . . . 1A 64
Nutter La. E11 . . . . . . 1E 41
Nutt St. SE15 . . . . 3B 92
Nutwell St. SW17 . . . 5A 116
Nye Bevan Est. E5 . . 5F 37
Nye Bevan Ho.
SW6 . . . . 3B 86
(off St Thomas's Way)
Nynehead St. SE14 . . 3A 94
Nyon Gro. SE6 . . . . . 2B 122
Nyssa Ct. E15 . . . . 2A 68
(off Teasel Way)
Nyton Cl. N19 . . . . . . 3A 34

O

Oak Apple Ct. SE12 . . 1C 124
Oakbank Gro. SE24 . . 2E 105
Oakbrook Cl.
BR1: Brom 4D 125
Oakbury Rd. SW6 . . . . 5D 87
Oak Cott. Cl. SE6 . . . 1B 124
Oak Ct. SE15 . . . . 3B 92
(off Sumner Rd.)
Oak Cres. E16 . . . . . . 4A 68
Oakcroft Rd. SE13 . . . 5F 95
Oakdale Rd. E7 . . . . . 4D 55
E11 . . . . 4F 39
N4 . . . . 1E 35
SE4 . . . . 1E 107
SE15 . . . . 1E 107
SW16 . . . . 5A 118
Oakdene SE15 . . . . . . 4D 93
Oakden St. SE11 . . . . 5C 76
Oake Ct. SW15 . . . . . 3A 100
Oakeford Ho. W14 . . . 4A 72
(off Russell Rd.)
Oakend Ho. N4 . . . . . 2F 35
Oakeshott Av. N6 . . . 4C 32
Oakey La.
SE1 . . . . 5B 24 (4C 76)
Oakfield Ct. N8 . . . . . 2A 34
NW2 . . . . 2F 29
Oakfield Gdns.
SE19 . . . . 5A 120
(not continuous)
Oakfield Ho. E3 . . . . . 4C 66
(off Gale St.)
Oakfield Rd. E6 . . . . . 5F 55
N4 . . . . 1C 34
SW19 . . . . 3F 113
Oakfields Rd. NW11 . . 1A 30
Oakfield St. SW10 . . . 2E 87
Oakford Rd. NW5 . . . . 1E 47
Oak Gro. NW2 . . . . . . 1A 44
Oakhall Ct. E11 . . . . . 1D 41
Oak Hall Rd. E11 . . . . 1D 41
Oakham Cl. SE6 . . . . 2B 122
Oakham Ho. W10 . . . . 3E 57
(off Sutton Way)
Oakhill Av. NW3 . . . . . 1D 45
Oakhill Ct. SW19 . . . 45 107
Oak Hill Pk. NW3 . . . . 1D 45
Oak Hill Pk. M.
NW3 . . . . 1E 45
Oakhill Pl. SW15 . . . . 3C 100
Oakhill Rd. SW15 . . . 3B 100

Oak Hill Way NW3 . . . 1D 45
(not continuous)
Oak Ho. W10 . . . . 3A 58
(off Sycamore Wlk.)
Oakhurst Gro. SE22 . . 2C 106
Oakington Rd. W9 . . . 3C 58
Oakington Way N8 . . . 2A 34
Oakland Rd. E15 . . . . 1F 53
Oaklands Ct. NW10 . . 5A 42
(off Nicoll Rd.)
Oaklands Est. SW4 . . 4E 103
Oaklands Gro. W12 . . 2C 70
Oaklands M. NW2 . . . 1F 43
(off Oaklands Rd.)
Oaklands Pas. NW2 . . 1F 43
(off Oaklands Rd.)
Oaklands Pl. SW4 . . . 2E 103
Oaklands Rd.
NW2 . . . . 1F 43
Oak La. E14 . . . . 1B 80
Oakley Cres. EC1 . . . 1D 63
Oakley Dr. SE13 . . . . 4F 109
Oakley Gdns. SW3 . . . 2A 88
Oakley Ho. SW1 . . . . . 5B 74
(off Sloane St.)
Oakley Pl. SE1 . . . . . . 1B 92
Oakley Rd. N1 . . . . . . 4F 49
Oakley Sq. NW1 . . . . . 1E 61
Oakley St. SW3 . . . . . 2A 88
Oakley Wlk. W6 . . . . . 2F 85
Oakley Yd. E2 . . . . . . 3B 64
Oak Lodge E11 . . . . . 1C 40
W8 . . . . 4D 73
(off Chantry Sq.)
Oakman Ho. SW19 . . . 1F 113
Oakmead Rd. SW12 . . 1C 116
Oak Pk. Gdns.
SW19 . . . . 1F 113
Oak Pk. M. N16 . . . . . 5B 36
Oak Pl. SW18 . . . . . . 3D 101
Oakridge La.
BR1: Brom 5F 123
Oakridge Rd.
BR1: Brom 4F 123
Oaks, The NW6 . . . . . 4F 43
(off Brondesbury Pk.)
NW10 . . . . 4D 43
Oaks Av. SE19 . . . . . . 5A 120
Oaksford Av. SE26 . . . 3D 121
Oakshade Rd.
BR1: Brom 4F 123
Oakshaw Rd. SW18 . . 5D 101
Oakshott Ct.
NW1 . . . . 1B 6 (1F 61)
(not continuous)
Oak St. E14 . . . . 3E 81
(off Stewart St.)
Oak Tree Gdns.
BR1: Brom 5D 125
Oak Tree Ho. W9 . . . . 3C 58
(off Shirland Rd.)
Oak Tree Rd. NW8 . . . 2A 60
Oakview Lodge
NW11 . . . . 2B 30
(off Beechcroft Av.)
Oakview Rd. SE6 . . . . 5D 123
Oak Village NW5 . . . . 1C 46
Oak Vs. NW11 . . . . . . 1B 30
(off Hendon Pk. Row)
Oak Way W3 . . . . 2A 70

Oakwood Bus. Pk.
NW10 . . . . 3A 56
Oakwood Ct. E6 . . . . . 5F 55
W14 . . . . 4B 72
Oakwood Dr. SE19 . . . 5F 119
Oakwood La. W14 . . . 4B 72
Oakworth Rd. W10 . . . 4E 57
Oasis Sports Cen.
. . . . 2D 15 (5A 62)
Oast Ct. E14 . . . . 1B 80
(off Newell St.)
Oast Lodge W4 . . . . . 3A 84
(off Corney Reach Way)
Oatfield Ho. N15 . . . . 1A 36
(off Perry Ct.)
Oat La. EC2 . . . 2A 18 (5E 63)
Oatwell Ho. SW3 . . . . 1A 88
(off Marlborough St.)
Oban Cl. E13 . . . . 3E 69
Oban Ho. E14 . . . . . . 5F 67
(off Oban St.)
Oban Rd. E13 . . . . . . 2E 69
Oban St. E14 . . . . 5F 67
Oberon Ho. N1 . . . . . . 1A 64
(off Arden Est.)
Oberstein Rd. SW11 . . 2F 101
Oborne Cl. SE24 . . . . 3D 105
O'Brien Ho. E2 . . . . . . 2F 65
(off Roman Rd.)
Observatory Gdns.
W8 . . . . 3C 72
Observatory M. E14 . . 5F 81
Occupation Rd. SE17 . . 1E 91
Ocean Est. E1 . . . . . . 3F 65
(Ernest St.)
E1 . . . . 4A 66
(Masters St.)
Ocean Music Venue . . 3D 51
(off Mare St.)
Ocean St. E1 . . . . 4F 65
Ocean Wharf E14 . . . 3B 80
Ockbrook E1 . . . . 4E 65
(off Hannibal Rd.)
Ockendon M. N1 . . . . 3F 49
Ockendon Rd. N1 . . . . 3F 49
Ockley Rd. SW16 . . . . 4A 118
Octagon, The SW10 . . 3D 87
(off Coleridge Gdns.)
Octagon Arc.
EC2 . . . . 1D 19 (4A 64)
Octagon Ct. SE16 . . . 2F 79
(off Rotherhithe St.)
Octavia Ho. SW1 . . . . 4F 75
(off Medway St.)
W10 . . . . 3A 58
Octavia M. W10 . . . . . 3B 58
Octavia St. SW11 . . . 4A 88
Octavius St. SE8 . . . . 3C 94
Odeon Cinema
Camden Town 5D 47
(off Parkway)
Edgware Rd. 3A 12
(off Edgware Rd.)
Holloway 5A 34
Kensington 4C 72
(off Kensington High St.)
Leicester Sq. 5C 14
(off Leicester Sq.)
Mezzanine 5C 14
(off Leicester Sq.)

Odeon Cinema
Panton St. 5C 14
(off Panton St.)
Putney 1A 100
Shaftesbury Av. . . . 3C 14
(off Shaftesbury Av.)
Streatham 3A 118
Streatham Hill 2A 118
Swiss Cen. 4B 14
(off Wardour St.)
Swiss Cottage 4F 45
Tottenham Ct. Rd. . 1B 14
(off Tottenham Ct. Rd.)
West End 5C 14
(off Leicester Sq.)
Odeon Ct. E16 . . . . . . 4C 68
NW10 . . . . 5A 42
(off St Albans Rd.)
Odessa Rd. E7 . . . . . . 5B 40
NW10 . . . . 1C 56
Odessa St. SE16. . . . . 3B 80
Odette Duval Ho. E1. . . 4E 65
(off Stepney Way)
Odger St. SW11 . . . . . 5B 88
Odhams Wlk.
WC2. . . . . 3E 15 (5A 62)
Odin Ho. SE5 . . . . 5E 91
O'Donnell Ct.
WC1. . . . . 3E 7 (3A 62)
Odontological Mus., The
. . . . 2A 16
(off Lincoln's Inn Flds.)
O'Driscoll Ho. W12 . . . 5D 57
Offa's Mead E9. . . . . . 1B 52
Offenbach Ho. E2. . . . . 1F 65
(off Mace St.)
Offerton Rd. SW4 . . . . 1E 103
Offham Ho. SE17 . . . . . 5A 78
(off Beckway St.)
Offley Rd. SW9. . . . . . 3C 90
Offord Rd. N1 . . . . 4B 48
Offord St. N1 . . . . 4B 48
Ogilvie Ho. E1. . . . . . . 5F 65
(off Stepney C'way.)
Oglander Rd. SE15. . . . 2B 106
Ogle St. W1 . . . . . . 5F 5 (4E 61)
O'Gorman Ho. SW10 . . 3E 87
(off King's Rd.)
Ohio Rd. E13 . . . . 3B 68
Oil Mill La. W6. . . . . . . 1C 84
Okeburn Rd. SW17 . . . 5C 116
Okehampton Rd.
NW10 . . . . 5E 43
Olaf St. W11 . . . . 1F 71
Oldacre M. SW12. . . . . 5C 102
Old Bailey
EC4 . . . . 3E 17 (5D 63)
Old Bailey
(Central Criminal Court)
. . . . 2E 17 (5D 63)
Old Barge Ho. All.
SE1. . . . . 5C 16
Old Barracks W8 . . . . . 3D 73
Old Barrack Yd.
SW1. . . . . 4B 20 (3C 74)
(not continuous)
Old Barrowfield E15. . . 5A 54
Old Bellgate Pl. E14. . . 4C 80
Old Bethnal Grn. Rd.
E2. . . . . 2C 64

Old Billingsgate Mkt.
EC3. . . . . 5C 18
(off Lwr. Thames St.)
Old Billingsgate Wlk.
EC3 . . . . 5D 19 (1A 78)
Old Bond St.
W1 . . . . 5F 13 (1E 75)
Old Brewer's Yd.
WC2. . . . . 3D 15 (5A 62)
Old Brewery M. NW3 . . 1F 45
Old Broad St.
EC2. . . . . 2C 18 (5F 63)
Old Bromley Rd.
BR1: Brom 5F 123
Old Brompton Rd.
SW5 . . . . 1C 86
SW7 . . . . 1C 86
Old Bldgs. WC2 . . . . . 2B 16
Old Burlington St.
W1 . . . . 4F 13 (1E 75)
Oldbury Pl.
W1 . . . . 5C 4 (4C 60)
Old Canal M. SE15. . . . 1B 92
(off Trafalgar Av.)
Old Castle St.
E1 . . . . 2F 19 (5B 64)
Old Cavendish St.
W1 . . . . 2D 13 (5D 61)
Old Change Ct. EC4 . . 3F 17
Old Chapel Pl. SW9 . . 5C 90
Old Chelsea M. SW3 . . 2A 88
Old Chiswick Yd.
W4 . . . . 2A 84
(off Pumping Sta. Rd.)
Old Church La. NW9 . . 4A 28
Old Church Rd. E1 . . . 5F 65
Old Church St. SW3 . . 1F 87
Old Compton St.
W1 . . . . 4B 14 (1F 75)
Old Ct. Ho. W8. . . . . . 3D 73
(off Old Ct. Pl.)
Old Ct. Pl. W8 . . . . . . 3D 73
Old Curiosity Shop . . 3A 16
(off Portsmouth St.)
Old Dairy M. NW5 . . . 3D 47
SW12 . . . . 1C 116
Old Devonshire Rd.
SW12 . . . . 5D 103
Old Dover Rd. SE3. . . 3C 96
Oldegate Ho. E6 . . . . 4F 55
Old Farm Ct. SW17 . . 2A 116
Oldfield Gro. SE16 . . . 5F 79
Oldfield Ho. W4 . . . . . 1A 84
(off Devonshire Rd.)
Oldfield M. N6 . . . . . . 2E 33
Oldfield Rd. N16 . . . . 5A 36
NW10 . . . . 4B 42
SW19 . . . . 5A 114
W3 . . . . 3B 70
Old Fish St. Hill EC4 . . 4F 17
(off Victoria St.)
Old Fleet La.
EC4 . . . . 2D 17 (5D 63)
OLD FORD 5C 52
Old Ford Rd. E2 . . . . . 2E 65
Old Forge M. W12. . . . 3D 71
Old Forge Rd. N19 . . . 4F 33
Old Gloucester St.
WC1. . . . . 5E 7 (4A 62)
Oldhill St. N16 . . . . . . 3C 36

Old Hospital Cl.
SW12 . . . . 1B 116
Old Ho. Cl. SW19. . . . 5A 114
Old Jamaica Rd.
SE16 . . . . 4C 78
Old James St.
SE15. . . . . 1D 107
Old Jewry
EC2. . . . . 3B 18 (5F 63)
Old Kent Rd. SE1 . . . . 5A 78
SE15. . . . . 5A 78
Old Mnr. Ct. NW8. . . . 1C 59
Old Mnr. Yd. SW5 . . . 5D 73
Old Mkt. Sq.
E2. . . . . 1F 11 (2B 64)
Old Marylebone Rd.
NW1 . . . . 4A 60
Old Mitre Ct.
EC4 . . . . 3C 16 (5C 62)
Old Montague St. E1 . . 4C 64
Old Nichol St.
E2. . . . . 3F 11 (3B 64)
Old Nth. St. WC1 . . . . 5F 7
OLD OAK COMMON . . 4A 56
Old Oak Comn. La.
NW10 . . . . 4A 56
W3 . . . . 4A 56
Old Oak La. NW10 . . . 2A 56
Old Oak Rd. W3. . . . . 1B 70
Old Orchard, The
NW3 . . . . 1B 46
Old Pal. Yd.
SW1. . . . . 5D 23 (4A 76)
Old Paradise St.
SE11. . . . . 5B 76
Old Pk. Av. SW12. . . . 4C 102
Old Pk. La.
W1 . . . . 2D 21 (2D 75)
Old Post Office La.
SE3. . . . . 1D 111
Old Pye St.
SW1. . . . . 5B 22 (4F 75)
Old Pye St. Est. SW1. . 5B 22
(off Old Pye St.)
Old Quebec St.
W1 . . . . 3A 12 (5B 60)
Old Queen St.
SW1. . . . . 4C 22 (3F 75)
Old Red Lion Theatre . 1C 8
(off St John St.)
Oldridge Rd. SW12 . . 5C 102
Old Royal Free Pl.
N1. . . . . 5C 48
Old Royal Free Sq.
N1. . . . . 5C 48
Old Royal Naval College
. . . . 1F 95
Old School Cl. SE10. . . 4A 82
Old School Cres. E7. . . 3C 54
Old School Sq. E14 . . . 5C 66
(off Pelling St.)
Old Seacoal La.
EC4 . . . . 3D 17 (5D 63)
Old Sth. Lambeth Rd.
SW8 . . . . 3A 90
Old Spitalfields Market
. . . . 5F 11 (4B 64)
Old Sq. WC2. . . . . 2B 16 (5B 62)
Old Stable M. N5 . . . . 5E 35

Oldstead Rd.
BR1: Brom 4E **123**
OLD STREET **3F 63**
Old St. E13 . . . . 1D **69**
EC1 . . . . **3F 9** (3E **63**)
Old Sun Wharf E14 . . . . 1A **80**
(off Narrow St.)
Old Swan Wharf
SW11 . . . . 4F **87**
Old Thackeray School
SW8 . . . . 5D **89**
Old Theatre Ct. SE1 . . . 1A **26**
(off Porter St.)
Old Town SW4 . . . . . . 1E **103**
Old Vic Theatre, The . . . **3C 24**
(off Cut, The)
Old Woolwich Rd.
SE10 . . . . 2F **95**
Old York Rd. SW18 . . 3D **101**
O'Leary Sq. E1 . . . . . . 4E **65**
Olga St. E3 . . . . 1A **66**
Olinda Rd. N16 . . . . . . 1B **36**
Oliphant St. W10 . . . . . 2F **57**
Oliver Goldsmith Est.
SE15 . . . . 4C **92**
Oliver Ho. SE16 . . . . . 3C **78**
(off George Row)
SW8 . . . . 3A **90**
(off Wyvil Rd.)
Oliver M. SE15 . . . . . . 5C **92**
Olive Rd. E13 . . . . 2E **69**
NW2 . . . . 1E **43**
Oliver Rd. E10 . . . . . . 4D **39**
Olivers Wharf E1 . . . . . 2D **79**
(off Wapping High St.)
Olivers Yd.
EC1 . . . . **3C 10** (3F **63**)
Olive Tree Ho. SE1 . . . . 2E **93**
(off Sharratt St.)
Olivette St. SW15 . . . . 1F **99**
Olive Waite Ho. NW6 . . 4C **44**
Olivier Theatre 1B **24**
Ollerton Grn. E3 . . . . . 5B **52**
Ollgar Cl. W12 . . . . . . 2B **70**
Olliffe St. E14 . . . . 4E **81**
Olmar St. SE1 . . . . 2C **92**
Olney Ho. NW8 . . . . . . 3A **60**
(off Tresham Cres.)
Olney Rd. SE17 . . . . . . 2D **91**
(not continuous)
Olympia 4A **72**
Olympia M. W2 . . . . . . 1D **73**
Olympian Ct. E14 . . . . 5C **80**
(off Homer Dr.)
Olympia Way W14 . . . . 4A **72**
Olympus Sq. E5 . . . . . 5C **36**
O'Mahoney Ct. SW17 . 3E **115**
Oman Av. NW2 . . . . . . 1E **43**
O'Meara St.
SE1 . . . . 2A **26** (2E **77**)
Omega Ct. E14 . . . . . . 4D **81**
Omega Pl. N1 . . . . 1E **7**
Omega St. SE14 . . . . . 4C **94**
Ommaney Rd. SE14 . . . 4F **93**
Ondine Rd. SE15 . . . . . 2B **106**
Onega Ga. SE16 . . . . . 4A **80**
O'Neill Ho. NW8 . . . . . 1A **60**
(off Cochrane St.)
One Owen St. EC1 . . . . 1D **9**
(off Goswell St.)

One Tree Cl. SE23 . . . 4E **107**
Ongar Rd. SW6 . . . . . 2C **86**
Onra Rd. E17 . . . . 2C **38**
Onslow Cl. W10 . . . . . 2B **58**
Onslow Gdns.
SW7 . . . . 5F **73**
Onslow M. E. SW7 . . . 5F **73**
Onslow M. W.
SW7 . . . . 5F **73**
Onslow Sq. SW7 . . . . . 5F **73**
Onslow St.
EC1 . . . . 4C **8** (3C **62**)
Ontario St.
SE1 . . . . 5E **25** (4D **77**)
Ontario Way E14 . . . . 1C **80**
(not continuous)
Onyx M. E15 . . . . 3B **54**
Opal Cl. E16 . . . . 5F **69**
Opal M. NW6 . . . . 5B **44**
Opal St. SE11 . . . . 1D **91**
Open Air Stage 3A **32**
Open Air Theatre
Roundwood Pk. 4C **42**
Open University, The
(Parsifal College) . . . 1C **44**
Openview SW18 . . . . 1E **115**
Opera Ct. N19 . . . . . . 5F **33**
(off Wedmore St.)
Operating Theatre Mus.
. . . . 2C **26**
Ophelia Gdns. NW2 . . . 5A **30**
Ophelia Ho. W6 . . . . . . 1F **85**
(off Fulham Pal. Rd.)
Ophir Ter. SE15 . . . . . 4C **92**
Opie Ho. NW8 . . . . . . 1A **60**
(off Townshend St.)
Oppenheim Rd. SE13 . . 5E **95**
Oppidans Rd. NW3 . . . 4B **46**
Orange Gro. E11 . . . . . 5A **40**
(not continuous)
Orange Pl. SE16 . . . . . 4E **79**
Orangery Gallery, The
. . . . 3B **72**
Orange St.
WC2 . . . . 5C **14** (1F **75**)
Orange Tree Ct. SE5 . . 3A **92**
(off Havil St.)
Orange Yd. W1 . . . . . . 3C **14**
Oransay Rd. N1 . . . . . 3E **49**
Oratory La. SW3 . . . . . 1F **87**
Orbain Rd. SW6 . . . . . 3A **86**
Orbel St. SW11 . . . . . 4A **88**
Orb St. SE17 . . . . 5F **77**
Orchard, The NW11 . . . 1C **30**
SE3 . . . . 5F **95**
W4 . . . . 5A **70**
Orchard Bus. Cen.
SE26 . . . . 5B **122**
Orchard Cl. N1 . . . . . . 4E **49**
NW2 . . . . 5C **28**
SE23 . . . . 4E **107**
W10 . . . . 4B **58**
Orchard Ct. E10 . . . . . 3D **39**
Orchard Dr. SE3 . . . . . 5F **95**
Orchard Hill SE13 . . . . 5D **95**
(off County Gro.)
SE16 . . . . 4E **79**
SW6 . . . . 3B **86**
(off Varna Rd.)

Orchard Ho. W1 . . . . . 2B **12**
(off Fitzhardinge St.)
W12 . . . . 2C **70**
Orchard Mead Ho.
NW2 . . . . 4C **30**
Orchard M. N1 . . . . . . 4F **49**
N6 . . . . 2D **33**
Orchard Pl. E5 . . . . . . 2D **51**
E14 . . . . 1A **82**
(not continuous)
Orchard Rd. N6 . . . . . 2D **33**
SE3 . . . . 5A **96**
Orchardson Ho. NW8 . . 3F **59**
(off Orchardson St.)
Orchardson St. NW8 . . 3F **59**
Orchard Sq. W14 . . . . 1B **86**
Orchard St.
W1 . . . . **3B 12** (5C **60**)
Orchard Studios W6 . . 5F **71**
(off Brook Grn.)
Orchard Ter. NW10 . . . 1B **42**
Orchard Wharf E14 . . . 1A **82**
(off Orchard Pl.)
Orchid Cl. E6 . . . . 4F **69**
Orchid St. W12 . . . . . . 1C **70**
Orde Hall St.
WC1 . . . . 4F **7** (3B **62**)
Ordell Rd. E3 . . . . 1B **66**
Ordnance Cres. SE10 . . 3F **81**
Ordnance Hill NW8 . . . 5F **45**
Ordnance M. NW8 . . . . 1F **59**
Ordnance Rd. E16 . . . . 4B **68**
Oregano Dr. E14 . . . . . 5F **67**
Orestes M. NW6 . . . . . 2C **44**
Orford Ct. SE27 . . . . . 2D **119**
Orford Ho. E17 . . . . . . 1C **38**
SE6 . . . . 3D **123**
Oriana Ho. E14 . . . . . . 1B **80**
(off Victory Pl.)
Oriel Ct. NW3 . . . . 1E **45**
Oriel Dr. SW13 . . . . . . 2E **85**
Oriel Pl. NW3 . . . . 1E **45**
(off Heath St.)
Oriel Rd. E9 . . . . 3F **51**
Oriental Rd. E16 . . . . . 2F **83**
Oriental St. E14 . . . . . 1C **80**
(off Pennyfields)
Orient Ind. Pk. E10 . . . 4C **38**
Orient St. SE11 . . . . . 5D **77**
Orient Way E5 . . . . . . 5F **37**
E10 . . . . 3A **38**
Orient Wharf E1 . . . . . 2E **79**
(off Wapping High St.)
Orion E14 . . . . 5C **80**
(off Crews St.)
Orion Bus. Cen. SE14 . . 1F **93**
Orion Ho. E1 . . . . 3D **65**
(off Coventry Rd.)
Orkney Ho. N1 . . . . . . 5B **48**
(off Bemerton Est.)
Orkney St. SW11 . . . . . 5C **88**
Orlando Rd. SW4 . . . . 1E **103**
Orleston M. N7 . . . . . . 3C **48**
Orleston Rd. N7 . . . . . 3C **48**
Orlop St. SE10 . . . . . . 1A **96**
Ormanton Rd. SE26 . . 4C **120**
Orme Ct. W2 . . . . 1D **73**
Orme Ct. M. W2 . . . . . 1D **73**
(off Orme La.)
Orme Ho. E8 . . . . 5B **50**

Orme La. W2 . . . . 1D 73
Ormeley Rd. SW12 . . 1D 117
Orme Sq. W2 . . . . 1D 73
Ormiston Gro. W12 . . . 2D 71
Ormiston Rd. SE10. . . 1C 96
Ormond Cl.
　WC1. . . . . 5E 7 (4A 62)
Ormonde Ct. NW8 . . . . . 5B 46
　(off St Edmund's Cl.)
　SW15 . . . . 2E 99
Ormonde Ga. SW3. . . . 1B 88
Ormonde Pl. SW1 . . . . . 5C 74
Ormonde Ter. NW8. . . . 5B 46
Ormond Ho. N16. . . . . . 4F 35
Ormond M.
　WC1. . . . . 4E 7 (3A 62)
Ormond Rd. N19 . . . . . 3A 34
Ormond Yd.
　SW1. . . . . 1A 22 (2E 75)
Ormsby Lodge W4 . . . . 4A 70
Ormsby Pl. N16 . . . . . . 5B 36
Ormsby St. E2 . . . . 1B 64
Ormside St. SE15 . . . . . 2E 93
Ornan Rd. NW3 . . . . . . 2A 46
Orpen Wlk. N16 . . . . . . 5A 36
Orpheus St. SE5 . . . . . . 4F 91
Orsett M. W2 . . . . 5D 59
　(not continuous)
Orsett St. SE11 . . . . . . 1B 90
Orsett Ter. W2 . . . . 5D 59
Orsman Rd. N1. . . . . . . 5A 50
Orton St. E1 . . . . 2C 78
Orville Rd. SW11 . . . . . 5B 87
Orwell Ct. E8 . . . . 5C 50
　(off Pownall Rd.)
　N5. . . . . 1E 49
Orwell Rd. E13 . . . . 1E 69
Osbaldeston Rd. N16. . 4C 36
Osberton Rd. SE12. . . 3C 110
Osbert St. SW1. . . . . . . 5F 75
Osborn Cl. E8 . . . . 5C 50
Osborne Ct. E10 . . . . . . 2D 39
Osborne Gro. N4 . . . . . 3C 34
Osborne Ho. E16 . . . . . 2C 82
　(off Wesley Av.)
Osborne Rd. E7 . . . . . . 2D 55
　E9. . . . . 3B 52
　E10. . . . . 4D 39
　N4. . . . . 3C 34
　NW2 . . . . 3D 43
Osborne Ter. SW17 . . . 5B 116
　(off Church La.)
Osborn La. SE23 . . . . . 5A 108
Osborn St. E1 . . . . 4B 64
Osborn Ter. SE3 . . . . . 2B 110
Oscar Faber Pl. N1. . . . 4A 50
Oscar St. SE8 . . . . 5C 94
　(Lewisham Way)
　SE8. . . . . 4C 94
　(Thornville St.)
Oseney Cres. NW5 . . . . 2E 47
O'Shea Gro. E3. . . . . . . 5B 52
Osier Cl. E1. . . . . 3F 65
　(off Osier St.)
Osier La. SE10 . . . . 4B 82
　(off School Bank Rd.)
Osier M. W4 . . . . 2A 84
Osiers Est., The
　SW18 . . . . 2C 100
Osiers Rd. SW18 . . . . . 2C 100

Osier St. E1 . . . . 3E 65
Osier Way E10 . . . . 5D 39
Oslac Rd. SE6 . . . . 5D 123
Oslo Ct. NW8 . . . . 1A 60
　(off Prince Albert Rd.)
Oslo Ho. SE5 . . . . 5E 91
　(off Carew St.)
Oslo Sq. SE16 . . . . 4A 80
Osman Cl. N15. . . . . . . 1F 35
Osmani School Sports Cen.
　. . . . . 4C 64
Osman Rd. W6 . . . . 4E 71
Osmington Ho. SW8 . . . 3B 90
　(off Dorset Rd.)
Osmund St. W12 . . . . . 4B 56
Osnaburgh St.
　NW1 . . . . 4E 5 (3D 61)
　(Longford St.)
　NW1 . . . . 2E 5
　(Robert St.)
Osnaburgh Ter.
　NW1 . . . . 3E 5 (3D 61)
Osprey Cl. E6 . . . . 4F 69
Osprey Ct. E1 . . . . 1C 78
　(off Star Pl.)
Osprey Est. SE16 . . . . . 5A 80
Osprey Ho. E14 . . . . . . 1A 80
　(off Victory Pl.)
Ospringe Ho. SE1 . . . . 3C 24
　(off Wootton St.)
Ospringe Rd. NW5 . . . . 1E 47
Osram Ct. W6. . . . . 4E 71
Osric Path N1 . . . . 1A 64
Ossian M. N4 . . . . 2B 34
Ossian Rd. N4 . . . . 2B 34
Ossington Bldgs.
　W1. . . . . 5B 4 (4C 60)
Ossington Cl. W2 . . . . . 1C 72
Ossington St. W2 . . . . . 1C 72
Ossory Rd. SE1 . . . . . . 2C 92
Ossulston St.
　NW1 . . . . 1C 6 (1F 61)
Ostade Rd. SW2. . . . . . 5B 104
Ostend Pl. SE11 . . . . . . 5E 77
Osten M. SW7 . . . . 4D 73
Osterley Ho. E14 . . . . . 5D 67
　(off Girauld St.)
Osterley Rd. N16. . . . . 1A 50
Oswald Bldg. SW8. . . . 2D 89
Oswald St. E5. . . . . 5E 37
Oswald Ter. NW2 . . . . . 5E 29
Osward Rd. SW17 . . . . 2B 116
Oswell Ho. E1 . . . . 2D 79
　(off Farthing Flds.)
Oswin St. SE11 . . . . . . 5D 77
Oswyth Rd. SE5 . . . . . . 5A 92
Otford Cres. SE4 . . . . . 4B 108
Otford Ho. SE1 . . . . 5C 26
　(off Staple St.)
　SE15. . . . . 2C 92
　(off Lovelinch Cl.)
Othello Cl. SE11 . . . . . . 1D 91
Other Cinema, The 4B 14
　(off Rupert St.)
Otis St. E3 . . . . 2E 67
Otley Ho. N5. . . . . 5C 34
Otley Rd. E16. . . . . 5E 69
Otley Ter. E5. . . . . 5F 37
Ottaway Ct. E5 . . . . 5C 36

Ottaway St. E5 . . . . 5C 36
Otterburn Ho. SE5 . . . . 3E 91
　(off Sultan St.)
Otterburn St. SW17 . . . 5B 116
Otter Cl. E15. . . . . 5E 53
Otterden St. SE6 . . . . . 4C 122
Otto Cl. SE26 . . . . 3D 121
Otto St. SE17 . . . . 2D 91
Oulton Cl. E5 . . . . 4E 37
Oulton Rd. N15. . . . . . . 1F 35
Ouseley Rd.
　SW12 . . . . 1B 116
Outer Circ.
　NW1 . . . . 1D 5 (1A 60)
Outgate Rd. NW10. . . . 4B 42
Outram Pl. N1 . . . . 5A 48
Outram Rd. E6. . . . . . . 5F 55
Outwich St. EC3 . . . . . . 2E 19
Outwood Ho. SW2 . . . . 5B 104
　(off Deepdene Gdns.)
Oval, The E2 . . . . 1D 65
Oval Cricket Ground, The
　. . . . . 2B 90
Oval House Theatre . . . 2C 90
　(off Kennington Oval)
Oval Mans. SE11 . . . . . 2B 90
Oval Pl. SW8 . . . . 3B 90
Oval Rd. NW1 . . . . 5D 47
Oval Way SE11. . . . . . . 1B 90
Overbrae BR3: Beck.. . 5C 122
Overbury Rd. N15. . . . . 1F 35
Overbury St. E5 . . . . . . 1F 51
Overcliff Rd. SE13 . . . 1C 108
Overdown Rd. SE6. . . . 4C 122
Overhill Rd. SE22 . . . . 5C 106
Overlea Rd. E5. . . . . . . 2C 36
Oversley Ho. W2 . . . . . 4C 58
　(off Alfred Rd.)
Overstone Ho. E14. . . . 5C 66
　(off E. India Dock Rd.)
Overstone Rd. W6 . . . . 4E 71
Overstrand Mans.
　SW11 . . . . 4B 88
Overton Ct. E11 . . . . . . 2C 40
Overton Dr. E11 . . . . . . 2C 40
Overton Rd. SW15 . . . . 5B 98
　(off Tangley Gro.)
Overton Rd. E10. . . . . . 3A 38
　SW9 . . . . 5C 90
Overy Ho.
　SE1 . . . . 4D 25 (3D 77)
Ovex Cl. E14. . . . . 3E 81
Ovington Gdns. SW3 . . 4A 74
Ovington M. SW3. . . . . 4A 74
　(off Ovington Gdns.)
Ovington Sq. SW3 . . . . 4A 74
Ovington St. SW3 . . . . . 5A 74
Owen Mans. W14. . . . . 2A 86
　(off Queen's Club Gdns.)
Owens M. E11. . . . . 4A 40
Owen's Row
　EC1 . . . . 1D 9 (2D 63)
Owen St. EC1 . . 1D 9 (1D 63)
　(not continuous)
Owens Way SE23 . . . . 5A 108
Owgan Cl. SE5 . . . . 3F 91
Oxberry Av. SW6 . . . . . 5A 86
Oxendon St.
　SW1 . . . . 5B 14 (1F 75)
Oxenford St. SE15 . . . 1B 106

Oxenham Ho. SE8 . . . . . 2C 94
(off Benbow St.)
Oxenholme NW1 . . . . 1F 5
(off Hampstead Rd.)
Oxestall's Rd. SE8 . . . . 1A 94
Oxford & Cambridge Mans.
NW1 . . . . 4A 60
(off Old Marylebone Rd.)
Oxford Av. W10 . . . . 2D 57
Oxford Cir. W1 . . . . 3F 13
Oxford Cir. Av.
W1 . . . . 3F 13 (5E 61)
Oxford Ct. EC4 . . . . 4B 18
W9 . . . . 4C 58
(off Elmfield Way)
Oxford Dr.
SE1 . . . . 2D 27 (2A 78)
Oxford Gdns. W10 . . . . . 5E 57
Oxford Ga. W6 . . . . 5F 71
Oxford Pl. NW10 . . . . . . 5A 28
(off Press Rd.)
Oxford Rd. E15 . . . . 3F 53
(not continuous)
N4 . . . . 3C 34
NW6 . . . . 1C 58
SE19 . . . . 5F 119
SW15 . . . . 2A 100
Oxford Sq. W2 . . . . 5A 60
Oxford St.
W1 . . . . 3B 12 (5C 60)
Oxgate Cen. NW2 . . . . . 4D 29
Oxgate Ct. NW2 . . . . . . 4C 28
Oxgate Ct. Pde.
NW2 . . . . 4C 28
Oxgate Gdns. NW2 . . . . 5D 29
Oxgate La. NW2 . . . . . . 4D 29
Oxgate Pde. NW2 . . . . . 4C 28
Oxley Cl. SE1 . . . . 1B 92
Oxleys Rd. NW2 . . . . . . 5D 29
Oxonian St. SE22 . . . . 2B 106
Oxo Tower Wharf
SE1 . . . . 5C 16 (1C 76)
Oxzygeem Sports Cen.
. . . . 4D 105
Oystercatcher Cl.
E16 . . . . 5D 69
Oystergate Wlk.
EC4 . . . . 5B 18
Oyster Row E1 . . . . 5E 65
Oyster Wharf SW11 . . . 5F 87
Ozolins Way E16 . . . . . . 5C 68

P

Pablo Neruda Cl.
SE24 . . . . 2D 105
Pace Pl. E1 . . . . 5D 65
Pacific Ho. E1 . . . . 3F 65
(off Ernest St.)
Pacific Rd. E16 . . . . 5C 68
Pacific Wharf SE16 . . . 2F 79
Packenham Ho. E2 . . . . 2B 64
(off Wellington Row)
Packington Sq. N1 . . . . . 5E 49
(not continuous)
Packington St. N1 . . . . . 5D 49
Padbury SE17 . . . . 1A 92
(off Bagshot St.)
Padbury Ct. E2 . . . . 2B 64

Padbury Ho. NW8 . . . . . 3A 60
(off Tresham Cres.)
Paddenswick Rd. W6 . . . 4C 70
PADDINGTON 5F 59
Paddington Bowling &
Sports Club 3D 59
Paddington Grn.
W2 . . . . 4F 59
Paddington St.
W1 . . . . 5B 4 (4C 60)
Paddington Wlk. W2 . . . 4F 59
(off Hermitage St.)
Paddock Cl. SE3 . . . . . . 5C 96
SE26 . . . . 4F 121
Paddock Rd. NW2 . . . . . 5C 28
Paddock Way SW15 . . . 5E 99
Padfield Rd. SE5 . . . . . 1E 105
Padstow Ho. E14 . . . . . 1B 80
(off Three Colt St.)
Pagden St. SW8 . . . . . . 4D 89
Pageant Cres. SE16 . . . 2A 80
Pageantmaster Ct.
EC4 . . . . 3D 17
Page Grn. Rd. N15 . . . . 1C 36
Page Grn. Ter. N15 . . . 1B 36
Page Ho. SE10 . . . . 2E 95
(off Welland St.)
Page St. SW1 . . . . 5F 75
Page's Wlk.
SE1 . . . . 5E 27 (5A 78)
Pages Yd. W4 . . . . 2B 84
Paget Ho. E2 . . . . 1E 65
(off Bishop's Way)
Paget Rd. N16 . . . . 3F 35
Paget St. EC1 . . . 1D 9 (2D 63)
Pagham Ho. W10 . . . . . 3E 57
(off Sutton Way)
Pagin Ho. N15 . . . . 1A 36
(off Braemar Rd.)
Pagnell St. SE14 . . . . . 3B 94
Pagoda Gdns. SE3 . . . . 5F 95
Paignton Rd. N15 . . . . . 1A 36
Painsthorpe Rd. N16 . . . 5A 36
Painswick Ct. SE15 . . . . 3B 92
(off Daniel Gdns.)
Painted Hall 2E 95
Painters M. SE16 . . . . . 5C 78
Pakeman Ho. SE1 . . . . . 3E 25
(off Surrey Row)
Pakeman St. N7 . . . . . . 5B 34
Pakenham Cl.
SW12 . . . . 1C 116
Pakenham St.
WC1 . . . . 2A 8 (2B 62)
Pakington Ho. SW9 . . . 5A 90
(off Stockwell Gdns. Est.)
Palace Av. W8 . . . . 3D 73
Palace Bingo 5E 77
(off Walworth Rd.)
Palace Ct. NW3 . . . . . . 2D 45
W2 . . . . 1D 73
(off Moscow Rd.)
. . . . not continuous)
Palace Gdns. Ter.
W8 . . . . 2C 72
Palace Ga. W8 . . . . 3E 73
Palace Grn. W8 . . . . . . 2D 73
Palace Mans. W14 . . . . 5A 72
(off Hammersmith Rd.)

Palace M. SW1 . . . . 5C 74
(off Eaton Ter.)
SW6 . . . . 3C 86
Palace Pl.
SW1 . . . . . . 5F 21 (4E 75)
Palace Pl. Mans. W8 . . . 3D 73
(off Kensington Rd.)
Palace Rd. N8 . . . . 1F 33
(not continuous)
SW2 . . . . 1B 118
Palace St.
SW1 . . . . . . 5F 21 (4E 75)
Palace Theatre
Soho 3C 14
(off Shaftesbury Av.)
Palace Vw. SE12 . . . . . 2C 124
Palace Wharf W6 . . . . . 3E 85
(off Rainville Rd.)
Palamon Ct. SE1 . . . . . 1B 92
(off Cooper's Rd.)
Palamos Rd. E10 . . . . . 3C 38
Palatine Av. N16 . . . . . 1A 50
Palatine Rd. N16 . . . . . 1A 50
Palemead Cl. SW6 . . . . 4F 85
Palermo Rd.
NW10 . . . . 1C 56
Palewell Comn. Dr.
SW14 . . . . 3A 98
Palfrey Pl. SW8 . . . . . . 3B 90
Palgrave Gdns. NW1 . . . 3A 60
Palgrave Ho. SE5 . . . . . 3E 91
(off Wyndham Est.)
Palgrave Rd. W12 . . . . . 4B 70
Palissy St.
E2 . . . . 2F 11 (2B 64)
(not continuous)
Palladino Ho.
SW17 . . . . 5A 116
(off Laurel Cl.)
Palladium Ct. E8 . . . . . 4B 50
(off Queensbridge Rd.)
Pallant Ho. SE1 . . . . . . 5C 26
Pallett Way SE18 . . . . . 4F 97
Palliser Ct. W14 . . . . . . 1A 86
(off Palliser Rd.)
Palliser Ho. E1 . . . . 3F 65
(off Ernest St.)
SE10 . . . . 2F 95
(off Trafalgar Rd.)
Palliser Rd. W14 . . . . . 1A 86
Pall Mall
SW1 . . . . . . 2A 22 (2E 75)
Pall Mall E.
SW1 . . . . . . 1C 22 (2F 75)
Pall Mall Pl. SW1 . . . . . 2A 22
Palm Cl. E10 . . . . 5D 39
Palm Ct. SE15 . . . . 3B 92
(off Garnies Cl.)
Palmer Pl. N7 . . . . 2C 48
Palmer Rd. E13 . . . . . . 3D 69
Palmer's Rd. E2 . . . . . . 1F 65
Palmerston Ct. E3 . . . . . 1F 65
(off Old Ford Rd.)
Palmerston Ho. SE1 . . . 4B 24
(off Westminster Bri. Rd.)
W8 . . . . 2C 72
(off Kensington Pl.)
Palmerston Mans.
W14 . . . . 2A 86
(off Queen's Club Gdns.)

Palmerston Rd. E7 . . . . . 3D 55
　(not continuous)
NW6 . . . . 4B 44
　(not continuous)
Palmerston Way
SW8 . . . . 3D 89
Palmer St.
SW1 . . . . 5B 22 (4F 75)
Palm Tree Ho. SE14 . . . . 3F 93
　(off Barlborough St.)
Pamela Ho. E8 . . . . 5B 50
　(off Haggerston Rd.)
Panama Ho. E1 . . . . 4F 65
　(off Beaumont Sq.)
Pancras La.
EC4 . . . . 3B 18 (5E 63)
Pancras Rd.
NW1 . . . . 1D 7 (1F 61)
Pandian Way NW5 . . . . 3F 47
Pandora Rd. NW6 . . . . . 3C 44
Pangbourne NW1 . . . . . . 2F 5
　(off Stanhope St.)
Pangbourne Av.
W10 . . . . 4E 57
Pankhurst Av. E16 . . . . 2D 83
Pankhurst Cl. SE14 . . . . 3F 93
Panmure Cl. N5 . . . . . . 1D 49
Panmure Rd. SE26. . . . . 3D 121
Panorama Ct. N6 . . . . . 1E 33
Pansy Gdns. W12 . . . . . 1C 70
Panton St.
SW1 . . . . 5B 14 (1F 75)
Paper Bldgs. EC4 . . . . . 4C 16
Papillons Wlk. SE3 . . . . 5C 96
Papworth Gdns. N7 . . . 2B 48
Papworth Way SW2 . . . 5C 104
Parade, The N4 . . . . . . 3C 34
SE4 . . . . 5B 94
　(off Up. Brockley Rd.)
SE26. . . . . 3D 121
　(off Wells Pk. Rd.)
SW11 . . . . 3B 88
Parade Mans. NW4 . . . . 1D 29
Parade M. SE27 . . . . . 2D 119
Paradise Pas. N7 . . . . . 2C 48
Paradise Rd. SW4 . . . . 5A 90
Paradise Row E2 . . . . . 2D 65
Paradise St. SE16 . . . . . 3D 79
Paradise Wlk. SW3 . . . . 2B 88
Paragon, The SE3 . . . . . 5B 96
Paragon Cl. E16 . . . . . . 5C 68
Paragon M. SE1 . . . . . . 5F 77
Paragon Pl. SE3 . . . . . . 5B 96
Paragon Rd. E9 . . . . . . 3E 51
Paramount Bldg. EC1 . . . 3D 9
　(off St John St.)
Paramount Ct. WC1 . . . . 4A 6
Parbury Rd. SE23 . . . . 4A 108
Pardoner Ho. SE1 . . . . . 5C 26
　(off Pardoner St.)
Pardoner St.
SE1 . . . . 5C 26 (4F 77)
　(not continuous)
Pardon St.
EC1 . . . . 3E 9 (3D 63)
Parfett St. E1 . . . . 4C 64
　(not continuous)
Parfitt Cl. NW3 . . . . . . 3E 31
Parfrey St. W6 . . . . . . 2E 85

Paris Gdn.
SE1 . . . . 1D 25 (2D 77)
Paris Ho. E2 . . . . 1D 65
　(off Old Bethnal Grn. Rd.)
Park, The N6 . . . . 1C 32
NW11 . . . . 3D 31
SE23 . . . . 1E 121
Park App. SE16 . . . . . . 4D 79
Park Av. E15 . . . . 3A 54
NW2 . . . . 2D 43
NW10 . . . . 2D 43
NW11 . . . . 3D 31
SW14 . . . . 2A 98
Park Av. Nth. NW10 . . . 2D 43
Park Bus. Cen. NW6 . . . 2C 58
Park Cl. E9 . . . . 5E 51
NW2 . . . . 5D 29
SW1 . . . . 3B 74
W4 . . . . 2A 84
W14 . . . . 4B 72
Park Club, The 2A 70
Park Ct. E17 . . . . 1D 39
SE26 . . . . 5D 121
SW11 . . . . 4D 89
W6 . . . . 5C 70
Park Cres. W1 . . 4D 5 (3D 61)
Park Cres. M. E.
W1 . . . . 4E 5 (3D 61)
Park Cres. M. W.
W1 . . . . 4D 5 (3D 61)
Parkcroft Rd. SE12. . . . 5B 110
Park Dr. NW11 . . . . . . 3D 31
SE7 . . . . 2F 97
SW14 . . . . 3A 98
Park Dwellings NW3 . . . 2B 46
Park End NW3 . . . . . . 1A 46
Parker Cl. E16 . . . . . . 2F 83
Parker Ho. E14 . . . . . . 3C 80
　(off Admirals Way)
Parker M.
WC2 . . . . 2E 15 (5A 62)
Parke Rd. SW13 . . . . . 4C 84
Parkers Row SE1 . . . . . 3C 78
Parker St. E16 . . . . . . 2F 83
WC2 . . . . 2E 15 (5A 62)
Parkfield Av. SW14 . . . 2A 98
Parkfield Rd. NW10 . . . 4D 43
SE14 . . . . 4B 94
　(off Parkfield Rd.)
Parkfield Ind. Est.
SW11 . . . . 5C 88
Parkfields SW15 . . . . . 2E 99
Parkfield St. N1 . . . . . . 1C 62
Park Gdns. E10 . . . . . . 3C 38
Park Ga. SE3 . . . . 1B 110
Parkgate M. N6 . . . . . . 2E 33
Parkgate Rd. SW11 . . . 3A 88
Park Gro. E15 . . . . 5C 54
Park Gro. Rd. E11 . . . . 4A 40
Park Hall SE10 . . . . . . 3F 95
　(off Crooms Hill)
Pk. Hall Rd. SE21 . . . . 3E 119
Pk. Hall Trad. Est.
SE21 . . . . 3E 119
Parkham St. SW11 . . . . 4A 88
Park Hill SE23 . . . . . . 2D 121
SW4 . . . . 3F 103
Pk. Hill Ct. SW17 . . . . 3B 116

Parkhill Rd. NW3 . . . . . 2B 46
Parkhill Wlk. NW3 . . . . 2B 46
Parkholme Rd. E8 . . . . 3B 50
Park Ho. E9 . . . . 4E 51
　(off Shore Rd.)
Park Ho. Pas. N6 . . . . . 2C 32
Parkhouse St. SE5 . . . . 3F 91
Parkhurst Ct. N7 . . . . . 1A 48
Parkhurst Rd. N7 . . . . . 1A 48
Parkinson Ho. E9 . . . . . 4E 51
　(off Frampton Pk. Rd.)
SW1 . . . . 5E 75
　(off Tachbrook St.)
Parkland Ct. E15 . . . . . 2A 54
　(off Maryland Pk.)
Parkland Gdns.
SW19 . . . . 1F 113
Parklands N6 . . . . 2D 33
Parklands Rd.
SW16 . . . . 5D 117
Park La. E15 . . . . 5F 53
W1 . . . . 4A 12 (1B 74)
Pk. Lee Ct. N16 . . . . . . 2A 36
Park Lodge NW8. . . . . . 4F 45
Park Lofts SW2 . . . . . . 3A 104
　(off Mandrell Rd.)
Park Lorne NW8. . . . . . 2A 60
　(off Park Rd.)
Park Mans. NW4 . . . . . 1D 29
NW8 . . . . 1A 60
　(off Allitsen Rd.)
SW1 . . . . 4A 20
　(off Knightsbridge)
SW8 . . . . 2A 90
SW11 . . . . 4B 88
　(off Prince of Wales Dr.)
Parkmead SW15 . . . . . 4D 99
Park M. SE24 . . . . 5E 105
W10 . . . . 1A 58
Park Pde. NW10 . . . . . . 1B 56
Park Pl. E14 . . . . 2C 80
N1 . . . . 4F 49
　(off Downham Rd.)
SW1 . . . . 2F 21 (2E 75)
Park Pl. Vs. W2 . . . . . . 4E 59
Park Ri. SE23 . . . . 1A 122
Park Ri. Rd. SE23 . . . . 1A 122
Park Rd. E6 . . . . 5E 55
E10 . . . . 3C 38
E12 . . . . 3D 41
E15 . . . . 5C 54
E17 . . . . 1B 38
N8 . . . . 1F 33
NW1 . . . . 3A 4 (2A 60)
NW4 . . . . 2C 28
NW8 . . . . 2A 60
NW10 . . . . 5A 42
SW19 . . . . 5A 116
W4 . . . . 2A 84
Park Rd. Nth. W4. . . . . 1A 84
Park Road Swimming Pool
　. . . . . 1F 33
Park Row SE10 . . . . . . 1F 95
SW2 . . . . 4C 104
Park Side NW2 . . . . . . 5C 28
Parkside SE3 . . . . 3B 96
SW1 . . . . 3A 20
SW19 . . . . 3F 113
W3 . . . . 2A 70
Parkside Av. SW19. . . . 5F 113

Parkside Bus. Est.
SE8 . . . . 2A 94
(Blackhorse Rd.)
SE8 . . . . 2A 94
(Childers St.)
Parkside Ct. E11 . . . . 1C 40
(off Wanstead Pl.)
Parkside Cres. N7 . . . . 5C 34
Parkside Est. E9 . . . . . 5E 51
Parkside Gdns.
SW19 . . . . 4F 113
Parkside Rd. SW11 . . 4C 88
Park Sq. E.
NW1 . . . . . . 3D 5 (3D 61)
Park Sq. M.
NW1 . . . . . 4D 5 (3C 60)
Park Sq. W.
NW1 . . . . . . 3D 5 (3D 61)
Parkstead Rd. SW15 . . 3C 98
Park Steps W2 . . . . . . 1A 74
(off St George's Flds.)
Parkstone Rd. SE15 . . 5C 92
Park St. SE1 . . . 1F 25 (2E 77)
W1 . . . . . . 4B 12 (1C 74)
Parkthorne Rd.
SW12 . . . . 5F 103
Park Towers W1 . . . . . 2D 21
(off Brick St.)
Park Vw. N5 . . . . 1E 49
SE8 . . . . 1F 93
(off Trundleys Rd.)
Park Vw. Apartments
SE16 . . . . 4D 79
(off Banyard Rd.)
Parkview Ct. SW6 . . . . 5A 86
SW18 . . . . 4C 100
Park Vw. Est. E2 . . . . . 1F 65
Park Vw. Gdns. NW4 . . 1E 29
Park Vw. Ho. SE24 . . . 4D 105
(off Hurst St.)
Pk. View Mans. N4 . . . 1D 35
Park Vw. M. SW9 . . . . 5B 90
Park Vw. Rd. NW10 . . 1B 42
Pk. Village E.
NW1 . . . . . . 1E 5 (1D 61)
Pk. Village W. NW1 . . 1D 61
Parkville Rd. SW6 . . . . 3B 86
Park Vista SE10 . . . . . 2F 95
Park Wlk. N6 . . . . 2C 32
SE10 . . . . 3F 95
SW10 . . . . 2E 87
Park Way NW11 . . . . . 1A 30
Parkway NW1 . . . . . . 5D 47
Park W. W2 . . . . 5A 60
(off Edgware Rd.)
Park W. Pl. W2 . . . . . . 5A 60
Park Wharf SE8 . . . . . 1A 94
(off Evelyn St.)
Parkwood NW8 . . . . . 5B 46
(off St Edmund's Ter.)
Parkwood M. N6 . . . . 1D 33
Parkwood Rd.
SW19 . . . . 5B 114
Parliament Ct. E1 . . . . 1E 19
Parliament Fields 5C 32
Parliament Hill. 5B 32
Parliament Hill NW3 . . 1A 46
Parliament Hill Lido . . 1C 46
Parliament Hill Mans.
NW5 . . . . 1C 46

Parliament Sq.
SW1 . . . . . . 4D 23 (3A 76)
Parliament St.
SW1 . . . . . . 3D 23 (3A 76)
Parliament Vw. SE1 . . . 5B 76
Parma Cres. SW11 . . 2B 102
Parmiter Ind. Est. E2 . . 1D 65
(off Parmiter St.)
Parmiter St. E2 . . . . . 1D 65
Parmoor Ct. EC1 . . . . . 3F 9
Parnell Cl. W12 . . . . . 4D 71
Parnell Ho.
WC1 . . . . . . 1C 14 (4F 61)
Parnell Rd. E3 . . . . . . 5B 52
(not continuous)
Parnham St. E14 . . . . . 5A 66
(not continuous)
Parolles Rd. N19 . . . . . 3E 33
Parr Ct. N1 . . . . 1F 63
(off Nth. Rd.)
Parr Ho. E16 . . . . 2D 83
(off Beaulieu Av.)
Parrington Ho. SW4 . . 4F 103
Parr Rd. E6 . . . . 5F 55
Parr St. N1 . . . . 1F 63
Parry Ho. E1 . . . . 2D 79
(off Green Bank)
Parry Rd. W10 . . . . . . 2A 58
(not continuous)
Parry St. SW8 . . . . . . 2A 90
Parsifal Rd. NW6 . . . . 2C 44
Parsonage St. E14 . . . . 5E 81
PARSONS GREEN 5B 86
Parson's Grn. SW6 . . . 4C 86
Parson's Grn. La.
SW6 . . . . 4C 86
Parsons Ho. W2 . . . . . 3F 59
(off Hall Pl.)
Parsons Lodge NW6 . . 4D 45
(off Priory Rd.)
Parson's Rd. E13 . . . . . 1E 69
Parthenia Rd. SW6 . . . 4C 86
Partington Cl. N19 . . . 3F 33
Partridge Cl. E16 . . . . 4F 69
Partridge Ct. EC1 . . . . 3D 9
Pascall Ho. SE17 . . . . . 2E 91
(off Draco St.)
Pascal St. SW8 . . . . . . 3F 89
Pascoe Rd. SE13 . . . . 3F 109
Pasley Cl. SE17 . . . . . 1D 91
Passfield Dr. E14 . . . . 4D 67
Passfields SE6 . . . . . 3D 123
W14 . . . . 1B 86
(off Star St.)
Passing All. EC1 . . . . . 4E 9
Passmore House E2 . . . 5B 50
(off Kingsland Rd.)
Passmore St. SW1 . . . . 1C 88
Paston Cl. E5 . . . . 5F 37
Paston Cres. SE12 . . . 5D 111
Pastor Ct. N6 . . . . 1E 33
Pastor St. SE11 . . . . . . 5D 77
(not continuous)
Pasture Rd. SE6 . . . . . 1B 124
Patcham Ter. SW8 . . . . 4D 89
Patent Ho. E14 . . . . . . 4D 67
(off Morris Rd.)
Patent Office, The
EC4 . . . . 3C 16
(off Bouverie St.)

Paternoster La.
EC4 . . . . . . 3E 17 (5D 63)
Paternoster Row
EC4 . . . . . . 3F 17 (5E 63)
Paternoster Sq.
EC4 . . . . . . 3E 17 (5D 63)
Paterson Ct. EC1 . . . . . 2B 10
Pater St. W8 . . . . 4C 72
Pathfield Rd. SW16 . . . 5F 117
Patience Rd. SW11 . . . 5A 88
Patio Cl. SW4 . . . . . . 4F 103
Patmore Est. SW8 . . . . 4E 89
Patmore Ho. N16 . . . . 2A 50
Patmore St. SW8 . . . . 4E 89
Patmos Lodge SW9 . . . 4D 91
(off Elliott Rd.)
Patmos Rd. SW9 . . . . . 3D 91
Paton Cl. E3 . . . . 2C 66
Paton Ho. SW9 . . . . . . 5B 90
(off Stockwell Rd.)
Paton St. EC1 . . . 2F 9 (2E 63)
Patrick Coman Ho.
EC1 . . . . 2D 9
(off St John St.)
Patrick Connolly Gdns.
E3 . . . . 2D 67
Patrick Pas. SW11 . . . . 5A 88
Patrick Rd. E13 . . . . . . 2E 69
Patriot Sq. E2 . . . . . . 1D 65
Patrol Pl. SE6 . . . . . . 4D 109
Pat Shaw Ho. E1 . . . . . 3F 65
(off Globe Rd.)
Patshull Pl. NW5 . . . . . 3E 47
Patshull Rd. NW5 . . . . 3E 47
Pattenden Rd. SE6 . . . 1B 122
Patten Ho. N4 . . . . . . 3E 35
Patten Rd. SW18 . . . . 5A 102
Patterdale NW1 . . . . . . 2E 5
(off Osnaburgh St.)
Patterdale Rd. SE15 . . . 3E 93
Pattern Ho.
EC1 . . . . . . 3D 9 (3D 63)
Pattina Wlk. SE16 . . . . 2A 80
(off Capstan Way)
Pattinson Point E16 . . . 4C 68
(off Fife Rd.)
Pattison Ho. E1 . . . . . . 5F 65
(off Wellesley St.)
SE1 . . . . 3A 26
(off Redcross Way)
Pattison Rd. NW2 . . . . 5C 30
Paul Cl. E15 . . . . 4A 54
Paulet Rd. SE5 . . . . . . 5D 91
Pauline Ho. E1 . . . . . . 4C 64
(off Old Montague St.)
Paul Julius Cl. E14 . . . . 1F 81
Pauls Ho. E3 . . . . 4B 66
(off Timothy Rd.)
Paul St. E15 . . . . 5A 54
EC2 . . . . . . 4C 10 (3F 63)
Paul's Wlk.
EC4 . . . . . . 4E 17 (1E 77)
Paultons Sq. SW3 . . . . 2F 87
Paultons St. SW3 . . . . 2F 87
Pauntley St. N19 . . . . . 3E 33
Pavan Ct. E2 . . . . 2E 65
(off Sceptre Rd.)
Paveley Dr. SW11 . . . . 3A 88
Paveley Ho. N1 . . . . . . 1B 62
(off Priory Grn. Est.)

Paveley St. NW8 . . . . . . 2A **60**
Pavement, The E11 . . . . . *3E* **39**
   (off Hainault Rd.)
SW4 . . . . 2E **103**
Pavilion NW8 . . . . 2F **59**
Pavilion, The SW8 . . . . 3F **89**
Pavilion Ct. *NW6* *2C* **58**
   (off Stafford Rd.)
Pavilion Pde. *W12* *5E* **57**
   (off Wood La.)
Pavilion Rd.
SW1 . . . . 4A **20** *(4B* **74***)*
Pavilion Sq. SW17 . . . 3B **116**
Pavilion St.
SW1 . . . . 5A **20** *(4B* **74***)*
Pavilion Ter. *W12* *5E* **57**
   (off Wood La.)
Pawsey Cl. E13 . . . . . . 5D **55**
Paxton Ct. SE12 . . . . . 3E **125**
SE26 . . . . *4A* **122**
   (off Adamsrill Rd.)
Paxton Pl. SE27 . . . . . 4A **120**
Paxton Rd. SE23 . . . . . 3A **122**
W4 . . . . 2A **84**
Paxton Ter. SW1 . . . . . 2D **89**
Paymal Ho. *E1* *4E* **65**
   (off Stepney Way)
Payne Ho. *N1* *5B* **48**
   (off Barnsbury Est.)
Paynell Ct. SE3 . . . . . 1A **110**
Payne Rd. E3 . . . . 1D **67**
Paynesfield Av.
SW14 . . . . 1A **98**
Payne St. SE8 . . . . 3B **94**
Paynes Wlk. W6 . . . . . 2A **86**
Peabody Av. SW1 . . . . . 1D **89**
Peabody Bldgs. E1 . . *1C* **78**
   (off John Fisher St.)
EC1 . . . . 4A **10**
   (off Roscoe St.)
SW3 . . . . 2A **88**
   (off Cheyne Row)
Peabody Cl. SE10 . . . . 4D **95**
SW1 . . . . 1D **89**
Peabody Ct. *EC1* *4A* **10**
   (off Roscoe St.)
SE5 . . . . *4F* **91**
   (off Kimpton Rd.)
Peabody Est. E1 . . . . *1F* **79**
   (off Glamis Pl.)
E2 . . . . *1D* **65**
   (off Minerva St.)
EC1 . . . . 4A **10**
   (off Dufferin St.,
   not continuous)
EC1 . . . . *4C* **8**
   (off Farringdon La.)
N1 . . . . 5E **49**
SE1 . . . . 2C **24** *(2C* **76***)*
   (Duchy St.)
SE1 . . . . 2F **25** *(2E* **77***)*
   (Gt. Guildford St.)
SE1 . . . . 3A **26**
   (Mint St.)
SE24 . . . . 5D **105**
SW1 . . . . *5E* **75**
   (off Vauxhall Bri. Rd.)
SW3 . . . . 2A **88**
Peabody Est. *SW6* *2C* **86**
   (off Lillie Rd.)

Peabody Est. SW11 . . . 2A **102**
W6 . . . . 1E **85**
W10 . . . . 4E **57**
Peabody Hill SE21 . . . 1D **119**
Peabody Sq.
SE1 . . . . 4D **25** *(3D* **77***)*
   (not continuous)
Peabody Ter. *EC1* *4C* **8**
   (off Farringdon La.)
Peabody Twr. *EC1* *4A* **10**
   (off Golden La.)
Peabody Trust *SE17* . . . *5F* **77**
   (off Rodney Rd.)
Peabody Yd. N1 . . . . . 5E **49**
Peachey Edwards Ho.
E2 . . . . 2D **65**
   (off Teesdale St.)
Peach Gro. E11 . . . . . 5F **39**
Peach Rd. W10 . . . . . 2F **57**
Peachum Rd. SE3 . . . 2B **96**
Peachwalk M. E3 . . . . 1F **65**
Peacock St. SE17 . . . 5D **77**
   (off Portugal St.)
Peacock Theatre *3F* **15**
   (off Portugal St.)
Peacock Wlk. E16 . . . . 5D **69**
   (off Mortlake Rd.)
N6 . . . . 2D **33**
Peacock Yd. *SE17* *5D* **77**
   (off Iliffe St.)
Peak, The SE26 . . . . . 3E **121**
Peak Fitness
Crossharbour 3D **81**
Peak Hill SE26 . . . . . 4E **121**
Peak Hill Av.
SE26 . . . . 4E **121**
Peak Hill Gdns.
SE26 . . . . 4E **121**
Peak Ho. *N4* *3E* **35**
   (off Woodberry Down Est.)
Pearcefield Av.
SE23 . . . . 1E **121**
Pear Cl. SE14 . . . . . . 3A **94**
Pear Ct. *SE15* *3B* **92**
   (off Thruxton Way)
Pearcroft Rd. E11 . . . . 4F **39**
Peardon St. SW8 . . . . 5D **89**
Pearfield Rd.
SE23 . . . . 3A **122**
Pearl Cl. NW2 . . . . . . 2F **29**
Pearl St. E1 . . . . 2D **79**
Pearman St.
SE1 . . . . 5C **24** *(4C* **76***)*
Pear Pl. SE1 . . . 3B **24** *(3C* **76***)*
Pear Rd. E11 . . . . 5F **39**
Pearscroft Ct. SW6 . . . 4D **87**
Pearscroft Rd. SW6 . . . 4D **87**
Pearse St. SE15 . . . . . 2A **92**
Pearson Cl. *SE5* *4E* **91**
   (off Camberwell New Rd.)
Pearson M. *SW4* *1F* **103**
   (off Slievemore Cl.)
Pearson's Av. SE14 . . . 4C **94**
Pearson St. E2 . . . . . . 1B **64**
Peartree SE26 . . . . . . 5A **122**
Peartree Av. SW17 . . . 3E **115**
Pear Tree Cl. E2 . . . . . 5B **50**
Pear Tree Ct.
EC1 . . . . 4C **8** *(3C* **62***)*
Pear Tree Ho. SE4 . . . 1B **108**
Peartree La. E1 . . . . . 1E **79**

Pear Tree St.
EC1 . . . . 3E **9** *(3E* **63***)*
Peartree Way SE10 . . . 5C **82**
Peary Ho. NW10 . . . . . 4A **42**
Peary Pl. E2 . . . . 2E **65**
Peckarmans Wood
SE26 . . . . 3C **120**
Peckett Sq. N5 . . . . . . 1E **49**
Peckford Pl. SW9 . . . . 5C **90**
PECKHAM 4C **92**
Peckham Gro. SE15 . . . 3A **92**
Peckham High St.
SE15 . . . . 4C **92**
Peckham Hill St.
SE15 . . . . 3C **92**
Peckham Pk. Rd.
SE15 . . . . 3C **92**
Peckham Pulse Health &
Leisure Cen. 4C **92**
Peckham Rd. SE5 . . . . 4A **92**
SE15 . . . . 4A **92**
Peckham Rye SE15 . . . 1C **106**
SE22 . . . . 2C **106**
Peckham Sq. SE15 . . . 4C **92**
Pecks Yd. *E1* *5F* **11**
   (off Hanbury St.)
Peckwater St. NW5 . . . 2E **47**
Pedlar's Wlk. N7 . . . . . 2B **48**
Pedley St. E1 . . . . 3B **64**
Pedro St. E5 . . . . 5F **37**
Pedworth Gdns.
SE16 . . . . 5E **79**
Peek Cres. SW19 . . . . 5F **113**
Peel Gro. E2 . . . . 1E **65**
   (not continuous)
Peel Pas. W8 . . . . 2C **72**
Peel Pct. NW6 . . . . . . 1C **58**
Peel St. W8 . . . . 2C **72**
Peerless St.
EC1 . . . . 2B **10** *(2F* **63***)*
Pegasus Cl. N16 . . . . . 1F **49**
Pegasus Ct. *NW10* *2D* **57**
   (off Trenmar Gdns.)
Pegasus Ho. *E1* *3F* **65**
   (off Beaumont Sq.)
Pegasus Pl. SE11 . . . . 2C **90**
SW6 . . . . 4C **86**
Pegley Gdns. SE12 . . . 2C **124**
Pekin Cl. *E14* *5C* **66**
   (off Pekin St.)
Pekin St. E14 . . . . 5C **66**
Peldon Wlk. *N1* *5D* **49**
   (off Popham St.)
Pelham Cl. SE5 . . . . . 1A **106**
Pelham Ct. *SW3* *5A* **74**
   (off Fulham Rd.)
Pelham Cres. SW7 . . . 5A **74**
Pelham Ho. *W14* *5B* **72**
   (off Mornington Av.)
Pelham Pl. SW7 . . . . . 5A **74**
Pelham St. SW7 . . . . . 5F **73**
Pelican Est. SE15 . . . . 4B **92**
Pelican Ho. SE8 . . . . . 5B **80**
Pelican Pas. E1 . . . . . 3E **65**
Pelican Wlk. SW9 . . . . 2D **105**
Pelican Wharf *E1* *2E* **79**
   (off Wapping Wall)
Pelier St. SE17 . . . . . . 2E **91**
Pelinore Rd. SE6 . . . . 2A **124**
Pella Ho. SE11 . . . . . . 1B **90**

Pellant Rd. SW6 . . . . 3A 86
Pellatt Rd. SE22 . . . . . . 3B 106
Pellerin Rd. N16 . . . . 2A 50
Pellew Ho. E1 . . . . 3D 65
  (off Somerford St.)
Pelling St. E14 . . . . 5C 66
Pelly Rd. E13 . . . . 5C 54
  (not continuous)
Pelter St. E2 . . . 1F 11 (2B 64)
  (not continuous)
Pelton Rd. SE10 . . . . 1A 96
Pember Rd. NW10 . . . . . . 2F 57
Pemberton Ct. E1 . . . . . . 2F 65
  (off Portelet Rd.)
Pemberton Gdns.
  N19 . . . . 5E 33
Pemberton Ho.
  SE26 . . . . 4C 120
  (off High Level Dr.)
Pemberton Pl. E8 . . . . . . 4D 51
Pemberton Rd. N4 . . . . . 1C 34
Pemberton Row
  EC4 . . . . 2C 16 (5C 62)
Pemberton Ter. N19 . . . . . 5E 33
Pembridge Cres.
  W11 . . . . 1C 72
Pembridge Gdns. W2 . . . 1C 72
Pembridge M. W11 . . . . . 1C 72
Pembridge Pl.
  SW15 . . . . 3C 100
  W2 . . . . 1C 72
Pembridge Rd. W11 . . . . 1C 72
Pembridge Sq. W2 . . . . . 1C 72
Pembridge Vs. W2 . . . . . 1C 72
  W11 . . . . 1C 72
Pembroke Av. N1 . . . . . . 5A 48
Pembroke Bldgs.
  NW10 . . . . 2C 56
Pembroke Cl.
  SW1 . . . . . . 4C 20 (3C 74)
Pembroke Cotts. W8 . . . 4C 72
  (off Pembroke Sq.)
Pembroke Gdns. W8 . . . 5B 72
Pembroke Gdns. Cl.
  W8 . . . . 4C 72
Pembroke Ho. W2 . . . . . 5D 59
  (off Hallfield Est.)
Pembroke M. E3 . . . . 2A 66
  W8 . . . . 4C 72
Pembroke Pl. W8 . . . . . . 4C 72
Pembroke Rd. E17 . . . . . 1D 39
  N15 . . . . 1B 36
  W8 . . . . 5B 72
Pembroke Sq. W8 . . . . . 4C 72
Pembroke St. N1 . . . . . . 4A 48
  (not continuous)
Pembroke Studios
  W8 . . . . 4B 72
Pembroke Ter. NW8 . . . . 5F 45
  (off Queen's Ter.)
Pembroke Vs. W8 . . . . . 5C 72
Pembroke Wlk. W8 . . . . . 5C 72
Pembroke M. CW11 . . . 2F 101
Pembry Cl. SW9 . . . . . . 4C 90
Pembury Cl. E5 . . . . 2D 51
Pembury Pl. E5 . . . . 2D 51
Pembury Rd. E5 . . . . 2D 51
Pemell Cl. E1 . . . . 3E 65
Pemell Ho. E1 . . . . 3E 65
  (off Pemell Cl.)

Penally Pl. N1 . . . . 5F 49
Penang Ho. E1 . . . . 2D 79
  (off Prusom St.)
Penang St. E1 . . . . 2D 79
Penarth Cen. SE15 . . . . . 2E 93
Penarth St. SE15 . . . . . . 2E 93
Penberth Rd. SE6 . . . . . 2E 123
Pencombe M. W11 . . . . . 1B 72
Pencraig Way SE15 . . . . 2D 93
Penda's Mead E9 . . . . . . 1A 52
Pendennis Ho. SE8 . . . . 5A 80
Pendennis Rd.
  SW16 . . . . 4A 118
Penderry Ri. SE6 . . . . . 2F 123
Penderyn Way N7 . . . . . . 1F 47
Pendle Ho. SE26 . . . . . 3C 120
Pendle Rd. SW16 . . . . . 5D 117
Pendlestone Rd. E17 . . . 1D 39
Pendragon Rd.
  BR1: Brom 3B 124
Pendragon Wlk. NW9 . . . 1A 28
Pendrell Ho. WC2 . . . . . 3C 14
  (off New Compton St.)
Pendrell Rd. SE4 . . . . . . 5A 94
Pendulum M. E8 . . . . . . 2B 50
Penerley Rd. SE6 . . . . . 1D 123
Penfield Lodge W9 . . . . 4C 58
  (off Admiral Wlk.)
Penfields Ho. N7 . . . . . . 3A 48
Penfold Pl. NW1 . . . . 4A 60
Penfold St. NW1 . . . . 4A 60
  NW8 . . . . 3F 59
Penford Gdns. SE9 . . . . 1F 111
Penford St. SE5 . . . . 5D 91
Penge Ho. SW11 . . . . . . 1F 101
Penge Rd. E13 . . . . 5E 55
Penhall Rd. SE7 . . . . 5F 83
Penhurst Pl. SE1 . . . . . . 5A 24
Peninsula Apartments
  W2 . . . . 4A 60
  (off Praed St.)
Peninsula Ct. E14 . . . . . 4D 81
  (off E. Ferry Rd.)
Peninsula Hgts. SE1 . . . 1A 90
Peninsular Pk. SE7 . . . . 5C 82
Peninsular Pk. Rd.
  SE7 . . . . 5C 82
Penley Ct.
  WC2 . . . . . . 4A 16 (1B 76)
Penmayne Ho. SE11 . . . 1C 90
  (off Kennings Way)
Pennack Rd. SE15 . . . . . 2B 92
Penn Almshouses
  SE10 . . . . 4E 95
  (off Greenwich Sth. St.)
Pennant M. W8 . . . . 5D 73
Pennard Mans. W12 . . . 3E 71
  (off Goldhawk Rd.)
Pennard Rd. W12 . . . . . . 3E 71
Penner Cl. SW19 . . . . . 2A 114
Pennethorne Cl. E9 . . . . 5E 51
Pennethorne Ho.
  SW11 . . . . 1F 101
Pennethorne Rd.
  SE15 . . . . 3D 93
Penn Ho. NW8 . . . . 3A 60
  (off Mallory St.)
Pennine Dr. NW2 . . . . . . 4F 29
Pennine La. NW2 . . . . . . 4A 30
Pennine Pde. NW2 . . . . . 4A 30

Pennington Cl.
  SE27 . . . . 4F 119
Pennington Ct. SE16 . . . 2A 80
Pennington St. E1 . . . . . 1D 79
Pennington Way
  SE12 . . . . 2D 125
Penn Rd. N7 . . . . 2A 48
Penn St. N1 . . . . 5F 49
Pennyfields E14 . . . . 1C 80
  (not continuous)
Pennyford Ct. NW8 . . . . 3F 59
  (off St John's Wood Rd.)
Penny M. SW12 . . . . . . 5D 103
Pennymoor Wlk. W9 . . . 3B 58
  (off Ashmore Rd.)
Penpoll Rd. E8 . . . . 3D 51
Penrith Cl. SW15 . . . . . 3A 100
Penrith Pl. SE27 . . . . . . 2D 119
Penrith Rd. N15 . . . . 1F 35
Penrith St. SW16 . . . . . 5E 117
Penrose Gro. SE17 . . . . 1E 91
Penrose Ho. SE17 . . . . . 1E 91
  (not continuous)
Penrose St. SE17 . . . . . . 1E 91
Penryn Ho. SE11 . . . . . . 1D 91
  (off Seaton Cl.)
Penryn St. NW1 . . . . 1F 61
Pensbury Pl. SW8 . . . . . 5E 89
Pensbury St. SW8 . . . . . 5E 89
Penshurst NW5 . . . . 3C 46
Penshurst Ho. SE15 . . . 2E 93
  (off Lovelinch Cl.)
Penshurst Rd. E9 . . . . . 4F 51
Pentland Cl. NW11 . . . . 4A 30
Pentland Gdns.
  SW18 . . . . 4E 101
Pentland St. SW18 . . . . 4E 101
Pentlow St. SW15 . . . . . 1E 99
Pentney Rd. SW12 . . . . 1E 117
Penton Gro. N1 . . . . 1C 62
Penton Ho. N1 . . . . 1B 8
  (off Pentonville Rd.)
Penton Pl. SE17 . . . . . . 1D 91
Penton Ri.
  WC1 . . . . 1A 8 (2B 62)
Penton St. N1 . . . . 1C 62
PENTONVILLE 1B 62
Pentonville Rd.
  N1 . . . . 1F 7 (1B 62)
Pentridge St. SE15 . . . . 3B 92
Penwith Rd. SW18 . . . . 2C 114
Penwood Ho. SW15 . . . 4B 98
Penwortham Rd.
  SW16 . . . . 5D 117
Penywern Rd. SW5 . . . . 1C 86
Penzance Ho. SE11 . . . 1C 90
  (off Seaton Cl.)
Penzance Pl. W11 . . . . . 2A 72
Penzance St. W11 . . . . . 2A 72
Peony Gdns. W12 . . . . . 1C 70
Peperfield WC1 . . . . 2F 7
  (off Cromer St.)
Pepler Ho. W10 . . . . 3A 58
  (off Wornington Rd.)
Pepler M. SE5 . . . . 1B 92
Pepler Rd. NW6 . . . . 1F 57
Peppermead Sq.
  SE13 . . . . 3C 108
Peppermint Pl. E11 . . . . 5A 40

Pepper St. E14 . . . . 4D **81**
SE1 . . . . 3F **25** (3E **77**)
Peppie Cl. N16 . . . . 4A **36**
Pepys Cres. E16 . . . . . . 2C **82**
Pepys Ho. E2 . . . . 2E **65**
(off Kirkwall Pl.)
Pepys Rd. SE14 . . . . 4F **93**
Pepys St.
EC3 . . . . . . 4E **19** (1A **78**)
Perceval Av. NW3 . . . . . 2A **46**
Perch St. E8 . . . . 1B **50**
Percival David Foundation of
Chinese Art 3C **6**
Percival St.
EC1 . . . . 3D **9** (3D **63**)
Percy Cir.
WC1 . . . . . . 1A **8** (2B **62**)
Percy Laurie Ho.
SW15 . . . . 2F **99**
(off Nursery Cl.)
Percy M. W1 . . . . 1B **14**
Percy Pas. W1 . . . . 1B **14**
Percy Rd. E11 . . . . 2A **40**
E16 . . . . 4A **68**
W12 . . . . 3C **70**
Percy St. W1 . . 1B **14** (4F **61**)
Percy Yd.
WC1 . . . . . . 1A **8** (2B **62**)
Peregrine Cl. NW10 . . . . 2A **42**
Peregrine Ho. SE8 . . . . . 2C **94**
(off Edward St.)
Peregrine Ho. EC1 . . . . . 1E **9**
SW16 . . . . 4B **118**
Perham Rd. W14 . . . . . . 1A **86**
Perifield SE21 . . . . 1E **119**
Periton Rd. SE9 . . . . 2F **111**
Perkins Ho. E14 . . . . 4B **66**
(off Wallwood St.)
Perkin's Rents
SW1 . . . . . . 5B **22** (4F **75**)
Perkins Sq.
SE1 . . . . . . 1A **26** (2E **77**)
Perks Cl. SE3 . . . . 1A **110**
Perley Ho. E3 . . . . 4B **66**
(off Weatherley Cl.)
Perran Rd. SW2 . . . . 1D **119**
Perren St. NW5 . . . . 3D **47**
Perrers Rd. W6 . . . . 5D **71**
Perring Est. E3 . . . . 4C **66**
(off Gale St.)
Perrin Ho. NW6 . . . . 2C **58**
(off Malvern Rd.)
Perrin's Ct. NW3 . . . . . . 1E **45**
Perrin's La. NW3 . . . . . . 1E **45**
Perrin's Wlk. NW3 . . . . . 1E **45**
Perronet Ho. SE1 . . . . . . 5E **25**
Perry Av. W3 . . . . 5A **56**
Perry Ct. E14 . . . . 1C **94**
(off Maritime Quay)
N15 . . . . 1A **36**
Perryfield Way NW9 . . . . 1B **28**
Perry Hill SE6 . . . . 3B **122**
Perry Lodge E12 . . . . . . 3F **41**
Perrymead St. SW6 . . . . 4C **86**
Perryn Ho. W3 . . . . 1A **70**
Perryn Rd. SE16 . . . . . . 4D **79**
W3 . . . . 2A **70**
Perry Ri. SE23 . . . . 3A **122**
Perry's Pl.
W1 . . . . 2B **14** (5F **61**)

Perry Va. SE23 . . . . 2E **121**
Persant Rd. SE6 . . . . . . 2A **124**
Perseverance Pl.
SW9 . . . . 3C **90**
Perseverance Works
E2 . . . . 1E **11**
(off Kingsland Rd.)
Perth Av. NW9 . . . . 2A **28**
Perth Cl. SE5 . . . . 2F **105**
Perth Ho. N1 . . . . 4B **48**
(off Bemerton Est.)
Perth Rd. E10 . . . . 3A **38**
E13 . . . . 1D **69**
N4 . . . . 3C **34**
Perystreete SE23 . . . . . . 2E **121**
Peter Av. NW10 . . . . 4D **43**
Peter Best Ho. E1 . . . . . . 5D **65**
(off Nelson St.)
Peterboat Cl. SE10 . . . . . 5A **82**
Peterborough Ct.
EC4 . . . . . . 3C **16** (5C **62**)
Peterborough M.
SW6 . . . . 5C **86**
Peterborough Rd.
E10 . . . . 1E **39**
SW6 . . . . 5C **86**
Peterborough Vs.
SW6 . . . . 4D **87**
Peter Butler Ho. SE1 . . . . 3C **78**
(off Wolseley St.)
Peterchurch Ho.
SE15 . . . . 2D **93**
(off Commercial Way)
Petergate SW11 . . . . . . 2E **101**
Peter Heathfield Ho.
E15 . . . . 5F **53**
(off Wise Rd.)
Peter Ho. SW8 . . . . 3A **90**
(off Luscombe Way)
Peterley Bus. Cen.
E2 . . . . 1D **65**
Peter Pan Statue 2F **73**
Peter Scott Vis. Cen., The
. . . . 4D **85**
Peters Ct. W2 . . . . 5D **59**
(off Porchester St.)
Petersfield Ri.
SW15 . . . . 1D **113**
Petersham Ho. SW7 . . . . 5F **73**
(off Kendrick M.)
Petersham La. SW7 . . . . 4E **73**
Petersham M. SW7 . . . . . 4E **73**
Petersham Pl. SW7 . . . . . 4E **73**
Peter's Hill
EC4 . . . . . . 4F **17** (1E **77**)
Peter Shore Ct. E1 . . . . . 4F **65**
(off Beaumont Sq.)
Peter's La.
EC1 . . . . 5E **9** (4D **63**)
(not continuous)
Peter's Path SE26 . . . . . 4D **121**
Peterstow Cl. SW19 . . . . 2A **114**
Peter St. W1 . . . 4B **14** (1F **75**)
Petherton Ct. NW10 . . . . 5F **43**
(off Tiverton Rd.)
Petherton Ho. N4 . . . . . . 3E **35**
(off Woodberry Down Est.)
Petherton Rd. N5 . . . . . . 2E **49**
Petiver Cl. E9 . . . . 4E **51**
Petley Rd. W6 . . . . 2F **85**

Peto Pl. NW1 . . . 3E **5** (3D **61**)
Peto St. Nth. E16 . . . . . . 5B **68**
Petrie Cl. NW2 . . . . 3A **44**
Petrie Mus. of
Egyptian Archaeology
. . . . 4B **6**
Petros Gdns. NW3 . . . . . 3E **45**
Petticoat La.
E1 . . . . 1F **19** (4A **64**)
Petticoat Lane Market
. . . . 2F **19**
(off Middlesex St.)
Petticoat Sq.
E1 . . . . 2F **19** (5B **64**)
Petticoat Twr. E1 . . . . . . 2F **19**
Pettiward Cl. SW15 . . . . 2E **99**
Pett St. SE18 . . . . 5F **83**
Petty France
SW1 . . . . . . 5A **22** (4E **75**)
Petworth St. SW11 . . . . . 4A **88**
Petyt Pl. SW3 . . . . 2A **88**
Petyward SW3 . . . . 5A **74**
Pevensey Ho. E1 . . . . . . 4F **65**
(off Ben Jonson Rd.)
Pevensey Rd. E7 . . . . . . 1B **54**
SW17 . . . . 4F **115**
Peveril Ho. SE1 . . . . 5C **26**
Peyton Pl. SE10 . . . . . . 3E **95**
Pharamond NW2 . . . . . . 3F **43**
Pheasant Cl. E16 . . . . . . 5D **69**
Phelp St. SE17 . . . . 2F **91**
Phene St. SW3 . . . . 2A **88**
Philadelphia Ct.
SW10 . . . . 3E **87**
(off Uverdale Rd.)
Philbeach Gdns. SW5 . . . 1C **86**
Phil Brown Pl. SW8 . . . . 1D **103**
(off Wandsworth Rd.)
Philchurch Pl. E1 . . . . . . 5C **64**
Philip Ct. W2 . . . . 4F **59**
(off Hall Pl.)
Philip Ho. NW6 . . . . 5D **45**
(off Mortimer Pl.)
Philip Jones Ct. N4 . . . . . 3B **34**
Philip Mole Ho. W9 . . . . . 3C **58**
(off Chippenham Rd.)
Philippa Gdns. SE9 . . . . 3F **111**
Philip St. E13 . . . . 3C **68**
Philip Wlk. SE15 . . . . . . 1C **106**
(not continuous)
Phillimore Gdns.
NW10 . . . . 5E **43**
W8 . . . . 3C **72**
Phillimore Gdns. Cl.
W8 . . . . 4C **72**
Phillimore Pl. W8 . . . . . . 3C **72**
Phillimore Ter. W8 . . . . . 4C **72**
(off Allen St.)
Phillimore Wlk. W8 . . . . . 4C **72**
Phillipp St. N1 . . . . 5A **50**
Philpot La.
EC3 . . . . . . 4D **19** (1A **78**)
Philpot Sq. SW6 . . . . . . 1D **101**
Philpot St. E1 . . . . 5D **65**
Phineas Pett Rd.
SE9 . . . . 1F **111**
Phipps Ho. SE7 . . . . 1D **97**
(off Woolwich Rd.)
W12 . . . . 1D **71**
(off White City Est.)

Phipp St.
EC2 . . . . 3D **11** (3A **64**)
Phoebeth Rd.
SE4 . . . . 3C **108**
Phoenix Bus. Cen.
E3 . . . . 4C **66**
(off Bow Comn. La.)
Phoenix Cl. E8 . . . . 5B **50**
Phoenix Ct. E1 . . . . 3D **65**
(off Buckhurst St.)
E14 . . . . 5C **80**
NW1 . . . . 1C **6**
(off Purchese St.)
SE14 . . . . 2A **94**
(off Chipley St.)
Phoenix Lodge Mans.
W6 . . . . 5F **71**
(off Brook Grn.)
Phoenix Pk. NW2 . . . . . 4C **28**
Phoenix Pl.
WC1 . . . . 3A **8** (3B **62**)
Phoenix Rd.
NW1 . . . . 1B **6** (2F **61**)
Phoenix Sports &
Fitness Cen. 1C **70**
Phoenix St.
WC2 . . . . 3C **14** (5F **61**)
Phoenix Theatre 3C **14**
(off Charing Cross Rd.)
Phoenix Wharf E1 . . . . 2D **79**
(off Wapping High St.)
Phoenix Wharf Rd.
SE1 . . . . 4F **27**
Phoenix Yd. WC1 . . . . . . 2A **8**
Photographers' Gallery
. . . . 4D **15**
(off Gt. Newport St.)
Physic Pl. SW3 . . . . . . 2B **88**
Piazza, The WC2 . . . . . 4E **15**
(not continuous)
Piccadilly
W1 . . . . 2E **21** (2D **75**)
Piccadilly Arc. SW1 . . . 1F **21**
Piccadilly Circus
. . . . 5B **14** (1F **75**)
Piccadilly Cir.
W1 . . . . 5B **14** (1F **75**)
Piccadilly Pl. W1 . . . . . 5A **14**
Piccadilly Theatre 4A **14**
(off Denman St.)
Pickard St.
EC1 . . . . 1E **9** (2D **63**)
Pickering Cl. E9 . . . . . . 4F **51**
Pickering Ho. W2 . . . . . 5E **59**
(off Hallfield Est.)
Pickering M. W2 . . . . . . 5D **59**
Pickering Pl. SW1 . . . . . 2A **22**
Pickering St. N1 . . . . . . 5D **49**
Pickets St. SW12 . . . . 5D **103**
Picketts Ter. SE22 . . . . 3C **106**
Pickfords Wharf N1 . . . . 1E **63**
SE1 . . . . 1B **26** (2F **77**)
Pickwick Ho. SE16 . . . . 3C **78**
(off George Row)
Pickwick Rd. SE21 . . . . 5F **105**
Pickwick St.
SE1 . . . . 4F **25** (3E **77**)
Pickworth Cl. SW8 . . . . 3A **90**

Picton Pl.
W1 . . . . 3C **12** (5C **60**)
Picton St. SE5. . . . . . . 3F **91**
Pied Bull Yard N1 . . . . 5D **49**
(off Theberton St.)
WC1 . . . . 1D **15**
Pier Head E1 . . . . 2D **79**
(not continuous)
Pierhead Wharf E1. . . . 2D **79**
(off Wapping High St.)
Piermont Grn. SE22 . . 3D **107**
Piermont Rd. SE22 . . . 3D **107**
Pierpoint Bldg. E14 . . . 3B **80**
Pierrepont Arc. N1 . . . . 1D **63**
(off Islington High St.)
Pierrepont Row N1 . . . . 1D **63**
(off Camden Pas.)
Pier St. E14 . . . . 5E **81**
(not continuous)
Pier Ter. SW18 . . . . . . 2D **101**
Pietra Lara Bldg. EC1 . . . 3F **9**
(off Pear Tree St.)
Piggott Ho. E2 . . . . 1F **65**
(off Sewardstone Rd.)
Pigott St. E14 . . . . 5C **66**
Pike Cl. BR1: Brom . . 5D **125**
Pikemans Ct. SW5 . . . . 5C **72**
(off W. Cromwell Rd.)
Pikethorne SE23 . . . . . 2F **121**
Pilgrimage St.
SE1 . . . . 4B **26** (3F **77**)
Pilgrim Hill SE27 . . . . 4E **119**
Pilgrim Ho. SE1 . . . . . . 5C **26**
(off Lansdowne Pl.)
Pilgrims Cloisters
SE5 . . . . 3A **92**
(off Sedgmoor Pl.)
Pilgrim's La. NW3 . . . . . 1F **45**
Pilgrims M. E14 . . . . . . 1A **82**
Pilgrim's Pl. NW3 . . . . . 1F **45**
Pilgrim St.
EC4 . . . . 3D **17** (5D **63**)
Pilgrims Way N19 . . . . . 3F **33**
Pilkington Rd. SE15 . . . 5D **93**
Pilot Cl. SE8 . . . . 2B **94**
Pilot Ind. Cen. NW10 . . 3A **56**
Pilsden Cl. SW19 . . . . 1F **113**
Pilton Pl. SE17 . . . . . . 1E **91**
(off King & Queen St.)
Pilton Pl. Est. SE17 . . . 1E **91**
PIMLICO 1E **89**
Pimlico Ho. SW1 . . . . . 1D **89**
(off Ebury Bri. Rd.)
Pimlico Rd. SW1 . . . . . 1C **88**
Pimlico Wlk. N1 . . . . . . 1D **11**
Pinchin & Johnsons Yd.
E1 . . . . 1C **78**
(off Pinchin St.)
Pinchin St. E1 . . . . 1C **78**
Pincombe Ho. SE17 . . . 1F **91**
(off Orb St.)
Pincott Pl. SE4 . . . . . . 1F **107**
Pindar St.
EC2 . . . . 5D **11** (4A **64**)
Pindock M. W9 . . . . . . 3D **59**
Pineapple Ct. SW1 . . . . 5A **22**
Pine Av. E15 . . . . 2F **53**
Pine Cl. E10 . . . . 4D **39**
N19 . . . . 4E **33**

Pinedene SE15 . . . . . . 4D **93**
Pinefield Cl. E14 . . . . . 1C **80**
Pine Gro. N4 . . . . 4A **34**
SW19 . . . . 5B **114**
Pine Ho. SE16 . . . . 3E **79**
(off Ainsty Est.)
W10 . . . . 3A **58**
(off Droop St.)
Pinehurst Ct. W11 . . . . 5B **58**
(off Colville Gdns.)
Pinemartin Cl. NW2 . . . 5E **29**
Pine M. NW10 . . . . 1F **57**
Pine Rd. NW2 . . . . 1E **43**
Pine St. EC1 . . . 3C **8** (3C **62**)
Pine Tree Ho. SE14 . . . 3F **93**
(off Reaston St.)
Pinewood Cl. SW4 . . . . 4F **103**
Pinfold Rd. SW16 . . . . 4A **118**
Pinkerton Pl. SW16 . . . 4F **117**
Pinnace Ho. E14. . . . . . 4E **81**
(off Manchester Rd.)
Pinnell Rd. SE9 . . . . . . 2F **111**
Pinner Ct. NW8 . . . . . . 3F **59**
(off St John's Wood Rd.)
Pinners Pas. EC2 . . . . . 2C **18**
(off Austin Friars)
Pintail Cl. E6 . . . . 4F **69**
Pintail Ct. SE8 . . . . 2B **94**
(off Pilot Cl.)
Pinter Ho. SW9 . . . . . . 5A **90**
(off Grantham Rd.)
Pinto Way SE3 . . . . 2D **111**
Pioneer St. SE15 . . . . . 4C **92**
Pioneer Way W12 . . . . 5D **57**
Piper Cl. N7 . . . . 2B **48**
Pipers Ho. SE10 . . . . . . 1F **95**
(off Collington St.)
Pippin Cl. NW2 . . . . . . 5C **28**
Pirbright Rd. SW18 . . . 1B **114**
Pirie Cl. SE5 . . . . 1F **105**
Pirie St. E16 . . . . 2D **83**
Pitcairn Ho. E9 . . . . 4E **51**
Pitchford St. E15 . . . . . 4F **53**
Pitfield Est.
N1 . . . . 1D **11** (2A **64**)
Pitfield St.
N1 . . . . 1D **11** (2A **64**)
Pitfold Cl. SE12 . . . . . . 4C **110**
Pitfold Rd. SE12. . . . . . 4C **110**
Pitman Ho. SE8 . . . . . . 4C **94**
Pitman St. SE5 . . . . 3E **91**
(not continuous)
Pitmaston Ho. SE13. . . . 5E **95**
(off Lewisham Rd.)
Pitsea Pl. E1 . . . . 5F **65**
Pitsea St. E1 . . . . 5F **65**
Pitt Cres. SW19 . . . . . 4D **115**
Pitt's Head M.
W1 . . . . 2C **20** (2C **74**)
Pitt St. W8 . . . . 3C **72**
Pixley St. E14 . . . . 5B **66**
Place, The 2C **6**
(off Duke's Rd.)
Plaisterers Highwalk
EC2 . . . . 1F **17**
(off Noble St.)
PLAISTOW 1D **69**
Plaistow Gro. E15 . . . . 5B **54**
Plaistow Pk. Rd. E13. . . 1D **69**
Plaistow Rd. E15 . . . . . 5B **54**

Plaistow Wharf E16 . . . . . 3C 82
Plane St. SE26 . . . . . . 3D 121
Planetree Ct. *W6* 5F 71
   (off Brook Grn.)
Plane Tree Ho. *SE8* 2A 94
   (off Etta St.)
Plane Tree Wlk.
  SE19 . . . . 5A 120
Plantain Gdns. *E11* 5F 39
   (off Hollydown Way,
   not continuous)
Plantain Pl.
  SE1 . . . . 3B 26 (3F 77)
Plantation, The SE3 . . . . 5C 96
Plantation Pl. EC3 . . . . 4D 19
Plantation Wharf
  SW11 . . . . 1E 101
Plasel Ct. *E13* 5D 55
   (off Pawsey Cl.)
PLASHET 3F 55
Plashet Gro. E6 . . . . 5E 55
Plashet Rd. E13 . . . . 5C 54
Plassy Rd. SE6 . . . . . . 5D 109
Plate Ho. *E14* 1D 95
   (off Burrells Wharf Sq.)
Platina St. EC2 . . . . 3C 10
Plato Rd. SW2 . . . . 2A 104
Platt, The SW15 . . . . . . 1F 99
Platt's La. NW3 . . . . 1C 44
Platt St. NW1 . . . . 1F 61
Plaxton Ct. E11 . . . . 5B 40
Playfair Ho. *E14* 5C 66
   (off Saracen St.)
Playfair Mans. *W14* 2A 86
   (off Queen's Club Gdns.)
Playfair St. W6 . . . . 1E 85
Playfield Cres. SE22 . . 3B 106
Playford Rd. N4 . . . . 4B 34
   (not continuous)
Playgreen Way SE6 . . 3C 122
Playhouse Ct. *SE1* 3F 25
   (off Southwark Bri. Rd.)
Playhouse Theatre *1E 23*
   (off Northumberland Av.)
Playhouse Yd.
  EC4 . . . . 3D 17 (5D 63)
Playscape Pro Racing
  Karting Track 5A 118
Plaza Cinema *5B 14*
   (off Regent St.)
Plaza Pde. NW6 . . . . . . 1D 59
Plaza Shop. Cen., The
  W1 . . . . 2A 14 (5E 61)
Pleasance, The
  SW15 . . . . 2D 99
Pleasance Rd. SW15 . . 3D 99
Pleasance Theatre *3A 48*
   (off Carpenters M.)
Pleasant Pl. N1 . . . . 4D 49
Pleasant Row NW1 . . . 5D 47
Plender Pl. *NW1* 5F 47
   (off Plender St.)
Plender St. NW1 . . . . . . 5F 47
Pleshey Rd. N7 . . . . 1F 47
Plevna Cres. N15 . . . . . 1A 36
Plevna St. E14 . . . . 4E 81
Pleydell Av. W6 . . . . 5B 70
Pleydell Ct. *EC4* 3C 16
   (off Lombard La.)
Pleydell Est. EC1 . . . . . 2A 10

Pleydell St. EC4 . . . . . . 3C 16
Plimsoll Cl. E14 . . . . . . 5D 67
Plimsoll Rd. N4 . . . . 5C 34
Plough Ct.
  EC3 . . . . 4C 18 (1F 77)
Plough La. SE22 . . . . . 4B 106
Ploughmans Cl.
  NW1 . . . . 5F 47
Plough M. SW11 . . . . . 2F 101
Plough Pl.
  EC4 . . . . 2C 16 (5C 62)
Plough Rd. SW11 . . . . . 1F 101
Plough St. E1 . . . . 5B 64
Plough Ter. SW11 . . . . . 2F 101
Plough Way SE16 . . . . . 5F 79
Plough Yd.
  EC2 . . . . 4E 11 (3A 64)
Plover Ho. *SW9* 3C 90
   (off Brixton Rd.)
Plover Way SE16 . . . . . 4A 80
Plowden Bldgs. EC4 . . 4B 16
Plumber's Row E1 . . . . 4C 64
Plumbridge St. SE10 . . 4E 95
Plume Ho. *SE10* 2D 95
   (off Creek Rd.)
Plummer Rd. SW4 . . . . 5F 103
Plumtree Ct.
  EC4 . . . . 2D 17 (5D 63)
Plymouth Ho. *SE10* 4D 95
   (off Devonshire Dr.)
Plymouth Rd. E16 . . . . 4C 68
Plymouth Wharf E14 . . 5F 81
Plympton Av. NW6 . . . . 4B 44
Plympton Pl. NW8 . . . . 3A 60
Plympton Rd. NW6 . . . . 4B 44
Plympton St. NW8 . . . . 3A 60
Pocklington Ct. *W12* . . 4C 70
   (off Ashchurch Pk. Vs.)
Pocklington St.
  SW15 . . . . 1C 112
Pocklington Lodge
  W12 . . . . 4C 70
Pocock St.
  SE1 . . . . 3D 25 (3D 77)
Podmore Rd. SW18 . . . 2E 101
Poet's Rd. N5 . . . . 2F 49
Point, The *W2*. 5F 59
   (off Nth. Wharf Rd.)
Point Cl. SE10 . . . . 4E 95
Pointers Cl. E14 . . . . . . 1D 95
Point Hill SE10 . . . . 3E 95
Point Pleasant
  SW18 . . . . 2C 100
Point Ter. *E7*. 2D 55
   (off Claremont Rd.)
Point W. SW7 . . . . 5D 73
Poland St.
  W1 . . . . 3A 14 (5B 61)
Polebrook Rd. SE3 . . . 1E 111
Polecroft La. SE6 . . . . 2B 122
Polesworth Ho. *W2* . . . 4C 58
   (off Alfred Rd.)
Pollard Cl. E16 . . . . 1C 82
  N7 . . . . 1B 48
Pollard Ho. *N1* 1F 7
   (off Northdown St.)
Pollard Row E2 . . . . . . 2C 64
Pollard St. E2 . . . . 2C 64

Pollen St.
  W1 . . . . 3F 13 (5E 61)
Pollitt Dr. NW8 . . . . 3F 59
Pollock Ho. *W10* 3A 58
   (off Kensal Rd.)
Pollock's Toy Mus.
   . . . . 5A 6 (4E 61)
Polperro M. SE11 . . . . . 5D 77
Polsted Rd. SE6 . . . . . 5B 108
Polworth Rd. SW16 . . . 5A 118
Polygon, The *NW8* 5F 45
   (off Avenue Rd.)
SW4 . . . . 2E 103
Polygon Rd.
  NW1. . . . . 1B 6 (1F 61)
Pomell Way
  E1. . . . . 2F 19 (5B 64)
Pomeroy Ho. *E2*. 1F 65
   (off St James's Av.)
  W11 . . . . 5A 58
   (off Lancaster Rd.)
Pomeroy St. SE14 . . . . . 3E 93
Pomfret Rd. SE5 . . . . . 1D 105
Pomoja La. N19. . . . . . . 4A 34
Pomona Ho. *SE8* 5A 80
   (off Evelyn St.)
Pond Cl. SE10 . . . . 5C 96
Pond Cotts. SE21 . . . . 1A 120
Ponder St. N7. . . . . 4B 48
   (not continuous)
Pond Farm Est. E5 . . . . . 5E 37
Pondfield Ho. SE27 . . . 5E 119
Pond Ho. SW3 . . . . 5A 74
Pond Mead SE21 . . . . . 4F 105
Pond Pl. SW3. . . . . 5A 74
Pond Rd. E15. . . . . 1A 68
  SE3. . . . . 5B 96
Pond Sq. N6. . . . . 3C 32
Pond St. NW3 . . . . 2A 46
Ponler St. E1 . . . . 5D 65
Ponsard Rd. NW10 . . . . 2D 57
Ponsford St. E9 . . . . 3E 51
Ponsonby Ho. *E2* 1E 65
   (off Bishop's Way)
Ponsonby Pl. SW1 . . . . 1F 89
Ponsonby Rd. SW15 . . 5D 99
Ponsonby Ter. SW1 . . . 1F 89
Pontefract Rd.
  BR1: Brom 5B 124
Ponton Rd. SW8 . . . . . . 3F 89
Pont St. SW1. . 5A 20 (4B 74)
Pont St. M.
  SW1. . . . . . . 5A 20 (4B 74)
Pontypool Pl.
  SE1 . . . . 3D 25 (3D 77)
Pool Cl. BR3: Beck. . . . 5C 122
Pool Ct. SE6 . . . . 2C 122
Poole Ct. *N1*. 4A 50
   (off St Peter's Way)
Poole Ho. SE11 . . . . 4C 76
   (off Lambeth Wlk.)
Poole Rd. E9. . . . . 3F 51
Pooles Bldgs. WC1 . . . . 4B 8
Pooles La. SW10 . . . . . . 3E 87
Pooles Pk. N4 . . . . 4C 34
Poole St. N1. . . . . 5F 49
Pooley Ho. E1. . . . . 2F 65
Pool Ho. *NW8*. 4F 59
   (off Penfold St.)
Poolmans St. SE16. . . . . 3F 79

Poonah St. E1. . . . . 5E 65
Pope Ho. SE5 . . . . 3F 91
(off Elmington Est.)
SE16. . . . . 5D 79
(off Manor Est.)
Pope's Head All.
EC3. . . . . 3C 18 (5F 63)
Pope's Rd. SW9 . . . . . . 1C 104
Pope St. SE1 . . . . 4E 27 (3A 78)
Popham Rd. N1 . . . . 5E 49
Popham St. N1 . . . . 5D 49
(not continuous)
POPLAR 1D 81
Poplar Bath St. E14 . . . . . 5D 67
Poplar Bus. Pk. E14 . . . . . 1E 81
Poplar Ct. E9 . . . . 2B 52
Poplar Ct. SW19. . . . . . 5C 114
Poplar Gro. W6. . . . . 3E 71
Poplar High St. E14 . . . . . 1D 81
Poplar Ho. SE4. . . . . . . 2B 108
(off Wickham Rd.)
SE16 . . . . 3F 79
(off Woodland Cres.)
Poplar M. W12 . . . . 2E 71
Poplar Pl. W2. . . . . 1D 73
Poplar Rd. E12 . . . . 4F 41
SE24 . . . . 2E 105
Poplars Av. NW2. . . . . . . 3E 43
Poplars Rd. E17. . . . . 1D 39
Poplar Wlk. SE24 . . . . . . 1E 105
(not continuous)
Poppins Ct.
EC4 . . . . 3D 17 (5D 63)
Poppleton Rd. E11 . . . . . 1A 40
Porchester Cl. SE5 . . . . . 2E 105
Porchester Ct. W2 . . . . . 1D 73
(off Porchester Gdns.)
Porchester Gdns.
W2 . . . . 1D 73
Porchester Gdns. M.
W2 . . . . 1D 73
Porchester Ga. W2. . . . . 1D 73
(off Bayswater Rd.,
not continuous)
Porchester Ho. SE5 5D 65
(off Philpot St.)
Porchester Leisure Cen.
. . . . 5D 59
Porchester Mead
BR3: Beck. 5D 123
Porchester M. W2 . . . . . 5D 59
Porchester Pl. W2 . . . . . 5A 60
Porchester Rd. W2. . . . . 5D 59
Porchester Sq. W2. . . . . 5D 59
Porchester Ter. W2. . . . . 1E 73
Porchester Ter. Nth.
W2 . . . . 5D 59
Porden Rd. SW2. . . . . . 2B 104
Porlock Ho. SE26 . . . . . 3C 120
Porlock St.
SE1. . . . . 3C 26 (3F 77)
Porson Ct. SE13. . . . . . 1D 109
Portal Q! SE27 . . . . . . 3C 118
Portal Way W3 . . . . 4A 56
Portbury Cl. SE15. . . . . . 4C 92
Port Cres. E13 . . . . 3D 69
Portcullis Ho. SW1 . . . . . 4D 23
Portelet Ct. N1 . . . . 5A 50
(off De Beauvoir Est.)
Portelet Rd. E1 . . . . 2F 65

Porten Ho's. W14. . . . . . 4A 72
(off Porten Rd.)
Porten Rd. W14 . . . . 4A 72
Porters Lodge, The
SW10 . . . . 3E 87
(off Coleridge Gdns.)
Porter Sq. N19. . . . . 3A 34
Porter St.
SE1 . . . . 1A 26 (2E 77)
W1. . . . . 5A 4 (4B 60)
Porters Wlk. E1. . . . . 1D 79
(off Balkan Wlk.)
Porteus Rd. W2 . . . . 4E 59
Portgate Cl. W9 . . . . 3B 58
Porthcawe Rd.
SE26. . . . . 4A 122
Port Ho. E14. . . . . 1D 95
(off Burrells Wharf Sq.)
Portia Ct. SE11 . . . . 1D 91
(off Opal St.)
Portia Way E3 . . . . 3B 66
Porticos, The
SW3 . . . . 2F 87
(off King's Rd.)
Portinscale Rd.
SW15 . . . . 3A 100
Portland Av. N16 . . . . . . 2B 36
Portland Ct. N1 . . . . 4A 50
(off St Peter's Way)
SE1 . . . . 5B 26
(off Gt. Dover St.)
SE14. . . . . 2A 94
(off Whitcher Cl.)
Portland Cres. SE9 . . . . . 2F 125
Portland Gdns. N4. . . . . 1D 35
Portland Gro. SW8. . . . . 4B 90
Portland Ho. SW1. . . . . . 5F 21
Portland M.
W1. . . . . 3A 14 (5E 61)
Portland Pl.
W1. . . . . 4D 5 (3D 61)
Portland Ri. N4 . . . . 3D 35
(not continuous)
Portland Rd.
BR1: Brom 4E 125
SE9 . . . . 2F 125
W11 . . . . 1A 72
Portland Sq. E1. . . . . . . 2D 79
Portland St. SE17. . . . . . 1F 91
Portman Av. SW14. . . . . 1A 98
Portman Cl.
W1. . . . . 2A 12 (5B 60)
Portman Ga. NW1 . . . . . 3A 60
Portman Mans. W1 . . . . 5A 4
(off Chiltern St.)
Portman M. Sth.
W1. . . . . 3B 12 (5C 60)
Portman Pl. E2. . . . . 2E 65
Portman Sq.
W1. . . . . 2B 12 (5C 60)
Portman St.
W1. . . . . 3B 12 (5C 60)
Portman Towers
W1 . . . . 2A 12 (5B 60)
Port Meers Cl. E17. . . . . 1D 38
Portnall Rd. W9. . . . . 1B 58
Portobello Ct. Est.
W11 . . . . 5B 58
Portobello M. W11. . . . . 1C 72

Portobello Rd. W10 . . . . 4A 58
W11 . . . . 5B 58
Portobello Road Market
. . . . 4A 58
Portpool La.
EC1 . . . . 5B 8 (4C 62)
Portree St. E14. . . . . 5F 67
Portsdown Av. NW11. . . 1B 30
Portsdown M. NW11 . . . 1B 30
Portsea Hall W2. . . . . . . 5B 60
(off Portsea Pl.)
Portsea M. W2. . . . . 5A 60
(off Portsea Pl.)
Portsea Pl. W2. . . . . 5A 60
Portslade Rd. SW8. . . . . 5E 89
Portsmouth M. E16 . . . . 2D 83
Portsmouth Rd. SW15. . 5D 99
Portsmouth St.
WC2. . . . . 3F 15 (5B 62)
Portsoken St.
E1. . . . . 4F 19 (1B 78)
Portswood Pl. SW15. . . . 4B 98
Portugal St.
WC2. . . . . 3F 15 (5B 62)
Portway E15. . . . . 5B 54
Portway Gdns. SE18. . . . 3F 97
Pory Ho. SE11. . . . . 5B 76
(off Lambeth Wlk.)
Poseidon Ct. E14. . . . . . 5C 80
(off Homer Dr.)
Postern, The EC2. . . . . . 1A 18
Post Office App. E17 . . . 2D 55
Post Office Ct. EC3. . . . . 3C 18
(off Barbican)
Post Office Way SW8. . . 3F 89
Potier St.
SE1. . . . . 5C 26 (4F 77)
Potterne Cl. SW19. . . . . 5F 99
Potters Flds.
SE1 . . . . 2E 27 (2A 78)
Potter's La. SW16 . . . . . 5F 117
Potters Lodge E14 . . . . . 1E 95
(off Manchester Rd.)
Potters Rd. SW6. . . . . . . 5E 87
Pottery La. W11. . . . . . . 2A 72
Pottery St. SE16. . . . . . . 3D 79
Pott St. E2 . . . . 2D 65
Poulton Cl. E8 . . . . 3D 51
Poultry EC2 . . . . . 3B 18 (5F 63)
Pound La. NW10 . . . . . . 3C 42
Pound Pk. Rd. SE7. . . . . 5F 83
Pountney Rd. SW11. . . . 1C 102
Povey Ho. SE17 . . . . 5A 78
(off Tatum St.)
Powell Ho. W2. . . . . 5D 59
(off Gloucester Ter.)
Powell Rd. E5 . . . . 5D 37
Powell's Wlk. W4. . . . . . 2A 84
Powergate Bus. Pk.
NW10 . . . . 2A 56
Powerleague Soccer Cen.
. . . . 1C 122
Powerscroft Rd. E5 . . . . 1E 51
Powis Ct. W11 . . . . 5B 58
(off Powis Gdns.)
Powis Gdns. NW11 . . . . 2B 30
W11 . . . . 5B 58
Powis M. W11. . . . . 5B 58
Powis Pl. WC1 . . . 4E 7 (3A 62)
Powis Rd. E3 . . . . 2D 67

Powis Sq. W11 . . . . 5B 58
(not continuous)
Powis Ter. W11 . . . . 5B 58
Powlesland Ct. E1 . . . . . 5A 66
(off White Horse Rd.)
Powlett Ho. NW1 . . . . . . 3D 47
(off Powlett Pl.)
Powlett Pl. NW1 . . . . . . 4C 46
(not continuous)
Pownall Rd. E8 . . . . 5B 50
Powster Rd.
BR1: Brom 5C 124
Poynders Ct. SW4 . . . . 4E 103
Poynders Gdns.
SW4 . . . . 5E 103
Poynders Rd. SW4 . . . . 4E 103
Poynings Rd. N19 . . . . . 5E 33
Poynter Ho. NW8 . . . . . 3F 59
(off Fisherton St.)
W11 . . . . 2F 71
(off Queensdale Cres.)
Poyntz Rd. SW11 . . . . . 5B 88
Poyser St. E2 . . . . 1D 65
Praed M. W2 . . . . 5F 59
Praed St. W2 . . . . 5F 59
Pragel St. E13 . . . . 1E 69
Pragnell Rd. SE12 . . . . 2D 125
Prague Pl. SW2 . . . . . . 3A 104
Prah Rd. N4 . . . . 4C 34
Prairie St. SW8 . . . . 5C 88
Pratt M. NW1 . . . . 5E 47
Pratt St. NW1 . . . . 5E 47
Pratt Wlk. SE11 . . . . 5B 76
Prayle Gro. NW2 . . . . . . 3F 29
Preachers Ct. EC1 . . . . . 5E 9
(off Charterhouse Sq.)
Prebend Gdns. W4 . . . . 5B 70
W6 . . . . 5B 70
(not continuous)
Prebend Mans. W4 . . . . 5B 70
(off Chiswick High Rd.)
Prebend St. N1 . . . . 5E 49
Precinct, The N1 . . . . . . 5E 49
Premier Cinema 5C 92
Premier Cnr. W9 . . . . . . 1B 58
Premiere Pl. E14 . . . . . . 1C 80
Premier Ho. N1 . . . . 4D 49
(off Waterloo Ter.)
Premier Pl. SW15 . . . . . 2A 100
Prendergast Rd.
SE3 . . . . 1A 110
Prentice Ct. SW19 . . . . . 5B 114
Prentis Rd. SW16 . . . . . 4F 117
Prentiss Ct. SE7 . . . . . . 5F 83
Presburg St. E5 . . . . 5F 37
Prescot St. E1 . . . . 1B 78
Prescott Ho. SE17 . . . . . 2D 91
(off Hillingdon St.)
Prescott Pl. SW4 . . . . . . 1F 103
Presentation M.
SW2 . . . . 2B 118
President Dr. E1 . . . . . . 2D 79
President Ho.
EC1 . . . . 2E 9 (2D 63)
President Quay E1 . . . . . 2B 78
(off St Katherine's Way)
President St. EC1 . . . . . . 1F 9
Press Ho. NW10 . . . . . . 5A 28
Press Rd. NW10 . . . . . . 5A 28
Prestage Way E14 . . . . . 1E 81

Prestbury Rd. E7 . . . . . . 4E 55
Prested Rd. SW11 . . . . . 2A 102
Preston Cl. SE1 . . . . 5A 78
Preston Dr. E11 . . . . 1E 41
Preston Gdns.
NW10 . . . . 3B 42
Preston Ho. SE1 . . . . . . 5A 78
(off Preston Cl.)
SE1 . . . . 5F 27
(off Stanworth St.)
Preston Pl. NW2 . . . . . . 3C 42
Preston Rd. E11 . . . . . . 1A 40
SE19 . . . . 5D 119
Preston's Rd. E14 . . . . . 1E 81
Preston St. E2 . . . . 1F 65
Prestwich Ter. SW4 . . . . 3E 103
Prestwood Ho. SE16 . . . 4D 79
(off Drummond Rd.)
Prestwood St.
N1 . . . . 1A 10 (1E 63)
Pretoria Rd. E11 . . . . . . 3F 39
E16 . . . . 3B 68
SW16 . . . . 5D 117
Priam Ho. E2 . . . . 1D 65
(off Old Bethnal Grn. Rd.)
Price Cl. SW17 . . . . 3B 116
Price Ho. N1 . . . . 5E 49
(off Britannia Row)
Price's Ct. SW11 . . . . . . 1F 101
Price's St.
SE1 . . . . 2E 25 (2D 77)
Price's Yd. N1 . . . . 5B 48
Prichard Ct. N7 . . . . 3B 48
Prideaux Pl. W3 . . . . . . 1A 70
WC1 . . . . 1A 8 (2B 62)
Prideaux Rd. SW9 . . . . . 1A 104
Priestfield Rd. SE23 . . . 3A 122
Priestley Cl. N16 . . . . . . 2B 36
Priestley Ho. EC1 . . . . . 3A 10
(off Old St.)
Priestley Way NW2 . . . . 3C 28
Priest's Bri. SW14 . . . . . 1A 98
Priest's Ct. EC2 . . . . . . 2F 17
(off Foster La.)
Prima Rd. SW9 . . . . 3C 90
Prime Meridian Line . . . 3F 95
Primrose Cl. E3 . . . . 1C 66
SE6 . . . . 5E 123
Primrose Ct. SW12 . . . . 5F 103
Primrose Gdns. NW3 . . . 3A 46
PRIMROSE HILL 5C 46
Primrose Hill
EC4 . . . . 3C 16 (5C 62)
Primrose Hill Ct.
NW3 . . . . 4B 46
Primrose Hill Rd.
NW3 . . . . 4B 46
Primrose Hill Studios
NW1 . . . . 5C 46
Primrose Mans.
SW11 . . . . 4C 88
Primrose M. NW1 . . . . . 4B 46
(off Sharpleshall St.)
SE3 . . . . 3C 96
Primrose Rd. E10 . . . . . 3D 39
Primrose Sq. E9 . . . . . . 4E 51
Primrose St.
EC2 . . . . 5D 11 (4A 64)
Primrose Wlk. SE14 . . . . 3A 94
Primula St. W12 . . . . . . 5C 56

Prince Albert Ct.
NW8 . . . . 5B 46
(off Prince Albert Rd.)
Prince Albert Rd.
NW1 . . . . 2A 60
NW8 . . . . 2A 60
Prince Arthur M.
NW3 . . . . 1E 45
Prince Arthur Rd.
NW3 . . . . 2E 45
Prince Charles Cinema
. . . . 4C 14
Prince Charles Dr.
NW4 . . . . 2E 29
Prince Charles Rd.
SE3 . . . . 5B 96
Prince Consort Rd.
SW7 . . . . 4E 73
Princedale Rd. W11 . . . . 2A 72
Prince Edward Mans.
W2 . . . . 1C 72
(off Moscow Rd.)
Prince Edward Rd.
E9 . . . . 3B 52
Prince Edward Theatre
. . . . 3C 14
(off Old Compton St.)
Prince George Rd.
N16 . . . . 1A 50
Prince Henry Rd. SE7 . . 3F 97
Prince John Rd.
SE9 . . . . 3F 111
Princelet St.
E1 . . . . 5F 11 (4B 64)
Prince of Orange La.
SE10 . . . . 3E 95
Prince of Wales Dr.
SW8 . . . . 3D 89
SW11 . . . . 4A 88
Prince of Wales Mans.
SW11 . . . . 4C 88
Prince of Wales Pas.
NW1 . . . . 2F 5
Prince of Wales Rd.
E16 . . . . 5E 69
NW5 . . . . 3C 46
SE3 . . . . 5B 96
Prince of Wales Ter.
W4 . . . . 1A 84
W8 . . . . 3D 73
Prince of Wales Theatre
. . . . 5B 14
(off Coventry St.)
Prince Regent Ct.
NW8 . . . . 1A 60
(off Avenue Rd.)
SE16 . . . . 1A 80
(off Edward Sq.)
Prince Regent La.
E13 . . . . 2D 69
E16 . . . . 2D 69
Prince Regent M.
NW1 . . . . 2F 5
Prince Regents Ga.
NW8 . . . . 3A 60
Princes Arc. SW1 . . . . . 1A 22
Princes Cir.
WC2 . . . . 2D 15 (5A 62)
Princes Cl. N4 . . . . 3D 35
SW4 . . . . 1E 103

Prince's Ct. SE16 . . . . . 4B 80
SW3 . . . . 4B 74
(off Brompton Rd.)
Princes Ct. Bus. Cen.
E1 . . . . 1D 79
Prince's Gdns. SW7 . . . 4F 73
Prince's Ga. SW7 . . . . . 3F 73
(not continuous)
Prince's Ga. Ct. SW7 . . 3F 73
Prince's Ga. M.
SW7 . . . . 4F 73
Princes M. W2 . . . . 1D 73
W6 . . . . 1D 85
(off Down Pl.)
Princes Pde. NW11 . . . . 1A 30
(off Golders Grn. Rd.)
Princes Pk. Av.
NW11 . . . . 1A 30
Princes Pl. SW1 . . . . . . 1A 22
W11 . . . . 2A 72
Prince's Ri. SE13 . . . . . 5E 95
Princes Riverside Rd.
SE16 . . . . 2F 79
Princes Rd. SW14 . . . . 1A 98
SW19 . . . . 5C 114
Princess Alice Ho.
W10 . . . . 3E 57
Princess Ct. N6 . . . . . . 2E 33
W1 . . . . 4B 60
(off Bryanston Pl.)
W2 . . . . 1D 73
(off Queensway)
Princess Cres. N4 . . . . 4D 35
Princess Louise Cl.
W2 . . . . 4F 59
Princess Mary Ho.
SW1 . . . . 5F 75
(off Vincent St.)
Princess May Rd.
N16 . . . . 1A 50
Princess M. NW3 . . . . . 2F 45
Princess Sq. W2 . . . . . 1D 73
(not continuous)
Princess Rd. NW1 . . . . 5C 46
NW6 . . . . 1C 58
Princess St.
SE1 . . . . . . 5E 25 (4D 77)
Princes St.
EC2 . . . . 3B 18 (5F 63)
W1 . . . . 3E 13 (5D 61)
Princes Ter. E13 . . . . . 5D 55
Prince's Twr. SE16 . . . . 3E 79
(off Elephant La.)
Prince St. SE8 . . . . 2B 94
Princes Way SW19 . . . . 5F 99
Prince's Yd. W11 . . . . . 2A 72
Princethorpe Ho. W2 . . 4D 59
(off Woodchester Sq.)
Princethorpe Rd.
SE26 . . . . 4F 121
Princeton Cl. SW15 . . . 1F 99
Princeton St.
WC1 . . . . 1F 15 (4B 62)
Principal Sq. E9 . . . . . . 2F 51
Pringle Gdns. SW16 . . . 4E 117
(not continuous)
Printers Inn Ct. EC4 . . 5C 62
Printers M. E3 . . . . 5A 52
Printer St.
EC4 . . . . 2C 16 (5C 62)

Printing Ho. Yd.
E2 . . . . 1E 11 (2A 64)
Printon Ho. E14 . . . . . . 4B 66
(off Wallwood St.)
Print Village SE15 . . . . 5B 92
Printwork Apartments
SE1 . . . . 5D 27
(off Long La.)
Priolo Rd. SE7 . . . . 1E 97
Prior Bolton St.
N1 . . . . 3D 49
Prioress Rd. SE27 . . . . 3D 119
Prioress St.
SE1 . . . . . . 5C 26 (4A 78)
Prior St. SE10 . . . . 3E 95
Priory, The SE3 . . . . . . 2B 110
Priory Apartments, The
SE6 . . . . 1D 123
Priory Av. W4 . . . . 5A 70
Priory Ct. E6 . . . . 5E 55
E9 . . . . 2F 51
EC4 . . . . 3E 17
(off Pilgrim St.)
SW8 . . . . 4F 89
Priory Gdns. N6 . . . . . . 1D 33
SW13 . . . . 1B 98
W4 . . . . 5A 70
Priory Grn. Est. N1 . . . . 1B 62
Priory Gro. SW8 . . . . . 4A 90
Priory Ho. E1 . . . . 5F 11
(off Folgate St.)
EC1 . . . . 3D 9
(off Sans Wlk.)
SW1 . . . . 1F 89
(off Rampayne St.)
Priory La. SW15 . . . . . 4A 98
Priory M. SW8 . . . . 4A 90
Priory Pk. SE3 . . . . 1B 110
Priory Pk. Rd.
NW6 . . . . 5B 44
(not continuous)
Priory Rd. E6 . . . . 5F 55
NW6 . . . . 5D 45
Priory St. E3 . . . . 2D 67
Priory Ter. NW6 . . . . . . 5D 45
Priory Wlk. SW10 . . . . . 1E 87
Pritchard Ho. E2 . . . . . 1D 65
(off Ada Pl.)
Pritchard's Rd. E2 . . . . 5C 50
Priter Rd. SE16 . . . . . . 4C 78
Priter Way SE16 . . . . . 4C 78
Probert Rd. SW2 . . . . . 3C 104
Probyn Ho. SW1 . . . . . 5F 75
(off Page St.)
Probyn Rd. SW2 . . . . . 2D 119
Procter Ho. SE1 . . . . . . 1C 92
(off Avondale Sq.)
SE5 . . . . 3F 91
(off Picton St.)
Procter St.
WC1 . . . . 1F 15 (4B 62)
Project Pk. E3 . . . . 3F 67
Prologis Pk. E16 . . . . . 3F 67
Promenade, The
W4 . . . . 5A 84
Promenade App. Rd.
W4 . . . . 3A 84
Prospect Cl. SE26 . . . . 4D 121
Prospect Cotts.
SW18 . . . . 2C 100

Prospect Ho. N1 . . . . . 1C 62
(off Donegal St.)
SE1 . . . . 5D 25
W10 . . . . 5F 57
(off Bridge Cl.)
Prospect Pl. E1 . . . . . . 2E 79
(not continuous)
N1 . . . . 1A 48
NW2 . . . . 5B 30
NW3 . . . . 1E 45
SE8 . . . . 2B 94
(off Evelyn St.)
W4 . . . . 1A 84
Prospect Quay
SW18 . . . . 2C 100
(off Lightermans Wlk.)
Prospect Rd. NW2 . . . . 5B 30
Prospect St. SE16 . . . . 4D 79
Prospect Va. SE18 . . . . 5F 83
Prospect Wharf E1 . . . . 1E 79
Prospero Rd. N19 . . . . 3F 33
Protea Cl. E16 . . . . 3B 68
Prothero Rd. SW6 . . . . 3A 86
Prout Gro. NW10 . . . . . 1A 42
Prout Rd. E5 . . . . 5D 37
Provence St. N1 . . . . . . 1E 63
Providence Cl. E9 . . . . . 5F 51
Providence Ct.
W1 . . . . 4C 12 (1C 74)
Providence Pl. N1 . . . . 5D 49
Providence Row N1 . . . 1F 7
Providence Row Cl.
E2 . . . . 2D 65
Providence Sq. SE1 . . . 3C 78
Providence Twr.
SE16 . . . . 3C 78
(off Bermondsey Wall W.)
Providence Yd. E2 . . . . 2C 64
(off Ezra St.)
Provost Ct. NW3 . . . . . 3B 46
(off Eton Rd.)
Provost Est. N1 . . . . . . 1B 10
Provost Rd. NW3 . . . . . 4B 46
Provost St.
N1 . . . . 1B 10 (1F 63)
Prowse Pl. NW1 . . . . . . 4E 47
Prudent Pas. EC2 . . . . 2A 18
Prusom's Island E1 . . . 2E 79
(off Cinnamon St.)
Prusom St. E1 . . . . 2D 79
Pryors, The NW3 . . . . . 5F 31
Pudding La.
EC3 . . . . 5C 18 (1F 77)
Pudding Mill La. E15 . . 5D 53
Puddle Dock
EC4 . . . . 4E 17 (1D 77)
(not continuous)
Pugin Ct. N1 . . . . 4C 48
(off Liverpool Rd.)
Pulborough Rd.
SW18 . . . . 5B 100
Pulford St. SW1 . . . . . . 1E 89
Pulham Ho. SW8 . . . . . 3B 90
(off Dorset Rd.)
Pullen's Bldgs. SE17 . . 1D 91
(off Iliffe St.)
Pullman Ct. SW2 . . . . . 1A 118
Pullman Gdns. SW15 . . 4E 99
Pullman M. SE12 . . . . . 3D 125
Pulross Rd. SW9 . . . . . 1B 104

Pulteney Cl. E3........5B 52
Pulteney Ter. N1.......5B 48
　(not continuous)
Pulton Ho. SE4........2A 108
　(off Turnham Rd.)
Pulton Pl. SW6........3C 86
Puma Ct. E1....5F 11 (4B 64)
Pump Ct.
　EC4........3B 16 (5C 62)
Pump Ho. Cl. SE16......3E 79
Pump House Gallery, The
　................3C 88
Pump Ho. M. E1........1C 78
　(off Hooper St.)
Pump House Steam &
　Transport Mus......1A 38
Pumping Ho. E14......1F 81
　(off Naval Row)
Pumping Sta. Rd.
　W4........3A 84
Pump La. SE14........3E 93
Punderson's Gdns.
　E2........2D 65
Purbeck Dr. NW2.......4F 29
Purbeck Ho. SW8......3B 90
　(off Bolney St.)
Purbrook Est.
　SE1........4E 27 (3A 78)
Purbrook St.
　SE1........5E 27 (4A 78)
Purcell Cres. SW6......3F 85
　(not continuous)
Purcell Ho. SW10......2F 87
　(off Milman's St.)
Purcell Mans. W14.....2A 86
　(off Queen's Club Gdns.)
Purcell M. NW10.......4A 42
Purcell Room........1A 24
　(in South Bank)
Purcell St. N1........1A 64
Purchese St.
　NW1........1C 6 (1F 61)
Purdon Ho. SE15......4C 92
　(off Peckham High St.)
Purdy St. E3........3D 67
Purelake M. SE13.....1F 109
　(off Mariscchal Rd.)
Purley Av. NW2.......4A 30
Purley Pl. N1........4D 49
Purneys Rd. SE9.....2F 111
Purser Ho. SW2......4C 104
　(off Tulse Hill)
Pursers Cross Rd.
　SW6........4B 86
　(not continuous)
Purves Rd. NW10......2D 57
Pusey Ho. E14........5C 66
　(off Saracen St.)
Puteaux Ho. E2........1F 65
　(off Mace St.)
PUTNEY........2F 99
Putney Arts Theatre...2F 99
Putney Bri. SW6.....1A 100
　SW15........1A 100
Putney Bri. App.
　SW6........1A 100
Putney Bri. Rd.
　SW15........2A 100
　SW18........2A 100
Putney Comn. SW15...1E 99

Putney Exchange Shop. Cen.
　SW15........2F 99
PUTNEY HEATH......4E 99
Putney Heath SW15...5D 99
Putney Heath La.
　SW15........4F 99
Putney High St.
　SW15........2F 99
Putney Hill SW15......5F 99
　(not continuous)
Putney Leisure Cen....2E 99
Putney Pk. Av. SW15...2C 98
Putney Pk. La. SW15...2D 99
　(not continuous)
PUTNEY VALE......3C 112
Putney Vale Crematorium
　SW15........2C 112
Putney Wharf
　SW15........1A 100
Pylon Trad. Est. E16....3A 68
Pymers Mead SE21...1E 119
Pynfolds SE16........3D 79
Pynnersmead SE24...3E 105
Pyrford Ho. SW9......2D 105
Pyrland Rd. N5........2F 49
Pyrmont Gro. SE27...3D 119
Pytchley Rd. SE22....1A 106

Q

Q Bldg., The E15......3A 54
　(off Grove, The)
Quadrangle, The
　E15........3A 54
　SE24........3E 105
　SW6........3A 86
　SW10........4E 87
　W2........5A 60
　W12........5D 57
　(off Du Cane Rd.)
Quadrangle Cl. SE1....5A 78
Quadrant, The W10....2F 57
Quadrant Arc. W1......5A 14
Quadrant Gro. NW5....2B 46
Quadrant Ho. SE1.....1D 25
Quaggy Wlk. SE3.....2C 110
Quain Mans. W14......2A 86
　(off Queen's Club Gdns.)
Quainton St. NW10....5A 28
Quaker Ct. E1.......4F 11
　(off Quaker St.)
　EC1........3B 10
Quakers Pl. E7........2F 55
Quaker St. E1...4F 11 (3B 64)
Quality Ct. WC2.......2B 16
Quantock Gdns. NW2...4F 29
Quantock Ho. N16......3B 36
Quarley Way SE15.....3B 92
Quarrendon St. SW6...5C 86
Quarry Rd. SW18......4E 101
Quarterdeck, The
　E14........3C 80
Quarter Mile La. E10...1D 53
Quastel Ho. SE1......4B 26
　(off Long La.)
Quay Ho. E14........3C 80
　(off Admirals Way)
Quayside Cotts. E1....2C 78
　(off Mews St.)

Quayside Ct. SE16.....2F 79
　(off Abbotshade Rd.)
Quayside Ho. E14.....2B 80
Quay Vw. Apartments
　E14........4C 80
　(off Arden Cres.)
Quebec M.
　W1........3A 12 (5B 60)
Quebec Way SE16......3F 79
Quebec Way Ind. Est.
　SE16........3A 80
Quebec Wharf E8......5A 50
　(off Kingsland Rd.)
　E14........5C 66
Quedgeley Ct. SE15...2B 92
　(off Ebley Cl.)
Queeens Ct. E11......2A 40
Queen Alexandra Mans.
　WC1........2D 7
　(off Bidborough St.)
Queen Alexandra's Ct.
　SW19........5B 114
Queen Anne Ho. E16...2C 82
　(off Hardy Av.)
Queen Anne M.
　W1........1E 13 (4D 61)
Queen Anne Rd. E9....3F 51
Queen Anne's Ct.
　SE10........1F 95
　(off Park Row)
Queen Anne's Gdns.
　W4........4A 70
Queen Anne's Ga.
　SW1....4B 22 (3F 75)
Queen Anne's Gro.
　W4........4A 70
Queen Anne M.
　W1........2D 13 (5D 61)
Queen Anne's Wlk.
　WC1........4E 7
Queen Anne Ter. E1...1D 79
　(off Sovereign Cl.)
Queenbridge Sports &
　Community Cen.....4B 50
Queen Caroline St.
　W6........1E 85
　(not continuous)
Queen Catherine Ho.
　SW6........3D 87
　(off Wandon Rd.)
Queen Elizabeth Bldgs.
　EC4........4B 16
Queen Elizabeth Hall
　................1A 24
Queen Elizabeth Ho.
　SW12........5C 102
Queen Elizabeth II
　Conference Cen.
　..........4C 22 (3F 75)
Queen Elizabeth's Cl.
　N16........4F 35
Queen Elizabeth's Coll.
　SE10........3E 95
Queen Elizabeth St.
　SE1.....3E 27 (3A 78)
Queen Elizabeth's Wlk.
　N16........3F 35
Queen Elizabeth Wlk.
　SW13........4C 84
　(not continuous)

Queenhithe
EC4 . . . . 4A **18** (1E **77**)
Queen Isabella Way
EC1 . . . . 2E **17**
(off King Edward St.)
Queen Margaret Flats
E2 . . . . 2D **65**
(off St Jude's Rd.)
Queen Margaret's Gro.
N1 . . . . 2A **50**
Queen Mary Ho. E16 . . 2D **83**
(off Wesley Av.)
Queen Mary Rd.
SE19 . . . . 5D **119**
Queen Marys Bldgs.
SW1 . . . . 5E **75**
(off Stillington St.)
Queen Mary's Ct.
SE10 . . . . 2F **95**
(off Park Row)
Queen Mother Sports Cen., The
. . . . 5E **75**
(off Vauxhall Bri. Rd.)
Queen of Denmark Ct.
SE16 . . . . 4B **80**
Queensberry M. W.
SW7 . . . . 5F **73**
Queensberry Pl. E12 . . 2F **55**
SW7 . . . . 5F **73**
Queensberry Way
SW7 . . . . 5F **73**
Queensborough M.
W2 . . . . 1E **73**
Queensborough Pas.
W2 . . . . 1E **73**
(off Queensborough M.)
Queensborough Studios
W2 . . . . 1E **73**
(off Queensborough M.)
Queensborough Ter.
W2 . . . . 1D **73**
Queensbridge Ct. E2 . . 5B **50**
(off Queensbridge Rd.)
Queensbridge Rd. E2 . . 3B **50**
E8 . . . . 4E **49**
Queensbury St. N1 . . . . 4E **49**
Queen's Chapel of the Savoy
. . . . 5F **15**
(off Savoy St.)
Queen's Cir. SW8 . . . . 3D **89**
Queen's Club Gdns.
W14 . . . . 2A **86**
Queens Club, The (Tennis)
. . . . 1A **86**
Queens Ct. NW6 . . . . . . 2D **45**
NW8 . . . . 1F **59**
(off Queen's Ter.)
NW11 . . . . 1B **30**
SE23 . . . . 2D **121**
W2 . . . . 1D **73**
(off Queensway)
Queen's Cres. NW5 . . . . 3C **46**
Queenscroft Rd.
SE9 . . . . 3F **111**
Queensdale Cres.
W11 . . . . 2F **71**
Queensdale Pl. W11 . . 2A **72**
Queensdale Rd. W11 . . 2F **71**
Queensdale Wlk.
W11 . . . . 2A **72**

Queensdown Rd. E5 . . 1D **51**
Queens Dr. E10 . . . . . . 2C **38**
N4 . . . . 4D **35**
Queen's Elm Pde.
SW3 . . . . 1F **87**
(off Old Chu. St.)
Queen's Elm Sq. SW3. . 1F **87**
Queen's Gallery
. . . . 4F **21** (3D **75**)
Queens Gdns. NW4 . . . 1E **29**
W2 . . . . 1E **73**
Queen's Ga. SW7 . . . . 3E **73**
Queens Ga. Gdns.
SW7 . . . . 4E **73**
SW15 . . . . 2D **99**
Queen's Ga. M. SW7 . . 4E **73**
Queen's Ga. Pl. SW7. . 4E **73**
Queensgate Pl. NW6 . . 4C **44**
Queen's Ga. Pl. M.
SW7 . . . . 4E **73**
Queen's Ga. Ter.
SW7 . . . . 4E **73**
Queen's Ga. Vs. E9. . . 4A **52**
Queen's Gro. NW8 . . . . 5F **45**
Queen's Gro. Studios
NW8 . . . . 5F **45**
Queen's Head Pas.
EC4 . . . . 2F **17** (5E **63**)
Queen's Head St.
N1 . . . . 5D **49**
Queen's Head Yd.
SE1 . . . . 2B **26**
Queens House, The . . 2F **95**
Queens Ho. SE18 . . . . 3A **90**
(off Sth. Lambeth Rd.)
Queen's Ice Bowl 1D **73**
(off Queensway)
Queensland Pl. N7 . . . . 1C **48**
Queensland Rd. N7 . . . 1C **48**
Queen's Mans. W6 . . . . 5F **71**
(off Brook Grn.)
Queen's Mkt. E13 . . . . 5E **55**
Queensmead NW8 . . . . 5F **45**
Queensmere Cl.
SW19 . . . . 2F **113**
Queensmere Ct.
SW13 . . . . 3B **84**
Queensmere Rd.
SW19 . . . . 2F **113**
Queen's M. W2 . . . . . . 1D **73**
(not continuous)
Queensmill Rd.
SW6 . . . . 3F **85**
Queens Pde. NW2 . . . . 3E **43**
(off Willesden La.)
NW4 . . . . 1E **29**
(off Queens Rd.)
Queens Pk. Ct. W10 . . 2F **57**
Queen's Pk. Rangers FC
. . . . 2D **71**
Queens Pk. School
Sports Cen. 5F **43**
(within school)
Queen Sq.
WC1 . . . . 4E **7** (3A **62**)
Queen Sq. Pl. WC1 . . . 4E **7**
Queen's Quay EC4 . . . . 4F **17**
(off Up. Thames St.)
Queens Ride SW13 . . . . 1C **98**
SW15 . . . . 1C **98**

Queens Rd. E11 . . . . . . 2F **39**
E13 . . . . 5D **55**
E17 . . . . 1B **38**
NW4 . . . . 1E **29**
SE14 . . . . 4E **93**
SE15 . . . . 4D **93**
SW14 . . . . 1A **98**
SW19 . . . . 5C **114**
Queens Rd. W. E13 . . . 1C **68**
Queen's Row SE17 . . . 2F **91**
Queens Ter. E1 . . . . . . 3E **65**
E13 . . . . 5D **55**
NW8 . . . . 5F **45**
Queen's Theatre
Westminster 4B **14**
(off Shaftesbury Av.)
Queensthorpe Rd.
SE26 . . . . 4F **121**
Queenstown M. SW8 . . 5D **89**
Queen St.
EC4 . . . . 4A **18** (1E **77**)
(not continuous)
W1 . . . . 1D **21** (2D **75**)
Queen St. Pl.
EC4 . . . . 4A **18** (1E **77**)
Queensville Rd.
SW12 . . . . 5F **103**
Queen's Wlk. N5 . . . . . . 2D **49**
SW1 . . . . 2F **21** (2E **75**)
Queen's Wlk., The
SE1 . . . . 1C **26** (2A **78**)
(Morgan's La.)
SE1 . . . . 5C **16** (1C **76**)
(Oxo Tower Wharf)
SE1 . . . . 1A **24** (2B **76**)
(Waterloo Rd.)
Queen's Way NW4 . . . . 1E **29**
Queensway W2 . . . . . . 5D **59**
Queens Wharf W6 . . . . 1E **85**
Queenswood Ct.
SE27 . . . . 4F **119**
SW4 . . . . 3A **104**
Queenswood Gdns.
E11 . . . . 3D **41**
Queens Wood Rd.
N10 . . . . 1D **33**
Queenswood Rd.
SE23 . . . . 3F **121**
Queen's Yd.
WC1 . . . . 4A **6** (4E **61**)
Queen Victoria Memorial
. . . . 4F **21** (3E **75**)
Queen Victoria Seaman's Rest
E14 . . . . 5D **67**
(off E. India Dock Rd.)
Queen Victoria St.
EC4 . . . . 4D **17** (1D **77**)
Queen Victoria Ter.
E1 . . . . 1D **79**
(off Sovereign Cl.)
Quemerford Rd. N7 . . . 2B **48**
Quendon Ho. W10 . . . . 3E **57**
(off Sutton Way)
Quenington Ct. SE15 . . 2B **92**
Quentin Ho. SE1 . . . . . . 4C **24**
(off Gray St., not continuous)
Quentin Pl. SE13 . . . . 1A **110**
Quentin Rd. SE13 . . . . 1A **110**
Quernmore Cl.
BR1: Brom 5C **124**

Quernmore Rd.
BR1: Brom 5C 124
N4 . . . . 1C 34
Querrin St. SW6 . . . . . 5E 87
Quested Ct. E8 . . . . . 2D 51
(off Brett Rd.)
Quex M. NW6 . . . . . 5C 44
Quex Rd. NW6 . . . . . 5C 44
Quick Rd. W4 . . . . . 1A 84
Quick St. N1 . . . . . 1D 63
Quick St. M. N1 . . . . . 1D 63
Quickswood NW3 . . . . 4A 46
Quill La. SW15 . . . . . 2F 99
Quill St. N4 . . . . 5C 34
Quilp St.
SE1 . . . . 3F 25 (3E 77)
(not continuous)
Quilter Ho. W10 . . . . . 2B 58
(off Dart St.)
Quilter St. E2 . . . . . 2C 64
Quilting Ct. SE16 . . . . 5F 79
(off Garter Way)
Quince Ho. SE13 . . . 5D 95
(off Quince Rd.)
Quinton St. SW8 . . . . 3A 90
(off Wyvil Rd.)
Quinton St. SW18 . . . . 2E 115
Quixley St. E14 . . . . . 1F 81
Quorn Rd. SE22 . . . . 2A 106

R

Rabbit Row W8 . . . . . 2C 72
Raby St. E14 . . . . . . 5A 66
Raceway, The (Go-Kart Track)
. . . . 5A 48
Racine SE5 . . . . 4A 92
(off Peckham Rd.)
Rackham M. SW16 . . . 5E 117
Rackstraw Ho. NW3 . . 4B 46
Racton Rd. SW6 . . . . 2C 86
RADA 5B 6
(off Chenies St.)
Radbourne Cl. E5 . . . . 1F 51
Radbourne Rd.
SW12 . . . . 5E 103
Radcliffe Av. NW10 . . 1C 56
Radcliffe Ho. SE16 . . 5D 79
(off Anchor St.)
Radcliffe Path SW8 . . 5D 89
Radcliffe Rd.
SE1 . . . . 5E 27 (4A 78)
Radcot St. SW15 . . . . 4F 99
Radcot St. SE11 . . . . 1C 90
Raddington Rd. W10 . . 4A 58
Radford Est. NW10 . . 2A 56
Radford Ho. E14 . . . . 4D 67
(off St Leonard's Rd.)
N7 . . . . 2B 48
Radford Rd. SE13 . . . 4E 109
Radipole Rd. SW6 . . . 4B 86
Radland Rd. E16 . . . . 5B 68
Radlet Av. SE26 . . . . 3D 121
Radlett Cl. E7 . . . . . . 3B 54
Radlett Pl. NW8 . . . . 5A 46
Radley Ct. SE16 . . . . 3F 79
Radley Ho. NW1 . . . . . 3A 4
(off Gloucester Pl.)

Radley M. W8 . . . . . 4C 72
Radley Sq. E5 . . . . . 4E 37
Radley Ter. E16 . . . . 4B 68
(off Hermit Rd.)
Radlix Rd. E10 . . . . . 3C 38
Radnor M. W2 . . . . . 5F 59
Radnor Pl. W2 . . . . . 5A 60
Radnor Rd. NW6 . . . . 5A 44
SE15 . . . . 3C 92
Radnor St.
EC1 . . . . 2A 10 (2E 63)
Radnor Ter. W14 . . . . 5B 72
Radnor Wlk. E14 . . . 5C 80
(off Barnsdale Av.)
SW3 . . . . 1A 88
Radstock St. SW11 . . . 3A 88
(not continuous)
Raeburn Cl. NW11 . . . 1E 31
Raeburn St. SW2 . . . 2A 104
Ragged School Mus.
. . . . 4A 66
Raglan Ct. SE12 . . . . 3C 110
Raglan Rd. E17 . . . . . 1E 39
Raglan St. NW5 . . . . 3D 47
Railey M. NW5 . . . . . 2E 47
Railton Rd. SE24 . . . 2C 104
Railway App. N4 . . . . 1C 34
SE1 . . . . 2C 26 (2F 77)
Railway Arches E2 . . . 5B 50
(off Laburnum St.)
E2 . . . . 1F 11
(off Geffrye St.)
E7 . . . . 1C 54
(off Winchelsea Rd.)
E8 . . . . 4D 51
(off Mentmore Ter.)
E10 . . . . 2D 39
(off Capworth St.)
E11 . . . . 4A 40
(off Leytonstone High Rd.)
E11 . . . . 3F 39
(off Sidings, The)
E17 . . . . 1C 38
(off Yunus Khan Cl.)
W12 . . . . 3E 71
(off Shepherd's Bush Mkt.)
Railway Av. SE16 . . . . 3E 79
(not continuous)
Railway Children Wlk.
BR1: Brom 2C 124
SE12 . . . . 2C 124
Railway Cotts. E15 . . . 1A 68
(off Baker's Row)
SW19 . . . . 4D 115
W6 . . . . 3E 71
(off Sulgrave Rd.)
Railway Gro. SE14 . . . 3B 94
Railway M. E3 . . . . . . 2C 66
(off Wellington Way)
W11 . . . . 5A 58
Railway Ri. SE22 . . . 2A 106
Railway Side SW13 . . 1A 98
(not continuous)
Railway St. N1 . . . . . 1A 62
Railway Ter. SE13 . . . 3D 109
Rainbow Av. E14 . . . . 1D 95
Rainbow Ct. SE14 . . . 2A 94
(off Chipley St.)
Rainbow Quay SE16 . . 4A 80
(not continuous)

Rainbow St. SE5 . . . . 3A 92
Rainbow Theatre 4C 34
Raines Est. Ct. N16 . . 4B 36
Raine St. E1 . . . . 2D 79
Rainham Cl. SW11 . . 4A 102
Rainham Ho. NW1 . . . 5E 47
(off Bayham Pl.)
Rainham Rd. NW10 . . 2E 57
Rainhill Way E3 . . . . 2C 66
(not continuous)
Rainsborough Av.
SE8 . . . . 5A 80
Rainsford St. W2 . . . . 5A 60
Rainton Rd. SE7 . . . . 1C 96
Rainville Rd. W6 . . . . 2E 85
Raleana Rd. E14 . . . . 2E 81
Raleigh Ct. SE16 . . . . 2F 79
(off Clarence M.)
W12 . . . . 3E 71
(off Scott's Rd.)
Raleigh Gdns. SW2 . . 4B 104
Raleigh Ho. E14 . . . . 3D 81
(off Admirals Way)
SW1 . . . . 2F 89
(off Dolphin Sq.)
Raleigh M. N1 . . . . . . 5D 49
(off Packington St.)
Raleigh St. N1 . . . . . 5D 49
Ralph Brook Ct. N1 . . 1C 10
(off Chart St.)
Ralph Ct. W2 . . . . . . 5D 59
(off Queensway)
Ralston St. SW3 . . . . 1B 88
Ramac Ind. Est. SE7 . . 5D 83
Ramac Way SE7 . . . . 5D 83
Ramar Ho. E1 . . . . . . 4C 64
(off Hanbury St.)
Rambler Cl. SW16 . . . 4E 117
Rame Cl. SW17 . . . . 5C 116
Ramilles Cl. SW2 . . . 4A 104
Ramilles Pl.
W1 . . . . 3F 13 (5E 61)
Ramillies Rd. W4 . . . . 5A 70
Ramillies St.
W1 . . . . 3F 13 (5E 61)
Rampart St. E1 . . . . . 5D 65
Rampayne St. SW1 . . 1F 89
Ram Pl. E9 . . . . 3E 51
Ramsay Ho. NW8 . . . . 1A 60
(off Townshend Est.)
Ramsay M. SW3 . . . . 2A 88
Ramsay Rd. E7 . . . . . 1A 54
Ramsdale Rd.
SW17 . . . . 5C 116
Ramsden Rd.
SW12 . . . . 4C 102
Ramsey Cl. NW9 . . . . 1B 28
Ramsey Ho. SW9 . . . 3C 90
Ramsey St. E2 . . . . . 3C 64
Ramsey Wlk. N1 . . . . 3F 49
(off Handa Wlk.)
Ramsfort Ho. SE16 . . 5D 79
(off Camilla Rd.)
Ramsgate Cl. E16 . . . 2D 83
Ramsgate St. E8 . . . . 3B 50
Ram St. SW18 . . . . 3D 101
Rancliffe Gdns.
SE9 . . . . 2F 111
Randall Av. NW2 . . . . 4A 28
Randall Cl. SW11 . . . . 4A 88

Randall Pl. SE10 . . . . . . 3E 95
Randall Rd. SE11 . . . . . . 1B 90
Randall Row SE11 . . . . . 5B 76
Randalls Rents SE16 . . . . 4B 80
 (off Gulliver St.)
Randell's Rd. N1 . . . . . . 5A 48
 (not continuous)
Randisbourne Gdns.
 SE6 . . . . 3D 123
Randlesdown Rd.
 SE6 . . . . 4C 122
 (not continuous)
Randolph App. E16 . . . . . 5E 69
Randolph Av. W9 . . . . . . 1D 59
Randolph Cres. W9 . . . . . 3E 59
Randolph Gdns.
 NW6 . . . . 1D 59
Randolph M. W9 . . . . 3E 59
Randolph Rd. E17 . . . . . . 1D 39
 W9 . . . . 3E 59
Randolph St. NW1 . . . . . 4E 47
Ranelagh Av. SW6 . . . . 1B 100
 SW13 . . . . 5C 84
Ranelagh Bri. W2 . . . . . . 4D 59
Ranelagh Gdns.
 SW6 . . . . 1A 100
 (not continuous)
 W6 . . . . 5B 70
Ranelagh Gdns. Mans.
 SW6 . . . . 1A 100
 (off Ranelagh Gdns.)
Ranelagh Gro.
 SW1 . . . . 1C 88
Ranelagh Ho. SW3 . . . . . 1B 88
 (off Elystan Pl.)
Rangbourne Ho. N7 . . . . 2A 48
Rangefield Rd.
 BR1: Brom 5A 124
Rangemoor Rd. N15 . . . . 1B 36
Rangers House 4F 95
Rangers Sq. SE10 . . . . . . 4F 95
Rangoon St. EC3 . . . . . . 3F 19
Rankine Ho. SE1 . . . . . . 5F 25
 (off Bath Ter.)
Ranmere St. SW12 . . . . 1D 117
Rannoch Rd. W6 . . . . . . 2E 85
Rannock Av. NW9 . . . . . . 2A 28
Ransome's Dock Bus. Cen.
 SW11 . . . . 3A 88
Ransom Rd. SE7 . . . . . . 5E 83
Ranston St. NW1 . . . . . . 4A 60
Ranulf Rd. NW2 . . . . 1B 44
Ranwell Cl. E3 . . . . 5B 52
Raphael Ct. SE16 . . . . . . 1D 93
 (off Stubbs Dr.)
Raphael St. SW7 . . . . . . 3B 74
Rapley Ho. E2 . . . . 2C 64
 (off Turin St.)
Raquel Ct. SE1 . . . . 3D 27
 (off Snowfields)
Rashleigh Ct. SW8 . . . . . 5B 68
Rashleigh Ho. WC1 . . . . . 2D 7
 (off Thanet St.)
Rastell Av. SW2 . . . . . . 2F 117
RATCLIFF 4A 66
Ratcliffe Cl. SE12 . . . . . 5C 110

Ratcliffe Ct. SE1 . . . . . . 4A 26
 (off Gt. Dover St.)
Ratcliffe Cross St. E1 . . . 5F 65
Ratcliffe Ho. E14 . . . . . . 5A 66
Ratcliffe La. E14 . . . . . . 5A 66
Ratcliffe Orchard E1 . . . . 1F 79
Ratcliff Rd. E7 . . . . 2E 55
Rathbone Ho. E16 . . . . . 5B 68
 (off Rathbone St.)
 NW6 . . . . 5C 44
Rathbone Mkt. E16 . . . . 4B 68
Rathbone Pl.
 W1 . . . . 1B 14 (4F 61)
Rathbone St. E16 . . . . . 4B 68
 W1 . . . . 1A 14 (4E 61)
Rathcoole Gdns. N8 . . . . 1B 34
Rathfern Rd. SE6 . . . . . 1B 122
Rathgar Rd. SW9 . . . . . 1D 105
Rathmell Dr. SW4 . . . . . 4F 103
Rathmore Rd. SE7 . . . . . 1D 97
Rattray Rd. SW2 . . . . . . 2B 104
Raul Rd. SE15 . . . . 5C 92
Raveley St. NW5 . . . . 1E 47
 (not continuous)
Ravenet St. SW11 . . . . . 4D 89
 (not continuous)
Ravenfield Rd.
 SW17 . . . . 3B 116
Ravenhill Rd. E13 . . . . . . 1E 69
Raven Ho. SE16 . . . . 5F 79
 (off Tawny Way)
Ravenna Rd. SW15 . . . . . 3F 99
Raven Row E1 . . . . 4D 65
 (not continuous)
Ravensbourne Ct.
 SE6 . . . . 5C 108
Ravensbourne Ho.
 BR1: Brom 5F 123
 NW8 . . . . 4A 60
 (off Broadley St.)
Ravensbourne Mans.
 SE8 . . . . 2C 94
 (off Berthon St.)
Ravensbourne Pk.
 SE6 . . . . 5C 108
Ravensbourne Pk. Cres.
 SE6 . . . . 5B 108
Ravensbourne Rd.
 SE6 . . . . 5B 108
Ravensbury Rd.
 SW18 . . . . 2C 114
Ravensbury Ter.
 SW18 . . . . 2D 115
Ravenscar NW1 . . . . 5E 47
 (off Bayham St.)
Ravenscar Rd.
 BR1: Brom 5A 124
Ravenscourt Av. W6 . . . . 5C 70
Ravenscourt Gdns.
 W6 . . . . 5C 70
Ravenscourt Pk. W6 . . . . 4C 70
Ravenscourt Pk. Mans.
 W6 . . . . 4D 71
 (off Paddenswick Rd.)
Ravenscourt Pl. W6 . . . . 5D 71
Ravenscourt Rd. W6 . . . . 5D 71
 (not continuous)

Ravenscourt Sq. W6 . . . . 4C 70
Ravenscroft Av.
 NW11 . . . . 2B 30
 (not continuous)
Ravenscroft Cl. E16 . . . . 4C 68
Ravenscroft Rd. E16 . . . . 4C 68
Ravenscroft St. E2 . . . . . 1B 64
Ravensdale Mans.
 N8 . . . . 1A 34
 (off Haringey Pk.)
Ravensdale Rd. N16 . . . . 2B 36
Ravensdon St. SE11 . . . . 1C 90
Ravenshaw St. NW6 . . . . 2B 44
Ravenslea Rd.
 SW12 . . . . 5B 102
Ravensleigh Gdns.
 BR1: Brom 5D 125
Ravensmede Way
 W4 . . . . 5B 70
Ravens M. SE12 . . . . . . 3C 110
Ravenstone SE17 . . . . . . 1A 92
Ravenstone Rd. NW9 . . . 1B 28
Ravenstone St.
 SW12 . . . . 1C 116
Ravens Way SE12 . . . . . 3C 110
Ravenswood Rd.
 SW12 . . . . 5D 103
Ravensworth Ct.
 SW6 . . . . 3C 86
 (off Fulham Rd.)
Ravensworth Rd.
 NW10 . . . . 2D 57
Ravent Rd. SE11 . . . . . . 5B 76
Raven Wharf SE1 . . . . . . 3F 27
 (off Lafone St.)
Ravey St.
 EC2 . . . . 3D 11 (3A 64)
Rav Pinter Cl. N16 . . . . . 2A 36
Rawalpindi Ho. E16 . . . . 3B 68
Rawchester Cl.
 SW18 . . . . 1B 114
Rawlings St. SW3 . . . . . . 5B 74
Rawlinson Ct. NW2 . . . . 2E 29
Rawlinson Ho. SE13 . . . . 2F 109
 (off Mercator Rd.)
Rawlinson Point E16 . . . . 4B 68
 (off Fox Rd.)
Rawreth Wlk. N1 . . . . . . 5E 49
 (off Basire St.)
Rawson St. SW11 . . . . . 4C 88
 (not continuous)
Rawstone Wlk. E13 . . . . 1C 68
Rawstorne Pl.
 EC1 . . . . 1D 9 (2D 63)
Rawstorne St.
 EC1 . . . . 1D 9 (2D 63)
 (not continuous)
Rayburne Ct. W14 . . . . . 4A 72
Raydon St. N19 . . . . 4D 33
Rayford Av. SE12 . . . . . . 5B 110
Ray Gunter Ho. SE17 . . . 1D 91
 (off Marsland Cl.)
Ray Ho. N1 . . . . 5A 50
 (off Colville Est.)
Rayleigh Rd. E16 . . . . . . 2D 83
Raymede Towers
 W10 . . . . 4F 57
 (off Treverton St.)
Raymond Bldgs.
 WC1 . . . . 5A 8 (4B 62)

Raymond Cl. SE26 . . . . 5E 121
Raymond Revuebar . . . *4B 14*
   (off Walkers Ct.)
Raymond Rd. E13. . . . . . 5E 55
SW19 . . . . 5A 114
Raymouth Ho. *SE16 . . . 5E 79*
   (off Raymouth Rd.)
Raymouth Rd. SE16. . . . 5D 79
Raynald Ho. SW16. . . . 3A 118
Rayne Ho. *W9 . . . . 3D 59*
   (off Delaware Rd.)
Rayner Ct. *W12 . . . . 3E 71*
   (off Bamborough Gdns.)
Rayners Rd. SW15. . . . 3A 100
Rayner Towers *E10. . . . 2C 38*
   (off Albany Rd.)
Raynes Av. E11. . . . . 2E 41
Raynham *W2 . . . . 5A 60*
   (off Norfolk Cres.)
Raynham Ho. *E1 . . . . . . 3F 65*
   (off Harpley Sq.)
Raynham Rd. W6. . . . . . 5D 71
Raynor Pl. N1. . . . . 4E 49
Ray St. EC1 . . . . 4C 8 (3C 62)
Ray St. Bri. EC1. . . . . 4C 8
Ray Wlk. N7 . . . . 4B 34
Reachview Cl. NW1. . . . . 4E 47
Read Ct. E17 . . . . 1C 38
Reade Ho. *SE10 . . . . . . 2F 95*
   (off Trafalgar Gro.)
Reade Wlk. NW10 . . . . . 4A 42
Read Ho. *SE11. . . . . . . 2C 90*
   (off Clayton St.)
Reading Ho. *SE15 . . . . 2C 92*
W2 . . . . 5E 59
   (off Hallfield Est.)
Reading La. E8 . . . . 3D 51
Reapers Cl. NW1 . . . . . . 5F 47
Reardon Ho. *E1 . . . . . . 2D 79*
   (off Reardon St.)
Reardon Path E1 . . . . . . 2D 79
   (not continuous)
Reardon St. E1. . . . . 2D 79
Reaston St. SE14 . . . . . . 3F 93
Reckitt Rd. W4 . . . . 1A 84
Record St. SE15 . . . . 2C 93
Recovery St. SW17 . . . . 5A 116
Recreation Rd.
  SE26 . . . . 4F 121
Rector St. N1 . . . . 5E 49
Rectory Cres. E11. . . . . . 1E 41
   (not continuous)
Rectory Fld. Cres.
  SE7 . . . . 3E 97
Rectory Gdns. SW4 . . . . 1E 103
Rectory Gro. SW4. . . . . 1E 103
Rectory La. SW17 . . . . 5C 116
Rectory Orchard
  SW19 . . . . 4A 114
Rectory Rd. N16. . . . . . . 4B 36
SW13 . . . . 5C 84
Rectory Sq. E1 . . . . 1F 65
Reculver Ho. *SE15 . . . . 2E 93*
   (off Lovelinch Cl.)
Reculver Rd. SE16. . . . . 1F 93
Red Anchor Cl. SW3 . . . 2F 87
Redan Pl. W2. . . . . 5D 59
Redan St. W14 . . . . 4F 71
Redan Ter. SE5. . . . . . . 5D 91

Redberry Gro. SE26 . . . . 3E 121
Redbourne Ho. *E14 . . . . 5B 66*
   (off Norbiton Rd.)
Redbourn Ho. *W10. . . . 3E 57*
   (off Sutton Way)
REDBRIDGE 1F 41
Redbridge Gdns. SE5. . . 3A 92
Redbridge La. E.
  IG4: IIf 1F 41
Redbridge La. W.
  E11. . . . . 1D 41
REDBRIDGE RDBT. 1F 41
Redburn St. SW3 . . . . . . 2B 88
Redcar St. SE5. . . . . 3E 91
Redcastle Cl. E1. . . . . . . 1E 79
Redchurch St.
  E2 . . . . 3F 11 (3B 64)
Redcliffe Cl. SW5 . . . . . . 1D 87
   (off Old Brompton Rd.)
Redcliffe Ct. E5 . . . . 5D 37
   (off Napoleon Rd.)
Redcliffe Gdns. SW10 . . 1D 87
Redcliffe M. SW10 . . . . . 1D 87
Redcliffe Pl. SW10 . . . . . 2E 87
Redcliffe Rd. SW10 . . . . 1E 87
Redcliffe Sq. SW10 . . . . 1D 87
Redcliffe St. SW10 . . . . . 2D 87
Redclyffe Rd. E6 . . . . . . 5E 55
Redclyf Ho. *E1 . . . . 3E 65*
   (off Cephas St.)
Red Cow La.
  EC1. . . . . 3F 9 (3E 63)
Redcross Way
  SE1 . . . . 3A 26 (3E 77)
Redding Ho. SE18 . . . . . 4F 83
Reddins Rd. SE15 . . . . . 2C 92
Redenham Ho. *SW15 . . 5C 98*
   (off Ellisfield Dr.)
Rede Pl. W2 . . . . 5C 58
Redesdale St. SW3 . . . . 2A 88
Redfern Ho. *E13. . . . . . 5B 54*
   (off Redriffe Rd.)
Redfern Rd. NW10. . . . . 4A 42
SE6 . . . . 5E 109
Redfield La. SW5. . . . . . 5C 72
Redfield M. SW5. . . . . . 5D 73
Redford Ho. *W10 . . . . . 2B 58*
   (off Dowland St.)
Redford Wlk. *N1. . . . . . 5E 49*
   (off Popham St.)
Redgate Ter. SW15. . . . . 4F 99
Redgrave Rd. SW15. . . . 1F 99
Redgrave Ter. *E2 . . . . . 2C 64*
   (off Derbyshire St.)
Redhill Ct. SW2 . . . . . . 2C 118
Redhill St.
  NW1. . . . . . . 1E 5 (1D 61)
Red Ho. Sq. N1 . . . . 3E 49
Redington Gdns.
  NW3 . . . . 1D 45
Redington Ho. *N1 . . . . . 1B 62*
   (off Priory Grn. Est.)
Redington Rd. NW3. . . . 5D 31
Redlands Way SW2 . . . . 5B 104
Red Lion Cl. *SE17 . . . . . 2F 91*
   (off Red Lion Row)
Red Lion Ct.
  EC4 . . . . 3C 16 (5C 62)
SE1 . . . . 1A 26 (2E 77)
Red Lion Row SE17 . . . . 2E 91

Red Lion Sq. SW18 . . . . 3C 100
WC1 . . . . 1F 15 (4B 62)
Red Lion St.
  WC1 . . . . 5F 7 (4B 62)
Red Lion Yd. W1 . . . . . . 1C 20
Redman Ho. *EC1 . . . . . . 5B 8*
   (off Bourne Est.)
  SE1 . . . . *4A 26*
   (off Borough High St.)
Redman's Rd. E1. . . . . . . 4E 65
Redmead La. E1 . . . . 2C 78
Redmill Ho. *E1 . . . . 3D 65*
   (off Headlam St.)
Redmond Ho. *N1 . . . . . . 5B 48*
   (off Barnsbury Est.)
Redmore Rd. W6. . . . . . 5D 71
Red Path E9 . . . . 3A 52
Red Pl. W1 . . . . 4B 12 (1C 74)
Red Post Hill SE21. . . . . 3F 105
SE24 . . . . 2F 105
Red Post Ho. E6. . . . . . . 4F 55
Redriffe Rd. E13 . . . . . . 5B 54
Redriff Est. SE16 . . . . . . 4B 80
Redriff Rd. SE16. . . . . . . 5F 79
RED ROVER 2C 98
Redrup Ho. *SE14 . . . . . 2F 93*
   (off John Williams Cl.)
Redruth Rd. E9. . . . . 5E 51
Red Sq. N16. . . . . 5F 35
Redstart Cl. E6 . . . . 4F 69
SE14 . . . . 3A 94
Redvers St. N1. . . . . 1E 11
Redwald Rd. E5 . . . . 1F 51
Redwing Ct. *SE1 . . . . . . 4A 26*
   (off Swan St.)
Redwood Cl. E3 . . . . 1C 66
SE16. . . . . 2A 80
Redwood Ct. N19 . . . . . . 2F 33
NW6 . . . . 4A 44
Redwood Mans. *W8 . . . 4D 73*
   (off Chantry Sq.)
Redwood M. SW4 . . . . . 1D 103
Redwoods SW15 . . . . . 1C 112
Reece M. SW7 . . . . 5F 73
Reed Cl. E16 . . . . 4C 68
SE12. . . . . 3C 110
Reedham St. SE15. . . . . 5C 92
Reedholm Vs. N16. . . . . 1F 49
Reed's Pl. NW1 . . . . 4E 47
Reedworth St. SE11. . . . 5C 76
Reef Ho. *E14 . . . . 4E 81*
   (off Manchester Rd.)
Rees St. N1 . . . . 5E 49
Reets Farm Cl. NW9 . . . 1A 28
Reeves Av. NW9 . . . . . . 2A 28
Reeves Ho. *SE1 . . . . . . 4B 24*
   (off Baylis Rd.)
Reeves M.
  W1. . . . . 5B 12 (1C 74)
Reeves Rd. E3. . . . . 3D 67
Reflection Ho. *E2. . . . . . 3C 64*
   (off Cheshire St.)
Reform St. SW11. . . . . . 5B 88
Regal Cl. E1. . . . . 4C 64
Regal Ct. NW6. . . . . 1B 58
   (off Malvern Rd.)
Regan Way N1. . . . . 5C 46
Regal Pl. E3. . . . . 2B 66
SW6 . . . . 3D 87
Regal Row SE15. . . . . . . 4E 93

Regan Way
N1 . . . . . . .1D **11** (1A **64**)
Regatta Point *E14* *3C 80*
(off Westferry Rd.)
Regency Ho. *E16* *2C 82*
(off Pepys Cres.)
NW1 . . . . *3E 5*
(off Osnaburgh St.)
Regency Lawn NW5. . .5D **33**
Regency Lodge
NW3 . . . . *4F 45*
(off Adelaide Rd.)
Regency M. NW10 . . .3C **42**
SW9 . . . . 3D **91**
Regency Pde. *NW3*. . . . *4F 45*
(off Finchley Rd.)
Regency Pl. SW1 . . . . .5F **75**
Regency St. NW10 . . .3A **56**
SW1 . . . . .5F **75**
Regency Ter. *SW7* 1F *87*
(off Fulham Rd.)
Regent Ct. *NW8* *2A 60*
(off North Bank)
Regent Ho. *W14* 5A *72*
(off Windsor Way)
Regent Pl. SW19 . . . . .5E **115**
W1 . . . . .4A **14** (1F **75**)
Regent Rd. SE24 . . . .4D **105**
Regent's Bri. Gdns.
SW8 . . . . .3A **90**
Regents Canal Ho.
E14 . . . . *4A 66*
(off Commercial Rd.)
Regents College. 3A 4
Regents Ct. *E8* *5B 50*
(off Pownall Rd.)
Regents Ga. Ho. *E14* . . .1A *80*
(off Horseferry Rd.)
Regents M. NW8 . . . . .1E **59**
REGENT'S PARK
. . . . .2E 5 (2D **61**)
Regent's Pk. . . .1A 4 (1B **60**)
Regent's Pk. Barracks . .1E 5
Regents Pk. Est. NW1 . .1F **5**
Regent's Pk. Gdns. M.
NW1. . . . . .5B **46**
Regents Pk. Golf &
Tennis School. 1B **60**
Regent's Pk. Ho.
NW8 . . . . *2A 60*
(off Park Rd.)
Regent's Pk. Open Air Theatre
. . . . .2B 4 (2C **60**)
Regent's Pk. Rd.
NW1 . . . . .4B **46**
(not continuous)
Regent's Pk. Ter.
NW1 . . . . .5D *47*
Regent's Pl. SE3 . . . . .5C **96**
Regents Plaza *NW6*. . . .1D *59*
(off Kilburn High Rd.)
Regent Sq. E3 . . . . . . .2D **67**
WC1 . . . . .2E 7 (2A **62**)
Regents Row E9 . . . . . .5C **50**
Regent St. NW10 . . . .2F *57*
SW1 . . . . .2E **13** (1F **75**)
W1 . . . . .2E **13** (5D **61**)
Regents Wharf E2 . . . .5D *51*
(off Wharf Pl.)
N1 . . . . .1B **62**

Reginald Pl. *SE8* *3C 94*
(off Deptford High St.)
Reginald Rd. E7. . . . .4C **54**
SE8 . . . . .3C **94**
Reginald Sorenson Ho.
E11 . . . . .2F **39**
Reginald Sq. SE8 . . . .3C **94**
Regina Point SE16. . . .4E **79**
Regina Rd. N4 . . . . . .3B **34**
Regis Ct. NW1 . . . . . . *4B 60*
(off Melcombe Pl.)
Regis Pl. SW2 . . . . . .2B **104**
Regis Rd. NW5 . . . . . .2D **47**
Regnart Bldgs. NW1 . . .3A 6
Reigate Rd.
BR1: Brom 3B **124**
Reighton Rd. E5 . . . . .5C **36**
Reizel Cl. N16 . . . . . . .3B **36**
Relay Rd. W12 . . . . . .2E **71**
Relf Rd. SE15. . . . . . .1C **106**
Reliance Arc. SW9 . . . .2C **104**
Reliance Sq.
EC2 . . . . .3E **11** (3A **64**)
Relton M. SW7 . . . . . .4A **74**
Rembold Ho. *SE10*. . . .4E *95*
(off Blissett St.)
Rembrandt Cl. E14. . . .4F **81**
SW1 . . . . *1C 88*
(off Graham Ter.)
Rembrandt Ct. *SE16* . .1D *93*
(off Stubbs Dr.)
Rembrandt Rd.
SE13 . . . . .2A **110**
Remembrance Rd.
E7 . . . . .1F **55**
Remington Rd. E6 . . . .5F **69**
N15. . . . . .1F **35**
Remington St. N1 . . . .1D **63**
Remnant St.
WC2 . . . . .2F **15** (5B **62**)
Remsted Ho. *NW6*. . . .5D *45*
(off Mortimer Cres.)
Remus Bldg., The *EC1*. .2C *8*
(off Hardwick St.)
Remus Rd. E3 . . . . . . .4C **52**
Renaissance Wlk.
SE10 . . . . *4B 82*
(off Teal St.)
Rendlesham Rd. E5. . . .1C **50**
Renforth St. SE16. . . . .4E **79**
Renfrew Rd. SE11 . . . .5D **77**
Renmuir St. SW17 . . . .5B **116**
Rennell St. SE13 . . . . .1E **109**
Rennie Cotts. *E1* 3E *65*
(off Pernell Cl.)
Rennie Ct. SE1. . . . . .1D **25**
Rennie Est. SE16. . . . .5D **79**
Rennie Ho. *SE1* 5F *25*
(off Bath Ter.)
Rennie St.
SE1 . . . . .1D **25** (2D **77**)
(not continuous)
Renoir Cinema . .3E 7 (3A **62**)
Renoir Ct. *SE16* 1D *93*
(off Stubbs Dr.)
Rensburg Rd. E17 . . . .1F **37**
Renters Av. NW4 . . . .1E **29**

Renton Cl. SW2 . . . . .4B **104**
Rephidim St.
SE1 . . . . .5D **27** (4A *78*)
Replingham Rd.
SW18 . . . . .1B **114**
Reporton Rd. SW6. . . .3A **86**
Repton Ho. *E14* 5A *66*
(off Repton St.)
SW1 . . . . *5E 75*
(off Charlwood St.)
Repton St. E14. . . . . .5A **66**
Reservoir Rd. SE4. . . . .5A **94**
Reservoir Studios
F1 . . . . *5F 65*
(off Cable St.)
Resolution Way *SE8* . . .3C *94*
(off Deptford High St.)
Restell Cl. SE3. . . . . . .2A **96**
Reston Pl. SW7 . . . . . .3E **73**
Restoration Sq.
SW11 . . . . .4F **87**
Restormel Ho. *SE11* . . .5C *76*
(off Chester Way)
Retcar Cl. N19. . . . . . .4D **33**
Retcar Pl. *N19* 4D *33*
(off Retcar Cl.)
Retford St.
N1 . . . . .1E **11** (1A *64*)
Retreat, The SW14 . . .1A **98**
Retreat Ho. E9. . . . . . .3E **51**
Retreat Pl. E9. . . . . . . .3E **51**
Reunion Row E1 . . . . .1D **79**
Reveley Sq. SE16 . . . . .3A **80**
Revelon Rd. SE4 . . . . .2A **108**
Revelstoke Rd.
SW18 . . . . .2B **114**
Reverdy Rd. SE1 . . . . .5C **78**
Review Rd. NW2 . . . . .4B **28**
Rewell St. SW6 . . . . . .3E **87**
Rex Pl. W1 . . . .5C **12** (1C *74*)
Reydon Av. E11 . . . . . .1E **41**
Reynard Cl. SE4. . . . . .1A **108**
Reynard Pl. SE14. . . . .2A **94**
Reynolah Gdns. SE7 . . .1D **97**
Reynolds Cl. NW11 . . . .2D **31**
Reynolds Ho. E2. . . . . .1E *65*
(off Approach Rd.)
NW8 . . . . *1F 59*
(off Wellington Rd.)
SW1 . . . . *5F 75*
(off Erasmus St.)
Reynolds Pl. SE3. . . . . .3D **97**
Reynolds Rd. SE15 . . . .2E **107**
Rheidol M. N1 . . . . . . .1E **63**
Rheidol Ter. N1 . . . . . .5E **49**
Rhoda St. E2 . . .3F **11** (3B **64**)
Rhodes Ho. *N1*. 1B *10*
(off Fairbank Est.)
Rhodesia Rd. E11. . . . .4F **39**
SW9 . . . . .5A **90**
Rhodes St. N7 . . . . . . .2B **48**
Rhodeswell Rd. E14 . . .4A **66**
(Ben Jonson Rd.)
E14. . . . . .5B **66**
(Norbiton Rd., not continuous)
Rhondda Gro. E3 . . . . .2A **66**
Rhyl St. NW5 . . . . . . .3C **46**
Ribblesdale Ho.
NW6 . . . . *5C 44*
(off Kilburn Va.)

Ribblesdale Rd.
SW16 . . . . 5D 117
Ribbon Dance M.
SE5 . . . . 4F 91
Ricardo St. E14 . . . . 5D 67
Ricards Rd. SW19 . . . . 5B 114
Riceyman Ho. WC1 . . . . . 2B 8
(off Lloyd Baker St.)
Richard Anderson Ct.
SE14 . . . . 3F 93
(off Monson Rd.)
Richard Burbidge Mans.
SW13 . . . . 2E 85
(off Brasenose Dr.)
Richard Ho. SE16 . . . . . . 5E 79
(off Silwood St.)
Richard Ho. Dr. E16 . . . . 5F 69
Richard Neale Ho. E1 . . 1D 79
(off Cornwall St.)
Richard Robert
Residence, The
E15 . . . . 3F 53
(off Salway Rd.)
Richardson Cl. E8 . . . . . 5B 50
Richardson Ct. SW4 . . . . 5A 90
(off Studley Rd.)
Richardson Rd. E15 . . . . 1A 68
Richardson's M. W1 . . . . . 4F 5
Richard's Pl. SW3 . . . . . 5A 74
Richard St. E1 . . . . 5D 65
Richbell Pl.
WC1 . . . . 5F 7 (4B 62)
Richborne Ter. SW8 . . . . 3B 90
Richborough Ho.
SE15 . . . . 2E 93
(off Sharratt St.)
Richborough Rd.
NW2 . . . . 1A 44
Richbourne Ct. W1 . . . . 5A 60
(off Harrowby St.)
Richford Ga. W6 . . . . . . 4E 71
Richford Rd. E15 . . . . . 5B 54
Richford St. W6 . . . . 3E 71
Rich Ind. Est.
SE1 . . . . 5E 27 (4A 78)
SE15 . . . . 2D 93
Rich La. SW5 . . . . 1D 87
Richman Ho. SE8 . . . . . 1B 94
(off Grove St.)
Richmond American
International University
in London, The 4D 73
(off Ansdell St.)
Richmond Av. N1 . . . . . 5B 48
NW10 . . . . 3E 43
Richmond Bldgs.
W1 . . . . 3B 14 (5F 61)
Richmond Cl. E17 . . . . . 1B 38
Richmond College
(American International
University in London, The)
. . . . 3D 73
Richmond Cotts. W14 . . 5A 72
(off Hammersmith Rd.)
Richmond Ct. E8 . . . . . . 4D 51
(off Mare St.)
NW6 . . . . 4F 43
(off Willesden La.)
SW1 . . . . 4A 20
(off Sloane St.)

Richmond Cres. N1 . . . . 5B 48
Richmond Gro. N1 . . . . . 4D 49
(not continuous)
Richmond Ho. NW1 . . . . 1E 5
(off Pk. Village E.)
SE17 . . . . 1F 91
(off Portland St.)
Richmond M.
W1 . . . . 3B 14 (5F 61)
Richmond Rd. E7 . . . . . 2D 55
(not continuous)
E8 . . . . 4B 50
E11 . . . . 4F 39
N15 . . . . 1A 36
Richmond St. E13 . . . . . 1C 68
Richmond Ter.
SW1 . . . . 3D 23 (3A 76)
Richmond Way E11 . . . . 4C 40
W12 . . . . 3F 71
W14 . . . . 3F 71
Richmount Gdns.
SE3 . . . . 1C 110
Rich St. E14 . . . . 1B 80
Rickard Cl. SW2 . . . . . 1C 118
Rickett St. SW6 . . . . . . 2C 86
Rickman Ho. E1 . . . . . . 2E 65
(off Rickman St.)
Rickman St. E1 . . . . 3E 65
Rick Roberts Way
E15 . . . . 5E 53
Rickthorne Rd. N19 . . . . 4A 34
Rickyard Path SE9 . . . . 2F 111
Riddell Ct. SE5 . . . . 1B 92
(off Albany Rd.)
Riddons Rd. SE12 . . . . 3E 125
Ridgdale St. E3 . . . . . . 1D 67
Ridgebrook Rd. SE3 . . 1F 111
Ridge Ct. SE22 . . . . . . 5C 106
Ridge Hill NW11 . . . . . . 3A 30
Ridge Rd. N8 . . . . 1B 34
NW2 . . . . 5B 30
Ridge Way SE19 . . . . . 5A 120
Ridgeway, The NW11 . . 2A 30
Ridgeway Dr.
BR1: Brom 4D 125
Ridgeway Gdns. N6 . . . . 2E 33
Ridgewell Cl. N1 . . . . . . 5E 49
SE26 . . . . 4B 122
Ridgmount Gdns.
WC1 . . . . 5B 6 (4F 61)
Ridgmount Pl.
WC1 . . . . 5B 6 (4F 61)
Ridgmount Rd.
SW18 . . . . 3D 101
Ridgmount St.
WC1 . . . . 5B 6 (4F 61)
Ridgway Pl. SW19 . . . . 5A 114
Ridgway Rd. SW9 . . . . 1D 105
Ridgwell Rd. E16 . . . . . 4E 69
Riding, The NW11 . . . . . 2B 30
Riding Ho. St.
W1 . . . . 1E 13 (4D 61)
Ridings, The N6 . . . . . . 2E 33
Ridley Ct. SW16 . . . . . 5A 118
Ridley Rd. E7 . . . . 1E 55
E8 . . . . 2B 50
NW10 . . . . 1C 56
Riffel Rd. NW2 . . . . 2E 43
Rifle Cl. SE11 . . . . 2C 90
Rifle St. E14 . . . . 4D 67

Riga Ho. E1 . . . . 4F 65
(off Shandy St.)
Rigault Rd. SW6 . . . . . . 5A 86
Rigden St. E14 . . . . 5D 67
Rigeley Rd. NW10 . . . . 2C 56
Rigg App. E10 . . . . 3F 37
Rigge Pl. SW4 . . . . 2F 103
Riggindale Rd.
SW16 . . . . 5F 117
Riley Ho. SW10 . . . . . . 3F 87
Riley Rd.
SE1 . . . . 5E 27 (4B 78)
Riley St. SW10 . . . . 2F 87
Rill Ho. SE5 . . . . 3F 91
(off Harris St.)
Rinaldo Rd. SW12 . . . . 5D 103
Ring, The
W2 . . . . 4A 12 (1F 73)
(not continuous)
Ringcroft St. N7 . . . . . . 2C 48
Ringford Rd. SW18 . . . . 3B 100
Ring Ho. E1 . . . . 1E 79
(off Sage St.)
Ringlet Cl. E16 . . . . 4D 69
Ringmer Av. SW6 . . . . . 4A 86
Ringmer Gdns. N19 . . . . 4A 34
Ringmore Ri. SE23 . . . . 5D 107
Ring Rd. W12 . . . . 2E 71
Ringsfield Ho. SE17 . . . . 1E 91
(off Bronti Cl.)
Ringstead Rd. SE6 . . . . 5D 109
Ringwood Gdns. E14 . . 5C 80
SW15 . . . . 1C 112
Ringwood Rd. E17 . . . . 1B 38
Rio Cinema 2A 50
(off Kingsland High St.)
Ripley Gdns. SW14 . . . . 1A 98
Ripley Ho. SW1 . . . . . . 2E 89
(off Churchill Gdns.)
Ripley M. E11 . . . . 1A 40
Ripley Rd. E16 . . . . 5E 69
Ripon Gdns. IG1: Ilf . . . 1F 41
Ripplevale Gro. N1 . . . . 4B 48
Risborough SE17 . . . . . 5E 77
(off Deacon Way)
Risborough Ho. NW8 . . 3A 60
(off Mallory St.)
Risborough St.
SE1 . . . . 3E 25 (3D 77)
Risdon Ho. SE16 . . . . . 3E 79
(off Risdon St.)
Risdon St. SE16 . . . . . . 4E 79
Rise, The E11 . . . . 1C 40
NW10 . . . . 1A 42
Riseholme Ct. E9 . . . . . 3B 52
Riseldine Rd. SE23 . . . 4A 108
Risinghill St. N1 . . . . . . 1B 62
Rising Sun Ct. EC1 . . . . 5E 9
Rita Rd. SW8 . . . . 2A 90
Ritches Rd. N15 . . . . . . 1E 35
Ritchie Ho. E14 . . . . . . 5F 67
(off Blair St.)
N19 . . . . 3F 33
SE16 . . . . 4E 79
(off Howland Est.)
Ritchie St. N1 . . . . 1C 62
Ritherdon Rd.
SW17 . . . . 2C 116
Ritson Ho. N1 . . . . 5B 48
(off Barnsbury Est.)

Ritson Rd. E8 . . . . 3C **50**
Riva Bingo 1A **118**
Rivaz Pl. E9 . . . . 3E **51**
Riven Ct. *W2* *5D 59*
    (off Inverness Ter.)
Riverbank Rd.
  BR1: Brom 3C **124**
River Barge Cl. E14 . . . 3E **81**
River Cl. E11 . . . . 1E **41**
River Ct.
  SE1 . . . . 5D **17** (1D **77**)
Rivercourt Rd. W6 . . . . 5D **71**
Riverdale SE13 . . . . . . 2E **109**
Riverdale Dr. SW18 . . 1D **115**
Riverdale Shop. Cen.
  SE13 . . . . 1E **109**
Riverfleet *WC1* *1E 7*
    (off Birkenhead St.)
River Ho. SE26. . . . . . 3D **121**
Rivermead Ct. SW6 . . 1B **100**
Rivermead Ho. E9 . . . . 2A **52**
River Pl. N1 . . . . 4E **49**
Riversdale Rd. N5 . . . . 5D **35**
Riverside NW4 . . . . 2D **29**
  SE7 . . . . 4D **83**
  WC1 . . . . *1E 7*
    (off Birkenhead St.)
Riverside Apartments
  SE1 . . . . 2F **27** (2B **78**)
Riverside Bus. Cen.
  SW18 . . . . 1D **115**
Riverside Cl. E5 . . . . . . 3E **37**
Riverside Cl. SE3 . . . . 2B **110**
  SW8 . . . . 2F **89**
Riverside Dr. NW11 . . 1A **30**
  W4 . . . . 3A **84**
Riverside Gdns. W6 . . 1D **85**
Riverside Ho. N1 . . . . . 4E **49**
    (off Canonbury St.)
Riverside Mans. E1 . . 2E **79**
    (off Milk Yd.)
Riverside Rd. E15 . . . . 1E **67**
  N15 . . . . 1C **36**
  SW17 . . . . 4D **115**
Riverside Studios *1E 85*
    (off River Ter.)
Riverside Twr. SW6 . . *5E 87*
    (off Boulevard, The)
Riverside Wlk. SE10 . . 4A **82**
    (Morden Wharf Rd.)
  SE10 . . . . 3F **81**
    (Tunnel Av.)
  SW6 . . . . 1A **100**
  W4 . . . . *2B 84*
    (off Chiswick Wharf)
Riverside Workshops
  SE1 . . . . 1A **26**
    (off Park St.)
Riverside Yd. SW17 . . 4E **115**
River St. EC1 . . . 1B **8** (2C **62**)
River Ter. W6 . . . . 1E **85**
  WC2 . . . . 5F **15**
Riverton Cl. W9 . . . . . . 2B **58**
Riverview Cl. F14. . . . . 4B **80**
Riverview Gdns.
  SW13 . . . . 2D **85**
River Vw. Hgts.
  SE16 . . . . 3C **78**
    (off Bermondsey Wall W.)
Riverview Pk. SE6 . . . 2C **122**

River Wlk. W6 . . . . 3E **85**
River Way SE10 . . . . . 4B **82**
Rivet Ho. *SE1* *1B 92*
    (off Coopers Rd.)
Rivington Ct.
  NW10 . . . . 5C **42**
Rivington Pl.
  EC2 . . . . . . 2E **11** (2A **64**)
Rivington St.
  EC2 . . . . . . 2D **11** (2A **64**)
Rivington Wlk. E8 . . . . 5C **50**
Rixon St. N7 . . . . 5C **34**
Ruach Rd. E3 . . . . 4C **52**
Roads Pl. N19 . . . . 4A **34**
Roan St. SE10 . . . . 2F **95**
Robert Adam St.
  W1 . . . . . . 2B **12** (5C **60**)
Roberta St. E2 . . . . 2C **64**
Robert Bell Ho. SE16. . 5C **78**
    (off Rouel Rd.)
Robert Burns M.
  SE24 . . . . 3D **105**
Robert Cl. W9 . . . . 3E **59**
Robert Dashwood Way
  SE17 . . . . 5E **77**
Robert Gentry Ho.
  W14 . . . . *1A 86*
    (off Gledstanes Rd.)
Robert Jones Ho.
  SE16 . . . . *5C 78*
    (off Rouel Rd.)
Robert Keen Cl.
  SE15 . . . . 4C **92**
Robert Lowe Cl.
  SE14 . . . . 3F **93**
Robert Owen Ho.
  SW6 . . . . 4F **85**
Robert Runcie Ct.
  SW2 . . . . 2B **104**
Roberts Cl. SE16 . . . . 3F **79**
Roberts Ct. *N1* *5D 49*
    (off Essex Rd.)
  NW10 . . . . 3A **42**
Roberts M.
  SW1 . . . . . . 5B **20** (4C **74**)
Robertson Gro.
  SW17 . . . . 5A **116**
Robertson Rd. E15. . . . 5E **53**
Robertson St. SW8 . . 1D **103**
Roberts Pl.
  EC1 . . . . 3C **8** (3C **62**)
Robert St.
  NW1 . . . . . . 2E **5** (2D **61**)
  WC2 . . . . . . 5E **15** (1A **76**)
Robert Sutton Ho. *E1* . . 5E **65**
    (off Tarling St.)
Robeson St. E3 . . . . . . 4B **66**
Robin Ct. E14 . . . . 3E **81**
  SE16 . . . . 5C **78**
Robin Cres. E6 . . . . . . 4F **69**
Robin Gro. N6 . . . . 4C **32**
ROBIN HOOD 3A **112**
Robin Hood Ct. EC4 . . 2C **16**
    (off Shoe La.)
Robin Hood Gdns.
  E14 . . . . *1E 81*
    (off Woolmore St.,
    not continuous)
Robin Hood La. E14. . . 1E **81**
  SW15 . . . . 3A **112**

Robin Hood Rd.
  SW19 . . . . 5C **112**
Robin Hood Way
  SW15 . . . . 3A **112**
  SW20 . . . . 3A **112**
Robin Ho. *NW8* *1A 60*
    (off Barrow Hill Est.)
Robin Howard Dance Theatre
  . . . . *2C 6*
    (in Place, The)
Robinia Cres. E10 . . . . 4D **39**
Robins Ct. SE12 . . . . . 3E **125**
Robinscroft M. SE10 . . 4E **95**
Robinson Cl. E11 . . . . 5A **40**
Robinson Ct. *N1* *5D 49*
    (off St Mary's Path)
Robinson Ho. E14 . . . . 4C **66**
    (off Selsey St.)
  W10 . . . . *5F 57*
    (off Bramley Rd.)
Robinson Rd. E2 . . . . . 1E **65**
  SW17 . . . . 5A **116**
Robinson St. SW3 . . . . 2B **88**
Robinwood Pl.
  SW15 . . . . 4A **112**
Robsart St. SW9 . . . . . 5B **90**
Robson Av. NW10 . . . . 4C **42**
Robson Cl. E6. . . . . . . 5F **69**
Robson Rd. SE27 . . . . 3D **119**
Roby Ho. *EC1* *3F 9*
    (off Mitchell St.)
Rocastle Rd. SE4 . . . . 3A **108**
Rochdale Rd. E17 . . . . 2C **38**
Rochdale Way SE8. . . . 3C **94**
    (not continuous)
Roche Ho. E14 . . . . . . *1B 80*
    (off Beccles St.)
Rochelle Cl. SW11 . . 2F **101**
Rochelle St.
  E2. . . . . 2F **11** (2B **64**)
    (not continuous)
Rochemont Wlk. *E8* . . *5C 50*
    (off Pownall Rd.)
Rochester Av. E13 . . . 5E **55**
Rochester Ct. E2 . . . . . 3D **65**
    (off Wilmot St.)
  NW1 . . . . *4E 47*
    (off Rochester Sq.)
Rochester Ho. SE1 . . . 4C **26**
    (off Manciple St.)
  SE15 . . . . *2E 93*
    (off Sharratt St.)
Rochester M. NW1 . . . 4E **47**
Rochester Pl. NW1 . . . 3E **47**
Rochester Rd. NW1 . . . 3E **47**
Rochester Row SW1 . . 5E **75**
Rochester Sq. NW1 . . . 4E **47**
Rochester St. SW1 . . . 4F **75**
Rochester Ter. NW1 . . . 3E **47**
Rochester Wlk.
  SE1 . . . . 1B **26** (2F **77**)
Rochester Way SE3 . . . 4D **97**
  SE9 . . . . 2E **111**
Rochester Way Relief Rd.
  SE3 . . . . 4D **97**
  SE9 . . . . 2E **111**
Rochford Cl. E6 . . . . . . 1F **69**
Rochford Wlk. E8 . . . . 4C **50**
Rochfort Ho. SE8 . . . . 1B **94**
Rock Av. SW14 . . . . . . 1A **98**

Rockbourne M.
SE23 . . . . 1F 121
Rockbourne Rd.
SE23 . . . . 1F 121
Rockell's Pl. SE22 . . . . 4D 107
Rockfield Ho. SE10 . . . . 2E 95
(off Welland St.)
Rock Gro. Way
SE16 . . . . 5C 78
(not continuous)
Rockhall Rd. NW2 . . . . 1F 43
Rockhall Way NW2 . . . . 5F 29
Rockhampton Cl.
SE27 . . . . 4C 118
Rockhampton Rd.
SE27 . . . . 4C 118
Rock Hill SE26 . . . . . . 4B 120
(not continuous)
Rockingham Cl.
SW15 . . . . 2B 98
Rockingham St.
SE1 . . . . 5F 25 (4E 77)
Rockland Rd.
SW15 . . . . 2A 100
Rockley Ct. W14 . . . . . . 3F 71
(off Rockley Rd.)
Rockley Rd. W14 . . . . . . 3F 71
Rocks La. SW13 . . . . . . 4C 84
Rock St. N4 . . . . 4C 34
Rockwell Gdns.
SE19 . . . . 5A 120
Rockwood Pl. W12 . . . . 3E 71
Rocliffe St. N1 . . . . . . 1D 63
Rocombe Cres.
SE23 . . . . 5E 107
Rocque Ho. SW6 . . . . . 3B 86
(off Estcourt Rd.)
Rocque La. SE3 . . . . . . 1B 110
Rodale Mans.
SW18 . . . . 4D 101
Rodborough Ct. W9 . . . . 3C 58
(off Hermes Cl.)
Rodborough Rd.
NW11 . . . . 3C 30
Roden Ct. N6 . . . . 2F 33
Rodenhurst Rd.
SW4 . . . . 4E 103
Roden St. N7 . . . . 5B 34
Roderick Ho. SE16 . . . . 5E 79
(off Raymouth Rd.)
Roderick Rd.
NW3 . . . . 1B 46
Rodgers Ho. SW4 . . . . 5F 103
(off Clapham Pk. Est.)
Rodin Ct. N1 . . . . 5D 49
(off Essex Rd.)
Roding Ho. N1 . . . . . . 5C 48
(off Barnsbury Est.)
Roding La. Sth.
IG4: Ilf, Wfd Grn 1F 41
(not continuous)
Roding M. E1 . . . . 2C 78
Roding Rd. E5 . . . . . . 1F 51
Rodmarton St.
W1 . . . . . . 1A 12 (4B 60)
Rodmell WC1 . . . . . . 2E 7
(off Regent Sq.)
Rodmere St. SE10 . . . . 1A 96
Rodmill La. SW2 . . . . . 5A 104
Rodney Ct. W9 . . . . . . 3E 59

Rodney Ho. E14 . . . . . 5D 81
(off Cahir St.)
N1 . . . . 1B 62
(off Donegal St.)
SW1 . . . . 1D 89
(off Dolphin Sq.)
W11 . . . . 1C 72
(off Pembridge Cres.)
Rodney Pl. SE17 . . . . . 5E 77
Rodney Rd. SE17 . . . . 5E 77
(not continuous)
Rodney St. N1 . . 1A 8 (1B 62)
Rodway Rd. SW15 . . . . 5C 98
Rodwell Rd. SE22 . . . . 4B 106
Roebuck Ho. SW1 . . . . 5F 21
(off Palace St.)
Roedean Cres. SW15 . . 4A 98
ROEHAMPTON 5C 98
Roehampton Cl.
SW15 . . . . 2C 98
Roehampton Ga.
SW15 . . . . 4A 98
Roehampton High St.
SW15 . . . . 5C 98
ROEHAMPTON LANE
. . . . 1D 113
Roehampton La.
SW15 . . . . 5C 98
Roehampton Recreation Cen.
. . . . 5C 98
Roehampton Va.
SW15 . . . . 3B 112
Roffey St. E14 . . . . . . 3E 81
Rogate Ho. E5 . . . . . . 5C 36
Roger Dowley Ct. E2 . . 1E 65
Roger Harriss Almshouses
E15 . . . . 5B 54
(off Gift La.)
Rogers Ct. E14 . . . . . . 1C 80
(off Premiere Pl.)
Rogers Est. E2 . . . . . . 2E 65
Rogers Ho. SW1 . . . . . 5F 75
(off Page St.)
Rogers Rd. E16 . . . . . 5B 68
SW17 . . . . 4F 115
Roger St.
WC1 . . . . . . 4A 8 (3B 62)
Rohere Ho.
EC1 . . . . . . 2F 9 (2E 63)
Rojack Rd. SE23 . . . . . 1F 121
Rokeby Ho. SW12 . . . . 5D 103
(off Lochinvar St.)
Rokeby Rd. SE4 . . . . . 5B 94
Rokeby St. E15 . . . . . 5F 53
Rokell Ho.
BR3: Beck 5D 123
(off Beckenham Hill Rd.)
Roland Gdns. SW7 . . . . 1E 87
Roland Ho. SW7 . . . . . 1E 87
(off Old Brompton Rd.)
Roland M. E1 . . . . 4F 65
Roland Way SE17 . . . . 1F 91
SW7 . . . . 1E 87
Rollins St. SE15 . . . . . 2E 93
Rollit St. N7 . . . . 2C 48
Rolls Bldgs.
EC4 . . . . . . 2B 16 (5C 62)
Rollscourt Av. SE24 . . . 3E 105
Rolls Pas. EC4 . . . . . . 2B 16
Rolls Rd. SE1 . . . . . . 1B 92

Rolt St. SE8 . . . . 2A 94
(not continuous)
Roman Ct. N7 . . . . . . 3B 48
Romanfield Rd.
SW2 . . . . 5B 104
Roman Ho. EC2 . . . . . 1A 18
Roman Ri. SE19 . . . . . 5F 119
Roman Rd. E2 . . . . . . 2E 65
E3 . . . . 5B 52
E6 . . . . 3F 69
NW2 . . . . 5E 29
W4 . . . . 5A 70
Roman Rd. Mkt. E3 . . . 5B 52
(off Roman Rd.)
Roman Way N7 . . . . . . 3B 48
SE15 . . . . 3E 93
Roman Way Ind. Est.
N7 . . . . 4B 48
(off Roman Way)
Roma Read Cl.
SW15 . . . . 5D 99
Romayne Ho. SW4 . . . . 1F 103
Romberg Rd. SW17 . . . 3C 116
Romborough Gdns.
SE13 . . . . 3E 109
Romborough Way
SE13 . . . . 3E 109
Romer Ho. W10 . . . . . 2B 58
(off Dowland St.)
Romero Cl. SW9 . . . . . 1B 104
Romero Sq. SE3 . . . . . 2E 111
Romeyn Rd. SW16 . . . . 3B 118
Romford Rd. E7 . . . . . 3A 54
E12 . . . . 2E 55
E15 . . . . 3A 54
Romford St. E1 . . . . . . 4C 64
Romilly Rd. N4 . . . . . . 4D 35
Romilly St.
W1 . . . . . . 4C 14 (1F 75)
Romilly St. SW6 . . . . . 5B 86
Rommany Rd. SE27 . . . 4F 119
(not continuous)
Romney Cl. NW11 . . . . 3E 31
SE14 . . . . 3E 93
Romney Ct. NW3 . . . . . 3A 46
W12 . . . . 3F 71
(off Shepherd's Bush Grn.)
Romney M.
W1 . . . . 5B 4 (4C 60)
Romney Rd. SE10 . . . . 2F 95
Romney Row NW2 . . . . 4F 29
(off Brent Ter.)
Romney St. SW1 . . . . . 4A 76
Romola Rd. SE24 . . . . 1D 119
Ronald Av. E15 . . . . . . 2A 68
Ronald Buckingham Ct.
SE16 . . . . 3E 79
(off Kenning St.)
Ronald Ho. SE3 . . . . . 2E 111
Ronaldshay N4 . . . . . . 2C 34
Ronalds Rd. N5 . . . . . 2C 48
(not continuous)
Ronald St. E1 . . . . . . 5E 65
Rona Rd. NW3 . . . . . . 1C 46
Rona Wlk. N1 . . . . 3F 49
(off Ramsey Wlk.)
Rondu Rd. NW2 . . . . . 2A 44
Ronver Rd. SE12 . . . . . 1B 124
Rood La.
EC3 . . . . . . 4D 19 (1A 78)

Roof Ter. Apartments, The
. . . . EC1 . . . . 4E 9
(off Gt. Sutton St.)
Rookery Rd. SW4 . . . . 2E 103
Rookery Way NW9 . . . . 1B 28
Rooke Way SE10 . . . . 1B 96
Rookstone Rd.
. . . SW17 . . . . 5B 116
Rookwood Rd. N16 . . . 2B 36
Roosevelt Memorial
. . . . 4C 12 (1C 74)
Rootes Dr. W10 . . . . . 4F 57
Ropemaker Rd.
. . . SE16 . . . . 3A 80
Ropemaker's Flds.
. . . E14 . . . . 1B 80
Ropemaker St.
. . . EC2 . . . . 5B 10 (4F 63)
Roper La.
. . . SE1 . . . . 4E 27 (3A 78)
Ropers Orchard SW3 . 2A 88
(off Danvers St.)
Ropers Wlk. SW2 . . . 5C 104
Ropery Bus. Pk. SE7 . . 5E 83
Ropery St. E3 . . . . 3B 66
Rope St. SE16 . . . . 5A 80
Rope Wlk. Gdns. E1 . . 5C 64
Ropewalk M. E8 . . . . . 4C 50
(off Middleton St.)
Ropley St. E2 . . . . 1C 64
Rosa Alba M. N5 . . . . 1E 49
Rosalind Ho. N1 . . . . . 1A 64
(off Arden St.)
Rosaline Rd. SW6 . . . . 3A 86
Rosaline Ter. SW6 . . . 3A 86
(off Rosaline Rd.)
Rosamond St. SE26 . . 3D 121
Rosary Gdns. SW7 . . . 5E 73
Rosaville Rd. SW6 . . . 3B 86
Roscoe St.
. . . EC1 . . . . 4A 10 (3E 63)
(not continuous)
Roscoe St. Est.
. . . EC1 . . . . 4A 10 (3E 63)
Rose All. EC2 . . . . 1E 19
(off Bishopsgate)
SE1 . . . . . . 1A 26 (2E 77)
Rose & Crown Ct.
. . . EC2 . . . . 2A 18
Rose & Crown Yd.
. . . SW1 . . . . 1A 22 (2E 75)
Rosebank SW6 . . . . . . 3E 85
Rosebank Gdns. E3 . . 1B 66
Rosebank Rd. E17 . . . 1D 39
Rosebank Wlk. NW1 . . 4F 47
Roseberry Gdns. N4 . . 1D 35
Roseberry Pl. E8 . . . . 3B 50
Roseberry St. SE16 . . 5D 79
Rosebery Av. E12 . . . . 3F 55
. . . EC1 . . . . 4B 8 (3C 62)
Rosebery Ct. EC1 . . . . 4B 8
(off Rosebery Av.)
Rosebery Gdns. N8 . . 1A 34
Rosebery Ho. E2 . . . . 1E 65
(off Sewardstone Rd.)
Rosebery Rd. SW2 . . 4A 104
Rosebery Sq. EC1 . . . 4B 8
Rosebury Rd. SW6 . . . 5D 87
Rose Bush Ct. NW3 . . 2B 46

Rose Ct. E1 . . . . 1F 19
E8 . . . . 4B 50
(off Richmond Rd.)
N1 . . . . 5D 49
(off Collin's Yd.)
SE8 . . . . 5F 79
Rosecroft Av. NW3 . . 5C 30
Rosecroft Gdns. NW2 . 5C 28
Rosedale Ct. N5 . . . . 1D 49
Rosedale Ho. N16 . . . 3F 35
Rosedale Rd. E7 . . . . 2E 55
Rosedale Ter. W6 . . . 4D 71
(off Dalling Rd.)
Rosedene NW6 . . . . . 5F 43
(not continuous)
Rosedene Av. SW16 . . 3B 118
Rosedene Ter. E10 . . . 4D 39
Rosedew Rd. W6 . . . . 2F 85
Rosefield Gdns. E14 . . 1C 80
Roseford Ct. W12 . . . . 3F 71
(off Shepherd's Bush Grn.)
Rosehart M. W11 . . . . 5C 58
Rosehill Rd. SW18 . . . 4E 101
Roseleigh Av. N5 . . . . 1D 49
Rosemary Branch Theatre
. . . . 5F 49
(off Penally Pl.)
Rosemary Ct. SE8 . . . . 2B 94
(off Dorking Cl.)
Rosemary Dr. E14 . . . 5F 67
IG4: Ilf 1F 41
Rosemary Ho. N1 . . . . 5F 49
(off Branch Pl.)
Rosemary Rd. SE15 . . 3B 92
SW17 . . . . 3E 115
Rosemary St. N1 . . . . 5F 49
Rosemead NW9 . . . . . 2B 28
Rosemont Rd. NW3 . . 3E 45
Rosemoor St. SW3 . . 5B 74
Rosemount Point
. . . SE23 . . . . 3F 121
Rosenau Cres. SW11 . 4B 88
Rosenau Rd. SW11 . . 4A 88
Rosendale Rd. SE21 . 3F 119
SE24 . . . . 5E 105
Roseneath Rd.
. . . SW11 . . . . 4C 102
Rosenthal Rd. SE6 . . 4D 109
Rosenthorpe Rd.
. . . SE15 . . . . 3F 107
Roserton St. E14 . . . . 3E 81
Rose Sq. SW7 . . . . . . 1F 87
Rose St. EC4 . . . 2E 17 (5D 63)
WC2 . . . . . . 4D 15 (1A 76)
(not continuous)
Rosethorn Cl. SW12 . 5F 103
Rosetta Cl. SW8 . . . . 3A 90
(off Kenchester Cl.)
Roseveare Rd.
. . . SE12 . . . . 4E 125
Rose Way SE12 . . . . 3C 110
Roseway SE21 . . . . . 4F 105
Rosewood Cl. E11 . . . 1F 53
Rosewood Gdns.
. . . SE13 . . . . 5E 95
Rosewood Ho. SW8 . . 2B 90
(off Sth. Lambeth Rd.)
Rosewood Sq. W12 . . 5C 56
Rosher Cl. E15 . . . . . 4F 53
Roshni Ho. SW17 . . . 5A 116

Rosina St. E9 . . . . 3F 51
Roskell Rd. SW15 . . . 1F 99
Roslin Ho. E1 . . . . . . 1F 79
(off Brodlove La.)
Roslin Way
. . . BR1: Brom 5C 124
Rosmead Rd. W11 . . . 1A 72
Rosoman Pl.
. . . EC1 . . . . 3C 8 (3C 62)
Rosoman St.
. . . EC1 . . . . 2C 8 (2C 62)
Ross Ct. E5 . . . . 1D 51
(off Napoleon St.)
SW15 . . . . 5F 99
Rosscourt Mans.
. . . SW1 . . . . 5F 21
(off Buckingham Pal. Rd.)
Rossdale Rd. SW15 . . 2E 99
Rosse M. SE3 . . . . . . 4D 97
Rossendale St. E5 . . . 4D 37
Rossendale Way
. . . NW1 . . . . 5E 47
Rossetti Ct. WC1 . . . . 5B 6
(off Ridgmount Pl.)
Rossetti Ho. SW1 . . . 5F 75
(off Erasmus St.)
Rossetti M. NW8 . . . . 5F 45
Rossetti Rd. SE16 . . . 1D 93
Ross Ho. E1 . . . . 2D 79
(off Prusom St.)
Rossington St. E5 . . . 4C 36
Rossiter Rd. SW12 . . 1D 117
Rosslyn Av. SW13 . . . 1A 98
Rosslyn Hill NW3 . . . 1F 45
Rosslyn Mans. NW6 . 4E 45
(off Goldhurst Ter.)
Rosslyn M. NW3 . . . . 1F 45
Rosslyn Pk. M. NW3 . 2F 45
Rosslyn Pk. RUFC . . 2B 98
Rossmore Cl. NW1 . . 3A 60
(off Rossmore Rd.)
Rossmore Ct. NW1 . . 3B 60
Rossmore Rd. NW1 . . 3A 60
Ross Way SE9 . . . . . 1F 111
Rostella Rd. SW17 . . 4F 115
Rostrevor Av. N15 . . . 1B 36
Rostrevor M. SW6 . . . 4B 86
Rostrevor Rd. SW6 . . 4B 86
SW19 . . . . 5C 114
Rotary St.
. . . SE1 . . . . 5D 25 (4D 77)
Rothay NW1 . . . . 1E 5
(off Albany St.)
Rothbury Hall SE10 . . 5A 82
Rothbury Rd. E9 . . . . 4B 52
Rotheley Ho. E9 . . . . 4E 51
(off Balcorne St.)
Rotherfield Ct. N1 . . . 4F 49
(off Rotherfield St.,
not continuous)
Rotherfield St. N1 . . . 4E 49
Rotherham Wlk. SE1 . 2D 25
ROTHERHITHE 3E 79
Rotherhithe New Rd.
. . . SE16 . . . . 1D 93
Rotherhithe Old Rd.
. . . SE16 . . . . 4E 79
Rotherhithe St. SE16 . 3E 79
Rotherhithe Tunnel
. . . SE16 . . . . 2F 79

Rother Ho. SE15 . . . . . .2D **107**
Rotherwick Ho. E1 . . . . . 1C **78**
(off Thomas More St.)
Rotherwick Rd.
NW11 . . . . .2C **30**
Rotherwood Rd.
SW15 . . . . .1F **99**
Rothery St. N1 . . . . .5D **49**
(off St Marys Path)
Rothesay Ct. SE6 . . . . .2B **124**
SE11 . . . . .2C **90**
(off Harleyford St.)
SE12 . . . . .3D **125**
Rothley Ct. NW8 . . . . . .3F **59**
(off St John's Wood Rd.)
Rothsay Rd. E7 . . . . . . .4E **55**
Rothsay St.
SE1 . . . . .5D **27** (4A **78**)
Rothsay Wlk. E14 . . . . . .5C **80**
(off Charnwood Gdns.)
Rothschild St. SE27 . . .4D **119**
Roth Wlk. N7 . . . . .4B **34**
Rothwell St. NW1 . . . . . .5B **46**
Rotten Row NW3 . . . . . . .3E **31**
SW1 . . . . . .3A **20** (3A **74**)
SW7 . . . . .3A **74**
Rotterdam Dr. E14 . . . . . .4E **81**
Rouel Rd. SE16 . . . . .4C **78**
(Dockley Rd.)
SE16 . . . . .5C **78**
(Southwark Pk. Rd.)
Roundacre SW19 . . . . . .2F **113**
Roundel Cl. SE4 . . . . . . .2B **108**
Roundhay Cl. SE23 . . . . .2F **121**
Round Hill SE26 . . . . . . .2E **121**
(not continuous)
Roundhouse, The 4C **46**
(off Chalk Farm Rd.)
Roundtable Rd.
BR1: Brom 3B **124**
Roundwood Rd.
NW10 . . . . .3B **42**
Rounton Rd. E3 . . . . .3C **66**
Roupell Rd. SW2 . . . . . .1B **118**
Roupell St.
SE1 . . . . .2C **24** (2C **76**)
Rousden St. NW1 . . . . . .4E **47**
Rouse Gdns. SE21 . . . . .4A **120**
Routemaster Cl.
E13 . . . . .2D **69**
Routh Rd. SW18 . . . . . .5A **102**
Rover Ho. N1 . . . . .5A **50**
(off Mill Row)
Rowallan Rd. SW6 . . . . . .3A **86**
Rowan Ct. E13 . . . . .1D **69**
(off High St.)
SE15 . . . . .3B **92**
(off Garnies Cl.)
SW11 . . . . .4B **102**
Rowan Ho. SE16 . . . . . . .3F **79**
(off Woodland Cres.)
Rowan Lodge W8 . . . . . .4D **73**
(off Chantry Sq.)
Rowan Rd. W6 . . . . .5F **71**
Rowans Complex N4 . . . .4C **34**
Rowan Ter. W6 . . . . .5F **71**
Rowan Wlk. N2 . . . . .1E **31**
N19 . . . . .4E **33**
W10 . . . . .3A **58**
Rowberry Cl. SW6 . . . . . .3E **85**

Rowcross St. SE1 . . . . . .1B **92**
Rowditch La. SW11 . . . . .5C **88**
Rowdon Av. NW10 . . . . . .4D **43**
Rowe Ho. E9 . . . . .3E **51**
Rowe La. E9 . . . . .2E **51**
Rowena Cres. SW11 . . . .5A **88**
Rowfant Rd. SW17 . . . . .1C **116**
Rowhill Rd. E5 . . . . .1D **51**
Rowington Cl. W2 . . . . . .4D **59**
Rowland Ct. E16 . . . . . . .3B **68**
Rowland Gro. SE26 . . . . .3D **121**
Rowland Hill Ho.
SE1 . . . . .3D **25** (3D **77**)
Rowland Hill St.
NW3 . . . . .2A **46**
Rowlands Cl. N6 . . . . . . .1C **32**
Rowley Gdns. N4 . . . . . . .2E **35**
Rowley Ho. SE8 . . . . .1C **94**
(off Watergate St.)
Rowley Rd. N15 . . . . .1E **35**
Rowley Way NW8 . . . . . .5D **45**
Rowntree Clifford Cl.
E13 . . . . .3C **68**
Rowntree Cl. NW6 . . . . . .3C **44**
Rowse Cl. E15 . . . . .5E **53**
Rowstock Gdns. N7 . . . . .2F **47**
Roxburgh Rd. SE27 . . . .5D **119**
Roxby Pl. SW6 . . . . .2C **86**
Roxley Rd. SE13 . . . . . . .4D **109**
Roxwell NW1 . . . . .3D **47**
(off Hartland Rd.)
Roxwell Rd. W12 . . . . . . .3C **70**
Roxwell Trad. Pk.
E10 . . . . .2A **38**
Royal Academy of Arts
(Burlington House)
. . . . .5F **13** (1E **75**)
Royal Academy of Music Mus.
. . . . .4C **4** (3C **60**)
Royal Air Force Memorial
. . . . .2E **23** (2A **76**)
Royal Albert Hall 3F **73**
Royal Albert Rdbt.
E16 . . . . .1F **83**
(off Royal Albert Way)
Royal Albert Way E16 . . .1F **83**
Royal Arc. W1 . . . . .5F **13**
Royal Av. SW3 . . . . .1B **88**
Royal Av. Ho. SW3 . . . . . .1B **88**
(off Royal Av.)
Royal Belgrave Ho.
SW1 . . . . .5D **75**
(off Hugh St.)
Royal Ceremonial Dress
Collection, The 2D **73**
(in Kensington Palace)
Royal Cir. SE27 . . . . .3C **118**
Royal Cl. N16 . . . . .3A **36**
SE8 . . . . .2B **94**
SW19 . . . . .3F **113**
Royal College of Art 3F **73**
Royal College of Music
. . . . .4F **73**
Royal College of Obstetricians
& Gynaecologists 3B **60**
Royal College of Physicians
. . . . .3D **5** (3D **61**)
Royal College of Surgeons
. . . . .2A **16** (5B **62**)
Royal Coll. St. NW1 . . . . .4E **47**

Royal Connaught Apartments
E16 . . . . .2F **83**
(off Connaught Rd.)
Royal Ct. EC3 . . . . .3C **18**
(off Finch La.)
SE16 . . . . .4B **80**
Royal Courts of Justice
. . . . .3A **16** (5C **62**)
Royal Court Theatre
. . . . .5C **74**
(off Sloane Sq.)
Royal Cres. W11 . . . . . . .2F **71**
Royal Cres. M. W11 . . . . .2F **71**
Royal Duchess M.
SW12 . . . . .5D **103**
Royal Exchange
. . . . .3C **18** (5F **63**)
Royal Exchange Av.
EC3 . . . . .3C **18**
Royal Exchange Bldgs.
EC3 . . . . .3C **18**
Royal Festival Hall
. . . . .2A **24** (2B **76**)
Royal Fusiliers Mus.
. . . . .5F **19**
(in Tower of London)
Royal Geographical Society
. . . . .3F **73**
(off Kensington Gore)
Royal Hill SE10 . . . . .3E **95**
Royal Hill Ct. SE10 . . . . .3E **95**
(off Greenwich High St.)
Royal Hospital Chelsea Mus.
. . . . .1C **88**
Royal Hospital Rd.
SW3 . . . . .2B **88**
Royal London Ind. Est.
NW10 . . . . .1A **56**
Royal Mews, The 5E **21** (4D **75**)
Royal M.
SW1 . . . . .5E **21** (4D **75**)
Royal Mint Ct.
EC3 . . . . .5F **19** (1B **78**)
Royal Mint Pl. E1 . . . . . . .1C **78**
Royal Mint St. E1 . . . . . . .1B **78**
Royal National Theatre
. . . . .1A **24** (2B **76**)
Royal Naval Pl. SE14 . . . .3B **94**
Royal Oak Ct. N1 . . . . . . .1D **11**
(off Pitfield St.)
Royal Oak Pl. SE22 . . . . .4D **107**
Royal Oak Rd. E8 . . . . . . .3D **51**
Royal Oak Yd.
SE1 . . . . .4D **27** (3A **78**)
Royal Observatory Greenwich
. . . . .3A **96**
Royal Opera Arc.
SW1 . . . . .1B **22** (2F **75**)
Royal Opera House
. . . . .3E **15** (5A **62**)
Royal Orchard Cl.
SW18 . . . . .5A **100**
Royal Pde. SE3 . . . . .5B **96**
SW6 . . . . .3A **86**
Royal Pde. M. SE3 . . . . . .5B **96**
(off Royal Pde.)
Royal Pl. SE10 . . . . .3E **95**
Royal Rd. E16 . . . . .5F **69**
SE17 . . . . .2D **91**

Royal St.
SE1 . . . . 5A **24** (4B **76**)
Royal Twr. Lodge *E1* . . *1C 78*
   (off Cartwright St.)
Royalty M.
W1 . . . . 3B **14** (5F **61**)
Royalty Studios *W11* . . *5A 58*
   (off Lancaster Rd.)
Royal Veterinary College
  Camden Town 5F 47
Royal Victoria Docks
  Watersports Cen. . . . 1C 82
Royal Victoria Patriotic Bldg.
  SW18 . . . . 4F **101**
Royal Victoria Pl.
  E16 . . . . 2D **83**
Royal Victoria Sq.
  E16 . . . . 1D **83**
Royal Victor Pl. E3 . . . 1F **65**
Royal Westminster Lodge
  SW1 . . . . *5F 75*
   (off Elverton St.)
Roycroft Cl. SW2 . . . . 1C **118**
Roydon Cl. SW11 . . . . *5B 88*
   (off Battersea Pk. Rd.)
Royle Bldg. *N1* *1E 63*
   (off Wenlock St.)
Roy Sq. E14 . . . . 1A **80**
Royston Cl. *E13* *5C 54*
   (off Stopford Rd.)
  SE24 . . . . 4E **105**
Royston Gdns.
  IG1: Ilf. 1F **41**
Royston Ho. *SE15* *2D 93*
   (off Friary Est.)
Royston Pde. IG1: Ilf. . . 1F **41**
Royston St. E2 . . . . . . 1E **65**
Rozel Ct. N1 . . . . 5A **50**
Rozel Rd. SW4 . . . . . . 1E **103**
Rq33 SW18. . . . . 2C **100**
Rubens Gdns. *SE22* . . *5C 106*
   (off Lordship La.)
Rubens Pl. SW4 . . . . . 2A **104**
Rubens St. SE6 . . . . . 2B **122**
Ruby St. SE15 . . . . 2D **93**
Ruby Triangle SE15 . . . 2D **93**
Ruckholt Cl. E10 . . . . . 5D **39**
Ruckholt Rd. E9 . . . . . 1C **52**
  E10 . . . . 1C **52**
Rucklidge Av. NW10. . . 1B **56**
Rucklidge Pas.
  NW10 . . . . *1B 56*
   (off Rucklidge Av.)
Rudall Cres. NW3. . . . . 1F **45**
Rudbeck Ho. *SE15* . . . *3C 92*
   (off Peckham Pk. Rd.)
Ruddington Cl. E5 . . . . 1A **52**
Rudge Ho. *SE16*. *4C 78*
   (off Jamaica Rd.)
Rudgwick Ter. NW8 . . . 5A **46**
Rudloe Rd. SW12 . . . . 5E **103**
Rudolf Pl. SW8. . . . . . . 2A **90**
Rudolf Ho. *E13* 1B **68**
  NW6 . . . . *1D 58*
Rufford St. N1 . . . . 5A **48**
Rufford Bus. Cen.
  SW18 . . . . 2D **115**
Rufus Ho. *SE1* *5F 27*
   (off Abbey St.)
Rufus St. N1 . . 2D **11** (2A **64**)

Rugby Mans. *W14* *5A 72*
   (off Bishop King's Rd.)
Rugby Rd. W4 . . . . 3A **70**
Rugby St.
  WC1 . . . . 4F **7** (3B **62**)
Rugg St. E14 . . . . 1C **80**
Rugless Ho. *E14*. *3E 81*
   (off E. Ferry Rd.)
Rugmere *NW1* *4C 46*
   (off Ferdinand St.)
Ruislip St. SW17 . . . . 4B **116**
Rumball Ho. *SE5* *3A 92*
   (off Harris St.)
Rumbold Rd. SW6 . . . . 3D **87**
Rumford Ho. *SE1* *5F 25*
   (off Tiverton St.)
Rumsey M. N4. . . . . . . 5D **35**
Rumsey Rd. SW9. . . . . 1B **104**
Runacres Ct. SE17 . . . . 1E **91**
Runbury Circ. NW9 . . . . 4A **28**
Runcorn Pl. W11 . . . . . 1A **72**
Rundell Cres.
  NW4 . . . . 1D **29**
Rundell Twr. SW8 . . . . . 4B **90**
Runnymede Ct.
  SW15 . . . . 1C **112**
Runnymede Ho. E9 . . . 1A **52**
Rupack St. SE16. . . . . . 3E **79**
Rupert Ct.
  W1 . . . . 4B **14** (1F **75**)
Rupert Gdns. SW9. . . . . 5D **91**
Rupert Ho. SE11 . . . . . 5C **76**
Rupert Rd. N19. . . . . . . 5F **33**
   (not continuous)
  NW6 . . . . 1B **58**
  W4 . . . . 4A **70**
Rupert St.
  W1 . . . . 4B **14** (1F **75**)
Rusbridge Cl. E8 . . . . . 2C **50**
Ruscoe Rd. E16 . . . . . . 5B **68**
Rusham Rd. SW12. . . . 4B **102**
Rush Comn. M.
  SW2 . . . . 5B **104**
   (Cotherstone Rd.)
  SW2 . . . . 5A **104**
   (New Pk. Rd.)
Rushcroft Rd. SW2 . . . 2C **104**
Rushcutters Ct. *SE16*. . *5A 80*
   (off Boat Lifter Way)
Rushey Grn. SE6 . . . . 5D **109**
Rushey Mead SE4 . . . 3C **108**
Rushford Rd. SE4. . . . . 4B **108**
Rushgrove Pde. NW9. . . 1A **28**
Rush Hill M. SW11 . . . *1C 102*
   (off Rush Hill Rd.)
Rush Hill Rd. SW11. . . 1C **102**
Rushmead E2 . . . . 2D **65**
Rushmere Pl. SW19. . . 5F **113**
Rushmore Cres. E5 . . . 1F **51**
Rushmore Ho. SW15. . . 5C **98**
  W14 . . . . *4A 72*
   (off Russell Rd.)
Rushmore Rd. E5. . . . . 1E **51**
   (not continuous)
Rusholme Gro.
  SE19. . . . . 5A **120**
Rusholme Rd. SW15 . . . 4F **99**
Rushton Ho. SW8 . . . . . 5F **89**
Rushton St. N1 . . . . 1F **63**

Rushworth St.
  SE1 . . . . 3E **25** (3D **77**)
Ruskin Av. E12 . . . . 3F **55**
Ruskin Cl. NW11 . . . . . 1D **31**
Ruskin Ct. *SE5* *1F 105*
   (off Champion Hill)
Ruskin Ho. *SW1* *5F 75*
   (off Herrick St.)
Ruskin Mans. *W14*. . . . *2A 86*
   (off Queen's Club Gdns.)
Ruskin Pk. Ho. SE5 . . 1F **105**
Ruskin Wlk. SE24. . . . . 3E **105**
Rusper Cl. NW2 . . . . . . 5E **29**
Rusper Ct. *SW9* *5A 90*
   (off Clapham Rd.)
Russell Cl. SE7 . . . . . . 3E **97**
  W4 . . . . 2B **84**
Russell Ct. E10 . . . . . . 2D **39**
  SE15. . . . . *5D 93*
   (off Heaton Rd.)
  SW1 . . . . 2A **22**
  SW16 . . . . 5B **118**
  WC1 . . . . 4D **7**
Russell Flint Ho. *E16*. . . *2D 83*
   (off Pankhurst St.)
Russell Gdns. NW11 . . . 1A **30**
  W14 . . . . 4A **72**
Russell Gdns. M.
  W14 . . . . 3A **72**
Russell Gro. SW9 . . . . . 3C **90**
Russell Ho. *E14*. *5C 66*
   (off Saracen St.)
  SW1 . . . . *1E 89*
   (off Cambridge St.)
Russell Lodge *SE1*. . . . *5B 26*
   (off Spurgeon St.)
Russell Pde. NW11 . . . *1A 30*
   (off Golders Grn. Rd.)
Russell Pl. NW3. . . . . . 2A **46**
  SE16 . . . . 4A **80**
Russell Rd. E10. . . . . . 1D **39**
  E16 . . . . 5C **68**
  N8. . . . . 1F **33**
  N15. . . . . 1A **36**
  NW9 . . . . 1B **28**
  W14 . . . . 4A **72**
Russell's Footpath
  SW16 . . . . 5A **118**
Russell Sq.
  WC1. . . . . 4D **7** (4A **62**)
Russell St.
  WC2 . . . . 4E **15** (1A **76**)
Russell Yd. SW15 . . . . 2A **100**
Russet Cres. N7. . . . . . 2B **48**
Russett Way SE13 . . . . 5D **95**
Russia Ct. EC2 . . . . 2A **18**
Russia Dock Rd.
  SE16 . . . . 2A **80**
Russia La. E2 . . . . 1E **65**
Russia Row
  EC2 . . . . 3A **18** (5E **63**)
Russia Wlk. SE16 . . . . 3A **80**
Rusthall Av. W4 . . . . . . 5A **70**
Rustic Wlk. *E16* *5D 69*
   (off Lambert Rd.)
Ruston M. W11 . . . . . . 5A **58**
Ruston Rd. SE18 . . . . . 4F **83**
Ruston St. E3 . . . . 5B **52**
Rust Sq. SE5. . . . . 3F **91**
Rutford Rd. SW16 . . . . 5A **118**

Ruth Ct. E3 . . . . 1A 66
Rutherford Ho. E1 . . . 3D 65
(off Brady St.)
Rutherford St. SW1 . . . 5F 75
Ruth Ho. W10 . . . . 3A 58
(off Kensal Rd.)
Ruthin Cl. NW9 . . . . . . 1A 28
Ruthin Rd. SE3 . . . . . . 2C 96
Ruthven St. E9 . . . . . . 5F 51
Rutland Ct. SE5 . . . . 2F 105
SW7 . . . . 3A 74
(off Rutland Gdns.)
Rutland Gdns. N4 . . . . 1D 35
SW7 . . . . 3A 74
Rutland Gdns. M.
SW7 . . . . 3A 74
Rutland Ga. SW7 . . . . . 3A 74
Rutland Ga. M. SW7 . . 3A 74
(off Rutland Ga.)
Rutland Gro. W6 . . . . . 1D 85
Rutland Ho. W8 . . . . . . 4D 73
(off Marloes Rd.)
Rutland M. NW8 . . . . . 5D 45
Rutland M. E. SW7 . . . 4A 74
(off Ennismore St.)
Rutland M. Sth. SW7 . . 4A 74
(off Ennismore St.)
Rutland M. W. SW7 . . . 4A 74
(off Rutland Ga.)
Rutland Pk. NW2 . . . . . 3E 43
SE6 . . . . 2B 122
Rutland Pk. Gdns.
NW2 . . . . 3E 43
(off Rutland Pk.)
Rutland Pk. Mans.
NW2 . . . . 3E 43
Rutland Pl.
EC1 . . . . 5E 9 (3D 63)
Rutland Rd. E7 . . . . . . 4F 55
E9 . . . . 5F 51
E17 . . . . 1C 38
Rutland St. SW7 . . . . . 4A 74
Rutland Wlk. SE6 . . . . 2B 122
Rutley Cl. SE17 . . . . . . 2D 91
Rutt's Ter. SE14 . . . . . 4F 93
Ruvigny Gdns. SW15 . . 1F 99
Ryan Cl. SE3 . . . . 2D 111
Rycott Path SE22 . . . . 5C 106
Ryculff Sq. SE3 . . . . . 5B 96
Rydal Gdns. NW9 . . . . 1A 28
SW15 . . . . 5A 112
Rydal Rd. SW16 . . . . . 4F 117
Rydal Water
NW1 . . . . 2F 5 (2E 61)
Rydens Ho. SE9 . . . . . 3E 125
Ryder Cl.
BR1: Brom 5D 125
Ryder Ct. E10 . . . . 4D 39
SW1 . . . . 1A 22
Ryder Dr. SE16 . . . . . . 1D 93
Ryder Ho. E1 . . . . 3E 65
(off Colebert Av.)
Ryder M. E9 . . . . 2E 51
Ryder's Ter. NW8 . . . . 1E 59
Ryder St.
SW1 . . . . . . 1A 22 (2E 75)
Ryder Yd.
SW1 . . . . . . 1A 22 (2E 75)
Ryde Va. Rd. SW12 . . 2E 117
Rydons Cl. SE9 . . . . . . 1F 111

Rydon St. N1 . . . . 5E 49
Rydston Cl. N7 . . . . . . 4A 48
Ryecotes Mead
SE21 . . . . 1A 120
Ryecroft Rd. SE13 . . . 3E 109
SW16 . . . . 5C 118
Ryecroft St. SW6 . . . . 4D 87
Ryedale SE22 . . . . 4D 107
Ryefield Path SW15 . . 1C 112
Ryefield Rd. SE19 . . . 5E 119
Rye Hill Pk. SE15 . . . . 2E 107
Rye Ho. SE16 . . . . 3E 79
(off Swan Rd.)
SW1 . . . . 1D 89
(off Ebury Bri. Rd.)
Ryelands Cres.
SE12 . . . . 4E 111
Rye La. SE15 . . . . 4C 92
Rye Pas. SE15 . . . . . . 1C 106
Rye Rd. SE15 . . . . 2F 107
Ryfold Rd. SW19 . . . . 3C 114
Rylandes Rd. NW2 . . . 5C 28
Ryland Rd. NW5 . . . . . 3D 47
Rylett Cres. W12 . . . . . 3B 70
Rylett Rd. W12 . . . . . . 3B 70
Rylston Rd. SW6 . . . . 2B 86
Rymer St. SE24 . . . . . 4D 105
Rysbrack St.
SW3 . . . . 5A 20 (4B 74)

S

Saatchi Collection . . . 3F 23
Sabbarton St. E16 . . . 5B 68
Sabella Ct. E3 . . . . 1B 66
Sabine Rd. SW11 . . . . 1B 102
Sable St. N1 . . . . 4D 49
Sach Rd. E5 . . . . 4D 37
Sackville Ho.
SW16 . . . . 3A 118
Sackville St.
W1 . . . . 5A 14 (1E 75)
Saddlers M. SW8 . . . . 4A 90
Saddle Yd.
W1 . . . . 1D 21 (2D 75)
Sadler Ho. EC1 . . . . . . 1C 8
(off Spa Grn. Est.)
Sadler's Wells Theatre
. . . . 1C 8
Saffron Av. E14 . . . . . . 1F 81
Saffron Cl. NW11 . . . . 1B 30
Saffron Ct. E15 . . . . . . 2A 54
(off Maryland Pk.)
Saffron Hill
EC1 . . . . 5C 8 (4C 62)
Saffron St.
EC1 . . . . 5C 8 (4C 62)
Saffron Wharf SE1 . . . 3B 78
(off Shad Thames)
Sage M. SE22 . . . . 3B 106
Sage St. E1 . . . . 1E 79
Sage Way WC1 . . . . . . 2F 7
Saigasso Cl. E16 . . . . . 5F 69
Sail Ct. E14 . . . . 1F 81
(off Newport Av.)
Sailmakers Ct. SW6 . . 5E 87
Sail St. SE11 . . . . 5B 76
Sainfoin Rd. SW17 . . . 2C 116

Sainsbury Rd. SE19 . . 5A 120
St Agnes Cl. E9 . . . . . . 5E 51
St Agnes Pl. SE11 . . . . 2C 90
St Agnes Well EC1 . . . 3C 10
St Aidan's Rd. SE22 . . 4D 107
St Alban's Av. W4 . . . . 4A 70
St Albans Cl. NW11 . . 3C 30
St Albans Ct. EC2 . . . . 1A 18
St Alban's Gro. W8 . . . 4D 73
St Albans La. NW11 . . 3C 30
St Albans Mans. W8 . . 4D 73
(off Kensington Ct. Pl.)
St Alban's Pl. N1 . . . . . 5D 49
St Albans Rd. NW5 . . . 5C 32
NW10 . . . . 5A 42
St Alban's St.
SW1 . . . . 5B 14 (1F 75)
(not continuous)
St Albans Studios
W8 . . . . 4D 73
(off St Albans Gro.)
St Albans Ter. W6 . . . . 2A 86
St Albans Vs. NW5 . . . 5C 32
St Alfege Pas. SE10 . . 2E 95
St Alfege Rd. SE7 . . . . 2F 97
St Alphage Gdn.
EC2 . . . . 1A 18 (4E 63)
St Alphage Highwalk
EC2 . . . . 1A 18
St Alphage Ho. EC2 . . 1B 18
St Alphonsus Rd.
SW4 . . . . 2E 103
St Amunds Cl. SE6 . . . 4C 122
St Andrews Chambers
W1 . . . . 1A 14
(off Wells St.)
St Andrews Cl. NW2 . . 5D 29
SE16 . . . . 1D 93
St Andrew's Ct.
SW18 . . . . 2E 115
St Andrew's Gro. N16 . 3F 35
St Andrew's Hill
EC4 . . . . 4E 17 (1D 77)
(not continuous)
St Andrews Mans.
W1 . . . . 1B 12
(off Dorset St.)
W14 . . . . 2A 86
St Andrews M. N16 . . . 3A 36
SE3 . . . . 3C 96
SW12 . . . . 1F 117
St Andrew's Pl.
NW1 . . . . 3E 5 (3D 61)
St Andrews Rd. E11 . . 1A 40
E12 . . . . 4F 41
E13 . . . . 2D 69
NW10 . . . . 3D 43
NW11 . . . . 1B 30
W3 . . . . 1A 70
W14 . . . . 2A 86
St Andrews Sq. W11 . . 5A 58
St Andrew St.
EC1 . . . . 1C 16 (4C 62)
St Andrews Way E3 . . 3D 67
St Andrew's Wharf
SE1 . . . . 3B 78
St Anne's Cl. N6 . . . . . 5C 32
St Anne's Ct. NW6 . . . 5A 44
W1 . . . . 3B 14 (5F 61)

St Anne's Flats NW1 . . . 1B 6
    (off Doric Way)
St Anne's Pas. E14. . . . . 5B 66
St Anne's Rd. E11. . . . . . 4F 39
St Anne's Row E14. . . . . 5B 66
St Anne's Trad. Est.
   E14. . . . . 5B 66
    (off St Anne's Row)
St Anne St. E14. . . . . . . 5B 66
St Ann's Cres.
   SW18 . . . . 4D 101
St Ann's Gdns.
   NW5 . . . . 3C 46
St Ann's Hill SW18. . . 3D 101
St Ann's Ho. WC1. . . . . . 2B 8
    (off Margery St.)
St Ann's La.
   SW1. . . . . 5C 22 (4F 75)
St Ann's Pk. Rd.
   SW18 . . . . 4E 101
St Ann's Pas. SW13. . . . 1A 98
St Ann's Rd. N15. . . . . . 1D 35
   SW13 . . . . 5B 84
   W11. . . . . 1F 71
St Ann's St.
   SW1. . . . . 5C 22 (4F 75)
St Ann's Ter. NW8. . . . . 1F 59
St Ann's Vs. W11. . . . . . 2F 71
St Anselm's Pl.
   W1. . . . . 4D 13 (1D 75)
St Anthony's Cl. E1. . . . 2C 78
   SW17 . . . . 2A 116
St Anthony's Ct.
   SW17 . . . . 2C 116
St Anthony's Flats
   NW1 . . . . 1B 6
    (off Aldenham St.)
St Antony's Rd. E7. . . . . 4D 55
St Asaph Rd. SE4 . . . . . 1F 107
St Aubins Ct. N1. . . . . . 5F 49
St Aubyn's Av.
   SW19 . . . . 5B 114
St Augustine's Ho.
   NW1 . . . . 1B 6
    (off Werrington St.)
St Augustine's Mans.
   SW1 . . . . 5E 75
    (off Bloomburg St.)
St Augustine's Path
   N5. . . . . 1E 49
St Augustine's Rd.
   NW1 . . . . 4F 47
St Austell Rd. SE13 . . . . 5E 95
St Barnabas Cl.
   SE22. . . . . 3A 106
St Barnabas Rd. E17 . . . 1C 38
St Barnabas St. SW1 . . . 1C 88
St Barnabas Ter. E9 . . . . 2F 51
St Barnabas Vs. SW8. . . 4A 90
St Bartholomew's Cl.
   SE26. . . . . 4D 121
St Bartholomew's
   Hospital Mus. 1E 17
St Benedict's Cl.
   SW17 . . . . 5C 116
St Benet's Pl.
   EC3. . . . . 4C 18 (1F 77)
St Bernard's Cl.
   SE27 . . . . 4F 119

St Bernards Ho. E14. . . . 4E 81
St Bernard's Rd. E6 . . . . 5F 55
St Botolph Row
   EC3. . . . . 3F 19 (5B 64)
St Botolph St.
   EC3. . . . . 2F 19 (5B 64)
St Brelades Ct. N1 . . . . . 5A 50
St Bride's Av. EC4 . . . . . 3D 17
St Bride's Crypt Mus.
   . . . . 3D 17
    (in St Bride's)
St Bride's Pas. EC4 . . . . 3D 17
St Bride St.
   EC4. . . . . 2D 17 (5D 63)
St Catherine's Cl.
   SW17 . . . . 2A 116
St Catherine's Ct. W4. . . 4A 70
St Catherine's Dr.
   SE14 . . . . 5F 93
St Catherines M.
   SW3 . . . . 5B 74
St Catherines Twr.
   E10. . . . . 2D 39
St Chad's Pl.
   WC1. . . . . 1E 7 (2A 62)
St Chad's St.
   WC1. . . . . 1E 7 (2A 62)
    (not continuous)
St Charles Pl. W10 . . . . 4A 58
St Charles Sq. W10 . . . . 4F 57
St Christopher's Ho.
   NW1 . . . . 1E 61
    (off Bridgeway St.)
St Christopher's Pl.
   W1. . . . . 2C 12 (5C 60)
St Clair Rd. E13. . . . . . . 1D 69
St Clare St.
   EC3. . . . . 3F 19 (5B 64)
St Clements Ct. EC4. . . . 4C 18
   N7. . . . . 3B 48
   SE14 . . . . 2F 93
    (off Myers La.)
   W11. . . . . 1F 71
    (off Stoneleigh St.)
St Clement's Hgts.
   SE26. . . . . 3C 120
St Clements Ho. E1 . . . . 1F 19
    (off Leyden St.)
St Clement's La.
   WC2. . . . . 3A 16 (5B 62)
St Clements Mans.
   SW6 . . . . 2F 85
    (off Lillie Rd.)
St Clements St. N7 . . . . 3C 48
St Clements Yd.
   SE22. . . . . 2B 106
St Cloud Rd. SE27 . . . . 4E 119
St Crispin's Cl. NW3 . . . 1A 46
St Cross St.
   EC1. . . . . 5C 8 (4C 62)
St Cuthbert's Rd.
   NW2 . . . . 3B 44
St Cyprian's St.
   SW17 . . . . 4B 116
St Davids Cl. SE16. . . . . 1D 93
    (off Masters Dr.)
St Davids M. E3 . . . . . . 2A 66
    (off Morgan St.)
St David's Pl. NW4 . . . . 2D 29

St Davids Sq. E14. . . . . 1D 95
St Denis Rd. SE27 . . . . . 4F 119
St Dionis Rd. E12. . . . . . 5F 41
   SW6 . . . . 5B 86
St Donatt's Rd. SE14 . . . 4B 94
St Dunstan's All.
   EC3. . . . . 4D 19
St Dunstans Av. W3 . . . 1A 70
St Dunstan's Ct.
   EC4. . . . . 3C 16 (5C 62)
St Dunstans Hill
   EC3. . . . . 5D 19 (1A 78)
St Dunstan's La.
   EC3. . . . . 5D 19 (1A 78)
St Dunstan's Rd. E7. . . . 3D 55
   W6. . . . . 1F 85
St Edmund's Cl. NW8. . . 5B 46
   SW17 . . . . 2A 116
St Edmund's Ct. NW8. . . 5B 46
    (off St Edmund's Ter.)
St Edmunds Cl.
   SW13 . . . . 2E 85
St Edmund's Ter.
   NW8 . . . . 5A 46
St Edward's Cl.
   NW11 . . . . 1C 30
St Edwards Ct. E10 . . . . 2D 39
   NW11 . . . . 1C 30
St Elizabeth Ct. E10. . . . 2D 39
St Elmo Rd. W12. . . . . . 2B 70
    (not continuous)
St Elmos Rd. SE16. . . . . 3A 80
St Ermin's Hill SW1 . . . . 5B 22
St Ervan's Rd. W10 . . . . 4B 58
St Eugene Ct. NW6 . . . . 5A 44
    (off Salusbury Rd.)
St Faith's Rd. SE21 . . . . 1D 119
St Fillans Rd. SE6 . . . . . 1E 123
St Francis' Ho. NW1 . . . . 1F 61
    (off Bridgeway St.)
St Francis Rd. SE22 . . . . 2A 106
St Frideswide's M.
   E14. . . . . 5E 67
St Gabriel's Cl. E11. . . . . 4D 41
   E14. . . . . 4D 67
St Gabriels Mnr. SE5. . . 4D 91
    (off Cormont Rd.)
St Gabriels Rd. NW2 . . . 2F 43
St George's Av. E7. . . . . 4D 55
   N7. . . . . 1F 47
St George's Bldgs.
   SE1. . . . . 4D 77
    (off St George's Rd.)
St George's Cathedral
   . . . . 1E 5 (2D 61)
St George's Cir.
   SE1 . . . . 5D 25 (4D 77)
St George's Cl.
   NW11 . . . . 1B 30
   SW8 . . . . 4E 89
St Georges Ct.
   EC4. . . . . 2D 17 (5D 63)
   SW1 . . . . 1E 89
    (off St George's Dr.)
   SW15 . . . . 2B 100
St George's Dr. SW1 . . . 5D 75
St George's Flds. W2 . . . 1A 74
St George's Flds. W2 . . . 5A 60
St George's Gro.
   SW17 . . . . 3F 115

St George's Ho. NW1 . . . 1F **61**
(off Bridgeway St.)
St George's La. EC3 . . . . 4C **18**
St George's Mans.
SW1 . . . . 1F **89**
(off Causton St.)
St George's M. NW1 . . . 4B **46**
SE1 . . . . 5C **24**
SE8 . . . . 5B **80**
St Georges Pde.
SE6 . . . . 2B **122**
St George's Path
SE4 . . . . 2C **108**
(off Adelaide Av.)
St George's RC Cathedral
. . . . 5C **24** (4C **76**)
E10 . . . . 5E **39**
NW11 . . . . 1B **30**
SE1 . . . . 5C **24** (4C **76**)
W4 . . . . 3A **70**
St Georges Sq. E7 . . . 4D **55**
E14 . . . . 1A **80**
SE8 . . . . 5B **80**
(not continuous)
SW1 . . . . 1F **89**
St George's Sq. M.
SW1 . . . . 1F **89**
St George's Ter. *E6* . . . 2F **69**
(off Masterman Rd.)
NW1 . . . . 4B **46**
SE15 . . . . 3C **92**
(off Peckham Hill St.)
St George's Theatre . . . 1F **47**
St George St.
W1 . . . . 3E **13** (1D **75**)
St George's Way
SE15 . . . . 2A **92**
St George's Wharf
SE1 . . . . 3F **27**
(off Shad Thames)
St George Wharf
SW8 . . . . 2A **90**
St Gerards Cl. SW4 . . 3E **103**
St German's Pl. SE3 . . 4C **96**
St German's Rd.
SE23 . . . . 1A **122**
St Giles Cir.
W1 . . . . 2C **14** (5F **61**)
St Giles Ct. WC2 . . . . 2D **15**
St Giles High St.
WC2 . . . . . . 2C **14** (5F **61**)
St Giles Pas. WC2 . . . 3C **14**
St Giles Rd. SE5 . . . . . 3A **92**
St Giles Ter. *EC2* 1A **18**
(off Beech St.)
St Giles Twr. *SE5* 4A **92**
(off Gables Cl.)
St Gilles Ho. *E2* 1F **65**
(off Mace St.)
St Gothard Rd.
SE27 . . . . 4F **119**
(not continuous)
St Helena Ho. *WC1* 2B **8**
(off Margery St.)
St Helena Rd. SE16 . . 5F **79**
St Helena St.
WC1. . . . . 2B **8** (2C **62**)
St Helen's Gdns.
W10. . . . . 4F **57**

St Helen's Pl.
EC3 . . . . 2D **19** (3A **64**)
St Helier Ct. *N1* 5A **50**
(off De Beauvoir Est.)
SE16 . . . . 3F **79**
(off Poolmans St.)
St Helier's Rd. E10. . . . 1E **39**
St Hilda's Cl. NW6 . . . 4F **43**
SW17 . . . . 2A **116**
St Hilda's Rd. SW13 . . 2D **85**
St Hilda's Wharf *E1* . . . 2E **79**
(off Wapping High St.)
St Hubert's Ho. *E14* . . . 4C **80**
(off Janet St.)
St Hughes Cl. SW17 . . 2A **116**
St James SE14 . . . . . . 4A **94**
St James App.
EC2 . . . . 4D **11** (3A **64**)
St James Ct. *E2* 2C **64**
(off Bethnal Grn. Rd.)
E12 . . . . 4E **41**
SE3 . . . . 4D **97**
SW1 . . . . 5A **22** (4E **75**)
St James Gro. SW11 . . 5B **88**
St James Mans.
NW6 . . . . 4C **44**
(off W. End La.)
St James M. E14 . . . . . 4E **81**
E17 . . . . 1A **38**
(off St James's St.)
St James Residences
W1 . . . . 4B **14**
(off Brewer St.)
St James' Rd. E15 . . . 2B **54**
ST JAMES'S . . . 1B **22** (2F **75**)
St James's
SW1 . . . . 1A **22** (2E **75**)
St James's Av. E2. . . . 1E **65**
St James's Chambers
SW1 . . . . 1A **22**
(off Jermyn St.)
St James's Cl. *NW8*. . . 5B **46**
(off St James's Ter. M.)
SW17 . . . . 2B **116**
St James's Cres.
SW9 . . . . 1C **104**
St James's Dr. SW17 . . 1B **116**
St James's Gdns.
W11 . . . . 2A **72**
(not continuous)
St James's Mkt.
SW1 . . . . . . 5B **14** (1F **75**)
St James's Palace
. . . . 2A **22** (3E **75**)
St James's Pk.
. . . . 3B **22** (3F **75**)
St James's Pas. EC3 . . 3E **19**
St James's Pl.
SW1 . . . . . . 2F **21** (2E **75**)
St James's Rd. SE1 . . 2C **92**
SE16 . . . . 4C **78**
St James's Sq.
SW1 . . . . . . 1A **22** (2E **75**)
St James's St. E17. . . . 1A **38**
SW1 . . . . . . 1F **21** (2E **75**)
St James's Ter. *NW8* . . 5B **46**
(off Prince Albert Rd.)
St James's Ter. M.
NW8 . . . . 5B **46**
St James St. W6 . . . . . 1E **85**

St James's Wlk.
EC1 . . . . 3D **9** (3D **63**)
St James Ter. SW12. . . 1C **116**
ST JOHNS 5C **94**
St John's Av. NW10 . . . 5B **42**
SW15 . . . . 3F **99**
St Johns Chu. Rd.
E9 . . . . 2E **51**
St John's Cl. SW6 . . . 3C **86**
St John's Ct. *E1* 2D **79**
(off Scandrett St.)
N4. . . . . 4D **35**
N5. . . . . 1D **49**
SE13 . . . . 5E **95**
W6 . . . . 5D **71**
(off Glenthorne Rd.)
St John's Cres.
SW9 . . . . 1C **104**
St Johns Dr. SW18. . . 1D **115**
St John's Est. N1 . . . . 1F **63**
SE1 . . . . 3F **27**
St John's Gdns. W11 . . 1A **72**
St John's Gate 4D **9**
St John's Gro. N19. . . . 4E **33**
SW13 . . . . 5B **84**
St John's Hill SW11 . . 3F **101**
St John's Hill Gro.
SW11 . . . . 2F **101**
St Johns Ho. *E14* 5E **81**
(off Pier St.)
SE17 . . . . 2F **91**
(off Lytham St.)
St John's La.
EC1 . . . . 4D **9** (3D **63**)
St John's M. W11. . . . . 5C **58**
St John's Pk. SE3. . . . 3B **96**
St John's Pk. Mans.
N19. . . . . 5E **33**
St John's Path EC1. . . . 4D **9**
St Johns Pathway
SE23 . . . . 1E **121**
St John's Pl.
EC1 . . . . 4D **9** (3D **63**)
St John's Rd. E16. . . . 5C **68**
N15. . . . . 1A **36**
NW11 . . . . 1B **30**
SW11 . . . . 2A **102**
St John's Sq.
EC1 . . . . 4D **9** (3D **63**)
St John's Ter. E7 . . . . 3D **55**
SW15 . . . . 3A **112**
(off Kingston Va.)
W10. . . . . 3F **57**
St John St.
EC1 . . . . 1C **8** (1C **62**)
St John's Va. SE8. . . . 5C **94**
St John's Vs. N19. . . . 4F **33**
W8 . . . . 4D **73**
(off St Mary's Pl.)
St John's Way N19 . . . 4E **33**
ST JOHN'S WOOD . . . 1F **59**
St John's Wood Ct.
NW8 . . . . 2F **59**
(off St John's Wood Rd.)
St John's Wood High St.
NW8 . . . . 1F **59**
St John's Wood Pk.
NW8 . . . . 5F **45**
St John's Wood Rd.
NW8 . . . . 3F **59**

St John's Wood Ter.
NW8 . . . . 1F **59**
St Josephs Almshouses
W6 . . . . 5F **71**
(off Brook Grn.)
St Joseph's College
Sports Cen. 5D **119**
St Joseph's Cotts.
SW3 . . . . 5B **74**
(off Cadogan St.)
St Joseph's Cl. SE7. . . 2D **97**
St Joseph's Flats
NW1 . . . . 1B **6**
(off Drummond Cres.)
St Joseph's Ho. W6 . . . 5F **71**
(off Brook Grn.)
St Joseph's St. SW8 . . 4D **89**
St Joseph's Va. SE3 . . 1F **109**
St Jude's Rd. E2. . . . . 1D **65**
St Jude St. N16 . . . . . 2A **50**
St Julian's Cl.
SW16 . . . . 4C **118**
St Julian's Farm Rd.
SE27 . . . . 4C **118**
St Julian's Rd. NW6. . . 5C **44**
St Katharine Docks
. . . . 5F **19** (2C **78**)
St Katharine's Pct.
NW1 . . . . 1D **61**
St Katharine's Way
E1 . . . . 1F **27** (2B **78**)
(not continuous)
St Katherine's Row
EC3 . . . . 4E **19**
St Katherines Wlk.
W11 . . . . 2F **71**
(off St Ann's Rd.)
St Kilda's Rd. N16 . . . 3F **35**
St Kitts Ter. SE19 . . . 5A **120**
St Laurence Cl. NW6 . . 5F **43**
St Lawrence Cotts.
E14 . . . . 2E **81**
(off St Lawrence St.)
St Lawrence Ct. N1. . . 4F **49**
St Lawrence Ho. SE1 . 5E **27**
(off Purbrook St.)
St Lawrence Ter. E14. . 2E **81**
St Lawrence Ter.
W10 . . . . 4A **58**
St Lawrence Way
SW9 . . . . 4C **90**
St Leonard M. N1. . . . 1A **64**
(off Hoxton St.)
St Leonard's Ct. N1 . . 1C **10**
St Leonard's Rd. E14. . 4D **67**
(not continuous)
NW10 . . . . 3A **56**
St Leonards Sq.
NW5 . . . . 3C **46**
St Leonard's St. E3 . . 2D **67**
St Leonard's Ter.
SW3 . . . . 1B **88**
St Loo Av. SW3 . . . . . . 2A **88**
St Louis Rd. SE27 . . . 4F **119**
St Lucia Dr. E15 . . . . 5B **54**
ST LUKE'S . . . 3A **10** (3E **63**)
St Luke's Av. SW4 . . . 2F **103**
St Luke's Cl.
EC1 . . . . 3A **10** (3E **63**)

St Lukes Ct. E10 . . . . . 2D **39**
(off Capworth St.)
St Luke's Est.
EC1 . . . . 2B **10** (2F **63**)
St Luke's M. W11 . . . . . 5B **58**
St Luke's Rd. W11 . . . . 4B **58**
St Luke's Sq. E16 . . . . 5B **68**
St Luke's St. SW3 . . . 1A **88**
St Luke's Yd. W9 . . . . . 1B **58**
(not continuous)
St Margarets Cl.
EC2 . . . . 5F **63**
St Margarels Ct.
SE1 . . . . 2A **26** (2E **77**)
SW15 . . . . 2D **99**
St Margaret's Cres.
SW15 . . . . 3D **99**
St Margaret's Gro.
E11 . . . . 5B **40**
St Margaret's La. W8 . . 4D **73**
St Margaret's Pas.
SE13 . . . . 1A **110**
(not continuous)
St Margarets Rd. E12. . 4E **41**
NW10 . . . . 2E **57**
SE4 . . . . 2B **108**
(not continuous)
St Margaret St.
SW1 . . . . 4D **23** (3A **76**)
St Marks Cl. SE10 . . . 1A **95**
SW6 . . . . 4C **86**
St Marks Ct. E10 . . . . . 2D **39**
(off Capworth St.)
NW8 . . . . 1E **59**
(off Abercorn Pl.)
St Mark's Cres. NW1 . . 5C **46**
St Mark's Gro. SW10 . . 3D **87**
St Marks Ho. SE17. . . . 2F **91**
(off Lytham St.)
St Marks Ind. Est.
E16 . . . . 2F **83**
St Mark's Pl.
SW19 . . . . 5B **114**
W11 . . . . 5A **58**
St Mark's Ri. E8 . . . . . 2B **50**
St Mark's Rd. W10 . . . 4F **57**
St Mark's Sq. NW1 . . . 5C **46**
St Mark St. E1 . . . . . . 5B **64**
St Mark's Vs. N4 . . . . . 4B **34**
(off Moray Rd.)
St Martin-in-the-Fields Church
. . . . 5D **15**
(off St Martin's Pl.)
St Martin's Almshouses
NW1 . . . . 5E **47**
St Martin's Av. E6. . . . 1F **69**
St Martin's Cl. NW1 . . . 5E **47**
St Martins Ct. EC4 . . . . 2F **17**
(off Paternoster Sq.)
N1 . . . . 5A **50**
(off De Beauvoir Est.)
WC2 . . . . 4D **15** (1A **76**)
St Martins Est. SW2. . 1C **118**
St Martin's La.
WC2 . . . . 4D **15** (1A **76**)
St Martin's le-Grand
EC1 . . . . 2F **17** (5E **63**)
St Martin's Pl.
WC2 . . . . 5D **15** (1A **76**)
St Martin's Rd. SW9 . . 5B **90**

St Martin's St.
WC2 . . . . 5C **14** (1F **75**)
(not continuous)
St Martin's Theatre. . . . 4D **15**
(off West St.)
St Martins Way
SW17 . . . . 3E **115**
St Mary Abbot's Ct.
W14 . . . . 4B **72**
(off Warwick Gdns.)
St Mary Abbot's Pl.
W8 . . . . 4B **72**
St Mary Abbot's Ter.
W14 . . . . 4B **72**
St Mary at Hill
EC3 . . . . 5D **19** (1A **78**)
St Mary Axe
EC3 . . . . 3D **19** (5A **64**)
St Marychurch St.
SE16 . . . . 3E **79**
St Mary Graces Ct.
E1 . . . . 1B **78**
St Marylebone Cl.
NW10 . . . . 5A **42**
St Mary le-Park Ct.
SW11 . . . . 3A **88**
(off Parkgate Rd.)
St Mary Newington Cl.
SE17 . . . . 1A **92**
(off Surrey Sq.)
St Mary's Av. E11. . . . . 2D **41**
St Mary's Ct. SE7 . . . . 3F **97**
W6 . . . . 4B **70**
St Mary's Est. SE16 . . . 3E **79**
(off St Marychurch St.)
St Mary's Flats NW1 . . 1B **6**
(off Drummond Cres.)
St Mary's Gdns.
SE11 . . . . 5C **76**
St Mary's Ga. W8. . . . . 4D **73**
St Mary's Gro. N1 . . . . 3D **49**
SW13 . . . . 1D **99**
St Mary's Ho. N1 . . . . . 5D **49**
(off St Mary's Path)
St Mary's Mans. W2. . . 4F **59**
St Mary's M. NW6 . . . . 4D **45**
St Mary's Path E1. . . . . 5C **64**
(off Adler St.)
N1 . . . . 5D **49**
St Mary's Pl. W8 . . . . . 4D **73**
St Mary's Rd. E10 . . . . 5E **39**
E13 . . . . 1D **69**
NW10 . . . . 5A **42**
NW11 . . . . 2A **30**
SE15 . . . . 4E **93**
SW19 . . . . 5A **114**
St Mary's Sq. W2 . . . . . 4F **59**
St Mary's Ter. W2. . . . . 4F **59**
St Mary's Twr. EC1. . . . 4A **10**
(off Fortune St.)
St Mary's Wlk. SE11 . . 5C **76**
St Matthews Ct. E10 . . 2D **39**
SE1 . . . . 4E **77**
(off Meadow Row)
St Matthews Ho.
SE17 . . . . 2F **91**
(off Phelp St.)
St Matthew's Lodge
NW1 . . . . 1E **61**
(off Oakley Sq.)

St Matthew's Rd.
SW2 . . . . 2B **104**
St Matthew's Row E2 . . 2C **64**
St Matthew St.
SW1 . . . . 5B **22** (4F **75**)
St Maur Rd. SW6 . . . . . 4B **86**
St Michael's All.
EC3 . . . . 3C **18** (5F **63**)
St Michaels Cl. E16 . . . . 4F **69**
St Michaels Ct. E14 . . . . 4E **67**
(off St Leonards Rd.)
SE1 . . . . 4A **26**
(off Trinity St.)
St Michael's Flats
NW1 . . . . 1B **6**
(off Aldenham St.)
St Michael's Gdns.
W10 . . . . 4A **58**
St Michaels M. SW1 . . 5C **74**
St Michael's Grn.
NW2 . . . . 1E **43**
SW9 . . . . 5F **59**
St Michael's St. W2 . . . 5F **59**
St Michaels Ter. N6 . . . 3C **32**
(off South Gro.)
St Mildred's Ct.
EC2 . . . . 3B **18** (5F **63**)
St Mildreds Rd.
SE6 . . . . 5A **110**
SE12 . . . . 5A **110**
St Nicholas' Flats
NW1 . . . . 1B **6**
(off Werrington St.)
St Nicholas Glebe
SW17 . . . . 5C **116**
St Nicholas Ho. SE8 . . . 2C **94**
(off Deptford Grn.)
St Nicholas St. SE8 . . . 4B **94**
St Norbert Grn. SE4 . . 2A **108**
St Norbert Rd. SE4 . . . 3F **107**
St Olaf Ho. SE1 . . . . . . 1C **26**
St Olaf's Rd. SW6 . . . . 3A **86**
St Olaf Stairs SE1 . . . . 1C **26**
St Olave's Ct.
EC2 . . . . 3B **18** (5F **63**)
St Olave's Est.
SE1 . . . . 3E **27** (3A **78**)
St Olave's Gdns.
SE11 . . . . 5C **76**
St Olave's Mans.
SE11 . . . . 5C **76**
(off Walnut Tree Wlk.)
St Olave's Ter. SE1 . . . 3E **27**
St Olav's Sq. SE16 . . . 3E **79**
St Oswald's Pl. SE11 . . 1B **90**
St Oswalds Studios
SW6 . . . . 2C **86**
(off Sedlescombe Rd.)
St Oswulf St. SW1 . . . 5F **75**
St Owen Ho. SE1 . . . . . 5F **27**
(off Fendall St.)
ST PANCRAS . . . 2E **7** (3B **62**)
St Pancras Commercial Cen.
NW1 . . . . 5E **47**
(off Pratt St.)
St Pancras Way NW1 . . 4E **47**
St Paul's All. EC4 . . . . . 3E **17**
(off St Paul's Chyd.)
St Paul's Arts Cen. 5C **80**
(off Westferry Rd.)

St Paul's Av. NW2 . . . 3D **43**
SE16 . . . . 2F **79**
St Paul's Bldgs. EC1 . . . 3E **9**
(off Dallington St.)
St Paul's Cathedral
. . . . 3F **17** (5E **63**)
St Paul's Chyd.
EC4 . . . . 3E **17** (5D **63**)
(not continuous)
St Pauls Cl. SE7 . . . . . 1F **97**
St Pauls Ct. SW4 . . . . 3F **103**
St Pauls Courtyard
SE8 . . . . 3C **94**
(off Crossfield St.)
St Paul's Cres. NW1 . . . 4F **47**
(not continuous)
St Paul's M. NW1 . . . . 4F **47**
St Paul's Pl. N1 . . . . . . 3F **49**
St Paul's Rd. N1 . . . . . 3D **49**
St Paul's Shrubbery
N1 . . . . 3F **49**
St Paul's Studios
W14 . . . . 1A **86**
(off Talgarth Rd.)
St Pauls Ter. SE17 . . . 2D **91**
St Pauls Twr. E10 . . . . 2D **39**
(off Beaumont Rd.)
St Paul Sta. N1 . . . . . . 5E **49**
(not continuous)
St Pauls Vw. Apartments
EC1 . . . . 2B **8**
(off Amwell St.)
St Pauls Way E3 . . . . . 4B **66**
St Peter's All. EC3 . . . . 3C **18**
(off Cornhill)
St Peter's Av. E2 . . . . . 1C **64**
St Petersburgh M.
W2 . . . . 1D **73**
St Petersburgh Pl.
W2 . . . . 1D **73**
St Peter's Cen. E1 . . . . 2D **79**
(off Reardon St.)
St Peter's Chu. Ct.
N1 . . . . 5D **49**
(off St Peter's St.)
St Peter's Cl. E2 . . . . . 1C **64**
SW17 . . . . 2A **116**
St Peters Ct. NW4 . . . . 1E **29**
SE12 . . . . 3B **110**
St Peter's Gdns.
SE27 . . . . 3C **118**
St Peter's Gro. W6 . . . 5C **70**
St Peters Ho. SE17 . . . 2F **91**
WC1 . . . . 2E **7**
(off Regent Sq.)
St Peters M. N8 . . . . . 1C **34**
St Peters Pl. W9 . . . . . 3D **59**
St Peter's Rd. W6 . . . . 1C **84**
St Peter's Sq. E2 . . . . . 1C **64**
W6 . . . . 5B **70**
St Peter's St. N1 . . . . . 5D **49**
St Peter's St. M. N1 . . . 1D **63**
(off St Peters St.)
St Peter's Ter. SW6 . . . 3B **86**
St Peter's Vs. W6 . . . . 5C **70**
St Peter's Way N1 . . . . 4A **50**
St Peter's Wharf W4 . . 1C **84**
St Philip Ho. WC1 . . . . . 2B **8**
(off Lloyd Baker St.)

St Philip Sq. SW8 . . . . 5D **89**
St Philip's Rd. E8 . . . . 3C **50**
St Philip St. SW8 . . . . 5D **89**
St Philip's Way N1 . . . . 5E **49**
St Quentin Ho.
SW18 . . . . 4F **101**
St Quintin Av. W10 . . . 4E **57**
St Quintin Gdns.
W10 . . . . 4E **57**
St Quintin Rd. E13 . . . 2D **69**
St Regis Hgts. NW3 . . . 5D **31**
St Richard's Ho.
NW1 . . . . 1B **6**
(off Eversholt St.)
St Rule St. SW8 . . . . . 5E **89**
St Saviour's Coll.
SE27 . . . . 4F **119**
St Saviour's Est.
SE1 . . . . 5F **27** (3B **78**)
St Saviour's Rd.
SW2 . . . . 3B **104**
St Saviour's Wharf
SE1 . . . . 3F **27**
(off Mill St.)
SE1 . . . . 3F **27**
(off Shad Thames)
Saints Cl. SE27 . . . . . 4D **119**
Saints Dr. E7 . . . . 2F **55**
St Silas Pl. NW5 . . . . . 3C **46**
St Simon's Av. SW15 . . 3E **99**
St Stephen's Av. E17 . . 1E **39**
W12 . . . . 2D **71**
(not continuous)
St Stephen's Cl. E17 . . 1D **39**
NW8 . . . . 5A **46**
St Stephens Ct. N8 . . . 1B **34**
St Stephen's Cres.
W2 . . . . 5C **58**
St Stephen's Gdns.
SW15 . . . . 3B **100**
W2 . . . . 5C **58**
(not continuous)
St Stephens Gro.
SE13 . . . . 1E **109**
St Stephens Ho.
SE17 . . . . 2F **91**
(off Lytham St.)
St Stephens M. W2 . . . 4C **58**
St Stephens Pde. E7 . . 4E **55**
St Stephen's Rd. E3 . . 5A **52**
E6 . . . . 4E **55**
E17 . . . . 1D **39**
St Stephen's Row
EC4 . . . . 3B **18**
St Stephen's Ter.
SW8 . . . . 3B **90**
St Stephen's Wlk.
SW7 . . . . 5E **73**
(off Southwell Gdns.)
St Swithins La.
EC4 . . . . 4B **18** (1F **77**)
St Swithun's Rd.
SE13 . . . . 4F **109**
St Thomas Ct. E10 . . . 2D **39**
(off Beaumont Rd.)
NW1 . . . . 4E **47**
(off Wrotham Rd.)
St Thomas Ho. E1 . . . . 5F **65**
(off W. Arbour St.)
St Thomas Rd. E16 . . . 5C **68**

St Thomas's Gdns.
NW5 . . . . 3C 46
St Thomas's Pl. E9 . . . . . 4E 51
St Thomas's Rd. N4 . . . . 4C 34
NW10 . . . . 5A 42
St Thomas's Sq. E9 . . . . 4E 51
St Thomas Ho.
SE1 . . . . 2C 26 (2F 77)
St Thomas's Way
SW6 . . . . 3B 86
St Vincent Cl. SE27 . . . 5D 119
St Vincent De Paul Ho.
E1 . . . . 4E 65
(off Jubilee St.)
St Vincent Ho. SE1 . . . . 5F 27
(off Fendall St.)
St Vincent St.
W1 . . . . 1C 12 (4C 60)
Sala Ho. SE3 . . . . 2D 111
Salamanca Pl. SE1 . . . 5B 76
Salamanca Sq. SE1 . . . 5B 76
(off Salamanca Pl.)
SE11 . . . . 5B 76
Salcombe Rd. E17 . . . . 2B 38
N16 . . . . 2A 50
Salcott Rd. SW11 . . . . 3A 102
Salehurst Rd. SE4 . . . . 4B 108
Salem Rd. W2 . . . . . . 1D 73
Sale Pl. W2 . . . . 4A 60
Sale St. E2 . . . . 3C 64
Salford Ho. E14 . . . . . 5E 81
(off Seyssel St.)
Salford Rd. SW2 . . . . 1F 117
Salisbury Cl. SE17 . . . 5F 77
Salisbury Ct.
EC4 . . . . 3D 17 (5D 63)
Salisbury Ho. E14 . . . . 5D 67
(off Hobday St.)
EC2 . . . . 1C 18
(off London Wall)
N1 . . . . 5D 49
(off St Mary's Path)
SW1 . . . . 1F 89
(off Drummond Ga.)
SW9 . . . . 3C 90
(off Cranmer Rd.)
Salisbury Mans. N15 . . 1D 35
Salisbury M. SW6 . . . . 3B 86
Salisbury Pas. SW6 . . . 3B 86
(off Dawes Rd.)
Salisbury Pavement
SW6 . . . . 3B 86
(off Dawes Rd.)
Salisbury Pl. SW9 . . . . 3D 91
W1 . . . . 5A 4 (4B 60)
Salisbury Rd. E7 . . . . . 3C 54
E10 . . . . 4E 39
E12 . . . . 2F 55
E17 . . . . 1E 39
N4 . . . . 1D 35
Salisbury Sq.
EC4 . . . . 3C 16 (5C 62)
Salisbury St. NW8 . . . . 3A 60
Salisbury Ter. SE15 . . . 1E 107
Salisbury Wlk. N19 . . . 4E 33
Salmen Rd. E13 . . . . . 1B 68
Salmon La. E14 . . . . . 5A 66
Salmon M. NW6 . . . . . 2C 44
Salmon St. E14 . . . . . 5B 66

Salomons Rd. E13 . . . . 4E 69
Salop Rd. E17 . . . . . . 1F 37
Saltcoats Rd. W4 . . . . 3A 70
Saltdene N4 . . . . 3B 34
Salterford Rd.
SW17 . . . . 5C 116
Salter Rd. SE16 . . . . . 2F 79
Salters Ct. EC4 . . . . . . 3A 18
Salter's Hall Ct. EC4 . . 4B 18
Salter's Hill SE19 . . . . 5F 119
Salters Rd. W10 . . . . . 3F 57
Salter St. E14 . . . . . . 1B 80
NW10 . . . . 2C 56
Salterton Rd. N7 . . . . . 5B 34
Saltoun Rd. SW2 . . . . 2C 104
Saltram Cres. W9 . . . . 2B 58
Saltwell St. E14 . . . . . 1C 80
Saltwood Gro. SE17 . . 1F 91
Saltwood Ho. SE15 . . . 2E 93
(off Lovelinch Cl.)
Salusbury Rd. NW6 . . . 5A 44
Salutation St. SE10 . . . 5A 82
Salvador SW17 . . . . . 5B 116
Salvin Rd. SW15 . . . . 1F 99
Salway Pl. E15 . . . . . . 3F 53
Salway Rd. E15 . . . . . 3F 53
Samantha Cl. E17 . . . . 2B 38
Sam Bartram Cl. SE7 . . 1E 97
Sambrook Ho. E1 . . . . 4E 65
(off Jubilee St.)
SE11 . . . . 5C 76
(off Hotspur St.)
Sambruck M. SE6 . . . . 1D 123
Samels Ct. W6 . . . . . . 1C 84
Samford Ho. N1 . . . . . 5C 48
(off Barnsbury Est.)
Samford St. NW8 . . . . 3F 59
Samira Cl. E17 . . . . . . 1C 38
Sam Manners Ho.
SE10 . . . . 1A 96
(off Tuskar St.)
Sam March Ho. E14 . . . 5F 67
(off Blair St.)
Sampson Ho.
SE1 . . . . 1D 25 (2D 77)
Sampson St. E1 . . . . . 2C 78
Samson St. E13 . . . . . 1E 69
Samuda Est. E14 . . . . 4E 81
Samuel Cl. E8 . . . . . . 5B 50
SE14 . . . . 2F 93
Samuel Ho. E8 . . . . . . 5B 50
(off Clarissa St.)
Samuel Johnson Cl.
SW16 . . . . 4B 118
Samuel Jones Ind. Est.
SE15 . . . . 3A 92
Samuel Lewis Bldgs.
N1 . . . . 3C 48
Samuel Lewis Trust Dwellings
N16 . . . . 1A 36
SE5 . . . . 4E 91
(off Warner Rd.)
SW3 . . . . 5A 74
SW6 . . . . 3C 86
(off Vanston Pl.)
W14 . . . . 5B 72
(off Lisgar Ter.)
Samuel Richardson Ho.
W14 . . . . 5B 72
(off Nth. End Cres.)

Samuel's Cl. W6 . . . . . 5E 71
Samuel St. SE15 . . . . . 3B 92
Sancroft Cl. NW2 . . . . 5D 29
Sancroft Ho. SE11 . . . 1B 90
(off Sancroft St.)
Sancroft St. SE11 . . . . 1B 90
Sanctuary, The SW1 . . . 5C 22
Sanctuary St.
SE1 . . . . 3A 26 (3E 77)
Sandale Cl. N16 . . . . . 5F 35
Sandall Ho. E3 . . . . . . 1A 66
Sandall Rd. NW5 . . . . 3E 47
Sandal St. E15 . . . . . . 5A 54
Sandalwood Cl. E1 . . . 3A 66
Sandalwood Mans.
W8 . . . . 4D 73
(off Stone Hall Gdns.)
Sandbourne NW8 . . . . 5D 45
(off Abbey Rd.)
W11 . . . . 5C 58
(off Dartmouth Cl.)
Sandbourne Rd. SE4 . . 5A 94
Sandbrook Rd. N16 . . . 5A 36
Sandby Ho. NW6 . . . . 5C 44
Sandell St.
SE1 . . . . 3B 24 (3C 76)
Sanderling Ct. SE8 . . . 2B 94
(off Abinger Gro.)
Sanderling Lodge E1 . . 1B 78
(off Star Pl.)
Sanders Ho. WC1 . . . . 1B 8
(off Gt. Percy St.)
Sanderson Ho. NW5 . . 1D 47
Sanderson Ho. SE8 . . . 1B 94
(off Grove St.)
Sanderstead Av.
NW2 . . . . 4A 30
Sanderstead Cl.
SW12 . . . . 5E 103
Sanderstead Rd. E10 . . 3A 38
Sanders Way N19 . . . . 3F 33
Sandfield WC1 . . . . . . 2E 7
(off Cromer St.)
Sandford Ct. N16 . . . . 3A 36
Sandford Row SE17 . . . 1F 91
Sandford St. SW6 . . . . 3D 87
Sandgate Ho. E5 . . . . . 2D 51
Sandgate La. SW18 . . . 1A 116
Sandgate St. SE15 . . . 2D 93
Sandgate Trad. Est.
SE15 . . . . 2D 93
(off Sandgate St.)
Sandham Ct. SW4 . . . . 4A 90
Sandhills, The SW10 . . 2E 87
(off Limerston St.)
Sandhurst Ct. SW2 . . . 2A 104
Sandhurst Ho. E1 . . . . 4E 65
(off Wolsy St.)
Sandhurst Mkt. SE6 . . 1E 123
(off Sandhurst Rd.)
Sandhurst Rd. SE6 . . . 1F 123
Sandifer Dr. NW2 . . . . 5F 29
Sandilands Rd. SW6 . . 4D 87
Sandison St. SE15 . . . 1C 106
Sandland St.
WC1 . . . . 1A 16 (4B 62)
Sandlings Cl. SE15 . . . 5D 93
Sandmere Rd. SW4 . . . 2A 104
Sandown St. SE26 . . . 3D 121
Sandpiper Cl. SE16 . . . 3B 80

Sandpiper Ct. *E1* *1C 78*
   (off Thomas More St.)
E14 . . . . *4E 81*
   (off New Union Cl.)
SE8 . . . . *2C 94*
   (off Edward Pl.)
Sandpiper Ho.
  SW18 . . . . 1E 101
Sandpit Rd.
  BR1: Brom 5A 124
Sandridge St. N19 . . . . 4E 33
Sandringham Cl.
  SW19 . . . . 1F 113
Sandringham Ct.
  SE16 . . . . *2F 79*
   (off King & Queen Wharf)
  W1 . . . . *3A 14*
   (off Dufour's Pl.)
  W9 . . . . *2E 59*
   (off Maida Va.)
Sandringham Flats
  WC2 . . . . *4C 14*
   (off Charing Cross Rd.)
Sandringham Gdns.
  N8 . . . . 1A 34
Sandringham Ho.
  W14 . . . . *5A 72*
   (off Windsor Way)
Sandringham Rd.
  BR1: Brom 5C 124
  E7 . . . . 2E 55
  E8 . . . . 2B 50
  E10 . . . . 1F 39
  NW2 . . . . 3D 43
  NW11 . . . . 2A 30
Sandrock Rd. SE13 . . . 1C 108
SANDS END 4E 87
Sand's End La. SW6 . . . 4D 87
Sandstone La. E16 . . . . 1D 83
Sandstone Pl. N19 . . . . 4D 33
Sandstone Rd.
  SE12 . . . . 2D 125
Sandtoft Rd. SE7 . . . . . 2D 97
Sandwell Cres. NW6 . . . 3C 44
Sandwich Ho. *SE16* *3E 79*
   (off Swan Rd.)
  WC1 . . . . *2D 7*
   (off Sandwich St.)
Sandwich St.
  WC1 . . . . 2D 7 (2A 62)
Sandy Rd. NW3 . . . . . . 4D 31
   (not continuous)
Sandys Row
  E1 . . . . 1E 19 (4A 64)
Sanford La. N16 . . . . . . 5B 36
Sanford St. SE14 . . . . . 2A 94
Sanford Ter. N16 . . . . . 5B 36
Sanford Wlk. N16 . . . . . 4B 36
  SE14 . . . . 2A 94
Sangley Rd. SE6 . . . . . 5D 109
Sangora Rd. SW11 . . . . 2F 101
Sankey Ho. *E2* *1E 65*
   (off St James's Av.)
Sansom Rd. E11 . . . . . . 4B 40
Sansom St. SE5 . . . . . . 4F 91
Sans Wlk.
  EC1 . . . . 3C 8 (3C 62)
Santley Ho.
  SE1 . . . . 4C 24 (3C 76)
Santley St. SW4 . . . . . . 2B 104

Santos Rd. SW18 . . . . . 3C 100
Sapcote Trad. Cen.
  NW10 . . . . 3B 42
Saperton Wlk. *SE11* . . . *5B 76*
   (off Juxon St.)
Sapperton Ho. EC1 . . . . 3F 9
Sapphire Ct. *E1* *1C 78*
   (off Cable St.)
Sapphire Rd. SE8 . . . . . 5A 80
Saracens Head Yd.
  EC3 . . . . 3F 19
Sarah Ho. *E1* *5D 65*
   (off Commercial Rd.)
Sarah St. N1 . . . 1E 11 (2A 64)
Sarah Swift Ho. *SE1* . . . *3C 26*
   (off Kipling St.)
Sara La. Ct. *N1* *1A 64*
   (off Stanway St.)
Saratoga Rd. E5 . . . . . . 1E 51
Sardinia St.
  WC2 . . . . 3F 15 (5B 62)
Sarjant Path *SW19* . . . *2F 113*
   (off Blincoe Cl.)
Sark Wlk. E16 . . . . 5D 69
Sarnesfield Ho. *SE15* . . *2D 93*
   (off Pencraig Way)
Sarratt Ho. *W10* *4E 57*
   (off Sutton Way)
Sarre Rd. NW2 . . . . 2A 44
Sarsfeld Rd. SW12 . . . . 1B 116
Sartor Rd. SE15 . . . . . . 2F 107
Sarum Ter. E3. . . . . 3B 66
Satanita Cl. E16 . . . . . . 5F 69
Satchwell Rd. E2 . . . . . . 2C 64
Satchwell St. E2. . . . . . . 2C 64
Sattar M. *N16*. *5F 35*
   (off Clissold Rd.)
Saul Ct. SE15 . . . . 2B 92
Sauls Grn. E11. . . . . 5A 40
Saunders Cl. *E14*. *1B 80*
   (off Limehouse C'way.)
Saunders Ho. *SE16* *3F 79*
   (off Quebec Way)
Saunders Ness Rd.
  E14 . . . . 1E 95
Saunders St. SE11 . . . . 5C 76
Savage Gdns.
  EC3 . . . . 4E 19 (1A 78)
   (not continuous)
Savannah Cl. SE15 . . . . 3B 92
Savernake Ho. N4 . . . . . 2E 35
Savernake Rd. NW3 . . . 1B 46
Savile Row
  W1 . . . . 4F 13 (1E 75)
Saville Rd. E16. . . . . 2F 83
Savill Ho. SW4 . . . . 4F 103
Savona Ho. *SW8* *3E 89*
   (off Savona St.)
Savona St. SW8 . . . . . . 3E 89
Savoy Bldgs. WC2 . . . . . 5F 15
SAVOY CIRCUS 1B 70
Savoy Cl. E15. . . . . 5A 54
Savoy Ct. NW3 . . . . 5E 31
  WC2 . . . . 5F 15 (1B 76)
Savoy Hill
  WC2 . . . . 5F 15 (1B 76)
Savoy Pl.
  WC2 . . . . 5F 15 (1A 76)
Savoy Row WC2 . . . . . . 4F 15

Savoy Steps WC2 . . . . . 5F 15
Savoy St.
  WC2 . . . . 5F 15 (1B 76)
Savoy Theatre *5E 15*
   (off Strand)
Savoy Way WC2 . . . . . . 5F 15
Sawkins Cl. SW19 . . . . . 2A 114
Sawley Rd. W12 . . . . . . 2C 70
Sawmill Yd. E3 . . . . 5A 52
Sawyer Ct. NW10 . . . . . 4A 42
Sawyer St.
  SE1 . . . . 3F 25 (3E 77)
Saxby Rd. SW2 . . . . 5A 104
Saxonbury Ct. N7 . . . . . 2A 48
Saxon Cl. E17. . . . . 2C 38
Saxonfield Cl.
  SW2 . . . . 1B 118
Saxon Ho. *E1* *1F 19*
   (off Thrawl St.)
Saxon Rd. E3. . . . . 1B 66
Saxon Ter. SE6. . . . . 2B 122
Saxton Cl. SE13 . . . . . . 1F 109
Sayes Ct. SE8. . . . . 2B 94
Sayes Ct. St. SE8. . . . . . 2B 94
Scafell *NW1* *1F 5*
   (off Stanhope St.)
Scala St. W1. . . . . 5A 6 (4E 61)
Scampston Rd. W10 . . . 5F 57
Scandrett St. E1. . . . . . . 2D 79
Scarba Wlk. *N1* *3F 49*
   (off Marquess Rd.)
Scarborough Rd. E11. . . 3F 39
  N4. . . . . 3C 34
Scarborough St. E1 . . . . 5B 64
Scarlet Rd. SE6 . . . . 3A 124
Scarlette Mnr. Way
  SW2 . . . . 5C 104
Scarsbrook Rd. SE3 . . . 1F 111
Scarsdale Pl. W8. . . . . . 4D 73
Scarsdale Studios
  W8 . . . . *4C 72*
   (off Stratford Rd.)
Scarsdale Vs. W8 . . . . . 4C 72
Scarth Rd. SW13 . . . . . 1B 98
Scawen Rd. SE8 . . . . . . 1A 94
Scawfell St. E2. . . . . 1B 64
Sceaux Gdns. SE5 . . . . . 4A 92
Sceptre Ct. *EC3* *5F 19*
   (off Tower Hill)
Sceptre Ho. *E1* *3E 65*
   (off Malcolm Rd.)
Sceptre Rd. E2. . . . . 2E 65
Schafer Ho.
  NW1. . . . . 2F 5 (2E 61)
Schiller International
  University *2B 24*
   (off Stamford St.)
Schofield Wlk. SE3 . . . . 3C 96
Scholars Pl. N16 . . . . . . 5A 36
Scholars Rd. SW12 . . . 1E 117
Scholefield Rd. N19 . . . 4F 33
Scholey Ho. SW11 . . . . 1A 102
Schomberg Ho. *SW1* . . *5F 75*
   (off Page St.)
Schonfeld Sq. N16 . . . . 4F 35
School App.
  E2 . . . . 1E 11 (2A 64)
Schoolbank Rd.
  SE10 . . . . 4B 82
Schoolbell M. E3 . . . . . . 1A 66

School Ho. *SE1* 5A *78*
(off Page's Wlk.)
School Ho. La. E1 . . . . . . 1F *79*
School of Hygiene &
Tropical Medicine 5C *6*
School of Oriental &
African Studies 4C *6*
School Rd. NW10 . . . . . . 3A *56*
School Sq. SE10 . . . . . . 4B *82*
Schooner Cl. E14 . . . . . . 4F *81*
SE16 . . . . 3F *79*
Schubert Rd.
SW15 . . . . 3B *100*
Science Mus. 4F *73*
Sclater St.
E1 . . . . 3F *11* (3B *64*)
Scoble Pl. N16 . . . . 1B *50*
Scoles Cres. SW2 . . . . . 1C *118*
Scoresby St.
SE1 . . . . 2D *25* (2D *77*)
Scorton Ho. *N1* 1A *64*
(off Whitmore Est.)
SCOTCH HOUSE 3B *74*
Scoter Ct. *SE8* 2B *94*
(off Abinger Gro.)
Scotia Bldg. *E1* 1F *79*
(off Jardine Rd.)
Scotia Ct. *SE16* 3E *79*
(off Canada St.)
Scotia Rd. SW2 . . . . . . 5C *104*
Scotland Pl.
SW1 . . . . 2D *23* (2A *76*)
Scotney Ho. E9 . . . . 3E *51*
Scotsdale Rd. SE12 . . . 3D *111*
Scotson Ho. *SE11* 5C *76*
(off Marylee Way)
Scotswood St.
EC1 . . . . 3C *8* (3C *62*)
Scott Ellis Gdns.
NW8 . . . . 2F *59*
Scott Ho. *E13* 1C *68*
E14 . . . . 3C *80*
(off Admirals Way)
N1 . . . . 5F *49*
(off Sherborne St.)
N7 . . . . 3B *48*
(off Caledonian Rd.)
NW8 . . . . 3A *60*
(off Broadley St.)
NW10 . . . . 4A *42*
(off Kingthorpe Rd.)
Scott Lidgett Cres.
SE16 . . . . 3C *78*
Scott Russell Pl. F14 . . 1D *95*
Scotts Ct. *W12* 3E *71*
(off Scott's Rd.)
Scott's Rd. E10 . . . . 3E *39*
W12 . . . . 3D *71*
Scott's Sufferance Wharf
SE1 . . . . 4F *27*
Scotts Ter. SE9 . . . . . . 2F *125*
Scott St. E1 . . . . 3D *65*
Scott's Yd.
EC4 . . . . 4B *18* (1F *77*)
Scoulding Ho.
E14 . . . . 4C *80*
(off Mellish St.)
Scoulding Rd. E16 . . . . . 5C *68*
Scouler St. E14 . . . . 1E *81*

Scout App. NW10 . . . . . . 1A *42*
Scout La. SW4 . . . . 1E *103*
Scovell Cres. SE1 . . . . . 4F *25*
Scovell Rd.
SE1 . . . . 4F *25* (3E *77*)
Screen on Baker Street
(Cinema) 5A *4*
(off Baker St.)
Screen on the Green Cinema
. . . . 5D *49*
(off Upper St.)
Screen on the Hill (Cinema)
Belsize Pk. 2A *46*
Scriven Ct. E8 . . . . 5B *50*
Scriven St. E8 . . . . 5B *50*
Scrooby St. SE6 . . . . . . 4D *109*
Scrope Ho. *EC1* 5B *8*
(off Bourne Est.)
Scrubs La. NW10 . . . . . 2C *56*
W10 . . . . 2C *56*
Scrutton Cl.
SW12 . . . . 5F *103*
Scrutton St.
EC2 . . . . 4D *11* (3A *64*)
Scutari Rd. SE22 . . . . . 3E *107*
Scylla Rd. SE15 . . . . . . 1C *106*
(not continuous)
Seabright St. E2 . . . . . . 2D *65*
Seacole Cl. W3 . . . . 5A *56*
Seacon Twr. E14 . . . . . . 3B *80*
Seaford Ho. *SE16* 3E *79*
(off Swan Rd.)
Seaford St.
WC1 . . . . 2E *7* (2B *62*)
Seaforth Cres. N5 . . . . . 2E *49*
Seaforth Pl. SW1 . . . . . 5A *22*
Seagar Pl. E3 . . . . 4B *66*
Seager Bldgs. SE8 . . . . . 4C *94*
Seagrave Cl. E1 . . . . . . 4F *65*
Seagrave Lodge *SW6* . . 2C *86*
(off Seagrave Rd.)
Seagrave Rd. SW6 . . . . . 2C *86*
Seagry Rd. E11 . . . . 2C *40*
Seagull La. E16 . . . . 1C *82*
Seal Ho. *SE1* 5C *26*
(off Pardoner St.)
Seal St. E8 . . . . 1B *50*
Searles Cl. SW11 . . . . . 3A *88*
Searles Rd. SE1 . . . . . . 5F *77*
Searson Ho. *SE17* 5D *77*
(off Canterbury Pl.)
Sears St. SE5 . . . . 3F *91*
Seaton Cl. E13 . . . . 3C *68*
SE11 . . . . 1C *90*
SW15 . . . . 1D *113*
Seaton Point *E5* 1C *50*
(off Nolan Way)
Sebastian Ho. *N1* 1D *11*
(off Hoxton St.)
Sebastian St.
EC1 . . . . 2E *9* (2D *63*)
Sebbon St. N1 . . . . 4D *49*
Sebert Rd. E7 . . . . 2D *55*
Sebright Ho. *E2* 1C *64*
(off Coate St.)
Sedgmere Pas. *E2* 1C *64*
Secker Ho. *SW9* 5D *91*
(off Loughborough Est.)
Secker St.
SE1 . . . . 2B *24* (2C *76*)

Second Av. E13 . . . . 2C *68*
SW14 . . . . 1A *98*
W3 . . . . 2B *70*
W10 . . . . 3A *58*
Sedan Way SE17 . . . . . 1A *92*
Sedding St. SW1 . . . . . . 5C *74*
Sedding Studios
SW1 . . . . 5C *74*
Seddon Highwalk *EC2* . . 5F *9*
(off Seddon Ho.)
Seddon Ho. EC2 . . . . . . 5F *9*
Seddon St.
WC1 . . . . 2A *8* (2B *62*)
Sedgebrook Rd. SE3 . . . 5F *97*
Sedgeford Rd. W12 . . . . 2B *70*
Sedgehill Rd. SE6 . . . . 4C *122*
Sedgeway SE6 . . . . 1B *124*
Sedgmoor Pl. SE5 . . . . . 3A *92*
Sedgwick Ho. *E3* 4C *66*
(off Gale St.)
Sedgwick Rd. E10 . . . . . 4E *39*
Sedgwick St. E9 . . . . . . 2F *51*
Sedleigh Rd. SW18 . . . 4B *100*
Sedlescombe Rd.
SW6 . . . . 2C *86*
Sedley Ct. SE26 . . . . . . 2D *121*
Sedley Ho. SE11 . . . . . . 1B *90*
(off Newburn St.)
Sedley Pl.
W1 . . . . 3D *13* (5D *61*)
Seeley Dr. SE21 . . . . . . 4A *120*
Seelig Av. NW9 . . . . 2C *28*
Seely Rd. SW17 . . . . . . 5C *116*
Seething La.
EC3 . . . . 4E *19* (1A *78*)
Sefton St. SW15 . . . . . . 1E *99*
Segal Cl. SE23 . . . . 5A *108*
Sekforde St.
EC1 . . . . 4D *9* (3D *63*)
Selbie Av. NW10 . . . . . . 2B *42*
Selborne Rd. SE5 . . . . . 5F *91*
Selbourne Ho. SE1 . . . . 4B *26*
Selby Cl. E6 . . . . 4F *69*
Selby Ho. *W10* 2A *58*
(off Beethoven St.)
Selby Rd. E11 . . . . 5A *40*
E13 . . . . 4D *69*
Selby St. E1 . . . . 3C *64*
Selcroft Ho. SE10 . . . . . 1B *96*
(off Glenister Rd.)
Selden Ho. SE15 . . . . . . 5E *93*
(off Selden Rd.)
Selden Rd. SE15 . . . . . . 5E *93*
Selden Wlk. N7 . . . . 4B *34*
Seldon Ho. SW1 . . . . . . 1E *89*
(off Churchill Gdns.)
SW8 . . . . 3E *89*
(off Stewart's Rd.)
Selfridges 3B *12*
(off Oxford St.)
Selhurst Cl. SW19 . . . . 1F *113*
Selina Ho. *NW8* 3F *59*
(off Frampton St.)
Selkirk Rd. SW17 . . . . . 4A *116*
Sellincourt Rd.
SW17 . . . . 5A *116*
Sellons Av. NW10 . . . . . 5B *42*
Selma Ho. *W12* 5D *57*
(off Du Cane Rd.)

Selman Ho. E9 . . . . 3A 52
Selsdon Rd. E11 . . . . . . 2C 40
   E13 . . . . 5E 55
   NW2 . . . . 4B 28
   SE27 . . . . 3C 118
Selsdon Way E14 . . . . . 4D 81
Selsea Pl. N16 . . . . 2A 50
Selsey St. E14 . . . . 4C 66
Selway Ho. SW8 . . . . 4A 90
   (off Sth. Lambeth Rd.)
Selwood Pl. SW7 . . . . . 1F 87
Selwoods SW2 . . . . . . 5C 104
Selwood Ter. SW7 . . . . 1F 87
Selworthy Cl. E11 . . . . . 1C 40
Selworthy Rd. SE6 . . . 3B 122
Selwyn Ct. E17 . . . . . . 1C 38
   (off Yunus Khan Cl.)
   SE3 . . . . 1B 110
Selwyn Rd. E3 . . . . 1B 66
   E13 . . . . 5D 55
   NW10 . . . . 4A 42
Semley Ga. E9 . . . . 3B 52
Semley Ho. SW1 . . . . . 5D 75
   (off Semley Pl.)
Semley Pl. SW1 . . . . . . 5C 74
Senate St. SE15 . . . . . . 5E 93
Senators Lodge E3 . . . 1A 66
   (off Roman Rd.)
Senior St. W2 . . . . 4D 59
Senlac Rd. SE12 . . . . . 1D 125
Senrab St. E1 . . . . 5F 65
Seraph Ct. EC1 . . . . 1F 9
   (off Moreland St.)
Serbin Cl. E10 . . . . 2E 39
Serenaders Rd. SW9 . . . 5C 90
Sergeant Ind. Est.
   SW18 . . . . 4D 101
Serica Ct. SE10 . . . . . . 3E 95
Serjeants Inn
   EC4 . . . . 3C 16 (5C 62)
Serle St.
   WC2 . . . . . . 2A 16 (5B 62)
Sermon La. EC4 . . . . . . 3F 17
Serpentine, The 2A 74
Serpentine Gallery 3F 73
Serpentine Rd.
   W2 . . . . 2A 20 (2A 74)
Setchell Rd. SE1 . . . . . . 5B 78
Setchell Way SE1 . . . . . 5B 78
Seth St. SE16 . . . . 3E 79
Settle Point E13 . . . . . . 1C 68
   (off London Rd.)
Settle Rd. E13 . . . . 1C 68
Settlers Ct. E14 . . . . 1F 81
Settles St. E1 . . . . 4C 64
Settrington Rd. SW6 . . . 5D 87
Seven Dials
   WC2 . . . . 3D 15 (5A 62)
Seven Dials Ct. WC2 . . . 3D 15
   (off Shorts Gdns.)
Seven Islands Leisure Cen.
   . . . . 4E 79
Sevenoaks Rd. SE4 . . . 4A 108
Seven Sisters Rd. N4 . . . 5B 34
   N7 . . . . 5B 34
   N15 . . . . 4C 34
Seven Stars Cnr. W6 . . . 4C 70
Seven Stars Yd. E1 . . . . 5F 11
Severnake Cl. E14 . . . . . 5C 80
Severn Way NW10 . . . . 2B 42

Severus Rd. SW11 . . . . 2A 102
Seville Ho. E1 . . . . 2C 78
   (off Hellings St.)
Seville M. N1 . . . . 4A 50
Seville St.
   SW1 . . . . . . 4A 20 (3B 74)
Sevington Rd. NW4 . . . . 1D 29
Sevington St. W9 . . . . . . 3D 59
Sewardstone Rd.
   E2 . . . . 1E 65
Seward St.
   EC1 . . . . 3E 9 (2D 63)
Sewdley St. E5 . . . . 5F 37
Sewell St. E13 . . . . 2C 68
Sextant Av. E14 . . . . . . 5F 81
Sexton Ct. E14 . . . . 1F 81
   (off Newport Av.)
Sextons Ho. SE10 . . . . . 2E 95
   (off Bardsley La.)
Seymour Ct. NW2 . . . . . 4D 29
Seymour Gdns.
   SE4 . . . . 1A 108
Seymour Ho. E16 . . . . . 2C 82
   (off De Quincey M.)
   NW1 . . . . 1C 6
   (off Churchway)
   WC1 . . . . 3D 7
   (off Tavistock Pl.)
Seymour M.
   W1 . . . . 2B 12 (5C 60)
Seymour Pl.
   W1 . . . . 2A 12 (4B 60)
Seymour Rd. E6 . . . . . . 1F 69
   E10 . . . . 3B 38
   N8 . . . . 1C 34
   SW18 . . . . 5B 100
   SW19 . . . . 3F 113
Seymour St.
   W1 . . . . 3A 12 (5B 60)
   W2 . . . . 5B 60
Seymour Wlk. SW10 . . . 2E 87
Seyssel St. E14 . . . . 5E 81
Shaa Rd. W3 . . . . 1A 70
Shabana Rd. W12 . . . . . 2D 71
Shackleton Cl.
   SE23 . . . . 2D 121
Shackleton Ct. E14 . . . . 1C 94
   (off Maritime Quay)
   W12 . . . . 3D 71
Shackleton Ho. E1 . . . . . 2E 79
   (off Prusom St.)
   NW10 . . . . 4A 42
SHACKLEWELL 1B 50
Shacklewell Grn. E8 . . . 1B 50
Shacklewell Ho. E8 . . . . 1B 50
Shacklewell La. E8 . . . . 2B 50
Shacklewell Rd. N16 . . . 1B 50
Shacklewell Row E8 . . . 1B 50
Shacklewell St. E2 . . . . 2B 64
Shad Thames
   SE1 . . . . 2F 27 (2B 78)
SHADWELL 1D 79
Shadwell Gdns. E1 . . . . 1E 79
Shadwell Pierhead
   E1 . . . . 1E 79
Shadwell Pl. E1 . . . . . . 1E 79
   (off Shadwell Gdns.)
Shaftesbury Av.
   W1 . . . . 5B 14 (1F 75)
   WC2 . . . . . . 2D 15 (5A 62)

Shaftesbury Cen.
   W10 . . . . 3F 57
   (off Barlby Rd.)
Shaftesbury Ct. N1 . . . . 1F 63
   (off Shaftesbury St.)
   SW6 . . . . 4D 87
   (off Maltings Pl.)
   SW16 . . . . 3F 117
Shaftesbury Gdns.
   NW10 . . . . 3A 56
Shaftesbury Lodge
   E14 . . . . 5D 67
   (off Up. North St.)
Shaftesbury M. SE1 . . . 5B 26
   SW4 . . . . 3E 103
   W8 . . . . 4C 72
   (off Stratford Rd.)
Shaftesbury Pl. EC2 . . . 1F 17
   (off London Wall)
   W14 . . . . 5B 72
   (off Warwick Rd.)
Shaftesbury Point
   E13 . . . . 1C 68
   (off High St.)
Shaftesbury Rd. E7 . . . . 4E 55
   E10 . . . . 3C 38
   E17 . . . . 1D 39
   N19 . . . . 3A 34
Shaftesbury St. N1 . . . . 1E 63
   (not continuous)
Shaftesbury Theatre . . . 2D 15
   (off Shaftesbury Av.)
Shafto M. SW1 . . . . 4B 74
Shafton M. E9 . . . . 5F 51
Shafton Rd. E9 . . . . 5F 51
Shaftsbury Ct. SE5 . . . . 2F 105
Shafts Ct.
   EC3 . . . . 3D 19 (5A 64)
Shahjalal Ho. E2 . . . . . 1C 64
   (off Pritchards Rd.)
Shakespeare Ho. E9 . . . 4E 51
   (off Lyme Gro.)
Shakespeare Rd.
   SE24 . . . . 3D 105
Shakespeare's Globe Theatre
& Exhibition
   . . . . 5F 17 (2E 77)
Shakespeare Twr.
   EC2 . . . . 5A 10
Shakspeare M. N16 . . . 1A 50
Shakspeare Wlk.
   N16 . . . . 1A 50
Shalbourne Sq. E9 . . . . 3B 52
Shalcomb St. SW10 . . . 2E 87
Shalden Ho. SW15 . . . . 4B 98
Shalfleet Dr. W10 . . . . . 1F 71
Shalford Ct. N1 . . . . 1D 63
   (off Charlton Pl.)
Shalford Ho.
   SE1 . . . . 5C 26 (4F 77)
Shamrock St. SW4 . . . . 1F 103
Shandon Rd. SW4 . . . . 4E 103
Shand St.
   SE1 . . . . 3E 27 (3A 78)
Shandy St. E1 . . . . 4F 65
Shanklin Rd. N8 . . . . . . 1F 33
Shannon Cl. NW2 . . . . . 5F 29
Shannon Ct. N16 . . . . . 5A 36
Shannon Gro. SW9 . . . 2B 104
Shannon Pl. NW8 . . . . . 1A 60

Shanti Ct. SW18. . . . . . .1C 114
Shap St. E2. . . . . .1B 64
Shardcroft Av. SE24 . . . .3D 105
Shardeloes Rd. SE14 . . . .5B 94
Shard's Sq. SE15 . . . . . . .2C 92
Sharnbrook Ho. W14 . . . .2C 86
Sharon Gdns. E9. . . . . . . .5E 51
Sharp Ho. SW8 . . . . . . .1D 103
Sharpleshall St.
     NW1. . . . . .4B 46
Sharpness (St. SF15 . . . .3B 92
     (off Daniel Gdns.)
Sharratt St. SE15 . . . . . .2F 93
Sharsted St. SE17 . . . . . .1D 91
Sharwood WC1. . . . . .1A 8
     (off Penton Ri.)
Shaver's Pl. SW1 . . . . . . .5B 14
Shawbrooke Rd.
     SE9. . . . . .3E 111
Shawbury Rd. SE22 . . . .3B 106
Shaw Cres. E14 . . . . .5A 66
Shawfield St. SW3 . . . . . .1A 88
Shawford Ct. SW15 . . . . .5C 98
Shaw Path
     BR1: Brom 3B 124
Shaw Rd.
     BR1: Brom 3B 124
     SE22 . . . . .2A 106
Shaws Cotts. SE23 . . . . .3A 122
Shaw Theatre . . . 2C 6 (2F 61)
Shearling Way N7 . . . . . .3A 48
Shearman Rd. SE3 . . . . .2B 110
Shearwater Ct. E1 . . . . . .1C 78
     (off Star Pl.)
     SE8. . . . . .2B 94
     (off Abinger Gro.)
Sheba Pl. E1 . . . . .4F 11 (3B 64)
Sheenewood SE26 . . . . .4D 121
Sheengate Mans.
     SW14 . . . . .2A 98
Sheen Gro. N1 . . . . .5C 48
Sheen Sports & Fitness Cen.
     . . . . .2A 98
Sheepcote La. SW11 . . . .5B 88
Sheep La. E8 . . . . .5D 51
Sheep Wlk. M.
     SW19 . . . . .5F 113
Sheerwater Rd. E16 . . . . .4F 69
Sheffield Sq. E3 . . . . .2B 66
Sheffield St.
     WC2. . . . . . . .3F 15 (5B 62)
Sheffield Ter. W8 . . . . . . .2C 72
Shelburne Rd. N7 . . . . . . .1B 48
Shelbury Rd. SE22 . . . . .3D 107
Sheldon Av. N6. . . . . .2A 32
Sheldon Cl. SE12 . . . . . .3D 111
Sheldon Ct. SW8 . . . . . . .3A 90
     (off Lansdowne Grn.)
Sheldon Ho. N1 . . . . .5A 50
     (off Kingsland Rd.)
Sheldon Pl. E2 . . . . .1C 64
     (not continuous)
Sheldon Rd. NW2 . . . . . . .1F 43
Sheldon Sq. W2 . . . . .4E 59
Sheldrake Ho. SE16 . . . . .5F 79
     (off Tawny Way)
Sheldrake Pl. W8 . . . . . . .3C 72
Shelduck Cl. E15 . . . . . . .2B 54
Shelduck Ct. SE8 . . . . . . .2B 94
     (off Pilot Cl.)

Shelford Pl. N16. . . . . . . .5F 35
Shelgate Rd.
     SW11 . . . . .3A 102
Shelley Av. E12 . . . . .3F 55
Shelley Cl. SE15 . . . . . . .5D 93
Shelley Ct. E10 . . . . .2D 39
     (off Skelton's La.)
     N19. . . . . .3B 34
     SW3 . . . . .2B 88
     (off Tite St.)
Shelley Ho. E2 . . . . .2E 65
     (off Cornwall Av.)
     N16. . . . . .1A 50
     SE17. . . . . .1E 91
     (off Browning St.)
     SW1 . . . . .2E 89
     (off Churchill Gdns.)
Shelley Rd. NW10 . . . . . .5A 42
Shelley Way SW19. . . . . .5F 115
Shellness Rd. E5. . . . . . . .2D 51
Shell Rd. SE13. . . . . . . .1D 109
Shellwood Rd.
     SW11 . . . . .5B 88
Shelmerdine Cl. E3 . . . . .4C 66
Shelton St.
     WC2. . . . . . . .3D 15 (5A 62)
     (not continuous)
Shene Ho. EC1. . . . . .5B 8
     (off Bourne Est.)
Shenfield Ho. SE18 . . . . .4F 97
     (off Portway Gdns.)
Shenfield St.
     N1 . . . . .1E 11 (1A 64)
     (not continuous)
Shenley Rd. SE5 . . . . . . .4A 92
Shenstone Ho.
     SW16 . . . . .5E 117
Shepherdess Pl.
     N1 . . . . .1A 10 (2E 63)
Shepherdess Wlk.
     N1 . . . . .1A 10 (1E 63)
Shepherd Ho. E14 . . . . . .5D 67
     (off Annabel Cl.)
     W1. . . . . .1D 21 (2D 75)
SHEPHERD'S BUSH 3E 71
Shepherds Bush
     Empire Theatre 3E 71
Shepherd's Bush Grn.
     W12 . . . . .3E 71
Shepherd's Bush Mkt.
     W12 . . . . .3E 71
     (not continuous)
Shepherd's Bush Pl.
     W12. . . . . .3F 71
Shepherd's Bush Rd.
     W6 . . . . .5E 71
Shepherds Cl. N6. . . . . . .1D 33
     (off Lees Pl.)
     W1 . . . . .4B 12
Shepherds Ct. W12 . . . . .3F 71
     (off Shepherd's Bush Grn.)
Shepherd's Hill N6. . . . . .1D 33
Shepherds La. E9. . . . . . .3F 51
Shepherd's Path NW3 . . . .2F 45
     (off Lyndhurst Rd.)
Shepherds Pl.
     W1. . . . . .4B 12 (1C 74)
Shepherd St.
     W1. . . . . .2D 21 (2D 75)

Shepherds Wlk.
     NW2 . . . . .4C 28
     NW3 . . . . .2F 45
     (not continuous)
Sheppard Dr. SE16 . . . . .1D 93
Sheppard Ho. E2 . . . . . . .1C 64
     (off Warner Pl.)
     SW2 . . . . .1C 118
Sheppard St. E16. . . . . . .3B 68
Shepperton Rd. N1. . . . . .5E 49
Shepton Ho's. E2 . . . . . . .2E 65
     (off Welwyn St.)
Sherard Ct. N7 . . . . .5A 34
Sherard Rd. E9. . . . . .4E 51
     (off Frampton Pk. Rd.)
Sheraton Ho. SW1. . . . . .2D 89
     (off Churchill Gdns.)
Sheraton St.
     W1 . . . . .3B 14 (5F 61)
Sherborne Ho. SW1. . . . .1D 89
     (off Winchester St.)
     SW8 . . . . .3B 90
     (off Bolney St.)
Sherborne La.
     EC4. . . . . .4B 18 (1F 77)
Sherborne St. N1 . . . . . . .5F 49
Sherboro Rd. N15 . . . . . .1E 36
Sherbrooke Ho. E2. . . . . .1E 65
     (off Bonner Rd.)
Sherbrooke Rd. SW6 . . . .3A 86
Sherbrooke Ter.
     SW6 . . . . .3A 86
     (off Sherbrook Rd.)
Shere Ho. SE1 . . . . .5B 26
Sherfield Gdns.
     SW15 . . . . .4B 98
Sheridan Bldgs. WC2. . . .3E 15
     (off Martlett Ct.)
Sheridan Ct. NW6 . . . . . .4E 45
     (off Belsize Rd.)
Sheridan Ho. E1 . . . . .5E 65
     (off Tarling St.)
     SE11. . . . . .5C 76
     (off Wincott St.)
Sheridan M. E11 . . . . . . .1D 41
Sheridan Pl. SW13 . . . . . .1B 98
Sheridan Rd. E7. . . . . . . .5B 40
Sheridan St. E1 . . . . .5D 65
Sheridan Wlk.
     NW11 . . . . .1C 30
Sheringham NW8 . . . . . . .5F 45
Sheringham Ho.
     NW1 . . . . .4A 60
     (off Lisson St.)
Sheringham Rd. N7 . . . . .3B 48
Sherington Rd. SE7. . . . .2D 97
Sherlock Ct. NW8. . . . . . .5F 45
     (off Dorman Way)
Sherlock Holmes Mus.
     . . . . .4A 4
Sherlock M.
     W1. . . . . .5B 4 (4C 60)
Shernhall St. E17. . . . . . .1E 39
Sherrard Rd. E7 . . . . .3E 55
     E12 . . . . .3E 55
Sherren Ho. E1 . . . . .3E 65
Sherrick Grn. Rd.
     NW10 . . . . .2D 43
Sherriff Rd. NW6 . . . . . . .3C 44
Sherrin Rd. E10. . . . . . . .1D 53

Sherston Ct. *SE1* 5D **77**
   (off Newington Butts)
WC1 . . . . 2B **8**
Sherwin Ho. *SE1* 2C **90**
   (off Kennington Rd.)
Sherwin Rd. SE14 . . . . . . 4F **93**
Sherwood NW6 . . . . 4A **44**
Sherwood Cl. SW13 . . . . 1D **99**
Sherwood Ct. SW11 . . . 1E **101**
W1 . . . . 4B **60**
   (off Bryanston Pl.)
Sherwood Gdns. E14 . . . . 5C **80**
SE16 . . . . 1C **92**
Sherwood St.
W1 . . . . 4A **14** (1E **75**)
Shetland Rd. E3 . . . . 1B **66**
Shifford Path SE23 . . . . 3F **121**
Shillaker Ct. W3 . . . . 2B **70**
Shillibeer Pl. *W1* 4A **60**
   (off Harcourt St.)
Shillingford St. N1 . . . . . 4D **49**
Shillingstone Ho.
W14 . . . . 4A **72**
   (off Russell Rd.)
Shinfield St. W12 . . . . . . 5E **57**
Ship & Mermaid Row
SE1 . . . . 3C **26** (3F **77**)
Shipka Rd. SW12 . . . . . 1D **117**
Shiplake Ho. *E2* 2F **11**
   (off Arnold Cir.)
Shipman Rd. E16 . . . . . . 5D **69**
SE23 . . . . 2F **121**
Ship St. SE8 . . . . 4C **94**
Ship Tavern Pas.
EC3 . . . . 4D **19** (1A **78**)
Shipton Ho. *E2* 1B **64**
   (off Shipton St.)
Shipton St. E2 . . . . 1B **64**
Shipway Ter. N16 . . . . . . 5B **36**
Shipwright Rd. SE16 . . . 3A **80**
Shipwright Yd.
SE1 . . . . 2D **27** (2A **78**)
Ship Yd. E14 . . . . 1D **95**
Shirburn Cl. SE23 . . . . . 5E **107**
Shirebrook Rd. SE3 . . . . 1F **111**
Shirehall Cl. NW4 . . . . . 1F **29**
Shirehall Gdns. NW4 . . . 1F **29**
Shirehall La. NW4 . . . . . 1F **29**
Shirehall Pk. NW4 . . . . . 1F **29**
Shire Pl. SW18 . . . . 5E **101**
Shirland M. W9 . . . . 2B **58**
Shirland Rd. W9 . . . . 2B **58**
Shirlbutt St. E14 . . . . . . 1D **81**
Shirley Gro. SW11 . . . . 1C **102**
Shirley Ho. *SE5* 3F **91**
   (off Picton St.)
Shirley Ho. Dr. SE7 . . . . 3E **97**
Shirley Rd. E15 . . . . 4A **54**
W4 . . . . 3A **70**
Shirley St. E16 . . . . 5B **68**
Shirlock Rd. NW3 . . . . . 1B **46**
Shobroke Cl. NW2 . . . . . 5E **29**
Shoe La.
EC4 . . . . 2C **16** (5C **62**)
Shona Ho. E13 . . . . 4E **69**
Shooters Hill Rd.
SE3 . . . . 4F **95**
SE10 . . . . 4F **95**
SE18 . . . . 3E **97**
Shoot Up Hill NW2 . . . . 2A **44**

Shore Bus. Cen. E9 . . . . 4E **51**
SHOREDITCH
. . . . 1D **11** (2A **64**)
Shoreditch Ct. *E8* 4B **50**
   (off Queensbridge Rd.)
Shoreditch High St.
E1 . . . . 4E **11** (3A **64**)
Shoreham Cl.
SW18 . . . . 3D **101**
Shore Ho. SW8 . . . . . . 1D **103**
Shore M. *E9* 4E **51**
   (off Shore Rd.)
Shore Pl. E9 . . . . 4E **51**
Shore Rd. E9 . . . . 4E **51**
Shorncliffe Rd. SE1 . . . . 1B **92**
Shorndean St. SE6 . . . . 1E **123**
Shorrold's Rd. SW6 . . . . 3B **86**
Shorter St. EC3 . . . . 1B **78**
Shortlands W6 . . . . 5F **71**
Shortlands Rd. E10 . . . . 2D **39**
Short Rd. E11 . . . . 4A **40**
W4 . . . . 2A **84**
Shorts Gdns.
WC2 . . . . 3D **15** (5A **62**)
Short St. SE1 . . 3C **24** (3C **76**)
Short Wall E15 . . . . 2E **67**
Short Way SE9 . . . . 1F **111**
Shottendane Rd.
SW6 . . . . 4C **86**
Shottery Cl. SE9 . . . . . . 3F **125**
Shottfield Av. SW14 . . . . 2A **98**
Shottsford *W2* 5C **58**
   (off Talbot Rd.)
Shoulder of Mutton All.
E14 . . . . 1A **80**
Shouldham St. W1 . . . . . 4A **60**
Shrewsbury Ct. EC1 . . . . 4A **10**
Shrewsbury Cres.
NW10 . . . . 5A **42**
Shrewsbury Ho. *SW8* . . . 2B **90**
   (off Kennington Oval)
Shrewsbury M. *W2* 4C **58**
   (off Chepstow Rd.)
Shrewsbury Rd. E7 . . . . 2F **55**
W2 . . . . 5C **58**
Shrewsbury St. W10 . . . 3E **57**
Shroffold Rd.
BR1: Brom 4A **124**
Shropshire Pl.
WC1 . . . . 4B **6** (3E **61**)
Shroton St. NW1 . . . . . . 4A **60**
Shrubbery, The E11 . . . . 1D **41**
Shrubbery Cl. N1 . . . . . . 5E **49**
Shrubbery Rd.
SW16 . . . . 4A **118**
Shrubland Rd. E8 . . . . . 5B **50**
E10 . . . . 2C **38**
E17 . . . . 1C **38**
Shrublands Cl.
SE26 . . . . 3E **121**
Shuna Wlk. N1 . . . . 3F **49**
Shurland Gdns. SE15 . . 3B **92**
Shuters Sq. W14 . . . . . . 1B **86**
Shuttle St. E1 . . . . 3C **64**
Shuttleworth Rd.
SW11 . . . . 5A **88**
Sibella Rd. SW4 . . . . . . 5F **89**
Sibthorpe Rd. SE12 . . . 4D **111**
Sicilian Av. WC1 . . . . . . 1E **15**
Sidbury St. SW6 . . . . . . 4A **86**

Sidcup Rd. SE9 . . . . . . 4E **111**
SE12 . . . . 4E **111**
Siddons La.
NW1 . . . . 4A **4** (3B **60**)
Siddons Rd. SE23 . . . . 2A **122**
Side Rd. E17 . . . . 1B **38**
Sidford Ho. SE1 . . . . . . 5A **24**
Sidford Pl.
SE1 . . . . 5A **24** (4C **76**)
Sidgwick Ho. *SW9* 5B **90**
   (off Lingham St.)
Sidings, The E11 . . . . . . 3E **39**
Sidings M. N7 . . . . 5C **34**
Sidlaw Ho. N16 . . . . 3B **36**
Sidmouth Ho. *SE15* 3C **92**
   (off Lympstone Gdns.)
W1 . . . . 5A **60**
   (off Cato St.)
Sidmouth Pde. NW2 . . . 4E **43**
Sidmouth Rd. E10 . . . . . 5E **39**
NW2 . . . . 4E **43**
Sidmouth St.
WC1 . . . . 2E **7** (2B **62**)
Sidney Boyd Ct.
NW6 . . . . 4C **44**
Sidney Est. E1 . . . . 5E **65**
   (Bromhead St.)
E1 . . . . 4E **65**
   (Lindley St.)
Sidney Godley (VC) Ho.
E2 . . . . 2E **65**
   (off Digby St.)
Sidney Gro.
EC1 . . . . 1D **9** (1D **63**)
Sidney Ho. *E2* 1F **65**
   (off Old Ford Rd.)
Sidney Rd. E7 . . . . 5C **40**
SW9 . . . . 5B **90**
Sidney Sq. E1 . . . . 4E **65**
Sidney St. E1 . . . . 4D **65**
Sidworth St. E8 . . . . 4D **51**
Siebert Rd. SE3 . . . . . . 2C **96**
Siege Ho. *E1* 5D **65**
   (off Sidney St.)
Siemens Rd. SE18 . . . . 4F **83**
Sienna Ter. NW2 . . . . . . 4C **28**
Sigdon Pas. E8 . . . . 2C **50**
Sigdon Rd. E8 . . . . 2C **50**
Sigmund Freud Statue
. . . . 3F **45**
Signal Ho. *E8* 4D **51**
   (off Martello Ter.)
Signmakers Yd.
NW1 . . . . 5D **47**
   (off Delancey St.)
Silbury Ho. SE26 . . . . . 3C **120**
Silbury St.
N1 . . . . 1B **10** (2F **63**)
Silchester Rd. W10 . . . . 5F **57**
Silesia Bldgs. E8 . . . . . . 4D **51**
Silex St. SE1 . . 4E **25** (3D **77**)
Silk Cl. SE12 . . . . 3C **110**
Silk Ct. *E2* 2C **64**
   (off Squirries St.)
Silk Mills Pas. SE13 . . . 5D **95**
Silk Mills Path SE13 . . . 5D **95**
   (not continuous)
Silk Mills Sq. E9 . . . . . . 3B **52**
Silks Ct. E11 . . . . 3B **40**
Silk St. EC2 . . . 5A **10** (4E **63**)

Sillitoe Ho. *N1* *5F 49*
(off Colville Est.)
Silsoe Ho. NW1 . . . . 1D **61**
Silver Birch Cl. SE6 . . 3B **122**
Silverbirch Wlk.
NW3 . . . . 3B **46**
Silverburn Ho. SW9 . . . . 4D **91**
(off Lothian Rd.)
Silver Cl. SE14 . . . . . . 3A **94**
Silverdale NW1 . . . . *1F 5*
(off Hampstead Rd.)
SE26 . . . . 4E **121**
Silverdale Ct. EC1 . . . . . . 3F **9**
Silverdale Dr. SE9 . . . . 2F **125**
Silvermere Rd. SE6 . . 5D **109**
Silver Pl. W1 . . 4A **14** (5E **61**)
Silver Rd. SE13 . . . . . . 1D **109**
(not continuous)
W12 . . . . 1F **71**
Silverthorn NW8 . . . . . . 5D **45**
(off Abbey Rd.)
Silverthorne Loft SF5 . . 2F **91**
(off Albany Rd.)
Silverthorne Rd. SW8 . 5D **89**
Silverton Rd. W6 . . . . . . 2F **85**
SILVERTOWN 2E **83**
Silvertown Viaduct
E16 . . . . 5B **68**
Silvertown Way E16 . . 5A **68**
(not continuous)
Silver Wlk. SE16 . . . . . . 2A **80**
Silvester Ho. E1 . . . . 5D **65**
(off Varden St.)
E2 . . . . 2E **65**
(off Sceptre Rd.)
W11 . . . . 5B **58**
(off Basing St.)
Silvester Rd. SE22 . . 3B **106**
Silvester St.
SE1 . . . . . 4B **26** (3F **77**)
Silvocea Way E14 . . . . . . 5F **67**
Silwood Est. SE16 . . . . 5E **79**
Silwood St. SE16 . . . . . . 5E **79**
(off Rotherhithe New Rd.)
Simla Ho. SE1 . . . . 4C **26**
(off Kipling Est.)
Simms Rd. SE1 . . . . . . 5C **78**
Simnel Rd. SE12 . . . . 5D **111**
Simon Cl. W11 . . . . . . 1B **72**
Simon Ct. W9 . . . . 2C **58**
(off Saltram Cres.)
Simonds Rd. E10 . . . . . . 4C **38**
Simone Ct. SE26 . . . . 3E **121**
Simons Ct. N16 . . . . . . 4B **36**
Simons Wlk. E15 . . . . . . 2F **53**
Simpson Dr. W3 . . . . . . 5A **56**
Simpson Ho. NW8 . . . . 5A **60**
SE11 . . . . 1B **90**
Simpson's Rd. E14 . . 1D **81**
Simpson St. SW11 . . 5A **88**
Simrose Ct. SW18 . . . . 3C **100**
Sims Wlk. SE3 . . . . . . 2B **110**
Sinclair Gdns. W14 . . 3F **71**
Sinclair Gro. NW11 . . 1F **29**
Sinclair Ho. WC1 . . . . . . *2D 7*
(off Sandwich St.)
Sinclair Mans. W12 . . . . 3F **71**
(off Richmond Way)
Sinclair Pl. SE4 . . . . . . 4C **108**
Sinclair Rd. W14 . . . . . . 3F **71**

Singer St.
EC2 . . . . 2C **10** (2F **63**)
Sir Abraham Dawes Cotts.
SW15 . . . . 2A **100**
Sir Alexander Cl. W3 . . 2B **70**
Sir Alexander Rd.
W3 . . . . 2B **70**
Sir Christopher France Ho.
E1 . . . . 2A **66**
Sirdar Rd. W11 . . . . . . 1F **71**
Sirinham Point SW8 . . 2B **90**
(off Meadow Rd.)
Sirius Bldg. E1 . . . . 1F **79**
(off Jardine Rd.)
Sir John Cass Hall E9 . . 4F **51**
(off Well St.)
Sir John Kirk Cl. SE5 . . 3E **91**
Sir John Soane's Mus.
. . . . 2F **15** (5B **62**)
Sir Nicholas Garrow Ho.
W10 . . . . 3A **58**
(off Kensal Rd.)
Sir Oswald Stoll
Foundation, The
SW6 . . . . 3D **87**
(off Fulham Rd.)
Sir Oswald Stoll Mans.
SW6 . . . . 3D **87**
(off Fulham Rd.)
Sir William Powell's
Almshouses SW6 . . 5A **86**
Sise La. EC4 . . 3B **18** (5F **63**)
Siskin Ho. SE16 . . . . . . 5F **79**
(off Tawny Way)
Sispara Gdns.
SW18 . . . . 4B **100**
Sissinghurst Cl.
BR1: Brom 5A **124**
Sissinghurst Ho.
SE15 . . . . 2E **93**
(off Sharratt St.)
Sissulu Ct. E6 . . . . 5E **55**
Sister Mabel's Way
SE15 . . . . 3C **92**
Sisters Av. SW11 . . . . 1B **102**
Sistova Rd. SW12 . . 1D **117**
Sisulu Pl. SW9 . . . . . . 1C **104**
Sitarey Ct. W12 . . . . . . 2D **71**
Sivill Ho. E2 . . . . 1F **11**
(off Columbia Rd.)
Siward Rd. SW17 . . . . 3E **115**
Six Acres Est. N4 . . . . 4B **34**
Six Bridges Ind. Est.
SE1 . . . . 1C **92**
Sixth Av. W10 . . . . . . 2A **58**
Skardu Rd. NW2 . . . . . . 2A **44**
Skeena Hill SW18 . . 5A **100**
Skeggs Ho. E14 . . . . . . 4E **81**
(off Glengall St.)
Skegness Ho. N7 . . . . . . 4B **48**
(off Sutterton St.)
Skelbrook St. SW18 . . 2E **115**
Skelgill Rd. SW15 . . 2B **100**
Skelley Rd. E15 . . . . . . 4B **54**
Skelton Cl. E8 . . . . . . 3B **50**
Skelton Rd. E7 . . . . . . 3C **54**
Skelton's La. E10 . . . . 2D **39**
Skelwith Rd. W6 . . . . . . 2E **85**
Skenfrith Ho. SE15 . . 2D **93**
(off Commercial Way)

Sketchley Gdns.
SE16 . . . . 1F **93**
Skiers St. E15 . . . . . . 5A **54**
Skiffington Cl. SW2 . . 1C **118**
Skinner Pl. SW1 . . . . . . 5C **74**
(off Bourne St.)
Skinners La.
EC4 . . . . 4A **18** (1E **77**)
Skinner's Row SE10 . . 4D **95**
Skinner St.
EC1 . . . . 2D **9** (2C **62**)
Skipsea Ho.
SW18 . . . . 4A **102**
Skipton Ho. SE4 . . . . 2A **108**
Skipwith Ho. EC1 . . . . . . 5B **8**
(off Bourne St.)
Skipworth Rd. E9 . . . . 5E **51**
Skua Ct. SE8 . . . . 2B **94**
(off Dorking Cl.)
Skylark Ct. SE1 . . . . . . 4A **26**
(off Swan St.)
Skyline Plaza Bldg.
E1 . . . . 5C **64**
(off Commercial Rd.)
Skylines E14 . . . . 3E **81**
Skylines Village E14 . . 3E **81**
Sladebrook Rd. SE3 . . 1F **111**
Sladen Pl. E5 . . . . 1D **51**
Slade Twr. E10 . . . . . . 4C **38**
(off Leyton Grange Est.)
Slade Wlk. SE17 . . . . 2D **91**
Slagrove Pl. SE13 . . 3C **108**
Slaidburn St. SW10 . . 2E **87**
Slaithwaite Rd.
SE13 . . . . 2E **109**
Slaney Ct. NW10 . . . . 4E **43**
Slaney Pl. N7 . . . . 2C **48**
Sleaford Ind. Est.
SW8 . . . . 3E **89**
Sleaford St. SW8 . . . . 3E **89**
Sleigh Ho. E2 . . . . 2E **65**
(off Bacton St.)
Slievemore Cl. SW4 . . 1F **103**
Sligo Ho. E1 . . . . 3F **65**
(off Beaumont Gro.)
Slindon Ct. N16 . . . . . . 5B **36**
Slingsby Pl.
WC2 . . . . 4D **15** (1A **76**)
Slipway Ho. E14 . . . . . . 1D **95**
(off Burrells Wharf Sq.)
Sloane Av. SW3 . . . . . . 5A **74**
Sloane Ct. E. SW3 . . 1C **88**
Sloane Ct. W. SW3 . . 1C **88**
Sloane Gdns.
SW1 . . . . 5C **74**
Sloane Ho. E9 . . . . 4E **51**
(off Loddiges Rd.)
Sloane Sq. SW1 . . . . . . 5C **74**
Sloane St.
SW1 . . . . . . 4A **20** (3B **74**)
Sloane Ter. SW1 . . . . 5C **74**
Sloane Ter. Mans.
SW1 . . . . 5C **74**
(off Sloane Ter.)
Sloman Ho. W10 . . . . 2A **58**
(off Beethoven St.)
Sly St. E1 . . . . 5D **65**
Smallbrook M. W2 . . . . 5F **59**
Smalley Cl. N16 . . . . . . 5B **36**

Smalley Rd. Est.
N16 . . . . 5B 36
(off Smalley Cl.)
Smallwood Rd.
SW17 . . . . 4F 115
Smart's Pl.
WC2 . . . . 2E 15 (5A 62)
Smart St. E2 . . . . 2F 65
Smeaton Ct.
SE1 . . . . 5F 25 (4E 77)
Smeaton Rd. SW18 . . 5C 100
Smeaton St. E1 . . . . . . 2D 79
Smedley St. SW4 . . . . . 5F 89
Smeed Rd. E3 . . . . 4C 52
Smiles Pl. SE13 . . . . . . 5E 95
Smith Cl. SE16 . . . . 2F 79
Smithfield (Central Markets)
. . . . 1D 17
Smithfield St.
EC1 . . . . 1D 17 (4D 63)
Smithies Ct. E15 . . . . . . 2E 53
Smith's Ct. W1 . . . . 4A 14
Smiths Point E13 . . . . . 5C 54
(off Brooks Rd.)
Smith Sq.
SW1 . . . . 5D 23 (4A 76)
Smith St. SW3 . . . . 1B 88
Smith's Yd. SW18 . . . . 2E 115
Smith Ter. SW3 . . . . . . 1B 88
Smithwood Cl.
SW19 . . . . 1A 114
Smithy St. E1 . . . . 4E 65
Smokehouse Yd. EC1 . . 5E 9
(off St John St.)
Smugglers Way
SW18 . . . . 2D 101
Smyrk's Rd. SE17 . . . . 1A 92
Smyrna Rd. NW6 . . . . . 4C 44
Smythe St. E14 . . . . . . 1D 81
SNARESBROOK 1C 40
Snarsgate St. W10 . . . . 4E 57
Sneath Av. NW11 . . . . . 2B 30
Sneyd Rd. NW2 . . . . . . 2E 43
Snowberry Cl. E15 . . . . 1F 53
Snowbury Rd. SW6 . . . 5D 87
Snowden St.
EC2 . . . . . . 4D 11 (3A 64)
Snowdon Aviary 5B 46
(in London Zoo)
Snowdon Dr. NW9 . . . . 1A 28
Snow Hill
EC1 . . . . 1D 17 (4D 63)
Snow Hill Ct.
EC1 . . . . 2E 17 (5D 63)
(not continuous)
Snowman Ho. NW6 . . . 5D 45
Snowsfields
SE1 . . . . 3C 26 (3F 77)
Snowshill Rd. E12 . . . . 2F 55
Soames St. SE15 . . . . . 1B 106
Soane Ct. NW1 . . . . . . 4E 47
(off St Pancras Way)
SOHO 3B 14 (5E 61)
Soho Sq. W1 . . 2B 14 (5F 61)
Soho St. W1 . . . 2B 14 (5F 61)
Soho Theatre & Writers Cen.
. . . . 3B 14
(off Dean St.)
Sojourner Truth Cl.
E8 . . . . 3D 51

Solander Gdns. E1 . . . . 1D 79
(off Cable St.)
E1 . . . . 1E 79
(Highway, The)
Solarium Ct. SE1 . . . . . 5B 78
(off Alscot Rd.)
Soldene Ct. N7 . . . . 2B 48
(off George's Rd.)
Solebay St. E1 . . . . 3A 66
Solent Ho. E1 . . . . 4A 66
(off Ben Jonson Rd.)
Solent Ri. E13 . . . . 2C 68
Solent Rd. NW6 . . . . . . 2C 44
Soley M. WC1 . . 1B 8 (2C 62)
Solna Av. SW15 . . . . . . 3E 99
Solomon's Pas.
SE15 . . . . 2D 107
Solon New Rd.
SW4 . . . . 2A 104
Solon New Rd. Est.
SW4 . . . . 2A 104
Solon Rd. SW2 . . . . . . 2A 104
Solway Cl. E8 . . . . 3B 50
(off Queensbridge Rd.)
Solway Ho. E1 . . . . 3F 65
(off Ernest St.)
Solway Rd. SE22 . . . . . 2C 106
Somali Rd. NW2 . . . . . . 2B 44
Sombourne Ho.
SW15 . . . . 5C 98
(off Fontley Way)
Somer Ct. SW6 . . . . 2C 86
(off Anselm Rd.)
Somerfield Ho. SE16 . . 1F 93
Somerfield Rd. N4 . . . . . 4D 35
(not continuous)
Somerfield St. SE16 . . . 1F 93
Somerford Gro. N16 . . . 1B 50
Somerford Gro. Est.
N16 . . . . 1B 50
Somerford St. E1 . . . . . 3D 65
Somerford Way SE16 . . 3A 80
Somerleyton Pas.
SW9 . . . . 2D 105
Somerleyton Rd.
SW9 . . . . 2C 104
Somers Cl. NW1 . . . . . . 1F 61
Somers Cres. W2 . . . . . 5A 60
Somerset Est. SW11 . . 4F 87
Somerset Gdns. N6 . . . 2C 32
SE13 . . . . 5D 95
Somerset House
. . . . 4F 15 (1B 76)
Somerset Ho. SW19 . . 3F 113
Somerset Rd. E17 . . . . 1C 38
SW19 . . . . 3F 113
Somers Pl. SW2 . . . . . . 5B 104
Somers Rd. SW2 . . . . . 4B 104
SOMERS TOWN
. . . . 1B 6 (2F 61)
Somers Town Community
Sports Cen. 1F 61
Somerton Rd. NW2 . . . 5A 30
SE15 . . . . 2D 107
Somertrees Av.
SE12 . . . . 2D 125
Somerville Av. SW13 . . 2D 85
Somerville Point
SE16 . . . . 3B 80

Sonderburg Rd. N7 . . . . 4B 34
Sondes St. SE17 . . . . . 2F 91
Sonia Gdns. NW10 . . . . 1B 42
Sonning Ho. E2 . . . . . . 2F 11
(off Swanfield St.)
Soper Cl. SE23 . . . . 1F 121
Sophia Cl. N7 . . . . 3B 48
Sophia Ho. W6 . . . . 1E 85
(off Queen Caroline St.)
Sophia Rd. E10 . . . . . . 3D 39
E16 . . . . 5D 69
Sophia Sq. SE16 . . . . . 1A 80
(off Sovereign Cres.)
Sopwith Way SW8 . . . . 3D 89
Sorensen Ct. E10 . . . . . 4D 39
(off Leyton Grange Est.)
Sorrel Gdns. E6 . . . . . . 4F 69
Sorrel La. E14 . . . . 5F 67
Sorrell Cl. SE14 . . . . . . 3A 94
SW9 . . . . 5C 90
Sotheby Rd. N5 . . . . . . 5D 35
Sotheran Cl. E8 . . . . . . 5C 50
Sotherby Lodge E2 . . . . 1E 65
(off Sewardstone Rd.)
Sotheron Rd. SW6 . . . . 3D 87
Soudan Rd. SW11 . . . . 4B 88
Souldern Rd. W14 . . . . 4F 71
Sth. Access Rd. E17 . . 2A 38
Southacre W2 . . . . 5A 60
(off Hyde Pk. Cres.)
Sth. Africa Rd. W12 . . . 2D 71
Southall Pl.
SE1 . . . . 4B 26 (3F 77)
Southampton Bldgs.
WC2 . . . . . . 1B 16 (4C 62)
Southampton M. E16 . . 2D 83
Southampton Pl.
WC1 . . . . 1E 15 (4A 62)
Southampton Rd.
NW5 . . . . 2B 46
Southampton Row
WC1 . . . . 5E 7 (4A 62)
Southampton St.
WC2 . . . . . . 4E 15 (1A 76)
Southampton Way
SE5 . . . . 3F 91
Southam St. W10 . . . . . 3A 58
Sth. Audley St.
W1 . . . . 5C 12 (1C 74)
South Av. NW10 . . . . . . 3E 57
South Bank . . . 1A 24 (2B 76)
Sth. Bank Bus. Cen.
SW8 . . . . 2F 89
Sth. Birkbeck Rd.
E11 . . . . 5F 39
Sth. Black Lion La.
W6 . . . . 1C 84
South Block SE1 . . . . . 4F 23
(off Westminster Bri. Rd.)
Sth. Bolton Gdns.
SW5 . . . . 1E 87
Southborough Ho.
SE17 . . . . 1A 92
(off Surrey Gro.)
Southborough Rd. E9 . . 5F 51
Southbourne Gdns.
SE12 . . . . 3D 111
Sth. Branch Av.
NW10 . . . . 3E 57
SOUTH BROMLEY 1E 81

Southbrook M.
　SE12 . . . . 4B 110
Southbrook Rd.
　SE12 . . . . 4B 110
Southbury NW8. . . . . 5E 45
　(off Loudoun St.)
Sth. Carriage Dr.
　SW1 . . . . . 3A 20 (3B 74)
　SW7 . . . . 3F 73
Sth. Circular Rd.
　SW15 . . . . 2C 98
Sth. City Ct. SE15. . . . . 3A 92
South Cl. N6. . . . . 1D 33
Sth. Colonnade, The
　E14 . . . . 2C 80
Southcombe St. W14 . . 5A 72
Southcote Rd. N19 . . . . 1E 47
Southcott M. NW8 . . . . 1A 60
South Cres. E16 . . . . . . 3F 67
　WC1 . . . . . . 1B 14 (4F 61)
Southcroft Rd.
　SW16 . . . . 5D 117
　SW17 . . . . 5C 116
Sth. Croxted Rd.
　SE21 . . . . 3F 119
Southdean Gdns.
　SW19 . . . . 2B 114
Southdown N7 . . . . 3A 48
South Eastern University
　. . . . . 5B 34
Sth. Eaton Pl. SW1 . . . 5C 74
Sth. Edwardes Sq.
　W8 . . . . 4B 72
SOUTHEND 4F 123
South End W8. . . . . 4D 73
Sth. End Cl. NW3 . . . . . 1A 46
Sth. End Grn. NW3 . . . . 1A 46
Southend La. SE6. . . . . 4B 122
　SE26 . . . . 4B 122
Sth. End Rd. NW3 . . . . 1A 46
Southend Rd.
　BR3: Beck. 5D 123
Sth. End Row W8 . . . . . 4D 73
Southengate Way
　SE14 . . . . 3A 94
Southern Gro. E3 . . . . . 2B 66
Southern Rd. E13. . . . . 1D 69
Southern Row W10 . . . 3A 58
Southern St. N1 . . . . . . 1B 62
Southern Way SE10 . . . 5B 82
　(off School Bank Rd.)
Southernwood Retail Pk.
　SE1 . . . . 1B 92
Southerton Rd. W6. . . . 5E 71
Sth. Esk Rd. E7. . . . . . . 3E 55
Southey Ho. SE17. . . . . 1E 91
　(off Browning St.)
Southey M. E16 . . . . . . 2C 82
Southey Rd. N15 . . . . . 1A 36
　SW9 . . . . 4C 90
Southfield Ct. E11 . . . . 5B 40
Southfield Rd. W4 . . . . 3A 70
SOUTHFIELDS 1B 114
Southfields M.
　SW18 . . . . 4C 100
Southfields Pas.
　SW18 . . . . 4C 100
Southfields Rd.
　SW18 . . . . 4C 100
Southfleet NW5 . . . . . . 3C 46

Southgate Ct. N1 . . . . . 4F 49
　(off Downham Rd.)
Southgate Gro. N1 . . . . 4F 49
South Ga. Rd. E12 . . . . 5F 41
Southgate Rd. N1. . . . . 5F 49
South Gro. E17. . . . . . . 1B 38
　N6. . . . . 3C 32
　N15. . . . . 1F 35
Sth Gro. Ho. N6 . . . . . . 3C 32
SOUTH HACKNEY 4F 51
SOUTH HAMPSTEAD . . 4E 45
Sth. Hill Pk. NW3. . . . . 1A 46
Sth. Hill Pk. Gdns.
　NW3 . . . . 5A 32
Southill St. E14 . . . . . . 5D 67
Sth. Island Pl. SW9 . . . 3B 90
SOUTH KENSINGTON
　. . . . . 5F 73
Sth. Kensington Sta. Arc.
　SW7 . . . . 5F 73
　(off Pelham St.)
SOUTH LAMBETH 3A 90
Sth. Lambeth Pl.
　SW8 . . . . 2A 90
Sth. Lambeth Rd.
　SW8 . . . . 2A 90
Southlands Dr.
　SW19 . . . . 2F 113
South Lodge E16 . . . . . 2D 83
　(off Audley Dr.)
　NW8 . . . . 1F 59
　SW7 . . . . 3A 74
　(off Knightsbridge)
South London Gallery
　. . . . . 4A 92
　(off Peckham Rd.)
South London Theatre
　. . . . . 3D 119
　(off Norwood High St.)
South Mall SW18. . . . . 4D 101
Southmead Rd.
　SW19 . . . . 1A 114
Sth. Molton La.
　W1. . . . . 3D 13 (5D 61)
Sth. Molton Rd. E16 . . . 5C 68
Sth. Molton St.
　W1. . . . . 3D 13 (5D 61)
Southmoor Way E9 . . . 3B 52
Sth. Oak Rd. SW16 . . . 4B 118
Southolm St. SW11 . . . 4D 89
Southover
　BR1: Brom 5C 124
South Pde. SW3 . . . . . . 1F 87
　W4 . . . . 5A 70
South Pk. Cres. SE6. . . 1A 124
South Pk. M. SW6 . . . . 1D 101
South Pk. Rd. SW19 . . 5E 115
South Pl. EC2 . . . 5C 10 (4F 63)
South Pl. M.
　EC2. . . . . . . 1C 18 (4F 63)
Sth. Quay Plaza E14 . . 3D 81
South Ri. W2 . . . . 1A 74
　(off St George's Flds.)
South Rd. SE23 . . . . . . 2F 121
South Row EC1 . . . . . . 5B 96
Sth. Sea St. SE16 . . . . . 1D 80
South Side W6 . . . . 4B 70
Southside N7 . . . . 1F 47
Southside Comn.
　SW19 . . . . 5E 113

Southside Ind. Est.
　SW8 . . . . 4E 89
　(off Havelock Ter.)
Southside Shop. Cen.
　SW18 . . . . 4D 101
South Sq. NW11 . . . . . 1D 31
　WC1 . . . . . . 1B 16 (4C 62)
South St. W1. . . 1C 20 (2C 74)
South Ter. SW7 . . . . . . 5A 74
SOUTH TOTTENHAM . . 1B 36
Southvale Rd. SE3 . . . . 5A 96
Southview Av. NW10 . . 2B 42
Southview Cl.
　SW17 . . . . 5C 116
Southview Rd.
　BR1: Brom 4F 123
South Vs. NW1 . . . . . . 3F 47
Southville SW8 . . . . . . 4F 89
SOUTHWARK
　. . . . . 3E 25 (2E 77)
Southwark Bri.
　SE1 . . . . 5A 18 (1E 77)
Southwark Bri. Bus. Cen.
　SE1 . . . . 2A 26
　(off Southwark Bri. Rd.)
Southwark Bri. Office Village
　SE1 . . . . 1A 26
Southwark Bri. Rd.
　SE1 . . . . 5E 25 (4D 77)
Southwark Cathedral
　. . . . . 1B 26 (2F 77)
Southwark Pk. Est.
　SE16 . . . . 4D 79
Southwark Pk. Rd.
　SE16 . . . . 5R 78
Southwark Pk. Sports Cen.
　. . . . . 5E 79
Southwark Pk. Sports Complex
　. . . . . 5E 79
Southwark Playhouse
　. . . . . 2F 25
　(off Gt. Guildford St.)
Southwark St.
　SE1 . . . . 1D 25 (2D 77)
Southwater Cl. E14 . . . 5B 66
Southway NW11 . . . . . 1D 31
Southway Cl. W12. . . . . 3D 71
　(off Scott's Rd.)
Southwell Gdns.
　SW7 . . . . 5E 73
Southwell Gro. Rd.
　E11 . . . . 4A 40
Southwell Ho. SE16. . . 5D 79
　(off Anchor St.)
Southwell Rd. SE5 . . . . 1E 105
South W. India Dock Entrance
　E14 . . . . 3E 81
Southwest Rd. E11 . . . 3F 39
Sth. Wharf Rd. W2. . . . 5F 59
Southwick M. W2. . . . . 5A 60
Southwick Pl. W2. . . . . 5A 60
Southwick St. W2. . . . . 5A 60
Southwick Yd. W2 . . . . 5A 60
　(off Titchborne Row)
SOUTH WIMBLEDON
　. . . . . 5D 115
Southwold Mans. W9 . . 2C 58
　(off Widley Rd.)
Southwold Rd. E5 . . . . 4D 37

Southwood Av. N6 . . . . . . 2D 33
Southwood Ct. E1 . . . . . . 2D 9
  (off Wynyatt St.)
NW11 . . . . 1D 31
Sth. Woodford to
Barking Relief Rd.
E11 . . . . 1F 41
IG4: Ilf 1F 41
Southwood Hall N6 . . . . 1D 33
Southwood Hgts. N6 . . . 2D 33
Southwood Ho. W11 . . 1A 72
  (off Avondale Pk. Rd.)
Southwood La. N6 . . . . . 3C 32
Southwood Lawn Rd.
N6 . . . . 2C 32
Southwood Mans. N6 . . 1C 32
  (off Southwood La.)
Southwood Pk. N6 . . . . . 2C 32
Southwood Smith Ho.
E2 . . . . 2D 65
  (off Florida St.)
Southwood Smith St.
N1 . . . . 5D 49
Sth. Worple Av.
SW14 . . . . 1A 98
Sth. Worple Way
SW14 . . . . 1A 98
Southwyck Ho.
SW9 . . . . 2D 105
Sovereign Cl. E1 . . . . . 1D 79
Sovereign Cres.
SE16 . . . . 1A 80
Sovereign Ho. E1 . . . . . 3D 65
  (off Cambridge Heath Rd.)
Sovereign M. E2 . . . . . . 1B 64
Spa Ct. SW16 . . . . 4B 118
Spafield St.
EC1 . . . . 3B 8 (3C 62)
Spa Grn. Est.
EC1 . . . . 1C 8 (2D 63)
Spalding Ho. SE4 . . . . . 2A 108
Spalding Rd. NW4 . . . . . 2E 29
SW17 . . . . 5D 117
Spanby Rd. E3 . . . . 3C 66
Spaniards Cl. NW11 . . . 3F 31
Spaniards End NW3 . . . 3E 31
Spaniards Rd. NW3 . . . 4E 31
Spanish Pl.
W1 . . . . 2C 12 (5C 60)
Spanish Rd. SW18 . . . . 3E 101
Sparkes Cotts. SW1 . . . 5C 74
  (off Graham Ter.)
Sparke Ter. E16 . . . . . . 5B 68
  (off Clarkson Rd.)
Spa Rd. SE16 . . 5F 27 (4B 78)
Sparrick's Row
SE1 . . . . 3C 26 (3F 77)
Sparrow Ho. E1 . . . . . . 3E 65
  (off Cephas Av.)
Sparsholt Rd. N19 . . . . 3B 34
Sparta St. SE10 . . . . . . 4E 95
Speakers' Corner
. . . . 4A 12 (1B 74)
Speakman Ho. SE4 . . . 1A 108
  (off Arica Rd.)
Spearman Ho. E14 . . . . 5C 66
  (off Up. North St.)
Spear M. SW5 . . . . 5C 72
Spears Rd. N19 . . . . . . 3A 34
Spectacle Works E13 . . 2E 69

Spectrum Pl. SE17 . . . . 2F 91
  (off Lytham St.)
Spedan Cl. NW3 . . . . . . 5E 31
Speechly M. E8 . . . . . . 2B 50
Speed Highwalk EC2 . . 5A 10
  (off Silk St.)
Speed Ho. EC2 . . . . 5A 10
Speedwell St. SE8 . . . . 3C 94
Speedy Pl. WC1 . . . . . . 2D 7
Speke's Monument . . . 2F 73
Speldhurst Rd. E9 . . . . 4F 51
W4 . . . . 4A 70
Spellbrook Wlk. N1 . . . 5E 49
Spelman Ho. E1 . . . . . . 4C 64
  (off Spelman St.)
Spelman St. E1 . . . . . . 4C 64
  (not continuous)
Spence Cl. SE16 . . . . . 3B 80
Spencer Dr. N2 . . . . . . 1E 31
Spencer House 2F 21
Spencer Ho. NW4 . . . . . 1D 29
Spencer Mans. W14 . . 2A 86
  (off Queen's Club Gdns.)
Spencer M. SW8 . . . . . 4B 90
  (off Sth. Lambeth Rd.)
. . . . 2A 86
SPENCER PARK 3F 101
Spencer Pk. SW18 . . . 3F 101
Spencer Pl. N1 . . . . . . 4D 49
Spencer Ri. NW5 . . . . . 1D 47
Spencer Rd. E6 . . . . . . 5F 55
N8 . . . . 1B 34
  (not continuous)
SW18 . . . . 2F 101
Spencer St.
EC1 . . . . 2D 9 (2D 63)
Spencer Wlk. NW3 . . . . 1E 45
  (off Perrin's Ct.)
NW3 . . . . 1F 45
  (Hampstead High St.)
SW15 . . . . 2F 99
Spenlow Ho. SE16 . . . . 4C 78
  (off Jamaica Rd.)
Spenser Gro. N16 . . . . 2A 50
Spenser M. SE21 . . . . . 2F 119
Spenser Rd. SE24 . . . . 3D 105
Spenser St.
SW1 . . . . 5A 22 (4E 75)
Spensley Wlk. N16 . . . . 5F 35
Spert St. E14 . . . . 1A 80
Spey St. E14 . . . . 4E 67
Spezia Rd. NW10 . . . . . 1C 56
Spice Cl. E1 . . . . 1C 78
Spice Quay Hgts.
SE1 . . . . 2B 78
Spicer Cl. SW9 . . . . . . 5D 91
Spindrift Av. E14 . . . . . 5C 80
Spinnaker Ho. E14 . . . . 3C 80
  (off Byng St.)
Spinney, The SW13 . . . 3D 85
SW16 . . . . 3E 117
Spinney Gdns. SE19 . . 5B 120
Spire Ho. W2 . . . . 1E 73
  (off Lancaster Ga.)
Spirit Quay E1 . . . . 2C 78
SPITALFIELDS
. . . . 5F 11 (4B 64)
Spital Sq. E1 . . 5E 11 (4A 64)
Spital St. E1 . . . . 4C 64
Spital Yd. E1 . . 5E 11 (4A 64)

Splendour Wlk.
SE16 . . . . 1E 93
  (off Verney Rd.)
Spode Ho. SE11 . . . . . 5B 24
Spode Wlk. NW6 . . . . . 2D 45
Sportsbank St. SE6 . . . 5E 109
Spratt Hall Rd. E11 . . . 1C 40
Spriggs Ho. N1 . . . . . . 4D 49
  (off Canonbury Rd.)
Sprimont Pl. SW3 . . . . 1B 88
Springall St. SE15 . . . . 3D 93
Springalls Wharf
SE16 . . . . 3C 78
  (off Bermondsey Wall W.)
Springbank Rd.
SE13 . . . . 4F 109
Springbank Wlk.
NW1 . . . . 4F 47
Springdale M. N16 . . . . 1F 49
Springdale Rd. N16 . . . 1F 49
Springfield E5 . . . . 3D 37
Springfield Ct. NW3 . . . 4A 46
  (off Eton Av.)
Springfield Gdns. E5 . . 3D 37
NW9 . . . . 1A 28
Springfield Gro. SE7 . . 2E 97
Springfield La. NW6 . . . 5D 45
Springfield Ri.
SE26 . . . . 3D 121
  (not continuous)
Springfield Rd. E15 . . . 2A 68
E17 . . . . 1B 38
NW8 . . . . 5E 45
SE26 . . . . 5D 121
SW19 . . . . 5B 114
Springfield Wlk.
NW6 . . . . 5D 45
Spring Gdns. N5 . . . . . 2E 49
SW1 . . . . 1C 22 (2F 75)
  (not continuous)
SE26 . . . . 4E 121
Springhill Cl. SE5 . . . . 1F 105
Spring Ho. WC1 . . . . . . 2B 8
Spring La. E5 . . . . 2D 37
Spring M. W1 . . 5A 4 (4B 60)
Spring Pk. Dr. N4 . . . . 3E 35
Spring Pas. SW15 . . . . 1F 99
Spring Path NW3 . . . . . 2F 45
Spring Pl. NW5 . . . . . . 2D 47
Springrice Rd. SE13 . . 4F 109
Spring St. W2 . . . . 5F 59
Spring Tide Cl. SE15 . . 4C 92
Spring Va. Ter. W14 . . . 4F 71
Spring Wlk. E1 . . . . . . 4C 64
Springwater WC1 . . . . 5F 7
Springwell Av. NW10 . . 5B 42
Springwell Cl.
SW16 . . . . 4B 118
Springwell Rd.
SW16 . . . . 4C 118
Springwood Cl. E3 . . . 1C 66
Sprowston M. E7 . . . . . 3C 54
Sprowston Rd. E7 . . . . 2C 54
Spruce Ho. SE16 . . . . . 3F 79
  (off Woodland Cres.)
Sprules Rd. SE4 . . . . . 5A 94
Spurgeon St. SE1 . . . . 5B 26
Spurling Rd. SE22 . . . . 2B 106

Spur Rd. SE1 . . . 3B **24** (3C **76**)
 SW1 . . . . . . 4F **21** (3E **75**)
Spurstowe Rd. E8 . . . . . 3D **51**
Spurstowe Ter. E8 . . . . . 2C **50**
Square, The E10 . . . . . . 5E **39**
 W6 . . . . 1E **85**
Square Rigger Row
 SW11 . . . . 1E **101**
Squarey St. SW17 . . . . 3E **115**
Squire Gdns. NW8 . . . . 2F **59**
 (off Grove End Rd.)
Squires Ct. SW4 . . . . . . 4A **90**
 SW19 . . . . 4C **114**
Squires Mt. NW3 . . . . . . 5F **31**
Squirrels, The SE13 . . . 1F **109**
Squirries St. E2 . . . . 2C **64**
Stable M. SE6 . . . . 1A **124**
Stables Gallery & Arts Cen.
 . . . . 5C **28**
Stables Lodge E8 . . . . . 4D **51**
 (off Mare St.)
Stables Mkt., The
 NW1 . . . . 4D **47**
Stables M. SE27 . . . . . 5E **119**
Stables Way SE11 . . . . 1C **90**
Stables Yd. SW18 . . . . 4C **100**
Stable Wlk. N1 . . . . 1A **62**
 (off Wharfdale Rd.)
Stable Way W10 . . . . . . 5E **57**
Stable Yd. SW1 . . . . 3F **21**
 SW15 . . . . 1E **99**
Stableyard, The SW9 . . 5B **90**
Stable Yd. Rd.
 SW1 . . . . 3A **22** (3E **75**)
 (not continuous)
Stacey Cl. E10 . . . . 1F **39**
Stacey St. N7 . . . . 5C **34**
 WC2 . . . . 3C **14** (5F **61**)
Stack Ho. SW1 . . . . 5C **74**
 (off Cundy St.)
Stackhouse St. SW3 . . 5A **20**
Stacy Path SE5 . . . . 3A **92**
Stadium Rd. E. NW4 . . . 2D **29**
Stadium St. SW10 . . . . . 3E **87**
Staffa Rd. E10 . . . . 3A **38**
Stafford Cl. E17 . . . . . . 1B **38**
 (not continuous)
 NW6 . . . . 2C **58**
Stafford Ct. SW8 . . . . . 3A **90**
Stafford Cripps Ho.
 E2 . . . . 2E **65**
 (off Globe Rd.)
 SW6 . . . . 2B **86**
 (off Clem Attlee Ct.)
Stafford Mans. SW1 . . . 5F **21**
 (off Stafford Pl.)
 SW4 . . . . 2A **104**
 SW11 . . . . 3B **88**
 (off Albert Bri. Rd.)
 W14 . . . . 4F **71**
 (off Haarlem Rd.)
Stafford Pl.
 SW1 . . . . 5F **21** (4E **75**)
Stafford Rd. E3 . . . . 1B **66**
 E7 . . . . 4E **55**
 NW6 . . . . 2C **58**
Staffordshire St.
 SE15 . . . . 4C **92**
Stafford St.
 W1 . . . . 1F **21** (2E **75**)

Stafford Ter. W8 . . . . . . 4C **72**
Staff St.
 EC1 . . . . 2C **10** (2F **63**)
STAG LANE 2B **112**
Stag La. SW15 . . . . 3B **112**
Stag Pl. SW1 . . 5F **21** (4E **75**)
Stainer Ho. SE3 . . . . . . 2E **111**
Stainer St.
 SE1 . . . . 2C **26** (2F **77**)
Staining La.
 EC2 . . . . 2A **18** (5E **63**)
Stainsbury St. E2 . . . . . 1E **65**
Stainsby Pl. E14 . . . . . . 5C **66**
Stainsby Rd. E14 . . . . . 5C **66**
Stainton Rd. SE6 . . . . . 4F **109**
Stalbridge Flats W1 . . . 3C **12**
 (off Lumley St.)
Stalbridge St. NW1 . . . . 4A **60**
Stalham St. SE16 . . . . . 4D **79**
Stamford Bridge 3D **87**
Stamford Brook Arches
 W6 . . . . 5C **70**
Stamford Brook Av.
 W6 . . . . 4B **70**
Stamford Brook Gdns.
 W6 . . . . 4B **70**
Stamford Brook Mans.
 W6 . . . . 5B **70**
 (off Goldhawk Rd.)
Stamford Brook Rd.
 W6 . . . . 4B **70**
Stamford Cl. NW3 . . . . . 5E **31**
 (off Heath St.)
Stamford Cotts.
 SW10 . . . . 3D **87**
 (off Billing St.)
Stamford Ct. W6 . . . . . . 5C **70**
Stamford Ga. SW6 . . . . 3D **87**
Stamford Gro. E. N16 . . 3C **36**
Stamford Gro. W.
 N16 . . . . 3C **36**
STAMFORD HILL 3B **36**
Stamford Hill N16 . . . . . 4B **36**
Stamford Lodge N16 . . . 2B **36**
Stamford Rd. E6 . . . . . . 5F **55**
 N1 . . . . 4A **50**
Stamford St.
 SE1 . . . . 2B **24** (2C **76**)
Stamp Pl. E2 . . 1F **11** (1B **64**)
Stanard Cl. N16 . . . . . . 2A **36**
Stanborough Pas. E8 . . 3B **50**
Stanbridge Rd. SW15 . . 1E **99**
Stanbury Ct. NW3 . . . . . 3B **46**
Stanbury Rd. SE15 . . . . 5D **93**
 (not continuous)
Standard Ct. SE6 . . . . . 1D **123**
Standard Pl. EC2 . . . . . 2E **11**
Standard Rd. NW10 . . . 3A **56**
Standen Rd. SW18 . . . . 5B **100**
Standish Ho. SE3 . . . . . 2D **111**
 (off Elford Cl.)
 W6 . . . . 5C **70**
 (off St Peter's Gro.)
Standish Rd. W6 . . . . . . 5C **70**
Standlake Point
 SE23 . . . . 3F **121**
Stane Pas. SW16 . . . . . 5A **118**
Stanesgate Ho. SE15 . . 3C **92**
 (off Friary Est.)
Stane Way SE18 . . . . . . 3F **97**

Stanifield Ho. NW8 . . . . 3F **59**
 (off Frampton St.)
Stanfield Rd. E3 . . . . . . 1A **66**
Stanford Ct. SW6 . . . . . 4D **87**
Stanford Pl. SE17 . . . . . 5A **78**
Stanford Rd. W8 . . . . . . 4D **73**
Stanford St. SW1 . . . . . 5F **75**
Stangate SE1 . . . . 5A **24**
Stanhope Cl. SE16 . . . . 3F **79**
Stanhope Gdns. N4 . . . 1D **35**
 N6 . . . . 1D **33**
 SW7 . . . . 5E **73**
Stanhope Ga.
 W1 . . . . 2C **20** (2C **74**)
Stanhope Ho. SE8 . . . . 3B **94**
 (off Adolphus St.)
Stanhope M. E. SW7 . . . 5E **73**
Stanhope M. Sth.
 SW7 . . . . 5E **73**
Stanhope M. W. SW7 . . 5E **73**
Stanhope Pde.
 NW1 . . . . 1F **5** (2E **61**)
Stanhope Pl. W2 . . . . . . 1B **74**
Stanhope Rd. E17 . . . . . 1D **39**
 N6 . . . . 1E **33**
Stanhope Row
 W1 . . . . 2D **21** (2D **75**)
Stanhope St.
 NW1 . . . . 1F **5** (1E **61**)
Stanhope Ter. W2 . . . . . 1F **73**
Stanier Cl. W14 . . . . . . 1B **86**
Stanlake M. W12 . . . . . 2E **71**
Stanlake Rd. W12 . . . . . 2E **71**
Stanlake Vs. W12 . . . . . 2E **71**
Stanley Cl. SW8 . . . . . . 2B **90**
Stanley Cohen Ho.
 EC1 . . . . 4F **9**
 (off Golden La. Est.)
Stanley Cres. W11 . . . . 1B **72**
Stanley Gdns. NW2 . . . . 2E **43**
 W3 . . . . 3A **70**
 W11 . . . . 1B **72**
Stanley Gdns. M.
 W11 . . . . 1B **72**
 (off Kensington Pk. Rd.)
Stanley Gro. SW8 . . . . . 5C **88**
Stanley Holloway Ct.
 E16 . . . . 5C **68**
 (off Coolfin Rd.)
Stanley Ho. E14 . . . . . . 5C **66**
 (off Saracen St.)
 SW10 . . . . 3E **87**
 (off Coleridge Gdns.)
Stanley M. SW10 . . . . . 3E **87**
 (off Coleridge Gdns.)
Stanley Rd. E10 . . . . . . 1D **39**
 E12 . . . . 2F **55**
 E15 . . . . 5F **53**
 NW9 . . . . 2C **28**
Stanley St. SE8 . . . . . . 3B **94**
Stanley Ter. N19 . . . . . . 4A **34**
Stanmer St. SW11 . . . . 4A **88**
Stanmore Pl. NW1 . . . . 5D **47**
Stanmore Rd. E11 . . . . 3B **40**
Stanmore St. N1 . . . . . . 5B **48**
Stanmore Cotts. E1 . . . 3E **65**
 (off Fox St.)
Stannard M. E8 . . . . . . 3C **50**
 (off Stannard Rd.)
Stannard Rd. E8 . . . . . . 3C **50**

Stannary Pl. SE11 . . . . . 1C 90
Stannary St. SE11 . . . . . 2C 90
Stansbury Ho. W10 . . . . . 2A 58
  (off Beethoven St.)
Stansfield Rd. E6 . . . . . 4F 69
  E16 . . . . 1F 83
Stansfield Ho. SE1 . . . . 5B 78
  (off Balaclava Rd.)
Stansfield Rd. SW9 . . . 1B 104
Stanstead Gro. SE6 . . . 1B 122
Stanstead Rd. E11 . . . . . 1D 41
  SE6 . . . . 1A 122
  SE23 . . . . 1F 121
Stanswood Gdns.
  SE5 . . . . 3A 92
Stanthorpe Cl.
  SW16 . . . . 5A 118
Stanthorpe Rd.
  SW16 . . . . 5A 118
Stanton Ho. SE10 . . . . . 2E 95
  (off Thames St.)
  SE16 . . . . 3B 80
  (off Rotherhithe St.)
Stanton Rd. SE26 . . . . 4B 122
  SW13 . . . . 5B 84
Stanton Sq. SE26 . . . . 4B 122
Stanton Way SE26 . . . . 4B 122
Stanway Ct. N1 . . . . 1A 64
  (not continuous)
Stanway St. N1 . . . . 1A 64
Stanwick Rd. W14 . . . . . 5B 72
Stanworth St.
  SE1 . . . . . 4F 27 (4B 78)
Stanyhurst SE23 . . . . . 1A 122
Staplefield Cl. SW2 . . . 1A 118
Stapleford Cl.
  SW19 . . . . 5A 114
Staplehurst Rd.
  SE13 . . . . 3F 109
Staple Inn WC1 . . . . . . 1B 16
Staple Inn Bldgs.
  WC1 . . . . 1B 16 (4C 62)
Staples Cl. SE16 . . . . . 2A 80
STAPLES CORNER . . . 3D 29
Staples Cnr. Bus. Pk.
  NW2 . . . . 3D 29
Staple St.
  SE1 . . . . . 4C 26 (3F 77)
Stapleton Hall Rd.
  N4 . . . . 3B 34
Stapleton Ho. E2 . . . . . 2D 65
  (off Ellsworth St.)
Stapleton Rd.
  SW17 . . . . 3C 116
Stapleton Vs. N16 . . . . . 1A 50
  (off Wordsworth Rd.)
Star All. EC3 . . . . 4E 19
  (off Fenchurch St.)
Starboard Way E14. . . . 4C 80
Starcross St.
  NW1 . . . . . 2A 6 (2E 61)
Starfield Rd. W12 . . . . . 3C 70
Star La. E16 . . . . 3A 68
Starling Ho. NW8 . . . . . 1A 60
  (off Barrow Hill Est.)
Star Pl. E1 . . . . 1C 78
Star Rd. W14 . . . . 2B 86
Star St. W2 . . . . 5A 60
Star Yd.
  WC2 . . . . 2B 16 (5C 62)

Statham Gro. N16 . . . . . 1F 49
Statham Ho.
  SW8 . . . . 4E 89
  (off Wadhurst Rd.)
Station App. E7 . . . . . . 1D 55
  NW1 . . . . . 4A 4 (3B 60)
  NW10 . . . . 2B 56
  SE3 . . . . 1D 111
  SE12 . . . . 4C 110
  (off Burnt Ash Hill)
  SE26 . . . . 4E 121
  SW6 . . . . 1A 100
  SW16 . . . . 5F 117
Station App. Rd.
  SE1 . . . . . 4A 24 (3C 76)
Station Arc. W1 . . . . 4E 5
  (off Gt. Portland St.)
Station Av. SW9 . . . . . 1D 105
Station Cres. SE3 . . . . . 1C 96
Stationer's Hall Ct.
  EC4 . . . . . 3E 17 (5D 63)
Station Pde. E13 . . . . . . 5E 55
  (off Green St.)
Station Pas. SE15 . . . . . 4E 93
Station Path E8 . . . . 3D 51
  (off Graham Rd.)
Station Pl. N4 . . . . 4C 34
Station Ri. SE27 . . . . . 2D 119
Station Rd. E7 . . . . 1C 54
  E12 . . . . 1F 55
  E17 . . . . 1A 38
  N19 . . . . 5E 33
  NW4 . . . . 1C 28
  NW10 . . . . 1B 56
  SE13 . . . . 1E 109
  SE20 . . . . 5E 121
  SW13 . . . . 5B 84
Station St. E15 . . . . 4F 53
Station Ter. NW10 . . . . . 1F 57
  SE5 . . . . 4E 91
Station Ter. M. SE3 . . . . 1C 96
Station Way SE15 . . . . . 5C 92
Staton Ct. E10 . . . . 2D 39
  (off Kings Cl.)
Staunton Ho. SE17 . . . . 5A 78
  (off Tatum St.)
Staunton St. SE8 . . . . . 2B 94
Staveley NW1 . . . . 1F 5
  (off Varndell St.)
Staveley Cl. E9 . . . . 2E 51
  N7 . . . . 1A 48
  SE15 . . . . 4D 93
Staveley Gdns. W4 . . . . 4A 84
Staveley Rd. W4 . . . . . . 3A 84
Staverton Rd. NW2 . . . . 4E 43
Stavordale Rd. N5 . . . . 1D 49
Stayner's Rd. E1 . . . . . . 3F 65
Steadman Ct. EC1 . . . . 3A 10
  (off Old St.)
Stead St. SE17 . . . . 5F 77
Stean St. E8 . . . . 5B 50
Stebbing Ho. W11 . . . . . 2F 71
  (off Queensdale Cres.)
Stebondale St. E14 . . . . 5E 81
Stedham Pl. WC1 . . . . . 2D 15
Steedman St. SE17 . . . . 5E 77

Steele Ho. E15 . . . . 1A 68
  (off Eve Rd.)
Steele Rd. E11 . . . . 1A 54
Steele's M. Nth.
  NW3 . . . . 3B 46
Steele's M. Sth.
  NW3 . . . . 3B 46
Steele's Rd. NW3 . . . . . 3B 46
Steele's Studios
  NW3 . . . . 3B 46
Steel's La. E1 . . . . 5E 65
Steelyard Pas. EC4 . . . . 5B 18
Steen Way SE22 . . . . . 3A 106
Steep Hill SW16 . . . . . . 3F 117
Steeple Cl. SW6 . . . . . . 5A 86
  SW19 . . . . 5A 114
Steeple Ct. E1 . . . . 3D 65
Steeple Wlk. N1 . . . . 5E 49
  (off New Nth. Rd.)
Steerforth St. SW18 . . . 2E 115
Steers Way SE16 . . . . . . 3A 80
Stelfox Ho. WC1 . . . . 1A 8
  (off Penton Ri.)
Stella Rd. SW17 . . . . . . 5B 116
Stellman Cl. E5 . . . . 5C 36
Stephan Cl. E8 . . . . 5C 50
Stephendale Rd.
  SW6 . . . . 1D 101
Stephen Fox Ho. W4 . . . 1A 84
  (off Chiswick La.)
Stephen M.
  W1 . . . . . . 1B 14 (4F 61)
Stephen Pl. SW4 . . . . . 1E 103
Stephens Ct. E16 . . . . . 3B 68
  SE4 . . . . 1A 108
Stephenson Ho.
  SE1 . . . . 5F 25 (4E 77)
Stephenson Rd. E17 . . . 1A 38
Stephenson St. E16 . . . . 3A 68
  NW10 . . . . 2A 56
Stephenson Way
  NW1 . . . . . 3A 6 (3E 61)
Stephen's Rd. E15 . . . . 5A 54
Stephen St.
  W1 . . . . . . 1B 14 (4F 61)
Stepney C'way. E1 . . . . . 5F 65
Stepney City Apartments
  E1 . . . . 4E 65
Stepney Grn. E1 . . . . . . 4E 65
Stepney Grn. Ct. E1 . . . 4F 65
  (off Stepney Grn.)
Stepney High St. E1 . . . 4F 65
Stepney Way E1 . . . . . . 4D 65
Sterling Cl. NW10 . . . . . 4C 42
Sterling Gdns. SE14 . . . 2A 94
Sterling Ho. SE3 . . . . . 2D 111
Sterling St. SW7 . . . . . . 4A 74
Sterndale Rd. W14 . . . . 4F 71
Sterne St. W12 . . . . 3F 71
Sternhall La. SE15 . . . . 1C 106
Sternhold Av. SW2 . . . . 2F 117
Sterry St.
  SE1 . . . . . 4B 26 (3F 77)
Steucers La. SE23 . . . . 1A 122
Steve Biko La. SE6 . . . . 4C 122
Steve Biko Lodge
  E13 . . . . 1C 68
  (off London Rd.)
Steve Biko Rd. N7 . . . . . 5C 34

Stevedore St. E1 . . . . . . 2D 79
Stevenage Rd. SW6 . . 3F 85
Stevens Av. E9 . . . . 3E 51
Stevens Cl.
  BR3: Beck 5C 122
Stevenson Cres.
  SE16 . . . . 1C 92
Stevenson Hu. NW8 . . 5E 45
  (off Boundary Rd.)
Stevens St.
  SE1 . . . . . . 5E 27 (4A 78)
Steventon Rd. W12 . . . 1B 70
Steward Ho.
  E1 . . . . . . 5E 11 (4A 64)
  (not continuous)
Stewart Rd. E15 . . . . . . 1F 53
Stewart's Gro. SW3 . . . 1F 87
Stewart's Rd. SW8 . . . . 3E 89
Stewart St. E14 . . . . . . 3E 81
Stew La. EC4 . . 4F 17 (1E 77)
Stifford Ho. E1 . . . . 4E 65
  (off Stepney Way)
Stileman Ho. E3 . . . . . . 4B 66
  (off Ackroyd Dr.)
Stillingfleet Rd.
  SW13 . . . . 2C 84
Stillington St. SW1 . . . 5E 75
Stillness Rd. SE23 . . 4A 108
Stirling Rd. E13 . . . . . . 1D 69
  SW9 . . . . 5A 90
Stockbeck NW1 . . . . . . 1A 6
  (off Ampthill Est.)
Stockfield Rd.
  SW16 . . . . 3B 118
Stockholm Ho. E1 . . . . 1C 78
  (off Swedenborg Gdns.)
Stockholm Rd. SE16 . . 1E 93
Stockholm Way E1 . . . 2C 78
Stockhurst Cl. SW15 . . 5E 85
Stockleigh Hall NW8 . . 1A 60
  (off Prince Albert Rd.)
Stock Orchard Cres.
  N7 . . . . 2B 48
Stock Orchard St. N7 . . 2B 48
Stocks Pl. E14 . . . . 1B 80
Stock St. E13 . . . . 1C 68
Stockton Ho. E2 . . . . . . 2D 65
  (off Ellsworth St.)
STOCKWELL 5B 90
Stockwell Av. SW9 . . . 1B 104
Stockwell Gdns.
  SW9 . . . . 4B 90
Stockwell Gdns. Est.
  SW9 . . . . 5A 90
Stockwell Grn. SW9 . . 5B 90
Stockwell Grn. Ct.
  SW9 . . . . 5B 90
Stockwell La. SW9 . . . . 5B 90
Stockwell M. SW9 . . . . 5B 90
Stockwell Pk. Cres.
  SW9 . . . . 5B 90
Stockwell Pk. Est.
  SW9 . . . . 5B 90
Stockwell Pk. Rd.
  SW9 . . . . 4B 90
Stockwell Pk. Wlk.
  SW9 . . . . 1C 104
Stockwell Rd. SW9 . . . 5B 90
Stockwell St. SE10 . . . 2E 95
Stockwell Ter. SW8 . . . 4B 90

Stoddart Ho. SW8 . . . . 2B 90
Stofield Gdns. SE9 . . . 3F 125
Stoford Cl. SW19 . . . . 5A 100
Stokenchurch St.
  SW6 . . . . 4D 87
STOKE NEWINGTON . . 5B 36
Stoke Newington Chu. St.
  N16 . . . . 5F 35
Stoke Newington Comn.
  N16 . . . . 4B 36
Stoke Newington High St.
  N16 . . . . 5B 36
Stoke Newington Rd.
  N16 . . . . 2B 50
Stoke Pl. NW10 . . . . . . 2B 56
Stokesley St. W12 . . . . 5B 56
Stokes Rd. E6 . . . . 3F 69
Stoll Cl. NW2 . . . . 5E 29
Stoms Path SE6 . . . . . 5C 122
  (off Maroons Way)
Stondon Ho. E15 . . . . . 5B 54
  (off John St.)
Stondon Pk. SE23 . . . 4A 108
Stondon Wlk. E6 . . . . . 1F 69
Stonebridge Cen.
  N15 . . . . 1B 36
Stonebridge Rd. N15 . . 1B 36
Stone Bldgs. WC2 . . . . 1A 16
Stone Cl. SW4 . . . . 5E 89
Stonecutter St.
  EC4 . . . . . . 2D 17 (5D 63)
Stonefield N4 . . . . 4B 34
Stonefield St. N1 . . . . . 5C 48
Stonefield Way SE7 . . . 3F 97
Stone Hall W8 . . . . 4D 73
  (off Stone Hall Gdns.)
Stonehall Av. IG1: Ilf . . 1F 41
Stone Hall Gdns. W8 . . 4D 73
Stone Hall Pl. W8 . . . . 4D 73
Stonehills Ct. SE21 . . . 3A 120
Stonehouse NW1 . . . . . 5E 47
  (off Plender St.)
Stone Ho. Ct. EC3 . . . . 2E 19
Stone Lake Ind. Pk.
  SE7 . . . . 5E 83
Stone Lake Retail Pk.
  SE7 . . . . 5E 83
Stoneleigh M. E3 . . . . . 1A 66
Stoneleigh Pl. W11 . . . 1F 71
Stoneleigh St. W11 . . . 1F 71
Stoneleigh Ter. N19 . . . 4D 33
Stonell's Rd. SW11 . . . 4B 102
Stonenest St. N4 . . . . . 3B 34
Stones End St.
  SE1 . . . . . . 4F 25 (3E 77)
Stoneyard La. E14 . . . . 1D 81
Stoneycroft Cl.
  SE12 . . . . 5B 110
Stoney La.
  E1 . . . . 2E 19 (5B 64)
Stoney St.
  SE1 . . . . . . 1B 26 (2F 77)
Stonhouse St. SW4 . . . 2F 103
Stonor Rd. W14 . . . . . . 5B 72
Stopes St. SE15 . . . . . 3B 92
Stopford Rd. E13 . . . . . 5C 54
  SE17 . . . . 1D 91
Stopher Ho. SE1 . . . . . 4E 25
  (off Webber St.)
Storers Quay E14 . . . . . 5F 81

Store St. E15 . . . . 2F 53
  WC1 . . . . . . 1B 14 (4F 61)
Storey Ct. NW8 . . . . . . 2F 59
  (off St John's Wood Rd.)
Storey Ho. E14 . . . . 1D 81
  (off Cottage St.)
Storey Rd. N6 . . . . 1B 32
Storey's Ga.
  SW1 . . . . . . 4C 22 (3F 75)
Stories M. SE5 . . . . 5A 92
Stories Rd. SE5 . . . . . 1A 106
Stork Rd. E7 . . . . 3B 54
Stork's Rd. SE16 . . . . . 4C 78
Stormont Lawn Tennis &
  Squash Club 1B 32
Stormont Rd. N6 . . . . . 2B 32
  SW11 . . . . 1C 102
Storrington WC1 . . . . . . 2E 7
  (off Regent Sq.)
Story St. N1 . . . . 4B 48
Stothard Ho. E1 . . . . . . 3E 65
  (off Amiel St.)
Stothard St. E1 . . . . . . 3E 65
Stott Cl. SW18 . . . . . . 4F 101
Stoughton Cl. SE11 . . . 5B 76
  (off Gibson Rd.)
  SW15 . . . . 1C 112
Stourcliffe Cl. W1 . . . . 5B 60
Stourcliffe St. W1 . . . . 5B 60
Stourhead Cl. SW19 . . 5F 99
Stourhead Ho. SW1 . . . 1F 89
  (off Tachbrook St.)
Stour Rd. E3 . . . . 4C 52
Stowage SE8 . . . . 2C 94
Stowe Ho. NW11 . . . . . 1E 31
Stowe Rd. W12 . . . . . . 3D 71
Stracey Rd. E7 . . . . 1C 54
  NW10 . . . . 5A 42
Stradbroke Rd. N5 . . . . 1E 49
Stradella Rd. SE24 . . . 4E 105
Strafford Ho. SE8 . . . . 1B 94
  (off Grove St.)
Strafford St. E14 . . . . . 3C 80
Strahan Rd. E3 . . . . . . 2A 66
Straightsmouth
  SE10 . . . . 3E 95
Strait Rd. E6 . . . . 1F 83
Strakers Rd. SE15 . . . . 2D 107
Strale Ho. N1 . . . . 5A 50
  (off Whitmore St.)
Strand WC2 . . 5E 15 (1A 76)
Strand La.
  WC2 . . . . . . 4A 16 (1B 76)
Strand Theatre 4F 15
  (off Aldwych)
Strang Ho. N1 . . . . 5E 49
Strang Print Room 3B 6
Strangways Ter. W14 . . 4B 72
Stranraer Way N1 . . . . 4A 48
Strasburg Rd. SW11 . . 4C 88
STRATFORD 4F 53
Stratford Cen., The
  E15 . . . . 4F 5
Stratford Circus
  (Performing Arts Cen.)
  . . . . 3F
Stratford Gro. SW15 . . 2
STRATFORD MARSH . . 4
STRATFORD NEW TOWN
  . . . .

Stratford Office Village, The
  E15 . . . . 4A **54**
  (off Romford Rd.)
Stratford Picture House
  . . . . 3F **53**
Stratford Pl.
  W1 . . . . 3D **13** (5D **61**)
Stratford Rd. E13 . . . . . . 5B **54**
  (not continuous)
  W8 . . . . 4C **72**
Stratford Shop. Cen.
  E15 . . . . 4F **53**
  (off Stratford Cen., The)
Stratford Studios W8 . . 4C **72**
Stratford Vs. NW1 . . . . 4E **47**
Stratham St. N19 . . . . . . 3A **34**
  (off Alexander Rd.)
Strathan Cl. SW18 . . . 4A **100**
Strathaven Rd.
  SE12 . . . . 4D **111**
Strathblaine Rd.
  SW11 . . . . 3F **101**
Strathdale SW16 . . . . . 5B **118**
Strathdon Dr. SW17 . . 3F **115**
Strathearn Pl. W2 . . . . . 5A **60**
Strathearn Rd.
  SW19 . . . . 5C **114**
Stratheden Pde. SE3 . . 3C **96**
Stratheden Rd. SE3 . . . 4C **96**
Strathleven Rd.
  SW2 . . . . 3A **104**
Strathmore Ct. NW8 . . . 2A **60**
  (off Park Rd.)
Strathmore Gdns.
  W8 . . . . 2C **72**
Strathmore Rd.
  SW19 . . . . 3C **114**
Strathnairn St. SE1 . . . 5C **78**
Strathray Gdns. NW3 . . 3A **46**
Strath Ter. SW11 . . . . 2A **102**
Strathville Rd.
  SW18 . . . . 2C **114**
  (not continuous)
Stratton Ct. N1 . . . . 4A **50**
  (off Hertford Rd.)
Strattondale St. E14 . . . 4E **81**
Stratton St.
  W1 . . . . 1E **21** (2D **75**)
Strauss Rd. W4 . . . . 3A **70**
Streakes Fld. Rd.
  NW2 . . . . 4C **28**
Streamline Ct.
  SE22 . . . . 1C **120**
  (off Streamline M.)
Streamline M. SE22 . . 1C **120**
STREATHAM 5A **118**
Streatham Cl.
  SW16 . . . . 2A **118**
STREATHAM COMMON
  . . . . 5A **118**
treatham Comn. Nth.
  SW16 . . . . 5A **118**
eatham Comn. Sth.
  SW16 . . . . 5A **118**
atham High Rd.
  W16 . . . . 3A **118**
tham High Rd.
  '16 . . . . 4A **118**
THAM HILL . . . 2A **118**
am Hill SW2 . . 2A **118**

Streatham Ice Arena
  . . . . 5F **117**
Streatham Leisure Cen.
  . . . . 5A **118**
STREATHAM PARK . . 5E **117**
Streatham Pl. SW2 . . 5A **104**
Streatham St.
  WC1 . . . . 2D **15** (5A **62**)
Streathbourne Rd.
  SW17 . . . . 2C **116**
Streatley Pl. NW3 . . . . 1E **45**
Streatley Rd. NW6 . . . 4B **44**
Streetfield M. SE3 . . 1C **110**
Streimer Rd. E15 . . . . 1E **67**
Strelley Way W3 . . . . . 1A **70**
Stretton Mans. SE8 . . . 1C **94**
Strickland Ct. SE15 . . 1C **106**
Strickland Ho. E2 . . . . . 2F **11**
  (off Chambord St.)
Strickland Row
  SW18 . . . . 5F **101**
Strickland St. SE8 . . . 5C **94**
Stride Rd. E13 . . . . 1B **68**
Stringer Ho. N1 . . . . . . 5A **50**
  (off Whitmore Est.)
Strode Rd. E7 . . . . 1C **54**
  NW10 . . . . 3C **42**
  SW6 . . . . 3A **86**
Strome Ho. NW6 . . . . . 1D **59**
  (off Carlton Va.)
Strone Rd. E7 . . . . 3E **55**
  E12 . . . . 3E **55**
Stronsa Rd. W12 . . . . . 3B **70**
Strood Ho. SE1 . . . . . . 4C **26**
  (off Staple St.)
Stroud Cres. SW15 . . 3C **112**
STROUD GREEN 2B **34**
Stroud Grn. Rd. N4 . . . 3B **34**
Stroudley Ho. SW8 . . . 4E **89**
Stroudley Wlk. E3 . . . . 2D **67**
Stroud Rd. SW19 . . . . 3C **114**
Strouts Pl. E2 . . 1F **11** (2B **64**)
Strudwick Ct. SW4 . . . 4A **90**
  (off Binfield Rd.)
Strutton Ground
  SW1 . . . . 5B **22** (4F **75**)
Strype St. E1 . . 1F **19** (4B **64**)
Stuart Av. NW9 . . . . . . 2C **28**
Stuart Ho. E16 . . . . 2D **83**
  (off Beaulieu Av.)
  W14 . . . . 5A **72**
  (off Windsor Way)
Stuart Mill Ho. N1 . . . . . 1F **7**
  (off Killick St.)
Stuart Rd. NW6 . . . . . . 2C **58**
  (not continuous)
  SE15 . . . . 2E **107**
  SW19 . . . . 3C **114**
Stuart Twr. W9 . . . . . . 2E **59**
  (off Maida Va.)
Stubbs Dr. SE16 . . . . . 1D **93**
Stubbs Ho. E2 . . . . 2F **65**
  (off Bonner St.)
  SW1 . . . . 5F **75**
  (off Erasmus St.)
Stubbs Point E13 . . . . 3C **68**
Stucley Pl. NW1 . . . . . . 4D **47**
Studdridge St. SW6 . . 5C **86**
  (not continuous)
Studd St. N1 . . . . 5D **49**

Studholme Ct. NW3 . . 1C **44**
Studholme St. SE15 . . 3D **93**
Studio Pl. SW1 . . . . . . 4A **20**
Studland SE17 . . . . 1F **91**
  (off Portland St.)
Studland Ho. E14 . . . . . 5A **66**
  (off Aston St.)
Studland Rd. SE26 . . . 5F **121**
Studland St. W6 . . . . . 5D **71**
Studley Cl. E5 . . . . 2A **52**
Studley Ct. E14 . . . . . . 1F **81**
  (off Jamestown Way)
Studley Dr. IG4: Ilf . . . 1F **41**
Studley Est. SW4 . . . . 4A **90**
Studley Rd. E7 . . . . 3D **55**
  SW4 . . . . 4A **90**
Stukeley Rd. E7 . . . . . . 4D **55**
Stukeley St.
  WC2 . . . . 2E **15** (5A **62**)
Stumps Hill La.
  BR3: Beck 5C **122**
Stunell Ho. SE14 . . . . . 2F **93**
  (off John Williams Cl.)
Sturdee Ho. E2 . . . . . . 1C **64**
  (off Horatio St.)
Sturdy Ho. E3 . . . . 1A **66**
  (off Gernon Rd.)
Sturdy Rd. SE15 . . . . . 5D **93**
Sturgeon Rd. SE17 . . . 1E **91**
Sturgess Av. NW4 . . . . 2D **29**
Sturge St.
  SE1 . . . . 3F **25** (3E **77**)
Sturmer Way N7 . . . . . 2B **48**
Sturminster Ho. SW8 . . 3B **90**
  (off Dorset Rd.)
Sturry St. E14 . . . . 5D **67**
Sturt St. N1 . . . 1A **10** (1E **63**)
Stutfield St. E1 . . . . . . 5C **64**
Styles Gdns. SW9 . . . 1D **105**
Styles Ho. SE1 . . . . . . 3D **25**
Sudbourne Rd.
  SW2 . . . . 3A **104**
Sudbrooke Rd.
  SW12 . . . . 4B **102**
Sudbury Ct. SW8 . . . . . 4F **89**
  (off Allen Edwards Dr.)
Sudbury Cres.
  BR1: Brom 5C **124**
Sudbury Ho. SW18 . . . 3D **101**
Sudeley St. N1 . . . . . . 1D **63**
Sudlow Rd. SW18 . . . 3C **100**
Sudrey St.
  SE1 . . . . 4F **25** (3E **77**)
Suffield Ho. SE17 . . . . 1D **91**
  (off Berryfield Rd.)
Suffolk Ct. E10 . . . . . . 2C **38**
Suffolk La.
  EC4 . . . . 4B **18** (1F **77**)
Suffolk Pl.
  SW1 . . . . 1C **22** (2F **75**)
Suffolk Rd. E13 . . . . . . 2C **68**
  N15 . . . . 1F **35**
  NW10 . . . . 4A **42**
  SW13 . . . . 3B **84**
Suffolk St. E7 . . . . 1C **54**
  SW1 . . . . 5C **14** (1F **75**)
Sugar Bakers Ct. EC3 . . 3E **19**
Sugar Ho. La. E15 . . . . 1E **67**
Sugar Loaf Wlk. E2 . . . 2E **65**
Sugar Quay EC3 . . . . . 5E **19**

Sugar Quay Wlk.
EC3 . . . . 5E **19** (1A **78**)
Sugden Rd. SW11 . . . 1C **102**
Sugden St. SE5 . . . . 2F **91**
Sulby Ho. SE4 . . . . 2A **108**
(off Turnham Rd.)
Sulgrave Gdns. W6 . . . . 3E **71**
Sulgrave Rd. W6 . . . . . 4E **71**
Sulina Rd. SW2 . . . . . 5A **104**
Sulivan Cl. SW6 . . . . . 5C **86**
Sulivan Ent. Cen.
SW6 . . . . 1D **101**
Sulivan Rd. SW6 . . . . 1C **100**
Sulkin Ho. E2 . . . . 2F **65**
(off Knottisford St.)
Sullivan Av. E16 . . . . . 4F **69**
Sullivan Cl. SW11 . . . . 1A **102**
Sullivan Ct. N16 . . . . . 2B **36**
Sullivan Ho. SE11 . . . . 5B **76**
(off Vauxhall St.)
SW1 . . . . 2D **89**
(off Churchill Gdns.)
Sullivan Rd. SE11 . . . . 5C **76**
Sultan St. SE5 . . . . 3E **91**
Sumatra Rd. NW6 . . . . 2C **44**
Sumburgh Rd.
SW12 . . . . 4C **102**
Summercourt Rd. E1 . . 5E **65**
Summerfield Av.
NW6 . . . . 1A **58**
Summerfield St.
SE12 . . . . 5B **110**
Summerhouse Rd.
N16 . . . . 4A **36**
Summerley St.
SW18 . . . . 2D **115**
Summersby Rd. N6 . . 1D **33**
Summerskill Cl.
SE15 . . . . 1D **107**
Summers St.
EC1 . . . . 4B **8** (3C **62**)
SUMMERSTOWN. 3E **115**
Summerstown
SW17 . . . . 3E **115**
Summit Av. NW9 . . . . 1A **28**
Summit Ct. NW2 . . . . 2A **44**
Summit Est. N16 . . . . 2C **36**
Summit Rd. SE15 . . . . 4B **92**
Sumner Bldgs. SE1 . . 1F **25**
Sumner Ct. SW8 . . . . 3A **90**
Sumner Est. SE15 . . . 3B **92**
Sumner Ho. E3 . . . . . . 4D **67**
(off Watts Gro.)
Sumner Pl. SW7 . . . . 5F **73**
Sumner Pl. M. SW7 . . 5F **73**
Sumner Rd. SE15 . . . . 2B **92**
Sumner St.
SE1 . . . . 1E **25** (2D **77**)
Sumpter Cl. NW3 . . . . 3E **45**
Sunbeam Cres. W10 . . 3E **57**
Sunbeam Rd. NW10. . . 3A **56**
Sunbury Av. SW14 . . . 2A **98**
Sunbury Av. Pas.
SW14 . . . . 2A **98**
Sunbury Ho. E2 . . . . . 2F **11**
(off Swanfield St.)
SE14 . . . . 2F **93**
(off Myers La.)
Sunbury La. SW11 . . . 4F **87**
(not continuous)

Sunbury Workshops
E2 . . . . 2F **11**
(off Swanfield St.)
Sun Ct. EC3 . . . . 3C **18**
Suncroft Pl. SE26 . . . 3E **121**
Sunderland Ct.
SE22 . . . . 5C **106**
Sunderland Mt.
SE23 . . . . 2F **121**
Sunderland Rd.
SF23 . . . . 1F **121**
Sunderland Ter. W2. . 5D **59**
Sunderland Way E12 . . 4F **41**
Sundew Av. W12 . . . . 1C **70**
Sundew Cl. W12 . . . . . 1C **70**
Sundorne Rd. SE7 . . . 1E **97**
Sundra Wlk. E1. . . . . . 3F **65**
SUNDRIDGE. 5D **125**
Sundridge Ho. E9 . . . . 4F **51**
(off Church Cres.)
Sunfields Pl. SE3. . . . 3D **97**
SUN-IN-THE-SANDS . . 3D **97**
Sun La. SE3 . . . . 3D **97**
Sunlight Cl. SW19 . . . 5E **115**
Sunlight Sq. E2 . . . . . 2D **65**
Sunningdale Av. W3 . . 1A **70**
Sunningdale Cl.
SE16 . . . . 1D **93**
Sunningdale Gdns.
W8 . . . . 4C **72**
(off Stratford Rd.)
Sunninghill Rd. SE13 . 5D **95**
Sunnydale Rd.
SE12 . . . . 3D **111**
Sunnydene St. SE26 . . 4A **122**
Sunnyhill Cl. E5 . . . . . 1A **52**
Sunnyhill Rd. SW16 . . 4A **118**
Sunnymead Rd. NW9 . . 2A **28**
SW15 . . . . 3D **99**
Sunnyside NW2 . . . . . 5B **30**
SW19 . . . . 5A **114**
Sunnyside Ho's.
NW2 . . . . 5B **30**
(off Sunnyside)
Sunnyside Pas.
SW19 . . . . 5A **114**
Sunnyside Pl.
SW19 . . . . 5A **114**
Sunnyside Rd. E10. . . 3C **38**
N19 . . . . 2F **33**
Sun Pas. SE16 . . . . . . 4C **78**
(off Old Jamaica Rd.)
Sunray Av. SE24 . . . . 2F **105**
Sun Rd. W14 . . . . 1B **86**
Sunset Rd. SE5 . . . . . 2E **105**
SW19 . . . . 5D **113**
Sun St. EC2 . . . 5C **10** (4F **63**)
(not continuous)
Sun St. Pas.
EC2 . . . . 1D **19** (4A **64**)
Sun Wlk. E1 . . . . 1B **78**
Sunwell Ct. SE15. . . . 4D **93**
Sun Wharf SE8. . . . . . 3D **95**
(off Creekside)
Surma Cl. E1 . . . . 3D **65**
Surrendale Pl. W9 . . . 3C **58**
Surrey Canal Rd.
SE15 . . . . 2E **93**
Surrey County Cricket Club
. . . . 2B **90**

Surrey Docks Stadium
. . . . 2F **79**
Surrey Docks Watersports Cen.
. . . . 4A **80**
Surrey Gdns. N4. . . . . 1E **35**
Surrey Gro. SE17 . . . . 1A **92**
Surrey Ho. SE16. . . . . 2F **79**
(off Rotherhithe St.)
Surrey La. SW11 . . . . 4A **88**
Surrey La. Est.
SW11 . . . . 4A **88**
Surrey M. SE27 . . . . . 4A **120**
Surrey Mt. SE23. . . . . 1D **121**
Surrey Quays Rd.
SE16 . . . . 4E **79**
Surrey Quays Shop. Cen.
SE16. . . . . 4F **79**
Surrey Rd. SE15 . . . . 3F **107**
Surrey Row
SE1 . . . . 3D **25** (3D **77**)
Surrey Sq. SE17. . . . . 1A **92**
Surrey Steps WC2 . . . 4A **16**
(off Surrey St.)
Surrey St. E13 . . . . . . 2D **69**
WC2 . . . . . . 4A **16** (1B **76**)
Surrey Ter. SE17 . . . . 1A **92**
Surrey Water Rd.
SE16 . . . . 2F **79**
Surridge Ct. SW9. . . . 5A **90**
(off Clapham Rd.)
Surr St. N7 . . . . 2A **48**
Susan Constant Ct.
E14 . . . . 1F **81**
(off Newport Av.)
Susannah St. E14 . . . 5D **67**
Susan Rd. SE3 . . . . . . 5D **97**
Sussex Cl. N19 . . . . . 4A **34**
Sussex Ct. SE10 . . . . 2E **95**
(off Roan St.)
Sussex Gdns. N4 . . . . 1E **35**
N6 . . . . 1B **32**
W2 . . . . 1F **73**
Sussex Ga. N6 . . . . . . 1B **32**
Sussex Lodge W2. . . . 5F **59**
(off Sussex Pl.)
Sussex Mans. SW7 . . . 5F **73**
(off Old Brompton Rd.)
WC2 . . . . 4E **15**
(off Maiden La.)
Sussex M. SE6. . . . . . 5C **108**
Sussex M. E. W2 . . . . 5F **59**
(off Clifton Pl.)
Sussex M. W. W2. . . . 1F **73**
Sussex Pl.
NW1. . . . . 3A **4** (3B **60**)
W2. . . . . 5F **59**
W6 . . . . 1E **85**
Sussex Sq. W2 . . . . . . 1F **73**
Sussex St. E13 . . . . . . 2D **69**
SW1 . . . . 1D **89**
Sussex Way N7 . . . . . 4A **34**
N19 . . . . 3F **33**
(not continuous)
Sutcliffe Cl. NW11. . . 1D **31**
Sutcliffe Pk. Athletics Track
. . . . 3E **111**
Sutherland Av. W9. . . 3C **58**
Sutherland Cl. N16. . . 5F **35**
W9 . . . . 3C **58**
(off Marylands Rd.)

Sutherland Gdns.
  SW14 . . . . 1A **98**
Sutherland Gro.
  SW18 . . . . 4A **100**
Sutherland Ho. W8 . . . . 4D **73**
Sutherland Pl. W2 . . . . 5C **58**
Sutherland Point E5 . . . . 5D **37**
  (off Brackenfield Cl.)
Sutherland Rd. E3 . . . . . 1B **66**
  W4 . . . . 2A **84**
Sutherland Row SW1 . . 1D **89**
Sutherland Sq. SE17 . . 1E **91**
Sutherland St. SW1 . . . 1D **89**
Sutherland Wlk.
  SE17 . . . . 1E **91**
Sutlej Rd. SE7 . . . . 3E **97**
Sutterton St. N7 . . . . . . 3B **48**
Sutton Ct. Rd. E13 . . . . 2E **69**
Sutton Est. EC1. . . . . . . 2C **10**
  W10 . . . . 2C **58**
Sutton Est., The N1 . . 4D **49**
Sutton La. EC1 . . . . 4E **9**
  (off Gt. Sutton St.)
Sutton Pl. E9. . . . . 2E **51**
Sutton Rd. E13 . . . . 3B **68**
Sutton Row
  W1 . . . . 2C **14** (5F **61**)
Sutton Sq. E9 . . . . 2E **51**
Sutton St. E1. . . . . 1E **79**
Sutton's Way
  EC1 . . . . 4A **10** (3E **63**)
Sutton Wlk.
  SE1 . . . . 2A **24** (2B **76**)
Sutton Way W10. . . . . . 3E **57**
Swaby Rd. SW18 . . . . . 1E **115**
Swaffield Rd.
  SW18 . . . . 5D **101**
Swains La. N6 . . . . 3C **32**
Swainson Rd. W3. . . . . 3B **70**
Swain St. NW8 . . . . 3A **60**
  (off Tresham Cres.)
Swallands Rd. SE6 . . . 3C **122**
  (not continuous)
Swallow Cl. SE14 . . . . . 4F **93**
Swallow Cl. SE1 . . . . . . 4A **26**
  (off Swan St.)
  SE12 . . . . 5C **110**
  W9 . . . . 4C **58**
  (off Admiral Wlk.)
Swallow Dr. NW10 . . . . 3A **42**
Swallowfield Rd.
  SE7 . . . . 1D **97**
Swallow Gdns.
  SW16 . . . . 5F **117**
Swallow Ho. NW8 . . . . 1A **60**
  (off Barrow Hill Est.)
Swallow Pas. W1 . . . . . 3E **13**
  (off Swallow Pl.)
Swallow Pl.
  W1 . . . . 3E **13** (5D **61**)
Swallow St.
  W1 . . . . 5A **14** (1E **75**)
Swanage Ct. N1 . . . . . . 4A **50**
  (off Hertford Rd.)
Swanage Ho. SW8 . . . . 3B **90**
  (off Dorset Rd.)
Swanage Rd. SW18 . . . 4E **101**
Swan App. E6 . . . . 4F **69**
Swanbourne SE17 . . . . 5E **77**
  (off Wansey St.)

Swanbourne Ho.
  NW8 . . . . 3A **60**
  (off Capland St.)
Swan Cen., The
  SW17 . . . . 3D **115**
Swan Ct. E1 . . . . 1C **78**
  (off Star Pl.)
  E14 . . . . 5B **66**
  (off Agnes St.)
  SW3 . . . . 1A **88**
  SW6 . . . . 3C **86**
  (off Fulham Rd.)
Swandon Way
  SW18 . . . . 3D **101**
Swanfield St.
  E2. . . . . 2F **11** (2B **64**)
Swan Ho. N1. . . . . 4F **49**
  (off Oakley Rd.)
Swan La.
  EC4. . . . . 5C **18** (1F **77**)
Swanley Ho.
  SE17 . . . . 1A **92**
  (off Kinglake Est.)
Swan Mead
  SE1 . . . . 5D **27** (4A **78**)
Swan M. SW6 . . . . 4B **86**
  SW9 . . . . 5B **90**
Swanne Ho. SE10. . . . . 3E **95**
  (off Gloucester Cir.)
Swan Pas. E1 . . . . 1B **78**
  (off Royal Mint Pl.)
Swan Pl. SW13 . . . . 5B **84**
Swan Rd. SE16. . . . . . . 3E **79**
  SE18 . . . . 4F **83**
Swanscombe Ho.
  W11 . . . . 2F **71**
  (off St Ann's Rd.)
Swanscombe Point
  E16 . . . . 4B **68**
  (off Clarkson Rd.)
Swanscombe Rd. W4 . . 1A **84**
  W11 . . . . 2F **71**
Swan St. SE1 . . 5A **26** (4E **77**)
Swanton Gdns.
  SW19 . . . . 1F **113**
Swan Wlk. SW3 . . . . . . 2B **88**
Swanwick Cl. SW15. . . 5B **98**
Swan Yd. N1 . . . . 3D **49**
Swathling Ho. SW15 . . 4B **98**
  (off Tunworth Cres.)
Swaton Rd. E3 . . . . 3C **66**
Swedeland Ct. E1. . . . . 1E **19**
Swedenborg Gdns.
  E1. . . . . 1D **79**
Swedenborg Pl. E1 . . . 1D **79**
  (off Swedenborg Gdns.)
Sweden Ga. SE16 . . . . 4A **80**
Swedish Quays SE16 . . 4A **80**
  (not continuous)
Sweeney Cres.
  SE1 . . . . 4F **27** (3B **78**)
Swell Ct. E17 . . . . 1C **38**
Swete St. E13 . . . . 1C **68**
Sweyn Pl. SE3 . . . . 5C **96**
Swift Lodge W9 . . . . . . 3C **58**
  (off Admiral Wlk.)
Swiftsden Way
  BR1: Brom 5A **124**
Swift St. SW6 . . . . 4B **86**
Swinbrook Rd. W10 . . . 4A **58**

Swinburne Ct. SE5 . . . . 2F **105**
  (off Basingdon Way)
Swinburne Ho. E2 . . . . 2E **65**
  (off Roman Rd.)
Swinburne Rd. SW15. . 2C **98**
Swindon St. W12. . . . . . 2D **71**
Swinford Gdns.
  SW9 . . . . 1D **105**
Swingfield Ho. E9 . . . . . 5E **51**
  (off Templecombe Rd.)
Swinley Ho. NW1. . . . . . 1E **5**
  (off Redhill St.)
Swinnerton St. E9 . . . . 2A **52**
Swinton Pl.
  WC1. . . . . . . 1F **7** (2B **62**)
Swinton St.
  WC1. . . . . . . 1F **7** (2B **62**)
Swiss Cen. W1. . . . . . . 5B **14**
SWISS COTTAGE 4F **45**
Swiss Cottage Sports Cen.
  . . . . 4F **45**
Swiss Ct. WC2 . . . . 5C **14**
Swiss Re. 2E **19**
Swiss Ter. NW6 . . . . . . 4F **45**
Switch Ho. E14. . . . . . . 1F **81**
Sybil M. N4 . . . . 1D **35**
Sybil Phoenix Cl. SE8 . 1F **93**
Sybil Thorndike Casson Ho.
  SW5 . . . . 1C **86**
  (off Kramer M.)
Sybourn St. E17 . . . . . . 2B **38**
Sycamore Av. E3 . . . . . 5B **52**
Sycamore Cl. E16 . . . . 3A **68**
  W3 . . . . 2A **70**
Sycamore Ct. E7 . . . . . 3C **54**
  NW6 . . . . 5C **44**
  (off Bransdale Cl.)
Sycamore Gdns. W6 . . 3D **71**
Sycamore Gro. SE6 . . . 4E **109**
Sycamore Ho. SE16 . . . 3F **79**
  (off Woodland Cres.)
  W6 . . . . 3D **71**
Sycamore Lodge W8 . . 4D **73**
  (off Stone Hall Pl.)
Sycamore M. SW4 . . . . 1E **103**
Sycamore Rd.
  SW19 . . . . 5E **113**
Sycamore St.
  EC1. . . . . 4F **9** (3E **63**)
Sycamore Wlk. W10 . . . 3A **58**
Sydcote SE21 . . . . 1E **119**
SYDENHAM 4E **121**
Sydenham Av. SE26. . . 5D **121**
Sydenham Cotts.
  SE12 . . . . 2E **125**
Sydenham Hill
  SE23 . . . . 1D **121**
  SE26 . . . . 4B **120**
Sydenham Pk. SE26 . . 3E **121**
Sydenham Pk. Mans.
  SE26 . . . . 3E **121**
  (off Sydenham Pk.)
Sydenham Pk. Rd.
  SE26 . . . . 3E **121**
Sydenham Pl. SE27. . . 3D **119**
Sydenham Ri. SE23. . . 2D **121**
Sydenham Rd.
  SE26 . . . . 4E **121**
Sydmons Ct. SE23 . . . 5E **107**
Sydner M. N16. . . . . . . 1B **50**

Sydner Rd. N16 . . . . 1B 50
Sydney Cl. SW3 . . . . 5F 73
Sydney Gro. NW4 . . . . . . 1E 29
Sydney M. SW3 . . . . 5F 73
Sydney Pl. SW7 . . . . 5F 73
Sydney Rd. E11 . . . . 1D 41
Sydney St. SW3 . . . . 1A 88
Sylvan Gro.
 NW2 . . . . 1F 43
 SE15 . . . . 2D 93
Sylvan Rd. E7 . . . . 3D 65
 E17 . . . . 1C 38
Sylvan Ter. SE15 . . . . . . 2D 93
 (off Sylvan Gro.)
Sylvester Path E8 . . . . . 3D 51
Sylvester Rd. E8 . . . . . . 3D 51
 E17 . . . . 2B 38
Sylvia Ct. N1 . . . . 1F 63
 (off Wenlock St.)
Symes M. NW1 . . . . 1E 61
Symington Ho. SE1 . . . . 5B 26
 (off Deverell St.)
Symington M.
 E9 . . . . 2F 51
Symister M. N1 . . . . 2D 11
Symons St. SW3 . . . . . . 5B 74
Symphony M. W10 . . . . . 2A 58
Syon Lodge SE12 . . . . . 5C 110
Syringa Ho. SE4 . . . . . . 1B 108

T

Tabard Ct. E14 . . . . 5E 67
 (off Lodore St.)
Tabard Gdn. Est.
 SE1 . . . . 4B 26 (4F 77)
Tabard Ho. SE1 . . . . 5C 26
 (off Manciple St.)
Tabard St.
 SE1 . . . . 3A 26 (3E 77)
Tabernacle Av. E13 . . . . 3C 68
Tabernacle St.
 EC2 . . . . 4C 10 (3F 63)
Tableer Av. SW4 . . . . . . 3E 103
Tabley Rd. N7 . . . . 1A 48
Tabor Rd. W6 . . . . 4D 71
Tachbrook Est. SW1 . . . . 1F 89
Tachbrook M. SW1 . . . . . 5E 75
Tachbrook St. SW1 . . . . 5E 75
 (not continuous)
Tack M. SE4 . . . . 1C 108
Tadema Ho. NW8 . . . . . . 3F 59
 (off Penfold St.)
Tadema Rd. SW10 . . . . . 3E 87
Tadmor St. W12 . . . . 2F 71
Tadworth Ho. SE1 . . . . . 4D 25
Tadworth Rd. NW2 . . . . . 4C 28
Taeping St. E14 . . . . 5D 81
Taffrail Ho. E14 . . . . 1D 95
 (off Burrells Wharf Sq.)
Taft Way E3 . . . . 2D 67
Tailor Ho. WC1 . . . . 4E 7
 (off Colonnade)
Tailworth St. E1 . . . . 4C 64
 (off Chicksand St.)
Tait Ct. E3 . . . . 5B 52
 (off St Stephen's Rd.)
 SW8 . . . . 4A 90
 (off Lansdowne Grn.)

Tait Ho. SE1 . . . . 2C 24
 (off Greet St.)
Takhar M. SW11 . . . . . . 5A 88
Talacre Community
 Sports Cen.
 Kentish Town 3C 46
Talacre Rd. NW5 . . . . . . 3C 46
Talbot Ct. EC3 . . . . 4C 18
Talbot Cres. NW4 . . . . . 1C 28
Talbot Gro. Ho.
 W11 . . . . 5A 58
 (off Lancaster Rd.)
Talbot Ho. E14 . . . . 5D 67
 (off Giraud St.)
 N7 . . . . 5C 34
Talbot Pl. SE3 . . . . 5A 96
Talbot Rd. E7 . . . . 1C 54
 N6 . . . . 1C 32
 SE22 . . . . 2A 106
 W2 . . . . 5C 58
 W11 . . . . 5B 58
 (not continuous)
Talbot Sq. W2 . . . . 5F 59
Talbot Wlk. NW10 . . . . . 3A 42
 W11 . . . . 5A 58
Talbot Yd.
 SE1 . . . . 2B 26 (2F 77)
Talcott Path SW2 . . . . . 1C 118
Talfourd Pl. SE15 . . . . . 4B 92
Talfourd Rd. SE15 . . . . . 4B 92
Talgarth Mans. W14 . . . 1A 86
 (off Talgarth Rd.)
Talgarth Rd. W6 . . . . . . 1F 85
 W14 . . . . 1F 85
Talia Ho. E14 . . . . 4E 81
 (off Manchester Rd.)
Talina Cen. SW6 . . . . . . 4E 87
Talisman Sq. SE26 . . . . 4C 120
Tallack Rd. E10 . . . . 3B 38
Talleyrand Ho. SE5 . . . . 5E 91
 (off Lilford Rd.)
Tallis Cl. E16 . . . . 5D 69
Tallis Gro. SE7 . . . . 2D 97
Tallis St. EC4 . . 4C 16 (1C 76)
Tallis Vw. NW10 . . . . . . 3A 42
Talmage Cl. SE23 . . . . . 5E 107
Talma Rd. SW2 . . . . 2C 104
Talwin St. E3 . . . . 2D 67
Tamar Cl. E3 . . . . 5B 52
Tamar Ho. E14 . . . . 3E 81
 (off Plevna St.)
 SE11 . . . . 1C 90
 (off Kennington La.)
Tamarind Ct. W8 . . . . . . 4D 73
 (off Stone Hall Gdns.)
Tamarind Yd. E1 . . . . . . 2C 78
 (off Kennet St.)
Tamarisk Sq. W12 . . . . . 1B 70
Tamar St. SE7 . . . . 4F 83
Tamplin Ho. W10 . . . . . . 2B 58
 (off Dowland St.)
Tamworth N7 . . . . 3A 48
Tamworth St. SW6 . . . . . 2C 86
Tancred Rd. N4 . . . . 1D 35
Tanfield Av. NW2 . . . . . . 1B 42
Tangley Gro. SW15 . . . . 4B 98
Tangmere WC1 . . . . 2F 7
 (off Sidmouth St.)
Tanhurst Ho. SW2 . . . . . 5B 104
 (off Redlands Way)

Tankerton Ho's. WC1 . . . 2E 7
 (off Tankerton St.)
Tankerton St.
 WC1 . . . . 2E 7 (2A 62)
Tankridge Rd. NW2 . . . . 4D 29
Tanner Ho. SE1 . . . . 4E 27
 (off Tanner St.)
Tanneries, The E1 . . . . . 3E 65
 (off Cephas Av.)
Tanner Point E13 . . . . . 5C 54
 (off Pelly Rd.)
Tanner's Hill SE8 . . . . . 4B 94
Tanner St.
 SE1 . . . . 4E 27 (3A 78)
 (not continuous)
Tannington Ter. N5 . . . . 5D 35
Tannsfeld Rd. SE26 . . . 5F 121
Tansley Cl. N7 . . . . 2F 47
Tanswell St.
 SE1 . . . . 4B 24 (3C 76)
Tantallon Rd. SW12 . . . 1C 116
Tant Av. E16 . . . . 5B 68
Tanza Rd. NW3 . . . . 1B 46
Tapley Ho. SE1 . . . . 3C 78
 (off Wolseley St.)
Taplow SE17 . . . . 1F 91
 (off Thurlow St.)
Taplow Ho. E2 . . . . 2F 11
 (off Palissy St.)
Taplow St.
 N1 . . . . 1A 10 (1E 63)
Tappesfield Rd.
 SE15 . . . . 1E 107
Tapp St. E1 . . . . 3D 65
Tara Arts Cen. 1D 115
 (off Garratt La.)
Tara M. N8 . . . . 1A 34
Taranto Rd. E1 . . . . 4F 65
 (off Master's St.)
Tarbert Rd. SE22 . . . . . 3A 106
Tarbert Wlk. E1 . . . . 1E 79
Tariff Cres. SE8 . . . . 5B 80
Tarleton Gdns.
 SE23 . . . . 2D 121
Tarling Ho. E1 . . . . 5D 65
 (off Tarling St.)
Tarling Rd. E16 . . . . 5B 68
Tarling St. E1 . . . . 5D 65
Tarling St. Est. E1 . . . . . 5E 65
Tarns, The NW1 . . . . . . 1F 5
 (off Varndell St.)
Tarn St. SE1 . . . . 4E 77
Tarplett Ho. SE14 . . . . . 2F 93
 (off John Williams Cl.)
Tarquin Ho. SE26 . . . . . 4C 120
 (off High Level Dr.)
Tarragon Cl. SE14 . . . . 3A 94
Tarragon Gro. SE26 . . . 5F 121
Tarranbrae NW6 . . . . . . 4A 44
Tarrant Ho. E2 . . . . 2E 65
 (off Roman Rd.)
Tarrant Pl. W1 . . . . 4B 60
Tarrington Cl. SW16 . . . 3F 117
Tartan Ho. E14 . . . . 5E 67
 (off Dee St.)
Tarver Rd. SE17 . . . . . . 1D 91
Tarves Way SE10 . . . . . 3D 95
Tasker Ho. E14 . . . . 4B 66
 (off Wallwood St.)
Tasker Rd. NW3 . . . . . . 2B 46

Tasman Ct. *E14* 5D *81*
   (off Westferry Rd.)
Tasman Ho. *E1* 2D *79*
   (off Clegg St.)
Tasman Rd. SW9 . . . . 1A *104*
Tasman Wlk. E16 . . . . . . 5F *69*
Tasso Rd. W6 . . . . 2A *86*
Tasso Yd. W6 . . . . 2A *86*
   (off Tasso Rd.)
Tatchbury Ho. *SW15* . . . 4B *98*
   (off Tunworth Cres.)
Tate Britain 5A *76*
Tate Ho. *E2* 1F *65*
   (off Mace St.)
Tate Modern . . 1E *76* (2D *77*)
Tatham Pl. NW8 . . . . 1F *59*
Tatnell Rd. SE23. . . . 4A *108*
Tatsfield Ho. *SE1* 5C *26*
   (off Pardoner St.)
Tatton Cres. N16. . . . . . . 2B *36*
Tatum St. SE17 . . . . 5F *77*
Tauheed Cl. N4. . . . . . . 4E *35*
Taunton Ho. *W2* 5E *59*
   (off Hallfield Est.)
Taunton M. NW1. . . . . . . 3B *60*
Taunton Pl. NW1 . . . . . . 3B *60*
Taunton Rd. SE12. . . . 3A *110*
Tavern Ct. *SE1* 4E *77*
   (off Falmouth St.)
Taverners Cl. W11 . . . . . 2A *72*
Taverners Ct. *E3* 2A *66*
   (off Grove Rd.)
Taverner Sq. N5 . . . . 1E *49*
Tavern La. SW9 . . . . . . 5C *90*
Tavern Quay SE16 . . . . 5A *80*
Tavistock Cl. N16 . . . . . 2A *50*
Tavistock Ct. *WC1* 3C *6*
   (off Tavistock Sq.)
WC2 . . . . 4E *15*
   (off Tavistock St.)
Tavistock Cres. W11. . . . 4B *58*
   (not continuous)
Tavistock Ho.
  WC1. . . . . 3C *6* (3F *61*)
Tavistock M. W11. . . . . . 5B *58*
Tavistock Pl.
  WC1. . . . . 3D *7* (3A *62*)
Tavistock Rd. E7. . . . . . 1B *54*
  E15. . . . . 3B *54*
  N4. . . . . 1F *35*
  NW10 . . . . 1B *56*
  W11 . . . . 5B *58*
   (not continuous)
Tavistock Sq.
  WC1. . . . . 3C *6* (3F *61*)
Tavistock St.
  WC2. . . . . 4E *15* (1A *76*)
   (not continuous)
Tavistock Ter. N19 . . . . . 5F *33*
Tavistock Twr. SE16 . . . . 4A *80*
Taviton St.
  WC1. . . . . 3B *6* (3F *61*)
Tavy Cl. *SE11* 1C *90*
   (off White Hart St.,
   not continuous)
Tawny Way SE16. . . . . . 5F *79*
Taybridge Rd.
  SW11 . . . . 1C *102*
Tay Bldgs. SE1 . . . . 5D *27*
Tayburn Cl. E14 . . . . . . 5E *67*

Taylor Ct. NW8 . . . . . . 5F *45*
Taylor Cl. SE8 . . . . 2B *94*
Taylors La. E15 . . . . . . 2E *53*
Taylors Grn. W3. . . . . . 5A *56*
Taylors La. NW10. . . . 4A *42*
  SE26. . . . . 4D *121*
Taymount Grange
  SE23. . . . . 2E *121*
Taymount Ri. SE23. . . 2E *121*
Tayport Cl. N1 . . . . 4A *48*
Tayside Ct. SE5 . . . . . . 2F *105*
Teak Cl. SE16. . . . . 2A *80*
Tealby Ct. N7 . . . . 2B *48*
   (off George's Rd.)
Teal Cl. E16 . . . . 4F *69*
Teal Ct. *E1* 1C *78*
   (off Star Pl.)
  SE8 . . . . 2B *94*
   (off Abinger Gro.)
Teale St. E2 . . . . 1C *64*
Teal St. SE10 . . . . 4B *82*
Teasel Way E15 . . . . . . 2A *68*
Tea Trade Wharf *SE1* . . . 3B *78*
   (off Shad Thames)
Ted Roberts Ho. *E2* . . . 1D *65*
   (off Parmiter St.)
Tedworth Gdns.
  SW3 . . . . 1B *88*
Tedworth Sq. SW3 . . . . 1B *88*
Tee, The W3 . . . . 5A *56*
Teesdale Cl. E2 . . . . . . 1C *64*
Teesdale Rd. E11. . . . . 1B *40*
Teesdale St. E2 . . . . . . 1C *64*
Teesdale Yd. E2 . . . . . . 1D *65*
   (off Teesdale St.)
Teignmouth Cl.
  SW4 . . . . 2F *103*
Teignmouth Rd. NW2. . . 2F *43*
Telegraph Hill NW3 . . . 5D *31*
Telegraph Pas. SW2 . . 5A *104*
   (off New Pk. Rd.)
Telegraph Pl. E14 . . . . . 5D *81*
Telegraph Quarters
  SE10 . . . . 1F *95*
   (off Park Row)
Telegraph Rd. SW15 . . . 5D *99*
Telegraph St.
  EC2. . . . . 2B *18* (5F *63*)
Telemann Sq. SE3 . . . . 2D *111*
Telephone Pl. SW6 . . . . 2B *86*
Telfer Ho. EC1 . . . . 2E *9*
Telferscot Rd. SW12. . . 1F *117*
Telford Av. SW2 . . . . . . 1F *117*
Telford Cl. E17 . . . . 2A *38*
Telford Ho. *SE1* 5F *25*
   (off Tiverton St.)
Telford Rd. NW9. . . . . . 1C *28*
  W10 . . . . 4A *58*
Telfords Yd. E1 . . . . . . 1C *78*
Telford Ter. SW1. . . . . . 2E *89*
Telford Way W3 . . . . . . 4A *56*
Tell Gro. SE22 . . . . 2B *106*
Tellson Av. SE18 . . . . . 4F *97*
Temair Ho. *SE10* 3D *95*
   (off Tarves Way)
Temeraire St. SE16 . . . . 3E *79*
Tempelhof Av. NW2 . . . 3E *29*
  NW4 . . . . 2E *29*
Temperley Rd.
  SW12 . . . . 5C *102*

Templar Ct. NW8 . . . . . 2F *59*
   (off St John's Wood Rd.)
Templar Ho. NW2 . . . . 3B *44*
Templars Av. NW11 . . . 1B *30*
Templars Ho. E15 . . . . 2D *53*
Templar St. SE5. . . . . . 5D *91*
Temple Av.
  EC4 . . . . 4C *16* (1C *76*)
Temple Bar 3B *16*
Temple Bar Gate 3E *17*
   (off Paternoster Sq.)
Temple Chambers
  EC4. . . . . 4C *16*
Temple Cl. E11. . . . . . . 2A *40*
Templecombe Rd. E9 . . 5E *51*
Temple Ct. *E1* 4F *65*
   (off Rectory Sq.)
  SW8 . . . . 3A *90*
   (off Thorncroft St.)
Temple Dwellings *E2*. . . 1D *65*
   (off Temple St.)
TEMPLE FORTUNE 1B *30*
Temple Fortune Hill
  NW11 . . . . 1C *30*
Temple Fortune La.
  NW11 . . . . 1B *30*
Temple Fortune Pde.
  NW11 . . . . 1B *30*
Temple Gdns. EC4 . . . . 4B *16*
   (off Middle Temple La.)
  NW11 . . . . 1B *30*
Temple Gro. NW11 . . . 1C *30*
Temple La.
  EC4 . . . . 4C *16* (5C *62*)
Templemead Cl. W3 . . 5A *56*
Templemead Ho. E9 . . 1A *52*
Temple Mill La. E10 . . 1D *53*
   (not continuous)
  E15. . . . . 1E *53*
TEMPLE MILLS 1D *53*
Temple Mills E10. . . . . 5E *39*
Temple of Mithras (remains)
  . . . . 3B *18*
   (off Queen Victoria St.)
Temple Pl.
  WC2. . . . . 4A *16* (1B *76*)
Temple Rd. E6 . . . . 5F *55*
  NW2 . . . . 1E *43*
Temple St. E2 . . . . 1D *65*
Templeton Cl. N15. . . . 1F *35*
  N16. . . . . 2A *50*
Templeton Pl. SW5 . . . 5C *72*
Templeton Rd. N15 . . . 1F *35*
Temple W. M.
  SE11 . . . . 5D *25* (4D *77*)
Templewood Av.
  NW3 . . . . 5D *31*
Templewood Gdns.
  NW3 . . . . 5D *31*
Templewood Point
  NW2 . . . . 4B *30*
   (off Granville Rd.)
Tempus Yd. *SE16*. 3C *78*
   (off Bermondsey Wall W.)
Tempus Wharf *SE16*. . . 3C *78*
   (off Temple St.)
Tenbury Cl. E7 . . . . 2F *55*
Tenbury Ct. SW2. . . . . 1F *117*
Tenby Ho. *W2*. 5E *59*
   (off Hallfield Est.)

Tenby Mans. *W1* *5C 4*
(off Nottingham St.)
Tench St. E1 . . . . 2D 79
Tenda Rd. SE16 . . . . . . 5D 79
Tenham Av. SW2 . . . . 1F 117
Tenison Ct.
W1 . . . . 4F 13 (1E 75)
Tenison Way
SE1 . . . . . . 2A 24 (2B 76)
Tenniel Cl. W2 . . . . 1E 73
Tennis St.
SE1 . . . . 3B 26 (3F 77)
Tennyson Av. E11 . . . . . 2C 40
E12 . . . . 4F 55
Tennyson Ct. *SW6* *4E 87*
(off Imperial Rd.)
Tennyson Ho. *SE17* *1E 91*
(off Browning St.)
Tennyson Mans.
W14 . . . . 2B 86
(off Queen's Club Gdns.)
Tennyson Rd. E10 . . . . . 3D 39
E15 . . . . 4A 54
E17 . . . . 1B 38
NW6 . . . . 5B 44
(not continuous)
SW19 . . . . 5E 115
Tennyson St. SW8 . . . . 5D 89
Tenterden Ho. *SE17* *1A 92*
(off Surrey Gro.)
Tenterden St.
W1 . . . . 3E 13 (5D 61)
Tenter Ground
E1 . . . . 1F 19 (4B 64)
Tenter Pas. *E1* *5B 64*
(off Nth. Tenter St.)
Tent St. E1 . . . . 3D 65
Terborch Way SE22 . . 3A 106
Teredo St. SE16 . . . . . . 4F 79
Terence McMillan Stadium
. . . . 3E 69
Terence Messenger Twr.
. . . . *4D 39*
(off Alpine Rd.)
Terling Cl. E11 . . . . 5B 40
Terling Ho. *W10* *4E 57*
(off Sutton Way)
Terling Wlk. *N1* *5E 49*
(off Popham St.)
Terminus Pl. SW1 . . . . 4D 75
Terrace, The *E2* *2E 65*
(off Old Ford Rd.)
EC4 . . . . 3C 16
NW6 . . . . 5C 44
SE8 . . . . *5B 80*
(off Longshore)
SE23 . . . . 5A 108
SW13 . . . . 5A 84
Terrace Av. NW10 . . . . 3E 57
Terrace Gdns. SW13 . . 5B 84
Terrace Rd. E9 . . . . 4E 51
E13 . . . . 1C 68
Terraces, The *NW8* *1F 59*
(off Queen's Ter.)
Terrace Wlk. *SW11* *3B 88*
(off Albert Bri. Rd.)
Terrapin Rd. SW17 . . . 3D 117
Terretts Pl. *N1* *4D 49*
(off Upper St.)
Terrick St. W12 . . . . . . 5D 57

Territorial Ho. *SE11* . . . *5C 76*
(off Reedworth St.)
Tessa Sanderson Pl.
SW8 . . . . *1D 103*
(off Daley Thompson Way)
Testerton Rd. W11 . . . . . 1F 71
Testerton Wlk. W11 . . . . 1F 71
Tetbury Pl. N1 . . . . 5D 49
Tetcott Rd. SW10 . . . . . 3E 87
(not continuous)
Teversham La. SW8 . . . 4A 90
Teviot Est. E14 . . . . 4D 67
Teviot St. E14 . . . . 3E 67
Tewkesbury Av.
SE23 . . . . 1D 121
Tewkesbury Cl. N15 . . . 1F 35
Tewkesbury Rd. N15 . . . 1F 35
Thackeray Ct. *SW3* *18 88*
(off Elystan Pl.)
W14 . . . . *4A 72*
(off Blythe Rd.)
Thackeray Ho. WC1 . . . . 3G 7
Thackeray M. E8 . . . . . 3C 50
Thackeray Rd. E6 . . . . . 1F 69
SW8 . . . . 5D 89
Thackeray St. W8 . . . . . 4D 73
Thakeham Cl. SE26 . . . 4D 121
Thalia Cl. SE10 . . . . . . 2F 95
Thame Rd. SE16 . . . . . . 3F 79
Thames Av. SW10 . . . . 4E 87
Thames Barrier Ind. Area
SE18 . . . . *4F 83*
(off Faraday Way)
Thames Barrier Vis. Cen.
. . . . 4F 83
Thamesbrook *SW3* *1A 88*
(off Dovehouse St.)
Thames Circ. E14 . . . . . 5C 80
Thames Ct. *SE15* *3B 92*
(off Daniel Gdns.)
Thames Cres. W4 . . . . . 3A 84
Thames Exchange Bldg.
EC4 . . . . 5A 18
Thames Ho. *EC4* *4A 18*
(off Up. Thames St.)
SW1 . . . . 5A 76
(off Millbank)
Thameside Ind. Est.
E16 . . . . 3F 83
Thames Pl. SW15 . . . . . 1F 99
(not continuous)
Thames Point SW6 . . . . 5E 87
Thames Quay E14 . . . . 3D 81
SW10 . . . . *4E 87*
(off Chelsea Harbour)
Thames Reach *W6* *2E 85*
(off Rainville Rd.)
Thames Rd. E16 . . . . . . 2F 83
Thames Rd. Ind. Est.
E16 . . . . 3F 83
Thames St. SE10 . . . . . 2D 95
Thames Wlk. SW11 . . . . 3A 88
W6 . . . . *2E 85*
(off Rainville Rd.)
Thames Wharf Studios
W6 . . . . *2E 85*
(off Rainville Rd.)
Thanet Ho. *WC1* *2D 7*
(off Thanet St.)
Thanet Lodge *NW2* . . . 3A 44
(off Mapesbury Rd.)

Thanet St.
WC1 . . . . 2D 7 (2A 62)
Thanet Wharf *SE8* *2D 95*
(off Copperas St.)
Thane Vs. N7 . . . . 5B 34
Thane Works N7 . . . . . . 5B 34
Thant Cl. E10 . . . . 5D 39
Thavie's Inn
EC1 . . . . 2C 16 (5C 62)
Thaxted Ct. *N1* *1C 10*
(off Fairbank Est.)
Thaxted Ho. *SE16* *5E 79*
(off Abbeyfield Est.)
Thaxton Rd. W14 . . . . . 2B 86
Thayer St.
W1 . . . . 1C 12 (5C 60)
Theatre Mus. 4E 15
Theatrerites 2D 115
Theatre Royal
Stratford 4F 53
Theatre Sq. E15 . . . . . . 3F 53
Theatre St. SW11 . . . . 1B 102
Theatro Technis *5E 47*
(off Crowndale Rd.)
Theberton St. N1 . . . . . 5C 48
Theed St.
SE1 . . . . 2C 24 (2C 76)
Thelma Gdns. SE3 . . . . 4F 97
Theobald Rd. E17 . . . . . 2B 38
Theobalds Ct. N4 . . . . . 5E 35
Theobald's Rd.
WC1 . . . . 5F 7 (4B 62)
Theobald St. SE1 . . . . . 4F 77
Theodore Ct. SE13 . . . 4F 109
Theodore Rd. SE13 . . . 4F 109
Therapia Rd. SE22 . . . 4E 107
Theresa Rd. W6 . . . . . . 5C 70
Therfield Ct. N4 . . . . . . 4E 35
Thermopylae Ga.
E14 . . . . 5D 81
Theseus Wlk. N1 . . . . . 1E 9
Thessaly Ho. *SW8* *3E 89*
(off Thessaly Rd.)
Thessaly Rd. SW8 . . . . 3E 89
(not continuous)
Thesus Ho. *E14* *5E 67*
(off Blair St.)
Thetford Ho. *SE1* *5F 27*
(off Maltby St.)
Theydon Rd. E5 . . . . . . 4E 37
Theydon St. E17 . . . . . . 2B 38
Third Av. E13 . . . . 2C 68
E17 . . . . 1C 38
W3 . . . . 2B 70
W10 . . . . 2A 58
Thirleby Rd.
SW1 . . . . 5A 22 (4E 75)
Thirlmere *NW1* *1E 5*
(off Cumberland Mkt.)
Thirlmere Rd.
SW16 . . . . 4F 117
Thirsk Rd. SW11 . . . . . 1C 102
Thistle Gro. SW10 . . . . 1E 87
Thistle Ho. *E14* *5E 67*
(off Dee St.)
Thistlewaite Rd. E5 . . . 5D 37
Thistlewood Cl. N7 . . . . 4B 34
Thistley Ct. *SE8* 2D 95
Thomas Baines Rd.
SW11 . . . . 1F 101

Thomas Burt Ho. *E2* 2D **65**
    (off Canrobert St.)
Thomas Darby Ct.
  W11 . . . . 5A **58**
    (off Lancaster Rd.)
Thomas Dean Rd.
  SE26 . . . . 4B **122**
Thomas Dinwiddy Rd.
  SE12 . . . . 2D **125**
Thomas Doyle St.
  SE1 . . . . 5D **25** (4D **77**)
Thomas Hollywood Ho.
  E2 . . . . 1E **65**
    (off Approach Rd.)
Thomas La. SE6. . . . . . 5C **108**
Thomas More Highwalk
  EC2 . . . . 1F **17**
    (off Beech St.)
Thomas More Ho.
  EC2 . . . . 1F **17**
Thomas More Sq. *E1* . . 1C **78**
    (off Thomas More St.)
Thomas More St.
  E1 . . . . 1C **78**
Thomas Neal's Shop. Mall
  WC2. . . . . . 3D **15** (5A **62**)
Thomas Nth. Ter.
  E16 . . . . 4B **68**
    (off Barking Rd.)
Thomas Pl. W8 . . . . 4D **73**
Thomas Rd. E14. . . . . . 5B **66**
Thomas Rd. Ind. Est.
  E14 . . . . 4C **66**
Thompson Ho. *SE14*. . . 2F **93**
    (off John Williams Cl.)
Thompson Rd.
  SE22 . . . . 4B **106**
Thompson's Av. SE5. . . 3E **91**
Thomson Ho. *E14*. 5C **66**
    (off Saracen St.)
  SE17. . . . . 5A **78**
    (off Tatum St.)
  SW1 . . . . 1F **89**
    (off Bessborough Pl.)
Thorburn Sq. SE1. . . . . 5C **78**
Thoresby St.
  N1 . . . . 1A **10** (2E **63**)
Thornaby Ho. *E2* 2D **65**
    (off Canrobert St.)
Thornbury Cl. N16 . . . . 2A **50**
Thornbury Ct. *W11*. . . . 1C **72**
    (off Chepstow Vs.)
Thornbury Rd.
  SW2 . . . . 4A **104**
Thornbury Sq. N6 . . . . . 3E **33**
Thornby Rd. E5. . . . . . . 5E **37**
Thorncliffe Rd.
  SW2 . . . . 4A **104**
Thorncombe Rd.
  SE22 . . . . 3A **106**
Thorncroft St. SW8. . . . 3A **90**
Thorndean St.
  SW18 . . . . 2E **118**
Thorndike Cl. SW10 . . . 3E **87**
Thorndike Ho.
  SW1 . . . . 1F **89**
    (off Vauxhall Bri. Rd.)
Thorndike St. SW1 . . . . 5F **75**
Thorne Cl. E11 . . . . 1F **53**
  E16 . . . . 5C **68**

Thorne Ho. *E2* 2E **65**
    (off Roman Rd.)
  E14 . . . . 4E **81**
    (off Launch St.)
Thorne Pas. SW13. . . . 5A **84**
Thorne Rd. SW8. . . . . . 3A **90**
Thorne St. SW13 . . . . . 1A **98**
Thornewill Ho. *E1* 1E **79**
    (off Cable St.)
Thorney Ct. *W8* 3E **73**
    (off Palace Ga.)
Thorney Cres. SW11 . . 3F **87**
Thorney St. SW1 . . . . . 5A **76**
Thornfield Ho. *E14*. . . . 1C **80**
    (off Rosefield Gdns.)
Thornfield Rd. W12. . . . 3D **71**
    (not continuous)
Thornford Rd. SE13 . . . 3E **109**
Thorngate Rd. W9 . . . . 3C **58**
Thorngrove Rd. E13. . . 5D **55**
Thornham Gro. E15. . . 2F **53**
Thornham Ind. Est.
  E15 . . . . 3F **53**
Thornham St. SE10 . . . 2D **95**
Thornhaugh M.
  WC1 . . . . 4C **6** (3F **61**)
Thornhaugh St.
  WC1 . . . . 4C **6** (3F **61**)
Thornhill Bri. Wharf
  N1 . . . . 5B **48**
Thornhill Cres. N1 . . . . 4B **48**
Thornhill Gdns. E10. . . 4D **39**
Thornhill Gro. N1. . . . . 4B **48**
Thornhill Ho. *W4* 1A **84**
    (off Wood St.)
Thornhill Ho's. N1 . . . . 4C **48**
Thornhill Rd. E10. . . . . 4D **39**
  N1 . . . . 4C **48**
Thornhill Sq. N1. . . . . . 4B **48**
Thornicroft Ho. *SW9* . . 5B **90**
    (off Stockwell Rd.)
Thornlaw Rd. SE27 . . . 4C **118**
Thornley Pl. SE10 . . . . 1A **96**
Thornsbeach Rd.
  SE6. . . . . 1E **123**
Thornsett Rd. SW18 . . 1D **115**
Thorn Ter. SE15 . . . . . 1E **107**
Thornton Av. SW2. . . . 1F **117**
  W4 . . . . 5A **70**
Thornton Gdns.
  SW12 . . . . 1F **117**
Thornton Ho. *SE17*. . . . 5A **78**
    (off Townsend St.)
Thornton Pl.
  W1 . . . . 5A **4** (4B **60**)
Thornton Rd.
  BR1: Brom 5C **124**
  E11 . . . . 4F **39**
  SW12 . . . . 5F **103**
Thornton St. SW9. . . . . 5C **90**
Thornton Way NW11 . . 1D **31**
Thorntree Rd. SE7 . . . . 1F **97**
Thornville St. SE8 . . . . 4C **94**
Thornwood Rd.
  SE13. . . . . 3A **110**
Thornycroft Ho. *W4* . . . 1A **84**
    (off Fraser St.)
Thorogood Gdns. E15 . 2A **54**
Thorold Ho. *SE1* 3F **25**
    (off Pepper St.)

Thorparch Rd. SW8 . . . 4F **89**
Thorpebank Rd. W12. . 2C **70**
Thorpe Cl. SE26. . . . . . 4F **121**
  W10 . . . . 5A **58**
Thorpedale Rd. N4. . . . 4A **34**
Thorpe Ho. *N1* 5B **48**
    (off Barnsbury Est.)
Thorpe Rd. E7 . . . . 1B **54**
  N15. . . . . 1A **36**
Thorpewood Av.
  SE26. . . . . 2D **121**
Thorsden Way SE19. . . 5A **120**
Thorverton Rd. NW2 . . 5A **30**
Thoydon Rd. E3 . . . . . . 1A **66**
Thrale Rd. SW16 . . . . . 4E **117**
Thrale St.
  SE1 . . . . 2A **26** (2E **77**)
Thrasher Cl. E8 . . . . . . 5B **50**
Thrawl St. E1. . . . 1F **19** (4B **64**)
Thrayle Ho. SW9 . . . . . 1B **104**
    (off Benedict Rd.)
Threadgold Ho. *N1*. . . . 3F **49**
    (off Dovercourt Est.)
Threadneedle St.
  EC2. . . . . 3C **18** (5F **63**)
Three Barrels Wlk.
  EC4 . . . . 5A **18**
    (off Queen St. Pl.)
Three Colt Cnr. *E2* 3C **64**
    (off Cheshire St.)
Three Colts La. E2 . . . . 3D **65**
Three Colt St. E14 . . . . 5B **66**
Three Cranes Wlk.
  EC4 . . . . 5A **18**
Three Cups Yd. WC1 . . 1A **16**
Three Kings Yd.
  W1. . . . . 4D **13** (1D **75**)
Three Mill La. E3 . . . . . 2E **67**
    (not continuous)
Three Mills 2E **67**
Three Oak La. SE1 . . . . 3F **27**
Three Quays EC3 . . . . . 5E **19**
Three Quays Wlk.
  EC3 . . . . 5E **19** (1A **78**)
Threshers Pl. W11. . . . 1A **72**
Thriftwood SE26. . . . . . 3E **121**
Thring Ho. *SW9* 5B **90**
    (off Stockwell Rd.)
Throckmorten Rd.
  E16 . . . . 5D **69**
Throgmorton Av.
  EC2. . . . . 2C **18** (5F **63**)
    (not continuous)
Throgmorton St.
  EC2. . . . . 2C **18** (5F **63**)
Thrush St. SE17 . . . . . 1E **91**
Thurbarn Rd. SE6 . . . . 5D **123**
Thurland Ho. *SE16*. . . . 5D **79**
    (off Camilla Rd.)
Thurland Rd. SE16. . . . 4C **78**
Thurlby Rd. SE27. . . . . 4C **118**
Thurleigh Av. SW12 . . . 4C **102**
Thurleigh Ct. SW12 . . . 4C **102**
Thurleigh Rd.
  SW12 . . . . 5B **102**
Thurlestone Rd.
  SE27 . . . . 3C **118**
Thurloe Cl. SW7. . . . . . 5A **74**
Thurloe Ct. SW3. . . . . . 5A **74**
    (off Fulham Ct.)

Thurloe Pl. SW7 . . . . . 5F 73
Thurloe Pl. M. SW7 . . . . 5F 73
  (off Thurloe Pl.)
Thurloe Sq. SW7 . . . . . 5A 74
Thurloe St. SW7 . . . . . 5F 73
Thurlow Hill SE21 . . . . 1E 119
Thurlow Ho. SW16 . . . 3A 118
Thurlow Pk. Rd.
  SE21 . . . . 2D 119
Thurlow Rd. NW3 . . . . . 2F 45
Thurlow St. SE17 . . . . . 1F 91
  (not continuous)
Thurlow Ter. NW5 . . . . . 2C 46
Thurlow Wlk. SE17 . . . . 1A 92
  (not continuous)
Thurnscoe NW1 . . . . . . 5E 47
  (off Pratt St.)
Thursley Gdns.
  SW19 . . . . 2F 113
Thursley Ho. SW2 . . . . 5B 104
  (off Holmewood Gdns.)
Thurso Ho. NW6 . . . . . . 1D 59
Thurso St. SW17 . . . . . 4F 115
Thurstan Dwellings
  WC2 . . . . 2E 15
  (off Newton St.)
Thurston Ind. Est.
  SE13 . . . . 1D 109
Thurston Rd. SE13 . . . . 5D 95
Thurtle Rd. E2 . . . . 1B 64
Thyme Cl. SE3 . . . . 1E 111
Tibbatt's Rd. E3 . . . . . . 3D 67
Tibbenham Pl. SE6 . . . 2C 122
Tibbenham Wlk.
  E13 . . . . 1B 68
Tibberton Sq. N1 . . . . . 5E 49
Tibbet's Cl. SW19 . . . . 1F 113
TIBBET'S CORNER 5F 99
Tibbet's Ride SW15 . . . 5F 99
Tiber Gdns. N1 . . . . 5A 48
Ticehurst Rd. SE23 . . . 2A 122
Tickford Ho. NW8 . . . . . 2A 60
Tidal Basin Rd. E16 . . . 1B 82
  (not continuous)
Tidbury Ct. SW8 . . . . . . 3E 89
  (off Stewart's St.)
Tideswell Rd. SW15 . . . 2E 99
Tideway Cl. SE16 . . . . . 2F 79
Tideway Ho. E14 . . . . . . 3C 80
  (off Strafford St.)
Tideway Ind. Est.
  SW8 . . . . 2E 89
Tideway Wlk. SW8 . . . . 2E 89
Tidey St. E3 . . . . 4C 66
Tidworth Rd. E3 . . . . . . 3C 66
Tierney Rd. SW2 . . . . . 1A 118
Tiffany Hgts. SW18 . . . 5C 100
Tiger Way E5 . . . . 1D 51
Tilbrook Rd. SE3 . . . . . 1E 111
Tilbury Cl. SE15 . . . . . . 3B 92
Tilbury Ho. SE14 . . . . . 2F 93
  (off Myers La.)
Tilbury Rd. E10 . . . . . . 2E 39
Tileyard Rd. SW15 . . . . 4E 99
Tilehurst Rd. SW18 . . . 1F 115
Tile Kiln La. N6 . . . . . . 3D 33
Tile Kiln Studios N6 . . . 2E 33
Tile Yd. E14 . . . . 5B 66
Tileyard Rd. N7 . . . . . . 4A 48
Tilford Gdns. SW19 . . . 1F 113

Tilford Ho. SW2 . . . . . . 5B 104
  (off Holmewood Gdns.)
Tilia Rd. E5 . . . . 1D 51
Tilia Wlk. SW9 . . . . 2D 105
Tilleard Ho. W10 . . . . . 2A 58
  (off Herries St.)
Tiller Leisure Cen., The
  . . . . 4C 80
Tiller Rd. E14 . . . . 4C 80
Tillett Sq. SE16 . . . . . . 3A 80
Tillet Way E2 . . . . 2C 64
Tilling Rd. NW2 . . . . . . 3E 29
Tillings Cl. SE5 . . . . . . 4E 91
Tillman St. E1 . . . . 5D 65
Tilloch St. N1 . . . . 4B 48
Tillotson Ct. SW8 . . . . . 3F 89
  (off Wandsworth Rd.)
Tilney Ct.
  EC1 . . . . 3A 10 (3E 63)
Tilney Gdns. N1 . . . . . . 3F 49
Tilney St.
  W1 . . . . 1C 20 (2C 74)
Tilson Cl. SE5 . . . . 3A 92
Tilson Gdns. SW2 . . . . 5A 104
Tilson Ho. SW2 . . . . . . 5A 104
Tilton St. SW6 . . . . 2A 86
Timberland Cl. SE15 . . . 3C 92
Timberland Rd. E1 . . . . 5D 65
Timber Mill Way
  SW4 . . . . 1F 103
Timber Pond Rd.
  SE16 . . . . 2F 79
Timber St.
  EC1 . . . . 3F 9 (3E 63)
Timberwharf Rd.
  N16 . . . . 1C 36
Timber Wharves Est.
  E14 . . . . 5C 80
  (off Copeland Dr.)
Timbrell Pl. SE16 . . . . . 2B 80
Time Sq. E8 . . . . 2B 50
Timor Ho. E1 . . . . 3A 66
  (off Duckett St.)
Timothy Cl. SW4 . . . . . 3E 103
Timothy Rd. E3 . . . . . . 4B 66
Timsbury Wlk.
  SW15 . . . . 1C 112
Tindal St. SW9 . . . . 4D 91
Tinderbox All. SW14 . . . 1A 98
Tinniswood Cl. N5 . . . . 2C 48
Tinsley Rd. E1 . . . . 4E 65
Tintagel Cres. SE22 . . . 2B 106
Tintagel Gdns. SE22 . . . 2B 106
Tintern Cl. SW15 . . . . . 3A 100
Tintern Ho. NW1 . . . . . 1E 5
  (off Augustus St.)
  SW1 . . . . 5D 75
  (off Abbots Mnr.)
Tintern Path NW9 . . . . 1A 28
  (off Fryent Gro.)
Tintern St. SW4 . . . . . 2A 104
Tinto Rd. E16 . . . . 3C 68
Tinworth St. SE11 . . . . 1A 90
Tiptree NW1 . . . . 4D 47
  (off Castlehaven Rd.)
Tisbury Ct. W1 . . . . 4B 14
Tisdall Pl. SE17 . . . . . . 5F 77
Tissington Ct. SE16 . . . 5E 79

Titan Bus. Est. SE8 . . . 3C 94
  (off Ffinch St.)
Titchborne Row W2 . . . 5A 60
Titchfield Rd. NW8 . . . . 5A 46
Titchwell Rd. SW18 . . . 1F 115
Tite St. SW3 . . . . 1B 88
Titmuss St. W12 . . . . . 3E 71
Tiverton Rd. N15 . . . . . 1F 35
  NW10 . . . . 5F 43
Tiverton St.
  SE1 . . . . 5F 25 (4E 77)
Tivoli Ct. SE16 . . . . 2B 80
Tivoli Gdns. SE18 . . . . 5F 83
  (not continuous)
Tivoli Rd. N8 . . . . 1F 33
  SE27 . . . . 5E 119
Tobacco Dock E1 . . . . . 1D 79
Tobacco Quay E1 . . . . . 1D 79
Tobago St. E14 . . . . . . 3C 80
Tobin Cl. NW3 . . . . 4A 46
Toby La. E1 . . . . 3A 66
Todds Wlk. N7 . . . . 4B 34
Tokenhouse Yd.
  EC2 . . . . 2B 18 (5F 63)
Token Yd. SW15 . . . . . 2A 100
Toland Sq. SW15 . . . . . 3C 98
Tolchurch W11 . . . . . . 5B 58
  (off Dartmouth Cl.)
Tollbridge Cl. W10 . . . . 3A 58
Tollet St. E1 . . . . 3F 65
Tollgate Dr. SE21 . . . . . 2A 120
Tollgate Gdns. NW6 . . . 1D 59
Tollgate Ho. NW6 . . . . . 1D 59
  (off Tollgate Gdns.)
Tollgate Rd. E6 . . . . 4E 69
  E16 . . . . 4E 69
Tollhouse Way N19 . . . 4E 33
Tollington Pk. N4 . . . . . 4B 34
Tollington Pl. N4 . . . . . 4B 34
Tollington Rd. N7 . . . . . 1B 48
Tollington Way N7 . . . . 5A 34
Tolmers Sq.
  NW1 . . . . 3A 6 (3E 61)
  (not continuous)
Tolpaide Ho. SE11 . . . . 5C 76
  (off Marylee Way)
Tolpuddle Av. E13 . . . . 5E 55
  (off Queens Rd.)
Tolpuddle St. N1 . . . . . 1C 62
Tolsford Rd. E5 . . . . . . 2D 51
Tom Allen Arts Cen. . . . 3F 53
Tom Blau Gallery 3F 27
  (off Queen Elizabeth St.)
Tom Groves Cl. E15 . . . 2F 53
Tom Hood Cl. E15 . . . . 2F 53
Tom Jenkinson Rd.
  E16 . . . . 2C 82
Tomkyns Ho. SE11 . . . . 5C 76
  (off Distin St.)
Tomlin's Gro. E3 . . . . . 2C 66
Tomlinson Cl. E2 . . . . . 2B 64
Tomlins Ter. E14 . . . . . 5A 66
Tomlins Wlk. N7 . . . . . 4B 34
Tom Nolan Cl. E15 . . . . 1A 68
Tompion Ho. EC1 . . . . . 3E 9
  (off Percival St.)
Tompion St.
  EC1 . . . . 2D 9 (2D 63)
  (not continuous)
Tom Smith Cl. SE10 . . . 2A 96

Tomson Ho. *SE1* 5F **27**
(off Riley Rd.)
Tom Williams Ho.
SW6 . . . . 2B **86**
(off Clem Attlee Ct.)
Tonbridge Ho's. *WC1* 2D **7**
(off Tonbridge St.)
Tonbridge St.
WC1 . . . . . . 1D **7** (2A **62**)
Tonbridge Wlk. WC1 . . . 1D **7**
Toneborough *NW8* 5D **45**
(off Abbey Rd.)
Tonsley Hill SW18 . . . . 3D **101**
Tonsley Pl. SW18 . . . . . 3D **101**
Tonsley Rd. SW18 . . . . . 3D **101**
Tonsley St. SW18 . . . . . 3D **101**
Tony Cannell M. E3 . . . . 2B **66**
Took's Ct.
EC4 . . . . . . 2B **16** (5C **62**)
Tooley St.
SE1 . . . . 1C **26** (2F **77**)
Toomy Cen. *E16* 2D **83**
(off Evelyn Rd.)
TOOTING 5A **116**
TOOTING BEC 3B **116**
Tooting Bec Gdns.
SW16 . . . . 4F **117**
(not continuous)
Tooting Bec Lido 4E **117**
Tooting Bec Rd.
SW16 . . . . 3C **116**
SW17 . . . . 3C **116**
Tooting B'way.
SW17 . . . . 5A **116**
TOOTING GRAVENEY
. . . . 5B **116**
Tooting Gro. SW17 . . . . 5A **116**
Tooting High St.
SW17 . . . . 5A **116**
Tooting Leisure Cen.
. . . . 4F **115**
Tooting Mkt. SW17 . . . . 4B **116**
Topaz Wlk. NW2 . . . . . . 2F **29**
Topham Ho. *SE10* 3E **95**
(off Prior St.)
Topham St.
EC1 . . . . 3B **8** (3C **62**)
Topley St. SE9 . . . . 2E **111**
Topmast Point E14 . . . . 3C **80**
Topp Wlk. NW2 . . . . 4E **29**
Topsfield Cl. N8 . . . . 1F **33**
Topsfield Pde. *N8* 1A **34**
(off Tottenham La.)
Topsfield Rd. N8 . . . . . . 1A **34**
Topsham Rd. SW17 . . . . 3B **116**
Torbay Ct. NW1 . . . . 4D **47**
Torbay Mans. *NW6* 5B **44**
(off Willesden La.)
Torbay Rd. NW6 . . . . 4B **44**
Torbay St. NW1 . . . . 4D **47**
Tor Ct. W8 . . . . 3C **72**
Torcross Dr. SE23 . . . . 2E **121**
Tor Gdns. W8 . . . . 3C **72**
Tor Ho. N6 . . . . 1D **33**
Tornay Ho. N1 . . . . 4E **51**
N1 . . . . 1B **62**
(off Priory Grn. Est.)
Torquay St. W2 . . . . 4D **59**
Torrance Ct. SE7 . . . . . . 2F **97**
Torrens Ct. SE5 . . . . . . 1F **105**

Torrens Rd. E15 . . . . . . 3B **54**
SW2 . . . . 3B **104**
Torrens Sq. E15 . . . . . . 3B **54**
Torrens St. EC1 . . . . 1C **62**
Torrey Dr. SW9 . . . . 5C **90**
Torriano Av. NW5 . . . . . 2F **47**
Torriano Cotts. NW5 . . . 2E **47**
Torriano M. NW5 . . . . . . 2E **47**
Torridge Gdns.
SE15 . . . . 2E **107**
Torridon Ho. *NW6* 1D **59**
(off Randolph Gdns.)
Torridon Rd. SE6 . . . . . 5F **109**
SE13 . . . . 5A **110**
Torrington Ct. *SE26* 5C **120**
(off Crystal Pal. Pk. Rd.)
Torrington Pl. E1 . . . . . . 2C **78**
WC1 . . . . . . 5B **6** (4F **61**)
Torrington Sq.
WC1 . . . . 4C **6** (3F **61**)
Tortington Ho. SE15 . . . . 3C **92**
(off Friary Est.)
Torwood Rd. SW15 . . . . 3C **98**
Tothill Ho. *SW1* 5F **75**
(off Page St.)
Tothill St.
SW1 . . . . . . 4C **22** (3F **75**)
Tottan Ter. E1 . . . . 5F **65**
Tottenhall *NW1* 4C **46**
(off Ferdinand St.)
Tottenham Ct. Rd.
W1 . . . . 4A **6** (3E **61**)
Tottenham La. N8 . . . . . 1A **34**
Tottenham M.
W1 . . . . 5A **6** (4E **61**)
Tottenham Rd. N1 . . . . . 3A **50**
Tottenham St.
W1 . . . . 1A **14** (4E **61**)
Totterdown St.
SW17 . . . . 4B **116**
Totteridge Ho. *SW11* . . . 5F **87**
(off Yelverton Rd.)
Toulmin St.
SE1 . . . . 4F **25** (3E **77**)
Toulon St. SE5 . . . . 3E **91**
Toulouse Ct. *SE16* 1D **93**
(off Rossetti Rd.)
Tourist Info. Cen.
City of London
. . . . 3F **17** (5E **63**)
Greenwich 2E **95**
Hackney 3D **51**
King's Cross 1D **7**
Leicester Sq.
. . . . 5C **14** (1F **75**)
Lewisham 2E **109**
Southwark
. . . . 1A **26** (2E **77**)
Waterloo International
Terminal 3A **24** (3C **76**)
Tournay Rd. SW6 . . . . . 3B **86**
Tours Pas. SW11 . . . . . 2E **101**
Toussaint Wlk. SE16 . . . 4C **78**
Tovy Ho. *SE1* 1C **92**
(off Avondale Sq.)
Towcester Rd. E3 . . . . . 3D **67**
Tower 42 . . . . 2D **19** (5A **64**)
Tower Bri. E1 . . . 1F **27** (2B **78**)
SE1 . . . . 2F **27** (2B **78**)

Tower Bri. App.
E1 . . . . 1F **27** (2B **78**)
Tower Bri. Bus. Complex
SE16 . . . . 4C **78**
Tower Bri. Bus. Sq.
SE16 . . . . 5D **79**
Tower Bridge Experience
. . . . 1F **27**
Tower Bri. Plaza
SE1 . . . . 2F **27** (2B **78**)
Tower Bri. Rd.
SE1 . . . . 5D **27** (4A **78**)
Tower Bri. Sq. SE1 . . . . 3F **27**
Tower Bri. Wharf E1 . . . 2C **78**
Tower Bldgs. *E1* 2D **79**
(off Brewhouse La.)
Tower Cl. NW3 . . . . 2F **45**
Tower Ct. E5 . . . . 2B **36**
N1 . . . . 4E **49**
(off Canonbury St.)
NW8 . . . . 1A **60**
(off Mackennal St.)
WC2 . . . . 3D **15**
Tower Hamlets Rd.
E7 . . . . 1B **54**
TOWER HILL 1B **78**
Tower Hill
EC3 . . . . 5E **19** (1A **78**)
Tower Hill Ter. EC3. . . . 5E **19**
Tower Ho. *E1* 4C **64**
(off Fieldgate St.)
Tower Mill Rd. SE15 . . . 2A **92**
(not continuous)
Tower of London, The
. . . . 5F **19** (1B **78**)
Tower of London Vis. Cen., The
. . . . 5E **19** (1A **78**)
Tower Pl.
EC3 . . . . 5E **19** (1A **78**)
Tower Pl. E. *EC3* 5E **19**
(off Lwr. Thames St.)
Tower Pl. W. *EC3* 5E **19**
(off Lwr. Thames St.)
Tower Rd. NW10 . . . . . . 4C **42**
Tower Royal
EC4 . . . . . . 4B **18** (1F **77**)
Tower St.
WC2 . . . . 3D **15** (5A **62**)
Towncourt Path N4 . . . . 3E **35**
Town Hall Rd.
SW11 . . . . 1B **102**
Town Hall Wlk. *N16* 1F **49**
(off Albion Rd.)
Townley Ct. E15 . . . . . . 3B **54**
Townley Rd. SE22 . . . . 3A **106**
Townley St. SE17 . . . . . 1F **91**
(not continuous)
Townmead Bus. Cen.
SW6 . . . . 1E **101**
Townmead Rd.
SW6 . . . . 1D **101**
Townsend Ho. *SE1* 5C **78**
(off Strathnairn St.)
Townsend La. NW9 . . . . 2A **28**
Townsend Rd. N15 . . . . 1B **36**
Townsend St. SE17 . . . . 5A **78**
Townsend Yd. N6 . . . . . 3D **33**
Townshend Ct. *NW8* . . . 1A **60**
(off Townshend Rd.)
Townshend Est. NW8 . . . 1A **60**

Townshend Rd. NW8 . . 5A **46**
(not continuous)
Towns Ho. SW4 . . . . 1F **103**
Towpath, The SW10 . . . . 4F **87**
Towpath Wlk. E9 . . . . . . 2B **52**
Towton Rd. SE27 . . . . . . 2E **119**
Toynbee St.
E1 . . . . .1F **19** (4B **64**)
Toyne Way N6 . . . . 1B **32**
Tracey Av. NW2 . . . . 2E **43**
Tradescant Ho. E9 . . . . 4F **51**
(off Frampton Pk. Rd.)
Tradescant Rd. SW8 . . . 3A **90**
Tradewinds Ct. E1 . . . . . 1C **78**
Trafalgar Av. SE15 . . . . . 1B **92**
Trafalgar Chambers
SW3 . . . . 1F **87**
(off South Pde.)
Trafalgar Cl. SE16 . . . . . 4A **80**
Trafalgar Ct. E1 . . . . 2E **79**
(off Wapping Wall)
Trafalgar Gdns. E1 . . . . 4F **65**
W8 . . . . 4D **73**
(off Sth. End Row)
Trafalgar Gro. SE10 . . . . 2F **95**
Trafalgar Ho. SE17 . . . . 1E **91**
(off Bronti Cl.)
Trafalgar M. E9 . . . . 3B **52**
Trafalgar Point N1 . . . . . 4F **49**
(off Downham Rd.)
Trafalgar Rd. SE10 . . . . 2F **95**
Trafalgar Square
. . . . 1D **23** (2A **76**)
Trafalgar Sq.
WC2 . . . . 1C **22** (2F **75**)
Trafalgar St. SE17 . . . . . 1F **91**
Trafalgar Way E14 . . . . . 2E **81**
Trafford Cl. E15 . . . . 2D **53**
Trafford Ho. N1 . . . . 1F **63**
(off Cranston Est.)
Trahorn Cl. E1 . . . . 3D **65**
Traitors' Gate
. . . . 1F **27** (2B **78**)
(in Tower of London, The)
Tralee Ct. SE16 . . . . 1D **93**
(off Masters Dr.)
Tramway Av. E15 . . . . . . 4A **54**
Tranley M. NW3 . . . . 1A **46**
(off Fleet Rd.)
Tranmere Rd. SW18 . . . 2E **115**
Tranquil Pas. SE3 . . . . . 5B **96**
(off Montpelier Va.)
Tranquil Va. SE3 . . . . . . 5A **96**
Transay Wlk. N1 . . . . . . 3F **49**
Transept St. NW1 . . . . . 4A **60**
Transom Cl. SE16 . . . . . 5A **80**
Transom Sq. E14 . . . . . 1D **95**
Tranton Rd. SE16 . . . . . 4C **78**
Trappes Ho. SE16 . . . . . 5D **79**
(off Camilla Rd.)
Travers Ho. SE10 . . . . . 2F **95**
(off Trafalgar Gro.)
Travers Rd. N7 . . . . 5C **34**
Travis Ho. SE10 . . . . 4E **95**
Treadgold Ho. W11 . . . . 1F **71**
(off Bomore Rd.)
Treadgold St. W11 . . . . . 1F **71**
Treadway St. E2 . . . . . . 1D **65**
Treasury Pas. SW1 . . . . 3D **23**
Treaty St. N1 . . . . 5B **48**

Trebeck St.
W1 . . . . 1D **21** (2D **75**)
Trebovir Rd. SW5 . . . . . 1C **86**
Treby St. E3 . . . . 3B **66**
Trecastle Way N7 . . . . . 1F **47**
Tredegar M. E3 . . . . 2B **66**
Tredegar Rd. E3 . . . . . . 1B **66**
Tredegar Sq. E3 . . . . . . 2B **66**
Tredegar Ter. E3 . . . . . . 2B **66**
Trederwen Rd. E8 . . . . . 5C **50**
Tredown Rd. SE26 . . . . 5E **121**
Tredwell Cl. SW2 . . . . . 2B **118**
Tredwell Rd. SE27 . . . . 4D **119**
Treen Av. SW13 . . . . . . 1B **98**
Tree Rd. E16 . . . . 5E **69**
Treewall Gdns.
BR1: Brom 4D **125**
Trefil Wlk. N7 . . . . 1A **48**
Trefoil Rd. SW18 . . . . . 3E **101**
Tregaron Av. N8 . . . . . . 1A **34**
Tregarvon Rd.
SW11 . . . . 2C **102**
Trego Rd. E9 . . . . 4C **52**
Tregothnan Rd.
SW9 . . . . 1A **104**
Tregunter Rd.
SW10 . . . . 2D **87**
Treherne Ct. SW9 . . . . . 4D **91**
SW17 . . . . 4C **116**
Trehern Rd. SW14 . . . . 1A **98**
Trehurst St. E5 . . . . 2A **52**
Trelawney Est. E9 . . . . . 3E **51**
Trelawney Ho. SE1 . . . . 3F **25**
(off Pepper St.)
Trelawn Rd. E10 . . . . . . 5E **39**
SW2 . . . . 3C **104**
Trellick Twr. W10 . . . . . 3B **58**
(off Golborne Rd.)
Trellis Sq. E3 . . . . 2B **66**
Tremadoc Rd. SW4 . . . 2F **103**
Tremaine Cl. SE4 . . . . . 5C **94**
Trematon Ho. SE11 . . . 1C **90**
(off Kennings Way)
Tremlett Gro. N19 . . . . . 5E **33**
Trenchard Ct. NW4 . . . . 1C **28**
Trenchard St. SE10 . . . . 1F **95**
Trenchold St. SW8 . . . . 2A **90**
Trendell Ho. E14 . . . . . . 5C **66**
(off Dod St.)
Trenmar Gdns. NW10 . . 2D **57**
Trent Ho. SE15 . . . . 2E **107**
Trent Rd. SW2 . . . . 3B **104**
Treport St. SW18 . . . . . 5D **101**
Tresco Ho. SE11 . . . . . . 1C **90**
(off Sancroft St.)
Tresco Rd. SE15 . . . . . 2D **107**
Tresham Cres.
NW8 . . . . 3A **60**
Tresham Wlk. E9 . . . . . . 2E **51**
Tresidder Ho. SW4 . . . . 5F **103**
Tressell Cl. N1 . . . . 4D **49**
Tressillian Cres.
SE4 . . . . 1C **108**
Tressillian Rd.
SE4 . . . . 2B **108**
Tress Pl. SE1 . . . . 1D **25**
Trevanion Rd. W14 . . . . 5A **72**
Trevelyan Gdns.
NW10 . . . . 5E **43**

Trevelyan Ho. E2 . . . . . . 2F **65**
(off Morpeth St.)
SE17 . . . . 3D **91**
(off John Ruskin St.)
Trevelyan Rd. E15 . . . . . 1B **54**
SW17 . . . . 5A **116**
Trevenna Ho. SE23 . . . . 3F **121**
(off Dacres Rd.)
Treveris St.
SE1 . . . . 2E **25** (2D **77**)
Treverton St. W10 . . . . . 3F **57**
Treverton Towers
W10 . . . . 4F **57**
(off Treverton St.)
Treves Ho. E1 . . . . 3C **64**
(off Vallance Rd.)
Treville St. SW15 . . . . . 5D **99**
Treviso Rd. SE23 . . . . . 2F **121**
Trevithick Ho. SE16 . . . 5D **79**
(off Rennie Est.)
Trevithick St. SE8 . . . . . 2C **94**
Trevone Ct. SW2 . . . . . 5A **104**
(off Doverfield Rd.)
Trevor Pl. SW7 . . . . 3A **74**
Trevor Sq. SW7 . . . . . . 3B **74**
Trevor St. SW7 . . . . 3A **74**
Trevor Wlk. SW7 . . . . . . 3A **74**
(off Trevor Pl., not continuous)
Trevose Ho. SE11 . . . . . 1B **90**
(off Orsett St.)
Trewint St. SW18 . . . . . 2E **115**
Trewsbury Rd. SE26 . . . 5F **121**
Triangle, The E8 . . . . . . 5D **51**
EC1 . . . . 3E **9**
Triangle Bus. Cen., The
NW10 . . . . 2B **56**
Triangle Ct. E16 . . . . . . 4F **69**
Triangle Pl. SW4 . . . . . 2F **103**
Triangle Rd. E8 . . . . 5D **51**
Tricycle Cinema 4B **44**
(in Tricycle Theatre)
Tricycle Theatre 4B **44**
(off Kilburn High Rd.)
Trident Bus. Cen.
SW17 . . . . 5B **116**
Trident Ho. E14 . . . . . . 5E **67**
(off Blair St.)
Trident Pl. SW3 . . . . . . 2F **87**
(off Old Chu. St.)
Trident St. SE16 . . . . . . 5F **79**
Trig La.
EC4 . . . . 4F **17** (1E **77**)
Trigon Rd. SW8 . . . . . . 3B **90**
Trilby Rd. SE23 . . . . . . 2F **121**
Trimdon NW1 . . . . 5E **47**
Trim St. SE14 . . . . 2B **94**
Trinder Gdns. N19 . . . . 3A **34**
Trinder Rd. N19 . . . . . . 3A **34**
Trinidad Ho. E14 . . . . . 1B **80**
(off Gill St.)
Trinidad St. E14 . . . . . . 1B **80**
Trinity Buoy Wharf
E14 . . . . 1A **82**
(off Orchard Pl.)
Trinity Chu. Pas.
SW13 . . . . 2D **85**
Trinity Chu. Rd.
SW13 . . . . 2D **85**
Trinity Chu. Sq.
SE1 . . . . 5A **26** (4E **77**)

Trinity Cl. E8 . . . . 3B 50
E11 . . . . 4A 40
NW3 . . . . 1F 45
SE13 . . . . 2F 109
SW4 . . . . 2E 103
Trinity College of Music
. . . . 2E 95
Trinity Ct. N1 . . . . 5A 50
(off Downham Rd.)
NW2 . . . . 2E 43
SE1 . . . . 5A 26
(off Brockham St.)
SE7 . . . . 5F 83
SE26 . . . . 3E 121
SW9 . . . . 1B 104
W2 . . . . 5E 59
(off Gloucester Ter.)
WC1 . . . . 3F 7
Trinity Cres. SW17 . . . . 3E 116
Trinity Gdns. E16 . . . . . 4B 68
(not continuous)
SW9 . . . . 2B 104
Trinity Grn. E1. . . . . 3E 65
Trinity Gro. SE10 . . . . . . 4E 95
Trinity Hospital (Almshouses)
SE10 . . . . 1F 95
Trinity Ho. SE1 . . . . 5A 26
(off Bath Ter.)
Trinity M. E1. . . . . 4E 65
(off Redman's Rd.)
W10. . . . . 5F 57
Trinity Path SE23 . . . . . 3E 121
Trinity Pl.
EC3. . . . . . 4F 19 (1B 78)
Trinity Ri. SW2. . . . . . . 1C 118
Trinity Rd. SW17 . . . . . 1A 116
SW18 . . . . 2E 101
SW19 . . . . 5C 114
Trinity Sq.
EC3 . . . . . . 5E 19 (1A 78)
Trinity St. E16. . . . . 4B 68
SE1 . . . . . . 4A 26 (3E 77)
(not continuous)
Trinity Twr. E1. . . . . 1C 78
(off Vaughan Way)
Trinity Wlk. NW3 . . . . . . 3E 45
Trinity Way W3 . . . . 1A 70
Trio Pl. SE1 . . . 4A 26 (3E 77)
Tristan Ct. SE8 . . . . 2B 94
(off Dorking Cl.)
Tristan Sq. SE3. . . . . . . 1A 110
Tristram Rd.
BR1: Brom 4B 124
Triton Ho. E14 . . . . 5D 81
(off Cahir St.)
Triton Sq.
NW1. . . . . . . 3F 5 (3E 61)
Tritton Rd. SE21 . . . . . . 3F 119
Trocadero Cen.
. . . . 5B 14 (1F 75)
Trocette Mans.
SE1 . . . . 5D 27
(off Bermondsey St.)
Trojan Ct. NW6 . . . . 4A 44
Trojan Ind. Est.
NW10 . . . . 3B 42
Troon Cl. SE16 . . . . 1D 93
Troon Ho. E1 . . . . 5A 66
(off White Horse Rd.)
Troon St. E1 . . . . 5A 66

Tropical Ct. W10 . . . . . . 2F 57
(off Kilburn La.)
Trossachs Rd. SE22 . . . 3A 106
Trothy Rd. SE1 . . . . 5C 78
Trotman Ho. SE14 . . . . . 4E 93
(off Pomeroy St.)
Trott St. SW11 . . . . 4A 88
Troughton Rd. SE7 . . . . . 1D 97
Troutbeck NW1 . . . . 2E 5
SE14 . . . . 4A 94
Trouville Rd. SW4 . . . . . 4E 103
Trowbridge Rd. E9 . . . . . 3B 52
Troy Ct. W8 . . . . 4C 72
(off Kensington High St.)
Troy Town SE15 . . . . . . 1C 106
Trumans Rd. N16. . . . . . 2B 50
Trumpington Rd. E7 . . . . 1B 54
Trump St.
EC2 . . . . . . 3A 18 (5E 63)
Trundle St.
SE1 . . . . . . 3F 25 (3E 77)
Trundleys Rd. SE8 . . . . . 1F 93
Trundley's Ter. SE8. . . . . 5F 79
Truro Rd. NW5. . . . . 3C 46
Truslove Rd. SE27 . . . . 5C 118
Trussley Rd. W6. . . . . . . 4E 71
Trust Wlk. SE21 . . . . . . 1D 119
Tryfan Cl. IG4: Ilf 1F 41
Tryon Cres. E9 . . . . 5E 51
Tryon St. SW3 . . . . 1B 88
Tubbs Rd. NW10 . . . . . . 1B 56
Tucklow Wlk. SW15 . . . . 5B 98
Tudor Cl. N6 . . . . 2E 33
NW3 . . . . 2A 46
SW2 . . . . 4B 104
Tudor Ct. E17 . . . . 2B 38
N1 . . . . 3A 50
SE16 . . . . 2F 79
(off Princes Riverside Rd.)
Tudor Gdns. SW13 . . . . . 1A 98
Tudor Gro. E9 . . . . 4E 51
Tudor Ho. E9. . . . . 4E 51
E16 . . . . 2D 83
(off Wesley Av.)
W14. . . . . 5F 71
(off Windsor Way)
Tudor Rd. E6. . . . . 5E 55
E9 . . . . 5D 51
Tudor Stacks SE24 . . . . 2E 105
Tudor St. EC4 . . 4C 16 (1C 76)
Tudway Rd. SE3. . . . . . 1D 111
TUFNELL PARK 1E 47
Tufnell Pk. Rd. N7 . . . . . 1E 47
N19 . . . . 1E 47
Tufton Ct. SW1. . . . . . . 5D 23
(off Tufton St.)
Tufton St.
SW1 . . . . . . 5D 23 (4A 76)
Tugela St. SE6 . . . . 2B 122
Tullis Ho. E9 . . . . 4E 51
(off Frampton Pk. Rd.)
TULSE HILL. 1D 119
Tulse Hill SW2 . . . . 4C 104
Tulse Hill Est. SW2 . . . . 4C 104
Tulse Ho. SW2 . . . . 4C 104
Tulsemere Rd. SE27 . . . . 2E 119
Tunbridge Ho. EC1 . . . . . 1C 8
Tunis Rd. W12 . . . . 2E 71
Tunley Grn. E14 . . . . . . 4B 66

Tunley Rd. NW10 . . . . . . 5A 42
SW17 . . . . 1C 116
Tunmarsh La. E13 . . . . . 2D 69
Tunnel App. E14 . . . . . . 1A 80
SE10 . . . . 3A 82
SE16 . . . . 3E 79
Tunnel Av. SE10 . . . . . . 3F 81
(not continuous)
Tunnel Av. Trad. Est.
SE10 . . . . 3F 81
Tunnel Rd. SE16. . . . . . . 3E 79
Tunstall Rd. SW9. . . . . . 2B 104
Tunworth Cres. SW15 . . . 4B 98
Tun Yd. SW8 . . . . 5D 89
(off Silverthorne Rd.)
Tupelo Rd. E10 . . . . 4D 39
Tupman Ho. SE16 . . . . . 3C 78
(off Scott Lidgett Cres.)
Turenne Cl. SW18 . . . . . 2E 101
Turin St. E2 . . . . 2C 64
Turk's Head Yd.
EC1 . . . . . . 5D 9 (4D 63)
Turk's Row SW3 . . . . . . 1B 88
Turle Rd. N4 . . . . 4B 34
Turlewray Cl. N4 . . . . . . 3B 34
Turley Cl. E15. . . . . 5A 54
Turnagain La. EC4 . . . . . 2D 17
Turnberry Cl. SE16. . . . . 1D 93
Turnberry Quay E14. . . . 4D 81
Turnbull Ho. N1 . . . . . . 5D 49
Turnchapel M. SW4 . . . 1D 103
Turner Cl. NW11 . . . . . . 1D 31
SW9 . . . . 3D 91
Turner Ct. SE16 . . . . . . 3E 79
(off Albion St.)
Turner Dr. NW11 . . . . . . 1D 31
Turner Ho. NW6 . . . . . . 2E 45
(off Dresden Cl.)
NW8 . . . . 1A 60
(off Townshend St.)
SW1 . . . . 5F 75
(off Herrick St.)
Turner Pl. SW11 . . . . . . 3A 102
Turner's All.
EC3 . . . . . . 4D 19 (1A 78)
Turners Cl. N15 . . . . . . 1F 35
Turners Rd. E3 . . . . 4B 66
Turner St. E1 . . . . 4D 65
E16 . . . . 5B 68
Turners Wood NW11 . . . 2E 31
Turneville Rd. W14 . . . . 2B 86
Turney Rd. SE21. . . . . . 5E 105
TURNHAM GREEN 5A 70
Turnham Grn. Ter.
W4 . . . . 5A 70
Turnham Grn. Ter. M.
W4 . . . . 5A 70
Turnham Rd. SE4 . . . . . 3A 108
Turnmill St.
EC1 . . . . . . 4D 9 (3D 63)
Turnour Ho. E1 . . . . 5D 65
(off Walburgh St.)
Turnpike Cl. SE8 . . . . . . 3B 94
Turnpike Ho.
EC1 . . . . . . 2E 9 (2D 63)
Turnpin La. SE10 . . . . . . 2E 95
Turnstone Cl. E13. . . . . . 2C 68
Turnstone Ho. E1 . . . . . . 1C 78
(off Star Pl.)
Turpentine La. SW1 . . . . 1D 89

Turpin Cl. E1 . . . . 1F 79
Turpin Ho. SW11 . . . . . . 4D 89
Turpin Way N19 . . . . . . 4F 33
(not continuous)
Turquand St. SE17 . . . . . . 5E 77
Turret Gro. SW4 . . . . . 1E 103
Turville Ho. NW8 . . . . 3A 60
(off Grendon St.)
Turville St. E2 . . . . 3F 11
Tuscan Ho. E2. . . . . 2E 65
(off Knottisford St.)
Tuskar St. SE10 . . . . 2A 96
Tustin Est. SE15 . . . . . . 2E 93
Tuttle Ho. SW1 . . . . 1F 89
(off Aylesford St.)
Tweedale Ct. E15 . . . . . . 2E 53
Tweed Ho. E3 . . . . 1E 67
(off Teviot St.)
Tweedmouth Rd. E13. . . 1D 69
Tweezer's All. W2 . . . . . 4B 16
Twelvetrees Cres. E3 . . . 3E 67
(not continuous)
E16 . . . . 3F 67
Twickenham Rd. E11 . . . 4E 39
Twig Folly Cl. E2. . . . . . . 1F 65
Twilley St. SW18 . . . . . 5D 101
Twine Ct. E1 . . . . 1E 79
Twine Ter. E3 . . . . 3B 66
(off Ropery St.)
Twisden Rd. NW5. . . . . . 1D 47
Twycross M. SE10 . . . . . 1A 96
Twyford Ho. N5. . . . . . . 5D 35
N15. . . . . 1A 36
(off Chisley Rd.)
Twyford Pl.
WC2 . . . . 2F 15 (5B 62)
Twyford St. N1 . . . . 5B 48
Tyas Rd. E16 . . . . 3B 68
Tyburn Tree (site of) . . . 4A 12
Tyburn Way
W1. . . . . 4A 12 (1B 74)
Tyers Est. SE1 . . . . 3D 27
Tyers Ga.
SE1 . . . . 4D 27 (3A 78)
Tyers St. SE11 . . . . 1B 90
Tyers Ter. SE11. . . . . 1B 90
Tyler Cl. E2 . . . . 1B 64
Tyler's Ct. W1. . . . . 3B 14
Tyler St. SE10. . . . . 1A 96
(not continuous)
Tylney Av. SE19 . . . . . . 5B 120
(not continuous)
Tylney Ho. E1 . . . . 5D 65
(off Nelson St.)
Tylney Rd. E7 . . . . 1E 55
Tyndale Ct. E14 . . . . 1D 95
(off Transom Sq.)
Tyndale La. N1. . . . . 4D 49
Tyndale Mans. N1 . . . . . 4D 49
(off Upper St.)
Tyndale Ter. N1 . . . . 4D 49
Tyndall Gdns. E10 . . . . . 4E 39
Tyndall Rd. E10 . . . . 4E 39
Tyneham Cl. SW11 . . . . 1C 102
Tyneham Rd. SW11 . . . . 1C 88
Tynemouth St. SW6 . . . 5E 87
Tyne St. E1. . . . . 5B 64
Tynsdale Rd. NW10. . . . 4A 42
Tynwald Ho. SE26 . . . . 3C 120
Type St. E2 . . . . 1F 65

Tyrawley Rd. SW6 . . . . . 4D 87
Tyrell Ho.
BR3: Beck. 5D 123
(off Beckenham Hill Rd.)
Tyrols Rd. SE23 . . . . 1F 121
Tyrrell Ho. SW1 . . . . 2E 89
(off Churchill Gdns.)
Tyrrell Rd. SE22. . . . . . . 2C 106
Tyrwhitt Rd. SE4 . . . . . . 1C 108
Tysoe St. EC1 . . . 2C 8 (2C 62)
Tyson Gdns. SE23 . . . . . 5E 107
Tyson Rd. SE23 . . . . 5E 107
Tyssen Pas. E8. . . . . 3B 50
Tyssen Rd. N16 . . . . 5B 36
Tyssen St. E8 . . . . 3B 50
N1. . . . . 1A 64
Tytherton E2 . . . . 1E 65
(off Cyprus St.)
Tytherton Rd. N19 . . . . . 5F 33

U

Uamvar St. E14 . . . . 4D 67
UCI Cinema
Rotherhithe 4F 79
Whiteleys Cen. 5D 59
(in Whiteleys Cen.)
UCI Filmworks 5B 82
Udall St. SW1. . . . . 5E 75
Udimore Ho. W10 . . . . . 4E 57
(off Sutton Way)
Uffington Rd. NW10. . . . 5C 42
SE27. . . . . 4C 118
Ufford St.
SE1 . . . . 3C 24 (3C 76)
Ufton Gro. N1. . . . . 4F 49
Ufton Rd. N1 . . . . 4F 49
(not continuous)
UGC Cinema
Fulham Rd. 1E 87
(off Fulham Rd.)
Hammersmith 5D 71
Haymarket 5B 14
(off Haymarket)
King's Rd. 5B 14
(off King's Rd.)
Staples Corner 3D 29
Trocadero 5B 14
(off Coventry St.)
West India Quay . . . 1C 80
Uhura Sq. N16 . . . . 5A 36
Ujima Ct. SW16 . . . . . . 4A 118
Ullathorne Rd. SW16. . . 4E 117
Ullin St. E14. . . . . 4E 67
Ullswater Cl. SW15 . . . . 4A 112
Ullswater Cres.
SW15 . . . . 4A 112
Ullswater Ho. SE15 . . . . 2E 93
(off Hillbeck Cl.)
Ullswater Rd. SE27 . . . 2D 119
SW13 . . . . 3C 84
Ulster Pl. NW1. . . . 4D 5 (3D 61)
Ulster Ter.
NW1 . . . . 3C 4 (3C 60)
Ulundi Rd. SE3. . . . . 2A 96
Ulva Rd. SW15. . . . . 3F 99
Ulverscroft Rd.
SE22 . . . . 3B 106

Ulverstone Rd.
SE27. . . . . 2D 119
Ulysses Rd. NW6. . . . . . 2B 44
Umberston St. E1 . . . . . 5C 64
Umbria St. SW15 . . . . . 4C 98
Umfreville Rd. N4 . . . . . 1D 35
Undercliff Rd. SE13. . . . 1C 108
Underhill Ho. E14 . . . . . 4C 66
(off Burgess St.)
Underhill Pas. NW1. . . . 5D 47
(off Camden High St.)
Underhill Rd. SE22 . . . . 3C 106
Underhill St. NW1 . . . . . 5D 47
Undershaft
EC3. . . . . 3D 19 (5A 64)
Undershaw Rd.
BR1: Brom 3B 124
Underwood Ct. E10 . . . 3D 39
(off Leyton Grange Est.)
Underwood Ho. W6. . . . 4D 71
(off Sycamore Gdns.)
Underwood Rd. E1. . . . . 3C 64
Underwood Row
N1 . . . . 1A 10 (2E 63)
Underwood St.
N1 . . . . 1A 10 (2E 63)
Undine Rd. E14. . . . . . . 5D 81
Undine St. SW17 . . . . . 5B 116
Unicorn Bldg. E1 . . . . . 1F 79
(off Jardine Rd.)
Union Canal Wlk.
W10 . . . . 3E 57
(off Canal Way)
Union Cl. E11 . . . . 1F 53
Union Cotts. E15 . . . . . . 4A 54
Union Ct. EC2. . . . . 2D 19
SW4 . . . . 5A 90
W9 . . . . 4C 58
(off Elmfield Way)
Union Dr. E1. . . . . 3A 66
Union Gro. SW8 . . . . . . 5F 89
Union M. SW4 . . . . 5A 90
Union Rd. SW4 . . . . 5F 89
SW8 . . . . 5F 89
Union Sq. N1 . . . . 5E 49
Union St. E15 . . . . 5F 53
SE1 . . . . 2D 25 (2D 77)
Union Theatre 2E 25
Union Wlk.
E2. . . . . 1E 11 (2A 64)
Union Wharf N1 . . . . . . 1E 63
(off Wenlock Rd.)
N1 . . . . 5E 49
(Arlington Av.)
Union Yd. W1. . . 3E 13 (5D 61)
Unit Workshops E1 . . . . 5C 64
(off Adler St.)
Unity Cl. NW10 . . . . 3C 42
SE19 . . . . 5E 119
Unity M. NW1 . . . . 1F 61
Unity Way SE18 . . . . . . 4F 83
Unity Wharf SE1. . . . . . 3B 78
(off Mill St.)
University College Department
of Geological Sciences
Collection 4B 6
University College London
Gower St. . . . 1B 6 (3F 61)
Campbell House . . . 3B 6
(off Taviton St.)

University College London
Chemistry Building . . . 3B 6
(off Gordon St.)
University of East London
Maryland Ho. 3A 54
Stratford Campus . . . 3A 54
University of Greenwich
Maritime Greenwich
Campus 2E 95
University of London
College Hall 4B 6
(off Malet St.)
Institute of Education
. . . . 3F 61
Institute of Latin
American Studies . . . 3F 61
Senate Ho. . . . 5C 6 (4F 61)
University of London Union
. . . . 4C 6
University of North London
Highbury Cres. 3C 48
Highbury Gro. 2C 48
Hornsey Rd. 1C 48
University of Surrey
Roehampton 4B 98
University of Westminster
Cavendish Campus
. . . . 5E 5 (4D 61)
Hanson St. . . 5F 5 (4E 61)
Marylebone Campus
. . . . 5B 4 (4C 60)
Regent Campus 1F 13
Regent St.
. . . . 2E 13 (5D 61)
Wells St. 1A 14
University St.
WC1 . . . . 4A 6 (3E 61)
Unwin Cl. SE15 . . . . . . 2C 92
Unwin Mans.
W14 . . . . 2B 86
(off Queen's Club Gdns.)
Unwin Rd. SW7 . . . . . . 4F 73
Upbrook M. W2 . . . . . . 5E 59
Upcerne Rd. SW10 . . . 3E 87
Upcott Ho. *E9* 4E 51
(off Frampton Pk. Rd.)
Upgrove Mnr. Way
SW2 . . . . 5C 104
Upham Pk. Rd.
W4 . . . . 5A 70
Upland M. SE22 . . . . . 3C 106
Upland Rd. E13 . . . . . . 3C 68
SE22 . . . . 3C 106
Uplands Rd. N8 . . . . . . 1B 34
Upnall Ho. SE15 . . . . . . 2E 93
Upnor Way SE17 . . . . . 1A 92
Up. Addison Gdns.
W14 . . . . 3A 72
Upper Bank St.
E14 . . . . 2D 81
Up. Bardsey Wlk.
N1 . . . . 3E 49
(off Douglas Rd. Nth.)
Up. Belgrave St.
SW1 . . . . . . 5C 20 (4C 74)
Up. Berenger Wlk.
SW10 . . . . 3F 87
(off Berenger Wlk.)
Up. Berkeley St.
W1 . . . . 3A 12 (5B 60)

Up. Blantyre Wlk.
SW10 . . . . 3F 87
(off Blantyre Wlk.)
Up. Brockley Rd.
SE4 . . . . 1B 108
(not continuous)
Up. Brook St.
W1 . . . . 4B 12 (1C 74)
Up. Caldy Wlk.
N1 . . . . 3E 49
(off Arran Wlk.)
Up. Camelford Wlk.
W11 . . . . 5A 58
(off Cambourne M.)
W11 . . . . 5A 58
(off St Mark's Rd.)
Up. Cheyne Row
SW3 . . . . 2A 88
(off Old Chu. St.)
UPPER CLAPTON 4D 37
Up. Clapton Rd. E5 . . . 3D 37
Up. Clarendon Wlk.
W11 . . . . 5A 58
(off Clarendon Rd.)
Up. Dartrey Wlk.
SW10 . . . . 3F 87
(off Whistler Wlk.)
Up. Dengie Wlk. *N1* . . . 5E 49
(off Baddow Wlk.)
Upper Feilde *W1* 4B 12
(off Park St.)
Up. Grosvenor St.
W1 . . . . 5B 12 (1C 74)
Upper Ground
SE1 . . . . 1B 24 (2C 76)
Up. Gulland Wlk.
N1 . . . . 4E 49
(off Church Rd.)
Up. Hampstead Wlk.
NW3 . . . . 1E 45
Up. Handa Wlk. *N1* . . . 3F 49
(off Handa Wlk.)
Up. Hawkwell Wlk.
N1 . . . . 5E 49
(off Maldon Cl.)
UPPER HOLLOWAY . . . 4E 33
Up. James St.
W1 . . . . 4A 14 (1E 75)
Up. John St.
W1 . . . . 4A 14 (1E 75)
Up. Lismore Wlk.
N1 . . . . 3E 49
(off Clephane Rd.)
Up. Lodge *W8* 2D 73
(off Palace Grn.)
Upper Mall W6 . . . . . . 1C 84
(not continuous)
Upper Marsh
SE1 . . . . 5A 24 (4B 76)
Up. Montagu St.
W1 . . . . 5A 4 (4B 60)
Up. North St. E14 . . . . 4C 66
Up. Park Rd. NW3 . . . . 2B 46
Up. Phillimore Gdns.
W8 . . . . 3C 72
Up. Ramsey Wlk.
N1 . . . . 3F 49
(off Ramsey Wlk.)
Up. Rawreth Wlk. *N1* . . 5E 49
(off Basire St.)

Up. Richmond Rd.
SW15 . . . . 2B 98
Up. Richmond Rd. W.
SW14 . . . . 2A 98
Upper Rd. E13 . . . . . . 2C 68
Up. St Martin's La.
WC2 . . . . 4D 15 (1A 76)
Upper St. N1 . . . . 1C 62
UPPER SYDENHAM . . 3D 121
Up. Tachbrook St.
SW1 . . . . 5E 75
Up. Talbot Wlk. *W11* . . 5A 58
(off Talbot Wlk.)
Upper Ter. NW3 . . . . . 5E 31
Up. Thames St.
EC4 . . . . 4E 17 (1D 77)
Up. Tollington Pk.
N4 . . . . 3C 34
(not continuous)
Upperton Rd. E. E13 . . 2E 69
Upperton Rd. W. E13 . . 2E 69
UPPER TOOTING 4B 116
Up. Tooting Pk.
SW17 . . . . 2B 116
Up. Tooting Rd.
SW17 . . . . 4B 116
Up. Tulse Hill SW2 . . . 5B 104
Up. Whistler Wlk.
SW10 . . . . 3E 87
(off Worlds End Est.)
Up. Wimpole St.
W1 . . . . 5C 4 (4C 60)
Up. Woburn Pl.
WC1 . . . . 2C 6 (2F 61)
Upstall St. SE5 . . . . . . 4D 91
UPTON 4C 54
Upton Av. E7 . . . . 4C 54
Upton Cl. NW2 . . . . . . 5A 30
Upton La. E7 . . . . 4C 54
Upton Lodge E7 . . . . . 3C 54
UPTON PARK 5F 55
Upton Pk. Boleyn Cinema
. . . . 1F 69
Upton Pk. Rd. E7 . . . . 4D 55
Upton Pk. Stadium . . . 1E 69
Upwey Ho. N1 . . . . 5A 50
Upwood Rd. SE12 . . . 4C 110
Urban M. N4 . . . . 1D 35
Urlwin St. SE5 . . . . . . 2E 91
Urlwin Wlk. SW9 . . . . . 4C 90
Urmston Dr. SW19 . . . 1A 114
Urmston Ho. *E14* 5E 81
(off Seyssel St.)
Ursula M. N4 . . . . 3E 35
Ursula St. SW11 . . . . . 4A 88
Urswick Rd. E9 . . . . . . 2E 51
Usborne M. SW8 . . . . 3B 90
Usher Rd. E3 . . . . 5B 52
Usk Rd. SW11 . . . . . . 2E 101
Usk St. E2 . . . . 2F 65
Utopia Village NW1 . . . 4C 46
Uverdale Rd. SW10 . . . 3E 87
Uxbridge Rd. W12 . . . . 2C 70
Uxbridge St. W8. . . . . . 2C 72

V

Vaine Ho. E9 . . . . 3A 52
Vaizeys Wharf SE7. . . . 4D 83

Vale, The NW11 . . . . . . 5F 29
  SW3 . . . . 2F 87
  W3 . . . . 2A 70
Vale Cl. W9 . . . . 2E 59
Vale Cotts. SW15 . . . . 3A 112
Vale Ct. W3 . . . . 2B 70
  W9 . . . . 2E 59
Vale Cres. SW15 . . . . . 4A 112
Vale End SE22 . . . . . . 2B 106
Vale Est., The W3 . . . . 2A 70
Vale Gro. N4 . . . . 2E 35
  W3 . . . . 3A 70
Vale Lodge SE23 . . . . 2E 121
Valentia Pl. SW9 . . . . 2C 104
Valentine Ct.
  SE23 . . . . 2F 121
    (not continuous)
Valentine Pl.
  SE1 . . . . 3D 25 (3D 77)
Valentine Rd. E9 . . . . . 3F 51
Valentine Row
  SE1 . . . . . . 4D 25 (3D 77)
VALE OF HEALTH 5E 31
Vale of Health NW3 . . . 5F 31
Vale Pde. SW15 . . . . . 3A 112
Valerian Way E15 . . . . 2A 68
Vale Ri. NW11 . . . . 3B 30
Vale Rd. E7 . . . . 3D 55
  N4 . . . . 2E 35
Vale Row N5 . . . . 5D 35
Vale Royal N7 . . . . 4A 48
Vale Royal Ho. WC2. . . 4C 14
    (off Charing Cross Rd.)
Vale St. SE27 . . . . 3F 119
Valeswood Rd.
  BR1: Brom 5B 124
Vale Ter. N4 . . . . 1E 35
Valetta Gro. E13 . . . . . 1C 68
Valetta Rd. W3 . . . . 3A 70
Valette Ho. E9 . . . . 3E 51
Valette St. E9 . . . . 3E 51
Valiant Ho. E14 . . . . 3E 81
    (off Plevna St.)
  SE7 . . . . 1E 97
Vallance Rd. E1 . . . . . . 2C 64
  E2 . . . . 2C 64
Valley, The 1E 97
Valleyfield Rd.
  SW16 . . . . 5B 118
Valley Gro. SE7 . . . . . . 1E 97
Valley Leisure Cen., The
  . . . . 1F 97
    (off Valley, The)
Valley Rd. SW16 . . . . . 5B 118
Valley Side SE7 . . . . . . 1F 97
Valliere Rd. NW10 . . . . 2C 56
Val McKenzie Av. N7 . . 5C 34
Valmar Rd. SE5 . . . . . . 4E 91
Valmar Trad. Est.
  SE5 . . . . 4E 91
Valnay St. SW17 . . . . . 5B 116
Valois Ho. SE1 . . . . 5F 27
    (off Grange, The)
Valonia Gdns.
  SW18 . . . . 4D 100
Vanbrugh Castle SE3 . . 2A 96
    (off Maze Hill)
Vanbrugh Cl. E16 . . . . 4F 69
Vanbrugh Ct. SE11 . . . 5C 76
    (off Wincott St.)

Vanbrugh Flds. SE3 . . . 2B 96
Vanbrugh Hill SE3 . . . . 2B 96
  SE10 . . . . 1B 96
Vanbrugh Ho. E9 . . . . . 4E 51
    (off Loddiges Rd.)
Vanbrugh Pk.
  SE3 . . . . 3B 96
Vanbrugh Pk. Rd.
  SE3 . . . . 3B 96
Vanbrugh Pk. Rd. W.
  SE3 . . . . 3B 96
Vanbrugh Rd. W4 . . . . 4A 70
Vanbrugh Ter. SE3 . . . 4B 96
Vanbrugh Ho. E1 . . . . . 5F 11
    (off Folgate St.)
Vancouver Ho. E1 . . . . 2D 79
    (off Reardon Path)
Vancouver Rd.
  SE23 . . . . 2A 122
Vanderbilt Rd.
  SW18 . . . . 1D 115
Vanderbilt Vs. W12 . . . 3F 71
    (off Sterne St.)
Vandome Cl. E16 . . . . . 5D 69
Vandon Ct. SW1. . . . . . 5A 22
    (off Petty France)
Vandon Pas.
  SW1 . . . . . . 5A 22 (4E 75)
Vandon St.
  SW1 . . . . . . 5A 22 (4E 75)
Vandyke Cl. SW15 . . . . 5F 99
Vandyke Cross SE9 . . . 3F 111
Vandy St.
  EC2 . . . . 4D 11 (3A 64)
Vane Cl. NW3 . . . . 2F 45
Vane St. SW1 . . . . 5E 75
Vange Ho. W10 . . . . . . 4E 57
    (off Sutton Way)
Van Gogh Cl. E14 . . . . 4F 81
Vanguard Bldg. E14 . . . 3B 80
Vanguard Cl. E16 . . . . 4C 68
Vanguard Ct. SE5 . . . . 4A 92
Vanguard St. SE8 . . . . 4C 94
Vanguard Trad. Est.
  E15 . . . . 1E 53
Vanneck Sq. SW15 . . . 3C 98
Vanoc Gdns.
  BR1: Brom 4C 124
Vansittart Rd. E7 . . . . . 1B 54
Vansittart St. SE14. . . . 3A 94
Vanston Pl. SW6 . . . . . 3C 86
Vantage M. E14 . . . . . . 2E 81
    (off Preston's Rd.)
Vantage Pl. W8 . . . . . . 4C 72
Vantrey Ho. SE11 . . . . 5C 76
    (off Marylee Way)
Vant Rd. SW17 . . . . . . 5B 116
Varcoe Rd. SE16 . . . . . 1D 93
Vardens Rd. SW11 . . . 2F 101
Varden St. E1 . . . . 5D 65
Vardon Cl. W3 . . . . 5A 56
Vardon Ho. SE10 . . . . . 4E 95
Varley Ho. NW6 . . . . . . 5C 44
Varley Rd. E16 . . . . 5D 69
Varna Rd. SW6 . . . . . . 3A 86
Varndell Pl.
  NW1 . . . . . . 1F 5 (2E 61)
Varnishers Yd. N1 . . . . 1E 7
    (off York Rd.)
Vartry Rd. N15 . . . . 1F 35

Vassall Ho. E3 . . . . 2A 66
    (off Antill Rd.)
Vassall Rd. SW9 . . . . . 3C 90
Vat Ho. SW8. . . . . 3A 90
    (off Rita Rd.)
Vauban Est. SE16. . . . . 4B 78
Vauban St. SE16 . . . . . 4B 78
Vaudeville Ct. N4 . . . . . 4C 34
Vaudeville Theatre 5E 15
    (off Strand)
Vaughan Av. NW4 . . . . 1C 28
  W6 . . . . 5B 70
Vaughan Est. E2. . . . . . 1F 11
Vaughan Ho. SE1 . . . . . 3D 25
    (off Blackfriars Rd.)
  SW4 . . . . 5E 103
Vaughan Rd. E15 . . . . . 3B 54
  SE5 . . . . 5E 91
Vaughan St. SE16 . . . . 3B 80
Vaughan Way E1 . . . . . 1C 78
Vaughan Williams Cl.
  SE8 . . . . 3C 94
VAUXHALL. 2A 90
Vauxhall Bri. SW1 . . . . 1A 90
Vauxhall Bri. Rd.
  SW1 . . . . 4E 75
VAUXHALL CROSS . . . 1A 90
Vauxhall Distribution Pk.
  SW8 . . . . 2F 89
    (off Post Office Way)
Vauxhall Gro. SW8 . . . 2B 90
Vauxhall St. SE11 . . . . 1B 90
Vauxhall Wlk. SE11 . . . 1B 90
Vawdrey Cl. E1 . . . . 3E 65
Veda Rd. SE13. . . . . . . 2C 108
Velde Way SE22 . . . . . 3A 106
Velletri Ho. E2 . . . . 1F 65
    (off Mace St.)
Venables St. NW8 . . . . 3F 59
Vencourt Pl. W6 . . . . . . 5C 70
Venetian Rd. SE5 . . . . . 5E 91
Venetia Rd. N4 . . . . 1D 35
Venice Ct. NW8 . . . . . . 3F 59
    (off Fisherton St.)
  SE5 . . . . 3E 91
    (off Bowyer St.)
Venner Rd. SE26 . . . . . 5E 121
    (not continuous)
Venn Ho. N1 . . . . 5B 48
    (off Barnsbury Est.)
Venn St. SW4 . . . . 2E 103
Ventnor Rd. SE14. . . . . 3F 93
Venture Ct. SE12 . . . . . 5C 110
Venture Ho. W10 . . . . . 5F 57
    (off Bridge Cl.)
Venue St. E14. . . . . 4E 67
Venus Ho. E14 . . . . 5C 80
    (off Westferry Rd.)
Vera Lynn Cl. E7 . . . . . 1C 54
Vera Rd. SW6 . . . . 4A 86
Verbena Cl. E16. . . . . . 3B 68
Verbena Gdns. W6. . . . 1C 84
Verdant Ct. SE6 . . . . . . 5A 110
    (off Verdant La.)
Verdant La. SE6 . . . . . . 5A 110
Verdi Ho. W10 . . . . 1A 58
    (off Herries St.)
Verdun Rd. SW13 . . . . 2C 84
Vereker Rd. W14 . . . . . 1A 86
Vere St. W1 . . . 3D 13 (5D 61)

Verity Cl. W11 . . . . 1A 72
Vermeer Ct. E14 . . . . 4F 81
Vermeer Gdns.
  SE15 . . . . 2E 107
Vermont Ho. SW18 . . . 4D 101
Verney Ho. NW8 . . . . 3A 60
  (off Jerome Cres.)
Verney Rd. SE16 . . . . 2C 92
Verney St. NW10 . . . . 5A 28
Verney Way SE16. . . . . 1D 93
Vernon Ct. NW2 . . . . 5B 30
Vernon Ho. SE11 . . . . 1B 90
  WC1 . . . . 1E 15
  (off Vauxhall St.)
  (off Vernon Pl.)
Vernon M. W14 . . . . 5A 72
Vernon Pl.
  WC1 . . . . 1E 15 (4A 62)
Vernon Ri.
  WC1 . . . . . . 1A 8 (2B 62)
Vernon Rd. E3 . . . . 1B 66
  E11 . . . . 3A 40
  E15 . . . . 4A 54
  SW14 . . . . 1A 98
Vernon Sq.
  WC1 . . . . . . 1A 8 (2B 62)
Vernon St. W14 . . . . 5A 72
Vernon Yd. W11 . . . . 1B 72
Verona Ct. SE14 . . . . 2F 93
  (off Myers La.)
  W4 . . . . 1A 84
Verona Rd. E7 . . . . 4C 54
Veronica Ho. SE4 . . . . . 1B 108
Veronica Rd. SW17 . . . 2D 117
Verran Rd. SW12 . . . . . 5D 103
Verulam Av. E17. . . . . . . 1B 38
Verulam Bldgs. WC1 . . . 5A 8
Verulam Ct. NW9 . . . . . . 2C 28
Verulam Ho. W6 . . . . 3E 71
  (off Hammersmith Gro.)
Verulam St.
  WC1 . . . . 5B 8 (4C 62)
Verwood Ho. SW8 . . . . . 3B 90
  (off Cobbett St.)
Verwood Lodge E14 . . . . 4F 81
  (off Manchester Rd.)
Veryan Ct. N8 . . . . 1F 33
Vesage Ct. EC1 . . . . 1C 16
  (off Leather La.)
Vesey Path E14 . . . . 5D 67
Vespan Rd. W12 . . . . 3C 70
Vesta Ct. SE1 . . . . 4D 27
Vesta Rd. SE4 . . . . 5A 94
Vestris Rd. SE23 . . . . . . 2F 121
Vestry Ct. SW1 . . . . 4F 75
  (off Monck St.)
Vestry M. SE5 . . . . 4A 92
Vestry Rd. SE5 . . . . 4A 92
Vestry St. N1 . . 1B 10 (2F 63)
Vevey St. SE6 . . . . 2B 122
Viaduct Bldgs.
  EC1 . . . . 1C 16 (4C 62)
Viaduct Pl. E2 . . . . 2D 65
Viaduct St. E2 . . . . 2D 65
Vian St. SE13 . . . . 1D 109
Vibart Gdns. SW2 . . . . . 5B 104
Vibart Wlk. N1 . . . . 5A 48
  (off Outram Pl.)
Vicarage Av. SE3 . . . . . . 3C 96
Vicarage Ct. W8 . . . . 3D 73

Vicarage Cres.
  SW11 . . . . 4F 87
Vicarage Gdns. W8 . . . . . 2C 72
Vicarage Ga. W8 . . . . 2D 73
Vicarage Gro.
  SE5 . . . . 4F 91
Vicarage La. E15 . . . . 4A 54
Vicarage Path N8 . . . . . . 2A 34
Vicarage Rd. E10. . . . . . . 2C 38
  E15 . . . . 4B 54
  NW4 . . . . 1C 28
  SW14 . . . . 3A 98
Vicarage Wlk. SW11 . . . . 4F 87
Vicarage Way
  NW10 . . . . 5A 28
Vicars Cl. E9 . . . . 5E 51
  E15 . . . . 5C 54
Vicar's Hill SE13 . . . . . 2D 109
Vicars Oak Rd.
  SE19 . . . . 5A 120
Vicar's Rd. NW5. . . . . 2C 46
Viceroy Ct. NW8 . . . . 1A 60
  (off Prince Albert Rd.)
Viceroy Rd. SW8 . . . . 4A 90
Vickery Ct. EC1 . . . . 3A 10
  (off Mitchell St.)
Victor Cazalet Ho.
  N1 . . . . 5D 49
  (off Gaskin St.)
Victoria & Albert Mus.
  . . . . 4F 73
Victoria Arc. SW1 . . . . . . 5E 21
  (off Victoria St.)
Victoria Av. E6 . . . . 5F 55
  EC2 . . . . 1E 19 (4A 64)
Victoria Bldgs. E8 . . . . . 5D 51
  (off Mare St.)
Victoria Colonnade
  WC1 . . . . 1E 15
  (off Southampton Row)
Victoria Cotts. E1 . . . . . . 4C 64
  (off Deal St.)
Victoria Ct. SE26 . . . . . . 5E 121
  SE19 . . . . 5A 120
Victoria Dock Rd.
  E16 . . . . 5B 68
Victoria Dr. SW19. . . . . . 5F 99
Victoria Emb.
  EC4 . . . . 5A 16 (3A 76)
  SW1 . . . 3E 23 (3A 76)
  WC2 . . . . 3E 23 (3A 76)
Victoria Gdns. W11 . . . . 2C 72
Victoria Gro. W8 . . . . 4E 73
Victoria Gro. M.
  W2 . . . . 1C 72
Victoria Hall E16 . . . . . . 2C 82
  (off Wesley Av.,
  not continuous)
Victoria Ho. SW1 . . . . . . 1D 89
  (off Ebury Bri. Rd.)
  SW1 . . . . 5E 75
  (off Francis St.)
  SW8 . . . . 3A 90
  (off Sth. Lambeth Rd.)
  W3 . . . . 4A 56
Victoria Ind. Est.
  W3 . . . . 4A 56
Victoria Mans. NW10 . . . 4D 43
  SW8 . . . . 3A 90
  (off Sth. Lambeth Rd.)

Victoria M. E8 . . . . 3C 50
  NW6 . . . . 5C 44
  SW4 . . . . 2D 103
  SW18 . . . . 1E 115
Victoria Mills Studios
  E15 . . . . 5F 53
Victorian Gro.
  N16 . . . . 1A 50
Victorian Rd. N16 . . . . . . 5A 36
Victoria Palace Theatre
  . . . . 5F 21
  (off Victoria St.)
Victoria Pk. Ct. E9 . . . . . 4E 51
  (off Well St.)
Victoria Pk. Ind. Cen.
  E9 . . . . 4C 52
  (off Rothbury Rd.)
Victoria Pk. Rd. E9 . . . . . 5E 51
Victoria Pk. Sq. E2. . . . . 2E 65
Victoria Pas. NW8 . . . . . 3F 59
  (off Fisherton St.)
Victoria Pl. Shop. Cen.
  SW1 . . . . 5D 75
  (off Buckingham Pal. Rd.)
Victoria Point E13 . . . . . 1C 68
  (off Victoria Rd.)
Victoria Ri. NW6 . . . . 4E 45
  (off Hilgrove Rd.)
  SW4 . . . . 1D 103
Victoria Rd. E11. . . . . . . 1A 54
  E13 . . . . 1C 68
  N4 . . . . 2B 34
  NW6 . . . . 1B 58
  NW10 . . . . 4A 56
  W3 . . . . 4A 56
  W8 . . . . 4E 73
Victoria Sq. SW1 . . . . . . 5E 21
Victoria St. E15 . . . . 4A 54
  SW1 . . . . . 5E 21 (4E 75)
Victoria Ter. N4 . . . . 3C 34
  NW10 . . . . 3B 56
  SW8 . . . . 5D 89
Victoria Way SE7 . . . . . 1D 97
Victoria Wharf E2 . . . . . 1F 65
  (off Palmers Rd.)
  E14 . . . . 1A 80
  SE8 . . . . 1B 94
  (off Dragoon Rd.)
Victoria Works NW2 . . . 4D 29
Victoria Yd. E1. . . . . 5C 64
Victor Rd. NW10 . . . . . . 2D 57
Victor Wharf SE1 . . . . . . 1B 26
  (off Clink St.)
Victory Ct. W9 . . . . 3C 58
  (off Hermes Cl.)
Victory Pl. E14. . . . . 1A 80
  SE17 . . . . 5F 77
Victory Wlk. SE8 . . . . . . 4C 94
Victory Way SE16. . . . . 3A 80
Video Ct. N4. . . . . 2B 34
View Cl. N6 . . . . 2B 32
View Ct. SE12. . . . . 3E 125
View Cres. N8. . . . . 1F 33
Viewfield Rd. SW18. . . . 4B 100
View Rd. N6 . . . . 2B 32
Vigilant Cl. SE26 . . . . . . 4C 120
Vigo St. W1 . . . 5F 13 (1E 75)
Viking Cl. E3 . . . . 1A 66
Viking Ct. SW6. . . . . 2C 86
Viking Gdns. E6 . . . . 3F 69

Viking Ho. *SE5* 5E **91**
(off Denmark Rd.)
Viking Pl. E10. . . . . 3B **38**
Village, The
NW3 . . . . 4E **31**
SE7 . . . . 2E **97**
Village Cl. *NW3* 2F **45**
(off Belsize La.)
Village Ct. *SE3* 1A **110**
(off Hurren Cl.)
Village Way NW10 . . . 1A **42**
SE21 . . . . 4F **105**
Villa Rd. SW9. . . . . . . 1C **104**
Villas on the Heath
NW3 . . . . 5E **31**
Villa St. SE17 . . . . 1F **91**
Villa Wlk. *SE17*. 1F **91**
(off Inville Rd.)
Villiers Cl. E10. . . . . . . 4C **38**
Villiers M. NW2 . . . . . . 3C **42**
Villiers Rd. NW2 . . . . . 3C **42**
Villiers St.
WC2 . . . . 5D **15** (2A **76**)
Vincennes Est.
SE27 . . . . 4F **119**
Vincent Cl. SE16 . . . . . 3A **80**
Vincent Ct. N4 . . . . 3A **34**
SW9 . . . . 4B **90**
W1 . . . . 2A **12**
(off Seymour Pl.)
Vincent Gdns. NW2 . . . 5B **28**
Vincent Ho. *SW1* 5F **75**
(off Vincent Sq.)
Vincent M. E3 . . . . 1C **66**
Vincent Sq. SW1. . . . . . 5F **75**
Vincent Sq. Mans.
SW1 . . . . 5E **75**
(off Walcott St.)
Vincent St. E16. . . . . . . 4B **68**
SW1 . . . . 5F **75**
Vincent Ter. N1 . . . . . . 1D **63**
Vince St. EC1. . 2C **10** (2F **63**)
Vine Cotts. *E1* 5E **65**
(off Sidney Sq.)
Vine Ct. E1 . . . . 4C **64**
Vinegar St. E1 . . . . 2D **79**
Vinegar Yd.
SE1 . . . . 3D **27** (3A **78**)
Vine Hill EC1 . . 4B **8** (3C **62**)
Vine La. SE1 . . . 2E **27** (2A **78**)
Vineries, The SE6 . . . 1C **122**
Vine Rd. E15 . . . . 4B **54**
SW13 . . . . 1B **98**
Vinery Row W6 . . . . . . 4D **71**
Vine Sq. *W14*. 1B **86**
(off Star Rd.)
Vine St. EC3. . . 3F **19** (5B **64**)
W1 . . . . 5A **14** (1E **75**)
Vine St. Bri.
EC1 . . . . 4C **8** (3C **62**)
Vine Yd. SE1 . . . . 3A **26**
Vineyard Cl. SE6 . . . . 1C **122**
Vineyard Hill Rd.
SW19 . . . . 4B **114**
Vineyard M. EC1 . . . . . 5C **8**
Vineyard Wlk.
EC1 . . . . 3B **8** (3C **62**)
Viney Rd. SE13 . . . . . . 1D **109**
Vining St. SW9. . . . . . . 2C **104**
Vinopolis 1A **26** (2E **77**)

Vinson Ho. *N1* 1F **63**
(off Cranston Est.)
Vintners Ct.
EC4 . . . . 5A **18** (1E **77**)
Vintner's Pl. EC4 . . . . . 1E **77**
Viola Sq. W12 . . . . 1B **70**
Violet Cl. E16. . . . . 3A **68**
SE8 . . . . 2B **94**
Violet Hill NW8 . . . . . . 1E **59**
Violet Hill Ho. *NW8* . . . 1E **59**
(off Violet Hill, not continuous)
Violet Rd. E3 . . . . 3D **67**
F17 . . . . 1C **38**
Violet St. E2. . . . . 3D **65**
VIP Trading Est. SE7 . . . 5E **83**
Virgil Pl. W1 . . . . 4B **60**
Virgil St.
SE1 . . . . 5A **24** (4B **76**)
Virginia Ct. *SE16* 3F **79**
(off Eleanor Cl.)
WC1 . . . . 3C **6**
(off Burton St.)
Virginia Ho. *E14*. 1E **81**
(off Newby Pl.)
Virginia Rd.
E2. . . . . 2F **11** (2B **64**)
Virginia St. E1 . . . . 1C **78**
Virginia Wlk. SW2 . . . . 4B **104**
Visage *NW3* 4F **45**
(off Winchester Rd.)
Viscount Ct. *W2* 5C **58**
(off Pembridge Vs.)
Viscount St.
EC1 . . . . 4F **9** (3E **63**)
Vista, The SE9 . . . . . . 4F **111**
Vista Dr. IG4: Ilf 1F **41**
Vitae Apartments W6. . . 4C **70**
Vittoria Ho. *N1*. 5B **48**
(off High Rd.)
Vivian Av. NW4 . . . . . . 1D **29**
Vivian Comma Cl.
N4. . . . . 5D **35**
Vivian Mans. *NW4*. 1D **29**
(off Vivian Av.)
Vivian Rd. E3 . . . . 1A **66**
Vivian Sq. SE15 . . . . . 1D **107**
Vixen M. *E8* 4B **50**
(off Haggerston Rd.)
Vogans Mill SE1. . . . . . 3B **78**
Vogler Ho. *E1* 1E **79**
(off Cable St.)
Vollasky Ho. *E1* 4C **64**
(off Daplyn St.)
Voltaire Rd. SW4 . . . . . 1F **103**
Volt Av. NW10 . . . . 2A **56**
Voluntary Pl. E11. . . . . . 1C **40**
Vorley Rd. N19. . . . . . . 4E **33**
Voss St. E2. . . . . 2C **64**
Voyager Bus. Est.
SE16. . . . . 4C **78**
(off Spa Rd.)
Vue Cinema
Finchley Rd.. . . . . 3E **45**
(in O2 Centre)
Fulham Broadway . . . 3C **86**
Islington 1C **62**
Leicester Sq. 4D **14**
(off Leicester Pl.)
Shepherds Bush 3F **71**
Vulcan Rd. SE4 . . . . . . 5B **94**

Vulcan Sq. E14 . . . . . . 5D **81**
Vulcan Ter. SE4 . . . . . . 5B **94**
Vulcan Way N7. . . . . . . 3B **48**
Vyner Rd. W3. . . . . 1A **70**
Vyner St. E2. . . . . 5D **51**

W

W12 W12 . . . . 3F **71**
Wadding St. SE17 . . . . . 5F **77**
Waddington Rd. E15 . . . 2F **53**
Waddington St. E15. . . . 3F **53**
Wade Ho. *SE1* 3C **78**
(off Parkers Row)
Wadeson St. E2 . . . . . . 1D **65**
Wade's Pl. E14 . . . . 1D **81**
Wadham Gdns. NW3 . . . 5A **46**
Wadham Rd.
SW15 . . . . 2A **100**
Wadhurst Rd. SW8. . . . . 4E **89**
W4 . . . . 4A **70**
Wadley Rd. E11 . . . . . . 2A **40**
Wager St. E3 . . . . 3B **66**
Waghorn Rd. E13. . . . . . 5E **55**
Waghorn St. SE15 . . . . 1C **106**
Wagner St. SE15 . . . . . 3E **93**
Wainford St. SW19 . . . . 1F **113**
Wainwright Ho. *E1*. 2E **79**
(off Garnet St.)
Waite Davies Rd.
SE12 . . . . 5B **110**
Waite St. SE15. . . . . . . 2B **92**
Waithman St. *EC4* 3D **17**
(off Apothecary St.)
Wakefield Ct. SE26 . . . 5E **121**
Wakefield Gdns.
IG1: Ilf 1F **41**
Wakefield Ho. SE15. . . . 4C **92**
Wakefield M.
WC1 . . . . 2E **7** (2A **62**)
Wakefield Rd. N15. . . . . 1B **36**
Wakefield St. E6. . . . . . 5F **55**
WC1 . . . . 2E **7** (2A **62**)
Wakeford Cl. SW4 . . . . 3E **103**
Wakeham St. N1 . . . . . . 3F **49**
Wakehurst Rd.
SW11 . . . . 3A **102**
Wakeling St. E14 . . . . . 5A **66**
Wakelin Ho. *N1* 4D **49**
(off Sebbon St.)
SE23 . . . . 5A **108**
(off Brockley Pk.)
Wakelin Rd. E15 . . . . . 1A **68**
Wakeman Ho. NW10 . . . 2F **57**
(off Wakeman Rd.)
Wakeman Rd. NW10 . . . 2E **57**
Wakley St.
EC1 . . . . 1D **9** (2D **63**)
Walberswick St.
SW8 . . . . 3A **90**
Walbrook
EC4 . . . . 4B **18** (1F **77**)
(not continuous)
Walbrook Ct. *N1*. 1A **64**
(off Hemsworth St.)
Walbrook Wharf EC4 . . . 5A **18**
(off Bell Wharf La.)
Walburgh St. E1. . . . . . 5D **65**
Walcorde Av. SE17. . . . . 5E **77**

Walcot Gdns. *SE11* 5C **76**
(off Kennington Rd.)
Walcot Sq. *SE11* 5C **76**
Walcot St. *SW1* 5E **75**
Waldeck Gro. *SE27* 3D **119**
Waldemar Av. *SW6* 4A **86**
Waldemar Rd.
SW19 . . . . 5C **114**
Walden Ct. *SW8* 4F **89**
Walden Ho. *SW1* 5C **74**
(off Pimlico Rd.)
Waldenshaw Rd.
SE23 . . . . 1E **121**
Walden St. E1 . . . . 5D **65**
(not continuous)
Waldo Cl. *SW4* 3E **103**
Waldo Ho. *NW10* 2D **57**
(off Waldo Rd.)
Waldo Rd. *NW10* 2C **56**
(not continuous)
Waldram Cres.
SE23 . . . . 1E **121**
Waldram Pk. Rd.
SE23 . . . . 1F **121**
Waldram Pl. *SE23* 1E **121**
Waldron M. *SW3* 2F **87**
Waldron Rd. *SW18* . . . 3E **115**
Walerand Rd. *SE13* 5E **95**
Waleran Flats *SE1* 5A **78**
Wales Cl. *SE15* 3D **93**
Wales Farm Rd. *W3* 4A **56**
Waley St. E1 . . . . 4A **66**
Walford Ho. *E1* 5C **64**
Walford Rd. N16 . . . . . . 1A **50**
WALHAM GREEN 4C **86**
Walham Grn. Ct.
SW6 . . . . 3D **87**
(off Waterford Rd.)
Walham Gro. *SW6* 3C **86**
Walham Yd. *SW6* 3C **86**
Walker Ho.
NW1 . . . . 1B **6** (1F **61**)
Walker M. *SW2* 3C **104**
Walker's Ct. *W1* 4B **14**
Walkerscroft Mead
SE21 . . . . 1E **119**
Walkers Lodge *E14* 3E **81**
(off Manchester Rd.)
Walkers Pl. *SW15* 2A **100**
Walkinshaw St. *N1* 4E **49**
(off Rotherfield St.)
Wallace Collection
. . . . 2C **12** (5C **60**)
Wallace Ct. *NW1* 4A **60**
(off Old Marylebone Rd.)
Wallace Ho. *N7* 3B **48**
(off Caledonian Rd.)
Wallace Rd. N1 . . . . 3E **49**
Wallace Way *N19* 4F **33**
(off St John's Way)
Wallbutton Rd. *SE4* 5A **94**
Wallcote Av. *NW2* 3F **29**
Wall Ct. *N4* 3B **34**
(off Stroud Grn. Rd.)
Waller Rd. *SE14* 4F **93**
Waller Way *SE10* 3D **95**
Wallflower St. *W12* 1B **70**
Wallgrave Rd. *SW5* 5D **73**
Wallingford Av. *W10* 4F **57**
Wallis All. *SE1* 3A **26**

Wallis Cl. *SW11* 1F **101**
Wallis Ho. *SE14* 4A **94**
Wallis Rd. E9 . . . . 3B **52**
Wallis's Cotts. *SW2* . . . 5A **104**
Wallorton Gdns.
SW14 . . . . 2A **98**
Wallside *EC2* 1A **18**
Wall St. N1 . . . . 3F **49**
Wallwood Rd. *E11* 2F **39**
Wallwood St. *E14* 4B **66**
Walmer Ho. *W10* 5F **57**
(off Bramley Rd.)
Walmer Pl. *W1* 4B **60**
(off Walmer St.)
Walmer Rd. *W10* 5E **57**
W11 . . . . 1A **72**
Walmer St. *W1* 4B **60**
Walm La. *NW2* 3E **43**
Walney Wlk. N1 . . . . 3E **49**
Walnut Cl. *SE8* 2B **94**
Walnut Ct. *W8* 4D **73**
(off St Mary's Ga.)
Walnut Gdns. *E15* 2A **54**
Walnut Rd. *E10* 4C **38**
Walnut Tree Ho.
SW13 . . . . 4B **84**
Walnut Tree Cotts.
SW19 . . . . 5A **114**
Walnut Tree Ho.
SW10 . . . . 2D **87**
(off Tregunter Rd.)
Walnut Tree Rd.
SE10 . . . . 1A **96**
(not continuous)
Walnut Tree Wlk.
SE11 . . . . 5C **76**
Walpole Ct. *W14* 4F **71**
(off Blythe Rd.)
Walpole Ho. *SE1* 4B **24**
(off Westminster Bri. Rd.)
Walpole M. *NW8* 5F **45**
Walpole Rd. E6 . . . . 4E **55**
SW19 . . . . 5F **115**
Walpole St. *SW3* 1B **88**
Walsham Cl. N16 . . . . . . 3C **36**
Walsham Ho. *SE14* 5F **93**
SE17 . . . . 1F **91**
(off Blackwood St.)
Walsham Rd. *SE14* 5F **93**
Walsingham *NW8* 5F **45**
Walsingham Lodge
SW13 . . . . 4C **84**
Walsingham Mans.
SW6 . . . . 3D **87**
(off Fulham Rd.)
Walsingham Pl.
SW4 . . . . 4C **102**
Walsingham Rd. E5 . . . . 5C **36**
Walston Ho. *SW1* 1F **89**
(off Aylesford St.)
Walter Besant Ho. *E1* . . 2F **65**
(off Bancroft Rd.)
Walter Grn. Ho.
SE15 . . . . 4E **93**
(off Lausanne Rd.)
Walter Langley Ct.
SE16 . . . . 3E **79**
(off Brunel Rd.)
Walter Savill Twr. *E17* . . 1C **38**
(off Colchester Rd.)

Walters Cl. *SE17* 5F **77**
(off Brandon St.)
Walters Ho. *SE17* 2D **91**
(off Otto St.)
Walter St. E2 . . . . 2F **65**
Walters Way *SE23* 4F **107**
Walter Ter. E1 . . . . 5F **65**
Walterton Rd. W9 . . . . . . 3B **58**
Waltham Ho. NW8 . . . . . 5E **45**
Walton Cl. E5 . . . . 5F **37**
NW2 . . . . 4D **29**
SW8 . . . . 3A **90**
Walton Dr. NW10 . . . . . . 3A **42**
Walton Ho. *E2* 3F **11**
(off Montclare St.)
Walton Pl.
SW3 . . . . 5A **20** (4B **74**)
Walton Rd. E13 . . . . 1E **69**
Walton St. SW3 . . . . 5A **74**
Walton Vs. *N1* 4A **50**
(off Downham Rd.)
Walt Whitman Cl.
SE24 . . . . 2D **105**
WALWORTH 1E **91**
Walworth Pl. *SE17* 1E **91**
Walworth Rd. SE1 . . . . . 5E **77**
SE17 . . . . 5E **77**
Wanborough Dr.
SW15 . . . . 1D **113**
Wandle Ho.
BR1: Brom 5F **123**
NW8 . . . . 4A **60**
(off Penfold St.)
Wandle Meadow Nature Pk.
. . . . 5E **115**
Wandle Recreation Cen.
. . . . 4D **101**
Wandle Rd. SW17 . . . . 3A **116**
Wandle Way SW18 . . . 1D **115**
Wandon Rd. SW6 . . . . . 3D **87**
(not continuous)
Wandsdown Pl. *SW6* . . 3D **87**
WANDSWORTH 3D **101**
Wandsworth Bri.
SW6 . . . . 1D **101**
Wandsworth Bri. Rd.
SW6 . . . . 4D **87**
WANDSWORTH COMMON
. . . . 1B **116**
Wandsworth Comn. W. Side
SW18 . . . . 3E **101**
WANDSWORTH GYRATORY
. . . . 3D **101**
Wandsworth High St.
SW18 . . . . 3C **100**
Wandsworth Mus. 3D **101**
Wandsworth Plain
SW18 . . . . 3D **101**
Wandsworth Rd.
SW8 . . . . 1D **103**
Wangford Ho. *SW9* . . . 2D **105**
(off Loughborough Pk.)
Wanless Rd. SE24 . . . . 1E **105**
Wanley Rd. SE5 . . . . . . 2F **105**
Wanlip Rd. E13 . . . . . . 3D **69**
Wansbeck Rd. E9 . . . . . 4B **52**
Wansey St. SE17 . . . . . 5E **77**
WANSTEAD 1D **41**
Wanstead Gdns.
IG4: Ilf 1F **41**

Wanstead La. IG1: Ilf . . . 1F **41**
Wanstead Leisure Cen.
. . . . 1E **41**
Wanstead Pk. Av.
E12 . . . . 3F **41**
Wanstead Pk. Rd.
IG1: Ilf 1F **41**
Wanstead Pl. E11. . . 1C **40**
Wantage Rd. SE12. . . 3B **110**
WAPPING 2D **79**
Wapping Dock St.
E1. . . . . 2D **79**
Wapping High St. E1 . . 2C **78**
Wapping La. E1 . . . . . 1D **79**
Wapping Wall E1 . . . . 2E **79**
Warbeck Rd. W12 . . . 3D **71**
Warburton Cl. N1. . . . 3A **50**
(off Culford Rd.)
Warburton Ho. E8. . . . 5D **51**
(off Warburton St.)
Warburton Rd. E8. . . . 5D **51**
Warburton St. E8 . . . . 5D **51**
Wardalls Gro. SE14 . . 3E **93**
Wardalls Ho. SE8. . . . 2B **94**
(off Staunton St.)
Wardell Ho. SE10. . . . 2E **95**
(off Welland St.)
Warden Rd. NW5 . . . . 3C **46**
Wardens Gro.
SE1. . . . . 2F **25** (2E **77**)
Wardle St. E9 . . . . . . 2F **51**
Wardley St. SW18 . . . 5D **101**
Wardo Av. SW6 . . . . . 4A **86**
Wardour M. W1 . . . . . 3A **14**
Wardour St.
W1. . . . . 2A **14** (5E **61**)
Ward Point SE11 . . . . 5C **76**
Ward Rd. E15 . . . . . . 5F **53**
N19. . . . . 5E **33**
Wardrobe Pl. EC4. . . . 3E **17**
Wardrobe Ter. EC4 . . . 4E **17**
Wards Wharf App.
E16 . . . . 2F **83**
Wareham Ct. N1. . . . . 4A **50**
(off Hertford Rd.)
Wareham Ho. SW8. . . 3B **90**
Warfield Rd. NW10. . . 2F **57**
Warfield Yd. NW10. . . 2F **57**
(off Warfield Rd.)
Wargrave Av. N15 . . . 1B **36**
Wargrave Ho. E2. . . . . 2F **11**
(off Navarre St.)
Warham Rd. N4 . . . . . 1C **34**
Warham St. SE5. . . . . 3D **91**
Waring St. SE27. . . . . 4E **119**
Warley Cl. E10 . . . . . 3B **38**
Warley St. E2 . . . . . . 2F **65**
Warlock Rd. W9 . . . . 3B **58**
Warlters Cl. N7 . . . . . 1A **48**
Warlters Rd. N7 . . . . . 1A **48**
Warltersville Mans.
N19. . . . . 2A **34**
Warltersville Rd.
N19. . . . . 2A **34**
Warmington Cl. E5 . . . 5F **37**
Warmington Rd.
SE24 . . . . 4E **105**
Warmington St. E13. . . 3D **68**
Warmington Twr.
SE14 . . . . 4A **94**

Warmsworth NW1 . . . . 5E **47**
(off Pratt St.)
Warndon St. SE16 . . . 5F **79**
Warneford St. E9 . . . . 5D **51**
Warner Cl. E15. . . . . . 2A **54**
NW9 . . . . 2B **28**
Warner Ho.
BR3: Beck. 5D **123**
NW8 . . . . 2E **59**
SE13. . . . . 5D **95**
(off Russett Way)
Warner Pl. E2. . . . . . . 1C **64**
Warner Rd. SE5 . . . . . 4E **91**
Warner St.
EC1 . . . . 4B **8** (3C **62**)
Warner Ter. E14. . . . . 4D **67**
(off Broomfield St.)
Warner Yd. EC1 . . . . . 4B **8**
Warnford Ho. SW15. . . 4A **98**
(off Tunworth Cres.)
Warnham WC1 . . . . . . 2F **7**
(off Sidmouth St.)
Warnham Ho.
SW2 . . . . 5B **104**
(off Up. Tulse Hill)
Warple M. W3 . . . . . . 3A **70**
Warple Way W3 . . . . . 3A **70**
(not continuous)
Warren, The SE7 . . . . 2E **97**
Warren Av. E10. . . . . . 5E **39**
Warren Cl. SE21 . . . . 5E **105**
Warren Ct. NW1. . . . . . 3A **6**
(off Warren St.)
Warrender Rd. N19 . . . 5E **33**
Warren Dr., The E11 . . 2E **41**
Warren Gdns. E15 . . . . 2F **53**
Warren Ho. W14 . . . . . 5B **72**
(off Beckford Cl.)
Warren M. W1 . . . 4F **5** (3E **61**)
Warren Pl. E1. . . . . . . 5F **65**
(off Caroline St.)
Warren Rd. E10 . . . . . 5E **39**
E11. . . . . 1E **41**
(not continuous)
NW2 . . . . 4B **28**
Warren St. W1. . . 4F **5** (3E **61**)
Warren Wlk. SE7 . . . . 2E **97**
Warriner Gdns.
SW11 . . . . 4B **88**
Warrington Cres. W9 . . 3E **59**
Warrington Gdns.
W9 . . . . 3E **59**
Warspite Ho. E14. . . . . 5D **81**
(off Cahir St.)
Warspite Rd. SE18. . . . 4F **83**
Warton Rd. E15 . . . . . 4E **53**
Warwick W14. . . . . . . 5B **72**
(off Kensington Village)
Warwick Av. W2. . . . . 3E **59**
W9 . . . . 3D **59**
Warwick Bldg. SW8. . . 2D **89**
Warwick Chambers
W8 . . . . 4C **72**
(off Pater St.)
Warwick Ct. EC4. . . . . 3E **17**
(off Warwick La.)
WC1. . . . . . . 1A **16** (1D **62**)
Warwick Cres. W2 . . . 4E **59**
Warwick Dr. SW15. . . . 1D **99**
Warwick Est. W2 . . . . 4D **59**

Warwick Gdns. N4 . . . . 1E **35**
W14 . . . . 4B **72**
Warwick Gro. E5 . . . . 3D **37**
Warwick Ho. E16 . . . . . 2C **82**
(off Wesley Av.)
SW9 . . . . 5C **90**
Warwick Ho. St.
SW1 . . . . 1C **22** (2F **75**)
Warwick La.
EC4 . . . . 2E **17** (5D **63**)
Warwick Pas. EC4 . . . . 2E **17**
(off Old Bailey)
Warwick Pl. W9 . . . . . 4E **59**
Warwick Pl. Nth.
SW1 . . . . 5E **75**
Warwick Rd. E12 . . . . 2F **55**
E15. . . . . 0B **54**
SW5 . . . . 5C **72**
W14 . . . . 5B **72**
Warwick Row
SW1 . . . . 5E **21** (4D **75**)
Warwickshire Path
SE8. . . . . 3B **94**
Warwickshire Rd.
N16. . . . . 1A **50**
Warwick Sq.
EC4 . . . . 2E **17** (5D **63**)
SW1 . . . . 1E **89**
(not continuous)
Warwick Sq. M. SW1. . . 5E **75**
Warwick St.
W1 . . . . 4A **14** (1E **75**)
Warwick Ter. E17. . . . . 1F **39**
(off Lea Bri. Rd.)
Warwick Way SW1 . . . 1D **89**
Warwick Yd.
EC1 . . . . 4A **10** (3E **63**)
Washington Cl. E3. . . . 2D **67**
Washington Rd. E6 . . . 4E **55**
SW13 . . . . 3C **84**
Wastdale Rd. SE23 . . . 1F **121**
Waterbank Rd.
SE6. . . . . 3D **123**
Water Brook La.
NW4 . . . . 1E **29**
Watercress Pl. N1 . . . . 4A **50**
Waterden Cres. E15. . . 2C **52**
Waterden Rd. E15. . . . 2C **52**
Waterer Ho. SE6 . . . . 4E **123**
Waterfall Cotts.
SW19 . . . . 5F **115**
Waterfall Rd. SW19. . . 5F **115**
Waterfall Ter. SW17. . . 5A **116**
Waterford Ho. W11 . . . 1B **72**
(off Kensington Pk. Rd.)
Waterford Rd. SW6 . . . 3D **87**
(not continuous)
Waterford Way
NW10 . . . . 2D **43**
Waterfront Studios Bus. Cen.
E16 . . . . 2C **82**
(off Dock Rd.)
Water Gdns., The W2 . . 5A **60**
Watergate
EC4 . . . . 4D **17** (1D **77**)
Watergate St. SE8 . . . . 2C **94**
Watergate Wlk.
WC2 . . . . 1E **23** (2A **76**)
Waterhead NW1 . . . . . . 1F **5**
(off Varndell St.)

Waterhouse Cl. E16 . . . . 4F 69
NW3 . . . . 2F 45
W6 . . . . 5F 71
Waterhouse Sq.
EC1 . . . . 1B 16 (4C 62)
Wateridge Cl. E14 . . . . . 4C 80
Water La. E15 . . . . 3A 54
EC3 . . . . 5E 19 (1A 78)
NW1 . . . . 4D 47
SE14 . . . . 3E 93
Waterloo Bri.
SE1 . . . . 5A 16 (1B 76)
Waterloo Cl. E9 . . . . 2E 51
Waterloo Gdns. E2 . . . . . 1E 65
Waterloo Pas. NW6 . . . . 4B 44
Waterloo Pl.
SW1 . . . . 1B 22 (2F 75)
Waterloo Rd. E6 . . . . 4E 55
E7 . . . . 2B 54
E10 . . . . 2C 38
NW2 . . . . 3C 28
SE1 . . . . 1A 24 (2B 76)
Waterloo Ter. N1 . . . . . . 4D 49
Waterlow Ct. NW11 . . . . 2D 31
Waterlow Rd. N19 . . . . . 3E 33
Waterman Bldg. E14 . . . . 3B 80
Waterman St. SW15 . . . . 1F 99
Watermans Wlk. EC4 . . . 5B 18
. . . . 3A 80
Waterman Way E1 . . . . . 2D 79
Watermead Ho. E9 . . . . . 2A 52
Watermead La.
SW6 . . . . 5E 87
Watermead Rd. SE6 . . . . 4E 123
Water M. SE13 . . . . 2E 107
Watermint Quay N16 . . . 2C 36
Water's Edge SW6 . . . . . 4E 85
(off Palemead Cl.)
Waterside E17 . . . . 1E 37
W2 . . . . 4F 59
(off Nth. Wharf Rd.)
Waterside Cl. E3 . . . . . . 5B 52
SE16 . . . . 3C 78
Waterside Ho. E14 . . . . . 3D 81
(off Admirals Way)
Waterside Pl. NW1 . . . . . 5C 46
Waterside Point
SW11 . . . . 3A 88
Waterside Twr. SW6 . . . . 5E 87
(off Boulevard, The)
Waterside Way
SW17 . . . . 4E 115
Waterson St.
E2 . . . . 1E 11 (2A 64)
Waters Pl. SW15 . . . . . . 5E 85
Waters Rd. SE6 . . . . 3A 124
Water St. WC2 . . . . 4B 16
Water Twr. Pl. N1 . . . . . . 5C 48
Waterview Ho. E14 . . . . . 4A 66
(off Carr St.)
Waterworks La. E5 . . . . . 4F 37
Waterworks Rd.
SW2 . . . . 4B 104
Watford Cl. SW11 . . . . . 4A 88
Watford Rd. E16 . . . . . . 4C 68
Watford Way NW4 . . . . . 1D 29
Watkins Ho. E14 . . . . . . 3E 81
(off Manchester Rd.)
Watkinson Rd. N7 . . . . . 3B 48
Watling Ct. EC4 . . . . 3A 18

Watling Gdns. NW2 . . . . 3A 44
Watling St.
EC4 . . . . 3A 18 (5E 63)
SE15 . . . . 2A 92
Watlington Gro.
SE26 . . . . 5A 122
Watney Mkt. E1 . . . . 5D 65
Watney St. E1 . . . . 5D 65
Watson Cl. N16 . . . . 2F 49
Watson's M. W1 . . . . 4A 60
Watsons St. SE8 . . . . . . 3C 94
Watson St. E13 . . . . 1D 69
Wattisfield Rd. E5 . . . . . 5E 37
Watts Gro. E3 . . . . 4C 66
Watts Point E13 . . . . 5C 54
(off Brooks Rd.)
Watts St. E1 . . . . 2D 79
SE15 . . . . 4B 92
Wat Tyler Rd. SE3 . . . . . 5E 95
SE10 . . . . 5E 95
Wavel Ct. E1 . . . . 2E 79
(off Garnet St.)
Wavelengths Leisure Pool
. . . . 3C 94
Wavel M. NW6 . . . . 4D 45
Wavel Pl. SE26 . . . . 4B 120
Wavendon Av. W4 . . . . . 1A 84
Waveney Av. SE15 . . . . . 2D 107
Waveney Cl. E1 . . . . 2C 78
Waveney Ho. SE15 . . . . . 2D 107
Waverley Ct. NW3 . . . . . 3B 46
NW6 . . . . 4A 44
SE26 . . . . 5E 121
Waverley Pl. N4 . . . . 4D 35
NW8 . . . . 1F 59
Waverley Rd. N8 . . . . . . 1A 34
Waverton Ho. E3 . . . . . . 5B 52
Waverton Rd. SW18 . . . . 5E 101
Waverton St.
W1 . . . . 1D 21 (2C 74)
Wavertree Ct. SW2 . . . . 1A 118
Wavertree Rd. SW2 . . . . 1B 118
Waxham NW3 . . . . 2B 46
Waxlow Rd. NW10 . . . . . 1A 56
Wayford St. SW11 . . . . . 5A 88
Wayland Av. E8 . . . . 2C 50
Wayland Ho. SW9 . . . . . 5C 90
(off Robsart St.)
Waylett Ho. SE11 . . . . . . 1B 90
(off Loughborough St.)
Waylett Pl. SE27 . . . . . . 3D 119
Wayman Ct. E8 . . . . 3D 51
Wayne Kirkum Way
NW6 . . . . 2B 44
Waynflete Sq. W10 . . . . 1F 71
Waynflete St. SW18 . . . . 2E 115
Wayside NW11 . . . . 3A 30
Weald Cl. SE16 . . . . 1D 93
Weald Sq. E5 . . . . 4C 36
Weardale Rd. SE13 . . . . 2F 109
Wearmouth Ho. E3 . . . . . 4B 66
(off Joseph St.)
Wear Pl. E2 . . . . 2D 65
(not continuous)
Wearside Rd. SE13 . . . . 2D 109
Weatherbury W2 . . . . . . 5C 58
(off Talbot Rd.)
Weatherbury Ho. N19 . . . 5F 33
(off Wedmore St.)
Weatherley Cl. E3 . . . . . 4B 66

Weavers Almshouses
E11 . . . . 1B 40
(off Cambridge Rd.)
Weavers Ho. E11 . . . . . . 1C 40
(off New Wanstead)
Weavers La.
SE1 . . . . 2E 27 (2A 78)
Weavers Ter. SW6 . . . . . 2C 86
(off Micklethwaite Rd.)
Weaver St. E1 . . . . 3C 64
Weavers Way NW1 . . . . . 5F 47
Weaver Wlk.
SE27 . . . . 4E 119
Webb Cl. W10 . . . . 3E 57
Webber Row SE1 . . . . . . 5C 24
Webber St.
SE1 . . . . 3C 24 (3C 76)
Webb Est. E5 . . . . 2C 36
Webb Gdns. E13 . . . . . . 3C 68
Webb Ho. SW8 . . . . 3F 89
Webb Pl. NW10 . . . . 2B 56
Webb Rd. SE3 . . . . 2B 96
Webb's Rd. SW11 . . . . . 2B 102
Webb St.
SE1 . . . . 5D 27 (4A 78)
Webheath NW6 . . . . 4B 44
(not continuous)
Webster Rd. E11 . . . . . . 5E 39
SE16 . . . . 4C 78
Weddell Ho. E1 . . . . 3F 65
(off Duckett St.)
Wedderburn Rd. NW3 . . 2F 45
Wedgewood Ho.
SW1 . . . . 1D 89
(off Churchill Gdns.)
Wedgewood M.
W1 . . . . 3C 14 (5F 61)
Wedgwood Ho. E2 . . . . . 2F 65
(off Warley St.)
SE11 . . . . 4C 76
(off Lambeth Wlk.)
Wedgwood Wlk.
NW6 . . . . 2D 45
(off Dresden Cl.)
Wedlake St. W10 . . . . . . 3A 58
Wedmore Gdns. N19 . . . 4F 33
Wedmore M. N19 . . . . . . 5F 33
Wedmore Rd. N19 . . . . . 5F 33
Weech Rd. NW6 . . . . 1C 44
Weedington Rd. NW5 . . . 2C 46
Weedon Ho. W12 . . . . . . 5C 56
Weekley Sq. SW11 . . . . . 1F 101
Weigall Rd. SE12 . . . . . . 3C 110
Weighhouse St.
W1 . . . . 3C 12 (5C 60)
Weimar St. SW15 . . . . . 1A 100
Weir Rd. SW12 . . . . 5E 103
SW19 . . . . 3D 115
Weir's Pas.
NW1 . . . . 1C 6 (2F 61)
Weiss Rd. SW15 . . . . . . 1F 99
Welbeck Av.
BR1: Brom 4C 124
Welbeck Cl. W14 . . . . . . 5B 72
(off Addison Bri. Pl.)
Welbeck Ho. W1 . . . . . . 2D 13
(off Welbeck St.)
Welbeck Rd. E6 . . . . 2F 69
Welbeck St.
W1 . . . . 1C 12 (4C 60)

Welbeck Way
W1. . . . . 2D **13** (5D **61**)
Welby Ho. N19 . . . . 2F **33**
Welby St. SE5 . . . . 4D **91**
Welcome Ct. E17. . . . . 2C **38**
(off Boundary Rd.)
Welfare Rd. E15. . . . . 4A **54**
Welford Cl. E5. . . . . . . 5F **37**
Welford Ct. NW1 . . . . 4D **47**
(off Castlehaven Rd.)
SW8 . . . . 5E **89**
W9 . . . . 4C **58**
(off Elmfield Way)
Welford Pl. SW19. . . . . 4A **114**
Welham Rd.
SW16 . . . . 5D **117**
SW17 . . . . 5C **116**
Welland Ct. SE6. . . . 2B **122**
(off Oakham Cl.)
Welland Ho. SE15 . . . 2E **107**
Welland M. E1 . . . . . . 2C **78**
Welland St. SE10 . . . . 2E **95**
Wellby Ct. E13 . . . . . . 5E **55**
Well Cl. NW6 . . . . . . 4B **118**
Wellclose Sq. E1 . . . . 1C **78**
Wellclose St. E1 . . . . . 1C **78**
E3 . . . . 1A **66**
(off Driffield Rd)
Wellcome Cen. for
Medical Science. 3B **6**
Wellcome Mus. 2A **16**
(off Portugal St.)
Well Cott. Cl. E11. . . . . 1E **41**
Well Ct. EC4 . . . 3A **18** (5E **63**)
(not continuous)
Weller Ho. SE16. . . . 3C **78**
(off George Row)
Weller St.
SE1. . . . . . . 3F **25** (3E **77**)
Welles Ct. E14 . . . . . 1C **80**
(off Premiere Pl.)
Wellesley Av. W6. . . . 4D **71**
Wellesley Cl. SE7. . . . 1E **97**
Wellesley Ct. NW2. . . . 4C **28**
W9 . . . . 2E **59**
Wellesley Ho. NW1 . . . 2C **6**
(off Wellesley Pl.)
SW1 . . . . 1D **89**
(off Ebury Bri. Rd.)
Wellesley Mans.
W14 . . . . 1B **86**
(off Edith Vs.)
Wellesley Pl.
NW1 . . . . . . 2B **6** (2F **61**)
NW5 . . . . 2C **46**
Wellesley Rd. E11 . . . . 1C **40**
E17 . . . . 1C **38**
NW5 . . . . 2C **46**
Wellesley St. E1 . . . . . 4F **65**
Wellesley Ter.
N1 . . . . 1A **10** (2E **63**)
Wellfield Rd. SW16 . . . 4A **118**
Wellfield Wlk.
SW16 . . . . 5B **118**
(not continuous)
Wellfit St. SE24 . . . . . 1D **10C**
Wellgarth Rd. NW11 . . . 3D **31**
Wellington Arch
. . . . 3C **20** (3C **74**)
Wellington Av. N15 . . . 1B **36**

Wellington Bldgs.
SW1 . . . . 1C **88**
Wellington Cl. SE14. . . 4F **93**
W11 . . . . 5C **58**
Wellington Ct. NW8 . . . 1F **59**
(off Wellington Rd.)
SW1 . . . . 3B **74**
(off Knightsbridge)
SW6 . . . . 4D **87**
(off Maltings Pl.)
Wellington Gdns.
SE7. . . . . 2E **97**
Wellington Gro. SE10. . 3F **95**
Wellington Ho. F16. . . 2C **82**
(off Pepys Cres.)
NW3 . . . . 3B **46**
(off Eton Rd.)
Wellington Mans.
E10. . . . . 3C **38**
Wellington M. N7. . . . 3B **48**
(off Roman Way)
SE7. . . . . 2E **97**
SE22 . . . . 2C **106**
SW16 . . . . 3F **117**
Wellington Monument
. . . . 3C **20**
Wellington Mus.
. . . . 3C **20** (3C **74**)
Wellington Pk. Est.
NW2 . . . . 4C **28**
Wellington Pas. E11 . . . 1C **40**
(off Wellington Rd.)
Wellington Pl. NW8 . . . 2F **59**
Wellington Rd. E7 . . . . 1B **54**
E10 . . . . 3A **38**
E11 . . . . 1C **40**
NW8 . . . . 1F **59**
NW10 . . . . 2F **57**
SW19 . . . . 2C **114**
Wellington Row E2 . . . 2B **64**
Wellington Sq. SW3 . . . 1B **88**
Wellington St.
WC2 . . . . . . 4F **15** (1B **76**)
Wellington Ter. E1 . . . 2D **79**
W2 . . . . 1C **72**
Wellington Way E3. . . 2C **66**
Wellmeadow Rd.
SE13 . . . . 4A **110**
(not continuous)
Well Pl. NW3 . . . . 5F **31**
Well Rd. NW3 . . . . 5F **31**
Wells Ct. NW6 . . . . . 1C **58**
(off Cambridge Av.)
Wells Gdns. IG1: IIf . . . 2F **41**
Wells Ho.
BR1: Brom 5D **125**
(off Pike Cl.)
EC1 . . . . 1C **8**
(off Spa Grn. Est.)
SE16. . . . . 4E **79**
(off Howland Est.)
Wells Ho. Rd. NW10 . . 4A **56**
Wells M. W1 . . . 1A **14** (4E **61**)
Wells Pk. Rd. SE26 . . . 3C **120**
Wells Pl. SW18 . . . . . . 5E **101**
Wells Ri. NW8 . . . . 5B **46**
Wells Rd. W12 . . . . 3E **71**
Wells Sq.
WC1 . . . . 2F **7** (2B **62**)
Wells St. W1 . . . 1F **13** (4E **61**)

Wells Ter. N4 . . . . 4C **34**
Well St. E9 . . . . 4E **51**
E15 . . . . 3A **54**
Wells Way SE5 . . . . . . 2F **91**
SW7 . . . . 4F **73**
Wells Yd. N7 . . . . 2C **48**
Well Wlk. NW3 . . . . . . 1F **45**
Welmar M. SW4 . . . . . 3F **103**
(off Northbourne Rd.)
Welsford St. SE1 . . . . 5C **78**
(not continuous)
Welsh Cl. E13 . . . . . . 2C **68**
Welsh Harp Nature Reserve
. . . . 3A **28**
Welsh Ho. F1. . . . . . . 2D **79**
(off Wapping La.)
Welshpool Ho. E8 . . . 5C **50**
(off Welshpool St.)
Welshpool St. E8 . . . . 5C **50**
(not continuous)
Welshside NW9 . . . . . 1A **28**
(off Ruthin Cl.)
Welshside Wlk. NW9. . . 1A **28**
Welstead Ho. E1 . . . . 5D **65**
(off Cannon St. Rd.)
Welstead Way
W4 . . . . 5B **70**
Weltje Rd. W6 . . . . . . 5C **70**
Welton Ct. SE5. . . . . . 4A **92**
Welton Ho. E1 . . . . . . 4F **65**
(off Stepney Way)
Welwyn St. E2 . . . . . . 2E **65**
Wembury M. N6. . . . . 2E **33**
Wembury Rd. N6 . . . . 2D **33**
Wendell Rd. W12. . . . . 4B **70**
Wendle Ct. SW8. . . . . 2A **90**
Wendling NW5 . . . . . . 2B **46**
Wendon St. E3 . . . . . . 5B **52**
Wendover SE17 . . . . . 1A **92**
(not continuous)
Wendover Ct. NW2 . . . 5C **30**
W1 . . . . 1B **12**
(off Chiltern St.)
Wendover Ho. W1 . . . . 1B **12**
(off Chiltern St.)
Wendover Rd. NW10 . . 1B **56**
SE9 . . . . 1F **111**
Wenham Ho. SW8 . . . . 3E **89**
Wenlake Ho. EC1 . . . . . 3F **9**
(off Old St.)
Wenlock Barn Est. N1 . . 1F **63**
(off Wenlock St.)
Wenlock Ct.
N1 . . . . 1C **10** (1F **63**)
Wenlock Rd.
N1 . . . . 1A **10** (1E **63**)
Wenlock St.
N1 . . . . 1A **10** (1E **63**)
Wennington Rd. E3 . . . 1F **65**
Wensdale Ho. E5 . . . . 4C **36**
Wentland Cl. SE6. . . . 2F **123**
Wentland Rd. SE6 . . . 2F **123**
Wentworth Ct.
SW18 . . . . 4D **101**
(off Garratt La.)
W6 . . . . 2A **86**
(off Rayner Wlk.)
Wentworth Cres.
SE15 . . . . 3C **92**

Wentworth Dwellings
E1 . . . . 2F **19**
(off Wentworth St.)
Wentworth M. E3 . . . . . 3A **66**
Wentworth Rd. E12. . . 1F **55**
NW11 . . . . 1B **30**
Wentworth St.
E1 . . . . 2F **19** (5B **64**)
Werrington St.
NW1 . . . . 1B **6** (1E **61**)
Werter Rd. SW15 . . . 2A **100**
Wesleyan Pl.
NW5 . . . . 1D **47**
Wesley Av. E16 . . . . . 2C **82**
NW10 . . . . 2A **56**
Wesley Cl. N7 . . . . . . 4B **34**
SE17 . . . . 5D **77**
Wesley Ct. SE16 . . . . 4D **79**
Wesley Rd. E10 . . . . . 2E **39**
Wesley's House, Chapel &
Mus. of Methodism
. . . . 3C **10** (3F **63**)
Wesley Sq. W11 . . . . . 5A **58**
Wesley St.
W1 . . . . 1C **12** (4C **60**)
Wessex Gdns. NW11 . . 3A **30**
Wessex Ho. SE1 . . . . 1B **92**
Wessex St. E2 . . . . . . 2E **65**
Wessex Way NW11 . . 3A **30**
Wesson Mead SE5 . . . 3E **91**
(off Camberwell Rd.)
Westacott Cl. N19 . . . 3F **33**
W. Arbour St. E1 . . . . 5F **65**
West Av. NW4 . . . . . . 1F **29**
West Bank N16 . . . . . 2A **36**
WEST BECKTON 5F **69**
Westbere Rd. NW2 . . 1A **44**
West Block SE1 . . . . . 4A **24**
(off Addington St.)
Westbourne Bri. W2 . . 4E **59**
Westbourne Cres.
W2 . . . . 1F **73**
Westbourne Cres. M.
W2 . . . . 1F **73**
(off Westbourne Cres.)
Westbourne Dr.
SE23 . . . . 2F **121**
Westbourne Gdns.
W2 . . . . 5D **59**
WESTBOURNE GREEN
. . . . 5B **58**
Westbourne Green
Sports Complex . . 4C **58**
Westbourne Gro. W2 . 5C **58**
W11 . . . . 1B **72**
Westbourne Gro. M.
W11 . . . . 5C **58**
Westbourne Gro. Ter.
W2 . . . . 5D **59**
Westbourne Ho.
SW1 . . . . 1D **89**
(off Ebury Bri. Rd.)
Westbourne Pk. Pas.
W2 . . . . 4C **58**
(not continuous)
Westbourne Pk. Rd.
W2 . . . . 4C **58**
W11 . . . . 5A **58**
Westbourne Pk. Vs.
W2 . . . . 4C **58**

Westbourne Rd. N7 . . . 3B **48**
SE26 . . . . 5F **121**
Westbourne St. W2 . . 1F **73**
Westbourne Ter.
SE23 . . . . 2F **121**
(off Westbourne Dr.)
W2 . . . . 5E **59**
Westbourne Ter. M.
W2 . . . . 5E **59**
Westbourne Ter. Rd.
W2 . . . . 4D **59**
Westbourne Ter. Rd. Bri.
W2 . . . . 4E **59**
(off Westbourne Ter. Rd.)
Westbridge Cl.
W12 . . . . 3C **70**
Westbridge Rd.
SW11 . . . . 4F **87**
WEST BROMPTON . . . 2E **87**
Westbrook Ho. E2 . . . . 2E **65**
(off Victoria Pk. Sq.)
Westbrook Rd. SE3 . . 4D **97**
Westbury Rd. E7 . . . . 3D **55**
Westbury St. SW8 . . . 5E **89**
(off Portslade Rd.)
Westbury Ter. E7 . . . . 3D **55**
W. Carriage Dr. W2 . . 1A **74**
(not continuous)
W. Central St.
WC1 . . . . . . 2D **15** (5A **62**)
West Cen. Av. NW10 . 3D **57**
Westcliffe Apartments
W2 . . . . 4F **59**
Westcombe Ct. SE3 . . 3B **96**
Westcombe Hill SE3 . . 3C **96**
SE10 . . . . 3C **96**
Westcombe Pk. Rd.
SE3 . . . . 3A **96**
Westcote Rd. SW16 . . 5E **117**
West Cotts. NW6 . . . . 2C **44**
Westcott Cl. N15 . . . . 1B **36**
Westcott Ho. E14 . . . . 1C **80**
Westcott Rd. SE17 . . . 2D **91**
Westcroft NW2 . . . . . 1A **44**
Westcroft Est. NW2 . . 1A **44**
Westcroft Sq. W6 . . . . 5C **70**
Westcroft Way NW2 . . 1A **44**
W. Cromwell Rd.
SW5 . . . . 1B **86**
W14 . . . . 1B **86**
W. Cross Route W10 . 1F **71**
W11 . . . . 1F **71**
W12 . . . . 1F **71**
Westdean Av. SE12 . . 1D **125**
Westdean Cl. SW18 . . 4D **101**
Westdown Rd. E15 . . . 1E **53**
SE6 . . . . 5C **108**
West Dr. SW16 . . . . . 4E **117**
WEST DULWICH 2F **119**
W. Eaton Pl. SW1 . . . . 5C **74**
W. Eaton Pl. M. SW1 . . 5C **74**
(off W. Eaton Pl.)
W. Ella Rd. NW10 . . . . 4A **42**
W. End Av. E10 . . . . . . 1F **39**
W. End Ct. NW6 . . . . . 4D **45**
W. End La. NW6 . . . . . 2C **44**
(not continuous)
W. End Quay W2 . . . . 4F **59**
(off Harbet Rd.)
Westerdale Rd. SE10 . . 1C **96**

Westerham NW1 . . . . . 5E **47**
(off Bayham St.)
Westerham Ho. SE1 . . 5C **26**
Westerham Rd. E10 . . 2D **39**
Westerley Cres.
SE26 . . . . 5B **122**
Western Av. NW11 . . . 1F **29**
W5 . . . . 5A **56**
Western Beach Apartments
E16 . . . . 1C **82**
Western Ct. NW6 . . . . 1B **58**
Western Gateway
E16 . . . . 1C **82**
Western La. SW12 . . . 5C **102**
Western M. W9 . . . . . . 3B **58**
Western Pl. SE16 . . . . 3E **79**
Western Rd. E13 . . . . 1E **69**
E17 . . . . 1F **39**
SW9 . . . . 1C **104**
Western Ter. W6 . . . . 1C **84**
(off Chiswick Mall)
Westferry Cir. E14 . . . 2B **80**
Westferry Rd. E14 . . . 1B **80**
Westfield Cl. SW10 . . 3E **87**
Westfield Ct. NW10 . . . 2F **57**
(off Chamberlayne Rd.)
Westfield Ho. SE16 . . . 5F **79**
(off Rotherhithe New Rd.)
Westfields SW13 . . . 1B **98**
Westfields Av. SW13 . . 1A **98**
Westfield St. SE18 . . . 4F **83**
Westfield Way E1 . . . . 2A **66**
West Gdn. Pl. W2 . . . . 5A **60**
West Gdns. E1 . . . . . . 1D **79**
SW17 . . . . 5A **116**
Westgate Cen., The
E8 . . . . 5D **51**
(off Bocking St.)
Westgate Cl. SE12 . . . 1C **124**
(off Burnt Ash Hill)
SW9 . . . . 1C **104**
(off Canterbury Cres.)
Westgate M. W10 . . . 3A **58**
(off West Row)
Westgate St. E8 . . . . . 5D **51**
Westgate Ter. SW10 . . 2D **87**
West Gro. SE10 . . . . . 4E **95**
Westgrove La. SE10 . . 4E **95**
W. Halkin St.
SW1 . . . . 5B **20** (4C **74**)
West Hallowes SE9 . . 1F **125**
WEST HAM 5B **54**
W. Ham La. E15 . . . . . 4F **53**
(not continuous)
WEST HAMPSTEAD . . 3D **45**
W. Hampstead M.
NW6 . . . . 3D **45**
West Ham United FC . . 1E **69**
W. Harding St.
EC4 . . . . 2C **16** (5C **62**)
W. Heath Av. NW11 . . 3C **30**
W. Heath Cl. NW3 . . . . 5C **30**
W. Heath Ct. NW11 . . . 3C **30**
W. Heath Dr. NW11 . . . 3C **30**
W. Heath Gdns. NW3 . 4C **30**
W. Heath Rd. NW3 . . . 4C **30**
WEST HENDON 2C **28**
WEST HILL 4B **100**
West Hill SW15 . . . . . 5F **99**

W. Hill Ct. N6 . . . . 5C 32
W. Hill Pk. N6 . . . . 4B 32
(not continuous)
W. Hill Rd. SW18 . . . . 4B 100
Westhope Ho. E2 . . . . . 2C 64
(off Derbyshire St.)
Westhorne Av. SE9 . . . 4E 111
SE12 . . . . 5C 110
Westhorpe Rd. SW15 . . 1E 99
West Ho. Cl. SW19 . . . 1A 114
W. India Av. E14 . . . . . 2C 80
W. India Dock Rd.
E14 . . . . 1B 80
(not continuous)
W. India Ho. E14 . . . . . 1C 80
(off W. India Dock Rd.)
WEST KENSINGTON . . 5B 72
W. Kensington Ct.
W14 . . . . 1B 86
(off Edith Vs.)
W. Kensington Mans.
W14 . . . . 1B 86
(off Beaumont Cres.)
WEST KILBURN 2B 58
Westlake SE16 . . . . . . 5E 79
(off Rotherhithe New Rd.)
Westland Pl.
N1 . . . . 1B 10 (2F 63)
Westlands Ter.
SW12 . . . . 4E 103
West La. SE16 . . . . 3D 79
Westleigh Av. SW15 . . 3D 99
Westleigh Ct. E11 . . . . 1C 40
West Lodge E16 . . . . . 2C 82
(off Britannia Ga.)
West Lodge Crematorium &
Chapel NW10 . . . . . . 3D 57
Westmacott Ho. NW8 . . 3F 59
(off Hatton St.)
West Mall W8 . . . . 2C 72
(off Palace Gdns. Ter.)
Westmark Point
SW15 . . . . 1D 113
(off Norley Vale)
Westmead SW15 . . . . . 4D 99
W. Mersea Cl. E16 . . . . 2D 83
West M. SW1 . . . . 5D 75
(off W. Warwick Pl.)
Westmill Ct. N4 . . . . . . 4E 35
WESTMINSTER
. . . . 4D 23 (3A 76)
Westminster Abbey
. . . . 5D 23 (4F 75)
Westminster Abbey
Chapter House 5D 23
(in Westminster Abbey)
Westminster Abbey Mus.
. . . . 5D 23
(in Westminster Abbey)
Westminster Abbey Pyx
Chamber 5D 23
(in Westminster Abbey)
Westminster Bri.
SW1 . . . . 4E 23 (3A 76)
Westminster Bri. Rd.
SE1 . . . . 4F 23 (3B 76)
Westminster Bus. Sq.
SE11 . . . . 1B 90
Westminster Children's
Sports Cen., The . . . 3F 59

Westminster Ct.
E11 . . . . 1C 40
(off Cambridge Pk.)
SE16 . . . . 2F 79
(off King & Queen Wharf)
Westminster Gdns.
SW1 . . . . 5A 76
(off Marsham St.)
Westminster Hall 4D 23
Westminster Ind. Est.
SE18 . . . . 4F 83
Westminster Mans.
SW1 . . . . 5C 22
(off Gt. Smith St.)
Westminster Pal. Gdns.
SW1 . . . . 5B 22
Westminster RC Cathedral
. . . . 4E 75
Westminster Theatre. . 5F 21
(off Palace St.)
Westmoor St. SE7 . . . . 4E 83
Westmore Ct.
SW15 . . . . 3A 100
Westmoreland Ho.
E16 . . . . 2C 82
(off Gatcombe Rd.)
Westmoreland Pl.
SW1 . . . . 1D 89
Westmoreland Rd.
SE17 . . . . 2F 91
(not continuous)
SW13 . . . . 4B 84
Westmoreland St.
W1 . . . . 1C 12 (4C 60)
Westmoreland Ter.
SW1 . . . . 1D 89
Westmoreland Wlk.
SE17 . . . . 2F 91
Westmorland Ct. E12 . . 4F 41
Westmorland Rd.
E17 . . . . 1C 38
WEST NORWOOD 4E 119
W. Norwood Crematorium
SE27 . . . . 3E 119
Westonbirt St. SE15 . . 2B 92
(off Ebley Cl.)
Weston Ct. N4 . . . . 5E 35
West One Ho. W1 . . . . . 1F 13
(off Wells St.)
W. One Shop. Cen.
W1 . . . . 3C 12
Weston Ho. E9 . . . . 5E 51
(off King Edward's Rd.)
NW6 . . . . 5A 44
Weston London Heliport
. . . . 5F 87
Weston Pk. N8 . . . . 1A 34
Weston Ri.
WC1 . . . . 1A 8 (2B 62)
Weston St.
SE1 . . . . 4C 26 (3A 78)
(not continuous)
Weston Wlk. E8 . . . . . . 4D 51
Westover Hill NW3 . . . 4C 30
Westover Rd. SW18 . . 5E 101
Westow Hill SE19 . . . . 5A 120
West Pk. SE9 . . . . 2F 125
West Pl. SW19 . . . . 5E 113

West Point E14 . . . . . . 1B 80
(off Grenade St.)
SE1 . . . . 1C 92
Westport Rd. E13 . . . . . 3D 69
Westport St. E1 . . . . . . 5F 65
W. Poultry Av.
EC1 . . . . 1D 17 (4D 63)
West Quarters W12 . . . 5C 56
West Quay W10 . . . . . . 3E 57
West Reservoir Cen.
. . . . 1A 74
West Ri. W2 . . . . 1A 74
(off St George's Flds.)
West Rd. E15 . . . . 5B 54
SE1 . . . . 3A 24 (3B 76)
SW3 . . . . 1B 88
SW4 . . . . 3F 103
West Row W10 . . . . 3A 58
Westrow SW15 . . . . . . 4E 99
W. Side Comn.
SW19 . . . . 5E 113
Westside Ct. W9 . . . . . 3C 58
(off Elgin Av.)
West Smithfield
EC1 . . . . 1D 17 (4D 63)
West Sq.
SE11 . . . . 5D 25 (4D 77)
West St. E2 . . . . 1D 65
E11 . . . . 5A 40
E17 . . . . 1D 39
WC2 . . . . 3C 14 (5F 61)
W. Tenter St.
E1 . . . . 3F 19 (5B 64)
Westvale M. W3 . . . . . . 3A 70
West Vw. Cl. NW10 . . . 2B 42
Westview Ct. W10 . . . . 5E 57
Westville Rd. W12 . . . . 3C 70
W. Warwick Pl. SW1 . . 5E 75
West Way NW10 . . . . . . 5A 28
Westway W2 . . . . 4B 58
W10 . . . . 4B 58
W11 . . . . 4B 58
W12 . . . . 1B 70
Westway Sports Cen.
. . . . 5F 57
Westwell M. SW16 . . . 5A 118
Westwell Rd. SW16 . . 5A 118
Westwell Rd. App.
SW16 . . . . 5A 118
Westwick Gdns. W14 . . 3F 71
Westwood Bus. Cen.
NW10 . . . . 3A 56
Westwood Gdns.
SW13 . . . . 1B 98
Westwood Hill SE26 . . 5C 120
Westwood Ho. W12 . . . 2E 71
(off Wood La.)
Westwood Pk.
SE23 . . . . 5D 107
Westwood Pl. SE26 . . . 4C 120
Westwood Rd. E16 . . . . 2D 83
SW13 . . . . 1B 98
Wetherby Gdns. SW5 . . 5E 73
Wetherby Mans.
SW5 . . . . 1D 87
(off Earls Court Sq.)
Wetherby M. SW5 . . . . 5D 73
Wetherby Pl. SW7 . . . . 5E 73
Wetherden St. E17 . . . . 2B 38
Wetherell Rd. E9 . . . . . 5F 51
Wevco Wharf SE15 . . . 2D 93

Wevell Ho. *N6* 2C **32**
    (off Hillcrest)
Wexford Ho. *E1*. 4E **65**
    (off Sidney St.)
Wexford Rd. *SW12*. . . 5B **102**
Weybourne St.
  SW18 . . . . 2E **115**
Weybridge Ct. *SE16*. . . 1D **93**
    (off Argyle Way)
Weybridge Point
  SW11 . . . . 5B **88**
Weydown Cl. *SW19* . . . 1A **114**
Weyhill Rd. *E1* 5C **64**
Weyman Rd. *SE3* 4E **97**
Weymouth Ct. *E2* 1B **64**
    (off Weymouth Ter.)
Weymouth Ho. *SW8*. . . 3B **90**
    (off Bolney St.)
Weymouth M.
  W1. . . . . 5D **5** (4D **61**)
Weymouth St.
  W1. . . . . 1C **12** (4C **60**)
Weymouth Ter.
  E2. . . . . 1F **11** (1B **64**)
Whadcoat St. *N4* 4C **34**
Whalebone Ct. *EC2* . . . 2B **18**
Whalebone La. *E15* . . . 4A **54**
Whales Yd. *E15* 4A **54**
    (off W. Ham La.)
Wharf, The
  EC3 . . . . 1E **27** (2B **78**)
Wharfdale Rd. *N1* 1A **62**
Wharfdale Ct. *E5* 1F **51**
Wharfedale Ho. *NW6*. . . 5D **45**
    (off Kilburn Va.)
Wharfedale St.
  SW10 . . . . 1D **87**
Wharfedale Yard *N1*. . . 1A **62**
    (off Wharfedale Rd.)
Wharf Pl. *E2*. 5D **51**
Wharf Rd. *N1* 1F **9** (1E **63**)
    (Angel)
  N1. . . . . 5F **47**
    (Camden Town)
Wharfside Rd. *E16*. . . . 4A **68**
Wharf St. *E16*. 4A **68**
Wharf Vw. Ct. *E14* 5E **67**
    (off Athol Sq.)
Wharton Cotts.
  WC1 . . . . 2B **8** (2C **62**)
Wharton Ho. *SE1* 5F **27**
    (off Maltby St.)
Wharton St.
  WC1 . . . . 2A **8** (2B **62**)
Whatcott's Yd. *N16* . . . 1A **50**
Wheatley Rd. *SE22* . . . 3B **106**
Wheatman Ho. *E14* . . . 5B **66**
    (off Wallwood St.)
Wheatsheaf Ho. *SE23* . . 5F **107**
Wheatland Ho.
  . . . . 1A **106**
Wheats Rd.
  . . . . 3C **116**
Wheatfield Ho. *SW15*. . . 5C **98**
    (off Ellisfield Dr)
. . . . 1C **12** (4C **60**)

Wheat Sheaf Cl. *E14* . . . 5D **81**
Wheatsheaf La.
  SW6 . . . . 3E **85**
  SW8 . . . . 3A **90**
    (not continuous)
Wheatsheaf Ter.
  SW6 . . . . 3B **86**
Wheatstone Rd.
  W10 . . . . 4A **58**
Wheeler Gdns. *N1* 5A **48**
    (off Outram Pl.)
Wheel Ho. *E14*. 1D **95**
    (off Burrells Wharf Sq.)
Wheelwright St. *N7* . . . 4B **48**
Wheler Ho. *E1* 4F **11**
    (off Quaker St.)
Wheler St.
  E1. . . . . 4F **11** (3B **64**)
Whellock Rd. *W4* 4A **70**
Whetstone Pk.
  WC2 . . . . 2F **15** (5B **62**)
Whetstone Rd. *SE3* . . . 5E **97**
Whewell Rd. *N19*. 4A **34**
Whidborne Bldgs.
  WC1 . . . . 2E **7**
    (off Whidborne St.)
Whidborne Cl. *SE8*. . . . 5C **94**
Whidborne St.
  WC1 . . . . 2E **7** (2A **62**)
    (not continuous)
Whinfell Cl. *SW16* 5F **117**
Whinyates Rd. *SE9*. . . . 1F **111**
Whipps Cross *E17* 1F **39**
Whipps Cross Rd.
  E11 . . . . 1F **39**
Whiskin St.
  EC1 . . . . 2D **9** (2D **63**)
Whistler M. *SE15*. 3B **92**
Whistlers Av. *SW11* . . . 3F **87**
Whistler St. *N5* 2D **49**
Whistler Twr. *SW10* . . . 3F **87**
    (off Worlds End Est.)
Whistler Wlk. *SW10*. . . 3F **87**
Whiston Ho. *N1*. 4D **49**
    (off Richmond Gro.)
Whiston Rd. *E2*. 1B **64**
Whitacre M. *SE11* 1C **90**
Whitbread Rd. *SE4* . . . 2A **108**
Whitburn Rd. *SE13* . . . 2D **109**
Whitby Cl. *N7* 1A **48**
Whitby Ho. *NW8*. 5E **45**
    (off Boundary Rd.)
Whitby St. *E1*. . . 3F **11** (3B **64**)
    (not continuous)
Whitcher Cl. *SE14* 2A **94**
Whitcher Pl. *NW1* 3E **47**
Whitchurch Ho. *W10* . . . 5F **57**
    (off Kingsdown Cl.)
Whitchurch Rd. *W11* . . . 1F **71**
Whitcomb Cl. *WC2*. . . . 5C **14**
Whitcomb St.
  WC2. . . . . . . 5C **14** (1F **75**)
Whiteadder Way *E14*. . . 5D **81**
Whitear Wlk. *E15* 3F **53**
Whitebeam Cl. *SW9* . . . 3B **90**
White Bear Pl. *NW3*. . . 1F **45**
White Bear Yd. *EC1*. . . . 4B **8**
    (off Clerkenwell Rd.)
WHITECHAPEL 4C **64**

Whitechapel Art Gallery
  . . . . 5B **64**
    (off Whitechapel High St.)
Whitechapel High St.
  E1. . . . . 2F **19** (5B **64**)
Whitechapel Rd. *E1*. . . 4C **64**
Whitechapel Sports Cen.
  . . . . 4D **65**
White Chu. La. *E1* 5C **64**
White Chu. Pas.
  E1. . . . . 5C **64**
    (off White Chu. La.)
WHITE CITY. 1D **71**
White City *W12*. 5E **57**
White City Cl. *W12*. . . . 1E **71**
White City Est. *W12*. . . 1D **71**
White City Rd. *W12*. . . 1E **71**
White Conduit St.
  N1. . . . . 1C **62**
Whitecross Pl.
  EC2. . . . . 5C **10** (4F **63**)
Whitecross St.
  EC1 . . . . 3A **10** (3E **63**)
Whitefield Av. *NW2* . . . 3E **29**
Whitefield Cl.
  SW15 . . . . 4A **100**
Whitefoot La.
  BR1: Brom 4E **123**
Whitefoot Ter.
  BR1: Brom 3A **124**
Whitefriars St.
  EC4 . . . . 3C **16** (5C **62**)
Whitehall
  SW1 . . . . 2D **23** (2A **76**)
Whitehall Ct.
  SW1. . . . . . . 2D **23** (2A **76**)
    (not continuous)
Whitehall Gdns.
  SW1 . . . . 2D **23**
Whitehall Pk. *N19* 3E **33**
Whitehall Pl. *E7*. 2C **54**
  SW1. . . . . . . 2D **23** (2A **76**)
Whitehall Theatre 1D **23**
    (off Whitehall)
White Hart Ct. *EC2*. . . . 1D **19**
White Hart La. *NW10* . . 3B **42**
  SW13 . . . . 1A **98**
White Hart St.
  EC4 . . . . 2E **17** (5D **63**)
  SE11 . . . . 1C **90**
White Hart Yd.
  SE1. . . . . . . 2B **26** (2F **77**)
Whitehaven St. *NW8* . . 3A **60**
Whitehead Cl.
  SW18 . . . . 5E **101**
Whiteheads Gro.
  SW3 . . . . 5A **74**
White Heather Ho.
  WC1 . . . . 2E **7**
    (off Cromer St.)
White Horse All. *EC1*. . . 5D **9**
White Horse La. *E1* . . . 3F **65**
Whitehorse M.
  SE1. . . . . 5C **24** (4C **76**)
White Horse Rd. *E1*. . . 4A **66**
    (not continuous)
White Horse St.
  W1. . . . . 2E **21** (2D **75**)
White Horse Yd.
  EC2. . . . . 2B **18** (5F **63**)

White Ho. SW4 . . . . . 5F 103
(off Clapham Pk. Est.)
SW11 . . . . 4F 87
White Ho., The
NW1 . . . . 3E 5
Whitehouse Est.
E10 . . . . 1E 39
White Kennett St.
E1 . . . . 2E 19 (5A 64)
Whitelands Ho. SW3 . . 1B 88
(off Cheltenham Ter.)
Whitelegg Rd. E13 . . . 1B 68
Whiteley Rd. SE19 . . . 5F 119
Whiteleys Cen. W2 . . . 5D 59
Whiteley's Cotts.
W14 . . . . 5B 72
White Lion Ct. EC3 . . . 3D 19
SE15 . . . . 2E 93
White Lion Hill
EC4 . . . . 4E 17 (1D 77)
White Lion St. N1 . . . . 1C 62
White Lodge Cl. N2 . . . 1F 31
White Lyon Ct. EC2 . . . 5F 9
White Post La. E9 . . . . 4B 52
White Post St. SE15 . . 3E 93
White Rd. E15 . . . . . . 4A 54
White's Grounds
SE1 . . . . 4E 27 (3A 78)
White's Grounds Est.
SE1 . . . . 3E 27
White's Row
E1 . . . . 1F 19 (4D 64)
Whites Sq. SW4 . . . . . 2F 103
Whitestone La. NW3 . . 5E 31
Whitestone Wlk.
NW3 . . . . 5E 31
Whiteswan M. W4 . . . . 1A 84
Whitethorn Ho. E1 . . . 2E 79
(off Prusom St.)
Whitethorn Pas. E3 . . . 3C 66
(off Whitethorn St.)
Whitethorn St. E3 . . . . 4C 66
White Tower 5F 19
(in Tower of London, The)
Whitfield Ho. NW8 . . . 3A 60
(off Salisbury St.)
Whitfield Pl. W1 . . . . . 4F 5
Whitfield Rd. E6 . . . . . 4E 55
SE3 . . . . 4F 95
Whitfield St.
W1 . . . . 4F 5 (3E 61)
Whitgift Ho. SE11 . . . . 5B 76
Whitgift St. SE11 . . . . 5B 76
Whitley Ho. SW1 . . . . 2E 89
(off Churchill Gdns.)
Whitlock Dr. SW19 . . . 5A 100
Whitman Ho. E2 . . . . . 2E 65
(off Cornwall Av.)
Whitman Rd. E3 . . . . . 3A 66
Whitmore Est. N1 . . . . 5A 50
Whitmore Gdns.
NW10 . . . . 1E 57
Whitmore Ho. N1 . . . . 5A 50
(off Whitmore Est.)
Whitmore Rd. N1 . . . . 5A 50
Whitnell Way SW15 . . . 3E 99
Whitney Rd. E10 . . . . . 2D 39
Whitstable Ho. W10 . . 5F 57
(off Silchester Rd.)
Whittaker Rd. E6 . . . . 4E 55

Whittaker St. SW1 . . . 5C 74
Whittaker Way SE1 . . . 5C 78
Whitta Rd. E12 . . . . . . 1F 55
Whittingham Ct. W4 . . 3A 84
Whittingstall Rd.
SW6 . . . . 4B 86
Whittington Av.
EC3 . . . . 3D 19 (5A 64)
Whittington Ct. N2 . . . 1B 32
Whittle Cl. E17 . . . . . . 1A 38
Whittlesey St.
SE1 . . . . 2B 24 (2C 76)
Whitton Wlk. E3 . . . . . 2C 66
Whitwell Rd. E13 . . . . 2C 68
Whitworth Ho.
SE1 . . . . 5A 26 (4E 77)
Whitworth St. SE10 . . 1A 96
Whorlton Rd. SE15 . . . 1D 107
Whychcote Point
NW2 . . . . 3E 29
(off Whitefield Av.)
Whyteville Rd. E7 . . . . 3D 55
Whytlaw Ho. E3 . . . . . 4B 66
(off Baythorne St.)
Wickersley Rd.
SW11 . . . . 5C 88
Wickers Oake SE19 . . 4B 120
Wicker St. E1 . . . . 5D 65
Wickfield Ho. SE16 . . . 3D 79
(off Wilson Gro.)
Wickford Ho. E1 . . . . . 3E 65
(off Wickford St.)
Wickford St. E1 . . . . . 3E 65
Wickham Cl. E1 . . . . . 4E 65
Wickham Gdns.
SE4 . . . . 1B 108
Wickham M. SE4 . . . . 5B 94
Wickham Rd. SE4 . . . . 2B 108
Wickham St. SE11 . . . 1B 90
Wick La. E3 . . . . 5C 52
Wicklow Ho. N16 . . . . 3B 36
Wicklow St.
WC1 . . . . 1F 7 (2B 62)
Wick M. E9 . . . . 3A 52
Wick Rd. E9 . . . . 3F 51
Wicks Cl. SE9 . . . . . . 4F 125
Wick Sq. E9 . . . . 3B 52
Wicksteed Ho. SE1 . . . 4E 77
Wickway Ct. SE15 . . . 2B 92
(off Cator St.)
Wickwood St. SE5 . . . 5D 91
Widdenham Rd. N7 . . . 1B 48
Widdin St. E15 . . . . . . 4A 54
Widegate St.
E1 . . . . 1E 19 (4A 64)
Widford NW1 . . . . . . 3D 47
(off Lewis St.)
Widford Ho. N1 . . . . . 1D 63
(off Colebrooke Rd.)
Widgeon Cl. E16 . . . . 5D 69
Widley Rd. W9 . . . . . . 2C 58
Wigan Ho. E5 . . . . . . 3D 37
Wightman Rd. N4 . . . . 1C 34
N8 . . . . 1C 34
Wigmore Hall 2D 13
Wigmore Pl.
W1 . . . . 2D 13 (5D 61)
Wigmore St.
W1 . . . . 2C 12 (5C 60)

Wigram Ho. E14 . . . . . 1D 81
(off Wade's Pl.)
Wigram Rd. E11 . . . . . 1E 41
Wigston Rd. E13 . . . . 3D 69
Wigton Pl. SE11 . . . . . 1C 90
Wilberforce M. SW4 . . 2F 103
Wilberforce Rd. N4 . . . 4D 35
(not continuous)
NW9 . . . . 1C 28
Wilberforce Way
SW19 . . . . 5F 113
Wilbraham Ho. SW8 . . 3A 90
(off Wandsworth Rd.)
Wilbraham Pl. SW1 . . 5B 74
Wilby M. W11 . . . . . . 2B 72
Wilcox Cl. SW8 . . . . . 3A 90
(not continuous)
Wilcox Ho. E3 . . . . . . 4B 66
(off Ackroyd Dr.)
Wilcox Pl.
SW1 . . . . 5A 22 (4E 75)
Wilcox Rd. SW8 . . . . . 3A 90
Wild Ct. WC2 . . 3F 15 (5B 62)
Wildcroft Mnr. SW15 . . 5E 99
Wildcroft Rd. SW15 . . 5E 99
Wilde Cl. E8 . . . . 5C 50
Wilde Ho. W2 . . . . . . 5D 59
(off Gloucester Ter.)
Wilde Pl. SW18 . . . . . 5F 101
Wilderness M. SW4 . . 2D 103
Wilderton Rd. N16 . . . 2A 36
Wildfell Rd. SE6 . . . . . 5D 109
Wild Goose Dr. SE14 . . 4E 93
Wild Hatch NW11 . . . . 1C 30
Wild's Rents
SE1 . . . . 5D 27 (4A 78)
Wild St. WC2 . . 3E 15 (5A 62)
Wildwood Cl. SE12 . . . 5B 110
Wildwood Gro. NW3 . . 3E 31
Wildwood Ri. NW11 . . 3E 31
Wildwood Rd. NW11 . . 1D 31
Wilfred Cl. N15 . . . . . . 1F 35
(off South Gro.)
Wilfred Owen Cl.
SW19 . . . . 5E 115
Wilfred St.
SW1 . . . . 5F 21 (4E 75)
Wilkes St. E1 . . 5F 11 (4B 64)
Wilkie Ho. SW1 . . . . . 1F 89
(off Cureton St.)
Wilkins Ho. SW1 . . . . 2D 89
(off Churchill Gdns.)
Wilkinson Ct. SW17 . . 4F 115
Wilkinson Ho. N1 . . . . 1F 63
(off Cranston Est.)
Wilkinson Rd. E16 . . . 5E 69
Wilkinson St. SW8 . . . 3B 90
Wilkin St. NW5 . . . . . 3C 46
Wilkin St. M. NW5 . . . 3D 47
Wilks Pl. N1 . . . . 1A 64
Willan Wall E16 . . . . . 1B 82
Willard St. SW8 . . . . . 1D 103
Will Crooks Gdns.
SE9 . . . . 2E 111
WILLESDEN 3C 42
Willesden Belle Vue Cinema
. . . . 3D 43
(off Grange Rd.)
WILLESDEN GREEN . . 3D 43

Willesden La. NW2 . . . . 3E **43**
   NW6 . . . . 3F **43**
Willesden Section Ho.
   NW2 . . . . 3F *43*
   (off Willesden La.)
Willesden Sports Cen.
   . . . . 5D **43**
Willesden Sports Stadium
   . . . . 5D **43**
Willes Rd. NW5 . . . . . . 3D **47**
Willett Ho. *E13.* 1D **69**
   (off Queens Rd. W.)
William IV St.
   WC2 . . . . . . 5D **15** (1A **76**)
William Banfield Ho.
   SW6 . . . . 5B *86*
   (off Munster Rd.)
William Blake Ho.
   SW11 . . . . 4A **88**
William Bonney Est.
   SW4 . . . . 2F **103**
William Caslon Ho.
   E2 . . . . 1D *65*
   (off Patriot Sq.)
William Channing Ho.
   E2 . . . . 2D *65*
   (off Canrobert St.)
William Cl. SE13 . . . . . 1E **109**
William Cobbett Ho.
   W8 . . . . 4D *73*
   (off Scarsdale Pl.)
William Dromey Ct.
   NW6 . . . . 4B **44**
William Dunbar Ho.
   NW6 . . . . 1B *58*
   (off Albert Rd.)
William Dyce M.
   SW16 . . . . 4F **117**
William Ellis Way
   SE16 . . . . 4C *78*
   (off St James's Rd.)
William Evans Ho.
   SE8 . . . . 5F *79*
   (off Bush Rd.)
William Farm La.
   SW15 . . . . 1D **99**
William Fenn Ho.
   E2 . . . . 2C *64*
   (off Shipton Rd.)
William Gdns. SW15 . . . 3D **99**
William Gibbs Ct.
   SW1 . . . . 5B *22*
   (off Old Pye St.)
William Gunn Ho.
   NW3 . . . . 2A **46**
William Guy Gdns.
   E3 . . . . 2D **67**
William Harvey Ho.
   SW19 . . . . 1A *114*
   (off Whitlock Dr.)
William Henry Wlk.
   SW8 . . . . 2F **89**
William Hunt Mans.
   SW13 . . . . 2E **85**
William Margrie Cl.
   SE15 . . . . 5C **92**
William M.
   SW1 . . . . . . 4A **20** (3B **74**)
William Morley Cl.
   E6 . . . . 5F **55**

William Morris Ho.
   W6 . . . . 2F **85**
William Morris Way
   SW6 . . . . 1E **101**
William Paton Ho.
   E16 . . . . 5D **69**
William Pl. E3 . . . . 1B **66**
William Rathbone Ho.
   E2 . . . . 2D *65*
   (off Florida St.)
William Rd.
   NW1 . . . . . . 2F **5** (2E **61**)
William Rushbrooke Ho.
   SE16 . . . . 5C *78*
   (off Rouel Rd.)
William Saville Ho.
   NW6 . . . . 1B *58*
   (off Denmark Rd.)
William's Bldgs. E2 . . . . 3E **65**
Williams Cl. N8 . . . . . . 1F **33**
   SW6 . . . . 3A **86**
Williams Ho. *E9.* 5D *51*
   (off King Edward's St.)
   NW2 . . . . 5E *29*
   (off Stoll Cl.)
Williamson Cl. SE10 . . . 1B **96**
Williamson Ct.
   SE17 . . . . 1E **91**
Williamson Rd. N4 . . . . 1D **35**
Williamson St. N7 . . . . 1A **48**
William Sq. SE16. . . . . . 1A *80*
   (off Sovereign Cres.)
William St. E10 . . . . . . 1D **39**
   SW1 . . . . . . 4A **20** (3B **74**)
William White Cl.
   E13 . . . . 5E *55*
   (off Green St.)
William Wood Ho.
   SE26 . . . . 3E *121*
   (off Shrublands Cl.)
Willifield Way NW11 . . . 1C **30**
Willingham Cl. NW5 . . . 2E **47**
Willingham Ter. NW5. . . 2E **47**
Willington Ct. E5 . . . . . 5A **38**
Willington Rd. SW9 . . . 1A **104**
Willis Ho. *E14* 1D *81*
   (off Hale St.)
Willis Rd. E15 . . . . 1B **68**
Willis St. E14. . . . . 5D **67**
Willoughby Highwalk
   EC2 . . . . 1B *18*
   (off Moor La.)
Willoughby Ho. *E1.* . . . 2D *79*
   (off Reardon Path)
   EC2 . . . . 5B **10**
Willoughby Pas. *E14.* . . 2C *80*
   (off W. India Av.)
Willoughby Rd. NW3 . . . 1F **45**
Willoughbys, The
   SW14 . . . . 1A **98**
Willoughby St. WC1 . . . 1D **15**
Willoughby Way 5D **83**
Willow Av. SW13 . . . . . 5B **84**
Willow Bank SW6 . . . . 1A **100**
Willow Bri. Rd. N1. . . . . 3E **49**
   (not continuous)
Willow Brook Rd.
   SE15 . . . . 3B **92**

Willow Bus. Pk.
   SE26 . . . . 3E **121**
Willow Cl. SE6 . . . . . . 1B **124**
Willow Ct. E11 . . . . 4A *40*
   (off Trinity Cl.)
   EC2 . . . . 3D **11**
   NW6 . . . . 4A **44**
   W4 . . . . 3A *84*
   (off Corney Reach Way)
   W9 . . . . 4C *58*
   (off Admiral Wlk.)
Willowdene N6. . . . . . . 2B **32**
   SE15 . . . . 3D **93**
Willow Gro. E13. . . . . . 1C **68**
Willow Ho. *W10.* 3F *57*
   (off Maple Wlk.)
Willow Lodge SW6. . . . 4F **85**
Willow Pl. SW1 . . . . . . 5E **75**
Willow Rd. NW3. . . . . . 1F **45**
Willows Ter. *NW10.* . . . 1B *56*
   (off Rucklidge Av.)
Willow St.
   EC2 . . . . . . 3D **11** (3A **64**)
Willow Tree Cl. E3. . . . . 5A **52**
   SW18 . . . . 1D **115**
Willow Va. W12 . . . . . . 2C **70**
Willow Wlk. SE1 . . . . . 4A **78**
Willow Way SE26 . . . . 3E **121**
   W11. . . . . 1F **71**
Willsbridge Ct.
   SE15 . . . . 2A **92**
Wilman Gro. E8 . . . . . . 4C **50**
Wilmcote Ho. *W2* 4D *59*
   (off Woodchester Sq.)
Wilment Ct. NW2 . . . . . 5E **29**
Wilmer Gdns. N1 . . . . . 5A **50**
   (not continuous)
Wilmer Lea Cl. E15 . . . 4E **53**
Wilmer Pl. N16 . . . . . . 4B **36**
Wilmers Ct. *NW10.* . . . 5A *42*
   (off Stracey Rd.)
Wilmington Sq.
   WC1 . . . . . . 2B **8** (2C **62**)
   (not continuous)
Wilmington St.
   WC1 . . . . . . 2B **8** (2C **62**)
Wilmot Cl. SE15 . . . . . 3C **92**
Wilmot Pl. NW1 . . . . . . 4E **47**
Wilmot Rd. E10 . . . . . . 4D **39**
Wilmot St. E2 . . . . 3D **65**
Wilna Rd. SW18 . . . . . 5E **101**
Wilsham St. W11 . . . . . 2F **71**
Wilshaw Ho. SE8 . . . . . 3C **94**
Wilshaw St. SE14 . . . . 4C **94**
Wilson Gro. SE16 . . . . 3D **79**
Wilson Rd. E6 . . . . 2F **69**
   SE5 . . . . 4A **92**
Wilson's Pl. E14. . . . . . 5B **66**
Wilson's Rd. W6 . . . . . 1F **85**
Wilson St.
   EC2 . . . . . . 5C **10** (4F **63**)
Wilson Wlk. *W4.* 5B *70*
   (off Prebend Gdns.)
Wiltern Ct. NW2 . . . . . 3A **44**
Wilton Av. W4 . . . . 1A **84**
Wilton Ct. *E1* 5D *65*
   (off Cavell St.)
Wilton Cres.
   SW1 . . . . . . 4B **20** (3C **74**)
Wilton Est. E8 . . . . 3C **50**

Wilton M. E8 . . . . 3D **51**
SW1 . . . . 5C **20** (4C **74**)
Wilton Pl.
SW1 . . . . 4B **20** (3C **74**)
Wilton Rd. SW1 . . . . 4D **75**
Wilton Row
SW1 . . . . 4B **20** (3C **74**)
Wilton Sq. N1 . . . . 5F **49**
Wilton St.
SW1 . . . . . . 5D **21** (4D **75**)
Wilton Ter.
SW1 . . . . 5B **20** (4C **74**)
Wilton Vs. N1 . . . . 5F **49**
(off Wilton Sq.)
Wilton Way E8 . . . . 3C **50**
Wiltshire Cl. SW3 . . . . . . 5B **74**
Wiltshire Ct. N4 . . . . 3B **34**
(off Marquis Rd.)
Wiltshire Gdns. N4 . . . . . 1E **35**
Wiltshire Rd. SW9 . . . . . 1C **104**
Wiltshire Row N1 . . . . . . 5F **49**
Wimbart Rd. SW2 . . . . . 5B **104**
WIMBLEDON 5B **114**
Wimbledon (All England Lawn
Tennis & Croquet Club)
. . . . 4A **114**
Wimbledon Common
. . . . 4C **112**
Wimbledon Greyhound &
Speedway Stadium
. . . . 4E **115**
Wimbledon Hill Rd.
SW19 . . . . 5A **114**
Wimbledon Lawn Tennis Mus.
. . . . 4A **114**
Wimbledon Mus. of
Local History 5A **114**
WIMBLEDON PK. 3C **114**
Wimbledon Pk. Ct.
SW19 . . . . 1B **114**
Wimbledon Pk. Rd.
SW18 . . . . 2A **114**
SW19 . . . . 2A **114**
Wimbledon Pk. Side
SW19 . . . . 3F **113**
Wimbledon Rd.
SW17 . . . . 4E **115**
Wimbledon Stadium Bus. Cen.
SW17 . . . . 3D **115**
Wimbledon Windmill Mus.
. . . . 2D **113**
Wimbolt St. E2 . . . . 2C **64**
Wimborne Cl. SE12 . . 3B **110**
Wimborne Ct.
SW12 . . . . 3E **117**
Wimborne Ho. E16 . . . . 1B **82**
(off Victoria Dock Rd.)
NW1 . . . . 3A **60**
(off Harewood Av.)
SW8 . . . . 3B **90**
(off Dorset Rd.)
SW12 . . . . 3E **117**
Wimbourne Cl. N1 . . . . . 1F **63**
(off Wimbourne St.)
Wimbourne St. N1 . . . . . 1F **63**
Wimpole M.
W1 . . . . 5D **5** (4D **61**)
Wimpole St.
W1 . . . . 1D **13** (4D **61**)
Winans Wlk. SW9 . . . . . 5C **90**

Winant Ho. E14 . . . . . . 1D **81**
(off Simpson's Rd.)
Wincanton Rd.
SW18 . . . . 5B **100**
Winchcomb Gdns.
SE9 . . . . 1F **111**
Winchelsea Cl.
SW15 . . . . 3F **99**
Winchelsea Ho.
SE16 . . . . 3E **79**
(off Swan Rd.)
Winchelsea Rd. E7 . . 5C **40**
NW10 . . . . 5A **42**
Winchendon Rd.
SW6 . . . . 4B **86**
Winchester Av. NW6 . . 5A **44**
Winchester Cl.
SE17 . . . . 5D **77**
Winchester Ct. W8 . . . . 3C **72**
(off Vicarage Ga.)
Winchester Ho. SE18 . . 3F **97**
(off Portway Gdns.)
SW3 . . . . 2F **87**
(off Beaufort St.)
SW9 . . . . 3C **90**
W2 . . . . 5C **59**
(off Hallfield Est.)
Winchester Pl. E8 . . . . 2B **50**
N6 . . . . 3D **33**
Winchester Rd. N6 . . 2D **33**
NW3 . . . . 4F **45**
Winchester Sq. SE1 . . 1B **26**
Winchester St. SW1 . . 1D **89**
Winchester Wlk.
SE1 . . . . . . 1B **26** (2F **77**)
Winchester Wharf
SE1 . . . . 1B **26**
(off Clink St.)
Winchfield Ho.
SW15 . . . . 4B **98**
Winchfield Rd.
SE26 . . . . 5A **122**
Winch Ho. E14 . . . . . . 4D **81**
(off Tiller Rd.)
SW10 . . . . 3E **87**
(off King's Rd.)
Winchilsea Ho. NW8 . . 2F **59**
(off St John's Wood Rd.)
Wincott St. SE11 . . . . . 5C **76**
Windermere NW1 . . . . . 2E **5**
(off Albany St.)
Windermere Av.
NW6 . . . . 5A **44**
Windermere Ct.
SW13 . . . . 2B **84**
Windermere Ho. E3 . . 3B **66**
Windermere Point
SE15 . . . . 3E **93**
(off Old Kent Rd.)
Windermere Rd. N19 . . 4E **33**
SW15 . . . . 4A **112**
Winders Rd. SW11 . . 5A **88**
(not continuous)
Windfield Cl. SE26 . . 4F **121**
Winding, The W2 . . . . . 4F **59**
(off Nth. Wharf Rd.)
Windlass Pl. SE8 . . . . 5A **80**
Windlesham Gro.
SW19 . . . . 1F **113**
Windley Cl. SE23 . . . . 2E **121**

Windmill WC1 . . . . 5F **7**
(off New Nth. St.)
Windmill Cl. SE1 . . . . . 5C **78**
(off Beatrice Rd.)
SE13 . . . . 5E **95**
Windmill Ct. NW2 . . . . 3A **44**
Windmill Dr. NW2 . . . . 5A **30**
SW4 . . . . 3D **103**
Windmill Hill NW3 . . . 5E **31**
Windmill Ho. E14 . . . . 5C **80**
Windmill La. E15 . . . . 3F **53**
Windmill M. W4 . . . . . 5A **70**
Windmill Pas. W4 . . . . 5A **70**
Windmill Rd. SW18 . . 4F **101**
SW19 . . . . 2D **113**
W4 . . . . 5A **70**
Windmill Row SE11 . . 1C **90**
Windmill St.
W1 . . . . 1B **14** (4F **61**)
(not continuous)
Windmill Wlk.
SE1 . . . . . . 2C **24** (2C **76**)
Windrose Cl. SE16 . . . 3F **79**
Windrush Cl. SW11 . . 2F **101**
Windrush La. SE23 . . 3F **121**
Windsock Cl. SE16 . . 5B **80**
Windsor Cen., The
N1 . . . . 5D **49**
(off Windsor St.)
Windsor Ct. SE27 . . 4E **119**
Windsor Cotts. SE14 . . 3B **94**
(off Amersham Va.)
Windsor Ct. NW2 . . . . 3A **44**
(off Chatsworth Rd.)
NW3 . . . . 1C **44**
NW11 . . . . 1A **30**
(off Golders Grn. Rd.)
SE16 . . . . 1F **79**
(off King & Queen Wharf)
SW3 . . . . 1A **88**
(off Jubilee Pl.)
SW11 . . . . 5F **87**
W2 . . . . 1D **73**
(off Moscow Rd.)
W10 . . . . 5F **57**
(off Bramley Rd.)
Windsor Gdns. W9 . . 4C **58**
Windsor Gro. SE27 . . 4E **119**
Windsor Hall E16 . . . . 2D **83**
(off Wesley Av.)
Windsor Ho. E2 . . . . . 2F **65**
(off Knottisford St.)
N1 . . . . 1E **63**
NW1 . . . . 1E **5**
Windsor M. SE6 . . . . 1E **123**
SE23 . . . . 1A **122**
SW18 . . . . 5E **101**
(off Wilna Rd.)
Windsor Pl. SW1 . . . . 4E **75**
Windsor Rd. E7 . . . . . 2D **55**
E10 . . . . 4D **39**
E11 . . . . 3C **40**
N7 . . . . 5A **34**
NW2 . . . . 3D **43**
Windsor St. N1 . . . . . 5D **49**
Windsor Ter.
N1 . . . . 1A **10** (2E **63**)
Windsor Wlk. SE5 . . . . 5F **91**
Windsor Way W14 . . . 5F **71**
Windsor Wharf E9 . . . 3C **52**

Windspoint Dr. SE15 . . . 2D 93
Windus Rd. N16 . . . . 3B 36
Windus Wlk. N16 . . . . . . 3B 36
Windy Ridge Cl.
  SW19 . . . . 5F 113
Wine Cl. E1 . . . . 1E 79
  (not continuous)
Wine Office Ct. EC4 . . . 5C 62
Winford Ct. SE15 . . . . . 4D 93
Winford Ho. E3 . . . . 4B 52
Winforton St. SE10 . . . . 4E 95
Winfrith Rd. SW18 . . . . 5E 101
Wingate Rd. W6 . . . . . . 4D 71
Wingfield Ct. E14 . . . . . . 1F 81
  (off John Smith M.)
Wingfield Ho. E2 . . . . . 2F 11
  (off Virginia Rd.)
  NW6 . . . . 1D 59
  (off Tollgate Gdns.)
Wingfield M. SE15 . . . 1C 106
Wingfield Rd. E15 . . . . 1A 54
  E17 . . . . 1D 39
Wingfield St. SE15 . . . 1C 106
Wingford Rd. SW2 . . . . 4A 104
Wingmore Rd. SE24 . . . 1E 105
Wingrad Ho. E1 . . . . 4E 65
  (off Jubilee St.)
Wingrave SE17 . . . . 5F 77
  (not continuous)
Wingrave Rd. W6 . . . . . 2E 85
Wingreen NW8 . . . . 5D 45
  (off Abbey Rd.)
Wingrove Rd. SE6 . . . . 2A 124
Winicotte Ho. W2 . . . . . 4F 59
  (off Paddington Grn.)
Winifred Ter. E13 . . . . . 1C 68
  (off Upper Rd.)
Winkfield Rd. E13 . . . . 1D 69
Winkley St. E2 . . . . 1D 65
Winkworth Cotts. E1 . . . 3E 65
  (off Cephas St.)
Winlaton Rd.
  BR1: Brom 4F 123
Winnett St.
  W1 . . . . 4B 14 (1F 75)
Winnington Cl. N2 . . . . 1F 31
Winnington Ho. SE5 . . . 3E 91
  (off Wyndham Est.)
Winnington Rd. N2 . . . . 1F 31
Winn Rd. SE12 . . . . 1C 124
Winscombe St. N19 . . . 4D 33
Winsford Rd. SE6 . . . . . 3B 122
Winsham Gro.
  SW11 . . . . 3C 102
Winsham Ho. NW1 . . . . . 1C 6
  (off Churchway)
Winslade Rd. SW2 . . . 3A 104
Winslade Way SE6 . . . 5D 109
Winsland M. W2 . . . . . . 5F 59
Winsland St. W2 . . . . . 5F 59
Winsley St.
  W1 . . . . 2A 14 (5E 61)
Winslow SE17 . . . . 1A 92
Winslow Cl. NW10 . . . 5A 28
Winslow Rd. W6 . . . . . . 2E 85
Winstanley Est.
  SW11 . . . . 1F 101
Winstanley Rd.
  SW11 . . . . 1F 101
  (not continuous)

Winston Av. NW9 . . . . . 2A 28
Winston Ho. WC1 . . . . . . 3C 6
Winston Rd. N16 . . . . . 1F 49
Winterbourne Ho.
  W11 . . . . 1A 72
  (off Portland Rd.)
Winterbourne Rd.
  SE6 . . . . 1B 122
Winterbrook Rd.
  SE24 . . . . 4E 105
Winterfold Cl.
  SW19 . . . . 2A 114
Wintergreen Cl. E6 . . . . 4F 69
Winterleys NW6 . . . . . . 1B 58
  (off Denmark Rd.)
Winter Lodge SE16 . . . 1C 92
  (off Fern Wlk.)
Winterslow Ho. SE5 . . . 5E 91
  (off Flaxman Rd.)
Winterstoke Rd.
  SE6 . . . . 1B 122
Winterton Ho. E1 . . . . . 5E 65
  (off Deancross St.)
Winterton Pl.
  SW10 . . . . 2E 87
Winterwell Rd.
  SW2 . . . . 3A 104
Winthorpe Rd.
  SW15 . . . . 2A 100
Winthrop Ho. W12 . . . . 1D 71
  (off White City Est.)
Winthrop St. E1 . . . . . . 4D 65
Winton Way SW16 . . . . 5C 118
Wirrall Ho. SE26 . . . . . 3C 120
Wisbech N4 . . . . 3B 34
  (off Lorne Rd.)
Wisden Ho. SW8 . . . . . . 2B 90
Wiseman Rd. E10 . . . . 4C 38
Wise Rd. E15 . . . . 5F 53
Wiseton Rd. SW17 . . . 1A 116
Wishart Rd. SE3 . . . . . . 5F 97
Wisley Ho. SW1 . . . . . . 1F 89
  (off Rampayne St.)
Wisley Rd. SW11 . . . . . 3C 102
Wisteria Rd. SE13 . . . . 2F 109
Witanhurst La. N6 . . . . 3C 32
Witan St. E2 . . . . 2D 65
Witham Ct. E10 . . . . 5D 39
  SW17 . . . . 3B 116
Witherington Rd. N5 . . 2C 48
Withers Pl.
  EC1 . . . . 3A 10 (3E 63)
Withycombe Rd.
  SW19 . . . . 5F 99
Withy Ho. E1 . . . . 3F 65
  (off Globe Rd.)
Witley Ct. WC1 . . . . 4D 7
Witley Ho. SW2 . . . . . 5A 104
Witley Point SW15 . . . 1D 113
  (off Wanborough Dr.)
Witney Path SE23 . . . . 3F 121
Wittersham Rd.
  BR1: Brom 5B 124
Wivenhoe Cl. SE15 . . . 1D 107
Wiverton Rd. SE26 . . . . 5E 121
Wixom Ho. SE3 . . . . 2E 111
Wix's La. SW4 . . . . 1D 103
Woburn Ct. SE16 . . . . . 1D 93
  (off Masters Dr.)

Woburn M.
  WC1 . . . . 4C 6 (3F 61)
Woburn Pl.
  WC1 . . . . 4D 7 (3A 62)
Woburn Sq.
  WC1 . . . . 4C 6 (3F 61)
Woburn Wlk.
  WC1 . . . . 2C 6 (2F 61)
Wodeham Gdns. E1 . . . 4C 64
Wodehouse Av. SE5 . . . 4B 92
Woking Cl. SW15 . . . . . 2B 98
Wolcot Ho. NW1 . . . . . . 1A 6
  (off Aldenham St.)
Wolfe Cres. SE7 . . . . . . 1F 97
  SE16 . . . . 3F 79
Wolfe Ho. W12 . . . . 1D 71
  (off White City Est.)
Wolffe Gdns. E15 . . . . . 3B 54
Wolfington Rd.
  SE27 . . . . 4D 119
Wolfram Cl. SE13 . . . . 3A 110
Wolftencroft Cl.
  SW11 . . . . 1A 102
Wollaston Cl. SE1 . . . . 5E 77
Wollett Ct. NW1 . . . . . . 4E 47
  (off St Pancras Way)
Wolseley Av. SW19 . . . 2C 114
Wolseley Rd. E7 . . . . . . 4D 55
  N8 . . . . 1F 33
Wolseley St. SE1 . . . . . 3C 78
Wolsey Cl. NW6 . . . . . . 4E 45
  SW11 . . . . 4A 88
  (off Westbridge Rd.)
Wolsey M. NW5 . . . . . . 3E 47
Wolsey Rd. N1 . . . . 2F 49
Wolsey St. E1 . . . . 4E 65
Wolverley St. E2 . . . . . 2D 65
Wolverton SE17 . . . . . . 1A 92
Wolverton Gdns. W6 . . 5F 71
Womersley Rd. N8 . . . . 1B 34
Wontner Cl. N1 . . . . 4E 49
Wontner Rd. SW17 . . . 2B 116
Woodall Cl. E14 . . . . . . 1D 81
Woodbank Rd.
  BR1: Brom 3B 124
Woodbastwick Rd.
  SE26 . . . . 5F 121
Woodberry Down N4 . . 2E 35
Woodberry Down Est.
  N4 . . . . 3E 35
  (Woodberry Down)
  N4 . . . . 2E 35
  (Woodberry Gro.)
Woodberry Gro. N4 . . . 2E 35
Woodbine Pl. E11 . . . . . 1C 40
Woodbine Ter. E9 . . . . . 3E 51
Woodborough Rd.
  SW15 . . . . 2D 99
Woodbourne Av.
  SW16 . . . . 3F 117
Woodbourne Cl.
  SW16 . . . . 3A 118
Woodbridge Cl. N7 . . . 4B 34
  NW2 . . . . 5C 28
Woodbridge Ho. E11 . . 3B 40
Woodbridge St.
  EC1 . . . . 3D 9 (3D 63)
  (not continuous)
Woodburn Cl. NW4 . . . 1F 29
Woodbury Ho. SE26 . . . 3C 120

Woodbury St. SW17...5A 116
Woodchester St. W2...4D 59
Woodchurch Rd.
NW6...........4C 44
Wood Cl. E2.......3C 64
NW9............2A 28
Woodcock Ho. E14...4C 66
(off Burgess St.)
Woodcocks E16......4E 69
Woodcombe Cres.
SE23...........1E 121
Woodcote Ho. SE8...2B 94
(off Prince St.)
Woodcote Pl. SE27...5D 119
Woodcote Rd. E11...2C 40
Woodcote Vs. SE27...5E 119
(off Woodcote Pl.)
Woodcroft M. SE8....5A 80
Wood Dene SE15....4D 93
(off Queen's Rd.)
Woodend SE19......1E 135
Wooder Gdns. E7....1C 54
Woodfall Rd. N4.....4C 34
Woodfall St. SW3....1B 88
Woodfarrs SE5.......2F 105
Wood Fld. NW3......2B 46
Woodfield Av. SW16..3F 117
Woodfield Gro.
SW16..........3F 117
Woodfield Ho. SE23...3F 121
(off Dacres Rd.)
Woodfield La.
SW16..........3F 117
Woodfield Pl. W9....3B 58
Woodfield Rd. W9....4B 58
Woodford Ct. W12....3F 71
(off Shepherd's Bush Grn.)
Woodford Rd. E7....5D 41
Woodger Rd. W12....3E 71
Woodget Cl. E6......5F 69
Woodgrange Rd. E7...2D 55
Woodhall NW1.......2F 5
(off Robert St.)
Woodhall Av. SE21...3B 120
Woodhall Dr. SE21...3B 120
Woodhall Ho. SW18...4F 101
Woodham Rd. SE6....3E 123
Woodhatch Cl. E6....4F 69
Woodheyes Rd.
NW10..........2A 42
Woodhouse Gro. E12..3F 55
Woodhouse Rd. E11...5B 40
Woodland Cl. SE19..5A 120
Woodland Ct. E11....1C 40
(off New Wanstead)
Woodland Cres.
SE10...........2A 96
SE16...........3F 79
Woodland Gro. SE10..1A 96
Woodland Hill SE19..5A 120
Woodland M. SW16..3A 118
Woodland Rd. SE19..5A 120
Woodlands NW11....1A 30
Woodlands, The N5...1E 49
SE13..........5F 109
Woodlands Art Gallery
.............2C 96
Woodlands Av. E11...3D 41
Woodlands Cl. NW11..1A 30

Woodlands Ct. NW10..5F 43
(off Wrentham Av.)
SE23..........5D 107
Woodlands Ga.
SW15..........3B 100
(off Woodlands Way)
Woodlands Hgts.
SE3...........2B 96
(off Vanburgh Hill)
Woodlands Ho. NW6..4A 44
Woodlands Pk. Rd.
N15...........1D 35
SF10..........2A 96
(not continuous)
Woodlands Rd. E11...4A 40
SW13..........1B 98
Woodlands St. SE13...5F 109
Woodland St. E8.....3B 50
Woodlands Way
SW15..........3B 100
Woodland Ter. SE7...5F 83
Wood Ter. NW2......5D 29
Woodland Wlk.
BR1: Brom......4F 123
(not continuous)
NW3...........2A 46
SE10..........1A 96
Wood La. N6........1D 33
NW9...........2A 28
W12...........5E 57
Woodlawn Cl.
SW15..........3B 100
Woodlawn Rd. SW6...3F 85
Woodlea Rd. N16....5A 36
Woodleigh Gdns.
SW16..........3A 118
Woodmans Gro.
NW10..........2B 42
Woodman's M.
W12...........4D 57
Woodmere Cl.
SW11..........1C 102
Woodnook Rd.
SW16..........5D 117
Woodpecker M.
SE13...........2F 109
(off Freshfield Cl.)
Woodpecker Rd.
SE14..........2A 94
Wood Point E16.....4C 68
(off Fife Rd.)
Woodquest Av.
SE24..........3E 105
Woodriffe Rd. E11...2F 39
Woodrush Cl. SE14...3A 94
Wood's Bldgs. E1....4D 65
(off Winthrop St.)
Woodseer St. E1.....4B 64
Woodsford SE17.....1F 91
(off Portland St.)
Woodsford Sq. W14...3A 72
Woodside SW19.....5B 114
Woodside Av. N6....1B 32
Woodside Ct. E12....3E 41
Woodside Ho.
SW19..........5B 114
Woodside M. SE24...3B 106
Woodside Rd. E13...3E 69
Woods M.
W1............4B 12 (1C 74)
Woodsome Rd. NW5...5C 32

Woods Pl.
SE1...........5E 27 (4A 78)
Woodspring Rd.
SW19..........2A 114
Woods Rd. SE15....4D 93
Woodstock Av. NW11..2A 30
Woodstock Ct. SE11...1B 90
SE12..........4C 110
Woodstock Gro. W12..3F 71
Woodstock M. W1....1C 12
Woodstock Rd. E7....4E 55
N4............3C 34
NW11..........2B 30
W4............5A 70
Woodstock St.
W1............3D 13 (5D 61)
Woodstock Ter. E14...1D 81
Wood St. E16.......1D 83
EC2...........2A 18 (5E 63)
W4............1A 84
Woodsyre SE26.....4B 120
Wood Va. N10......1E 33
SE23..........1D 121
Wood Va. Est. SE23..5E 107
Woodvale Wlk.
SE27..........5E 119
Woodvale Way NW11..5F 29
Woodview Cl. N4....2D 35
SW15..........4A 112
Woodville SE3......3D 97
Woodville Cl. SE12..3C 110
Woodville Gdns.
NW11..........2F 29
Woodville Ho. SE1...5F 27
(off Grange Wlk.)
Woodville Rd. E11...3B 40
N16...........2A 50
NW6...........1B 58
NW11..........2F 29
Woodward Av. NW4...1C 28
Woodwarde Rd.
SE22..........4A 106
Woodwell St. SW18...3E 101
Wood Wharf SE10....2E 95
Wood Wharf Bus. Pk.
E14...........2D 81
(not continuous)
Woodyard Cl. NW5...2C 46
Woodyard La. SE21..5A 106
Woodyates Rd.
SE12..........4C 110
Woolacombe Rd. SE3..4E 97
Woolcombes Ct.
SE16..........2F 79
(off Princes Riverside Rd.)
Wooler St. SE17....1F 91
Woolf M. WC1.......3C 6
(off Burton Pl.)
Woolgar M. N16.....2A 50
(off Gillett St.)
Woollaston Rd. N4...1D 35
Woolley Ho. SW9....1D 105
(off Loughborough Rd.)
Woolmead Av. NW9..2D 28
Woolmore St. E14...1E 81

Woolneigh St. SW6 . . . . . 1D **101**
Woolridge Way E9 . . . . . . 4E **51**
Woolstaplers Way
SE16 . . . . 4C **78**
Woolstone Rd.
SE23 . . . . 2A **122**
Woolwich Chu. St.
SE18 . . . . 4F **83**
Woolwich Dockyard Ind. Est.
SE18 . . . . 4F **83**
Woolwich Rd. SE7 . . . . . . 1C **96**
SE10 . . . . 1B **96**
Wooster Gdns. E14 . . . . . 5F **67**
Wooster Pl. SE1 . . . . 5F **77**
(off Searles Rd.)
Wootton St.
SE1 . . . . 2C **24** (2C **76**)
Worcester Cl. NW2 . . . . . 5D **29**
Worcester Cl. W9 . . . . . . 4C **58**
(off Elmfield Way)
Worcester Dr. W4 . . . . . . 3A **70**
Worcester Gdns.
SW11 . . . . 3B **102**
(off Grandison Rd.)
Worcester Ho. SE11 . . . . 5B **24**
(off Kennington Rd.)
SW9 . . . . 3C **90**
(off Cranmer Rd.)
W2 . . . . 5E **59**
(off Hallfield Est.)
Worcester M. NW6 . . . . . 3D **45**
Worcester Rd.
SW19 . . . . 5B **114**
Wordsworth Av. E12 . . . . 4F **55**
Wordsworth Ho.
NW6 . . . . 2C **58**
(off Stafford Rd.)
Wordsworth Pl. NW3 . . . . 2B **46**
Wordsworth Rd. N16 . . . 1A **50**
SE1 . . . . 5B **78**
Worfield St. SW11 . . . . . 3A **88**
Worgan St. SE11 . . . . . . 1B **90**
SE16 . . . . 5F **79**
Worland Rd. E15 . . . . . . 4A **54**
Worlds End Est.
SW10 . . . . 3F **87**
World's End Pas.
SW10 . . . . 3F **87**
(off Worlds End Est.)
World's End Pl.
SW10 . . . . 3F **87**
(off Worlds End Est.)
Worlidge St. W6 . . . . 1E **85**
Worlingham Rd.
SE22 . . . . 2B **106**
Wormholt Rd. W12 . . . . . 1C **70**
Wormwood St.
EC2 . . . . 2D **19** (5A **64**)
Wornington Rd. W10 . . . 3A **58**
(not continuous)
Wornum Ho. W10 . . . . . . 1A **58**
(off Kilburn La.)
Woronzow Rd. NW8 . . . . 5F **45**
Worple Rd. SW19 . . . . . 5B **114**
Worple Rd. M.
SW19 . . . . 5B **114**
Worple St. SW14 . . . . . . 1A **98**
Worship St.
EC2 . . . . 4C **10** (3F **63**)
Worslade Rd. SW17 . . . . 4F **115**

Worsley Bri. Rd.
BR3: Beck 5C **122**
SE26 . . . . 4B **122**
Worsley Gro. E5 . . . . 1C **50**
Worsley Ho. SE23 . . . . . 2E **121**
Worsley Rd. E11 . . . . . . 1A **54**
Worsopp Dr. SW4 . . . . . 3E **103**
Worth Gro. SE17 . . . . . . 1F **91**
Worthing Cl. E15 . . . . . . 5A **54**
Worthington Ho. EC1 . . . 1C **8**
(off Myddelton Pas.)
Wortley Rd. E6 . . . . 4F **55**
Wotton E14 . . . . 1F **81**
(off Jamestown Way)
Wotton Rd. NW2 . . . . . . 5E **29**
SE8 . . . . 2B **94**
Wouldham Rd. E16 . . . . . 5B **68**
Wragby Rd. E11 . . . . 5A **40**
Wrayburn Ho. SE16 . . . . 3C **78**
(off Llewellyn St.)
Wray Cres. N4 . . . . 4A **34**
Wren Av. NW2 . . . . 2E **43**
Wren Cl. E16 . . . . 5B **68**
Wren Ho. E3 . . . . 1A **66**
(off Gernon Rd.)
SW1 . . . . 1F **89**
(off Aylesford St.)
Wren Landing E14 . . . . . 2C **80**
Wrenn Ho. SW13 . . . . . . 2E **85**
Wren Rd. SE5 . . . . 4F **91**
Wren's Pk. Ho. E5 . . . . . 4D **37**
Wren St. WC1 . . . 3A **8** (3B **62**)
Wrentham Av. NW10 . . . 1F **57**
Wrenthorpe Rd.
BR1: Brom 4A **124**
Wren Vw. N6 . . . . 2E **33**
Wrestlers Ct. EC3 . . . . . 2D **19**
Wrexham Rd. E3 . . . . . . 1C **66**
Wricklemarsh Rd.
SE3 . . . . 5D **97**
(not continuous)
Wrigglesworth Rd.
SE14 . . . . 3F **93**
Wright Cl. SE13 . . . . 2F **109**
Wright Rd. N1 . . . . 3A **50**
Wrights Grn. SW4 . . . . . 2F **103**
Wright's La. W8 . . . . 4D **73**
Wright's Rd. E3 . . . . 1B **66**
(not continuous)
Wrotham Ho. SE1 . . . . . 5C **26**
(off Law St.)
Wrotham Rd. NW1 . . . . . 4E **47**
Wrottesley Rd.
NW10 . . . . 1C **56**
Wroughton Rd.
SW11 . . . . 3B **102**
Wroxton Rd. SE15 . . . . . 5E **93**
Wulfstan St. W12 . . . . . . 4B **56**
Wyatt Cl. SE16 . . . . 3B **80**
Wyatt Dr. SW13 . . . . 2D **85**
Wyatt Ho. NW8 . . . . 3F **59**
(off Frampton St.)
SE3 . . . . 5B **96**
Wyatt Pk. Rd. SW2 . . . . 2A **118**
Wyatt Rd. E7 . . . . 3C **54**
N5 . . . . 5E **35**
Wybert St.
NW1 . . . . 3F **5** (3E **61**)
Wychcombe Studios
NW3 . . . . 3B **46**

Wycherley Cl. SE3 . . . . . 3B **96**
Wychwood End N6 . . . . . 2E **33**
Wychwood Way
SE19 . . . . 5F **119**
Wyclif Ct. EC1 . . . . 2D **9**
(off Wyclif St.)
Wycliffe Rd. SW11 . . . . . 5C **88**
Wyclif St. EC1 . . 2D **9** (2D **63**)
Wycombe Gdns.
NW11 . . . . 4C **30**
Wycombe Ho. NW8 . . . . 3A **60**
(off Grendon St.)
Wycombe Pl. SW18 . . . . 4E **101**
Wycombe Sq. W8 . . . . . 2B **72**
Wydeville Mnr. Rd.
SE12 . . . . 4D **125**
Wye St. SW11 . . . . 5F **87**
Wyfold Rd. SW6 . . . . . . 3A **86**
Wykeham Cl. NW4 . . . . . 1E **29**
(off Wykeham Rd.)
Wykeham Rd. NW4 . . . . 1E **29**
Wyke Rd. E3 . . . . 4C **52**
Wyldes Cl. NW11 . . . . . . 3E **31**
Wyleu St. SE23 . . . . 5A **108**
Wyllen Cl. E1 . . . . 3E **65**
Wymans Way E7 . . . . . . 1E **55**
Wymering Mans. W9 . . . 2C **58**
(off Wymering Rd.,
not continuous)
Wymering Rd. W9 . . . . . 2C **58**
Wymond St. SW15 . . . . . 1E **99**
Wynan Rd. E14 . . . . 1D **95**
Wyndcliff Rd. SE7 . . . . . 2D **97**
Wyndham Cres. N19 . . . 5E **33**
Wyndham Deedes Ho.
E2 . . . . 1C **64**
(off Hackney Rd.)
Wyndham Est. SE5 . . . . 3E **91**
Wyndham Ho. E14 . . . . . 3D **81**
(off Marsh Wall)
Wyndham M. W1 . . . . . . 4B **60**
Wyndham Pl.
W1 . . . . 1A **12** (4B **60**)
Wyndham Rd. E6 . . . . . . 4F **55**
SE5 . . . . 3E **91**
Wyndhams Ct. E8 . . . . . 4B **50**
(off Celandine Dr.)
Wyndham's Theatre 4D **15**
(off St Martin's La.)
Wyndham St. W1 . . . . . . 4B **60**
Wyndham Yd. W1 . . . . . 4B **60**
Wyneham Rd. SE24 . . . . 3F **105**
Wynell Rd. SE23 . . . . . . 3F **121**
Wynford Ho. N1 . . . . 1B **62**
(off Wynford Rd.)
Wynford Rd. N1 . . . . 1B **62**
Wynne Ho. SE14 . . . . . . 4F **93**
Wynne Rd. SW9 . . . . . . 5C **90**
Wynnstay Gdns. W8 . . . 4C **72**
Wynter St. SW11 . . . . . . 2E **101**
Wynyard Ho. SE11 . . . . 1B **90**
(off Newburn St.)
Wynyard Ter. SE11 . . . . 1B **90**
Wynyatt St.
EC1 . . . . 2D **9** (2D **63**)
Wythburn Ct. W1 . . . . . . 2A **12**
(off Wythburn Pl.)
Wythburn Pl.
W1 . . . . 3A **12** (5B **60**)
Wythes Rd. E16 . . . . . . 2F **83**

Wyvil Rd. SW8 . . . . 3A 90
Wyvis St. E14 . . . . 4D 67

Y

Yabsley St. E14 . . . . 2E 81
Yalding Rd. SE16 . . . . . . 4C 78
Yale Ct. NW6 . . . . 2D 45
Yard, The. N1 . . . . 1E 7
(off Caledonian Rd.)
Yardley St.
WC1 . . . . 2B 8 (2C 62)
(not continuous)
Yarmouth Pl.
W1 . . . . 2D 21 (2D 75)
Yarnfield Sq. SE15 . . . . . 4C 92
Yarrow Cres. E6 . . . . . . 4F 69
Yarrow Ho. E14 . . . . 4E 81
(off Stewart St.)
W10 . . . . 4E 57
(off Sutton Way)
Yateley St. SE18 . . . . . . 4F 83
Yates Ct. NW2 . . . . 3F 43
Yates Ho. E2 . . . . 2C 64
(off Roberta St.)
Yatton Ho. W10 . . . . 4E 57
(off Sutton Way)
Yeadon Ho. W10 . . . . . . 4E 57
(off Sutton Way)
Yearby Ho. W10 . . . . 3E 57
(off Sutton Way)
Yeate St. N1 . . . . 4F 49
Yeatman Rd. N6 . . . . . . 1B 32
Yeats Cl. NW10 . . . . 2A 42
SE13 . . . . 5F 95
Yeldham Ho. W6 . . . . 1F 85
(off Yeldham Rd.)
Yeldham Rd. W6 . . . . . . 1F 85
Yeldham Vs. W6 . . . . 1F 85
(off Yeldham Rd.)
Yelverton Rd. SW11 . . . . 5F 87
Yeoman Cl. SE27 . . . . . . 3D 119
Yeoman Ct. SE1 . . . . . . 1B 92
(off Cooper's Rd.)
Yeoman's Row
SW3 . . . . 4A 74
Yeoman St. SE8 . . . . . . 5A 80
Yeoman's Yd. E1 . . . . . . 1B 78
(off Chamber St.)
Yeo St. E3 . . . . 4D 67
Yeovil Ho. W10 . . . . 3E 57
(off Sutton Way)

Yerbury Rd. N19 . . . . . . 5F 33
(not continuous)
Yetev Lev Ct. E5 . . . . . . 3C 36
Yewfield Rd. NW10 . . . . 3B 42
Yew Gro. NW2 . . . . 1F 43
Yew Ho. SE16 . . . . 3F 79
(off Woodland Cres.)
Yew Tree Ct. NW11 . . . 1B 30
(off Bridge La.)
Yew Tree Lodge
SW16 . . . . 4E 117
Yew Tree Rd. W12 . . . . . 1B 70
Yoakley Rd. N16 . . . . . . 4A 36
Yoke Cl. N7 . . . . 3A 48
Yolande Gdns. SE9 . . . . 3F 111
Yonge Pk. N4 . . . . 5C 34
York Av. SE17 . . . . 1E 91
York Bri. NW1 . . . 3B 4 (3C 60)
York Bldgs.
WC2 . . . . 5E 15 (1A 76)
York Cl. SE5 . . . . 5E 91
(off Lilford Rd.)
York Ga. NW1 . . . 4B 4 (3C 60)
York Gro. SE15 . . . . 4E 93
York Hill SE27 . . . . 3D 119
York Ho. E16 . . . . 2C 82
(off De Quincey M.)
SE1 . . . . 5A 24 (4B 76)
W1 . . . . 5A 4
(off York St.)
York Ho. Pl. W8 . . . . 3D 73
Yorkley Ho. W10 . . . . . . 3E 57
(off Sutton Way)
York Mans. SW5 . . . . . . 1D 87
(off Earls Ct. Rd.)
SW11 . . . . 4C 88
(off Prince of Wales Dr.)
W1 . . . . 5B 4
(off Chiltern St.)
York M. NW5 . . . . 2D 47
York Pas. W8 . . . . 3D 73
(off York Ho. Pl.)
York Pl. SW11 . . . . 1F 101
WC2 . . . . 5E 15
York Pl. Mans. W1 . . . . . 5A 4
(off Baker St.)
York Ri. NW5 . . . . 5D 33
York Rd. E7 . . . . 3C 54
E10 . . . . 5E 39
E17 . . . . 1F 37
SE1 . . . . 3A 24 (3B 76)
SW11 . . . . 2E 101
SW18 . . . . 2E 101
SW19 . . . . 5E 115

Yorkshire Cl. N16 . . . . . 5A 36
YORKSHIRE GREY . . . 3F 111
Yorkshire Grey Pl.
NW3 . . . . 1E 45
Yorkshire Grey Yd.
WC1 . . . . 1F 15
Yorkshire Rd. E14 . . . . . 5A 66
York St. W1 . . . 1A 12 (4B 60)
York St. Chambers
W1 . . . . 4B 60
(off York St.)
York Ter. E.
NW1 . . . . 4C 4 (3C 60)
York Ter. W.
NW1 . . . . 4B 4 (3C 60)
Yorkton St. E2 . . . . 1C 64
York Way N1 . . . 1E 7 (3A 48)
N7 . . . . 3F 47
York Way Ct. N1 . . . . . . 5A 48
York Way Est. N7 . . . . . 3A 48
Young Cl. NW6 . . . . 4A 44
Young Rd. E16 . . . . 5E 69
Youngs Bldgs. EC1 . . . 3A 10
Youngs Ct. SW11 . . . . . 4C 88
Young St. W8 . . . . 3D 73
Young Vic Theatre, The
. . . . 3C 24
Yoxall Ho. W10 . . . . 3E 57
(off Sutton Way)
Yukon Rd. SW12 . . . . . 5D 103
Yunus Khan Cl. E17 . . . 1C 38

Z

Zampa Rd. SE16 . . . . . . 1E 93
Zander Ct. E2 . . . . 2C 64
Zangwill Rd. SE3 . . . . . . 4F 97
Zealand Ho. SE5 . . . . . . 5E 91
(off Denmark Rd.)
Zealand Rd. E3 . . . . 1A 66
Zennor Rd. SW12 . . . . . 1E 117
Zennor Rd. Ind. Est.
SW12 . . . . 1E 117
Zenoria St. SE22 . . . . . 2B 106
Zetland Ho. W8 . . . . 4D 73
(off Marloes Rd.)
Zetland St. E14 . . . . 4D 67
(off Jubilee St.)
Zion Ho. E1 . . . . 5E 65
(off Jubilee St.)
Zoar St. SE1 . . . 1F 25 (2E 77)
Zoffany St. N19 . . . . 4F 33

HOSPITALS and HOSPICES
covered by this atlas.

N.B. Where Hospitals and Hospices are not named on the map,
the reference given is for the road in which they are situated.

ABBEY CHURCHILL LONDON, THE
.................................4C **76** (5C **24**)
22 Barkham Terrace
LONDON
SE1 7PW
Tel: 020 79285633

ATHLONE HOUSE 3B **32**
Hampstead Lane
LONDON
N6 4RX
Tel: 020 83485231

BARNES HOSPITAL 1A **98**
South Worple Way
LONDON
SW14 8SU
Tel: 020 88784981

BELVEDERE DAY HOSPITAL 5C **42**
341 Harlesden Road
LONDON
NW10 3RX
Tel: 020 84593562

BLACKHEATH BMI HOSPITAL, THE 1B **110**
40-42 Lee Terrace
LONDON
SE3 9UD
Tel: 020 83187722

BOLINGBROKE HOSPITAL. 3A **102**
Bolingbroke Grove
LONDON
SW11 6HN
Tel: 020 72237411

BRITISH HOME 5D **119**
Crown Lane
LONDON
SW16 3JB
Tel: 020 86708261

CAMDEN MEWS DAY HOSPITAL 4E **47**
1-5 Camden Mews
LONDON
NW1 9DB
Tel: 020 75304780

CHARING CROSS HOSPITAL 2F **85**
Fulham Palace Road
LONDON
W6 8RF
Tel: 020 88461234

CHELSEA & WESTMINSTER HOSPITAL
.................................2E **87**
369 Fulham Road
LONDON
SW10 9NH
Tel: 020 87468000

CHILDREN'S HOSPITAL, THE (LEWISHAM)
.................................3D **109**
Lewisham University Hospital
Lewisham High Street
LONDON
SE13 6LH
Tel: 020 83333000

CROMWELL HOSPITAL, THE 5D **73**
162-174 Cromwell Road
LONDON
SW5 0TU
Tel: 020 74602000

DULWICH COMMUNITY HOSPITAL 2A **106**
East Dulwich Grove
LONDON
SE22 8PT
Tel: AWAITING NEW T

EASTMAN DENTAL HOSPITAL &
  DENTAL INSTITUTE, THE 3B **62** (3F **7**)
256 Gray's Inn Road
LONDON
WC1X 8LD
Tel: 020 79151000

EDENHALL MARIE CURIE CENTRE 2F **45**
11 Lyndhurst Gardens
LONDON
NW3 5NS
Tel: 020 78533400

ELIZABETH GARRETT ANDERSON &
  OBSTETRIC HOSPITAL, THE 3E **61** (4A **6**)
Huntley Street
LONDON
WC1E 6DH
Tel: 020 73879300

EVELINA CHILDREN'S HOSPITAL
.................................4B **76** (5F **23**)
St Thomas' Hospital
Lambeth Palace Road
LONDON
SE1 7EH
Tel: 0207 1887188

FLORENCE NIGHTINGALE DAY HOSPITAL
.................................4A **60**
1B Harewood Row
LONDON
NW1 6SE
Tel: 020 77259940

FLORENCE NIGHTINGALE HOSPITAL 4A **60**
11-19 Lisson Grove
LONDON
NW1 6SH
Tel: 020 75357700

FORDWYCH ROAD DAY HOSPITAL 2B **44**
85-87 Fordwych Road
LONDON
NW2 3TL
Tel: 020 82081612

GORDON HOSPITAL 5F **75**
Bloomburg Street
LONDON
SW1V 2RH
Tel: 020 87468733

GREAT ORMOND STREET HOSPITAL FOR
CHILDREN 3A **62** (4E **7**)
Great Ormond Street
LONDON
WC1N 3JH
Tel: 020 74059200

GUY'S HOSPITAL 2F **77** (2C **26**)
St Thomas Street
LONDON
SE1 9RT
Tel: 020 71887188

GUY'S NUFFIELD HOUSE 3F **77** (3B **26**)
Newcomen Street
LONDON
SE1 1YR
Tel: 020 79554257

HAMMERSMITH HOSPITAL 5C **56**
Du Cane Road
LONDON
W12 0HS
Tel: 020 83831000

HARLEY STREET CLINIC, THE 4D **61** (5D **5**)
35 Weymouth Street
LONDON
W1G 8BJ
Tel: 020 79357700

HEART HOSPITAL, THE 4C **60** (1C **12**)
16-18 Westmoreland Street
LONDON
W1G 8PH
Tel: 020 75738888

HIGHGATE HOSPITAL 1B **32**
17 View Road
LONDON
N6 4DJ
Tel: 020 83414182

HOMERTON UNIVERSITY HOSPITAL 2F **51**
Homerton Row
LONDON
E9 6SR
Tel: 020 85105555

HOSPITAL FOR TROPICAL DISEASES
. . . . 3E **61** (4A **6**)
Mortimer Market,
Capper Street
LONDON
WC1E 6AU
Tel: 020 7387 9300

HOSPITAL OF ST JOHN & ST ELIZABETH
. . . . 1F **59**
60 Grove End Road
LONDON
NW8 9NH
Tel: 020 78064000

KING EDWARD VII'S HOSPITAL SISTER AGNES
. . . . 4C **60** (5C **4**)
5-10 Beaumont Street
LONDON
W1G 6AA
Tel: 020 74864411

KING'S COLLEGE HOSPITAL 5F **91**
Denmark Hill
LONDON
SE5 9RS
Tel: 020 77374000

LAMBETH HOSPITAL 1B **104**
108 Landor Road
LONDON
SW9 9NT
Tel: 020 74116100

LATIMER DAY HOSPITAL 4E **61** (5F **5**)
40 Hanson Street
LONDON
W1W 6UL
Tel: 020 73809187

LEWISHAM UNIVERSITY HOSPITAL . . . 3D **109**
Lewisham High Street
LONDON
SE13 6LH
Tel: 020 83333000

LISTER HOSPITAL, THE 1D **89**
Chelsea Bridge Road
LONDON
SW1W 8RH
Tel: 020 77303417

LONDON BRIDGE HOSPITAL . . . 2F **77** (1C **26**)
27 Tooley Street
LONDON
SE1 2PR
Tel: 020 74073100

LONDON CHEST HOSPITAL 1E **65**
Bonner Road
LONDON
E2 9JX
Tel: 020 73777000

LONDON CLINIC, THE 3C **60** (4C **4**)
20 Devonshire Place
LONDON
W1G 6BW
Tel: 020 79354444

LONDON FOOT HOSPITAL 3E **61** (4F **5**)
33 & 40 Fitzroy Square
LONDON
W1T 6AY
Tel: 020 75304500

LONDON INDEPENDENT BMI HOSPITAL, THE 4F **65**
1 Beaumont Square
LONDON
E1 4NL
Tel: 020 77802400

LONDON LIGHTHOUSE 5A **58**
111-117 Lancaster Road
LONDON
W11 1QT
Tel: 020 77921200

LONDON WELBECK HOSPITAL
. . . . 4D **61** (1D **13**)
27 Welbeck Street
LONDON
W1G 8EN
Tel: 020 72242242

MAUDSLEY HOSPITAL, THE 5F **91**
Denmark Hill
LONDON
SE5 8AZ
Tel: 0207 7036333

MIDDLESEX HOSPITAL, THE 4E **61** (1A **14**)
Mortimer Street
LONDON
W1T 3AA
Tel: 020 76368333

MILDMAY MISSION HOSPITAL . . 2B **64** (2F **11**)
Hackney Road
LONDON
E2 7NA
Tel: 020 76136300

MILE END HOSPITAL 3F **65**
Bancroft Road
LONDON
E1 4DG
Tel: 020 73777000

MOORFIELDS EYE HOSPITAL 2F **63** (2B **10**)
162 City Road
LONDON
EC1V 2PD
Tel: 020 72533411

**NATIONAL HOSPITAL FOR NEUROLOGY &
NEUROSURGERY, THE** 3A **62** (4E **7**)
Queen Square
LONDON
WC1N 3BG
Tel: 020 78373611

NEWHAM GENERAL HOSPITAL 3E **69**
Glen Road
LONDON
E13 8SL
Tel: 020 74764000

NHS WALK-IN CENTRE (CHARING CROSS)
. . . . 1F **85**
Charing Cross Hospital
Fulham Palace Road
LONDON
W6 8RF
Tel: 020 8383 0904

NHS WALK-IN CENTRE (HACKNEY) 2F **51**
Homerton University Hospital
Homerton Row
LONDON
E9 6SR
Tel: 020 8510 5342 / 7121

**NHS WALK-IN CENTRE
(LEYTONSTONE - WHIPPS CROSS)** 1F **39**
Whipps Cross Hospital
Whipps Cross Road
LONDON
E11 1NR
Tel: 020 8558 8965 / 4229

NHS WALK-IN CENTRE (NEW CROSS) . . . 3A **94**
Henderson House
40 Goodwood Road
LONDON
SE14 6BL
Tel: 020 7206 3100

NHS WALK-IN CENTRE (NEWHAM) 3E **69**
Glen Road
LONDON
E13 8SH
Tel: 020 7363 9200

NHS WALK-IN CENTRE (PARSONS GREEN)
. . . . 4C **86**
5-7 Parsons Green
LONDON
SW6 4UL
Tel: 020 8846 6758

NHS WALK-IN CENTRE (SOHO) . . 5F **61** (3B **14**)
1 Frith Street
LONDON
W1D 3HZ
Tel: 020 7534 6500

NHS WALK-IN CENTRE (TOOTING) 5A **116**
Clare House
St. Georges Hospital
Blackshaw Road
LONDON
SW17 0QT
Tel: 020 8700 0505

NHS WALK-IN CENTRE (WHITECHAPEL)
. . . . 4D **65**
Royal London Hospital
174 Whitechapel Road
LONDON
E1 1BZ
Tel: 020 7943 1333

NHS WALK-IN CENTRE (WHITTINGTON)
. . . . 4E **33**
Whittington Hospital, Sterling Way
LONDON
N18 1QX
Tel: 020 7288 5216

PARKSIDE HOSPITAL 3F **113**
53 Parkside
LONDON
SW19 5NX
Tel: 020 89718000

PLAISTOW HOSPITAL 1E **69**
Samson Street
LONDON
E13 9EH
Tel: 020 85866200

PORTLAND HOSPITAL, THE FOR WOMEN &
CHILDREN, THE 3D **61** (4E **5**)
209 Great Portland Street
LONDON
W1W 5AH
Tel: 020 75804400

PRINCESS GRACE HOSPITAL 3C **60** (4B **4**)
42-52 Nottingham Place
LONDON
W1U 5NY
Tel: 020 74861234

PRINCESS GRACE HOSPITAL ANNEXE
. . . . .4C **60** (5C **4**)
29-31 Devonshire Street
LONDON
W1G 6PU
Tel: 020 74861234

PRINCESS LOUISE DAY HOSPITAL 4F **57**
St. Quintin Avenue
LONDON
W10 6DL
Tel: 020 89690133

QUEEN CHARLOTTE'S & CHELSEA HOSPITAL
. . . . .5C **56**
Du Cane Road
LONDON
W12 0HS
Tel: 020 83831111

QUEEN MARY'S HOUSE 5E **31**
23 East Heath Road
LONDON
NW3 1DU
Tel: 020 74314111

QUEEN MARY'S UNIVERSITY HOSPITAL
. . . . .4C **98**
Roehampton Lane
LONDON
SW15 5PN
Tel: 020 87896611

RAVENSCOURT PARK HOSPITAL 5C **70**
Ravenscourt Park
LONDON
W6 0NT
Tel: 020 88467777

RICHARD HOUSE CHILDREN'S HOSPICE
. . . . .1F **83**
Richard House Drive
LONDON
E16 3RG
Tel: 020 75110222

ROEHAMPTON HUNTERCOMBE HOSPITAL
. . . . .5C **98**
Holybourne Avenue
LONDON
SW15 4JL
Tel: 0208 7806155

ROEHAMPTON PRIORY HOSPITAL 2B **98**
Priory Lane
LONDON
SW15 5JJ
Tel: 020 88768261

ROYAL BROMPTON HOSPITAL 1A **88**
Sydney Street
LONDON
SW3 6NP
Tel: 020 73528121

ROYAL BROMPTON HOSPITAL (ANNEXE)
. . . . .1F **87**
Fulham Road
LONDON
SW3 6HP
Tel: 020 73528121

ROYAL FREE HOSPITAL, THE 2A **46**
Pond Street
LONDON
NW3 2QG
Tel: 020 77940500

ROYAL HOSPITAL FOR NEURO-DISABILITY
. . . . .4A **100**
West Hill
LONDON
SW15 3SW
Tel: 020 87804500

ROYAL LONDON HOMOEOPATHIC HOSPITAL,
THE .4A **62** (5E **7**)
Great Ormond Street
LONDON
WC1N 3HR
Tel: 020 73918864

ROYAL LONDON HOSPITAL 4D **65**
Whitechapel Road
LONDON
E1 1BB
Tel: 020 73777000

ROYAL MARSDEN HOSPITAL (FULHAM), THE
. . . . .1F **87**
Fulham Road
LONDON
SW3 6JJ
Tel: 020 73528171

ROYAL NATIONAL ORTHOPAEDIC HOSPITAL
(OUTPATIENTS) 3D **61** (4E **5**)
45-51 Bolsover Street
LONDON
W1W 5AQ
Tel: 020 73875070

ROYAL NATIONAL THROAT, NOSE &
EAR HOSPITAL 2B **62** (1F **7**)
330 Gray's Inn Road
LONDON
WC1X 8DA
Tel: 020 79151300

ST ANDREW'S HOSPITAL 3D **67**
Devas Street
LONDON
E3 3NT
Tel: 020 74764000

ST ANN'S HOSPITAL 1E **35**
St Ann's Road
LONDON
N15 3TH
Tel: 020 84426000

ST BARTHOLOMEW'S HOSPITAL
. . . . .4D **63** (1E **17**)
West Smithfield
LONDON
EC1A 7BE
Tel: 020 73777000

ST CHARLES HOSPITAL 4F **57**
Exmoor Street
LONDON
W10 6DZ
Tel: 020 89692488

ST CHRISTOPHER'S HOSPICE 5E **121**
51-59 Lawrie Park Road
LONDON
SE26 6DZ
Tel: 020 87789252

ST CLEMENT'S HOSPITAL 2B **66**
2A Bow Road
LONDON
E3 4LL
Tel: 020 73777000

ST GEORGE'S HOSPITAL (TOOTING) . . . 5A **116**
Blackshaw Road
LONDON
SW17 0QT
Tel: 020 86721255

ST JOHN'S HOSPICE 1F **59**
Hospital of St John & St Elizabeth,
60 Grove End Road
LONDON
NW8 9NH
Tel: 020 78064040

ST JOSEPH'S HOSPICE 5D **51**
Mare Street
LONDON
E8 4SA
Tel: 020 85256000

ST LUKE'S HOSPITAL FOR THE CLERGY
. . . . .3E **61** (4F **5**)
14 Fitzroy Square
LONDON
W1T 6AH
Tel: 020 73884954

ST MARY'S HOSPITAL 5F **59**
Praed Street
LONDON
W2 1NY
Tel: 020 77256666

ST PANCRAS HOSPITAL 5F **47**
4 St Pancras Way
LONDON
NW1 0PE
Tel: 020 75303500

ST THOMAS' HOSPITAL 4B **76** (5F **23**)
Lambeth Palace Road
LONDON
SE1 7EH
Tel: 0207 1887188

SPRINGFIELD UNIVERSITY HOSPITAL. . .3A **116**
61 Glenburnie Road
LONDON
SW17 7DJ
Tel: 020 86826000

TRINITY HOSPICE 2D **103**
30 Clapham Common North Side
LONDON
SW4 0RN
Tel: 020 77871000

UNIVERSITY COLLEGE HOSPITAL
. . . . .3E **61** (3A **6**)
Gower Street
LONDON
WC1E 6AU
Tel: 020 73879300

WELLINGTON HOSPITAL, THE 2F **59**
8a Wellington Place
LONDON
NW8 9LE
Tel: 0207 5865959

WESTERN EYE HOSPITAL 4B **60**
171 Marylebone Road
LONDON
NW1 5QH
Tel: 020 78866666

WHIPPS CROSS UNIVERSITY HOSPITAL
. . . . 1F **39**
Whipps Cross Road
LONDON
E11 1NR
Tel: 020 85395522

WHITTINGTON HOSPITAL 4E **33**
Highgate Hill
LONDON
N19 5NF
Tel: 020 72723070

WILLESDEN COMMUNITY HOSPITAL 4C **42**
Harlesden Road
LONDON
NW10 3RY
Tel: 020 84518017

RAIL, CROYDON TRAMLINK, DOCKLANDS LIGHT RAILWAY, RIVERBUS AND LONDON UNDERGROUND STATIONS

with their map square reference

A

Acton Central (Rail) 2A 70
Aldgate East (Tube) 2F 19 (5B 64)
Aldgate (Tube) 3F 19 (5B 64)
All Saints (DLR) 1D 81
Angel (Tube) 1C 62
Archway (Tube) 4E 33
Arsenal (Tube) 5C 34

B

Baker Street (Tube) 4A 4 (3B 60)
Balham (Rail & Tube) 1D 117
Bankside Pier (Riverbus) 5F 17 (1E 77)
Bank (Tube & DLR) 3B 18 (5F 63)
Barbican (Rail & Tube) 5F 9 (4E 63)
Barnes (Rail) 1C 98
Barnes Bridge (Rail) 5B 84
Barons Court (Tube) 1A 86
Battersea Park (Rail) 3D 89
Bayswater (Tube) 1D 73
Beckenham Hill (Rail) 5E 123
Bellingham (Rail) 3D 123
Belsize Park (Tube) 2A 46
Bermondsey (Tube) 4C 78
Bethnal Green (Rail). 3D 65
Bethnal Green (Tube) 2E 65
Blackfriars Millennium Pier (Riverbus)
. . . . 4C 16 (1C 76)
Blackfriars (Rail & Tube) 4D 17 (1D 77)
Blackheath (Rail) 1B 110
Blackwall (DLR) 1E 81
Bond Street (Tube) 3D 13 (5D 61)
Borough (Tube) 4A 26 (3E 77)
Bow Church (DLR) 2C 66
Bow Road (Tube) 2C 66
Brent Cross (Tube) 2F 29
Brixton (Rail & Tube) 2C 104
Brockley (Rail) 1A 108
Bromley-by-Bow (Tube). 2D 67
Brondesbury Park (Rail) 5A 44
Brondesbury (Rail) 4B 44

C

Cadogan Pier (Riverbus) 2A 88
Caledonian Road & Barnsbury (Rail)
. . . . 4B 48
Caledonian Road (Tube) 3B 48
Cambridge Heath (Rail) 1D 65
Camden Road (Rail) 4E 47
Camden Town (Tube) 5D 47
Canada Water (Tube) 3E 79
Canary Wharf (Tube). 2D 81
Canary Wharf (DLR) 2C 80

Canary Wharf Pier (Riverbus) 2B 80
Canning Town (Rail, Tube & DLR)
. . . . 5A 68
Cannon Street (Rail & Tube)
. . . . 4B 18 (1F 77)
Canonbury (Rail) 2E 49
Catford (Rail). 5C 108
Catford Bridge (Rail) 6C 108
Chalk Farm (Tube) 4C 46
Chancery Lane (Tube) 1B 16 (4C 62)
Charing Cross (Rail & Tube). . . 1D 23 (2A 76)
Charlton (Rail) 1E 97
City Thameslink (Rail)
Holborn Viaduct 2D 17 (5D 63)
Clapham Common (Tube) 2E 103
Clapham High Street (Rail) 1F 103
Clapham Junction (Rail) 1A 102
Clapham North (Rail) 1A 104
Clapham South (Tube) 4D 103
Clapton (Rail) 4D 37
Covent Garden (Tube) 4E 15 (1A 76)
Cricklewood (Rail) 1F 43
Crofton Park (Rail) 3B 108
Crossharbour & London Arena (DLR)
. . . . 4D 81
Crouch Hill (Rail) 2B 34
Custom House for ExCeL (Rail & DLR)
. . . . 1D 83
Cutty Sark for Maritime Greenwich (DLR)
. . . . 2E 95

D

Dalston Kingsland (Rail) 2A 50
Denmark Hill (Rail) 5F 91
Deptford (Rail). 3C 94
Deptford Bridge (DLR) 4C 94
Devons Road (DLR) 3D 67
Dollis Hill (Tube) 2C 42
Drayton Park (Rail) 1C 48

E

Earl's Court (Tube) 5D 73
Earlsfield (Rail) 1E 115
East Acton (Tube) 5B 56
East Dulwich (Rail) 2A 106
East India (DLR) 1F 81
East Putney (Tube) 3A 100
Edgware Road (Tube) 4A 60
Elephant & Castle (Rail & Tube). 5E 77
Elmstead Woods (Rail) 5F 125
Elverson Road (DLR) 5D 95
Embankment Pier (Riverbus)
. . . . 1E 23 (2A 76)
Embankment (Tube). 1E 23 (2A 76)
Essex Road (Rail) 4E 49

Index to Stations

Euston Square (Tube) 3A 6 (3E 61)
Euston (Rail & Tube) 2B 6 (2F 61)

F

Farringdon (Rail & Tube) 5D 9 (4D 63)
Fenchurch Street (Rail)
. . . . 4F 19 (1B 78)
Festival Pier (Riverbus) 2B 76
Finchley Road (Tube) 3E 45
Finchley Road & Frognal (Rail) 2E 45
Finsbury Park (Rail & Tube) 4C 34
Forest Gate (Rail) 2C 54
Forest Hill (Rail) 2E 121
Fulham Broadway (Tube) 3C 86

G

Gipsy Hill (Rail) 5A 120
Gloucester Road (Tube) 5E 73
Golders Green (Tube) 3C 30
Goldhawk Road (Tube) 3E 71
Goodge Street (Tube) 5B 6 (4F 61)
Gospel Oak (Rail) 1C 46
Great Portland Street (Tube)
. . . . 4E 5 (3D 61)
Greenland Pier (Riverbus) 4B 80
Green Park (Tube) 1E 21 (2E 75)
Greenwich (Rail & DLR) 3D 95
Greenwich Pier (Riverbus) 1E 95
Grove Park (Rail) 3D 125

H

Hackney Central (Rail) 3D 51
Hackney Downs (Rail) 2D 51
Hackney Wick (Rail) 3C 52
Hammersmith (Tube) 5E 71
Hampstead (Tube) 1E 45
Hampstead Heath (Rail) 1A 46
Harlesden (Rail & Tube) 1A 56
Harringay Green Lanes (Rail) 1D 35
Harringay (Rail) 1C 34
Haydons Road (Rail) 5E 115
Hendon (Rail) 1C 28
Hendon Central (Tube) 1D 29
Herne Hill (Rail) 4D 105
Heron Quays (DLR) 2C 80
Highbury & Islington (Rail & Tube) . . . 3D 49
Highgate (Tube) 1D 33
High Street Kensington (Tube) 3D 73
Hilton Docklands Pier (Riverbus) 2B 80
Hither Green (Rail) 4A 110
Holborn (Tube) 1F 15 (5B 62)
Holland Park (Tube) 2B 72
Holloway Road (Tube) 2B 48
Homerton (Rail) 3F 51
Honor Oak Park (Rail) 4F 107
Hyde Park Corner (Tube) 3C 20 (3C 74)

I

Imperial Wharf (Rail) 4E 87
Island Gardens (DLR) 5E 81

K

Kennington (Tube) 1D 91
Kensal Green (Rail & Tube) 2E 57
Kensal Rise (Rail) 1F 57
Kensington Olympia (Rail & Tube) . . . 4A 72
Kentish Town (Rail & Tube) 2E 47
Kentish Town West (Rail) 3D 47
Kidbrooke (Rail) 1D 111
Kilburn (Tube) 3B 44
Kilburn High Road (Rail) 5D 45
Kilburn Park (Tube) 1C 58
King's Cross (Rail) 1E 7 (1A 62)
King's Cross St Pancras (Tube)
. . . . 1D 7 (2A 62)
King's Cross Thameslink (Rail)
. . . . 1E 7 (2A 62)
Knightsbridge (Tube) 4A 20 (3B 74)

L

Ladbroke Grove (Tube) 5A 58
Ladywell (Rail) 3D 109
Lambeth North (Tube) 5B 24 (4C 76)
Lancaster Gate (Tube) 1F 73
Latimer Road (Tube) 1F 71
Lee (Rail) 4C 110
Leicester Square (Tube) 4C 14 (1A 76)
Lewisham (Rail & DLR) 1E 109
Leyton (Tube) 5E 39
Leyton Midland Road (Rail) 3E 39
Leytonstone High Road (Rail) 4A 40
Leytonstone (Tube) 3A 40
Limehouse (Rail & DLR) 5A 66
Liverpool Street (Rail & Tube)
. . . . 1D 19 (4A 64)
London Bridge (Rail & Tube) . . 2C 26 (2F 77)
London Bridge City Pier (Riverbus)
. . . . 1D 27 (2A 78)
London Fields (Rail) 4D 51
Loughborough Junction (Rail) 1D 105
Lower Sydenham (Rail) 5B 122

M

Maida Vale (Tube) 2D 59
Manor Park (Rail) 1F 55
Mansion House (Tube) 4A 18 (1E 77)
Marble Arch (Tube) 3A 12 (5B 60)
Maryland (Rail) 3A 54
Marylebone (Rail & Tube) 3B 60
Masthouse Terrace Pier (Riverbus) . . . 1C 94
Maze Hill (Rail) 2A 96
Mile End (Tube) 3B 66
Millbank Millennium Pier (Riverbus) . . 5A 76
Monument (Tube) 4C 18 (1F 77)
Moorgate (Rail & Tube) 1B 18 (4F 63)
Mornington Crescent (Tube) 1E 61
Mudchute (DLR) 5D 81

N

Neasden (Tube) 2A 42
New Cross (Rail & Tube) 3B 94

New Cross Gate (Rail & Tube) 4A 94
North Acton (Tube) 4A 56
North Dulwich (Rail) 3F 105
North Greenwich (Tube) 3A 82
Notting Hill Gate (Tube) 2C 72
Nunhead (Rail) 5E 93

O

Old Street (Rail & Tube) 2C 10 (3F 63)
Oval (Tube) 2C 90
Oxford Circus (Tube) 3F 13 (5E 61)

P

Paddington (Rail & Tube) 5F 59
Parsons Green (Tube) 4C 86
Peckham Rye (Rail) 5C 92
Penge East (Rail) 5E 121
Piccadilly Circus (Tube) 5B 14 (1F 75)
Pimlico (Tube) 1F 89
Plaistow (Tube) 1B 68
Pontoon Dock (DLR) 2E 83
Poplar (DLR) 1D 81
Prince Regent (DLR) 1E 83
Pudding Mill Lane (DLR) 5D 53
Putney (Rail) 2A 100
Putney Bridge (Tube) 1B 100

Q

Queen's Park (Rail & Tube) 1B 58
Queens Road (Peckham) (Rail) 4E 93
Queenstown Road (Battersea) (Rail)
. . . . 4D 89
Queensway (Tube) 1D 73

R

Ravenscourt Park (Tube) 5D 71
Rectory Road (Rail) 5B 36
Redbridge (Tube) 1F 41
Regent's Park (Tube) 4D 5 (3D 61)
Rotherhithe (Tube) 3E 79
Royal Albert (DLR) 1F 83
Royal Oak (Tube) 4D 59
Royal Victoria (DLR) 1C 82
Russell Square (Tube) 4D 7 (3A 62)

S

St James's Park (Tube) 5B 22 (3F 75)
St James Street Walthamstow (Rail)
. . . . 1A 38
St Johns (Rail) 5C 94
St John's Wood (Tube) 1F 59
St Katharine's Pier (Riverbus)
. . . . 1F 27 (2B 78)
St Pancras (Rail) 1D 7 (2A 62)
St Paul's (Tube) 2F 17 (5E 63)
Savoy Pier (Riverbus) 5F 15 (1B 76)
Seven Sisters (Rail & Tube) 1B 36
Shadwell (Tube & DLR) 1D 79

Shepherd's Bush (Rail & Tube)
  Central Line 3F 71
Shepherd's Bush (Tube)
  Hammersmith & City Line 2E 71
Shoreditch (Tube) 3B 64
Silvertown (Rail) 2F 83
Sloane Square (Tube) 5C 74
Snaresbrook (Tube) 1C 40
South Bermondsey (Rail) 1E 93
Southfields (Tube) 1B 114
South Hampstead (Rail) 4E 45
South Kensington (Tube) 5F 73
South Quay (DLR) 3D 81
South Tottenham (Rail) 1B 36
Southwark (Tube) 2D 26 (2D 77)
Stamford Brook (Tube) 5B 70
Stamford Hill (Rail) 2A 36
Stepney Green (Tube) 3F 65
Stockwell (Tube) 4A 90
Stoke Newington (Rail) 4B 36
Stratford Low Level (Rail, Tube & DLR)
. . . . 4F 53
Stratford (Rail) 3F 53
Streatham Hill (Rail) 2A 118
Streatham (Rail) 5F 117
Surrey Quays (Tube) 5F 79
Swiss Cottage (Tube) 4F 45
Sydenham Hill (Rail) 3B 120
Sydenham (Rail) 4E 121

T

Temple (Tube) 4B 16 (1B 76)
Tooting Bec (Tube) 3C 116
Tooting Broadway (Tube) 5A 116
Tottenham Court Road (Tube)
. . . . 2C 14 (5F 61)
Tower Gateway (DLR) 4F 19 (1B 78)
Tower Hill (Tube) 4F 19 (1B 78)
Tower Millennium Pier (Riverbus)
. . . . 1E 27 (2A 78)
Tufnell Park (Tube) 1E 47
Tulse Hill (Rail) 2D 119
Turnham Green (Tube) 5A 70

U

Upper Holloway (Rail) 4F 33
Upton Park (Tube) 5E 55

V

Vauxhall (Rail & Tube) 1A 90
Victoria (Rail & Tube) 5D 75
Victoria Coach (Bus) 5D 75

W

Walthamstow Queens Road (Rail)
. . . . 1C 38
Wandsworth Common (Rail) 1B 116
Wandsworth Road (Rail) 5E 89
Wandsworth Town (Rail) 2D 101
Wanstead (Tube) 1D 41

Index to Stations

Wanstead Park (Rail) 1D 55
Wapping (Tube) 2E 79
Warren Street (Tube) 3F 5 (3E 61)
Warwick Avenue (Tube) 3E 59
Waterloo East (Rail) 2C 24 (2C 76)
Waterloo International (Rail)
. . . . 3B 24 (3C 76)
Waterloo Millennium Pier (Riverbus)
. . . . 3F 23 (3B 76)
Waterloo (Rail & Tube) 3B 24 (3C 76)
Westbourne Park (Tube) 4B 58
West Brompton (Rail & Tube) 2C 86
Westcombe Park (Rail) 1C 96
West Dulwich (Rail) 2F 119
Westferry (DLR) 1C 80
West Hampstead (Rail) 3C 44
West Hampstead (Tube) 3D 45
West Hampstead Thameslink (Rail) . . . 3C 44
West Ham (Rail & Tube) 2A 68
West India Quay (DLR) 1C 80
West Kensington (Tube) 1B 86
Westminster (Tube) 4D 23 (3A 76)
Westminster Millennium Pier (Riverbus)
. . . . 3E 23 (3A 76)
West Norwood (Rail) 4D 119
West Silvertown (DLR) 2C 82
Whitechapel (Tube) 4D 65
White City (Tube) 1E 71
Willesden Green (Tube) 3E 43
Willesden Junction (Rail & Tube)
. . . . 2B 56
Wimbledon (Rail, Tube & CT) 5B 114
Wimbledon Park (Tube) 3C 114
Woodgrange Park (Rail) 2F 55